T0319726

Econometrics

Econometrics

FRANCO PERACCHI

JOHN WILEY & SONS, LTD
Chichester · New York · Weinheim · Brisbane · Singapore · Toronto

Baffins Lane, Chichester,
West Sussex, PO19 1UD, England

National 01243 779777
International (+44) 1243 779777

e-mail (for orders and customer service enquiries): cs-books@wiley.co.uk

Visit our Home Page on http://www.wiley.co.uk

Other Wiley Editorial Offices

John Wiley & Sons, Inc., 605 Third Avenue,
New York, NY 10158-0012, USA

Wiley-VCH Verlag GmbH, Pappelallee 3,
D-69469 Weinheim, Germany

Jacaranda Wiley Ltd, 33 Park Road, Milton,
Queensland 4064, Australia

John Wiley & Sons (Asia) Pte Ltd, 2 Clementi Loop #02-01,
Jin Xing Distripark, Singapore 129809

John Wiley & Sons (Canada) Ltd, 22 Worcester Road,
Rexdale, Ontario, M9W 1L1, Canada

Library of Congress Cataloging-in-Publication Data

Peracchi, Franco
Econometrics / Franco Peracchi
p. cm
Includes bibliogaphical references and index.
ISBN 0-471-98764-6 (alk.paper)
1. Econometrics. I. Title.

HB139 .P43 2000
330'.01'5195—dc21

00-043915

British Library Cataloguing in Publication Data

A catalogue record for this book is available from the British Library

ISBN 0-471-98764-6

Contents

Preface

This book is based on lecture notes for the econometrics courses I taught at UCLA, New York University and, in more recent years, at the Universities of Udine, Pescara and Rome "Tor Vergata".

The book is divided into three parts. The first part (Chapters 1–5) contains review material on statistical modeling (Chapters 1–3) and statistical inference (Chapters 4 and 5). These five chapters provide basic concepts and results used in the rest of the book. They also introduce in a simplified setting some of the ideas developed later. In particular, Chapters 1 and 2 present the elements of statistical models constructed by combining a model for the variability of the population of interest with a model for the sampling process. These kind of models are typically used to analyze cross-section and panel data. Chapter 3 discusses a number of models for time series data. Chapter 4 discusses various methods for estimating the parameters of a statistical model (method of moments, least squares, least absolute deviations, maximum likelihood, Bayes methods), whereas Chapter 5 is devoted to confidence intervals and hypothesis testing, distinguishing between classical, bootstrap and Bayes methods.

The second part (Chapters 6–14) covers linear methods. It begins with the classical linear model and ordinary least squares (OLS), and then examines various departures from the ideal conditions for OLS. Generalized least squares and linear instrumental variables procedures are introduced, along with various generalizations of the linear model (linear panel data models, linear simultaneous equation models) and nonparametric regression. The results presented in Chapters 6–9 are exact but tend to rely on the assumptions of the Gaussian linear model. Chapters 10–13 go beyond the Gaussian case but the results presented here tend to be valid only in large samples. Chapter 14 discusses in some detail nonparametric methods that free the researcher from the need for assuming a parametric model for the regression function.

The third part (Chapters 15–18) covers nonlinear methods. After a discussion of the general class of M-estimators and their large sample properties (consistency, asymptotic normality, robustness), I present nonlinear estimators for the linear model (Chapter 16), methods for categorical data and generalized linear models (Chapter 17), and methods for truncated and censored data (Chapter 18).

With respect to other textbooks, the main novelties of this book are as follows.

1. A unified approach to statistical estimation emphasizing the analogy (or bootstrap) principle.
2. An introduction to bootstrap and jackknife methods for assessing the

accuracy of an estimator.

3. An extensive discussion of nonparametric methods for estimating density and regression functions.
4. Emphasis on diagnostic procedures (residuals, influence, etc.) and on prediction criteria for evaluating the results of a statistical analysis.
5. Enough references to linear exponential family models to make the treatment of generalized linear models in Chapter 17 fairly straightforward.
6. Some room for Bayesian methods and methods based on statistical decision theory.
7. A careful discussion of robustness in the statistical sense.

The book is at the level of an advanced undergraduate or a first-year graduate econometrics course. The prerequisites are fairly standard. I only assume some background in probability and familiarity with calculus and linear algebra. Most of the linear algebra and the probability used in the book is contained in the Appendices A, C and D. The style of the presentation is sometimes a little dry, but I felt that this was necessary in order to keep the size of the book under control.

The book is suitable for econometric courses emphasizing problems related to the analysis of cross-section and panel data (sampling schemes, sample selection, heterogeneity, nonparametrics, etc.). The book does contain some material on the analysis of time series data, but this is definitely not its main focus.

To conclude, I would like to thank all the people, colleagues and students, who made comments on the various drafts of the book, with a very special thank you to Carlo Giannini.

Franco Peracchi

Notation

Unless stated otherwise, vectors are always interpreted as column vectors. Thus, to denote an m-dimensional column vector we simply write $x = (x_1, \ldots, x_m)$ instead of $x = (x_1, \ldots, x_m)^\top$. If y is an n-dimensional vector, we write $z = (x, y)$ instead of $z = (x^\top, y^\top)^\top$ to denote the $(m+n)$-dimensional column vector obtained by stacking x and y on top of each other.

Random variables or random vectors are denoted by upper-case letters (for example Z). Realizations of a random variable or a random vector are denoted by lower-case letters (for example z).

A data set is represented either as a vector or matrix, in which case bold-face letters are used (for example $\mathbf{Z}$), or as a list of elements (for example $Z_1, \ldots, Z_n$).

The conclusion of a proof, a definition or an example is marked by the symbol $\Box$. Theorems or corollaries for which no proof is presented are left to the reader as an exercise.

The remainder of this section lists the symbols and abbreviations most frequently used.

MATHEMATICAL SYMBOLS

$\approx$	approximately equal to
$\propto$	proportional to
$\otimes$	Kronecker product
$A \times B$	Cartesian product of sets A and B
$\Re$	the set of real numbers (the real line)
$\Re_+$	the set of positive real numbers
$\Re^p$	real Euclidean p-dimensional space
$f \circ g$	composition of two functions
$g'(x)$, $g''(x)$, etc.	vector or matrix of first, second, etc., derivatives of a function g
$\frac{\partial}{\partial x} g(x, y)$, $g_x(x, y)$	vector or matrix of partial derivatives of a function $g(x, y)$ with respect to x
e^x, $\exp x$	exponential of x
$\ln x$	natural logarithm of x
$\operatorname{sign} x$	sign of x
$\|\|x\|\|$	norm of a vector x
$\det A$	determinant of a matrix A

$\operatorname{rank} A$	rank of a matrix A
$\operatorname{tr} A$	trace of a matrix A
$A^\top$	transpose of a matrix A
A^{-1}	inverse of a matrix A
$A^{-\top}$	inverse of the transpose of a matrix A
$\operatorname{diag}[a_{ii}]$	diagonal matrix with ith diagonal element equal to a_{ii}
ι_n	n-vector whose components are all equal to one
e_j	jth unit vector (its jth component is equal to one and all the others are equal to zero)
I_n	identity matrix of order n

STATISTICAL SYMBOLS

$\sim$	is distributed as
F, f	distribution function and density of a probability distribution
$1\{A\}$	indicator function of the event A (is equal to one or zero depending on whether the event A is true or false)
$\Pr\{A\}$	probability of the event A with respect to the relevant probability distribution
$\ell(u)$	loss function
$\mathrm{E}\, Z$, μ_Z	mean (expected value) of a random variable Z
$\operatorname{Med} Z$	median of a random variable Z
$\operatorname{Var} Z, \sigma_Z^2$	variance of a random variable Z
$\operatorname{Corr}(X, Y)$, ρ_{XY}	correlation between X and Y
$\operatorname{Cov}(X, Y)$, σ_{XY}	covariance between X and Y
E_F, Var_F, Cov_F	mean, variance, covariance with respect to a distribution with distribution function F
E_θ, $\operatorname{Var}_\theta$, $\operatorname{Cov}_\theta$	mean, variance, covariance with respect to a distribution with density function $f(z;\theta)$
$l(\theta)$	expected log-likelihood
$L(\theta)$	sample log-likelihood
$\mathcal{I}(\theta)$	expected information about the parameter θ
$\mathcal{P}_\Theta$	parametric family of probability distributions with parameter space Θ
$\mathcal{F}_\Theta$	parametric family of density functions with parameter space Θ
$\mathcal{B}(\alpha, \beta)$	beta distribution with parameter (α, β)
$\operatorname{Bi}(m, \theta)$	binomial distribution with index m and parameter θ
χ_n^2	(central) chi-square distribution with n degrees of freedom
$\chi_{n,\lambda}^2$	noncentral chi-square distribution with n degrees of freedom and noncentrality parameter λ
$\mathcal{E}(\theta)$	exponential distribution with parameter θ
$F_{m,n}$	(central) F-distribution with (m, n) degrees of freedom
$F_{m,n,\lambda}$	noncentral F-distribution with (m, n) degrees of freedom and noncentrality parameter λ
$\mathcal{G}(\alpha, \beta)$	gamma distribution with parameter (α, β)

$\mathcal{M}(n, \theta)$	multinomial distribution with index n and parameter θ
$\mathcal{N}(\mu, \sigma^2)$	Gaussian (normal) distribution with mean μ and variance σ^2
$\Phi(\cdot), \phi(\cdot)$	distribution and density function of a $\mathcal{N}(0,1)$ distribution
$\mathcal{N}_m(\mu, \Sigma)$	m-variate Gaussian (normal) distribution with mean vector μ and variance matrix Σ
$\mathcal{P}(\theta)$	Poisson distribution with parameter θ
t_n	(central) t-distribution with n degrees of freedom
$t_{n,\lambda}$	noncentral t-distribution with n degrees of freedom and noncentrality parameter λ
$\mathcal{U}(a, b)$	uniform distribution on the interval $[a, b]$
$\{X_t\}$, $\{Y_t\}$, $\{Z_t\}$	time series
$\mathrm{WN}(0, \sigma^2)$	white noise with mean zero and variance σ^2
$\mathrm{AR}(p)$	autoregressive process of order p
$\mathrm{MA}(q)$	moving average of order q
$\mathrm{ARMA}(p, q)$	autoregressive–moving average process of order (p, q)
n	sample size
$\bar{X}$, $\bar{Y}$, $\bar{Z}$	sample averages
$\hat{\theta}$, $\hat{F}$, $\hat{f}$	estimates or estimators of θ, F, f
$\tilde{\theta}$, $\widetilde{F}$, $\widetilde{f}$	other estimates or estimators of θ, F, f
$\mathrm{AV}(\hat{\theta}_n)$	asymptotic variance of an estimator sequence $\{\hat{\theta}_n\}$
$\mathrm{Bias}\,\hat{\theta}$	bias of an estimator $\hat{\theta}$
$\stackrel{\mathrm{d}}{\to}$	convergence in distribution
$\stackrel{\mathrm{p}}{\to}$	convergence in probability
$\stackrel{\mathrm{ms}}{\to}$	mean square convergence
$\stackrel{\mathrm{as}}{\to}$	almost sure convergence
O_p, o_p	orders in probability

ABBREVIATIONS

AIC	Akaike information criterion
ALAD	asymmetric least absolute deviations
ARE	asymptotic relative efficiency
BLP	best linear predictor
BLU	best linear unbiased
CLT	central limit theorem
CMF	conditional mean function
CV	cross-validation
CVF	conditional variance function
GLM	generalized linear model
GLS	generalized least squares
GMM	generalized method of moments
IF	influence function
i.i.d.	independently and identically distributed
IV	instrumental variables
LAD	least absolute deviations

LS	least squares
MD	minimum distance
MISE	mean integrated squared error
ML	maximum likelihood
MM	method of moments
MS	maximum score
MSE	mean squared error
n.d.	negative definite
NLLS	nonlinear least squares
n.n.d.	non-negative definite
OLS	ordinary least squares
p.d.	positive definite
SLLN	strong law of large numbers
SRS	simple random sampling
SURE	seemingly unrelated regression equations
UMVU	uniformly minimum variance unbiased
WLLN	weak law of large numbers
WLS	weighted least squares

1

Regression Models

Consider a data matrix $\mathbf{z}$ of order $n \times q$, consisting of n observations on q variables that are numerical or can be represented as numerical. In most cases, the data display a certain degree of variability. In the theory of statistical inference, this is taken into account by treating $\mathbf{z}$ as the outcome of a chance experiment, that is, as a realization of a random $n \times q$ matrix $\mathbf{Z}$ or, stacking the n rows of $\mathbf{Z}$ on top of each other, of a random nq-vector.

The variables in $\mathbf{Z}$ are often treated asymmetrically, in the sense that the probabilistic behavior of one subset of them, called *response variables*, is related to the values taken by another subset of variables, called *covariates*. The data matrix may then be partitioned as $\mathbf{Z} = [\mathbf{X}, \mathbf{Y}]$, where the $n \times k$ matrix $\mathbf{X}$ represents the observations on the covariates and the $n \times m$ matrix $\mathbf{Y}$ ($m = q - k$) represents the observations on the response variables. The response variables are also called *dependent variables* when their relationship with the covariates is interpreted in terms of causal dependence. In this case, the covariates are also called *explanatory variables*. In broad terms, regression analysis is the study of the conditional distribution of $\mathbf{Y}$ given $\mathbf{X}$.

The generality of this definition raises a number of problems. Are we interested in the whole conditional distribution or only in some aspects of it? In the first case, we have to select the particular characterization of the distribution that we want to focus on. Is it the cumulative distribution function, the density, the quantile function, or the hazard? Looking only at certain aspects of the distribution may be simpler, but we still have to decide which ones. Is it the center, the spread, or the skewness? And what measure of center? What measure of spread? What measure of skewness?

The answers to these questions depend on the purposes of the analysis. Are we interested in exploratory data analysis or in prediction? Or do we want instead to fit a well defined model, possibly suggested by economic theory? The answer also depends on the nature of the data. For example, if the response variable is a 0–1 random variable, then its conditional distribution is entirely characterized by its conditional mean. In other cases, the sample size, the accuracy of the data, etc., may also be relevant. Finally, the set of available statistical techniques may restrict our decisions.

A second set of issues has to do with how we want to model the functional relationship between $\mathbf{X}$ and the aspects of the conditional distribution of $\mathbf{Y}$ which are of interest. Do we want to leave this relationship essentially unrestricted, or do we want to place restrictions on it, and if so, of what kind? The answer here depends on the strength of our prior information (our past experience, theoretical knowledge of the subject, results obtained by others, etc.), but also on the purposes of the analysis, the sample size, the available statistical techniques, etc.

If we are mainly interested in exploring or describing the data, we may want to restrict the relationship of interest as little as possible. At the end of the study, however, we ought to ask the question of how we go from data description to interpretation and prediction. What kind of data do we need? What kind of restrictions do we have to impose on the model?

On the other hand, when we choose a specific model we should always be aware that the model assumptions are useful, because they simplify the problem and help in organizing and interpreting the results, but they may also be straightjackets that prevent us from seeing certain features of the data. Further, the choice of a specific model is often dictated by mathematical tractability or simply by convention. In this case, we are really dealing with an approximation problem, and this may change our interpretation of the statistical results.

1.1 PARAMETRIC STATISTICAL MODELS

In the theory of statistical inference, the chance experiment that generates the observed data vector $\mathbf{z}$ is formally represented by a random vector $\mathbf{Z}$ taking values in a probability space $(\mathcal{Z}, \mathcal{A}, P_0)$, where $(\mathcal{Z}, \mathcal{A})$ is a measurable space consisting of a set $\mathcal{Z}$ of elementary events, called the *sample space*, and a suitable σ-algebra $\mathcal{A}$ of subsets of $\mathcal{Z}$. In what follows, $\mathcal{Z}$ is a subset of the real Euclidean space $\Re^{nq}$ of dimension nq and the σ-algebra $\mathcal{A}$ is the Borel field on $\Re^{nq}$. The fundamental characteristic of $\mathbf{Z}$ is its probability distribution P_0 defined on $(\mathcal{Z}, \mathcal{A})$.

In a statistical problem, the only thing that is known about P_0 is that it may belong to a family $\mathcal{P}$ of probability distributions on $(\mathcal{Z}, \mathcal{A})$. The triple $(\mathcal{Z}, \mathcal{A}, \mathcal{P})$ is called the *statistical model*. When the reference to the underlying sample space is obvious, a statistical model is simply indicated by $\mathcal{P}$. Given the statistical model and the observed data, one is required to draw certain inferences concerning P_0. A statistical model is said to be *correctly specified* if $P_0 \in \mathcal{P}$. The choice of a statistical model depends both on the available prior information, that is, the information available before the data are observed (this information may come from previous studies, from the economic theory, etc.), and the purposes for which the model is built.

The family $\mathcal{P}$ of distributions may sometimes be put in a one-to-one correspondence with a subset Θ of the real p-dimensional Euclidean space $\Re^p$ and represented as a *parametric statistical model* $\mathcal{P}_\Theta = \{P_\theta, \theta \in \Theta\}$, where the index set Θ is called the *parameter space*. A parametric statistical model is said to be *correctly specified* if $P_0 = P_{\theta_0}$ for some $\theta_0 \in \Theta$. If the model is correctly specified, then the problem of drawing inferences about the distribution P_0 reduces to that of drawing inferences about the "true" parameter θ_0.

A parametrization is generally not unique. To see this, let $\mathcal{P}$ be a family of distributions indexed by the elements of a parameter space Θ. If $g \colon \Theta \to \Gamma$ is any one-to-one function, then $\mathcal{P}$ and Γ are also in a one-to-one correspondence and therefore the parameter space Γ may be used instead of Θ to index the elements of $\mathcal{P}$. The original parametrization of $\mathcal{P}$ in terms of θ and the one in terms of $\gamma = g(\theta)$ are equivalent in the sense that P_θ and P_γ represent the same element of $\mathcal{P}$. The choice of a particular parametrization may be justified on the grounds of its interpretability or mathematical tractability. For example, the parameter θ may be chosen such that it corresponds to interesting features of the distribution, or it may be chosen in order to simplify some formal aspect of the statistical problem.

Under general conditions, a parametric statistical model $\mathcal{P}_\Theta$ may be characterized by a family $\mathcal{F}_\Theta = \{f(\mathbf{z};\theta), \theta \in \Theta\}$ of density functions defined on $\mathcal{Z}$, where the term "density function" is used, depending on the context, to denote either a probability mass function or a probability density function. The statistical model is correctly specified if the density f_0 of $\mathbf{Z}$ may be represented as $f_0(\mathbf{z}) = f(\mathbf{z};\theta_0)$ for some $\theta_0 \in \Theta$. If there is no ambiguity, from now on, a parametric statistical model will simply be called a parametric model and denoted by $\mathcal{F}_\Theta$. Probabilities and expectations with respect to an element $f(\mathbf{z};\theta)$ of $\mathcal{F}_\Theta$ are denoted by P_θ and E_θ respectively.

Example 1.1 An important example is when the observed data correspond to a single cross-section. In this case, the data vector $\mathbf{z} = (z_1, \ldots, z_n)$ may often be viewed as the outcome of n independent replications of the same chance experiment, that is, as n distinct realizations of the same random variable. If the chance experiment that results in a single data point is represented by the parametric model $(\mathcal{Z}, \mathcal{A}, \{P_\theta, \theta \in \Theta\})$, then the statistical model for the data is the parametric model $(\mathcal{Z}^n, \mathcal{A}^n, \{P_\theta^n, \theta \in \Theta\})$, where $\mathcal{Z}^n = \mathcal{Z} \times \cdots \times \mathcal{Z}$, $\mathcal{A}^n = \mathcal{A} \times \cdots \times \mathcal{A}$ and $P_\theta^n = P_\theta \times \cdots \times P_\theta$. If $f(z;\theta)$ is the density of P_θ, then the joint density of the data is $f(\mathbf{z};\theta) = \prod_i f(z_i;\theta)$. □

The previous example illustrates the fact that the statistical model is often obtained by combining a model that describes the variability of the characteristic of interest in the population under examination, or *model of the statistical population*, with one that describes the way in which the data have been obtained, or *model of the sampling process*. In our example, the former is represented by the density $f(z_i, \theta)$, whereas the latter corresponds to the assumption that the data come from n independent replications of the same chance experiment.

In this chapter, we leave aside the problem of how to represent the sampling process and concentrate instead on some models of the statistical population that are frequently used in the analysis of economic data.

1.1.1 *EXAMPLES OF PARAMETRIC MODELS*

We first review some important examples of parametric models.

Example 1.2 Let Z be a 0–1 random variable, that is, a binary random variable taking value one ("success") with probability θ and value zero ("failure") with probability $1 - \theta$, where $0 < \theta < 1$. The random variable Z is often the indicator of the occurrence of a particular event, such as the decision by a consumer to purchase a certain good, the decision by a bank to grant a loan to a customer, the decision by a worker to accept a new job offer. The chance experiment corresponding to Z is called a *Bernoulli trial*. The distribution of Z belongs to the family of *Bernoulli distributions* with parameter θ and probability function

$$f(z;\theta) = \begin{cases} \theta^z(1-\theta)^{1-z}, & \text{if } z = 0, 1, \\ 0, & \text{otherwise.} \end{cases}$$

By standard results, $\mathrm{E}\, Z = \Pr\{Z = 1\} = \theta$ and $\mathrm{Var}\, Z = \theta(1-\theta)$. Notice that $\mathrm{Var}\, Z$ is a quadratic function of θ and attains its maximum of $1/4$ when $\theta = 1/2$.

Figure 1 Probability function of a binomial distribution with index $m = 20$ and parameter $\theta = .20$.

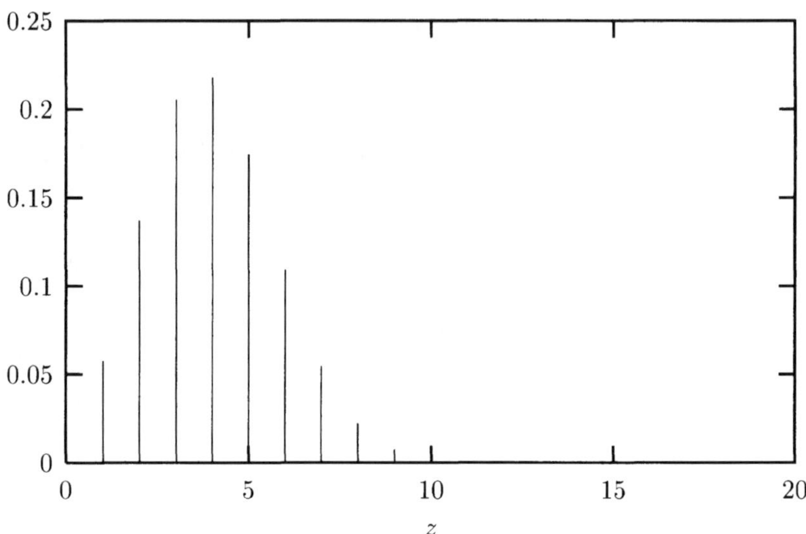

Now let $Z_1, \ldots, Z_m$ be independent random variables with a common Bernoulli distribution with parameter θ. The random variable $Z = \sum_{j=1}^{m} Z_j$ is a discrete random variable which can take the values $0, 1, \ldots, m$ and represents the number of successes in m independent Bernoulli trials. Its distribution belongs to the family $\{\mathrm{Bi}(m, \theta), 0 < \theta < 1\}$ of *binomial distributions* with index m and parameter θ, with probability function (Figure 1)

$$f(z; \theta) = \begin{cases} \binom{m}{z} \theta^z (1-\theta)^{m-z}, & \text{if } z = 0, 1, \ldots, m, \\ 0, & \text{otherwise,} \end{cases}$$

where $\binom{m}{z} = m!/[z!(m-z)!]$ is the binomial coefficient. In this case, $\mathrm{E}\, Z = m\theta$ and $\mathrm{Var}\, Z = m\theta(1-\theta)$. A Bernoulli distribution is a binomial with index $m = 1$. □

Example 1.3 Let Z be a discrete random variable which can take the values $0, 1, 2, \ldots$ and represents the number of times that a particular event occurs during a specified time period. For example, Z may represent the number of strikes in an industry during a year, or the number of purchases of a given good by a household during a month, or the number of patents registered by a firm during a semester.

A possible parametric model for Z is the family $\{\mathcal{P}(\theta), \theta > 0\}$ of *Poisson distributions* with parameter θ and probability function (Figure 2)

$$f(z; \theta) = \begin{cases} \dfrac{\theta^z}{z!} e^{-\theta}, & \text{if } z = 0, 1, 2, \ldots, \\ 0, & \text{otherwise.} \end{cases}$$

By standard results, $\mathrm{E}\, Z = \mathrm{Var}\, Z = \theta$. □

Figure 2 Probability function of a Poisson distribution with parameter $\theta = 4$.

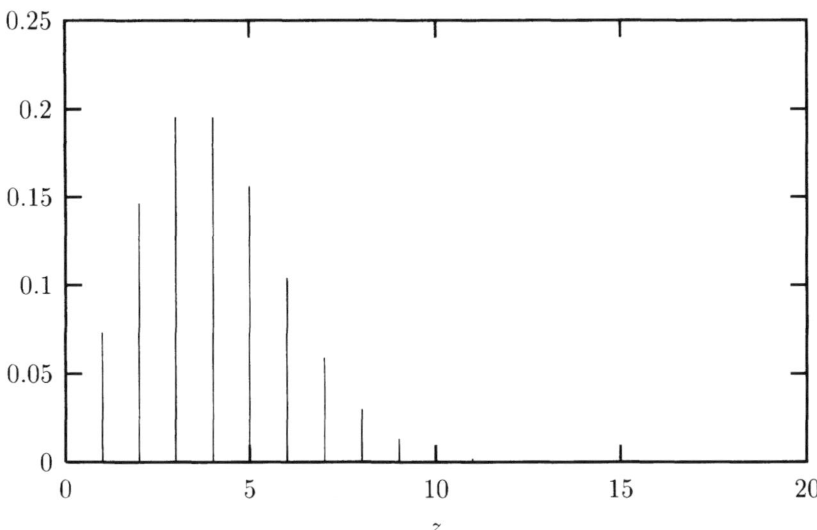

Example 1.4 If Z is a continuous non-negative random variable, then a possible parametric model for Z is the family $\{\mathcal{E}(\theta), \theta > 0\}$ of *exponential distributions* with parameter θ and probability density function (Figure 3)

$$f(z;\theta) = \begin{cases} \theta e^{-\theta z}, & \text{if } z \geq 0, \\ 0, & \text{otherwise.} \end{cases}$$

The distribution function of Z is

$$F(z;\theta) = \int_0^z f(u;\theta)\, du = 1 - e^{-\theta z}, \qquad z \geq 0,$$

and its first two moments are $\mathrm{E}\, Z = 1/\theta$ and $\mathrm{Var}\, Z = 1/\theta^2 = (\mathrm{E}\, Z)^2$. The distribution $\mathcal{E}(1)$ is called *unit exponential*.

An exponential distribution may be reparametrized by letting $\lambda = 1/\theta$. In this case, its probability density function becomes

$$f(z;\lambda) = \frac{1}{\lambda} e^{-z/\lambda}, \qquad z \geq 0,$$

and therefore $\mathrm{E}\, Z = \lambda$ and $\mathrm{Var}\, Z = \lambda^2$. □

Example 1.5 If Z is a continuous random variable that can take any value on the real line $\Re$, then a possible parametric model for Z is the family $\{\mathcal{N}(\mu, \sigma^2), \mu \in \Re, \sigma^2 > 0\}$ of *Gaussian* or *normal distributions* with mean μ, variance σ^2 and probability density function (Figure 4)

$$f(z;\theta) = \frac{1}{\sigma\sqrt{2\pi}} \exp\left[-\frac{1}{2}\left(\frac{z-\mu}{\sigma}\right)^2\right], \qquad \theta = (\mu, \sigma^2).$$

Figure 3 Probability density functions of exponential distributions.

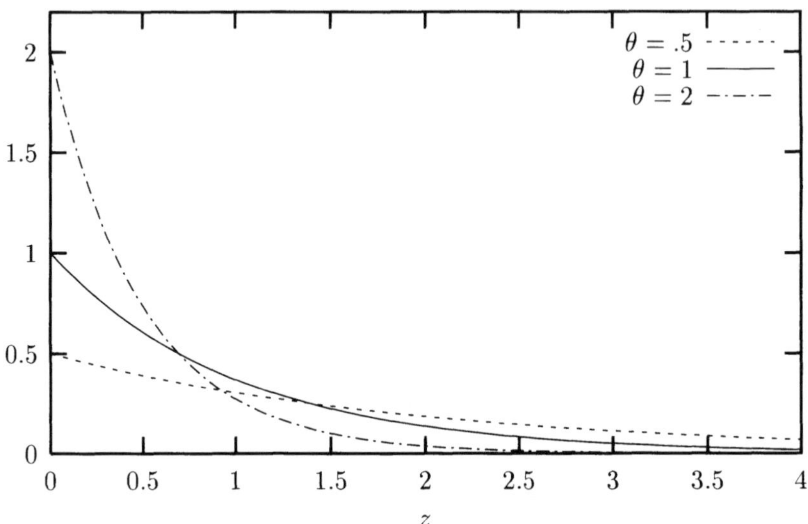

Alternative parametrizations are sometimes adopted where σ^2 is replaced by σ, $1/\sigma^2$ or $\ln\sigma$. The $\mathcal{N}(0,1)$ distribution is also called *standard Gaussian*. In what follows, its distribution function and density will generally be denoted by Φ and ϕ respectively.

The use of the Gaussian model is often justified with reference to a central limit theorem (Appendix D.5), for example as an approximation to the distribution of the sum of a large number of independent random variables, none of which dominates the others. □

When $Z = (Z_1, \ldots, Z_q)$ is a random vector, modeling each individual element in isolation generally implies a loss of information, for it ignores the possible lack of independence between the elements of Z. In this case, multivariate representations are more adequate. Some of the models described in the previous examples are easily generalized to the multivariate case.

Example 1.6 Let Z be a random q-vector whose elements are discrete random variables that add up to m and can take any of the values $0, 1, \ldots, m$. A possible parametric model for Z is the family $\{\mathcal{M}_q(m, \theta)\}$ of *multinomial distributions* with index m and parameter $\theta = (\theta_1, \ldots, \theta_q)$, with probability function

$$f(z;\theta) = \frac{m!}{z_1! \cdots z_q!}\theta_1^{z_1} \cdots \theta_q^{z_q}, \qquad z_j = 0, 1, \ldots, m; \qquad j = 1, \ldots, q.$$

The parameter space Θ is the unit simplex in $\Re^q$

$$\Theta = \left\{ (\theta_1, \ldots, \theta_q) \colon \theta_j > 0,\ j = 1, \ldots, q;\ \sum_{j=1}^{q} \theta_j = 1 \right\},$$

Figure 4 Probability density functions of Gaussian distributions.

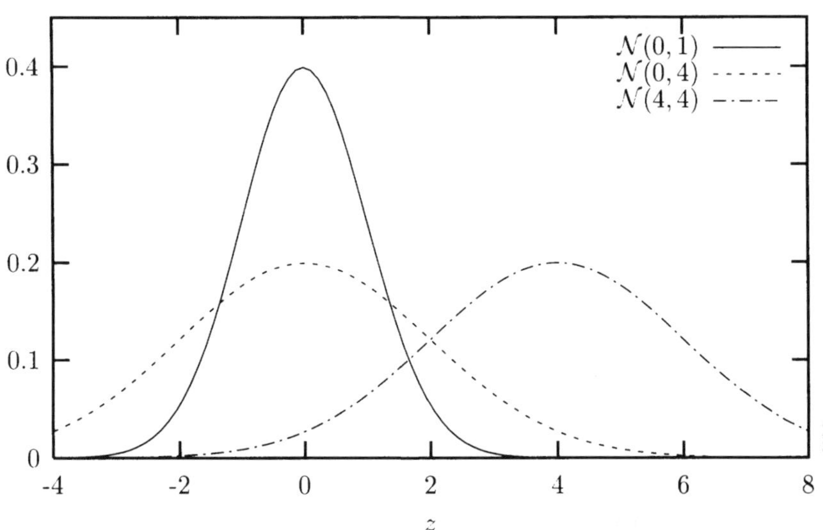

that is, it consists of all q-vectors whose elements are positive and add up to one. Formally, the multinomial distribution arises as the distribution by type of m elements randomly drawn with replacement from a population consisting of q types, where θ_j indicates the fraction of elements of type j in the population. The case when $q = 2$, $\theta_1 = 1 - \pi$ and $\theta_2 = \pi$, corresponds to the $\mathrm{Bi}(m, \pi)$ distribution.

Because the marginal distribution of every element Z_j of Z is $\mathrm{Bi}(m, \theta_j)$, one has $\mathrm{E}\, Z_j = m\theta_j$ and $\mathrm{Var}\, Z_j = m\theta_j(1 - \theta_j)$ for every j. Further, because the distribution of $Z_i + Z_j$ is $\mathrm{Bi}(m, \theta_i + \theta_j)$, it follows that $\mathrm{Cov}(Z_i, Z_j) = -m\theta_i\theta_j$ for all $i \neq j$. □

Example 1.7 If Z is a random q-vector whose elements can take any value in $\Re$, then a possible parametric model for Z is the family $\{\mathcal{N}_q(\mu, \Sigma)\}$ of *q-variate Gaussian* or *normal distributions* with mean μ, variance Σ, and probability density function

$$f(z; \theta) = (2\pi)^{-q/2} (\det \Sigma)^{-1/2} \exp\left[-\frac{1}{2}(z - \mu)^\top \Sigma^{-1} (z - \mu)\right],$$

where μ is a q-vector and Σ is a $q \times q$ symmetric p.d. matrix. In this case, θ consists of the vector μ and the $q(q + 1)/2$ distinct elements of the matrix Σ. The $\mathcal{N}_q(0, I_q)$ distribution, where I_q is the unit matrix of order q, is also called *standard* q-variate Gaussian distribution. □

1.1.2 LOCATION AND SCALE MODELS

Parametric models may often be interpreted as the result of certain transformations applied to some basic distribution. This allows one to decompose the model into a deterministic part, more closely related to specific knowledge of the problem under examination, and a stochastic part.

An important class of transformations is the class of affine transformations. Given a random variable U, this class corresponds to all random variables that may be represented as $Z = \mu + \sigma U$ for some $\mu \in \Re$ and $\sigma > 0$. If F is the distribution function of U, then the distribution function of any member Z of this class is

$$F(z;\mu,\sigma) = \Pr\{Z \le z\} = \Pr\left\{U \le \frac{z-\mu}{\sigma}\right\} = F\left(\frac{z-\mu}{\sigma}\right).$$

The parametric family $\mathcal{F} = \{F(z;\mu,\sigma), \mu \in \Re, \sigma > 0\}$ is called a *location and scale model*, μ is called the *location parameter*, σ is called the *scale parameter*, and we say that U *generates* $\mathcal{F}$. Clearly, F is the member of $\mathcal{F}$ corresponding to $\mu = 0$ and $\sigma = 1$. In the special case when $\sigma = 1$, the model is called a *location model* and denoted by $\{F(z;\mu), \mu \in \Re\}$. When $\mu = 0$, it is called a *scale model* and denoted by $\{F(z;\sigma), \sigma > 0\}$.

If U is a continuous random variable with density function f, then the density function of Z is

$$f(z;\mu,\sigma) = \frac{1}{\sigma} f\left(\frac{z-\mu}{\sigma}\right).$$

If U has finite variance, then $\mathrm{E}\, Z = \mu + \sigma\, \mathrm{E}\, U$ and $\mathrm{Var}\, Z = \sigma^2\, \mathrm{Var}\, U$. If U has zero mean and unit variance, then $\mathrm{E}\, Z = \mu$ and $\mathrm{Var}\, Z = \sigma^2$. In general, however, μ and σ^2 need not correspond to the mean and variance of Z.

The location and scale model $\mathcal{F}$ has an important property. If $g(Z) = \alpha + \beta Z$ is an affine transformation of Z and $\beta > 0$, then the distribution function of $g(Z)$ is

$$F(z;\mu',\sigma') = \Pr\{g(Z) \le z\} = F\left(\frac{z-\mu'}{\sigma'}\right),$$

where $\mu' = \alpha + \beta\mu$ and $\sigma' = \beta\sigma$. Because the distribution of $g(Z)$ also belongs to $\mathcal{F}$, we say that model $\mathcal{F}$ is *invariant* under the class of affine transformations.

Example 1.8 A location model is a typical model for measurement errors. Under this interpretation, μ represents the quantity to be measured, the random variable U represents the probabilistic description of the accuracy of the measurement device, and the random variable Z represents the probabilistic description of the variability of the recorded measurements of μ. □

Example 1.9 The random variable Z has an $\mathcal{E}(\theta)$ distribution if and only if $Z = U/\theta$, where $U \sim \mathcal{E}(1)$. The family $\{\mathcal{E}(\theta)\}$ is therefore a scale model generated by the unit exponential distribution and $1/\theta$ is the scale parameter. □

Example 1.10 The random variable Z has a $\mathcal{N}(\mu,\sigma^2)$ distribution if and only if $Z = \mu + \sigma U$, where $\sigma > 0$ and $U \sim \mathcal{N}(0,1)$. The family $\{\mathcal{N}(\mu,\sigma^2)\}$ is therefore a location and scale model generated by the standard Gaussian distribution. Thus, if $Z \sim \mathcal{N}(\mu,\sigma^2)$, its distribution function and density are respectively

$$F(z;\theta) = \Phi\left(\frac{z-\mu}{\sigma}\right), \qquad f(z;\theta) = \frac{1}{\sigma}\phi\left(\frac{z-\mu}{\sigma}\right),$$

where $\theta = (\mu,\sigma^2)$, and Φ and ϕ denote the distribution function and the density of the $\mathcal{N}(0,1)$ distribution. □

An alternative parametrization of an affine transformation is sometimes useful. If $\gamma = \mu/\sigma$ and $\delta = 1/\sigma$, then Z may equivalently be represented as $Z = (\gamma + U)/\delta$. Under this parametrization, the distribution function and the density of Z are respectively $F(z; \gamma, \delta) = F(\delta z - \gamma)$ and $f(z; \gamma, \delta) = \delta\, f(\delta z - \gamma)$.

1.1.3 THE QUANTILE FUNCTION

The distribution function and the density function are mathematically equivalent ways of representing the distribution of a random variable. Other representations are possible, however, and sometimes more convenient to work with.

Given a real number p in the interval $(0, 1)$, a pth *quantile* of Z is any number ζ_p such that

$$\Pr\{Z < \zeta_p\} \leq p \leq \Pr\{Z \leq \zeta_p\}. \tag{1.1}$$

It is easily verified that a solution to (1.1) always exists but need not be unique, and that the set of solutions to (1.1) is a closed interval of the real line. Quantiles increase monotonically with p, that is, $\zeta_{p'} \geq \zeta_p$ whenever $p' > p$. Unlike probabilities, which range between 0 and 1, they are on the same scale as Z.

Quantiles are often employed to provide summaries of the distribution of a random variable. A *median*, corresponding to $p = .5$, is a well known measure of location, whereas the *interquartile range* IQR $= \zeta_{.75} - \zeta_{.25}$ and the *interdecile range* IDR $= \zeta_{.90} - \zeta_{.10}$ are well known measures of spread. A measure of symmetry is the ratio $(\zeta_{.75} - \zeta_{.50})/(\zeta_{.50} - \zeta_{.25})$, while a measure of tail weight is the ratio IDR/IQR, or some normalized version of it.

If Z is a continuous random variable with distribution function F, then $\Pr\{Z < z\} = \Pr\{Z \leq z\} = F(z)$ for every z, and a pth quantile is any number ζ_p such that

$$F(\zeta_p) = p. \tag{1.2}$$

If F is continuous and strictly increasing or, equivalently, Z has a strictly positive density, then the inverse F^{-1} exists and equation (1.2) has the unique solution $\zeta_p = F^{-1}(p)$. In this case ζ_p, viewed as a function of p, is called the *quantile function* of Z. To stress the interpretation of the quantile function as a function defined on $(0, 1)$, the notation $\zeta_p = Q(p)$ is also used. The distribution function and the quantile function of selected distributions are shown in Table 1.

The quantile function $Q(p)$ has several interesting properties. First, if g is any monotonically increasing and left-continuous function, then

$$p = \Pr\{Z \leq Q(p)\} = \Pr\{g(Z) \leq g(Q(p))\}$$

for every p in the interval $(0, 1)$. Hence, the quantile function of the random variable $g(Z)$ is equal to $g(Q(p))$. In particular, if $g(z) = \alpha + \beta z$, with $\beta \geq 0$, then the quantile function of $g(Z)$ is equal to $\alpha + \beta Q(p)$.

Example 1.11 If $Z \sim \mathcal{E}(\theta)$, then the quantile function of Z is obtained from the quantile function of the unit exponential distribution in Table 1 through the relationship

$$Q(p; \theta) = \frac{1}{\theta} Q(p) = -\frac{1}{\theta} \ln(1 - p).$$

Table 1 Distribution function $F(z)$ and quantile function $Q(p)$ of selected distributions.

Distribution	$F(z)$	$Q(p)$
Cauchy	$\frac{1}{2}+\frac{1}{\pi}\arctan z$	$\tan[\pi(p-\frac{1}{2})]$
Chi-square(1)	$2\Phi(\sqrt{z})-1$	$[\Phi^{-1}((p+1)/2)]^2$
Exponential	$1-e^{-z}$	$-\ln(1-p)$
Gaussian	$\Phi(z)$	$\Phi^{-1}(p)$
Gumbel	$1-\exp(-e^{z})$	$\ln[-\ln(1-p)]$
Laplace	$\frac{1}{2}e^{z},\ z<0$	$\ln 2p,\ p<\frac{1}{2}$
	$1-\frac{1}{2}e^{-z},\ z\geq 0$	$-\ln 2(1-p),\ p\geq\frac{1}{2}$
Logistic	$\dfrac{e^{z}}{1+e^{z}}$	$\ln\dfrac{p}{1-p}$
Log-normal	$\Phi(\ln z)$	$\exp[\Phi^{-1}(p)]$
Pareto	$1-(\alpha/z)^{\beta}$	$\alpha(1-p)^{-1/\beta}$
Uniform	z	p
Weibull	$1-\exp(-\gamma z^{\alpha})$	$[-\frac{1}{\gamma}\ln(1-p)]^{1/\alpha}$

If $Z \sim \mathcal{N}(\mu, \sigma^2)$, then the quantile function of Z is obtained from the quantile function of the standard normal distribution in Table 1 through the relationship

$$Q(p; \theta) = \mu + \sigma Q(p) = \mu + \sigma \Phi^{-1}(p), \qquad \theta = (\mu, \sigma^2).$$

□

Next notice that, if U is a uniform random variable on $[0, 1]$ and u is any number between 0 and 1 then, by the monotonicity of Q,

$$u = \Pr\{U \leq u\} = \Pr\{Q(U) \leq Q(u)\}.$$

Because $\Pr\{Z \leq Q(u)\} = u$ by the definition of quantile function, it follows that Z and $Q(U)$ have the same distribution.

Finally, if Z has a continuous positive density f in a neighborhood of $Q(p)$, then it can be shown that the derivative of the quantile function at u exists and is $Q'(p) = 1/f(Q(p))$. The slope Q' is known as the *sparsity function* or the *quantile-density function*, whereas the composition $f \circ Q$ is known as *density-quantile function*. The quantile-density function is well defined whenever the density is strictly positive and is strictly positive whenever the density is bounded.

1.1.4 HAZARD RATE MODELS

If Z is a continuous non-negative random variable with distribution function F and density function f, then the following limit

$$\lim_{\epsilon \to 0} \frac{\Pr\{z \leq Z < z + \epsilon \,|\, Z \geq z\}}{\epsilon} = \lim_{\epsilon \to 0} \frac{\Pr\{z \leq Z < z + \epsilon\}}{\epsilon \Pr\{Z \geq z\}}$$

exists and is equal to

$$h(z) = \frac{f(z)}{1 - F(z)},$$

called the *hazard rate* of Z at z. Hence, for sufficiently small ϵ, the conditional probability $\Pr\{z \leq Z < z + \epsilon \,|\, Z \geq z\}$ is well approximated by $\epsilon h(z)$.

In typical applications, Z represents the length of time between the occurrence of two events. For example, Z may represent the survival time of a patient in a clinical trial, the lifetime of a marriage, the length of an unemployment spell, or the duration of a strike. With this interpretation, Z is often called the *failure time* or *duration of stay*, and the hazard rate $h(z)$ describes the instantaneous rate of failure or the instantaneous rate of exit from a given state after z time units. The larger is $h(z)$, the more likely it is that failure or exit will occur immediately after time z.

Viewed as a function of z, $h(z)$ is called the *hazard function* of Z. The hazard function is necessarily non-negative and may be represented as $h(z) = f(z)/S(z)$, where $S(z) = 1 - F(z)$ is called the *survivor function* of Z. Notice that $S(0) = 1$ since Z is continuous and non-negative.

Under appropriate conditions, the hazard function completely characterizes the distribution of Z, in the sense that knowledge of the hazard function is equivalent to knowledge of the distribution or the density functions of Z. To see this, notice that if $h(z)$ is the hazard function of Z, then it must satisfy the relationship

$$h(z) = -\frac{d}{dz} \ln S(z), \qquad z > 0.$$

Solving this differential equation, using the initial condition $S(0) = 1$, gives

$$S(z) = e^{-H(z)}, \tag{1.3}$$

where the function $H(z) = \int_0^z h(u)\,du$ is called the *integrated hazard.* Obvious candidates for the distribution and density functions of Z are therefore

$$F(z) = 1 - e^{-H(z)}, \qquad f(z) = F'(z) = h(z)\,e^{-H(z)}.$$

Notice that $F(\infty) = 1$ only if $H(\infty) = \infty$. Also notice that, for $F(z)$ to be a nondecreasing function, $H(z)$ must be nondecreasing in z and therefore the hazard function must be non-negative.

Relationship (1.3), together with the fact that $H(z)$ is nondecreasing, implies that

$$e^{-H(z)} = \Pr\{Z \geq z\} = \Pr\{H(Z) \geq H(z)\}.$$

The integrated hazard $H(Z)$, viewed as a transformation of Z, is therefore a random variable with a unit exponential distribution.

There are several reasons why working with the hazard may be preferable to working with the density or the distribution function. First, certain economic models make predictions directly in terms of the hazard. Second, working with the hazard may sometimes be mathematically more convenient than working with the density or the distribution functions.

Example 1.12 Let $Z_1, \ldots, Z_m$ be independent non-negative continuous random variables, let h_j and S_j denote respectively the hazard and the survivor function of Z_j, and consider the distribution of the random variable $Z = \min(Z_1, \ldots, Z_m)$. Because $Z \geq z$ if and only if $Z_j \geq z$ for all j, the survivor function of Z is

$$S(z) = \Pr\{Z \geq z\} = \Pr\{Z_1 \geq z, \ldots, Z_m \geq z\} = \prod_{j=1}^m S_j(z).$$

Since $\ln S(z) = \sum_j \ln S_j(z)$, the hazard function of Z is

$$h(z) = -\frac{d}{dz} \ln S(z) = \sum_{j=1}^m \left[-\frac{d}{dz} \ln S_j(z) \right] = \sum_{j=1}^m h_j(z).$$

The random variable Z may represent the duration of stay in a given state when exit from that state may be due to m independent causes. With this interpretation, the model is known as the *competing risks model.* □

A third reason for working with the hazard function is that comparison with the exponential distribution is particularly simple.

Figure 5 Hazard functions of Weibull distributions.

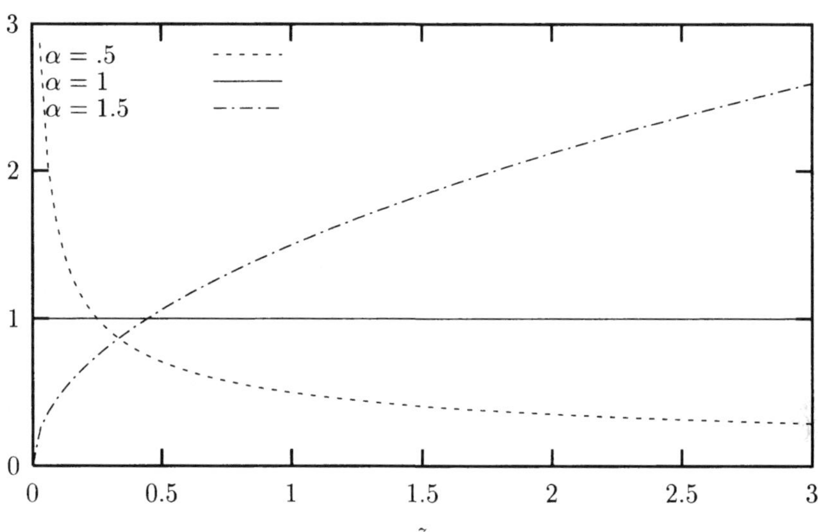

Example 1.13 If Z has an $\mathcal{E}(\theta)$ distribution, then its density and survivor function are respectively $f(z) = \theta e^{-\theta z}$ and $S(z) = e^{-\theta z}$, $z \geq 0$. Hence, the hazard function of Z is

$$h(z) = \frac{\theta e^{-\theta z}}{e^{-\theta z}} = \theta,$$

that is, the exponential distribution has a constant hazard. For this reason, it is sometimes said that the exponential distribution is *memoryless* or shows *no duration dependence*. It is easily verified that the converse is also true, that is, a continuous non-negative random variable Z has an exponential distribution if it has a constant hazard. Thus, the memoryless property characterizes the exponential distribution. □

Example 1.14 The exponential distribution, having a constant hazard, may be inappropriate in some cases. For example, one may convincingly argue that for an unemployed person the probability of finding a job depends on the length of his unemployment spell. The Weibull distribution (see Appendix C.6) provides a statistical model that allows for this possibility.

If Z has a Weibull distribution with parameter $\theta = (\alpha, \gamma)$, then its density function is

$$f(z) = \begin{cases} \gamma\alpha z^{\alpha-1}\exp(-\gamma z^{\alpha}), & \text{if } z \geq 0, \\ 0, & \text{otherwise,} \end{cases}$$

and its survivor function is

$$S(z) = \exp(-\gamma z^{\alpha}), \qquad z \geq 0.$$

The Weibull distribution reduces to the $\mathcal{E}(\gamma)$ when $\alpha = 1$. The hazard function of a Weibull distribution (Figure 5) is

$$h(z) = \gamma\alpha z^{\alpha-1},$$

which is constant if and only if $\alpha = 1$. Because

$$h'(z) = \gamma\alpha(\alpha - 1)z^{\alpha-2}$$

the Weibull hazard is monotonically increasing or decreasing, that is, the model exhibits positive or negative duration dependence, depending on whether $\alpha > 1$ or $0 < \alpha < 1$. □

1.1.5 *IDENTIFIABILITY*

Let the random variable Z represent the variability of some numerical characteristic of the population. Suppose that the investigator decides to parametrize the model for the probability distribution of Z in terms of a finite-dimensional parameter $\theta \in \Theta$, and let $\mathcal{F}_\Theta$ denote the family of densities that comprise the model. It may happen that, given the chosen parametrization, distinct parameter points in Θ are associated with the same element of $\mathcal{F}_\Theta$. Formally, the mapping that associates with each element of Θ an element of $\mathcal{F}_\Theta$ is not invertible. In this case, one says that the model is *not identifiable* because, even if the density of Z were known, it would be impossible in the absence of further information to single out a unique element of Θ. This difficulty is due to the chosen parametrization and could be avoided by restricting the parameter space.

Example 1.15 Let $\mathcal{F}_\Theta$ be the parametric model generated by the random variable $U \sim \mathcal{N}_2(0, I_2)$ through the class of linear transformations of the form $g(U) = \Gamma U$, where Γ is a 2×2 p.d. matrix. This model does not ensure that distinct parameter points in Θ are associated with distinct elements of $\mathcal{F}_\Theta$ and so it is not identifiable in general. For example, the two parameter points

$$\Gamma_0 = \begin{bmatrix} 2 & 1 \\ 1 & 2 \end{bmatrix}, \qquad \Gamma_1 = \begin{bmatrix} \sqrt{5} & 0 \\ 4/\sqrt{5} & 3/\sqrt{5} \end{bmatrix}$$

are associated with the same $N_2(0, \Sigma)$ distribution, with

$$\Sigma = \Gamma_0\Gamma_0^\top = \Gamma_1\Gamma_1^\top = \begin{bmatrix} 5 & 4 \\ 4 & 5 \end{bmatrix}.$$

One way out, in this case, is to restrict the class of admissible transformations of U by imposing the restriction that Γ is a diagonal matrix. □

More generally, a model is not identifiable if distinct parameter points in Θ are associated with elements of $\mathcal{F}_\Theta$ that only differ on a set having zero probability.

Definition 1.1 Given a parametric model $\mathcal{F}_\Theta = \{f(z;\theta), \theta \in \Theta\}$, a parameter point $\theta_0 \in \Theta$ is said to be *identifiable* if, for every other parameter point $\theta \in \Theta$,

$$P_0\{z\colon f(z;\theta_0) \neq f(z;\theta)\} = \mathrm{E}_0\, 1\left\{\frac{f(Z;\theta_0)}{f(Z;\theta)} \neq 1\right\} > 0, \tag{1.4}$$

where P_0 and E_0 respectively denote probability and expectations with respect to the density function $f(z;\theta_0)$ and $1\{A\}$ is the indicator function of the event A ($1\{A\}$ is equal to one or zero depending on whether the event A is true or false). Model $\mathcal{F}_\Theta$ is said to be *identifiable* if all its parameter points are identifiable. □

Checking the identifiability of a parameter point on the basis of the above definition may look like a hard task. Consider, however, as a measure of dissimilarity between the density $f(z;\theta_0)$ and any other density $f(z;\theta)$ in $\mathcal{F}_\Theta$, the expectation with respect to $f(z;\theta_0)$ of the logarithm of the ratio of the two densities, or *likelihood ratio*,

$$\mathcal{K}(\theta,\theta_0) = \mathrm{E}_0 \ln \frac{f(Z;\theta_0)}{f(Z;\theta)} = \mathrm{E}_0[\ln f(Z;\theta_0)] - \mathrm{E}_0[\ln f(Z;\theta)].$$

If the expectation does not exist, put $\mathcal{K}(\theta,\theta_0) = \infty$. This index of dissimilarity between densities is known as the *Kullback–Leibler index.*

Theorem 1.1 (Kullback–Leibler inequality) *Given a parametric model* $\mathcal{F}_\Theta = \{f(z;\theta), \theta \in \Theta\}$, *for any* $\theta, \theta_0 \in \Theta$ *one has:*

(i) $\mathcal{K}$ *is well defined;*
(ii) $0 \le \mathcal{K} \le \infty$;
(iii) $\mathcal{K}(\theta,\theta_0) = 0$ *if and only if* $P_0\{z\colon f(z;\theta_0) = f(z;\theta)\} = 1$.

Proof. Part (i) is trivial. Because the logarithmic function is strictly concave, Jensen inequality implies

$$-\mathcal{K}(\theta,\theta_0) = \mathrm{E}_0 \ln \frac{f(Z;\theta)}{f(Z;\theta_0)} \le \ln \mathrm{E}_0 \frac{f(Z;\theta)}{f(Z;\theta_0)},$$

with equality if and only if $f(Z;\theta_0)/f(Z;\theta)$ is a degenerate random variable, that is, $f(Z;\theta_0)/f(Z;\theta) = c$ with probability one for some $c > 0$. Because densities must integrate to one, one has that $c = 1$ and so equality holds if and only if $P_0\{z\colon f(z;\theta_0) = f(z;\theta)\} = 1$. Finally,

$$\ln \mathrm{E}_0 \frac{f(Z;\theta)}{f(Z;\theta_0)} = \ln \sum_j f(z_j;\theta) = 0$$

when Z is discrete, and

$$\ln \mathrm{E}_0 \frac{f(Z;\theta)}{f(Z;\theta_0)} = \ln \int f(z;\theta)\, dz = 0$$

when Z is continuous. □

Since $\mathcal{K}(\theta_0,\theta_0) = 0$, as a corollary we obtain the following.

Corollary 1.1 *Given a parametric model* $\mathcal{F}_\Theta$, *a parameter point* $\theta_0 \in \Theta$ *is identifiable if and only if* $\mathcal{K}(\theta,\theta_0)$ *attains its unique minimum on* Θ *at* $\theta = \theta_0$.

Proof. It follows from Theorem 1.1 that, if $\theta \ne \theta_0$, then $\mathcal{K}(\theta,\theta_0) > 0$ if and only if $P_0\{z\colon f(z;\theta_0) = f(z;\theta)\} = 1 - P_0\{z\colon f(z;\theta_0) \ne f(z;\theta)\} < 1$, that is, if and only if (1.4) holds. Hence, the parameter point θ_0 is identifiable if and only if $0 = \mathcal{K}(\theta_0,\theta_0) < \mathcal{K}(\theta,\theta_0)$ for all $\theta \ne \theta_0$. □

The function $\ln f(z;\theta)$, viewed as a function of θ for given z, is called the *log-likelihood* of θ. More generally, we call log-likelihood any function that differs from

Figure 6 Expected log-likelihood of a $\mathcal{N}(\mu, \sigma^2)$ distribution.

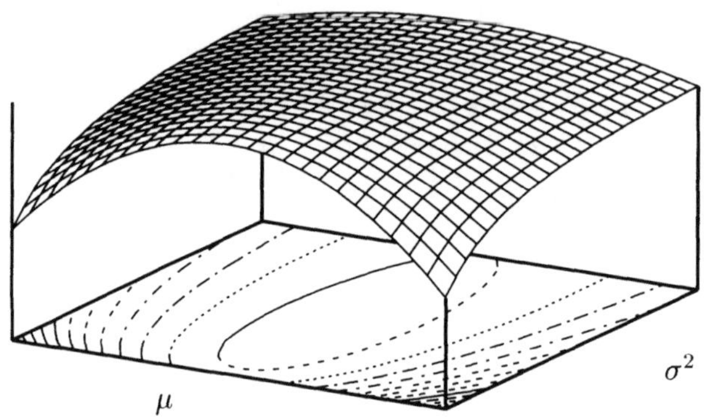

$\ln f(z;\theta)$ up to an additive constant. Searching for a minimum of the Kullback–Leibler index is therefore equivalent to searching for a maximum of the *expected log-likelihood*

$$l(\theta) = c + \mathrm{E}_0 \ln f(Z;\theta),$$

where c is an arbitrary constant. We conclude that a parameter point θ_0 is identifiable if and only if it corresponds to the unique point of maximum of l on Θ. For example, if the parameter space Θ is a convex set and the expected log-likelihood l is a strictly concave function, then l attains a unique maximum on Θ and we only have to verify that it coincides with θ_0.

Example 1.16 Let $\mathcal{F}_\Theta$ be the family of $\mathcal{N}(\mu, \sigma^2)$ distributions, with $\mu \in \Re$ and $\sigma^2 > 0$, and let $\theta_0 = (\mu_0, \sigma_0^2)$ and $\theta = (\mu, \sigma^2)$ be distinct parameter points in Θ. Because the logarithm of the density function is

$$\ln f(z;\theta) = -\frac{1}{2}\ln \sigma^2 - \frac{1}{2}\left(\frac{z-\mu}{\sigma}\right)^2,$$

the expected log-likelihood is of the form

$$l(\theta) = c - \frac{1}{2}\left[\ln \sigma^2 + \frac{\sigma_0^2 + (\mu_0 - \mu)^2}{\sigma^2}\right]$$

(Figure 6), where c is an arbitrary constant and we used the fact that $\mathrm{E}_0(Z-\mu)^2 = \sigma_0^2 + (\mu_0 - \mu)^2$.

For $\sigma^2 > 0$ fixed, maximizing the expected log-likelihood with respect to μ is equivalent to minimizing $(\mu_0 - \mu)^2$. Hence, $\mu = \mu_0$ is the unique point of maximum of

l for all $\sigma^2 > 0$. Substituting $\mu = \mu_0$ in the expected log-likelihood gives

$$l_*(\sigma^2) = l(\mu_0, \sigma^2) = c_* - \frac{1}{2}\left(\ln \sigma^2 + \frac{\sigma_0^2}{\sigma^2}\right),$$

where c_* is an arbitrary constant. It is easily verified that the function $l_*(\sigma^2)$ attains a unique maximum on $(0, \infty)$ at the point where

$$0 = l_*'(\sigma^2) = -\frac{1}{2}\frac{\sigma^2 - \sigma_0^2}{\sigma^4},$$

whose solution is $\sigma^2 = \sigma_0^2$. Because θ_0, whatever its value, is the unique maximum of $l(\theta)$ on Θ, the model is identifiable. □

1.1.6 *REGULAR PARAMETRIC MODELS*

It is often easier to check that a parametric model is identifiable in a weaker sense than the one discussed in the previous section.

Definition 1.2 Given a parametric model $\mathcal{F}_\Theta$, a parameter point $\theta_0 \in \Theta$ is said to be *locally identifiable* if there exists an open neighborhood $\mathcal{O} \subset \Theta$ of θ_0 such that $l(\theta_0) > l(\theta)$ for every other $\theta \in \mathcal{O}$. Model $\mathcal{F}_\Theta$ is said to be *locally identifiable* if all its parameter points are locally identifiable. □

Thus, a parameter point θ_0 is locally identifiable if it corresponds to a unique local maximum of the expected log-likelihood.

We now give sufficient conditions for local identifiability of a wide class of parametric models. This class consists of models that are smooth in the following sense.

Definition 1.3 A parametric model $\mathcal{F}_\Theta$ is said to be *smooth* if:

(i) Θ is an open subset of $\Re^p$;
(ii) the set $\mathcal{S} = \{z\colon f(z;\theta) > 0\}$ does not depend on θ;
(iii) the density $f(z;\theta)$ is twice continuously differentiable with respect to θ for almost all $z \in \mathcal{S}$;
(iv) $\mathrm{E}_\theta\,|\ln f(Z;\theta)| < \infty$ for every $\theta \in \Theta$;
(v) if $g(z)$ is any function of Z such that $\mathrm{E}_\theta\,|g(Z)| < \infty$ for every $\theta \in \Theta$, then the operations of integration and differentiation with respect to θ can be interchanged in $\int g(z) f(z;\theta)\,dz$, that is,

$$\frac{\partial}{\partial\theta}\int g(z) f(z;\theta)\,dz = \int g(z)\,\frac{\partial}{\partial\theta} f(z;\theta)\,dz.$$

□

If a parametric model is smooth, then its log-likelihood is differentiable with respect to θ. The function

$$s(z;\theta) = \frac{\partial}{\partial\theta}\ln f(z;\theta) = \frac{f'(z;\theta)}{f(z;\theta)}$$

is called the *likelihood score*, and plays a fundamental role in statistics. Some of its properties are collected in Theorem 1.2. Here and in what follows, $f'(z;\theta)$ denotes the gradient of $f(z;\theta)$ with respect to θ.

Example 1.17 The family of $\mathcal{N}(\mu, \sigma^2)$ distributions, with $\mu \in \Re$ and $\sigma^2 > 0$, is a smooth parametric model. The components of the likelihood score are, in this case,

$$s_\mu(z;\theta) = \frac{\partial}{\partial \mu} \ln f(z;\theta) = \frac{z-\mu}{\sigma^2},$$
$$s_{\sigma^2}(z;\theta) = \frac{\partial}{\partial \sigma^2} \ln f(z;\theta) = \frac{1}{2\sigma^2}\left[\frac{(z-\mu)^2}{\sigma^2} - 1\right].$$

□

Theorem 1.2 (Information equality) *If $\mathcal{F}_\Theta$ is a smooth parametric model, then:*

(i) $\mathrm{E}_\theta\, s(Z;\theta) = 0$;

(ii) *if $g(z;\theta)$ is any function that is continuously differentiable with respect to θ for almost all $z \in \mathcal{S}$ and such that $\mathrm{E}_\theta\, g(Z;\theta) = 0$ for every $\theta \in \Theta$, then*

$$\mathrm{Cov}_\theta[g(Z;\theta), s(Z;\theta)] = -\,\mathrm{E}_\theta\, g'(Z;\theta);$$

(iii) $\mathrm{Var}_\theta\, s(Z;\theta) = -\,\mathrm{E}_\theta\, s'(Z;\theta)$.

Proof. We only give the proof for the case when Z is a continuous random variable. The proof for the case when Z is discrete is left to the reader as an exercise.

Differentiating with respect to θ both sides of the identity $1 = \int f(z;\theta)\,dz$ gives

$$0 = \frac{\partial}{\partial\theta}\int f(z;\theta)\,dz = \int \frac{f'(z;\theta)}{f(z;\theta)} f(z;\theta)\,dz = \mathrm{E}_\theta\, s(Z;\theta).$$

Further differentiating with respect to θ both sides of the identity $0 = \mathrm{E}_\theta\, g(Z;\theta)$ gives

$$\begin{aligned} 0 &= \frac{\partial}{\partial\theta}\int g(z;\theta) f(z;\theta)\,dz \\ &= \int g'(z;\theta) f(z;\theta)\,dz + \int g(z;\theta)\left[\frac{f'(z;\theta)}{f(z;\theta)}\right]^\top f(z;\theta)\,dz \\ &= \mathrm{E}_\theta\, g'(Z;\theta) + \mathrm{E}_\theta\, g(Z;\theta) s(Z;\theta)^\top \\ &= \mathrm{E}_\theta\, g'(Z;\theta) + \mathrm{Cov}_\theta[g(Z;\theta), s(Z;\theta)], \end{aligned}$$

from which we immediately get conclusion (ii). Given (i) and (ii), one obtains (iii) by simply putting $g(z;\theta) = s(z;\theta)$. □

The $p \times p$ matrix

$$\mathcal{I}(\theta) = \mathrm{E}_\theta\, s(Z;\theta)\, s(Z;\theta)^\top = \mathrm{Var}_\theta\, s(Z;\theta)$$

is called the *expected* or *Fisher information* on θ. By Theorem 1.2

$$\mathcal{I}(\theta) = -\,\mathrm{E}_\theta\, s'(Z;\theta) = -\,\mathrm{E}_\theta \frac{\partial^2}{\partial\theta\partial\theta^\top} \ln f(Z;\theta).$$

Thus, the Fisher information is also equal to (minus) the expectation of the Hessian of the log-likelihood, that is, $\mathcal{I}(\theta)$ is also a measure of the average curvature of the log-likelihood at θ.

If $\mathcal{F}_\Theta$ is a smooth parametric model, then the expected log-likelihood $l(\theta)$ is twice continuously differentiable on Θ. Because Θ is an open set, the following conditions are necessary and sufficient for the parameter point θ_0 to be locally identifiable:

1. $l'(\theta_0) = 0$;
2. the Hessian matrix $l''(\theta_0)$ is finite and n.d.

Since $\mathcal{F}_\Theta$ is sufficiently smooth, we have

$$l'(\theta) = \int \frac{f'(z;\theta)}{f(z;\theta)} f(z;\theta_0)\, dz = \mathrm{E}_0\, s(Z;\theta).$$

Part (i) of Theorem 1.2 implies that $l'(\theta_0) = \mathrm{E}_0\, s(Z;\theta_0) = 0$, and so the first condition is always satisfied. Further,

$$l''(\theta) = \frac{\partial}{\partial\theta} \mathrm{E}_0\, s(Z;\theta) = \mathrm{E}_0\, s'(Z;\theta)$$

is a finite $p \times p$ matrix. Evaluating $l''(\theta)$ at the point $\theta = \theta_0$ gives

$$l''(\theta_0) = \mathrm{E}_0\, s'(Z;\theta_0) = -\mathcal{I}(\theta_0).$$

Except for the sign, the Fisher information is therefore equal to the Hessian of the expected log-likelihood. This result establishes an important relationship between the rank of the Fisher information of a smooth parametric model and the local identifiability of a point θ_0 in the parameter space. In particular, if $\mathcal{I}(\theta_0)$ is a p.d. matrix, then there exists an open neighborhood of θ_0 on which the expected log-likelihood $l(\theta)$ attains its unique maximum at the point θ_0, that is, θ_0 is locally identifiable. Further, if Θ is a convex set and $\mathcal{I}(\theta)$ is p.d. on Θ, then $l(\theta)$ is a strictly concave function and all points in Θ are identifiable.

A parametric model $\mathcal{F}_\Theta$ is called *regular* if it is sufficiently smooth and the Fisher information is continuous and p.d. on Θ. If a parametric model is regular, then every parameter point is locally identifiable.

Example 1.18 To illustrate the above results, consider again the smooth parametric model $\{\mathcal{N}(\mu,\sigma^2), \mu \in \Re, \sigma^2 > 0\}$. The expected log-likelihood has been derived in Example 1.16 and the components of the likelihood score in Example 1.17. It is easy to verify that

$$\frac{\partial l}{\partial \mu} = \frac{\mu_0 - \mu}{\sigma^2} = \mathrm{E}_0\, s_\mu(Z;\theta)$$

and

$$\frac{\partial l}{\partial \sigma^2} = \frac{1}{2\sigma^2}\left[\frac{\sigma_0^2 + (\mu_0 - \mu)^2}{\sigma^2} - 1\right] = \mathrm{E}_0\, s_{\sigma^2}(Z;\theta).$$

Because the components of the likelihood score have mean zero when $\theta = \theta_0$, such a parameter point solves the equation $l'(\theta) = 0$. The elements of the Hessian of the log-likelihood are

$$\frac{\partial^2 \ln f}{\partial \mu^2} = -\frac{1}{\sigma^2}, \qquad \frac{\partial^2 \ln f}{\partial \mu \partial \sigma^2} = -\frac{z-\mu}{\sigma^4}, \qquad \frac{\partial^2 \ln f}{\partial \sigma^4} = \frac{1}{2\sigma^4}\left[\frac{1}{2} - \frac{(z-\mu)^2}{\sigma^2}\right],$$

and it is easy to verify that the expectation of the Hessian of the log-likelihood is equal to the Hessian $l''(\theta)$ of the expected log-likelihood. Evaluating $l''(\theta)$ at the point $\theta = \theta_0$, we get

$$l''(\theta_0) = -\frac{1}{\sigma_0^2}\begin{bmatrix} 1 & 0 \\ 0 & 1/(2\sigma_0^2) \end{bmatrix} = -\mathcal{I}(\theta_0).$$

Since the Hessian of the expected log-likelihood is n.d. at θ_0, such a parameter point corresponds to a local maximum of l and is therefore locally identifiable. □

1.1.7 EXPONENTIAL FAMILIES

An important class of smooth parametric models is the one characterized by density functions of the form

$$f(z;\theta) = \exp\left[\sum_{j=1}^{p} a_j(\theta)T_j(z) + b(\theta) + c(z)\right]$$
$$= \exp\left[a(\theta)^\top T(z) + b(\theta) + c(z)\right],$$

at all points in the support of the distribution, where a: $\Re^p \to \Re^p$ is an invertible function, b: $\Re^p \to \Re$ is a concave function, both functions are twice continuously differentiable, and the vectors $a(\theta)$ and $T(z)$ have the same number p of components. For the model to be regular, the parameter space Θ must be an open subset of $\Re^p$ and the support of the distribution corresponding to $f(z;\theta)$ must not depend on θ. A model in this class is called a *p-parameter (linear) exponential family.*

All parametric models considered in Section 1.1.1 belong to this class.

Example 1.19 For the binomial distribution with index m and parameter θ we have

$$f(z;\theta) = \binom{m}{z}\theta^z(1-\theta)^{m-z} = \exp\left[z\ln\frac{\theta}{1-\theta} + m\ln(1-\theta) + \ln\binom{m}{z}\right].$$

The family of $\mathrm{Bi}(m,\theta)$ distributions is therefore a one-parameter exponential family with $a(\theta) = \ln[\theta/(1-\theta)]$, $T(z) = z$, $b(\theta) = m\ln(1-\theta)$ and $c(z) = \ln\binom{m}{z}$.

For the Poisson distribution with parameter θ we have

$$f(z;\theta) = \frac{\theta^z}{z!}e^{-\theta} = \exp(z\ln\theta - \theta - \ln z!).$$

The family of $\mathcal{P}(\theta)$ distributions is therefore a one-parameter exponential family with $a(\theta) = \ln\theta$, $T(z) = z$, $b(\theta) = -\theta$ and $c(z) = -\ln(z!)$.

For the exponential distribution with parameter θ we have

$$f(z;\theta) = \theta e^{-\theta z} = \exp(-\theta z + \ln\theta).$$

The family of $\mathcal{E}(\theta)$ distributions is therefore a one-parameter exponential family with $a(\theta) = -\theta$, $T(z) = z$, $b(\theta) = \ln\theta$ and $c(z) = 0$.

For the Gaussian distribution with mean μ and variance σ^2, letting $\theta = (\mu,\sigma)$, we have

$$f(z;\theta) = \frac{1}{\sigma\sqrt{2\pi}}\exp\left[-\frac{1}{2}\left(\frac{z-\mu}{\sigma}\right)^2\right]$$
$$= \exp\left\{\frac{\mu z}{\sigma^2} - \frac{z^2}{2\sigma^2} - \frac{1}{2}\left[\frac{\mu^2}{\sigma^2} + \ln(2\pi\sigma^2)\right]\right\}.$$

The family of $\mathcal{N}(\mu,\sigma^2)$ distributions is therefore a two-parameter exponential family with $a_1(\theta) = \mu/\sigma^2$, $a_2(\theta) = -1/(2\sigma^2)$, $T_1(z) = z$, $T_2(z) = z^2$, $c(z) = 0$ and

$$b(\theta) = -\frac{1}{2}\left[\frac{\mu^2}{\sigma^2} + \ln(2\pi\sigma^2)\right].$$

□

It can be shown that the family of beta and gamma distributions are both two-parameter exponential families. The family $\{\mathcal{M}_q(m,\theta)\}$ of multinomial distributions is an exponential family with $p = q-1$ parameters, whereas the family $\{\mathcal{N}_q(\mu,\Sigma)\}$ of q-variate Gaussian distributions is an exponential family with $p = q(q+3)/2$ parameters. Thus, for example, the bivariate Gaussian distribution is a five-parameter exponential family.

An important and useful reparametrization of an exponential family is obtained by putting $\eta = a(\theta)$. With this parametrization, the exponential family is said to be *in canonical form* and the parameter η is called the *canonical* or *natural parameter*. The density function of a model in canonical form is

$$f(z;\eta) = \exp\left[\eta^\top T(z) + d(\eta) + c(z)\right],$$

where $d(\eta) = b(a^{-1}(\eta))$. The main advantage of the canonical form is that the log-density

$$\ln f(z;\eta) = \eta^\top T(z) + d(\eta) + c(z)$$

is a concave function of the parameter η, whereas the likelihood score takes the simple form

$$s(z;\eta) = \frac{\partial}{\partial\eta}\ln f(z;\eta) = T(z) + d'(\eta). \tag{1.5}$$

Regularity of a p-parameter exponential family is easy to verify when the model is in canonical form. Because the Hessian of the log-likelihood is the $p \times p$ matrix $s'(z;\eta) = d''(\eta)$, which does not depend on z, the Fisher information is simply $\mathcal{I}(\eta) = -d''(\eta)$. If d is a strictly concave function, then $-d''$ is a p.d. matrix for all η and so the parametric model is regular.

Example 1.20 The canonical form of the $\mathrm{Bi}(m,\theta)$ distribution is

$$f(z;\eta) = \exp\left[\eta z - m\ln(1+e^\eta) + c(z)\right],$$

where the canonical parameter $\eta = \ln[\theta/(1-\theta)]$ is the logarithm of the *odds-ratio*, that is, the logarithm of the ratio between the probability of success and the probability of failure. Thus, the log-likelihood is

$$\ln f(z;\eta) = \eta z - m\ln(1+e^\eta),$$

where we omitted the arbitrary constant, the likelihood score is

$$s(z;\eta) = z - m\,\frac{e^\eta}{1+e^\eta},$$

and the Fisher information is

$$\mathcal{I}(\eta) = m\,\frac{e^\eta}{(1+e^\eta)^2},$$

which is positive for all η. □

Figure 7 Log-likelihood (solid line) and likelihood score (broken line) of a binomial model with index $m = 20$ and of a Poisson model. Both models are in canonical form and $z = 10$ in both cases. The log-likelihood is shown up to an additive constant.

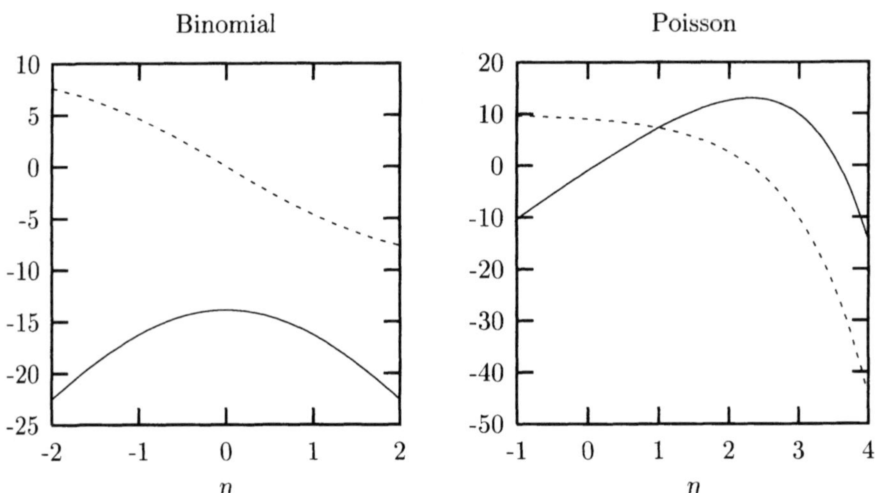

Example 1.21 The canonical form of the $\mathcal{P}(\theta)$ distribution is

$$f(z;\eta) = \exp\left[\eta z - e^\eta - \ln(z!)\right],$$

where $\eta = \ln\theta$. Thus, the log-likelihood is

$$\ln f(z;\eta) = \eta z - e^\eta,$$

where we omitted the arbitrary constant, the likelihood score is $s(z;\eta) = z - e^\eta$, and the Fisher information is $\mathcal{I}(\eta) = e^\eta$, which is positive for all η. The log-likelihood and the likelihood score for this and the previous model are shown in Figure 7. □

If the model is in canonical form, two important relationships may be derived which connect the moments of $T(Z)$ to the derivatives of the function d. The first two moments of the likelihood score (1.5) are

$$\mathrm{E}_\eta\, s(Z;\eta) = \mathrm{E}_\eta\, T(Z) + d'(\eta), \qquad \mathrm{Var}_\eta\, s(Z;\eta) = \mathrm{Var}_\eta\, T(Z).$$

The fact that the likelihood score has mean zero implies

$$\mathrm{E}_\eta\, T(Z) = -d'(\eta),$$

whereas the information equality (Theorem 1.2) implies

$$\mathrm{Var}_\eta\, T(Z) = -d''(\eta).$$

In the case of a one-parameter exponential family with $T(z) = z$, it then follows that $\mathrm{E}_\eta\, Z = -d'(\eta)$ and $\mathrm{Var}_\eta\, Z = -d''(\eta)$.

Figure 8 Bivariate Gaussian density corresponding to $(\sigma_X^2, \sigma_Y^2, \sigma_{XY}) = (1, 1, 0)$.

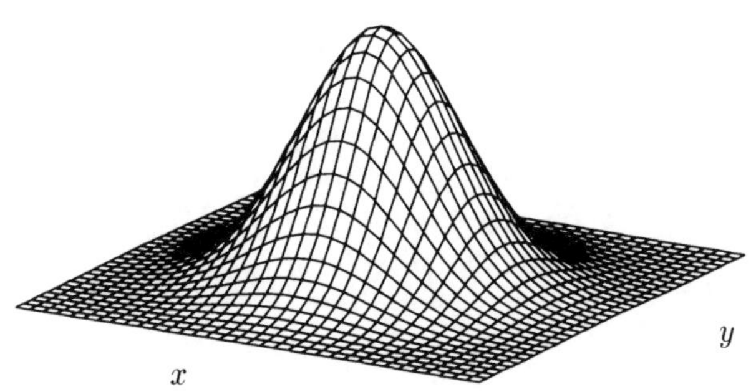

1.2 CONDITIONAL PARAMETRIC MODELS

The q variables under study are often treated asymmetrically, in the sense that the probabilistic behavior of a subset of them, called the ***response variables*** and denoted by $Y = (Y_1, \dots, Y_m)$, is related to the values taken by the other $k = q - m$ variables, called the ***covariates*** and denoted by $X = (X_1, \dots, X_k)$. In this case, the statistical problem typically consists of drawing inferences about the conditional distribution of Y given X. A parametric model for this conditional distribution, or *conditional parametric model*, is a family of conditional distributions of Y given $X = x$ indexed by a finite-dimensional parameter θ. We now consider ways of constructing models of this kind.

1.2.1 CONDITIONING

The first method is to start directly from the joint distribution of $Z = (X, Y)$. Given a family $\{f(z; \theta), \theta \in \Theta\}$ of joint density functions, a conditional parametric model for Y is a family $\{f(y \mid x; \theta), \theta \in \Theta\}$ of density functions such that

$$f(y \mid x; \theta) = \frac{f(x, y; \theta)}{\int f(x, u; \theta)\, du}.$$

Example 1.22 Let the random vector $Z = (X, Y)$ have a bivariate Gaussian distribution with mean μ and variance (dispersion matrix) Σ, where

$$\mu = \begin{pmatrix} \mu_X \\ \mu_Y \end{pmatrix}, \qquad \Sigma = \begin{bmatrix} \sigma_X^2 & \sigma_{XY} \\ \sigma_{XY} & \sigma_Y^2 \end{bmatrix},$$

and $\sigma_{XY}^2 \leq \sigma_Y^2 \sigma_X^2$. If $\sigma_X^2 > 0$, then the conditional distribution of Y given $X = x$ is also Gaussian with mean

$$\mu(x) = \mu_Y + \frac{\sigma_{XY}}{\sigma_X^2}(x - \mu_X) = \mu_Y + \rho_{XY}\,\frac{\sigma_Y}{\sigma_X}(x - \mu_X), \tag{1.6}$$

where $\rho_{XY} = \operatorname{Corr}(X, Y)$, and variance

$$\sigma^2(x) = \sigma_Y^2 - \frac{\sigma_{XY}^2}{\sigma_X^2} = \sigma_Y^2(1 - \rho_{XY}^2) \leq \sigma_Y^2.$$

If $\rho_{XY} = 0$ (Figure 8), then X and Y are independent and the conditional distribution of Y given $X = x$ is equal to the marginal distribution of Y. If $\rho_{XY} = \pm 1$, then X and Y are perfectly correlated and the conditional distribution of Y given $X = x$ is degenerate for it gives all its mass to the point $y = \mu(x)$.

The conditional mean $\mu(x)$ is linear in x, that is, of the form $\mu(x) = \alpha + \beta x$ (Figure 9), with

$$\alpha = \mu_Y - \beta\mu_X, \qquad \beta = \frac{\sigma_{XY}}{\sigma_X^2} = \rho_{XY}\,\frac{\sigma_Y}{\sigma_X},$$

whereas the conditional variance $\sigma^2(x)$ does not depend on x. Notice that the three parameters of the conditional distribution of Y, namely α, β and $\sigma^2 = \sigma_Y^2(1 - \rho_{XY}^2)$, are functions of the five parameters of the joint distribution of X and Y.

These results generalize to the case when Y and X are random vectors of order m and $k = q - m$ respectively and

$$\Sigma = \begin{bmatrix} \Sigma_{XX} & \Sigma_{XY} \\ \Sigma_{YX} & \Sigma_{YY} \end{bmatrix}$$

is a $q \times q$ matrix with $\Sigma_{YX} = \Sigma_{XY}^\top$. If Σ_{XX} is nonsingular, then the conditional distribution of Y given $X = x$ is Gaussian with mean

$$\mu(x) = \mu_Y + \Sigma_{YX}\Sigma_{XX}^{-1}(x - \mu_X)$$

and variance

$$\Sigma(x) = \Sigma_{YY} - \Sigma_{XY}^\top \Sigma_{XX}^{-1} \Sigma_{XY}.$$

The conditional mean of Y is again linear in x, that is, of the form $\mu(x) = \alpha + B^\top x$, where $\alpha = \mu_Y - B^\top \mu_X$ and $B = \Sigma_{XX}^{-1}\Sigma_{XY}$ are an m-vector and a $k \times m$ matrix respectively, whereas the conditional variance $\Sigma(x)$ does not depend on x. □

1.2.2 EXOGENEITY

Focusing attention on the conditional model for Y, as is often done in econometrics, is justified when the relationship between X and Y is stable, in the sense that the conditional distribution of Y given X does not change with changes in the marginal distribution of X.

To formalize this idea, consider a regular parametric model $\mathcal{F}_\Theta$ for the joint distribution of $Z = (X, Y)$. The joint density $f(z; \theta)$ may always be decomposed as

$$f(z; \theta) = f(y \mid x; \theta)\, f_X(x; \theta),$$

Figure 9 Level curves of bivariate Gaussian densities corresponding to $(\sigma_X^2, \sigma_Y^2, \sigma_{XY}) = (1, 1, .5)$ and $(\sigma_X^2, \sigma_Y^2, \sigma_{XY}) = (1, 1, -.5)$. The dotted line denotes the conditional mean of Y given $X = x$.

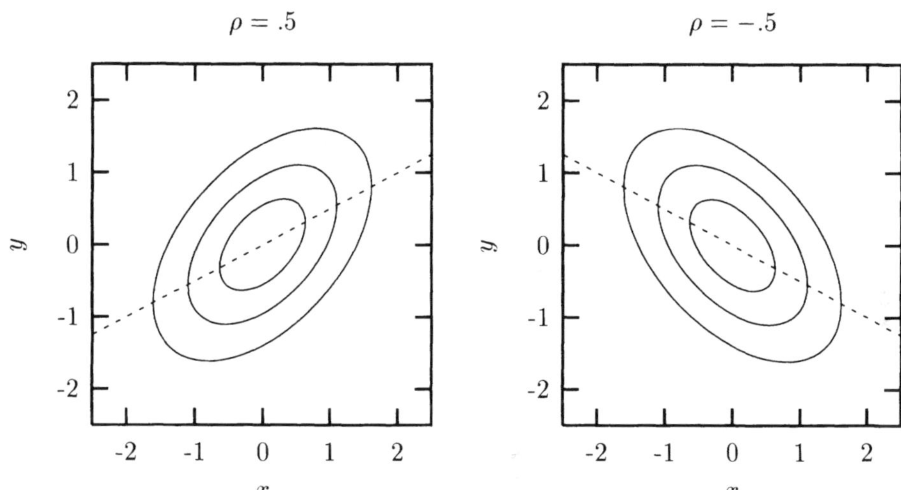

where $f(y \mid x; \theta)$ is the conditional density of Y given $X = x$ and $f_X(x; \theta)$ is the marginal density of X. Corresponding to this decomposition, we have the following decomposition of the log-likelihood

$$\ln f(z; \theta) = \ln f(y \mid x; \theta) + \ln f_X(x; \theta).$$

Suppose that the parameter θ consists of two functionally unrelated components, that is, $\theta = (\theta_1, \theta_2)$ with $\theta_1 \in \Theta_1$, $\theta_2 \in \Theta_2$ and $\Theta = \Theta_1 \times \Theta_2$. In this case it is sometimes said that θ_1 and θ_2 are *variation free.* If

$$\ln f(z; \theta) = \ln f(y \mid x; \theta_1) + \ln f_X(x; \theta_2),$$

then the random vector X is said to be *ancillary* or *exogenous for* θ_1. From now on, we shall follow the econometric practice of using the term exogeneity for this case.

Exogeneity of X for θ_1 corresponds to a decomposition of the log-likelihood into two separate parts: the conditional log-likelihood $\ln f(y \mid x; \theta_1)$ of θ_1 given $X = x$ and the log-likelihood $\ln f_X(x; \theta_2)$ of θ_2, with no functional relationship linking θ_1 and θ_2. A sufficient condition is invariance of the conditional distribution of Y given X to changes in the marginal distribution of X.

Example 1.23 Consider again Example 1.22. The conditional distribution of Y given X is $\mathcal{N}(\alpha + \beta X, \sigma^2)$, where

$$\alpha = \mu_Y - \beta\mu_X, \qquad \beta = \frac{\sigma_{XY}}{\sigma_X^2}, \qquad \sigma^2 = \sigma_Y^2 - \frac{\sigma_{XY}^2}{\sigma_X^2}.$$

Exogeneity of X for the parameter $\theta_1 = (\alpha, \beta, \sigma^2)$ in the conditional distribution of Y requires the absence of any functional relationship between θ_1 and the parameter $\theta_2 = (\mu_X, \sigma_X^2)$ in the marginal distribution of X. This means that changes in θ_2 can only affect the parameters μ_Y and σ_Y^2 of the marginal distribution of Y and the covariance σ_{XY} between X and Y through the relations $\mu_Y = \alpha + \beta\mu_X$, $\sigma_Y^2 = \beta^2\sigma_X^2 + \sigma^2$, and $\sigma_{XY} = \beta\sigma_X^2$. □

If the random vector X is exogenous for θ_1, then the elements of the likelihood score are

$$\frac{\partial}{\partial\theta_1}\ln f(z;\theta) = \frac{\partial}{\partial\theta_1}\ln f(y \mid x;\theta_1),$$
$$\frac{\partial}{\partial\theta_2}\ln f(z;\theta) = \frac{\partial}{\partial\theta_2}\ln f_X(x;\theta_2),$$

which we denote by $s(y \mid x;\theta_1)$ and $s(x;\theta_2)$ respectively. The function $s(y \mid x;\theta_1)$ is called the *conditional likelihood score*, while the matrix

$$\mathcal{I}(\theta_1 \mid x) = \mathrm{E}_{\theta_1}[s(Y \mid X;\theta_1)\, s(Y \mid X;\theta_1)^\top \mid X = x],$$

where the expectation is with respect to the conditional distribution of Y given $X = x$, is called the *Fisher information on θ_1 given $X = x$*.

Under exogeneity, the cross-derivatives of the log-likelihood are equal to zero, which implies that the two components of the likelihood score are uncorrelated.

Theorem 1.3 *Suppose that the distribution of the random vector $Z = (X, Y)$ belongs to a regular parametric model with parameter $\theta = (\theta_1, \theta_2)$ and parameter space $\Theta = \Theta_1 \times \Theta_2$. If X is exogenous for θ_1, then the Fisher information on θ is block diagonal with respect to θ_1 and θ_2, that is,*

$$\mathcal{I}(\theta) = \begin{bmatrix} \mathcal{I}_1(\theta) & 0 \\ 0 & \mathcal{I}_2(\theta_2) \end{bmatrix},$$

where $\mathcal{I}_1(\theta) = \int \mathcal{I}(\theta_1 \mid x)\, f_X(x;\theta_2)\, dx$ is the expectation of $\mathcal{I}(\theta_1 \mid X)$ with respect to the marginal distribution of X.

Thus, if X is exogenous for θ_1, then no information about θ_1 is lost by focusing attention on the conditional model for Y disregarding the marginal model for X.

1.2.3 CONDITIONAL LOCATION AND SCALE MODELS

If the joint distribution of (X, Y) is unknown, one may sometimes assume, on the basis of specific knowledge of the problem under study, that there exist transformations $\mu(X)$ and $\sigma(X) > 0$ of X and a random variable U distributed independently of X such that $Y = \mu(X) + \sigma(X)\, U$. The interpretation of the random variable U depends on the nature of the problem. A common interpretation is that U represents measurement errors in Y.

Because U generates the conditional distribution of Y given $X = x$ through a location and scale transformation, the conditional density of Y given $X = x$ is

$$f(y \mid x) = \frac{1}{\sigma(x)}\, f\left(\frac{y - \mu(x)}{\sigma(x)}\right),$$

where f denotes the density of U. If $\operatorname{E} U = 0$ and $\operatorname{Var} U = 1$, then $\operatorname{E}(Y \mid X) = \mu(X)$ and $\operatorname{Var}(Y \mid X) = \sigma(X)^2$.

When $\mu(x) = h(x;\beta)$ and $\sigma(x) = s(x;\psi)$ are known parametric functions of x, letting $\theta = (\beta, \psi)$ gives a conditional parametric model for Y. In this context, it is quite natural to assume that X is exogenous for θ. The special case when $h(x;\beta) = \beta_1 + \beta_2 x$, $\beta = (\beta_1, \beta_2)$, is an example of a *linear model*. Notice that one should always check whether the chosen parametrization of $\sigma(x)$ is *admissible*, that is, satisfies the condition $\sigma(x) > 0$ for all x.

Example 1.24 If Y is a continuous random variable that can take values on the whole real line, then a conditional parametric model for Y may be generated by the standard Gaussian distribution by letting $\mu(x) = \beta_1 + \beta_2 x$ and $\sigma(x) = \exp(\psi_1 + \psi_2 x)$, where the exponential function is used to ensure that $\sigma(x) > 0$. □

1.2.4 CONDITIONAL PARAMETRIZATIONS

A third method of constructing a conditional parametric model is to start from a parametric family $\mathcal{F}_\Theta = \{f(y;\theta), \theta \in \Theta\}$ of densities of Y and generate a parametric family $\{f(y \mid x;\beta), \beta \in B\}$ of conditional densities of Y given $X = x$ by specifying θ as a known parametric function $\theta(x;\beta)$ of x. The choice of the parametric family $\mathcal{F}_\Theta$ depends on the nature of the problem. In any case, it is important to check that the chosen parametrization is *admissible*, that is, does not violate the admissible range of θ.

Example 1.25 Let Y be a continuous non-negative random variable that represents the duration of stay in a given state. One way of generating a conditional parametric model for Y is to consider the family of exponential distributions with parameter θ and specify θ as a known parametric function of X. Letting $\theta(x;\beta) = \beta_1 + \beta_2 x$, where $\beta = (\beta_1, \beta_2)$, is not appropriate in this case for it violates the condition that $\theta > 0$. An admissible parametrization is obtained instead by letting $\ln \theta(x;\beta) = \beta_1 + \beta_2 x$, which is equivalent to the assumption that $\operatorname{E}(Y \mid X = x) = \exp(-\beta_1 - \beta_2 x)$. Because

$$\frac{\partial}{\partial x} \ln \operatorname{E}(Y \mid X = x) = -\beta_2,$$

the parameter β_2 may be interpreted as the proportional effect of a unit change in x on the conditional mean of Y. □

Example 1.26 Consider the family of Weibull distributions with parameter $\theta = (\alpha, \gamma)$. Parametrizing the non-negative parameter γ as $\gamma(x;\beta) = \exp(\beta_1 + \beta_2 x)$, where $\beta = (\beta_1, \beta_2)$, gives the conditional hazard function $h(y \mid x;\beta) = \alpha y^{\alpha-1} \exp(\beta_1 + \beta_2 x)$. This model retains the proportional effect of the covariate on the hazard, but it allows for dependence on the duration y through the term $\alpha y^{\alpha-1}$. □

1.3 NONPARAMETRIC AND SEMIPARAMETRIC PROBLEMS

A statistical model $\mathcal{P}$ for the probability distribution P_0 of Z is called *nonparametric* when it is impossible to index the elements of $\mathcal{P}$ by a finite-dimensional parameter.

An example is the case when the only known thing about P_0 is that it belongs to the family of continuous distributions on $\Re$.

A statistical problem is called *nonparametric* when one is required to draw inferences about some function associated with the distribution P_0 and this function belongs to a class of functions that cannot be indexed by a finite number of parameters.

Example 1.27 Consider the problem of drawing inferences about the density of a distribution P_0. The statistical problem is nonparametric when the only known thing about P_0 is that it belongs to the family of probability distributions defined on $\Re$ that are continuous and have a twice continuously differentiable density. □

A statistical problem is called *semiparametric* when one is required to draw inferences about a finite-dimensional parameter $\theta_0 \in \Theta$ which does not characterize the distribution P_0. The parameter point θ_0 can generally be represented as $\theta_0 = T(P_0)$, that is, as the value corresponding to P_0 of a noninvertible transformation $T\colon \mathcal{P} \to \Theta$, called the *statistical functional*.

Example 1.28 Consider the problem of drawing inferences about the mean and the variance of a distribution P_0 with density function f_0. The statistical problem is semiparametric if the only thing which is known about P_0 is that it belongs to the family $\mathcal{P}$ of probability distributions on $\Re$ that are continuous and have finite variance. In this case, the parameter of interest is the value corresponding to f_0 of the statistical functional $T = (T_1, T_2)$ defined on $\mathcal{P}$ by

$$T_1(f) = \int z f(z)\, dz, \qquad T_2(f) = \int z^2 f(z)\, dz - [\theta_1(f)]^2.$$

□

Semiparametric statistical problems often arise when one is only interested in certain aspects of a distribution and the available information is not sufficient to restrict P_0 to a parametric family. In a predictive context, which are the interesting aspects of a distribution ultimately depends on the way in which the consequences of prediction error are evaluated.

1.3.1 UNCONDITIONAL PREDICTION PROBLEMS

Consider the problem of predicting a random variable Z knowing its probability distribution. A *predictor* is simply a number $c \in \Re$ which is used to approximate the value taken by Z. The difference $z - c$ is the error made when z is the realized value of Z and c is the chosen predictor. Given c, the variability of the prediction error is represented by the random variable $U = Z - c$.

In order to choose a predictor optimally, let the loss or negative utility when c is the predictor and z is a particular realization of Z be represented by the number $\ell(z - c)$, where ℓ is a non-negative function, called the *loss function*, which satisfies the following conditions:

(L.1) $\ell(0) = 0$;
(L.2) if $0 < u < u'$, then $\ell(0) \leq \ell(u) \leq \ell(u')$ and $\ell(0) \leq \ell(-u) \leq \ell(-u')$;

(L.3) $\ell\colon \Re \to \Re_+$ is integrable with respect to the distribution of Z.

Condition (L.1) is only an innocuous normalization. Condition (L.2) requires the loss function to be nondecreasing for $u > 0$ and nonincreasing for $u < 0$. The integrability condition (L.3) is satisfied if the loss function is bounded from above, but otherwise restricts the class of problems that may be considered. Notice that the loss function is not required to be continuous, nor convex, nor symmetric, nor differentiable.

For a given c, the loss $\ell(Z - c)$ is a transformation of the random variable Z. The expected loss $r(c) = \mathrm{E}\,\ell(Z - c)$ is called the *risk* associated with the predictor c. A *best predictor* of Z is a number $c_* \in \Re$ such that $r(c_*) \le r(c)$ for all other c. Notice that we do not require c_* to coincide with one of the possible values of Z.

Clearly, a best predictor depends on both the distribution of Z and the particular loss function adopted. The next result characterizes the best predictor under two different loss functions: the quadratic loss function $\ell(u) = u^2$ and the absolute loss function $\ell(u) = |u|$. Figure 10 shows the difference between the two loss functions. Notice that the quadratic loss is smooth, whereas the absolute loss is not differentiable at the origin. The absolute loss exceeds the quadratic loss for $|u| < 1$, whereas the opposite is true for $|u| > 1$. Finally, the absolute loss weights the errors proportionally to their size, whereas the quadratic loss penalizes larger errors proportionally more than smaller errors. The risk of a predictor under the quadratic loss is also called its *mean squared error (MSE)*, whereas its risk under the absolute loss is also called its *mean absolute error (MAE)*.

Theorem 1.4 *Let Z be a random variable with mean μ and variance $0 < \sigma^2 < \infty$. If $\ell(u) = u^2$, then the unique best predictor of Z is equal to μ and its associated risk is equal to σ^2. If $\ell(u) = |u|$, then a best predictor of Z is equal to a median of Z and its associated risk is equal to the mean absolute deviation from the median.*

Proof. If $\ell(u) = u^2$, then the risk of a predictor c is $r(c) = \mathrm{E}(Z - c)^2 = \sigma^2 + (\mu - c)^2$. Because σ^2 does not depend on c, the function $r(c)$ attains its minimum value of σ^2 when $c = \mu$.

If $\ell(u) = |u|$, then the risk of a predictor c is

$$\mathrm{E}\,|Z - c| = \mathrm{E}(Z - c \,|\, Z > c)\,\Pr\{Z > c\} + \mathrm{E}(c - Z \,|\, Z \le c)\,\Pr\{Z \le c\}.$$

Recall now that the set of medians of Z is a closed interval $[m_0, m_1]$. If ζ is a median of Z and $\zeta \le m_1 < c$, then

$$\begin{aligned}\mathrm{E}(Z - c \,|\, Z > c)\,\Pr\{Z > c\} = {}& \mathrm{E}(Z - c \,|\, Z > \zeta)\,\Pr\{Z > \zeta\} \\ & - \mathrm{E}(Z - c \,|\, \zeta < Z \le c)\,\Pr\{\zeta < Z \le c\},\end{aligned}$$

whereas

$$\begin{aligned}\mathrm{E}(c - Z \,|\, Z \le c)\,\Pr\{Z \le c\} = {}& \mathrm{E}(c - Z \,|\, \zeta < Z \le c)\,\Pr\{\zeta < Z \le c\} \\ & + \mathrm{E}(c - Z \,|\, Z \le \zeta)\,\Pr\{Z \le \zeta\}.\end{aligned}$$

Letting $d(c) = \mathrm{E}\,|Z - c| - \mathrm{E}\,|Z - \zeta|$, we get

$$d(c) = (c - \zeta)[\Pr\{Z \le \zeta\} - \Pr\{Z > \zeta\}] + 2\,\mathrm{E}(c - Z \,|\, \zeta < Z \le c)\,\Pr\{\zeta < Z \le c\},$$

Figure 10 Quadratic and absolute loss functions.

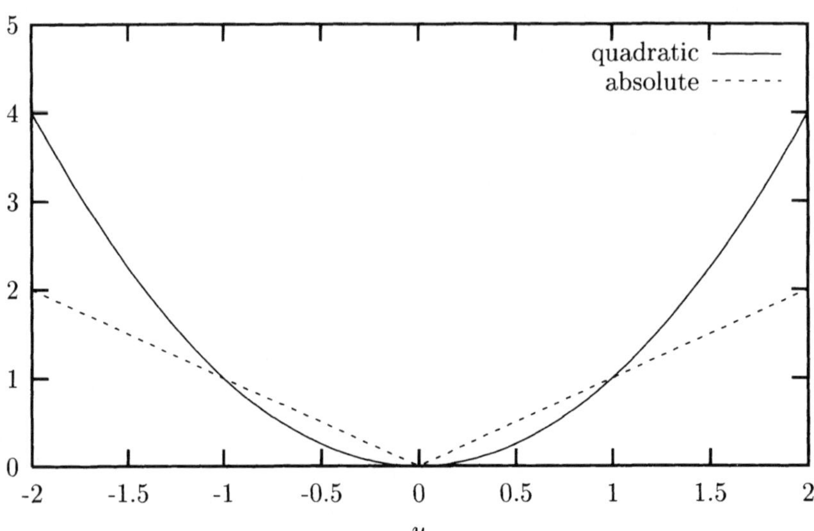

and therefore $d(c) > d(\zeta) = 0$ for all $c > m_1$. By a similar argument, $d(c) > d(\zeta) = 0$ for all $c < m_0$, which completes the proof. □

If Z has a continuous and symmetric distribution with finite mean and strictly positive density, then the median is unique and coincides with the mean. More generally, one can show that, if the distribution of Z is symmetric about μ, then μ is a best predictor of Z for every loss function that is convex and symmetric about zero (see e.g. Lehmann 1983, p. 55).

The quadratic and absolute loss functions are convex and symmetric about zero. A loss function that is convex but not symmetric is

$$\ell_p(u) = [p\,1\{u \geq 0\} + (1-p)\,1\{u < 0\}]\,|u| = [p - 1\{u < 0\}]\,u,$$

with $0 < p < 1$, called the *asymmetric absolute loss function.* This loss function is shown in Figure 11 for various values of p. Unless $p = 1/2$, which corresponds to symmetric absolute loss, prediction errors are now penalized differently depending on whether they are positive (underprediction) or negative (overprediction). When $p > 1/2$, positive errors are penalized more heavily, and increasingly so as p increases. When $p < 1/2$, negative errors are penalized instead more heavily. By an argument similar to that used for the symmetric absolute loss, one can show that a best predictor of Z is in this case a pth quantile of Z.

1.3.2 CONDITIONAL PREDICTION PROBLEMS

Let $Z = (X, Y)$, where Y is a random variable and X is a random k-vector. If X and Y are not independent and X is observable, then it is reasonable to predict Y through a transformation of X, that is, through a rule $h\colon \Re^k \to \Re$ which associates

Figure 11 Asymmetric absolute loss functions.

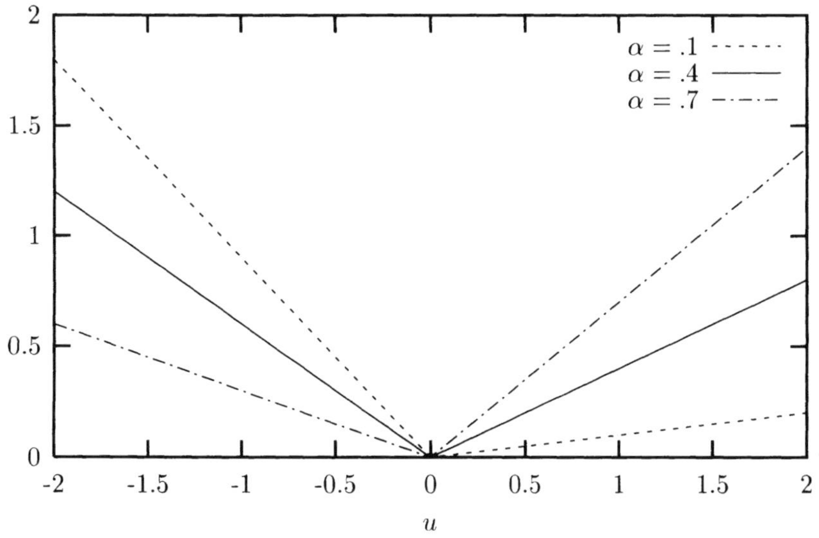

with each realization x of X a number $h(x)$. Because the predictor is now a random variable $h(X)$, its associated risk is $r(h) = \mathrm{E}\,\ell(Y - h(X))$, where the expectation is with respect to the joint distribution of X and Y. A best conditional predictor of Y given X is a function h_* such that $r(h_*) \leq r(h)$ for every other function h. In particular, because this must be true if g is a constant function, the risk of a best conditional predictor cannot exceed that of an unconditional predictor.

In order to construct a best conditional predictor notice that, by the law of iterated expectations,

$$\mathrm{E}\,\ell(Y - h(X)) = \mathrm{E}\{\mathrm{E}[\ell(Y - h(X)) \,|\, X = x]\},$$

where the first expectation on the right-hand side is with respect to the marginal distribution of X and the second is with respect to the conditional distribution of Y given $X = x$. Therefore, a function h_* is a best conditional predictor if, for every x in the support of X, $h_*(x)$ solves the problem

$$\min_{c \in \Re} \mathrm{E}[\ell(Y - c) \,|\, X = x].$$

We can now use the results of Section 1.3.1. For example, conditionally on $X = x$, a minimum MSE predictor of Y is a solution to the problem

$$\min_{c \in \Re} \mathrm{E}[(Y - c)^2 \,|\, X = x].$$

If Y has finite variance σ_Y^2, the unique solution to this problem is the mean $\mu(x) = \mathrm{E}(Y \,|\, X = x)$ of the conditional distribution of Y given $X = x$, and the risk associated with $\mu(x)$ is equal to the variance $\sigma^2(x) = \mathrm{Var}(Y \,|\, X = x)$ of the conditional distribution of Y given $X = x$. Because this must hold for all x in the support of X, the minimum MSE predictor of Y conditionally on X is the random variable $\mu(X) = E(Y \mid X)$, and its associated risk is equal to $\mathrm{E}\,\sigma^2(X)$. By the law of total variance

$$\mathrm{E}\,\sigma^2(X) = \sigma_Y^2 - \mathrm{Var}\,\mu(X) \leq \sigma_Y^2. \tag{1.7}$$

This is a direct proof of the fact that the risk associated with $\mu(X)$ cannot exceed that associated with the best unconditional predictor μ_Y. Notice that the gain, in terms of reduced risk, from using $\mu(X)$ increases with its variability.

The prediction error $U = Y - \mu(X)$ necessarily satisfies

$$\mathrm{E}(U \mid X) = \mathrm{E}(Y \mid X) - \mu(X) = 0,$$

which implies that U is mean independent of X. Thus, by the law of iterated expectations,

$$\mathrm{E}\,g(X)\,U = \mathrm{E}\{\mathrm{E}[g(X)\,U \mid X]\} = \mathrm{E}[g(X)\,\mathrm{E}(U \mid X)] = 0$$

for every function g: $\Re \to \Re$, that is, the prediction error U must be uncorrelated with every function of X. In particular, $\mathrm{E}\,U = 0$, $\mathrm{E}\,XU = 0$ and $\mathrm{E}\,\mu(X)\,U = 0$, that is, U must have mean zero and be uncorrelated with X and $\mu(X)$. Further

$$\mathrm{Var}(U \mid X) = \mathrm{Var}[Y - \mu(X) \mid X] = \sigma^2(X),$$

and so $\mathrm{Var}\,U = \mathrm{E}[\mathrm{Var}(U \mid X)] = \mathrm{E}\,\sigma^2(X)$.

By a similar argument one can show that a minimum MAE conditional predictor of Y given X is a median of the conditional distribution of Y given X, denoted by $\zeta(X)$ or by $\mathrm{Med}(Y \mid X)$, whereas a best conditional predictor under the asymmetric absolute loss function ℓ_p is a pth quantile $\zeta_p(X)$ of the conditional distribution of Y given X, where $\zeta_p(x)$ is a number such that

$$\Pr\{Y < \zeta_p(x) \mid X = x\} \leq p \leq \Pr\{Y \leq \zeta_p(x) \mid X = x\}.$$

There is no necessary relationship between all these conditional predictors. For example, $\mu(X)$ may be linear in X even when $\zeta_p(X)$ is not, or they can both be linear in X but have a different slope. It is even possible that one is increasing in X and the other decreasing.

1.3.3 MODELS OF THE CONDITIONAL MEAN

Classical regression analysis focuses on $\mu(x) = \mathrm{E}(Y \mid X = x)$. Viewed as a function of x, this is called the *conditional mean function (CMF)* or *(mean) regression function* of Y. We have seen that, in a predictive context, interest in the CMF of Y may be justified with reference to quadratic loss. Of course, using loss functions different from quadratic loss leads us to emphasize other aspects of the conditional distribution of Y given X, such as the median or a set of quantiles.

A *regression model* assumes that the CMF of Y belongs to a known family $\mathcal{H}$ of functions of x. A regression model is called *parametric* or *nonparametric* depending on whether or not the family $\mathcal{H}$ can be put in a one-to-one correspondence with a subset Θ of the real Euclidean space $\Re^p$ and represented as $\mathcal{H}_\Theta = \{h(x;\theta), \theta \in \Theta\}$. A parametric regression model $\mathcal{H}_\Theta$ is said to be *correctly specified* if there exists a $\theta_0 \in \Theta$

such that $\mu(\cdot) = h(\cdot;\theta_0)$ or, equivalently, $\mathrm{E}[Y - h(x;\theta_0)]^2 = \mathrm{E}\,\sigma^2(X)$. A parameter point θ_0 is said to be *identifiable* if $\mathrm{E}[Y - h(x;\theta)]^2 > \mathrm{E}[Y - h(x;\theta_0)]^2$ for any other $\theta \in \Theta$. Thus, θ_0 is identifiable if $\mathrm{E}[Y - h(x;\theta)]^2$ attains its unique minimum on Θ at $\theta = \theta_0$.

An important class of parametric regression models specifies $h(x;\theta)$ as a linear function of a finite-dimensional parameter θ. Thus, $\mu(x)$ is assumed to be of the form

$$h(x;\theta) = \alpha + \beta_1 h_1(x) + \cdots + \beta_q h_q(x),$$

where $h_1, \ldots, h_q$ are known functions of x and $\theta = (\alpha, \beta_1, \ldots, \beta_q)$. A model of this kind is called a *linear regression model*. An important special case is when $h(x;\theta)$ is linear in both θ and x, that is, of the form

$$h(x;\theta) = \alpha + \beta_1 x_1 + \cdots + \beta_k x_k = \alpha + \beta^\top x.$$

Example 1.29 Let X be a scalar random variable. A model that is linear in both θ and x is the *simple regression model* $h(x;\theta) = \alpha + \beta x$, $\theta = (\alpha, \beta)$. The model parameters have a simple interpretation as $\alpha = \mu(0)$ and $\beta = \mu'(x)$. In fact, this model is equivalent to the assumption that the derivative of the CMF with respect to x is constant and equal to β. From Example 1.22, this model is perfectly appropriate when the joint distribution of (X, Y) is Gaussian.

A model that is linear in θ but not in x is $h(x;\theta) = \alpha + \beta_1 x + \beta_2 x^2$, $\theta = (\alpha, \beta_1, \beta_2)$, which corresponds to the assumption that the derivative of the CMF with respect to x varies linearly with x. This model allows for more flexibility in the shape of the CMF and reduces to the previous model when $\beta_2 = 0$. If $\beta_2 \neq 0$, the function m is strictly concave or convex in x depending on $\beta_2 < 0$ or $\beta_2 > 0$, and has a unique inflexion point at $x = -\beta_1/2\beta_2$. □

There are cases when using a linear regression model implies no loss of generality from the statistical viewpoint.

Example 1.30 If D is a discrete random variable that can only take a finite number of values, then it is always possible to represent the conditional mean Y given D by a linear regression model. Specifically, if $0, 1, \ldots, k$ are the possible values of D and $\mu_j = \mathrm{E}(Y \mid D = j)$, then one may represent $\mathrm{E}(Y \mid D)$ either by the vector $(\mu_0, \mu_1, \ldots, \mu_k)$, or by the linear regression model $\mathrm{E}(Y \mid D) = \alpha + \sum_{j=1}^k \beta_j X_j$, where $\alpha = \mu_0$, $\beta_j = \mu_j - \mu_0$, and X_j is a 0–1 random variable that takes value one when $D = j$ and value zero otherwise.

If C and D are 0–1 random variables and $\mu_{hj} = \mathrm{E}(Y \mid C = h, D = j)$, then $\mathrm{E}(Y \mid C, D)$ may be represented either by the matrix

$$\begin{bmatrix} \mu_{00} & \mu_{01} \\ \mu_{10} & \mu_{11} \end{bmatrix},$$

or by the linear regression model $\mathrm{E}(Y \mid C, D) = \alpha + \beta_1 X_1 + \beta_2 X_2 + \beta_3 X_3$, where $\alpha = \mu_{00}$ and

$$\begin{aligned} \beta_1 &= \mu_{10} - \mu_{00}, & X_1 &= C, \\ \beta_2 &= \mu_{01} - \mu_{00}, & X_2 &= D, \\ \beta_3 &= \mu_{11} - \mu_{10} - \mu_{01} + \mu_{00}, & X_3 &= CD. \end{aligned}$$

Restrictions on the conditional mean $\mathrm{E}(Y \mid C, D)$ imply restrictions on the parameters of the linear model, and vice versa. For example, $\mathrm{E}(Y \mid C, D) = \mathrm{E}(Y \mid D)$ (that is, Y is mean independent of C given D) if and only if $\beta_1 = \beta_3 = 0$, $\mathrm{E}(Y \mid C, D) = \mathrm{E}(Y \mid C)$ (that is, Y is mean independent of D given C) if and only if $\beta_2 = \beta_3 = 0$, whereas the difference $\mathrm{E}(Y \mid C, D = 1) - \mathrm{E}(Y \mid C, D = 0)$ does not depend on C if and only if $\beta_3 = 0$. □

There are also cases when a linear regression model may be justified on the basis of some economic theory. This has two main advantages: the restrictions on the behavior of the CMF are theoretically grounded and the model parameters have an economic interpretation.

Example 1.31 Consider a household that maximizes preferences represented by a utility function of the form $\nu(q_1, \ldots, q_J) = \prod_{j=1}^J (q_j - \gamma_j)^{\beta_j}$, under the linear budget constraint $\sum_j p_j q_j \leq x$, where q_j denotes the quantity consumed of the jth good, p_j denotes its market price and x denotes money income. It can be shown that, if $x > \sum_k p_k \gamma_k$, then expenditures on each good must satisfy the set of relationships

$$p_j q_j = p_j \gamma_j + \beta_j (x - \sum_k p_k \gamma_k), \qquad j = 1, \ldots, J,$$

called the *linear expenditure system.* If all households face the same set of prices, then the variability of expenditures across households may be entirely attributed to the variability of income and tastes. Treating x as a realization of a random variable X and setting $Y_j = p_j q_j$ and $\gamma_j = \mu_j + U_j$, where U_j is a random variable such that $\mathrm{E}(U_j \mid X) = 0$, gives a system of J linear regression equations of the form

$$\mathrm{E}(Y_j \mid X) = \alpha_j + \beta_j X, \qquad j = 1, \ldots, J,$$

where $\alpha_j = p_j \mu_j - \beta_j \sum_k p_k \mu_k$. □

A linear regression model is convenient because it simplifies considerably the statistical problem and makes it easy to interpret the results of an analysis. If however, as sometimes happens, such a model is only chosen because of convenience, then it is important to ask whether it makes sense given the nature of the statistical problem.

Example 1.32 Let the random variable Y be an indicator of labor force participation and let the random vector X represent personal characteristics such as age, schooling level, etc. Specifically, let $Y = 1$ if a person is in the labor force and $Y = 0$ otherwise. A simple probabilistic model for the conditional distribution of Y given $X = x$ is the Bernoulli model where $\mu(x) = \mathrm{E}(Y \mid X = x) = \Pr\{Y = 1 \mid X = x\}$ and $\sigma^2(x) = \mathrm{Var}(Y \mid X = x) = \mu(x)[1 - \mu(x)]$. Since $\mu(x)$ coincides with a conditional probability, we must have that $0 \leq \mu(x) \leq 1$ for all x in the support of X, with strict inequality if the conditional distribution of Y is nondegenerate. Further, it is easily seen that $0 \leq \sigma^2(x) \leq 1/4$ for all x in the support of X.

Specifying $\mu(x)$ as linear gives the so-called *linear probability model.* Although sometimes used in practice, this model is inadmissible because it violates the conditions on the range of $\mu(x)$ and $\sigma^2(x)$. An admissible model is obtained by assuming that the CMF is of the form

$$h(x; \theta) = G(\alpha + \beta^\top x), \qquad \theta = (\alpha, \beta), \tag{1.8}$$

Figure 12 Comparison between the probit $\Phi(\alpha + \beta x)$ and the logit model $\Lambda(\pi(\alpha + \beta x)/\sqrt{3})$ for $\alpha = \beta = 1$. The reparametrization of the logit model is necessary because the standard logistic distribution has variance equal to $\pi^2/3$.

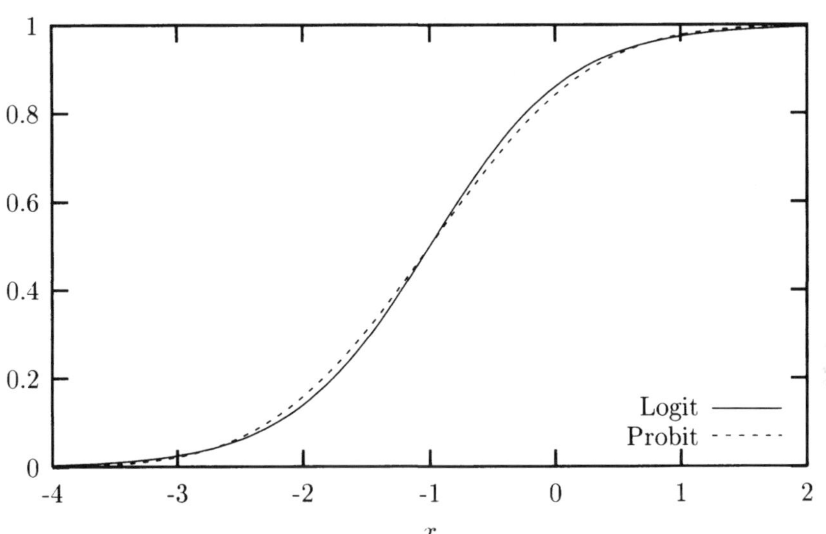

where G is some monotonic function mapping $\Re$ into the unit interval $(0, 1)$. Monotonicity is important for it guarantees that the model is identifiable. Notice that $h(x;\theta)$ depends on x and θ only through the linear combination or "index" $\alpha + \beta^\top x$. This implies that, although nonlinear in θ, model (1.8) has two properties in common with linear models. First, since the function G is non-negative, β_j and $\partial h(x;\theta)/\partial x_j$ have the same sign. Second, the ratio of partial derivatives

$$\frac{\partial h(x;\theta)/\partial x_j}{\partial h(x;\theta)/\partial x_l}, \qquad j, l = 1, \ldots, k$$

is constant and equal to β_j/β_l. Models of this kind are called *single-index models.*

When $G = \Phi$, where Φ is the distribution function of the $\mathcal{N}(0, 1)$ distribution, we obtain the *probit model.* When $G = \Lambda$, where Λ is the distribution function of the standard logistic, we obtain the *logit model*

$$h(x;\theta) = \Lambda(\alpha + \beta^\top x) = \frac{\exp(\alpha + \beta^\top x)}{1 + \exp(\alpha + \beta^\top x)}, \qquad \theta = (\alpha, \beta).$$

As shown in Figure 12, the logistic distribution is very similar to the Gaussian except in the tails, which are slightly thicker. If

$$\eta(x) = \ln \frac{\mu(x)}{1 - \mu(x)}$$

denotes the log-odds, then the logit model implies that $\eta(x) = \alpha + \beta^\top x$, that is, the log-odds are linear in x. This parametrization is admissible because $\eta(x)$ can take any value on the real line. □

Nonlinear regression models arise quite naturally when a random variable with a linear CMF is subject to censoring or truncation.

Example 1.33 Let the random variable Y^* be distributed as $\mathcal{N}(\alpha + \beta x, \sigma^2)$ conditionally on $X = x$, and consider the distribution of the random variable $Y = \max(0, Y^*)$, which coincides with Y^* when $Y^* > 0$ and is equal to zero otherwise. The random variable Y is called the *left-censored version* of Y^* with fixed censoring at zero, whereas the random variable which coincides with Y^* when $Y^* > 0$ but is otherwise undefined is called the *left-truncated version* of Y^* with fixed truncation at zero. For example, Y^* may represent desired expenditure on a particular good by a household, while Y may represent actual expenditure, which cannot be negative. With this interpretation, the model is known in the economic literature as the *tobit model*, after Tobin (1958) who first applied this model to the demand for cars in the USA.

First notice that the conditional distribution of Y given $X = x$ is of the mixed continuous–discrete type, for the conditional probability of the event that $Y = 0$ is

$$\Pr\{Y = 0 \,|\, X = x\} = \Pr\{Y^* \leq 0 \,|\, X = x\} = 1 - \Phi\left(\frac{\alpha + \beta x}{\sigma}\right) > 0.$$

Now let $D = 1\{Y > 0\}$ be the binary indicator of the event that $Y > 0$ and notice that the CMF of Y is

$$\mu(x) = \mu_0(x) \Pr\{D = 0 \,|\, X = x\} + \mu_1(x) \Pr\{D = 1 \,|\, X = x\},$$

where $\mu_d(x) = \mathrm{E}(Y \,|\, X = x, D = d)$, $d = 0, 1$. Because $\mu_0(x)$ is identically equal to zero, it follows that $\mu(x) = \mu_1(x) \Pr\{D = 1 \,|\, X = x\}$, where

$$\Pr\{D = 1 \,|\, X = x\} = \Phi\left(\frac{\alpha + \beta x}{\sigma}\right).$$

In order to compute $\mu_1(x)$, it is convenient to exploit the representation $Y^* = \alpha + \beta X + \sigma U$, where U is distributed independently of X as $\mathcal{N}(0, 1)$. Using this representation, the event that $D = 1$ is equivalent to the event that $U > -(\alpha + \beta X)/\sigma$. Putting $c(x) = (\alpha + \beta x)/\sigma$, we therefore obtain

$$\mu_1(x) = \alpha + \beta x + \sigma\, \mathrm{E}(U \,|\, U > -c(x)).$$

Next notice that, for any constant c,

$$\mathrm{E}(U \,|\, U > -c) = \int_{-c}^{\infty} u \,\frac{\phi(u)}{\Phi(c)}\, du = -\frac{1}{\Phi(c)} \int_{-c}^{\infty} \phi'(u)\, du = \lambda(c),$$

where $\lambda(c) = \phi(c)/\Phi(c)$ is called the *inverse Mill's ratio* and we exploited the fact that $\phi'(u) = -u\phi(u)$ and $\phi(-c) = \phi(c)$. Thus

$$\mu_1(x) = \alpha + \beta x + \sigma\, \lambda(c(x)),$$

whereas

$$\mu(x) = \mu_1(x)\, \Phi(c(x)) = (\alpha + \beta x)\, \Phi(c(x)) + \sigma\, \phi(c(x)).$$

Because $\mu_1(x)$ and $\mu(x)$ depend on x only through the linear combination $\alpha + \beta x$, both are examples of single-index models. Notice that both CMFs are greater than that of Y^* and both are nonlinear in x, as shown in Figure 13. Also notice that, for a fixed σ^2, their difference from the CMF of Y^* tends to zero as $\alpha + \beta x \to \infty$. □

Figure 13 Comparison between $\mu^*(x) = \mathrm{E}(Y^* \mid X = x)$, $\mu(x) = \mathrm{E}(Y \mid X = x)$ and $\mu_1(x) = \mathrm{E}(Y \mid Y > 0, X = x)$ in Example 1.33. The conditional distribution of Y^* given $X = x$ is $\mathcal{N}(1 + x,\, 1)$.

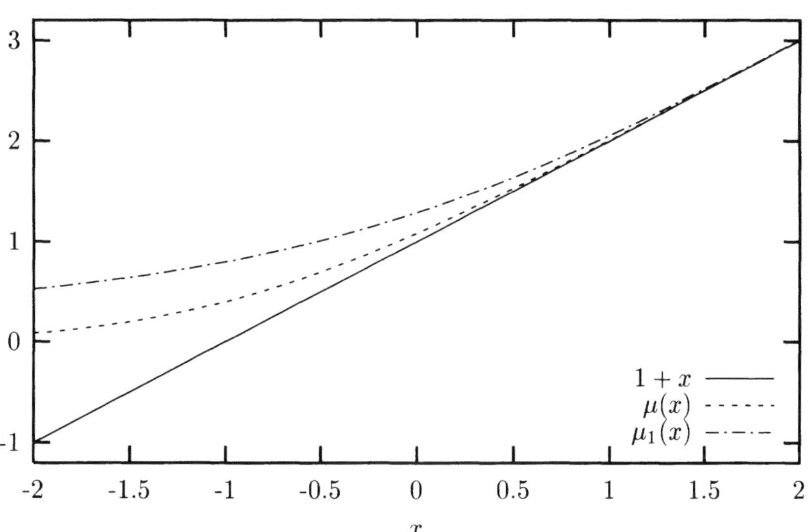

1.3.4 MODELS OF THE CONDITIONAL VARIANCE

Classical regression analysis is often concerned also with $\sigma^2(x) = \mathrm{Var}(Y \mid X = x)$. Viewed as a function of x, this is called the *conditional variance function (CVF)* of Y. We have seen that, under quadratic loss, the CVF of Y measures the risk associated with the best conditional predictor $\mu(x)$. Further, because of (1.7), the ratio

$$\eta^2_{Y\mid X} = 1 - \frac{\mathrm{E}\,\sigma^2(X)}{\sigma^2_Y} = \frac{\mathrm{Var}\,\mu(X)}{\sigma^2_Y}$$

measures how much the variability of $\mu(X)$ helps explain the total variance of Y. Of course, using alternative loss functions leads us to emphasize other measures of dispersion of the conditional distribution of Y, such as the mean absolute deviation from the median.

In many cases, $\sigma^2(x)$ is assumed to belong to a known family $\mathcal{V}$ of non-negative functions of x. We distinguish between parametric and nonparametric models depending on whether or not the family $\mathcal{V}$ can be put in a one-to-one correspondence with a subset Ψ of a finite-dimensional Euclidean space and represented as $\mathcal{V}_\Psi = \{v(x;\psi), \psi \in \Psi\}$.

A common parametric assumption is *homoskedasticity*, that is, $v(x;\psi)$ is assumed to be a constant function $v(x;\psi) = \psi^2 > 0$. A class of parametric models that allows for *conditional heteroskedasticity*, that is, for dependence of $\sigma^2(x)$ on x, consists of models of the form

$$v(x;\psi) = g(\gamma + \delta^\top x), \qquad \psi = (\gamma, \delta),$$

where g is a non-negative function, such as the quadratic or the exponential.

Although the Gaussian model in principle excludes any relationship between the CMF and the CVF, this is not true for other models. In addition to the Bernoulli model in Example 1.32, where $\sigma^2(x) = \mu(x)[1 - \mu(x)]$, other important examples where there exists an explicit relationship between the CVF and the CMF are the Poisson model, where $\sigma^2(x) = \mu(x)$, and the exponential model, where $\sigma^2(x) = \mu(x)^2$. More complicated types of dependence between the CVF and the CMF may arise when a random variable is subject to censoring or truncation.

Example 1.34 Continuing with Example 1.33, the CVF of Y is

$$\sigma^2(x) = \mathrm{E}(Y^2 \mid X = x) - \mu(x)^2,$$

where

$$\mathrm{E}(Y^2 \mid X = x) = \mathrm{E}(Y^2 \mid X = x, D = 1) \Pr\{D = 1 \mid X = x\},$$

with $D = 1\{Y > 0\}$. Using the fact that $\mu(x) = \mu_1(x) \Pr\{D = 1 \mid X = x\}$ and rearranging terms gives

$$\sigma^2(x) = \sigma_1^2(x) \, \mathrm{E}(D \mid X = x) + \mu_1(x)^2 \, \mathrm{Var}(D \mid X = x),$$

where

$$\sigma_1^2(x) = \mathrm{Var}(Y \mid X = x, D = 1) = \sigma^2 \, \mathrm{Var}(U \mid U > -c(x))$$

is the CVF of the truncated version of Y^* and $c(x) = (\alpha + \beta x)/\sigma$. Next notice that, for any constant c,

$$\mathrm{Var}(U \mid U > -c) = \mathrm{E}(U^2 \mid U > -c) - \mathrm{E}(U \mid U > -c)^2.$$

Integrating by parts,

$$\mathrm{E}(U^2 \mid U > -c) = \int_{-c}^{\infty} u^2 \frac{\phi(u)}{\Phi(c)} \, du = -\frac{1}{\Phi(c)} \int_{-c}^{\infty} u \, \phi'(u) \, du = 1 - c\lambda(c),$$

with $\lambda(c) = \phi(c)/\Phi(c)$, whereas $\mathrm{E}(U \mid U > -c) = \lambda(c)$ from Example 1.33. Hence,

$$\sigma_1^2(x) = \sigma^2[1 - c(x)\lambda(c(x)) - \lambda(c(x))^2].$$

The CVFs of the censored and the truncated version of Y^* are both smaller than the CVF of Y^* and both depend on x, as shown in Figure 14. However, their difference from the CVF of Y^* tends to zero as $c \to \infty$.

There is an interesting relationship between the CMF $\mu_1(x)$ and the CVF $\sigma_1^2(x)$. The slope of $\mu_1(x)$ is

$$\mu_1'(x) = \beta[1 - c(x)\lambda(c(x)) - \lambda(c(x))^2] = \beta \, \frac{\sigma_1^2(x)}{\sigma^2}.$$

Since

$$0 \leq \frac{\sigma_1^2(x)}{\sigma^2} = \frac{\mathrm{Var}(Y \mid Y > 0, X = x)}{\mathrm{Var}(Y^* \mid X = x)} \leq 1,$$

it follows that $|\mu_1'(x)| \leq |\beta|$, a result which is sometimes referred to as the *attenuation bias* due to censoring. □

Figure 14 Comparison between $\sigma^2(x) = \mathrm{Var}(Y \mid X = x)$ and $\sigma_1^2(x) = \mathrm{Var}(Y \mid Y > 0, X = x)$ in Example 1.34. The conditional distribution of Y^* given $X = x$ is $\mathcal{N}(1 + x, 1)$.

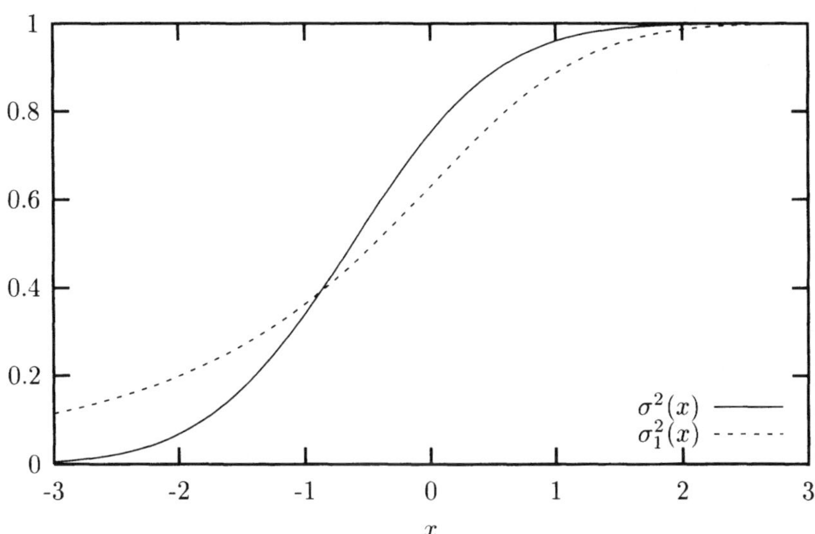

1.3.5 MODELS OF CONDITIONAL QUANTILES

Under the asymmetric absolute loss function ℓ_p, a best predictor of Y given $X = x$ is a pth conditional quantile $\zeta_p(x)$. If $\zeta_p(x)$ is unique then, viewed as a function of x for p fixed, it is called the pth *conditional quantile function (CQF)* or the pth *quantile regression* of Y. The conditional quantile function corresponding to $p = 1/2$ is also called the *median regression function* of Y.

A *quantile regression model* assumes that the CQF of Y is well defined and belongs to a known family $\mathcal{Q}$ of functions of x. As usual, we distinguish between parametric and nonparametric models depending on whether or not the family $\mathcal{Q}$ can be put in a one-to-one correspondence with a subset Θ of a finite-dimensional Euclidean space and represented as $\mathcal{Q}_\Theta = \{q(x;\theta), \theta \in \Theta\}$. For example, if X is a scalar random variable, a simple parametric model for quantile regression is the linear model $q(x;\theta) = \alpha + \beta x$, $\theta = (\alpha, \beta)$.

We say that a parametric quantile regression model $\mathcal{Q}_\Theta$ is *correctly specified* if $\zeta_p(x) = q(x;\theta_0)$ for some $\theta_0 \in \Theta$, and is *identifiable* if the problem

$$\min_{\theta \in \Theta} \mathrm{E}_F\, \ell_p(Y - q(x;\theta)), \qquad 0 < p < 1$$

has a unique solution at $\theta = \theta_0$.

Which model is appropriate for a set of conditional quantiles depends on the nature of the statistical problem. Consider, for example, the case when Y is a continuous random variable whose conditional distribution given $X = x$ depends on x only through a location parameter $\mu(x)$, that is, the conditional distribution function of Y is of the form $F(y \mid x) = F(y - \mu(x))$, where F is some univariate distribution function with strictly positive density. By definition, $\zeta_p(x)$ is such that

$$p = F(\zeta_p(x) \,|\, x) = F(\zeta_p(x) - \mu(x)).$$

Inverting this relationship gives $\zeta_p(x) = \zeta_p + \mu(x)$, where $\zeta_p = F^{-1}(p)$ is the pth quantile of F. Hence, for any $q \neq p$, $\zeta_q(x) - \zeta_p(x) = \zeta_q - \zeta_p$, that is, the vertical distance between any pair of conditional quantiles does not depend on x. In particular, if $\mu(x) = \alpha + \beta x$, then $\zeta_p(x) = (\alpha + \zeta_p) + \beta x$, and so the conditional quantiles of Y form a family of parallel lines with a common slope equal to β.

Now consider the case when the conditional distribution of Y given $X = x$ is symmetric, with location parameter that is linear in x and scale parameter that also depends on x, that is

$$F(y \,|\, x) = F\left(\frac{y - \alpha - \beta x}{\sigma(x)}\right), \qquad \sigma(x) > 0,$$

where $F(0) = 1/2$ and therefore $\zeta_{1/2} = 0$. Because now $\zeta_p(x) = \alpha + \sigma(x)\zeta_p + \beta x$, the conditional quantiles of Y are no longer parallel and, with the exception of the conditional median, not even linear in x. Figure 15 illustrates the difference between the homoskedastic and the heteroskedastic case.

1.4 STATISTICAL MODELS AS APPROXIMATIONS

It is often more appropriate to consider a statistical model as an approximation to a particular aspect of a distribution, rather than a complete characterization of it. For example, economic theory may sometimes provide qualitative information about the CMF, such as monotonicity, convexity or concavity, homogeneity, etc., while it is much less likely to provide "credible" parametric specifications. If the assumed model is not correctly specified, how can we interpret the problem of statistical inference?

1.4.1 PARAMETRIC MODELS AS APPROXIMATIONS

Let Z be a random vector with density function f_0. A parametric model $\mathcal{F}_\Theta = \{f(z;\theta), \theta \in \Theta\}$ for the distribution of Z is said to be *incorrectly specified*, or simply *misspecified*, if f_0 does not belong to $\mathcal{F}_\Theta$, that is, $f_0(Z) \neq f(Z;\theta)$ with probability one for all $\theta \in \Theta$.

As a measure of discrepancy between f_0 and any element $f(z;\theta)$ of $\mathcal{F}_\Theta$, consider again the Kullback–Leibler index $\mathcal{K}(\theta, f_0) = \mathrm{E}_0[\ln f_0(Z) - \ln f(Z;\theta)]$, where the expectation is with respect to the density f_0. It is easy to verify, by the same argument used in Theorem 1.1, that $\mathcal{K}(\theta, f_0) \geq 0$ for every $\theta \in \Theta$, with equality if and only if there exists a parameter point $\theta_0 \in \Theta$ such that $f_0(Z) = f(Z;\theta_0)$ with probability one, that is, if and only if $\mathcal{F}_\Theta$ is correctly specified.

If $\mathcal{F}_\Theta$ is misspecified, suppose that there exists a parameter point θ_* at which $\mathcal{K}(\theta, f_0)$ attains its minimum on Θ. Such a parameter point is also a point of maximum of the expected log-likelihood $\ell(\theta) = c + \mathrm{E}_0 \ln f(Z;\theta)$, where c is an arbitrary constant. If θ_* is unique, it is called the *pseudo true parameter* and the associated density $f(z;\theta_*)$ is called the *best Kullback–Leibler approximation* to f_0. In this case, we may interpret the statistical problem as one of drawing inferences about the element of the assumed

Figure 15 Family of conditional quantiles of Y given $X = x$. The conditional distribution is Gaussian with CMF $\mu(x) = 1 + x$. The top part of the figure shows the homoskedastic case when the CVF is constant. The bottom part shows the heteroskedastic case when $\sigma^2(x) = 1 + .5x^2$.

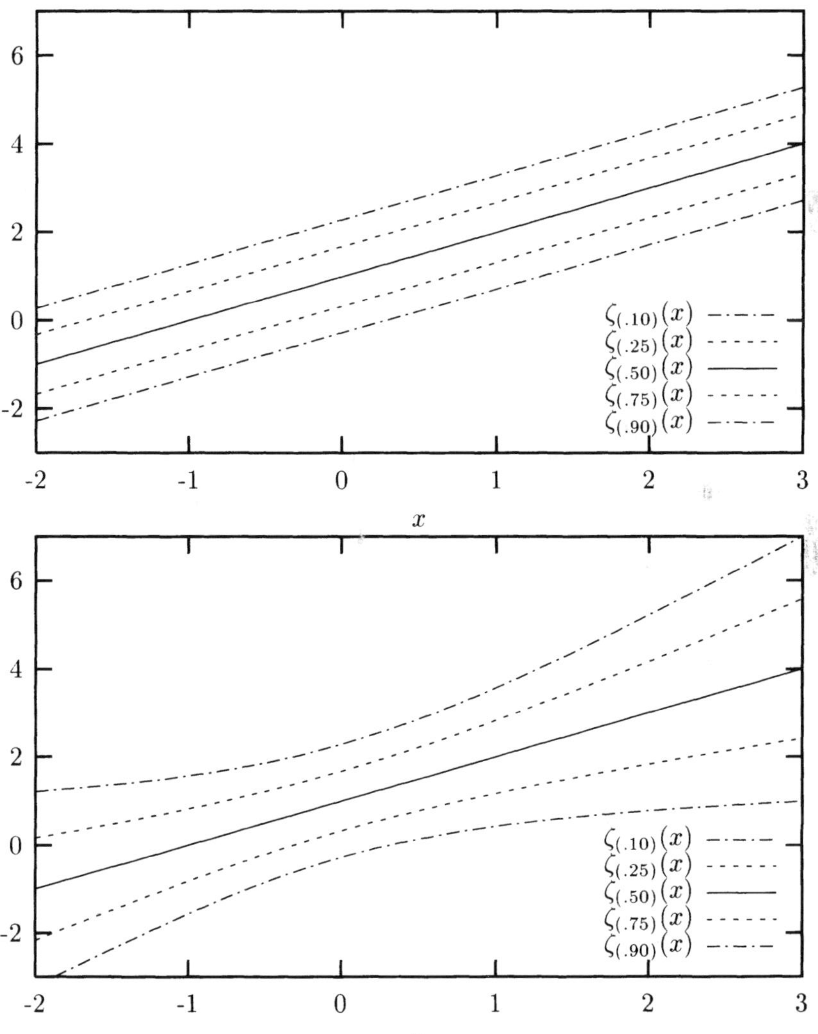

model $\mathcal{F}_\Theta$ that best approximates, in the Kullback–Leibler sense, the density of Z. Except for this interpretation, the pseudo true parameter θ_* may not correspond to any interesting or meaningful aspect of the distribution of Z.

If $\mathcal{F}_\Theta$ is a smooth parametric model, then $\mathcal{K}(\theta, f_0)$ has a unique local maximum at the point θ_* if and only if $\mathcal{K}'(\theta_*, f_0) = 0$ and $\mathcal{K}''(\theta_*, f_0)$ is a finite p.d. matrix. Because

$$\mathcal{K}'(\theta, f_0) = -\int \frac{f'(z;\theta)}{f(z;\theta)} f_0(z)\,dz = -\operatorname{E}_0 s(Z;\theta),$$

the pseudo true parameter θ_* must be a root of the equation $\operatorname{E} s(Z;\theta) = 0$. However, the information equality no longer holds because $\mathcal{K}''(\theta_*, f_0) = -\operatorname{E}_0 s'(Z;\theta_*)$ is in general different from $\operatorname{Var}_0 s(Z;\theta_*)$.

Now consider the case when $Z = (X, Y)$, and let $\mu(x)$ and $\sigma^2(x)$ denote, respectively, the CMF and the CVF of Y given X. A parametric regression model $\mathcal{H}_\Theta = \{h(x;\theta), \theta \in \Theta\}$ is said to be *misspecified* if $\operatorname{E}(Y - h(x;\theta)]^2 > \operatorname{E}\sigma^2(X)$ for every $\theta \in \Theta$. If the model $\mathcal{H}_\Theta$ is misspecified, consider the problem of approximating the CMF of Y by an element of $\mathcal{H}_\Theta$. Under quadratic loss such a problem becomes

$$\min_{\theta\in\Theta} \operatorname{E}[\mu(X) - h(X;\theta)]^2. \tag{1.9}$$

If problem (1.9) has a unique solution θ_*, then the function $h(x;\theta_*)$ is called the *minimum MSE approximation* to $\mu(x)$. In this case, we may interpret the statistical problem as one of drawing inferences about the parameter θ_* which characterizes the best approximation, in the MSE sense, to the CMF of Y.

The minimum MSE approximation $h(x;\theta_*)$ may also be regarded as the minimum MSE predictor of Y in the class $\mathcal{H}_\Theta$.

Theorem 1.5 *Problem (1.9) is equivalent to the problem*

$$\min_{\theta\in\Theta} \operatorname{E}[Y - h(X;\theta)]^2. \tag{1.10}$$

Proof. By Theorem C.1, the MSE of $h(X;\theta)$ is

$$\operatorname{E}[Y - h(X;\theta)]^2 = \operatorname{E}\sigma^2(X) + \operatorname{E}[\mu(X) - h(X;\theta)]^2.$$

Because $\operatorname{E}\sigma^2(X)$ does not depend on θ, problems (1.10) and (1.9) are equivalent. □

The next section presents a characterization of θ_* when the class $\mathcal{H}_\Theta$ consists of functions which are linear in x.

1.4.2 LINEAR PREDICTION

If the joint distribution of X and Y is not Gaussian, then the CMF of Y is not necessarily linear and may be complicated to compute. In this case one may still give a meaningful interpretation to a linear regression model.

A linear predictor of Y given X is a random variable of the form $h(X) = \alpha + \beta X$. Given a loss function ℓ, we say that a linear predictor $h_*(X) = \alpha_* + \beta_* X$ is optimal, and we call it a *best linear predictor (BLP)*, if α_* and β_* solve the problem

$$\min_{(\alpha,\beta)\in\Re^2} \operatorname{E}\ell(Y - \alpha - \beta X).$$

We say that the parameter point (α_*, β_*) is *identifiable* if it represents the unique solution to the above problem. Clearly, for any given loss function, the risk associated with a BLP is necessarily intermediate between the ones associated, respectively, with the best unconditional predictor and the best conditional predictor.

The characterization of α_* and β_* depends on the particular loss function adopted. For example, under quadratic loss, α_* and β_* solve the minimum MSE linear prediction problem

$$\min_{(\alpha,\beta)\in\Re^2} \mathrm{E}(Y - \alpha - \beta X)^2. \tag{1.11}$$

Quadratic loss is usually preferred because, as we shall see immediately, it leads to a simple closed form solution that only requires knowledge of the first two moments of the joint distribution of X and Y. From now on, by BLP we always mean the minimum MSE linear predictor.

Theorem 1.6 *If the joint distribution of X and Y has finite second moments, then the function $Q(\alpha, \beta) = \mathrm{E}(Y - \alpha - \beta X)^2$ attains a minimum on $\Re^2$. Necessary and sufficient conditions for (α_*, β_*) to be a point of minimum of $Q(\alpha, \beta)$ are*

$$0 = \mathrm{E}(Y - \alpha_* - \beta_* X), \tag{1.12}$$

$$0 = \mathrm{E}\, X(Y - \alpha_* - \beta_* X). \tag{1.13}$$

Proof. Write the function $Q(\alpha, \beta)$ as

$$Q(\alpha, \beta) = \mathrm{E}\, Y^2 - 2\alpha\, \mathrm{E}\, Y - 2\beta\, \mathrm{E}\, XY + \alpha^2 + 2\alpha\beta\, \mathrm{E}\, X + \beta^2\, \mathrm{E}\, X^2.$$

The function Q attains a minimum on $\Re^2$ because it is quadratic and its Hessian

$$Q''(\alpha, \beta) = 2 \begin{bmatrix} 1 & \mathrm{E}\, X \\ \mathrm{E}\, X & \mathrm{E}\, X^2 \end{bmatrix}$$

is a n.n.d. matrix for all (α, β), The minimum is attained at the point (α_*, β_*) if and only if

$$0 = \frac{\partial}{\partial\alpha} Q(\alpha_*, \beta_*) = -2\,\mathrm{E}\, Y + 2\alpha_* + 2\beta_*\, \mathrm{E}\, X,$$

$$0 = \frac{\partial}{\partial\beta} Q(\alpha_*, \beta_*) = -2\,\mathrm{E}\, XY + 2\alpha_*\, \mathrm{E}\, X + 2\beta_*\, \mathrm{E}\, X^2,$$

that is, if and only if (1.12) and (1.13) hold. □

The linear equations (1.12) and (1.13) are called *normal equations* of the linear prediction problem. From (1.12) we have

$$\alpha_* = \mu_Y - \beta_* \mu_X.$$

Substituting this expression back into (1.13) gives

$$0 = \mathrm{E}\, X(Y - \mu_Y) - \beta_*\, \mathrm{E}\, X(X - \mu_X) = \sigma_{XY} - \beta_* \sigma_X^2.$$

If $\sigma_X^2 > 0$, solving the above equation with respect to β_* gives the unique solution

$$\beta_* = \frac{\sigma_{XY}}{\sigma_X^2} = \rho_{XY} \frac{\sigma_Y}{\sigma_X}.$$

Thus, if $\sigma_X^2 > 0$, the intercept α_* and the slope β_* of the BLP are both identifiable.

Notice that, if $\sigma_X^2 > 0$, then β_* and ρ_{XY} have the same sign. In particular, $\beta_* = 0$ if $\rho_{XY} = 0$, in which case the BLP does not depend on X and coincides with the mean of Y. If X and Y are perfectly correlated then, except for the sign, β_* is equal to the ratio of the standard deviations of Y and X. Also notice that the expressions obtained for α_* and β_* when $\sigma_X^2 > 0$ exactly coincide with those derived in Example 1.22. This should not be surprising, for the BLP coincides with the CVF whenever the latter is linear in X.

Now let $\mathrm{E}^*(Y \mid X) = \alpha_* + \beta_* X$ denote the BLP of Y given X and consider the stochastic properties of the associated prediction error

$$V = Y - \mathrm{E}^*(Y \mid X) = (Y - \mu_Y) - \beta_*(X - \mu_X).$$

The normal equations show that $\mathrm{E}\, V = 0$ and $\mathrm{E}\, XV = 0$, that is, V has mean zero and is uncorrelated with X. These two conditions together imply that V and $\mathrm{E}^*(Y \mid X)$ are uncorrelated. The conditional mean of V given X is instead

$$\mathrm{E}(V \mid X) = \mathrm{E}(Y - \alpha_* - \beta_* X \mid X) = \mu(X) - \mathrm{E}^*(Y \mid X),$$

which is different from zero, unless the CMF of Y is linear in X. Hence, the stochastic properties of V are generally different from the ones of the regression error, that is, the error associated with the best conditional predictor.

Using the fact that $Y = \mathrm{E}^*(Y \mid X) + V$, where $\mathrm{E}^*(Y \mid X)$ and V are uncorrelated, we also get

$$\mathrm{Var}\, V = \sigma_Y^2 - \mathrm{Var}[\mathrm{E}^*(Y \mid X)] = \sigma_Y^2 - \beta_*^2 \sigma_X^2. \tag{1.14}$$

If $\sigma_X^2 > 0$, then

$$\mathrm{Var}\, V = \sigma_Y^2 - \frac{\sigma_{XY}^2}{\sigma_X^2} = \sigma_Y^2 (1 - \rho_{XY}^2),$$

that is, the variance of the prediction error V is a fraction equal to $1 - \rho_{XY}^2$ of the variance of Y. Notice that the normal equations imply nothing about the conditional variance of V given X. In particular, $\mathrm{Var}(V \mid X)$ may well depend on X.

The above results generalize without difficulty to the case when X or Y are random vectors. Suppose first that Y is a random variable and $X = (X_1, \ldots, X_k)$ is a random k-vector. A BLP of Y given X is any random variable

$$\mathrm{E}^*(Y \mid X) = \alpha_* + \sum_j \beta_{j*} X_j = \alpha_* + \beta_*^\top X$$

such that the scalar α_* and the k-vector β_* solve the problem

$$\min_{(\alpha,\beta) \in \Re^{k+1}} \ \mathrm{E}(Y - \alpha - \beta^\top X)^2.$$

Instead of a pair of normal equations, α_* and β_* must now satisfy the system of $k+1$ normal equations

$$0 = \mathrm{E}(Y - \alpha - \beta^\top X),$$
$$0 = \mathrm{E}\, X(Y - \alpha - \beta^\top X).$$

Since $\alpha_* = \mu_Y - \beta_*^\top \mu_X$, we get

$$X(Y - \alpha_* - \beta_*^\top X) = X(Y - \mu_Y) - X(X - \mu_X)^\top \beta_*.$$

Substituting back into the normal equations gives the system of k linear equations

$$0 = \mathrm{Cov}(X, Y) - (\mathrm{Var}\, X)\beta_*.$$

If $\mathrm{Var}\, X$ is a nonsingular matrix, we obtain the unique solution

$$\beta_* = (\mathrm{Var}\, X)^{-1} \mathrm{Cov}(X, Y).$$

Suppose next that $Y = (Y_1, \ldots, Y_m)$ and $X = (X_1, \ldots, X_k)$ is a random k-vector. A BLP of Y given X is any random vector $\mathrm{E}^*(Y \mid X) = \alpha_* + B_* X$ such that the m-vector α_* and the $m \times k$ matrix B_* solve the problem

$$\min_{\alpha, B} \mathrm{E}(Y - \alpha - X)^\top (Y - \alpha - BX). \tag{1.15}$$

The elements of α_* and B_* must now satisfy the system of $m(k+1)$ normal equations

$$\begin{aligned} 0 &= \mathrm{E}(Y - \alpha - BX), \\ 0 &= \mathrm{E}\, X_j (Y - \alpha - BX), \qquad j = 1, \ldots, k. \end{aligned}$$

Because necessarily $\alpha_* = \mu_Y - B_* \mu_X$, substituting back into the normal equations gives

$$0 = \mathrm{Cov}(X, Y) - (\mathrm{Var}\, X) B_*^\top.$$

If $\mathrm{Var}\, X$ is a nonsingular matrix, we obtain the unique solution

$$B_*^\top = (\mathrm{Var}\, X)^{-1} \mathrm{Cov}(X, Y).$$

The jth element of the vector α_* and the jth row of the matrix B_* are respectively

$$\alpha_{j*} = \mathrm{E}\, Y_j - \beta_{j*}^\top (\mathrm{E}\, X), \qquad \beta_{j*} = (\mathrm{Var}\, X)^{-1} \mathrm{Cov}(X, Y_j), \qquad j = 1, \ldots, m,$$

and therefore coincide with the coefficients that define the BLP of the random variable Y_j given X.

1.4.3 RELATION BETWEEN THE BLP AND THE CMF

We first look at the relationship between the regression error $U = Y - \mu(X)$ and the prediction error $V = Y - \mathrm{E}^*(Y \mid X)$ associated with the BLP. The latter may be decomposed as

$$V = U + [\mu(X) - \mathrm{E}^*(Y \mid X)] = U + \mathrm{E}(V \mid X), \tag{1.16}$$

where both U and the approximation error $\mu(X) - \mathrm{E}^*(Y \mid X)$ have zero mean. Because the approximation error depends only on X, it is necessarily uncorrelated with U. This shows that the two components in (1.16) are orthogonal. If the CMF is linear in X, then the approximation error is identically equal to zero and so V and U coincide.

Using (1.16) and (1.14), we obtain the following decomposition of the variance of Y

$$\sigma_Y^2 = \mathrm{Var}[\mathrm{E}^*(Y \mid X)] + \mathrm{Var}[\mathrm{E}(V \mid X)] + \mathrm{Var}\, U,$$

where $\mathrm{Var}[\mathrm{E}^*(Y \mid X)]$ is the variance of the BLP and $\mathrm{Var}[\mathrm{E}(V \mid X)]$ is the variance of the approximation error $\mathrm{E}(V \mid X) = \mu(X) - \mathrm{E}^*(Y \mid X)$.

Now suppose, for simplicity, that Y and X are scalar random variables and consider the following question. If the CMF is nonlinear, what is the relation between its gradient and the slope β_* of the BLP? The next theorem shows that, if $\mu(x)$ is a smooth function, then β_* may be viewed as a weighted average of the gradient $\mu'(x)$ of the CMF at all points in the support of X.

Theorem 1.7 *Let F_X denote the distribution function of X. If X has finite variance and $\mu(x) = \mathrm{E}(Y \mid X = x)$ is continuously differentiable, then*

$$\beta_* = \int \mu'(x)\, w(x)\, dx,$$

where

$$w(x) = \frac{F_X(x)}{\sigma_X^2} [\mu_X - \mathrm{E}(X \mid X \leq x)]$$

is a non-negative function such that $\int w(x)\, dx = 1$.

Proof. By the law of iterated expectations

$$\sigma_{XY} = \mathrm{E}\{\mathrm{E}[Y(X - \mu_X) \mid X = x]\} = \int \mu(x)(x - \mu_X)\, f_X(x)\, dx.$$

Letting

$$v(x) = \int_{-\infty}^{x} (t - \mu_X) f_X(t)\, dt = F_X(x)[\mathrm{E}(X \mid X \leq x) - \mu_X]$$

and integrating by parts gives

$$\sigma_{XY} = [\mu(x)v(x)]_{-\infty}^{\infty} - \int_{-\infty}^{\infty} \mu'(x)v(x)\, dx,$$

where $[\mu(x)v(x)]_{-\infty}^{\infty} = 0$. Therefore

$$\sigma_{XY} = \int \mu'(x)\, F_X(x)[\mu_X - \mathrm{E}(X \mid X \leq x)]\, dx.$$

The fact that $\mu'(x) = 1$ when $Y = X$ also gives

$$\sigma_X^2 = \mathrm{Cov}(X, X) = \int F_X(x)[\mu_X - \mathrm{E}(X \mid X \leq x)]\, dx.$$

Hence, $\beta_* = \sigma_{XY}/\sigma_X^2 = \int \mu'(x) w(x)\, dx$, where

$$w(x) = \frac{F_X(x)[\mu_X - \mathrm{E}(X \mid X \leq x)]}{\int F_X(x)[\mu_X - \mathrm{E}(X \mid X \leq x)]\, dx}$$

is a function that integrates to one. Because $\mu_X \geq \mathrm{E}(X \mid X \leq x)$, $w(x)$ is a nonnegative function. □

By Theorem 1.7, if the CMF $\mu(x)$ is nonlinear in x, then the intercept and the slope of the BLP are generally different from those of a first-order Taylor series expansion of $\mu(x)$ about any point in the support of X. For this reason, the BLP does not necessarily provide reliable information on the local properties (derivatives, elasticities, etc.) of an unknown CMF.

BIBLIOGRAPHIC NOTES

For an extensive treatment of the concept of invariance of a statistical model under certain classes of transformation, see Lehmann (1983).

For an introduction to hazard rate models see Cox and Oakes (1984) and Lancaster (1990).

The Kullback–Leibler index was introduced by Kullback and Leibler (1951). For a detailed discussion of its properties see Bahadur (1971). For other measures of dissimilarity between probability distributions see Maasumi (1993). The relevance of the properties of the Kullback–Leibler index for identification of parametric models is discussed in Bowden (1973). On the relationship between local identifiability and nonsingularity of the Fisher information matrix also see Rothenberg (1971).

A nice introduction to exponential families is the book by McCullagh and Nelder (1989). A more advanced treatment is in Barndorff-Nielsen (1978) and Brown (1986).

For an interpretation of regression as a conditional prediction problem see Manski (1991). On the properties of conditional quantile functions see Bassett and Koenker (1982).

For a thorough discussion of pseudo true parameters and best Kullback–Leibler approximations see Sawa (1978), White (1982a) and Gourieroux, Monfort and Trognon (1984a,b).

On the difference between the BLP and the CMF of Y given X see White (1980b).

PROBLEMS

1.1 In a sequence of independent Bernoulli trials with probability π of success, what is the probability that there are r successes before the kth failure?

1.2 Let Z_1 and Z_2 be independent Poisson random variables with parameters θ_1 and θ_2 respectively. Show that the distribution of $Z_1 + Z_2$ is also Poisson with parameter $\theta_1 + \theta_2$ and that the conditional distribution of Z_1 given $Z_1 + Z_2 = m$ is binomial with index m and parameter $\theta = \theta_1/(\theta_1 + \theta_2)$.

1.3 Given a continuous random variable U with distribution function F and density function f, compute the distribution function and the density function of the random variable $Z = \mu - \sigma U$, where $\mu \in \Re$ and $\sigma > 0$.

1.4 Let

$$f(z) = \begin{cases} (1 + \alpha z)/2, & \text{if } -1 \leq z \leq 1, \\ 0, & \text{otherwise,} \end{cases}$$

where $-1 \leq \alpha \leq 1$. Show that f is a density and find the associated distribution function. Compute the quantiles of the distribution in terms of α.

1.5 Let X and Y be independent $\mathcal{E}(\lambda)$ random variables. The distribution of the random variable $Z = Y - X$ is called *Laplace*. Compute the mean, the variance and the density of Z.

1.6 Show that if $Z \sim \mathcal{E}(\lambda)$, then the conditional probability $\Pr\{z \leq Z < z + \epsilon \,|\, Z \geq z\}$ depends on ϵ but not on z. Interpret this result.

1.7 Let Z be a continuous non-negative random variable. Show that

$$\mathrm{E}\, Z = \int_0^\infty e^{-H(z)}\, dz,$$

where $H(z)$ is the integrated hazard of Z.

1.8 Show that the distribution of a memoryless random variable is necessarily exponential.

1.9 Let Z be a non-negative random variable with log-logistic distribution, that is, the distribution of $\ln Z$ is logistic with distribution function

$$F(z) = \frac{\exp[(\mu - z)/\sigma]}{1 + \exp[(\mu - z)/\sigma]}, \qquad \sigma > 0.$$

Derive the survivor function, the density and the hazard function of Z, and show that the hazard function is nonmonotone in z.

1.10 Show that the Kullback–Leibler index is not a proper distance between two distributions.

1.11 Let $\mathcal{F}_\Theta$ be a smooth parametric model and let Θ be a subspace of $\Re^p$ defined by a set of q linear equality restrictions, that is,

$$\Theta = \{\theta \in \Re^p : R\theta = r\},$$

where R is a $q \times p$ matrix and r is a q-vector. Derive conditions under which a parameter point in Θ is identifiable (*Hint:* Consider the problem of maximizing the expected log-likelihood subject to the restriction that $R\theta = r$).

1.12 Prove the information equality (Theorem 1.2) for the case when Z is a discrete random variable.

1.13 Write the density of $\mathcal{N}(\mu, \sigma^2)$ distribution in canonical form and check that the resulting log-likelihood is a concave function of the canonical parameter.

1.14 Suppose that the distribution function of Y given $X = x$ is of the form $F(y - \mu(x))$, where F is any distribution function which has finite mean and is symmetric about zero. Show that $\mathrm{Med}(Y \,|\, X) = \mathrm{E}(Y \,|\, X)$.

1.15 Let Z be a continuous random variable with density function f and consider the asymmetric absolute loss function

$$\ell_p(u) = [p\, 1\{u \geq 0\} + (1 - p)\, 1\{u < 0\}]\, |u|, \qquad 0 < p < 1.$$

Show that the best predictor of Z is unique and coincides with the pth quantile of Z.

1.16 (Newey & Powell 1987) Study the properties (continuity, differentiability, convexity) of the loss function

$$\ell_p(u) = [p\,1\{u \geq 0\} + (1-p)\,1\{u < 0\}]\,u^2, \qquad 0 < p < 1.$$

Given a continuous random variable Z with density function f, show that a best predictor μ_* under the above loss function satisfies the relationship

$$\frac{\int_{\mu_*}^{\infty}(z-\mu_*)f(z)\,dz}{\int_{-\infty}^{\mu_*}(\mu_*-z)f(z)\,dz} = \frac{1-p}{p}.$$

What happens if $p = .5$?

1.17 (Lee 1989) Study the properties (continuity, differentiability, convexity) of the loss function $\ell_p(u) = 1\{|u| \geq \alpha\}$, where $\alpha > 0$. Given a continuous random variable Z with density function f, show that a best predictor μ_* under the above loss function is equal to the midpoint of the interval of length 2α which contains most of the probability mass of Z. What is the relationship between μ_* and the mode of Z? Given $Z = (X, Y)$, what is the best predictor of Y given X?

1.18 Given two predictors c_1 and c_2 of a random variable Z and a loss $\ell_j = |Z - c_j|^q$, $j = 1, 2$, with $q > 0$, show that c_1 is preferred to c_2 whenever

$$\frac{P(c_1, c_2)}{P(c_2, c_1)} > \frac{\mathrm{E}(\ell_1 - \ell_2 \,|\, \ell_2 < \ell_1)}{\mathrm{E}(\ell_2 - \ell_1 \,|\, \ell_1 < \ell_2)},$$

where $P(c_i, c_j) = \Pr\{|Z - c_i| < |Z - c_j|\}$, $i, j = 1, 2$. Comment on the appropriateness of $P(c_1, c_2)$ as an alternative to risk as a criterion for comparing two predictors.

1.19 Derive the following result, which led to the expression "regression towards the mean", coined last century by Sir Francis Galton. Let (X, Y) have a joint Gaussian distribution with positive correlation coefficient and let $\mu(x) = \mathrm{E}(Y \,|\, X = x)$. If X and Y have the same marginal distribution with mean μ and variance σ^2, then

$$\begin{cases} \mu \leq \mu(x) \leq x, & \text{if } x \geq \mu, \\ x \leq \mu(x) \leq \mu, & \text{if } x \leq \mu. \end{cases}$$

1.20 Let C and D be 0–1 random variables and let $\mu_{hj} = \mathrm{E}(Y \,|\, C = h, D = j)$, $h, j = 0, 1$. Represent $\mathrm{E}(Y \,|\, C, D)$ as a double array and as a linear regression model, and derive the restrictions on the linear regression model implied by the following assumptions:

(i) $\mathrm{E}(Y \,|\, C, D) = \mathrm{E}(Y \,|\, C)$;
(ii) $\mathrm{E}(Y \,|\, C, D) = \mathrm{E}(Y \,|\, D)$;
(iii) $\mathrm{E}(Y \,|\, C, D = 1) - \mathrm{E}(Y \,|\, C, D = 2)$ is constant.

1.21 Compare the derivative with respect to x of the CMF of the linear probability model with those of the logit and probit models.

1.22 Consider Example 1.33 and compute the derivative of $E(Y \,|\, X = x)$ with respect to x.

1.23 Show that the ratio $\eta^2_{Y|X} = \mathrm{Var}\,\mu(X)/\sigma^2_Y$ satisfies:

(i) $0 \leq \eta^2_{Y|X} \leq 1$;

(ii) $\eta^2_{Y|X} = 0$ if Y is mean independent of X;
(iii) $\eta^2_{Y|X} = 0$ if $Y = h(X)$ for some function h.

Interpret these results.

1.24 Let X and Y be binary random variables with mean zero, and let U be the prediction error associated with the BLP of Y given X. Show that U is mean independent of X. Are U and X independent?

1.25 A fair die is rolled. Let Y be the face number showing and define X by the rule

$$X = \begin{cases} Y, & \text{if } Y \text{ is even,} \\ 0, & \text{if } Y \text{ is odd.} \end{cases}$$

Find the minimum MSE predictor and the minimum MSE linear predictor of Y based on X and compare their MSE.

1.26 Consider the random variable $Y = X^2 + U$, where X and U are independent $\mathcal{N}(0,1)$ random variables. Compute the conditional mean and the BLP of Y given X and compare their MSE.

1.27 Use the classical projection theorem (Theorem A.8) to prove Theorem 1.6.

1.28 Define $R^2_{Y|X} = \text{Var}[\text{E}^*(Y\,|\,X)]/\sigma^2_Y$ and show that:

(i) $0 \leq R^2_{Y|X} \leq 1$;
(ii) $R^2_{Y|X} \leq \eta^2_{Y|X}$, where $\eta^2_{Y|X} = \text{Var}\,\mu(X)/\sigma^2_Y$ is the coefficient introduced in Problem 1.23;
(iii) $\eta^2_{Y|X} - R^2_{Y|X} \leq 1 - R^2_{Y|X}$;
(iv) $R^2_{Y|X} = \rho^2_{XY}$.

Interpret these results.

1.29 Let $E^*(Y\,|\,X) = \alpha_* + \beta_* Y$ be the BLP of Y given X and let $E^*(X\,|\,Y) = \gamma_* + \delta_* Y$ be the BLP of X given Y. Show that β_* and δ_* must have the same sign, which is that of σ_{XY}. Also show that $|\beta_*| \leq 1/|\delta_*|$.

1.30 Given jointly distributed random variables (X,Y), a *best kth order polynomial approximation* $\text{E}^*(Y\,|\,X)$ to $\text{E}(Y\,|\,X)$, in the MSE sense, is a solution to the problem

$$\min_{\alpha,\beta_1,\ldots,\beta_k} \text{E}[\text{E}(Y\,|\,X) - \alpha - \beta_1 X - \cdots - \beta_k X^k]^2.$$

Find conditions on the joint distribution of (X,Y) under which $\text{E}^*(Y\,|\,X)$ exists. If $\text{E}^*(Y\,|\,X)$ exists, find its characterization and derive the properties of the prediction error $U = Y - \text{E}^*(Y\,|\,X)$.

1.31 Let X, Y and Z be jointly distributed random variables with finite second moments. Show that

$$\sigma_{XY} = \text{E}[\text{Cov}(X,Y\,|\,Z)] + \text{Cov}[\text{E}(Y\,|\,Z), \text{E}(X\,|\,Z)].$$

1.32 Suppose that the CMF of Y is quadratic

$$\mu(x) = \alpha + \beta x + \gamma x^2.$$

Let $\mu_*(x)$ denote a first-order Taylor series expansion of $\mu(x)$ about the mean of X and let $\text{E}^*(Y\,|\,X) = \alpha_* + \beta_* X$ denote the BLP of Y given X. Compare β_* with the slope of $\mu_*(x)$.

2

Sampling

Most of statistical inference amounts to describing the relationship between a sample and the population from which the sample is drawn. We typically rely on a sample because obtaining information about a large population by complete enumeration of its units, as in the case of a census, may be very costly or even impossible. Sampling usually costs less and the quality of the data can be more easily controlled.

What can be learned about a population characteristic of interest ultimately depends on the *sampling scheme*, that is, the way in which the data are gathered. When the sampling scheme is known, it is usually possible to assess how well a certain sample statistic does in estimating a given population parameter and to estimate the error due to sampling.

A variety of sampling schemes are available. In this chapter, we consider only sampling schemes that are *probabilistic*, that is, may be represented as the result of a chance experiment. Among them, a central role is played by *simple random sampling (SRS)*, in which all population units receive the same probability of being selected into the sample. SRS makes it especially easy to use the sample information to draw valid inferences about the population under study. Although many sampling schemes of practical importance deviate from SRS, the latter remains the natural yardstick to consider when evaluating the properties of a statistical procedure.

2.1 SAMPLING FROM A FINITE POPULATION

Consider a finite population consisting of N units and let $z_1, \ldots, z_N$ denote the values of a single numeric characteristic for each of the N population units. Define the population mean and variance, respectively, as

$$\mu = \frac{1}{N}\sum_{j=1}^{N} z_j, \qquad \sigma^2 = \frac{1}{N}\sum_{j=1}^{N}(z_j - \mu)^2.$$

The parameters μ and σ^2 are examples of population parameters.

A *sample of size n* is an unordered set of n units drawn from the population. In what follows, the sample size n is assumed to be fixed at the outset and the sample is identified with the values $z_1, \ldots, z_n$ of the numeric characteristic for the n sample units. Under probabilistic sampling, the sample observations may be represented as a realization of a collection $Z_1, \ldots, Z_n$ of random variables whose properties depend on the sampling scheme. The issue discussed in this section is how the nature of the sampling scheme affects the information carried by the sample about the population parameters μ and σ^2.

2.1.1 SRS WITH REPLACEMENT

SRS *with replacement* corresponds to n independent random draws, with replacement, of a single unit from the finite population.

Let the random variable T_j represent the number of times that the jth unit is selected in a sample of size n. Clearly, T_j may take any of the values $0, 1, \ldots, n$. Because in any given draw each population unit has probability N^{-1} of being selected and because the n draws are independent, the distribution of T_j is $\mathrm{Bi}(n, N^{-1})$ for all j. Therefore, the probability of sample selection, or *first-order inclusion probability*, is

$$\Pr\{T_j > 0\} = 1 - \Pr\{T_j = 0\} = 1 - \left(1 - \frac{1}{N}\right)^n, \qquad j = 1, \ldots, N,$$

and is the same for all population units. This probability tends to one as $n \to \infty$ and to zero as $N \to \infty$.

The next result records some properties of the sample values $Z_1, \ldots, Z_n$.

Theorem 2.1 *Under SRS with replacement:*

(i) $\mathrm{E}\, Z_i = \mu$ *for all* i*;*
(ii) $\mathrm{Var}\, Z_i = \sigma^2$ *for all* i*;*
(iii) $\mathrm{Cov}(Z_i, Z_j) = 0$ *for all* $i \neq j$*.*

If the population parameters μ and σ^2 are unknown, one may try to estimate them using some *statistic*, that is, some function $T(Z_1, \ldots, Z_n)$ that depends only on the data. Viewed as a transformation of the random variables $Z_1, \ldots, Z_n$, a statistic T is itself a random variable. Its probability distribution, induced by the sampling process, is called the *sampling distribution* of T and the characteristics of such a distribution (e.g. its moments or quantiles) are called the sampling characteristics of T.

Natural statistics to consider, in our case, are the sample mean $\bar{Z} = n^{-1} \sum_i Z_i$ and the sample mean squared deviation $\hat{\sigma}^2 = n^{-1} \sum_i (Z_i - \bar{Z})^2$. The next corollary derives the *sampling mean* of $\bar{Z}$ and $\hat{\sigma}^2$ and the *sampling variance* of $\hat{\sigma}^2$, that is, the average values of $\bar{Z}$ and $\hat{\sigma}^2$ and the variance of $\bar{Z}$ over all possible samples of size n from the given population.

Corollary 2.1 *Under SRS with replacement*

$$\mathrm{E}\, \bar{Z} = \mu, \qquad \mathrm{Var}\, \bar{Z} = \frac{\sigma^2}{n}, \qquad \mathrm{E}\, \hat{\sigma}^2 = \sigma^2 \left(1 - \frac{1}{n}\right).$$

This corollary implies that, no matter what the population mean μ is, the sampling mean of $\bar{Z}$ is equal to μ. For this reason, $\bar{Z}$ is said to be an *unbiased* estimator of μ. The corollary also implies that the sampling variance of $\bar{Z}$ tends to vanish as the sample size increases. Because the sampling distribution of $\bar{Z}$ becomes more and more concentrated around the target parameter μ as the sample size increases, $\bar{Z}$ becomes an increasingly precise estimator of μ. It then follows from the results in Appendix D.1

that the sequence of estimators $\{\bar{Z}_n\} = \{\bar{Z}_1, \bar{Z}_2, \ldots\}$, corresponding to increasing sample sizes, converges in mean square and therefore in probability to μ, that is, the sample mean is a consistent estimator of the population mean μ.

When σ^2 is unknown, a simple way of obtaining information about the sampling variance of $\bar{Z}$ consists of dividing by n an estimate of the population variance, such as the mean squared deviation $\hat{\sigma}^2$. Notice however that $\mathrm{E}\,\hat{\sigma}^2 \neq \sigma^2$ for any σ^2, that is, $\hat{\sigma}^2$ is a ***biased*** estimator of σ^2. In turn, this implies that $\hat{\sigma}^2/n$ is a biased estimator of the sampling variance of $\bar{Z}$. The difference

$$\mathrm{E}\,\hat{\sigma}^2 - \sigma^2 = -\frac{\sigma^2}{n}$$

is called the ***bias*** of $\hat{\sigma}^2$ as an estimator of σ^2 and is denoted by $\mathrm{Bias}\,\hat{\sigma}^2$. Since the bias of $\hat{\sigma}^2$ is negative, $\hat{\sigma}^2$ is said to be ***downward biased*** for σ^2. It is clear from Corollary 2.1 that an unbiased estimator of σ^2 is the sample variance

$$s^2 = \hat{\sigma}^2 \frac{n}{n-1} = \frac{1}{n-1} \sum_{i=1}^{n} (Z_i - \bar{Z})^2.$$

Hence, an unbiased estimator of the sampling variance of $\bar{Z}$ is given by s^2/n.

2.1.2 SRS WITHOUT REPLACEMENT

Under sampling with replacement, the same population unit may be included more than once in a sample of size $n > 1$. For this reason, more frequently used in practice is SRS *without replacement*, corresponding to the random draw of a set of $n < N$ distinct population units or, equivalently, to n successive random draws, without replacement, of a single population unit.

Since we disregard the order of the elements in a sample, the number of samples of size n that can be obtained in this way is equal to the number of combinations of N elements taken n at a time

$$\binom{N}{n} = \frac{N!}{n!(N-n)!}.$$

All these samples have the same probability $n!(N-n)!/N!$ of being drawn. Thus, under SRS without replacement, the probability of selecting a sample, or *sampling design*, is described by a uniform distribution on the set of possible samples. Since the jth population unit shows up in $\binom{N-1}{n-1}$ of the possible samples, all population units have first-order inclusion probabilities equal to

$$\frac{\binom{N-1}{n-1}}{\binom{N}{n}} = \frac{n}{N},$$

where n/N is called the *sampling fraction* and its reciprocal N/n is called the *inflation factor*. Unlike SRS with replacement, however, the sample observations are no longer uncorrelated.

Theorem 2.2 *Under SRS without replacement:*

(i) $\mathrm{E}\, Z_i = \mu$ *for all* i;
(ii) $\mathrm{Var}\, Z_i = \sigma^2$ *for all* i;
(iii) $\mathrm{Cov}(Z_i, Z_j) = -\sigma^2/(N-1)$ *for all* $i \neq j$.

Corollary 2.2 *Under SRS without replacement*

$$\mathrm{E}\, \bar{Z} = \mu, \qquad \mathrm{Var}\, \bar{Z} = \frac{\sigma^2}{n}\left(\frac{N-n}{N-1}\right), \qquad \mathrm{E}\, \hat{\sigma}^2 = \sigma^2 \frac{N}{N-1}\left(1 - \frac{1}{n}\right).$$

The sample mean $\bar{Z}$ remains an unbiased estimator of μ. However, because the ratio $(N-n)/(N-1)$, called *finite population correction*, is less than one for $n > 1$, the sampling variance of $\bar{Z}$ is smaller than under sampling with replacement. The bias of $\hat{\sigma}^2$ is now

$$\mathrm{Bias}\, \hat{\sigma}^2 = -\frac{\sigma^2}{n}\left(\frac{N-n}{N-1}\right),$$

and an unbiased estimator of σ^2 is

$$\tilde{\sigma}^2 = \hat{\sigma}^2 \frac{n(N-1)}{(n-1)N} = s^2 \left(1 - \frac{1}{N}\right).$$

An unbiased estimator of the sampling variance of $\bar{Z}$ is therefore

$$\widehat{\mathrm{Var}}\, \bar{Z} = \frac{\tilde{\sigma}^2}{n}\left(\frac{N-n}{N-1}\right) = \frac{s^2}{n}\left(1 - \frac{n}{N}\right).$$

Notice that, for a fixed sample size n, the sampling variance of $\bar{Z}$ declines linearly with the sampling fraction n/N and is equal to zero when $n = N$. If the sampling fraction is very small, then $\mathrm{Var}\, \bar{Z} \approx \sigma^2/n$, which depends only on the population variance σ^2 and the sample size n, but not on the population size N.

2.1.3 UNEQUAL PROBABILITY SAMPLING

SRS, with or without replacement, is an example of *equal probability sampling*, that is, a sampling design whose first-order inclusion probabilities are the same for all population units. In practice, however, decisions by the survey statisticians as well as self-selection or nonresponse decisions by the economic agents being studied, or both, may lead to sampling schemes that differ from equal probability sampling. In these cases, ignoring the nature of the sampling process may lead to estimates of the target parameters that are biased no matter how large the sample size.

Let D_j be a random variable that takes value one if the jth population unit is included in the sample and value zero otherwise. The random variable D_j is called the *sample membership indicator* of the jth population unit. Clearly, $\pi_j = \Pr\{D_j = 1\}$ is its first-order inclusion probability. The probability $\pi_{jk} = \Pr\{D_j = 1, D_k = 1\}$ that the jth and kth population units are both included in the sample is called their *second-order inclusion probability.* In practice, a sampling design is often chosen to attain certain desired first- and second-order inclusion probabilities.

The next result gathers some properties of the sample membership indicators.

Theorem 2.3 *For an arbitrary sampling design and for all $j, k = 1, \dots, N$:*

(i) $\mathrm{E}\, D_j = \pi_j$;
(ii) $\mathrm{Var}\, D_j = \pi_j(1 - \pi_j)$;
(iii) $\mathrm{Cov}(D_j, D_k) = \pi_{jk} - \pi_j \pi_k$, $j \neq k$.

Proof. Conclusions (i) and (ii) follow from the fact that D_j is a Bernoulli random variable. Conclusion (iii) follows from the fact that $\mathrm{Cov}(D_j, D_k) = \mathrm{E}\, D_j D_k - (\mathrm{E}\, D_j)(\mathrm{E}\, D_k)$, where $\mathrm{E}\, D_j D_k = \Pr\{D_j = 1, D_k = 1\} = \pi_{jk}$. □

Now consider the problem of estimating the population total $\tau = \sum_{j=1}^N z_j$. The sample total $n\bar{Z} = \sum_{i=1}^n Z_i$ is clearly downward biased for τ. Intuitively, since the sample contains fewer units than the population, an expansion is required to reach the level of the whole population. When the N population units have positive but possibly different first-order inclusion probabilities, an alternative to the sample total is the *Horvitz–Thompson estimator*

$$\hat{\tau} = \sum_{i=1}^n \frac{Z_i}{\pi_i},$$

where the ith sample unit represents $1/\pi_i$ population units. The Horvitz–Thompson estimator may also be written as a linear combination of the sample membership indicators

$$\hat{\tau} = \sum_{j=1}^N D_j \frac{z_j}{\pi_j}.$$

This is the key to establishing its sampling properties.

Corollary 2.3 *For an arbitrary sampling design,* $\mathrm{E}\,\hat{\tau} = \tau$ *and*

$$\mathrm{Var}\,\hat{\tau} = \sum_{j=1}^N \sum_{k=1}^N \mathrm{Cov}(D_j, D_k) \frac{z_j z_k}{\pi_j \pi_k}.$$

Since the Horvitz–Thompson estimator is unbiased for the population total, $\hat{\mu} = \hat{\tau}/N$ is unbiased for the population mean μ. This need not be true for the sample mean, however, because $\mathrm{E}\,\bar{Z} = n^{-1} \sum_{j=1}^N \pi_j z_j$ may differ from μ if $\pi_j \neq n/N$, that is, the sampling scheme differs from SRS.

2.1.4 STRATIFIED SAMPLING

We now consider the case when a survey is *stratified*, that is, the population units have inclusion probabilities that differ depending on what population subgroup or *stratum* they belong to. Specifically, we discuss the case of *stratified random sampling with replacement*, where a finite population of size N is first partitioned into $S > 1$ strata $\mathcal{A}_1, \dots, \mathcal{A}_S$, each containing $N_s \geq 1$ units, and then a simple random sample of size $n_s \geq 1$ is separately drawn, with replacement, from each stratum. Thus, first-order inclusion probabilities are equal for units belonging to the same stratum but may differ for units belonging to different strata.

Partition of the population into strata is carried out before collecting the data and is generally based on the value of some known characteristic of the sample units. Notice, however, that the presence of stratification need not imply heterogeneity across strata. For example, the population may be completely homogeneous and the strata simply reflect the branches or administrative divisions of the agency running the survey.

Let $\pi_s = N_s/N$ denote the relative importance of the sth stratum in the population, or sth *population stratum weight*, and let μ_s and σ_s^2 denote, respectively, the population mean and variance for the sth stratum. Our parameter of interest is the overall population mean, defined as the weighted sum $\mu_* = \sum_{s=1}^S \pi_s \mu_s$ of the population stratum means, where the weights π_s are such that $\sum_s \pi_s = 1$. If all strata have the same mean, that is, $\mu_s = \mu$ for all s, then $\mu_* = \mu$.

The sth *sample stratum weight* is defined as $p_s = n_s/n$, where $n = \sum_s n_s$. If $\omega_s = n_s/N_s$ denotes the sampling fraction for the sth stratum, then the relationship between the sample stratum weights and the population stratum weights is

$$p_s = \frac{n_s}{\sum_{j=1}^S n_j} = \frac{\omega_s N_s}{\sum_{j=1}^S \omega_j N_j} = \frac{\omega_s (N_s/N)}{\sum_{j=1}^S \omega_j (N_j/N)} = w_s \pi_s,$$

where

$$w_s = \frac{\omega_s}{\sum_{j=1}^S \omega_j \pi_j}.$$

We want to compare the sampling properties of the simple average $\bar{Z} = n^{-1} \sum_i Z_i$, where $\bar{Z}_s = n_s^{-1} \sum_{i \in \mathcal{A}_s} Z_i$ is the sth sample stratum mean, with those of the stratified average $\bar{Z}_* = \sum_{s=1}^S \pi_s \bar{Z}_s$, which is based on the knowledge of the population stratum weights. The next result gives the essential properties of the sample stratum means. The proof follows immediately from Theorem 2.2 and the fact that sampling is carried out separately across strata.

Theorem 2.4 *Under stratified random sampling:*

(i) $\mathrm{E}\, \bar{Z}_s = \mu_s$, $s = 1, \ldots, S$;
(ii) $\mathrm{Var}\, \bar{Z}_s = \sigma_s^2/n_s$, $s = 1, \ldots, S$;
(iii) $\bar{Z}_1, \ldots, \bar{Z}_S$ *are uncorrelated.*

We can now compare the sampling properties of $\bar{Z}$ and $\bar{Z}_*$.

Corollary 2.4 *Under stratified random sampling:*

(i) $\mathrm{E}\, \bar{Z} = \sum_s p_s \mu_s$;
(ii) $\mathrm{E}\, \bar{Z}_* = \mu_*$;
(iii) $\mathrm{Var}\, \bar{Z} = n^{-1} \sum_s p_s \sigma_s^2$;
(iv) $\mathrm{Var}\, \bar{Z}_* = \sum_s \pi_s^2 \sigma_s^2 / n_s$.

Proof. Immediate from the definition of $\bar{Z}_*$ and the fact that $\bar{Z} = \sum_{s=1}^S p_s \bar{Z}_s$. □

This shows that knowledge of the population stratum weights is essential in order to obtain good estimates of the μ_*, the population parameter of interest. More precisely, while the stratified average $\bar{Z}_*$ is an unbiased estimator of μ_*, the simple average $\bar{Z}$

is biased unless all strata have the same mean or the sampling scheme is such that $p_s = \pi_s$ for all strata, in which case $\bar{Z} = \bar{Z}_*$. When the latter condition holds, which is equivalent to the fact that the sampling fractions ω_s are the same for all strata, we say that there is *self-weighting* or *probability proportional to size (PPS)*.

It is worth stressing that, in order to obtain an unbiased estimator of the target parameter μ_*, three conditions are necessary: (i) the stratification $\mathcal{A}_1, \ldots, \mathcal{A}_S$ must correspond to a partition of the population, that is, $\sum_s \pi_s = 1$; (ii) the population stratum weights π_s must all be known; and (iii) the sampling scheme must be such that $n_s > 0$ for each stratum, so that $\bar{Z}_s$ can be computed for all s.

Example 2.1 Consider a heterogeneous population consisting of $S = 2$ strata and suppose that data are available for the first stratum but not for the second, that is, $n_1 > 0$ but $n_2 = 0$. In this case, the sample mean $\bar{Z}_1$ for the first stratum is a biased estimator of the population mean $\mu_* = \pi_1\mu_1 + \pi_2\mu_2$. Its bias is equal to $\mathrm{E}\,\bar{Z}_1 - \mu_* = \mu_1 - \mu_* = \pi_2(\mu_1 - \mu_2)$, which increases with the population weight of the second stratum and with the difference $\mu_1 - \mu_2$ between the population stratum means. □

2.1.5 OPTIMAL SAMPLE ALLOCATION

Why not always using PPS? The answer depends on both the cost differentials in data collection and the presence of heterogeneity across strata.

Suppose that the cost of a sample survey consists of a fixed cost c_0 and variable unit costs $c_s > 0$, which may differ across strata. We want to determine an *optimal sample allocation*, that is, a set $n_1, \ldots, n_S$ of sample sizes, one for each stratum, such that the sampling variance of the stratified average $\bar{Z}_*$ is minimized subject to a total budget C to carry out the survey. Formally, the problem is

$$\min_{\{n_s\}} \quad V = \sum_{s=1}^{S} \frac{\pi_s^2 \sigma_s^2}{n_s}$$

$$\text{such that} \quad c_0 + \sum_{s=1}^{S} c_s n_s \leq C.$$

If the budget constraint is satisfied with equality, then minimizing the sampling variance of the stratified average is equivalent to minimizing the product $V(C - c_0)$ with respect to the choice of the n_s. Given two vectors $a, b \in \Re^S$, the Cauchy–Schwarz inequality implies that

$$\left(\sum_{s=1}^{S} a_s b_s\right)^2 \leq \left(\sum_{s=1}^{S} a_s^2\right)\left(\sum_{s=1}^{S} b_s^2\right),$$

with equality if and only if there exists a constant k such that $a_s = kb_s$, $s = 1, \ldots, S$. Letting

$$a_s = (c_s n_s)^{1/2}, \qquad b_s = \left(\frac{\pi_s^2 \sigma_s^2}{n_s}\right)^{1/2}, \qquad s = 1, \ldots, S,$$

it then follows that the function $V(C - c_0)$ attains its minimum if and only if

$$(c_s n_s)^{1/2} = k \left(\frac{\pi_s^2 \sigma_s^2}{n_s} \right)^{1/2}, \qquad s = 1, \ldots, S.$$

Solving for n_s gives the optimal sample allocation

$$\tilde{n}_s = k \frac{\sigma_s}{\sqrt{c_s}} \pi_s, \qquad s = 1, \ldots, S, \tag{2.1}$$

where the constant k may be obtained by substituting into the budget constraint.

If the variances σ_s^2 and the unit costs c_s are the same for all strata, then we obtain PPS. Otherwise, the optimal sample allocation oversamples the strata with higher variance or lower unit costs, and undersamples the strata with lower variance or higher unit costs. In particular, even when the population stratum variances are all the same, PPS may not be optimal in the presence of cost differentials across strata.

Now suppose that all strata have the same mean μ and the same unit costs, but there are differences in the population stratum variances. We want to quantify the advantage of using the optimal sampling allocation instead of PPS. Under the optimal sample allocation

$$\frac{\tilde{n}_s}{\tilde{n}} = \frac{\pi_s \sigma_s}{\sum_{j=1}^S \pi_j \sigma_j} = \frac{\pi_s \sigma_s}{\bar{\sigma}}, \qquad s = 1, \ldots, S,$$

where $\tilde{n} = \sum_s \tilde{n}_s$ and $\bar{\sigma} = \sum_j \pi_j \sigma_j$. In this case

$$\operatorname{Var} \bar{Z}_* = \sum_s \pi_s^2 \frac{\sigma_s^2}{\tilde{n}_s} = \frac{1}{\tilde{n}} \sum_s \pi_s^2 \sigma_s^2 \frac{\tilde{n}}{\tilde{n}_s} = \frac{1}{\tilde{n}} \sum_s \pi_s^2 \sigma_s^2 \frac{\bar{\sigma}}{\pi_s \sigma_s} = \frac{\bar{\sigma}^2}{\tilde{n}}.$$

Under self-weighting, one instead has that $\bar{Z}_* = \bar{Z}$. If the total sample size is equal to $\tilde{n}$, then

$$\operatorname{Var} \bar{Z} = \sum_s \pi^2 \frac{\sigma_s^2}{n_s} = \frac{1}{\tilde{n}} \sum_s \pi_s \sigma_s^2,$$

because $n_s = \tilde{n}\pi_s$ in this case. Hence

$$\begin{aligned} \operatorname{Var} \bar{Z} - \operatorname{Var} \bar{Z}_* &= \frac{1}{\tilde{n}} \left(\sum_s \pi_s \sigma_s^2 - \bar{\sigma}^2 \right) \\ &= \frac{1}{\tilde{n}} \sum_s \pi_s (\sigma_s^2 - 2\sigma_s \bar{\sigma} + \bar{\sigma}^2) = \frac{1}{\tilde{n}} \sum_s \pi_s (\sigma_s - \bar{\sigma})^2 \geq 0, \end{aligned}$$

with equality if and only if all strata have the same variance.

2.2 SAMPLING FROM AN INFINITE POPULATION

The distinction between SRS with and without replacement disappears when the size of a finite population is very large. In this case, it simplifies matters considerably to treat the population as infinite, for we can drop any reference to the individual population units and represent the variability of a numeric characteristic of the population by a random variable Z defined on a suitable probability space $(\mathcal{Z}, \mathcal{A}, P)$.

In the infinite population case, SRS may be formalized by representing the data as n independent realizations of the parent random variable Z or, equivalently, as one of the possible realizations of a collection $Z_1, \ldots, Z_n$ of *independently and identically distributed (i.i.d.)* random variables (or vectors), whose common distribution is equal to that of Z. In this case we also say that the data are a *sample from the distribution of the random variable* Z. The probability distribution of Z is also called the *parent distribution* and its distribution function is also called the *parent distribution function.*

2.2.1 PROPERTIES OF THE SAMPLE MEAN AND VARIANCE

This section reviews well known properties of the sample mean $\bar{Z}$ and the sample variance s^2 under sampling from a probability distribution.

Theorem 2.5 *If $Z_1, \ldots, Z_n$ is a sample from a distribution with mean μ and variance $0 < \sigma^2 < \infty$, then:*

(i) $\mathrm{E}\,\bar{Z} = \mu$;
(ii) $\mathrm{Var}\,\bar{Z} = \sigma^2/n$;
(iii) $\mathrm{E}\,s^2 = \sigma^2$ *for all* $n > 1$;
(iv) **(Gauss–Markov theorem)** *$\bar{Z}$ has smallest sampling variance in the class of estimators of μ that are unbiased and linear, that is, of the form $\hat{\mu} = \sum_{i=1}^n c_i Z_i$, where the c_i are constant.*

By properties (i) and (iii), the sample mean and variance are unbiased estimators of the population mean and variance. By property (ii), the precision of the sample mean increases as the sample size increases. Because convergence in mean square implies convergence in probability, this implies that the sequence of estimators $\{\bar{Z}_n\} = (\bar{Z}_1, \bar{Z}_2, \ldots)$, corresponding to increasing sample sizes, is consistent for μ. Further, because of property (iv), the sample mean is said to be a minimum variance linear unbiased or simply a *best linear unbiased (BLU)* estimator of μ.

Theorem 2.5 gives information only on the first and second moments of the sampling distribution of $\bar{Z}$ and the first moment of the sampling distribution of s^2. In the important special case when the population is well described by a Gaussian distribution, it is possible to completely characterize the sampling distribution of $\bar{Z}$ and s^2.

Theorem 2.6 *If $Z_1, \ldots, Z_n$ is a sample from a $\mathcal{N}(\mu, \sigma^2)$ distribution, then:*

(i) $\bar{Z} \sim \mathcal{N}(\mu, \sigma^2/n)$;
(ii) $(n-1)s^2/\sigma^2 \sim \chi^2_{n-1}$ *for all* $n > 1$;
(iii) *$\bar{Z}$ and s^2 are indepedent;*
(iv) *$\bar{Z}$ and s^2 have smallest sampling variance in the class of estimators that are unbiased for μ and σ^2;*
(v) $T = \sqrt{n}\,(\bar{Z} - \mu)/s \sim t_{n-1}$;
(vi) $F = T^2 \sim F_{1,n-1}$.

Result (iv) of Theorem 2.6 is stronger than the Gauss–Markov theorem. We shall refer to this result by saying that, under sampling from a Gaussian population with finite variance, the sample mean and the sample variance are best unbiased or *minimum variance unbiased (MVU)* estimators of the population mean and variance.

The next result shows that, even without the normality assumption, Theorem 2.6 provides a good approximation to the sampling properties of the sample mean and variance when the sample size is very large. We denote by $\{\bar{Z}_n\}$, $\{s_n^2\}$, $\{T_n\}$, $\{F_n\}$ sequences of estimators and test statistics corresponding to increasing sample sizes.

Theorem 2.7 *If $Z_1, \ldots, Z_n$ is a sample from a distribution with mean μ and variance $0 < \sigma^2 < \infty$, then:*

(i) $\sqrt{n}\,(\bar{Z}_n - \mu) \xrightarrow{\text{d}} \mathcal{N}(0, \sigma^2)$;
(ii) $\sqrt{n}\,(s_n^2 - \sigma^2) \xrightarrow{\text{d}} \mathcal{N}(0, 2\sigma^4)$;
(iii) $\bar{Z}_n$ *and* s_n^2 *are asymptotically independent;*
(iv) $T_n = \sqrt{n}\,(\bar{Z}_n - \mu)/s_n \xrightarrow{\text{d}} \mathcal{N}(0, 1)$;
(v) $F_n = T_n^2 \xrightarrow{\text{d}} \chi_1^2$.

2.2.2 THE EMPIRICAL DISTRIBUTION FUNCTION

Let $Z_1, \ldots, Z_n$ be a sample from the distribution of a random variable Z with distribution function F, and consider the problem of estimating F and not just some of its characteristics such as the mean and the variance. Estimating F is usually the first step in the exploratory analysis of the data and is often an essential component of more complex statistical procedures.

If the population distribution function belongs to a known parametric family $\mathcal{F}_\Theta$ of distributions, then the problem reduces to estimating a point in the parameter space Θ. This problem is discussed in Section 4.4. Here we consider the case when the available information is not enough to restrict F to a particular parametric family. How can F be estimated in this case? The solution to this problem is not only of practical importance but, as we shall see in Chapter 4, also helps in clarifying the common nature of apparently different approaches to statistical estimation.

The key to estimating F is the fact that, for any z, $F(z) = \Pr\{Z \le z\} = \mathrm{E}\,1\{Z \le z\}$, that is, $F(z)$ is just the mean of the Bernoulli random variable $1\{Z \le z\}$. This suggests estimating $F(z)$ by its sample counterpart

$$\hat{F}(z) = n^{-1} \sum_{i=1}^{n} 1\{Z_i \le z\}, \tag{2.2}$$

namely the fraction of sample points for which $Z_i \le z$. Viewed as a function of z, $\hat{F}$ is called the *empirical* or *sample distribution function.* Figure 16 shows the empirical distribution function of a sample of size 50 from the $\mathcal{N}(0, 1)$ distribution.

It is easy to verify that $\hat{F}$ is the distribution function of a discrete probability measure, called the *empirical measure* of Z_i, which assigns to a set A a probability equal to the fraction of sample points contained in A. In particular, each distinct sample point receives probability equal to $1/n$, whereas each sample point repeated $m \le n$ times receives probability equal to m/n.

Suppose that all the observations are distinct and let $Z_{[1]} < \cdots < Z_{[n]}$ be the ordered sample values, or sample *order statistics.* Then the empirical distribution function may

Figure 16 Empirical distribution function $\hat{F}$ of a sample of size 50 from the $\mathcal{N}(0,1)$ distribution. The population distribution function is denoted by Φ.

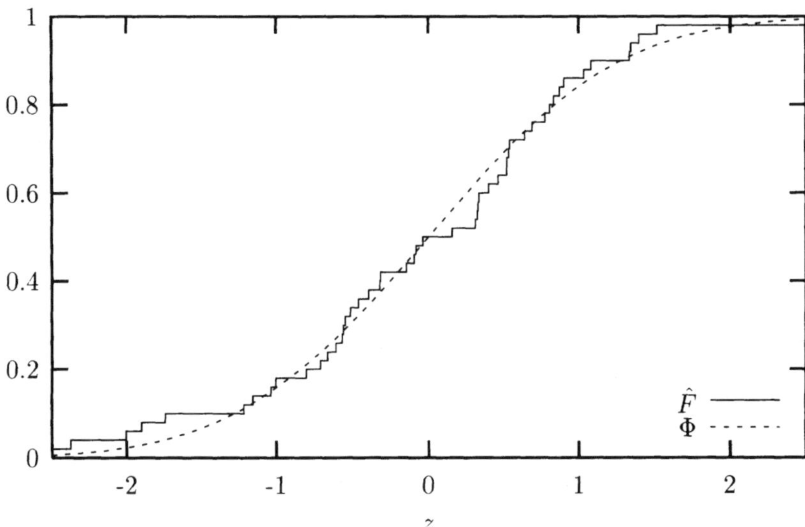

also be written

$$\hat{F}(z) = \begin{cases} 0, & \text{if } z < Z_{[1]}, \\ i/n, & \text{if } Z_{[i]} \leq z < Z_{[i+1]}, \qquad i = 1, \ldots, n-1, \\ 1 & \text{if } z \geq Z_{[n]}. \end{cases}$$

This shows that the empirical distribution function contains all the information carried by the sample, except the order in which the observations are arranged.

The fact that $\hat{F}(z)$ is just an average of n i.i.d. random variables with a common Bernoulli distribution is also the key to establishing its sampling properties.

Theorem 2.8 *If $Z_1, \ldots, Z_n$ is a sample from a distribution with distribution function F, then for all z:*

(i) $n\hat{F}(z) \sim \mathrm{Bi}(n, F(z))$;
(ii) $\mathrm{E}\,\hat{F}(z) = F(z)$;
(iii) $\mathrm{Var}\,\hat{F}(z) = n^{-1}F(z)[1 - F(z)]$;
(iv) $\mathrm{Cov}[\hat{F}(z), \hat{F}(z')] = n^{-1}F(z)[1 - F(z')]$ *for any* $z' > z$.

Hence, for any z, $\hat{F}(z)$ is an unbiased estimator of $F(z)$. Notice that, because of the correlation between $\hat{F}(z)$ and $\hat{F}(z')$, some care is needed in drawing inference about the shape of F. As the sample size increases, however, the sampling variance of $\hat{F}(z)$ and the correlation between $\hat{F}(z)$ and $\hat{F}(z')$ both tend to vanish. As a result, the sequence $\{\hat{F}_n(z)\}$ of estimators, corresponding to increasing sample sizes, is consistent for $F(z)$, while $\hat{F}(z)$ and $\hat{F}(z')$ are asymptotically uncorrelated. Being the average of n i.i.d. random variables with finite variance, $\hat{F}_n(z)$ also satisfies the standard CLT and is therefore asymptotically normal.

Theorem 2.9 *If $Z_1, \ldots, Z_n$ is a sample from a distribution with distribution function F, then $\hat{F}_n(z) \xrightarrow{p} F(z)$ for all z. Further, given any two distinct points $z_j < z_k$, let $\mathbf{F} = (F(z_j), F(z_k))$ and $\hat{\mathbf{F}}_n = (\hat{F}_n(z_j), \hat{F}_n(z_k))$. Then, as $n \to \infty$, $\sqrt{n}\,(\hat{\mathbf{F}}_n - \mathbf{F}) \xrightarrow{d} \mathcal{N}_2(0, \Sigma)$ with $\Sigma = [\sigma_{jk}]$, where $\sigma_{jk} = F(z_j)[1 - F(z_k)]$ can be estimated consistently by $\hat{\sigma}_{jk} = \hat{F}_n(z_j)[1 - \hat{F}_n(z_k)]$.*

A much stronger result is that, as the sample size increases, convergence of $\hat{F}$ to F is uniform in the following sense. As a measure of distance between the random function $\hat{F}$ and F consider the *Kolmogorov–Smirnov statistic*

$$D_n = \sup_{-\infty < z < \infty} |\hat{F}(z) - F(z)|.$$

Since $\hat{F}$ depends on the data, D_n is itself a random variable. A fundamental result, known as the *Glivenko–Cantelli theorem* (see e.g. van der Vaart 1998), shows that if $Z_1, \ldots, Z_n$ are i.i.d. with distribution function F, then $D_n \xrightarrow{as} 0$ as $n \to \infty$, that is, the event that D_n does not converge to zero as the sample size increases without bounds occurs with zero probability under repeated sampling. This implies that the entire probabilistic structure of Z can almost certainly be uncovered from the sample data provided that the sample size is large enough.

The definition of empirical distribution function and its sampling properties are easily generalized to the case when Z is a random vector. In particular, if $Z_i = (X_i, Y_i)$, then the *joint empirical distribution function* is defined as

$$\hat{F}(x, y) = n^{-1} \sum_{i=1}^{n} 1\{X_i \le x, Y_i \le y\} = n^{-1} \sum_{i=1}^{n} 1\{X_i \le x\}\, 1\{Y_i \le y\}, \tag{2.3}$$

that is, $\hat{F}(x, y)$ is the fraction of sample points such that X_i is at most equal to x and Y_i is at most equal to y. The empirical marginal distribution function of, say, X may be obtained from $\hat{F}(x, y)$ through the relationship $\hat{F}(x) = \lim_{y \to \infty} \hat{F}(x, y)$.

When X is discrete and x is one of its possible values, the conditional distribution function of Y given $X = x$ is defined as

$$F(y \,|\, x) = \Pr\{Y \le y \,|\, X = x\} = \frac{\Pr\{Y \le y, X = x\}}{\Pr\{X = x\}}.$$

If $\mathcal{O}(x) = \{i\colon X_i = x\}$ is the set of sample points such that $X_i = x$ and $n(x)$ is their number, then the sample counterpart of $\Pr\{X = x\}$ is the fraction $n(x)/n$ of sample points such that $X_i = x$. Hence, if $n(x) > 0$, a reasonable estimate of $F(y \,|\, x)$ is the fraction of sample points in $\mathcal{O}(x)$ such that $Y_i \le y$

$$\hat{F}(y \,|\, x) = n(x)^{-1} \sum_{i=1}^{n} 1\{Y_i \le y, X_i = x\} = n(x)^{-1} \sum_{i \in \mathcal{O}(x)} 1\{Y_i \le y\}. \tag{2.4}$$

Viewed as a function of y for x fixed, $\hat{F}(y \,|\, x)$ is called the *conditional empirical distribution function of Y_i given $X_i = x$.*

2.3 SELECTIVE SAMPLING

SRS is of fundamental importance in theoretical statistics, because it guarantees perfect coincidence between the model that represents variability at the population level and the one that represents variability at the sample level. As already seen, however, many sampling schemes of practical importance are quite far from this ideal.

To formalize the distinction between the models of variability at the population and the sample level, we represent the population by a random variable (or vector) Z with density function f and the sample by a collection $Z_1, \ldots, Z_n$ of i.i.d. random variables (or vectors) with common density function $g(z) = w(z)\, f(z)$, where $w(z)$ is a non-negative function that represents the sampling scheme. Because the density function g must integrate to one, the weight function w must satisfy the further restriction that $\mathrm{E}\, w(Z) = 1$. In order to incorporate this restriction, $w(z)$ may also be represented as

$$w(z) = \frac{\omega(z)}{\mathrm{E}\, \omega(Z)},$$

where $\omega(z)$ is a non-negative function with a finite mean.

This formulation assumes that the sampling scheme consists of n independent replications of the same chance experiment, but allows the model of variability to be different at the sample and the population level. SRS corresponds to the case when $w(z) = 1$. A more general sampling scheme introduces a systematic difference between the probability distribution of a single sample observation and that of the population. When this occurs, we say that sampling is *selective*. In particular, values of Z such that $w(z) > 1$ are oversampled, values such that $0 < w(z) < 1$ are undersampled, whereas values such that $w(z) = 0$ are systematically missing in the data.

Suppose that the following three conditions are met:

1. the support of Z is known;
2. the weight function w is known and different from zero;
3. the density function g is known or may accurately be estimated from the available data.

Under these conditions, the population density f can be recovered from the knowledge of w and g through the relationship

$$f(z) = \frac{g(z)}{w(z)}. \tag{2.5}$$

Condition 2. may be weakened by allowing $w(z)$ to be equal to zero on a set of points with zero probability. In this case, the relationship (2.5) allows the population density f to be recovered at essentially any point z on the support of Z. When $\Pr\{w(Z) = 0\} > 0$, however, knowledge of w and g is no longer sufficient to recover f. If neither the support of Z nor the function w are known, then one cannot determine whether the absence of a set of values in the sample is due to the sampling scheme or instead to the fact that this set of values is impossible at the population level.

Now consider the case when $Z = (X, Y)$, where Y is the response variable and X is a vector of covariates, and let $w(z) = w(x, y)$. A sampling scheme is called *exogenously stratified* when the weight function w depends on x but not on y, that is, $w(x, y) = w(x)$ for all y. Under exogenously stratified sampling, sample selection depends only on the value of the variables in X. Sampling schemes of this kind are routinely applied in controlled experiments, where one first selects a value x of the covariate vector and then observes the value of the response variable that results from a chance experiment represented by the conditional distribution of Y given $X = x$.

Exogenously stratified sampling enjoys the following important property.

Theorem 2.10 *Let $f(y \mid x)$ denote the population conditional density of Y given $X = x$ and let $g(y \mid x)$ denote the conditional density of Y_i given $X_i = x$. Then, under exogenously stratified sampling $g(y \mid x) = f(y \mid x)$.*

Proof. Because the weight function w depends only on x, the marginal density of a sample value X_i is

$$g_X(x) = \int g(x, y)\, dy = w(x) \int f(x, y)\, dy = w(x) f_X(x),$$

where $f_X(x) = \int f(x, y)\, dy$ is the population marginal density of X. The conditional density of Y_i given $X_i = x$ is therefore

$$g(y \mid x) = \frac{g(x, y)}{g_X(x)} = \frac{w(x) f(x, y)}{w(x) f_X(x)} = f(y \mid x).$$

□

Because the conditional density of a sample observation coincides with the population conditional density of Y given X, exogenously stratified sampling schemes are said to *preserve the regression of* Y *on* X. In particular, if Y possesses a CMF and a CVF, then both coincide with those of the sampled data. Of course, the population joint distribution of X and Y and the population marginal distributions of X and Y need not coincide with those of the sampled data.

A sampling scheme is said to be *endogenously stratified* when the weight function w depends on y, or on both x and y. In general, endogenously stratified sampling does not preserve the regression of Y on X. In the remainder of this section we consider a few important examples of endogenously stratified sampling. In all these examples, the key problem is one of *identifiability*: knowledge of the distribution of the sample observations is generally not enough to recover, or "identify", the population distribution.

2.3.1 *CENSORED AND TRUNCATED SAMPLING*

In this section we consider sampling schemes that systematically exclude a fraction of the population depending on the value of Z, that is, $w(Z) = 0$ with positive probability. This may reflect design decisions by the survey statisticians as well as self-selection or nonresponse by the population units under investigation.

Let D be a binary random variable that takes value zero if $w(Z) = 0$ and value one otherwise, that is, D is the indicator of the event that $w(Z) > 0$. The fraction of the population that is subject to sampling is equal to $\Pr\{D = 1\} = \mathrm{E}\, D$. We say that sampling is *censored* if $\Pr\{D = 1\}$ is known or may accurately be estimated from the available data, otherwise we say that sampling is *truncated.* In the case of a censored sample, we further distinguish between fixed and random censoring. Censoring is said to be *fixed* if $D = 0$ over a fixed range, and is said to be *random* if the set of points for which $D = 0$ is itself random. The next two examples illustrate these concepts.

Example 2.2 To guarantee anonymity in a household survey, income data are often subject to *top-coding*, that is, the actual income amount is recorded if it falls below a certain threshold $c > 0$, otherwise the survey only contains a flag indicating that the household income is at least equal to c. If the population proportion of households with income below c is known or may be accurately estimated, then sampling is censored, otherwise it is truncated.

Let the variability of income in the population be represented by a continuous latent random variable Z^* with distribution function F, and let $D = 1\{Z^* < c\}$. The fraction of the population for which the actual income amount may be observed is equal to $\Pr\{D = 1\} = \Pr\{Z^* < c\} = F(c)$. Although the actual income amount is unobservable when it exceeds c, we may conventionally set measured income equal to c in this case. With this convention, measured income may be represented by the random variable $Z = \min(Z^*, c)$, corresponding to a *right-censored* version of Z^* with *fixed censoring at the point* c.

Let the data $(Z_1, D_1), \ldots, (Z_n, D_n)$ correspond to n independent observations on (Z, D). A truncated sample only contains households whose income is below the threshold c, that is, $D_i = 1$. Conditionally on $D_i = 1$, the distribution function of a single observation Z_i is equal to $F(z \mid Z^* < c) = F(z)/F(c)$ whenever $z < c$ and is equal to one otherwise (Figure 17), that is,

$$G(z \mid D_i = 1) = 1\{z < c\} \frac{F(z)}{F(c)} + 1\{z \geq c\}. \tag{2.6}$$

Since $F(c)$ is unknown, it is generally impossible to identify F on the basis of a truncated sample. Thus, for example, the empirical distribution function of the observed data provides a good estimate of the ratio $F(z)/F(c)$ for $z < c$, but not of $F(z)$.

A censored sample instead contains households with income both below and above the threshold c. Although in the latter case we only know that the income is not less than c, the data provide sufficient information for estimating $\Pr\{D = 1\}$, for example by $\bar{D} = n^{-1} \sum_i D_i$. The conditional distribution function of Z_i given $D_i = 1$ is equal to (2.6), while the distribution of a top-coded observation is degenerate with all its mass concentrated at the point c. Hence $G(z \mid D_i = 0) = 1\{z \geq c\}$. Because the marginal distribution of D_i is

$$\Pr\{D_i = d\} = F(c)^d \, [1 - F(c)]^{1-d}, \qquad d = 0, 1,$$

the joint distribution function of (Z_i, D_i) is

$$\begin{aligned} G(z, d) &= G(z \mid D_i = d) \Pr\{D_i = d\} \\ &= \begin{cases} 1\{z \geq c\}[1 - F(c)], & \text{if } d = 0, \\ 1\{z < c\}F(z) + 1\{z \geq c\}F(c), & \text{if } d = 1. \end{cases} \end{aligned}$$

Figure 17 Distribution function $G(z \mid D_i = 1)$ of a single observation under censored sampling from a $\mathcal{N}(0,1)$ distribution with fixed censoring at the point $c = .5$.

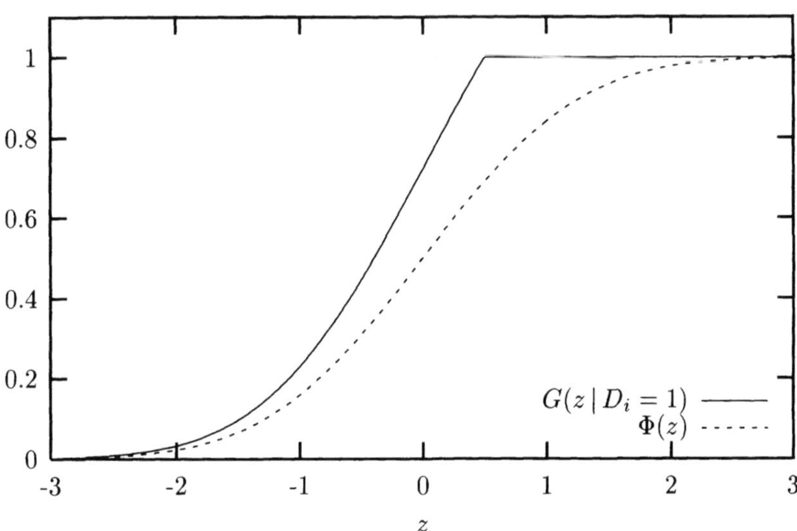

The marginal distribution function of a single observation Z_i is therefore

$$G(z) = G(z, 0) + G(z, 1) = \begin{cases} F(z), & \text{if } z < c, \\ 1, & \text{if } z \geq c. \end{cases}$$

This is the distribution function of a mixed (continuous–discrete) distribution assigning probability mass $1 - F(c)$ to the single point $z = c$ and spreading the remaining mass over the interval $(-\infty, c)$ according to the distribution function $F(z)$. It is easily seen that, if $\mu = \mathrm{E}\, Z^*$ exists, then the mean of Z_i is

$$\mathrm{E}\, Z_i = \int_{-\infty}^{c} z f(z)\, dz + c[1 - F(c)] = \mu - \int_{c}^{\infty} [1 - F(z)]\, dz < \mu.$$

Notice that a censored sample provides the investigator with enough information to identify $F(z)$ for $z < c$, but with no information to identify the shape of the population distribution function for income values above c. Although knowledge of $F(z)$ for $z < c$ is generally insufficient to identify the mean of Z^*, it is nevertheless sufficient to recover all the quantiles ζ_p of Z^* for which $p \leq F(c)$. In particular, it is enough to identify the median of Z^* whenever $F(c) > 1/2$, that is, less than half of the observations are censored. □

Example 2.3 Following Gronau (1973) and Heckman (1974), let Z^* and W^* be latent continuous non-negative random variables representing, respectively, a person's offered wage and her reservation wage, that is, the wage at which she is indifferent between working and not working. Also let D be a binary indicator representing the person's decision whether or not to work. The person works ($D = 1$) if the offered wage exceeds her reservation wage, that is, $C = W^* - Z^* < 0$, in which case her offered wage is observable and coincides with the measured wage Z. The probability of this event is $\Pr\{D = 1\} = \Pr\{C < 0\}$. Although wage data are unavailable for those who do not work ($D = 0$), wages are conventionally set equal to zero in this case. With this convention, measured wage is represented by the non-negative random variable $Z = D\,Z^*$. Notice that Z is just a left-censored version of Z^*. Unlike the fixed censoring case, however, the range of censored values of Z^* is now random since it depends on the unobservable reservation wage W^*. Denoting by $F(z, c)$ the joint distribution function of (Z^*, C), the distribution function of Z for those who work is

$$G(z \mid D = 1) = \Pr\{Z^* \leq z \mid D = 1\} = \frac{\Pr\{Z^* \leq z, C < 0\}}{\Pr\{C < 0\}} = \frac{F(z, 0)}{F_C(0)}, \qquad (2.7)$$

where $F_C(0) = \lim_{z\to\infty} F(z, 0)$. Let the data $(Z_1, D_1), \ldots, (Z_n, D_n)$ correspond to n independent observations on (Z, D). A truncated sample only contains people who work, that is, $D_i = 1$ for all i. A censored sample contains instead both people who work and people who do not work, and therefore provides enough information to estimate $\Pr\{D = 1\}$. The distribution function of Z_i for those who work is equal to (2.7), whereas for those who do not work is degenerate with all its mass concentrated at zero, that is,

$$G(z \mid D_i = 0) = \Pr\{Z_i \leq z \mid D_i = 0\} = 1\{z > 0\}.$$

The joint distribution function of (Z_i, D_i) in a censored sample is therefore

$$G(z, d) = G(z \mid D_i = d)\, \Pr\{D_i = d\} = 1\{z > 0\}\, F(z, 0)^d [1 - F_C(0)]^{1-d}.$$

Given $G(z, d)$, one can easily compute the marginal distribution of measured wages in a censored sample and compare it with the marginal distribution $F(z) = \lim_{c\to\infty} F(z, c)$ of offered wages. This model is an example of the economic models of self-selection discussed in Chapter 18. □

2.3.2 THE KAPLAN–MEIER ESTIMATOR

If the data are uncensored, then all the sample information about the population distribution function is contained in the empirical distribution function $\hat{F}(z)$. It is easily verified that the associated empirical survivor function is

$$\hat{S}(z) = 1 - \hat{F}(z) = \prod_{i: Z_{[i]} \leq z} \frac{n - i}{n - i + 1},$$

where $Z_{[i]}$ denotes the ith sample order statistic. For censored data, the analogue of the empirical survivor function is the *product limit* or *Kaplan–Meier (KM) estimator*.

Assume that the observed data Z_i are randomly right-censored, that is $Z_i = \min(Z_i^*, C_i)$, where C_i is a random variable distributed independently of the latent random variable Z_i^*. Fixed censoring (Example 2.2) corresponds to the case when C_i has a degenerate distribution with all its mass concentrated at c. Let D_i be a censoring

Table 2 Censored data (Basu 1984).

obs.	Z_i	D_i	$Z_{[i]}$	$D_{[i]}$
1	4	1	4	1
2	90	0	9	1
3	55	1	9	0
4	15	1	15	1
5	20	0	20	0
6	35	0	35	0
7	9	1	45	1
8	9	0	55	1
9	45	1	90	0
10	100	1	100	1

indicator that takes value zero if the observation is censored and value one otherwise, let $Z_{[i]}$ denote the ordered sample values of Z_i and let $D_{[i]}$ denote the associated values of the censoring indicator. The KM estimator of the survivor function is defined as

$$\tilde{S}(z) = \prod_{i:Z_{[i]}\le z} \left(\frac{n-i}{n-i+1}\right)^{D_{[i]}}.$$

Notice that $\tilde{S}$ is discrete, taking jumps only at the values of the uncensored Z_i. If there is no censoring, then $\tilde{S}$ reduces to the empirical survivor function. If the largest Z_i is censored, then $\tilde{S}(z)$ will not tend to 0 as $z \to \infty$. In this case, the convention is to set $\tilde{S}(z) = 0$ for $z \ge Z_{[n]}$.

Example 2.4 Consider the data in Table 2, which is taken from Basu (1984). The Kaplan–Meier estimator is given by

$$\tilde{S}(z) = \begin{cases} 1, & \text{if } 0 \le z < 4, \\ \tilde{S}(0)\,(1-1/10) = .9, & \text{if } 4 \le z < 9, \\ \tilde{S}(4)\,(1-1/9) = .8, & \text{if } 9 \le z < 15, \\ \tilde{S}(9)\,(1-1/7) = .69, & \text{if } 15 \le z < 45, \\ \tilde{S}(15)\,(1-1/4) = .52, & \text{if } 45 \le z < 55, \\ \tilde{S}(45)\,(1-1/3) = .35, & \text{if } 55 \le z < 100, \\ 0, & \text{otherwise.} \end{cases}$$

□

Assuming no ties, the sampling variance of $\tilde{S}(z)$ may be estimated by

$$\widehat{\text{Var}}\,\tilde{S}(z) = \tilde{S}(z)^2 \sum_{i:Z_{[i]}\le z} \frac{D_{[i]}}{(n-i)(n-i+1)},$$

which is known as *Greenwood's formula.* Asymptotic confidence bands for $\tilde{S}(z)$ have been obtained by Hall and Wellner (1980). These confidence bands reduce to the standard bands in the uncensored case.

2.3.3 BOUNDS ON THE REGRESSION FUNCTION UNDER CENSORING

Being a case of endogenously stratified sampling, censored sampling does not generally preserve the regression of Y on X. It is interesting, however, to ask what information it carries about the CMF of Y.

To answer this question notice that, if it exists, the CMF of Y can always be decomposed as

$$\mu(x) = \mu_0(x)[1 - \pi(x)] + \mu_1(x)\pi(x),$$

where $\mu_0(x) = \mathrm{E}(Y \mid X = x, D = 0)$ and $\mu_1(x) = \mathrm{E}(Y \mid X = x, D = 1)$ are respectively the CMF of Y for the censored and the uncensored data, $\pi(x) = \Pr\{D = 1 \mid X = x\} = \mathrm{E}(D \mid X = x)$ is the fraction of the population, in the stratum corresponding to $X = x$, for which Y is observable. Censored samples provide direct information on $\mu_1(x)$ and $\pi(x)$, but no information on $\mu_0(x)$. Because of this, the sample information is not sufficient to recover $\mu(x)$.

In order to deal with this problem, nonsample or prior information must be available. One assumption is clearly sufficient to identify $\mu(x)$, namely that $\mu_0(x) = \mu_1(x)$. This assumption is very restrictive, however, for it corresponds to independence between Y and D conditionally on X.

An alternative, proposed by Manski (1989), is to exploit prior information about the support of Y. Assume, specifically, that the available prior information restricts the support of Y, conditionally on $X = x$ and $D = 0$, to the closed interval $[a(x), b(x)]$, that is, $a(x) \leq \mu_0(x) \leq b(x)$. This implies that

$$\mu_1(x)\pi(x) + a(x)(1 - \pi(x)) \leq \mu_1(x)\pi(x) + \mu_0(x)(1 - \pi(x))$$

and

$$\mu_1(x)\pi(x) + \mu_0(1 - \pi(x)) \leq \mu_1(x)\pi(x) + b(x)(1 - \pi(x)),$$

that is, the population CMF $\mu(x)$ must necessarily belong to the closed interval $[\mu_L(x), \mu_U(x)]$, where

$$\begin{aligned} \mu_L(x) &= \mu_1(x)\pi(x) + a(x)(1 - \pi(x)), \\ \mu_U(x) &= \mu_1(x)\pi(x) + b(x)(1 - \pi(x)). \end{aligned} \tag{2.8}$$

The lower bound $\mu_L(x)$ is the value that $\mu_0(x)$ would take if Y was always equal to $a(x)$ for the censored population, while the upper bound $\mu_U(x)$ is the value that $\mu_0(x)$ would take if Y was always equal to $b(x)$. The length of the interval is equal to $[b(x) - a(x)]\,[1 - \pi(x)]$ and may be interpreted as a measure of how informative a censored sample can be about $\mu(x)$. The smaller is the range of $\mu_0(x)$, or the censoring probability $1 - \pi(x)$, the more informative are the data.

An important special case is when Y is a 0–1 random variable, and therefore $\mu(x) = \Pr\{Y = 1 \mid X = x\}$ and $\mu_d(x) = \Pr\{Y = 1 \mid X = x, D = d\}$, $d = 0, 1$. Because natural bounds for $\mu_0(x)$ are in this case $a(x) = 0$ and $b(x) = 1$, we obtain

$$\mu_L(x) = \mu_1(x)\pi(x), \qquad \mu_U(x) = \mu_1(x)\pi(x) + 1 - \pi(x). \tag{2.9}$$

Notice that the length of the interval $[\mu_L(x), \mu_U(x)]$ is now equal to the censoring probability $1 - \pi(x)$.

Figure 18 Bounds on the conditional median of a random variable Y under censoring. The conditional median of Y is equal to zero, the censoring probability is 20 percent, and the conditional distribution of Y is $\mathcal{N}(0,1)$ for the uncensored population and $\mathcal{N}(0,1.5)$ for the censored one.

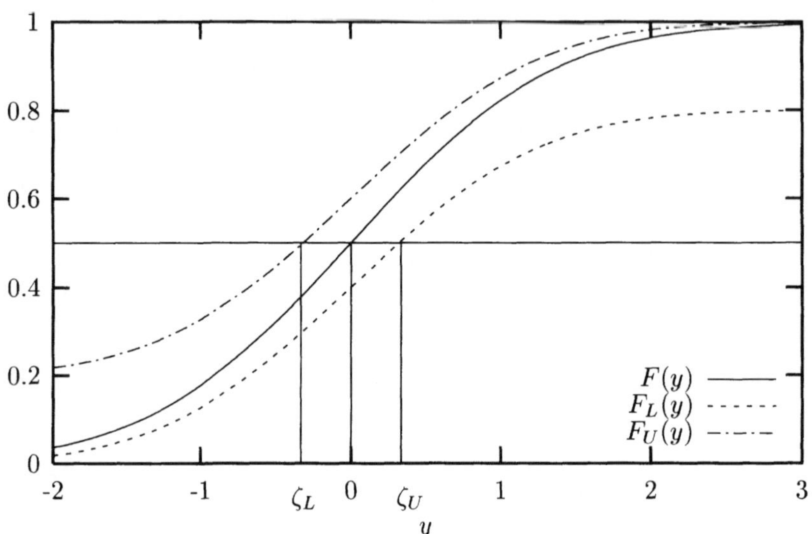

Example 2.5 If $1\{Y \in A\}$ is the indicator function of the event $\{Y \in A\}$, then (2.9) gives an interval to which the conditional probaility $\Pr\{Y \in A \,|\, X = x\}$ must necessarily belong. In particular, putting $A = (-\infty, y]$ gives bounds for $F(y \,|\, x) = \Pr\{Y \leq y \,|\, X = x\}$, namely $F_L(y \,|\, x) \leq F(y \,|\, x) \leq F_U(y \,|\, x)$, where

$$F_L(y \,|\, x) = F_1(y \,|\, x)\pi(x), \qquad F_U(y \,|\, x) = F_1(y \,|\, x)\pi(x) + 1 - \pi(x),$$

and $F_1(y \,|\, x)$ is the conditional probability that $Y \leq y$ for the uncensored population ($D = 1$). By varying y, one obtains bounds for the conditional distribution function of Y given $X = x$.

Manski (1995) noticed that, if Y is a continuous random variable, then the bounds for the conditional distribution function may be inverted to obtain bounds for the conditional quantile $\zeta_p(x)$ of Y. The key is the fact that, since $F(\zeta_p(x) \,|\, x) = p$, the conditional quantile $\zeta_p(x)$ must lie in the interval $[\zeta_{pL}(x), \zeta_{pU}(x)]$, where the lower bound $\zeta_{pL}(x)$ satisfies

$$F_U(\zeta_{pL}(x) \,|\, x) = F_1(\zeta_{pL}(x) \,|\, x)\, \pi(x) + 1 - \pi(x) = p,$$

and the upper bound $\zeta_{pU}(x)$ satisfies

$$F_L(\zeta_{pU}(x) \,|\, x) = F_1(\zeta_{pU}(x) \,|\, x)\, \pi(x) = p.$$

Thus

$$\zeta_{pL}(x) = F_1^{-1}\left(\frac{p - 1 + \pi(x)}{\pi(x)} \,|\, x\right), \qquad \zeta_{pU}(x) = F_1^{-1}\left(\frac{p}{\pi(x)} \,|\, x\right)$$

(Figure 18). Notice that the bounds for the population quantile are well defined only if $1 - \pi(x) < p < \pi(x)$. □

The interval (2.8) may also be used to obtain information from a censored sample about the effect on $\mu(x)$ of a finite variation in x. Let x and x' be distinct points in the support of X, and consider the difference $\mu(x) - \mu(x')$. Because the inequalities $a \le y \le b$ and $c \le y' \le d$ imply the inequality $a - d \le y - y' \le b - c$, the difference $\mu(x) - \mu(x')$ must necessarily belong to an interval whose lower bound is equal to

$$\psi(x) - \psi(x') + a(x)[1 - \pi(x)] - b(x')[1 - \pi(x')],$$

where $\psi(x) = \mu_1(x)\pi(x)$, and whose upper bound is equal to

$$\psi(x) - \psi(x') + b(x)[1 - \pi(x)] - a(x')[1 - \pi(x')].$$

The length of this interval is equal to the sum of the length of the intervals for $\mu(x)$ and $\mu(x')$.

2.3.4 RESPONSE-BASED SAMPLING

Let $Z = (X, Y)$ be a vector of discrete random variables, where Y may take the values $1, \ldots, S$, and let $\mathcal{A}_s = \{(x, y)\colon y = s\}$ be the population stratum for which $Y = s$. *Response-based sampling* consists in drawing at random n_s units from each stratum $\mathcal{A}_s$ and recording the associated value of X.

A typical situation is when the response Y represents the choice of alternative modes of transportation (automobile, bus, train, etc.) and $\mathcal{A}_s$ is the population stratum that chooses the sth mode. Sampling bus riders at a bus stop, train riders at a train station or car drivers at a parking lot is often simpler and much less expensive than interviewing people at their homes. More generally, whenever the population units are physically clustered on the basis of the alternative that they choose, response-based sampling offers economies of scale that may not be possible under random sampling.

Denoting by $\omega(s)$ the sampling fraction from the sth population stratum, the probability that $Y = y$ in the data is

$$g_Y(y) = \frac{\omega(y) f_Y(y)}{\sum_{s=1}^{S} \omega(s) f_Y(s)} = w(y)\, f_Y(y),$$

where the weight function

$$w(y) = \frac{\omega(y)}{\sum_{s=1}^{S} \omega(s) f_Y(s)}$$

is generally different from one, unless the sampling fraction is the same for all strata, which corresponds to PPS. Because the probability that $X = x$ conditionally on $Y = y$ is equal to $f(x \mid y)$, the joint probability of $Y = y$ and $X = x$ is

$$g(x, y) = f(x \mid y)\, g_Y(y) = \frac{\omega(y) f(x \mid y)\, f_Y(y)}{\sum_{s=1}^{S} \omega(s) f_Y(s)} = w(y) f(x, y),$$

while the probability that $X = x$ is

$$g_X(x) = \sum_{s=1}^{S} g(x,y) = \sum_{s=1}^{S} w(s) f(s,x).$$

The probability that $Y = y$ conditionally on $X = x$ is therefore

$$g(y \,|\, x) = \frac{g(x,y)}{g_X(x)} = \frac{w(y) f(y \,|\, x)}{\sum_s w(s) f(s \,|\, x)},$$

where we used the fact that $f(x,y) = f(y \,|\, x)\, f_X(x)$. Because $w(y) = g_Y(y)/f_Y(y)$, this probability may equivalently be written

$$g(y \,|\, x) = \frac{f(y \,|\, x)\, g_Y(y)/f_Y(y)}{\sum_s f(s \,|\, x)\, g_Y(s)/f_Y(s)}.$$

Therefore, unless there is self-weighting, the regression of Y on X is not preserved under response-based sampling. The hypothesis that $\mathcal{A}_1, \ldots, \mathcal{A}_S$ form a partition of the support of Y is crucial. When this is not true, $g(y \,|\, x)$ may differ from $f(y \,|\, x)$ even when $\omega(s)$ is the same for all strata. If $g(y \,|\, x) \neq f(y \,|\, x)$, then the knowledge of $g(y \,|\, x)$ enables one to identify $f(y \,|\, x)$ provided that the union of $\mathcal{A}_1, \ldots, \mathcal{A}_S$ is equal to the support of Y and the marginal probabilities $f_Y(s)$ are known.

2.3.5 FLOW AND STOCK SAMPLING

Let Z be a non-negative continuous random variable with distribution function F and density function f. For concreteness, let Z represent the duration of an unemployment spell.

There are two ways of gathering information about the distribution of Z. The first, called *flow sampling*, consists in drawing a random sample from the population of those who become unemployed during a specified period of time. The other, called *stock sampling*, consists in drawing a random sample from the population of those who are unemployed at a given point in time.

Let $Z_1, \ldots, Z_n$ be the observed data on unemployment duration. For simplicity, assume that they correspond to completed unemployment spells. It is easy to show that, under flow sampling, Z_i has the same distribution as Z.

The case of stock sampling is a little more complicated. The completed duration of an unemployment spell for the ith person included in the survey may be decomposed as $Z_i = U_i + V_i$, where U_i denotes the elapsed duration, that is, duration up to the time of the survey, and V_i denotes the successive duration. For an interviewed person to be registered as unemployed it is necessary that $U_i > 0$, that is, observed duration must be left-censored. If $U_i = u$ and $t = 0$ denotes the time of the survey, then the person must have entered unemployment at time $t = -u$.

To compute the distribution of elapsed duration U_i in the sample data, suppose that the rate of entry into unemployment is constant and equal to $\lambda > 0$. Of those who entered into unemployment at time $t = -u$, only the fraction for whom $Z > u$ remains unemployed at time $t = 0$. This fraction is equal to $\Pr\{Z > u\} = 1 - F(u)$. Therefore, aggregating over the different cohorts of unemployed people and integrating by parts, the fraction of the population that is unemployed at time $t = 0$ is

$$P_0 = \lambda \int_0^\infty [1 - F(u)]\, du = \lambda \int_0^\infty u f(u)\, du = \lambda\mu,$$

under the additional assumption that Z has a finite mean μ. On the other hand, the fraction of the population that, at the time of the survey, has been unemployed for a period not greater than u is

$$\lambda \int_0^u [1 - F(z)]\, dz.$$

The distribution function of elapsed duration U_i is therefore

$$G_U(u) = \Pr\{U_i \leq u\} = \frac{\lambda \int_0^u [1 - F(z)]\, dz}{P_0} = \frac{\int_0^u [1 - F(z)]\, dz}{\mu},$$

whereas its density function is $g_U(u) = G'_U(u) = [1 - F(u)]/\mu$. Because the conditional density of Z_i given $U_i = u$ is $f(z \mid u) = f(z)/[1 - F(u)]$, $0 < u < z$, the joint density of Z_i and U_i in the sampled data is

$$g(z, u) = f(z \mid u)\, g_U(u) = \frac{f(z)}{1 - F(u)} \frac{1 - F(u)}{\mu} = \frac{f(z)}{\mu}.$$

Integrating the joint density with respect to u and using the fact that $u < z$, one obtains the density of the completed duration of an unemployment spell in the sample data

$$g(z) = \int_0^z g(z, u)\, du = \frac{f(z)}{\mu} \int_0^z du = \frac{z f(z)}{\mu}.$$

This distribution is known as the *first moment distribution* corresponding to $f(z)$. Notice that $g(z) = w(z) f(z)$ with $w(z) = z/\mu$, that is, sampling from those who are unemployed at the time of the survey leads to oversampling the longer spells and undersampling the shorter spells. For this reason, stock sampling is said to be *length-biased.* This may lead to incorrect inferences about the distribution of Z at the population level. For example, the mean of the observed durations is

$$\mathrm{E}\, Z_i = \int_0^\infty \frac{z^2 f(z)}{\mu}\, dz = \mu \left(1 + \frac{\sigma^2}{\mu^2}\right) > \mu,$$

where $\sigma^2 = \mathrm{Var}\, Z$. Thus, stock sampling leads to an upward biased measure of mean unemployment duration and the relative bias $(\mathrm{E}\, Z_i - \mu)/\mu$ is simply proportional to the squared coefficient of variation of Z.

2.4 UNOBSERVED HETEROGENEITY AND MIXTURE MODELS

Conditioning on observed covariates is a way of controlling for heterogeneity in observed response across sample units. In general, however, the available covariates represent at best only a partial list of the many factors that influence the variability of the phenomenon under investigation. In these cases, failure to adequately control for unobservable sources of heterogeneity may produce severe biases in estimates of the population characteristics of interest.

Example 2.6 Let $h_i(z)$ be the hazard of leaving unemployment for the ith member of a population of unemployed people. Suppose that the individual hazards exhibit no duration dependence but are not all the same. Specifically, let $h_i(z) = \lambda U_i$, where U_i reflects unobservable differences across individuals. The individual survivor function is then $S_i(z) = \exp(-\lambda z U_i)$. The variability of the hazard in the population may be modeled by treating the U_i as i.i.d. random variables with a common $\mathcal{E}(\gamma)$ distribution. The population survivor function is then

$$S(z) = \mathrm{E}\, S_i(z) = \int_0^\infty e^{-\lambda z u}\, \gamma e^{-\gamma u}\, du$$
$$= \int_0^\infty \gamma e^{-(\lambda z + \gamma)u}\, du = \frac{1}{(\lambda/\gamma)z + 1}.$$

Therefore, the population hazard is

$$h(z) = -\frac{d}{dz} \ln S(z) = \frac{\lambda/\gamma}{(\lambda/\gamma)z + 1},$$

where the numerator is the conditional hazard evaluated at the mean $1/\gamma$ of the distribution of U_i. Hence

$$h'(z) = -\left[\frac{\lambda/\gamma}{(\lambda/\gamma)z + 1}\right]^2 < 0,$$

that is, the population hazard exhibits negative duration dependence despite the absence of duration dependence at the individual level. Intuitively, the individuals with the highest hazards exit first, and so the population hazard falls as the fraction of low hazard members increases. □

Unobserved heterogeneity is typically dealt with by letting certain parameters of the model vary across sample units. This variability may be modeled explicitly by assuming that the individual parameters come from a common distribution, either discrete or continuous, called the *mixing distribution*. The case of a discrete mixing distribution corresponds to a countable number of "types" in the population. After specifying a parametric model for the conditional distribution of the observables given the unobservables, the model for the marginal distribution of the observables may be obtained by integrating out the unobservables using the mixing distribution.

Thus, let $\{F(z \,|\, u; \beta)\}$ be the model for the conditional distribution function of Z_i given $U_i = u$, where U_i is a scalar random variable which represents unobserved heterogeneity. For simplicity we ignore the presence of observed covariates. If the distribution of U_i (the mixing distribution) were known, then the unconditional distribution of Z_i would be

$$G(z; \beta) = \mathrm{E}\, F(z \,|\, U_i; \beta),$$

where the expectation is taken with respect to the mixing distribution. Models of this kind are known as *mixture models* or *random coefficient models.*

Since the mixing distribution is generally unknown, a common approach is to assume that it belongs to some known parametric family $\{p(u; \gamma)\}$. Coupled with the parametric model for the conditional distribution of Z_i given U_i, this assumption leads to a parametric model for the unconditional distribution function of Z_i, namely

$$G(z;\theta) = \sum_u F(z \mid u; \beta)\, p(u; \gamma) \tag{2.10}$$

if U_i is discrete, and

$$G(z;\theta) = \int F(z \mid u; \beta)\, p(u; \gamma)\, du \tag{2.11}$$

if U_i is continuous. In either case, $\theta = (\beta, \gamma)$. The choice of model for the mixing distribution is important. This choice is often justified on the basis of computational simplicity or by appeal to familiarity with special functional forms. While economic theory can sometimes suggest a parametric model for the conditional distribution of Z_i given the unobservables, it rarely offers guidance on the appropriate parametric model for the distribution of the unobservables. Further, estimates obtained by the above strategy are often very sensitive to the essentially arbitrary assumptions made about this distribution.

The key problem with mixture models is one of identifiability: from the knowledge of G, is it possible to solve (2.10) or (2.11) for unique $F(z \mid u)$ and $p(u)$? The example below shows that, in general, the answer is negative.

Example 2.7 Heckman and Singer (1984) produce two different models which generate the same exponential distribution of observed duration. Suppose first that $Z_i \sim \mathcal{E}(u)$, with distribution function $F_1(z \mid u) = 1 - e^{-uz}$, $z \geq 0$. If there is no population heterogeneity, that is, the mixing distribution has all its mass concentrated at the point $u = \eta$, then the distribution function of the observed duration is $G_1(z) = 1 - e^{-\eta z}$, that is, exponential with parameter η.

Now suppose that

$$F_2(z \mid u) = 2\Phi\left(\frac{z}{\sqrt{2u}}\right) - 1, \qquad z \geq 0,$$

where Φ denotes the $\mathcal{N}(0,1)$ distribution function. If $U_i \sim \mathcal{E}(\eta^2)$ with density $p(u) = \eta^2 e^{-\eta^2 u}$, $u > 0$, then it is easy to verify that

$$G_2(z) = \int_0^\infty F_2(z \mid u)\, p(u)\, dv = 1 - e^{-\eta z} = G_1(z). \tag{2.12}$$

Although they imply the same distribution for the observed data, the two models are quite different. The first exhibits no duration dependence at the individual level, and no population heterogeneity. The second model is characterized by positive duration dependence at the individual level which, contaminated by population heterogeneity, generates a distribution of observed durations which exhibits no duration dependence. Without further identifying assumptions, one cannot choose between these two observationally equivalent explanations of the same data. □

2.5 MEASUREMENT ERRORS

We have assumed so far that the data correspond to exact measurements of certain characteristics of a population. In practice, however, the data may be subject to measurement errors or can be contaminated in various ways. The nature of the measurement errors or the form of the contamination process may affect the information contained in the data about the aspects of interest of the population.

2.5.1 *THE CLASSICAL MEASUREMENT ERROR MODEL*

In the *classical measurement error model*, the data are regarded as realizations of a random vector $Z = Z^* + U$, where Z^* and U are independent random vectors that represent, respectively, the correct measurement or "signal" and a measurement error. The assumption of independence between Z^* and U implies that $\operatorname{Var} Z = \operatorname{Var} Z^* + \operatorname{Var} U$, that is, the data tend to display larger variability than the correct measurements. This model is often motivated with reference to the inaccuracy of the instruments with which Z^* is measured. The additional assumption that U has mean zero implies that $\mathrm{E}(Z \mid Z^*) = Z^*$, that is, the measurements of Z^* are inaccurate but not systematically distorted.

If f and h denote the densities of Z^* and U respectively, then the density g of Z is the convolution of f and h, that is, $g(z) = \int_{-\infty}^{\infty} f(z-u)\, h(u)\, du$. In particular, if $Z = (X, Y)$, $Z^* = (X^*, Y^*)$ and $U = (U_X, U_Y)$, where U_X has a nondegenerate distribution, then the conditional distribution of Y given $X = x$ is generally different from the conditional distribution of Y^* given $X^* = x$.

Example 2.8 Let the random vector $Z^* = (X^*, Y^*)$ have a Gaussian distribution with mean (μ_X, μ_Y) and variance matrix

$$\Sigma = \begin{bmatrix} \sigma_X^2 & \sigma_{XY} \\ \sigma_{XY} & \sigma_Y^2 \end{bmatrix},$$

and let U be a measurement error vector that is distributed independently of Z^* as Gaussian with mean zero and variance matrix

$$\Omega = \begin{bmatrix} \omega_X^2 & 0 \\ 0 & \omega_Y^2 \end{bmatrix}.$$

The distribution of the random vector $Z = Z^* + U$ is therefore Gaussian with mean (μ_X, μ_Y) and variance matrix

$$\Sigma + \Omega = \begin{bmatrix} \sigma_X^2 + \omega_X^2 & \sigma_{XY} \\ \sigma_{XY} & \sigma_Y^2 + \omega_Y^2 \end{bmatrix}.$$

Thus, Z and Z^* have a Gaussian distribution with the same mean but different variance matrix. The assumption that the random vector U has a distribution of the continuous type implies that $\Pr\{Z \neq Z^*\} = 1$, that is, measurement errors occur almost surely.

If $\sigma_X^2 > 0$, then the conditional distribution of Y^* given $X^* = x$ is $\mathcal{N}(\alpha_* + \beta_* x, \sigma_*^2)$, where

$$\alpha_* = \mu_Y - \beta_* \mu_X, \qquad \beta_* = \frac{\sigma_{XY}}{\sigma_X^2}, \qquad \sigma_*^2 = \sigma_Y^2 - \frac{\sigma_{XY}^2}{\sigma_X^2}.$$

The conditional distribution of Y given $X = x$ is instead $\mathcal{N}(\alpha + \beta x, \sigma^2)$, where

$$\alpha = \mu_Y - \beta\mu_X = \alpha_* - (\beta - \beta_*)\mu_X,$$

$$\beta = \frac{\sigma_{XY}}{\sigma_X^2 + \omega_X^2} = \beta_* \frac{\sigma_X^2}{\sigma_X^2 + \omega_X^2},$$

$$\sigma^2 = \sigma_Y^2 + \omega_Y^2 - \frac{\sigma_{XY}^2}{\sigma_X^2 + \omega_X^2} = \sigma_*^2 + \frac{\sigma_{XY}^2}{\sigma_X^2} \frac{\omega_X^2}{\sigma_X^2 + \omega_X^2} + \omega_Y^2.$$

Thus, the classical measurement error model preserves the CMF of Y^* only in two cases. The first is when X^* and Y^* are uncorrelated, the other is when $\omega_X^2 = 0$, that is, X^* is observed without error. While β and β_* have the same sign, we have

$$|\beta| \leq |\beta_*|, \tag{2.13}$$

that is, β is smaller than β_* in absolute value. If $\mu_X \neq 0$, then $|\alpha| \geq |\alpha_*|$. Thus, the presence of measurement errors in X^* biases β towards zero and α away from zero. Further, it makes σ^2 larger than σ_*^2. The effect on β is sometimes referred to as the *attenuation bias* caused by measurement error.

Notice that (2.13) is not the only information that the data contain about the parameter β_*. Consider the conditional mean of X given Y. This is of the form $\mathrm{E}(X \mid Y) = \gamma + \delta Y$, where

$$\delta = \frac{\mathrm{Cov}(X, Y)}{\mathrm{Var}\, Y} = \frac{\sigma_{XY}}{\sigma_Y^2 + \omega_Y^2} = \beta_* \frac{\sigma_X^2}{\sigma_Y^2 + \omega_Y^2}.$$

If X^* and Y^* are correlated, then $\sigma_{XY}^2 \leq \sigma_X^2 \sigma_Y^2$ and therefore $\beta_*^2 \leq \sigma_Y^2/\sigma_X^2$. Hence

$$\frac{1}{\delta} = \frac{\sigma_Y^2 + \omega_Y^2}{\beta_* \sigma_X^2} \geq \beta_* + \frac{\omega_Y^2}{\beta_* \sigma_X^2},$$

that is, $|1/\delta| \geq |\beta_*|$. Combining this result with inequality (2.13) gives

$$|\beta| \leq |\beta_*| \leq \left|\frac{1}{\delta}\right|. \tag{2.14}$$

Thus, although the classical measurement error model does not preserve the CMF of Y^*, it nevertheless provides some information about the parameter β_* through the inequality (2.14). □

2.5.2 *OTHER MEASUREMENT ERROR MODELS*

The classical measurement error model is widely used but it may be inappropriate in certain situations. For example, the assumption that the "signal" Z^* and the measurement error U are independent is inappropriate when Z^* is a discrete random variable. In this case, a different model should be considered.

Example 2.9 Consider the following model of classification errors. Let Z^* be a binary random variable that takes values zero and one with probability $1 - \pi$ and

π respectively, where $0 < \pi < 1$. The observed value of Z^* is another 0–1 random variable Z that depends on Z^* through the relationships

$$\Pr\{Z = 0 \mid Z^* = 1\} = \eta, \qquad \Pr\{Z = 1 \mid Z^* = 0\} = \nu.$$

This model may also be written $Z = Z^* + U$, where $U = Z - Z^*$. Because

$$\begin{aligned} E(Z \mid Z^* = 0) &= \Pr\{Z = 1 \mid Z^* = 0\} = \nu, \\ E(Z \mid Z^* = 1) &= \Pr\{Z = 1 \mid Z^* = 1\} = 1 - \eta, \end{aligned}$$

we have

$$E(U \mid Z^* = z) = \mathrm{E}(Z \mid Z^* = z) - Z^* = \begin{cases} \nu, & \text{if } z = 0, \\ -\eta, & \text{if } z = 1. \end{cases}$$

The mean of U is therefore

$$\begin{aligned} \mathrm{E}\, U &= E(U \mid Z^* = 0) \Pr\{Z^* = 0\} + \mathrm{E}(U \mid Z^* = 1) \Pr\{Z^* = 1\} \\ &= \nu(1 - \pi) - \eta\pi, \end{aligned}$$

whereas

$$\mathrm{E}\, U Z^* = \mathrm{E}(U \mid Z^* = 1) \Pr\{Z^* = 1\} = -\eta\pi.$$

Hence

$$\mathrm{Cov}(U, Z^*) = \mathrm{E}\, U Z^* - (\mathrm{E}\, U)(\mathrm{E}\, Z^*) = -\pi(1 - \pi)(\eta + \nu).$$

Thus, the measurement error U is not independent of Z^*. In particular, the measurement error U is negatively correlated with Z^* and its conditional mean given Z^* is different from zero. □

2.5.3 CONTAMINATED SAMPLING

The *contaminated sampling model* regards the data as realizations of a random variable Z which is equal to the "signal" Z^* with probability $1 - \epsilon$, and with probability ϵ is equal to some extraneous random variable W. Formally

$$Z = (1 - U)Z^* + UW = Z^* + U(W - Z^*),$$

where U is an unobservable binary random variable, distributed independently of Z^* and W, which takes the values zero and one with probability $1 - \epsilon$ and ϵ respectively ($0 \leq \epsilon < 1$). Realizations of Z such that $U = 0$ correspond to error-free measurements of Z^*. Of some importance, especially for the theory of robust statistics discussed in Chapter 15, is the special case when W is a degenerate random variable giving unit mass to some point in the sample space. This is known as the *gross-error model.*

The contaminated sampling model is often motivated with reference to coding errors, such as digit transposition, and may be useful in situations where measurement errors occur with positive probability but not always. Alternatively, this model may be used to represent the fact that a statistical model is only an approximation to the actual data generation process. As such, it may be good for the bulk of the data but not for the whole sample.

If F and H are the distribution functions of Z^* and W respectively, then the distribution function of Z is

$$G(z) = (1-\epsilon)\,F(z) + \epsilon\,H(z), \qquad 0 \le \epsilon < 1.$$

The distribution of Z is therefore a mixture of the distributions of Z^* and W, with mixing parameter ϵ that is equal to the probability of measurement error. If both Z^* and W have finite mean, then the mean of an observed data point is

$$\mathrm{E}\,Z = (1-\epsilon)\,\mathrm{E}\,Z^* + \epsilon\,\mathrm{E}\,W.$$

If both Z^* and W have finite variance, then the variance of an observed data point can be shown to be

$$\mathrm{Var}\,Z = (1-\epsilon)\,\mathrm{Var}(Z^*) + \epsilon\,\mathrm{Var}\,W + \epsilon(1-\epsilon)(\mathrm{E}\,Z^* - \mathrm{E}\,W)^2.$$

If Z^* and W have the same mean, then

$$\mathrm{Var}\,Z = (1-\epsilon)\,\mathrm{Var}\,Z^* + \epsilon\,\mathrm{Var}\,W.$$

Thus, unless both ϵ and the distribution of W are known, contaminated sampling does not enable one to identify the distribution of Z^* or interesting aspects of this distribution, such as the mean and the variance.

The contaminated sampling model assumes that the occurrence of errors is independent of the sampling realization of the population of interest, that is,

$$\Pr\{Z^* \le z \,|\, U = u\} = \Pr\{Z^* \le z\}, \qquad u = 0, 1. \tag{2.15}$$

The *corrupted sampling model* corresponds to the case when (2.15) does not hold. This model permits arbitrary corruption of an arbitrary selected fraction of the data and underlies most of the literature on high-breakdown estimation discussed in Chapters 15 and 16.

BIBLIOGRAPHIC NOTES

A standard reference on sampling methods is Cochran (1977). Another useful reference is Wolter (1985), while a more technical one is Särndal, Swensson and Wretman (1992).

For a generalization of the Kaplan–Meier estimator to the case of double censoring (both left and right), see Turnbull (1974). The asymptotic properties of the Kaplan–Meier estimator are surveyed in Basu (1984).

For a general discussion of response-based sampling see Manski and Lerman (1977) and Manski and McFadden (1981). For a nice introduction to the general problem of identification in the social sciences see Manski (1995).

On the problems posed by various aspects of economic data see Griliches (1986). Lessler and Kalsbeek (1992) and Deaton (1997) provide excellent introductions to sources and implications of nonsampling errors in surveys. On the statistical problems that arise in the presence of missing data see Little and Rubin (1987) and Schafer (1997).

For an extensive treatment of the theory and applications of measurement error models, see Aigner *et al.* (1984) and Fuller (1987). On general approximations to the distribution of data subject to measurement error see Chesher (1991).

On the contaminated sampling model and its connection to robust statistics see Huber (1981) and Hampel *et al.* (1986).

PROBLEMS

2.1 Given a sample of size n drawn at random with replacement from a population of N units, show that the probability that the sample contains no repetition is equal to

$$\prod_{i=1}^{n-1}\left(1-\frac{i}{N}\right).$$

2.2 Prove Theorem 2.1.

2.3 Prove Corollary 2.1.

2.4 Prove Theorem 2.2.

2.5 Prove Corollary 2.2.

2.6 Consider a finite population consisting of N units and let $z_1,\dots,z_N$ denote the values of a numeric characteristic for each of the N population units. Given a sample of size n, the sample mean $\bar{Z}$ can be represented as $\bar{Z}=n^{-1}\sum_{j=1}^{N}T_jz_j$, where $T_1,\dots,T_N$ are random variables.

(i) Show that, under SRS with replacement, the distribution of the random vector $(T_1,\dots,T_N)$ is multinomial with index n and parameter $(N^{-1},\dots,N^{-1})$, and therefore

$$\operatorname{E}T_j=\frac{n}{N},\qquad \operatorname{Var}T_j=\frac{n(N-1)}{N^2},\qquad \operatorname{Cov}(T_j,T_h)=-\frac{n}{N^2},\ h\neq j.$$

(ii) Show that, under SRS without replacement, $T_1,\dots,T_N$ are 0–1 random variables such that

$$\operatorname{E}T_j=\frac{n}{N},\qquad \operatorname{Var}T_j=\frac{n(N-n)}{N^2},\qquad \operatorname{Cov}(T_j,T_h)=-\frac{n(N-n)}{N^2(N-1)},\ h\neq j.$$

(iii) Use the above results to prove Corollaries 2.1 and 2.2.

2.7 Compare the sampling properties of the sample mean $\bar{Z}$ and the Horvitz–Thompson estimator $\hat{\mu}=N^{-1}\sum_i(Z_i/\pi_i)$ in the case of SRS with replacement.

2.8 Determine the value of the constant k in (2.1).

2.9 Determine sample sizes $n_1,\dots,n_S$ to minimize the total cost of a stratified random survey, $C=c_0+\sum_{s=1}^{S}c_sn_s$, under the constraint that the sampling variance of the stratified average $\bar{Z}^*=\sum_s\pi_s\bar{Z}_s$ does not exceed a given number $V>0$.

2.10 Consider a heterogeneous population consisting of two strata, each with weight equal to π_j $(\pi_1+\pi_2=1)$, mean equal to μ_j and variance equal to σ_j^2 $(j=1,2)$. Suppose that sample data are only available for the first stratum and not for the second. Compute the bias of the sample variance s_1^2 for the first stratum as an estimator of the population variance.

2.11 Prove Theorem 2.5.

2.12 Prove Theorem 2.6.

2.13 Prove Theorem 2.7.

2.14 Let $\hat{F}$ be the empirical distribution function for a sample of size n. Show that $\hat{F}$ is also the empirical distribution function of every permutation of the elements of the sample.

2.15 Let Z^* be a random variable with finite mean μ and distribution function F, and let $Z = \min(Z^*, c)$. Show that $\mathrm{E}\, Z = \mu - \int_c^\infty [1 - F(z)]\, dz$.

2.16 Show that the survivor function associated with the empirical distribution function is

$$\hat{S}(z) = \prod_{i:Z_{[i]} \leq z} \frac{n-i}{n-i+1},$$

where $Z_{[i]}$ denotes the ith sample order statistic.

2.17 Prove Theorem 2.8.

2.18 Show that if a sampling scheme preserves the regression of Y on X, then it generally does not preserve the regression of X on Y.

2.19 Compare the marginal distribution of offered wages in Example 2.3 with the marginal distribution of measured wages in a censored sample.

2.20 Show that the bounds (2.8) may equivalently be written

$$\mu_L(x) = \mathrm{E}(YD \mid X = x) + a(x)[1 - \pi(x)], \qquad \mu_U(x) = \mathrm{E}(YD \mid X = x) + b(x)[1 - \pi(x)].$$

2.21 Consider a population where everybody chooses between two mutually exclusive modes of transportation: bus and train. Let $Y = 1, 2$ be an indicator of choice between the two modes and let q_y, $y = 1, 2$, denote the population frequency with which mode y is chosen. The statistical problem is to draw inference about the conditional probability $f(y \mid x)$ that mode y is chosen given that $X = x$, where X is a discrete random variable, such as a person's sex or age. Consider the following sampling strategies.

(i) Data on (X, Y) are collected for a large sample of size n drawn at random from the population. Is it possible to obtain good estimates of $f(y \mid x)$ on the basis of the information obtained in this way?

(ii) Data on $(Y = 1, X)$ are collected by interviewing n_1 persons chosen at random at the bus stops, and on $(Y = 2, X)$ by interviewing n_2 persons chosen at random at the train station, with $n_1 + n_2 = n$, where n is the same sample size as in (i). Is it now possible to obtain good estimates of $f(y \mid x)$? May it help to have information about the distribution of X in the population?

(iii) Discuss the costs and benefits of the sampling schemes described in (i) and (ii).

2.22 (Flinn & Heckman 1982) Show that if Z has a Gaussian distribution, then it is possible to identify its distribution function on the basis of a censored or truncated sample. Show that this is no longer true if Z has a Pareto distribution with density

$$f(z) = \frac{\beta - 1}{\gamma^{1-\beta}}\, z^{-\beta}, \qquad z \geq \gamma > 0, \qquad \beta \geq 2.$$

2.23 Verify formula (2.12) in Example 2.7.

2.24 Consider a sample of size $n = qS$, which consists of q observations drawn at random from each of the S regions into which a country is divided. Let Y_s be the number of employed people sampled from the sth region and let $Y = \sum_{s=1}^{S} Y_s$ be the total number of employed people in the sample.

(i) Compute the mean and the variance of Y when all regions have the same employment rate.

(ii) Compute the mean and the variance of Y when the employment rates differ across regions.

(iii) Suppose that the regional employment rates $\pi_1, \ldots, \pi_S$ are realizations of a random variable with mean π and variance $\tau^2\pi(1-\pi)$, where $0 < \tau^2 \leq 1$. Show that Y has mean equal to $n\pi$ and variance equal to $n\omega^2\pi(1-\pi)$, where $\omega^2 = 1 + (q-1)\tau^2$.

(iv) Discuss the implications of this result for the problem of estimating the dependence of π on a vector X of covariates.

2.25 Let Z be a random variable which is equal to Z^* with probability $1-\epsilon$ and is equal to W with probability ϵ, where Z^* and W are random variables with finite variance. Compute the mean and variance of Z.

3

Time Series

A *time series* consists of a collection of observations, made sequentially through time, on a variable that is or may be represented as numerical. Examples of economic time series include the series of a country's national income accounts, the time series of a company's sales, the time series of prices and returns on a financial asset, etc.

Three important aspects make the analysis of time series somewhat different from the sampling situations considered in the previous chapter. First, usually one can only observe a single history of a given time series. Second, the elements of a time series are naturally ordered by the value of a time index. Third, most observed time series exhibit a certain degree of regularity or persistence. Many concepts in the statistical analysis of time series are a simple consequence of these three observations.

3.1 UNIVARIATE TIME SERIES

We begin by considering the case of a single time series. In a multivariate context this corresponds to the case when a particular time series is analyzed in isolation of all the others.

3.1.1 STOCHASTIC PROCESSES

A convenient mathematical representation of a time series is through the notion of stochastic processes.

Definition 3.1 A *stochastic process* is a function Z defined on a space $\Omega \times \mathcal{T}$, such that, for every $t \in \mathcal{T}$, $Z(\cdot, t)$ is a random variable defined on a probability space $(\Omega, \mathcal{A}, P)$. □

A stochastic process is therefore a collection $\{Z(\cdot, t), t \in \mathcal{T}\}$ of random variables defined on a common probability space $(\Omega, \mathcal{A}, P)$. The range of $Z(\cdot, t)$ is called the *state space* of the process. Given an event $\omega \in \Omega$, $Z(\omega, t)$ is simply a function of t and the set $\{Z(\omega, t), t \in \mathcal{T}\}$ is called the *realization* or *sample path* of the process. To simplify the notation, an element of a stochastic process is henceforth simply denoted by $Z_t = Z(\cdot, t)$ and the stochastic process by $\{Z_t, t \in \mathcal{T}\}$.

One may distinguish between various classes of stochastic process depending on the nature of their state space and their index space $\mathcal{T}$. A process whose state space is a subset of the real line $\Re$ and whose index space is the set of the integers $0, \pm 1, \pm 2, \ldots$, or a subset of it, is called a *real valued, discrete time, equally spaced time series*, or simply a *time series*. The index space of a time series corresponds to points in time that are equally spaced with respect to a given time unit. Unless otherwise indicated, a time series is assumed to have started in the infinite past and to continue indefinitely into the future. In this case, it is simply represented as $\{Z_t\} = (\ldots, Z_{-1}, Z_0, Z_1, Z_2, \ldots)$.

Example 3.1 A *Markov process* is a stochastic process such that the knowledge of its current state contains all the information needed to determine the probabilities of its future states. Formally, $\{Z_t, t \in \mathcal{T}\}$ is a Markov process if

$$\Pr\{Z_t \in A \,|\, Z_{t_1} = z_1, \ldots, Z_{t_n} = z_n\} = \Pr\{Z_t \in A \,|\, Z_{t_n} = z_n\},$$

for every subset A of the state space and every subset of indices $\{t_1, \ldots, t_n\}$ such that $t_1 < \cdots < t_n < t$.

A *Markov chain* is a Markov process whose index space is the set of the integers and whose state space is discrete. Thus, a Markov chain is a time series whose elements are discrete random variables. In typical applications, the random variable Z_t represents the particular state in which the process is at time t. For example, Z_t may represent the labor force status (employed, looking for a job, not in the labor force) of a person at a given point in time.

Given a Markov chain $\{Z_t\}$, the probability that the process occupies state i at time t is called the ith *state probability* and denoted by $\pi_{it} = \Pr\{Z_t = i\}$. Clearly, $\sum_i \pi_{it} = 1$ for every t. The probability that the process occupies state j at time $t+1$, conditionally on occupying state i at time t, is called instead the *one-step transition probability* and denoted by $\lambda_{ijt} = \Pr\{Z_{t+1} = j \,|\, Z_t = i\}$. Clearly, $\sum_j \lambda_{ijt} = 1$ for all i and every t.

State probabilities at adjacent points in time are linked through the relationship

$$\pi_{j,t+1} = \sum_i \lambda_{ijt}\, \pi_{it}.$$

If there is a finite number J of states, the above relationship may be written more compactly as

$$\pi_{t+1} = \Lambda_t^\top \pi_t,$$

where $\pi_t = (\pi_{1t}, \ldots, \pi_{Jt})$ is a J-vector and

$$\Lambda_t = \begin{bmatrix} \lambda_{11t} & \cdots & \lambda_{1Jt} \\ \vdots & & \vdots \\ \lambda_{J1t} & \cdots & \lambda_{JJt} \end{bmatrix}$$

is a $J \times J$ matrix, called the *transition probability matrix* of the process, with the property that its rows add up to one. State probabilities at time $t+h$, $h = 2, 3, \ldots$, are simply computed by repeatedly substituting backwards

$$\pi_{t+h} = \Lambda_{t+h-1}^\top \pi_{t+h-1} = \Lambda_{t+h-1}^\top (\Lambda_{t+h-2}^\top \pi_{t+h-2}) = \cdots = \Big(\prod_{j=1}^{h} \Lambda_{t+h-j}^\top\Big)\, \pi_t.$$

If transition probabilities are time-invariant, that is, $\Lambda_t = \Lambda$ does not depend on t, then $\pi_{t+h} = (\Lambda^\top)^h\, \pi_t$. □

Besides discrete time series, other classes of stochastic process are of some importance in the analysis of economic data.

Example 3.2 Let $\{Z_t, t \in \Re\}$ be a continuous time, continuous state space, stochastic process with the following properties:

(i) for any h, the increment $Z_{t+h} - Z_t$ is distributed as $\mathcal{N}(0, \sigma^2 h)$, where σ^2 is finite and positive;
(ii) for any pair of disjoint time intervals $[t_1, t_2]$, $[t_3, t_4]$, with $t_1 < t_2 \leq t_3 < t_4$, the increments $Z_{t_4} - Z_{t_3}$ and $Z_{t_2} - Z_{t_1}$ are uncorrelated random variables;
(iii) $Z_0 = 0$ and Z_t is continuous at $t = 0$.

This process is called *Brownian motion* with variance σ^2. When $\sigma^2 = 1$, the process is called *standard Brownian motion* or the *Wiener process*. Because of (ii), Brownian motion is another example of a Markov process. Notice that, because of (i) and (iii), the variance of Z_t is equal to $\sigma^2 t$.

It is not difficult to see that, given arbitrary points $t_1 < \ldots < t_n$, the joint density of $Z_{t_1}, \ldots, Z_{t_n}$ given the initial condition $Z_0 = 0$ is equal to the joint density of $Z_{t_1}, Z_{t_2} - Z_{t_1}, \ldots, Z_{t_n} - Z_{t_{n-1}}$, which is

$$f(z_1, \ldots, z_n) = p(z_1, t_1)\, p(z_2 - z_1, t_2 - t_1) \cdots p(z_n, t_n),$$

where

$$p(z, t) = \frac{1}{\sigma\sqrt{2\pi t}} \exp\left(-\frac{z^2}{2\sigma^2 t}\right).$$

Further, for any $t_1 < t < t_2$, the conditional density of Z_t given $Z_{t_1} = z_1$ and $Z_{t_2} = z_2$ is Gaussian with mean equal to

$$z_1 + \frac{z_2 - z_1}{t_2 - t_1}(t - t_1),$$

and variance equal to

$$\sigma^2 \frac{(t_2 - t_1)(t - t_1)}{t_2 - t_1}.$$

□

Example 3.3 Consider an event that repeats itself through time and let $\mathcal{B}$ be the family of intervals of the positive half-line $\Re_+$. These intervals are interpreted as time intervals. Given $B \in \mathcal{B}$, let Z_B be a discrete random variable representing the number of times that the given event occurs during the time interval B. The stochastic process $\{Z_B, B \in \mathcal{B}\}$ is called a *point process*. The state space of this process is the discrete set $0, 1, 2, \ldots$.

A point process $\{Z_B, B \in \mathcal{B}\}$ is called a *Poisson process* with intensity $\lambda > 0$ if:

(i) for every $B \in \mathcal{B}$, the random variable Z_B has a Poisson distribution with parameter $\lambda\mu_B$, where μ_B denotes the length of the interval B;
(ii) for every finite collection $B_1, \ldots, B_n$ of disjoint intervals of $\Re_+$, the random variables $Z_{B_1}, \ldots, Z_{B_n}$ are independent.

By the properties of the Poisson distribution, (i) implies that $\mathrm{E}\, Z_B = \lambda \mu_B$, that is, the expected number of events in the interval B is proportional to the length of B.

There exists an important relationship between the Poisson process and the exponential distribution. Consider an event that repeats itself through time according to a Poisson process with intensity λ, and suppose that an event occurred at time t_0. Denoting by H the length of the time interval until a second event occurs, we have

$$\Pr\{H \geq h\} = \Pr\{\text{no event in the interval } [t_0, t_0 + h)\} = e^{-\lambda h}, \qquad h \geq 0,$$

where we used the assumption that the number of events occurring in a time interval of length h follows a Poisson distribution with parameter λh. The random variable H therefore has an exponential distribution with parameter λ.

Now suppose that the second event occurred at time t_1. Proceeding as before, it can be shown that the length of the time interval until a third event occurs also has an exponential distribution with parameter λ. Hence, given a Poisson process, the length of the time interval until the next event occurs has a distribution that does not depend on the origin of the time scale. Further, given assumption (ii), the length of the time interval until the next event occurs is independent of the length of the time interval between any two consecutive events. The time intervals between successive events in a Poisson process are therefore a collection of i.i.d. exponential random variables. □

3.1.2 STATIONARITY

A stochastic process $\{Z_t, t \in \mathcal{T}\}$ is characterized by the relationships between its component random variables. In particular, under appropriate regularity conditions, a stochastic process is completely characterized by prescribing, for each integer $n \geq 1$ and every set $t_1, \ldots, t_n$ of n distinct time indices, the joint distribution function

$$F_{t_1,\ldots,t_n}(z_1, \ldots, z_n) = \Pr\{Z_{t_1} \leq z_1, \ldots, Z_{t_n} \leq z_n\} \tag{3.1}$$

of a finite subset $Z_{t_1}, \ldots, Z_{t_n}$ of its elements.

Given the joint distribution function of any pair (Z_t, Z_s) of elements of a process, one may define the first moments $\mu_t = \mathrm{E}\, Z_t$ and $\mu_s = \mathrm{E}\, Z_s$, and the second moments or *autocovariances*

$$\mathrm{Cov}(Z_t, Z_s) = \mathrm{E}(Z_t - \mu_t)(Z_s - \mu_s),$$

provided that the appropriate integrals converge. These moments, if they exist, contain important information about the structure of a process. In particular, the set of first and second moments completely characterizes a *Gaussian process*, that is, one for which (3.1) is Gaussian for each integer $n \geq 1$ and every set $t_1, \ldots, t_n$ of time indices.

Analyzing the collection of distribution functions (3.1) may be quite complicated. This task is simplified considerably if we assume that (3.1) satisfies the following form of time homogeneity.

Definition 3.2 A stochastic process $\{Z_t, t \in \mathcal{T}\}$ is called *strictly stationary* if

$$F_{t_1+h,\ldots,t_n+h}(z_1, \ldots, z_n) = F_{t_1,\ldots,t_n}(z_1, \ldots, z_n) \tag{3.2}$$

for all $h > 0$ and every finite set of indices $t_1, \ldots, t_n$. □

Figure 19 Three sample paths of a Gaussian random walk starting at time $t = 0$ with $Z_0 = 0$.

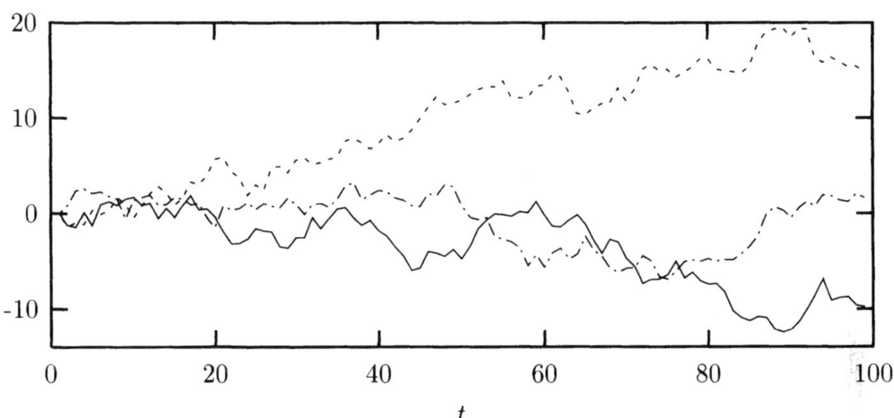

If a process is strictly stationary then the joint distribution of any finite set $Z_{t_1}, \ldots, Z_{t_n}$ of its elements is invariant under translation of the time indices. In particular, the marginal distribution of Z_t is the same for all t and therefore the mean and the variance of Z_t, if they exist, do not depend on t. Analogously, strict stationarity implies that the bivariate distribution of Z_t and Z_s and the autocovariance $\text{Cov}(Z_t, Z_s)$, if it exists, depend on the two time indices only through their distance $|t - s|$.

Example 3.4 Consider a time series starting at time $t = 0$ with $Z_0 = 0$ and evolving through time according to the relationship

$$Z_t = Z_{t-1} + U_t, \qquad t = 1, 2, \ldots,$$

where $U_1, U_2, \ldots$ are uncorrelated random variables with mean zero and variance $\sigma^2 > 0$. Such a time series is called a *random walk* and represents a classical model for the behavior of the logarithm of the price of an asset in an efficient asset market. Since $U_t = Z_t - Z_{t-1}$, a random walk is a process with uncorrelated increments. Figure 19 shows three different sample paths of the same random walk.

Repeated backward substitution gives

$$Z_t = \sum_{j=0}^{t-1} U_{t-j}. \tag{3.3}$$

Thus, a random walk may be represented as a sequence of partial sums.

It follows from (3.3) that, although the unconditional mean of Z_t is equal to zero and therefore does not depend on t, a random walk is not a stationary process for $\text{Var}\, Z_t = \sigma^2 t$, that is, the variability of a component of a random walk increases linearly with its distance from the time origin, implying that $\text{Var}\, Z_t \to \infty$ as $t \to \infty$.

It also follows from (3.3) that $\mathrm{E}\, Z_{t-j}U_t = 0$ for all $j \geq 1$, that is, U_t is uncorrelated with all past values of Z_t, which implies that Z_{t-1} is the BLP of Z_t given the entire past history of the process and U_t is the associated prediction error.

When $U_1, U_2, \ldots$ are either Gaussian or independent, we obtain the stronger conclusion

$$\mathrm{E}(Z_t \mid Z_{t-1}, \ldots, Z_0) = Z_{t-1}.$$

A process with the latter property is called a *martingale*.

Suppose now that $U_1, U_2, \ldots$ are Gaussian, and consider partitioning the time interval into m equally spaced subintervals defined by $t-1, t-1+1/m, \ldots, t-1/m, t$. Let $Z_{t-1}, Z_{t-1+1/m}, \ldots, Z_{t-1/m}, Z_t$ be the value of the process at this finer grid of dates and assume that

$$Z_{t-1+j/m} = Z_{t-1+(j-1)/m} + U_{jt}, \qquad j = 1, \ldots, m,$$

where the U_{jt} are i.i.d. with a common $\mathcal{N}(0, \sigma^2/m)$ distribution. It is easily verified that the process retains its original properties on the finer grid of dates. In particular, for any h, the increment $Z_{t+h} - Z_t$ is distributed as $\mathcal{N}(0, \sigma^2 h)$ and, for any pair of disjoint time intervals $[t_1, t_2]$, $[t_3, t_4]$, with $t_1 < t_2 \leq t_3 < t_4$, the increments $Z_{t_4} - Z_{t_3}$ and $Z_{t_2} - Z_{t_1}$ are uncorrelated. Letting $m \to \infty$ gives a continuous time, continuous state process which satisfies properties (i)–(iii) in Example 3.2 and is therefore a Brownian motion. Thus, a random walk may be viewed as a Brownian motion sampled at equally spaced dates. □

A property that, in a sense, is weaker than strict stationarity is the following.

Definition 3.3 A stochastic process $\{Z_t, t \in \mathcal{T}\}$ is called *weakly stationary*, or simply *stationary*, if its first and second moments are finite, and $\mu_t = \mu_s$ and $\mathrm{Cov}(Z_t, Z_{t+h}) = \mathrm{Cov}(Z_s, Z_{s+h})$ for every pair of indices (t, s) and all h. □

There is no necessary relationship between weak and strict stationarity. In fact, neither does strict stationarity imply the existence of second moments, nor weak stationarity guarantee that (3.2) holds. An important special case when these two notions of stationarity are equivalent is the case of a Gaussian process.

3.1.3 AUTOCOVARIANCES AND AUTOCORRELATIONS

Given a stationary time series $\{Z_t\}$, the number $\gamma_h = \mathrm{Cov}(Z_t, Z_{t+h})$ is called the hth *autocovariance* of $\{Z_t\}$. The sequence $\{\gamma_h\}$, viewed as a function defined on the integers, is called the *autocovariance function* of $\{Z_t\}$.

If $\gamma_0 > 0$, the standardized version of γ_h, defined as

$$\rho_h = \frac{\gamma_h}{\gamma_0} = \mathrm{Corr}(Z_t, Z_{t+h}),$$

is called the hth *autocorrelation* of $\{Z_t\}$. Clearly, $\rho_0 = 1$ and $|\rho_h| \leq 1$ for all h. The sequence $\{\rho_h\}$, viewed as a function defined on the integers, is called the *autocorrelation function* of $\{Z_t\}$. Autocorrelations are convenient to work with because they are scale-invariant.

Figure 20 Sample path of a Gaussian white noise with $\sigma^2 = 1$.

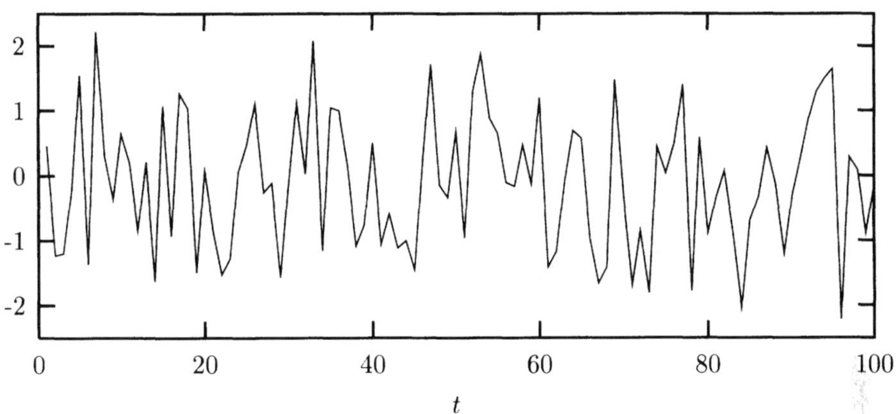

Example 3.5 A time series $\{Z_t\}$ consisting of uncorrelated random variables with mean zero and variance $\sigma^2 > 0$ is stationary with autocovariance function

$$\gamma_h = \begin{cases} \sigma^2, & \text{if } h = 0, \\ 0, & \text{otherwise,} \end{cases}$$

and autocorrelation function

$$\rho_h = \begin{cases} 1, & \text{if } h = 0, \\ 0, & \text{otherwise.} \end{cases}$$

This time series is called a *white noise*, written $\{Z_t\} \sim \text{WN}(0, \sigma^2)$, and represents the extreme case of a purely random process. If the elements of $\{Z_t\}$ are i.i.d., then the time series is strictly stationary and we write $\{Z_t\} \sim \text{IID}(0, \sigma^2)$. The two definitions coincide in the case of a Gaussian white noise (Figure 20). A process $\{Z_t\}$ is a white noise with mean μ if $\{Z_t - \mu\} \sim \text{WN}(0, \sigma^2)$. □

A white noise, defined in the previous example, is the building block of many time series models.

Example 3.6 A time series $\{Z_t\}$ such that

$$Z_t = U_t - \theta U_{t-1}, \qquad \{U_t\} \sim \text{WN}(0, \sigma^2), \tag{3.4}$$

where $\theta \neq 0$, is called a *first-order moving average*, written $\{Z_t\} \sim \text{MA}(1)$ (Figure 21). This time series is stationary for every value of θ, with zero mean, autocovariance function

$$\gamma_h = \begin{cases} (1 + \theta^2)\sigma^2, & \text{if } h = 0, \\ -\theta\sigma^2, & \text{if } |h| = 1, \\ 0, & \text{otherwise,} \end{cases} \tag{3.5}$$

Figure 21 Sample paths of Gaussian MA(1) processes.

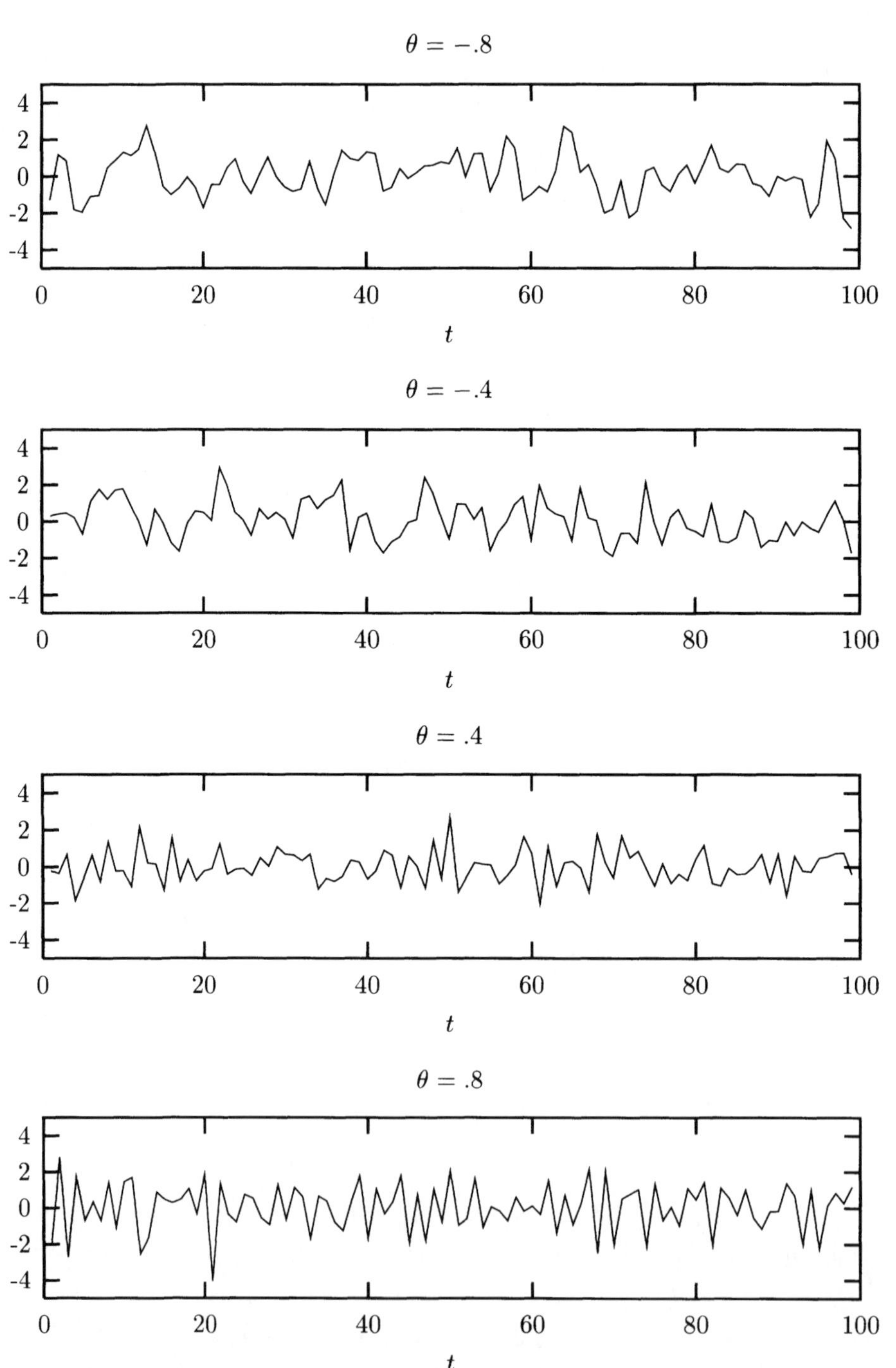

and autocorrelation function

$$\rho_h = \begin{cases} 1, & \text{if } h = 0, \\ -\theta/(1+\theta^2), & \text{if } |h| = 1, \\ 0, & \text{otherwise.} \end{cases}$$

Unlike the case of a white noise, the autocovariance and the autocorrelation functions of an MA(1) process do not vanish immediately but only after one lag. It is not difficult to show that $|\rho_1| \leq .5$.

An MA(1) process is the simplest example of a *linear filter*. Filtering the white noise $\{U_t\}$ through the moving average operator produces a time series $\{Z_t\}$ that differs from $\{U_t\}$ because of its larger variance and the fact that adjacent elements of the process are correlated. □

Example 3.7 A time series $\{Z_t\}$ that satisfies the relationship

$$Z_t = \phi Z_{t-1} + U_t, \qquad \{U_t\} \sim \mathrm{WN}(0, \sigma^2), \tag{3.6}$$

where $\phi \neq 0$, is called a *first-order autoregressive process*, written $\{Z_t\} \sim \mathrm{AR}(1)$. The relationship (3.6) is an example of a *stochastic difference equation*, that is, a nonhomogeneous difference equation "driven" by a stochastic process, in this case a white noise. The existence and the nature of a stationary solution to (3.6) depend on the value of the parameter ϕ. We distinguish three cases, depending on whether ϕ is equal to, smaller or greater than one, in absolute value.

First notice that, when $|\phi| = 1$, no stationary solution exists because the process is a random walk. Next notice that repeated backward substitution in (3.6) gives

$$Z_t = \phi(\phi Z_{t-2} + U_{t-1}) + U_t = \cdots = \phi^h Z_{t-h} + \sum_{j=0}^{h-1} \phi^j U_{t-j}.$$

If $|\phi| < 1$ and the process started in the infinite past then

$$\lim_{h\to\infty} \mathrm{E}\left(Z_t - \sum_{j=0}^{h-1} \phi^j U_{t-j}\right)^2 = \lim_{h\to\infty} \phi^{2h}\, \mathrm{E}\, Z_t^2 = 0.$$

On the other hand, because $Z_t = \phi^{-1}(Z_{t+1} - U_{t+1})$, repeated forward substitution in (3.6) gives

$$Z_t = \phi^{-1}[\phi^{-1}(Z_{t+2} - U_{t+2}) - U_{t+1}] = \cdots = \phi^{-h} Z_{t+h} - \sum_{j=1}^{h} \phi^{-j} U_{t+j}.$$

If $|\phi| > 1$ and the process continues indefinitely into the future then

$$\lim_{h\to\infty} \mathrm{E}\left(Z_t + \sum_{j=1}^{h} \phi^{-j} U_{t+j}\right)^2 = \lim_{h\to\infty} \phi^{-2h}\, \mathrm{E}\, Z_t^2 = 0.$$

Figure 22 Sample paths of Gaussian AR(1) processes.

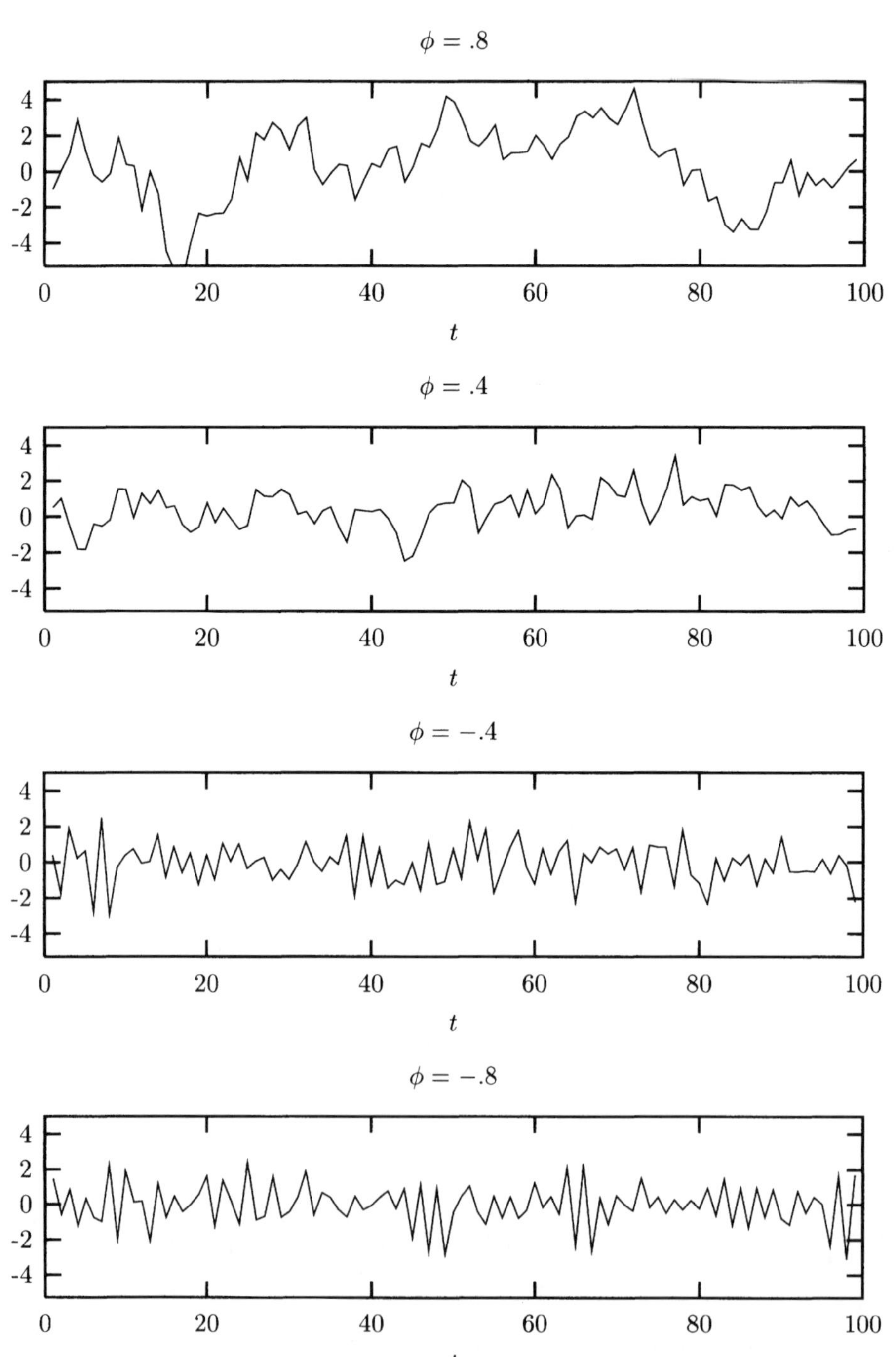

This justifies two alternative representations of Z_t, depending on whether $|\phi| < 1$ or $|\phi| > 1$. If $|\phi| < 1$, then Z_t may be represented as

$$Z_t = \sum_{j=0}^{\infty} \phi^j U_{t-j},$$

where the sequence of weights $\{\phi^j\}$ is absolutely summable, that is, $\sum_{j=0}^{\infty} |\phi^j| < \infty$. This representation is a stationary solution to (3.6) for it satisfies equation (3.6) and is such that

$$\mathrm{E}\, Z_t = 0 \cdot \sum_{j=0}^{\infty} \phi^j = 0 \cdot \frac{1}{1-\phi} = 0$$

and

$$\mathrm{Cov}(Z_t, Z_{t+h}) = \sigma^2 \sum_{j=0}^{\infty} \phi^j \phi^{j+|h|} = \sigma^2 \phi^{|h|} \sum_{j=0}^{\infty} \phi^{2j} = \sigma^2 \frac{\phi^{|h|}}{1-\phi^2}.$$

The autocovariance function of $\{Z_t\}$ is therefore

$$\gamma_h = \sigma^2 \frac{\phi^{|h|}}{1-\phi^2}, \qquad |h| = 0, 1, 2, \ldots, \tag{3.7}$$

while its autocorrelation function, shown in Figure 23, is

$$\rho_h = \phi^{|h|}, \qquad |h| = 0, 1, 2, \ldots.$$

Notice that autocovariances and autocorrelations tend to zero exponentially fast as $|h|$ increases. Figure 22 shows the sample paths of Gaussian AR(1) processes for different values of θ, whereas Figure 23 shows the autocorrelation functions of two AR(1) processes, respectively with $\phi = .8$ and $\phi = -.8$.

If $|\phi| > 1$, then Z_t may instead be represented as

$$Z_t = -\sum_{j=1}^{\infty} \alpha^j U_{t+j},$$

where $\alpha = \phi^{-1}$ and the sequence of weights $\{\alpha^j\}$ is absolutely summable, that is, $\sum_{j=1}^{\infty} |\alpha^j| < \infty$. This representation is a stationary solution to (3.6) for it satisfies equation (3.6) and is such that $\mathrm{E}\, Z_t = 0$ and

$$\mathrm{Cov}(Z_t, Z_{t+h}) = \sigma^2 \sum_{j=1}^{\infty} \alpha^j \alpha^{j+|h|} = \sigma^2 \alpha^{2+|h|} \sum_{j=0}^{\infty} \alpha^{2j} = \sigma^2 \alpha^2 \frac{\alpha^{|h|}}{1-\alpha^2}.$$

In this case, the autocovariance function of $\{Z_t\}$ is

$$\gamma_h = \sigma^2 \alpha^2 \frac{\alpha^{|h|}}{1-\alpha^2} = \sigma^2 \frac{\phi^{-|h|}}{\phi^2 - 1}, \qquad |h| = 0, 1, 2, \ldots,$$

while the autocorrelation function is $\rho_h = \phi^{-|h|}$, $|h| = 0, 1, 2, \ldots$. □

Figure 23 Autocorrelation functions of AR(1) processes.

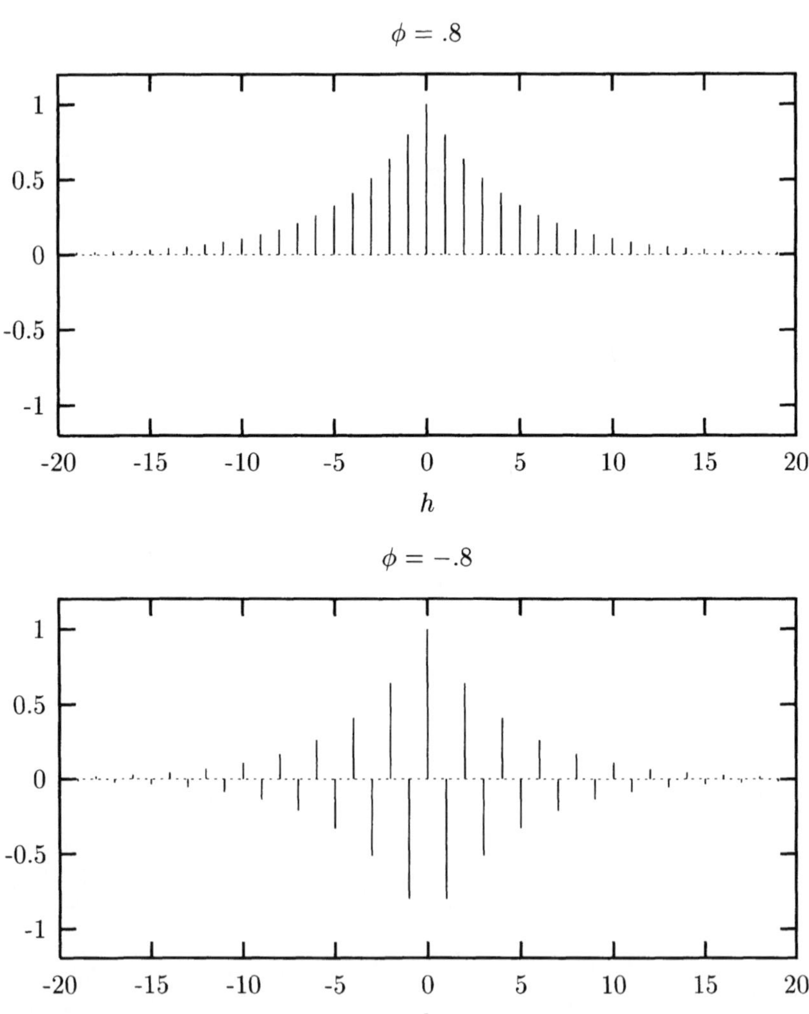

The autocovariance and autocorrelation functions contain important information about the nature of a time series. In particular, the speed at which the autocorrelation function ρ_h tends to zero as $|h|$ increases may be used to measure the degree of "persistence" or "memory" of a process. Thus, a white noise has no memory, an MA(1) process has a short memory, since ρ_h vanishes after one time period, while a stationary AR(1) process has an infinite memory which, however, declines exponentially fast and is effectively zero after a number of time periods that depends on the size of ϕ. These persistence properties are important when it comes to deciding how to model a particular time series.

If $\rho_h \to 0$ as $|h| \to \infty$, as in the white noise, MA(1) and stationary AR(1) cases, then elements of the process far apart in time from each other are approximately uncorrelated. It is important to notice that stationarity, by itself, is not sufficient to guarantee this property.

Example 3.8 Consider a time series $\{Z_t\}$ such that

$$Z_t = \mu + V + U_t, \qquad \{U_t\} \sim \mathrm{WN}(0, \sigma^2),$$

where V is a zero-mean random variable with variance $\omega^2 > 0$. Suppose further that V and $\{U_t\}$ are uncorrelated. The time series $\{Z_t\}$ is stationary with mean μ and autocorrelation function

$$\rho_h = \begin{cases} 1, & \text{if } h = 0, \\ \dfrac{\omega^2}{\sigma^2 + \omega^2}, & \text{otherwise.} \end{cases}$$

This process therefore has an infinite memory that never dies out. □

The next theorem collects some properties of the autocovariance function of a stationary time series. Analogous properties hold for the autocorrelation function.

Theorem 3.1 *If $\{\gamma_h\}$ is the autocovariance function of a stationary time series, then:*

(i) $0 \le |\gamma_h| \le \gamma_0$ *for all* h;
(ii) *the autocovariance function is an even function of* h, *that is,* $\gamma_h = \gamma_{-h}$;
(iii) *the autocovariance function is n.n.d., that is,*

$$\sum_{h=1}^{n} \sum_{j=1}^{n} a_h a_j \, \gamma_{|h-j|} \ge 0$$

for all $n = 1, 2, \ldots$ *and every set of constants* $a_1, \ldots, a_n$.

Proof. Property (i) follows from the fact that $\gamma_0 = \operatorname{Var} Z_t \ge 0$ and the Cauchy–Schwarz inequality

$$|\gamma_h| = |\operatorname{Cov}(Z_t, Z_{t+h})| \le (\operatorname{Var} Z_t)^{1/2} (\operatorname{Var} Z_{t+h})^{1/2} = \gamma_0.$$

Property (ii) follows from the symmetry of covariances, while property (iii) follows from the fact that

$$0 \le \operatorname{Var}\left(\sum_{h=1}^{n} a_h Z_{t+h} \right) = \sum_{h=1}^{n} \sum_{j=1}^{n} a_h a_j \, \gamma_{|h-j|}$$

for all $n = 1, 2, \ldots$ and every set of constants $a_1, \ldots, a_n$. □

It may be shown that properties (ii) and (iii) of Theorem 3.1 completely characterize the autocovariance function of a stationary time series (see for example Brockwell & Davis 1987, Theorem 1.5.1).

If $\{Z_t\}$ is a stationary time series, the $n \times n$ matrix

$$\Gamma_n = \begin{bmatrix} \gamma_0 & \gamma_1 & \cdots & \gamma_{n-1} \\ \gamma_1 & \gamma_0 & \cdots & \gamma_{n-2} \\ \vdots & \vdots & & \vdots \\ \gamma_{n-1} & \gamma_{n-2} & \cdots & \gamma_0 \end{bmatrix}$$

is called the *autocovariance matrix* associated with a finite portion $Z_{t+1}, \ldots, Z_{t+n}$ of the time series. If $\gamma_0 > 0$, the matrix

$$\mathrm{R}_n = \frac{1}{\gamma_0}\Gamma_n = \begin{bmatrix} 1 & \rho_1 & \cdots & \rho_{n-1} \\ \rho_1 & 1 & \cdots & \rho_{n-2} \\ \vdots & \vdots & & \vdots \\ \rho_{n-1} & \rho_{n-2} & \cdots & 1 \end{bmatrix}$$

is called the *autocorrelation matrix* associated with $Z_{t+1}, \ldots, Z_{t+n}$. The matrices Γ_n and R_n are symmetric and have a band diagonal structure, that is, the elements along the same diagonal are all equal, and therefore contain only n distinct elements. Matrices of this kind are also called *Toeplitz matrices.* Further, by conclusion (iii) of Theorem 3.1, they are n.n.d. The latter property places a number of constraints on these two matrices, namely the fact that, for every n, the determinant and all the principal minors must be non-negative.

We now give sufficient conditions for the matrices Γ_n and R_n to be nonsingular for every n.

Theorem 3.2 *If an autocovariance function $\{\gamma_h\}$ is such that $\gamma_0 > 0$ and $\gamma_h \to 0$ as $|h| \to \infty$, then the autocovariance matrix Γ_n and the autocorrelation matrix R_n are nonsingular for every n.*

Proof. See Brockwell and Davis (1987), Proposition 5.1.1. □

3.1.4 STABILITY AND INVERTIBILITY

We have seen that every stationary time series has a mean and an autocovariance function associated with it. Without loss of generality, we now consider the class of zero-mean stationary time series and ask the following question which is crucial for identifiability of a process: Given an autocovariance function $\{\gamma_h\}$, is there a unique time series that has $\{\gamma_h\}$ as its autocovariance function?

Example 3.9 If $\theta \neq 0$, then the following MA(1) processes

$$X_t = U_t - \theta U_{t-1}, \qquad \{U_t\} \sim \mathrm{WN}(0, \sigma^2),$$

$$Y_t = V_t - \frac{1}{\theta} V_{t-1}, \qquad \{V_t\} \sim \mathrm{WN}(0, \theta^2\sigma^2),$$

both have autocovariance function equal to (3.5). □

Example 3.10 From Example 3.7, if $|\phi| < 1$, then the following stationary AR(1) processes

$$X_t = \phi X_{t-1} + U_t, \qquad \{U_t\} \sim \mathrm{WN}(0, \sigma^2),$$
$$Y_t = -\frac{1}{\phi} Y_{t-1} + V_t, \qquad \{V_t\} \sim \mathrm{WN}\left(0, \frac{\sigma^2}{\phi^2}\right),$$

both have autocovariance function equal to (3.7). □

Thus, it is generally impossible to establish a one-to-one correspondence between the class of stationary time series with a given mean and the class of autocovariance functions. The typical solution to this problem consists of restricting attention to stationary time series that possess the following additional properties.

Definition 3.4 A time series $\{Z_t\}$ is said to be *invertible* if it satisfies the relationship

$$\sum_{j=0}^{\infty} \pi_j Z_{t-j} = U_t, \qquad \{U_t\} \sim \mathrm{WN}(0, \sigma^2), \tag{3.8}$$

where $\{\pi_j\}$ is a sequence of constants such that $\pi_0 = 1$ and $\sum_{j=0}^{\infty} |\pi_j| < \infty$. □

Definition 3.5 A time series $\{Z_t\}$ is said to be *stable* or *future–independent* if it possesses the representation

$$Z_t = \sum_{j=0}^{\infty} \psi_j U_{t-j}, \qquad \{U_t\} \sim \mathrm{WN}(0, \sigma^2), \tag{3.9}$$

where $\{\psi_j\}$ is a sequence of constants such that $\psi_0 = 1$ and $\sum_{j=0}^{\infty} |\psi_j| < \infty$. □

The representations (3.8) and (3.9) are called, respectively, the *infinite autoregressive* or AR(∞) *representation* or the *infinite moving average* or MA(∞) *representation* of a time series.

The notion of stability seems appropriate for time series produced by mechanisms where the future cannot influence the present and the past. In fact, if $\{Z_t\}$ is stable, then

$$\mathrm{Cov}(U_{t+h}, Z_t) = \mathrm{Cov}\left(U_{t+h}, \sum_{j=0}^{\infty} \psi_j U_{t-j}\right) = 0, \qquad h = 1, 2, \ldots.$$

It is easy to verify that a stable process is stationary. The sequence of weights $(1, \psi_1, \psi_2, \ldots)$, viewed as a function defined on the integers, is called the *impulse response function* of $\{Z_t\}$ in terms of $\{U_t\}$. The impulse response function may be interpreted as a sequence of dynamic multipliers that describe the effect of a unit change in U_t on $Z_t, Z_{t+1}, Z_{t+2}, \ldots$.

An AR(1) process is always invertible, but is stable only if $|\phi| < 1$. This is equivalent to the condition that the root of the equation $1 - \phi z = 0$ is greater than one in absolute value, that is, $1 - \phi z \neq 0$ for all $|z| \leq 1$. After imposing this condition, there exists a unique zero-mean AR(1) process with autocovariance function equal to (3.7).

On the contrary, an MA(1) process is always stable. To establish conditions under which it is also invertible, substitute backwards in (3.4) to obtain

$$Z_t = U_t - \theta(Z_{t-1} + \theta U_{t-2}),$$

that is,

$$U_t - Z_t - \theta Z_{t-1} = \theta^2 U_{t-2}.$$

Repeated backward substitution gives

$$U_t - \sum_{j=0}^{h-1} \theta^j Z_{t-j} = \theta^h U_{t-h}.$$

If $|\theta| < 1$ and the process started in the infinite past, then

$$\lim_{h\to\infty} \mathrm{E}\left(U_t - \sum_{j=0}^{h-1} \theta^j Z_{t-j}\right)^2 = \lim_{h\to\infty} \theta^{2h}\sigma^2 = 0.$$

In this case, $\{Z_t\}$ may be represented as

$$\sum_{j=0}^{\infty} \theta^j Z_{t-j} = U_t,$$

where the sequence of weights $\{\theta^j\}$ is absolutely summable. This representation is not available when $|\theta| > 1$ or, equivalently, when the root of the equation $1 - \theta z = 0$ is less than one in absolute value. Thus, after imposing the condition that $|\theta| < 1$, there exists a unique zero-mean MA(1) process with autocovariance function equal to (3.5).

3.1.5 PREDICTION

Let $\{Z_t\}$ be a stationary time series with mean μ and autocovariance function $\{\gamma_h\}$, and consider the problem of predicting Z_t given quadratic loss.

From Chapter 1, the unconditional predictor of Z_t is $\mathrm{E}\, Z_t$ and its associated risk or MSE of prediction is just $\mathrm{Var}\, Z_t = \gamma_0$. If the elements of the process are correlated, then the unconditional predictor is generally inefficient, for it neglects the information contained in the past history of Z_t. This information should instead be exploited in order to reduce the MSE of prediction. Notice a distinctive feature of time series: the set of conditioning variables (namely the past values of Z_t) grows with time.

From Section 1.4.2, the BLP of Z_t given $Z_{t-1}, \ldots, Z_{t-k}$ exists and is of the form

$$\mathrm{E}^*(Z_t \mid Z_{t-1}, \ldots, Z_{t-k}) = \alpha_k + \beta_{k1} Z_{t-1} + \cdots + \beta_{kk} Z_{t-k},$$

where

$$\alpha_k = \mathrm{E}\, Z_t - \beta_{k1}\, \mathrm{E}\, Z_{t-1} - \cdots - \beta_{kk}\, \mathrm{E}\, Z_{t-k} = (1 - \sum_{j=1}^{k} \beta_{kj})\, \mu,$$

and the coefficients $\beta_{k1}, \ldots, \beta_{kk}$ satisfy the system of k linear equations

$$\beta_{k1} \operatorname{Cov}(Z_{t-j}, Z_{t-1}) + \cdots + \beta_{kk} \operatorname{Cov}(Z_{t-j}, Z_{t-k}) = \operatorname{Cov}(Z_{t-j}, Z_t), \tag{3.10}$$

for $j = 1, \ldots, k$. Clearly, $\alpha_k = 0$ if the process has zero mean. If the process is Gaussian, then the BLP coincides with the conditional mean of Z_t given $Z_{t-1}, \ldots, Z_{t-k}$.

The set of equations (3.10) may be represented more compactly as

$$\Gamma_k \beta = \gamma,$$

where $\beta = (\beta_{k1}, \ldots, \beta_{kk})$, $\gamma = (\gamma_1, \ldots, \gamma_k)$ and Γ_k is the autocovariance matrix associated with $Z_{t-1}, \ldots, Z_{t-k}$. If Γ_k is nonsingular, solving for the vector β gives the unique solution

$$\beta = \Gamma_k^{-1} \gamma = \mathrm{R}_k^{-1} \rho,$$

where $\rho = (\rho_1, \ldots, \rho_k)$. The kth element of β is called the kth *partial autocorrelation* of $\{Z_t\}$ and denoted by η_k. The sequence $\{\eta_k\}$, viewed as a function defined on the integers, is called the *partial autocorrelation function* of $\{Z_t\}$.

Example 3.11 If $\{Z_t\}$ is a zero-mean stationary time series, then the BLP of Z_t given Z_{t-1} is $\mathrm{E}^*(Z_t \,|\, Z_{t-1}) = \beta_{11} Z_{t-1}$, where $\beta_{11} = \rho_1$. If R_2 is p.d., then the BLP of Z_t given Z_{t-1} and Z_{t-2} is

$$\mathrm{E}^*(Z_t \,|\, Z_{t-1}, Z_{t-2}) = \beta_{21} Z_{t-1} + \beta_{22} Z_{t-2},$$

where

$$\begin{pmatrix} \beta_{21} \\ \beta_{22} \end{pmatrix} = \mathrm{R}_2^{-1} \begin{pmatrix} \rho_1 \\ \rho_2 \end{pmatrix} = \frac{1}{1-\rho_1^2} \begin{pmatrix} \rho_1 - \rho_1 \rho_2 \\ \rho_2 - \rho_1^2 \end{pmatrix}.$$

Hence, the first two elements of the partial autocorrelation function are

$$\eta_1 = \rho_1, \qquad \eta_2 = \frac{\rho_2 - \rho_1^2}{1 - \rho_1^2}.$$

For an MA(1) process, $\rho_2 = 0$ and so $\eta_2 = -\rho_1^2/(1-\rho_1^2) \neq 0$. For a stationary AR(1) process, $\rho_2 = \rho_1^2$ and so $\eta_2 = 0$. In fact, in this case, $\eta_k = 0$ for all $k \geq 2$. □

The risk associated with the BLP $Z_t^* = \mathrm{E}^*(Z_t \,|\, Z_{t-1}, \ldots, Z_{t-k})$ is

$$\begin{aligned} r(Z_t^*) &= \mathrm{E}(Z_t - \alpha - \beta_{k1} Z_{t-1} - \cdots - \beta_{kk} Z_{t-k})^2 \\ &= (1 \; -\beta) \begin{bmatrix} \gamma_0 & \gamma^\top \\ \gamma & \Gamma_k \end{bmatrix} \begin{pmatrix} 1 \\ -\beta \end{pmatrix} \\ &= \gamma_0 - 2\gamma^\top \beta + \beta^\top \Gamma_k \beta. \end{aligned}$$

Since $\beta = \Gamma_k^{-1}\gamma$, the risk difference between the unconditional and the conditional predictors is

$$\gamma_0 - r(Z_t^*) = \gamma^\top \Gamma_k^{-1} \gamma \geq 0,$$

with equality only if all elements of the vector γ are equal to zero, as in the white noise case.

3.1.6 THE LAG OPERATOR

It is often convenient to translate the time indices of a time series $\{Z_t\}$ forward or backward. The *lag* or *backward shift* operator L operates on the entire time series $\{Z_t\}$ shifting back each time index by one unit, that is,

$$LZ_t = Z_{t-1}$$

for all t. Because $Z_{t-2} = LZ_{t-1} = L(LZ_t)$, we define

$$L^k Z_t = Z_{t-k}, \qquad k = 1, 2, \ldots,$$

and put $L^0 Z_t = Z_t$. It is easily verified that L is a linear operator, that is, if $\{Y_t\}$ and $\{X_t\}$ are time series defined on the same probability space, then

$$L(aY_t + bX_t) = a\, LY_t + b\, LX_t.$$

One may therefore define the polynomial lag operator of degree s as

$$B(L) = b_0 + b_1 L + \cdots + b_s L^s,$$

which operates on the entire time series $\{Z_t\}$ by transforming Z_t into

$$B(L)\, Z_t = b_0 Z_t + b_1 Z_{t-1} + \cdots + b_s Z_{t-s}.$$

If the operator $B(L)$ is applied to a time series that always assumes the constant value c, then $B(L)\, c = c(b_0 + b_1 + \cdots + b_s)$.

It may be shown that there is a one-to-one correspondence between the space of polynomial lag operators of degree s and the space of polynomial functions of the same degree $B(z) = b_0 + b_1 z + \cdots + b_s z^s$. Because of this correspondence, common operations such as the sum, multiplication and division of polynomials, and their expansion in convergent series, may all be extended to polynomial lag operators.

Example 3.12 Using the lag operator notation, a stable AR(1) process may be represented either as

$$\Phi(L)\, Z_t = U_t, \qquad \{U_t\} \sim \mathrm{WN}(0, \sigma^2),$$

where $\Phi(L) = 1 - \phi L$, or as

$$Z_t = \Psi(L)\, U_t, \qquad \{U_t\} \sim \mathrm{WN}(0, \sigma^2),$$

where

$$\Psi(L) = \sum_{j=0}^{\infty} \psi_j L^j,$$

with $\psi_j = \phi^j$, $j = 0, 1, 2, \ldots$, and $\sum_{j=0}^{\infty} |\psi_j| < \infty$. The fact that $|\phi| < 1$ implies that $\Phi(z) \neq 0$ for all $|z| \leq 1$. It also implies that the infinite-degree polynomial $\Psi(z)$ converges (is finite) for all $|z| \leq 1$. Because the following identity holds

$$\Phi(L)\, \Psi(L)\, U_t = U_t,$$

we formally define

$$\Psi(L) = \Phi(L)^{-1} = \frac{1}{1 - \phi L}.$$

□

Two related operators are the *first difference* operator Δ, defined by the relationship

$$\Delta Z_t = Z_t - Z_{t-1} = (1 - L)Z_t,$$

and the *forward shift* operator L^{-1}, defined by the relationship $L^{-1}Z_t = Z_{t+1}$. Because

$$(1 - L)(Z_t + Z_{t-1} + Z_{t-2} + \cdots) = 1$$

if the process started in the infinite past, we formally define $(1-L)^{-1} = 1+L+L^2+\cdots$.

3.1.7 GENERATING FUNCTIONS

Generating functions offer a compact and convenient way of recording the information contained in a sequence. Let $\{a_j\}$ be a (possibly doubly-infinite) sequence of real numbers and let z be a (possibly complex) number. If the limit

$$\lim_{n\to\infty} \sum_{j=-n}^{n} a_j z^j$$

is finite for all z with modulus less than or equal to one, then we write

$$a(z) = \sum_{j=-\infty}^{\infty} a_j z^j$$

and call $a(z)$ the *generating function* of the sequence. The generating function exists if the sequence is *absolutely summable*, that is, $\sum_{j=-\infty}^{\infty} |a_j| < \infty$. If the generating function exists, then the individual elements of the sequence can easily be recovered from the coefficients associated with the powers of z. Further, putting $z = 0$ and $z = 1$ gives respectively $a(0) = a_0$ and $a(1) = \sum_{j=-\infty}^{\infty} a_j$. If z is a complex number, then the modulus of $a(z)$ is the real number

$$|a(z)| = [a(z)\, a(z^{-1})]^{1/2}.$$

Two useful properties of generating functions are:

1. if $\{c_j\}$ is the sum of $\{a_j\}$ and $\{b_j\}$, then $c(z) = a(z) + b(z)$;
2. if $\{c_j\}$ is the convolution of $\{a_j\}$ and $\{b_j\}$, that is, $c_j = \sum_{h=-\infty}^{\infty} a_h b_{j-h}$, then $c(z) = a(z)\, b(z)$.

We now consider an important example of a generating function. If $\{Z_t\}$ is a stationary time series with absolutely summable autocovariance sequence $\{\gamma_h\}$, then

$$\gamma(z) = \sum_{h=-\infty}^{\infty} \gamma_h z^h = \gamma_0 + \sum_{h=1}^{\infty} \gamma_h (z^h + z^{-h})$$

exists for all z with modulus less than or equal to one and is called the *autocovariance generating function* of $\{Z_t\}$.

Example 3.13 If $\{Z_t\} \sim \text{WN}(0, \sigma^2)$, then its autocovariance and autocorrelation generating functions are $\gamma(z) = \sigma^2$ and $\rho(z) = 1$ respectively. If $\{Z_t\} \sim \text{MA}(1)$, then

$$\gamma(z) = \sigma^2[1 + \theta^2 - \theta(z + z^{-1})], \qquad \rho(z) = 1 - \frac{\theta}{1+\theta^2}(z + z^{-1}).$$

□

The concept of a generating function may be extended to sequences of random variables. Given a finite segment $Z_1, \ldots, Z_n$ of a time series, its associated *z-transform* is defined as

$$Z_n(z) = \sum_{t=1}^{n} Z_t z^t.$$

There exists a simple relationship between the autocovariance generating function and the z-transform of a zero-mean stationary time series $\{Z_t\}$. Because

$$\mathrm{E}\,|Z_n(z)|^2 = \sum_{h=-n}^{n} (n - |h|)\, \gamma_h z^h,$$

we have that

$$\frac{1}{n}\mathrm{E}\,|Z_n(z)|^2 = \sum_{h=-n}^{n} \left(1 - \frac{|h|}{n}\right) \gamma_h z^h \to \gamma(z) \tag{3.11}$$

as $n \to \infty$.

3.1.8 LINEAR PROCESSES

A time series $\{Y_t\}$ is said to be obtained from a time series $\{Z_t\}$ by applying a *linear filter* with a finite set of weights $\psi_s, \psi_{s+1}, \ldots, \psi_m$ if

$$Y_t = \sum_{j=s}^{m} \psi_j Z_{t-j}.$$

A simple example, which we already encountered, is the MA(1) process. Using the lag operator, a linear filter may be written $Y_t = \Psi(L)\, Z_t$, where the polynomial

$$\Psi(z) = \sum_{j=s}^{m} \psi_j z^j$$

is called the *transfer function* of the filter. The modulus $|\Psi(z)|$ is called the *gain* of the filter, whereas the squared modulus $|\Psi(z)|^2$ is called its *power transfer function.* The time series $\{Y_t\}$ is clearly stationary if $\{Z_t\}$ is stationary and m and s are finite. A linear filter is called *two-sided* if $s < 0 < m$, *backward looking* or *future independent* if $0 \le s \le m$, and *forward looking* if $s \le m \le 0$.

Let $\{Z_t\}$ be a stationary time series with autocovariance generating function $\gamma(z)$. The next theorem gives the autocovariance generating function of any time series $\{Y_t\}$ obtained from $\{Z_t\}$ through linear filtering.

Theorem 3.3 *Given a stationary time series $\{Z_t\}$ with autocovariance generating function $\gamma(z)$ and transfer function $\Psi(z) = \sum_{j=s}^{m} \psi_j z^j$, the autocovariance generating function of the time series $Y_t = \Psi(L)\, Z_t$ is $\gamma^*(z) = |\Psi(z)|^2\, \gamma(z)$.*

Proof. By the convolution property of generating functions, the z-transform of a finite sequence $Y_1, \ldots, Y_n$ is given by $Y_n(z) = \Psi(z)\, Z_n(z)$. Therefore, from (3.11), the autocovariance generating function of $\{Y_t\}$ is

$$\begin{aligned}\gamma^*(z) &= \lim_{n\to\infty} n^{-1}\, \mathrm{E}\, |\Psi(z)\, Z_n(z)|^2 \\ &= |\Psi(z)|^2 \lim_{n\to\infty} n^{-1}\, \mathrm{E}\, |Z_n(z)|^2 = |\Psi(z)|^2\, \gamma(z).\end{aligned}$$

□

Theorem 3.3 generalizes to the case when the transfer function of the filter is of the form $\Psi(z) = \sum_{j=-\infty}^{\infty} \psi_j z^j$, where the doubly-infinite sequence $\{\psi_j\}$ is absolutely summable.

Example 3.14 The transfer function of a stable AR(1) process is equal to

$$\sum_{j=0}^{\infty} \phi^j z^j = \frac{1}{1 - \phi z}$$

for all $|z| \leq 1$. Because the sequence $\{\phi^j\}$ is absolutely summable whenever $|\phi| < 1$, the autocovariance generating function of $\{Z_t\}$ is

$$\gamma(z) = \frac{\sigma^2}{|1 - \phi z|^2} = \frac{\sigma^2}{(1 + \phi z)(1 + \phi z^{-1})}.$$

To check that this is indeed the autocovariance generating function of the process, notice that

$$\frac{\sigma^2}{(1 + \phi z)(1 + \phi z^{-1})} = \sigma^2 (1 + \phi z + \phi^2 z^2 + \cdots)(1 + \phi z^{-1} + \phi^2 z^{-2} + \cdots),$$

and so the coefficient on the hth power of z is

$$\sigma^2 (\phi^h + \phi^{h+1}\phi + \phi^{h+2}\phi^2 + \cdots) = \frac{\sigma^2 \phi^h}{1 - \phi^2},$$

which corresponds to the hth autocovariance of the process. □

We now introduce a general class of stationary processes obtained from an i.i.d. noise sequence by applying a two-sided linear filter with a doubly-infinite set of weights.

Definition 3.6 A time series $\{Z_t\}$ is said to be a *linear process* if it satisfies the relationship

$$Z_t = \mu + \sum_{j=-\infty}^{\infty} \psi_j U_{t-j}, \qquad \{U_t\} \sim \mathrm{IID}(0, \sigma^2),$$

where $\{\psi_j\}$ is a sequence of constants such that $\psi_0 = 1$ and $\sum_{j=-\infty}^{\infty} |\psi_j| < \infty$. □

Clearly, a linear process is stable if $\psi_j = 0$ for all $j \leq 1$. The fact that, for a linear process, the sequence $\{\psi_j\}$ is absolutely summable implies

$$\sum_{j=-\infty}^{\infty} \psi_j < \infty, \qquad \sum_{j=-\infty}^{\infty} \psi_j^2 < \infty.$$

Hence, a linear process $\{Z_t\}$ has mean μ and autocovariance function

$$\gamma_h = \mathrm{E}(\sum_{j=-\infty}^{\infty} \psi_j U_{t-j})(\sum_{k=-\infty}^{\infty} \psi_k U_{t+h-k}) = \sigma^2 \sum_{j=-\infty}^{\infty} \psi_j \psi_{j+|h|}.$$

In particular, $\gamma_0 = \operatorname{Var} Z_t = \sigma^2 \sum_{j=-\infty}^{\infty} \psi_j^2$. Since both the mean and the autocovariances of $\{Z_t\}$ are finite and independent of t, a linear process is stationary. Absolute summability of the sequence $\{\psi_j\}$ also implies that the autocovariance generating function of $\{Z_t\}$ exists and is

$$\gamma(z) = \sigma^2 |\Psi(z)|^2 = \sigma^2 \Psi(z) \Psi(-z).$$

3.1.9 THE SPECTRAL DENSITY

Let $\{Z_t\}$ be a stationary time series with absolutely summable autocovariance sequence $\{\gamma_h\}$ and autocovariance generating function $\gamma(z)$, and consider the case when z is a complex number with modulus equal to one. Recall that the exponential form of such a complex number is $z = e^{i\omega}$, where $i = \sqrt{-1}$ and ω is an angular frequency in the interval $[-\pi, \pi]$. Also recall that the conjugate of $e^{i\omega}$ is $e^{-i\omega}$ and that $e^{i\omega} + e^{-i\omega} = 2\cos\omega$. The real function

$$\begin{aligned} f(\omega) = \frac{1}{2\pi}\gamma(e^{-i\omega}) &= \frac{1}{2\pi} \sum_{h=\infty}^{\infty} \gamma_h e^{-i\omega h} \\ &= \frac{1}{2\pi} [\gamma_0 + \sum_{h=1}^{\infty} \gamma_h (e^{-i\omega h} + e^{i\omega h})] \\ &= \frac{1}{2\pi} (\gamma_0 + 2\sum_{h=1}^{\infty} \gamma_h \cos \omega h), \end{aligned}$$

defined on the interval $[-\pi, \pi]$, is called the ***spectral density*** of the time series and corresponds to the Fourier transform of its autocovariance sequence $\{\gamma_h\}$. It is easy to verify that $f(\omega)$ is bounded and continuous, which implies that its integral on the interval $[-\pi, \pi]$ is finite. Further, $f(\omega) = f(-\omega)$, that is, the spectral density is symmetric about zero, and

$$f(0) = \frac{1}{2\pi} \sum_{-\infty}^{\infty} \gamma_h = \frac{1}{2\pi} (\gamma_0 + 2\sum_{h=1}^{\infty} \gamma_h), \tag{3.12}$$

that is, the value of the spectral density at the origin is proportional to the sum of the autocovariances. Finally, the spectral density function can be shown to be non-negative (see e.g. Fuller 1976, Theorem 3.1.9).

It follows from Theorem 3.3 that, if $\{Z_t\}$ is a stationary time series with spectral density $f(\omega)$, then the spectral density of the filtered time series $Y_t = \Psi(L)\, Z_t$, where $\Psi(z) = \sum_{j=s}^{m} \psi_j z^j$, is

$$f^*(\omega) = |\Psi(e^{-i\omega})|^2 \, f(\omega), \qquad -\pi \leq \omega \leq \pi.$$

This result generalizes to the case when the transfer function $\Psi(z)$ is absolutely summable.

Example 3.15 The spectral density of a white noise with variance σ^2 is the constant function

$$f(\omega) = \frac{\sigma^2}{2\pi}, \qquad -\pi \leq \omega \leq \pi.$$

Hence, the spectral density of an MA(1) process is

$$f^*(\omega) = |1 - \theta e^{-i\omega}|^2 \, f(\omega) = \frac{\sigma^2}{2\pi}\,(1 + \theta^2 - 2\theta \cos\omega), \qquad -\pi \leq \omega \leq \pi.$$

Notice that $f^*(\omega)$ is finite at all frequencies. At $\omega = 0$, the spectral density is

$$f^*(0) = \frac{\sigma^2}{2\pi}\,(1 - \theta)^2.$$

This corresponds to the global maximum of the spectral density when $\theta < 0$, and to its global minimum when $\theta > 0$. If $\theta = 1$, then $f^*(0) = 0$. At $\omega = \pm\pi$, the spectral density is

$$f^*(\pm\pi) = \frac{\sigma^2}{2\pi}\,(1 + \theta)^2.$$

This corresponds to the global minimum of the spectral density when $\theta < 0$ and to its global maximum when $\theta > 0$. If $\theta = -1$, then $f^*(\pm\pi) = 0$.

Now consider an AR(1) process with $|\phi| < 1$. Because $\Psi(z) = (1 - \phi z)^{-1}$ in this case, the spectral density of such a process is

$$f^*(\omega) = \frac{f(\omega)}{|1 - \phi e^{-i\omega}|^2} = \frac{\sigma^2}{2\pi(1 + \phi^2 - 2\phi\cos\omega)}, \qquad -\pi \leq \omega \leq \pi,$$

which is just the reciprocal of the spectral density of an MA(1) process with parameter ϕ. Notice that $f^*(\omega)$ is strictly positive at all frequencies. At $\omega = 0$, the spectral density is

$$f^*(0) = \frac{\sigma^2}{2\pi(1 - \phi)^2}.$$

This corresponds to the global maximum of the spectral density when $0 < \phi < 1$, and to its global minimum when $-1 < \phi < 0$. At $\omega = \pm\pi$, the spectral density is

$$f^*(\pm\pi) = \frac{\sigma^2}{2\pi(1 + \phi)^2}.$$

This corresponds to the global minimum of the spectral density when $0 < \phi < 1$ and to its global maximum when $-1 < \phi < 0$. Notice that $f^*(0)$ is unbounded when $\phi = 1$, whereas $f^*(\pm\pi)$ is unbounded when $\phi = -1$.

Figure 24 shows examples of spectral density functions of MA(1) and AR(1) processes. □

Figure 24 Spectral densities of MA(1) and AR(1) processes.

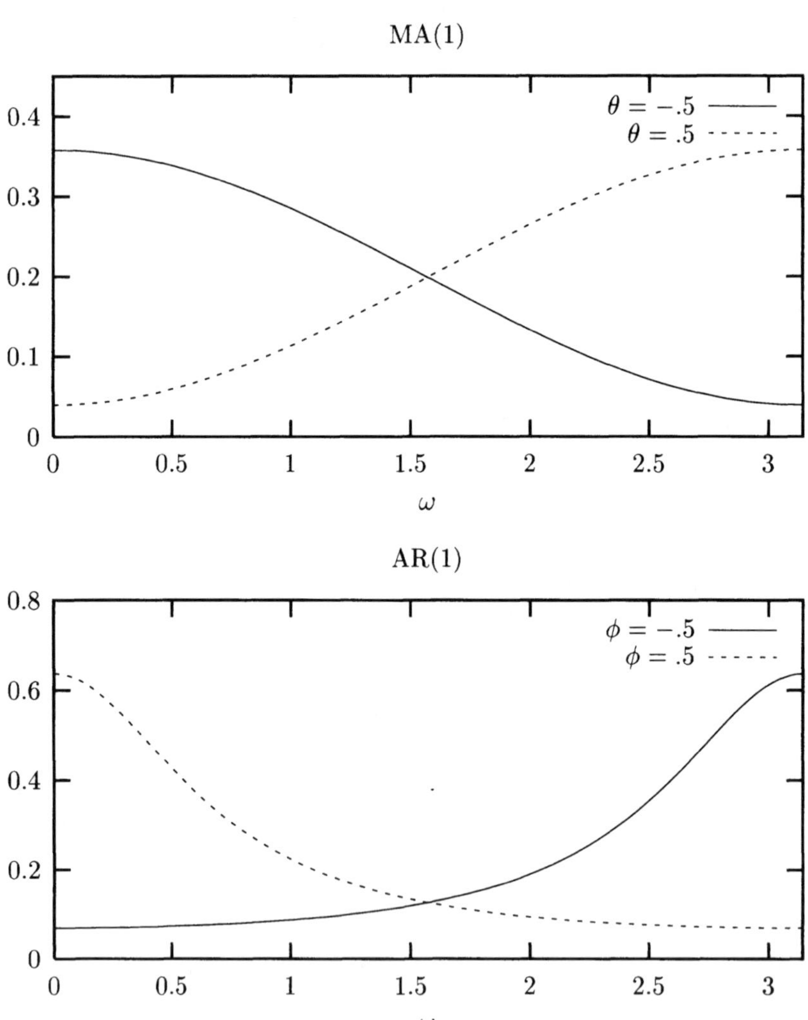

Given a spectral density f, the individual autocovariances may be obtained by integration. First notice that

$$\int_{-\pi}^{\pi} \cos(\omega h)\,\cos(\omega k)\,d\omega = \begin{cases} 2\pi, & \text{if } h = k = 0, \\ \pi, & \text{if } h = k \neq 0, \\ 0, & \text{if } h \neq k. \end{cases}$$

In particular, since $\cos(\omega k) = 1$ whenever $k = 0$, we have that $\int_{-\pi}^{\pi} \cos(\omega h)\,d\omega = 0$ whenever $h \neq 0$. Thus, integrating the function $f(\omega)\cos(\omega h)$ over the interval $[-\pi, \pi]$ gives

$$\begin{aligned}
\int_{-\pi}^{\pi} f(\omega)\,\cos(\omega h)\,d\omega &= \int_{-\pi}^{\pi} \frac{1}{2\pi}[\gamma_0 + 2\sum_{k=1}^{\infty} \gamma_k \cos(\omega k)] \cos(\omega h)\,d\omega \\
&= \frac{\gamma_0}{2\pi}\int_{-\pi}^{\pi} \cos(\omega h)\,d\omega + \frac{1}{\pi}\sum_{k=1}^{\infty} \gamma_k \int_{-\pi}^{\pi} \cos(\omega k)\,\cos(\omega h)\,d\omega \\
&= \gamma_h,
\end{aligned}$$

that is, the hth autocovariance is the inverse transform of the spectral density. In particular

$$\gamma_0 = \int_{-\pi}^{\pi} f(\omega)\,d\omega,$$

which provides a decomposition of the variance of the process into the contribution of the different angular frequencies in the interval $[-\pi, \pi]$.

3.2 ARMA PROCESSES

This section introduces an important class of stochastic processes which is frequently used to model a stationary time series.

Definition 3.7 A time series $\{Z_t\}$ is a *mixed autoregressive–moving average process of order* (p, q), written $\{Z_t\} \sim \text{ARMA}(p, q)$, if it satisfies the relationship

$$Z_t - \phi_1 Z_{t-1} - \cdots - \phi_p Z_{t-p} = U_t - \theta_1 U_{t-1} - \cdots - \theta_q U_{t-q}, \qquad \{U_t\} \sim \text{WN}(0, \sigma^2),$$

where $\phi_p \neq 0$ and $\theta_q \neq 0$. A process $\{Z_t\}$ is ARMA(p, q) with mean μ if $\{Z_t - \mu\}$ is an ARMA(p, q) process. □

An ARMA(p, q) process may be represented more compactly as

$$\Phi(L)\,Z_t = \Theta(L)\,U_t, \qquad \{U_t\} \sim \text{WN}(0, \sigma^2), \tag{3.13}$$

where $\Phi(L) = 1 - \phi_1 L - \cdots - \phi_p L^p$ is a polynomial lag operator of degree p, called the *autoregressive polynomial*, and $\Theta(L) = 1 - \theta_1 L - \cdots - \theta_q L^q$ is a polynomial lag operator of degree q, called the *moving average polynomial*. An ARMA(p, q) process with mean μ may also be represented as

$$\Phi(L)\,Z_t = \alpha + \Theta(L)\,U_t, \qquad \{U_t\} \sim \text{WN}(0, \sigma^2),$$

where $\alpha = \mu(1 - \phi_1 - \cdots - \phi_p) = \mu\,\Phi(1)$.

The autoregressive and moving average polynomials are often factorized in terms of the roots of the associated characteristic equations. Thus, for example, the autoregressive polynomial may also be written

$$\Phi(L) = \prod_{j=1}^{p}(1 - \lambda_j L),$$

where $\lambda_1, \ldots, \lambda_j$ are the roots of the characteristic equation $0 = z^p - \phi_1 z^{p-1} - \ldots - \phi_p$. These roots are just the reciprocal of the roots of the polynomial equation $0 = \Phi(z) = 1 - \phi_1 z - \ldots - \phi_p z^p$. We say that the autoregressive polynomial contains unit roots if some of the λ_j are equal to one in modulus. In particular, if one such root is equal to one then $\Phi(1) = 0$, which implies that $\sum_{j=1}^{p} \phi_j = 1$. We also say that the autoregressive and moving average polynomials have no root in common if their ratio $\Phi(z)/\Theta(z)$ cannot be reduced to the ratio $\Phi^*(z)/\Theta^*(z)$ of polynomials of lower degree.

We now consider two important special cases in the general ARMA class.

Example 3.16 An ARMA$(0, q)$ or MA(q) process is a simple generalization of the MA(1) process introduced in Example 3.6. Thus, a time series $\{Z_t\}$ is an MA(q) process if it satisfies the relationship

$$Z_t = U_t - \theta_1 U_{t-1} - \cdots - \theta_q U_{t-q}, \qquad \{U_t\} \sim \mathrm{WN}(0, \sigma^2),$$

where $\theta_q \neq 0$. We say that $\{Z_t\}$ is an MA(q) process with mean μ if $\{Z_t - \mu\}$ is an MA(q) process. An MA(q) process is stable with autocovariance function

$$\gamma_h = \begin{cases} \sigma^2(1 + \theta_1^2 + \cdots + \theta_q^2), & \text{if } h = 0, \\ \sigma^2(-\theta_h + \theta_1\theta_{h+1} + \cdots + \theta_{q-h}\theta_q), & \text{if } |h| = 1, \ldots, q, \\ 0, & \text{otherwise}, \end{cases}$$

where $\theta_0 = 1$. Since γ_h vanishes for all h such that $|h| > q$, elements of the process farther apart than q periods are uncorrelated. □

Example 3.17 An ARMA$(p, 0)$ or AR(p) process is a simple generalization of the AR(1) process introduced in Example 3.7. Thus, a time series $\{Z_t\}$ is an AR(p) process if it satisfies the relationship

$$Z_t - \phi_1 Z_{t-1} - \cdots - \phi_p Z_{t-p} = U_t, \qquad \{U_t\} \sim \mathrm{WN}(0, \sigma^2),$$

where $\phi_p \neq 0$. We say that $\{Z_t\}$ is an AR(p) process with mean μ if $\{Z_t - \mu\}$ is an AR(p) process. □

ARMA processes often arise by aggregating lower order processes. If $\{Y_t\}$ and $\{X_t\}$ are independent stationary processes, respectively ARMA(p, q) and ARMA(p', q'), then it can be shown that $Z_t = Y_t + X_t$ is a stationary ARMA(r, s) process with

$$r \leq p + p', \qquad s \leq \max(p + q', p' + q).$$

In particular, if $\{Y_t\} \sim$ AR(p) and $\{X_t\} \sim \mathrm{WN}(0, \sigma^2)$, then $\{Z_t\} \sim$ ARMA(p, p). If $\{Y_t\} \sim$ AR(p) and $\{X_t\} \sim$ AR(p'), where $p \geq p'$, then $\{Z_t\} \sim$ ARMA$(p + p', p)$. If $\{Y_t\} \sim$ MA(q) and $\{X_t\} \sim$ MA(q'), where $q \geq q'$, then $\{Z_t\} \sim$ MA(q).

3.2.1 STATIONARITY, STABILITY AND INVERTIBILITY

For an ARMA process to be stationary, stable or invertible, the autoregressive and moving average polynomials must satisfy certain restrictions.

Theorem 3.4 *If $\{Z_t\}$ is an ARMA(p,q) process such that the polynomials $\Phi(z)$ and $\Theta(z)$ have no roots in common, then:*

(i) *$\{Z_t\}$ is stationary if and only if $\Phi(z) \neq 0$ for all $|z| = 1$;*
(ii) *$\{Z_t\}$ is stable if and only if $\Phi(z) \neq 0$ for all $|z| \leq 1$, and the coefficients $\{\psi_j\}$ in its MA(∞) representation are determined by the relationship*

$$\Psi(z) = \sum_{j=0}^{\infty} \psi_j z^j = \frac{\Theta(z)}{\Phi(z)}, \qquad |z| \leq 1;$$

(iii) *$\{Z_t\}$ is invertible if and only if $\Theta(z) \neq 0$ for all $|z| \leq 1$, and the coefficients $\{\pi_j\}$ in its AR(∞) representation are determined by the relationship*

$$\Pi(z) = \sum_{j=0}^{\infty} \pi_j z^j = \frac{\Phi(z)}{\Theta(z)}, \qquad |z| \leq 1.$$

Proof. See e.g. Brockwell and Davis (1987), pp. 85–87. □

Theorem 3.4 implies that, for a stable invertible ARMA process, the transfer function $\Psi(z)$ and the AR(∞) polynomial $\Pi(z)$ are both *rational*, that is, they can be represented as the ratio of finite-degree polynomials. This is one of the main practical advantages of ARMA models, for it allows approximation of complicated transfer functions simply by the ratio of two polynomials of low degree.

Corollary 3.1 *If $\{Z_t\}$ is a stable ARMA(p,q) process, then:*

(i) *its autocovariance generating function is*

$$\gamma(z) = \sigma^2 \, |\Psi(z)|^2 = \sigma^2 \, \frac{|\Theta(z)|^2}{|\Phi(z)|^2}, \qquad |z| \leq 1;$$

(ii) *its spectral density function is*

$$f(\omega) = \frac{\sigma^2}{2\pi} \, |\Psi(e^{-i\omega})|^2 = \frac{\sigma^2}{2\pi} \, \frac{|\Theta(e^{-i\omega})|^2}{|\Phi(e^{-i\omega})|^2}, \qquad -\pi \leq \omega \leq \pi.$$

Being the ratio of two trigonometric polynomials, the spectral density of a stable ARMA process is often called a *rational spectral density*.

Example 3.18 A time series $\{Z_t\}$ is an ARMA(1,1) process if it satisfies the relationship

$$Z_t - \phi Z_{t-1} = U_t - \theta U_{t-1}, \qquad \{U_t\} \sim \text{WN}(0, \sigma^2), \tag{3.14}$$

where $\phi \neq 0$ and $\theta \neq 0$ (Figure 25). Suppose that the autoregressive and the moving average polynomials have no root in common, that is, $\phi \neq \theta$. Since $\Phi(z) = 1 - \phi z$ and

Figure 25 Sample paths of Gaussian ARMA(1,1) processes.

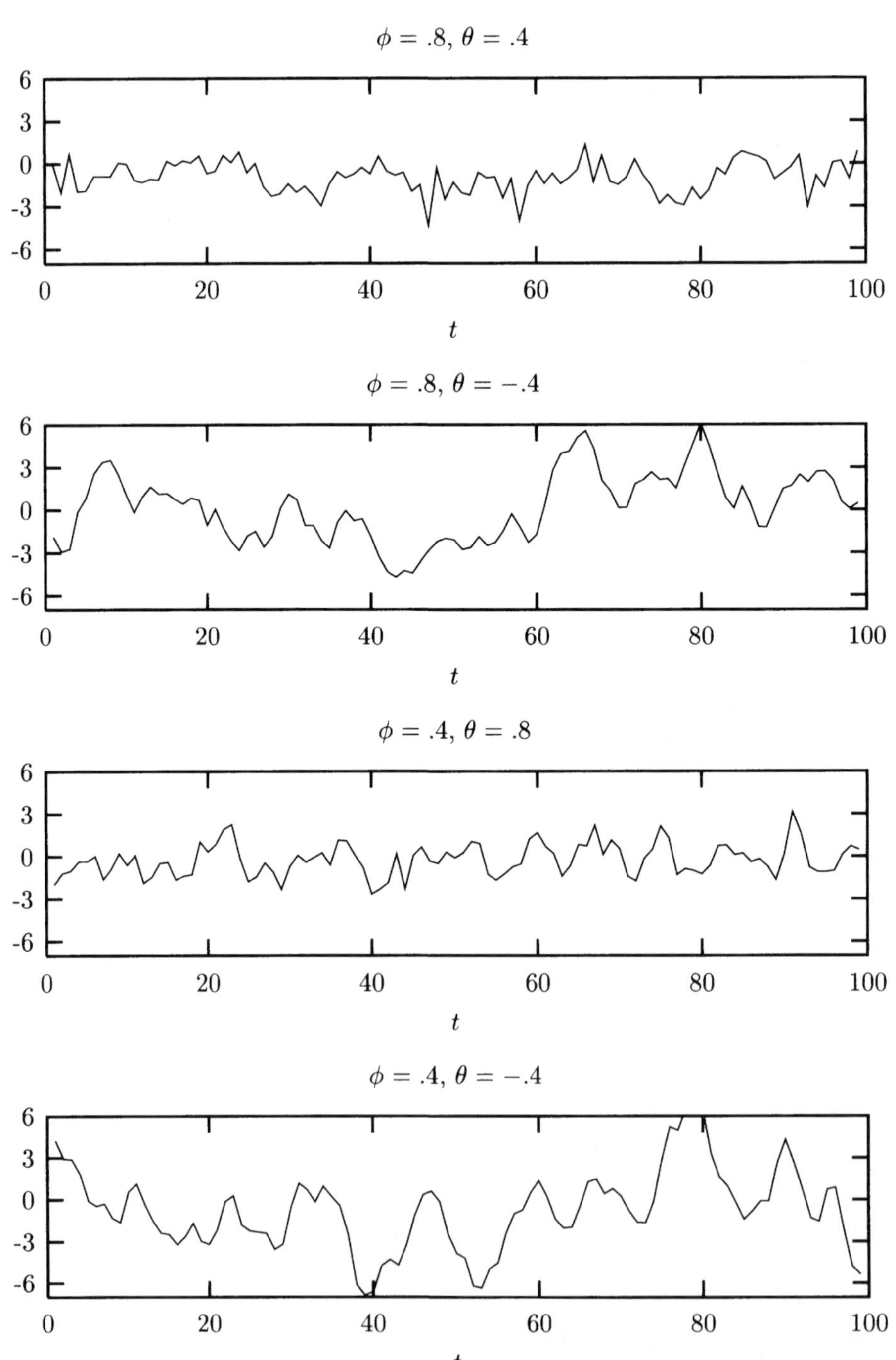

Figure 26 Impulse response functions of ARMA(1,1) processes for different values of (ϕ, θ).

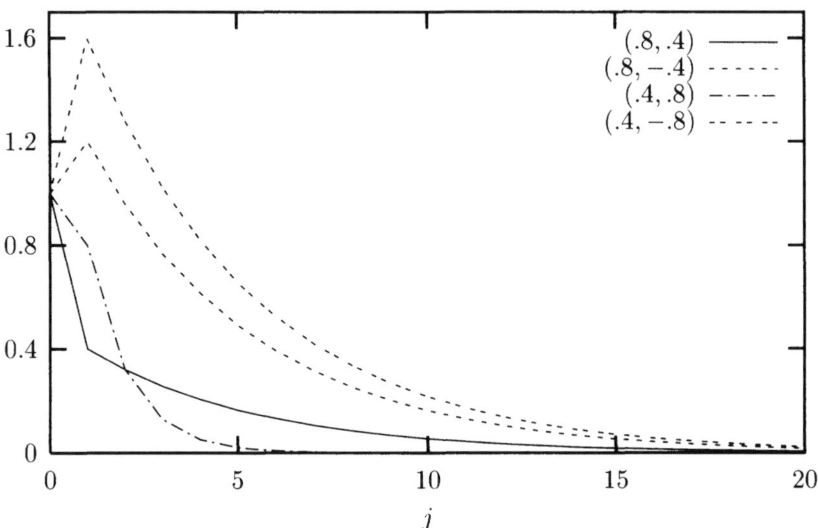

$\Theta(z) = 1 - \theta z$, the process is stationary if and only if $|\phi| \neq 1$, stable if and only if $|\phi| < 1$, and invertible if and only if $|\theta| < 1$.

If $\{Z_t\}$ is stable, its autocovariance function may be obtained through multiplying (3.14) by Z_{t+h}, $h = 0, 1, 2, \ldots$, and then taking expectations of the resulting expressions. This gives the equation system

$$\begin{aligned} \gamma_0 - \phi\gamma_1 &= \sigma^2(1 + \theta^2 - \phi\theta), \\ \gamma_1 - \phi\gamma_0 &= -\sigma^2\theta, \\ \gamma_h - \phi\gamma_{h-1} &= 0, \qquad h \geq 2. \end{aligned}$$

The last equation of this system is a homogeneous first-order linear difference equation with solution

$$\gamma_h = c\phi^h, \qquad h \geq 1,$$

where the constant c is determined by solving with respect to γ_0 and γ_1 the first two equations of the system. The autocovariance function of $\{Z_t\}$ is therefore

$$\gamma_h = \begin{cases} \sigma^2 \dfrac{1 + \theta^2 - 2\phi\theta}{1 - \phi^2}, & \text{if } h = 0, \\ \sigma^2(1 - \phi\theta)(\phi - \theta)\dfrac{\phi^{|h-1|}}{1 - \phi^2}, & \text{if } |h| \geq 1. \end{cases}$$

The impulse response function of the process, that is, the sequence of coefficients $\{\psi_j\}$ in its MA(∞) representation, may be obtained by equating the coefficients of powers of z of the same order on both sides of the identity

$$\begin{aligned}1-\theta z &= (1-\phi z)(\psi_0+\psi_1 z+\psi_2 z^2+\cdots)\\ &= \psi_0+(\psi_1-\phi\psi_0)z+(\psi_2-\phi\psi_1)z^2+\cdots.\end{aligned}$$

This method, known as the *method of indeterminate coefficients*, results in the equation system

$$\psi_0 = 1, \qquad \psi_1-\phi\psi_0 = -\theta, \tag{3.15}$$

$$\psi_j-\phi\psi_{j-1} = 0, \qquad j\geq 2. \tag{3.16}$$

Notice that (3.16) is the same difference equation which determines the autocovariances of $\{Z_t\}$ for all $|h|\geq 1$. Solving for $\{\psi_j, j\geq 2\}$, given the initial conditions $\psi_0=1$ and $\psi_1=\phi-\theta$ obtained from (3.15), we get

$$\psi_j = \begin{cases} 1, & \text{if } j=0,\\ \phi^{j-1}(\phi-\theta), & \text{if } j\geq 1\end{cases}$$

(Figure 26).

Analogously, the coefficients $\{\pi_j\}$ in the AR(∞) representation may be obtained by equating the coefficients of powers of z of the same order on both sides of the identity

$$\begin{aligned}1-\phi z &= (1-\theta z)(\pi_0+\pi_1 z+\pi_2 z^2+\cdots)\\ &= \pi_0+(\pi_1-\theta\pi_0)z+(\pi_2-\theta\pi_1)z^2+\cdots.\end{aligned}$$

This results in the equation system

$$\pi_0 = 1, \qquad \pi_1-\theta\pi_0 = -\phi, \tag{3.17}$$

$$\pi_j-\theta\pi_{j-1} = 0, \qquad j\geq 2. \tag{3.18}$$

Solving the difference equation (3.18) for $\{\pi_j, j\geq 2\}$, given the initial conditions $\pi_0=1$ and $\pi_1=\theta-\phi$ obtained from (3.17), we get

$$\pi_j = \begin{cases} 1, & \text{if } j=0,\\ \theta^{j-1}(\theta-\phi), & \text{if } j\geq 1.\end{cases}$$

Finally, if the process is stable, its spectral density is

$$f(\omega) = \frac{\sigma^2}{2\pi}\frac{|1-\theta e^{-i\omega}|^2}{|1-\phi e^{-i\omega}|^2} = \frac{\sigma^2}{2\pi}\frac{1+\theta^2-2\theta\cos\omega}{1+\phi^2-2\phi\cos\omega}, \qquad -\pi\leq\omega\leq\pi.$$

The spectral density is finite at all frequencies if $|\phi|\neq 1$, and strictly positive at all frequencies if $|\theta|\neq 1$. □

3.2.2 PREDICTION

This section provides the general solution to the linear prediction problem for a stable invertible ARMA process. In what follows, we indicate with $\mathcal{Z}_t$ the information about the process accumulated up to time t, that is, $\mathcal{Z}_t=\{Z_s, s\leq t\}$.

Theorem 3.5 *If $\{Z_t\}$ is a stable invertible* ARMA(p,q) *process, then*

$$\mathrm{E}^*(Z_{t+h} \mid \mathcal{Z}_t) = -\sum_{j=1}^{\infty} \pi_j \, \mathrm{E}^*(Z_{t+h-j} \mid \mathcal{Z}_t) = \sum_{j=h}^{\infty} \psi_j U_{t+h-j}, \qquad h = 1, 2, \ldots,$$

where $\mathrm{E}^*(Z_{t+h-j} \mid \mathcal{Z}_t) = Z_{t+h-j}$ *for* $j \geq h$. *Further*

$$\mathrm{E}[Z_{t+h} - \mathrm{E}^*(Z_{t+h} \mid \mathcal{Z}_t)]^2 = \sigma^2 \sum_{j=0}^{h-1} \psi_j^2. \tag{3.19}$$

Proof. Since $\{Z_t\}$ is stable and invertible, we have

$$Z_{t+h} = \sum_{j=0}^{\infty} \psi_j U_{t+h-j}, \qquad U_{t+h} = Z_{t+h} + \sum_{j=1}^{\infty} \pi_j Z_{t+h-j}.$$

Hence $\mathrm{E}^*(U_{t+h} \mid \mathcal{Z}_t) = 0$ for all $h \geq 1$, and therefore

$$0 = \mathrm{E}^*(Z_{t+h} \mid \mathcal{Z}_t) + \sum_{j=1}^{\infty} \pi_j \, \mathrm{E}^*(Z_{t+h-j} \mid \mathcal{Z}_t),$$

where $\mathrm{E}^*(Z_{t+h-j} \mid \mathcal{Z}_t) = Z_{t+h-j}$ for $j \geq h$. Further, since $\mathrm{E}^*(U_{t+h-j} \mid \mathcal{Z}_t) = U_{t+h-j}$ for any $j \geq h$, we get

$$\mathrm{E}^*(Z_{t+h} \mid \mathcal{Z}_t) = \sum_{j=h}^{\infty} \psi_j U_{t+h-j},$$

and therefore

$$Z_{t+h} - \mathrm{E}^*(Z_{t+h} \mid \mathcal{Z}) = \sum_{j=0}^{h-1} \psi_j U_{t+h-j},$$

from which (3.19) follows immediately. □

The risk (3.19) of the BLP $Z_{t+h}^* = \mathrm{E}^*(Z_{t+h} \mid \mathcal{Z}_t)$ cannot exceed that of the unconditional predictor $\mu = \mathrm{E}\, Z_{t+h}$, for which $r(\mu) = \mathrm{Var}\, Z_{t+h} = \sigma^2 \sum_{j=0}^{\infty} \psi_j^2$. The risk difference between the two predictors decreases as the predictive horizon h increases and tends to zero as $h \to \infty$.

Example 3.19 If $\{Z_t\} \sim$ AR(p) then

$$\pi_j = \begin{cases} -\phi_j, & \text{if } j = 1, \ldots, p, \\ 0, & \text{otherwise.} \end{cases}$$

Hence

$$\mathrm{E}^*(Z_{t+1} \mid \mathcal{Z}_t) = \phi_1 Z_t + \cdots + \phi_p Z_{t-p+1} = \mathrm{E}^*(Z_{t+1} \mid Z_{t-1}, \ldots, Z_{t-p+1}).$$

This has three important implications. First, the BLP of Z_{t+1} given $Z_t, \ldots, Z_{t-p+1}$ coincides with that based on the whole history of the process up to time t. Second, U_{t+1} may be interpreted as the prediction error associated with the BLP of Z_{t+1}. Third, the partial autocorrelation function of an AR(p) process vanishes for $k > p$. □

3.2.3 ARMA-ARCH PROCESSES

The main interest for ARMA processes as models for stationary time series is due to the fact that they provide a simple and parsimonious way of approximating the conditional mean of Z_{t+h} given the information contained in the history of the process $\mathcal{Z}_t = \{Z_s, s \leq t\}$ up to time t. As shown by Theorem 3.5, conditioning on this past history is useful because it leads to a lower prediction error variance with respect to the unconditional prediction case.

Theorem 3.5 also reveals an important limitation of ARMA models, namely the fact that, while allowing for a flexible dependence of the conditional mean of Z_{t+h} on $\mathcal{Z}_t$, they treat the conditional variance of Z_{t+h} too rigidly, by letting it depend only on the predictive horizon h and not on the accumulated information. The class of *ARMA processes with autoregressive conditional heteroskedasticity* or *ARMA-ARCH processes* allows the conditional variance of Z_t to depend on the past history of the process. This class of models, and its generalizations, have been applied extensively to the analysis of financial data, where predicting the variability of a time series is as important as predicting its level.

A zer-mean time series $\{Z_t\}$ is a pure ARCH(1) process, written $\{Z_t\} \sim$ ARCH(1), if

$$Z_t = \sigma_t U_t, \qquad \{U_t\} \sim \text{IID}(0, 1),$$

where σ_t, called the *stochastic volatility*, is an element of a stochastic process that obeys the relationship

$$\sigma_t^2 = \omega^2 + \alpha Z_{t-1}^2,$$

with $\omega \neq 0$ and $\alpha > 0$ (Figure 27). Since $\{U_t\}$ is an i.i.d. sequence with unit variance we have

$$\text{E}(Z_t^2 \mid \mathcal{Z}_{t-1}) = \sigma_t^2 = \omega^2 + \alpha Z_{t-1}^2.$$

Thus, an ARCH(1) process for Z_t corresponds to an AR(1) process for Z_t^2.

If $0 \leq \alpha < 1$, then an ARCH(1) process is stationary and its unconditional variance is equal to $\bar{\sigma}^2 = \omega^2/(1 - \alpha)$. The difference between the conditional and the unconditional variance is

$$\sigma_t^2 - \bar{\sigma}^2 = \omega^2 + \alpha Z_{t-1}^2 - \frac{\omega^2}{1-\alpha} = \alpha Z_{t-1}^2 - \frac{\alpha}{1-\alpha}\omega^2 = \alpha(Z_{t-1}^2 - \bar{\sigma}^2),$$

which is proportional to the difference between the squared prediction error at time $t-1$ (equal to Z_{t-1}^2 in this case) and its unconditional expectation. By the law of iterated expectations,

$$\begin{aligned} \text{E}(Z_{t+1}^2 \mid \mathcal{Z}_{t-1}) - \bar{\sigma}^2 &= \text{E}(\sigma_{t+1}^2 - \bar{\sigma}^2 \mid \mathcal{Z}_{t-1}) \\ &= \text{E}[\alpha(Z_t^2 - \bar{\sigma}^2) \mid \mathcal{Z}_{t-1}] \\ &= \alpha(\sigma_t^2 - \bar{\sigma}^2). \end{aligned}$$

Repeatedly applying this recursive formula gives

$$\text{E}(Z_{t+h}^2 \mid \mathcal{Z}_{t-1}) - \bar{\sigma}^2 = \alpha^{h+1}(Z_{t-1}^2 - \bar{\sigma}^2), \qquad h = 1, 2, \ldots. \tag{3.20}$$

Thus, $\text{E}(Z_{t+h}^2 \mid \mathcal{Z}_{t-1}) \to \bar{\sigma}^2$ as $h \to \infty$.

Figure 27 Sample paths of Gaussian ARCH(1) processes.

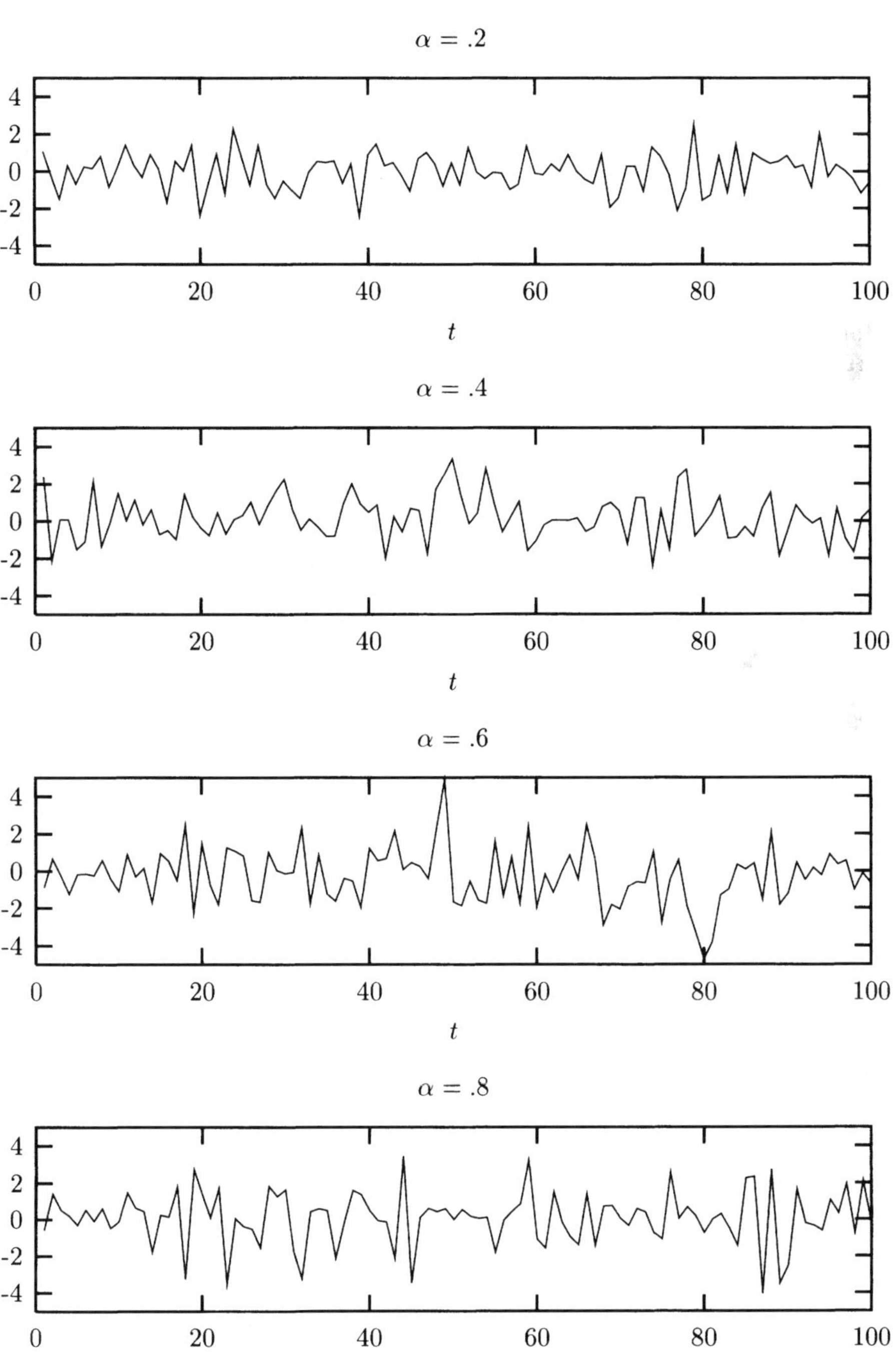

Another interesting property of this process is that its marginal distribution exhibits fatter tails than its conditional distribution. To see this, assume that Z_t is stationary with finite fourth moments and notice that, conditionally on $\mathcal{Z}_{t-1}$, the coefficient of kurtosis of Z_t is

$$\kappa_{t|t-1} = \frac{\mathrm{E}(Z_t^4 \mid \mathcal{Z}_{t-1})}{[\mathrm{E}(Z_t^2 \mid \mathcal{Z}_{t-1})]^2} = \frac{\mathrm{E}\, U_t^4}{(\mathrm{E}\, U_t^2)^2} = \mathrm{E}\, U_t^4.$$

On the other hand, the unconditional coefficient of kurtosis of Z_t is

$$\kappa_t = \frac{\mathrm{E}\, Z_t^4}{(\mathrm{E}\, Z_t^2)^2} = \frac{(\mathrm{E}\, \sigma_t^4)(\mathrm{E}\, U_t^4)}{(\mathrm{E}\, Z_t^2)^2} > \frac{(\mathrm{E}\, \sigma_t^2)^2(\mathrm{E}\, U_t^4)}{(\mathrm{E}\, Z_t^2)^2} = \frac{(\mathrm{E}\, Z_t^2)^2(\mathrm{E}\, U_t^4)}{(\mathrm{E}\, Z_t^2)^2} = \kappa_{t|t-1},$$

where we used Jensen's inequality and the fact that, by the law of iterated expectations, $\mathrm{E}\, Z_t^2 = \mathrm{E}\, \sigma_t^2$.

A simple generalization of the pure ARCH(1) process is the pure ARCH(m) process, where

$$\sigma_t^2 = \omega^2 + \alpha_1 Z_{t-1}^2 + \cdots + \alpha_m Z_{t-m}^2,$$

with $\alpha_j \geq 0$, $j = 1, \ldots, m-1$, and $\alpha_m > 0$, which corresponds to an AR(m) process for Z_t^2.

A time series $\{Z_t\}$ is called an ARMA(p, q)-ARCH(m) process if it satisfies the relationship

$$\Phi(L)\, Z_t = \Theta(l)\, U_t, \qquad \{U_t\} \sim \mathrm{ARCH}(m),$$

where $\Phi(L)$ and $\Theta(L)$ are polynomials in the lag operator of order p and q respectively.

Example 3.20 A time series $\{Z_t\}$ is a stationary AR(1)-ARCH(1) process if it satisfies the relationship

$$Z_t = \phi Z_{t-1} + U_t, \qquad \{U_t\} \sim \mathrm{ARCH}(1),$$

where $|\phi| < 1$. In this case

$$\mathrm{E}(Z_{t+1} \mid \mathcal{Z}_t) = \phi Z_t, \qquad \mathrm{Var}(Z_{t+1} \mid \mathcal{Z}_t) = \omega^2 + \alpha(Z_t - \phi Z_{t-1})^2.$$

Since $Z_{t+h} = \sum_{j=0}^{\infty} \phi^j U_{t+h-j}$, we have

$$Z_{t+h} - \mathrm{E}(Z_{t+h} \mid \mathcal{Z}_t) = \sum_{j=0}^{h-1} \phi^j U_{t+h-j}, \qquad h = 1, 2 \ldots.$$

Hence, by the recursive formula (3.20), the conditional variance of Z_{t+h} is

$$\begin{aligned}\mathrm{Var}(Z_{t+h} \mid \mathcal{Z}_t) &= \sum_{j=0}^{h-1} \phi^{2j}\, \mathrm{E}(U_{t+h-j}^2 \mid \mathcal{Z}_t) \\ &= \bar{\sigma}^2 \sum_{j=0}^{h-1} \phi^{2j} + \alpha^h (U_t^2 - \bar{\sigma}^2) \sum_{j=0}^{h-1} \phi^{2j} \alpha^{-j},\end{aligned}$$

which depends on both the predictive horizon h and the deviation of the quadratic error $U_t^2 = (Z_t - \phi Z_{t-1})^2$ from $\bar{\sigma}^2$. □

A further generalization is a process exhibiting *generalized autoregressive conditional heteroskedasticity (GARCH)* of order (r, m), where

$$\sigma_t^2 = \omega^2 + \delta_1 \sigma_{t-1}^2 + \cdots + \delta_r \sigma_{t-r}^2 + \alpha_1 Z_{t-1}^2 + \cdots + \alpha_m Z_{t-m}^2,$$

with $\delta_r, \alpha_m > 0$, $\delta_h \geq 0$, $h = 1, \ldots, r-1$, and $\alpha_j \geq 0$, $j = 1, \ldots, m-1$. An ARCH(m) process corresponds to a GARCH$(0, m)$. If $V_t = Z_t^2 - \sigma_t^2$ denotes the forecast error in predicting Z_t^2 using its conditional predictor σ_t^2, then a GARCH(r, m) process may be written

$$Z_t^2 = \omega^2 + \gamma_1 Z_{t-1}^2 + \cdots + \gamma_p Z_{t-p}^2 + V_t - \alpha_1 V_{t-1} - \cdots - \alpha_r V_{t-r},$$

where $p = \max(m, r)$, $\gamma_j = \alpha_j + \delta_j$, $\alpha_j = 0$ for $j > m$ and $\delta_j = 0$ for $j > r$. Thus, a GARCH(r, m) process for Z_t corresponds to an ARMA(p, r) process for Z_t^2, with $p = \max(m, r)$.

A time series $\{Z_t\}$ is called an ARMA(p, q)-GARCH(r, m) process if it satisfies the relationship

$$\Phi(L)\, Z_t = \Theta(l)\, U_t, \qquad \{U_t\} \sim \text{GARCH}(r, m),$$

where $\Phi(L)$ and $\Theta(L)$ are polynomials in the lag operator of order p and q respectively.

3.3 MULTIVARIATE TIME SERIES

Very often, the data consist of observations on multiple time series. Thus consider the case when $\{Z_t\}$ is an m-variate time series, that is, $Z_t = (Z_{t1}, \ldots, Z_{tm})$ is a random m-vector. If there is correlation between the component series of $\{Z_t\}$, modeling each of them separately is likely to be inefficient for it ignores the information contained in these correlations. This suggests modeling the elements of $\{Z_t\}$ jointly.

3.3.1 STATIONARITY AND AUTOCOVARIANCES

The definitions of weak and strong stationarity are the same as in the univariate case. Because $\mu_t = \text{E}\, Z_t$ is now an m-vector and

$$\text{Cov}(Z_t, Z_s) = \text{E}(Z_t - \mu_t)(Z_s - \mu_s)^\top$$

is now an $m \times m$ matrix, the multivariate process $\{Z_t\}$ is stationary if all elements of μ_t do not depend on t and all elements of the autocovariance matrix $\text{Cov}(Z_t, Z_s)$ depend on the time indices t and s only through their distance $|t - s|$. Clearly, if $\{Z_t\}$ is stationary, then all its components are also stationary. The converse is not true in general, for stationarity of all components of $\{Z_t\}$ does not guarantee by itself that the cross-covariances, that is, the off-diagonal elements of $\text{Cov}(Z_t, Z_s)$, depend only on $|t - s|$.

If $\{Z_t\}$ is a stationary m-variate time series with mean μ, then the $m \times m$ matrix

$$\Gamma_h = \text{E}(Z_t - \mu)(Z_{t+h} - \mu)^\top = [\gamma_{ijh}]$$

is called the hth *autocovariance matrix*. The ith diagonal element γ_{iih} of Γ_h is the hth autocovariance of the ith component of $\{Z_t\}$, while γ_{ijh} is the cross-covariance between Z_{ti} and $Z_{t+h,j}$. Because

$$\gamma_{ijh} = \text{E}(Z_{ti} - \mu_i)(Z_{t+h,j} - \mu_j) = \text{E}(Z_{tj} - \mu_j)(Z_{t-h,i} - \mu_i) = \gamma_{ji,-h},$$

the autocovariance matrix Γ_h is not an even function of h. We have instead $\Gamma_{-h} = \Gamma_h^\top$.

Example 3.21 An m-variate time series $\{Z_t\}$ consisting of uncorrelated random vectors with mean zero and variance matrix $\Sigma = [\sigma_{ij}]$ is stationary and its autocovariance matrix is

$$\Gamma_h = \begin{cases} \Sigma, & \text{if } h = 0, \\ 0, & \text{otherwise.} \end{cases}$$

This time series is called a *m-variate white noise*, written $\{Z_t\} \sim \mathrm{WN}_m(0, \Sigma)$. Notice that Σ need not be diagonal, that is, the components of a multivariate white noise may be contemporaneously correlated. □

A multivariate white noise, defined in the previous example, is the building block of many multivariate time series models.

Example 3.22 An m-variate time series $\{Z_t\}$ is called multivariate MA(1) process, written $\{Z_t\} \sim \mathrm{MA}_m(1)$, if

$$Z_t = U_t - \Theta U_{t-1}, \qquad \{U_t\} \sim \mathrm{WN}_m(0, \Sigma), \tag{3.21}$$

where $\Theta = [\theta_{ij}]$ is an $m \times m$ matrix. An $\mathrm{MA}_m(1)$ process is stationary with mean zero and autocovariance matrix

$$\Gamma_h = \begin{cases} \Sigma + \Theta\Sigma\Theta^\top, & \text{if } h = 0, \\ -\Theta\Sigma, & \text{if } h = 1, \\ -\Sigma\Theta^\top, & \text{if } h = -1, \\ 0, & \text{otherwise.} \end{cases}$$

Repeated backward substitution in (3.21) gives

$$\sum_{j=0}^{k-1} \Theta^j Z_{t-j} = U_t - \Theta^k U_{t-k}.$$

Assume, for simplicity, that the eigenvalues of the matrix Θ are all distinct. If Λ is the diagonal matrix whose diagonal elements are the eigenvalues of Θ, and Q is the orthonormal matrix of the associated eigenvectors, then $\Theta = Q\Lambda Q^\top$ and $Q^k = Q\Lambda^k Q^\top$. Hence, $\lim_{k\to\infty} \Theta^k = 0$ if and only if all eigenvalues of Θ are less than one in modulus. In this case

$$\lim_{k\to\infty} \mathrm{E} \,\| U_t - \sum_{j=0}^{k-1} \Theta^j Z_{t-j} \|^2 = 0,$$

which justifies the representation

$$\sum_{j=0}^{\infty} \Theta^j Z_{t-j} = U_t,$$

called the *infinite autoregressive* or $\mathrm{AR}_m(\infty)$ *representation* of $\{Z_t\}$.

An $\mathrm{MA}_m(1)$ process is therefore invertible, namely possesses an $\mathrm{AR}_m(\infty)$ representation, if and only if all eigenvalues of Θ are less than one in modulus. This is equivalent to the condition that all roots of the equation $\det[I_m - \Theta z] = 0$ are greater than one in modulus, that is, $\det[I_m - \Theta z] \neq 0$ for all $|z| \leq 1$. In such a case we have that the infinite-degree polynomial matrix

$$\Pi(z) = \sum_{j=0}^{\infty} \Pi_j z^j = [I_m - \Theta z]^{-1}$$

converges for all $|z| \leq 1$. □

Example 3.23 An m-variate time series $\{Z_t\}$ is called a multivariate or vector AR(1) process, written $\{Z_t\} \sim \mathrm{AR}_m(1)$, if it satisfies the relationship

$$Z_t - \Phi Z_{t-1} = U_t, \qquad \{U_t\} \sim \mathrm{WN}_m(0, \Sigma), \tag{3.22}$$

where $\Phi = [\phi_{ij}]$ is an $m \times m$ matrix. The existence and the nature of a stable solution to (3.22) depend on the eigenvalues of the matrix Φ. Proceeding as in Example 3.22, it can be shown that, if all eigenvalues of Φ are less than one in modulus, then the only stable solution to (3.22) is

$$Z_t = \sum_{j=1}^{\infty} \Phi^j U_{t-j},$$

where $\sum_{j=1}^{\infty} \Phi^j z^j = (I_m - \Phi z)^{-1}$ converges for all $|z| \leq 1$. If all eigenvalues of Φ are greater than one in modulus, then (3.22) possesses the stationary but nonstable solution

$$Z_t = -\sum_{j=1}^{\infty} \Phi^{-j} U_{t+j}.$$

If some eigenvalue of Φ is equal to one in modulus, then neither representation exists and $\{Z_t\}$ is nonstationary. Hence, the unique stable multivariate AR(1) processes are those for which all eigenvalues of Φ have modulus less than one. This is equivalent to the condition that all roots of the equation $\det(I_m - \Phi z) = 0$ are greater than one in modulus, that is, $\det(I_m - \Phi z) \neq 0$ for all $|z| \leq 1$.

If $\{Z_t\}$ is stable, postmultiplying both sides of (3.22) by $Z_{t-h}^\top$ and taking expectations gives

$$\Gamma_h^\top - \Phi \Gamma_{h-1}^\top = \mathrm{E}\, U_t Z_{t-h}^\top, \qquad h = 0, 1, 2, \ldots.$$

For $h \geq 1$, we obtain the matrix difference equation

$$\Gamma_h^\top - \Phi \Gamma_{h-1}^\top = 0,$$

whose solution is

$$\Gamma_h^\top = \Phi^h \Gamma_0^\top, \qquad h \geq 1,$$

where Γ_0 is determined by the initial condition

$$\Gamma_0 = \Phi \Gamma_1 + \Sigma = \Phi \Gamma_0 \Phi^\top + \Sigma.$$

Using the fact that $\mathrm{vec}\,(A + B) = \mathrm{vec}\, A + \mathrm{vec}\, B$ and $\mathrm{vec}\,(ABC) = (A \otimes C^\top)\mathrm{vec}\,(B)$ (see Appendix A.8), an explicit solution for Γ_0 is

$$\mathrm{vec}\,(\Gamma_0) = [I_{m^2} - (\Phi \otimes \Phi)]^{-1}\, \mathrm{vec}\,(\Sigma).$$

When $m = 1$, this coincides with formula (3.7) for a univariate AR(1) process. □

3.3.2 MULTIVARIATE ARMA PROCESSES

An m-variate time series $\{Z_t\}$ is called a *multivariate* ARMA(p,q) *process*, written $\{Z_t\} \sim \text{ARMA}_m(p,q)$, if it satisfies the relationship

$$Z_t - \Phi_1 Z_{t-1} - \cdots - \Phi_p Z_{t-p} = U_t - \Theta_1 U_{t-1} - \cdots - \Theta_q U_{t-q}, \qquad \{U_t\} \sim \text{WN}_m(0,\Sigma),$$

where $\Phi_1,\ldots,\Phi_q$ and $\Theta_1,\ldots,\Theta_q$ are $m \times m$ matrices, with $\Phi_p \neq 0$ and $\Theta_q \neq 0$. We say that $\{Z_t\}$ is an ARMA$_m(p,q)$ process with mean μ if $\{Z_t - \mu\} \sim \text{ARMA}_m(p,q)$.

An m-variate ARMA(p,q) process may be represented more compactly as

$$\Phi(L)\, Z_t = \Theta(L)\, U_t, \qquad \{U_t\} \sim \text{WN}_m(0,\Sigma), \tag{3.23}$$

where $\Phi(L) = I_m - \Phi_1 L - \cdots - \Phi_p L^p$ and $\Theta(L) = I_m - \Theta_1 L - \cdots - \Theta_q L^q$ are $m \times m$ matrices whose elements are polynomial lag operators of degree at most equal to p and q respectively. If the matrices Σ, $\Phi(L)$ and $\Theta(L)$ are all diagonal, then an m-variate ARMA process reduces to a collection of m unrelated univariate ARMA processes of order not greater than (p,q).

Two important special cases in the general multivariate ARMA class are the class of multivariate MA(q) processes, with $\Phi(z) = I_m$ for all z, and the class of multivariate AR(p) processes, with $\Theta(z) = I_m$ for all z. These are simple generalizations of the multivariate MA(1) and AR(1) processes introduced in Examples 3.22 and 3.23.

In fact, Example 3.23 is more general than it may seem at first, since every AR(p) process, univariate or multivariate, may be represented as a multivariate AR(1). For example, putting

$$\mathbf{Z}_t = \begin{pmatrix} Z_t \\ Z_{t-1} \\ \vdots \\ Z_{t-p+1} \end{pmatrix}, \qquad \mathbf{U}_t = \begin{pmatrix} U_t \\ 0 \\ \vdots \\ 0 \end{pmatrix}, \qquad \Phi = \begin{bmatrix} \Phi_1 & \cdots & \Phi_{p-1} & \Phi_p \\ I_m & \cdots & 0 & 0 \\ \vdots & \ddots & \vdots & \vdots \\ 0 & \cdots & I_m & 0 \end{bmatrix},$$

an AR$_m(p)$ process may be represented as the mp-variate AR(1) process

$$\mathbf{Z}_t - \Phi \mathbf{Z}_{t-1} = \mathbf{U}_t,$$

where $\{\mathbf{U}_t\}$ is an mp-variate white noise with singular variance matrix equal to

$$\Omega = \begin{bmatrix} \Sigma & 0 & \cdots & 0 \\ 0 & 0 & \cdots & 0 \\ \vdots & \vdots & \ddots & \vdots \\ 0 & 0 & \cdots & 0 \end{bmatrix}.$$

In particular, every univariate AR(p) process may be represented as a p-variate AR(1).

It can be shown that an m-variate ARMA process is stationary if all roots of the equation

$$0 = \det \Phi(z) = \det(I_m - \Phi_1 z - \cdots - \Phi_p z^p)$$

are different from one in modulus, that is, $\det \Phi(z) \neq 0$ for all z such that $|z| = 1$.

An m-variate ARMA process is stable if all roots of the equation $0 = \det \Phi(z)$ are greater than one in modulus, that is, $\det \Phi(z) \neq 0$ for all $|z| \leq 1$. In this case, $\{Z_t\}$ possesses the $\mathrm{MA}_m(\infty)$ representation

$$Z_t = \Psi(L)\, U_t,$$

where

$$\Psi(z) = \sum_{j=0}^{\infty} \Psi_j z^j = \Phi^{-1}(z)\, \Theta(z)$$

converges for all $|z| \leq 1$. The sequence of matrices $\{\Psi_j\}$ is the impulse response function of the multivariate process, and its elements may be computed by applying the method of indeterminate coefficients to the identity $\Phi(z)\, \Psi(z) = \Theta(z)$.

Finally, an m-variate ARMA process is invertible if all roots of the equation

$$0 = \det \Theta(z) = \det(I_m - \Theta_1 z - \cdots - \Theta_q z^q)$$

are greater than one in modulus, that is, $\det \Theta(z) \neq 0$ for all z such that $|z| \leq 1$. In this case, $\{Z_t\}$ possesses the $\mathrm{AR}_m(\infty)$ representation

$$\Pi(L)\, Z_t = U_t,$$

where

$$\Pi(z) = \sum_{j=0}^{\infty} \Pi_j z^j = \Theta^{-1}(z)\, \Phi(z)$$

converges for all $|z| \leq 1$. The coefficients in $\Pi(z)$ may be computed by applying the method of indeterminate coefficients to the identity $\Phi(z) = \Theta(z)\, \Pi(z)$.

Given a stable $\mathrm{ARMA}_m(p, q)$ process, the inverse of the autoregressive polynomial $\Phi(z)$ exists for all $|z| \leq 1$ and is equal to

$$\Phi^{-1}(z) = \phi^{-1}(z)\, \Phi^*(z),$$

where $\phi(z) = \det \Phi(z)$ is a polynomial of degree mp and $\Phi^*(z)$ denotes the adjoint matrix of $\Phi(z)$. The process may therefore be represented in the equivalent form

$$\phi(L)\, Z_t = \Theta^*(L)\, U_t, \tag{3.24}$$

where $\Theta^*(L) = \Phi^*(L)\, \Theta(z)$ is a matrix whose elements are polynomial lag operators of degree at most equal to $p+q$. Representation (3.24) is called the *autoregressive final form* of $\{Z_t\}$.

The term on the right side of (3.24) is a vector of m components, each consisting of a linear combination of univariate MA processes of order at most equal to $p+q$. From Section 3.2, each of these linear combinations may be represented as a univariate MA process of order at most equal to $p+q$. Each component of $\{Z_t\}$ may therefore be represented as a univariate ARMA process of order at most equal to $(mp, p+q)$, that is,

$$\phi(L)\, Z_{tj} = \theta_j^*(L)\, U_{tj}, \qquad j = 1, \ldots, m,$$

where $\{U_{tj}\}$ is a univariate white noise. Unless $\phi(L)$ and $\theta_j^*(L)$ have some root in common, the autoregressive operator $\phi(L)$ is the same for each component of $\{Z_t\}$, whereas the moving average operators $\theta_j^*(L)$ depend on all the parameters in $\Phi(L)$ and $\Theta(L)$. Further, the white noise processes $\{U_{tj}\}$ driving each component are correlated with each other.

3.3.3 IMPULSE RESPONSE ANALYSIS

Let $\{Z_t\}$ be a stable $\mathrm{ARMA}_m(p,q)$ process. It follows from its $\mathrm{MA}_m(\infty)$ representation that

$$Z_{t+h} = \Psi_0 U_{t+h} + \Psi_1 U_{t+h-1} + \cdots + \Psi_{h-1} U_{t+1} + \sum_{j=h}^{\infty} \Psi_j U_{t+h-j}, \qquad h = 1, 2, \ldots,$$

where $\Psi_0 = I_m$, $\Psi_k = [\psi_{ijk}]$ and $\{U_t\} \sim \mathrm{WN}_m(0, \Sigma)$. By a straightforward generalization of Theorem 3.5, the BLP of Z_{t+s} given the information $\mathcal{Z}_t = \{Z_s, s \leq t\}$ accumulated up to time t is

$$\mathrm{E}^*(Z_{t+h} \,|\, \mathcal{Z}_t) = \sum_{j=h}^{\infty} \Psi_j U_{t+h-j}.$$

The associated prediction error is therefore

$$V_{t+h} = Z_{t+h} - \mathrm{E}^*(Z_{t+h} \,|\, \mathcal{Z}_t) = \sum_{k=0}^{h-1} \Psi_k U_{t+h-k}.$$

Clearly, V_{t+h} has mean zero and variance equal to $\sum_{k=0}^{h-1} \Psi_k \Sigma \Psi_k^\top$.

Without loss of generality, suppose that all components of the vector U_t have unit variance and consider the special case when $\Sigma = I_m$, that is, the elements of U_t are contemporaneously uncorrelated. In this case, the fact that $\Psi_0 = I_m$ implies that U_{tj} may be regarded as the shock specific to the jth variable at time t. The generic element ψ_{ijk} of the matrix Ψ_k may therefore be interpreted as the effect on Z_{ti} of a unit shock to the jth variable at time $t - k$. Further, the ratio

$$\frac{\sum_{k=0}^{h-1} \psi_{ijk}^2}{\sum_{s=1}^{m} \sum_{k=0}^{h-1} \psi_{isk}^2} \tag{3.25}$$

measures how much of the risk associated with the BLP of $Z_{t+h,i}$ is due to the sequence of shocks $U_{t+1,j}, \ldots, U_{t+h,j}$ specific to the jth variable. The impulse response functions $\{\psi_{ijk}\}$ and the variance decompositions of the form (3.25) are important tools for studying the dynamic properties of a multivariate time series $\{Z_t\}$. In particular, they enable one to analyze the mechanisms through which shocks to a specific variable are transmitted to all the other variables in the system.

The possibility of identifying $\{U_{tj}\}$ as the sequence of shocks specific to the jth variable is lost when the components of U_t are contemporaneously correlated. Notice however that, if $H = [h_{ij}]$ is a nonsingular matrix such that $H^\top H = \Sigma^{-1}$ and we put $V_t = HU_t$, then the process $\{V_t\}$ is also a white noise, but its components are contemporaneously uncorrelated for

$$\mathrm{Var}\, V_t = H \Sigma H^\top = H(H^\top H)^{-1} H^\top = I_m.$$

The $\mathrm{MA}(\infty)$ representation of Z_t in terms of the transformed white noise $\{V_t\}$ is

$$Z_t = \Psi^*(L)\, V_t, \qquad \{V_t\} \sim \mathrm{WN}_m(0, I_m),$$

where $\Psi^*(z) = \Psi(z)H^{-1}$. The impulse response functions and the variance decompositions based on this new representation may now be interpreted without ambiguity.

The problem with this approach is that, since H is not unique in general, the conclusions obtained about the dynamic properties of $\{Z_t\}$ may depend crucially on the particular choice of H. It can be shown that H is unique if it is restricted in some way. A common approach is to select a particular ordering of the components of the process and require H to be a lower triangular matrix with diagonal elements all equal to one. This corresponds to requiring H to be a *Cholesky factorization* of Σ. In this case we have

$$
\begin{aligned}
V_{t1} &= U_{t1}, \\
V_{t2} &= h_{21}U_{t1} + U_{t2}, \\
&\cdots \\
V_{tm} &= h_{m1}U_{t1} + h_{m2}U_{t2} + \cdots + h_{m,m-1}U_{t,m-1} + U_{tm}.
\end{aligned}
$$

In other words, U_{t1} affects the current value of all components of $\{Z_t\}$, U_{t2} affects the current value of all components except the first, and so on. The last component U_{tm} of U_t affects only the current value of Z_{tm}. A system with such a property is called *recursive*.

In practice, the dynamic properties of $\{Z_t\}$ may be quite sensitive to the way in which the components of Z_t are ordered. If Z_t is an m-vector, then its components may be ordered in $m!$ distinct ways. It is clear that choosing between these different recursive models requires some prior information about the structure of the system represented by $\{Z_t\}$.

3.3.4 GRANGER NONCAUSALITY

Let $\{X_t\}$ and $\{Y_t\}$ be any two components of a multivariate time series $\{Z_t\}$. Define

$$
\mathcal{Z}_{t-1} = \{Z_s, s \le t-1\}, \qquad \mathcal{X}_{t-1} = \{X_s, s \le t-1\}, \qquad \mathcal{Y}_{t-1} = \{Y_s, s \le t-1\}.
$$

Denote by $E^*(Y_t \mid \mathcal{Z}_{t-1})$ the BLP of Y_t given $\mathcal{Z}_{t-1}$ and by

$$
\sigma^2(Y_t \mid \mathcal{Z}_{t-1}) = \mathrm{E}[Y_t - \mathrm{E}^*(Y_t \mid \mathcal{Z}_{t-1})]^2
$$

the associated MSE of prediction. If $\{Z_t\}$ is a Gaussian process, then $\mathrm{E}^*(Y_t \mid \mathcal{Z}_{t-1}) = \mathrm{E}(Z_t \mid \mathcal{Z}_{t-1})$ and $\sigma^2(Y_t \mid \mathcal{Z}_{t-1}) = \mathrm{Var}(Y_t \mid \mathcal{Z}_{t-1})$.

Definition 3.8 (Granger) $\{X_t\}$ *does not cause* $\{Y_t\}$, relative to $\{Z_t\}$, if

$$
\sigma^2(Y_t \mid \mathcal{Z}_{t-1}) = \sigma^2(Y_t \mid \mathcal{Z}_{t-1} - \mathcal{X}_{t-1}).
$$

It *does not instantaneously cause* $\{Y_t\}$, relative to $\{Z_t\}$, if

$$
\sigma^2(Y_t \mid X_t, \mathcal{Z}_{t-1}) = \sigma^2(Y_t \mid \mathcal{Z}_{t-1}).
$$

□

Thus, $\{X_t\}$ does not (Granger) cause $\{Y_t\}$, relative to $\{Z_t\}$, if the information contained in the past of $\{X_t\}$ does not help to better predict Y_t one period ahead. Similarly, $\{X_t\}$ does not instantaneously (Granger) cause $\{Y_t\}$, relative to $\{Z_t\}$, if knowledge of the current value of X_t does not help to better predict the current value of Y_t.

Example 3.24 Let $\{Z_t\} = \{(Y_t, X_t)\}$ be the stable bivariate AR(1) process

$$\begin{bmatrix} 1-\phi_{11}L & -\phi_{12}L \\ -\phi_{21}L & 1-\phi_{22}L \end{bmatrix} \begin{pmatrix} Y_t \\ X_t \end{pmatrix} = \begin{pmatrix} U_t \\ V_t \end{pmatrix},$$

where $\{(U_t, V_t)\}$ is a bivariate white noise with variance matrix

$$\Sigma = \begin{bmatrix} \sigma_1^2 & \sigma_{12} \\ \sigma_{12} & \sigma_2^2 \end{bmatrix}.$$

The BLP of Y_t given $\mathcal{Z}_{t-1}$ is

$$\mathrm{E}^*(Y_t \,|\, \mathcal{Z}_{t-1}) = \phi_{11} Y_{t-1} + \phi_{12} X_{t-1},$$

and so $\{X_t\}$ does not (Granger) cause $\{Y_t\}$ if and only if $\phi_{12} = 0$. On the other hand, the BLP of Y_t given X_t and $\mathcal{Z}_{t-1}$ is

$$\mathrm{E}^*(Y_t \,|\, X_t, \mathcal{Z}_{t-1}) = \phi_{11} Y_{t-1} + \phi_{12} X_{t-1} + \frac{\sigma_{12}}{\sigma_2^2} V_t,$$

and so $\{X_t\}$ does not instantaneously (Granger) cause $\{Y_t\}$ if and only if $\sigma_{12} = 0$, that is, U_t and V_t are uncorrelated. □

Granger's definitions of noncausality are based on the assumption that the future has no influence on the past. Further, they are entirely in terms of predictability and this must be taken into account in the interpretation.

Notice that (Granger) noncausality is defined with reference to a given "universe" $\{Z_t\}$. Adding or subtracting components to Z_t may therefore modify the relationships of noncausality between $\{Y_t\}$ and $\{X_t\}$.

Example 3.25 Let $X_t = U_t$, $Y_t = V_{t-1}$ and $W_t = U_t + V_t$, where $\{U_t\}$ and $\{V_t\}$ are independent white noises. If $Z_t = (X_t, Y_t)$, then $\{X_t\}$ does not (Granger) cause $\{Y_t\}$, for

$$\mathrm{E}(Y_t \,|\, \mathcal{Y}_{t-1}) = \mathrm{E}(Y_t \,|\, \mathcal{Z}_{t-1}) = 0.$$

This is no longer true if instead $Z_t = (X_t, Y_t, W_t)$, for then

$$\mathrm{E}(Y_t \,|\, \mathcal{X}_t, \mathcal{W}_t) = \frac{\mathrm{Cov}(Y_t, W_{t-1})}{\mathrm{Var}\, W_{t-1}} W_{t-1} = \frac{W_{t-1}}{2} = \frac{U_{t-1} + V_{t-1}}{2},$$

whereas $\mathrm{E}(Y_t \,|\, \mathcal{Z}_t) = Y_{t-1} = V_{t-1}$. □

Also notice that there is no necessary relationship between the concepts of noncausality and instantaneous noncausality.

Example 3.26 If $\{X_t\}$ and $\{Y_t\}$ are correlated white noises and $Z_t = (X_t, Y_t)$, then $\{X_t\}$ (Granger) causes $\{Y_t\}$ but only instantaneously. If instead $Z_t = (Y_t, W_t)$, with $W_t = X_{t-1}$, then $\{Y_t\}$ causes $\{W_t\}$ although not instantaneously. □

3.3.5 EXOGENEITY

The concept of exogeneity of a random vector X for the parameters of the conditional distribution of Y given X was introduced in Section 1.2.2. We now extend this definition to the case when $\{X_t\}$ and $\{Y_t\}$ are time series defined on the same probability space.

A regular parametric model for a multivariate time series $\{Z_t\} = \{(X_t, Y_t)\}$ is generally defined by a parametric family $\mathcal{F}_\Theta$ of conditional densities of Z_t given $\mathcal{Z}_{t-1}$. Under general conditions, every density in $\mathcal{F}_\Theta$ may be decomposed as

$$f(Z_t \mid \mathcal{Z}_{t-1};\theta) = f(Y_t \mid X_t, \mathcal{Z}_{t-1};\theta)\, f(X_t \mid \mathcal{Z}_{t-1};\theta), \qquad \theta \in \Theta.$$

The corresponding decomposition of the log-likelihood is

$$\ln f(Z_t \mid \mathcal{Z}_{t-1};\theta) = \ln f(Y_t \mid X_t, \mathcal{Z}_{t-1};\theta) + \ln f(X_t \mid \mathcal{Z}_{t-1};\theta), \qquad \theta \in \Theta.$$

If the parameter θ consists of two functionally unrelated components, that is, $\theta = (\theta_1, \theta_2)$, where $\theta_1 \in \Theta_1$, $\theta_2 \in \Theta_2$ and $\Theta = \Theta_1 \times \Theta_2$, and if

$$\ln f(Z_t \mid \mathcal{Z}_{t-1};\theta) = \ln f(Y_t \mid X_t, \mathcal{Z}_{t-1};\theta_1) + \ln f(X_t \mid \mathcal{Z}_{t-1};\theta_2) \tag{3.26}$$

for all t, then the time series $\{X_t\}$ is said to be *weakly exogenous for* θ_1. Thus, weak exogeneity of $\{X_t\}$ for θ_1 corresponds to a decomposition of the log-likelihood of θ into two separate parts: the conditional log-likelihood $\ln f(Y_t \mid X_t, \mathcal{Z}_{t-1};\theta_1)$ of θ_1 given X_t and $\mathcal{Z}_{t-1}$, and the conditional log-likelihood $\ln f(X_t \mid \mathcal{Z}_{t-1};\theta_2)$ of θ_2 given $\mathcal{Z}_{t-1}$, with no functional relationship between θ_1 and θ_2. Given $\mathcal{Z}_{t-1}$, a sufficient condition is invariance of the conditional distribution of Y_t given X_t to changes in the distribution of X_t.

If the process $\{X_t\}$ is weakly exogenous for θ_1, then the components of the likelihood score are

$$\frac{\partial}{\partial\theta_1} \ln f(Y_t \mid X_t, \mathcal{Z}_{t-1};\theta) = \frac{\partial}{\partial\theta_1} \ln f(Y_t \mid X_t, \mathcal{Z}_{t-1};\theta_1),$$
$$\frac{\partial}{\partial\theta_2} \ln f(X_t \mid \mathcal{Z}_{t-1};\theta) = \frac{\partial}{\partial\theta_2} \ln f(X_t \mid \mathcal{Z}_{t-1};\theta_2).$$

Because the second cross-derivatives of the log-likelihood vanish, the components of the likelihood score relative to θ_1 and θ_2 are uncorrelated conditionally on $\mathcal{Z}_{t-1}$. The proof is completely analogous to that of Theorem 1.3.

Even when $\{X_t\}$ is weakly exogenous for θ_1, the conditional density of X_t given $\mathcal{Z}_{t-1}$ depends on the whole past history of Y_t. In order to be able to treat X_t as "fixed" in the conditional model for Y_t it is therefore necessary to have the stronger condition that

$$f(X_t \mid \mathcal{Z}_{t-1};\theta_2) = f(X_t \mid \mathcal{X}_{t-1};\theta_2) \tag{3.27}$$

for all t. This condition, which represents an adaptation to the parametric case of the notion that $\{Y_t\}$ does not (Granger) cause $\{X_t\}$, makes it possible to predict X_t using only its past history and then predict Y_t conditionally on the predicted value of X_t.

Definition 3.9 Given the parametric model (3.26), the time series $\{X_t\}$ is said to be *strongly exogenous for* θ_1 if it is weakly exogenous and condition (3.27) is satisfied. □

Verifying the definition of strong exogeneity requires knowledge not only of the conditional distribution of Y_t given $(X_t, \mathcal{Z}_{t-1})$, but also of the conditional distribution of X_t given $\mathcal{Z}_{t-1}$.

Example 3.27 Consider again the case of Example 3.24, but now assume that $\{(U_t, V_t)\}$ is a Gaussian white noise. The conditional distribution of Y_t given X_t and $\mathcal{Z}_{t-1}$ is $\mathcal{N}(\alpha Y_{t-1} + \beta X_t + \gamma X_{t-1}, \sigma^2)$, where

$$\alpha = \phi_{11} - \beta\phi_{21}, \qquad \beta = \frac{\sigma_{12}}{\sigma_2^2}, \qquad \gamma = \phi_{12} - \beta\phi_{22}, \qquad \sigma^2 = \sigma_1^2 - \beta^2\sigma_2^2,$$

while the conditional distribution of X_t given $\mathcal{Z}_{t-1}$ is $\mathcal{N}(\phi_{21}Y_{t-1} + \phi_{22}X_{t-1}, \sigma_2^2)$. Exogeneity of $\{X_t\}$ for $\theta_1 = (\alpha, \beta, \gamma, \sigma^2)$ requires this parameter to be functionally unrelated to the parameter $\theta_2 = (\phi_{21}, \phi_{22}, \sigma_2^2)$ which characterizes the conditional distribution of X_t given $\mathcal{Z}_{t-1}$. This means that changes in θ_2 can only affect the parameters ϕ_{11}, ϕ_{12}, σ_U^2 and σ_{12} through the relationships

$$\phi_{11} = \alpha + \beta\phi_{21}, \qquad \phi_{12} = \gamma + \beta\phi_{22}, \qquad \sigma_1^2 = \beta^2\sigma_2^2 + \sigma^2, \qquad \sigma_{12} = \beta\sigma_2^2.$$

In order to be able to treat X_t as "fixed" in the conditional model for Y_t, it must be the case that $\{Y_t\}$ does not (Granger) cause $\{X_t\}$, that is, we must have $\phi_{21} = 0$. The process $\{X_t\}$ is therefore strongly exogenous for θ_1 if it is weakly exogenous and the conditional distribution of X_t given $\mathcal{Z}_{t-1}$ is $\mathcal{N}(\phi_{22}X_{t-1}, \sigma_2^2)$. □

3.4 MODELS FOR NONSTATIONARY TIME SERIES

From the practical viewpoint, the assumption of stationarity is very strong. Many observed time series, such as a country's GDP, capital stock, aggregate consumption, etc., display trends or seasonal components in the levels and sometimes also in their variability. Figure 28 shows an example of a time series with a strong trend in the levels, whereas Figure 29 shows an example of one with both a trend and a strong seasonal component.

3.4.1 DETERMINISTIC COMPONENT MODELS

Nonstationarity in the levels of a time series $\{Z_t\}$ may be modeled in various ways. In the univariate case, the classical approach assumes the following decomposition

$$Z_t = T_t + S_t + U_t,$$

where T_t and S_t are deterministic functions representing, respectively, the "trend" and the "seasonality", and $\{U_t\}$ is a zero-mean stationary process representing the irregular component of $\{Z_t\}$. Because $Z_t - T_t - S_t$ follows a stationary process, $\{Z_t\}$ is sometimes said to be *trend stationary*.

The trend T_t is often modelled as a polynomial or an exponential function of t, while the seasonal component S_t is often taken to be a periodic function of period h, namely such that $S_{t+jh} = S_t$, $|j| = 1, 2, \ldots$. For example, in the case of monthly data with a seasonal pattern that repeats itself every year, one may put $h = 12$. Once the trend

Figure 28 Logarithm of real GDP at market prices, Italy. Quarterly data, 1970:I–1998:I.

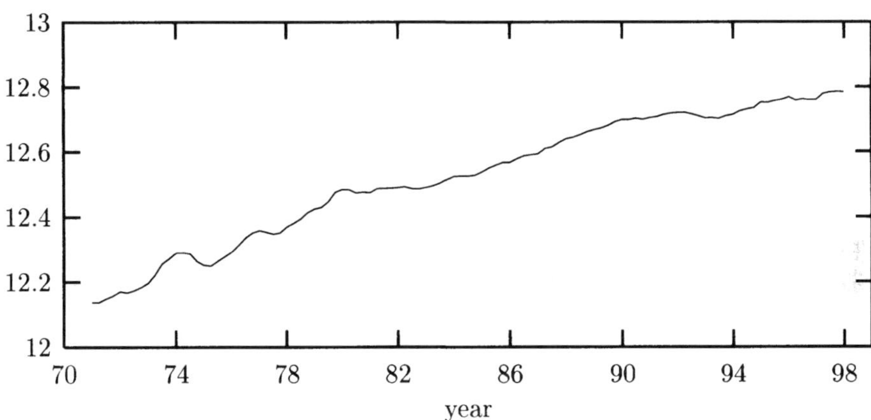

Figure 29 Logarithm of the industrial production index, Italy. Monthly data, 1980:1–1998:12.

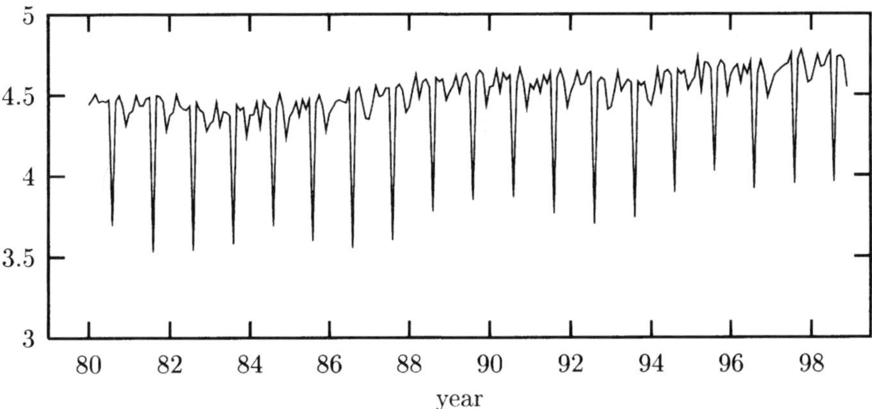

and the seasonality have been removed, the resulting time series $U_t = Z_t - T_t - S_t$ may be analyzed using any of the models discussed in the previous sections.

Although these kind of models are widely used and may provide useful descriptive summaries of the data, the lack of flexibility limits considerably their usefulness for prediction purposes.

Example 3.28 Let $\{Z_t\}$ be a time series such that

$$Z_t = T_t + U_t, \qquad \{U_t\} \sim \mathrm{WN}(0, \sigma^2),$$

where T_t is a deterministic function. If $T_t = \alpha + \beta t$, the time series is said to contain a *deterministic linear trend.* In this case

$$Z_{t+k} = \alpha + \beta(t+k) + U_{t+k}, \qquad k \geq 0.$$

Since $\mathrm{E}\, Z_{t+k} U_t = 0$ for $k > 0$, the BLP of Z_{t+k} given the information contained in the history of the process up to time t is

$$\mathrm{E}^*(Z_{t+k} \mid \mathcal{Z}_t) = (\alpha + \beta t) + \beta k = \alpha_t + \beta k, \qquad k \geq 1,$$

where the intercept $\alpha_t = \alpha + \beta t$ is a deterministic function of t. This model is not well suited for prediction, because it implies that

$$\mathrm{E}^*(Z_{t+k} \mid \mathcal{Z}_{t+1}) = \mathrm{E}^*(Z_{t+k} \mid \mathcal{Z}_t), \qquad k > 1,$$

that is, the arrival of the new information contained in Z_{t+1} does not lead to any revision of the BLP of Z_{t+k}. □

3.4.2 INTEGRATED PROCESSES

Let the time series $\{Z_t\}$ be nonstationary in the levels. A more flexible alternative to deterministic trend models consists of modeling as stationary the time series obtained by applying to $\{Z_t\}$ the first difference operator $\Delta = 1 - L$ a finite number of times.

Definition 3.10 A time series $\{Z_t\}$ is said to be *integrated of order* d, written $\{Z_t\} \sim \mathrm{I}(d)$, if $\{\Delta^d Z_t\}$ is a stationary time series. □

Thus, a random walk is I(1), while a stationary time series is I(0). For simplicity, we shall only consider the case when the order of integration d is a non-negative integer. Because $\Delta^d Z_t$ follows a stationary process whenever $\{Z_t\} \sim \mathrm{I}(d)$, $\{Z_t\}$ is sometimes said to be *difference stationary.*

Notice that if $Z_t = \ln X_t$ then

$$\Delta Z_t = \ln \frac{X_t}{X_{t-1}} = \ln\left(1 + \frac{X_t - X_{t-1}}{X_{t-1}}\right) \approx \frac{X_t - X_{t-1}}{X_{t-1}}.$$

Thus, the first difference of the logarithm of a time series (see Figure 30 for an example) has a natural interpretation as an approximation to the growth rate of the series over the given time interval. In particular, if a time series represents the price of an asset,

Figure 30 Time series obtained by applying the first difference operator $\Delta = 1 - L$ to the data in Figure 28. It is approximately equal to the quarterly growth rate of real GDP at market prices in Italy.

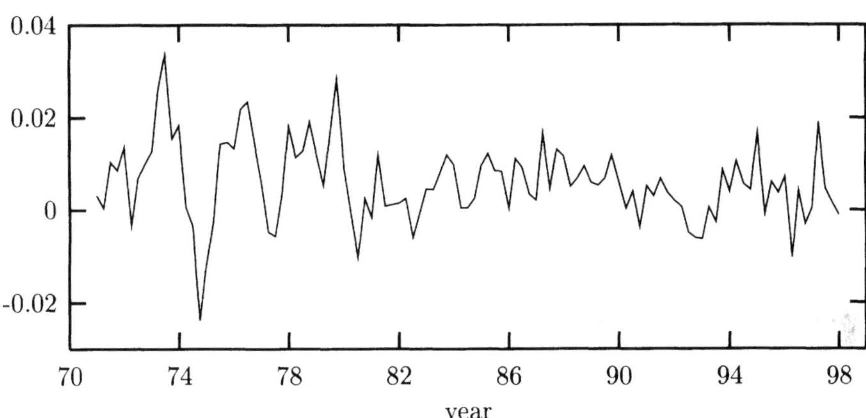

then taking the first difference of its logarithm gives the continuously compounded rate of return on the asset.

Of particular practical importance is the class of *autoregressive integrated moving averages* or *ARIMA processes*, that is, processes that may be represented as stationary ARMA processes after applying the first difference operator a finite number of times.

Definition 3.11 A time series $\{Z_t\}$ is called an *ARIMA process of order* (p, d, q), written $\{Z_t\} \sim \text{ARIMA}(p, d, q)$, if it satisfies the relationship

$$\Phi(L)(\Delta^d Z_t - \mu) = \Theta(L)U_t, \qquad \{U_t\} \sim WN(0, \sigma^2),$$

where $d = 1, 2, \ldots$, $\Phi(z) = 1 - \phi_1 z - \cdots - \phi_p z^p$ and $\Theta(z) = 1 - \theta_1 z - \cdots - \theta_q z^q$, with $\phi_p, \theta_q \neq 0$ and $\Phi(z) \neq 0$ for all $|z| = 1$. □

Hence, $\{Z_t\} \sim \text{ARIMA}(p, d, q)$ if $\{\Delta^d Z_t\}$ is a stationary $\text{ARMA}(p, q)$ process with mean μ. The inclusion of a constant μ allows for a deterministic polynomial trend of degree d. If $\mu = 0$, then an $\text{ARIMA}(p, d, q)$ process may equivalently be represented as a nonstationary $\text{ARMA}(p + d, q)$ process, where the autoregressive operator is equal to $\Phi(L)(1 - L)^d$ and therefore contains d unit roots.

Example 3.29 A time series $\{Z_t\}$ such that

$$Z_t = Z_{t-1} + \beta + U_t, \qquad \{U_t\} \sim \text{WN}(0, \sigma^2)$$

is called a *random walk with drift* β. This is an $\text{ARIMA}(0, 1, 0)$ process since $\{\Delta Z_t\}$ is a white noise with mean β and variance σ^2. Repeated backward substitution gives

$$Z_{t+k} = Z_t + \beta k + \sum_{h=1}^{k} U_{t+h}, \qquad k > 0.$$

Figure 31 Sample paths of a Gaussian ARIMA(0, 2, 0) process starting at time $t = 0$ with $Z_0 = 0$.

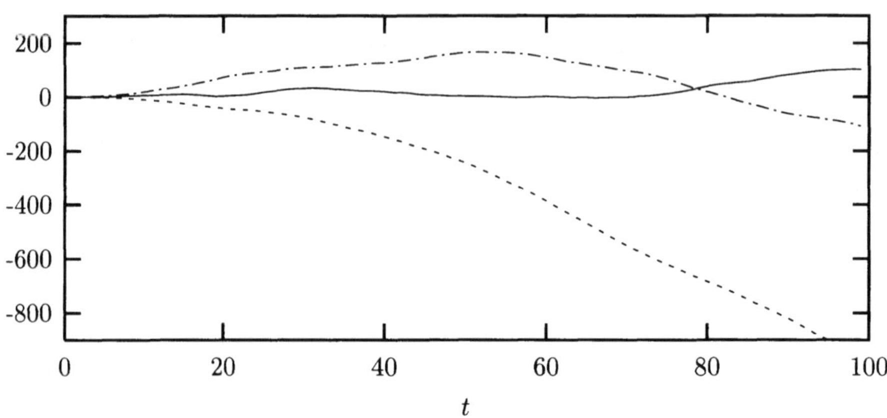

Hence, the process $\{Z_t\}$ contains a deterministic linear trend. The BLP of Z_{t+k} given the information available up to time t is

$$\mathrm{E}^*(Z_{t+k} \mid \mathcal{Z}_t) = \alpha_t + \beta k, \qquad k > 0,$$

where $\alpha_t = Z_t$. Thus, the model corresponds to a linear trend model with an intercept α_t that follows a random walk with drift. In this case, the arrival of the new information contained in Z_{t+1} leads one to revise the BLP of Z_{t+k}, which becomes

$$\mathrm{E}^*(Z_{t+k} \mid \mathcal{Z}_{t+1}) = \alpha_{t+1} + \beta(k-1), \qquad k > 1,$$

with $\alpha_{t+1} = Z_{t+1}$. This model is an example of a *stochastic linear trend model.* □

Example 3.30 A time series $\{Z_t\}$ such that

$$Z_t - 2Z_{t-1} + Z_{t-2} = U_t, \qquad \{U_t\} \sim \mathrm{WN}(0, \sigma^2)$$

is an ARIMA(0, 2, 0) process, for applying the difference operator twice produces a white noise with variance σ^2 (Figure 31). Repeated backward substitution gives

$$Z_{t+k} = Z_t + (Z_t - Z_{t-1})k + \sum_{h=1}^{k}(k-h+1)\,U_{t+h}, \qquad k > 0.$$

Hence

$$E^*(Z_{t+k} \mid \mathcal{Z}_t) = Z_t + (Z_t - Z_{t-1})k = \alpha_t + \beta_t k, \qquad k > 0,$$

where $\beta_t = Z_t - Z_{t-1}$ and $\alpha_t = Z_t$. This process therefore corresponds to a linear trend where both the intercept and the slope evolve stochastically. □

Figure 32 Time series obtained by applying the seasonal difference operator $(1 - L^4)$ to the data in Figure 28. It is approximately equal to the annual growth rate of real GDP at market prices in Italy.

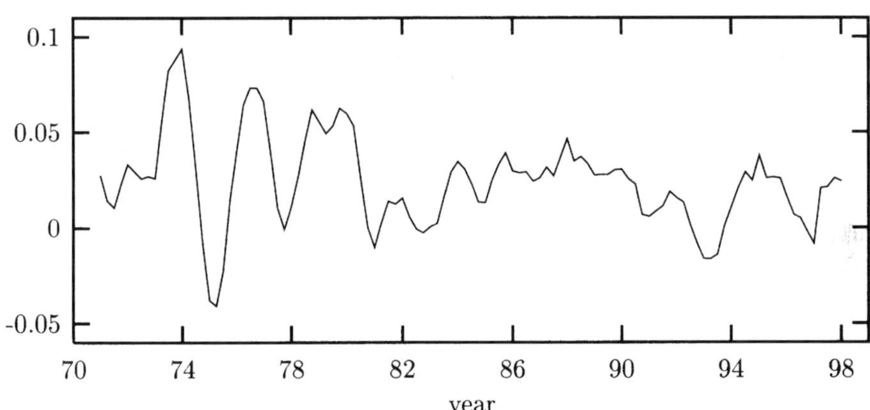

Figure 33 Time series obtained by applying the seasonal difference operator $(1 - L^{12})$ to the data in Figure 29. It is approximately equal to the annual growth rate of the Italian index of industrial production.

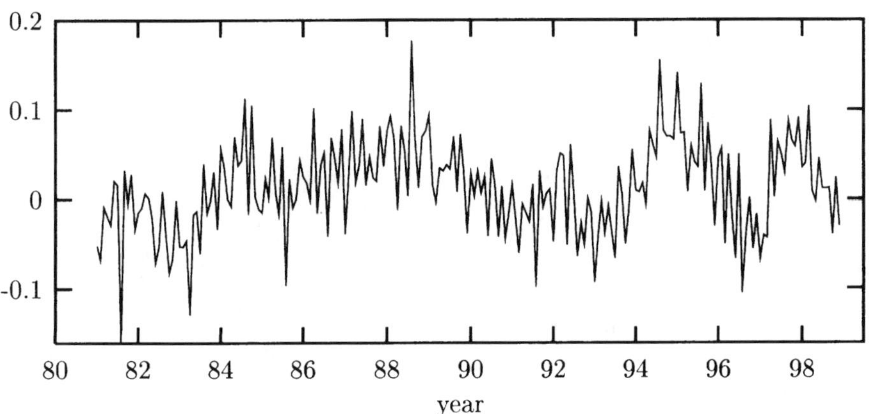

By analogy, a more flexible alternative to models with deterministic seasonal components of period h is the class of *seasonal ARIMA processes*, where the difference operator Δ^d is replaced by the seasonal difference operator $(1 - L^h)^d$. Figures 32 and 33 show examples of time series obtained by applying seasonal difference operators.

In general, given an ARIMA process, the variance of the time series obtained after repeated application of the difference operator first tends to decrease, reaches a minimum when a stationary and invertible process is obtained, and then increases again. This suggests some care is required in applying the first difference operator: overdifferencing may introduce a noninvertible MA component that increases the variance of the series and may create problems at the estimation stage.

Example 3.31 Applying the difference operator to a random walk $\{Z_t\}$ gives $\Delta Z_t = U_t$, with $\operatorname{Var}\Delta Z_t = \sigma^2$. Applying the difference operator further, gives

$$\Delta^k Z_t = \Delta^{k-1} U_t, \qquad \operatorname{Var}\Delta^k Z_t = k\sigma^2, \qquad k > 1.$$

Although $\{\Delta^k Z_t\}$ is an MA$(k-1)$ process, and therefore stationary, it is not invertible since all roots of the moving average polynomial $(1 - z)^k$ are equal to one. □

An m-variate time series $\{Z_t\}$ is a multivariate ARIMA(p, d, q) process, written $\{Z_t\} \sim \text{ARIMA}_m(p, d, q)$, if it satisfies the relationship

$$\Phi(L)\, D^d Z_t = \Theta(L)\, U_t, \qquad \{U_t\} \sim \text{WN}_m(0, \Sigma),$$

with

$$D^d = \begin{bmatrix} \Delta^{d_1} & & \\ & \ddots & \\ & & \Delta^{d_m} \end{bmatrix},$$

where $d = \max(d_1, \ldots, d_m)$ and $\det \Phi(z) \neq 0$ for all z such that $|z| = 1$. Hence, $\{Z_t\}$ is an ARIMA$_m(p, d, q)$ process if $\{\Delta^d Z_t\}$ is a stationary ARMA$_m(p, q)$ process. Since the order of differentiation needed to achieve stationarity may be different for each of the components of $\{Z_t\}$, applying the difference operator the same number d of times to all series in $\{Z_t\}$ may result in a noninvertible process, unless $d_1 = \cdots = d_m$.

3.4.3 COINTEGRATION

In practice, one often faces the problem of modeling a set of time series which, although individually nonstationary, tend nevertheless to move together, in the sense that they tend deviate little from each other. One example is shown in Figure 34.

Definition 3.12 An m-variate time series $\{Z_t\}$ is called a *cointegrated system of order* (d, b), written $\{Z_t\} \sim \text{CI}(d, b)$, if all its components are I(d) and there exists a vector $\alpha \neq 0$ such that $\alpha^\top Z_t \sim I(d - b)$, with $b > 0$. The vector α is called the *cointegrating vector.* □

If a random walk is a model for a drunkard's walk, a cointegrated system of order (1,1) is a model for the walk of a drunkard and his dog.

Figure 34 Logarithm of real consumption (C) and real GDP (Y), Italy. Quarterly data, 1970:I–1998:I.

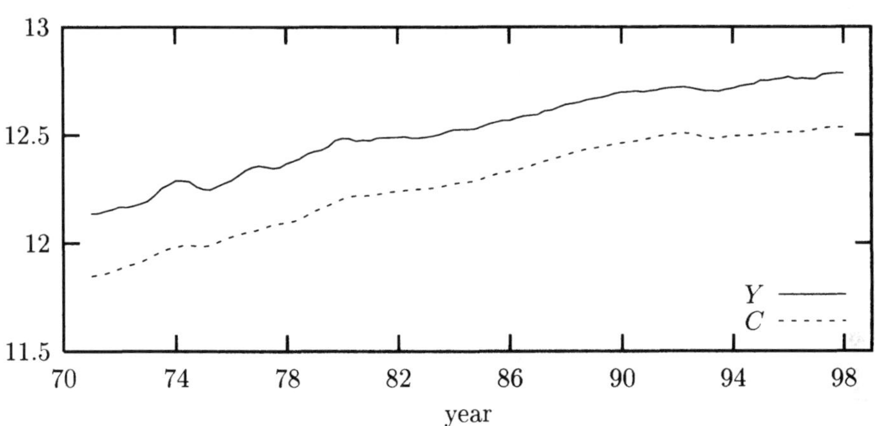

Example 3.32 Consider the bivariate time series $\{(X_t, Y_t)\}$, where both $\{X_t\}$ and $\{Y_t\}$ are I(1) processes. If

$$Y_t = \beta X_t + U_t, \qquad \{U_t\} \sim \text{MA}(q),$$

where $\beta \neq 0$, then $\{Y_t\}$ and $\{X_t\}$ form a cointegrated system of order $(1,1)$ with cointegrating vector equal to $(1, -\beta)$. □

Under what conditions is $\{Z_t\}$ a cointegrated system? Suppose, for simplicity that all components of $\{Z_t\}$ are $I(1)$ and that $\{\Delta Z_t\}$ is a stable ARMA process. In this case, ΔZ_t possesses the MA(∞) representation

$$\Delta Z_t = \Psi(L)\, U_t, \qquad \{U_t\} \sim \text{WN}_m(0, \Sigma),$$

where $\Psi(z) = \sum_{j=0}^{\infty} \Psi_j z^j = \Phi^{-1}(z)/\Theta(z)$ converges for all $|z| \leq 1$. The latter condition implies that $\Psi(1) = \sum_{j=1}^{\infty} \Psi_j$ exists and therefore allows us to define the polynomial operator $B(z) = \Psi(z) - \Psi(1)$. Since $B(1) = 0$, such an operator may also be written as $B(z) = (1 - L)B^*(z)$, where $B^*(1) \neq 0$, and therefore

$$\Psi(z) = \Psi(1) + B(z) = \Psi(1) + (1 - z)B^*(z).$$

Hence, an alternative representation of ΔZ_t is

$$(1 - L)Z_t = \Psi(1)\, U_t + (1 - L)\, B^*(L)\, U_t, \qquad \{U_t\} \sim \text{WN}_m(0, \Sigma), \tag{3.28}$$

Suppose that the matrix $\Psi(1)$ is singular. Then there exists a vector $\alpha \neq 0$ such that $\alpha^\top \Psi(1) = 0$. Premultiplying (3.28) by $\alpha^\top$ gives

$$(1 - L)\, \alpha^\top Z_t = (1 - L)\, \alpha^\top B^*(L)\, U_t,$$

which implies that $\{\alpha^\top Z_t\}$ is a stationary process provided that $\{B^*(L)\,U_t\}$ is stationary. Since $\{\Delta Z_t\}$ is a stable ARMA process, the latter condition is satisfied and we conclude that $\{Z_t\}$ is a cointegrated system of order $(1,1)$ whenever the matrix $\Psi(1)$ is singular, that is, has rank $k < m$. Because the dimension of the null space of $\Psi(1)$ is in this case equal to $m - k$, there exists a matrix A of order $m \times k$, whose columns are the eigenvectors associated with the zero eigenvalues of $\Psi(1)$, such that $X_t = A^\top Z_t$ is a k-variate stationary process. The columns of A are the k cointegrating vectors of the process $\{Z_t\}$.

From the practical viewpoint, an important consequence of the property of being a cointegrated system is that $\{Z_t\}$ possesses the representation

$$C(L)\,\Delta Z_t = GA^\top Z_{t-1} + U_t, \tag{3.29}$$

called an *error correction model*, where the expressions for the $m \times k$ matrices $C(z)$ and G, the latter of rank k, may be found in Engle and Granger (1987). The representation (3.29) establishes a relationship between the short-term dynamics of the system and the deviations $GA^\top Z_{t-1} + U_t$ from the long-run equilibrium relationship. This relationship is excluded by a simple m-variate AR model for ΔZ_t, which is therefore incompatible with the assumption that $\{Z_t\}$ is a cointegrated system.

BIBLIOGRAPHIC NOTES

For an introduction to stochastic processes see Karlin and Taylor (1975). A classical treatment is Doob (1953).

Standard references on the statistical analysis of time series are Anderson (1971), Fuller (1975), Box and Jenkins (1977), Priestley (1981) and Brockwell and Davis (1987). Granger and Newbold (1986), Lütkepohl (1991) and Hamilton (1994) present several economic examples.

For a thorough discussion of aggregation of economic time series see Forni and Lippi (1997).

ARCH models were introduced by Engle (1982), GARCH models by Bollerslev (1986). For a survey of this class of models see Engle and Bollerslev (1986), Bera and Higgins (1993) and Bollerslev, Engle and Nelson (1994). For a review of their applications to studying the variability of financial data see Bollerslev, Chou and Kroner (1992). The book by Gourieroux (1997) provides a comprehensive presentation of the statistical theory and financial applications of ARCH-type models.

Impulse response analysis and variance decomposition based on small-scale multivariate AR models have been advocated by Sims (1980).

The notions of noncausality discussed in Section 3.3.4 have been proposed by Granger (1969). See Dufour and Renault (1998) for a generalization of the original notions in terms of predictability one period ahead to predictability h periods ahead. Based on these more general definitions, a distinction is made between short run causality (h small) and long run causality (h large). The concepts of weak and strong exogeneity are discussed in Engle, Hendry and Richard (1983).

For a study of the properties of integrated processes where the order of integration is a non-negative real number see Granger and Joyeux (1980) and Hosking (1981).

On the relationship between ARIMA models and models with stochastic linear trends see Beveridge and Nelson (1981) and Stock and Watson (1988).

The concept of cointegration has been introduced by Granger (1981). Some important contributions to the theory of cointegrated processes are collected in Engle and Granger (1991).

PROBLEMS

3.1 Let $\{Z_t\}$ be a sequence of independent random variables such that Z_t has an $\mathcal{E}(1)$ distribution if t is even and a $\mathcal{N}(1,1)$ distribution if t is odd. Show that the process $\{Z_t\}$ is stationary but not strictly stationary.

3.2 Let $\{X_t\}$ and $\{Y_t\}$ be stationary time series that are uncorrelated with each other. Show that $\{X_t + Y_t\}$ and $\{X_t - Y_t\}$ are also stationary and determine their autocovariance functions.

3.3 Show that a time series that starts at time $t = 0$ with $Z_0 = 0$ and evolves through time according to the relationship $Z_t = -Z_{t-1} + U_t$, where $\{U_1\} \sim \text{WN}(0, \sigma^2)$, is nonstationary.

3.4 Let $\{Z_t\}$ be a random walk. Compute the correlation between Z_t and Z_{t+h} and show that $\text{Cov}(Z_t, Z_{t+h}) \to 0$ as $h \to \infty$ with t fixed and $\text{Cov}(Z_t, Z_{t+h}) \to 1$ as $t \to \infty$ with h fixed.

3.5 Give sufficient conditions for stationarity of the time series $Z_t = \alpha\cos(\lambda t) + \beta\sin(\lambda t)$, where α and β are random variables with zero mean and finite variance.

3.6 Determine the constraints that the stationarity hypothesis places on the autocovariance matrix Γ_n when $n = 2$ and $n = 3$.

3.7 Consider a time series $\{Z_t\}$ that satisfies the relationship

$$Z_t = \mu + V + U_t, \qquad \{U_t\} \sim \text{WN}(0, \sigma_U^2),$$

where the random variable V has mean zero, finite variance and is uncorrelated with the process $\{U_t\}$. Given a finite segment $Z_1, \ldots, Z_n$ of the time series, is the sample mean $\bar{Z} = n^{-1}\sum_t Z_t$ unbiased for μ? Compute the variance of $\bar{Z}$ and study its behavior as $n \to \infty$. Comment on this result.

3.8 Check that the AR(∞) representation of an invertible MA(1) process satisfies (3.4).

3.9 Verify that the MA(∞) representation of a stationary AR(1) process satisfies (3.6).

3.10 Show that $|\rho_1| \leq .5$ for an MA(1) process and that $|\rho_1| \leq \cos[\pi/(q+2)]$ for an MA(q) process.

3.11 Compare the autocovariance functions of the following processes:

$$X_t = U_t - \theta_1 U_{t-1} - \theta_2 U_{t-2}, \qquad \{U_t\} \sim \text{WN}(0, \sigma^2),$$
$$Y_t = \phi_1 Y_{t-1} + \phi_2 Y_{t-2} + U_t, \qquad \{U_t\} \sim \text{WN}(0, \sigma^2).$$

3.12 Determine which of the following processes is stable or invertible:

(i) $Z_t + .2Z_{t-1} - .48Z_{t-2} = U_t$;

(ii) $Z_t + 1.9Z_{t-1} + .88Z_{t-2} = U_t + .2U_{t-1} + .7U_{t-2}$;
(iii) $Z_t + .6Z_{t-2} = U_t + 1.2U_{t-1}$;
(iv) $Z_t + 1.8Z_{t-1} - .81Z_{t-2} = U_t$;
(v) $Z_t + 1.6Z_{t-1} + .88Z_{t-2} = U_t - .4U_{t-1} + .4U_{t-2}$.

3.13 Verify formula (3.12) for an MA(1) and an AR(1) process.

3.14 Verify that the second-order polynomial $\Phi(z) = 1 - \phi_1 z - \phi_2 z^2$ may equivalently be written as

$$\Phi(z) = (1 - \lambda_1 L)(1 - \lambda_2 L),$$

where λ_1 and λ_2 are the roots of the characteristic equation $0 = z^2 - \phi_1 z - \phi_2$.

3.15 Study the behavior of the autocovariance function and the sequence of coefficients $\{\psi_j\}$ and $\{\pi_j\}$ of a stable invertible ARMA(1, 1) process if, alternatively, $\theta = 0$, $\phi = 0$, and $\theta = \phi$.

3.16 An investigator assumes that the observed data have been generated by a stationary AR(6) process and, using an appropriate procedure, obtains the following parameter estimates

$$\hat{\phi}_1 = .4, \quad \hat{\phi}_2 = -.36, \quad \hat{\phi}_3 = .32, \quad \hat{\phi}_4 = -.29, \quad \hat{\phi}_5 = .26, \quad \hat{\phi}_6 = -.23.$$

Show that these six parameters could as well be represented in terms of the two parameters of an ARMA(1,1) model. Discuss the relative advantages of the two models.

3.17 Using the parameters computed for the ARMA(1,1) model of the previous problem, calculate its first autocorrelations. What feature of the estimated autocorrelations would lead you to immediately reject an AR(1) specification for the process?

3.18 Compute the coefficients $\{\psi_j\}$ in the $AR(\infty)$ representation of the process

$$Z_t - .5Z_{t-1} + .4Z_{t-2} = U_t + .25U_{t-1}, \qquad \{U_t\} \sim \text{WN}(0, \sigma^2).$$

3.19 Given a zero-mean stationary process $\{Z_t\}$, define the processes

$$X_t = Z_t - 2.5Z_{t-1}, \qquad Y_t = Z_{t-1} - .4Z_{t-1}.$$

(i) Express the autocovariance functions of $\{X_t\}$ and $\{Y_t\}$ in terms of that of $\{Z_t\}$.
(ii) Show that $\{X_t\}$ and $\{Y_t\}$ have the same autocovariance function.
(iii) Show that the process $U_t = -\sum_{j=1}^{\infty} (.4)^j Z_{t+j}$ satisfies the relationship $U_t - 2.5U_{t-1} = Z_t$.

3.20 Show that instantaneous (Granger) noncausality is necessarily symmetric, that is, $\{X_t\}$ does not instantaneously cause $\{Y_t\}$ if and only if $\{Y_t\}$ does not instantaneously cause $\{X_t\}$.

3.21 Draw the autocorrelation function of the first difference of an AR(1) process with $\phi = .5$.

3.22 Show that if m_t is a polynomial in t of degree p, that is, $m_t = \sum_{j=0}^{p} c_j t^j$, $t = 0, \pm 1, \ldots$, then Δm_t is a polynomial in t of degree $p - 1$, and therefore that $\Delta^{p+1} m_t = 0$.

3.23 Consider the time series

$$Z_t = \mu + S_t + U_t, \qquad \{U_t\} \sim \text{WN}(0, \sigma^2),$$

where S_t is a periodic function with period h, that is, $S(t + jh) = S_t$ for $|j| = 1, 2, \ldots$. Show that the time series $X_t = (1 - L^h)Z_t$ contains no periodic component but is noninvertible.

3.24 Suppose that the time series $\{Z_t\}$ satisfies

$$Z_t = \sum_{j=0}^{\infty} \psi_j U_{t-j}, \qquad \{U_t\} \sim \text{WN}(0, \sigma^2).$$

Define

$$V_h = \frac{1}{h+1} \frac{\text{Var}(Z_{t+h+1} - Z_t)}{\text{Var}(Z_{t+1} - Z_t)},$$

and consider the following measures of persistence of the series

$$A = \lim_{h \to \infty} \psi_h, \qquad V = \lim_{h \to \infty} V_h.$$

Show that:

(i) if $\{Z_t\}$ is a stationary process, then $A = V = 0$;
(ii) if $\{Z_t\}$ is a random walk, then $A = V = 1$;
(iii) if $\Delta Z_t = Z_t - Z_{t-1}$ is a stationary process, then $A_h = \sum_{j=0}^{h} \varphi_h$, where φ_j is the jth coefficient in the MA(∞) representation of ΔZ_t, and

$$V_h = 1 + 2 \sum_{j=1}^{h} \left(1 - \frac{j}{h+1}\right) \rho_j,$$

where ρ_j is the jth autocorrelation of ΔZ_t.

4

Point Estimation

The problem of point estimation is one of using the sample information in order to obtain a plausible approximation to some aspect of the population from which the sample has been drawn. Once the population aspect of interest is defined, various estimation methods are often available. Given a statistical model, we distinguish between two broad classes of method. The first class consists of methods that are based only on the sample information and the assumed statistical model. The second class consists of Bayes methods, which combine the sample information with prior information that goes beyond that contained in the specification of the statistical model.

4.1 THE ANALOGY PRINCIPLE

The empirical distribution function introduced in Section 2.2.2 is the basis of a wide class of methods for point estimation. These methods share the feature of approximating a population aspect of interest by its sample counterpart, obtained by substituting the population distribution function F with the empirical distribution function $\hat{F}$ in the definition of the population aspect of interest. This idea, simple and extremely fruitful, is known as the *analogy principle* (Manski 1988b, 1994), or the *bootstrap principle* (Hall 1992, 1994), or the *plug-in principle* (Efron & Tibshirani 1993).

More precisely, suppose that the population aspect of interest is a parameter $\theta = T(F)$, defined as the value corresponding to F of a statistical functional $T(\cdot)$. If the data are a sample from the population, then the analogy principle suggests estimating $\theta(F)$ by the value corresponding to $\hat{F}$ of the statistical functional $T(\cdot)$, namely $\hat{\theta} = T(\hat{F})$. Because, as $n \to \infty$, $\hat{F}$ converges to F under general conditions (Section 2.2.2), $\hat{\theta}$ may be expected to converge to the target parameter θ provided that $T(\cdot)$ is a continuous functional.

It is important to observe that, while the analogy principle provides a general method for constructing plausible estimators, it does not ensure by itself that an estimator obtained in this way has particular desirable properties, except the obvious one that computing the estimator using the population distribution function F instead of the empirical distribution function $\hat{F}$ gives the population parameter θ. This property is sometimes called *Fisher consistency*. Formally, a statistical functional $\hat{\theta}$ is Fisher consistent for a parameter $\theta = T(F)$ if $\hat{\theta}(F) = T(F)$. If $\hat{\theta}$ is a continuous functional, then Fisher consistency implies consistency, that is, $\hat{\theta}(\hat{F}) \xrightarrow{p} \theta(F)$.

In what follows we shall sometimes use the notation of the Stieltjes integral (see e.g. Apostol 1974). Given a distribution function F and an integrable function g, we define

$$\mathrm{E}_F\, g(Z) = \int g(z)\, dF(z) = \int g(z) f(z)\, dz$$

if F is continuous with probability density function $f(z)$, and

$$\mathrm{E}_F\, g(Z) = \int g(z)\, dF(z) = \sum_j g(z_j) f(z_j)$$

if F is discrete with probability mass function $f(z_j)$. In particular, because the empirical distribution function $\hat{F}$ is discrete, with a probability function that assigns probability mass $1/n$ to each distinct sample point, we have

$$\mathrm{E}_{\hat{F}}\, g(Z) = \int g(z)\, d\hat{F}(z) = n^{-1} \sum_{i=1}^{n} g(Z_i).$$

If $\theta = T(F) = \mathrm{E}_F\, g(Z)$ is the target parameter and $\hat{\theta} = T(\hat{F}) = \mathrm{E}_{\hat{F}}\, g(Z)$ is an estimate of θ based on the analogy principle, then the estimation error is equal to

$$\hat{\theta} - \theta = T(\hat{F}) - T(F) = \int g(z)\, [d\hat{F}(z) - dF(z)],$$

which shows that the estimation error ultimately depends on how close $\hat{F}$ is to F.

The next sections discuss various applications of the bootstrap principle.

4.2 ESTIMATING MOMENTS AND QUANTILES

The estimation of moments or quantiles often represents one of the first steps of a statistical analysis. It is an important step, both for exploratory purposes and because it may suggest a particular parametric model for the data. Further, estimated moments and quantiles may be used to derive simple estimates of the parameters of a parametric model.

4.2.1 SAMPLE MOMENTS

Given a random variable Z with distribution function F and a positive integer k, the kth (noncentral or raw) moment of Z is defined as

$$\mu_k = \mathrm{E}_F\, Z^k = \int z^k\, dF(z),$$

assuming that the integral is finite. The moment corresponding to $k = 1$ is just the mean of Z. If $Z_1, \ldots, Z_n$ is a sample from the distribution of Z, then the analogy principle suggests estimating μ_k by the corresponding moment of the empirical distribution function, namely

$$\hat{\mu}_k = \mathrm{E}_{\hat{F}}\, Z^k = \int z^k\, d\hat{F}(z) = n^{-1} \sum_{i=1}^{n} Z_i^k,$$

called the kth (noncentral or raw) *empirical* or *sample moment.*

It follows from Chapter 1 that, if Z has finite moments up to order $2k$, then its kth moment μ_k is also the unique solution to the prediction problem

$$\min_{c\in\Re} \mathrm{E}_F(Z^k - c)^2. \tag{4.1}$$

It is easily verified that the kth sample moment $\hat{\mu}_k$ is the unique solution to the sample counterpart of problem (4.1), that is,

$$\min_{c\in\Re} \mathrm{E}_{\hat{F}}(Z^k - c)^2 = n^{-1}\sum_{i=1}^n (Z_i^k - c)^2.$$

This problem is called a *least squares (LS)* problem.

Two of the sampling properties of $\hat{\mu}_k$ are immediate. First,

$$\mathrm{E}_F\,\hat{\mu}_k = n^{-1}\sum_{i=1}^n \mathrm{E}_F\,Z_i^k = \mu_k,$$

that is, $\hat{\mu}_k$ is an unbiased estimator of μ_k. Second, if Z has finite moments up to order $2k$, then the sampling variance of $\hat{\mu}_k$ is

$$\mathrm{Var}_F\,\hat{\mu}_k = n^{-1}\,\mathrm{Var}_F\,Z_i^k,$$

where

$$\mathrm{Var}_F\,Z_i^k = \mathrm{E}_F\,Z_i^{2k} - (\mathrm{E}_F\,Z_i^k)^2 = \mu_{2k} - \mu_k^2,$$

which shows that the precision of $\hat{\mu}_k$ increases with the sample size n. This implies that the sequence of estimators $\{\hat{\mu}_{nk}\}$ corresponding to increasing sample sizes is *consistent* for μ_k.

Except in special cases, exact results on the shape of the sampling distribution of empirical moments are not available and one typically relies on approximations valid for large samples, such as the theorem below.

Theorem 4.1 *Let $Z_1, \ldots, Z_n$ be a sample from a distribution with finite moments up to order $2k$. Let $\boldsymbol{\mu} = (\mu_1, \ldots, \mu_k)$ and let $\hat{\boldsymbol{\mu}}_n$ be the corresponding vector of sample moments. Then $\sqrt{n}\,(\hat{\boldsymbol{\mu}}_n - \boldsymbol{\mu}) \xrightarrow{\mathrm{d}} \mathcal{N}_k(0, \mathrm{AV}(\hat{\boldsymbol{\mu}}_n))$, where*

$$\mathrm{AV}(\hat{\boldsymbol{\mu}}_n) = \begin{bmatrix} \mathrm{Var}\,Z_i & \mathrm{Cov}(Z_i, Z_i^2) & \ldots & \mathrm{Cov}(Z_i, Z_i^k) \\ \mathrm{Cov}(Z_i^2, Z_i) & \mathrm{Var}\,Z_i^2 & \ldots & \mathrm{Cov}(Z_i^2, Z_i^k) \\ \vdots & \vdots & & \vdots \\ \mathrm{Cov}(Z_i^k, Z_i) & \mathrm{Cov}(Z_i^k, Z_i^2) & \ldots & \mathrm{Var}\,Z_i^k \end{bmatrix}.$$

4.2.2 ESTIMATING THE MOMENTS OF A STATIONARY TIME SERIES

Estimating the mean and the autocovariances or autocorrelations is often the first step in the process of specifying a model for a time series that appears stationary, possibly after differencing or some other transformation. For example, if the estimated autocorrelations are all approximately equal to zero after q lags, then it seems reasonable to consider an MA(q) model. If the estimated autocorrelations decline exponentially starting from the origin, then an AR(1) model may be considered. If the exponential decline starts from the first lag, then an ARMA(1,1) model may be considered instead. In this section we discuss estimates based on the analogy principle.

If $\{Z_t\}$ is a strictly stationary time series, then its mean and its hth autocovariance are defined respectively as

$$\mu = \mathrm{E}_F\, Z_t = \int z\, dF(z),$$

$$\gamma_h = \mathrm{E}_{\hat{F}}(Z_t - \mu)(Z_{t+h} - \mu) = \int (z - \mu)(z' - \mu)\, dF_h(z, z'),$$

where F denotes the marginal distribution function of Z_t and F_h denotes the bivariate distribution function of Z_t and Z_{t+h}. Under the strict stationarity assumption, F does not depend on t and F_h only depends on the distance h between the two time indices.

If $Z_1, \ldots, Z_n$ is a finite segment of this time series, then the sample counterpart of F is the empirical distribution function $\hat{F}(z) = \frac{1}{n}\sum_t 1\{Z_t \leq z\}$. If $n > h$, the sample counterpart of F_h is

$$\hat{F}_h(z, z') = \frac{1}{n-h}\sum_{t=1}^{n-h} 1\{Z_t \leq z, Z_{t+h} \leq z'\},$$

that is, the fraction of pairs (Z_t, Z_{t+h}) of sample observations (there are $n-h$ of them) such that $Z_t \leq z$ and $Z_{t+h} \leq z'$. The analogy principle then gives, as estimates of μ and γ_h, the following time averages

$$\bar{Z} = \frac{1}{n}\sum_{t=1}^{n} Z_t,$$

$$\tilde{\gamma}_h = \frac{1}{n-h}\sum_{t=1}^{n-h}(Z_t - \bar{Z})(Z_{t+h} - \bar{Z}), \qquad h = 0, 1, \ldots, n-1.$$

Because $\rho_h = \gamma_h/\gamma_0$, the hth autocorrelation may be estimated by

$$\tilde{\rho}_h = \frac{\tilde{\gamma}_h}{\tilde{\gamma}_0} = \frac{n}{n-h}\,\frac{\sum_{t=1}^{n-h}(Z_t - \bar{Z})(Z_{t+h} - \bar{Z})}{\sum_{t=1}^{n}(Z_t - \bar{Z})^2}, \qquad h = 1, \ldots, n-1.$$

Alternatively, γ_h and ρ_h may be estimated by

$$\hat{\gamma}_h = \frac{1}{n}\sum_{t=1}^{n-h}(Z_t - \bar{Z})(Z_{t+h} - \bar{Z}),$$

$$\hat{\rho}_h = \frac{\hat{\gamma}_h}{\hat{\gamma}_0} = \frac{\sum_{t=1}^{n-h}(Z_t - \bar{Z})(Z_{t+h} - \bar{Z})}{\sum_{t=1}^{n}(Z_t - \bar{Z})^2}.$$

Now consider some of the sampling properties of these estimates. The sample mean $\bar{Z}$

is clearly unbiased for μ. Its sampling variance is

$$\begin{aligned}\operatorname{Var}\bar{Z} &= \frac{1}{n^2}\sum_{t=1}^{n-h}\sum_{s=1}^{n-h}\gamma_{t-s} \\ &= \frac{1}{n^2}[n\gamma_0 + (n-1)(\gamma_1+\gamma_{-1}) + \cdots + (\gamma_{n-1}+\gamma_{1-n})] \\ &= \frac{1}{n}\sum_{h=1-n}^{n-1}\left(1-\frac{|h|}{n}\right)\gamma_h,\end{aligned}$$

where we used the fact that the autocovariance matrix Γ_n associated with $Z_1, \ldots, Z_n$ is band diagonal. To guarantee that $\operatorname{Var}\bar{Z} \to 0$ as $n \to \infty$, implying that the precision of $\bar{Z}$ increases with the length n of the observed time series, some restrictions must be placed on the behavior of the autocovariance function $\{\gamma_h\}$.

Because $\operatorname{Var}\bar{Z} \leq n^{-1}\sum_{h=1-n}^{n-1}\gamma_h$, a sufficient condition is $\sum_{h=-\infty}^{\infty}\gamma_h < \infty$, that is, the autocovariance function must decline fast enough. If this condition is satisfied, as in the case of a stationary ARMA process, then the mean μ may be estimated to an arbitrary degree of accuracy by the time average of a single sample path, and the process $\{Z_t\}$ is said to be *ergodic*. Ergodicity ensures that increasing the number of periods for which the time series is observed gives increasingly precise estimates of μ even when we cannot observe different sample paths of the process.

Example 4.1 Let the data consist of n consecutive observations on the stationary process introduced in Example 3.8, namely

$$Z_t = \mu + V + U_t, \qquad \{U_t\} \sim \mathrm{WN}(0, \sigma^2),$$

where V is a zero-mean random variable with variance $\omega^2 > 0$ and $\mathrm{E}\, VU_t = 0$ for all t. In this case, the sampling variance of the sample mean $\bar{Z}$ is

$$\operatorname{Var}\bar{Z} = \frac{1}{n^2}[n(\omega^2+\sigma^2) + n(n-1)\omega^2] = \omega^2 + \frac{\sigma^2}{n}.$$

Because $\operatorname{Var}\bar{Z} \to \omega^2 > 0$ as $n \to \infty$ this process is not ergodic. □

Turning to the sample autovariances, assume first that μ is known and without loss of generality let $\mu = 0$. In this case

$$\mathrm{E}\,\tilde{\gamma}_h = \frac{1}{n-h}\sum_{t=1}^{n-h}\mathrm{E}\, Z_t Z_{t+h} = \gamma_h,$$

that is, $\tilde{\gamma}_h$ is unbiased for γ_h. Since $\hat{\gamma}_h = [1-(h/n)]\,\tilde{\gamma}_h$, the estimator $\hat{\gamma}_h$ is instead biased for γ_h unless $h = 0$ or $\gamma_h = 0$, and its bias is equal to $-(h/n)\gamma_h$. When h is large relative to n, this downward bias is sizeable. For this reason, Box and Jenkins (1977) recommend using $\hat{\gamma}_h$ only when $n \geq 50$ and $h/n \leq 1/4$. Although biased, $\hat{\gamma}_h$ has one advantage over $\tilde{\gamma}_h$, namely the fact that the sample autocovariance matrix

$$\hat{\Gamma}_n = \begin{bmatrix}\hat{\gamma}_0 & \cdots & \hat{\gamma}_{n-1} \\ \vdots & & \vdots \\ \hat{\gamma}_{n-1} & \cdots & \hat{\gamma}_0\end{bmatrix}$$

is n.n.d., and is nonsingular if $\hat{\gamma}_0 > 0$.

The sample autocovariances are quadratic forms in random variables that are correlated in general. This creates a number of problems:

1. for the variance of a quadratic form to be finite, the fourth order moments of the elements of $\{Z_t\}$ must exist, but the (weak) stationarity assumption is not enough to guarantee this;
2. even if the fourth moments of $\{Z_t\}$ exist and agree with strict stationarity, the expressions for the second moments of the sample autocovariances are quite complicated (see e.g. Anderson 1971, Section 8.2);
3. because the sample autocovariances and autocorrelations are generally correlated, interpreting a sample autocovariance or autocorrelation function requires some care.

Things become even more complicated when μ is unknown and must be estimated by $\bar{Z}$, as is usually the case in practice. It can be shown that $\hat{\gamma}_h$ and $\tilde{\gamma}_h$ are now both biased for γ_h in general, although $\hat{\gamma}_h$ may have a smaller bias than $\tilde{\gamma}_h$ for all $h \neq 0$ for which the two estimators are defined (Percival 1993).

Important simplifications are obtained if we consider the behavior of $\hat{\gamma}_h$ and $\tilde{\gamma}_h$ in large samples, where they are essentially equivalent. The next result provides a large sample approximation to the joint distribution of a finite set of sample autocovariances when the underlying time series is a Gaussian linear process. The result is independent of whether μ is estimated by $\bar{Z}$ or is known.

Theorem 4.2 *If $Z_1, \ldots, Z_n$ is a finite segment of a Gaussian linear process $\{Z_t\}$ then, as $n \to \infty$, the $(m+1)$-vector $\sqrt{n}\,[(\tilde{\gamma}_0 - \gamma_0), (\tilde{\gamma}_1 - \gamma_1), \ldots, (\tilde{\gamma}_m - \gamma_m)]$ has a limiting multivariate Gaussian distribution with mean zero and covariance matrix $\Sigma = [\sigma_{hk}]$, where*

$$\sigma_{hk} = \sum_{j=-\infty}^{\infty} (\gamma_j \gamma_{j+h-k} + \gamma_{j+h} \gamma_{j-k}).$$

Proof. See Anderson (1971), Theorem 8.3.2. □

It follows from Theorem 4.2 that the asymptotic variance of $\tilde{\gamma}_h$ is

$$\sigma_{hh} = \sum_{j=-\infty}^{\infty} (\gamma_j^2 + \gamma_{j+h} \gamma_{j-h}).$$

If $\{Z_t\}$ is not Gaussian, v_{hk} has a slightly more complicated expression which involves the fourth moments of $\{Z_t\}$.

We now present a result on the limiting distribution of the sample autocorrelations $\tilde{\rho}_h = \tilde{\gamma}_h / \tilde{\gamma}_0$.

Theorem 4.3 *Let $Z_1, \ldots, Z_n$ be a finite segment of a linear process $\{Z_t\}$ whose sequence of weights $\{\psi_j\}$ satisfies $\sum_{j=-\infty}^{\infty} |j|\, \psi_j^2 < \infty$. Then, as $n \to \infty$, the m-vector $\sqrt{n}\,[(\tilde{\rho}_1 - \rho_1), \ldots, (\tilde{\rho}_1 - \rho_m)]$ has a limiting multivariate Gaussian distribution with mean zero and covariance matrix $\Omega = [\omega_{hk}]$, where*

$$\omega_{hk} = \sum_{j=-\infty}^{\infty} (\rho_{j+h}\rho_{j+k} + \rho_{j-h}\rho_{j+k} - 2\rho_h\rho_j\rho_{j+k} - 2\rho_k\rho_j\rho_{j+h} + 2\rho_h\rho_k\rho_j^2). \tag{4.2}$$

Proof. See Anderson (1971), Theorem 8.4.6. □

Expression (4.2) is often referred to as the *Bartlett formula.* It implies that the asymptotic variance of $\tilde{\rho}_h$ is given by

$$\omega_{hh} = \sum_{j=-\infty}^{\infty} (\rho_j^2 - \rho_{j-h}\rho_{j+h} - 4\rho_h\rho_j\rho_{h+j} + 2\rho_h^2\rho_j^2).$$

Notice that, unlike the case of sample autocovariances, we require neither $\{Z_t\}$ to be Gaussian nor conditions on its fourth moments.

For a time series with a correlation function that approaches zero rapidly, convenient approximations to (4.2) are available. For large values of h, the asymptotic covariance between $\tilde{\rho}_h$ and $\tilde{\rho}_k$ may be approximated by

$$\omega_{hk}^* = \sum_{j=-\infty}^{\infty} \rho_j\rho_{j+|h-k|}.$$

The corresponding approximation to the asymptotic variance of $\tilde{\rho}_h$ is

$$\omega_{hh}^* = \sum_{j=-\infty}^{\infty} \rho_j^2 = 1 + 2\sum_{j=1}^{\infty} \rho_j^2.$$

4.2.3 THE METHOD OF MOMENTS

It may sometimes be known that certain population moments are themselves functions of a p-dimensional parameter $\theta \in \Theta$. One may then construct an estimate of θ by first inverting the relationship between θ and the selected population moments, and then replacing the latter by estimates based on the analogy principle. This method is called the *method of moments (MM).*

Example 4.2 Let $Z_1, \ldots, Z_n$ be a sample from the distribution of a random variable Z with finite mean μ. If Z has an exponential distribution with parameter θ, then $\theta = 1/\mu$. Provided that $\bar{Z} > 0$, a MM estimate of θ is therefore $\hat{\theta} = 1/\bar{Z}$. Although $\bar{Z}$ is an unbiased estimator of $\mu = 1/\theta$, Jensen inequality gives

$$\mathrm{E}\,\hat{\theta} = \mathrm{E}\,\frac{1}{\bar{Z}} > \frac{1}{\mathrm{E}\,\bar{Z}} = \theta,$$

that is, $\hat{\theta}$ is an upward biased estimator of θ. In the exponential case, the variance of Z is $\sigma^2 = 1/\theta^2$ and so another MM estimate of θ is $\tilde{\theta} = 1/\hat{\sigma}$, where $\hat{\sigma}^2$ is the sample mean squared deviation of Z_i. Which estimate should one pick?

We have a similar problem if Z has a Poisson distribution with parameter θ. Because $\theta = \mu = \sigma^2$ in this case, both the sample mean and the sample variance may be used to estimate θ. □

The two problems raised in the last example are typical of the MM. First, this method does not guarantee that the proposed estimator of θ is unbiased. Second, the method may suggest more than one estimator for the same parameter. Chapter 11 discusses generalized MM estimators for the case when the number of restrictions on the population moments is greater than the number of parameters to be estimated.

We now present two examples of MM estimators of the parameters of a stationary time series model.

Example 4.3 Suppose that the data consist of n consecutive observations on the MA(1) process

$$Z_t = U_t - \theta U_{t-1}, \qquad \{U_t\} \sim \mathrm{WN}(0, \sigma^2),$$

where θ and σ^2 are unknown parameters. Given estimates $\hat{\gamma}_0$ and $\hat{\gamma}_1$ of γ_0 and γ_1 respectively, MM estimates of the unknown parameters may be obtained by solving with respect to θ and σ^2 the pair of nonlinear equations

$$\begin{aligned} \hat{\gamma}_0 - \sigma^2(1+\theta^2) &= 0, \\ \hat{\gamma}_1 + \theta\sigma^2 &= 0. \end{aligned}$$

If the invertibility condition is imposed, then this method gives unique estimates of θ and σ^2. □

Example 4.4 Suppose that the data consist of n consecutive observations on the stable AR(p) process

$$Z_t = \phi_1 Z_{t-1} + \cdots + \phi_p Z_{t-p} + U_t, \qquad \{U_t\} \sim \mathrm{WN}(0, \sigma^2), \tag{4.3}$$

where $\phi_1, \ldots, \phi_p$ and σ^2 are unknown parameters. Multiplying both sides of (4.3) by Z_{t-h}, $h = 1, 2, \ldots, p$, and taking expectations using the fact that $\mathrm{E}\, U_t Z_{t-h} = 0$, gives the following set of relationships between the autocovariances and the model parameters

$$\gamma_h = \phi_1 \gamma_{h-1} + \cdots + \phi_p \gamma_{h-p}, \qquad h = 1, 2, \ldots, p.$$

Viewed as a system of p linear equations in the p-vector $\phi = (\phi_1, \ldots, \phi_p)$, these relationships are called *Yule–Walker equations.* Replacing the autocovariances γ_h by the sample autocovariances $\hat{\gamma}_h$ gives the equation system

$$\begin{bmatrix} \hat{\gamma}_0 & \cdots & \hat{\gamma}_{p-1} \\ \vdots & & \vdots \\ \hat{\gamma}_{p-1} & \cdots & \hat{\gamma}_0 \end{bmatrix} \begin{pmatrix} \phi_1 \\ \vdots \\ \phi_p \end{pmatrix} = \begin{pmatrix} \hat{\gamma}_1 \\ \vdots \\ \hat{\gamma}_p \end{pmatrix},$$

whose solution provides a MM estimate $\hat{\phi} = (\hat{\phi}_1, \ldots, \hat{\phi}_p)$ of ϕ. Using the biased estimator $\hat{\gamma}_h$ guarantees that the matrix on the left-hand side is p.d. whenever $\hat{\gamma}_0 > 0$. Further, because

$$\sigma^2 = \gamma_0 - \phi_1 \gamma_1 - \cdots - \phi_p \gamma_p,$$

the variance of the white noise process $\{U_t\}$ may be estimated by

$$\hat{\sigma}^2 = \hat{\gamma}_0 - \hat{\phi}_1 \hat{\gamma}_1 - \cdots - \hat{\phi}_p \hat{\gamma}_p.$$

It can be shown that the AR(p) process corresponding to these estimates, namely

$$Z_t = \hat{\phi}_1 Z_{t-1} + \cdots + \hat{\phi}_p Z_{t-p} + U_t, \qquad \{U_t\} \sim \mathrm{WN}(0, \hat{\sigma}^2),$$

is stable and its autocovariances coincide, for $h = 0, 1, \ldots, p$, with the sample autocovariances.

The simplicity with which the parameters of an AR(p) model may be estimated and the fact that, for sufficiently large p, such a model provides a good approximation to any invertible ARMA process, explain its widespread use in empirical applications. □

Obtaining the sampling properties of a function $\hat{\theta} = h(\hat{\boldsymbol{\mu}})$ of a k-vector of sample moments is straightforward when $h\colon \Re^k \to \Re^p$ is a linear function, that is, $h(\hat{\boldsymbol{\mu}}) = C\hat{\boldsymbol{\mu}}$ for some $p \times k$ matrix C. In this case, if $\mathrm{E}\,\hat{\boldsymbol{\mu}} = \boldsymbol{\mu}$ and $\mathrm{Var}\,\hat{\boldsymbol{\mu}} = \Sigma$, then $\mathrm{E}\,\hat{\theta} = C\boldsymbol{\mu}$ and $\mathrm{Var}\,\hat{\theta} = C\Sigma C^\top$. Further, if $\hat{\boldsymbol{\mu}} \sim \mathcal{N}_k(\boldsymbol{\mu}, \Sigma)$, then $\hat{\theta} \sim \mathcal{N}_p(C\boldsymbol{\mu}, C\Sigma C^\top)$.

The following result is useful when the function h is nonlinear but smooth, or we can only assess the large sample behavior of a sequence $\{\hat{\boldsymbol{\mu}}_n\}$ of empirical moments.

Theorem 4.4 *Let the function $h\colon \Re^k \to \Re^p$ be differentiable at the point $\boldsymbol{\mu}$. If the Jacobian matrix $h'(\boldsymbol{\mu})$ has rank $p \leq k$ and $\sqrt{n}\,(\hat{\boldsymbol{\mu}}_n - \boldsymbol{\mu}) \xrightarrow{\mathrm{d}} \mathcal{N}_k(0, \Sigma)$, then $\sqrt{n}\,[h(\hat{\boldsymbol{\mu}}_n) - h(\boldsymbol{\mu})] \xrightarrow{\mathrm{d}} \mathcal{N}_p(0, h'(\boldsymbol{\mu})\,\Sigma\,h'(\boldsymbol{\mu})^\top)$.*

Proof. Immediate using Theorem D.21. □

Example 4.5 To appreciate the condition on the rank of the gradient matrix $h'(\boldsymbol{\mu})$, consider the limiting distribution of $h(\bar{Z}_n) = \bar{Z}_n^2$ when $\sqrt{n}\,(\bar{Z}_n - \mu) \xrightarrow{\mathrm{d}} \mathcal{N}(0, \sigma^2)$. Because $h'(x) = 2x$, Theorem 4.4 gives $\sqrt{n}\,(\bar{Z}_n^2 - \mu^2) \xrightarrow{\mathrm{d}} \mathcal{N}(0, 4\mu^2\sigma^2)$ for all μ except $\mu = 0$, for which $h(0) = 0$. □

4.2.4 SAMPLE QUANTILES

Recall that a pth quantile of a random variable Z, with $0 < p < 1$, is any number ζ_p such that

$$\Pr\{Z < \zeta_p\} \leq p \leq \Pr\{Z \leq \zeta_p\}.$$

If $Z_1, \ldots, Z_n$ is a sample from the distribution of Z, then the analogy principle suggests estimating ζ_p by the corresponding *empirical* or *sample quantile*, that is, a number $\hat{\zeta}_p$ such that

$$n^{-1} \sum_{i=1}^n 1\{Z_i < \hat{\zeta}_p\} \leq p \leq n^{-1} \sum_{i=1}^n 1\{Z_i \leq \hat{\zeta}_p\}$$

or, equivalently,

$$\sum_{i=1}^n 1\{Z_i < \hat{\zeta}_p\} \leq np \leq \sum_{i=1}^n 1\{Z_i \leq \hat{\zeta}_p\}.$$

It is easily verified that such a $\hat{\zeta}_p$ always exists, and is unique if np is not an integer. In particular, the sample quantile corresponding to $p = 1/2$ is the *sample median*, denoted here by $\hat{\zeta}$. In fact, if $Z_{[1]} \leq \cdots \leq Z_{[n]}$ are the sample order statistics, then the sample median is equal to $Z_{[k]}$, with $k = (n+1)/2$, when n is even, and is a point in the closed interval $[Z_{[k]}, Z_{[k+1]}]$, with $k = n/2$, when n is odd.

Figure 35 Criterion function of a LAD problem. The vertical bars on the x-axis denote the data points. The figure shows how the criterion function changes by adding to the first five observations the point $Z_6 = 2.5$.

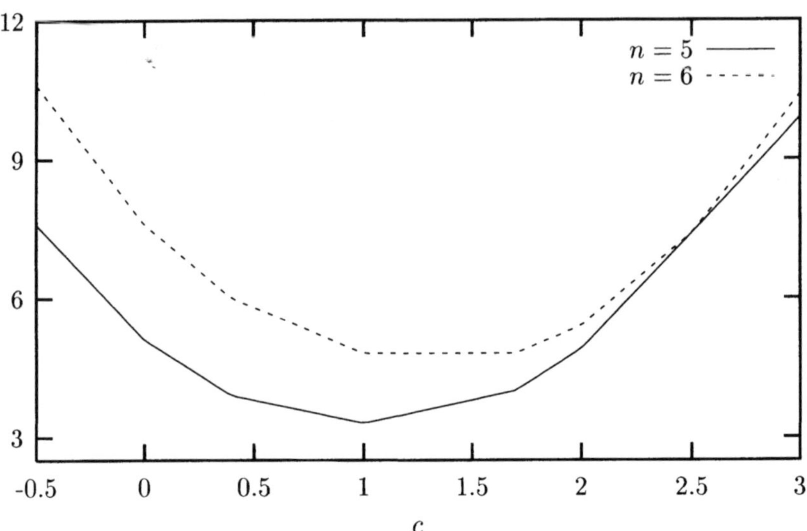

Recall from Section 1.3.1 that a pth quantile of Z may equivalently be defined as a solution to the problem

$$\min_{c \in \Re} \mathrm{E}_F \, \ell_p(Z - c), \qquad 0 < p < 1,$$

where ℓ_p is the asymmetric absolute loss function. In particular, a median of Z corresponds to $p = 1/2$. A pth sample quantile of Z_i may therefore also be defined as a solution to the problem

$$\min_{c \in \Re} \mathrm{E}_{\hat{F}} \, \ell_p(Z - c) = n^{-1} \sum_{i=1}^{n} \ell_p(Z_i - c), \qquad 0 < p < 1,$$

called an *asymmetric least absolute deviations (ALAD)* problem. In particular, a sample median may be defined as a solution to the problem

$$\min_{c \in \Re} n^{-1} \sum_{i=1}^{n} |Z_i - c|.$$

called a *least absolute deviations (LAD)* problem. Figure 35 shows an example of a criterion function for a LAD problem.

To verify the equivalence between the two definitions of sample median, notice that, if n is odd and $k = (n+1)/2$, then the function

$$\sum_{i=1}^{n} |Z_i - c| = \sum_{i=1}^{k-1} (|Z_{[i]} - c| + |Z_{[n-i+1]} - c|) + |Z_{[k]} - c|$$
$$= \sum_{i=1}^{k-1} (Z_{[n-i+1]} - Z_{[i]}) + |c - Z_{[k]}|$$

attains its minimum at the point $c = Z_{[k]}$. If instead n is even and $k = n/2$, then

$$\sum_{i=1}^{n} |Z_i - c| = \sum_{i=1}^{k-1} (|Z_{[i]} - c| + |Z_{[n-i+1]} - c|) + |Z_{[k]} - c| + |Z_{[k+1]} - c|$$
$$= \sum_{i=1}^{k-1} (Z_{[n-i+1]} - Z_{[i]}) + |Z_{[k]} - c| + |Z_{[k+1]} - c|$$

attains its minimum at any point in the closed interval $[Z_{[k]}, Z_{[k+1]}]$.

To illustrate how to derive the sampling distribution of an empirical quantile, we focus on the sample median $\hat{\zeta}$ for a sample $Z_1, \ldots, Z_n$ from a continuous distribution with distribution function F. Consider first the case when n is odd and therefore $\hat{\zeta} = Z_{[k]}$, where $k = (n+1)/2$. In this case, the event $\hat{\zeta} \leq a$ is equivalent to the event that exactly k observations do not exceed a. Because $\Pr\{Z_i \leq a\} = F(a)$, the probability of the latter event is equal to the probability of k successes in n independent Bernoulli trials where the probability of success is equal to $F(a)$. Hence,

$$\Pr\{\hat{\zeta} \leq a\} = \Pr\{Z_{[k]} \leq a\} = \Pr\{X = k\} = \binom{n}{k} F(a)^k [1 - F(a)]^{n-k},$$

where $X \sim \text{Bi}(n, F(a))$. If n is even, $\hat{\zeta}$ is any point in the interval $[Z_{[k]}, Z_{[k+1]}]$. In this case, the event $\hat{\zeta} \leq a$ is equivalent to the event that at least $k = n/2$ and not more than $k+1$ observations do not exceed a. Hence,

$$\Pr\{\hat{\zeta} \leq a\} = \Pr\{k \leq X \leq k+1\} = \Pr\{X = k+1\}$$
$$= \binom{n}{k+1} F(a)^{k+1} [1 - F(a)]^{n-k-1}.$$

Interest often centers not just on a single quantile, but on a set of them. This is typically the case when we seek a detailed description of the shape of a probability distribution, or we are interested in constructing some *L-estimate*, that is, a linear combination of sample quantiles such as the interquartile range or a trimmed mean. It is clear that sample quantiles corresponding to different values of p must be dependent. Hence, from a practical point of view, what matters is their joint distribution, or some approximation thereof. We now present an approximation valid for the case when the data are a sample from a continuous distribution whose density is continuous and strictly positive in a neighborhood of the population quantiles of interest.

Theorem 4.5 *Let $Z_1, \ldots, Z_n$ be a sample from a continuous distribution whose density $f(z)$ is continuous and strictly positive in a neighborhood of the quantiles ζ_{p_r}*

Table 3 Asymptotic efficiency of the sample median relative to the sample mean for t-distributions with $m \geq 3$ degrees of freedom. The t-distribution converges to the $\mathcal{N}(0,1)$ as $m \to \infty$.

m	3	4	5	8	∞
ARE	1.62	1.12	.96	.80	.64

and ζ_{p_s}, with $0 < p_r, p_s < 1$. Let $\zeta = (\zeta_{p_r}, \zeta_{p_s})$ and let $\hat{\zeta}_n$ be the corresponding vector of sample quantiles. Then $\sqrt{n}\,(\hat{\zeta}_n - \zeta) \xrightarrow{d} \mathcal{N}_2(0, \Omega)$, where Ω is a matrix with generic element

$$\omega_{rs} = \frac{\min(p_r, p_s) - p_r p_s}{f(\zeta_{p_r})\, f(\zeta_{p_s})}.$$

Proof. See, for example, Ferguson (1996), pp. 87–91. □

From Theorem 4.5, the asymptotic variance of a pth sample quantile is equal to $p(1-p)/[f(\zeta_p)]^2$. In particular, the asymptotic variance of the sample median is equal to $[4f(\zeta_{1/2})^2]^{-1}$.

Example 4.6 In order to compare the large sample properties of the sample mean and the sample median, assume that the population distribution is symmetric about zero with variance $0 < \sigma^2 < \infty$. Let $\bar{Z}_n$ and $\hat{\zeta}_n$ denote the sample mean and the sample median for a sample of size n. Under our assumptions, $\sqrt{n}\,\bar{Z}_n \xrightarrow{d} \mathcal{N}(0, \sigma^2)$ whereas $\sqrt{n}\,\hat{\zeta}_n \xrightarrow{d} \mathcal{N}(0, [4f(0)^2]^{-1})$. Because the two estimators are asymptotically normal and have the same asymptotic mean, a comparison between them may be based on the ratio of their asymptotic variances

$$\text{ARE}(\hat{\zeta}_n, \bar{Z}_n) = \frac{\text{AV}(\bar{Z}_n)}{\text{AV}(\hat{\zeta}_n)} = [2f(0)\sigma]^2,$$

called the *asymptotic efficiency* of the sample median relative to the sample mean. Because $\text{Var}\,\bar{Z}_n \approx n\,\text{AV}(\bar{Z}_n)$ and $\text{Var}\,\hat{\zeta}_n \approx n\,\text{AV}(\hat{\zeta}_n)$, $\text{ARE}(\hat{\zeta}_n, \bar{Z}_n)$ is equal to the ratio of the sample sizes needed for the two estimators to have approximately the same sampling variance.

The asymptotic relative efficiency of the sample median increases with the "peakedness" of the density f at the origin. It is easy to verify that $\text{ARE}(\hat{\zeta}_n, \bar{Z}_n) = 2/\pi \approx .64$ for the Gaussian distribution, whereas $\text{ARE}(\hat{\zeta}_n, \bar{Z}_n) = \pi^2/12 \approx .82$ for the logistic one. The higher relative efficiency of the sample median in the logistic case reflects the fact that this distribution has somewhat heavier tails than the Gaussian case. Table 3 shows the asymptotic efficiency of $\hat{\zeta}_n$ relative to $\bar{Z}_n$ for t-distributions with $m \geq 3$ degrees of freedom, for which the variance exists. □

In practice, the asymptotic variance of sample quantiles has to be estimated from the data. This requires estimating the density f at ζ_p. A consistent estimator of $[f(\zeta_p)]^{-1}$ (see e.g. Cox & Hinkley 1974, p. 470) is given by

$$\frac{Z_{([np]+h_n)} - Z_{([np]-h_n)}}{2h_n/n},$$

where $[x]$ denotes the integer part of x and h_n is a bandwidth parameter that goes to zero as $n \to \infty$.

4.3 ESTIMATING CONDITIONAL MOMENTS AND QUANTILES

This section considers the case when $Z = (X, Y)$, where X and Y are scalar random variables, and introduces the problem of estimating the conditional mean function (CMF), the conditional variance function (CVF) and the pth conditional quantile function (CQF) of Y given a sample $(X_1, Y_1), \ldots, (X_n, Y_n)$ from the distribution of (X, Y). We assume, of course, that the CMF, the CVF and the CQF are all well defined.

4.3.1 NONPARAMETRIC METHODS

If Y is a continuous random variable and X is a discrete random vector, then the analogy principle suggests estimating the CMF $\mu(x) = \mathrm{E}(Y \,|\, X = x)$ by

$$\hat{\mu}(x) = \int y \, d\hat{F}(y \,|\, x),$$

where $\hat{F}(y \,|\, x)$ is the conditional empirical distribution function (2.4). By the definition of $\hat{F}(y \,|\, x)$ we have

$$\hat{\mu}(x) = \frac{1}{n(x)} \sum_{i \in \mathcal{O}(x)} Y_i,$$

that is, $\hat{\mu}(x)$ is the average of the $n(x)$ sample values of Y corresponding to $X = x$. Because $\mathrm{E}[\hat{\mu}(x)] = \mu(x)$, the estimator $\hat{\mu}(x)$ is unbiased. If the conditional variance $\sigma^2(x)$ is finite, then $\mathrm{Var}\,\hat{\mu}(x) = \sigma^2(x)/n(x)$, that is, the precision of $\hat{\mu}(x)$ increases with $n(x)$. Notice that $\hat{\mu}(x) = \sum_i w_i(x) Y_i$, where

$$w_i(x) = \begin{cases} 1/n(x), & \text{if } \ i \in \mathcal{O}(x), \\ 0, & \text{otherwise}, \end{cases}$$

that is, $\hat{\mu}(x)$ is a "local" weighted average of the sample values of Y, with weights that add up to one and are equal to zero for observations outside $\mathcal{O}(x)$. An analogous approach based on "local" sample quantiles may be adopted for the estimation of conditional quantiles.

Turning to the problem of estimating the CVF $\sigma^2(x) = \mathrm{Var}(Y \,|\, X = x)$, two alternative approaches may be followed. If $\sigma^2(x)$ is known to depend on x, then one may consider the "local" estimate

$$\hat{\sigma}^2(x) = n(x)^{-1} \sum_{i \in \mathcal{O}(x)} [Y_i - \hat{\mu}(x)]^2.$$

If it is known that $\sigma^2(x)$ does not depend on x, then one may instead consider the "global" estimate

$$\tilde{\sigma}^2 = n^{-1} \sum_x \sum_{i \in \mathcal{O}(x)} [Y_i - \hat{\mu}(x)]^2 = \sum_x \frac{n(x)}{n} \hat{\sigma}^2(x).$$

Although fully nonparametric, the approach sketched here has some drawbacks. First, one cannot estimate the CMF, the CVF or a CQF for values of X that do not correspond to sample values. Second, the estimates are only sensible when the number of sample points for which $X = x$ is sufficiently large. Hence, if X is a continuous random vector, this approach breaks down.

If X is continuous, the analogy principle again leads to a simple way of proceeding. Because the CMF of Y is defined as

$$\mu(x) = \int y\, f(y \,|\, x)\, dy = \int y\, \frac{f(x,y)}{f_X(x)}\, dy,$$

where f_X denotes the marginal probability density of X, a nonparametric estimate of $\mu(x)$ may be obtained by replacing the population densities $f(x,y)$ and $f_X(x)$ by empirical densities $\hat{f}(x,y)$ and $\hat{f}_X(x) = \int \hat{f}(x,y)\, dy$. This gives

$$\hat{\mu}(x) = \int y\, \frac{\hat{f}(x,y)}{\hat{f}_X(x)}\, dy. \tag{4.4}$$

Further, because the CVF of Y is defined as $\sigma^2(x) = \mathrm{E}(Y^2 \,|\, X = x) - \mu(x)^2$, a nonparametric estimate of $\sigma^2(x)$ is easily obtained from nonparametric estimates of the CMF of Y and Y^2. This approach is further developed in Chapter 14.

4.3.2 PARAMETRIC METHODS

The parametric approach to estimating a CMF starts by restricting $\mu(x)$ to a known parametric family $\mathcal{H}_\Theta = \{h(x;\theta)\}$ of functions of x, indexed by a p-dimensional parameter $\theta \in \Theta \subseteq \Re^p$. Recall from Chapter 1 that, if the model is correctly specified and identifiable, then there exists a unique solution $\theta_0 \in \Theta$ to the problem

$$\min_{\theta\in\Theta} \mathrm{E}_F[Y - h(X;\theta)]^2.$$

Given a sample from the distribution of (X, Y), replacing the parent distribution function F by the bivariate empirical distribution function (2.3) gives the LS problem

$$\min_{\theta\in\Theta} \mathrm{E}_{\hat{F}}[Y - h(X;\theta)]^2 = n^{-1} \sum_{i=1}^{n} [Y_i - h_i(\theta)]^2, \tag{4.5}$$

where $h_i(\theta) = h(X_i;\theta)$. This is a simple generalization of the problem introduced in Section 4.2.1. If problem (4.5) admits a solution, this is called a LS estimate of θ. Given a LS estimate $\hat{\theta}$, a parametric estimate of $\mu(x)$ is $\hat{\mu} = h(x;\hat{\theta})$. If the parameter space Θ is an open set and $h_i(\theta)$ is a smooth function of θ, then a LS estimate $\hat{\theta}$ is a root of the *normal equations*

$$0 = n^{-1} \sum_{i=1}^{n} [Y_i - h_i(\theta)]\, h_i'(\theta).$$

When the model includes an intercept, these normal equations equate to zero the sample correlation between the estimated gradient $h_i'(\hat{\theta})$ of the CMF and the regression residuals $\hat{U}_i = Y_i - h_i(\hat{\theta})$. Unless the function $h_i(\theta)$ is linear, it may be complicated or even impossible to obtain a closed form solution to (4.5) and numerical methods become necessary (see Appendix B.3.4). When $h_i(\theta)$ is nonlinear, we shall refer to (4.5) as a *nonlinear least squares (NLLS)* problem and to its solution as a NLLS estimate of θ.

The special case when $\theta = (\alpha, \beta)$ and $h(x;\theta) = \alpha + \beta x$ (simple linear regression) corresponds to the *ordinary least squares (OLS)* problem

$$\min_{(\alpha,\beta)\in\Re^2} \mathrm{E}_{\hat{F}}(Y - \alpha - \beta X)^2 = n^{-1}\sum_{i=1}^{n}(Y_i - \alpha - \beta X_i)^2. \tag{4.6}$$

The OLS problem is just the sample counterpart of problem (1.11) which defines the BLP of Y given X. As we shall see in the next section, the OLS problem admits a simple closed form solution.

A similar approach may be followed to estimate conditional quantiles. Recall from Chapter 1 that, if a parametric quantile regression model $\mathcal{Q}_\Theta = \{q(x;\theta)\}$ is correctly specified and identifiable, then there exists a unique solution $\theta_0 \in \Theta$ to the problem

$$\min_{\theta\in\Theta} \mathrm{E}_F\, \ell_p(Y - q(x;\theta)), \qquad 0 < p < 1.$$

Given a sample from the distribution of (X, Y), replacing the parent distribution function F by the bivariate empirical distribution function (2.3) gives the ALAD problem

$$\min_{\theta\in\Theta} \mathrm{E}_{\hat{F}}\, \ell_p(Y - q(X;\theta)) = n^{-1}\sum_{i=1}^{n}\ell_p(Y_i - q_i(\theta)), \tag{4.7}$$

where $q_i(\theta) = q(X_i;\theta)$. This is a simple generalization of the problem introduced in Section 4.2.4. Given a solution $\hat{\theta}_p$ to (4.7), a parametric estimate of $\zeta_p(x)$ is $q(x;\hat{\theta}_p)$. When $p = 1/2$, problem (4.7) is equivalent to the LAD problem

$$\min_{\theta\in\Theta} n^{-1}\sum_{i=1}^{n}|Y_i - q_i(\theta)|,$$

and the corresponding estimate of $\zeta_{1/2}(x)$ is also called a *median regression estimate*.

In the special case when a quantile regression model is linear, problem (4.7) becomes

$$\min_{(\alpha,\beta)} n^{-1}\sum_{i=1}^{n}\ell_p(Y_i - \alpha - \beta X_i).$$

As shown in Chapter 16, this problem has a nice representation as a linear program for which simple and fast computational algorithms are available. Chapter 16 also discusses the sampling properties of the resulting estimates.

A linear combination $\psi(x) = \sum_j c_j\,\zeta_{p_j}(x)$ of conditonal quantiles is easily estimated by $\hat{\psi}(x) = \sum_j c_j\,\hat{\zeta}_{p_j}(x)$. If the estimated conditonal quantiles are linear in x, that is, $\hat{\zeta}_{pj}(x) = \hat{\alpha}_{p_j} + \hat{\beta}_{p_j}x$, then we get

$$\hat{\psi}(x) = \sum_j c_j\,\hat{\alpha}_{p_j} + (\sum_j c_j\,\hat{\beta}_{p_j})x.$$

For example, the conditional interquartile range is simply estimated by

$$\widehat{\mathrm{IQR}} = (\hat{\alpha}_{.75} - \hat{\alpha}_{.25}) + (\hat{\beta}_{.75} - \hat{\beta}_{.25})x.$$

4.3.3 ORDINARY LEAST SQUARES

Recall from Chapter 1 that the BLP of Y given X may equivalently be characterized through the normal equations (1.12) and (1.13). When $\mathrm{Var}_F X > 0$, these equations have the unique solution

$$\alpha = \mathrm{E}_F Y - \beta \, \mathrm{E}_F X, \qquad \beta = \frac{\mathrm{Cov}_F(X,Y)}{\mathrm{Var}_F X}. \tag{4.8}$$

Given a sample from the distribution of (X, Y), estimates of the parameters α and β are obtained by solving the OLS problem (4.6). Replacing the parent distribution function F with the empirical distribution function (2.3) shows that these estimates, called *OLS estimates* and denoted by $\hat{\alpha}$ and $\hat{\beta}$, must also satisfy the normal equations

$$0 = \mathrm{E}_{\hat{F}}(Y - \hat{\alpha} - \hat{\beta}X) = n^{-1} \sum_{i=1}^{n} (Y_i - \hat{\alpha} - \hat{\beta}X_i),$$

$$0 = \mathrm{E}_{\hat{F}} X(Y - \hat{\alpha} - \hat{\beta}X) = n^{-1} \sum_{i=1}^{n} X_i(Y_i - \hat{\alpha} - \hat{\beta}X_i).$$

These normal equations require the *OLS residuals* $\hat{U}_i = Y_i - \hat{\alpha} - \hat{\beta}X_i$ to mimic the basic properties of the underlying regression errors, that is, both their sample mean and their sample correlation with the X_i must vanish. When $\mathrm{Var}_{\hat{F}} X = n^{-1} \sum_i (X_i - \bar{X})^2 > 0$, the normal equations have the unique solution

$$\hat{\alpha} = \mathrm{E}_{\hat{F}} Y - \hat{\beta} \, \mathrm{E}_{\hat{F}} X = \bar{Y} - \hat{\beta}\bar{X},$$

$$\hat{\beta} = \frac{\mathrm{Cov}_{\hat{F}}(X,Y)}{\mathrm{Var}_{\hat{F}} X} = \frac{n^{-1} \sum_i (X_i - \bar{X})(Y_i - \bar{Y})}{n^{-1} \sum_i (X_i - \bar{X})^2}.$$

In this case, the OLS estimates $\hat{\alpha}$ and $\hat{\beta}$ coincide with the estimates of α_* and β_* based on the analogy principle applied directly to (4.8).

The properties of the OLS estimates will be discussed in detail in Chapters 6, 7 and 10. The rest of this section deals with their sampling properties under two simplifying assumptions: (i) $(X_1, Y_1), \ldots, (X_n, Y_n)$ is a sample from the distribution of (X, Y); and (ii) the conditional mean and variance of Y given X are equal, respectively, to $\alpha + \beta X$ and σ^2.

First notice that, if we condition on the observed values of the covariates, namely on the n-vector $\mathbf{X} = (X_1, \ldots, X_n)$, then $\mathrm{E}(Y_i \,|\, \mathbf{X}) = \mathrm{E}(Y_i \,|\, X_i) = \alpha + \beta X_i$. Hence

$$\mathrm{E}(\hat{\beta} \,|\, \mathbf{X}) = \frac{\sum_i (X_i - \bar{X})(\alpha + \beta X_i)}{\sum_i (X_i - \bar{X})^2} = \beta \, \frac{\sum_i (X_i - \bar{X})X_i}{\sum_i (X_i - \bar{X})^2} = \beta,$$

where we used the fact that $\sum_i (X_i - \bar{X}) = 0$. Therefore

$$\mathrm{E}(\hat{\alpha} \,|\, \mathbf{X}) = \mathrm{E}(\bar{Y} \,|\, \mathbf{X}) - \mathrm{E}(\hat{\beta} \,|\, \mathbf{X})\, \bar{X} = \alpha + \beta\bar{X} - \beta\bar{X} = \alpha.$$

Since the conditional means of $\hat{\alpha}$ and $\hat{\beta}$ do not depend on $\mathbf{X}$, we conclude that $\mathrm{E}\,\hat{\alpha} = \alpha$ and $\mathrm{E}\,\hat{\beta} = \beta$, that is, $\hat{\alpha}$ and $\hat{\beta}$ are both unbiased under assumptions (i) and (ii).

To derive the sampling variance of $\hat{\alpha}$ and $\hat{\beta}$ and their sampling covariance, notice that the two estimators may equivalently be written $\hat{\alpha} = \sum_{i=1}^n a_i Y_i$ and $\hat{\beta} = \sum_{i=1}^n b_i Y_i$, where

$$a_i = \frac{1}{n}\left(1 - \frac{X_i - \bar{X}}{\hat{\sigma}_X^2}\,\bar{X}\right), \qquad b_i = \frac{1}{n}\left(\frac{X_i - \bar{X}}{\hat{\sigma}_X^2}\right),$$

with $\hat{\sigma}_X^2 = n^{-1}\sum_i (X_i - \bar{X})^2$. Thus, both $\hat{\alpha}$ and $\hat{\beta}$ are weighted averages of the Y_i. Because of random sampling and the assumption that $\mathrm{Var}(Y_i \,|\, \mathbf{X}) = \sigma^2$, we have

$$\mathrm{Var}(\hat{\beta} \,|\, \mathbf{X}) = \sigma^2 \sum_{i=1}^n a_i^2, \qquad \mathrm{Var}(\hat{\alpha} \,|\, \mathbf{X}) = \sigma^2 \sum_{i=1}^n b_i^2, \qquad \mathrm{Cov}(\hat{\alpha}, \hat{\beta} \,|\, \mathbf{X}) = \sigma^2 \sum_{i=1}^n a_i b_i,$$

where

$$\sum_{i=1}^n a_i^2 = \sum_{i=1}^n \frac{1}{n^2}\left[1 + \frac{(X_i - \bar{X})^2}{\hat{\sigma}_X^4}\,\bar{X}^2 - 2\,\frac{X_i - \bar{X}}{\hat{\sigma}_X^2}\,\bar{X}\right] = \frac{1}{n}\left(1 + \frac{\bar{X}^2}{\hat{\sigma}_X^2}\right),$$

$$\sum_{i=1}^n b_i^2 = \sum_{i=1}^n \frac{1}{n^2}\,\frac{(X_i - \bar{X})^2}{\hat{\sigma}_X^4} = \frac{1}{n\hat{\sigma}_X^2},$$

and

$$\sum_{i=1}^n a_i b_i = -\sum_{i=1}^n \frac{1}{n^2}\,\frac{(X_i - \bar{X})^2}{\hat{\sigma}_X^4}\,\bar{X} = -\frac{\bar{X}}{n\hat{\sigma}_X^2}.$$

Therefore

$$\mathrm{Var}(\hat{\alpha} \,|\, \mathbf{X}) = \frac{\sigma^2}{n}\left(1 + \frac{\bar{X}^2}{\hat{\sigma}_X^2}\right), \qquad \mathrm{Var}(\hat{\beta} \,|\, \mathbf{X}) = \frac{\sigma^2}{n}\,\frac{1}{\hat{\sigma}_X^2},$$

and

$$\mathrm{Cov}(\hat{\alpha}, \hat{\beta} \,|\, \mathbf{X}) = -\frac{\sigma^2}{n}\,\frac{\bar{X}}{\hat{\sigma}_X^2}.$$

For a given sample size, $\hat{\alpha}$ and $\hat{\beta}$ are correlated and this correlation has opposite sign to $\bar{X}$. If $\bar{X} = 0$, then $\hat{\alpha}$ and $\hat{\beta}$ are uncorrelated and the sampling variance of $\hat{\alpha}$ attains its minimum. Notice that the sampling variance of $\hat{\alpha}$ and $\hat{\beta}$ and their sampling covariance are all proportional to the variance of the Y_i and inversely related to the sample size n and the sample variability of the X_i, as measured by $\hat{\sigma}_X^2$.

The second moments of the unconditional sampling distribution are obtained by applying the law of total variance. This gives

$$\mathrm{Var}\,\hat{\alpha} = \frac{\sigma^2}{n}\left(1 + \mathrm{E}\,\frac{\bar{X}^2}{\hat{\sigma}_X^2}\right), \qquad \mathrm{Var}\,\hat{\beta} = \frac{\sigma^2}{n}\left(\mathrm{E}\,\frac{1}{\hat{\sigma}_X^2}\right),$$

and

$$\mathrm{Cov}(\hat{\alpha}, \hat{\beta}) = -\frac{\sigma^2}{n}\left(\mathrm{E}\,\frac{\bar{X}}{\hat{\sigma}_X^2}\right).$$

4.4 MAXIMUM LIKELIHOOD ESTIMATION

Maximum likelihood (ML) is a general method of estimation for parametric problems. Application of this method requires the specification of a parametric model $\{P_\theta, \theta \in \Theta\}$ for the probability distribution P_0 of the data. In what follows, we assume that such a model is correctly specified and identifiable, that is, $P_0 = P_{\theta_0}$ for a unique $\theta_0 \in \Theta$. The term *pseudo* or *quasi maximum likelihood* will be used to denote the application of the ML method in situations where the assumed parametric model is not correctly specified.

Because the ML method requires information that goes beyond what is needed by the methods discussed in Sections 4.2 and 4.3, we should expect the method to produce estimators that are more precise when all the model assumptions are correct, but also less robust, that is, more sensitive to deviations from the model assumptions.

4.4.1 ML ESTIMATES

To simplify the presentation, suppose first that the observed data $\mathbf{Z} = (Z_1, \ldots, Z_n)$ are a sample from the distribution of a random vector Z whose density belongs to a known parametric family $\mathcal{F}_\Theta = \{f(z;\theta), \theta \in \Theta\}$, with Θ a subset of $\Re^p$. Recall from Section 1.1.5 that a parameter point $\theta_0 \in \Theta$ is identifiable if and only if it corresponds to the unique maximum on Θ of the expected log-likelihood $l(\theta) = c + \mathrm{E}_0 \ln f(Z;\theta)$, where c is an arbitrary constant and E_0 denotes expectations with respect to $f(z;\theta_0)$. Because this condition implicitly defines the target parameter θ_0, the analogy principle suggests estimating θ_0 by a point in Θ that maximizes the sample counterpart of $l(\theta)$, namely the *average log-likelihood*

$$\bar{l}(\theta) = c + \mathrm{E}_{\hat{F}} \ln f(Z;\theta) = c + n^{-1} \sum_{i=1}^{n} \ln f(Z_i;\theta),$$

where c is an arbitrary constant. Such a point, if it exists, is called a *global maximum likelihood estimate* or, for short, a *ML estimate.*

Example 4.7 If $Z_1, \ldots, Z_n$ is a sample from a $\mathrm{Bi}(1,\theta)$ distribution, with $0 < \theta < 1$, then

$$n^{-1} \sum_{i=1}^{n} \ln f(Z_i;\theta) = n^{-1} \sum_{i=1}^{n} [Z_i \ln\theta + (1 - Z_i)\ln(1-\theta)].$$

Hence, an average log-likelihood is any function of the form

$$\bar{l}(\theta) = c + p\ln\theta + (1-p)\ln(1-\theta),$$

where c is an arbitrary constant and $p = n^{-1}\sum_i Z_i$ is the sample proportion of successes. If $\hat\theta$ maximizes $\bar{l}(\theta)$ on $(0,1)$, then necessarily

$$0 = \bar{l}'(\hat\theta) = \frac{p}{\hat\theta} - \frac{1-p}{1-\hat\theta} = \frac{p-\hat\theta}{\hat\theta(1-\hat\theta)},$$

whose unique solution is $\hat\theta = p$. This is indeed the ML estimate, for

$$\bar{l}''(p) = -\frac{p}{p^2} - \frac{1-p}{(1-p)^2} = \frac{1}{p(1-p)}$$

is negative whenever $0 < p < 1$. □

It is often convenient to work with a monotone transformation of $\bar{l}$, namely $L(\theta) = n\,\bar{l}(\theta)$, called the *sample log-likelihood.* Of course, maximizing L on Θ is equivalent to maximizing $\bar{l}$. More generally, given a parametric model $\{f(\mathbf{z};\theta), \theta \in \Theta\}$ for the data $\mathbf{Z}$, a sample log-likelihood is any function $L(\theta)$ that is equal to $\ln f(\mathbf{Z};\theta)$ up to an additive constant. Given a conditional parametric model $\{f(\mathbf{y} \,|\, \mathbf{x};\theta), \theta \in \Theta\}$ for the data $\mathbf{Z} = (\mathbf{X}, \mathbf{Y})$, a (conditional) sample log-likelihood is any function $L(\theta)$ that is equal to $\ln f(\mathbf{Y} \,|\, \mathbf{X};\theta)$ up to an additive constant.

By standard results, a ML estimate exists if the function L is bounded above on Θ or L is a continuous function and the parameter space Θ is compact, that is, closed and bounded. Even in this case, however, a ML estimate need not be unique.

Example 4.8 Let $Z_1, \ldots, Z_n$ be a sample from a Laplace distribution with density

$$f(z;\theta) = \frac{1}{2\sigma} \exp\left(-\frac{|z-\mu|}{\sigma}\right), \qquad \theta = (\mu, \sigma),$$

where $\theta \in \Theta = \Re \times \Re_+$. The sample log-likelihood is

$$L(\theta) = c - n \ln \sigma - \sigma^{-1} Q(\mu),$$

where c is an arbitrary constant and $Q(\mu) = \sum_i |Z_i - \mu|$. For σ fixed, maximizing the sample log-likelihood with respect to μ is equivalent to minimizing $Q(\mu)$. Because this is just the LAD problem introduced in Section 4.2.4, a ML estimate of μ always exists and corresponds to a sample median $\hat{\zeta}$, which is clearly not unique.

Putting $\mu = \hat{\zeta}$ in $L(\theta)$ gives the function

$$L_*(\sigma) = L(\hat{\zeta}, \sigma) = c - n \ln \sigma - \sigma^{-1} Q(\hat{\zeta}),$$

called the *concentrated* or *profile sample log-likelihood* of σ (Figure 36). If $Q(\hat{\zeta}) = 0$, then no ML estimate of σ exists because the function $L_*(\sigma) = c - n \ln \sigma$ is unbounded. This occurs when $n = 1$, or when $n > 1$ but $Z_1 = \cdots = Z_n$. If $Q(\hat{\zeta}) > 0$, then L_* attains a unique maximum on the interval $(0, \infty)$. Such a maximum is characterized by the equation

$$0 = -\frac{n}{\sigma} + \frac{Q(\hat{\zeta})}{\sigma^2},$$

whose unique solution is $\hat{\sigma} = n^{-1} Q(\hat{\zeta}) = n^{-1} \sum_i |Z_i - \hat{\zeta}|$. The ML estimates of μ and σ are therefore, respectively, a sample median and the average absolute deviation from a median. □

If L is a strictly concave function and Θ is a convex set, then a ML estimate is unique. An important special case is when the sample log-likelihood is quadratic, namely of the form

$$L(\theta) = c - \frac{1}{2}(b - \theta)^\top Q (b - \theta), \tag{4.9}$$

where the scalar c, the p-vector b and the $p \times p$ matrix Q may be functions of the data. It is easily seen that $\hat{\theta} = b$ is a ML estimate if Q is a n.n.d. matrix, and is the unique ML estimate if Q is p.d.

Figure 36 Profile sample log-likelihood $L_*(\sigma)$ of the Laplace location and scale model for $n = 10$ and $Q(\hat{\zeta}) = 5$.

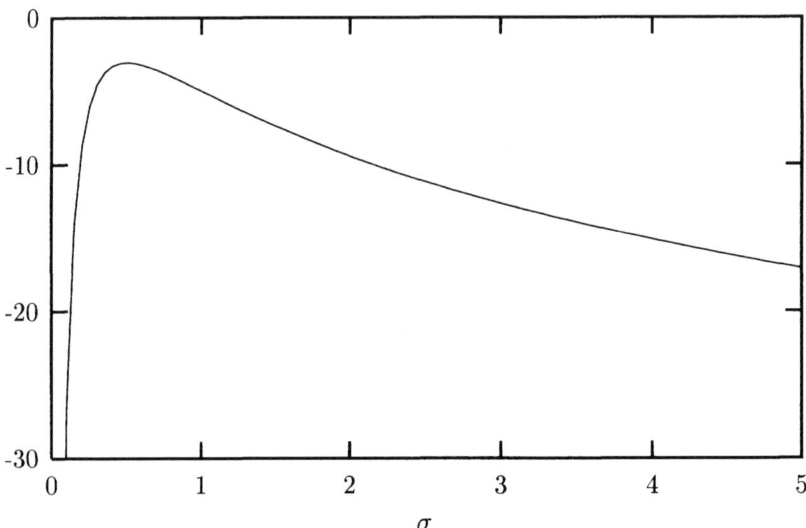

Example 4.9 Given a sample $Z_1, \ldots, Z_n$ from a $\mathcal{N}(\mu, \sigma^2)$ distribution, the sample log-likelihood is

$$L(\theta) = c - \frac{n}{2} \ln \sigma^2 - \frac{1}{2\sigma^2} \sum_{i=1}^{n} (Z_i - \mu)^2, \qquad \theta = (\mu, \sigma^2),$$

where c is an arbitrary constant. Because $n^{-1} \sum_i (Z_i - \mu)^2 = \hat{\sigma}^2 + (\bar{Z} - \mu)^2$, where $\bar{Z}$ and $\hat{\sigma}^2$ are respectively the sample mean and the sample mean squared deviation of Z_i, the sample log-likelihood may be written

$$L(\theta) = c - \frac{n}{2} \ln \sigma^2 - \frac{n}{2\sigma^2} [\hat{\sigma}^2 + (\bar{Z} - \mu)^2].$$

Since $L(\theta)$ is quadratic in μ for σ^2 fixed, the sample mean $\bar{Z}$ is the unique ML estimate of μ for this model. Now putting $\mu = \bar{Z}$ in $L(\theta)$ gives the profile sample log-likelihood

$$L_*(\sigma^2) = L(\bar{Z}, \sigma^2) = c - \frac{n}{2} \left(\ln \sigma^2 + \frac{\hat{\sigma}^2}{\sigma^2} \right).$$

If $\hat{\sigma}^2 > 0$, then L_* attains a unique maximum on the interval $(0, \infty)$ at $\sigma^2 = \hat{\sigma}^2$.

To check that the function $L(\theta)$ attains its maximum at $\hat{\theta} = (\bar{Z}, \hat{\sigma}^2)$, provided that $\hat{\sigma}^2 > 0$, consider the Hessian of the sample log-likelihood

$$L''(\theta) = -\frac{n}{\sigma^2} \begin{bmatrix} 1 & (\bar{Z} - \mu)/\sigma^2 \\ (\bar{Z} - \mu)/\sigma^2 & [\hat{\sigma}^2 + (\bar{Z} - \mu)^2]/\sigma^4 - 1/(2\sigma^2) \end{bmatrix}.$$

Evaluating L'' at the point $\hat{\theta}$ gives

$$L''(\hat{\theta}) = -\frac{n}{\hat{\sigma}^2} \begin{bmatrix} 1 & 0 \\ 0 & 1/(2\hat{\sigma}^2) \end{bmatrix}.$$

Since $L''(\hat{\theta})$ is n.d. if $\hat{\sigma}^2 > 0$, $\hat{\theta}$ is indeed the ML estimate of θ. □

As will be shown in the proof of Theorem 4.14, a quadratic log-likelihood provides a good approximation to the shape of a smooth log-likelihood for sufficiently large n. Further, quadratic approximations of some sort are often very useful when exact calculations are tedious or even impossible.

Example 4.10 Let $\mathbf{Z} = (Z_1, \ldots, Z_n)$ be a finite segment of the Gaussian AR(1) process

$$(1 - \rho L)Z_t = U_t,$$

where $|\rho| < 1$ and $\{U_t\}$ is a Gaussian WN$(0, \sigma^2)$ process. Because the conditional distribution of Z_t given $Z_{t-1}, Z_{t-2}, \ldots$ is $\mathcal{N}(\rho Z_{t-1}, \sigma^2)$ and the marginal distribution of Z_t is $\mathcal{N}(0, \gamma_0)$, with $\gamma_0 = \sigma^2/(1-\rho^2)$, the joint density of $\mathbf{Z}$ may be factorized as

$$\begin{aligned} f(\mathbf{Z};\theta) &= f(Z_1;\theta) \prod_{t=2}^n f(Z_t \mid Z_{t-1};\theta) \\ &= \frac{\sqrt{1-\rho^2}}{\sigma} \phi\left(\frac{Z_1\sqrt{1-\rho^2}}{\sigma}\right) \prod_{t=2}^n \frac{1}{\sigma} \phi\left(\frac{Z_t - \rho Z_{t-1}}{\sigma}\right), \end{aligned}$$

where $\theta = (\rho, \sigma^2)$ and $\phi(\cdot)$ denotes the $\mathcal{N}(0,1)$ density. The sample log-likelihood of the Gaussian AR(1) model is therefore

$$L(\theta) = c - \frac{n}{2} \ln \sigma^2 + \ln \sqrt{1-\rho^2} - \frac{1}{2\sigma^2} \left[(1-\rho^2) Z_1^2 + \sum_{t=2}^n (Z_t - \rho Z_{t-1})^2 \right],$$

where c is an arbitrary constant. Notice that, through the presence of the term $\ln \sqrt{1-\rho^2}$, the log-likelihood explicitly incorporates the restriction that $|\rho| < 1$. Letting

$$g(\rho) = \sqrt{1-\rho^2}, \qquad Q(\rho) = \sum_{t=2}^n (Z_t - \rho Z_{t-1})^2, \qquad G(\rho) = (1-\rho^2)Z_1^2 + Q(\rho),$$

one may write $L(\theta)$ more compactly as

$$L(\theta) = c - \frac{n}{2} \ln \sigma^2 + \ln g(\rho) - \frac{1}{2\sigma^2} G(\rho). \tag{4.10}$$

For ρ fixed, $L(\theta)$ attains its maximum at the point $\sigma^2(\rho) = n^{-1} G(\rho)$. Substituting back into $L(\theta)$ gives the profile sample log-likelihood

$$L_*(\rho) = L(\rho, \sigma^2(\rho)) = c - \frac{n}{2} [\ln G(\rho) - \ln n] + \ln g(\rho) - \frac{n}{2}$$

(Figure 37). This is a function of ρ only, although not a quadratic one due to the presence of the term $\ln g(\rho)$. A necessary condition for a maximum of L_* is

$$0 = L_*'(\rho) = -\frac{n}{2} \frac{G'(\rho)}{G(\rho)} + \frac{g'(\rho)}{g(\rho)},$$

Figure 37 Profile sample log-likelihood $L_*(\rho)$ and its approximations L_U and L_C based on $n = 8$ consecutive observations of a Gaussian AR(1) process with $\rho = .5$. The approximations considered correspond, respectively, to the unconditional and the conditional LS estimates.

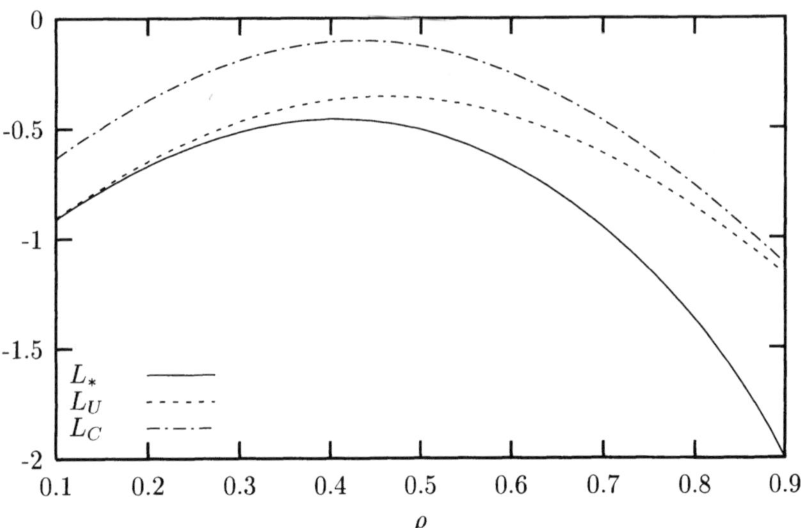

which can be shown to be a cubic equation in ρ with a unique real root in the interval $(-1, 1)$. An explicit expression for such a root may be obtained from the formulae for the roots of cubic equations (see, for example, Beach & MacKinnon 1978).

The calculations required to estimate ρ by the ML method may be reduced substantially if one considers certain approximations to L_*. Observe first that, if n is sufficiently large and $|\rho|$ is not too close to one, then the contribution to the log-likelihood of the term $\ln g(\rho)$ is negligible. Maximizing L_* ignoring this term is equivalent to minimizing with respect to ρ the quadratic function G. A necessary condition for a minimum of G is

$$0 = G'(\rho) = -2\rho Z_1^2 - 2\sum_{t=2}^{n}(Z_t - \rho Z_{t-1})Z_{t-1}.$$

If $\sum_{t=2}^{n-1} Z_t^2 > 0$, the above equation has the unique solution

$$\hat{\rho} = \frac{\sum_{t=2}^{n} Z_t Z_{t-1}}{\sum_{t=3}^{n} Z_{t-1}^2},$$

called the *unconditional LS estimate* of ρ.

If the first term in G is also ignored (or, equivalently, $Z_1 = 0$), then the problem reduces to minimizing $Q(\rho)$. If $\sum_{t=2}^{n} Z_{t-1}^2 > 0$, we get the unique solution

$$\tilde{\rho} = \frac{\sum_{t=2}^{n} Z_t Z_{t-1}}{\sum_{t=2}^{n} Z_{t-1}^2},$$

called the *conditional LS estimate* of ρ. In large samples, the ML estimate and the LS estimates $\hat{\rho}$ and $\tilde{\rho}$ should all be very close to each other, although in small samples they may differ considerably.

If ρ_0 denotes the true value of ρ, then all three estimators are biased for ρ_0. This is more easily seen in the case of the conditional LS estimator, for

$$\tilde{\rho} - \rho_0 = \frac{\sum_{t=2}^n U_t Z_{t-1}}{\sum_{t=2}^n Z_{t-1}^2} = \frac{T_1}{T_2},$$

where $T_1 = \sum_{t=2}^n U_t Z_{t-1}$ and $T_2 = \sum_{t=2}^n Z_{t-1}^2$. Although $\mathrm{E}\, T_1 = 0$, the fact that $\mathrm{E}(T_1/T_2) \neq (\mathrm{E}\, T_1)/(\mathrm{E}\, T_2)$ implies that $\mathrm{E}\, \tilde{\rho} \neq \rho_0$ in general. Analytical approximations to the bias of $\tilde{\rho}$ may be obtained by the δ-method (Section 5.1.5). On the other hand, by the strong law of large numbers for linear processes (Theorem D.13), $n^{-1}T_1 \overset{\text{as}}{\to} \mathrm{E}\, U_t Z_{t-1} = 0$ and $n^{-1}T_2 \overset{\text{as}}{\to} \mathrm{E}\, Z_{t-1}^2 \neq 0$ as $n \to \infty$. Hence, $\tilde{\rho} - \rho_0 \overset{\text{as}}{\to} 0$, that is, $\hat{\rho}$ is a strongly consistent estimator of the autoregressive parameter. □

The above example shows that if the sample log-likelihood is unimodal and bounded above but not quadratic, then it may be complicated or even impossible to obtain a closed form solution to a ML problem. In this case, finding a ML estimate requires numerical methods, such as those reviewed in Appendix B.

In all the examples discussed so far, the sample log-likelihood was constructed starting from either the probability mass function or the probability density function. There is no conceptual difficulty in constructing the log-likelihood for cases where the distribution of the data is of the mixed (continuous–discrete) type.

Example 4.11 Consider again the model of top-coding in Example 2.2. If the latent random variable Z^* is distributed as $\mathcal{N}(\mu, \sigma^2)$, with $\sigma^2 > 0$, then the fraction of the population for which income is unobserved is equal to $\Pr\{Z^* \geq c\} = 1 - \Phi((c-\mu)/\sigma)$ and the distribution function of a top-coded value $Z = \min(Z^*, c)$ is

$$F(z) = \begin{cases} \Phi\left(\dfrac{z-\mu}{\sigma}\right), & \text{if } z < c, \\ 1, & \text{if } z \geq c. \end{cases}$$

The sample log-likelihood of this model is the sum of two components, one corresponding to the continuous part of the distribution and the other to the discrete part with mass point at c. Up to an additive constant, the log-likelihood for a sample $Z_1, \ldots, Z_n$ from the distribution of Z is therefore

$$L(\theta) = \sum_1 \ln\left[\frac{1}{\sigma}\phi\left(\frac{Z_i - \mu}{\sigma}\right)\right] + n_0 \ln\left[1 - \Phi\left(\frac{c-\mu}{\sigma}\right)\right], \qquad \theta = (\mu, \sigma^2),$$

where $\sum_1$ denotes summation over the uncensored observations and n_0 denotes the number of censored (top-coded) observations. Since L is smooth and bounded and the parameter space is an open subset of $\Re^2$, a ML estimator $\hat{\theta} = (\hat{\mu}, \hat{\sigma}^2)$ must necessarily satisfy the pair of equations

$$0 = \frac{\partial L}{\partial \mu} = \sum_1 \frac{Z_i - \mu}{\sigma^2} + \frac{n_0}{\sigma}\, h\left(\frac{c-\mu}{\sigma}\right),$$

$$0 = \frac{\partial L}{\partial \sigma^2} = \frac{1}{2\sigma^2} \sum_1 \left[\left(\frac{Z_i - \mu}{\sigma}\right)^2 - 1\right] + \frac{n_0}{\sigma}\, \frac{c-\mu}{2\sigma^2}\, \lambda\left(-\frac{c-\mu}{\sigma}\right),$$

where $\lambda(-u) = \phi(-u)/\Phi(-u) = \phi(u)/[1 - \Phi(u)]$. The first equation shows that $\hat{\mu}$ is implicitly defined by

$$\hat{\mu} = \bar{Z}_1 + \hat{\sigma}\, \frac{n_0}{n_1}\, \lambda\left(-\frac{c-\hat{\mu}}{\hat{\sigma}}\right),$$

where $\bar{Z}_1$ is the average of the $n_1 = n - n_0$ uncensored observations. Because

$$\mathrm{E}(Z_i \,|\, Z_i < c) = \mu - \sigma\, \frac{\Pr\{Z_i \geq c\}}{\Pr\{Z_i < c\}}\, \lambda\left(-\frac{c-\hat{\mu}}{\sigma}\right),$$

where the ratio $\Pr\{Z_i \geq c\}/\Pr\{Z_i < c\}$ may simply be estimated by n_0/n_1, the ML estimator of μ may be interpreted as a way of correcting $\bar{Z}_1$ for its bias. Multiplying the first equation by $(c-\mu)/(2\sigma^2)$ and subtracting the result from the second one gives

$$0 = \frac{1}{2\sigma^2} \sum_1 \left[\frac{(Z_i - \mu)(Z_i - c)}{\sigma^2} - 1\right].$$

Therefore, evaluating at $\mu = \hat{\mu}$, the ML estimator of σ^2 is

$$\hat{\sigma}^2 = \frac{1}{n_1} \sum_1 (Z_i - \hat{\mu})(Z_i - c).$$

□

It should be clear from all the examples presented in this section that the ML method does not necessarily produce unbiased estimators of the target parameter. As shown in Section 4.6, the main justification for this method lies in its statistical properties when the sample size is large.

4.4.2 LIKELIHOOD EQUATIONS AND LOCAL ML ESTIMATES

The examples in the previous section show that if the parameter space Θ is an open set and the sample log-likelihood L is smooth and bounded, then a ML estimate may be obtained as follows:

1. compute the derivative L' of L;
2. solve with respect to θ the system of *likelihood equations* $L'(\theta) = 0$.

Unless $L(\theta)$ is strictly convex, this method does not guarantee that a root of the likelihood equations corresponds to a ML estimate, for L may have several local maxima, as well as local minima and saddlepoints. Any root of the likelihood equations corresponding to a local maximum of L is called a *local ML estimate*. A sufficient condition for $\hat{\theta}$ to be a local ML estimate is that the Hessian of L, evaluated at the point $\hat{\theta}$, is a n.d. matrix.

Notice the complete analogy between these conditions and the results in Section 1.1.6. Given a regular parametric model $\mathcal{F}_\Theta = \{f(z;\theta), \theta \in \Theta\}$ for a random vector Z, the likelihood score

$$s(Z;\theta) = \frac{\partial}{\partial\theta} \ln f(Z;\theta)$$

has mean zero. If $Z_1, \ldots, Z_n$ is a sample from the distribution of Z, then the sample log-likelihood is $L(\theta) = c + \sum_i \ln f(Z_i;\theta)$, where c is an arbitrary constant, and the sample counterpart of the above condition is the system of likelihood equations

$$0 = \mathrm{E}_{\hat{F}}\, s(Z;\theta) = n^{-1} \sum_{i=1}^{n} s_i(\theta) = n^{-1} L'(\theta),$$

where $s_i(\theta) = s(Z_i;\theta)$. Recall that a parameter point θ is locally identifiable if the Fisher information is a p.d. matrix at the point θ. The sample counterpart of this condition requires the matrix

$$-\bar{l}''(\theta) = -n^{-1} \sum_{i=1}^{n} s_i'(\theta) = -n^{-1} L''(\theta)$$

to be p.d. at the point $\hat{\theta}$, which guarantees that $\hat{\theta}$ is a local ML estimate. The matrix $-n^{-1}L''(\hat{\theta})$ is sometimes called the *observed information* (Efron & Hinkley 1978).

Example 4.12 Let $Z_1, \ldots, Z_n$ be a sample from a p-parameter exponential family. In terms of the canonical parameter η, the sample log-likelihood is

$$L(\eta) = \sum_{i=1}^{n} \eta^\top T(Z_i) + nd(\eta) + \sum_{i=1}^{n} c(Z_i),$$

and therefore the likelihood equations are

$$0 = \sum_{i=1}^{n} T(Z_i) + nd'(\eta).$$

Solving this equation may require numerical methods. Notice that the Hessian of $L(\theta)$ is $L''(\eta) = nd''(\eta) = -n\mathcal{I}(\eta)$, where $\mathcal{I}(\eta)$ is the Fisher information on η. Because $\mathcal{I}(\eta)$ is p.d. since the model is regular, the sample log-likelihood is strictly concave and so the ML estimate is unique.

The form of the likelihood equations for this class of models suggests an interesting interpretation of the ML estimator. Since the likelihood score $s_i(\eta) = T(Z_i) + d'(\eta)$ has mean zero, we have $d'(\eta) = -\mathrm{E}_\eta\, T(Z_i)$. Hence, the likelihood equations may also be written

$$0 = n^{-1} \sum_{i=1}^{n} s_i(\eta) = n^{-1} \sum_{i=1}^{n} T(Z_i) - E_\eta T(Z_i).$$

This relationship provides an interpretation of the ML estimate $\hat{\eta}$ as a MM estimate obtained by equating the sample mean of $T(Z_i)$ with its expectation under $\hat{\eta}$. □

4.5 MINIMUM VARIANCE UNBIASEDNESS

Let $\mathbf{Z}$ be a data vector (or matrix) and let $\hat{\theta} = \hat{\theta}(\mathbf{Z})$ be some estimator of a p-dimensional parameter $\theta \in \Theta$. The classical criterion for judging an estimator is the degree of concentration of its sampling distribution about the population parameter θ. The most common scalar measure of such a degree of concentration is the mean squared error (MSE) $\mathrm{E}_\theta(\hat{\theta}-\theta)^\top(\hat{\theta}-\theta)$, which coincides with the risk $r(\hat{\theta},\theta)$ of $\hat{\theta}$ under the quadratic loss function $\ell(u) = u^\top u$, where u is a p-vector. Another measure of the degree of concentration of the sampling distribution of $\hat{\theta}$ is the $p \times p$ matrix

$$R(\hat{\theta},\theta) = \mathrm{E}_\theta(\hat{\theta}-\theta)(\hat{\theta}-\theta)^\top = \mathrm{Var}_\theta\,\hat{\theta} + (\mathrm{Bias}_\theta\,\hat{\theta})(\mathrm{Bias}_\theta\,\hat{\theta})^\top,$$

called the *risk matrix* of the estimator. The two measures are related, for

$$r(\hat{\theta},\theta) = \sum_{j=1}^{p} r(\hat{\theta}_j,\theta) = \mathrm{tr}\,R(\hat{\theta},\theta).$$

Clearly, $r(\hat{\theta},\theta) = R(\hat{\theta},\theta)$ if θ is a scalar parameter.

In what follows, given two matrices A and B, we denote by $A - B \geq 0$ the fact that the difference $A - B$ is a n.n.d. matrix. If $\tilde{\theta} = \tilde{\theta}(\mathbf{Z})$ is any other estimator of θ such that $R(\hat{\theta},\theta) - R(\tilde{\theta},\theta) \geq 0$ for all $\theta \in \Theta$, then the MSE of any linear combination of the elements of $\hat{\theta}$ cannot be smaller than that of the corresponding linear combination of the elements of $\tilde{\theta}$. We say in this case that $\tilde{\theta}$ is *efficient* relative to $\hat{\theta}$. Notice that, while the risk matrix only provides a partial ordering of estimators, the MSE criterion gives a complete ordering.

Because θ is unknown, an ideal estimator $\tilde{\theta}$ on the basis of the above criterion should have minimum risk matrix uniformly on Θ, that is, should be such that $R(\hat{\theta},\theta) - R(\tilde{\theta},\theta) \geq 0$ for all $\theta \in \Theta$ and every other estimator $\hat{\theta}$. Because an estimator that takes the constant value θ_0 for all $\mathbf{Z}$ has zero risk matrix when $\theta = \theta_0$, the ideal estimator should have zero risk matrix for all $\theta \in \Theta$, which is generally impossible. By the same argument, to have minimum MSE uniformly on Θ, an estimator should have zero MSE for all θ, which is also generally impossible.

One way to circumvent this problem is to confine our attention to a smaller class of estimators that satisfy certain requirements. A popular choice is the class of unbiased estimators, whose risk matrix coincides with the sampling variance. If the class of unbiased estimators of θ is nonempty and contains more than one estimator, and if $\tilde{\theta}$ is an unbiased estimator such that $\mathrm{Var}_\theta\,\hat{\theta} - \mathrm{Var}_\theta\,\tilde{\theta} \geq 0$ for all $\theta \in \Theta$ and every other unbiased estimator $\hat{\theta}$, then $\hat{\theta}$ is said to be *uniformly minimum variance unbiased (UMVU)*. In what follows, we look at criteria for finding UMVU estimators.

Notice that the unbiasedness criterion, although popular, may be criticized on several grounds. First, there are cases when the class of unbiased estimators is empty or contains only one element. Second, as shown in Example 4.2, the property of unbiasedness is not preserved under nonlinear transformations. Third, the unbiasedness criterion may rule out estimators that are quite respectable, or select estimators that are hardly recommendable.

4.5.1 SUFFICIENCY

In the next two sections we assume that the density of the data belongs to a parametric family $\mathcal{F}_\Theta = \{f(\mathbf{z};\theta), \theta \in \Theta\}$ of densities on the sample space.

It is intuitively clear that, in drawing inferences about the population parameter θ, nothing is lost by neglecting those aspects of the data that provide no information on θ. This idea may be formalized as follows.

Definition 4.1 A statistic $T = T(\mathbf{Z})$ is said to be *sufficient* for a parameter θ if and only if the conditional distribution of $\mathbf{Z}$ given $T = t$ does not depend on θ. □

Theorem 4.6 (Factorization criterion) *Given a parametric model $\mathcal{F}_\Theta$ for the data, a statistic $T(\mathbf{Z})$ is sufficient if and only if $f(\mathbf{z};\theta) = g(T(\mathbf{z});\theta)\, h(\mathbf{z})$ for all $\theta \in \Theta$.*

Proof. See for example Lehmann (1988). □

If a parametric model for the data admits a sufficient statistic $T(\mathbf{Z})$, then the factorization criterion implies that the ratio between the value of the density at two sample points $\mathbf{z} \neq \mathbf{z}'$

$$\frac{f(\mathbf{z};\theta)}{f(\mathbf{z}';\theta)} = \frac{g(T(\mathbf{z});\theta)}{g(T(\mathbf{z}');\theta)}\,\frac{h(\mathbf{z})}{h(\mathbf{z}')}$$

does not depend on θ whenever $T(\mathbf{z}) = T(\mathbf{z}')$. Intuitively, once the value of T is known, the data contain no additional information on θ.

In general, a sufficient statistic is not unique. Further, the data vector $\mathbf{Z}$ is always sufficient. It is therefore interesting to ask whether there exist sufficient statistics that provide the greatest possible reduction of the data. Formally, a sufficient statistic T is called *minimal* if, for every other sufficient statistic $T_* = T_*(\mathbf{Z})$, there exists a function h such that $T = h(T_*)$.

Example 4.13 Let $\mathbf{Z} = (Z_1, \ldots, Z_n)$ be a sample from a $\mathcal{N}(\mu, \sigma^2)$ distribution. Writing the joint density of the data as

$$f(\mathbf{z};\theta) = \left(\frac{1}{\sigma\sqrt{2\pi}}\right)^n \exp\left[-\frac{1}{2\sigma^2}(\sum_i z_i^2 - 2\mu\sum_i z_i + n\mu^2)\right],$$

it is clear that the statistics

$$\begin{aligned} T_1 &= (z_1, \ldots, z_n), \\ T_2 &= \left(\sum_{i=1}^m z_i,\ \sum_{j=m+1}^n z_j,\ \sum_{i=1}^m z_i^2,\ \sum_{j=m+1}^n z_j^2\right), \\ T_3 &= \left(\sum_{i=1}^n z_i,\ \sum_{i=1}^n z_i^2\right), \\ T_4 &= \left(\bar{z},\ n^{-1}\sum_{i=1}^n (z_i - \bar{z})^2\right), \end{aligned}$$

with $\bar{z} = n^{-1}\sum_i z_i$, are all sufficient for $\theta = (\mu, \sigma^2)$, although only T_3 and T_4 are minimal sufficient. □

Example 4.14 Let $\mathbf{Z} = (Z_1, \ldots, Z_n)$ be a sample from a distribution in a p-parameter exponential family. The joint density of the data is of the form

$$f(\mathbf{z};\theta) = \exp\{a(\theta)^\top T(\mathbf{z}) + b(\theta) + c(\mathbf{z})\}, \tag{4.11}$$

where $T(\mathbf{z}) = \sum_i T(z_i)$ is a p-vector and $c(\mathbf{z}) = \sum_i c(z_i)$. Thus, for any n, the joint distribution of the data belongs to the same exponential family as the distribution of a single observation.

The statistic $T(\mathbf{Z})$ is sufficient, for we can identify the terms $\exp\{a(\theta)^\top T(\mathbf{z}) + b(\theta)\}$ and $\exp c(\mathbf{z})$ with, respectively, $g(T(\mathbf{z});\theta)$ and $h(\mathbf{z})$ in Theorem 4.6. In fact, $T(\mathbf{Z})$ is minimal sufficient and is called the *natural sufficient statistic* for θ. The dimension of this statistic is equal to p and does not change with the sample size, thus affording a considerable reduction of the data. □

It is easy to verify that, if a parametric model admits a minimal sufficient statistic T and the ML estimate is unique, then the latter must be a function of T. This result represents one justification for the ML method.

The relevance of the concept of sufficiency in searching for UMVU estimators of a parameter θ is due to the fact that an estimator $\hat\theta$ may be improved upon, in the MSE sense, by conditioning on a sufficient statistic.

Theorem 4.7 (Rao–Blackwell) *Let $\mathcal{F}_\Theta$ be a parametric model that admits a sufficient statistic T. If $\hat\theta$ is an estimator with finite sampling variance and $\tilde\theta = \mathrm{E}_\theta(\hat\theta \,|\, T)$, then $R(\hat\theta,\theta) - R(\tilde\theta,\theta) \geq 0$ for all $\theta \in \Theta$, with equality if and only if $\tilde\theta = \hat\theta$.*

Proof. By the law of iterated expectations $\mathrm{E}_\theta\,\hat\theta = \mathrm{E}_\theta[\mathrm{E}_\theta(\hat\theta \,|\, T)] = \mathrm{E}_\theta\,\tilde\theta$, and by the law of total variance

$$\mathrm{Var}\,\hat\theta - \mathrm{Var}_\theta\,\tilde\theta = \mathrm{Var}\,\hat\theta - \mathrm{Var}_\theta[\mathrm{E}_\theta(\hat\theta \,|\, T)] \geq 0.$$

Hence $R(\hat\theta,\theta) - R(\tilde\theta,\theta) = \mathrm{Var}_\theta\,\hat\theta - \mathrm{Var}_\theta\,\tilde\theta \geq 0$. □

Unless $\tilde\theta = \mathrm{E}_\theta(\hat\theta \,|\, T)$ is unique, one cannot conclude from the Rao–Blackwell theorem that $\tilde\theta$ has minimum MSE. For this conclusion to be true, one needs to verify that the family of distributions of T, obtained by varying θ over Θ, satisfies a further property.

Definition 4.2 Given a parametric model $\mathcal{F}_\Theta$ for the data, a statistic T is called *complete* if the only function g that satisfies $\mathrm{E}_\theta\, g(T) = 0$ for all $\theta \in \Theta$ is such that $\Pr_\theta\{g(T) = 0\} = 1$. □

Theorem 4.8 (Lehmann–Scheffè) *Let $\mathcal{F}_\Theta$ be a parametric model that admits a complete sufficient statistic T and let $\hat\theta$ be an unbiased estimator of θ. If $\hat\theta$ has finite sampling variance, then $\tilde\theta = \mathrm{E}_\theta(\hat\theta \,|\, T)$ is the unique UVMU estimator of θ.*

Proof. By the law of iterated expectations, if $\hat\theta$ is unbiased and has finite variance then $\tilde\theta = \mathrm{E}_\theta(\hat\theta \,|\, T)$ is also unbiased and has finite sampling variance. Further $\mathrm{Var}_\theta\,\hat\theta - \mathrm{Var}_\theta\,\tilde\theta \geq 0$ by the Rao–Blackwell theorem, with equality if and only if $\tilde\theta = \hat\theta$.

We now show that $\tilde{\theta}$ is unique, that is, $\tilde{\theta}$ does not depend on which particular unbiased estimator we started from. Thus suppose that $\tilde{\theta}_1 = g_1(T)$ and $\tilde{\theta}_2 = g_2(T)$ are both unbiased for θ. Then

$$\mathrm{E}_\theta[g_1(T) - g_2(T)] = \mathrm{E}_\theta\, g_1(T) - \mathrm{E}_\theta\, g_2(T) = 0.$$

Because the statistic T is complete, $\Pr_\theta\{g_1(T) - g_2(T) = 0\} = 1$, that is, $g_1(T) = g_2(T)$. □

In particular, if T is a complete sufficient statistic and $\hat{\theta} = h(T)$ is unbiased for θ and has finite sampling variance, then $\hat{\theta}$ is UMVU since $\mathrm{E}_\theta(\hat{\theta}\,|\,T) = \hat{\theta}$ in this case.

The next theorem provides a wide class of models for which there exists a complete sufficient statistic.

Theorem 4.9 *If the distribution of* $\mathbf{Z}$ *belongs to a p-parameter exponential family whose parameter space has a nonempty interior, then the natural sufficient statistic* $T(\mathbf{Z})$ *is complete.*

Proof. See for example Lehmann (1988). □

Example 4.15 Let $Z_1, \ldots, Z_n$ be a sample from a $\mathcal{N}(\mu, \sigma^2)$ distribution. The Gaussian model is a two-parameter exponential family whose parameter space $\Theta = \Re \times \Re_+$ has a nonempty interior. It then follows from Theorem 4.9 that the natural sufficient statistic $T = (\sum_i Z_i, \sum_i Z_i^2)$ is complete. Because the sample mean $\bar{Z}$ and the sample variance $s^2 = (n-1)^{-1} \sum_i (Z_i - \bar{Z})^2$ are functions of T and are unbiased, they are UMVU by the Lehmann–Scheffè theorem. □

4.5.2 THE CRAMÉR–RAO BOUND

When a sufficient statistic does not exist, or it exists but is not complete, one can establish a lower bound for the sampling variance of unbiased estimators which may be used to show that a given estimator is UMVU. Although this approach is less powerful than the previous one, it is important in the asymptotic optimality theory discussed in Section 4.6.

If the parametric model for the data is regular, then the likelihood score

$$S(\theta) = \frac{\partial}{\partial \theta} \ln f(\mathbf{Z}; \theta)$$

has mean zero and variance $I(\theta) = \mathrm{Var}_\theta\, S(\theta)$, called the *expected total information on* θ contained in the sample. In particular, given a sample $Z_1, \ldots, Z_n$ from a distribution in a regular parametric family $\{f(z;\theta), \theta \in \Theta\}$, the likelihood score is

$$S(\theta) = \sum_{i=1}^{n} \frac{\partial}{\partial \theta} \ln f(Z_i; \theta) = \sum_i s_i(\theta),$$

where $s_i(\theta) = s(Z_i;\theta)$ is the likelihood score for the ith observation, and the expected total information is $I(\theta) = \sum_i \mathrm{Var}_\theta\, s_i(\theta) = n\mathcal{I}(\theta)$, where $\mathcal{I}(\theta)$ is the Fisher information contained in a single observation.

The next theorem shows that, under appropriate regularity conditions, there exists a lower bound for the sampling variance of an estimator of a scalar parameter θ.

Theorem 4.10 (Cramér–Rao inequality) *Let $\mathcal{F}_\Theta$ be a regular parametric model with $\Theta \subseteq \Re$. If $\hat\theta$ is an estimator whose sampling variance is finite for all $\theta \in \Theta$ and whose bias $b(\theta) = \mathrm{E}_\theta\,\hat\theta - \theta$ is continuously differentiable on Θ, then*

$$\mathrm{Var}_\theta\,\hat\theta \geq \frac{[1+b'(\theta)]^2}{I(\theta)}.$$

Proof. Let $S = S(\mathbf{Z};\theta)$. Differentiating with respect to θ both sides of the identity $\theta + b(\theta) = \mathrm{E}_\theta\,\hat\theta$, using the fact that $\mathrm{E}_\theta(S) = 0$, gives

$$1 + b'(\theta) = \int \hat\theta(\mathbf{z}) f'(\mathbf{z};\theta)\,d\mathbf{z} = \mathrm{E}_\theta(\hat\theta S) = \mathrm{Cov}_\theta(\hat\theta, S),$$

The conclusion of the theorem then follows from the Cauchy–Schwarz inequality

$$[1+b'(\theta)]^2 = [\mathrm{Cov}_\theta(\hat\theta, S)]^2 \leq (\mathrm{Var}_\theta\,\hat\theta)\,(\mathrm{Var}_\theta\,S)$$

and the fact that $\mathrm{Var}_\theta\,S = I(\theta) \neq 0$ since the model is regular. □

If $\hat\theta$ is unbiased, then $b'(\theta) = 0$ and we have the following result.

Corollary 4.1 *Let $\mathcal{F}_\Theta$ be a regular parametric model with $\Theta \subseteq \Re$. If $\hat\theta$ is unbiased and has finite sampling variance for all $\theta \in \Theta$, then*

$$\mathrm{Var}_\theta\,\hat\theta \geq \frac{1}{I(\theta)}.$$

The generalization of the above corollary to the case of a vector-valued parameter is straightforward. If $\hat\theta$ is an unbiased estimator of a p-dimensional parameter θ and its sampling variance is finite for all $\theta \in \Theta$, then $\mathrm{Var}_\theta\,\hat\theta - I(\theta)^{-1} \geq 0$ (for a proof, see e.g. Silvey 1975, Section 2.12). The sampling variance of an unbiased estimator of the jth element of θ is therefore bounded below by the jth diagonal element of the inverse matrix of $I(\theta)$. In particular, if $I(\theta)$ is a diagonal matrix, the lower bound is equal to the jth diagonal element of $I(\theta)$.

Corollary 4.1 and its generalization to the vector parameter case imply that, if $\hat\theta$ is unbiased and such that $\mathrm{Var}\,\hat\theta = I(\theta)^{-1}$, then it is UMVU. Notice that this approach is less powerful than the one in Section 4.5.1 because a UMVU estimator may exist even if a parametric model is not regular. Even worse, a model may be regular and a UMVU estimator exist, but its sampling variance need not be equal to the Cramér–Rao bound.

Example 4.16 Given a sample of size n from a $\mathcal{N}(\mu, \sigma^2)$ distribution, the Cramér–Rao bound for unbiased estimation of (μ, σ^2) is

$$I(\theta)^{-1} = [n\mathcal{I}(\theta)]^{-1} = \frac{1}{n}\begin{bmatrix} \sigma^2 & 0 \\ 0 & 2\sigma^4 \end{bmatrix}.$$

The bound is attained by the sample mean $\bar Z$ but not by the unbiased estimator s^2, whose sampling variance is equal to $2\sigma^2/(n-1)$. This estimator is nevertheless UMVU for σ^2 as seen in Example 4.15. □

In fact, the Cramér–Rao bound is attained only in special cases.

Theorem 4.11 *Suppose that the conditions of Theorem 4.10 are satisfied. Then there exists an unbiased estimator $\hat\theta$ that attains the Cramér–Rao bound if and only if $S(\theta) = I(\theta)\,(\hat\theta - \theta)$.*

Proof. Consider for simplicity the scalar parameter case. The crucial step in the proof of the Cramér–Rao bound is the fact that

$$\mathrm{Cov}_\theta(\hat\theta, S)^2 \le (\mathrm{Var}_\theta\,\hat\theta)\,(\mathrm{Var}_\theta\,S).$$

If $\hat\theta$ and S are not constant, equality holds if and only if $\hat\theta$ and S are linearly related, that is, if and only if there exists a function $A(\theta)$ such that $S - \mathrm{E}_\theta\,S = A(\theta)\,(\hat\theta - \mathrm{E}_\theta\,\hat\theta)$ or, since $\mathrm{E}_\theta\,S = 0$ and $\hat\theta$ is unbiased for θ, if and only if $S = A(\theta)\,(\hat\theta - \theta)$. In this case, $1 = \mathrm{Cov}_\theta(\hat\theta, S)^2 = \mathrm{Var}_\theta\,S/A(\theta)$ and therefore $A(\theta) = \mathrm{Var}_\theta\,S = I(\theta)$. □

As a consequence of Theorem 4.11, if there exists an unbiased estimator $\hat\theta$ that attains the Cramér–Rao bound, then the ML estimator must coincide with it. This is because the likelihood score for the sample must be of the form $S(\theta) = I(\theta)\,(\hat\theta - \theta)$. Since $I(\theta)$ is a p.d. matrix, the likelihood equation $S(\theta) = 0$ has the unique solution $\theta = \hat\theta$.

Because the conditions of Theorem 4.11 are very special, the Cramér–Rao lower bound may not look particularly useful. As shown in Section 4.6, however, the bound is typically attained by ML estimators in large samples. This result provides one of the most important justifications for the ML method.

4.6 ASYMPTOTIC PROPERTIES OF ML ESTIMATORS

We now derive approximations to the sampling properties of a ML estimator. These approximations are valid for the case when the data $Z_1, \ldots, Z_n$ consist of a large sample from a distribution whose density $f_0(z)$ is known to belong to a regular parametric family $\mathcal{F}_\Theta = \{f(z;\theta), \theta \in \Theta\}$, that is, $f_0(z) = f(z;\theta_0)$ for some $\theta_0 \in \Theta$. For simplicity we only consider the case when θ_0 is a scalar parameter. More general results, also valid for the case when the assumed model is misspecified, are discussed in Chapter 15.

In what follows, we denote the likelihood score by $s_i(\theta)$, the Fisher information on θ by $\mathcal{I}(\theta) = \mathrm{Var}_\theta\,s_i(\theta)$, and the sample log-likelihood by $L_n(\theta) = c + \sum_{i=1}^n \ln f(Z_i;\theta)$, where c is an arbitrary constant. Probabilities and expectations taken with respect to θ_0 are denoted by P_0 and E_0 respectively.

4.6.1 CONSISTENCY

We first show that if θ_0 is identifiable then, with probability approaching one as $n \to \infty$, the sample log-likelihood attains its maximum at θ_0.

Theorem 4.12 *Let $Z_1, \ldots, Z_n$ be a sample from a distribution whose density $f(z;\theta_0)$ belongs to a parametric family $\mathcal{F}_\Theta$. If θ_0 is identifiable then, for all other $\theta \in \Theta$, $P_0\{L_n(\theta_0) > L_n(\theta)\} \to 1$ as $n \to \infty$.*

Proof. For all $\theta \in \Theta$, $\{\ln f(Z_i;\theta)\}$ is a sequence of i.i.d. random variables with finite mean. Therefore, by Khinchine WLLN,

$$n^{-1}[L_n(\theta_0) - L_n(\theta)] = n^{-1} \sum_{i=1}^{n} \ln \frac{f(Z_i;\theta_0)}{f(Z_i;\theta)} \xrightarrow{\text{p}} \mathrm{E}_0 \ln \frac{f(Z_i;\theta_0)}{f(Z_i;\theta)}.$$

The conclusion of the theorem then follows from the fact that, since θ_0 is identifiable, $\mathrm{E}_0 \ln f(Z_i;\theta_0) > \mathrm{E}_0 \ln f(Z_i;\theta)$ for all $\theta \neq \theta_0$. □

In the light of the above result, one may conjecture that a ML estimator, which maximizes the sample log-likelihood, ought to converge as $n \to \infty$ to the "true" value θ_0 of θ, which maximizes the expected log-likelihood. The next result gives a simple set of conditions under which this conjecture is valid.

Theorem 4.13 *Let $Z_1, \ldots, Z_n$ be a sample from a distribution whose density belongs to a regular parametric family $\{f(z;\theta), \theta \in \Theta\}$ and suppose that the likelihood equation*

$$0 = L_n'(\theta) = \sum_{i=1}^{n} s_i(\theta)$$

has a unique root $\hat{\theta}_n \in \Theta$ with probability approaching one as $n \to \infty$. Then $\hat{\theta}_n$ is the ML estimate with probability approaching one as $n \to \infty$. If $\theta_0 \in \Theta$ is the true value of θ, then $\hat{\theta}_n \xrightarrow{\text{p}} \theta_0$.

Proof. Let $\epsilon > 0$ be any number such that the open neighborhood $\mathcal{O} = (\theta_0 - \epsilon, \theta_0 + \epsilon)$ of θ_0 is contained in Θ, and let C_n be the set of points in the sample space such that $L_n(\theta_0) > L_n(\theta_0 - \epsilon)$ and $L_n(\theta_0) > L_n(\theta_0 + \epsilon)$. For each point in C_n there exists a parametric point $\hat{\theta}_n \in \mathcal{O}$ at which L_n attains a local maximum. Under our set of assumptions, $\hat{\theta}_n$ is necessarily a root of the likelihood equation and is unique with probability approaching one as $n \to \infty$. Theorem 4.12 implies that $P_0\{C_n\} \to 1$ as $n \to \infty$, and therefore the sequence $\{\hat{\theta}_n\}$ of roots must satisfy $P_0\{|\hat{\theta}_n - \theta_0| < \epsilon\} \to 1$ as $n \to \infty$. Since ϵ is arbitrary, we have that $\hat{\theta}_n \xrightarrow{\text{p}} \theta_0$.

Now suppose that the probability that $\hat{\theta}_n$ is the ML estimate does not approach one as $n \to \infty$. Since $\hat{\theta}_n$ is a local maximum of the log-likelihood L_n then, with positive probability as $n \to \infty$, L_n must also possess a local minimum, which contradicts the assumption that the root of the likelihood equation is unique with probability approaching one. □

4.6.2 ASYMPTOTIC NORMALITY

We now show that a consistent sequence of roots of the likelihood equation has a limiting Gaussian distribution. In addition to regularity of the parametric model, we assume that the density $f(z;\theta)$ is three times differentiable with respect to θ and that its third derivative is uniformly bounded by an integrable function, that is, for every $\theta_0 \in \Theta$ there exist a number $\epsilon > 0$ and a function $M(z)$ with $\mathrm{E}_0\, M(Z_i) < \infty$ such that

$$\left| \frac{\partial^3}{\partial \theta^3} \ln f(z;\theta) \right| \leq M(z)$$

for all z in the support of Z_i and every $\theta \in (\theta_0 - \epsilon, \theta_0 + \epsilon)$. This condition is used in the proof of the next theorem to bound the remainder in a second-order Taylor expansion of $L'_n(\hat{\theta}_n)$ about θ_0.

Theorem 4.14 *Let $Z_1, \ldots, Z_n$ be a sample from a distribution whose density $f(z;\theta_0)$ belongs to a regular parametric family $\{f(z;\theta), \theta \in \Theta\}$. If $f(z;\theta)$ is three times differentiable with respect to θ, with third derivative that is uniformly bounded in z by an integrable function, then any consistent sequence $\{\hat{\theta}_n\}$ of roots of the likelihood equation satisfies $\sqrt{n}\,(\hat{\theta}_n - \theta_0) \xrightarrow{d} \mathcal{N}(0, 1/\mathcal{I}(\theta_0))$.*

Proof. Expanding $L'_n(\hat{\theta}_n)$ in Taylor series about θ_0 gives

$$0 = L'_n(\hat{\theta}_n) = L'_n(\theta_0) + L''_n(\theta_0)\,(\hat{\theta}_n - \theta_0) + \frac{1}{2}\,L'''_n(\theta_n^*)\,(\hat{\theta}_n - \theta_0)^2,$$

where θ_n^* is a point between θ_0 and $\hat{\theta}_n$. The random variable $\sqrt{n}\,(\hat{\theta}_n - \theta_0)$ may then be represented as the ratio X_n/Y_n of two random variables, where

$$X_n = \frac{1}{\sqrt{n}} L'_n(\theta_0) = \frac{1}{\sqrt{n}} \sum_{i=1}^n s_i(\theta_0), \qquad Y_n = -\frac{1}{n} L''_n(\theta_0) - \frac{1}{2n}\,L'''_n(\theta_n^*)\,(\hat{\theta}_n - \theta_0).$$

Now consider the behavior of the sequences $\{X_n\}$ and $\{Y_n\}$ as $n \to \infty$. Since $\{s_i(\theta_0)\}$ is a sequence of random variables with mean zero and variance equal to $\mathcal{I}(\theta_0)$, the Lindeberg-Lévy CLT implies that $X_n \xrightarrow{d} X$, where $X \sim \mathcal{N}(0, \mathcal{I}(\theta_0))$. On the other hand, since $-\operatorname{E}_0 s'_i(\theta_0) = \mathcal{I}(\theta_0)$ is finite, Khinchine WLLN implies

$$-\frac{1}{n}\,L''_n(\theta_0) = -n^{-1} \sum_{i=1}^n s'_i(\theta_0) \xrightarrow{p} \mathcal{I}(\theta_0).$$

Further, because

$$\frac{1}{n}\,L'''_n(\theta) = n^{-1} \sum_{i=1}^n \frac{\partial^3}{\partial \theta^3} \ln f(Z_i;\theta),$$

it follows that, with probability approaching one as $n \to \infty$,

$$|n^{-1} L'''_n(\theta)| \le n^{-1} \sum_{i=1}^n M(Z_i)$$

for every θ sufficiently near θ_0. Since $n^{-1}\sum_i M(Z_i) \xrightarrow{p} \operatorname{E}_0 M(Z_i)$, we have that $n^{-1} L'''_n(\theta_n^*) = O_p(1)$ and so $n^{-1} L'''_n(\theta_n^*)\,(\hat{\theta}_n - \theta_0) = O_p(1)\,o_p(1) = o_p(1)$ by the consistency of $\hat{\theta}_n$. Hence, $Y_n = -n^{-1} L''_n(\theta_0) + o_p(1) \xrightarrow{p} \mathcal{I}(\theta_0)$, where $\mathcal{I}(\theta_0) \neq 0$ since the parametric model is regular. The conclusion of the theorem then follows from Slutzky's lemma (Corollary D.4). □

It is clear from the proof of Theorem 4.14 that the difference between $\hat{\theta}_n$ and θ_0 may be represented as

$$\hat{\theta}_n - \theta_0 = n^{-1} \sum_{i=1}^n \psi(Z_i;\theta_0) + R_n, \tag{4.12}$$

where $\psi(Z_i;\theta_0) = \mathcal{I}(\theta_0)^{-1} s_i(\theta_0)$ and the remainder term R_n is $o_p(1/\sqrt{n})$. The sequence $\{\psi(Z_i;\theta_0)\}$ is a sequence of i.i.d. random variables that have zero mean, finite variance equal to the inverse of the Fisher information, and satisfy all the conditions for the Lindeberg-Lévy CLT. The representation (4.12) is called the *linear asymptotic representation* of $\hat{\theta}_n$, and the function $\psi(z;\theta_0)$, viewed as a function of z for fixed θ_0, is called the *influence function* of $\hat{\theta}_n$. Its role will be discussed in more detail in Chapter 15.

Theorem 4.14 is one of the main justifications for the ML method because it shows that, under appropriate regularity conditions, the asymptotic variance of a consistent root of the likelihood equation attains the Cramér–Rao lower bound for unbiased estimators of θ. In this sense, a ML estimator is said to be *asymptotically efficient.*

Notice the difference with respect to Corollary 4.1, which states that if $\tilde{\theta}_n$ is an unbiased estimator with finite variance then $\text{Var}_\theta\, \tilde{\theta}_n \geq I(\theta_0)^{-1}$, where $I(\theta_0) = n\mathcal{I}(\theta_0)$ is the expected total information. Theorem 4.14 refers instead to the asymptotic variance of $\hat{\theta}_n$ and only requires the estimator to be consistent. Also notice that the variance $\mathcal{I}(\theta_0)^{-1}$ of the limiting distribution of the rescaled difference $\sqrt{n}\,(\hat{\theta}_n - \theta_0)$ need not coincide with the limit of its sampling variance.

For a generalization of Theorems 4.13 and 4.14 to the case when θ is a p-dimensional parameter, see for example Lehmann (1983).

4.7 BAYES METHODS

The elements of a Bayesian statistical model are: (i) a parametric model $\mathcal{F}_\Theta$ on the sample space, and (ii) a probability distribution p on the parameter space Θ. The distribution p, called the *prior distribution*, is introduced to represent the information available about the target parameter θ before observing the data. This prior information may come from previous studies, economic theory, etc.

The Bayesian inference problem is to determine how the assignment of probability to the parameter space Θ changes after the data $\mathbf{z}$ have been observed. Bayes theorem provides a way of combining the sample information and the prior information contained in a Bayesian statistical model. The result is a new assignment $p(\theta\,|\,\mathbf{z})$ of probability to the parameter space Θ, called the *posterior distribution* of θ, which represents the uncertainty about θ after the data $\mathbf{z}$ have been observed. The posterior distribution is the solution to the Bayesian inference problem.

Because the prior distribution may be difficult to specify and it is generally different for different subjects, a Bayesian analysis based on particular prior distribution is of limited interest. Whenever possible, the analysis should instead report the mapping from the space of prior distributions to the space of posterior distributions induced by the statistical model and the observed data. This mapping is ultimately the "message" of a Bayesian analysis.

4.7.1 BAYES THEOREM

To stress the fact that the target parameter θ is now regarded as a realization of a random vector with values in Θ, the density of the data is denoted by $f(\mathbf{z}\,|\,\theta)$. The density of the prior distribution on Θ is simply called the *prior density* of θ and denoted by $p(\theta)$. According to Bayes theorem, the conditional density of θ given the observed data $\mathbf{Z} = \mathbf{z}$, or *posterior density* of θ, is

$$p(\theta \mid \mathbf{z}) = \frac{f(\mathbf{z} \mid \theta)\, p(\theta)}{f(\mathbf{z})},$$

where $f(\mathbf{z} \mid \theta)$ is interpreted as the sample likelihood, that is, as a function of θ for $\mathbf{z}$ fixed, and

$$f(\mathbf{z}) = \int_\Theta f(\mathbf{z} \mid \theta)\, p(\theta)\, d\theta$$

is the marginal density of $\mathbf{Z}$, also called the *marginal likelihood* or *prior predictive density* of $\mathbf{Z}$. In a Bayesian analysis, $p(\theta \mid \mathbf{z})$ represents what can be inferred from the observed data about the parameter θ. The posterior density is simply proportional to $f(\mathbf{z} \mid \theta)\, p(\theta)$ and depends on the data only through the likelihood $f(\mathbf{z} \mid \theta)$.

Bayes theorem may be interpreted as a model of sequential learning. For example, if $\mathbf{z}_1$ and $\mathbf{z}_2$ are two independent samples from the same population and $\mathbf{z} = (\mathbf{z}_1, \mathbf{z}_2)$, repeated application of Bayes theorem gives

$$\begin{aligned} p(\theta \mid \mathbf{z}) \propto f(\mathbf{z}_1, \mathbf{z}_2 \mid \theta)\, p(\theta) &= f(\mathbf{z}_2 \mid \theta)\, f(\mathbf{z}_1 \mid \theta)\, p(\theta) \\ &= f(\mathbf{z}_2 \mid \theta)\, p(\theta \mid \mathbf{z}_1). \end{aligned}$$

Hence, $p(\theta \mid \mathbf{z})$ may be interpreted as the result of updating the posterior density $p(\theta \mid \mathbf{z}_1)$ in the light of the information on θ contained in the new sample $\mathbf{z}_2$.

A measure of the gain of information provided by the observed data $\mathbf{z}$ is the logarithm of the ratio of the posterior and the prior densities

$$\mathrm{I}(\theta \mid \mathbf{z}) = \ln \frac{p(\theta \mid \mathbf{z})}{p(\theta)}.$$

Because θ is regarded as a realization of a random vector, a summary measure of the information contained in the data is the Fisher information gain

$$\mathrm{E}\,\mathrm{I}(\theta \mid \mathbf{z}) = \int_\Theta \mathrm{I}(\theta \mid \mathbf{z})\, p(\theta)\, d\theta,$$

which is simply the Kullback–Leibler index of dissimilarity between the prior and the posterior density.

Bayes theorem is only a consequence of the definition of conditional probability and, as such, its validity is without discussion. What has been discussed, however, is its applicability to problems of statistical inference. The main difficulties have to do with two problems. The first one is the interpretation of prior probabilities, in particular when one cannot appeal to the concept of repeated sampling. The second is the elicitation and representation of prior probabilities.

Without going into details, it appears of limited usefulness to rely on an objective interpretation of prior probabilities as the limit of frequency distributions generated by a stable mechanism. As an alternative, prior probabilities have been interpreted either as rational degrees of belief given an initial state of ignorance about a target parameter (see e.g. Jeffreys 1961), or as degrees of belief held by a particular subject at a given point in time (see e.g. Raiffa & Schlaifer 1961, Savage 1972 and Leamer 1978).

4.7.2 CONJUGATE PRIORS

A subject is rarely able to specify every detail of her prior assignment of probability to the parameter space and, in any case, a Bayesian analysis based on a particular prior distribution would be of limited interest. These considerations suggest restricting attention to some suitable parametric family $\mathcal{P}_\Gamma = \{p(\theta;\gamma), \gamma \in \Gamma\}$ of distributions on Θ, and then selecting the particular element of $\mathcal{P}_\Gamma$ that better represents the available prior information. Proceeding in this way offers yet another advantage. Given a parametric family of prior distributions, it now becomes possible to investigate the general properties of the family of posterior distributions on Θ generated by the application of Bayes theorem.

In selecting a parametric family $\mathcal{P}_\Gamma$ of prior distributions, it seems reasonable to require the following:

1. $\mathcal{P}_\Gamma$ should be mathematically tractable, that is, the posterior density should be easily determined given the prior density and the likelihood. Further, if the prior density belongs to $\mathcal{P}_\Gamma$, then the posterior density should also belong to $\mathcal{P}_\Gamma$;
2. the family $\mathcal{P}_\Gamma$ should be rich enough to contain an element capable of accurately representing the available prior information;
3. the parametrization of $\mathcal{P}_\Gamma$ should be easy to interpret.

Taking these requisites into account, consider a parametric model $\{f(\mathbf{z}\,|\,\theta)\}$ for the data that admits a sufficient statistic $T = T(\mathbf{z})$. By Theorem 4.6 we have $f(\mathbf{z}\,|\,\theta) \propto g(T(\mathbf{z})\,|\,\theta)$, which implies that the posterior density $p(\theta\,|\,\mathbf{z})$ must be proportional to $g(T(\mathbf{z})\,|\,\theta)\,p(\theta)$. If the prior density of θ depends on a parameter γ in such a way that

$$p(\theta;\gamma) \propto g(\gamma\,|\,\theta), \tag{4.13}$$

then the posterior density of θ is proportional to $g(T(\mathbf{z})\,|\,\theta)\,g(\gamma\,|\,\theta)$. If $g(\cdot\,|\,\theta)$ belongs to a class of functions that is closed with respect to the product of its elements, then the posterior and the prior density will have the same form.

Definition 4.3 Let $\mathcal{F}_\Theta = \{f(\mathbf{z}\,|\,\theta)\}$ be a parametric model for the data that admits the factorization $f(\mathbf{z}\,|\,\theta) = g(T(\mathbf{z})\,|\,\theta)\,h(\mathbf{z})$, where $\{g(\cdot\,|\,\theta)\}$ is a class of functions that is closed with respect to the product of its elements. A parametric family $\mathcal{P}_\Gamma = \{p(\theta;\gamma), \gamma \in \Gamma\}$ of densities on Θ is said to be *conjugate* with respect to $\mathcal{F}_\Theta$ if each of its elements satisfies (4.13), with the proportionality factor depending on γ but not on θ. □

The condition (4.13) requires the prior density of θ to have the same functional form of $g(T\,|\,\theta)$, but with the parameter γ replacing the sufficient statistic T. The parameter γ may therefore be interpreted as the value of the sufficient statistic for a preliminary sample drawn from the same statistical model.

Example 4.17 Given a sample of size n from a $\mathcal{N}(\mu,\sigma^2)$ distribution, the sample likelihood may be written

$$f(\mathbf{z}\,|\,\theta) = (2\pi\sigma^2)^{-n/2}\exp\left\{-\frac{1}{2\sigma^2}[n\hat\sigma^2 + n(\bar z - \mu)^2]\right\}, \qquad \theta = (\mu,\sigma^2).$$

If σ^2 is known, then

$$f(\mathbf{z} \mid \mu) \propto \exp\left[-\frac{n}{2\sigma^2}(\bar{z}-\mu)^2\right],$$

where the proportionality factor depends on $\bar{z}$ and n, but not on μ. Because $T(\mathbf{z}) = (\bar{z}, n)$ is sufficient for μ, a family of distributions that is conjugate with respect to the Gaussian location model consists of densities of the form

$$p(\mu;\gamma) \propto \exp\left[-\frac{1}{2\nu^2}(\mu-\bar{\mu})^2\right], \qquad \gamma = (\bar{\mu}, \nu^2),$$

namely the $\{\mathcal{N}(\bar{\mu}, \nu^2)\}$ family of distributions on the parameter space. The parameters of the prior density may in this case be interpreted as the values of the sample mean and variance for a preliminary sample of size from a $\mathcal{N}(\mu, \sigma^2)$ distribution. □

4.7.3 DIFFUSE PRIORS

Consider now the problem of selecting a *noninformative* prior distribution, that is, a prior distribution that represents an initial state of "complete ignorance" about the target parameter θ. In the case of a scalar parameter, Jeffreys (1961) proposed the following rule:

1. if θ can take any real value, then select as noninformative prior for θ the uniform distribution on the whole real line;
2. if θ can only take positive values, then select as noninformative prior for $\ln\theta$ a uniform distribution on the whole real line.

A uniform distribution on the whole real line is not a proper distribution because the integral of its density over the interval $(-\infty, \infty)$ is not finite. In a sense, Jeffreys is using ∞ rather than 1 to represent the probability of the sure event $\{-\infty < \theta < \infty\}$. Prior distributions of this type are called *improper*.

Box and Tiao (1973) interpret the use of an improper prior density as a local approximation to the behavior of a proper prior density that is *dominated* by the likelihood, that is, varies very little on the region of Θ where the likelihood is appreciable and assumes negligible values outside that region. Formally, a prior density p is dominated by the likelihood if

$$p(\theta \mid \mathbf{z}) = \frac{f(\mathbf{z} \mid \theta)\, p(\theta)}{\int_\Theta f(\mathbf{z} \mid t)\, p(t)\, dt} = \frac{f(\mathbf{z} \mid \theta)}{\int_\Theta f(\mathbf{z} \mid t)\, dt}.$$

Using improper priors to represent a state of complete ignorance raises yet another problem. If the prior distribution for a scalar parameter θ is uniform, then the distribution of $\ln\theta$, $1/\theta$, or any other nontrivial reparametrization $g(\theta)$ is not uniform in general. Not taking this into account and using the same uniform prior for alternative parametrizations of the model results in posterior distributions for θ which, although based on the same sample information and the same initial state of complete ignorance, are inconsistent with each other. Consistency requires that if, for some reason, one chooses $p(\theta)$ as prior density for θ and g is a continuously differentiable function, then the prior distribution of $\alpha = g(\theta)$ should satisfy

$$q(\alpha) = p(g^{-1}(\alpha)) \left|\frac{\partial\theta}{\partial\alpha}\right|.$$

To reduce the effects of the arbitrariness of the parametrization in terms of which a prior is assumed to be noninformative, Jeffreys (1961) introduced the following principle.

Jeffreys' invariance principle *The prior distribution of a scalar parameter θ is approximately noninformative if its density is proportional to the square root of the Fisher information on θ, that is, $p(\theta)$ is proportional to $\mathcal{I}(\theta)^{1/2}$.*

We now show that Jeffreys' invariance principle guarantees consistency between alternative parametrizations of the same model. First notice that the relationship between the Fisher information for the model parametrized by α and that for the model parametrized by θ is

$$\mathcal{I}(\alpha) = \mathrm{E}\left(\frac{\partial \ln f}{\partial \theta}\frac{\partial \theta}{\partial \alpha}\right)^2 = \mathcal{I}(\theta)\left(\frac{\partial \theta}{\partial \alpha}\right)^2 .$$

If the prior distributions of α and θ are chosen following Jeffreys' principle, then

$$q(\alpha) \propto \mathcal{I}(\alpha)^{1/2} = \mathcal{I}(\theta)^{1/2}\left|\frac{\partial \theta}{\partial \alpha}\right| \propto p(\theta)\left|\frac{\partial \theta}{\partial \alpha}\right| .$$

Consistency of the prior distributions in turn implies consistency of the posterior distributions corresponding to alternative parametrizations of the model.

Example 4.18 Given a sample from a $\mathcal{N}(\mu, \sigma^2)$ distribution, Jeffreys' invariance principle leads us to select a uniform prior for the conditional distribution of μ given σ, and a density proportional to σ^{-1} for the marginal distribution of σ. The latter is nothing but a uniform prior for $\ln \sigma$. □

4.7.4 THE BINOMIAL MODEL

To illustrate the Bayes method, suppose that one is interested in the probability θ of success in a single Bernoulli trial and one observes the number z of successes in n independent trials. In this case, an appropriate parametric model for the data is the family $\{\mathrm{Bi}(n, \theta), 0 < \theta < 1\}$ of binomial distributions. The prior distribution on the parameter space $\Theta = (0, 1)$ is represented by a $\mathcal{B}(a, b)$ distribution (Appendix C.5), whose mean and variance are

$$\mathrm{E}\,\theta = \frac{a}{a+b}, \qquad \mathrm{Var}\,\theta = \frac{ab}{(a+b)^2(a+b+1)}.$$

By Bayes theorem, the posterior density on Θ is

$$p(\theta \mid z) \propto \theta^{a+z-1}(1-\theta)^{b+n-z-1},$$

which corresponds to a $\mathcal{B}(a+z, b+n-z)$ distribution. Thus, the class of beta distributions forms a conjugate family with respect to the binomial model. The effect of the observed data on the uncertainty about θ is illustrated in Figure 38.

Figure 38 The solid curve is the density of a prior $\mathcal{B}(2,2)$ distribution for the probability of success θ in a single Bernoulli trial. The broken curve is the posterior $\mathcal{B}(3,6)$ density based on $z = 1$ successes in $n = 5$ independent trials. The prior mean and variance are equal to 1/2 and 1/20 respectively, whereas the posterior mean and variance are equal to 1/3 and 1/90 respectively.

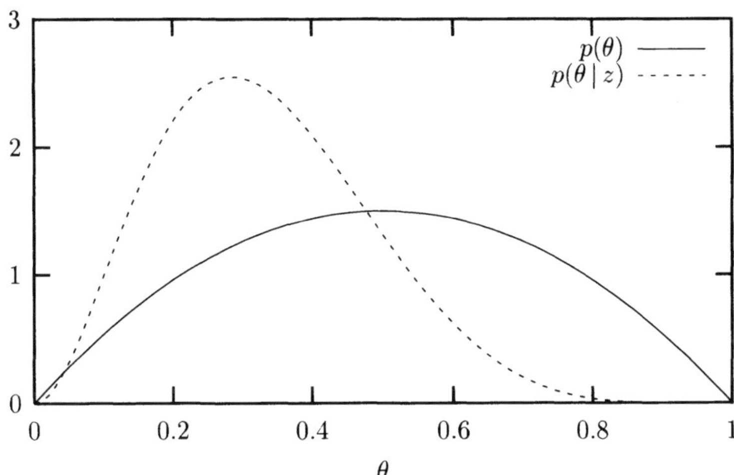

The posterior mean and variance of θ are

$$\mathrm{E}(\theta \mid z) = \frac{a+z}{n+a+b}, \qquad \mathrm{Var}(\theta \mid z) = \frac{(z+a)(n-z+b)}{(n+a+b)^2(n+a+b+1)}.$$

The posterior mean of θ is a convex combination of the prior mean and the fraction of "successes" z/n in the n trials, that is,

$$\mathrm{E}(\theta \mid z) = \lambda \, \mathrm{E}\, \theta + (1-\lambda)\frac{z}{n},$$

where $\lambda = (a+b)/(n+a+b)$ is a number between 0 and 1. In particular, if the sample fraction of successes is greater than the prior mean, then $\mathrm{E}(\theta \mid z) > E\theta$.

If z and n both tend to infinity at the same rate, then $\lambda \to 0$ and so $\mathrm{E}(\theta \mid z) \to z/n$ and $\mathrm{Var}(\theta \mid z) \to 0$, that is, the posterior distribution becomes more and more concentrated about the observed fraction of successes, which is the classical estimate of the success probability θ. From the Bayesian viewpoint, therefore, the classical result corresponds to the case when, because of the large sample size, the likelihood completely dominates the prior density.

If $a = b = 1$, then the prior density is uniform on the interval $(0, 1)$, while the posterior density becomes $p(\theta \mid z) \propto \theta^z (1-\theta)^{n-z}$. In this case, the posterior mean and variance are

$$\mathrm{E}(\theta \mid z) = \frac{z+1}{n+2}, \qquad \mathrm{Var}(\theta \mid z) = \frac{1}{n+3}\left(\frac{z}{n}\right)\left(1-\frac{z}{n}\right).$$

We get instead the classical results if a and b both tend to zero, that is, the prior distribution tends to $[\theta(1-\theta)]^{-1}$, corresponding to a uniform distribution on the whole real line for the logarithm of the odds-ratio, $\eta = \ln[\theta/(1-\theta)]$, which is the canonical parameter for the binomial model.

4.7.5 BAYES POINT ESTIMATES

Although the posterior distribution represents the complete solution to a Bayesian inference problem, point estimates of the parameter of interest are often required. Given a posterior density $p(\theta \,|\, \mathbf{z})$ on the parameter space Θ and a loss function $\ell(t,\theta)$, a *Bayes point estimate* is a parameter point $\hat{\theta} \in \Theta$ that minimizes the *posterior expected loss*, that is, the expected loss with respect to the posterior distribution given $\mathbf{Z} = \mathbf{z}$. Formally, a Bayes point estimate $\hat{\theta} = \hat{\theta}(\mathbf{z})$ is a solution to the problem

$$\min_{t \in \Theta} \int_{\Theta} \ell(t,\theta)\, p(\theta \,|\, \mathbf{z})\, d\theta,$$

provided that the integral is finite. Given the posterior density, a Bayes point estimate depends on the choice of loss function. For example, if $\ell(t,\theta) = (t-\theta)^2$ (quadratic loss), then $\hat{\theta}$ is the posterior mean of θ, whereas if $\ell(t,\theta) = |t-\theta|$ (absolute loss), then $\hat{\theta}$ is a posterior median. If the problem does not have an analytic solution, then numerical integration techniques can be used.

Example 4.19 Suppose that $\Theta = \Re$ and let $p(\theta \,|\, \mathbf{z}) \propto f(\mathbf{z} \,|\, \theta)$, that is, the prior distribution is noninformative. When the loss function is $\ell(t,\theta) = 1\{|t-\theta| \geq c\}$, where $c > 0$ is a sufficiently small number, a Bayes point estimate is a mode of the posterior distribution. Since a posterior mode is obtained by maximizing the likelihood $f(\mathbf{z} \,|\, \theta)$ with respect to θ, a Bayes point estimate coincides in this case with a ML estimate.

Under quadratic loss, a Bayes point estimate $\hat{\theta}$ is the mean of the posterior distribution, that is,

$$\hat{\theta} = \int_{\Re} \theta\, p(\theta \,|\, \mathbf{z})\, d\theta = \frac{\int_{\Re} \theta\, f(\mathbf{z} \,|\, \theta)\, d\theta}{\int_{\Re} f(\mathbf{z} \,|\, \theta)\, d\theta},$$

which is also known as the *Pitman estimate* of θ. If the family of distributions $\mathcal{F}_{\Theta}$ admits a sufficient statistic $T = T(\mathbf{z})$, that is, $f(\mathbf{z} \,|\, \theta) = g(T \,|\, \theta)\, h(\mathbf{z})$, where $h(\mathbf{z})$ does not depend on θ, then

$$\hat{\theta} = \frac{\int_{\Re} \theta\, g(T \,|\, \theta)\, d\theta}{\int_{\Re} g(T \,|\, \theta)\, d\theta},$$

that is, $\hat{\theta}$ is a function of the sufficient statistic T. □

The sampling properties of a Bayes estimator $\hat{\theta} = \hat{\theta}(\mathbf{Z})$ may be analyzed just like those of a classical estimator. In particular, for θ fixed, the risk associated with $\hat{\theta}$ is

$$r(\hat{\theta},\theta) = \int_{\mathcal{Z}} \ell(\hat{\theta}(\mathbf{z}),\theta)\, f(\mathbf{z} \,|\, \theta)\, d\mathbf{z}.$$

Since $f(\mathbf{z} \mid \theta)\, p(\theta) = p(\theta \mid \mathbf{z})\, f(\mathbf{z})$, integrating the risk of $\hat{\theta}$ with respect to the prior distribution over Θ gives the *Bayes risk of $\hat{\theta}$ relative to p*

$$\rho(\hat{\theta}, p) = \int_\Theta r(\hat{\theta}, \theta)\, p(\theta)\, d\theta = \int_\Theta \left[\int_\mathcal{Z} \ell(\hat{\theta}(\mathbf{z}), \theta)\, f(\mathbf{z} \mid \theta)\, d\mathbf{z}\right] p(\theta)\, d\theta$$
$$= \int_\mathcal{Z} \left[\int_\Theta \ell(\hat{\theta}(\mathbf{z}), \theta)\, p(\theta \mid \mathbf{z})\, d\theta\right] f(\mathbf{z})\, d\mathbf{z},$$

where we assumed regularity conditions sufficient to interchange the order of integration. Because the term in square brackets is the posterior expected loss $\hat{\theta}$ given $\mathbf{Z} = \mathbf{z}$, a Bayes estimator has, by definition, smallest Bayes risk among all estimators of θ.

4.7.6 THE GAUSSIAN LOCATION MODEL

Let $\mathbf{Z}$ be a random sample of size n from a $\mathcal{N}(\mu, \sigma^2)$ distribution with μ unknown and σ^2 known. The sample likelihood for this model is

$$f(\mathbf{Z} \mid \mu) \propto \exp\left[-\frac{n}{2}\left(\frac{\bar{Z} - \mu}{\sigma}\right)^2\right],$$

where the sample mean $\bar{Z}$ is a sufficient statistic for μ. If the prior density of μ is $\mathcal{N}(\bar{\mu}, \nu^2)$, then the posterior density of μ conditionally on the observed data is

$$p(\mu \mid \mathbf{Z}) \propto \exp\left\{-\frac{1}{2}\left[\left(\frac{\mu - \bar{\mu}}{\nu}\right)^2 + n\left(\frac{\bar{Z} - \mu}{\sigma}\right)^2\right]\right\}.$$

In order to evaluate the expression in square brackets we use the identity

$$A(z - a)^2 + B(z - b)^2 = (A + B)(z - c)^2 + \frac{AB}{A + B}(a - b)^2, \tag{4.14}$$

where $c = (Aa + Bb)/(A + B)$. Thus we obtain

$$\left(\frac{\mu - \bar{\mu}}{\nu}\right)^2 + n\left(\frac{\bar{Z} - \mu}{\sigma}\right)^2 = (h_0 + h_n)(\mu - \hat{\mu})^2 + d,$$

where $h_0 = 1/\nu^2$, $h_n = n/\sigma^2$, d is a constant that does not depend on μ, and

$$\hat{\mu} = \frac{1}{h_0 + h_n}(h_0 \bar{\mu} + h_n \bar{Z}).$$

The parameters h_0 and h_n, called the *prior* and *sample precision* respectively, are the reciprocal of the prior variance ν^2 and the sampling variance of $\bar{Z}$. Because d does not depend on μ, we have

$$p(\mu \mid \mathbf{Z}) \propto \exp\left[-\frac{1}{2}\left(\frac{\mu - \hat{\mu}}{\tau}\right)^2\right],$$

Figure 39 Risk of the sample mean $\bar{Z}$ and the posterior mean $\hat{\mu}$ given $n = 4$ observations from a $\mathcal{N}(0, 1)$ distribution, with a prior $\mathcal{N}(0, 1)$ distribution for μ.

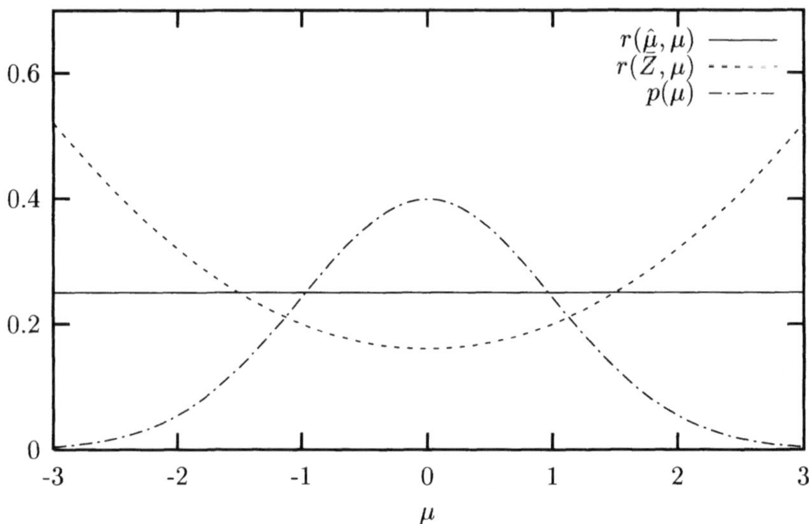

where $\tau^2 = (h_0 + h_n)^{-1}$, that is, the posterior distribution of μ is $\mathcal{N}(\hat{\mu}, \tau^2)$. Notice that the posterior mean $\hat{\mu}$ may be written $\hat{\mu} = \lambda\bar{\mu} + (1-\lambda)\bar{Z}$, where $\lambda = h_0/(h_0 + h_n)$ is a number between 0 and 1. Thus, the posterior mean $\hat{\mu}$ is a convex combination of the prior mean $\bar{\mu}$ and the sample mean $\bar{Z}$, with weights equal to their relative precision. Also notice that the posterior precision $1/\tau^2$ is just the sum of the prior and the sample precision.

The posterior mean $\hat{\mu}$ is the Bayes estimator under a quadratic loss function. In fact, because the posterior distribution of μ is Gaussian, $\hat{\mu}$ is the Bayes estimator for every symmetric and convex loss function. If $\lambda \to 0$ or, equivalently, $h_0/h_n \to 0$, then the posterior mean tends to the sample mean. This occurs in two cases. The first is when the sample size n is fixed and $h_0 \to 0$, that is, the prior information on μ becomes more and more vague. The second is when ν^2 is fixed and $n \to \infty$. These results are not surprising because in both cases the prior density is completely dominated by the likelihood. Thus, the sample mean may be viewed either as a Bayes estimator relative to a noninformative prior or as the limit, as $n \to \infty$, of a sequence of Bayes estimators relative to a proper prior.

Because $\bar{Z} \sim \mathcal{N}(\mu, \sigma^2/n)$, the risk associated with the posterior mean $\hat{\mu}$ under the quadratic loss function is

$$r(\hat{\mu}, \mu) = \mathrm{E}(\mu - \hat{\mu})^2 = \lambda^2(\mu - \bar{\mu})^2 + (1-\lambda)^2\,\frac{\sigma^2}{n},$$

and assumes its minimum of $(1-\lambda)^2/h_n$ when μ is equal to the prior mean $\bar{\mu}$. The expectation of $r(\hat{\mu}, \mu)$ with respect to the prior distribution, or Bayes risk of $\hat{\mu}$, is

$$\rho(\hat{\mu}) = \lambda^2\nu^2 + (1-\lambda)^2\,\frac{\sigma^2}{n} = \frac{1}{h_0 + h_n}.$$

The risk associated with the sample mean is instead

$$r(\bar{Z},\mu) = \mathrm{E}(\mu - \bar{Z})^2 = \frac{\sigma^2}{n} = \frac{1}{h_n}.$$

The risk of these two estimators is shown in Figure 39. Since $r(\bar{Z},\mu)$ is constant, it coincides with the Bayes risk $\rho(\bar{Z})$ of the sample mean. Hence $\rho(\bar{Z}) \geq \rho(\hat{\mu})$, with equality only if $h_0/h_n = 0$. Although there are regions in the parameter space where the sample mean has a smaller risk than the Bayes estimator, these regions receive very low prior probability.

4.8 STATISTICAL DECISION PROBLEMS

The theory of statistical decisions provides a general formulation of the problem of finding inference procedures with desirable properties. Despite its relatively abstract character, such a formulation has two advantages. On the one hand, it makes it possible to treat in a unified way the problems of statistical estimation and hypothesis testing. On the other hand, its reliance on classical noncooperative game theory and the Pareto criterion should make it quite natural for a public of economists.

4.8.1 STATISTICAL GAMES

The theory of statistical decisions represents the statistical problem as a sequential noncooperative game between two players: the statistician and chance or *Nature*. Nature moves first by choosing both a point θ in a state space Θ and a sample $\mathbf{z}$, that is, a realization of a random variable (vector) $\mathbf{Z}$ which takes values in a probability space $(\mathcal{Z}, \mathcal{B}, P_\theta)$. A point θ is also called a state. Then, after observing $\mathbf{z}$ but not knowing θ, the statistician chooses an action a out of a set $\mathcal{A}$ of available actions.

A parametric estimation problem corresponds to the case when Θ is a finite-dimensional Euclidean space and $\mathcal{A} = \Theta$. Classical hypothesis testing, discussed in Chapter 5, corresponds instead to the case when Θ and $\mathcal{A}$ consist only of two points: given a hypothesis H_0, the elements of Θ are the events "H_0 is true" and "H_0 is false", while the elements of $\mathcal{A}$ are the actions "reject H_0" and "do not reject H_0".

In deciding on how to move, the statistician evaluates the consequences of every available action on the basis of a loss function ℓ defined on $\mathcal{A} \times \Theta$. The function ℓ is non-negative and normalized in such a way that, given a state $\theta \in \Theta$, there always exists an action $a(\theta) \in \mathcal{A}$ for which $\ell(a(\theta), \theta) = 0$. Given an action $a \in \mathcal{A}$ and a state θ, the loss to the statistician is a number $\ell(a, \theta)$ that is interpreted as the negative utility she obtains from the game. A *statistical decision problem* is a triple $(\Theta, \mathcal{A}, \ell)$ associated with the chance experiment represented by the random vector $\mathbf{Z}$, whose probability distribution P_θ depends on the state θ.

In addition to the game form just described, called *extensive form*, a statistical decision problem has another equivalent representation. Since the action of the statistician depends in general on the observed sample, varying $\mathbf{z}$ gives a *decision function* δ: $\mathcal{Z} \to \mathcal{A}$, which specifies what action the statistician will choose for each of the possible samples. Thus, the statistician's problem becomes one of selecting, before actually observing the data, a decision function d (for example, an estimator of θ). Given a decision function d, the loss is now represented by the random variable

$\ell(d(\mathbf{Z}), \theta)$. For a fixed $\theta \in \Theta$, one may associate with a decision function d the non-negative number

$$r(d, \theta) = \int_{\mathcal{Z}} \ell(d(\mathbf{z}), \theta)\, f(\mathbf{z} \,|\, \theta)\, d\mathbf{z},$$

where $f(\mathbf{z} \,|\, \theta)$ is the conditional density of $\mathbf{Z}$ given θ. The number $r(d, \theta)$ is called the expected loss or *risk* of d conditional on θ. In what follows, we shall confine ourselves to the class $\mathcal{D}$ of decision functions for which the risk $r(d, \theta)$ is well defined for all $\theta \in \Theta$. In this case, varying θ over Θ gives a non-negative function $r(d, \cdot)$, defined on Θ and called the *risk function* of d, which represents the negative utility of the statistician when d is the decision function selected. The extensive form $(\Theta, \mathcal{A}, \ell)$ of the game can now be replaced by the new form $(\Theta, \mathcal{D}, r)$, called the *normal form*, where r is a non-negative function defined on $\mathcal{D} \times \Omega$ and the structure of $\mathcal{D}$ and r depend on $\mathcal{A}$, ℓ and the distribution of $\mathbf{Z}$.

In both game forms, the strategy set of Nature is the state space Θ. The strategy set of the statistician is the set $\mathcal{A}$ of actions in the extensive form of the game, and the set $\mathcal{D}$ of decision functions in the normal form. The problem for the statistician is to choose a "best" strategy, either an action or a decision function.

Notice that in the extensive form of the game the statistician need not plan ahead what the best action should be for each possible sample. It is enough that she chooses the best action given the particular sample $\mathbf{z}$ at hand. This consideration is of a certain importance in cases where the statistician cannot repeat or has no control over the chance experiment that generated the data.

4.8.2 THE MINIMAX AND BAYES PRINCIPLES

Uniformly best strategies for the statistican, that is, strategies that are best for all $\theta \in \Theta$, do not exist in general. The reason is essentially the same as why no uniformly minimum MSE estimator exists, namely the fact that, given a state θ_0 and an action a such that $\ell(a, \theta_0) > 0$, one can always find an action a_0 such that $\ell(a_0, \theta_0) = 0$.

To circumvent this problem, two general methods have been proposed. The first method consists of restricting the strategy set to a smaller class of strategies which satisfy certain requirements, such as unbiasedness. The second method consists of introducing some principle for ordering strategies. Two such principles are the minimax and the Bayes principles. Both lead to a complete ordering of the statistician's strategy set.

The minimax principle assumes that the statistician has no prior knowledge of the state θ chosen by Nature. The statistician is supposed to proceed in the following way. First she considers, for all $\theta \in \Theta$, the maximal loss that results from each strategy. She then selects a strategy that gives the smallest maximal loss. Such a strategy, called *minimax*, has the feature of preparing the statistician against all conceivable states, particularly the worst.

Definition 4.4 A decision function $d_0 \in \mathcal{D}$ is said to be *minimax* if

$$\sup_{\theta \in \Theta} r(d_0, \theta) = \inf_{d \in \mathcal{D}} \sup_{\theta \in \Theta} r(d, \theta),$$

where the number on the right-hand side is called the *minimax* or *upper value* of the game. □

Thus, a decision function d_0 is minimax if and only if $r(d_0, \theta') \leq \sup_{\theta \in \Theta} r(d, \theta)$ for all $d \in \mathcal{D}$ and every $\theta' \in \Theta$. The definition of a minimax action is completely analogous. There are situations where a minimax strategy does not exist or is not unique. Methods for finding a minimax strategy are discussed, for example, in Ferguson (1967). One of them is presented in Theorem 4.16 below.

The second principle assumes that there is pre-play information available to the statistician. Formally, Nature is supposed to follow a mixed strategy, that is, choose θ randomly according to a probability distribution defined on Θ. Nature's mixed strategy is assumed to be known to the statistician, for whom it represents a prior distribution on Θ. For simplicity, we shall consider the case when such a distribution is absolutely continuous with density function p.

In the normal form of the game, the statistician is assumed to know only the mixed strategy p chosen by Nature. She exploits this information by computing the expected loss or *Bayes risk* resulting from any available decision function d, where the Bayes risk of d relative to the prior density p is defined as

$$\rho(d, p) = \int_\Theta r(d, \theta)\, p(\theta)\, d\theta.$$

She then selects a decision function that minimizes Bayes risk.

Definition 4.5 A decision function $d_0 \in \mathcal{D}$ is said to be *Bayes relative to a prior density p on Θ* if

$$\rho(d_0, p) = \inf_{d \in \mathcal{D}} \rho(d, p),$$

where the number on the right-hand side is called the *minimum Bayes risk.* □

In the extensive form of the game, besides knowing the mixed strategy p followed by Nature, the statistician observes a sample $\mathbf{z}$. She first combines the prior and the sample information on θ by computing the posterior density $p(\theta \mid \mathbf{z})$. She then selects an action that minimizes the posterior expected loss or *posterior Bayes risk*

$$\varrho(a, p(\cdot \mid \mathbf{z})) = \int_\Theta \ell(a, \theta)\, p(\theta \mid \mathbf{z})\, d\theta.$$

Definition 4.6 An action $a_0 \in \mathcal{A}$ is said to be *Bayes relative to a posterior density $p(\theta \mid \mathbf{z})$ on Θ* if $\varrho(a_0, p(\cdot \mid \mathbf{z})) = \inf_{a \in \mathcal{A}} \varrho(a, p(\cdot \mid \mathbf{z}))$. □

Of course, Bayes strategies need not exist nor, if they exist, be unique. However, if Bayes solutions to both the normal and the extensive form of the game exist, then they are essentially equivalent.

Theorem 4.15 *For d_0 to be a Bayes decision function relative to a prior density p, it is enough that $d_0(\mathbf{z}) = a_0$ for almost every $\mathbf{z} \in \mathcal{Z}$, where a_0 is a Bayes action relative to the posterior density $p(\cdot \mid \mathbf{z})$.*

Proof. Consider minimizing

$$\rho(d, p) = \int_\Theta r(d, \theta)\, p(\theta)\, d\theta = \int_\Theta \left[\int_{\mathcal{Z}} \ell(d(\mathbf{z}), \theta)\, f(\mathbf{z} \mid \theta)\, d\mathbf{z} \right] p(\theta)\, d\theta$$

over the class $\mathcal{D}$ of decision functions. Since $f(\mathbf{z}\,|\,\theta)p(\theta) = p(\theta\,|\,\mathbf{z})f(\mathbf{z})$, we have

$$\rho(d,p) = \int_{\mathcal{Z}} \left[\int_{\Theta} \ell(a,\theta)\, p(\theta\,|\,\mathbf{z})\, d\theta\right] f(\mathbf{z})\, d\mathbf{z} = \int_{\mathcal{Z}} \varrho(a, p(\cdot\,|\,\mathbf{z}))\, f(\mathbf{z})\, d\mathbf{z},$$

where we assumed regularity conditions sufficient to allow interchanging the order of integration. To minimize $\rho(d,p)$ with respect to d it is therefore enough to minimize $\varrho(a, p(\cdot\,|\,z))$ with respect to a for almost every $\mathbf{z} \in \mathcal{Z}$. □

One important advantage of the Bayes principle over the minimax or other principles is that it often leads to solutions that are relatively easy to compute.

When is a Bayes strategy minimax? A minimax strategy, by minimizing the maximum risk, tries to do as well as possible in the worst case. One might therefore expect a minimax strategy to be Bayes relative to the prior distribution on Θ that causes the statistician the greatest Bayes risk.

Definition 4.7 A prior density p_0 on Θ is said to be *least favorable* if

$$\inf_{d\in\mathcal{D}} \rho(d, p_0) = \sup_{p} \inf_{d\in\mathcal{D}} \rho(d,p),$$

where the number on the right-hand side is called the *maximin* or *lower value* of the game. □

A density p_0 is least favorable if and only if, for all prior densities p,

$$\inf_{d\in\mathcal{D}} \rho(d, p_0) \geq \inf_{d\in\mathcal{D}} \rho(d,p).$$

Theorem 4.16 *Let d_0 be a Bayes decision function relative to the prior density p_0. If d_0 is such that $\rho(d_0,p_0) = \sup_{\theta\in\Theta} r(d_0,\theta)$, then d_0 is minimax and p_0 is the least favorable prior density. If d_0 is unique, then it is also the unique minimax decision function.*

Proof. For every $d \in \mathcal{D}$

$$\sup_{\theta\in\Theta} r(d,\theta) \geq \rho(d,p_0) \geq \rho(d_0,p_0) = \sup_{\theta\in\Theta} r(d_0,\theta).$$

Hence d_0 is minimax. If d_0 is unique, then the second inequality is strict. Finally, since

$$\inf_{d\in\mathcal{D}} \rho(d,p) \leq \rho(d_0,p) \leq \sup_{\theta\in\Theta} r(d_0,\theta) = \rho(d_0,p_0)$$

for every other prior p, p_0 is least favorable. □

Theorem 4.16 may be generalized to the case when a decision function d_0 can be represented as the limit, as $n \to \infty$, of a sequence $\{d_n\}$ of Bayes decision functions relative to prior distributions of the proper type.

Theorem 4.17 *Let d_0 be the limit, as $n \to \infty$, of a sequence $\{d_n\}$ of Bayes decision functions relative to a sequence $\{p_n\}$ of prior densities on Θ. If $\rho(d_n,p_n) \to c$ as $n \to \infty$ and $r(d_0,\theta) \leq c$ for all $\theta \in \Theta$, then d_0 is minimax.*

Proof. If $d \in \mathcal{D}$ is any other decision function then, for every n,

$$\sup_{\theta \in \Theta} r(d, \theta) \geq \rho(d, p_n) \geq \rho(d_n, p_n).$$

Taking the limit as $n \to \infty$ gives that $\sup_{\theta \in \Theta} r(d, \theta) \geq c \geq \sup_{\theta \in \Theta} r(d_0, \theta)$. □

An important special case where the conditions of Theorems 4.16 or 4.17 are satisfied is when d_0 has constant risk, that is, $r(d_0, \theta) = c$ for all $\theta \in \Theta$. Thus, if a decision function with constant risk is Bayes or is the limit, as $n \to \infty$, of Bayes decision functions relative to a sequence of proper priors, then it is minimax.

Example 4.20 Let $\bar{Z}$ be the sample mean of a random sample of size n from a $\mathcal{N}(\mu, \sigma^2)$ distribution with $\mu \in \Re$ unknown and σ^2 known. The risk of $\bar{Z}$ under the quadratic loss function is $r(\bar{Z}, \mu) = \mathrm{E}(\mu - \bar{Z})^2 = \sigma^2/n$. Because the risk of $\bar{Z}$ does not depend on μ, it coincides with the Bayes risk. We have seen in Section 4.7.6 that the sample mean is the limit, as $n \to \infty$, of Bayes decision functions relative to a sequence of proper priors. Hence $\bar{Z}$ is minimax. □

4.8.3 THE COMPLETE CLASS THEOREM

We first introduce a weak principle of optimality that corresponds to the classical Pareto criterion.

Definition 4.8 Let r be a risk function defined on $\mathcal{D} \times \Theta$. A decision function $d \in \mathcal{D}$ is said to be *strictly dominated* by another decision function $d_0 \in \mathcal{D}$ if $r(d, \theta) \geq r(d_0, \theta)$ for all $\theta \in \Theta$, with strict inequality for some $\theta \in \Theta$. A decision function $d \in \mathcal{D}$ is said to be *admissible* if it is not strictly dominated by another decision function in $\mathcal{D}$. A subset $D \subset \mathcal{D}$ of decision functions is said to form a *complete class* if every decision function $d \in \mathcal{D} - D$ is strictly dominated by one in D. A complete class D is said to be *minimal* if no proper subset of D is a complete class. □

Thus, a minimal complete class coincides with the class of decision functions that are admissible, that is, cannot be dominated in the sense of Pareto. Because of this, there is no disadvantage in restricting attention to a minimal complete class.

We now show that, under appropriate conditions, a Bayes decision function is admissible. This result represents an important justification for Bayes methods. In this section we shall consider two cases. The first case is straightforward.

Theorem 4.18 *Given a prior distribution, if a Bayes decision function is unique, then it is admissible.*

The second case is when the state space is a finite set $\Theta = \{\theta_1, \ldots, \theta_m\}$. In this case, the risk function associated with a decision function d may be represented by an m-vector $r(d) = (r_1(d), \ldots, r_m(d))$, where $r_j(d) = r(d, \theta_j)$. The set $\mathcal{R} = \{r(d)\colon d \in \mathcal{D}\}$ of all risk functions is a subset of $\Re^m$. It can be shown that if $\mathcal{R}$ is closed and bounded below, then any point on its lower boundary is an admissible decision function.

A prior distribution on the finite set Θ may also be represented as an m-vector $p = (p_1, \ldots, p_m)$, where p_j is the prior probability assigned to the state θ_j. The vector

p represents a valid assignment of probabilities to the elements of Θ if all its elements are non-negative and such that $\sum_j p_j = 1$. Given a decision function d and a prior distribution p, the Bayes risk $\rho(d, p) = p^\top r(d)$ is the value of the hyperplane through the point $r(d)$ with normal equal to p.

Theorem 4.19 *Let Θ be a finite state space and let p be a prior distribution on Θ such that $p_j > 0$ for all $j = 1, \ldots, m$. If $d_0 \in \mathcal{D}$ is a Bayes decision function relative to p, then it is admissible.*

Proof. Suppose, on the contrary, that d_0 is inadmissible. Then there exists a decision function $d \in \mathcal{D}$ such that $r_j(d) \leq r_j(d_0)$ for all $j = 1, \ldots, m$, and $r_j(d) < r_j(d_0)$ for some j. Since $p_j > 0$ for all j, we have

$$\rho(d, p) = \sum_j p_j r_j(d) < \sum_j p_j r_j(d_0) = \rho(d_0, p),$$

which is a contradiction. □

The converse of Theorem 4.19 is the following.

Theorem 4.20 *If d_0 is an admissible decision and Θ is a finite state space, then d_0 is a Bayes decision function relative to a proper prior distribution on Θ.*

Proof. See Ferguson (1967), Theorem 2.10.1. □

The next theorem gives conditions under which the class of Bayes decision functions is minimal complete.

Theorem 4.21 (Complete class theorem) *If Θ is a finite set and the set $\mathcal{R} = \{r(d)\colon d \in \mathcal{D}\}$ is closed and bounded below, then the class of Bayes decision functions is complete and the class of admissible Bayes decision functions is minimal complete.*

Proof. See Ferguson (1967), Section 2.10. □

BIBLIOGRAPHIC NOTES

On the concept of Fisher consistency see Cox and Hinkley (1974). For a detailed discussion of statistical estimation based on the analogy principle see Vapnik (1982) and Manski (1988a, 1994). Standard references for the classical theory of point estimation are Cox and Hinkley (1974) and Lehmann (1983).

Estimation of conditional quantiles by least absolute deviations was first proposed by Koenker and Bassett (1978). On efficient algorithms for estimating quantile regression models see Koenker and d'Orey (1987).

For a thorough discussion of the concepts of sufficiency and UMVU see Lehmann (1983). On the comparison of estimators using criteria other than MSE see Keating, Mason and Sen (1993).

The classical proof of the consistency of the ML estimator goes back to Wald (1949). A general reference for the results in Section 4.6 is Ferguson (1996). These results may be generalized along several directions. First, one may relax the assumption that the log-likelihood is smooth. A general method is discussed in Chapter 15. Further, Theorems 4.13 and 4.14 may be generalized to the case of observations that are independent but not identically distributed (Hoadley 1971) or dependent (Crowder 1976). In both cases, a crucial condition is that the expected total information must become arbitrarily large as $n \to \infty$.

Classical introductions to Bayes methods are Zellner (1971), Lindley (1972) and Box and Tiao (1973). Zellner (1988) presents an interesting interpretation of Bayes theorem as an optimal rule for information processing.

Wald (1950) was the first to point out the close connection between game theory and statistical theory. The proof of the complete class theorem for the case when the parameter space is discrete may be found in Ferguson (1967). A very general complete class theorem may be found in LeCam (1986).

PROBLEMS

4.1 Prove Theorem 4.1.

4.2 Given n consecutive observations on a stationary time series $\{Z_t\}$, let $\hat{\gamma}_h = n^{-1}\sum_{t=1}^{n-h}(Z_t - \bar{Z})(Z_{t+h} - \bar{Z})$. Show that the associated sample autocovariance matrix $\hat{\Gamma}_n$ is n.d.d., and is nonsingular if $\hat{\gamma}_0 > 0$.

4.3 Given n consecutive observations on a stationary time series $\{Z_t\}$ with mean zero, let $\tilde{\gamma}_h = (n-h)^{-1}\sum_{t=1}^{n-h} Z_t Z_{t+h}$. Show that the associated sample autocovariance matrix $\tilde{\Gamma}_n$ need not be n.n.d.

4.4 (Percival 1993) Given n consecutive observations on a stationary time series $\{Z_t\}$, let $\gamma_0 = \operatorname{Var} Z_t$ and $\tilde{\gamma}_0 = n^{-1}\sum_t (Z_t - \bar{Z})$. Show that $0 \leq \mathrm{E}\,\tilde{\gamma}_0 \leq \gamma_0$.

4.5 Use Bartlett's formula to approximate the sampling variances and covariances of sample autocorrelations from a stable AR(1) process.

4.6 Use Bartlett's formula to approximate the sampling variances and covariances of sample autocorrelations from an MA(1) process.

4.7 Derive MM estimates of the parameters of MA(2) and ARMA(1,1) processes.

4.8 Show that if $\hat{\theta}$ is a ML estimate of θ, then $\hat{\alpha} = g(\hat{\theta})$ is a ML estimate of $\alpha = g(\theta)$.

4.9 Given a sample from a $\mathcal{N}(\mu, \sigma^2)$ distribution, show that the sample log-likelihood is concave over the region of the parameter space for which $\sigma^2 < 2\hat{\sigma}^2$, where $\hat{\sigma}^2$ is the sample mean squared deviation.

4.10 Consider the problem of estimating the parameter ϕ of the Gaussian AR(1) model. Let $\hat{\pi}$, $\tilde{\phi}$ and $\bar{\phi}$ denote, respectively, the unconditional LS estimate, the conditional LS estimate and that obtained by solving the Yule–Walker equations. Show that $|\bar{\phi}| \leq 1$ and $\hat{\pi} \geq \tilde{\phi} \geq \bar{\phi}$.

4.11 Write down the sample log-likelihood of the Gaussian AR(p) model and derive the unconditional and the conditional LS estimates. Compare these estimates with those obtained by solving the Yule–Walker equations.

4.12 Show that if the sample log-likelihood is quadratic, that is, of the form (4.9) where Q is a p.d. matrix, then the Newton–Raphson algorithm converges to the ML estimate in one iteration, no matter what the starting point is.

4.13 Show that, if the parametric model belongs to a linear exponential family in canonical form, then the Newton–Raphson and the scoring algorithm coincide.

4.14 Let Z be the indicator of success in a Bernoulli trial with probability of success π. Show that $\hat{\theta} = Z$ is the unique unbiased estimator of π.

4.15 Let $Z_1, \ldots, Z_n$ be indicators of success in n independent Bernoulli trials with probability of success π. Show that there exists no unbiased estimator of the logarithm of the odds-ratio $\theta = \ln[\pi/(1-\pi)]$.

4.16 An estimator $\hat{\theta}$ with a continuous sampling distribution is called *median unbiased* for a parameter θ if $\Pr_\theta\{\hat{\theta} \leq \theta\} = \Pr_\theta\{\hat{\theta} \geq \theta\}$ for every θ. This property is distinct from (mean) unbiasedness. Assume that $Z \sim \mathcal{E}(\lambda)$ and show that:

(i) although $\hat{\theta} = Z$ is (mean) unbiased for $\theta = 1/\lambda$, it is not median unbiased;
(ii) although $\tilde{\theta} = Z/(\ln 2)$ is median unbiased for $\theta = 1/\lambda$, it is not (mean) unbiased.

4.17 Suppose that $Z \sim \mathcal{P}(\lambda)$ and consider the problem of estimating the parameter $\theta = \exp(-3\lambda)$. Show that $\hat{\theta} = (-2)^Z$ is unbiased for θ and discuss whether this is a reasonable estimator.

4.18 Show that, if a parametric model admits a sufficient statistic T and the ML estimate of θ is unique, then it must be a function of T.

4.19 Given a sample $Z_1, \ldots, Z_n$ from an exponential distribution with density

$$f(z;\tau) = \frac{1}{\tau} e^{-z/\tau}, \qquad z \geq 0,$$

show that the ML estimator of τ is unbiased. Compute its sampling variance and compare it with the Cramér–Rao lower bound.

4.20 Given a sample $Z_1, \ldots, Z_n$ from an $\mathcal{E}(\theta)$ distribution, determine the Cramér–Rao lower bound for an unbiased estimator of θ. As an estimator of θ, consider the statistic $\hat{\theta} = (n-1)/(\sum_i Z_i)$. Is it sufficient for θ? Is it unbiased for θ? Determine whether $\hat{\theta}$ attains the Cramér–Rao bound.

4.21 Let Z be a random variable with a $\mathrm{Bi}(n, \theta)$ distribution, where $0 < \theta < 1$. Use Jeffreys' invariance principle to select a noninformative prior distribution for θ. Compute the posterior distribution of θ and compare the properties of the posterior mean and mode of θ with the sampling properties of the classical estimator of θ.

4.22 Let the observed data consist of sample frequencies $z = (z_1, \ldots, z_J)$, with $z_j = 0, 1, \ldots, n$ and $\sum_j z_j = n$. As a model for the data consider the family of multinomial distributions with density

$$f(z;\theta) \propto \prod_{j=1}^{J} \theta_j^{z_j}, \qquad \theta = (\theta_1, \ldots, \theta_J),$$

where $0 \leq \theta_j \leq 1$ and $\sum_j \theta_j = 1$. Let the prior distribution on the parameter space be a *Dirichlet distribution*, with density

$$p(\theta) = \frac{\Gamma(\sum_j \beta_j)}{\prod_j \Gamma(\beta_j)} \prod_{i=j}^{J} \theta_j^{\beta_j - 1},$$

and mean

$$\mathrm{E}\,\theta_j = \frac{\beta_j}{\sum_{i=1}^{J} \beta_i}, \qquad j = 1, \ldots, J,$$

where Γ is the gamma function (Appendix C.5) and $\beta_j > 0$ for all j. This family of distributions generalizes the beta family. Show that the Dirichlet family is conjugate with respect to the multinomial model and compute the posterior mean of θ_j.

5

Statistical Accuracy and Hypothesis Testing

Given an estimate $\hat{\theta}$ of a parameter of interest θ, two problems often arise. The first is assessing the accuracy of our estimate of θ. The second is determining whether or not certain hypotheses about θ are inconsistent with the sample evidence.

5.1 ASSESSING VARIABILITY AND BIAS

Important measures of the statistical accuracy of an estimator are its sampling variability and its bias. The most common measure of an estimator's sampling variability is its sampling variance, either the exact one or some large sample approximation to it. In the scalar case, the (positive) square root of an estimator's sampling variance is called its *standard error*. The most common measure of the bias of an estimator $\hat{\theta}$ is the difference $\operatorname{Bias}\hat{\theta} = \mathrm{E}\,\hat{\theta} - \theta$, where θ is the target parameter.

5.1.1 *ASSESSING VARIABILITY*

Except in special cases, the sampling variance of an estimator $\hat{\theta}$ depends on unknown parameters and must therefore be estimated. The classical approach relies on knowledge of the form of $\operatorname{Var}\hat{\theta}$. We shall distinguish two cases.

The first case is when $\hat{\theta}$ is a ML estimator. Recall from Theorem 4.14 that if $Z_1, \ldots, Z_n$ is a large sample from a distribution whose density $f(z; \theta_0)$ belongs to a regular parametric family then, under some conditions, the sampling variance of $\hat{\theta}$ is well approximated by $n\mathcal{I}(\theta_0)$, where $\mathcal{I}(\theta_0)$ is the Fisher information on θ evaluated at the true parameter θ_0. Thus, if the assumed parametric model is correctly specified, the problem of estimating $\operatorname{Var}\hat{\theta}$ reduces to the problem of estimating $\mathcal{I}(\theta_0)$.

One possibility is the "plug-in" estimator obtained by evaluating the Fisher information matrix at $\hat{\theta}$. A second possibility is to estimate $\mathcal{I}(\theta_0)$ by the sample variance of the score evaluated at $\hat{\theta}$, that is, $\hat{\mathcal{I}} = n^{-1} \sum_i s_i(\hat{\theta}) s_i(\hat{\theta})^\top$. A third possibility exploits the fact that, by the information equality, $\mathcal{I}(\theta_0) = -\mathrm{E}[n^{-1} L''(\theta_0)]$, where $L''(\theta)$ is the Hessian of the log-likelihood. Dispensing with the expectation operator, $\mathcal{I}(\theta_0)$ may then be estimated by the observed information $\tilde{\mathcal{I}} = -n^{-1} L''(\hat{\theta})$. When the parametric model is correctly specified, all three estimators can be shown to be consistent for $\mathcal{I}(\theta_0)$. This result, however, does not provide a basis for choosing between the various alternatives. In practice, the choice largely depends on computational ease, with more refined asymptotic arguments also playing some role. On the basis of these arguments, the third estimator is usually considered as more precise than the other two (Efron & Hinkley 1978).

The second case is when $\hat{\theta}$ can be represented as $\hat{\theta} = h(T)$, where T is a vector-valued statistic with mean μ and variance Σ, and there exists an unbiased (or consistent) estimator $\hat{\Sigma}$ of Σ. If h is a linear function, that is, $h(T) = CT$ for some matrix C, then the sampling variance of $\hat{\theta}$ may be estimated unbiasedly (or consistently) by $\widehat{\operatorname{Var}}\,\hat{\theta} = C\hat{\Sigma}C^\top$.

When the function h is nonlinear but sufficiently smooth over a region that contains most of the probability distribution of T, then one may approximate $\hat{\theta}$ by a linear function of T and the sampling variance of $\hat{\theta}$ by the sampling variance of this linear approximation. This method is known as the *delta method.* Specifically, if h is differentiable in a neighborhood of μ with first derivative $h'(\mu)$ at μ, then a first-order Taylor series expansion about μ gives

$$h(t) \approx h(\mu) + h'(\mu)^\top (t - \mu).$$

Hence, to a first approximation,

$$\operatorname{Var}\hat{\theta} \approx h'(\mu)^\top \Sigma\, h'(\mu).$$

One may then estimate the sampling variance of $\hat{\theta}$ by replacing μ with T and Σ with its estimate $\hat{\Sigma}$. For a precise statement of the necessary regularity conditions, see e.g. Oehlert (1992).

Example 5.1 Let $\hat{\theta} = T_1/T_2$, where

$$\mathrm{E}\begin{pmatrix} T_1 \\ T_2 \end{pmatrix} = \begin{pmatrix} \mu_1 \\ \mu_2 \end{pmatrix}, \qquad \operatorname{Var}\begin{pmatrix} T_1 \\ T_2 \end{pmatrix} = \begin{bmatrix} \sigma_1^2 & \sigma_{12} \\ \sigma_{12} & \sigma_2^2 \end{bmatrix},$$

with $\mu_2 \neq 0$. For example, $\hat{\theta}$ may be the empirical correlation coefficient between two random variables X and Y, or the estimated slope of the regression of Y on X. If $\mu_2 \neq 0$, then

$$h'(\mu) = \begin{pmatrix} 1/\mu_2 \\ -\mu_1/\mu_2^2 \end{pmatrix}, \qquad \mu = (\mu_1, \mu_2).$$

Hence, to a first approximation,

$$\operatorname{Var}\hat{\theta} \approx \frac{\sigma_1^2}{\mu_2^2} - 2\sigma_{12}\frac{\mu_1}{\mu_2^3} + \sigma_2^2\,\frac{\mu_1^2}{\mu_2^4}.$$

One may now estimate the sampling variance of $\hat{\theta}$ replacing μ_j by T_j, $j = 1, 2$, and σ_1^2, σ_2^2 and σ_{12} by appropriate estimates. □

Despite its conceptual simplicity, the delta method may lead to very complicated calculations. As a result, classical econometric and statistical theory have traditionally focused on a rather limited class of problems for which relatively tractable results are available. Things have changed substantially in the last two decades due to the introduction of a variety of computer-based methods for assessing the accuracy of an estimator. The payoff from these methods is a considerable increase in the type of statistical problems that can be analyzed, a reduction in the assumptions required, and the elimination of routine but tedious theoretical calculations. The two basic methods are presented in the next sections.

5.1.2 THE NONPARAMETRIC BOOTSTRAP

Let $\mathbf{Z} = (Z_1, \ldots, Z_n)$ be a sample from a distribution with distribution function F, let $\hat\theta = \hat\theta(\mathbf{Z})$ be an estimator that does not depend on the order in which the observations are arranged, and let the precision of $\hat\theta$ be measured by its sampling variance, which we write as $\sigma^2(F) = \operatorname{Var}_F \hat\theta$ to stress its dependence on the parent distribution function F.

If F is unknown, then the analogy principle suggests estimating $\sigma^2(F)$ by replacing F with some estimate. When F is estimated by the empirical distribution function $\hat F$, the resulting estimate of $\sigma^2(F)$ is $\sigma^2(\hat F) = \operatorname{Var}_{\hat F} \hat\theta$. Because $\hat F$ is a nonparametric estimate of F, $\sigma^2(\hat F)$ is a nonparametric estimate of $\sigma^2(F)$.

Example 5.2 Let $\mathbf{Z} = (Z_1, \ldots, Z_n)$ be a sample from a distribution with distribution function F and finite moments up to order $2k$. The sampling variance of the kth empirical moment $\hat\mu_k$ is $\sigma^2(F) = n^{-1} \operatorname{Var}_F Z_i^k$. Because $\operatorname{Var}_F Z_i^k = \mu_{2k} - \mu_k^2$, a nonparametric estimate of $\sigma^2(F)$ is

$$\sigma^2(\hat F) = n^{-1} \operatorname{Var}_{\hat F} Z_i^k = n^{-1}(\hat\mu_{2k} - \hat\mu_k^2).$$

By Jensen's inequality, $\hat\mu_k^2$ is an upward biased estimator of μ_k^2 and so $\operatorname{Var}_{\hat F} \hat\mu_k$ is a downward biased estimator of the sampling variance of $\hat\mu_k$, although the bias is negligible for large enough n. □

More generally, if the functional $\psi(F)$ describes some aspect of the sampling distribution of $\hat\theta$ under F, then a nonparametric estimate of $\psi(F)$ is just $\psi(\hat F)$. Because $\hat F$ converges to the parent distribution function F under general conditions, $\psi(\hat F)$ ought to converge to $\psi(F)$ provided that ψ is a continuous functional.

Unfortunately, except in special cases such as Example 5.2, evaluating $\psi(\hat F)$ is complicated and some form of approximation becomes necessary.

Example 5.3 Let $\mathbf{Z}$ be a sample from a distribution with distribution function F. The analogy principle suggests estimating

$$\psi(F) = \mathrm{E}_F \hat\theta = \int \cdots \int \hat\theta(z_1, \ldots, z_n)\, dF(z_1) \cdots dF(z_n)$$

by its sample counterpart

$$\psi(\hat F) = \mathrm{E}_{\hat F} \hat\theta = \int \cdots \int \hat\theta(z_1, \ldots, z_n)\, d\hat F(z_1) \cdots d\hat F(z_n).$$

Because the empirical distribution function $\hat F$ is the distribution function of a discrete distribution that gives probability mass n^{-1} to each of the n sample values $Z_1, \ldots, Z_n$, we get

$$\mathrm{E}_{\hat F} \hat\theta = \frac{1}{n^n} \sum_{i_1=1}^{n} \cdots \sum_{i_n=1}^{n} \hat\theta(Z_{i_1}, \ldots, Z_{i_n}), \tag{5.1}$$

which is generally complicated to compute because the number of terms in the summation is equal to n^n. This number becomes rapidly astronomical. For example, if $n = 5$ then $n^n = 3,125$, if $n = 10$ then $n^n = 10,000,000,000$, and so on.

The generic term $\hat\theta(Z_{i_1}, \ldots, Z_{i_n})$ on the right-hand side of (5.1) corresponds to the value of the estimator $\hat\theta$ for one of the n^n samples that may be obtained by randomly drawing with replacement n elements from the original data $\mathbf{Z}$. Thus, an alternative to (5.1) consists in randomly selecting B of the possible samples obtained by drawing with replacement n elements from the set $\mathbf{Z}$. Denoting these samples by $\mathbf{Z}_1^*, \ldots, \mathbf{Z}_B^*$, one may then approximate $\mathrm{E}_{\hat F}\,\hat\theta$ by $\hat\theta_{(\cdot)} = B^{-1}\sum_b \hat\theta_b^*$, where $\hat\theta_b^* = \hat\theta(\mathbf{Z}_b^*)$. It can be shown that this approximation to the nonparametric estimate $\mathrm{E}_{\hat F}\,\hat\theta$ becomes increasingly accurate as B increases. Of course, this does not necessarily mean that $\mathrm{E}_{\hat F}\,\hat\theta$ is a good approximation to $\mathrm{E}_F\,\hat\theta$. □

Given a sample $\mathbf{Z} = (Z_1, \ldots, Z_n)$, a *resample* $\mathbf{Z}^* = (Z_1^*, \ldots, Z_n^*)$ is a random sample of size n drawn with replacement from $\mathbf{Z}$, so that Z_i^* has probability n^{-1} of being equal to any distinct element of $\mathbf{Z}$ and probability m/n of being equal to any element of $\mathbf{Z}$ that is repeated m times. A resample is therefore a sample of size n from the empirical distribution function $\hat F$. Even when all elements of $\mathbf{Z}$ are distinct, a resample may contain repeats.

Given a resample $\mathbf{Z}^*$, the estimate $\hat\theta^* = \hat\theta(\mathbf{Z}^*)$ is called a *replicate* of $\hat\theta$. Because the estimator is assumed not to depend on the order in which the data are arranged, some of the n^n possible resamples are really indistinguishable. It can be shown (Hall 1992) that the chance of drawing the same unordered resample more than once is less than $\frac{1}{2}B(B-1)n!/n^n$.

The argument in Example 5.3 motivates the following algorithm, called *nonparametric bootstrap*, for numerically approximating the nonparametric estimate of any aspect of the sampling distribution of $\hat\theta$.

Algorithm 5.1

(1) *Compute the empirical distribution function* $\hat F$ *of the sample* $\mathbf{Z}$.
(2) *Draw a sample* $\mathbf{Z}^*$ *of size* n *from* $\hat F$.
(3) *Compute* $\hat\theta^* = \hat\theta(\mathbf{Z}^*)$.
(4) *Repeat steps* (2) *and* (3) *a sufficiently large number* B *of times, obtaining bootstrap replicates* $\hat\theta_1^*, \ldots, \hat\theta_B^*$.
(5) *Use the empirical distribution of* $\hat\theta_1^*, \ldots, \hat\theta_B^*$ *to estimate any aspect of the sampling distribution of* $\hat\theta$.

Thus, the estimate of $\mathrm{E}_F\,\hat\theta$ based on Algorithm 5.1 is $\hat\theta_{(\cdot)} = B^{-1}\sum_{b=1}^B \hat\theta_b^*$, the estimate of $\mathrm{Var}_F\,\hat\theta$ is

$$\widehat{\mathrm{Var}}_B\,\hat\theta = B^{-1}\sum_{b=1}^B [\hat\theta_b^* - \hat\theta_{(\cdot)}]^2,$$

while the estimate of $\Pr_F\{\hat\theta \le c\}$ is

$$\widehat{\Pr}_B\{\hat\theta \le c\} = B^{-1}\sum_{b=1}^B 1\{\hat\theta_b^* \le c\}.$$

It can be shown that $\hat{\theta}_{(\cdot)} \to \mathrm{E}_{\hat{F}}\,\hat{\theta}$, $\widehat{\mathrm{Var}}_B\,\hat{\theta} \to \mathrm{Var}_{\hat{F}}\,\hat{\theta}$ and $\widehat{\Pr}_B\{\hat{\theta} \le c\} \to \Pr_{\hat{F}}\{\hat{\theta} \le c\}$ as $B \to \infty$.

The amount of computer time required by Algorithm 5.1 depends linearly on the number B of resamples. According to Efron and Tibshirani (1993), if one seeks estimates of $\mathrm{Var}_F\,\hat{\theta}$, then: (i) a number of resamples as small as $B = 25$ is usually informative, whereas $B = 50$ is often enough for a good estimate; (ii) very seldom is it necessary to draw more than 200 resamples.

5.1.3 THE PARAMETRIC BOOTSTRAP

Let $\mathbf{Z}$ be a sample from a distribution whose distribution function is known to belong to a parametric family $\{F(z;\theta), \theta \in \Theta\}$, and let $\hat{\theta} = \hat{\theta}(\mathbf{Z})$ be a ML estimate of θ. In this case, instead of using the empirical distribution function $\hat{F}$, which is a nonparametric estimate of the parent distribution function, the bootstrap may be based on the parametric estimate $F(z;\hat{\theta})$. This leads to the following algorithm.

Algorithm 5.2

(1) *Compute the parametric estimate* $F(z;\hat{\theta})$.
(2) *Draw a sample* $\mathbf{Z}^*$ *of size* n *from* $F(z;\hat{\theta})$.
(3) *Compute* $\hat{\theta}^* = \hat{\theta}(\mathbf{Z}^*)$.
(4) *Repeat steps* (2)–(3) *a sufficiently large number* B *of times obtaining bootstrap replicates* $\hat{\theta}^*_1, \ldots, \hat{\theta}^*_B$.
(5) *Use the empirical distribution of* $\hat{\theta}^*_1, \ldots, \hat{\theta}^*_B$ *to estimate any aspect of the sampling distribution of* $\hat{\theta}$.

5.1.4 JACKKNIFE ESTIMATES OF VARIANCE

We now present another method that may be used to estimate the sampling variance of an estimator $\hat{\theta}$. This method, which may be interpreted as an approximation to the nonparametric bootstrap, works well for estimators that are not far from being linear in the data.

Given a sample $Z_1, \ldots, Z_n$, the ith *jackknife sample* is the subset of $n-1$ elements obtained by excluding the ith data point Z_i. Let $\hat{\theta}_{(i)}$ denote the value of the estimator $\hat{\theta}$ for the ith jackknife sample and let $\hat{\theta}_{(\cdot)} = n^{-1}\sum_i \hat{\theta}_{(i)}$ be the average of $\hat{\theta}_{(i)}$ over the n jackknife samples. Tukey (1958) suggested estimating the sampling variance of $\hat{\theta}$ by

$$\widehat{\mathrm{Var}}_J\,\hat{\theta} = \frac{n-1}{n}\sum_{i=1}^{n}[\hat{\theta}_{(i)} - \hat{\theta}_{(\cdot)}][\hat{\theta}_{(i)} - \hat{\theta}_{(\cdot)}]^\top,$$

called the *jackknife estimate* of the sampling variance of $\hat{\theta}$.

The motivation for this method is easiest to see by considering the problem of estimating the sampling variance of the sample mean.

Example 5.4 Let $\bar{Z}$ be the mean of a sample $Z_1, \ldots, Z_n$ from a distribution with finite variance. The value of the sample mean for the ith jackknife sample is

$$\bar{Z}_{(i)} = (n-1)^{-1}(n\bar{Z} - Z_i).$$

Because $\bar{Z}_{(\cdot)} = \bar{Z}$, we have $\bar{Z}_{(i)} - \bar{Z}_{(\cdot)} = (n-1)^{-1}(\bar{Z} - Z_i)$. The jackknife estimate of the sampling variance of $\bar{Z}$ is therefore

$$\widehat{\mathrm{Var}}_J\,\hat{\theta} = \frac{n-1}{n}\sum_{i=1}^{n}\left(\frac{Z_i - \bar{Z}}{n-1}\right)^2 = \frac{1}{n(n-1)}\sum_{i=1}^{n}(Z_i - \bar{Z})^2 = \frac{s^2}{n}.$$

In this case, the jackknife estimate exactly coincides with the unbiased estimate of $\mathrm{Var}\,\bar{Z}$. □

When the sample size is small, the jackknife estimate is generally easier to compute than that based on the bootstrap, because it only requires n evaluations. Further, for estimators that are linear in the data, $\hat{\theta}_{(i)}$ may usually be computed through simple recursive formulae.

The jackknife suffers, however, from some limitations. First, it tends to be conservative, that is, the expectation of $\widehat{\mathrm{Var}}_J\,\hat{\theta}$ tends to exceed the actual variance of $\hat{\theta}$ (Efron & Stein 1981). Second, it may give poor answers when $\hat{\theta}$ is a highly nonlinear function of the data. One example is its failure to correctly estimate the sampling variance of the sample median (Efron 1982).

A way of improving the quality of the jackknife estimates is to use the *delete-d jackknife*, which excludes not a single data point but subsets of $d > 1$ data points. Because the number of jackknife samples is in this case equal to $\binom{n}{d}$, the method tends to lose its simplicity, especially when the sample size is large. Instead of computing $\hat{\theta}$ for each of the possible jackknife samples, an alternative is to randomly select a subset of them. With this modification, the jackknife tends to resemble more the bootstrap.

5.1.5 *ASSESSING BIAS*

Although unbiasedness plays an important role in statistical theory, unbiased estimators are rather rare. Given a biased estimator $\hat{\theta}$ of a target parameter θ, an important measure of statistical accuracy is the magnitude of its (mean) bias $\mathrm{Bias}\,\hat{\theta} = \mathrm{E}\,\hat{\theta} - \theta$. When $\theta = h(\mu)$ and $\hat{\theta} = h(T)$, where h is a nonlinear function and T is a vector-valued statistic with mean μ and variance Σ, the first-order approximation discussed in Section 5.1.1 would give as a result $\mathrm{Bias}\,\hat{\theta} = h(\mu) - \theta = 0$, which is clearly incorrect. If h is twice differentiable in a neighborhood of μ, then the bias of $\hat{\theta}$ may be approximated by carrying out the delta method up to the second order. A second-order Taylor expansion about μ gives

$$h(t) \approx \theta + h'(\mu)^\top(t-\mu) + \frac{1}{2}(t-\mu)^\top h''(\mu)\,(t-\mu).$$

Hence, up to second order,

$$\mathrm{Bias}\,\hat{\theta} = \mathrm{E}\,h(T) - \theta \approx \frac{1}{2}\,\mathrm{E}[(t-\mu)^\top h''(\mu)\,(t-\mu)] = \frac{1}{2}\,\mathrm{tr}[h''(\mu)\,\Sigma],$$

where we used the fact that $x^\top Ax = \mathrm{tr}\,x^\top Ax = \mathrm{tr}(Axx^\top)$. In the scalar parameter case, the bias of $\hat{\theta}$ is approximately proportional to the sampling variance of T. Given an estimate $\widehat{\mathrm{Bias}}\,\hat{\theta}$ of the bias of $\hat{\theta}$, a ***bias corrected estimate*** of θ is $\tilde{\theta} = \hat{\theta} - \widehat{\mathrm{Bias}}\,\hat{\theta}$.

Example 5.5 In the case of Example 5.1 we get

$$h''(\mu) = \begin{bmatrix} 0 & -1/\mu_2^2 \\ -1/\mu_2^2 & 2\mu_1/\mu_2^3 \end{bmatrix}.$$

Hence, up to second order, the bias of $\hat{\theta} = T_1/T_2$ as an estimator of $\theta = \mu_1/\mu_2$ is

$$\operatorname{Bias}\hat{\theta} \approx \frac{1}{2}\left(-2\frac{\sigma_{12}}{\mu_2^2} + 2\sigma_2^2\frac{\mu_1}{\mu_2^3}\right) = \theta\left(-\frac{\sigma_{12}}{\mu_1\mu_2} + \frac{\sigma_2^2}{\mu_2^2}\right).$$

A bias corrected estimate of θ is therefore

$$\tilde{\theta} = \hat{\theta}\left(1 + \frac{\hat{\sigma}_{12}}{T_1T_2} - \frac{\hat{\sigma}_2^2}{T_2^2}\right),$$

where $\hat{\sigma}_{12}$ and $\hat{\sigma}_2^2$ are estimates of σ_{12} and σ_2^2 respectively. If $\mu_1 = 0$, then $\operatorname{Bias}\hat{\theta} \approx -\sigma_{12}/\mu_2^2$ and a bias corrected estimate of θ is simply $\tilde{\theta} = \hat{\theta} + \hat{\sigma}_{12}^2/T_2^2$. □

When theoretical bias calculations are analytically complicated, one may rely on the nonparametric bootstrap. Because the bootstrap estimate of $\mathrm{E}_F\,\hat{\theta}$ is $\mathrm{E}_{\hat{F}}\,\hat{\theta}$, the bootstrap estimate of the bias of $\hat{\theta}$ is

$$\widehat{\operatorname{Bias}}_B\,\hat{\theta} = \mathrm{E}_{\hat{F}}\,\hat{\theta} - \hat{\theta}.$$

A bias corrected estimate of θ is therefore

$$\tilde{\theta} = \hat{\theta} - \widehat{\operatorname{Bias}}_B\,\hat{\theta} = 2\hat{\theta} - \mathrm{E}_{\hat{F}}\,\hat{\theta}.$$

Another alternative is the jackknife estimate of bias

$$\widehat{\operatorname{Bias}}_J\,\hat{\theta} = (n-1)(\hat{\theta}_{(\cdot)} - \hat{\theta}).$$

In this case, the bias corrected estimate of θ is

$$\tilde{\theta} = \hat{\theta} - \widehat{\operatorname{Bias}}_J\,\hat{\theta} = \hat{\theta}_{(\cdot)} + n(\hat{\theta} - \hat{\theta}_{(\cdot)}).$$

As for variance estimation, using the jackknife is problematic when $\hat{\theta}$ is a highly nonlinear estimator.

5.2 CONFIDENCE SETS

Let $\mathbf{Z}$ be a data matrix and let Θ be a parameter space. A particular realization $\mathbf{z}$ of $\mathbf{Z}$ divides Θ into two disjoint subsets: a "plausible" set given the observed data $\mathbf{z}$ and its complement. Rather than focusing attention on just a point estimate of θ, one may want to determine what this plausible set is. We shall consider two alternative ways of formalizing this idea: the classical and the Bayesian.

5.2.1 CLASSICAL CONFIDENCE SETS

Let $\{P_\theta, \theta \in \Theta\}$ be a parametric family of probability distributions on a sample space $\mathcal{Z}$. If there exists a family $\{C(\mathbf{z}), \mathbf{z} \in \mathcal{Z}\}$ of subsets of Θ with the property that, for all $\theta \in \Theta$,

$$P_\theta\{\mathbf{z}\colon \theta \in C(\mathbf{z})\} \geq 1 - \alpha, \qquad 0 < \alpha < 1,$$

then the random subset $C(\mathbf{Z})$ is called a *confidence set for* θ *with coverage level* $1 - \alpha$ or, for short, a $(1 - \alpha)$*-level confidence set for* θ. The interpretation of a confidence set is as follows. Suppose that one can draw repeated samples from the probability distribution P_θ. If for each sample $\mathbf{z}$ one computes a $(1 - \alpha)$-level confidence set $C(\mathbf{z})$ for θ, then approximately $1 - \alpha$ percent of these sets cover the true value of θ.

Example 5.6 Let $Z_1, \ldots, Z_n$ be a sample from a continuous distribution with distribution function F, and let $Z_{[k]}$ denote the kth sample order statistic. To derive a confidence set for the pth population quantile ζ_p $(0 < p < 1)$ of F, notice that the relation $Z_{[r]} \leq \zeta_p \leq Z_{[s]}$, for $1 \leq r < s \leq n$, is satisfied if and only if the number of sample observations that are not greater than ζ_p is at least r but not more than s. Because $\Pr\{Z_i \leq \zeta_p\} = F(\zeta_p) = p$, the probability that exactly k observations are not greater than ζ_p is equal to the probability of k successes in n independent Bernoulli trials where the probability of success is equal to p. Thus

$$\Pr\{Z_{[k]} \leq \zeta_p\} = \Pr\{X = k\} = \binom{n}{k} p^k (1 - p)^{n-k},$$

where $X \sim \mathrm{Bi}(n, p)$. Hence

$$\Pr\{Z_{[r]} \leq \zeta_p \leq Z_{[s]}\} = \Pr\{r \leq X \leq s\}, \tag{5.2}$$

which provides the basis for constructing confidence sets for ζ_p of a given level. Given (n, p, r, s), the value on the right-hand side of (5.2) is easily computed from the tables of the binomial distribution. For the population median $\zeta_{.5}$, we simply get

$$\Pr\{Z_{[r]} \leq \zeta_{.5} \leq Z_{[s]}\} = \sum_{k=r}^{s} \binom{n}{k} \left(\frac{1}{2}\right)^n.$$

When n is large, the Gaussian normal approximation to binomial probabilities may be used instead. □

Construction of a confidence set simplifies considerably if one can find a scalar statistic $T(\mathbf{Z}; \theta)$ whose sampling distribution does not depend on θ and has the property that, for all $\theta \in \Theta$,

$$P_\theta\{\mathbf{z}\colon T(\mathbf{z}; \theta) \leq c\} \geq 1 - \alpha \tag{5.3}$$

for some c. Such a statistic is sometimes called a ***pivot***. Given a pivot $T(\mathbf{Z}; \theta)$, consider the family of subsets of Θ of the form $C(\mathbf{z}) = \{\theta \in \Theta\colon T(\mathbf{z}; \theta) \leq c\}$. Because the event that $\theta \in C(Z)$ is equivalent to the event that $T(\mathbf{Z}; \theta) \leq c$, which by (5.3) has probability at least equal to $1 - \alpha$, the random subset $C(\mathbf{Z})$ is a $(1 - \alpha)$-level confidence set for θ.

In the special case when θ is a scalar parameter, it is often possible to find a finite interval $[a, b]$ such that

$$P_\theta\{\mathbf{z}: a \le T(\mathbf{z}; \theta) \le b\} \ge 1 - \alpha.$$

If the pivot $T(\mathbf{Z}; \theta)$ is strictly monotone in θ, inverting the above relationship gives the following two-sided $(1 - \alpha)$-level *confidence interval* for θ

$$C(\mathbf{Z}) = \{\theta \in \Theta: \hat{\theta}_L(\mathbf{Z}) \le \theta \le \hat{\theta}_U(\mathbf{Z})\},$$

where $\hat{\theta}_L = T^{-1}(a)$ and $\hat{\theta}_U = T^{-1}(b)$.

Example 5.7 Let $\mathbf{Z}$ be a sample of size n from a $\mathcal{N}(\mu, \sigma^2)$ distribution, and let $\bar{Z}$ and s^2 be the sample mean and the sample variance. As a pivot, consider the statistic

$$T(\mathbf{Z}; \mu) = \frac{\bar{Z} - \mu}{s/\sqrt{n}},$$

which is known to have a t-distribution with $n - 1$ degrees of freedom. In fact, without knowing μ and σ^2, one can always find a finite interval $[a, b]$ such that

$$P_\theta\left\{a \le \frac{\bar{Z} - \mu}{s/\sqrt{n}} \le b\right\} = 1 - \alpha,$$

where $0 < \alpha < 1$. Inverting the above relationship using the fact that $T^{-1}(\mu) = \bar{Z} - \mu s/\sqrt{n}$ gives

$$P_\theta\left\{\bar{Z} - b\frac{s}{\sqrt{n}} \le \mu \le \bar{Z} - a\frac{s}{\sqrt{n}}\right\} = 1 - \alpha.$$

The random interval

$$C(\mathbf{Z}) = \left\{\mu \in \Re: \bar{Z} - b\frac{s}{\sqrt{n}} \le \mu \le \bar{Z} - a\frac{s}{\sqrt{n}}\right\} \tag{5.4}$$

covers the population mean μ with probability $1-\alpha$ and is therefore a two-sided $(1-\alpha)$-level confidence interval for μ. Its length $(b - a)s/\sqrt{n}$ is an increasing transformation of the random variable s^2 and is a decreasing function of the sample size n. Because of the symmetry of the t-distribution, the shortest of these confidence intervals is the one that is symmetric about $\bar{Z}$. This is obtained by choosing $b = t_{(\alpha/2)}$ and $a = -b$, where $t_{(\alpha/2)}$ denotes the upper $(\alpha/2)$th quantile of the t-distribution with $n-1$ degrees of freedom, that is, $G(t_{(\alpha/2)}) = 1 - \alpha/2$, where G is the distribution function of the t-distribution with $n - 1$ degrees of freedom.

The length of a symmetric $(1 - \alpha)$-level confidence interval is equal to $2t_{(\alpha/2)}s/\sqrt{n}$ and is a decreasing function of α. Thus, a symmetric 99%-level confidence interval always contains a 95%-level one. □

5.2.2 BOOTSTRAP CONFIDENCE INTERVALS

Since its introduction, a major use of the nonparametric bootstrap has been in the construction of confidence intervals. In this section we consider three alternative methods for constructing bootstrap confidence intervals for a scalar parameter θ.

The first method assumes that a pivotal or approximately pivotal statistic $T = T(\mathbf{Z};\theta)$ is available. In typical situations, the pivot is of the form

$$T(\mathbf{Z};\theta) = \frac{\hat{\theta}(\mathbf{Z}) - \theta}{\widehat{\mathrm{SE}}(\hat{\theta})},$$

where $\hat{\theta}$ is an estimator of θ and $\widehat{\mathrm{SE}}(\hat{\theta})$ is some estimate of the standard error of $\hat{\theta}$. For each resample $\mathbf{Z}^*$, construct the replicate

$$T^* = T(\mathbf{Z}^*;\hat{\theta}) = \frac{\hat{\theta}^* - \hat{\theta}}{\widehat{\mathrm{SE}}^*(\hat{\theta})},$$

where $\widehat{\mathrm{SE}}^*(\hat{\theta})$ denotes the estimated standard error of $\hat{\theta}$. Given replicates $T_1^*, \ldots, T_B^*$, one may approximate a two-sided $(1-\alpha)$-level confidence interval for θ by the bootstrap interval

$$[\hat{\theta} - \hat{t}_{1-\alpha/2}\,\widehat{\mathrm{SE}}(\hat{\theta}),\ \hat{\theta} - \hat{t}_{\alpha/2}\,\widehat{\mathrm{SE}}(\hat{\theta})],$$

where $\hat{t}_p$ denotes a pth quantile of the empirical distribution of T_b^*. This method is called the *T-method.* Because α is usually very small, for example $\alpha = .01$ or $\alpha = .05$, to attain sufficiently accurate estimates of the tail probabilities, many more replicates are needed than for a bootstrap estimate of variance. The T-method tends to produce a confidence interval whose coverage probability is close to $1-\alpha$ on average but whose behavior is rather erratic.

The second method constructs confidence intervals directly from the bootstrap distribution of the estimator $\hat{\theta}$ of θ. Given B replicates $\hat{\theta}_1^*, \ldots, \hat{\theta}_B^*$, it is reasonable to consider, as an approximate $(1-\alpha)$-level confidence interval for θ, the interval $[\hat{t}_{\alpha/2}, \hat{t}_{1-\alpha/2}]$, where $\hat{t}_p$ now denotes a pth quantile of the empirical distribution of $\hat{\theta}_b^*$. This method, called the *percentile method,* tends to be less erratic than the previous one but also less accurate.

The third method (Efron 1987) is an attempt to improve upon the previous two. As an approximate $(1-\alpha)$-level confidence interval for θ, this method suggests the interval

$$[\hat{t}_{\alpha_1}, \hat{t}_{1-\alpha_2}], \tag{5.5}$$

where $\hat{t}_{\alpha_1}$ and $\hat{t}_{1-\alpha_2}$ are quantiles of the empirical distribution of $\hat{\theta}_b^*$, with

$$\alpha_1 = \Phi\left(\hat{z}_0 + \frac{\hat{z}_0 + z_\alpha}{1 - \hat{a}(\hat{z}_0 + z_\alpha)}\right),$$

$$\alpha_2 = \Phi\left(\hat{z}_0 + \frac{\hat{z}_0 + z_{1-\alpha}}{1 - \hat{a}(\hat{z}_0 + z_{1-\alpha})}\right),$$

and Φ and $z_\alpha = \Phi^{-1}(\alpha)$ denote respectively the distribution function and the αth quantile of the $\mathcal{N}(0,1)$ distribution. When $\hat{a} = \hat{z}_0 = 0$, the confidence interval (5.5) coincides with that obtained from the percentile method. The number $\hat{z}_0$ is a bias correction such that $\widehat{\Pr}_B\{\hat{\theta}^* \leq \hat{\theta}\} = \Phi(\hat{z}_0)$. Clearly, the correction is equal to zero when the distribution of $\hat{\theta}^*$ is symmetric about $\hat{\theta}$, in which case $\widehat{\Pr}_B\{\hat{\theta}^* \leq \hat{\theta}\} = 1/2$. The number $\hat{a}$, called the *acceleration*, is an estimate of the rate of change of the standard error of $\hat{\theta}$ as the population parameter θ varies. Efron (1987) suggests computing $\hat{a}$ as

$$\hat{a} = \frac{\sum_{i=1}^{n} (\hat{\theta}_{(\cdot)} - \hat{\theta}_{(i)})^3}{6\,[\sum_{i=1}^{n} (\hat{\theta}_{(\cdot)} - \hat{\theta}_{(i)})^2]^{3/2}},$$

where $\hat{\theta}_{(i)}$ denotes the value of $\hat{\theta}$ obtained from the ith jackknife sample and $\hat{\theta}_{(\cdot)} = n^{-1}\sum_i \hat{\theta}_{(i)}$. This method, called the *bias corrected and accelerated percentile method* or BC$_a$ *method*, has several theoretical advantages discussed in Efron (1987) and Efron and Tibshirani (1993).

5.2.3 BAYESIAN CONFIDENCE SETS

Given a posterior distribution $p(\theta \,|\, \mathbf{z})$ on the parameter space Θ, it is always possible to find a family $\mathcal{C} = \{C(\mathbf{z})\}$ of subsets of Θ such that

$$\Pr\{\theta \in C(\mathbf{z}) \,|\, \mathbf{z}\} = 1 - \alpha, \qquad 0 < \alpha < 1$$

for every $C(\mathbf{z}) \in \mathcal{C}$. Each element of $\mathcal{C}$ contains a fraction equal to $1-\alpha$ of the posterior probability on Θ and may therefore be interpreted as a Bayesian confidence set with coverage level equal to $1 - \alpha$.

The family $\mathcal{C}$ generally contains an infinite number of elements. In order to choose one of them, it seems reasonable to further require the posterior density at any point inside the set to be higher than the posterior density at any point outside it or, equivalently, the chosen set to occupy the smallest volume of Θ for a given probability content. Formally

Definition 5.1 Let $p(\theta \,|\, \mathbf{z})$ be a posterior density on a parameter space Θ. A subset $C(\mathbf{z})$ of Θ such that:

(i) $\Pr\{\theta \in C(\mathbf{z}) \,|\, \mathbf{z}\} = 1 - \alpha$;
(ii) $p(\theta_1 \,|\, \mathbf{z}) \geq p(\theta_2 \,|\, \mathbf{z})$ for all $\theta_1 \in C(\mathbf{z})$ and $\theta_2 \notin C(\mathbf{z})$

is called a *maximal posterior density set* with probability content $1 - \alpha$. □

Example 5.8 Given a sample $\mathbf{Z}$ of size n from a $\mathcal{N}(\mu, \sigma^2)$ distribution, the sample likelihood may be written in the form

$$f(\mathbf{Z} \,|\, \theta) \propto \frac{1}{\sigma^n} \exp\left\{-\frac{1}{2\sigma^2}[\nu s^2 + n(\mu - \bar{Z})^2]\right\}, \qquad \theta = (\mu, \sigma),$$

where $\nu = n - 1 > 0$. Assume that μ and σ are independent and, following Jeffreys' invariance principle, that μ and $\ln \sigma$ have a uniform distribution on the whole real line. The two assumptions together imply that the prior density of θ is of the form $p(\theta) \propto 1/\sigma$, and is therefore an improper density. By Bayes theorem, the posterior density of θ is

$$p(\theta \,|\, \mathbf{Z}) \propto \frac{1}{\sigma^{n+1}} \exp\left\{-\frac{1}{2\sigma^2}[\nu s^2 + n(\mu - \bar{Z})^2]\right\}. \tag{5.6}$$

Inspection of (5.6) reveals that the conditional posterior density of μ given σ is

$$p(\mu \,|\, \sigma; \mathbf{Z}) \propto \frac{1}{\sigma} \exp\left[-\frac{n}{2\sigma^2}(\mu - \bar{Z})^2\right],$$

which is the density of a $\mathcal{N}(\bar{Z}, \sigma^2/n)$ distribution. Given the relationship $p(\theta \,|\, \mathbf{Z}) = p(\mu \,|\, \sigma; \mathbf{Z})\, p(\sigma \,|\, \mathbf{Z})$, the marginal posterior density of σ is

$$p(\sigma \,|\, \mathbf{Z}) = \frac{p(\mu, \sigma \,|\, \mathbf{Z})}{p(\mu \,|\, \sigma; \mathbf{Z})} \propto \frac{1}{\sigma^{\nu+1}} \exp\left(-\frac{\nu s^2}{2\sigma^2}\right),$$

which is the density of an inverted gamma distribution with parameter $(\nu/2, \nu s^2/2)$. The marginal posterior density of μ is obtained by integrating the joint density $p(\theta \,|\, \mathbf{Z})$ with respect to σ

$$p(\mu \,|\, \mathbf{Z}) = \int_0^\infty p(\mu, \sigma \,|\, \mathbf{Z})\, d\sigma.$$

To compute this integral, we use the following formula

$$\int_0^\infty x^{-(m+1)} \exp(-a x^{-\lambda})\, dx = \frac{1}{\lambda} a^{-m/\lambda} \Gamma\left(\frac{m}{\lambda}\right), \tag{5.7}$$

where $\Gamma(\cdot)$ is the gamma function. Putting $m = \nu + 1 = n$, $\lambda = 2$ and a equal to the term in square brackets in the exponential part of (5.6) gives

$$p(\mu \,|\, \mathbf{Z}) \propto \left[\nu + \frac{n(\mu - \bar{Z})^2}{s^2}\right]^{-n/2}.$$

Finally, after a change of variable from μ to $t = \sqrt{n}(\mu - \bar{Z})/s$, we get

$$p(t \,|\, \mathbf{Z}) \propto \left(1 + \frac{t^2}{\nu}\right)^{-n/2},$$

which is the density of a t-distribution with $\nu = n - 1$ degrees of freedom. A maximal posterior density set with probability content $1 - \alpha$ is therefore

$$C(\mathbf{Z}) = \left\{\mu \colon \bar{Z} - t_{(\alpha/2)} \frac{s}{\sqrt{n}} \le \mu \le \bar{Z} + t_{(\alpha/2)} \frac{s}{\sqrt{n}}\right\},$$

where $t_{(\alpha/2)}$ denotes the upper αth quantile of a t distribution with $n - 1$ degrees of freedom. This interval has exactly the same form as the classical confidence interval (5.4), although its interpretation is completely different. □

5.3 HYPOTHESIS TESTING

A *statistical hypothesis* is a statement about the probability distribution of the data $\mathbf{Z}$. A statistical hypothesis that completely specifies the probability distribution of $\mathbf{Z}$ is called *simple*, otherwise it is called *composite*.

The theory of hypothesis testing is concerned with the problem of determining whether or not a statistical hypothesis is inconsistent with the sample evidence. The particular hypothesis to be tested is called the *null hypothesis* and is denoted by H_0. In addition to H_0, one may also be interested in a particular set of deviations from H_0, called the *alternative hypothesis* and denoted by H_1. Usually, the null and the alternative hypotheses are not on an equal footing: H_0 is clearly specified and of intrinsic interest, whereas H_1 serves only to indicate what types of departure from H_0 are of interest.

In a parametric context, such as that considered in the remainder of this chapter, a hypothesis implies that the distribution of $\mathbf{Z}$ belongs to a proper subset of a parametric family $\{P_\theta, \theta \in \Theta\}$ of distributions on the sample space or, equivalently, that the target parameter belongs to a proper subset of the parameter space Θ. Thus, H_0 and H_1 can be represented by two disjoint subsets, Θ_0 and Θ_1, of Θ. When $\Theta_1 = \Theta - \Theta_0$, we sometimes say that the null hypothesis is *nested* within the alternative one.

Example 5.9 Given a parametric model $\{P_\theta, \theta \in \Theta\}$, an example of a simple null is the hypothesis H_0: $\theta = \theta_0$ that the target parameter is equal to θ_0, while an example of a composite alternative is the hypothesis H_1: $\theta \neq \theta_0$ that the target parameter is different from θ_0. In this case, $\Theta_0 = \{\theta_0\}$ and $\Theta_1 = \{\theta \in \Theta\colon \theta \neq \theta_0\} = \Theta - \Theta_0$. If θ is a scalar parameter, the composite hypothesis that $\theta > \theta_0$ is called *one-sided*, whereas the composite hypothesis that $\theta \neq \theta_0$ is called *two-sided.* □

5.3.1 *STATISTICAL TESTS*

A *statistical test* is a partition of the sample space into two regions: the set $\mathcal{K}$ of observations that are regarded as inconsistent with H_0, called the *critical* or *rejection region*, and its complement $\mathcal{K}^c$, called the *nonrejection region*. Associated with a statistical test, is a decision rule that rejects H_0 as inconsistent with the data if the realized value $\mathbf{z}$ of $\mathbf{Z}$ falls in the critical region K, and does not reject H_0 if $\mathbf{z}$ belongs to $\mathcal{K}^c$. Clearly, there are as many statistical tests of a given hypothesis H_0 as there are ways of partitioning the sample space into two subsets. In simple situations, however, there is often a small class of tests which seem intuitively reasonable.

A statistical test is often defined through a scalar statistic $T(\mathbf{Z})$, called the *test statistic*, whose sampling distribution under H_0 is known, at least approximately. In this case, a typical critical region is of the form $\mathcal{K} = \{\mathbf{z}\colon T(\mathbf{z}) > k\}$, where the constant $k > 0$ is called the *critical value* of the test.

Example 5.10 Given a sample $\mathbf{Z}$ of size n from a $\mathcal{N}(\mu, \sigma^2)$ distribution, consider the problem of testing the simple hypothesis that the population mean μ is equal to μ_0 against the two-sided alternative that μ is different from μ_0. In this case, it is reasonable to consider the class of tests that reject H_0 for large values of the statistic $T(\mathbf{Z}) = |\bar{Z} - \mu_0|$. The critical region of this class of test is of the form $\mathcal{K} = \{\mathbf{z}\colon |\bar{z} - \mu_0| > k\}$, where k is the critical value of the test and $\bar{z}$ is the value of the sample mean for a particular realization $\mathbf{z}$ of $\mathbf{Z}$. □

For any test of H_0, two types of error are possible:

1. reject H_0 when it is true, that is, when $\theta \in \Theta_0$ (*Type I error*);
2. do not reject H_0 when it is false, that is, when $\theta \in \Theta_1$ (*Type II error*).

If $\mathcal{K}$ is the critical region of a test, the probability of both types of error may be described by the single function $\pi(\theta) = P_\theta\{\mathcal{K}\}$, $\theta \in \Theta$, called the *power function* of

Figure 40 Power function of a two-sided 10%-level test of the hypothesis H_0: $\mu = 0$ in the $\mathcal{N}(\mu, 1)$ model for increasing sample sizes. The test is based on the critical region $\{|\bar{Z}| > z_{(.05)}/\sqrt{n}\}$.

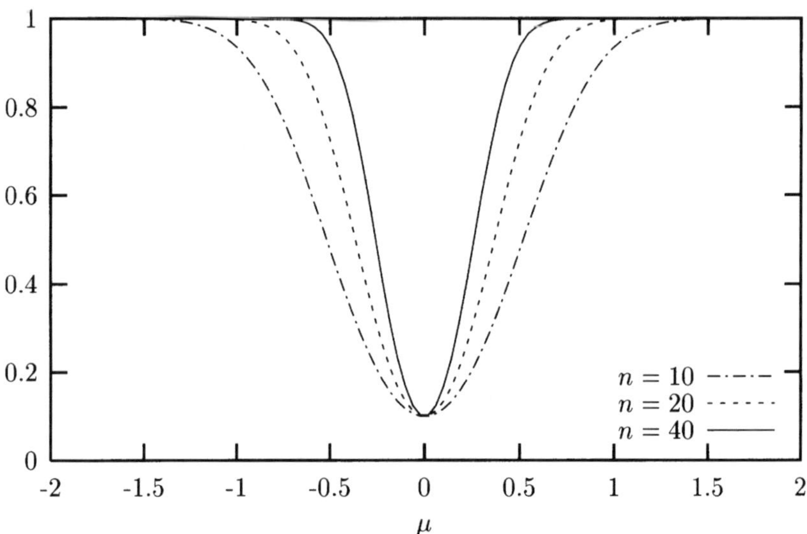

the test, which gives the probability of rejecting H_0 as a function of θ. If $\theta \in \Theta_0$, then $\pi(\theta)$ describes the probability of Type I error. The maximal probability of Type I error

$$\sup_{\theta \in \Theta_0} \pi(\theta)$$

is called the *size* of the test. A test is said to be of *level* α if its size does not exceed α. On the other hand,

$$1 - \pi(\theta) = 1 - P_\theta\{\mathcal{K}\} = P_\theta\{\mathcal{K}^c\}, \qquad \theta \in \Theta_1$$

describes the probability of Type II error.

Example 5.11 Consider again the class of tests introduced in Example 5.10. Because $\bar{Z} \sim \mathcal{N}(\mu, \sigma^2/n)$, their power function is

$$\begin{aligned} \pi(\mu) &= P_\mu\{|\bar{Z} - \mu_0| > k\} \\ &= 1 - \Phi\left(\frac{\mu_0 - \mu + k}{\sigma/\sqrt{n}}\right) + \Phi\left(\frac{\mu_0 - \mu - k}{\sigma/\sqrt{n}}\right). \end{aligned}$$

This power function has the following properties:

1. it is symmetric about μ_0, that is, $\pi(\mu_0 + \mu) = \pi(\mu_0 - \mu)$;
2. it is strictly increasing in $|\mu - \mu_0|$ and tends to one as $|\mu - \mu_0| \to \infty$, that is, the test rejects H_0 with a probability that increases with the distance between the population mean μ and the hypothesis μ_0, rejection becoming almost certain when μ is far enough from μ_0;

3. it attains its minimum at the point $\mu = \mu_0$, where

$$\pi(\mu_0) = 2\left[1 - \Phi\left(\frac{k\sqrt{n}}{\sigma}\right)\right];$$

4. it becomes more and more concentrated about μ_0 as the sample size n increases.

When σ^2 is known, an α-level test is obtained by choosing a critical value k such that

$$\alpha = 2\left[1 - \Phi\left(\frac{k\sqrt{n}}{\sigma}\right)\right].$$

Solving for k gives

$$k_\alpha = \Phi^{-1}(1-\alpha/2)\,\frac{\sigma}{\sqrt{n}} = z_{(\alpha/2)}\,\frac{\sigma}{\sqrt{n}},$$

where $z_{(\alpha/2)}$ denotes the upper $\alpha/2$th quantile of the $\mathcal{N}(0,1)$ distribution, that is, $\Phi(z_{(\alpha/2)}) = 1-\alpha/2$. Since $z_{(\alpha'/2)} > z_{(\alpha/2)}$ when $\alpha' < \alpha$, the critical region of an α-level test always contains that of a test of level $\alpha' < \alpha$. The power function of an α-level test (Figure 40) is

$$\pi(\mu) = 1 - \Phi\left(\frac{\sqrt{n}\,(\mu_0-\mu) + z_{(\alpha/2)}}{\sigma}\right) + \Phi\left(\frac{\sqrt{n}\,(\mu_0-\mu) - z_{(\alpha/2)}}{\sigma}\right).$$

□

Consider a test that rejects H_0 for large values of some statistic $T(\mathbf{Z})$. If $T(\mathbf{z})$ is the value of the test statistic for a realization $\mathbf{z}$ of $\mathbf{Z}$, then the number

$$p(\mathbf{z}) = \sup_{\theta\in\Theta_0} P_\theta\{T(\mathbf{Z}) \geq T(\mathbf{z})\}$$

is called the *observed significance level* or *p-value* of the test. Because $p(\mathbf{z})$ is the maximal probability of Type I error if one rejects H_0 on the basis of the observed data $\mathbf{z}$, the p-value may be interpreted as a measure of the strength of the sample evidence against H_0: the smaller is $p(\mathbf{z})$, the stronger is the evidence against H_0.

If H_0 is a simple hypothesis and F denotes the distribution function of the statistic $T(\mathbf{Z})$ under H_0, then $p(\mathbf{z}) = 1 - F(T(\mathbf{z}))$. If F is of the continuous type, then the distribution of the random variable $p(\mathbf{Z})$ under H_0 is

$$\begin{aligned}\Pr\{p(\mathbf{Z}) < c \,|\, H_0\} &= \Pr\{1 - F(T(\mathbf{Z})) < c \,|\, H_0\}\\ &= \Pr\{T(\mathbf{Z}) > F^{-1}(1-c) \,|\, H_0\}\\ &= 1 - F(F^{-1}(1-c)) = c.\end{aligned}$$

Since, under H_0, the p-value therefore has a uniform distribution on the interval $(0,1)$, an α-level test rejects H_0 whenever $p(\mathbf{Z})$ is less than α.

Example 5.12 The p-value of the class of tests introduced in Example 5.10 is

$$p(\mathbf{z}) = P_{\mu_0}\{|\bar{Z} - \mu_0| > |\bar{z} - \mu_0|\} = 2\left[1 - \Phi\left(\frac{|\bar{z}-\mu_0|}{\sigma/\sqrt{n}}\right)\right].$$

Viewed as a function of $\mathbf{z}$, the p-value has the following properties:

1. it is symmetric about μ_0;
2. it attains its maximum of one at the point $\bar{z} = \mu_0$;
3. it is decreasing in n and $|\mu - \mu_0|$, and tends to zero as $n \to \infty$ or $|\bar{z} - \mu_0| \to \infty$.

□

5.3.2 *DUALITY BETWEEN CONFIDENCE SETS AND CRITICAL REGIONS*

There is complete duality between confidence sets and critical regions, in the sense that families of confidence sets can always be used to construct critical regions and vice versa.

Given a family $\{C(\mathbf{z})\}$ of $(1 - \alpha)$-level confidence sets for θ, we necessarily have

$$P_\theta\{\mathbf{z}\colon \theta \in C(\mathbf{z})\} \geq 1 - \alpha.$$

For a fixed $\theta \in \Theta$, define the region in the sample space

$$\mathcal{K}(\theta) = \{\mathbf{z}\colon \theta \notin C(\mathbf{z})\}.$$

For any $\theta \in \Theta$, we then have

$$P_\theta\{\mathcal{K}(\theta)\} = 1 - P_\theta\{\mathbf{z}\colon \theta \in C(\mathbf{z})\} \leq 1 - (1 - \alpha) = \alpha.$$

Hence, $\mathcal{K}(\theta_0)$ is the critical region of an α-level test of the hypothesis $\mathrm{H}_0\colon \theta = \theta_0$ against the alternative that $\theta \neq \theta_0$. One may therefore reject $\mathrm{H}_0\colon \theta = \theta_0$ whenever θ_0 lies outside a $(1 - \alpha)$-level confidence set for θ.

Now consider the opposite case. Given a family $\{\mathcal{K}(\theta)\}$ of α-level critical regions, let $\mathcal{K}(\theta_0)$ be the critical region of an α-level test of the hypothesis $\mathrm{H}_0\colon \theta = \theta_0$ against the alternative that $\theta \neq \theta_0$. Clearly $P_{\theta_0}\{\mathcal{K}(\theta_0)\} \leq \alpha$. For a fixed $\mathbf{z}$, define the subset of Θ

$$C(\mathbf{z}) = \{\theta \in \Theta\colon \mathbf{z} \notin \mathcal{K}(\theta)\},$$

which corresponds to the set of hypotheses that could not be rejected if we observed $\mathbf{Z} = \mathbf{z}$ and used the given family of critical regions. Clearly

$$P_\theta\{\mathbf{z}\colon \theta \in C(\mathbf{z})\} = P_\theta\{\mathbf{z}\colon \mathbf{z} \notin \mathcal{K}(\theta)\} = 1 - P_\theta\{\mathbf{z}\colon \mathbf{z} \in \mathcal{K}(\theta)\} \geq 1 - \alpha.$$

Hence, $C(\mathbf{Z})$ is a $(1 - \alpha)$-level confidence set for θ.

Example 5.13 Let $\mathbf{Z}$ be a sample of size n from a $\mathcal{N}(\mu, 1)$ distribution. From Example 5.10, the critical region of an α-level test of the hypothesis $\mathrm{H}_0\colon \mu = \mu_0$ against the alternative $\mathrm{H}_1\colon \mu \neq \mu_0$ is

$$\mathcal{K}(\mu_0) = \left\{\mathbf{z}\colon |\bar{z} - \mu_0| > \frac{z_{(\alpha/2)}}{\sqrt{n}}\right\},$$

where $\bar{z}$ is the value of the sample mean for $\mathbf{Z} = \mathbf{z}$. The random interval

$$C(\mathbf{Z}) = \left\{\mu\colon |\bar{Z} - \mu| \leq \frac{z_{(\alpha/2)}}{\sqrt{n}}\right\}$$

is therefore a $(1 - \alpha)$-level confidence interval for μ. □

5.3.3 OPTIMALITY IN TESTING

In this section we introduce the problem of optimally choosing a test of a given hypothesis H_0. From the abstract viewpoint of statistical decision theory (Section 4.8), this problem may be represented as a sequential noncooperative game between the statistician and *Nature*.

Nature moves first by selecting a sample $\mathbf{z}$, that is, a realization of a random vector $\mathbf{Z}$, and one of two possible states, namely "H_0 is true" and "H_0 is false". Then, after observing the sample $\mathbf{z}$ but not knowing the state of Nature, the statistician chooses between two possible actions, namely a_0 = "do not reject H_0" and a_1 = "reject H_0". The consequences of each action under the different states of Nature are described by the 2×2 matrix

$$\begin{bmatrix} 0 & l_0 \\ l_1 & 0 \end{bmatrix}, \tag{5.8}$$

where the rows correspond to the actions and the columns to the states of Nature. The payoffs from taking the correct action are normalized to zero, whereas l_1 and l_0 are positive numbers representing the losses associated with Type I and Type II errors respectively.

Since the action of the statistician depends in general on the observed sample, varying $\mathbf{z}$ gives a decision function, that is, a mapping from the sample space into the set $\{a_0, a_1\}$, which specifies what action the statistician will choose for each of the possible samples. Given a decision function d, its risk is

$$r(d, \cdot) = \begin{cases} l_1 \Pr\{d(\mathbf{Z}) = a_1 \,|\, \mathrm{H}_0\}, & \text{if } \mathrm{H}_0 \text{ is true,} \\ l_0 \Pr\{d(\mathbf{Z}) = a_0 \,|\, \mathrm{H}_1\}, & \text{if } \mathrm{H}_1 \text{ is true,} \end{cases}$$

where $\Pr\{d(\mathbf{Z}) = a_1 \,|\, \mathrm{H}_0\}$ and $\Pr\{d(\mathbf{Z}) = a_0 \,|\, \mathrm{H}_1\}$ are the probabilities of Type I and Type II error, respectively. In general, for a given sample size, the probability of Type I error can only be made smaller by increasing the probability of Type II error, and vice versa.

To be specific, let $\mathbf{Z}$ be a sample of size n from a $\mathcal{N}(\mu, 1)$ distribution, and consider the problem of testing the simple hypothesis H_0: $\mu = \mu_0$ against the two-sided alternative H_1: $\mu \neq \mu_0$. The class of tests introduced in Example 5.10 rejects H_0 whenever $|\bar{Z} - \mu_0| > k$. The power function of an α-level test in this class was derived in Example 5.11. Rearranging such an expression gives the following relationship between the level α of the test and the probability β of Type II error

$$\beta = \Phi(\sqrt{n}\,(\mu_0 - \mu) + z_{(\alpha/2)}) - \Phi(\sqrt{n}\,(\mu_0 - \mu) - z_{(\alpha/2)}). \tag{5.9}$$

The form of this relationship is shown in Figure 41 for a fixed alternative μ and increasing values of n. Each point corresponds to a particular test, that is, a particular choice of the critical value.

We may now formulate the problem of selecting an optimal test within this class in a manner that is familiar to economists. Let $g_n(\alpha, \beta) = 0$ represent the relationship (5.9) between the probabilities of the two error types for a fixed sample size n, and let the function $u(\alpha, \beta)$ represent the preferences of a researcher about the likelihood

Figure 41 Trade-off between Type I (α) and Type II error probability (β) for a fixed alternative and increasing sample sizes. The test considered is a two-sided test of the hypothesis H$_0$: $\mu = \mu_0$ in the $\mathcal{N}(\mu, 1)$ model and is based on the critical region $\{|\bar{Z} - \mu_0| > z_{(\alpha/2)}/\sqrt{n}\}$.

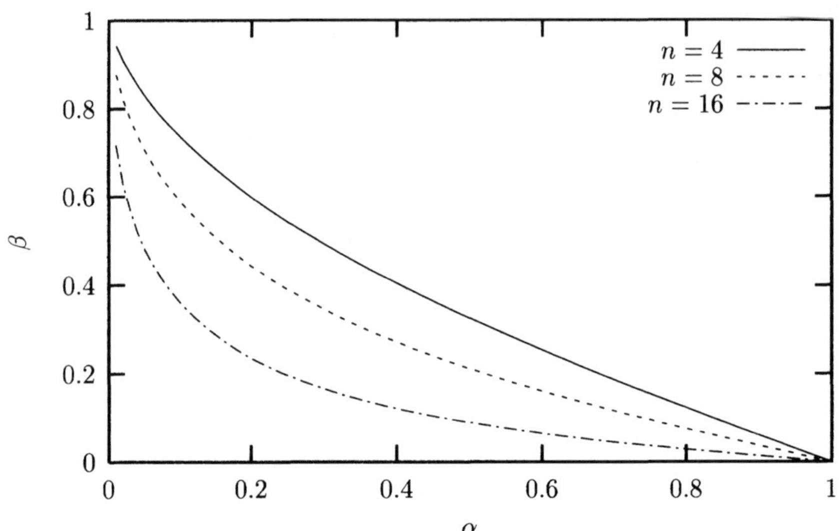

of the two error types. We may define an optimal test as a solution to the problem

$$\max_{0<\alpha,\beta<1} \quad u(\alpha, \beta)$$
$$\text{s.t.} \quad g_n(\alpha, \beta) = 0.$$

If u and g_n are smooth functions, then an optimal test (α_*, β_*) must satisfy the condition

$$\frac{\partial u/\partial \alpha}{\partial u/\partial \beta} = \frac{\partial g_n/\partial \alpha}{\partial g_n/\partial \beta}.$$

Unless preferences are of a special form, we would expect an optimal test to depend on the sample size n. In particular, we would expect tests of smaller and smaller size to be selected as n increases.

To choose an optimal test in a given class, various principles may be adopted. Each of them may be regarded as a particular specification of the preferences over the probabilities of the two error types. In the rest of this chapter we discuss two such principles.

1. *Classical hypothesis testing* corresponds to lexicographic preferences, with Type I error considered as the most important.
2. *Bayesian hypothesis testing* corresponds to preferences that can be represented in terms of the Bayes risk

$$\rho(d, \pi) = l_1 \Pr\{d(\mathbf{Z}) = a_1 \mid \mathrm{H}_0\}\, \pi + l_0 \Pr\{d(\mathbf{Z}) = a_0 \mid \mathrm{H}_1\}\, (1 - \pi),$$

where π is the prior probability assigned to H_0.

Because $\rho(d, \pi) = l_1 \alpha \pi + l_0 (1 - \beta)(1 - \pi)$, Bayesian hypothesis testing corresponds to preferences represented by a function $u(\alpha, \beta)$ which is linear.

5.3.4 *THE NEYMAN-PEARSON THEOREM*

The classical theory of hypothesis testing suggests controlling for Type I error by restricting attention to tests of a given level α, usually a small number such as $\alpha = .01$ or $\alpha = .05$. An optimal test in this class is one, if it exists, for which the probability of Type II error is uniformly minimized on Θ_1 or, equivalently, the power $\pi(\theta)$ is uniformly maximized on Θ_1. Such a test is called *uniformly most powerful (UMP)*.

Consider a parametric family $\{P_\theta, \theta \in \Theta\}$ of distributions on the sample space and the problem of testing a simple hypothesis H_0: $\theta = \theta_0$. We consider two cases, depending on whether the alternative hypothesis is simple or composite. The case of a composite alternative will be discussed in the next section.

When the alternative is simple, that is, $\Theta_1 = \{\theta_1\}$, the existence of a most powerful test is guaranteed by the following result.

Theorem 5.1 (Neyman–Pearson) *Let $\{P_\theta, \theta \in \Theta\}$ be a parametric family of distributions on the sample space, with density function $f(\mathbf{z}; \theta)$, and let $\mathcal{K}$ be a region of the sample space such that $P_{\theta_0}\{\mathcal{K}\} \leq \alpha$. If there exists a region $\mathcal{K}^*$ of the form*

$$\mathcal{K}^* = \left\{\mathbf{z}\colon \frac{f(\mathbf{z}; \theta_1)}{f(\mathbf{z}; \theta_0)} > k\right\}$$

and such that $P_{\theta_0}\{\mathcal{K}^*\} = \alpha$, then $P_{\theta_1}\{\mathcal{K}^*\} \geq P_{\theta_1}\{\mathcal{K}\}$.

Proof. Suppose that $f(\mathbf{z}; \theta)$ is a probability density function. If $f(\mathbf{z}; \theta)$ is a probability function, simply replace integration with summation.

Notice first that $\mathcal{K}$ is the union of the disjoint sets $\mathcal{K} \cap \mathcal{K}^*$ and $\mathcal{K} - \mathcal{K}^*$, while $\mathcal{K}^*$ is the union of the disjoint sets $\mathcal{K} \cap \mathcal{K}^*$ and $\mathcal{K}^* - \mathcal{K}$. Since $\alpha = P_{\theta_0}\{\mathcal{K}^*\} \geq P_{\theta_0}\{\mathcal{K}\}$, subtracting from both sides of this inequality the integral of $f(\mathbf{z}; \theta_0)$ over $\mathcal{K} \cap \mathcal{K}^*$ gives

$$\int_{\mathcal{K}^* - \mathcal{K}} f(\mathbf{z}; \theta_0)\, d\mathbf{z} \geq \int_{\mathcal{K} - \mathcal{K}^*} f(\mathbf{z}; \theta_0)\, d\mathbf{z}. \tag{5.10}$$

Next notice that $f(\mathbf{z}; \theta_1) > k f(\mathbf{z}; \theta_0)$ for all $\mathbf{z}$ in the subset $\mathcal{K}^* - \mathcal{K}$, while $f(\mathbf{z}; \theta_1) \leq k f(\mathbf{z}; \theta_0)$ for all $\mathbf{z}$ in the subset $\mathcal{K} - \mathcal{K}^*$. Multiplying (5.10) by k and using the above two inequalities we get

$$\int_{\mathcal{K}^* - \mathcal{K}} f(\mathbf{z}; \theta_1)\, d\mathbf{z} \geq \int_{\mathcal{K} - \mathcal{K}^*} f(\mathbf{z}; \theta_1)\, d\mathbf{z}. \tag{5.11}$$

Finally, adding to both sides of (5.11) the integral of $f(\mathbf{z}; \theta_1)$ over $\mathcal{K} \cap \mathcal{K}^*$ gives the desired result

$$P_{\theta_1}\{\mathcal{K}^*\} = \int_{\mathcal{K}^*} f(\mathbf{z}; \theta_1)\, d\mathbf{z} \geq \int_{\mathcal{K}} f(\mathbf{z}; \theta_1) d\mathbf{z} = P_{\theta_1}\{\mathcal{K}\}.$$

□

The region $\mathcal{K}^*$ is the critical region of a most powerful α-level test of the hypothesis $\mathrm{H}_0\colon \theta = \theta_0$ against the alternative $\mathrm{H}_1\colon \theta = \theta_1$. This provides a basis for choosing a critical value k, namely choose k such that, if possible, $P_{\theta_0}\{\lambda(\mathbf{Z}) > k\} = \alpha$, where the statistic

$$\lambda(\mathbf{Z}) = \frac{f(\mathbf{Z};\theta_1)}{f(\mathbf{Z};\theta_0)}$$

is called the *likelihood ratio.*

5.3.5 *COMPOSITE ALTERNATIVES*

When the alternative hypothesis is composite, a UMP α-level test exists if and only if the critical region is the same for each of the simple alternatives that make up H_1. This is sometimes the case for one-sided alternatives, but not when alternatives in more than one direction are of interest, as in the case of two-sided tests or composite hypotheses about a parameter vector.

Example 5.14 Let $\mathbf{Z}$ be a sample of size n from a $\mathcal{N}(\mu, \sigma^2)$ distribution. Because

$$f(\mathbf{z};\mu) = \left(\frac{1}{\sigma\sqrt{2\pi}}\right)^n \exp\left\{-\frac{n}{2\sigma^2}[\hat{\sigma}^2 + (\bar{z}-\mu)^2]\right\},$$

where $\bar{z}$ denotes the value of the sample mean corresponding to $\mathbf{Z} = \mathbf{z}$, the likelihood ratio for two distributions with the same variance but different means $\mu_0 \neq \mu_1$ is

$$\lambda(\mathbf{z}) = \frac{f(\mathbf{z};\mu_1)}{f(\mathbf{z};\mu_0)} = \exp\left[\frac{n\bar{z}}{\sigma^2}(\mu_1-\mu_0) + \frac{n}{2\sigma^2}(\mu_0^2-\mu_1^2)\right].$$

Suppose now that σ^2 is known and consider two cases, depending on whether $\mu_1 > \mu_0$ or $\mu_1 < \mu_0$. In the first case, $\lambda(\mathbf{z}) > k$ if and only if $\bar{z} > c$, where the critical value c is such that

$$\alpha = P_{\mu_0}\{\bar{Z} > c\} = P_{\mu_0}\left\{\frac{\bar{Z}-\mu_0}{\sigma/\sqrt{n}} \geq \frac{c-\mu_0}{\sigma/\sqrt{n}}\right\} = 1 - \Phi\left(\frac{c-\mu_0}{\sigma/\sqrt{n}}\right).$$

Hence

$$\frac{c-\mu_0}{\sigma/\sqrt{n}} = \Phi^{-1}(1-\alpha) = z_{(\alpha)},$$

and therefore $c = \mu_0 + z_{(\alpha)}\sigma/\sqrt{n}$. Thus, a most powerful α-level test of the hypothesis $\mathrm{H}_0\colon \mu = \mu_0$ against the simple alternative $\mathrm{H}_1\colon \mu = \mu_1$ is based on the critical region

$$\mathcal{K}_1 = \left\{\mathbf{z}\colon \bar{z} - \mu_0 > z_{(\alpha)}\frac{\sigma}{\sqrt{n}}\right\}.$$

Since this critical region does not depend on μ_1, it is also the critical region of a UMP α-level test of H_0 against the one-sided alternative $\mathrm{H}_1\colon \mu > \mu_0$.

When $\mu_0 < \mu_1$, an analogous argument shows that a UMP α-level test of the hypothesis H_0 against the one-sided alternative $\mathrm{H}_1\colon \mu < \mu_0$ is based on the critical region

$$\mathcal{K}_2 = \left\{\mathbf{z}\colon \bar{z} - \mu_0 < -z_{(\alpha)}\frac{\sigma}{\sqrt{n}}\right\}.$$

The fact that $\mathcal{K}_1 \neq \mathcal{K}_2$ implies that, even when σ^2 is known, there exists no UMP α-level test of H_0 against the two-sided alternative H_1: $\mu \neq \mu_0$. In particular, the test that rejects H_0 whenever

$$|\bar{Z} - \mu_0| > z_{(\alpha/2)} \frac{\sigma}{\sqrt{n}}, \tag{5.12}$$

although quite reasonable, is not UMP. □

When a UMP test does not exist, optimal tests may sometimes be found by restricting the class of tests. A widely used criterion is to require that $P_\theta\{\mathcal{K}\} \geq P_{\theta_0}\{\mathcal{K}\}$ for every $\theta \in \Theta_1$ and all $\theta_0 \in \Theta_0$, that is, the probability of Type I error cannot exceed the power of the test under any alternative in Θ_1. A test satisfying this criterion is called *unbiased*. In the case of Example 5.10, with σ^2 known, the critical region (5.12) can be shown to define a UMP unbiased α-level test of the hypothesis H_0: $\mu = \mu_0$ against the two-sided alternative H_1: $\mu \neq \mu_0$ (see e.g. Lehmann 1988).

Another possibility when a UMP test cannot be found is to consider alternatives that represent small deviations from the null hypothesis and look for a test that maximizes the power locally in a neighborhood of H_0. Given a regular parametric model $\{f(\mathbf{z};\theta), \theta \in \Theta\}$, where Θ is an open subset of the real line, let $L(\theta) = \ln f(\mathbf{Z};\theta)$ and let $S(\theta) = L'(\theta)$ be the likelihood score. By the Neyman–Pearson theorem, a most powerful test of H_0: $\theta = \theta_0$ against the simple alternative H_1: $\theta = \theta_1$, where $\theta_1 = \theta_0 + \delta$ and δ is a small number, rejects H_0 for large values of the logarithm of the likelihood ratio

$$\ln \lambda(\mathbf{Z}) = \ln f(\mathbf{Z};\theta_0 + \delta) - \ln f(\mathbf{Z};\theta_0) \approx \delta\, S(\theta_0).$$

Thus, for δ positive and sufficiently small, a critical region consists of large positive values of the likelihood score $S(\theta_0)$, whereas for δ negative and sufficiently small, it consists of large negative values of $S(\theta_0)$. It can be shown that the resulting test is *locally most powerful*, in the sense that it maximizes the slope of the power function at $\theta = \theta_0$ (see e.g. Cox & Hinkley 1974).

5.4 LIKELIHOOD-BASED TESTS

We have seen that UMP tests of a given level exist only for a limited class of problems, namely when θ is a scalar parameter and the set of alternatives is one-sided. In the case of two-sided alternatives or when θ is a parameter vector, no UMP test exists. We now introduce three testing principles which, although not UMP, have the advantage of general applicability.

Assume that the distribution of the observed data $\mathbf{Z}$ belongs to a regular parametric model $\{f(\mathbf{z};\theta), \theta \in \Theta\}$, where Θ is an open subset of $\Re^p$, and that the null hypothesis restricts the parameter θ to a subset Θ_0 of Θ defined by a set of $q \leq p$ linear equality constraints of the form $R\theta = r$, that is

$$\Theta_0 = \{\theta \in \Theta \colon R\theta = r\}, \tag{5.13}$$

where

$$R = \begin{bmatrix} R_1^\top \\ \vdots \\ R_q^\top \end{bmatrix}, \qquad r = \begin{pmatrix} r_1 \\ \vdots \\ r_q \end{pmatrix}$$

are, respectively, a known $q \times p$ matrix of rank q and a known q-vector. The alternative hypothesis is H_1: $R\theta \neq r$.

Example 5.15 The formulation (5.13) encompasses many important cases. If $R = I_p$ and $r = \theta_0$, where I_p denotes the unit matrix of order p, then (5.13) corresponds to the simple hypothesis H_0: $\theta = \theta_0$.

If $q < p$, then (5.13) does not specify the distribution of $\mathbf{Z}$ completely. An important special case is when H_0 only restricts some components of θ leaving the others completely unrestricted. For example, if $\theta = (\beta, \gamma)$, where the vectors β and γ are functionally independent, with dimension q and $p-q$ respectively, then the hypothesis H_0: $\beta = \beta_0$ may be written in the form (5.13) after putting $R = [I_q, 0]$ and $r = \beta_0$, where 0 denotes here the null matrix of order $q \times (p-q)$. □

Let $L(\theta) = c + \ln f(\mathbf{Z}; \theta)$, where c is an arbitrary constant, be the sample log-likelihood, let $S(\theta) = L'(\theta)$ be the likelihood score, and suppose that a ML estimator $\hat{\theta} = \hat{\theta}(\mathbf{Z})$ exists, is unique and corresponds to the unique root of the likelihood equation $S(\theta) = 0$. Imposing the constraint (5.13) on the estimation problem leads to the *constrained ML estimate*, defined as a solution $\tilde{\theta} = \tilde{\theta}(\mathbf{Z})$ to the problem of maximizing $L(\theta)$ over Θ_0 or, equivalently, to the problem

$$\begin{aligned} &\max_{\theta \in \Theta} L(\theta) \\ &\text{s.t. } R\theta = r. \end{aligned}$$

By Lagrange theorem, if $\tilde{\theta}$ is a constrained ML estimate, then there exists a non-negative vector $\tilde{\nu} = (\tilde{\nu}_1, \ldots, \tilde{\nu}_q)$ of Lagrange multipliers such that $\tilde{\theta}$ and $\tilde{\nu}$ together satisfy the *constrained likelihood equations*

$$\begin{aligned} 0 &= S(\tilde{\theta}) - R^\top \tilde{\nu}, \\ 0 &= R\tilde{\theta} - r. \end{aligned} \tag{5.14}$$

Under our set of assumptions, $\tilde{\theta}$ and $\tilde{\nu}$ are the unique solutions to this equation system.

Notice that $L(\hat{\theta}) \geq L(\tilde{\theta})$, with equality if and only if the unconstrained ML estimate $\hat{\theta}$ satisfies the constraints exactly or, equivalently, the Lagrange multiplier vector $\tilde{\nu}$ is identically equal to zero. This suggests three plausible measures of "distance" between H_0 and the sample evidence, namely:

1. the difference between $L(\hat{\theta})$ and $L(\tilde{\theta})$;
2. the norm of the vector $R\hat{\theta} - r$;
3. the norm of the likelihood score vector $S(\tilde{\theta})$ or, equivalently given (5.14), the norm of the vector $R^\top \tilde{\nu}$.

These three measures, illustrated in Figure 42, represent the basis for three alternative testing principles: the likelihood ratio, the Wald, and the score or Lagrange multiplier principles.

5.4.1 THE LIKELIHOOD RATIO PRINCIPLE

A *likelihood ratio test* rejects H_0 for large values of the statistic

$$\xi^R = 2[L(\hat{\theta}) - L(\tilde{\theta})].$$

Figure 42 The likelihood ratio (LR), Wald (W) and score (S) principles. The null hypothesis is H_0: $\theta = \theta_0$, and so the constrained ML estimator is $\tilde{\theta} = \theta_0$, whereas $R\hat{\theta} - r = \hat{\theta} - \theta_0$.

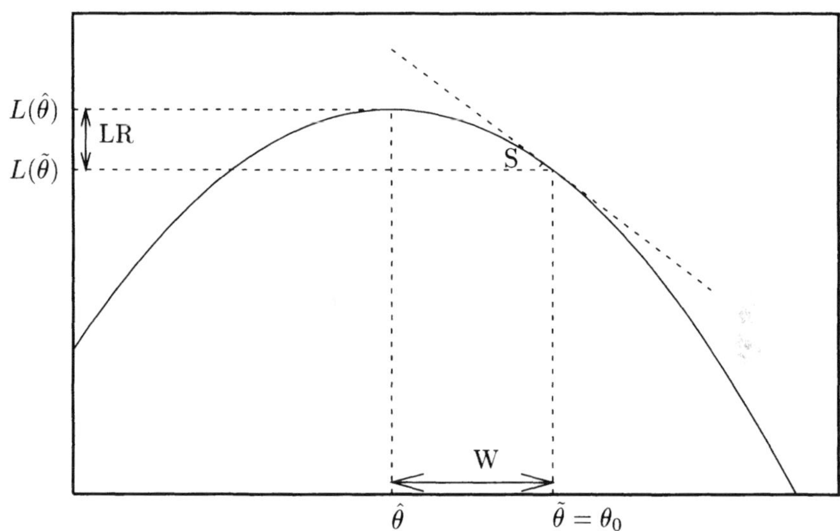

Example 5.16 Consider a population partitioned in S strata, let π_s denote the unemployment rate for the sth stratum and let $\pi = (\pi_1, \ldots, \pi_S)$. Suppose that the data consist of the S-vector $\mathbf{Z} = (Z_1, \ldots, Z_S)$, where Z_s is the number of unemployed in a random sample of size n_s from the sth stratum. Then the sample log-likelihood is

$$L(\pi) = c + \sum_{s=1}^{S} [Z_s \ln \pi_s + (n_s - Z_s) \ln(1 - \pi_s)],$$

where c is an arbitrary constant, the likelihood score is an S-vector with generic element

$$\frac{\partial L}{\pi_s} = \frac{Z_s - n_s \pi_s}{\pi_s(1 - \pi_s)}, \qquad s = 1, \ldots, S,$$

the ML estimate of π is $\hat{\pi} = (p_1, \ldots, p_S)$, where $p_s = Z_s/n_s$ is the sth stratum sample unemployment rate, and the maximized value of the sample log-likelihood is

$$L(\hat{\pi}) = c + \sum_{s=1}^{S} [Z_s \ln p_s + (n_s - Z_s) \ln(1 - p_s)].$$

Under the hypothesis H_0: $\pi_1 = \cdots = \pi_S$ of population homogeneity, the constrained ML estimate is $\tilde{\pi} = (p, \ldots, p)$, where $p = Z/n$, with $Z = \sum_s Z_s$ and $n = \sum_s n_s$. Notice that $p = \sum_s (n_s/n) p_s$ is a weighted average of the stratum sample unemployment rates p_s, with weights equal to the sample stratum weights n_s/n. The value of the log-likelihood at $\tilde{\pi}$ is therefore

$$L(\tilde{\pi}) = c + Z \ln p + (n - Z) \ln(1 - p).$$

Hence, a likelihood ratio test rejects H_0 for large values of the statistic

$$\xi^R = 2[L(\hat{\pi}) - L(\tilde{\pi})] = 2\sum_{s=1}^{S}\left[Z_s \ln\frac{p_s}{p} + (n_s - Z_s)\ln\frac{1-p_s}{1-p}\right].$$

□

5.4.2 THE WALD PRINCIPLE

Given a random m-vector Z with mean zero and finite nonsingular variance matrix Σ, the random variable

$$d(Z) = (Z^\top \Sigma^{-1} Z)^{1/2}$$

is called the *Mahalanobis norm* of Z or the *Mahalanobis distance* of Z from the origin. If $Z \sim \mathcal{N}_m(\mu, \Sigma)$, then $d(Z-\mu)^2 \sim \chi^2_m$.

An estimate of the Mahalanobis norm of the vector $R\hat{\theta} - r$ represents the basis of a *Wald test* of H_0. This test rejects H_0 for large values of the statistic

$$\xi^W = (R\hat{\theta} - r)^\top [R(\widehat{\operatorname{Var}}\,\hat{\theta})R^\top]^{-1}(R\hat{\theta} - r),$$

where $\widehat{\operatorname{Var}}\,\hat{\theta}$ is a p.d. estimate of the sampling variance of $\hat{\theta}$.

Example 5.17 Continuing with Example 5.16, the hypothesis of population homogeneity may be represented as H_0: $R\pi = 0$, where R is the $(S-1)\times S$ matrix

$$R = \begin{bmatrix} -1 & 1 & 0 & & \\ -1 & 0 & 1 & \ddots & \\ \vdots & & \ddots & \ddots & 0 \\ -1 & & & 0 & 1 \end{bmatrix}.$$

Because the sampling variance of the ML estimator $\hat{\pi}$ is a diagonal matrix whose diagonal elements $\pi_s(1-\pi_s)/n_s$ may be estimated by $\hat{V}_s = p_s(1-p_s)/n_s$, $s = 1, \ldots, S$, the Wald test statistic is $\xi^W = \hat{\pi}^\top R^\top [R(\widehat{\operatorname{Var}}\,\hat{\pi})R^\top]^{-1} R\hat{\pi}$, where

$$R\hat{\pi} = \begin{pmatrix} p_1 - p_2 \\ \vdots \\ p_1 - p_S \end{pmatrix}, \qquad R(\widehat{\operatorname{Var}}\,\hat{\pi})R^\top = \begin{bmatrix} \hat{V}_1 + \hat{V}_2 & \hat{V}_1 & \cdots & \hat{V}_1 \\ \hat{V}_1 & \hat{V}_1 + \hat{V}_3 & \cdots & \hat{V}_1 \\ \vdots & \vdots & & \vdots \\ \hat{V}_1 & \hat{V}_1 & \cdots & \hat{V}_1 + \hat{V}_S \end{bmatrix}.$$

□

5.4.3 THE SCORE PRINCIPLE

An estimate of the Mahalanobis norm of the vector $S(\tilde{\theta})$ represents the basis of a *score test* of H_0. This test rejects H_0 for large values of the statistic

$$\xi^S = \tilde{S}^\top \tilde{I}^{-1} \tilde{S},$$

where $\tilde{S} = S(\tilde{\theta})$ and $\tilde{I} = I(\tilde{\theta})$ are, respectively, the likelihood score and the expected total information, both evaluated at the constrained ML estimate. Because $\tilde{S} = R^\top \tilde{\nu}$ from the constrained likelihood equations, the test statistic may equivalently be represented as

$$\xi^S = \tilde{\nu}^\top R \tilde{I}^{-1} R^\top \tilde{\nu}.$$

For this reason, score tests are also called *Lagrange multiplier tests.*

Example 5.18 In the case of Example 5.16, the likelihood score evaluated at the constrained ML estimate $\tilde{\pi}$ is an S-vector with generic element

$$\frac{\partial L(\tilde{\pi})}{\partial \pi_s} = \frac{Z_s - n_s p}{p(1-p)}, \qquad s = 1, \ldots, S.$$

Because the expected total information is diagonal with diagonal elements equal to

$$I_{ss}(\pi) = \frac{n_s}{\pi_s(1-\pi_s)}, \qquad s = 1, \ldots, S,$$

the score test statistic is

$$\xi^S = \sum_{s=1}^{S} \frac{(Z_s - n_s p)^2}{n_s p(1-p)}.$$

□

5.4.4 PARTITIONED PARAMETERS

An important special case is when the null hypothesis only constrains a subset of the model parameters. Thus consider the case when $\theta = (\beta, \gamma)$, where β is a vector with $k < p$ elements, and H_0: $R\beta = r$, where R is a $q \times k$ matrix of rank $q \leq k$ and r is a q-vector. Partition the unconstrained and the constrained ML estimates of θ as $\hat{\theta} = (\hat{\beta}, \hat{\gamma})$ and $\tilde{\theta} = (\tilde{\beta}, \tilde{\gamma})$ respectively. Also partition the likelihood score and the expected total information, both evaluated at the constrained ML estimate, as as

$$\tilde{S} = \begin{pmatrix} \tilde{S}_\beta \\ \tilde{S}_\gamma \end{pmatrix}, \qquad \tilde{I} = \begin{bmatrix} \tilde{I}_{\beta\beta} & \tilde{I}_{\beta\gamma} \\ \tilde{I}_{\gamma\beta} & \tilde{I}_{\gamma\gamma} \end{bmatrix}.$$

In this case, a Wald test rejects H_0 for large values of the statistic

$$\xi^W = (R\hat{\beta} - r)^\top [R(\widehat{\operatorname{Var}}\,\hat{\beta})R^\top]^{-1}(R\hat{\beta} - r),$$

where $\widehat{\operatorname{Var}}\,\hat{\beta}$ is a p.d. estimate of the sampling variance of $\hat{\beta}$.

Since γ is unconstrained, $\tilde{S}_\gamma = 0$ and a score test rejects H_0 for large values of the statistic

$$\xi^S = \tilde{S}_\beta^\top \tilde{I}^{\beta\beta} \tilde{S}_\beta,$$

where $\tilde{I}^{\beta\beta}$ denotes the top-left block of $\tilde{I}^{-1}$. By the formulae for the inverse of a partitioned matrix (see Appendix A.7), we have that

$$\tilde{I}^{\beta\beta} = (\tilde{I}_{\beta\beta} - \tilde{I}_{\beta\gamma}\tilde{I}_{\gamma\gamma}^{-1}\tilde{I}_{\gamma\beta})^{-1}.$$

If the two components of the likelihood score are uncorrelated, then $I_{\beta\gamma} = 0$ and the score test statistic simplifies to

$$\xi^S = \tilde{S}_\beta^\top \tilde{I}_{\beta\beta}^{-1} \tilde{S}_\beta.$$

5.4.5 SAMPLING DISTRIBUTION

An important consideration in choosing between the three principles is the ease with which the relevant test statistics can be constructed. The Wald test statistic only requires computing the unconstrained ML estimator, the score test statistic only requires computing the constrained one, while the likelihood ratio test statistic requires computing both.

Usually, the difficult task is determining the distribution of the various test statistics and therefore the critical region of a test of a given level.

Example 5.19 Let $\mathbf{Z}$ be a sample of size n from a $\mathcal{N}(\mu, \sigma^2)$ distribution with $\theta = (\mu, \sigma^2)$ unknown, and consider the problem of testing the hypothesis H_0: $\mu = \mu_0$ against the two-sided alternative H_1: $\mu \neq \mu_0$. Because the parameter σ^2 is left unconstrained, H_0 is of the form (5.13) with $R = (1, 0)$ and $r = \mu_0$. The sample log-likelihood is

$$L(\theta) = c - \frac{n}{2} \ln \sigma^2 - \frac{n}{2\sigma^2}[\hat{\sigma}^2 + (\bar{Z} - \mu)^2],$$

where c is an arbitrary constant and $\hat{\theta} = (\bar{Z}, \hat{\sigma}^2)$ is the unconstrained ML estimate of θ. The constrained ML estimate of θ is $\tilde{\theta} = (\mu_0, \tilde{\sigma}^2)$, where

$$\tilde{\sigma}^2 = n^{-1} \sum_{i=1}^{n} (Z_i - \mu_0)^2 = \hat{\sigma}^2 + (\bar{Z} - \mu_0)^2 \geq \hat{\sigma}^2.$$

Hence, a likelihood ratio test rejects H_0 for large values of the statistic

$$\xi^R = 2[L(\hat{\theta}) - L(\tilde{\theta})] = n \ln \frac{\tilde{\sigma}^2}{\hat{\sigma}^2} = n \ln \left[1 + \frac{(\bar{Z} - \mu_0)^2}{\hat{\sigma}^2}\right].$$

The critical region of a likelihood ratio test corresponds to large values of the statistic

$$\frac{(\bar{Z} - \mu_0)^2}{\hat{\sigma}^2} = \frac{1}{n-1} \frac{(\bar{Z} - \mu_0)^2}{s^2/n} = \frac{F(\mathbf{Z})}{n-1},$$

where $F(\mathbf{Z}) = n(\bar{Z} - \mu_0)^2/s^2$. Because under H_0 the statistic $F(\mathbf{Z})$ has a (central) F-distribution with $(1, n-1)$ degrees of freedom, an α-level likelihood ratio test rejects H_0 whenever $F(\mathbf{Z}) > F_{(\alpha)}$, where $F_{(\alpha)}$ denotes the upper αth quantile of the $F_{1,n-1}$ distribution. One may also construct a one-sided test because, under H_0, the statistic $T(\mathbf{Z}) = \sqrt{F(\mathbf{Z})}$ has a t-distribution with $n - 1$ degrees of freedom.

Next observe that

$$R\hat{\theta} - r = \bar{Z} - \mu_0, \qquad R(\widehat{\operatorname{Var}} \,\hat{\theta})R^\top = \widehat{\operatorname{Var}} \,\bar{Z} = \hat{\sigma}^2/n.$$

Hence, a Wald test rejects H_0 for large values of the statistic

$$\xi^W = \frac{(\bar{Z} - \mu_0)^2}{\hat{\sigma}^2/n} = \frac{n}{n-1} F(\mathbf{Z}).$$

A Wald and a likelihood ratio test therefore have the same critical regions. Finally, since

$$S(\tilde{\theta}) = \begin{pmatrix} n(\bar{Z} - \mu_0)/\tilde{\sigma}^2 \\ 0 \end{pmatrix}, \qquad I(\tilde{\theta}) = \begin{bmatrix} n/\tilde{\sigma}^2 & 0 \\ 0 & n/(2\tilde{\sigma}^4) \end{bmatrix},$$

the score test statistic is

$$\xi^S = \frac{(\bar{Z} - \mu_0)^2}{\tilde{\sigma}^2/n} = \frac{\xi^W}{1 + n^{-1}\xi^W}.$$

Because ξ^S is a strictly monotone transformation of ξ^W, all three principles lead in this case to critical regions based on the $F_{1,n-1}$ distribution. □

Exact sampling results are generally not available, except for the important special case when the sample log-likelihood is quadratic.

Theorem 5.2 *If the sample log-likelihood L is quadratic, that is, of the form $L(\theta) = c - \frac{1}{2}(b - \theta)^\top Q^{-1}(b - \theta)$, where $\mathrm{E}_\theta\, b = \theta$ and $\mathrm{Var}_\theta\, b = Q$, then:*

(i) *the likelihood ratio, Wald and score statistics for testing the hypothesis H_0: $R\theta = r$ are all equal to $\xi = (R\hat{\theta} - r)^\top (RQR^\top)^{-1}(R\hat{\theta} - r)$;*
(ii) *if $b \sim \mathcal{N}_p(\theta, Q)$, then the sampling distribution of ξ is noncentral chi-square with q degrees of freedom and noncentrality parameter*

$$\lambda = (R\theta - r)^\top (RQR^\top)^{-1}(R\theta - r).$$

Proof. Observe first that $S(\theta) = L'(\theta) = Q^{-1}(b - \theta)$ and $-L''(\theta) = Q^{-1} = I(\theta)$. Since the unconstrained ML estimate $\hat{\theta}$ is equal to b, a Wald test rejects H_0 for large values of the statistic

$$\xi = (R\hat{\theta} - r)^\top (RQR^\top)^{-1}(R\hat{\theta} - r).$$

If $\tilde{\theta}$ and $\tilde{\nu}$ are the roots of the constrained likelihood equations, then

$$0 = Q^{-1}(b - \tilde{\theta}) - R^\top \tilde{\nu},$$
$$0 = R\tilde{\theta} - r.$$

Solving with respect to $(\tilde{\theta}, \tilde{\nu})$ gives

$$\tilde{\theta} = \hat{\theta} - QR^\top (RQR^\top)^{-1}(R\hat{\theta} - r),$$
$$\tilde{\nu} = (RQR^\top)^{-1}(R\hat{\theta} - r),$$
$$S(\tilde{\theta}) = R^\top (RQR^\top)^{-1}(R\hat{\theta} - r).$$

Hence, a score test is also based on ξ. Substituting the expression for $\tilde{\theta}$ into the sample log-likelihood gives

$$L(\tilde{\theta}) = c - \frac{1}{2}(b - \tilde{\theta})^\top Q^{-1}(b - \tilde{\theta}) = c - \frac{1}{2}(R\hat{\theta} - r)^\top (RQR^\top)^{-1}(R\hat{\theta} - r).$$

Because $L(\hat{\theta}) = c$, a likelihood ratio test is also based on ξ. Finally, if $b \sim \mathcal{N}_p(\theta, Q)$, then $R\hat{\theta} - r \sim \mathcal{N}(R\theta - h, RQR^\top)$, and so part (ii) follows. □

If the log-likelihood is quadratic and the statistic b is normally distributed, then Theorem 5.2 gives the sampling distribution of the test statistic ξ under the null hypothesis and any fixed alternative. Under H_0, the statistic ξ is a pivot because its distribution is (central) chi-square with q degrees of freedom and therefore does not depend on the parameter θ. This result is the basis for constructing critical regions of tests of a given level. Thus, an α-level test rejects H_0 whenever $\xi > c_{(\alpha)}$, where $c_{(\alpha)}$ is the upper αth quantile of the χ^2_q-distribution.

Under H_1, the sampling distribution of ξ is noncentral chi-square with q degrees of freedom and noncentrality parameter λ. The noncentrality parameter is equal to the squared norm of the vector $R\theta - r$ in the metric of the matrix $(RQR^\top)^{-1}$ and is therefore a measure of the distance between the null and the alternative hypotheses. Because the probability that ξ exceeds the critical value $c_{(\alpha)}$ is an increasing function of λ, the power of the test is greater than α under any alternative, that is, the test is unbiased. Further, the test rejects the null hypothesis with probability close to one for alternatives that are very far from H_0.

If the log-likelihood is not quadratic, then the likelihood ratio, Wald and score test statistics are no longer identical and their sampling distribution tends to be quite complicated. As is clear from the proof of Theorem 4.14, however, for sufficiently large n the sample log-likelihood $L_n(\theta)$ is approximately quadratic in a neighborhood of $\hat\theta_n$, that is,

$$L_n(\theta) - L_n(\hat\theta_n) + \frac{n}{2}(\hat\theta_n - \theta)^\top \mathcal{I}(\theta_0)\,(\hat\theta_n - \theta) \xrightarrow{\mathrm{p}} 0.$$

It therefore seems plausible that, in large samples, an analogue of Theorem 5.2 may hold. In fact, one can show the following.

Theorem 5.3 *Suppose that the assumptions of the multivariate generalization of Theorem 4.14 hold. If ξ_n^R, ξ_n^W and ξ_n^S are, respectively, the likelihood ratio, Wald and score test statistics for testing the hypothesis* H_0: $R\theta = r$, *where R is a $q \times p$ matrix of rank q, then:*

(i) *the likelihood ratio, Wald and score test statistics are asymptotically equivalent, that is, $\xi_n^R - \xi_n^W \xrightarrow{\mathrm{p}} 0$ and $\xi_n^R - \xi_n^S \xrightarrow{\mathrm{p}} 0$;*
(ii) *the limiting distribution of any of the three test statistics is noncentral chi-square with q degrees of freedom and noncentrality parameter*

$$\lambda = (R\theta_0 - r)^\top [R\mathcal{I}(\theta_0)^{-1}R^\top]^{-1}(R\theta_0 - r).$$

Thus, for large samples and under appropriate regularity conditions, the chi-square distribution still provides a good approximation in all three cases. One important regularity condition requires the parameter space to be an open subset of $\Re^p$. This implies that Theorem 5.3 is not applicable in cases involving parameters on the boundary of the parameter space.

5.4.6 BOOTSTRAP HYPOTHESIS TESTING

If the sampling distribution of a test statistic is not known exactly, then the bootstrap provides an alternative to approximate tests based on the assumption of a large sample size. This section considers two approaches to the bootstrap.

The first is applicable when θ is a scalar parameter and H_0 is a simple hypothesis of the form H_0: $\theta = \theta_0$. Given the duality between confidence sets and critical regions, an approximate α-level test may be obtained by first constructing a bootstrap $(1-\alpha)$-level confidence interval for θ and then rejecting H_0 if such an interval does not contain θ_0.

This method is easily generalized to the case when θ is a vector of parameters and the null hypothesis constrains a specific linear combination $\lambda^\top\theta$ of the parameters, that is, H_0: $\lambda^\top\theta = h$, where h is a known constant. In this case, an approximate α-level test is obtained by first constructing a bootstrap $(1-\alpha)$-level confidence interval for $\lambda^\top\theta$ and then rejecting H_0 if such an interval does not contain the value h.

While the first approach may be based on the nonparametric bootstrap, that discussed now requires the parametric bootstrap. Suppose that $\mathbf{Z}$ is a sample of size n from a distribution in a parametric family $\{F(z;\theta), \theta \in \Theta\}$ and that the null hypothesis consists of a set of linear equality constraints of the form $R\theta = r$. Let $\xi(\mathbf{Z})$ denote a test statistic that is pivotal or approximately so, such as the likelihood ratio, Wald or score test statistics. We have seen that, when the sampling distribution of $\xi(\mathbf{Z})$ under H_0 is known, an α-level test may be based on the p-value

$$p(\mathbf{z}) = \Pr\{\xi(\mathbf{Z}) \geq \xi(\mathbf{z}) \,|\, H_0\},$$

and rejects H_0 whenever $p(\mathbf{z}) < \alpha$. When the sampling distribution of $\xi(\mathbf{Z})$ under H_0 is unknown, a test may be based on an estimate of the p-value obtained from the parametric bootstrap. Algorithm 5.2 is inappropriate in this case because the ML estimate $\hat{\theta}$ does not satisfy H_0 in general and therefore does not give a good estimate of the distribution function of $\mathbf{Z}$ under H_0. The following modification of the bootstrap algorithm may be used instead.

Algorithm 5.3

(1) *Compute the parametric estimate $F(z;\tilde{\theta})$ using the constrained ML estimate.*
(2) *Draw a sample $\mathbf{Z}^*$ of size n from $F(z;\tilde{\theta})$.*
(3) *Compute $\xi^* = \xi(\mathbf{Z}^*)$.*
(4) *Repeat steps (2) and (3) a sufficiently high number B of times, obtaining bootstrap replicates $\xi_1^*, \ldots, \xi_B^*$.*
(5) *Use the empirical distribution of $\xi_1^*, \ldots, \xi_B^*$ to approximate the p-value by $\hat{p}_B(\mathbf{z}) = \widehat{\Pr}_B\{\xi^* \geq \xi(\mathbf{z})\}$.*

The bootstrap Algorithm 5.3 resamples from the parametric estimate $F(z\,|\,\tilde{\theta})$ of the parent distribution function under H_0 in order to compute an estimate of the p-value. This estimate is just the fraction of bootstrap replicates ξ^* that exceed the observed value of the test statistic for the given sample $\mathbf{Z} = \mathbf{z}$.

5.5 BAYESIAN HYPOTHESIS TESTING

What characterizes Bayesian hypothesis testing is the fact that prior probabilities are assigned to the hypotheses to be compared. These prior probabilities summarize the information available to the investigator before the data are observed.

5.5.1 SIMPLE HYPOTHESES

Consider first the case when there are only two simple hypotheses, H_0 and H_1, each specifying an alternative probability model for the data. If π denotes the prior probability assigned to H_0, then the *prior odds-ratio* in favor of H_1 is equal to $(1-\pi)/\pi$. Suppose that the investigator can only take one of two actions: a_0 = "accept H_0" or a_1 = "reject H_0". Given the loss matrix (5.8), the prior expected loss from each action is

$$\rho(a, \pi) = \begin{cases} l_0(1-\pi), & \text{if } a = a_0, \\ l_1 \pi, & \text{if } a = a_1. \end{cases}$$

By Bayes theorem, the posterior probability of H_0 is

$$\pi(\mathbf{z}) = \Pr\{H_0 \,|\, \mathbf{z}\} = \frac{f(\mathbf{z} \,|\, H_0)\pi}{f(\mathbf{z})},$$

where $f(\mathbf{z}) = f(\mathbf{z} \,|\, H_0)\pi + f(\mathbf{z} \,|\, H_1)(1-\pi)$. The *posterior odds-ratio* in favor of H_1 is then

$$\frac{1-\pi(\mathbf{z})}{\pi(\mathbf{z})} = \frac{1-\pi}{\pi} \frac{f(\mathbf{z} \,|\, H_1)}{f(\mathbf{z} \,|\, H_0)}.$$

Thus, the posterior odds-ratio is the product of the prior odds-ratio and the likelihood ratio $f(\mathbf{z} \,|\, H_1)/f(\mathbf{z} \,|\, H_0)$. Given the loss function and the posterior probabilities for the two hypotheses, the posterior expected loss associated with the two actions is

$$\rho(a, \pi(\mathbf{z})) = \begin{cases} l_0(1-\pi(\mathbf{z})), & \text{if } a = a_0, \\ l_1 \pi(\mathbf{z}), & \text{if } a = a_1. \end{cases}$$

The investigator will therefore reject H_0 whenever $\rho(a_1, \pi(\mathbf{z})) < \rho(a_0, \pi(\mathbf{z}))$, that is, whenever

$$\frac{1-\pi(\mathbf{z})}{\pi(\mathbf{z})} > \frac{l_1}{l_0}$$

or, equivalently, whenever

$$\frac{f(\mathbf{z} \,|\, H_1)}{f(\mathbf{z} \,|\, H_0)} > \frac{l_1 \pi}{l_0(1-\pi)},$$

where the likelihood ratio is compared with the ratio of prior expected losses. Thus, the Bayesian approach provides a justification for tests based on the likelihood ratio. At the same time, it indirectly solves the problem of choosing the significance level of a test, a problem left unresolved by the classical approach, by selecting the ratio of the prior expected losses as the critical value of the likelihood ratio. In particular, if the loss matrix is symmetric, that is, $l_0 = l_1$, then the critical value of the likelihood ratio is simply equal to the prior odds-ratio in favor of H_0. If in addition the two hypotheses are equally probable on a priori grounds, then the critical value of the likelihood ratio is equal to one.

Example 5.20 Let $\mathbf{Z}$ be a sample of size n from a $\mathcal{N}(\mu, 1)$ distribution. If H_0: $\mu = \mu_0$ and H_1: $\mu = \mu_1 > \mu_0$, then

$$\frac{f(\mathbf{Z} \,|\, \mu_1)}{f(\mathbf{Z} \,|\, \mu_0)} = \exp\left\{\frac{n}{2}[2\bar{Z}(\mu_1 - \mu_0) - (\mu_1^2 - \mu_0^2)]\right\}.$$

Hence, H_0 is rejected whenever

$$2\bar{Z}(\mu_1 - \mu_0) - (\mu_1^2 - \mu_0^2) > \frac{2}{n} \ln \frac{l_1 \pi}{l_0(1-\pi)}.$$

As $n \to \infty$, the last term converges to zero and so H_0 is rejected whenever $\bar{Z} > \frac{1}{2}(\mu_0 + \mu_1) > \mu_0$. This result differs from that obtained in Example 5.14, where the critical region of the UMP test converged to $\{\bar{Z} > \mu_0\}$ as $n \to \infty$, which is wider than that obtained from the Bayesian approach. □

5.5.2 *COMPOSITE HYPOTHESES*

Now suppose that the model for the data is the parametric family $\{f(\mathbf{z}\,|\,\theta), \theta \in \Theta\}$ under H_0, and a different parametric family $\{g(\mathbf{z}\,|\,\gamma), \gamma \in \Gamma\}$ under H_1. The prior probabilities assigned to H_0 and H_1 are π and $1 - \pi$, as before.

Bayes theorem gives posterior probabilities which are exactly as in Section 5.5.1, except that now

$$f(\mathbf{z}\,|\,\mathrm{H}_0) = \int_\Theta f(\mathbf{z}\,|\,\theta)\, p(\theta)\, d\theta,$$

$$f(\mathbf{z}\,|\,\mathrm{H}_1) = \int_\Gamma g(\mathbf{z}\,|\,\gamma)\, q(\gamma)\, d\gamma,$$

where p and q denote the prior distributions over Θ and Γ respectively, and the functions $f(\mathbf{z}\,|\,\mathrm{H}_0)$ and $f(z\,|\,\mathrm{H}_1)$ are the marginal likelihoods under the two hypotheses. In this case, the posterior odds-ratio is

$$\frac{1-\pi(\mathbf{z})}{\pi(\mathbf{z})} = \frac{1-\pi}{\pi} \frac{\int_\Gamma g(\mathbf{z}\,|\,\gamma)\, q(\gamma)\, d\gamma}{\int_\Theta f(\mathbf{z}\,|\,\theta)\, p(\theta)\, d\theta},$$

which is the product of the prior odds-ratio and the ratio of the marginal likelihoods. The latter is also called the *Bayes factor* in favor of model H_1 against model H_0. When the Bayes factor is greater than one, the posterior odds-ratio exceeds the prior odds-ratio and we say that the data favor H_1 over H_0. If the loss function is symmetric, that is $l_0 = l_1$, and the two hypotheses are equally probable, then the investigator will reject H_0 whenever the Bayes factor is greater than one.

Example 5.21 (Lindley paradox) Let $\mathbf{Z} = (Z_1, \ldots, Z_n)$ be a sample from a $\mathcal{N}(\mu, 1)$ distribution. Let $\mathrm{H}_0\colon \mu = 0$, $\mathrm{H}_1\colon \mu \neq 0$, and suppose that the prior distribution of μ gives mass π at $\mu = 0$ and allocates the rest according to a $\mathcal{N}(0, 1/h_0)$ distribution. It can be shown (see e.g. Leamer 1978, Section 4.3) that the posterior odds-ratio in favor of H_1 is

$$\frac{1-\pi(\mathbf{Z})}{\pi(\mathbf{Z})} = \frac{1-\pi}{\pi} \left(1 + \frac{n}{h_0}\right)^{-1/2} \exp\left[\frac{T^2}{2}\left(1 + \frac{h_0}{n}\right)^{-1}\right],$$

where $T^2 = n\bar{Z}^2$ is the classical F-test statistic. Thus, the posterior odds-ratio is equal to the prior odds-ratio times the Bayes factor

$$B(T^2, n, h_0) = \left(1 + \frac{n}{h_0}\right)^{-1/2} \exp\left[\frac{T^2}{2}\left(1 + \frac{h_0}{n}\right)^{-1}\right].$$

Since the Bayes factor is an increasing function of T^2 for a fixed sample size n, the larger is T^2, the more the data cast doubts on H_0. However, the Bayes factor is also a function of the sample size. In particular, for a fixed T^2, one can make the Bayes factor arbitrarily small by choosing n large enough. In this case, rather than concluding that the data are inconsistent with H_0, as the classical approach based on T^2 would do, we conclude that they quite strongly favor H_0. □

5.5.3 MULTIPLE HYPOTHESES

Unlike the classical approach, the Bayesian approach is straightforward to generalize to more than two hypotheses. Suppose there are J hypotheses $H_1, \ldots H_J$, and J available actions $a_1, \ldots, a_J$, where $a_j =$ "accept H_j". The loss function for this problem may be represented by a $J \times J$ matrix whose ijth element l_{ij} is the loss from action a_i when hypothesis H_j is true. The prior probabilities assigned to the hypotheses may be represented by a J-vector p whose jth element p_j is the probability that H_j is true. The vector p represents a proper prior if $\sum_j p_j = 1$.

Given the loss matrix $[l_{ij}]$, the prior expected loss from each available action is

$$\rho(a_i, p) = \sum_j l_{ij} p_j, \qquad i = 1, \ldots, J.$$

By Bayes theorem, the posterior probability of H_j is

$$p_j(\mathbf{z}) = \frac{f(\mathbf{z} \,|\, H_j)\, p_j}{f(\mathbf{z})}, \qquad j = 1, \ldots, J,$$

where $f(\mathbf{z}) = \sum_j f(\mathbf{z} \,|\, H_j)\, p_j$. Given the loss matrix and the posterior probabilities of the J hypotheses, one can evaluate the posterior expected loss associated with each available action

$$\rho(a_i, p(\mathbf{z})) = \sum_j l_{ij} p_j(\mathbf{z}), \qquad i = 1, \ldots, J.$$

The investigator will therefore choose H_i whenever

$$\rho(a_i, p(\mathbf{z})) \leq \rho(a_h, p(\mathbf{z})), \qquad \text{for all } h = 1, \ldots, J,$$

or, equivalently, whenever

$$\sum_j (l_{ij} - l_{hj}) f(\mathbf{z} \,|\, H_j)\, p_j \leq 0, \qquad \text{for all } h = 1, \ldots, J.$$

BIBLIOGRAPHIC NOTES

The bootstrap was introduced by Efron (1979). The jackknife goes back to Quenouille (1949) and Tukey (1958). Good introductions to both methods are the volume of Efron and Tibshirani (1993) and the review article of Hall (1994). A more advanced treatment is Shao and Tu (1995). An advanced treatment of the bootstrap is Hall (1992).

The best way of constructing bootstrap confidence intervals is still an unresolved issue. For a discussion of various solutions proposed in the literature, see Di Ciccio and Efron (1996).

Standard references for classical hypothesis testing are Cox and Hinkley (1974) and Lehmann (1988). For an elegant early presentation see Wald (1947). Wald (1950) was also the first to point out the formal analogy between hypothesis testing and noncooperative games.

The Wald test goes back to Wald (1943), the score test to Rao (1948). The Lagrange multiplier formulation of the score test was introduced by Aitcheson and Silvey (1958) and Silvey (1959).

Our discussion of the Bayesian approach to hypothesis testing is based on Box and Tiao (1973) and Leamer (1978).

PROBLEMS

5.1 Given a random variable Z with finite fourth moments and a smooth function h, use the delta method up to the second order to find an approximation to the variance of $h(Z)$. What happens if the distribution of Z is symmetric?

5.2 Derive jackknife estimates of the sampling variance of the mean squared deviation and the sample variance.

5.3 Let $\hat{\theta}$ be an estimator of a parameter θ based on a sample of size n and suppose that

$$\mathrm{E}\,\hat{\theta} = \theta + \frac{a_1}{n} + \frac{a_2}{n^2} + \cdots$$

for some constants $a_1, a_2, \ldots$. Show that the jackknife bias corrected estimator $\tilde{\theta} = \hat{\theta}_{(\cdot)} + n(\hat{\theta} - \hat{\theta}_{(\cdot)})$ is biased for θ, but its bias is only $O(n^2)$.

5.4 Consider the class of tests introduced in Example 5.10. Show that a test of level $\alpha' > \alpha$ has uniformly lower power than one of level α.

5.5 Given a sample from a $\mathcal{N}(\mu, \sigma^2)$ distribution with μ and σ^2 unknown, derive an α-level likelihood ratio test of the hypothesis that $\sigma^2 = \sigma_0^2$ against the alternative that $\sigma^2 \neq \sigma_0^2$.

5.6 Given a sample from an exponential distribution with parameter θ, construct a most powerful α-level test of the hypothesis H_0: $\theta = \theta_0$ against the simple alternative H_1: $\theta = \theta_1$, with $\theta_1 > \theta_0$. Determine whether this is a UMP test of the hypothesis H_0 against the one-sided hypothesis H_1: $\theta > \theta_0$.

5.7 Show that the Mahalanobis norm $d(\cdot)$ is invariant under nonsingular linear transformations, that is, if Z is a random vector with finite nonsingular variance matrix and $Y = AZ$, where A is a nonsingular matrix, then $d(Z) = d(Y)$.

5.8 Given a sequence of n Bernoulli trials, consider the hypothesis that the probability of success in a single trial is equal to π_0. Derive the Wald and score test statistics and show that they are identical.

5.9 Given a sample **Z** from a $\mathcal{N}(\mu, 1)$ distribution with μ unknown, construct a 5%-level test of H_0: $\mu = 0$ against the alternative H_1: $\mu = 1$. Write down the posterior odds-ratio $p(\mathrm{H}_0 \,|\, \mathbf{Z})/p(\mathrm{H}_1 \,|\, \mathbf{Z})$. If $p(\mathrm{H}_0)/p(\mathrm{H}_1) = 1$, what is the significance level of a test that rejects H_0 if $p(\mathrm{H}_0 \,|\, \mathbf{Z})/p(\mathrm{H}_1 \,|\, \mathbf{Z}) \leq 1$ and does not reject otherwise?

5.10 Let **Z** be a sample of size n from a $\mathcal{N}(\mu, 1)$ distribution. Let $\mathrm{H}_0\colon \mu = 0$ and $\mathrm{H}_1\colon \mu \neq 0$. The prior distribution of μ gives mass π at $\mu = 0$ and allocates the remaining probability mass $1 - \pi$ according to a $\mathcal{N}(0, 1/h_0)$ distribution with $h_0 > 0$. Show that the posterior odds-ratio in favor of the alternative is

$$\frac{p(\mathrm{H}_1 \,|\, \mathbf{Z})}{p(\mathrm{H}_0 \,|\, \mathbf{Z})} = \frac{1-\pi}{\pi}\left(1 + \frac{n}{h_0}\right)^{-1/2} \exp\left[\frac{T^2}{2}\left(1 + \frac{h_0}{n}\right)^{-1}\right],$$

where $T^2 = n\bar{Z}^2$ and $\bar{Z}$ is the sample mean.

6

The Classical Linear Model: Estimation

The OLS estimator of a linear regression model was introduced in Section 4.3.3 as the solution to the sample analogue of the problem which defines the BLP of a random variable Y given another random variable X. In this chapter we discuss some of its properties for the general case when the model contains a finite but arbitrary number of parameters.

6.1 ELEMENTS OF A LINEAR REGRESSION MODEL

Suppose that the data consist of n observations $\{(X_i, Y_i)\}$ on (X, Y), where Y is a scalar response variable and X is a k-vector of covariates. Notice that $X_i = (X_{i1}, \ldots, X_{ik})$, where X_{ij} denotes the ith observation on the jth covariate. We shall sometimes use the term ith *case* to denote the vector (X_i, Y_i) when we do not want to commit ourselves to a probabilistic model for the data.

The term *linear regression model*, or simply *linear model*, denotes a relationship between Y_i and X_i of the form

$$Y_i = \alpha + \sum_{j=1}^{k} \beta_j X_{ij} + U_i = \alpha + \beta^\top X_i + U_i, \qquad i = 1, \ldots, n,$$

where α and $\beta = (\beta_1, \ldots, \beta_k)$ are unknown parameters to be estimated from the data and $U_i = Y_i - \alpha - \beta^\top X_i$. The model may be represented more compactly by stacking the observations on Y into the n-vector

$$\mathbf{Y} = \begin{pmatrix} Y_1 \\ \vdots \\ Y_n \end{pmatrix},$$

and the observations on X into the $n \times k$ matrix

$$\mathbf{X} = \begin{bmatrix} X_1^\top \\ \vdots \\ X_n^\top \end{bmatrix} = \begin{bmatrix} X_{11} & \cdots & X_{1k} \\ \vdots & & \vdots \\ X_{n1} & \cdots & X_{nk} \end{bmatrix},$$

sometimes called the *design matrix*. The above set of n relationships may be written

$$\mathbf{Y} = \iota_n \alpha + \mathbf{X}\beta + \mathbf{U}, \tag{6.1}$$

where ι_n is an n-vector with elements all equal to one and $\mathbf{U} = \mathbf{Y} - \iota_n\alpha - \mathbf{X}\beta$ is an n-vector whose generic element is equal to U_i. We refer to the linear combination $\iota_n\alpha + \mathbf{X}\beta$ as the *structural* or *systematic* part of the model.

As it stands, the relationship (6.1) is simply an identity. It becomes a statistical model when assumptions are made about the nature of the relationship between $\mathbf{Y}$ and $\mathbf{X}$ or, equivalently, about the stochastic properties of the error vector $\mathbf{U}$. Three alternative interpretations of (6.1) are possible:

1. $\iota_n\alpha + \mathbf{X}\beta$ is the BLP of $\mathbf{Y}$ given $\mathbf{X}$, that is, for any i, $\alpha + \beta^\top X_i$ is the BLP of Y_i given $X_1, \ldots, X_n$;
2. $\iota_n\alpha + \mathbf{X}\beta$ is the conditional mean of $\mathbf{Y}$ given $\mathbf{X}$, that is, for any i, $\alpha + \beta^\top X_i$ is the conditional mean of Y_i given $X_1, \ldots, X_n$;
3. $\Pr\{\mathbf{Y} \leq \mathbf{y} \,|\, \mathbf{X}\} = F_n(\mathbf{y} - \iota_n\alpha - \mathbf{X}\beta)$, where $\mathbf{y} = (y_1, \ldots, y_n)$ and F_n is some n-variate distribution function. In particular, if the data are a simple random sample, then

$$F_n(\mathbf{y} - \iota_n\alpha - \mathbf{X}\beta) = \prod_{i=1}^{n} F(y_i - \alpha - \beta^\top X_i),$$

   where F is some univariate distribution function.

The second interpretation implies the first. Both of them require the mean of $\mathbf{Y}$ to exist, while the third does not. If $\mathbf{Y}$ has finite mean, however, then the third interpretation implies the other two. The three interpretations coincide in the special case when the conditional distribution of $\mathbf{Y}$ given $\mathbf{X}$ is n-variate Gaussian with mean equal to $\iota_n\alpha + \mathbf{X}\beta$ and scalar variance matrix.

Although the statistical problem always consists of drawing inferences about the parameters α and β, the three interpretations have quite different implications for the stochastic properties of the error vector $\mathbf{U}$. The first interpretation only implies that the elements of $\mathbf{U}$ have mean zero and are uncorrelated with the elements of $\mathbf{X}$. The second interpretation corresponds to the assumption that $\mathrm{E}(\mathbf{U} \,|\, \mathbf{X}) = 0$, that is, the elements of $\mathbf{U}$ have mean zero and are mean independent of the elements of $\mathbf{X}$, which in turn implies that they are uncorrelated with any transformation of the elements of $\mathbf{X}$. The third interpretation is the most restrictive, for it corresponds to the assumption that $\Pr\{\mathbf{U} \leq \mathbf{u} \,|\, \mathbf{X}\} = F_n(\mathbf{u})$, that is, the elements of $\mathbf{U}$ are independent of the elements of $\mathbf{X}$.

6.1.1 TYPES OF COVARIATE

To simplify the notation, we shall generally represent a linear model as

$$Y_i = \beta^\top X_i + U_i, \qquad i = 1, \ldots, n,$$

or equivalently

$$\mathbf{Y} = \mathbf{X}\beta + \mathbf{U}.$$

If the vector $\beta = (\beta_1, \dots, \beta_k)$ of regression coefficients includes an intercept, then one of the columns of the design matrix $\mathbf{X}$ must be equal to ι_n. By convention, we take such a column to be the first, which implies that the first element of the parameter vector β corresponds to the intercept.

The other columns of the design matrix may correspond to variables of the continuous type, or to indicators for categorical variables (such as the sex or the schooling level of a person), or to interactions between continuous variables and categorical indicators.

A categorical variable is usually represented by a set of binary 0–1 indicators, called *dummy variables*, each corresponding to a distinct level of the variable. If a categorical variable has q levels, then the number of corresponding dummy variables is equal to q when the model does not include an intercept and to $q-1$ otherwise.

Models with dummy variables arise quite naturally when the regression coefficients are allowed to depend on the level of a categorical variable.

Example 6.1 Let Y_i and H_i denote, respectively, annual earnings and annual hours worked by a person, and let S_i be an indicator of schooling attainment which takes value 1 for a high-school dropout, 2 for a high-school graduate, 3 for a person with some college, and 4 for a college graduate. Suppose that the model for the dependence of Y_i on H_i and S_i is

$$\mathrm{E}(Y_i \mid H_i, S_i = s) = \alpha_s + \beta_s H_i, \qquad s = 1, \dots, 4,$$

where both the intercept and the slope of the CMF are allowed to vary by schooling attainment. The corresponding linear regression model is

$$Y_i = \sum_{s=1}^{4} D_{is}(\alpha_s + \beta_s H_i) + U_i = \sum_{s=1}^{4} \alpha_s D_{is} + \sum_{s=1}^{4} \beta_s D_{is} H_i + U_i,$$

where $D_{is} = 1\{S_i = s\}$ is a dummy variable associated with the sth level of the categorical indicator and U_i is a regression error with zero mean conditional on H_i and S_i. The coefficient α_s is the intercept of the earnings–hours relationship for the sth schooling level, whereas the coefficient β_s is its slope. This model does not include an intercept.

Because $\sum_s D_{is} = 1$ for all i, and therefore $D_1 = 1 - \sum_{j=2}^{d} D_s$, an equivalent parametrization of the model is

$$Y_i = \alpha_1 + \beta_1 H_i + \sum_{s=2}^{4} \gamma_s D_{is} + \sum_{s=2}^{4} \delta_s D_{is} H_i + U_i,$$

where $\gamma_s = \alpha_s - \alpha_1$ and $\delta_s = \beta_s - \beta_1$. The model now includes an intercept α_1 which is equal to the intercept of the earnings–hours relationship for the baseline schooling level (in this case, high-school not completed). The coefficient β_1 on the variable H_i is just the slope of the earnings–hours relationship for the baseline schooling level, whereas the coefficients γ_s and δ_s represent the differences, in the intercepts and the slopes respectively, between the sth schooling level and the baseline. □

6.1.2 EQUIVARIANCE PROPERTIES

The coefficients of a linear regression model satisfy some properties of symmetry or *equivariance* under certain types of transformation of the data.

Suppose that $\mathbf{Y}$ satisfies the linear model $\mathbf{Y} = \mathbf{X}\beta + \mathbf{U}$. If $\tilde{\mathbf{Y}} = \mathbf{Y} + \mathbf{X}\gamma$, then $\tilde{\mathbf{Y}}$ satisfies the linear model $\tilde{\mathbf{Y}} = \mathbf{X}\alpha + \mathbf{U}$, where $\alpha = \beta + \gamma$. This property is called *regression equivariance.* A special case is when the model includes the intercept and $\gamma = (\gamma_1, 0, \ldots, 0)$. In this case $\tilde{Y}_i = Y_i + \gamma_1$ and so $\alpha_1 = \beta_1 + \gamma_1$, whereas $\alpha_j = \beta_j$ for $j = 2, \ldots, k$. This property is called *location* or *shift equivariance.*

If $\tilde{\mathbf{Y}} = \sigma\mathbf{Y}$, then $\tilde{\mathbf{Y}}$ satisfies the linear model $\tilde{\mathbf{Y}} = \mathbf{X}\alpha + \sigma\mathbf{U}$, where $\alpha = \sigma\beta$. This property is called *scale equivariance.*

Finally, if A is a nonsingular matrix and $\mathbf{W} = \mathbf{X}A$, then $\mathbf{Y}$ satisfies the linear model $\mathbf{Y} = \mathbf{W}\alpha + \mathbf{U}$, where $\alpha = A^{-1}\beta$.

These three transformations correspond, respectively, to a translation of the response variable, a change of its units of measurement, and a change of the coordinate system in which the covariates are measured. In order to free the estimation problem from the essentially arbitrary way in which the variables are expressed, it seems reasonable to require an estimate of β to satisfy the same equivariance properties.

Example 6.2 Continuing with Example 6.1, let $\mathbf{X}$ be the design matrix associated with the model

$$Y_i = \sum_{s=1}^{4} \alpha_s D_{is} + U_i, \qquad i = 1, \ldots, n,$$

and let $\mathbf{W}$ be that associated with the model

$$Y_i = \alpha_1 + \sum_{s=2}^{4} \gamma_s D_{is} + U_i, \qquad i = 1, \ldots, n.$$

In this case, $\mathbf{W} = \mathbf{X}A$, where A is the nonsingular matrix

$$A = \begin{bmatrix} 1 & & & \\ 1 & 1 & & \\ 1 & & 1 & \\ 1 & & & 1 \end{bmatrix}.$$

Hence, the relationship between the parameters of the two models is

$$\begin{pmatrix} \alpha_1 \\ \gamma_2 \\ \gamma_3 \\ \gamma_4 \end{pmatrix} = A^{-1} \begin{pmatrix} \alpha_1 \\ \alpha_2 \\ \alpha_3 \\ \alpha_4 \end{pmatrix},$$

where

$$A^{-1} = \begin{bmatrix} 1 & & & \\ -1 & 1 & & \\ -1 & & 1 & \\ -1 & & & 1 \end{bmatrix}.$$

□

6.2 ORDINARY LEAST SQUARES

This section considers the OLS estimate of a general k-dimensional regression parameter and examines some of its algebraic properties.

6.2.1 THE OLS ESTIMATE

An OLS estimate is a solution to the problem of minimizing with respect to $\beta \in \Re^k$ the criterion function

$$Q(\beta) = n^{-1} \sum_{i=1}^{n} (Y_i - \beta^\top X_i)^2 = n^{-1}(\mathbf{Y} - \mathbf{X}\beta)^\top(\mathbf{Y} - \mathbf{X}\beta)$$

(Figure 43). Because the OLS criterion $Q(\beta)$ is a smooth function, a solution must necessarily satisfy the first-order conditions

$$0 = Q'(\beta) = -\frac{2}{n}\sum_{i=1}^{n} X_i(Y_i - \beta^\top X_i) = -\frac{2}{n}\mathbf{X}^\top(\mathbf{Y} - \mathbf{X}\beta)$$

or, equivalently, the system of linear equations

$$0 = n^{-1}\sum_{i=1}^{n} X_i(Y_i - \beta^\top X_i) = n^{-1}\mathbf{X}^\top(\mathbf{Y} - \mathbf{X}\beta), \tag{6.2}$$

called the *OLS normal equations.* The set of points $\{(x, y) \in \Re^{k+1}\colon \hat\beta^\top x = y\}$ forms the *OLS hyperplane.*

Let $\hat\beta$ be an OLS estimate. Using the normal equations, the OLS criterion may be rewritten

$$Q(\beta) = n^{-1}\hat{\mathbf{U}}^\top\hat{\mathbf{U}} + (\beta - \hat\beta)^\top(\mathbf{X}^\top\mathbf{X}/n)(\beta - \hat\beta),$$

where $\hat{\mathbf{U}} = \mathbf{Y} - \mathbf{X}\hat\beta$ is the *OLS residual vector.* By Theorem A.6, the level curves of the function Q form a family of ellipsoids centered at $\hat\beta$, with the ith axis having the same direction as the ith eigenvector of $\mathbf{X}^\top\mathbf{X}$ and length inversely proportional to the ith eigenvalue of $\mathbf{X}^\top\mathbf{X}$.

If $\mathbf{X}^\top\mathbf{X}$ is a nonsingular matrix, that is, the design matrix $\mathbf{X}$ has rank k, then the function Q is strictly convex and so the OLS estimate is unique. Because $\mathbf{X}$ is of order $n \times k$, a necessary (but not sufficient) condition is that $k \le n$, that is, the number of regression coefficients cannot exceed the sample size. In this case, solving the OLS normal equations with respect to β gives the unique solution

$$\hat\beta = (n^{-1}\sum_i X_i X_i^\top)^{-1}(n^{-1}\sum_i X_i Y_i) = (\mathbf{X}^\top\mathbf{X})^{-1}\mathbf{X}^\top\mathbf{Y}. \tag{6.3}$$

We shall sometimes use the term *OLS coefficient vector* to denote the vector $\hat\beta$ when we do not want to make any reference to a statistical estimation problem.

When the data are a sample from the distribution of (X, Y), the OLS criterion Q, the normal equations (6.2) and expression (6.3) are just the sample counterpart of the corresponding population concepts introduced in Section 1.4.2.

The OLS estimate, although introduced here with reference to random sampling, is quite natural for other types of data as well.

Figure 43 The OLS criterion for $k = 2$.

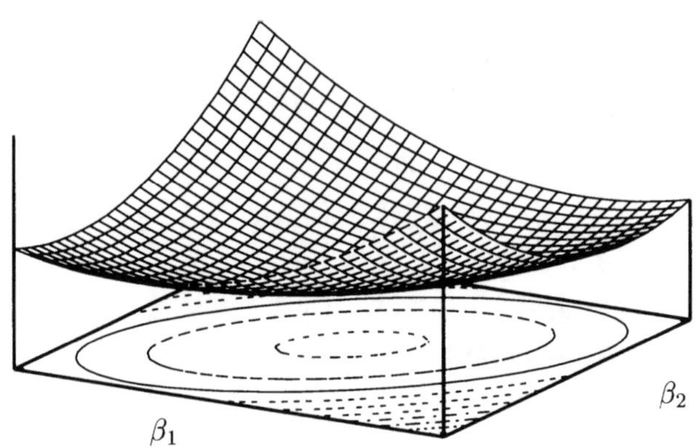

Example 6.3 If $\{Z_t\}$ is an AR(k) process, that is,

$$Z_t = \rho_1 Z_{t-1} + \cdots + \rho_k Z_{t-k} + U_t, \qquad \{U_t\} \sim \mathrm{WN}(0, \sigma^2),$$

then the BLP of Z_t given $Z_{t-1}, \ldots, Z_{t-k}$ is

$$\mathrm{E}^*(Z_t \,|\, Z_{t-1}, \ldots, Z_{t-k}) = \rho_1 Z_{t-1} + \cdots + \rho_k Z_{t-k}.$$

Given a finite segment $Z_1, \ldots, Z_T$ of this process, it is therefore natural to estimate the parameter $\rho = (\rho_1, \ldots, \rho_k)$ by solving the sample analogue of the problem that defines the BLP, namely the OLS problem

$$\begin{aligned} \min_{\rho \in \Re^k} Q(\rho) &= \frac{1}{T-k} \sum_{t=k+1}^{T} (Z_t - \rho_1 Z_{t-1} - \cdots - \rho_k Z_{t-k})^2 \\ &= \frac{1}{T-k} (\mathbf{Y} - \mathbf{X}\rho)^\top (\mathbf{Y} - \mathbf{X}\rho), \end{aligned}$$

where

$$\mathbf{Y} = \begin{pmatrix} Z_{k+1} \\ \vdots \\ Z_T \end{pmatrix}, \qquad \mathbf{X} = \begin{bmatrix} Z_k & \cdots & Z_1 \\ \vdots & & \vdots \\ Z_{T-1} & \cdots & Z_{T-k} \end{bmatrix},$$

respectively an n-vector and an $n \times k$ matrix, with $n = T - k$. □

6.2.2 GEOMETRIC INTERPRETATION

Rather than by calculus, the solution to the OLS problem may also be obtained by a geometric argument.

Figure 44 Geometric interpretation of OLS.

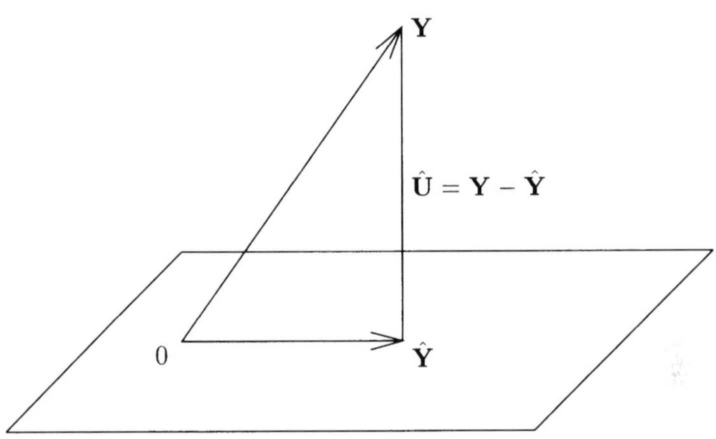

First notice that $\mathbf{Y}$ and the columns of $\mathbf{X}$ are vectors in $\Re^n$, a complete vector space for which the concept of inner product is well defined. Given two vectors $\mathbf{x}, \mathbf{y} \in \Re^n$, their inner product is in fact defined as $\mathbf{x}^\top \mathbf{y} = \sum_{i=1}^n x_i y_i$, and we say that $\mathbf{x}$ and $\mathbf{y}$ are *orthogonal* if $\mathbf{x}^\top \mathbf{y} = 0$. This inner product induces on $\Re^n$ the *Euclidean* or *L_2-norm* $||\mathbf{x}|| = (\mathbf{x}^\top \mathbf{x})^{1/2}$. Given the Euclidean norm, the *Euclidean distance* between $\mathbf{x}$ and $\mathbf{y}$ is defined as $d(\mathbf{x}, \mathbf{y}) = ||\mathbf{x} - \mathbf{y}|| = [(x - y)^\top (x - y)]^{1/2}$.

Now let $\mathcal{M}(\mathbf{X})$ be the k-dimensional subspace of $\Re^n$ consisting of all vectors that are linear combinations of the columns of $\mathbf{X}$, that is, can be represented as $\mathbf{X}\beta$ for some $\beta \in \Re^k$. Because

$$nQ(\beta) = ||\mathbf{Y} - \mathbf{X}\beta||^2 = d(\mathbf{Y}, \mathbf{X}\beta)^2,$$

the OLS problem is equivalent to finding a vector in $\mathcal{M}(\mathbf{X})$ that is at shortest distance from $\mathbf{Y}$. Since $\mathcal{M}(\mathbf{X})$ is a closed subspace of $\Re^n$, the classical projection theorem (Theorem A.8) implies that the OLS problem has a unique solution $\hat{\mathbf{Y}} \in \mathcal{M}(\mathbf{X})$, called the *OLS projection vector* or the vector of *OLS fitted values*. Further, such a solution is characterized by the condition that the residual vector $\hat{\mathbf{U}} = \mathbf{Y} - \hat{\mathbf{Y}}$ is orthogonal to any linear combination of the columns of $\mathbf{X}$, that is,

$$\hat{\mathbf{U}}^\top \mathbf{X} b = 0 \tag{6.4}$$

for any vector $b \in \Re^k$. Replacing b by the unit vectors in $\Re^k$, one obtains the OLS normal equations.

The orthogonality condition (6.4), illustrated in Figure 44, has two important implications. First, $\hat{\mathbf{U}}$ is orthogonal to the OLS projection vector $\hat{\mathbf{Y}}$, that is, $\hat{\mathbf{U}}^\top \hat{\mathbf{Y}} = 0$. Since $\hat{\mathbf{Y}} + \hat{\mathbf{U}} = \mathbf{Y}$, this provides a decomposition of $\mathbf{Y}$ into orthogonal components. Second, if the regression model includes an intercept, then $\hat{\mathbf{U}}^\top i_n = 0$, that is, the elements of the residual vector $\hat{\mathbf{U}}$ add up to zero. In turns, this implies that $\bar{Y} = \hat{\beta}^\top \bar{X}$, where $\bar{Y}$ and $\bar{X}$ denote the sample mean of Y and X respectively, that is, the point $(\bar{X}, \bar{Y})$ lies on the OLS hyperplane.

If the norm of the error vector $\mathbf{Y} - \mathbf{X}\beta$ is defined in some other way, then one obtains a different problem and therefore a different estimate of β. One of the arguments in favor of the Euclidean norm is undoubtedly its mathematical simplicity. For example, if one chooses instead the ***absolute*** or *L_1-norm* $\|\mathbf{x}\| = \sum_i |x_i|$, the problem becomes one of minimizing with respect to β the function $Q_*(\beta) = \sum_i |Y_i - \beta^\top X_i|$. This problem, which is a simple generalization of the least absolute deviations problem introduced in Section 4.2, always has a solution $\tilde{\beta}$, but this solution is no longer characterized by the orthogonality between the residual vector $\tilde{\mathbf{U}} = \mathbf{Y} - \mathbf{X}\tilde{\beta}$ and the columns of $\mathbf{X}$.

6.2.3 FITTED VALUES AND RESIDUALS

We shall henceforth assume that the matrix $\mathbf{X}^\top\mathbf{X}$ is nonsingular, which implies that the OLS coefficient is unique. Under this assumption, the vector of OLS fitted values $\hat{\mathbf{Y}} = \mathbf{X}\hat{\beta}$ may be written $\hat{\mathbf{Y}} = H\mathbf{Y}$, where $H = \mathbf{X}(\mathbf{X}^\top\mathbf{X})^{-1}\mathbf{X}^\top$ is an $n \times n$ matrix with the following properties:

1. (symmetry) $H = H^\top$;
2. (idempotency) $HH = H$;
3. $H\mathbf{X} = \mathbf{X}$.

The fact that the matrix H is symmetric and idempotent has a number of useful implications. First, its rank is equal to its trace

$$\operatorname{tr} H = \operatorname{tr}[(\mathbf{X}^\top\mathbf{X})^{-1}\mathbf{X}^\top\mathbf{X}] = \operatorname{tr} I_k = k.$$

Second, if $n > k$, then the matrix H is singular and so the linear transformation from $\mathbf{Y}$ to $\hat{\mathbf{Y}}$ is noninvertible. Third, denoting by $h_{ij} = X_i^\top(\mathbf{X}^\top\mathbf{X})^{-1}X_j$ the ijth element of H, one has $n^{-1}\sum_{i=1}^n h_{ii} = k/n$, that is, the elements on the main diagonal of H are on average equal to k/n. The number h_{ii} may be interpreted as the norm of the vector X_i in the metric of the matrix $(\mathbf{X}^\top\mathbf{X})^{-1}$. Finally, $h_{ii} = \sum_{j=1}^n h_{ij}^2$, which implies that $h_{ii} \geq h_{ii}^2$ and therefore $0 \leq h_{ii} \leq 1$ for every i.

When $\mathbf{X}^\top\mathbf{X}$ is nonsingular, the OLS residual vector may also be written

$$\hat{\mathbf{U}} = \mathbf{Y} - \hat{\mathbf{Y}} = (I_n - H)\mathbf{Y} = M\mathbf{Y},$$

where $M = I_n - H$ is an $n \times n$ symmetric idempotent matrix whose rank and trace are both equal to $n - k$. Notice that $M\mathbf{X} = 0$ and therefore $MH = 0$. The properties of the OLS residuals are discussed in more detail in Chapter 8.

6.2.4 GOODNESS-OF-FIT AND EQUIVARIANCE PROPERTIES

Orthogonality of $\hat{\mathbf{Y}}$ and $\hat{\mathbf{U}}$ implies the relationship

$$\mathbf{Y}^\top\mathbf{Y} = (\hat{\mathbf{Y}} + \hat{\mathbf{U}})^\top(\hat{\mathbf{Y}} + \hat{\mathbf{U}}) = \hat{\mathbf{Y}}^\top\hat{\mathbf{Y}} + \hat{\mathbf{U}}^\top\hat{\mathbf{U}},$$

that is,

$$\|\mathbf{Y}\|^2 = \|\hat{\mathbf{Y}}\|^2 + \|\hat{\mathbf{U}}\|^2.$$

Viewed geometrically, this is just Pythagoras theorem. If α denotes the angle between the vectors $\mathbf{Y}$ and $\hat{\mathbf{Y}}$, then a natural measure of goodness-of-fit is the ratio

$$(\cos\alpha)^2 = \frac{\|\hat{\mathbf{Y}}\|^2}{\|\mathbf{Y}\|^2} = \frac{\hat{\mathbf{Y}}^\top\hat{\mathbf{Y}}}{\mathbf{Y}^\top\mathbf{Y}} = 1 - \frac{\hat{\mathbf{U}}^\top\hat{\mathbf{U}}}{\mathbf{Y}^\top\mathbf{Y}},$$

called the *uncentered regression* R^2. This measure is dimensionless and ranges between zero and one, with the endpoints of the range corresponding to, respectively, complete lack of fit and perfect fit.

A more common measure of goodness-of-fit is the square of the sample correlation coefficient between Y_i and $\hat{Y}_i$

$$\hat{R}^2 = \frac{\widehat{\mathrm{Cov}}(Y_i, \hat{Y}_i)^2}{(\widehat{\mathrm{Var}}\, Y_i)\,(\widehat{\mathrm{Var}}\, \hat{Y}_i)},$$

called the *coefficient of determination* or *centered regression* R^2. Being a correlation coefficient, the coefficient of determination is also dimensionless and ranges between zero (complete lack of fit) and one (perfect fit).

Because the sample mean of Y_i may be represented as $\bar{Y} = n^{-1}\iota_n^\top\mathbf{Y}$, the vector of deviations $Y_i - \bar{Y}$ may be represented as

$$\mathbf{Y} - \iota_n\bar{Y} = (I_n - n^{-1}J_n)\mathbf{Y} = L\mathbf{Y},$$

where $J_n = \iota_n\iota_n^\top$ is a symmetric matrix whose elements are all equal to one and $L = I_n - n^{-1}J_n$ is a symmetric idempotent matrix which transforms a vector into deviations from the average of its elements. Thus

$$\widehat{\mathrm{Var}}\, Y_i = n^{-1}\sum_{i=1}^{n}(Y_i - \bar{Y})^2 = n^{-1}(L\mathbf{Y})^\top L\mathbf{Y} = n^{-1}\mathbf{Y}^\top L\mathbf{Y}.$$

Analogously, it can be shown that

$$\widehat{\mathrm{Var}}\, \hat{Y}_i = n^{-1}\mathbf{Y}^\top HLH\mathbf{Y}, \qquad \widehat{\mathrm{Cov}}(Y_i, \hat{Y}_i) = n^{-1}\mathbf{Y}^\top LH\mathbf{Y}.$$

Hence

$$\hat{R}^2 = \frac{(\mathbf{Y}^\top LH\mathbf{Y})^2}{(\mathbf{Y}^\top L\mathbf{Y})(\mathbf{Y}^\top HLH\mathbf{Y})}.$$

If the model includes an intercept, then $H\iota_n = \iota_n$ and $M\iota_n = 0$. This implies that $HL = LH$, $LM = M$, and therefore

$$\hat{R}^2 = \frac{\mathbf{Y}^\top LH\mathbf{Y}}{\mathbf{Y}^\top L\mathbf{Y}} = \frac{\mathbf{Y}^\top L(I_n - M)\mathbf{Y}}{\mathbf{Y}^\top\mathbf{Y} - \bar{Y}^2} = 1 - \frac{\hat{\mathbf{U}}^\top\hat{\mathbf{U}}}{S_Y},$$

where $S_Y = \sum_i(Y_i - \bar{Y})^2$. Because $n^{-1}\hat{\mathbf{U}}^\top\hat{\mathbf{U}}$ is the average squared deviation of the OLS residuals, while $n^{-1}S_Y$ is the average squared deviation of the Y_i, the regression R^2 may be interpreted as a measure of how much of the variability of Y_i is "explained" by the covariates. It is easy to verify that the centered and uncentered R^2 coincide when the regression model includes the intercept and $\bar{Y} = 0$.

The OLS estimate satisfies all the equivariance properties listed in Section 6.1.2. If $\tilde{\mathbf{Y}} = \mathbf{Y} + \mathbf{X}\gamma$, then

$$\tilde{\beta} = (\mathbf{X}^\top \mathbf{X})^{-1}\mathbf{X}^\top \tilde{\mathbf{Y}} = \hat{\beta} + \gamma,$$

that is, the OLS estimate is regression equivariant. This implies that $\tilde{\mathbf{Y}} - \mathbf{X}\tilde{\beta} = \mathbf{Y} - \mathbf{X}\hat{\beta}$, that is, the OLS residuals are invariant under this type of transformation of the data. This property holds, more generally, for any statistic that depends on the data only through the value of the OLS residuals.

If $\tilde{\mathbf{Y}} = \sigma \mathbf{Y}$, then

$$\tilde{\beta} = (\mathbf{X}^\top \mathbf{X})^{-1}\mathbf{X}^\top \tilde{\mathbf{Y}} = \sigma\hat{\beta},$$

that is, the OLS estimate is scale equivariant. This implies that the ratio between any two elements of $\hat{\beta}$, as well as the measures of goodness-of-fit in Section 6.2.4, are all independent of the choice of the units in which the response variable is measured.

Finally, if $\mathbf{W} = \mathbf{X}A$ is a nonsingular linear transformation of $\mathbf{X}$, then

$$\tilde{\beta} = (\mathbf{W}^\top \mathbf{W})^{-1}\mathbf{W}^\top \mathbf{Y} = A^{-1}\hat{\beta}.$$

Hence, $\tilde{\mathbf{Y}} = \mathbf{W}\tilde{\beta} = \mathbf{X}\hat{\beta} = \hat{\mathbf{Y}}$ and $\tilde{\mathbf{U}} = \mathbf{Y} - \tilde{\mathbf{Y}} = \mathbf{Y} - \hat{\mathbf{Y}} = \hat{\mathbf{U}}$, that is, the OLS projection vector $\hat{\mathbf{Y}}$ and the OLS residual vector $\hat{\mathbf{U}}$ do not depend on the choice of coordinates for the covariates.

6.2.5 MULTIVARIATE OLS

Now consider the case when $Y_i = (Y_{i1}, \ldots, Y_{im})$ is an m-vector. For example, Y_i may consist of observations on the same variable at different points in time, as in the case of longitudinal data, or it may consist of different variables, such as expenditures by the ith sample unit on different consumption categories. Our basic model for this case is the *multivariate linear regression model*

$$Y_i = BX_i + U_i, \qquad i = 1, \ldots, n,$$

where B is an $m \times k$ parameter matrix which solves the prediction problem (1.15) and $U_i = Y_i - BX_i$ is an m-vector whose components are uncorrelated with the elements of X_i. The sample analogue of this problem is the *multivariate* OLS problem, which consists of minimizing with respect to B the quadratic function

$$Q(B) = n^{-1} \sum_{i=1}^{n} (Y_i - BX_i)^\top (Y_i - BX_i).$$

Defining the $n \times m$ matrix

$$\mathbf{Y} = \begin{bmatrix} Y_1^\top \\ \vdots \\ Y_n^\top \end{bmatrix},$$

and using the fact that

$$\sum_{i=1}^{n} (Y_i - BX_i)^\top (Y_i - BX_i) = [\mathrm{vec}\,(\mathbf{Y} - \mathbf{X}B^\top)]^\top [\mathrm{vec}\,(\mathbf{Y} - \mathbf{X}B^\top)]$$

and $\text{vec}\,(\mathbf{X}B^\top) = (\mathbf{X} \otimes I_m)\beta$, where $\beta = \text{vec}\, B^\top$ is a km-vector, the multivariate OLS criterion may be written

$$Q(\beta) = n^{-1}(\tilde{\mathbf{Y}} - \tilde{\mathbf{X}}\beta)^\top(\tilde{\mathbf{Y}} - \tilde{\mathbf{X}}\beta),$$

where $\tilde{\mathbf{Y}} = \text{vec}\,\mathbf{Y}$ is an nm-vector and $\tilde{\mathbf{X}} = \mathbf{X} \otimes I_m$ is an $nm \times km$ matrix. The normal equations are

$$\begin{aligned} 0 &= \tilde{\mathbf{X}}^\top(\tilde{\mathbf{Y}} - \tilde{\mathbf{X}}\beta) \\ &= (\mathbf{X}^\top \otimes I_m)(\text{vec}\,\mathbf{Y}) - (\mathbf{X}^\top\mathbf{X} \otimes I_m)\beta \\ &= \text{vec}\,(\mathbf{X}^\top\mathbf{Y} - \mathbf{X}^\top\mathbf{X}B^\top), \end{aligned}$$

that is,

$$0 = \mathbf{X}^\top\mathbf{Y} - \mathbf{X}^\top\mathbf{X}B^\top.$$

If $\mathbf{X}^\top\mathbf{X}$ is a nonsingular matrix, then the multivariate OLS estimate is

$$\hat{B}^\top = (\mathbf{X}^\top\mathbf{X})^{-1}\mathbf{X}^\top\mathbf{Y} = (n^{-1}\sum_i X_i X_i^\top)(n^{-1}\sum_i X_i Y_i^\top),$$

which is the sample analogue of the expression obtained in Section 1.4.2 for the BLP. The jth row of $\hat{B}$ is

$$\hat{\beta}_j = (\mathbf{X}^\top\mathbf{X})^{-1}\mathbf{X}^\top\mathbf{Y}_j, \qquad j = 1, \ldots, m,$$

where $\mathbf{Y}_j$ denotes the jth column of $\mathbf{Y}$. Therefore, $\hat{\beta}_j$ coincides with the OLS coefficient in the regression of $\mathbf{Y}_j$ on $\mathbf{X}$.

The multivariate OLS projection matrix and residual matrix are $\hat{\mathbf{Y}} = \mathbf{X}\hat{B} = H\mathbf{Y}$ and $\hat{\mathbf{U}} = \mathbf{Y} - \hat{\mathbf{Y}} = M\mathbf{Y}$ respectively, where $H = \mathbf{X}(\mathbf{X}^\top\mathbf{X})^{-1}\mathbf{X}^\top$ and $M = I_n - H$ are the usual $n \times n$ symmetric idempotent matrices.

6.2.6 *PARTITIONED REGRESSION*

Suppose that the design matrix is partitioned as $\mathbf{X} = [\mathbf{X}_1, \mathbf{X}_2]$, where $\mathbf{X}_j$ is an $n \times k_j$ matrix ($j = 1, 2$) and $k_1 + k_2 = k$. Partition the vector of OLS coefficients correspondingly as $\hat{\beta} = (\hat{\beta}_1, \hat{\beta}_2)$. It is sometimes convenient to be able to compute one component of $\hat{\beta}$, say $\hat{\beta}_1$, without having to invert the full matrix $\mathbf{X}^\top\mathbf{X}$. Notice first that

$$\begin{pmatrix} \hat{\beta}_1 \\ \hat{\beta}_2 \end{pmatrix} = \begin{bmatrix} \mathbf{X}_1^\top\mathbf{X}_1 & \mathbf{X}_1^\top\mathbf{X}_2 \\ \mathbf{X}_2^\top\mathbf{X}_1 & \mathbf{X}_2^\top\mathbf{X}_2 \end{bmatrix}^{-1} \begin{pmatrix} \mathbf{X}_1^\top\mathbf{Y} \\ \mathbf{X}_2^\top\mathbf{Y} \end{pmatrix}.$$

By the properties of partitioned inverses (Appendix A.7), the upper-right element of $(\mathbf{X}^\top\mathbf{X})^{-1}$ is equal to $F^{-1} = (\mathbf{X}_1^\top M_2 \mathbf{X}_1)^{-1}$, where $M_2 = I_n - H_2$ and $H_2 = \mathbf{X}_2(\mathbf{X}_2^\top\mathbf{X}_2)^{-1}\mathbf{X}_2^\top$, while the upper-right element is equal to $F^{-1}\mathbf{X}_1^\top H_2$. Hence

$$\begin{aligned} \hat{\beta}_1 &= F^{-1}\mathbf{X}_1^\top\mathbf{Y} - F^{-1}\mathbf{X}_1^\top H_2\mathbf{Y} \\ &= F^{-1}\mathbf{X}_1^\top M_2\mathbf{Y} = (\mathbf{X}_1^\top M_2\mathbf{X}_1)^{-1}\mathbf{X}_1^\top M_2\mathbf{Y}. \end{aligned}$$

Because M_2 is a symmetric idempotent matrix, $\hat{\beta}_1$ may simply be computed by an OLS regression of $M_2\mathbf{Y}$ on $M_2\mathbf{X}_1$, where $M_2\mathbf{Y}$ is the OLS residual vector in the regression of $\mathbf{Y}$ on $\mathbf{X}_2$, and $M_2\mathbf{X}_1$ is the OLS residual matrix in the multivariate regression of $\mathbf{X}_1$ on $\mathbf{X}_2$, a result which is also known as the *Frisch–Waugh theorem* or *double residual regression method.* Notice that $\hat{\beta}_1$ is equal to the OLS coefficient $\tilde{\beta}_1 = (\mathbf{X}_1{}^\top\mathbf{X}_1)^{-1}\mathbf{X}_1{}^\top\mathbf{Y}$ in the regression of $\mathbf{Y}$ on $\mathbf{X}_1$ only when $\mathbf{X}_1$ and $\mathbf{X}_2$ are orthogonal, that is, $\mathbf{X}_1^\top\mathbf{X}_2 = 0$.

We illustrate the usefulness of this result with two examples.

Example 6.4 Consider a regression model that includes an intercept and let $\mathbf{X}_1 = \iota_n$. Because in this case $M_1 = I_n - \iota_n(\iota_n^\top\iota_n)^{-1}\iota_n^\top = L$, we get

$$\hat{\beta}_2 = [\sum_i (X_{i2} - \bar{X}_2)(X_{i2} - \bar{X}_2)^\top]^{-1} \sum_i (X_{i2} - \bar{X}_2)(Y_i - \bar{Y}),$$

that is, $\hat{\beta}_2$ is equal to the OLS coefficient in the regression of the deviations of Y_i from its sample mean on the deviations of X_{i2} from its sample mean. □

Example 6.5 Let $\{(Y_t, X_t)\}$ be a bivariate time series and assume that the relationship between $\{Y_t\}$ and $\{X_t\}$ includes a deterministic linear trend

$$Y_t = \alpha_1 + \alpha_2 t + \beta^\top X_t + U_t, \qquad \{U_t\} \sim \mathrm{WN}(0, \sigma^2),$$

where the term $\alpha_1 + \alpha_2 t$ represents the linear trend. Given T consecutive observations of the process $\{(Y_t, X_t)\}$, let $\tilde{Y}_t$ be the OLS residual in a regression of Y_t on the linear trend, that is, on a constant term and on t. Similarly, let $\tilde{X}_t$ be the OLS residual in a regression of X_t on the linear trend. These residuals may be interpreted as transformations of the original time series obtained by removing the trend. The OLS estimate of β in the original model is then equal to the OLS coefficient in the regression of the detrended series $\tilde{Y}_t$ on the detrended series $\tilde{X}_t$. □

By the properties of partitioned inverses, an equivalent expression for $\hat{\beta}_1$ is

$$\begin{aligned} \hat{\beta}_1 &= \tilde{\beta}_1 - (\mathbf{X}_1^\top\mathbf{X}_1)^{-1}\mathbf{X}_1^\top\mathbf{X}_2(\mathbf{X}_2^\top M_1\mathbf{X}_2)^{-1}\mathbf{X}_2^\top M_1\mathbf{Y} \\ &= \tilde{\beta}_1 - (\mathbf{X}_1{}^\top\mathbf{X}_1)^{-1}\mathbf{X}_1{}^\top\mathbf{X}_2\hat{\beta}_2, \end{aligned} \tag{6.5}$$

where $M_1 = I_n - \mathbf{X}_1(\mathbf{X}_1^\top\mathbf{X}_1)^{-1}\mathbf{X}_1^\top$ is a symmetric idempotent matrix and

$$\hat{\beta}_2 = (\mathbf{X}_2^\top M_1\mathbf{X}_2)^{-1}\mathbf{X}_2^\top M_1\mathbf{Y}.$$

Formula (6.5) gives a simple way of evaluating the effect of adding or dropping covariates from the regression. In particular, if the covariates in $\mathbf{X}_2$ are dropped, then the change in the OLS coefficients is

$$\tilde{\beta}_1 - \hat{\beta}_1 = (\mathbf{X}_1{}^\top\mathbf{X}_1)^{-1}\mathbf{X}_1{}^\top\mathbf{X}_2\hat{\beta}_2,$$

which is equal to the OLS coefficient in a regression of $\mathbf{X}_2\hat{\beta}_2$ on $\mathbf{X}_1$. There is no change when either $\hat{\beta}_2 = 0$ or $\mathbf{X}_1$ and $\mathbf{X}_2$ are orthogonal.

6.2.7 ADDING AND EXCLUDING OBSERVATIONS

We now want to study how sensitive the OLS coefficient is to the addition and exclusion of single data points. Besides providing information on the robustness properties of OLS, the formulae obtained in this section are also useful for constructing jackknife estimates of the accuracy of the OLS estimator.

Let $\hat{\beta}$ be the OLS coefficient computed for a set $[\mathbf{X}, \mathbf{Y}]$ of n observations. The OLS coefficient computed for the set of $n+1$ observations obtained by adding the arbitrary point (x, y) to the original data is

$$\hat{\beta}_{n+1} = (\mathbf{X}^\top\mathbf{X} + xx^\top)^{-1}(\mathbf{X}^\top\mathbf{Y} + xy).$$

The inverse of the matrix $\mathbf{X}^\top\mathbf{X} + xx^\top$ may be evaluated using Lemma A.1 in the Appendix. Letting $A = \mathbf{X}^\top\mathbf{X}$, $B = x$, $C = x^\top$ and $D = 1$ in the statement of the lemma gives

$$(\mathbf{X}^\top\mathbf{X} + xx^\top)^{-1} = (\mathbf{X}^\top\mathbf{X})^{-1} - \frac{(\mathbf{X}^\top\mathbf{X})^{-1}xx^\top(\mathbf{X}^\top\mathbf{X})^{-1}}{1+h},$$

where $h = x^\top(\mathbf{X}^\top\mathbf{X})^{-1}x$. Hence

$$\begin{aligned}\hat{\beta}_{n+1} &= \left[(\mathbf{X}^\top\mathbf{X})^{-1} - \frac{(\mathbf{X}^\top\mathbf{X})^{-1}xx^\top(\mathbf{X}^\top\mathbf{X})^{-1}}{1+h}\right](\mathbf{X}^\top\mathbf{Y} + xy) \\ &= \hat{\beta} - \frac{(\mathbf{X}^\top\mathbf{X})^{-1}xx^\top\hat{\beta}}{1+h} + \frac{(\mathbf{X}^\top\mathbf{X})^{-1}xy}{1+h} \\ &= \hat{\beta} + (\mathbf{X}^\top\mathbf{X})^{-1}\frac{x(y - \hat{\beta}^\top x)}{1+h},\end{aligned}$$

where $y - \hat{\beta}^\top x$ is the error made in predicting the new observation y on the basis of x and the original set of n observations. Thus, $\hat{\beta}_{n+1} = \hat{\beta}$ whenever the point (x, y) lies on the OLS hyperplane based on the original data.

Since $\mathbf{X}^\top\mathbf{X}$ grows without bounds with increasing sample size, the difference $\hat{\beta}_{n+1} - \hat{\beta}$ becomes arbitrarily small as $n \to \infty$. Thus, as a quantitative measure of robustness of $\hat{\beta}$, it is preferable to consider the normalized difference

$$\text{EIF}(x, y) = n(\hat{\beta}_{n+1} - \hat{\beta}) = \left(\frac{\mathbf{X}^\top\mathbf{X}}{n}\right)^{-1}\frac{x(y - \hat{\beta}^\top x)}{1+h},$$

called the *empirical influence function* of $\hat{\beta}$. Given the original set of n observations, $\text{EIF}(x, y)$ can be made arbitrarily large by appropriately choosing the additional point (x, y). This lack of robustness of the OLS estimator will be further discussed in later chapters.

Now consider the OLS coefficient computed by excluding the ith case (X_i, Y_i)

$$\hat{\beta}_{(i)} = (\mathbf{X}^\top\mathbf{X} - X_iX_i^\top)^{-1}(\mathbf{X}^\top\mathbf{Y} - X_iY_i).$$

Applying again Lemma A.1 gives

$$\hat{\beta}_{(i)} = \hat{\beta} - (\mathbf{X}^\top\mathbf{X})^{-1}\frac{X_i\hat{U}_i}{1 - h_{ii}}, \tag{6.6}$$

Figure 45 The left figure shows a sample of 100 observations from the joint distribution of (X, Y, W), where the conditional distribution of Y given (X, W) is $\mathcal{N}(1 + 2X + W, 1)$. The solid line is the OLS line in the regression of Y_i on X_i, with W_i omitted. The right figure shows the values of the difference $\tilde{\beta}_{(i)} = \hat{\beta} - \hat{\beta}_{(i)}$ for the OLS coefficient associated with X_i in the above regression.

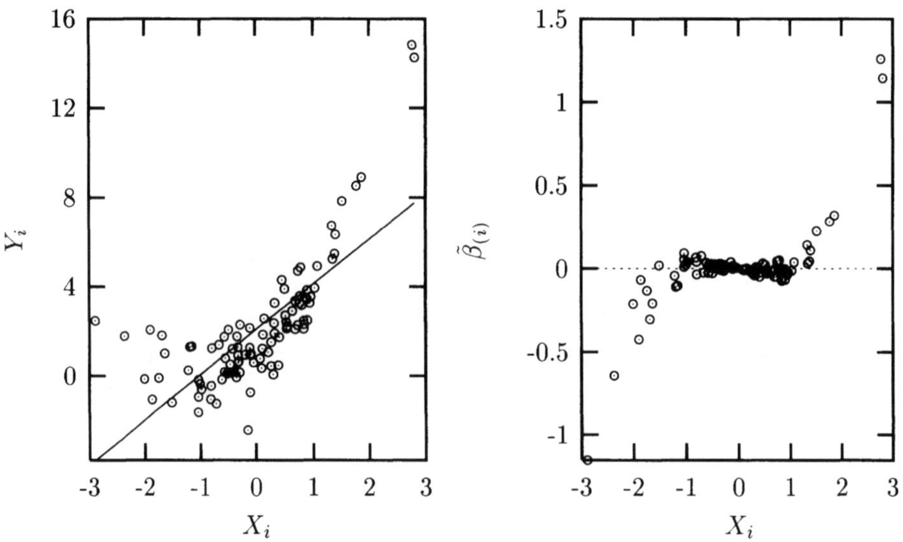

where $\hat{U}_i = Y_i - \hat{\beta}^\top X_i$ is the ith OLS residual and h_{ii} is the ith diagonal element of the projection matrix H. The k-vector $\hat{\beta} - \hat{\beta}_{(i)}$, viewed as a function of $i = 1, \ldots, n$, is called the ***sensitivity curve*** of $\hat{\beta}$ (Tukey 1977) and the ith case is called *influential* if the distance $\| \hat{\beta} - \hat{\beta}_{(i)} \|$ is large. An example of a sensitivity curve is shown in Figure 45.

Formula (6.6) reveals that the influence of the ith case on the OLS coefficient depends on both the residual $\hat{U}_i$ and the squared norm h_{ii} of the vector X_i. In particular, if $h_{ii} \to 1$, then $\| \hat{\beta} - \hat{\beta}_{(i)} \| \to \infty$. For this reason, if h_{ii} is near one, the ith case is said to exert a *high leverage*. A design matrix $\mathbf{X}$ is said to be *perfectly balanced* when all observations exert the same leverage, that is, $h_{ii} = k/n$ for all i. The notions of influence and leverage may be generalized without conceptual difficulty to pairs, triples, etc., of cases.

6.3 SAMPLING PROPERTIES OF THE OLS ESTIMATOR

When the design matrix $\mathbf{X}$ has rank k, the OLS estimate is a linear function of $\mathbf{Y}$, that is, of the form $\hat{\beta} = C\mathbf{Y}$, where $C = (\mathbf{X}^\top \mathbf{X})^{-1}\mathbf{X}^\top$ is a $k \times n$ matrix that depends on $\mathbf{X}$ but not on $\mathbf{Y}$. This representation is the basis for deriving the sampling properties of $\hat{\beta}$ from those of the vector $\mathbf{Y}$ for, if $\mathbf{X}$ is fixed (or can be treated as such) and $\mathrm{E}\,\mathbf{Y} = \mu$ and $\mathrm{Var}\,\mathbf{Y} = \Sigma$, then $\mathrm{E}\,\hat{\beta} = C\mu$ and $\mathrm{Var}\,\hat{\beta} = C\Sigma C^\top$. Of course, the structure of μ and Σ depends on both the model of the statistical population and the sampling process.

6.3.1 THE CLASSICAL LINEAR MODEL

The *classical linear model* corresponds to the following set of assumptions.

Assumption 6.1 $\mathbf{X}$ *is a nonstochastic* $n \times k$ *matrix of rank* k.

Assumption 6.2 *The mean of* $\mathbf{Y}$ *is equal to* $\mathbf{X}\beta$ *for some* $\beta \in \Re^k$.

Assumption 6.3 *The variance of* $\mathbf{Y}$ *is equal to* $\sigma^2 I_n$ *for some positive and finite* σ^2.

Assumption 6.1 implies that the elements of $\mathbf{X}$ are not random variables but just fixed numbers and that the columns of $\mathbf{X}$ are linearly independent. Assumption 6.2 implies that the mean of Y_i and Y_j may be different but they all lie on the same k-dimensional hyperplane in $\Re^n$. Assumption 6.3 that $\mathbf{Y}$ has a scalar variance matrix implies that the random variables $Y_1, \ldots, Y_n$ are uncorrelated and *homoskedastic*, that is, they all have the same variance. If $\mathbf{U} = \mathbf{Y} - \mathbf{X}\beta$ denotes the vector of regression errors, then Assumptions 6.2 and 6.3 imply that $\mathrm{E}\,\mathbf{U} = 0$ and $\mathrm{Var}\,\mathbf{U} = \sigma^2 I_n$, that is, the regression errors have mean zero and are homoskedastic and uncorrelated.

The classical linear model may be interpreted in several ways. One possible interpretation is that each Y_i represents an error-ridden measurement of some fixed quantity $\mu_i = \beta^\top X_i$. Although these measurements are generally inaccurate, the measurement errors $U_i = Y_i - \mu_i$ are not systematic, that is, they have zero mean, constant variance σ^2, and are uncorrelated.

A second interpretation is in terms of exogenously stratified random sampling and corresponds to the following controlled experiment.

1. Select n possible realizations $x_1, \ldots, x_n$ of a random k-vector X. These realizations correspond to the rows of the design matrix $\mathbf{X}$ and need not all be distinct, although Assumption 6.1 requires k of them to be linearly independent.
2. After partitioning the statistical population into n strata, with the ith stratum corresponding to a particular value $X = x_i$, a single independent random draw is made from each stratum.

Thus, Y_i is randomly drawn from the conditional distribution of Y given $X = x_i$, whereas Y_j is randomly drawn from the conditional distribution of Y given $X = x_j$. Because each draw is carried out independently of the others, $\mathrm{Cov}(Y_i, Y_j) = 0$ for $i \neq j$. If the CMF of Y is linear in X then $\mu_i = \mathrm{E}(Y \mid X = x_i) = \beta^\top x_i$, whereas $\mu_j = \mathrm{E}(Y \mid X = x_j) = \beta^\top x_j$. If the CVF of Y is constant and equal to σ^2, then $\mathrm{Var}\, Y_i = \mathrm{Var}\, Y_j = \sigma^2$.

Theorem 6.1

(i) *Under Assumption 6.1,* $\hat\beta = (\mathbf{X}^\top \mathbf{X})^{-1} \mathbf{X}^\top \mathbf{Y}$ *exists for all* $n \geq k$.

(ii) *Under the Assumptions 6.1 and 6.2,* $\mathrm{E}\, \hat\beta = \beta$.

(iii) *Under Assumptions 6.1–6.3,* $\mathrm{Var}\, \hat\beta = \sigma^2 (\mathbf{X}^\top \mathbf{X})^{-1}$.

(iv) **(Gauss–Markov theorem)** *Under Assumptions 6.1–6.3,* $\mathrm{Var}\, \tilde\beta - \mathrm{Var}\, \hat\beta \geq 0$ *for every other estimator* $\tilde\beta$ *which is linear in* $\mathbf{Y}$ *and unbiased for* β.

Proof. Conclusions (i)–(iii) are left to the reader as an exercise. To prove the Gauss–Markov theorem, consider the class of linear estimators $\tilde\beta = C\mathbf{Y}$, where C is any $k \times n$ matrix. The OLS estimator belongs to this class and corresponds to choosing $C = C_*$, where $C_* = (\mathbf{X}^\top \mathbf{X})^{-1} \mathbf{X}^\top$. A linear estimator $\tilde\beta$ is unbiased if

$$\mathrm{E}\, \tilde\beta = C\, \mathrm{E}\, \mathbf{Y} = C\mathbf{X}\beta = \beta.$$

This requires that $C\mathbf{X} = I_k$ and therefore that $C_* C^\top = (\mathbf{X}^\top \mathbf{X})^{-1} = C_* C_*^\top$.

Now consider estimating some linear combination $\lambda^\top \beta$ of the regression coefficients. If $\tilde\beta$ is unbiased for β and $\mathrm{Var}\, \mathbf{Y} = \sigma^2 I_n$, then

$$\begin{aligned}
\mathrm{Var}(\lambda^\top \tilde\beta) &= \sigma^2 \lambda^\top C C^\top \lambda \\
&= \sigma^2 \lambda^\top (C_* + C - C_*)(C_* + C - C_*)^\top \lambda \\
&= \sigma^2 [\lambda^\top (\mathbf{X}^\top \mathbf{X})^{-1} \lambda + \lambda^\top (C - C_*)(C - C_*)^\top \lambda] \\
&= \mathrm{Var}(\lambda^\top \hat\beta) + \sigma^2 \lambda^\top (C - C_*)(C - C_*)^\top \lambda,
\end{aligned}$$

where we used the fact that $C_*(C - C_*)^\top = 0$. This shows that the difference $\mathrm{Var}\, \lambda^\top \tilde\beta - \mathrm{Var}\, \lambda^\top \hat\beta$ is non-negative. Because the vector λ is arbitrary, the difference $\mathrm{Var}\, \tilde\beta - \mathrm{Var}\, \hat\beta$ is a n.n.d. matrix, which completes the proof. □

Part (iii) of Theorem 6.1 implies that $\mathrm{Cov}(\hat\beta_h, \hat\beta_j) = \sigma^2 q_{hj}$, where q_{hj} denotes the hjth element of the matrix $(\mathbf{X}^\top \mathbf{X})^{-1}$. The elements of the vector $\hat\beta$ are therefore correlated, except when $\mathbf{X}^\top \mathbf{X}$ is a diagonal matrix, that is, the columns of $\mathbf{X}$ are mutually orthogonal.

The Gauss–Markov theorem implies that, if the classical linear model holds, then the OLS estimator $\hat\beta$ is BLU for β. It also implies that, if one is interested in predicting the value of Y corresponding to $X = x$, then

$$\hat y = x^\top \hat\beta = x^\top (\mathbf{X}^\top \mathbf{X})^{-1} \mathbf{X}^\top \mathbf{Y}$$

is BLU for $y = \mathrm{E}(Y \mid X = x)$, in the sense that $\mathrm{Var}\,\hat y = \sigma^2\, x^\top (\mathbf{X}^\top\mathbf{X})^{-1} x \le \mathrm{Var}(\tilde y)$ for any other predictor $\tilde y$ that is linear in $\mathbf{Y}$ and unbiased for y.

6.3.2 STOCHASTIC REGRESSORS

Economic data are seldom the result of a controlled experiment where one records the values of the response variable corresponding to a given set of covariate values. For this reason, we also consider the following set of assumptions.

Assumption 6.4 $\mathbf{X}$ *is a random* $n \times k$ *matrix whose rank is equal to* k *with probability one, and* $\mathrm{E}(\mathbf{X}^\top\mathbf{X})^{-1}$ *is a finite matrix.*

Assumption 6.5 *The conditional mean of* $\mathbf{Y}$ *given* $\mathbf{X}$ *is equal to* $\mathbf{X}\beta$*, where* $\beta \in \Re^k$.

Assumption 6.6 *The conditional variance of* $\mathbf{Y}$ *given* $\mathbf{X}$ *is equal to* $\sigma^2 I_n$*, where* $0 < \sigma^2 < \infty$.

Given Assumptions 6.4–6.6, all the results of the previous section remain valid conditionally on $\mathbf{X}$.

Theorem 6.2

(i) *Under Assumption 6.4,* $\hat\beta = (\mathbf{X}^\top\mathbf{X})^{-1}\mathbf{X}^\top\mathbf{Y}$ *exists with probability one.*

(ii) *Under Assumptions 6.4 and 6.5,* $\mathrm{E}\,\hat\beta = \beta$.

(iii) *Under Assumptions 6.4–6.6,* $\mathrm{Var}\,\hat\beta = \sigma^2\, \mathrm{E}(\mathbf{X}^\top\mathbf{X})^{-1}$.

(iv) **(Gauss–Markov theorem)** *Under Assumptions 6.4–6.6,* $\mathrm{Var}(\tilde\beta \mid \mathbf{X}) - \mathrm{Var}(\hat\beta \mid \mathbf{X}) \ge 0$ *for any other estimator* $\tilde\beta$ *which is linear in* $\mathbf{Y}$ *and unbiased for* β.

Proof. We confine ourselves to the proof of (ii) and (iii). By the law of iterated expectations $\mathrm{E}\,\hat\beta = \mathrm{E}[\mathrm{E}(\hat\beta \mid \mathbf{X})]$, and by the law of total variance

$$\mathrm{Var}\,\hat\beta = \mathrm{E}[\mathrm{Var}(\hat\beta \mid \mathbf{X})] + \mathrm{Var}[\mathrm{E}(\hat\beta \mid \mathbf{X})].$$

The desired conclusions then follow from the fact that, under the stated assumptions, the sampling distribution of $\hat\beta$ given $\mathbf{X}$ has mean equal to β and variance equal to $\sigma^2(\mathbf{X}^\top\mathbf{X})^{-1}$. □

Assumptions 6.4–6.6 correspond to the case when the classical linear model holds for all values of $\mathbf{X}$, except possibly a set with probability zero. This set of assumptions may be interpreted in terms of random sampling from the distribution of a random vector (X, Y) with finite second moments. In this case, since the observations are i.i.d., we have

$$\mathrm{E}(Y_i \mid \mathbf{X}) = \mathrm{E}(Y_i \mid X_i),$$

$$\mathrm{Cov}(Y_i, Y_j \mid \mathbf{X}) = \begin{cases} \mathrm{Var}(Y_i \mid X_i), & \text{if } i = j, \\ 0, & \text{otherwise.} \end{cases}$$

In particular, since the rows of the data matrix $[\mathbf{X}, \mathbf{Y}]$ are identically distributed, it follows that $\mathrm{E}\, Y_i = \mathrm{E}\, Y$ and $\mathrm{E}\, X_i = \mathrm{E}\, X$ for all i. Notice the difference with respect to the classical linear model where the rows of $\mathbf{X}$ are instead nonstochastic vectors and $\mathrm{E}\, Y_i$ is different from $\mathrm{E}\, Y_j$ in general. If the CMF of Y is linear in X and the CVF is constant, then

$$\mathrm{E}(Y_i \,|\, X_i) = \beta^\top X_i, \qquad \mathrm{Var}(Y_i \,|\, X_i) = \sigma^2, \qquad i = 1, \ldots, n.$$

Other sampling schemes may be consistent with Assumptions 6.4–6.6. In general, however, Assumption 6.5 rules out the case of dynamic regression models where lagged values of the response variable are included among the covariates. No exact result is generally available for this case and inference is largely based on the asymptotic results discussed in Chapter 10.

Example 6.6 As an example of why Assumption 6.5 rules out the case of dynamic regression models, let $Z_1, \ldots, Z_T$ be a finite segment of the AR(1) process

$$Z_t = \rho Z_{t-1} + U_t, \qquad \{U_t\} \sim \mathrm{WN}(0, \sigma^2).$$

Let $\mathbf{Y} = (Z_2, \ldots, Z_T)$ and $\mathbf{X} = (Z_1, \ldots, Z_{T-1})$ be vectors of dimension $n = T - 1$. Because

$$\mathrm{E}(Z_t \,|\, Z_1, \ldots, Z_{T-1}) = \begin{cases} Z_t, & \text{if } t = 1, \ldots, T-1, \\ \rho Z_{T-1}, & \text{if } t = T, \end{cases}$$

we have

$$\mathrm{E}(\mathbf{Y} \,|\, \mathbf{X}) = \begin{pmatrix} Z_2 \\ \vdots \\ Z_{T-1} \\ \rho Z_{T-1} \end{pmatrix} \neq \begin{pmatrix} \rho Z_1 \\ \vdots \\ \rho Z_{T-2} \\ \rho Z_{T-1} \end{pmatrix} = \mathbf{X}\rho.$$

□

6.3.3 *ESTIMATES OF PRECISION*

The parameter of interest in the classical linear model is β, while σ^2 is usually treated as a nuisance parameter, that is, a parameter that is not of primary interest. Knowledge of σ^2 is nevertheless necessary in order to assess the sampling variability of the OLS estimator.

Because the classical linear model implies $\sigma^2 = \mathrm{Var}\, Y_i = \mathrm{E}(Y_i - \beta^\top X_i)^2$, an analogue estimator of σ^2 is

$$\hat{\sigma}^2 = n^{-1} \sum_{i=1}^{n} (Y_i - \hat{\beta}^\top X_i)^2 = n^{-1} \hat{\mathbf{U}}^\top \hat{\mathbf{U}}.$$

By the properties of the trace operator

$$\mathrm{E}\, \hat{\mathbf{U}}^\top \hat{\mathbf{U}} = \mathrm{E}\, \mathbf{Y}^\top M \mathbf{Y} = \mathrm{E}[\mathrm{tr}(M \mathbf{Y}\mathbf{Y}^\top)] = \mathrm{tr}[M(\mathrm{E}\, \mathbf{Y}\mathbf{Y}^\top)].$$

If the classical linear model holds, then

$$M[\mathrm{E}\, \mathbf{Y}\mathbf{Y}^\top] = M[\sigma^2 I_n + \mathbf{X}\beta\beta^\top \mathbf{X}^\top] = \sigma^2 M,$$

where we used the fact that $M\mathbf{X} = 0$. Hence

$$\mathrm{E}\,\hat{\sigma}^2 = \left(1 - \frac{k}{n}\right)\sigma^2.$$

The estimator $\hat{\sigma}^2$ is therefore biased for σ^2. Its bias can be serious if k is large relative to n, but tends to vanish as $k/n \to 0$. If $n > k$, an unbiased estimator of σ^2 is the *OLS estimator of scale*

$$s^2 = \frac{n}{n-k}\hat{\sigma}^2 = \frac{1}{n-k}\sum_i \hat{U}_i^2 = \frac{\hat{\mathbf{U}}^\top \hat{\mathbf{U}}}{n-k}.$$

Because $\mathbf{X}$ is a nonstochastic matrix, an unbiased estimator of $\sigma^2(\mathbf{X}^\top\mathbf{X})^{-1}$ is therefore $\widehat{\mathrm{Var}}\,\hat{\beta} = s^2(\mathbf{X}^\top\mathbf{X})^{-1}$. It is easy to verify that both s^2 and $\widehat{\mathrm{Var}}\,\hat{\beta}$ remain unbiased when the design matrix is stochastic.

6.4 THE GAUSSIAN LINEAR MODEL

So far, we used the information on the mean and the variance of $\mathbf{Y}$ to derive the sampling mean of $\hat{\beta}$ and s^2 and the sampling variance of $\hat{\beta}$. These results, although important, do not characterize the sampling distribution of the two estimators and therefore fall short of what is needed in order to construct confidence sets for the model parameters or critical regions of tests of statistical hypotheses.

One way of dealing with the above problem is to assume that the distribution of $\mathbf{Y}$ belongs to a known parametric family $\mathcal{F}_\Theta$. Whether the available information justifies such an assumption is often an issue. At any rate, knowledge of $\mathcal{F}_\Theta$ makes it possible, at least in principle, to determine the exact shape of the sampling distribution of $\hat{\beta}$ and s^2. Except for a few special cases, however, the formulae tend to be rather messy. This section discusses the important special case when $\mathcal{F}_\Theta$ is the family of n-variate Gaussian distributions with scalar variance matrix.

6.4.1 SAMPLING DISTRIBUTION OF THE OLS ESTIMATOR

We consider the sampling properties of the OLS estimator under the following set of assumpions.

Assumption 6.7 *The conditional distribution of* $\mathbf{Y}$ *given* $\mathbf{X}$ *is n-variate Gaussian with mean* $\mathbf{X}\beta$ *and variance* $\sigma^2 I_n$*, where* $\mathbf{X}$ *is a random $n \times k$ matrix whose rank is equal to k with probability one,* $\beta \in \Re^k$ *and* $0 < \sigma^2 < \infty$.

When $\mathbf{X}$ is a nonstochastic matrix of full column rank k, we refer to the above model as the *classical Gaussian linear model.* The next result gives the joint distributions of $\hat{\beta}$ and $\hat{\mathbf{U}}^\top\hat{\mathbf{U}}$.

Theorem 6.3 *Under the classical Gaussian linear model:*

(i) $\hat{\beta} \sim \mathcal{N}_k(\beta, \sigma^2(\mathbf{X}^\top\mathbf{X})^{-1})$;
(ii) $\hat{\mathbf{U}}^\top\hat{\mathbf{U}}/\sigma^2 \sim \chi^2_{n-k}$;

(iii) *$\hat\beta$ and $\hat{\mathbf{U}}$ are independent.*

Proof. Part (i) is immediate. Part (ii) follows from Result C.19 and the fact that $\mathbf{U}/\sigma = (\mathbf{Y} - \mathbf{X}\beta)/\sigma \sim \mathcal{N}_n(0, I_n)$ and M is an idempotent matrix with trace equal to $n-k$. Finally, since $\hat\beta - \beta = (\mathbf{X}^\top\mathbf{X})^{-1}\mathbf{X}^\top\mathbf{U}$, $\hat{\mathbf{U}} = M\mathbf{U}$ and $(\mathbf{X}^\top\mathbf{X})^{-1}\mathbf{X}^\top M = 0$, it follows from Result C.18 that $\hat\beta - \beta$ and $\hat{\mathbf{U}}$ are independent, and so are $\hat\beta$ and $\hat{\mathbf{U}}$. □

Thus, under the classical Gaussian linear model,

$$2(n-k) = \operatorname{Var}\frac{\hat{\mathbf{U}}^\top\hat{\mathbf{U}}}{\sigma^2} = \frac{(n-k)^2}{\sigma^4}\operatorname{Var} s^2,$$

which implies

$$\operatorname{Var} s^2 = \frac{2\sigma^4}{n-k}.$$

Further, because any function of $\hat\beta$ is independent of any function of $\hat{\mathbf{U}}$, $\hat\beta$ is independent of $\hat{\mathbf{U}}^\top\hat{\mathbf{U}}$ and therefore also of s^2.

When the design matrix is stochastic, the conclusions of Theorem 6.3 still hold conditionally on $\mathbf{X}$. In particular, the conditional distribution of $\hat\beta$ given $\mathbf{X}$ is $\mathcal{N}_k(\beta, \sigma^2(\mathbf{X}^\top\mathbf{X})^{-1})$. The marginal distribution of $\hat\beta$, however, being a mixture of Gaussian distributions, need not be Gaussian. On the other hand, since the conditional distribution of $(n-k)s^2/\sigma^2$ does not depend on $\mathbf{X}$, its marginal distribution remains chi-square with $n-k$ degrees of freedom.

6.4.2 THE GAUSSIAN ML ESTIMATOR

Given the classical Gaussian linear model, one may apply the ML method to estimate (β, σ^2). The sample log-likelihood of this model is

$$L(\beta, \sigma^2) = c - \frac{n}{2}\ln\sigma^2 - \frac{n}{2\sigma^2}Q(\beta),$$

where c is an arbitrary constant and $Q(\beta)$ is the OLS criterion. Because maximizing L with respect to β is equivalent to minimizing the OLS criterion, the Gaussian ML and the OLS estimates coincide. In particular, if $\mathbf{X}^\top\mathbf{X}$ is a p.d. matrix, the ML estimate of β is unique and is equal to $\hat\beta = (\mathbf{X}^\top\mathbf{X})^{-1}\mathbf{X}^\top\mathbf{Y}$.

For a fixed β, the ML estimate of σ^2 is a root of the equation

$$0 = \frac{\partial L}{\partial\sigma^2} = -\frac{n}{2\sigma^2} + \frac{n}{2\sigma^4}Q(\beta),$$

whose unique solution is $\sigma^2(\beta) = Q(\beta)$. The ML estimate of σ^2 is therefore

$$\sigma^2(\hat\beta) = Q(\hat\beta) = \frac{\hat{\mathbf{U}}^\top\hat{\mathbf{U}}}{n},$$

which coincides with the average squared deviation $\hat\sigma^2$ of the OLS residuals. It is interesting to notice that under the Gaussian linear model

$$\operatorname{Var}\hat\sigma^2 = \left(1 - \frac{k}{n}\right)^2 \operatorname{Var} s^2 < \operatorname{Var} s^2.$$

Thus, although downward biased, $\hat\sigma^2$ has smaller sampling variance than the unbiased estimator s^2.

6.4.3 MINIMUM VARIANCE UNBIASED ESTIMATION

If the assumptions of the Gauss–Markov theorem hold, the OLS estimator $\hat{\beta}$ has the weak optimality property of being a BLU or, more precisely, a minimum variance linear unbiased estimator of the regression parameter β. The next result provides a somewhat stronger justification for the OLS estimator when the classical Gaussian linear model holds.

Theorem 6.4 *Under the classical Gaussian linear model, the OLS estimator* $\hat{\theta} = (\hat{\beta}, s^2)$ *is UMVU for* $\theta = (\beta, \sigma^2)$.

Proof. It is enough to verify the conditions of the Lehmann–Scheffè theorem (Theorem 4.8). Since the design matrix is nonstochastic and $\mathbf{Y} \sim \mathcal{N}_n(\mathbf{X}\beta, \sigma^2 I_n)$, the density of $\mathbf{Y}$ is

$$\begin{aligned} f(\mathbf{Y} \mid \theta) &= (2\pi\sigma^2)^{-n/2} \exp\left[-\frac{n}{2\sigma^2} Q(\beta)\right] \\ &= (2\pi\sigma^2)^{-n/2} \exp\left[-\frac{1}{2\sigma^2}(\mathbf{Y}^\top\mathbf{Y} - 2\beta^\top\mathbf{X}^\top\mathbf{Y} + \beta^\top\mathbf{X}^\top\mathbf{X}\beta)\right]. \end{aligned}$$

By Theorem 4.6, the statistics $\mathbf{Y}^\top\mathbf{Y}$ and $\mathbf{X}^\top\mathbf{Y}$ are jointly sufficient for (β, σ^2). Because the classical Gaussian linear model is a linear exponential family of order $k + 1$ and the parameter space $\Theta = \Re^k \times \Re_+$ has a nonempty interior, the family of distributions of these sufficient statistics is complete. Since the OLS estimators $\hat{\beta}$ and s^2 are unbiased and are functions of the sufficient statistics, the Lehmann–Scheffè theorem implies that they are UMVU. □

It is instructive to compare the conclusions of Theorem 6.4 with the Cramér–Rao lower bound for the sampling variance of an unbiased estimator of $\theta = (\beta, \sigma^2)$ in the classical Gaussian linear model. It can easily be shown that the expected total information on θ contained in a sample of n observations from the model is

$$I(\theta) = \frac{1}{\sigma^2}\begin{bmatrix} \mathbf{X}^\top\mathbf{X} & 0 \\ 0 & n/(2\sigma^2) \end{bmatrix}. \tag{6.7}$$

If the matrix $\mathbf{X}^\top\mathbf{X}$ is nonsingular, the Cramér–Rao lower bound is

$$I(\theta)^{-1} = \begin{bmatrix} \sigma^2(\mathbf{X}^\top\mathbf{X})^{-1} & 0 \\ 0 & 2\sigma^4/n \end{bmatrix}.$$

This lower bound is clearly attained by $\hat{\beta}$. On the contrary, the UMVU estimator s^2 does not attain the bound, for $\operatorname{Var} s^2 = 2\sigma^4/(n-k) > 2\sigma^4/n$.

When the design matrix is stochastic, showing that $(\hat{\beta}, s^2)$ is UMVU for (β, σ^2) requires an additional assumption. In order to apply the Lehmann–Scheffè theorem, we must now be sure that no information on $\theta = (\beta, \sigma^2)$ is lost by neglecting the marginal distribution of $\mathbf{X}$ and only considering the conditional distribution of $\mathbf{Y}$ given $\mathbf{X}$. The joint density of $[\mathbf{X}, \mathbf{Y}]$ can always be decomposed as

$$f(\mathbf{x}, \mathbf{y}; \psi) = f(\mathbf{y} \mid \mathbf{x}; \theta)\, h(\mathbf{x}; \gamma),$$

where $\psi \in \Psi$ is a finite-dimensional parameter vector, $f(\mathbf{y} \mid \mathbf{x}; \theta)$ is the conditional density of $\mathbf{Y}$ given $\mathbf{X} = \mathbf{x}$, $h(\mathbf{x}; \gamma)$ is the marginal density of $\mathbf{X}$, and $\theta \in \Theta$ and $\gamma \in \Gamma$ are functions of ψ. The essential requirement is therefore the absence of a functional relationship between θ and γ, that is, we must have that $\Psi = \Theta \times \Gamma$, which corresponds to exogeneity of $\mathbf{X}$ with respect to θ.

6.4.4 CONFIDENCE SETS

In this section we assume that the classical Gaussian linear model holds and consider ways of using the OLS estimators $\hat{\beta}$ and s^2 to construct classical confidence sets for a finite number of linear combinations $\theta = R\beta$ of the regression parameters.

We first consider the case of a single linear combination of the elements of β.

Theorem 6.5 *Let $\theta = R\beta$, where $R \neq 0$ is a k-dimensional row vector. Under the classical Gaussian linear model*

$$Z(\mathbf{Y}; \theta) = \frac{R\hat{\beta} - \theta}{\sigma[R(\mathbf{X}^\top \mathbf{X})^{-1} R^\top]^{1/2}} \sim \mathcal{N}(0, 1),$$

$$T(\mathbf{Y}; \theta) = \frac{R\hat{\beta} - \theta}{s[R(\mathbf{X}^\top \mathbf{X})^{-1} R^\top]^{1/2}} \sim t_{n-k}.$$

Proof. The first conclusion follows from the fact that, under our set of assumptions, $R\hat{\beta} \sim \mathcal{N}_q(\theta, \sigma^2 R(\mathbf{X}^\top \mathbf{X})^{-1} R^\top)$. Observe next that $T = Z/[S/(n-k)]^{1/2}$, where $S = (n-k)s^2/\sigma^2$ has a (central) chi-square distribution with $n-k$ degrees of freedom. Because $\hat{\beta}$ and s^2 are independent, so are Z and S. The statistic $T(\mathbf{Y}; \beta)$ therefore has a t-distribution with $n-k$ degrees of freedom. □

The statistic $Z(\mathbf{Y}; \theta)$ is the ratio between $R\hat{\beta} - \theta$ and its standard error, whereas $T(\mathbf{Y}; \theta)$ is the ratio between $R\hat{\beta} - \theta$ and the square root of the unbiased estimator of its sampling variance. The second part of Theorem 6.5 implies that the random interval

$$C(\mathbf{Y}) = \{\theta \in \Re\colon |T(\mathbf{Y}; \theta)| \leq t_{(\alpha)}\}$$

or, equivalently,

$$C(\mathbf{Y}) = \left[R\hat{\beta} - t_{(\alpha)} s[R(\mathbf{X}^\top \mathbf{X})^{-1} R^\top]^{1/2},\ R\hat{\beta} + t_{(\alpha)} s[R(\mathbf{X}^\top \mathbf{X})^{-1} R^\top]^{1/2}\right],$$

where $t_{(\alpha)}$ denotes the upper αth quantile of the t-distribution with $n-k$ degrees of freedom, is a $(1-2\alpha)$-level symmetric confidence interval for the linear combination $\theta = R\beta$ of the elements of β. In particular, if R is a vector whose jth element is equal to one and all others are equal to zero, then $R\beta$ is equal to the jth element β_j of β, while $R(\mathbf{X}^\top \mathbf{X})^{-1} R^\top$ is equal to the jth diagonal element c_{jj} of the matrix $(\mathbf{X}^\top \mathbf{X})^{-1}$. The random interval

$$C(\mathbf{Y}) = \left[\hat{\beta}_j - t_{(\alpha)} s\sqrt{c_{jj}},\ \hat{\beta}_j + t_{(\alpha)} s\sqrt{c_{jj}}\right]$$

is therefore a $(1-2\alpha)$-level symmetric confidence interval for β_j.

Now consider the case of $q \geq 1$ linear combinations of the elements of β.

Theorem 6.6 *Let $\theta = R\beta$, where R is a $q \times k$ matrix of rank $q \geq 1$. Under the classical Gaussian linear model*

$$W(\mathbf{Y};\theta) = \frac{(R\hat{\beta} - \theta)^\top [R(\mathbf{X}^\top\mathbf{X})^{-1}R^\top]^{-1}(R\hat{\beta} - \theta)}{\sigma^2} \sim \chi^2_q,$$

$$F(\mathbf{Y};\theta) = \frac{(R\hat{\beta} - \theta)^\top [R(\mathbf{X}^\top\mathbf{X})^{-1}R^\top]^{-1}(R\hat{\beta} - \theta)}{qs^2} \sim F_{q,n-k}.$$

Proof. The first conclusion follows from the fact that, under our set of assumptions,

$$\sigma^{-1}[R(\mathbf{X}^\top\mathbf{X})^{-1}R^\top]^{-1/2}R(\hat{\beta} - \beta) \sim \mathcal{N}_q(0, I_q).$$

Now observe that

$$F = \frac{W/q}{S/(n-k)},$$

where $S = (n-k)s^2/\sigma^2$ has a chi-square distribution with $n-k$ degrees of freedom. Since $\hat{\beta} - \beta$ and s^2 are independent, so are W and S. Hence, the statistic F has an F-distribution with $(q, n-k)$ degrees of freedom. □

The statistic $W(\mathbf{Y};\theta)$ is the squared Mahalanobis norm of the random vector $R\hat{\beta}-\theta$, whereas $qF(\mathbf{Y};\theta)$ is an estimate of the squared Mahalanobis norm of $R\hat{\beta} - \theta$. The second part of Theorem 6.6 implies that the random set

$$C(\mathbf{Y}) = \{\theta \in \Re^q \colon F(\mathbf{Y};\theta) \leq F_{(\alpha)}\},$$

where $F_{(\alpha)}$ denotes the upper αth quantile of the $F_{q,n-k}$ distribution, is a $(1-\alpha)$-level confidence region for the vector $\theta = R\beta$ of $q \leq k$ nonsingular linear combinations of the elements of β. In particular, if $R = I_k$, then

$$C(\mathbf{Y}) = \{\beta \in \Re^k \colon F(\mathbf{Y};\beta) \leq F_{(\alpha)}\},$$

is a $(1-\alpha)$-level confidence set for the whole vector β. Notice that $C(\mathbf{Y})$ is an ellipsoid in $\Re^k$ centered at $\hat{\beta}$. If $\mathbf{X}^\top\mathbf{X} = I_k$, then $C(\mathbf{Y})$ is a hypersphere with center at $\hat{\beta}$.

When $q = 1$, the confidence regions based on Theorems 6.5 and 6.6 coincide. When $q > 1$, however, a confidence ellipsoid based on Theorem 6.6 differs from the multidimensional box obtained by taking the Cartesian product of the separate confidence intervals for the q linear combinations of β.

The confidence sets based on the t- and F-distributions lose their validity when $\mathbf{Y}$ is not Gaussian. As shown in Chapter 10, they remain approximately valid in large samples if all the assumptions of the linear model are satisfied. Of course, instead of relying on approximations that are only valid in large samples, an alternative is to construct bootstrap confidence intervals in the way described in Section 5.2.2.

6.5 CONSTRAINED OLS

Specific knowledge of the problem under examination or previous experience with similar problems sometimes provide prior information on the regression parameter β. In this section we discuss one way of incorporating this kind of information into the estimation problem. Specifically, we consider the special case when the prior information on β is exact, that is, not subject to any uncertainty.

Thus suppose that the regression parameter β belongs to a subset of $\Re^k$ defined by a set of $q \leq k$ linear inequalities of the form

$$R\beta \geq r, \tag{6.8}$$

where R is a known $q \times k$ matrix of rank q and r is a known q-vector. This formulation enables us to incorporate prior information on the sign of the regression coefficients or linear combinations thereof. A large variety of constraints on the regression coefficients may be subsumed under (6.8).

Example 6.7 Let $\beta = (\beta_1, \ldots, \beta_k)$. Putting $r = 0$ and $R = e_j^\top$, where e_j denotes the jth unit vector, corresponds to the non-negativity constraint $\beta_j \geq 0$. Putting $r = 0$ and $R = -e_j^\top$ corresponds to the nonpositivity constraint $\beta_j \leq 0$. Combining these two constraints corresponds to the single equality constraint $\beta_j = 0$, which excludes the jth covariate from the regression. Putting $R = (1, -1, 0, \ldots, 0)$ and $r = 0$ corresponds to the constraint $\beta_1 \geq \beta_2$. Putting $R = I_k$ and $r = 0$ corresponds to the constraints that all elements of β are non-negative. □

An important special case is when $R\beta = r$, that is, β is assumed to belong to a proper subspace of $\Re^k$ defined by a set of linear equality constraints.

An *inequality constrained OLS estimate* is a solution to the problem

$$\begin{aligned} &\min_{\beta \in \Re^k} \ (\mathbf{Y} - \mathbf{X}\beta)^\top (\mathbf{Y} - \mathbf{X}\beta) \\ &\text{s.t.} \qquad R\beta - r \geq 0. \end{aligned}$$

By the Kuhn–Tucker theorem, if $\bar{\beta}$ is a constrained OLS estimate, then there exists a non-negative vector of Kuhn–Tucker multipliers $\bar{\nu} = (\bar{\nu}_1, \ldots, \bar{\nu}_q)$ such that $\bar{\beta}$ and $\bar{\nu}$ together satisfy

$$\begin{aligned} 0 &= -2\mathbf{X}^\top \mathbf{Y} + 2\mathbf{X}^\top \mathbf{X}\bar{\beta} - R^\top \bar{\nu}, \\ 0 &\leq R\bar{\beta} - r, \\ 0 &= \bar{\nu}^\top (R\bar{\beta} - r), \end{aligned}$$

with $\bar{\nu}_j = 0$ whenever the jth constraint is not binding and $\bar{\nu}_j > 0$ otherwise. If all constraints are of the equality type, then $\bar{\nu}$ is the usual vector of Lagrange multipliers. The first of the above three conditions implies that

$$\mathbf{X}^\top \mathbf{X}\bar{\beta} - \mathbf{X}^\top \mathbf{Y} - R^\top \bar{\nu}/2 = 0.$$

Therefore, assuming that $\mathbf{X}^\top \mathbf{X}$ is nonsingular,

$$\bar{\beta} = \hat{\beta} + (\mathbf{X}^\top \mathbf{X})^{-1} R^\top \bar{\nu}/2, \tag{6.9}$$

where $\hat{\beta}$ is the unconstrained OLS estimate. If $\bar{\nu} = 0$, that is, none of the constraints is binding, then $\bar{\beta} = \hat{\beta}$.

Now consider the special case when all constraints are of the equality type, that is, $R\beta = r$ (Figure 46). In this case, the equality constrained OLS estimate $\tilde{\beta}$ must satisfy

Figure 46 The constrained OLS problem for $k = 2$ and $q = 1$. The family of ellipses represents the level curves of the OLS criterion whereas the dotted line represents a single linear constraint on the parameters (β_1, β_2).

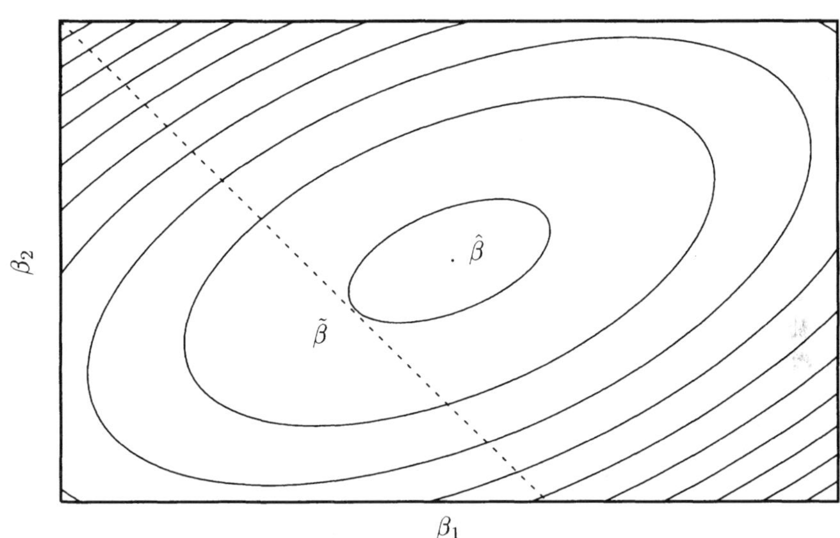

the constraint $R\tilde{\beta} = r$. When R has full rank and $q = k$, solving for $\tilde{\beta}$ gives $\tilde{\beta} = R^{-1}r$, a fixed (nonstochastic) vector. When $q < k$, $\tilde{\beta}$ depends on the unconstrained OLS estimate $\hat{\beta}$ and the Lagrange multiplier vector $\tilde{\nu}$ through a relationship of the same form as (6.9). Substituting into the constraint then gives

$$R\hat{\beta} + R(\mathbf{X}^\top\mathbf{X})^{-1}R^\top\tilde{\nu}/2 = r.$$

Since the matrix $R(\mathbf{X}^\top\mathbf{X})^{-1}R^\top$ is p.d. under the stated assumptions, solving for $\tilde{\nu}$ gives

$$\tilde{\nu} = -2[R(\mathbf{X}^\top\mathbf{X})^{-1}R^\top]^{-1}(R\hat{\beta} - r).$$

The equality constrained OLS estimate is therefore

$$\tilde{\beta} = \hat{\beta} - (\mathbf{X}^\top\mathbf{X})^{-1}R^\top[R(\mathbf{X}^\top\mathbf{X})^{-1}R^\top]^{-1}(R\hat{\beta} - r),$$

and the associated residual vector is

$$\tilde{\mathbf{U}} = \mathbf{Y} - \mathbf{X}\tilde{\beta} = \hat{\mathbf{U}} + \mathbf{X}(\mathbf{X}^\top\mathbf{X})^{-1}R^\top[R(\mathbf{X}^\top\mathbf{X})^{-1}R^\top]^{-1}(R\hat{\beta} - r).$$

Because $\mathbf{X}^\top\hat{\mathbf{U}} = 0$, it follows that

$$\begin{aligned}\tilde{\mathbf{U}}^\top\tilde{\mathbf{U}} - \hat{\mathbf{U}}^\top\hat{\mathbf{U}} &= (\tilde{\beta} - \hat{\beta})^\top\mathbf{X}^\top\mathbf{X}(\tilde{\beta} - \hat{\beta}) \\ &= (R\hat{\beta} - r)^\top[R(\mathbf{X}^\top\mathbf{X})^{-1}R^\top]^{-1}(R\hat{\beta} - r).\end{aligned} \tag{6.10}$$

Notice that $\tilde{\mathbf{U}}^\top\tilde{\mathbf{U}} \geq \hat{\mathbf{U}}^\top\hat{\mathbf{U}}$, with equality if and only if the unconstrained estimate $\hat{\beta}$ satisfies the constraints exactly.

Now consider the sampling properties of the equality constrained estimator. This is straightforward because $\tilde{\beta}$ is a linear transformation of $\hat{\beta}$ and therefore of $\mathbf{Y}$. Although the next result only gives the sampling mean and variance of $\tilde{\beta}$, it is clear that $\tilde{\beta}$ has a Gaussian distribution whenever the distribution of $\mathbf{Y}$ is Gaussian.

Theorem 6.7 *Under the classical linear model:*

(i) $\mathrm{E}\,\tilde{\beta} = \beta - (\mathbf{X}^\top\mathbf{X})^{-1}R^\top[R(\mathbf{X}^\top\mathbf{X})^{-1}R^\top]^{-1}(R\beta - r)$;
(ii) $\mathrm{Var}\,\tilde{\beta} = \mathrm{Var}\,\hat{\beta} - \sigma^2(\mathbf{X}^\top\mathbf{X})^{-1}R^\top[R(\mathbf{X}^\top\mathbf{X})^{-1}R^\top]^{-1}R(\mathbf{X}^\top\mathbf{X})^{-1}$.

Proof. Part (i) is trivial. To prove (ii), notice that

$$\tilde{\beta} - \mathrm{E}\,\tilde{\beta} = \hat{\beta} - \beta - (\mathbf{X}^\top\mathbf{X})^{-1}R^\top[R(\mathbf{X}^\top\mathbf{X})^{-1}R^\top]^{-1}R(\hat{\beta} - \beta).$$

Thus, after some algebra, we get

$$\begin{aligned}\mathrm{E}(\tilde{\beta} - \mathrm{E}\,\tilde{\beta})(\tilde{\beta} - \mathrm{E}\,\tilde{\beta})^\top &= \sigma^2(\mathbf{X}^\top\mathbf{X})^{-1} \\ &\quad - \sigma^2(\mathbf{X}^\top\mathbf{X})^{-1}R^\top[R(\mathbf{X}^\top\mathbf{X})^{-1}R^\top]^{-1}R(\mathbf{X}^\top\mathbf{X})^{-1}.\end{aligned}$$

□

Part (i) of Theorem 6.7 implies that the equality constrained OLS estimator is unbiased for β if and only if $R\beta = r$, that is, if and only if the constraints are valid. Part (ii) implies that, if $\hat{\beta} \neq \tilde{\beta}$, then $\mathrm{Var}\,\tilde{\beta} - \mathrm{Var}\,\hat{\beta}$ is a n.d. matrix, that is, the constrained estimator is more precise than the unconstrained one. Thus, even when the constraints are not valid, the constrained estimator may be more efficient (in the MSE sense) than the unconstrained one if its bias is more than offset by the smaller variance.

The counterpart of Theorem 6.7 for the case of a random design matrix follows immediately from the law of iterated expectations.

A class of constrained estimates of σ^2 is easily obtained by suitably rescaling the constrained OLS residual sum of squares. Assume for simplicity that the design matrix is nonstochastic. Given the relationship

$$\mathrm{E}(R\hat{\beta} - r)(R\hat{\beta} - r)^\top = \sigma^2 R(\mathbf{X}^\top\mathbf{X})^{-1}R^\top + (R\beta - r)(R\beta - r)^\top,$$

it is easily verified that

$$\mathrm{E}\,\tilde{\mathbf{U}}^\top\tilde{\mathbf{U}} = \sigma^2(n - k + q) + (R\beta - r)^\top[R(\mathbf{X}^\top\mathbf{X})^{-1}R^\top]^{-1}(R\beta - r).$$

If $n + q > k$ and the constraints are correct, that is, $R\beta = r$, then

$$\tilde{s}^2 = \frac{\tilde{\mathbf{U}}^\top\tilde{\mathbf{U}}}{n - k + q}$$

is an unbiased estimator of σ^2.

6.6 BAYESIAN ESTIMATORS

We now use Bayes theorem to combine the sample information contained in the observed data $\mathbf{Z} = [\mathbf{X}, \mathbf{Y}]$ with the prior information contained in the assumptions of the classical Gaussian linear model and a prior distribution on the parameter space $\Theta = \Re^k \times \Re_+$. The result is a posterior distribution on Θ conditional on the observed data.

In what follows we assume that the matrix $\mathbf{X}^\top\mathbf{X}$ is nonsingular and use the fact that the sample likelihood implied by the Gaussian linear model may be written

$$f(\mathbf{Y} \mid \theta) \propto \frac{1}{\sigma^n} \exp\left\{-\frac{1}{2\sigma^2}[\nu s^2 + (\beta - \hat{\beta})^\top \mathbf{X}^\top \mathbf{X}(\beta - \hat{\beta})]\right\}, \qquad \theta = (\beta, \sigma),$$

where the statistics $\hat{\beta}$ and $\nu s^2 = \hat{\mathbf{U}}^\top\hat{\mathbf{U}}$ are jointly sufficient for θ and $\nu = n - k > 0$.

6.6.1 *UNINFORMATIVE PRIORS*

In this section we consider the case of an initial state of complete ignorance about the model parameter $\theta = (\beta, \sigma)$. We therefore assume that the elements of θ are mutually independent and, following Jeffreys' invariance principle, let $\ln \sigma$ and all elements of β be uniformly distributed on the real line. The prior density of θ is therefore of the form $p(\theta) \propto 1/\sigma$, which is not a proper density. By Bayes theorem, the posterior density of θ is

$$p(\theta \mid \mathbf{Z}) \propto \frac{1}{\sigma^{n+1}} \exp\left\{-\frac{1}{2\sigma^2}[\nu s^2 + (\beta - \hat{\beta})^\top \mathbf{X}^\top \mathbf{X}(\beta - \hat{\beta})]\right\}. \tag{6.11}$$

Inspection of (6.11) reveals that the conditional posterior density of β given σ is

$$p(\beta \mid \sigma; \mathbf{Z}) \propto \frac{1}{\sigma^k} \exp\left[-\frac{1}{2\sigma^2}(\beta - \hat{\beta})^\top \mathbf{X}^\top \mathbf{X}(\beta - \hat{\beta})\right],$$

which corresponds to the density of a k-variate Gaussian distribution with mean $\hat{\beta}$ and variance $\sigma^2(\mathbf{X}^\top\mathbf{X})^{-1}$. Thus, under an uninformative prior, the OLS estimate corresponds to the mean of the conditional posterior distribution of β given σ. Because $p(\theta \mid \mathbf{Z}) = p(\beta \mid \sigma; \mathbf{Z})\, p(\sigma \mid \mathbf{Z})$, the marginal posterior density of σ is

$$p(\sigma \mid \mathbf{Z}) = \frac{p(\beta, \sigma \mid \mathbf{Z})}{p(\beta \mid \sigma; \mathbf{Z})} \propto \frac{1}{\sigma^{\nu+1}} \exp\left(-\frac{\nu s^2}{2\sigma^2}\right),$$

which is the density of an inverted gamma distribution with parameter $(\nu/2, \nu s^2/2)$.

The marginal posterior density of β may be obtained by integrating (6.11) with respect to σ

$$p(\beta \mid \mathbf{Z}) = \int_0^\infty p(\beta, \sigma \mid \mathbf{Z})\, d\sigma.$$

This integral may be computed using the formula (5.7), with $m = \nu + k = n$ and $\lambda = 2$, after setting a equal to the term in square brackets in the exponential part of (6.11). This gives

$$p(\beta \mid \mathbf{Z}) \propto \left[\nu + \frac{(\beta - \hat{\beta})^\top \mathbf{X}^\top \mathbf{X}(\beta - \hat{\beta})}{s^2}\right]^{-n/2}, \tag{6.12}$$

which is the density of a k-variate t-distribution with parameter $(\hat{\beta}, s^{-2}\mathbf{X}^\top\mathbf{X}, \nu)$. The properties of the marginal distribution of β follow immediately from those of the multivariate t-distribution.

1. Because (6.12) is a monotonically decreasing function of the quadratic form
$$Q_*(\beta) = (\beta - \hat{\beta})^\top \mathbf{X}^\top\mathbf{X}(\beta - \hat{\beta}),$$
the marginal posterior distribution of β is symmetric with a unique mode equal to the OLS estimate $\hat{\beta}$. This result should not be surprising, for the prior density is completely dominated by the Gaussian likelihood. The level curves of the posterior density (6.12) are a family of ellipsoids centered at $\hat{\beta}$. If $n - k > 1$, then the posterior mean of β exists and coincides with $\hat{\beta}$.
2. The marginal distribution of a subset of elements of β is also multivariate t. In particular, the marginal distribution of
$$T_j = \frac{\beta_j - \hat{\beta}_j}{s\sqrt{c_{jj}}}, \qquad j = 1, \ldots, k,$$
where c_{jj} is the jth diagonal element of the matrix $(\mathbf{X}^\top\mathbf{X})^{-1}$, is univariate t with $n - k$ degrees of freedom.
3. The posterior distribution of $Q_*(\beta)/(ks^2)$ is $F_{k,n-k}$. Denoting by $F_{(\alpha)}$ the upper αth quantile of the $F_{k,n-k}$ distribution, the region
$$\left\{\beta \in \Re^k \colon \frac{Q_*(\beta)}{ks^2} \le F_{(\alpha)}\right\}$$
contains a fraction equal to $1 - \alpha$ of the posterior distribution of β and is therefore a Bayesian confidence set for β.

Except for the interpretation, all these results correspond to those obtained with the classical approach.

6.6.2 *CONJUGATE PRIORS*

The prior distribution of $\theta = (\beta, \sigma)$ is called *gamma-Gaussian* with parameter $(\bar{\beta}, \Sigma, m, \lambda)$ if the conditional distribution of β given σ is $\mathcal{N}_k(\bar{\beta}, \sigma^2\Sigma^{-1})$ and the marginal distribution of σ is an inverted gamma with parameter $(m/2, m\lambda/2)$, where m is a positive integer, and probability density
$$p(\sigma) \propto \frac{1}{\sigma^{m+1}} \exp\left(-\frac{m\lambda}{2\sigma^2}\right).$$
The prior density of θ is therefore
$$p(\theta) \propto \frac{1}{\sigma^{m+k+1}} \exp\left\{-\frac{1}{2\sigma^2}[m\lambda + (\beta - \bar{\beta})^\top\Sigma(\beta - \bar{\beta})]\right\}. \tag{6.13}$$
Thus, unlike the previous section, β and σ are not independent. In other words, beliefs about β change with the information available on σ^2. The uninformative prior density in Section 6.6.1 corresponds to the limit of (6.13) as $\bar{\beta} \to 0$, $\Sigma \to 0$ and $m \to 0$.

The parameters of a gamma-Gaussian prior may be interpreted as the result of a Bayesian analysis of a preliminary sample $[\mathbf{Y}_0, \mathbf{X}_0]$ of size $n_0 > k$, starting from an initial state of complete ignorance about (β, σ). With this interpretation, $\bar{\beta}$ is the OLS coefficient in a regression of $\mathbf{Y}_0$ on $\mathbf{X}_0$, $m = n_0 - k$ is the number of degrees of freedom in the preliminary sample, $\lambda = s_0^2 = (n_0 - k)^{-1} \parallel \mathbf{Y}_0 - \mathbf{X}_0\bar{\beta} \parallel$ is the OLS estimate of scale, and $\Sigma^{-1} = s_0^2(\mathbf{X}_0^\top \mathbf{X}_0)^{-1}$ is the classical estimate of the sampling variance of $\bar{\beta}$. Alternatively, the parameters of the prior distribution (6.13) may be interpreted, in terms of subjective probability, as a convenient representation of the researcher's degrees of belief about statements concerning (β, σ).

The following theorem shows that the gamma-Gaussian family is conjugate with the Gaussian linear model.

Theorem 6.8 *If the classical Gaussian linear model holds and the prior distribution of (β, σ) is gamma-Gaussian with parameter $(\bar{\beta}, \Sigma, m, \lambda)$, then:*

(i) *the posterior distribution of (β, σ) is gamma-Gaussian with parameter $(\bar{\beta}_*, \Sigma_*, m_*, \lambda_*)$, where*

$$
\begin{aligned}
\bar{\beta}_* &= (\mathbf{X}^\top \mathbf{X} + \Sigma)^{-1}(\mathbf{X}^\top \mathbf{X}\hat{\beta} + \Sigma\bar{\beta}), \\
\Sigma_* &= \mathbf{X}^\top \mathbf{X} + \Sigma, \\
m_* &= \nu + m, \\
m_*\lambda_* &= \nu s^2 + m\lambda + (\bar{\beta} - \hat{\beta})^\top \Sigma\Sigma_*^{-1}\Sigma(\bar{\beta} - \hat{\beta});
\end{aligned}
$$

(ii) *the posterior distribution of β is k-variate t with parameter $(\bar{\beta}_*, \lambda^{*-2}\Sigma_*, m_*)$.*

Proof. The conditional distribution of (β, σ) given $\mathbf{Z} = [\mathbf{X}, \mathbf{Y}]$ is

$$
p(\beta, \sigma \,|\, \mathbf{Z}) \propto \frac{1}{\sigma^{n+m+k+1}} \exp\left[-\frac{1}{2\sigma^2} A(\mathbf{Z})\right],
$$

where

$$
A(\mathbf{Z}) = \nu s^2 + m\lambda + (\beta - \hat{\beta})^\top \mathbf{X}^\top \mathbf{X}(\beta - \hat{\beta}) + (\beta - \bar{\beta})^\top \Sigma(\beta - \bar{\beta}).
$$

Completing the square using the matrix generalization of formula (4.14), $A(\mathbf{Z})$ may be represented as

$$
A(\mathbf{Z}) = m_*\lambda_* + (\beta - \bar{\beta}_*)^\top \Sigma_*(\beta - \bar{\beta}_*),
$$

where $\bar{\beta}_*$, Σ_*, m_* and $m_*\lambda_*$ are defined in the statement of the theorem. Part (ii) then follows by exactly the argument applied in Section 6.6.1. □

The marginal posterior distribution of β is symmetric with a unique mode at the point $\bar{\beta}_*$, which may be represented as a matrix weighted average of the OLS estimate $\hat{\beta}$ and the prior mean $\bar{\beta}$, that is, $\bar{\beta}_* = D\hat{\beta} + (I_k - D)\bar{\beta}$, where $D = (\mathbf{X}^\top \mathbf{X} + \Sigma)^{-1}\mathbf{X}^\top \mathbf{X}$. If $m_* > 1$, that is, if $n + m > k + 1$, then the posterior mean of β exists and coincides with the posterior mode. Here, the symmetry of the posterior distribution of β implies that $\bar{\beta}_*$ is a Bayes estimate for every symmetric and convex loss function.

As the sample size increases, $\mathbf{X}^\top \mathbf{X}$ tends to dominate Σ and so $\beta_* \to \hat{\beta}$. On the other hand, for a fixed sample size, we have that $\beta_* \to \hat{\beta}$ as $\Sigma \to 0$, that is, the posterior mode converges to the OLS estimate when the prior information on β becomes more and more vague. The OLS estimate may therefore be interpreted either as the limit as $n \to \infty$ of a sequence of Bayes estimates with respect to a proper prior, or as a Bayes estimate with respect to an improper prior distribution.

By varying the parameter $(\bar{\beta}, \Sigma, m\lambda)$ of the prior distribution, one obtains a whole class of posterior distributions. In particular, varying the matrix Σ holding $\bar{\beta}$ and $m\lambda$ fixed defines a mapping from the class of symmetric p.d. matrices into the space $\Re^k$ of posterior modes of β. Such a mapping has been studied by Chamberlain and Leamer (1976). They show that, when only $\hat{\beta}$ and $\bar{\beta}$ are known, the posterior mode $\bar{\beta}_*$ may be anywhere in $\Re^k$. When the matrix $\mathbf{X}^\top\mathbf{X}$ is also known, then the posterior mode must belong to the ellipsoid

$$\{\beta \in \Re^k\colon 4(\beta - c)^\top \mathbf{X}^\top \mathbf{X}(\beta - c) < (\hat{\beta} - \bar{\beta})^\top \mathbf{X}^\top \mathbf{X}(\hat{\beta} - \bar{\beta})\},$$

where $c = (\hat{\beta} + \bar{\beta})/2$.

Leamer (1978) argues that unimodality of the posterior distribution of β is an undesirable feature because, if the prior and the sample information strongly disagree, then the posterior distribution should instead be bimodal, with the two modes corresponding to the OLS estimate and the prior mean. In order to get this result, he suggests replacing the gamma-Gaussian family of prior distributions by the *gamma-t* family, where β and σ are independent, β has a k-variate t-distribution and the distribution of σ is inverted gamma. One can show the posterior distribution of β obtained in this way is a mixture of t-distributions.

6.7 SHRINKAGE ESTIMATORS

If the prior distribution for β in a classical Gaussian linear model is $\mathcal{N}_k(0, \sigma^2\Sigma^{-1})$, then the posterior mode of β is $\bar{\beta}_* = (\mathbf{X}^\top\mathbf{X} + \Sigma)^{-1}\mathbf{X}^\top\mathbf{X}\hat{\beta}$. The posterior mode may therefore be interpreted as a way of "shrinking" the OLS estimate $\hat{\beta}$ towards the null vector. We now discuss a general class of non-Bayesian estimators with a similar property.

6.7.1 STEIN ESTIMATORS

The class of *Stein estimators* (Stein 1956) is defined as

$$\bar{\beta} = [I_k - h(T)A]\hat{\beta},$$

where $T = \hat{\beta}^\top B\hat{\beta}/s^2$, A and B are square matrices of order k, and $h\colon \Re \to \Re$ is a function satisfying $0 \leq h(T) \leq c/T$ for some $c > 0$. The basic idea of this class of estimators is to "correct" the OLS estimator by subtracting the quantity $h(u)A\hat{\beta}$, which depends on $\hat{\beta}$ itself and s^2. The OLS estimator is the Stein estimator corresponding to $h(T) = 0$ for all T.

A Stein estimator, being a nonlinear transformation of $\mathbf{Y}$, is generally biased. In order to compare its sampling properties with those of the OLS estimator, consider the quadratic loss function $\ell(u) = u^\top u$, where u is a k-vector. The risk of an estimator $\tilde{\beta}$ is

$$r(\tilde{\beta}, \beta) = \mathrm{E}\,\ell(\tilde{\beta}, \beta) = \mathrm{tr}[\mathrm{E}(\tilde{\beta} - \beta)(\tilde{\beta} - \beta)^\top],$$

where the expectation is with respect to the distribution of $\mathbf{Y}$. Hence, under the Gaussian linear model, the risk of the OLS estimator $\hat{\beta}$ is

$$r(\hat{\beta}, \beta) = \sigma^2 \operatorname{tr}[(\mathbf{X}^\top \mathbf{X})^{-1}],$$

which does not depend on β. Because $\bar{\beta} - \beta = (\hat{\beta} - \beta) - h(T)A\hat{\beta}$, the risk of a Stein estimator is instead

$$r(\bar{\beta}, \beta) = r(\hat{\beta}, \beta) - 2\,\mathrm{E}[h(T)(\hat{\beta} - \beta)^\top A\hat{\beta}] + \mathrm{E}[h(T)^2 \hat{\beta}^\top A^\top A\hat{\beta}].$$

It can be shown (see for example Judge & Bock 1978) that the second term on the right-hand side of the above expression can be made large enough to dominate the last term, in such a way that $r(\bar{\beta}, \beta) < r(\hat{\beta}, \beta)$ for every $\beta \in \Re^k$. A Stein estimator may therefore exists which strictly dominates the OLS estimator. The next section presents one such estimator.

6.7.2 JAMES-STEIN ESTIMATORS

We have seen in Section 4.8.3 that an estimator is admissible if it corresponds to a Bayes estimator with respect to some proper prior. The fact that the OLS estimator is Bayes with respect to an improper prior opens the possibility that it may be inadmissible, that is, it may be dominated by some other estimator. In this section we show that, under the standard assumptions of a classical Gaussian linear model and a quadratic loss function, one can find an estimator that dominates OLS when $k > 2$, that is, when the model contains more than two covariates.

A *James–Stein estimate* is defined as

$$\bar{\beta}_c = \left(1 - \frac{cs^2}{\hat{\beta}^\top \mathbf{X}^\top \mathbf{X}\hat{\beta}}\right)\hat{\beta},$$

for some $c \geq 0$. It is therefore a Stein estimate corresponding to $A = I_k$, $B = \mathbf{X}^\top \mathbf{X}$ and $h(T) = c/T$. As shown in Section 9.1.2, the statistic

$$\frac{T}{k} = \frac{\hat{\beta}^\top \mathbf{X}^\top \mathbf{X}\hat{\beta}}{ks^2}$$

is the classical test statistic for testing the null hypothesis H_0: $\beta = 0$. Thus, the correction operated by the James–Stein estimate on OLS is negligible when T is large and therefore H_0 is rejected. It may be appreciable, however, when T is close to zero and therefore H_0 is not rejected.

A James–Stein estimate may be interpreted as an *empirical Bayes estimate*. Assume that the conditional prior distribution of β given σ^2 is $\mathcal{N}_k(0, \sigma^2\tau^2(\mathbf{X}^\top \mathbf{X})^{-1})$, where the fact that the prior variance of β is proportional to $(\mathbf{X}^\top \mathbf{X})^{-1}$ may be justified when the design matrix is fixed in repeated samples. The mode of the posterior distribution of β is in this case

$$\left(1 + \frac{1}{\tau^2}\right)^{-1}\hat{\beta} = \left(1 - \frac{1}{\tau^2 + 1}\right)\hat{\beta}.$$

The empirical Bayesian approach assumes that τ^2 is unknown and tries to estimate it using the available data. Efron and Morris (1973) show that $cs^2/(\hat{\beta}^\top \mathbf{X}^\top \mathbf{X}\hat{\beta})$ may in fact be interpreted as an estimate of $1/(\tau^2 + 1)$.

In order to assess the sampling properties of a James–Stein estimator, consider the canonical form of the classical linear model. Because $\mathbf{X}^\top\mathbf{X}$ is a symmetric p.d. matrix, Theorem A.5 implies the existence of a nonsingular matrix S such that $S^\top S = (\mathbf{X}^\top\mathbf{X})^{-1}$. The *canonical form* of the linear model is then

$$\mathrm{E}\,\mathbf{Y} = \mathbf{W}\gamma, \tag{6.14}$$

where $\mathbf{W} = \mathbf{X}S^\top$ and $\gamma = S^{-\top}\beta$. Since $\mathbf{W}^\top\mathbf{W} = S\mathbf{X}^\top\mathbf{X}S^\top = SS^{-1}S^{-\top}S^\top = I_k$ and therefore $\mathrm{E}\,\mathbf{W}^\top\mathbf{Y} = \gamma$, the canonical form of the linear model corresponds to a location model for the k-vector $\mathbf{W}^\top\mathbf{Y}$.

The OLS and James–Stein estimators of the canonical parameter γ are respectively

$$\hat{\gamma} = \mathbf{W}^\top\mathbf{Y}, \qquad \bar{\gamma}_c = \left(1 - \frac{cs^2}{\hat{\gamma}^\top\hat{\gamma}}\right)\hat{\gamma}.$$

Given the quadratic loss function, the OLS estimator has the constant risk

$$r(\hat{\gamma},\gamma) = \operatorname{tr}\mathbf{W}^\top\mathbf{W} = k\sigma^2,$$

whereas the risk of a James–Stein estimator is given by the following theorem.

Theorem 6.9 *If the classical Gaussian linear model holds and $k > 2$, then the risk of a James–Stein estimator is*

$$r(\bar{\gamma}_c,\gamma) = r(\hat{\gamma},\gamma) + \sigma^2\left[c^2\left(\frac{2}{n-k}+1\right) - 2c(k-2)\right]\mathrm{E}\,\frac{1}{\chi^2_{k,\lambda}},$$

where $\lambda = \gamma^\top\gamma/\sigma$.

Proof. Because $\hat{\gamma}$ and s^2 are independent, the risk of a James–Stein estimator is

$$\begin{aligned} r(\bar{\gamma}_c,\gamma) &= \mathrm{E}\left(\hat{\gamma} - \gamma - \frac{cs^2}{\hat{\gamma}^\top\hat{\gamma}}\hat{\gamma}\right)^\top\left(\hat{\gamma} - \gamma - \frac{cs^2}{\hat{\gamma}^\top\hat{\gamma}}\hat{\gamma}\right) \\ &= r(\hat{\gamma},\gamma) - 2c\,\mathrm{E}(s^2)\left(1 - \mathrm{E}\,\frac{\gamma^\top\hat{\gamma}}{\hat{\gamma}^\top\hat{\gamma}}\right) + c^2\,\mathrm{E}(s^4)\left(\mathrm{E}\,\frac{1}{\hat{\gamma}^\top\hat{\gamma}}\right). \end{aligned}$$

To evaluate this expression, we use the fact that, if $Z \sim \mathcal{N}_k(\mu, I_k)$, then $Z^\top Z \sim \chi^2_{k,\lambda}$ with $\lambda = \mu^\top\mu$, and

$$\mathrm{E}\,\frac{\mu^\top Z}{Z^\top Z} = \lambda\,\mathrm{E}\,\frac{1}{\chi^2_{k+2,\lambda}}$$

(see Judge & Bock 1978, Appendix B.2, Theorem 1). Letting $Z = \hat{\gamma}/\sigma$ and $\mu = \gamma/\sigma$, it then follows that $\hat{\gamma}^\top\hat{\gamma}/\sigma^2 \sim \chi^2_{k,\lambda}$ with $\lambda = \gamma^\top\gamma/\sigma^2$, and

$$\mathrm{E}\,\frac{\gamma^\top\hat{\gamma}}{\hat{\gamma}^\top\hat{\gamma}} = \mathrm{E}\,\frac{\gamma^\top\hat{\gamma}/\sigma^2}{\hat{\gamma}^\top\hat{\gamma}/\sigma^2} = \lambda\,\mathrm{E}\,\frac{1}{\chi^2_{k+2,\lambda}}.$$

Because $(n-k)s^2/\sigma^2 \sim \chi^2_{n-k}$, we further have

$$\mathrm{E}\,s^2 = \sigma^2, \qquad \mathrm{E}\,s^4 = \operatorname{Var}s^2 + (\mathrm{E}\,s^2)^2 = \frac{2\sigma^4}{n-k} + \sigma^4.$$

Figure 47 Risk of the OLS estimator $\hat{\gamma}$ and of the best James–Stein estimator $\bar{\gamma}_*$ for $k = 4$ and $n = 10$.

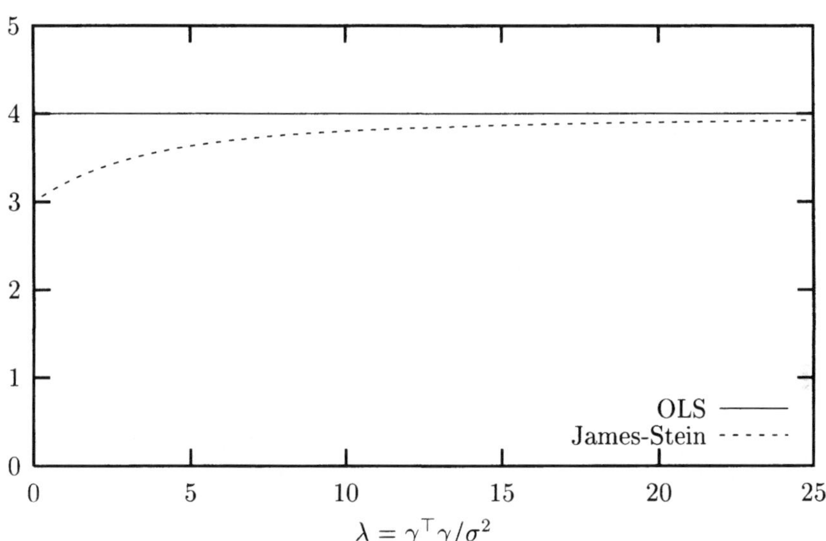

Hence, the risk of a James–Stein estimator is

$$r(\bar{\gamma}_c, \gamma) = r(\hat{\gamma}, \gamma) - 2c\sigma^2 \left(1 - \lambda \operatorname{E} \frac{1}{\chi^2_{k+2,\lambda}}\right) + c^2 \left(\frac{2\sigma^2}{n-k} + \sigma^2\right) \operatorname{E} \frac{1}{\chi^2_{k,\lambda}}.$$

If $k > 2$, the following relationship holds

$$(k-2) \operatorname{E} \frac{1}{\chi^2_{k,\lambda}} + \lambda \operatorname{E} \frac{1}{\chi^2_{k+2,\lambda}} = 1.$$

Substituting this expression in $r(\bar{\gamma}_c, \gamma)$, we obtain the conclusion of the theorem. □

Because $r(\bar{\gamma}_c, \gamma)$ is a quadratic function of c, the value of c that minimizes the risk of a James–Stein estimator is

$$c_* = \frac{(k-2)(n-k)}{n-k+2}, \qquad k > 2,$$

and the risk of the best estimator $\bar{\gamma}_* = \bar{\gamma}_{c_*}$ is

$$r(\bar{\gamma}_*, \gamma) = r(\hat{\gamma}, \gamma) - \sigma^2 c_* (k-2) \operatorname{E} \frac{1}{\chi^2_{k,\lambda}}.$$

Hence, if $k > 2$, the best James–Stein estimator uniformly dominates the OLS estimator which is therefore inadmissible.

To compute exactly the risk of $\bar{\gamma}_*$ one needs to evaluate the mean of the reciprocal of a random variable with a $\chi^2_{k,\lambda}$-distribution. Since $\operatorname{E}(1/\chi^2_k) = 1/(k-2)$ for $k > 2$, it then follows that $r(\bar{\gamma}_*, \gamma) = \sigma^2(k - c_*)$ when $\gamma = 0$. The general formula for the case when $\lambda > 0$ is rather messy (see for example Judge & Bock 1978). If k is even, this formula reduces to

$$\mathrm{E}\,\frac{1}{\chi^2_{k,\lambda}} = \frac{1}{2}\left(\frac{k}{2} - 1\right)!\left(-\frac{2}{\lambda}\right)^{(k/2)-1}\left[e^{-\lambda/2} - \sum_{j=0}^{(k/2)-2} \frac{(-\lambda/2)^j}{j!}\right].$$

Because $\mathrm{E}(1/\chi_{k,\lambda}) \to 0$ as $\lambda \to \infty$, we have that $r(\bar{\gamma}_*, \gamma) \to r(\hat{\gamma}, \gamma)$ as $\gamma^\top \gamma / \sigma^2 \to \infty$. The risk of two estimators is shown in Figure 47 for $k = 4$ and $n = 10$.

A James–Stein estimate has the property that its elements may change sign with respect to the OLS estimate. This occurs when $c/T > 1$, that is, when $T < c$. If this is regarded as inconvenient, then an alternative is the *positive-rule James–Stein estimate*

$$\bar{\beta}_c^+ = \begin{cases} \bar{\beta}_c, & \text{if } T > c, \\ 0, & \text{otherwise.} \end{cases}$$

This estimator is equal to $\bar{\beta}_c$ if the F-test statistic T/k exceeds the critical value c/k, otherwise it is equal to the value of β under the null hypothesis, H_0: $\beta = 0$.

BIBLIOGRAPHIC NOTES

For an introduction to the modern symbolic expressions for the formulation of a model see McCullagh and Nelder (1989) and Chambers and Hastie (1992).

Algorithms for the solution of quadratic linear programs with inequality constraints are discussed in Judge and Takayama (1966), Liew (1976) and Gill, Murray and Wright (1981).

Standard references for Section 6.6 are Zellner (1971) and Box and Tiao (1973).

The book by Judge and Bock (1978) contains a thorough discussion of the class of Stein estimators. For an interpretation of the best James–Stein estimator as an empirical Bayes estimator see Efron and Morris (1973). Zaman (1996) presents several examples of applications of empirical Bayes methods.

PROBLEMS

6.1 Show that, if the only parameter in a regression model is an intercept, then the OLS estimate is unique and coincides with the sample mean of Y_i.

6.2 Determine the form of the level curves of the OLS criterion function when the matrix $\mathbf{X}^\top \mathbf{X}$ is singular.

6.3 Show that if the number of covariates is equal to the number of observations and $\mathbf{X}^\top \mathbf{X}$ is nonsingular, then $\hat{\beta} = \mathbf{X}^{-1}\mathbf{Y}$, $\hat{\mathbf{Y}} = \mathbf{Y}$ and $\hat{\mathbf{U}} = 0$, that is, OLS reproduces the observations exactly.

6.4 Show that

$$\widehat{\mathrm{Var}}\, Y_i = \frac{1}{n}\mathbf{Y}^\top L \mathbf{Y}, \qquad \widehat{\mathrm{Var}}\, \hat{Y}_i = \frac{1}{n}\mathbf{Y}^\top H L H \mathbf{Y}, \qquad \widehat{\mathrm{Cov}}(Y_i, \hat{Y}_i) = \frac{1}{n}\mathbf{Y}^\top L H \mathbf{Y},$$

where $L = I_n - n^{-1}\iota_n \iota_n^\top$ is a matrix symmetric idempotent matrix.

6.5 Show that the coefficient of determination and the uncentered R^2 coincide when the regression model includes an intercept and $\bar{Y} = 0$.

6.6 Let $[\mathbf{X}_1, \mathbf{Y}_1]$ and $[\mathbf{X}_2, \mathbf{Y}_2]$ be two separate sets of observations on X and Y, where $\mathbf{X}_1$ and $\mathbf{X}_2$ both have rank k. Show that the OLS estimate for the pooled data is of the form

$$\hat{\beta} = D\hat{\beta}_1 + (I_k - D)\hat{\beta}_2,$$

where D is a nonsingular matrix and $\hat{\beta}_j$ is the OLS estimate in the regression of $\mathbf{Y}_j$ on $\mathbf{X}_j$, $j = 1, 2$. Interpret this result.

6.7 Let $[\mathbf{X}_s, \mathbf{Y}_s]$ be any of the $S = \binom{n}{k}$ subsets of k observations that can be obtained from a data matrix $[\mathbf{X}, \mathbf{Y}]$, where $\mathbf{Y}$ is an n-vector and $\mathbf{X}$ is an $n \times k$ matrix of rank k. Show that the OLS estimate in the regression of $\mathbf{Y}$ on $\mathbf{X}$ is equal to the weighted average

$$\hat{\beta} = \sum_{s=1}^{S} \frac{\det \mathbf{X}_s^\top \mathbf{X}_s}{\det \mathbf{X}^\top \mathbf{X}} \hat{\beta}_s,$$

where $\hat{\beta}_s = \mathbf{X}_s^{-1}\mathbf{Y}_s$.

6.8 Show that the matrix $H = \mathbf{X}(\mathbf{X}^\top\mathbf{X})^{-1}\mathbf{X}^\top$ is symmetric, idempotent and such that $H\mathbf{X} = \mathbf{X}$. Denoting by h_{ij} the ijth element of H, conclude that

$$0 \le h_{ii} \le 1, \qquad \sum_i h_{ii} = k, \qquad h_{ii} = \sum_j h_{ij}^2.$$

6.9 Show that the generic element h_{ij} of the projection matrix $H = \mathbf{X}(\mathbf{X}^\top\mathbf{X})^{-1}\mathbf{X}^\top$ is equal to the partial derivative of the ith OLS fitted value $\hat{Y}_i$ with respect to Y_j. Comment on this result.

6.10 Show that, if a linear regression model includes an intercept, then $\hat{R}^2 = S_{\hat{Y}}/S_Y$, where $S_{\hat{Y}} = \sum_i (\hat{Y}_i - \bar{Y})^2$, $S_Y = \sum_i (Y_i - \bar{Y})^2$, and $\bar{Y} = n^{-1}\sum_i Y_i$.

6.11 Consider the multivariate linear model $\mathrm{E}\,\mathbf{Y}_i = \mathbf{X}\beta_i$, $i = 1, \ldots, n$, where $\mathbf{Y}_i$ is a vector of dimension $m \ge k$ and $\mathbf{X}$ is a constant $m \times k$ matrix. Assume that $\sum_{i=1}^n \alpha_i \mathbf{Y}_i = \gamma$, where γ is an m-vector, and show that:

(i) the OLS predictor $\hat{\mathbf{Y}}_i = \mathbf{X}\hat{\beta}_i$ satisfies the constraints if $\gamma = 0$;
(ii) if $\gamma \ne 0$, then $\hat{\mathbf{Y}}_i$ satisfies the constraints if and only if γ is a linear combination of the columns of $\mathbf{X}$.

6.12 Prove the conclusions (i)–(iii) of Theorem 6.1.

6.13 This problem represents an alternative proof of the Gauss–Markov theorem. The class of estimators of β of the form

$$\tilde{\beta} = (\mathbf{W}^\top\mathbf{X})^{-1}\mathbf{W}^\top\mathbf{Y},$$

where $\mathbf{W}$ is a nonstochastic matrix such that $\mathbf{W}^\top\mathbf{X}$ is nonsingular, is called the class of *instrumental variables (IV) estimators.* Assume that the classical linear model holds and show that:

(i) the difference between the sampling variance of an IV estimator and that of the OLS estimator is a n.n.d. matrix;

(ii) the class of IV estimators coincides with the class of linear unbiased estimators of β.

6.14 Prove the following generalization of the Gauss–Markov theorem. Under Assumptions 6.1–6.3, $\operatorname{Var} A\tilde{\beta} - \operatorname{Var} A\hat{\beta} \geq 0$ for every $r \times k$ matrix A and any other estimator $\tilde{\beta}$ that is linear in $\mathbf{Y}$ and unbiased for β.

6.15 You want to draw a sample of 10 observations from the conditional distribution of Y given X, which is known to have mean $\alpha + \beta X$ and variance σ^2. The problem is to choose the design matrix optimally.

(i) Which values of X between zero and one should be selected in order to estimate β with the highest precision?
(ii) Which should be selected in order to estimate α with the highest precision?
(iii) Which should be selected if you want to predict Y conditionally on $X = x$?

6.16 Assume that the classical linear model holds and evaluate the effect of adding or excluding a single data point on (i) the sampling variance of the OLS estimator, and (ii) its unbiased estimator.

6.17 Assume that the classical Gaussian linear model holds and consider the class of estimators of σ^2 of the form $\tilde{\sigma}_a^2 = \hat{\mathbf{U}}^\top \hat{\mathbf{U}}/a$, where $\hat{\mathbf{U}}$ is the OLS residual vector and $a > 0$. Show that the estimator with minimum MSE in this class is the one for which $a = n - k + 2$.

6.18 Let Y_1 and Y_2 be i.i.d. random variables with density f. Compute the density of $X = c_1 Y_1 + c_2 Y_2$. Use this result to derive the sampling density of the OLS estimator of the classical linear model when $Y_1, \ldots, Y_n$ are independent with mean $\mu_i = X_i^\top \beta$, variance σ_i^2 and density $f_i(y) = f((y - \mu_i)/\sigma_i)/\sigma_i$.

6.19 Derive formula (6.7).

6.20 Assume that the data satisfy the Gaussian linear model $\mathbf{Y} \sim \mathcal{N}_n(\beta \mathbf{X}, \beta^2 I_n)$, where β is a scalar parameter. Obtain the ML estimator of β and compare its sampling variance with the Cramér–Rao lower bound for an unbiased estimator of β.

6.21 Let $Z_1, \ldots, Z_T$ be a finite segment of the stable AR(k) process

$$Z_t = \rho_1 Z_{t-1} + \cdots + \rho_k Z_{t-k} + U_t,$$

where $\{U_t\}$ is a Gaussian WN$(0, \sigma^2)$ process.

(i) Show that the sample log-likelihood is exactly of the form (4.10), with $\rho = (\rho_1, \ldots, \rho_k)$.
(ii) Show that the estimate obtained by solving the OLS problem in Example 6.3 coincides with the conditional LS estimate obtained by ignoring the term $g(\rho)$ and by appropriately simplifying the term $G(\rho)$ in the log-likelihood.

6.22 A researcher carries out an OLS regression and obtains

$$\hat{\beta} = \begin{pmatrix} \hat{\beta}_1 \\ \hat{\beta}_2 \\ \hat{\beta}_3 \end{pmatrix} = \begin{pmatrix} 5 \\ -4 \\ 2 \end{pmatrix}, \qquad s^2(\mathbf{X}^\top \mathbf{X})^{-1} = \begin{bmatrix} 3 & 1 & 1 \\ 1 & 2 & 1 \\ 1 & 1 & 2 \end{bmatrix},$$

where s^2 is the usual unbiased estimator of σ^2. On the basis of this information, how would you estimate β if it were known that $\beta_1 + \beta_2 = \beta_3$?

6.23 Prove formula (6.10).

6.24 This problem illustrates an equivalent way of estimating a classical linear model under a set of q linear equality constraints of the form $R\beta = r$, where R is a $q \times k$ matrix of rank q.

(i) Consider the representation $\beta = G\alpha + g$, where G is a $k \times (k-q)$ matrix and α is a vector of dimension $k-q$. Show that this representation satisfies the constraints if $RG = 0$ and $Rg = r$.

(ii) Consider the transformed model $\tilde{\mathbf{Y}} = \tilde{\mathbf{X}}\alpha + \mathbf{U}$, where $\tilde{\mathbf{Y}} = \mathbf{Y} - \mathbf{X}g$ and $\tilde{\mathbf{X}} = \mathbf{X}G$. Derive the BLU estimator of α.

(iii) Denoting by $\hat{\alpha}$ the estimator obtained in (ii), show that $\tilde{\beta} = G\hat{\alpha} + g$ is the constrained OLS estimator of β.

6.25 Given a classical linear model, show that imposing the set of linear constraints $R\beta = r$, where R is a $q \times k$ matrix of rank q, is equivalent to excluding q variables from a suitably redefined linear model.

6.26 Given a set of linear constraints $R\beta = r$, derive the sampling properties of the constrained OLS estimator when R is a nonsingular $k \times k$ matrix.

6.27 Let $\mathbf{Y}$ have an m-variate t-distribution with parameter (μ, Σ^{-1}, n). Show that

$$\frac{(\mathbf{Y} - \mu)^\top \Sigma (\mathbf{Y} - \mu)}{m} \sim F_{m,n}.$$

6.28 Consider the classical Gaussian linear model $\mathbf{Y} \sim \mathcal{N}_n(\mathbf{X}\beta, \sigma^2 I_n)$. Show that, if the prior distribution of β is $\mathcal{N}_k(\bar{\beta}, \omega^2\Sigma^{-1})$, then the conditional posterior distribution of β given σ is $\mathcal{N}_k(\bar{\beta}_*, \sigma^2(\mathbf{X}^\top\mathbf{X} + \gamma\Sigma)^{-1})$, where $\gamma = \sigma^2/\omega^2$ and

$$\bar{\beta}_* = (\mathbf{X}^\top\mathbf{X} + \gamma\Sigma)^{-1}(\mathbf{X}^\top\mathbf{Y} + \gamma\Sigma\bar{\beta}).$$

Show that the posterior mean $\bar{\beta}_*$ is also the solution to the penalized OLS problem

$$\min_{\beta \in \Re^k} \; (\mathbf{Y} - \mathbf{X}\beta)^\top(\mathbf{Y} - \mathbf{X}\beta) + \gamma\,(\beta - \bar{\beta})^\top\Sigma(\beta - \bar{\beta}).$$

6.29 Assume that the distribution of $\mathbf{Y}$ and the prior distribution of β are symmetric, with densities of the form

$$f(\mathbf{Y} \mid \beta) \propto g((\mathbf{Y} - \mathbf{X}\beta)^\top(\mathbf{Y} - \mathbf{X}\beta)), \qquad p(\beta) \propto h((\beta - \bar{\beta})^\top\Sigma(\beta - \bar{\beta})).$$

Compute the posterior distribution of β and find the expression for its mode. Show that the set of possible posterior modes is equal to the set of tangency points, in the parameter space, between the level curves of $f(\mathbf{Y} \mid \beta)$ and of $p(\beta)$.

6.30 Suppose that $\mathbf{Y} \sim \mathcal{N}_n(\mathbf{X}\beta, \sigma^2 I_n)$, $\beta = (\beta_1, \beta_2)$, $n = 12$, and

$$\mathbf{X}^\top\mathbf{X} = \frac{1}{3}\begin{bmatrix} 1 & -1 \\ -1 & 4 \end{bmatrix}, \qquad \mathbf{X}^\top\mathbf{Y} = \begin{pmatrix} 1 \\ 1 \end{pmatrix}, \qquad \mathbf{Y}^\top\mathbf{Y} = 8.$$

Suppose that the prior distribution of β is gamma-Gaussian with parameter $(\bar{\beta}, \Sigma, m, \lambda)$, where $\bar{\beta} = (0, 0)$, $\Sigma = I_2$, $m = 10$ and $\lambda = 1$. Compute the OLS estimate of β. Draw a 95%-level confidence set for β and trace out the set of points in the parameter space such that $\beta_1 + \beta_2 = 0$. Compute the constrained OLS estimate of β under the constraint that $\beta_1 + \beta_2 = 0$. Draw the Bayesian 95%-level confidence sets for β based, respectively, on the prior and the posterior distribution. Draw the prior and the posterior distributions of β_1, β_2, and $\beta_1 + \beta_2$, and the associated 95%-level confidence intervals.

7

Violations of the Ideal Conditions for OLS

This chapter studies the properties of the OLS estimator, in particular its bias and precision, when the assumptions of the classical linear model do not hold. It also shows that, in some cases, simple transformations of the data are enough to restore the ideal conditions for OLS. This makes it possible to widen considerably the applicability of the method.

7.1 COLLINEARITY

We say that there is *collinearity* when the k columns of the design matrix $\mathbf{X}$ are linearly dependent, that is, the (column) rank of $\mathbf{X}$ is less than k or, equivalently, $\mathbf{X}^\top\mathbf{X}$ is a singular matrix.

In this case, an OLS estimate of β exists but is not unique as the normal equations $\mathbf{X}^\top(\mathbf{Y} - \mathbf{X}\beta) = 0$ admit an infinite number of solutions. More precisely, suppose that the normal equations have a solution $\hat{\beta}$ (methods for finding one such solution are discussed in Appendix A.10) and let $c \neq 0$ be any vector in the null space of $\mathbf{X}$, that is, c is such that $\mathbf{X}c = 0$. Then the vector $\tilde{\beta} = \hat{\beta} + c$ is also a root of the normal equations since

$$\mathbf{X}^\top(\mathbf{Y} - \mathbf{X}\tilde{\beta}) = \mathbf{X}^\top(\mathbf{Y} - \mathbf{X}\hat{\beta}) - \mathbf{X}^\top\mathbf{X}c = 0.$$

Although the normal equations do not have a unique solution, the vector of fitted values is unique because $\mathbf{X}\tilde{\beta} = \mathbf{X}(\hat{\beta} + c) = \mathbf{X}\hat{\beta}$. Hence, the OLS residual vector and the classical estimate of scale are also unique.

Far from being a mere algebraic problem with OLS, collinearity reflects the basic lack of identifiability of the regression parameter β. To see this, notice that the BLP of the random vector $\mathbf{Y}$ given the fixed matrix $\mathbf{X}$ is a linear combination $\mathbf{X}\beta$ of the columns of $\mathbf{X}$ such that $\mathrm{E}(\mathbf{Y} - \mathbf{X}\beta)^\top(\mathbf{Y} - \mathbf{X}\beta)$ attains a minimum. The normal equations for this problem are $0 = \mathbf{X}^\top(\mathrm{E}\,\mathbf{Y} - \mathbf{X}\beta)$ and have a unique solution, equal to $\beta_* = (\mathbf{X}^\top\mathbf{X})^{-1}\mathbf{X}^\top(\mathrm{E}\,\mathbf{Y})$, only when $\mathbf{X}^\top\mathbf{X}$ is nonsingular. Thus, the BLP of $\mathbf{Y}$ given $\mathbf{X}$ has a unique representation as a linear combination of the columns of $\mathbf{X}$ only when $\mathbf{X}^\top\mathbf{X}$ is nonsingular.

Because collinearity reflects the fact that the regression coefficients are not all identifiable, the natural approach is to respecify the model reducing the dimensionality of the parameter space.

Example 7.1 Consider the model

$$\mathrm{E}\, Y_i = \beta_0 + \beta_1 X_{i1} + \beta_2 X_{i2}, \qquad i = 1, \ldots, n.$$

There is collinearity when $X_{i2} = \gamma + \delta X_{i1}$ for every i. In this case, the model may be respecified as

$$\mathrm{E}\, Y_i = \alpha_0 + \alpha_1 X_{i1}, \qquad i = 1, \ldots, n,$$

where $\alpha_0 = \beta_0 + \beta_2\gamma$ and $\alpha_1 = \beta_1 + \beta_2\delta$. This new model is not equivalent to the original one, for the transformation from $(\beta_0, \beta_1, \beta_2)$ to (α_0, α_1) is noninvertible. □

7.1.1 QUASI-COLLINEARITY

The matrix $\mathbf{X}^\top\mathbf{X}$ can always be represented as $\mathbf{X}^\top\mathbf{X} = \sum_{s=1}^k \lambda_s p_s p_s^\top$, where λ_s is the sth eigenvalue of $\mathbf{X}^\top\mathbf{X}$ and p_s is the associated eigenvector. We say that there is *quasi-collinearity* when the matrix $\mathbf{X}^\top\mathbf{X}$ is quasi singular, that is, its eigenvalues are all positive but some of them are close to zero.

Although the OLS estimator is unique in this case, the presence of eigenvalues near zero tends to inflate its sampling variance. To see this, notice that

$$(\mathbf{X}^\top\mathbf{X})^{-1} = \sum_{s=1}^k \frac{1}{\lambda_s} p_s p_s^\top,$$

and therefore the sampling variance of the jth element of $\hat\beta$ is

$$\operatorname{Var}\hat\beta_j = \sigma^2 \sum_{s=1}^k \frac{p_{sj}^2}{\lambda_s},$$

where p_{sj} denotes the jth element of the eigenvector p_s. The presence of eigenvalues near zero may affect the elements of $\hat\beta$ in different ways. For example, the fact that λ_s is near zero may have no effect on $\operatorname{Var}\hat\beta_j$ if p_{sj} is also very small.

Another useful way of looking at quasi-collinearity is the following. By the partitioned inverse formulae, the jth diagonal element c_{jj} of the matrix $(\mathbf{X}^\top\mathbf{X})^{-1}$ may be represented as

$$c_{jj} = \frac{1}{\mathbf{X}_j^\top[I_n - \mathbf{X}_{(j)}(\mathbf{X}_{(j)}^\top\mathbf{X}_{(j)})^{-1}\mathbf{X}_{(j)}^\top]\mathbf{X}_j},$$

where $\mathbf{X}_j$ and $\mathbf{X}_{(j)}$ denote respectively the jth column of $\mathbf{X}$ and the $n \times (k-1)$ matrix obtained by excluding from $\mathbf{X}$ its jth column. The element c_{jj} is therefore equal to the inverse of the residual sum of squares in the OLS regression of the jth column on all the other columns. If the jth column is nearly a linear combination of the other columns, then the residual sum of squares of this regression is very small and the sampling variance of $\hat\beta_j$ is very high.

As in the perfect collinearity case, one approach to the problem consists of reducing the dimensionality of the parameter space by exploiting prior information in the form of constraints on the regression coefficients.

Example 7.2 In time series analysis it is often necessary to represent situations where variations in the covariates take time to produce their full effect on the response variable. A model with this feature is

$$Y_t = \beta(L)\, X_t + U_t, \qquad \{U_t\} \sim \mathrm{WN}(0, \sigma^2), \qquad t = 1, \ldots, n, \tag{7.1}$$

where $\beta(L) = \sum_{j=0}^{\infty} \beta_j L^j$ is a polynomial in the lag operator and $\{X_t\}$ is a stationary process uncorrelated with $\{U_t\}$. This is called a *linear model with distributed lags*. The coefficients in $\beta(L)$ may be interpreted as dynamic multipliers that describe the effect on $Y_t, Y_{t+1}, Y_{t+2}, \ldots$ of a unit change in X_t.

In the absence of prior information, it is clearly impossible to estimate the distributed lag coefficients if there is an infinite number of them. When their number is finite and equal to k, one needs k not to exceed the effective sample size $n-k+1$. Even when $\beta(L)$ contains only $k < n-k+1$ coefficients, that is $k < (n+1)/2$, accurate estimation may be difficult if $\{X_t\}$ is characterized by a high degree of persistence, that is, its elements tend to be highly correlated with each other.

The problem of quasi-collinearity may be dealt with if there exists prior information on $\beta(L)$. In this example, we consider the case when it is known that $\beta(L) = \sum_{j=0}^{k-1} \beta_j L^j$ and the coefficients in $\beta(L)$ satisfy a polynomial of lower degree, that is, there exists a polynomial $\alpha(z) = \sum_{j=0}^{m-1} \alpha_j z^j$ of degree $m-1 < k-1$ such that

$$\beta_h = \alpha(h) = \sum_{j=0}^{m-1} \alpha_j h^j, \qquad h = 0, \ldots, k-1. \tag{7.2}$$

This model is called a *linear model with polynomial distributed lags*. Imposing the constraint (7.2) on model (7.1) gives

$$Y_t = \sum_{h=0}^{k-1} \beta_h X_{t-h} + U_t = \sum_{h=0}^{k-1} \sum_{j=0}^{m-1} \alpha_j h^j X_{t-h} + U_t = \sum_{j=0}^{m-1} \alpha_j W_{jt} + U_t, \tag{7.3}$$

where $W_{jt} = \sum_{h=0}^{k-1} h^j X_{t-h}$. When $m-1$ is sufficiently small, the resulting model is easily estimated by OLS.

The assumption of polynomial distributed lags is equivalent to imposing a set of $q = k - m \geq 1$ linear constraints on the vector $\beta = (\beta_0, \ldots, \beta_{k-1})$. To see this, recall that a polynomial of degree $m-1$ vanishes after applying the first difference operator m times, that is, $\Delta^m \alpha(z) = 0$. In particular, since $\beta_h = \alpha(h)$, we get

$$0 = \Delta^m \beta_h = (1-L)^m \beta_h, \qquad h = m, \ldots, k-1.$$

The vector β must therefore satisfy a set of $q = k - m$ linear constraints of the form $R\beta = 0$, where R is a $q \times k$ matrix whose rows contain the coefficients of the powers of L in the polynomial $\Delta^m = (1-L)^m$. Thus, a procedure which is equivalent to directly estimating model (7.3) is to estimate model (7.1) by constrained OLS, where the constraints correspond to the assumption of polynomial distributed lags.

As an illustration, if $k = 5$ and the coefficients of $\beta(L)$ lie on the quadratic polynomial $\alpha(h) = 2 + 4h - h^2$, then $\beta_0 = \alpha(0) = 2$, $\beta_1 = \alpha(1) = 5$, $\beta_2 = \alpha(2) = 6$, $\beta_3 = \alpha(3) = 5$, and $\beta_4 = \alpha(4) = 2$. Because $m = 3$ and $\Delta^3 = 1 - 3L + 3L^2 - L^3$, the vector of coefficients β must satisfy a set of linear constraints of the form $R\beta = 0$, where

$$R = \begin{bmatrix} -1 & 3 & -3 & 1 & 0 \\ 0 & -1 & 3 & -3 & 1 \end{bmatrix}.$$

□

Example 7.3 Shiller (1973) proposed a Bayesian approach to the problem in the previous example. This approach is motivated by the fact that the polynomial specification is, in most cases, only a convenient way of representing the prior belief that the sequence of distributed lag coefficients does not vary too wildly.

Uncertainty about the validity of the polynomial specification may be represented by a prior distribution for $R\beta$, where R is the $q \times k$ matrix introduced in the previous example. Under the assumption of a classical Gaussian linear model, a convenient choice of priors is the family of $\mathcal{N}_k(0,\, \omega^2 I_k)$ distributions, where the variance ω^2 may be interpreted as a measure of the strength of the prior information on the sequence of coefficients in $\beta(L)$. If ω is small, the prior information assigns high probability to distributed lag shapes that satisfy a polynomial of degree $m-1$ (the case when $R\beta = 0$) and low probability to more irregular shapes. The specification in Example 7.2 may be viewed as the limiting case corresponding to $\omega^2 \to 0$.

It is easy to see that the conditional posterior distribution of β given σ is

$$\begin{aligned} f(\beta \,|\, \sigma; \mathbf{Z}) &\propto \exp\left[-\frac{1}{2\omega^2}\beta^\top R^\top R\beta\right] \exp\left[-\frac{1}{2\sigma^2}(\mathbf{Y} - \mathbf{X}\beta)^\top(\mathbf{Y} - \mathbf{X}\beta)\right] \\ &= \exp\left[-\frac{1}{2\sigma^2}(\beta - \tilde{\beta})^\top \tilde{\mathbf{X}}^\top \tilde{\mathbf{X}}(\beta - \tilde{\beta})\right], \end{aligned}$$

where

$$\tilde{\mathbf{X}} = \begin{bmatrix} \mathbf{X} \\ \sqrt{\gamma} R \end{bmatrix}, \qquad \gamma = \frac{\sigma^2}{\omega^2},$$
$$\tilde{\mathbf{Y}} = \begin{pmatrix} \mathbf{Y} \\ 0 \end{pmatrix}, \qquad \tilde{\beta} = (\tilde{\mathbf{X}}^\top \tilde{\mathbf{X}})^{-1} \tilde{\mathbf{X}}^\top \tilde{\mathbf{Y}}.$$

The posterior distribution of β is therefore k-variate Gaussian with mean

$$\tilde{\beta} = (\mathbf{X}^\top \mathbf{X} + \gamma R^\top R)^{-1} \mathbf{X}^\top \mathbf{Y} = (\mathbf{X}^\top \mathbf{X} + \gamma R^\top R)^{-1} \mathbf{X}^\top \mathbf{X} \hat{\beta},$$

where $\hat{\beta}$ is the OLS estimate, and variance matrix

$$\sigma^2\, (\tilde{\mathbf{X}}^\top \tilde{\mathbf{X}})^{-1} = \sigma^2\, (\mathbf{X}^\top \mathbf{X} + \gamma R^\top R)^{-1}.$$

The posterior mean $\tilde{\beta}$ is therefore the Bayes estimate for every convex and symmetric loss function.

□

7.1.2 RIDGE-REGRESSION ESTIMATORS

The case of quasi-collinearity is often taken as an example of the advantage of employing a biased estimator of β when its bias is more than compensated by a smaller sampling variance relative to OLS.

Estimators of β of the form

$$\tilde{\beta}_\gamma = (\mathbf{X}^\top \mathbf{X} + \gamma I_k)^{-1} \mathbf{X}^\top \mathbf{Y} = (\mathbf{X}^\top \mathbf{X} + \gamma I_k)^{-1} \mathbf{X}^\top \mathbf{X} \hat{\beta},$$

for $\gamma \geq 0$, are called *ridge-regression estimators.* This class of estimators is yet another example of the kind of shrinkage estimators introduced in Section 6.7. A ridge-regression estimator is linear in $\mathbf{Y}$ and corresponds to a linear transformation of the OLS estimator, which is the ridge estimator corresponding to $\gamma = 0$. The reason for adding the matrix γI_k to $\mathbf{X}^\top \mathbf{X}$ is to make $\mathbf{X}^\top \mathbf{X} + \gamma I_k$ "more p.d." than $\mathbf{X}^\top \mathbf{X}$. For this reason, using a ridge estimator is sometimes recommended when $\mathbf{X}^\top \mathbf{X}$ is nearly singular.

A ridge estimator has a simple Bayesian interpretation. It is easy to verify that, if the prior distribution of β is $\mathcal{N}_k(0, \gamma^{-1} I_k)$, with $\gamma > 0$, then the mode of the posterior distribution of β coincides with the ridge estimator. The scalar γ may therefore be interpreted as a measure of the degree of concentration about zero of the prior distribution of β. If $\gamma \to 0$, then the prior information on β becomes more and more vague and the Bayes estimate converges to the OLS estimate.

Under the classical linear model, the first two moments of the sampling distribution of $\tilde{\beta}_\gamma$ are

$$\begin{aligned} \mathrm{E}\, \tilde{\beta}_\gamma &= (\mathbf{X}^\top \mathbf{X} + \gamma I_k)^{-1} \mathbf{X}^\top \mathbf{X} \beta, \\ \mathrm{Var}\, \tilde{\beta}_\gamma &= \sigma^2 \, (\mathbf{X}^\top \mathbf{X} + \gamma I_k)^{-1} \mathbf{X}^\top \mathbf{X} (\mathbf{X}^\top \mathbf{X} + \gamma I_k)^{-1}. \end{aligned}$$

The ridge estimator is therefore biased for all $\gamma > 0$. However, we also have the following result.

Theorem 7.1 *Under the classical linear model,* $\mathrm{Var}\, \hat{\beta} - \mathrm{Var}\, \tilde{\beta}_\gamma \geq 0$ *for all* $\gamma > 0$.

Proof. The proof is based on the fact that if A and B are nonsingular matrices, then $A - B \geq 0$ if and only if $B^{-1} - A^{-1} \geq 0$. Letting $A = (\mathbf{X}^\top \mathbf{X})^{-1}$ and $B = (\mathbf{X}^\top \mathbf{X} + \gamma I_k)^{-1} \mathbf{X}^\top \mathbf{X} (\mathbf{X}^\top \mathbf{X} + \gamma I_k)^{-1}$ then gives

$$\begin{aligned} B^{-1} - A^{-1} &= (\mathbf{X}^\top \mathbf{X} + \gamma I_k)(\mathbf{X}^\top \mathbf{X})^{-1} (\mathbf{X}^\top \mathbf{X} + \gamma I_k) - \mathbf{X}^\top \mathbf{X} \\ &= \gamma \, [2 I_k + \gamma (\mathbf{X}^\top \mathbf{X})^{-1}], \end{aligned}$$

which is a n.n.d. matrix. □

One may also show that the bias of $\tilde{\beta}_\gamma$ is an increasing function of γ, while its sampling variance is decreasing. Further, given β, there always exists a $\gamma > 0$ such that $\tilde{\beta}_\gamma$ has a lower MSE than the OLS estimator. Unfortunately, the value of γ depends on the unknown parameter β and so this result is of limited practical usefulness. When the parameter γ is chosen on the basis of the data, the resulting ridge estimator is called *adaptive.* The sampling properties of an adaptive ridge estimator are more complicated to analyze than those of a ridge estimator based on a value of γ which has been selected a priori.

7.2 MISSPECIFICATION OF THE REGRESSION FUNCTION

The crucial assumption of the classical linear model is that concerning the form of the regression function of $\mathbf{Y}$, that is, the form of $\mathrm{E}\, \mathbf{Y}$ when $\mathbf{X}$ is a nonstochastic matrix or of $\mathrm{E}(\mathbf{Y} \mid \mathbf{X})$ when $\mathbf{X}$ is stochastic. If the regression function may be represented as a linear combination $\mathbf{X}\beta$ of the columns of $\mathbf{X}$, then the OLS estimator is unbiased for β. What happens if this assumption is violated?

Theorem 7.2 *If* $\mathrm{E}\,\mathbf{Y} = \mathbf{X}\beta + \zeta$ *and* $\mathrm{Var}\,\mathbf{Y} = \sigma^2 I_n$, *where* $\mathbf{X}$ *is an* $n \times k$ *matrix of rank* k *and* ζ *is an* n*-vector, then:*

(i) $\mathrm{E}\,\hat{\beta} = \beta + (\mathbf{X}^\top\mathbf{X})^{-1}\mathbf{X}^\top\zeta$;
(ii) $\mathrm{Var}\,\hat{\beta} = \sigma^2\,(\mathbf{X}^\top\mathbf{X})^{-1}$;
(iii) $\mathrm{E}\,s^2 = \sigma^2 + (n-k)^{-1}\zeta^\top M\zeta$, *where* $M = I_n - \mathbf{X}(\mathbf{X}^\top\mathbf{X})^{-1}\mathbf{X}^\top$.

The vector ζ represents the specification error. Part (i) of the above theorem implies that the OLS estimator $\hat{\beta}$ is generally biased for β and its bias is equal to the OLS estimate in the regression of ζ on $\mathbf{X}$. There is no bias only when $\mathbf{X}^\top\zeta = 0$. This may occur in two cases. The first is when $\zeta = 0$, that is, the regression model is correctly specified. The second is when $\zeta \neq 0$ but $\mathbf{X}^\top\zeta = 0$, that is, the regression model is misspecified but $\mathbf{X}$ and ζ are orthogonal.

Unless $\zeta = 0$ or $n \to \infty$, the scale estimator s^2 is also biased. Since M is idempotent, $\zeta^\top M\zeta \geq 0$ and so s^2 is upward biased for σ^2. Hence, the classical estimator $s^2\lambda^\top(\mathbf{X}^\top\mathbf{X})^{-1}\lambda$ of the sampling variance of a linear combination $\lambda^\top\hat{\beta}$ of the OLS coefficients is also upward biased. Notice that, unless $n \to \infty$, s^2 remains biased even when $\mathbf{X}$ and ζ are orthogonal. Although $\hat{\beta}$ is unbiased in this case, inference about β based on the classical formula is incorrect unless the sample size is very large. It is worth noticing that confidence sets based on the classical formula are conservative, that is, their actual coverage level is higher than the nominal one.

Example 7.4 If the assumed model does not include an intercept, then $\zeta = \alpha\iota_n$. In this case, the bias of $\hat{\beta} = (\mathbf{X}^\top\mathbf{X})^{-1}\mathbf{X}^\top\mathbf{Y}$ is

$$\mathrm{Bias}\,\hat{\beta} = \alpha(\mathbf{X}^\top\mathbf{X})^{-1}\mathbf{X}^\top\iota_n,$$

which is equal to zero if $\alpha = 0$ or $\mathbf{X}^\top\iota_n = \sum_i X_i = 0$, that is, if the regression does not include an intercept or else all covariates have mean zero.

More generally, if $\zeta = \mathbf{W}\gamma$, where $\mathbf{W}$ is a nonstochastic $n \times q$ matrix of full (column) rank q, then the bias of $\hat{\beta}$ is

$$\mathrm{Bias}\,\hat{\beta} = (\mathbf{X}^\top\mathbf{X})^{-1}\mathbf{X}^\top\mathbf{W}\gamma,$$

where $(\mathbf{X}^\top\mathbf{X})^{-1}\mathbf{X}^\top\mathbf{W}$ is the matrix of OLS coefficients in the multivariate regression of $\mathbf{W}$ on $\mathbf{X}$. There is no bias only when $\mathbf{X}^\top\mathbf{W}\gamma = 0$. This may occur in three cases. The first is when $\gamma = 0$, that is, the assumed regression model is correctly specified. The second is when $\gamma \neq 0$ but $\mathbf{X}^\top\mathbf{W} = 0$, that is, the assumed model is misspecified but $\mathbf{X}$ and $\mathbf{W}$ are orthogonal. The third is when the columns of $\mathbf{X}^\top\mathbf{W}$ are linearly dependent and $\gamma \neq 0$ is a vector belonging to the null space of the matrix $\mathbf{X}^\top\mathbf{W}$. Since $\mathbf{X}^\top\mathbf{W}$ is of order $k \times q$, this can only occur when $q > k$, that is, the number of excluded variables is greater than the number of variables included in the model.

The bias of the scale estimator s^2 is

$$\mathrm{Bias}\,s^2 = \frac{\gamma^\top\mathbf{W}^\top M\mathbf{W}\gamma}{n-k}.$$

In finite samples, the only case when $\hat{\beta}$ and s^2 are both unbiased is when $\mathbf{W}\gamma = 0$. If the columns of $\mathbf{W}$ are linearly independent, this can only happen when $\gamma = 0$.

Now suppose that the matrix $[\mathbf{X}, \mathbf{W}]$ is of rank $k + q$ and compare the sampling variance $\sigma^2 (\mathbf{X}^\top \mathbf{X})^{-1}$ of the biased estimator $\hat{\beta}$ with that one of the unbiased estimator $\tilde{\beta} = (\mathbf{X}^\top M_W \mathbf{X})^{-1} \mathbf{X}^\top M_W \mathbf{Y}$, where $M_W = I_n - \mathbf{W}(\mathbf{W}^\top \mathbf{W})^{-1} \mathbf{W}^\top$. By Lemma A.1 in the Appendix

$$\begin{aligned}
\operatorname{Var} \tilde{\beta} &= \sigma^2 (\mathbf{X}^\top M_W \mathbf{X})^{-1} \\
&= \sigma^2 [\mathbf{X}^\top \mathbf{X} - \mathbf{X}^\top \mathbf{W}(\mathbf{W}^\top \mathbf{W})^{-1} \mathbf{W}^\top \mathbf{X}]^{-1} \\
&= \operatorname{Var} \hat{\beta} + \sigma^2 (\mathbf{X}^\top \mathbf{X})^{-1} \mathbf{X}^\top \mathbf{W}(\mathbf{W}^\top M \mathbf{W})^{-1} \mathbf{W}^\top \mathbf{X}(\mathbf{X}^\top \mathbf{X})^{-1}.
\end{aligned}$$

Although biased, $\hat{\beta}$ has smaller sampling variance than the unbiased estimator $\tilde{\beta}$. On the basis of quadratic loss, one would therefore prefer $\hat{\beta}$ to $\tilde{\beta}$ if its smaller sampling variance more than offsets its bias. The difference in the risk matrices of the two estimators is

$$R(\hat{\beta}) - R(\tilde{\beta}) = \operatorname{Var} \hat{\beta} - \operatorname{Var} \tilde{\beta} + (\operatorname{Bias} \hat{\beta})(\operatorname{Bias} \hat{\beta})^\top = -\sigma^2 Q Q^\top + Q\theta\theta^\top Q^\top,$$

where $Q = (\mathbf{X}^\top \mathbf{X})^{-1} \mathbf{X}^\top \mathbf{W}(\mathbf{W}^\top M \mathbf{W})^{-1/2}$ and $\theta = (\mathbf{W}^\top M \mathbf{W})^{1/2} \gamma$. Magnus and Durbin (1999) give precise conditions under which the above difference is n.p.d. or n.n.d. □

Example 7.5 Empirical macroeconomics is often based on "representative agent" models, which interpret aggregate data as the result of the decisions made by a single "representative" or "average" economic agent. These models ignore the potentially distortive effects of heterogeneity even in cases when the basic relationship is indeed linear.

As an illustration, consider a stratified population consisting of S strata and suppose that, for a randomly chosen individual from the sth population stratum at time t, the relationship between X and Y is of the form

$$Y = \alpha_{st} + \beta_{st} X + U, \tag{7.4}$$

where the regression coefficients α_{st} and β_{st} vary systematically both across strata and over time, and U is a random error such that $\operatorname{E}(U \mid X, S = s, T = t) = 0$.

The mean of the random variable Y, computed for the sth stratum at time t, is

$$Y^*_{st} = \alpha_{st} + \beta_{st} X^*_{st},$$

where $X^*_{st} = \operatorname{E}(X \mid S = s, T = t)$. Denoting by ω_{st} the sth population stratum weight at time t, the weighted mean of the stratum relationships (7.4), constructed using $\{\omega_{st}\}$ as weights, is

$$Y^*_t = \alpha^*_t + \beta^*_t X^*_t + \operatorname{Cov}(\beta_{st}, X^*_{st}), \tag{7.5}$$

with $Y^*_t = \sum_s \omega_{st} Y^*_{st}$, $\beta^*_t = \sum_s \omega_{st} \beta_{st}$, and

$$\operatorname{Cov}(\beta_{st}, X^*_{st}) = \sum_s \omega_{st} (\beta_{st} - \beta^*_t)(X^*_{st} - X^*_t),$$

where we used the fact that $\mathrm{E}(\beta_{st} X^*_{st}) = \mathrm{Cov}(\beta_{st}, X^*_{st}) + (\mathrm{E}\,\beta_{st})(\mathrm{E}\,X^*_{st})$.

A representative agent model with time-varying parameters assumes that the relation between X and Y is of the form

$$Y = \alpha_t + \beta_t X + V. \tag{7.6}$$

If (7.4) holds, then (7.6) is consistent with (7.5) only when $\mathrm{Cov}(\beta_{st}, X^*_{st}) = 0$. If the latter condition does not hold, then we say that there is *heterogeneity bias*. The source of the bias is the omission of the term $\mathrm{Cov}(\beta_{st}, X^*_{st})$ from the regression.

Observe that, even when there is no heterogeneity bias, the parameters of the representative agent model need not be time-invariant if the distribution of the population across strata, and therefore the population stratum weights ω_{st}, change over time. This is true even when the relationships at the stratum level are time invariant, that is, even when $\alpha_{st} = \alpha_s$ and $\beta_{st} = \beta_s$. □

It is important to notice that the problem of misspecification of $\mathrm{E}\,\mathbf{Y}$ may arise from two different sources. One is misspecification of the population regression function, the other is failure to take properly into account the nature of the sampling process from which the data have been obtained. The latter problem is discussed in Chapter 18.

Observe that an OLS regression of $\mathbf{Y}$ on $\mathbf{X}$ always gives an unbiased estimate of $\mathrm{E}(\mathbf{Y}\,|\,\mathbf{X})$ if this conditional mean is linear in $\mathbf{X}$. Assume, for example, that $\mathrm{E}(\mathbf{Y}\,|\,\mathbf{X}, \zeta) = \mathbf{X}\beta + \zeta$ and that $\mathrm{E}(\zeta\,|\,\mathbf{X}) = \mathbf{X}\delta$, where δ is a k-vector. By the law of iterated expectations

$$\mathrm{E}(\mathbf{Y}\,|\,\mathbf{X}) = \mathrm{E}[\mathrm{E}(\mathbf{Y}\,|\,\mathbf{X}, \zeta)\,|\,\mathbf{X}] = \mathbf{X}\beta + \mathrm{E}(\zeta\,|\,\mathbf{X}) = \mathbf{X}(\beta + \delta),$$

and therefore

$$\mathrm{E}(\hat\beta\,|\,\mathbf{X}) = (\mathbf{X}^\top\mathbf{X})^{-1}\mathbf{X}^\top\,\mathrm{E}(\mathbf{Y}\,|\,\mathbf{X}) = \beta + \delta.$$

Although the OLS estimator $\hat\beta$ is biased for β, the OLS predictor $\hat{\mathbf{Y}} = \mathbf{X}\hat\beta$ is unbiased in the sense that $\mathrm{E}(\hat{\mathbf{Y}}\,|\,\mathbf{X}) = \mathrm{E}(\mathbf{Y}\,|\,\mathbf{X})$.

7.3 MISSPECIFICATION OF THE VARIANCE FUNCTION

Assume now that $\mathrm{E}\,\mathbf{Y} = \mathbf{X}\beta$ but let $\mathrm{Var}\,\mathbf{Y} = \Sigma$, where the matrix Σ is symmetric and p.d. but not necessarily scalar. This allows the observations on the response variable to have unequal variance or to be correlated.

If this is the only change to the classical assumptions, then the OLS estimator $\hat\beta$ remains unbiased for β. If Σ is not a scalar matrix, there are however some less pleasant consequences. First, the sampling variance of $\hat\beta$ is

$$\begin{aligned}\mathrm{Var}\,\hat\beta &= (\mathbf{X}^\top\mathbf{X})^{-1}\mathbf{X}^\top(\mathrm{Var}\,\mathbf{Y})\mathbf{X}(\mathbf{X}^\top\mathbf{X})^{-1}\\ &= (\mathbf{X}^\top\mathbf{X})^{-1}\,\mathbf{X}^\top\Sigma\mathbf{X}\,(\mathbf{X}^\top\mathbf{X})^{-1},\end{aligned}$$

which is generally different from the classical formula. Second,

$$\mathrm{E}\,s^2 = \mathrm{E}\,\frac{\mathbf{Y}^\top M\mathbf{Y}}{n-k} = \frac{\mathrm{tr}(M\Sigma)}{n-k}.$$

These two reasons together imply that the classical estimator $s^2(\mathbf{X}^\top\mathbf{X})^{-1}$ of the sampling variance of $\hat\beta$ is generally biased. As a result, using this estimator to construct confidence intervals or statistical tests may lead to invalid inferences about the regression parameter β. Third, a crucial step in the proof of the Gauss–Markov theorem breaks down and therefore it is no longer necessarily true that $\hat\beta$ is BLU for β.

We now present some important classes of model where Σ is not constrained to be a scalar matrix. In the first class of models Σ is diagonal, in the second it is band-diagonal, whereas in the third it has a block structure.

7.3.1 PURE HETEROSKEDASTICITY

A linear model is said to be ***purely heteroskedastic*** when the matrix Σ is diagonal but not scalar, that is, the observations on the response variable are uncorrelated but have unequal variance

$$\operatorname{Cov}(Y_j, Y_i) = \begin{cases} \sigma_i^2, & \text{if } j = i, \\ 0, & \text{otherwise,} \end{cases}$$

where $\sigma_i^2 \neq \sigma_j^2$ for some pair of indices. Clearly, the number of distinct elements of Σ is at most n.

The sampling variance of the OLS estimator is in this case

$$\operatorname{Var}\hat\beta = (\mathbf{X}^\top\mathbf{X})^{-1}(\sum_i \sigma_i^2 X_i X_i^\top)(\mathbf{X}^\top\mathbf{X})^{-1}. \tag{7.7}$$

To better understand the difference with respect to the classical formula for the sampling variance of $\hat\beta$, let $\bar\sigma^2 = n^{-1}\sum_i \sigma_i^2$ and compare (7.7) with $\bar\sigma^2\,(\mathbf{X}^\top\mathbf{X})^{-1}$, which coincides with the classical formula when the variance of $\mathbf{Y}$ is a scalar matrix. The difference between the two expressions is

$$\operatorname{Var}\hat\beta - \bar\sigma^2\,(\mathbf{X}^\top\mathbf{X})^{-1} = (\mathbf{X}^\top\mathbf{X})^{-1}[\sum_i(\sigma_i^2 - \bar\sigma^2)X_i X_i^\top](\mathbf{X}^\top\mathbf{X})^{-1}.$$

This matrix is p.d., that is, the classical formula underestimates the true sampling variability of $\hat\beta$, when values of σ_i^2 larger than average are associated with large values of $X_i X_i^\top$.

We now consider two examples of how heteroskedasticity may arise.

Example 7.6 Consider a random sample from a statistical population for which

$$\operatorname{E}Y = \beta^\top X, \qquad \operatorname{Var}Y = \sigma^2.$$

If the investigator has no access to the individual data but only to the average values $\{(\bar X_s, \bar Y_s)\}$ for S groups, each consisting of $n_s > 0$ sampling units, then the appropriate regression model is

$$\operatorname{E}\bar Y_s = \beta^\top \bar X_s, \qquad s = 1, \ldots, S,$$

$$\operatorname{Cov}(\bar Y_r, \bar Y_s) = \begin{cases} \sigma^2/n_s, & \text{if } r = s, \\ 0, & \text{otherwise.} \end{cases}$$

We therefore have a heteroskedastic linear model unless all groups have the same sample size. □

Example 7.7 Let $Y_1, \ldots, Y_n$ be independent observations from a statistical population that is heterogeneous in the sense that

$$\mathrm{E}\, Y_i = \beta_i^\top X_i, \qquad i = 1, \ldots, n,$$

where β_i are unknown coefficients that may differ across population units. As discussed in Chapter 2, one way of taking this kind of heterogeneity into account consists of treating $\beta_1, \ldots, \beta_n$ as realizations of a random vector β with mean $\bar{\beta}$ and variance $\Gamma = [\gamma_{rs}]$. This is an example of a *random coefficient model.* With this interpretation, the statistical model becomes

$$\mathrm{E}(Y_i \,|\, \beta = \beta_i) = \beta_i^\top X_i, \qquad i = 1, \ldots, n.$$

By the law of iterated expectations,

$$\mathrm{E}\, Y_i = \mathrm{E}_\beta[\mathrm{E}(Y_i \,|\, \beta)] = \mathrm{E}_\beta(\beta^\top X_i) = \bar{\beta}^\top X_i,$$

where E_β denotes expectations with respect to the distribution of β. Further, by the law of total variance,

$$\mathrm{Var}\, Y_i = \mathrm{E}_\beta[\mathrm{Var}(Y_i \,|\, \beta)] + \mathrm{Var}_\beta[\mathrm{E}(Y_i \,|\, \beta)].$$

Even if the basic model is homoskedastic, namely $\mathrm{Var}(Y_i \,|\, \beta = \beta_i) = \sigma^2$ for all i, we obtain the heteroskedastic model

$$\mathrm{Var}\, Y_i = \sigma^2 + X_i^\top \Gamma X_i,$$

where

$$X_i^\top \Gamma X_i = \sum_{r=1}^{k} \sum_{s=1}^{k} \gamma_{rs} X_{ir} X_{is},$$

that is, the variance of Y_i is a linear function of all the covariates in X_i, their squares and their cross-products. In particular, if the elements of β are uncorrelated, then $\mathrm{Var}\, Y_i = \sigma^2 + \sum_r \gamma_{rr} X_{ir}^2$. Notice that no heteroskedasticity arises if the intercept is the only random coefficient in the model. □

7.3.2 AUTOCORRELATION

Consider the case when the observations on the response variable are correlated. Allowing for completely unrestricted patterns of autocorrelation would complicate the analysis substantially, for the matrix Σ would then contain $n(n+1)/2$ distinct elements. The task of analyzing Σ is simplified considerably if we instead assume that the behavior of the second moments of the response variable agrees with stationarity.

Thus, suppose that the data consist of a finite segment $\mathbf{Y} = (Y_1, \ldots, Y_n)$ of a time series with a time-varying mean $\mathrm{E}\, Y_t = \beta^\top X_t$, where $\{X_t\}$ is a sequence of nonstochastic vectors corresponding, for example, to a deterministic polynomial trend or a set of seasonal dummies. Also suppose that the deviations of Y_t from its mean follow a stationary process with mean zero and autocovariance sequence $\{\gamma_h\}$. Then

$\mathrm{E}\,\mathbf{Y} = \mathbf{X}\beta$ and $\mathrm{Var}\,\mathbf{Y} = \gamma_0\,\mathrm{R}_n$, where

$$\mathrm{R}_n = \begin{bmatrix} 1 & \rho_1 & \cdots & \rho_{n-1} \\ \rho_1 & 1 & \cdots & \rho_{n-2} \\ \vdots & \vdots & & \vdots \\ \rho_{n-1} & \rho_{n-2} & \cdots & 1 \end{bmatrix},$$

with $\rho_h = \gamma_h/\gamma_0$. Notice that $\mathrm{Var}\,\mathbf{Y}$ is now a band-diagonal matrix with at most n distinct elements. In this case, the sampling variance of the OLS estimator $\hat\beta$ is

$$\mathrm{Var}\,\hat\beta = \gamma_0\,(\mathbf{X}^\top\mathbf{X})^{-1}\mathbf{X}^\top\mathrm{R}_n\mathbf{X}(\mathbf{X}^\top\mathbf{X})^{-1},$$

where the matrix

$$\begin{aligned}\mathbf{X}^\top\mathrm{R}_n\mathbf{X} &= \sum_{t=1}^n\sum_{h=1}^n \rho_{t-h}X_tX_h^\top \\ &= \mathbf{X}^\top\mathbf{X} + \sum_{h=1}^{n-1}\sum_{t=h+1}^{n} \rho_h(X_tX_{t-h}^\top + X_{t-h}X_t^\top)\end{aligned}$$

is different from $\mathbf{X}^\top\mathbf{X}$ unless $\rho_h = 0$ for $|h| \geq 1$. We illustrate this result with two important examples.

Example 7.8 Suppose that the data consist of a finite segment $\mathbf{Y} = (Y_1, \ldots, Y_n)$ of a MA(1) process with mean βX_t, that is,

$$Y_t - \beta X_t = (1 - \theta L)V_t, \qquad \{V_t\} \sim \mathrm{WN}(0, \sigma^2),$$

where $\{X_t\}$ is a sequence of costants. Because the deviations of Y_t from its mean follow a MA(1) process with mean zero, this model is often represented in the form

$$\begin{aligned} Y_t &= \beta X_t + U_t, \\ U_t &= V_t - \theta V_{t-1}, \end{aligned}$$

and called the *linear model with* MA(1) *errors*. The error process $\{U_t\}$ is always stationary, and is invertible if $|\theta| < 1$. Because $\gamma_0 = \sigma^2(1+\theta^2)$ and $\gamma_h = 0$ for $|h| > 1$, the autocorrelation matrix of $\mathbf{Y}$ is

$$\mathrm{R}_n = \begin{bmatrix} 1 & \rho_1 & & & \\ \rho_1 & 1 & & & \\ & \ddots & \ddots & \ddots & \\ & & & 1 & \rho_1 \\ & & & \rho_1 & 1 \end{bmatrix},$$

where $\rho_1 = -\theta/(1+\theta^2)$. Hence, the sampling variance of $\hat\beta$ is

$$\mathrm{Var}\,\hat\beta = \frac{\mathrm{Var}(\sum_{t=1}^n X_tY_t)}{(\sum_{t=1}^n X_t^2)^2} = \frac{\gamma_0}{\sum_{t=1}^n X_t^2}\left(1 - 2\frac{\theta}{1+\theta^2}\frac{\sum_{t=1}^{n-1} X_tX_{t+1}}{\sum_{t=1}^n X_t^2}\right).$$

Thus, the classical formula underestimates the sampling variance of the OLS estimator, and therefore overestimates its precision, when θ and the first-order autocorrelation coefficient of X_t have opposite sign. □

Example 7.9 Suppose that the data consist of a finite segment $\mathbf{Y} = (Y_1, \ldots, Y_n)$ of an AR(1) process with mean βX_t, that is,

$$(1 - \phi L)(Y_t - \beta X_t) = V_t, \qquad \{V_t\} \sim \mathrm{WN}(0, \sigma^2),$$

where $\{X_t\}$ is a sequence of constants. Because the deviations of Y_t from its mean follow an AR(1) process with mean zero, this model is often represented in the form

$$Y_t = \beta X_t + U_t,$$
$$U_t = \phi U_{t-1} + V_t,$$

and called the *linear model with* AR(1) *errors.* The error process $\{U_t\}$ is stationary if $|\phi| \neq 1$, and stable if $|\phi| < 1$. If $|\phi| < 1$, then $\gamma_0 = \sigma^2/(1 - \phi^2)$ and the autocorrelation matrix of $\mathbf{Y}$ is

$$\mathrm{R}_n = \begin{bmatrix} 1 & \phi & \cdots & \phi^{n-1} \\ \phi & 1 & \cdots & \phi^{n-2} \\ \vdots & \vdots & & \vdots \\ \phi^{n-1} & \phi^{n-2} & \cdots & 1 \end{bmatrix}.$$

Hence, the sampling variance of $\hat{\beta}$ is

$$\begin{aligned} \mathrm{Var}\,\hat{\beta} &= \frac{\mathrm{Var}(\sum_{t=1}^n X_t Y_t)}{(\sum_t X_t^2)^2} \\ &= \frac{\gamma_0}{\sum_{t=1}^n X_t^2}\left(1 + 2\phi \frac{\sum_{t=1}^{n-1} X_t X_{t+1}}{\sum_{t=1}^n X_t^2} + \cdots + 2\phi^{n-1}\frac{X_1 X_n}{\sum_{t=1}^n X_t^2}\right), \end{aligned}$$

which is different from $\gamma_0/(\sum_t X_t^2)$ in general. Thus, the classical formula overestimates the precision of the OLS estimator whenever the powers of ϕ and the autocorrelation coefficients of X_t have the same sign.

As an illustration, let $\{X_t\}$ follow the AR(1) process

$$(1 - \alpha L)X_t = \epsilon_t, \qquad \{\epsilon_t\} \sim \mathrm{WN}(0, \sigma_\epsilon^2),$$

where $|\alpha| < 1$. It can be shown that, in large samples, $n\,\mathrm{Var}\,\hat{\beta}$ is well approximated by

$$\begin{aligned} V(\hat{\beta}) &= \frac{\gamma_0}{\mathrm{Var}\,X_t}\,[1 + 2\phi\,\mathrm{Corr}(X_t, X_{t+1}) + 2\phi^2\,\mathrm{Corr}(X_t, X_{t+2}) + \cdots] \\ &= \frac{\gamma_0}{\mathrm{Var}\,X_t}\,(1 + 2\phi\alpha + 2\phi^2\alpha^2 + \cdots) \\ &= \frac{\gamma_0}{\mathrm{Var}\,X_t}\left(1 + \frac{2\phi\alpha}{1 - \phi\alpha}\right) = \frac{\gamma_0}{\mathrm{Var}\,X_t}\,\frac{1 + \phi\alpha}{1 - \phi\alpha}. \end{aligned}$$

In large samples, the ratio between the classical formula for the sampling variance of $\hat{\beta}$ and its actual value is therefore

$$\frac{\gamma_0/(\mathrm{Var}\,X_t)}{V(\hat{\beta})} = \frac{1 - \phi\alpha}{1 + \phi\alpha}, \tag{7.8}$$

which is equal to one if $\phi = 0$ or $\alpha = 0$. If ϕ and α have the same sign (a reasonable assumption for many economic time series), then the classical formula tends to overestimate the precision of $\hat{\beta}$. For example, the ratio (7.8) is equal to .22 if $\phi = \alpha = .8$, and to .105 if $\phi = \alpha = .9$. □

7.3.3 SEEMINGLY UNRELATED REGRESSION EQUATIONS

Consider a panel or longitudinal data set consisting of T consecutive observations on n sample units, and let (X_{it}, Y_{it}) be the observations on the ith sample unit in the tth period. In some cases, despite the absence of heteroskedasticity or autocorrelation at the level of the individual sample units, it may be important to allow for both heterogeneity and dependence across sample units. Thus consider the following model

$$\mathrm{E}\, Y_{it} = \beta_i^\top X_{it}, \qquad i = 1, \dots, n; \qquad t = 1, \dots, T, \tag{7.9}$$

where β_i and X_{it} are nonstochastic vectors of dimension k_i and

$$\mathrm{Cov}(Y_{it}, Y_{js}) = \begin{cases} \gamma_{ij}, & \text{if } s = t, \\ 0, & \text{otherwise.} \end{cases} \tag{7.10}$$

This model was introduced by Zellner (1962) and is called a *system of seemingly unrelated regression equations (SURE)*. It differs from the classical linear model for two reasons. First, β_i and γ_{ii} differ across sample units, thus allowing for unrestricted patterns of heterogeneity. Second, γ_{ij} may be different from zero for $i \neq j$, thus allowing for contemporaneous correlation between sample units.

The SURE model may be derived by assuming that Y_{it} obeys a classical linear model conditionally on some unobservable random variable V_t, that is,

$$\mathrm{E}(Y_{it} \mid V_t) = \alpha_i V_t + \beta_i^\top X_{it}$$

and

$$\mathrm{Cov}(Y_{it}, Y_{js} \mid V_t) = \begin{cases} \sigma^2, & \text{if } i = j \text{ and } s = t, \\ 0, & \text{otherwise.} \end{cases}$$

For example, when the sample consists of firms belonging to the same industry, V_t may be an unobservable time-varying "macro shock" specific to the industry. If $\{V_t\}$ is a white noise process with zero mean and unit variance, then it is easy to verify that $\mathrm{E}\, Y_{it}$ is equal to (7.9) and $\mathrm{Cov}(Y_{it}, Y_{js})$ is equal to (7.10) with $\gamma_{ii} = \alpha_i^2 + \sigma^2$ and $\gamma_{ij} = \alpha_i \alpha_j$ for $i \neq j$.

Now let $\mathbf{Y}_i$ and $\mathbf{X}_i$ denote respectively the T-vector and the $T \times k_i$ matrix obtained by stacking the T observations on the response variable and the covariates for the ith sample unit, that is,

$$\mathbf{Y}_i = \begin{pmatrix} Y_{i1} \\ \vdots \\ Y_{iT} \end{pmatrix}, \qquad \mathbf{X}_i = \begin{bmatrix} X_{i1}^\top \\ \vdots \\ X_{iT}^\top \end{bmatrix}, \qquad i = 1, \dots, n.$$

The SURE model can then be written as

$$\begin{aligned} \mathrm{E}\, \mathbf{Y}_i &= \mathbf{X}_i \beta_i, \\ \mathrm{Cov}(\mathbf{Y}_i, \mathbf{Y}_j) &= \gamma_{ij} I_T, \qquad i, j = 1, \dots, n. \end{aligned}$$

Stacking the observations on the n sample units into a vector $\mathbf{Y}$ of dimension nT and a matrix $\mathbf{X}$ of order $nT \times k$, where $k = \sum_i k_i$, gives

$$\mathbf{Y} = \begin{pmatrix} \mathbf{Y}_1 \\ \vdots \\ \mathbf{Y}_n \end{pmatrix}, \qquad \mathbf{X} = \begin{bmatrix} \mathbf{X}_1 & & \\ & \ddots & \\ & & \mathbf{X}_n \end{bmatrix}.$$

The model can now be written more compactly as

$$\mathrm{E}\,\mathbf{Y} = \mathbf{X}\beta,$$

$$\mathrm{Var}\,\mathbf{Y} = \begin{bmatrix} \gamma_{11} I_T & \cdots & \gamma_{1n} I_T \\ \vdots & & \vdots \\ \gamma_{n1} I_T & \cdots & \gamma_{nn} I_T \end{bmatrix} = \Gamma \otimes I_T,$$

where

$$\beta = \begin{pmatrix} \beta_1 \\ \vdots \\ \beta_n \end{pmatrix}, \qquad \Gamma = \begin{bmatrix} \gamma_{11} & \cdots & \gamma_{1n} \\ \vdots & & \vdots \\ \gamma_{n1} & \cdots & \gamma_{nn} \end{bmatrix}$$

are respectively a k-vector and an $n \times n$ matrix. Notice that the multivariate regression model in Section 6.2.5 is a special case where each equation has exactly the same design matrix, that is, $\mathbf{X}_i = \bar{\mathbf{X}}$ for all i or, equivalently, $\mathbf{X} = I_n \otimes \bar{\mathbf{X}}$.

7.4 GENERALIZED LEAST SQUARES

Suppose that all the assumptions of the classical linear model hold except Assumption 6.3, which is replaced by the assumption that $\mathrm{Var}\,\mathbf{Y} = \Sigma$, a symmetric p.d. matrix. We now show that when Σ is known, except possibly for a factor of proportionality, it is generally possible to construct an estimator that is more efficient than OLS in the Gauss–Markov sense. The basic idea is to use the knowledge of Σ to suitably transform the data in order to restore the ideal conditions of the classical linear model, and then apply OLS to the transformed data. This result is also useful in cases when the matrix Σ is unknown because it suggests ways of constructing relatively simple alternatives to the OLS estimator.

7.4.1 AITKEN THEOREM

Without loss of generality, let $\Sigma = \sigma^2\Omega$, where $0 < \sigma^2 < \infty$ and Ω is a symmetric p.d. matrix. When Ω is known, it is sufficient to appropriately transform the data in order to get back to a situation where all assumptions of the classical linear model hold.

Given a nonsingular matrix Γ such that $\Gamma^\top\Gamma = \Omega^{-1}$, consider the following linear transformation of the data

$$\mathbf{X}^* = \Gamma\mathbf{X}, \qquad \mathbf{Y}^* = \Gamma\mathbf{Y}.$$

The existence of the matrix Γ is guaranteed by Theorem A.5. The linear transformation induced by Γ corresponds to a change of the coordinate system in which $\mathbf{Y}$ and $\mathbf{X}$ are represented. Because Γ is nonsingular, such a transformation leaves the rank of the design matrix unchanged. Further, because $\mathrm{E}\,\mathbf{Y}^* = \mathbf{X}^*\beta$, neither the linearity of the regression function nor the regression parameter are affected. The transformation does however modify the structure of the second moments of the observations, for

$$\mathrm{Var}\,\mathbf{Y}^* = \sigma^2\,\Gamma\Omega\Gamma^\top = \sigma^2\,\Gamma(\Gamma^\top\Gamma)^{-1}\Gamma^\top = \sigma^2 I_n.$$

Because, in the new coordinate system, the observations satisfy all the assumptions of the classical linear model, the BLU estimator of β is the OLS estimator for the transformed data

$$\begin{aligned}\tilde{\beta} &= (\mathbf{X}^{*\top}\mathbf{X}^*)^{-1}\mathbf{X}^{*\top}\mathbf{Y}^* \\ &= (\mathbf{X}^\top\Gamma^\top\Gamma\mathbf{X})^{-1}\Gamma^\top\Gamma\mathbf{Y} \\ &= (\mathbf{X}^\top\Omega^{-1}\mathbf{X})^{-1}\mathbf{X}^\top\Omega^{-1}\mathbf{Y}.\end{aligned}$$

This estimators is called the *generalized least squares (GLS)* or *Aitken estimator*. The GLS estimator $\tilde{\beta}$ solves the problem

$$\min_{\beta\in\Re^k} Q(\beta) = (\mathbf{Y} - \mathbf{X}\beta)^\top\Omega^{-1}(\mathbf{Y} - \mathbf{X}\beta).$$

Thus, like the OLS estimator, $\tilde{\beta}$ is a solution to a minimum norm problem. The difference is that the norm of the error vector is now defined in the more general metric of the p.d. matrix Ω^{-1}. Notice that the vector of GLS fitted values is $\tilde{\mathbf{Y}} = \mathbf{X}\tilde{\beta} = H_\Omega\mathbf{Y}$, where the matrix $H_\Omega = \mathbf{X}(\mathbf{X}^\top\Omega^{-1}\mathbf{X})^{-1}\mathbf{X}^\top\Omega^{-1}$ is idempotent but not symmetric, and the vector of GLS residuals is $\tilde{\mathbf{U}} = \mathbf{Y} - \tilde{\mathbf{Y}} = (I_n - H_\Omega)\mathbf{Y} = M_\Omega\mathbf{Y}$, where the matrix $M_\Omega = I_n - \mathbf{X}(\mathbf{X}^\top\Omega^{-1}\mathbf{X})^{-1}\mathbf{X}^\top\Omega^{-1}$ is also idempotent but not symmetric. It is easily seen that the GLS estimator coincides with the ML estimator of β for the Gaussian linear model $\mathbf{Y} \sim \mathcal{N}(\mathbf{X}\beta, \sigma^2\Omega)$, where Ω is a known matrix.

Example 7.10 If $\Omega = \text{diag}[\omega_i]$, with $\omega_i > 0$ for all i, then the matrix Γ exists, is unique, and is itself diagonal with ith diagonal element equal to $1/\sqrt{\omega_i}$. In this case, the GLS criterion reduces to

$$Q(\beta) = \sum_{i=1}^n w_i\,(Y_i - \beta^\top X_i)^2,$$

where the weight $w_i = 1/\omega_i$ is just the reciprocal of the variance of Y_i. Unlike the OLS criterion, which assigns the same weight to all observations, the higher is the variance of Y_i, the smaller the weight given to the ith observation. The GLS estimator of β is

$$\tilde{\beta} = (\sum_i w_i X_i X_i^\top)^{-1}\sum_i w_i X_i Y_i,$$

which is also called the *weighted least squares (WLS) estimator*. □

Example 7.11 Consider the linear model with AR(1) errors introduced in Example 7.9, and put $\Omega = (1-\phi^2)^{-1}\mathrm{R}_n$, where R_n is the autocorrelation matrix of $\mathbf{Y}$. It is easily verified that

$$\Omega^{-1} = \begin{bmatrix} 1 & -\phi & & & \\ -\phi & 1+\phi^2 & -\phi & & \\ & \ddots & \ddots & \ddots & \\ & & -\phi & 1+\phi^2 & -\phi \\ & & & -\phi & 1 \end{bmatrix},$$

and therefore

$$\Gamma = \begin{bmatrix} \sqrt{1-\phi^2} & & & & \\ -\phi & 1 & & & \\ & -\phi & \ddots & & \\ & & \ddots & 1 & \\ & & & -\phi & 1 \end{bmatrix}.$$

Hence, the transformed data are

$$X_t^* = \begin{cases} \sqrt{1-\phi^2}\, X_1, & \text{if } t = 1, \\ X_t - \phi X_{t-1}, & \text{otherwise,} \end{cases}, \qquad Y_t^* = \begin{cases} \sqrt{1-\phi^2}\, Y_1, & \text{if } t = 1, \\ Y_t - \phi Y_{t-1}, & \text{otherwise.} \end{cases}$$

This is known as the *exact GLS* or *Prais–Winsten transformation*. Dropping the first observation, or equivalently assuming that $U_1 = 0$, the GLS estimator coincides with the OLS estimator in the regression of the quasi-difference $Y_t - \phi Y_{t-1}$ on the quasi-difference $X_t - \phi X_{t-1}$. This transformation is known as the *approximate GLS* or *Cochrane–Orcutt transformation*. In large samples, dropping the first observation is only going to have a marginal effect on the estimates. This, however, need not be true in small samples. □

Given the GLS estimator $\tilde{\beta}$, as an estimator of scale consider

$$\tilde{s}^2 = \frac{Q(\tilde{\beta})}{n-k} = \frac{\tilde{\mathbf{U}}^\top \Omega^{-1} \tilde{\mathbf{U}}}{n-k},$$

where $\tilde{\mathbf{U}}$ is the vector of GLS residuals. It is easy to verify that $\tilde{s}^2$ is simply the OLS estimator of scale for the transformed data.

The sampling properties of $\tilde{\beta}$ and $\tilde{s}^2$ are a simple consequence of the equivalence between the GLS estimator and the OLS estimator for the transformed data. Thus, if $\mathrm{E}\,\mathbf{Y} = \mathbf{X}\beta$, where $\mathbf{X}$ is a nonstochastic matrix of full rank, and $\mathrm{Var}\,\mathbf{Y} = \sigma^2\Omega$, where Ω is a nonsingular matrix, then $\tilde{\beta}$ is unbiased for β, $\tilde{s}^2$ is unbiased for σ^2, and the sampling variance of $\tilde{\beta}$ is

$$\mathrm{Var}\,\tilde{\beta} = \sigma^2\, (\mathbf{X}^\top \Omega^{-1} \mathbf{X})^{-1}.$$

Further, $\mathrm{Var}\,\hat{\beta} - \mathrm{Var}\,\bar{\beta} \geq 0$ for every other estimator $\bar{\beta}$ which is linear in $\mathbf{Y}$ and unbiased for β. The latter result, known as the *Aitken theorem*, implies that the difference between the sampling variances of the OLS and the GLS estimator is a n.n.d. matrix. This may also be verified directly.

Theorem 7.3 *If $\hat{\beta}$ is the OLS estimator and $\tilde{\beta}$ is the GLS estimator, then*

$$\mathrm{Var}\,\hat{\beta} - \mathrm{Var}\,\tilde{\beta} \geq 0.$$

Proof. The proof is again based on the fact that if A and B are nonsingular matrices, then $A - B \geq 0$ if and only if $B^{-1} - A^{-1} \geq 0$. Put $A = (\mathbf{X}^\top\mathbf{X})^{-1}\mathbf{X}^\top\Omega\mathbf{X}(\mathbf{X}^\top\mathbf{X})^{-1}$, $B = (\mathbf{X}^\top\Omega^{-1}\mathbf{X})^{-1}$, and $\Omega^{-1} = \Gamma^\top\Gamma$. Because the matrix

$$\begin{aligned} &\mathbf{X}^\top\Omega^{-1}\mathbf{X} - \mathbf{X}^\top\mathbf{X}(\mathbf{X}^\top\Omega\mathbf{X})^{-1}\mathbf{X}^\top\mathbf{X} \\ &\qquad = \mathbf{X}^\top\Gamma^\top[I_n - \Gamma^{-\top}\mathbf{X}(\mathbf{X}^\top\Omega\mathbf{X})^{-1}\mathbf{X}^\top\Gamma^{-1}]\Gamma\mathbf{X} \end{aligned}$$

is symmetric and idempotent, it is n.n.d. □

There are cases, however, where the situation is not at all unfavorable to OLS.

Example 7.12 Consider the SURE model introduced in Section 7.3.3. If Γ is a p.d. matrix, then the GLS estimator $\tilde{\beta}$ is a solution to the problem of minimizing with respect to β the function

$$Q(\beta) = (\mathbf{Y} - \mathbf{X}\beta)^\top (\Gamma \otimes I_T)^{-1} (\mathbf{Y} - \mathbf{X}\beta).$$

For the multivariate regression model, where $\mathbf{X} = I_n \otimes \bar{\mathbf{X}}$, the GLS estimator is

$$\begin{aligned}\tilde{\beta} &= [(I_n \otimes \bar{\mathbf{X}})^\top (\Gamma \otimes I_T)^{-1} (I_n \otimes \bar{\mathbf{X}})]^{-1} (I_n \otimes \bar{\mathbf{X}})^\top (\Gamma \otimes I_T)^{-1} \mathbf{Y} \\ &= [I_n \otimes (\bar{\mathbf{X}}^\top \bar{\mathbf{X}})^{-1} \bar{\mathbf{X}}^\top]\, \mathbf{Y},\end{aligned}$$

by the properties of the Kronecker product. Hence

$$\tilde{\beta}_i = (\bar{\mathbf{X}}^\top \bar{\mathbf{X}})^{-1} \bar{\mathbf{X}}^\top \mathbf{Y}_i, \qquad i = 1, \ldots, n,$$

which coincides with the OLS estimator in the regression of $\mathbf{Y}_i$ on $\bar{\mathbf{X}}$.

This algebraic result is also useful in other contexts. Suppose that the data consist of a finite segment $Z_1, \ldots, Z_T$ of the m-variate Gaussian AR(1) process

$$Z_t = \Phi Z_{t-1} + U_t,$$

where Φ is an $m \times m$ matrix and $\{U_t\}$ is an m-variate Gaussian white noise with mean zero and variance Σ. Proceeding as in Example 4.10 shows that, for a fixed Σ, the Gaussian sample log-likelihood is of the form

$$L(\phi) = c - \frac{1}{2} \ln g(\phi) - \frac{1}{2} [Z_1^\top \Gamma_0^{-1} Z_1 + Q(\phi)], \qquad \phi = \operatorname{vec} \Phi,$$

where c is a constant that does not depend on ϕ, Γ_0 is the matrix derived in Example 3.23, $g(\phi) = \ln \det \Gamma_0$ and

$$Q(\phi) = \sum_{t=2}^{T} (Z_t - \Phi Z_{t-1})^\top \Sigma^{-1} (Z_t - \Phi Z_{t-1}).$$

The conditional LS estimator of ϕ is obtained by minimizing the function $Q(\phi)$, which may also be written more compactly as

$$Q(\phi) = (\mathbf{Y} - \mathbf{X}\phi)^\top (\Sigma^{-1} \otimes I_{T-1}) (\mathbf{Y} - \mathbf{X}\phi),$$

where

$$\mathbf{Y} = \begin{pmatrix} \mathbf{Y}_1 \\ \vdots \\ \mathbf{Y}_m \end{pmatrix}, \qquad \mathbf{X} = \begin{bmatrix} \bar{\mathbf{X}} & & \\ & \ddots & \\ & & \bar{\mathbf{X}} \end{bmatrix},$$

with

$$\mathbf{Y}_j = \begin{pmatrix} Z_{2j} \\ \vdots \\ Z_{Tj} \end{pmatrix}, \qquad \bar{\mathbf{X}} = \begin{bmatrix} Z_{11} & Z_{12} & \cdots & Z_{1m} \\ Z_{21} & Z_{22} & & Z_{2m} \\ \vdots & \vdots & & \vdots \\ Z_{T-1,1} & Z_{T-1,2} & \cdots & Z_{T-1,m} \end{bmatrix}.$$

The conditional LS problem is therefore formally equivalent to the problem that defines the GLS estimator for a SURE model where the design matrix is exactly the same in each equation. Hence, the conditional LS estimator for the jth row of $\mathbf{\Phi}$ coincides with the OLS estimator in the regression of Z_{tj} on $Z_{t-1,1}, \ldots, Z_{t-1,m}$. □

Example 7.13 Let A be an orthonormal $n \times k$ matrix whose columns consist of k eigenvectors of Ω, say the first k, and assume that $\mathbf{X} = AB$ for some nonsingular matrix B. Because $A^\top A = I_k$, we have

$$(\mathbf{X}^\top \mathbf{X})^{-1}\mathbf{X}^\top \Omega \mathbf{X}(\mathbf{X}^\top \mathbf{X})^{-1} = (B^\top B)^{-1} B^\top A^\top \Omega A B (B^\top B)^{-1}$$
$$= B^{-1} \Lambda B^{-\top},$$

where $\Lambda = A^\top \Omega A$ is a diagonal matrix that contains the first k eigenvalues of Ω on its main diagonal. Further

$$\mathbf{X}^\top \Omega^{-1} \mathbf{X} = B^\top A^\top \Omega^{-1} A B = B^\top \Lambda^{-1} B,$$

and therefore $\operatorname{Var} \hat{\beta} = \operatorname{Var} \tilde{\beta}$. Finally, since $\Omega A = A\Lambda$, it is easy to verify that

$$(\mathbf{X}^\top \mathbf{X})^{-1}\mathbf{X}^\top = B^{-1} A^\top = (\mathbf{X}^\top \Omega^{-1} \mathbf{X})^{-1} \mathbf{X}^\top \Omega^{-1}.$$

In this case, the OLS and the GLS estimators are numerically the same. For more general results, see Amemiya (1985), Section 6.1.3. □

7.4.2 FEASIBLE GLS ESTIMATORS

The Aitken estimator requires the matrix Ω to be known, at least up to a proportionality factor. Usually, this knowledge is only available in special circumstances, such as Example 7.6. Most often, Ω is unknown.

When $\mathbf{Y}$ is an n-vector, the matrix Ω contains $n(n+1)/2$ distinct elements (because of symmetry). If all these elements were free to vary, it would then be impossible to estimate them, jointly with σ^2 and the elements of β, on the basis of the sample information only. The existence of prior information on the structure of Ω is therefore essential.

A typical hypothesis is that $\Omega^{-1} = G(\psi)$, where $\psi \in \Psi$ is a finite-dimensional parameter and $G(\cdot)$ is an $n \times n$ matrix whose elements are functions of ψ. The examples presented in Sections 7.3.2 and 7.3.3 are all of this type. If $\hat{\psi}$ is a "good" estimate of ψ, it is plausible that $\hat{\Omega}^{-1} = G(\hat{\psi})$ is also a "good" estimate of Ω^{-1}. One may then use $\hat{\Omega}^{-1}$ to construct the *feasible* or GLS estimator

$$\bar{\beta} = (\mathbf{X}^\top \hat{\Omega}^{-1} \mathbf{X})^{-1} \mathbf{X}^\top \hat{\Omega}^{-1} \mathbf{Y}.$$

Example 7.14 It was seen in Example 7.11 that, if the first observation is dropped, then the GLS estimator of β in a linear model with AR(1) errors is equivalent to the OLS estimator in a regression of $Y_t - \phi Y_{t-1}$ on $X_t - \phi X_{t-1}$. A plausible estimate of ϕ is the first-order autocorrelation coefficient $\hat{\phi}$ of the OLS residuals. A feasible GLS estimator of β is the OLS estimator $\bar{\beta}$ in the regression of $Y_t - \hat{\phi} Y_{t-1}$ on $X_t - \hat{\phi} X_{t-1}$. This procedure may be iterated replacing $\hat{\phi}$ by the first-order autocorrelation coefficient of the residuals $Y_t - \bar{\beta} X_t$, and so on. This iterative scheme is known as the *Cochrane–Orcutt iterative procedure*. □

When the matrix Ω^{-1} is estimated from the data, the sampling properties of the feasible GLS estimator $\bar{\beta}$ are complicated to analyze and do not generally coincide with those of the GLS estimator $\tilde{\beta}$ based on the exact knowledge of Ω^{-1}. In particular, there is no guarantee that $\bar{\beta}$ is unbiased or more efficient than OLS. If the sample size is not large, using $\bar{\beta}$ may even imply an efficiency loss with respect to OLS.

Exact statistical results for $\bar{\beta}$ are generally not available. Some large sample results are discussed in Section 10.3.

7.5 ESTIMATING THE PRECISION OF THE OLS ESTIMATOR

The fact that the variance of **Y** is not a scalar matrix does not necessarily imply that one should lose interest in the OLS estimator. Such an estimator remains attractive for two reasons. First, there may be considerable uncertainty about the structure of the second moments of **Y**. Second, even when this structure is known with certainty, the need to rely on a feasible estimator may be a source of concern, especially when the sample size is small. It is therefore legitimate to keep using the OLS estimator, provided that inference about β is based on a correct assessment of its precision.

Recall from Section 7.3 that the classical estimator $\widehat{\text{Var}}\,\hat{\beta} = s^2(\mathbf{X}^\top\mathbf{X})^{-1}$ of the sampling variance of $\hat{\beta}$ is biased when the observations on the response variable are heteroskedastic or autocorrelated. We show in this section how the bootstrap and the jackknife may be used to derive alternative estimates of the sampling variance of $\hat{\beta}$. A theoretical justification for these methods is presented in Section 10.2.3.

7.5.1 *HETEROSKEDASTICITY*

The nonparametric bootstrap, introduced in Section 5.1.2, may be applied without changes. A resample $[\mathbf{X}^*, \mathbf{Y}^*]$ is in this case a sample of size n from the joint empirical distribution of (X_i, Y_i). Given B independent resamples, the bootstrap estimate of the sampling variance of $\hat{\beta}$ is

$$\widehat{\text{Var}}_B\,\hat{\beta} = B^{-1}\sum_{b=1}^{B}[\hat{\beta}_b^* - \hat{\beta}_{(\cdot)}][\hat{\beta}_b^* - \hat{\beta}_{(\cdot)}]^\top,$$

where $\hat{\beta}_b^*$ is the OLS estimate for the bth resample $[\mathbf{Y}_b^*, \mathbf{X}_b^*]$ and $\hat{\beta}_{(\cdot)} = B^{-1}\sum_b \hat{\beta}_b^*$. This estimate is nonparametric because it does not require the regression function to be linear nor the observations on the response variable to be homoskedastic. What is necessary, however, is that such observations are independent and not only uncorrelated.

It is instructive to compare this estimate with the one obtained by the following version of the bootstrap.

Algorithm 7.1

(1) *Compute the empirical distribution function* $\hat{F}$ *of the OLS residuals* $\hat{U}_i$*. If the regression model does not include an intercept, replace the original residuals by the centered residuals* $\hat{U}_i - \bar{U}$*, where* $\bar{U} = n^{-1}\sum_i \hat{U}_i$.

(2) *Draw a sample* $\hat{\mathbf{U}}^*$ *of size* n *from* $\hat{F}$.

(3) *Construct the pseudo data* $\mathbf{Y}^* = \mathbf{X}\hat{\beta} + \hat{\mathbf{U}}^*$.

(4) *Compute the OLS estimate* $\hat\beta^* = (\mathbf{X}^\top\mathbf{X})^{-1}\mathbf{X}\mathbf{Y}^*$ *for the pseudo data* $[\mathbf{Y}^*, \mathbf{X}]$.
(5) *Repeat steps* (2)–(4) *a sufficiently high number* B *of times, obtaining bootstrap replications* $\hat\beta^{*1}, \ldots, \hat\beta^{*B}$.
(6) *Use the empirical distribution of* $\hat\beta^{*1}, \ldots, \hat\beta^{*B}$ *to estimate any aspect of the sampling distribution of* $\hat\beta$.

Because Algorithm 7.1 takes advantage of the assumptions of the classical linear model, it may lose its validity when these assumptions do not hold. Under $\hat F$, it follows from the properties of the residuals that

$$\mathrm{E}_{\hat F}\, \hat U_i^* = n^{-1}\sum_{i=1}^n \hat U_i = 0, \qquad \mathrm{Var}_{\hat F}\, \hat U_i^* = n^{-1}\sum_{i=1}^n \hat U_i^2 = \hat\sigma^2.$$

Notice that, if the regression model does not include an intercept, centering is needed to ensure that they have zero mean. Because the distribution of the pseudo data $\mathbf{Y}^*$ has mean $\mathbf{X}\hat\beta$ and variance $\hat\sigma^2 I_n$ under $\hat F$, a bootstrap replication $\hat\beta^* = (\mathbf{X}^\top\mathbf{X})^{-1}\mathbf{X}^\top\mathbf{Y}^*$ is unbiased for $\hat\beta$ and its sampling variance is equal to $\hat\sigma^2(\mathbf{X}^\top\mathbf{X})^{-1}$. Therefore, when the number of bootstrap replications is sufficiently high, the bootstrap Algorithm 7.1 produces an estimate of the sampling variance of $\hat\beta$ that coincides with the classical estimate $s^2(\mathbf{X}^\top\mathbf{X})^{-1}$ and is therefore biased if the data are heteroskedastic.

The jackknife estimate of the sampling variance of $\hat\beta$ is

$$\widehat{\mathrm{Var}}_J\, \hat\beta = \frac{n-1}{n}\sum_{i=1}^n [\hat\beta_{(i)} - \hat\beta_{(\cdot)}][\hat\beta_{(i)} - \hat\beta_{(\cdot)}]^\top,$$

where $\hat\beta_{(i)}$ is the OLS estimate obtained by excluding the ith case and $\hat\beta_{(\cdot)} = n^{-1}\sum_i \hat\beta_{(i)}$. In practice, there is no need to recompute the OLS estimate for each of the n jackknife samples. It is easy to verify, using the results in Section 6.2.7, that

$$\hat\beta_{(i)} - \hat\beta_{(\cdot)} = -(\mathbf{X}^\top\mathbf{X})^{-1}\left(X_i\hat U_{(i)} - \frac{1}{n}\sum_{j=1}^n X_j\hat U_{(j)}\right),$$

where $\hat U_{(i)} = \hat U_i/(1-h_{ii})$ and $h_{ii} = X_i^\top(\mathbf{X}^\top\mathbf{X})^{-1}X_i$. The jackknife estimate of the sampling variance of $\hat\beta$ is therefore

$$\widehat{\mathrm{Var}}_J\, \hat\beta = \frac{n-1}{n}(\mathbf{X}^\top\mathbf{X})^{-1}\left[\sum_{i=1}^n \frac{\hat U_i^2}{(1-h_{ii})^2}X_iX_i^\top - \frac{1}{n}\mathbf{X}^\top D\hat{\mathbf{U}}\hat{\mathbf{U}}^\top D\mathbf{X}\right](\mathbf{X}^\top\mathbf{X})^{-1},$$

where $D = \mathrm{diag}[1/(1-h_{ii})]$. The jackknife estimate is itself a nonparametric estimate of $\mathrm{Var}\,\hat\beta$, because it does not require the regression function to be linear nor the observations on the response variable to be homoskedastic.

In large samples, if $h_{ii} \to 0$ for all i, then the jackknife estimate becomes

$$\widehat{\mathrm{Var}}_I\, \hat\beta = (\mathbf{X}^\top\mathbf{X})^{-1}(\sum_i \hat U_i^2 X_iX_i^\top)(\mathbf{X}^\top\mathbf{X})^{-1},$$

which is called the *infinitesimal jackknife* estimate of the sampling variance of $\hat\beta$. Notice the similarity with formula (7.7) for the sampling variance of $\hat\beta$ under heteroskedasticity.

7.5.2 AUTOCORRELATION

If the regression errors in a linear model follow a low-order MA(q) process, then their autocorrelation function dies after q lags. A natural estimate of the sampling variance of $\hat\beta$ is therefore

$$\widehat{\operatorname{Var}}\,\hat\beta = \hat\gamma_0\,(\mathbf{X}^\top\mathbf{X})^{-1} + (\mathbf{X}^\top\mathbf{X})^{-1}\left[\sum_{h=1}^{q}\sum_{t=h+1}^{n}\hat\gamma_h(X_tX_{t-h}^\top + X_{t-h}X_t^\top)\right](\mathbf{X}^\top\mathbf{X})^{-1}, \tag{7.11}$$

where $\hat\gamma_h$ is an estimate of γ_h obtained from the OLS residuals. When the regression errors follow instead an AR or ARMA process, this approach cannot be followed because it would require estimating autocorrelations of order too high to maintain an acceptable degree of accuracy. In this case, one may consider versions of the bootstrap for dependent data.

Example 7.15 Let the data consist of n consecutive observations $\{(X_t, Y_t)\}$ on a linear model with AR(1) errors

$$(1-\phi L)(Y_t - \beta X_t) = V_t, \qquad \{V_t\} \sim \mathrm{IID}(0,\sigma^2),$$

where $|\phi| < 1$. Notice that the assumption that the innovations are a white noise process has been replaced here by the stronger assumption that $\{V_t\}$ form a sequence of i.i.d. random variables. If β and ϕ were known, one might then compute $V_t = U_t - \phi U_{t-1}$, where $U_t = Y_t - \beta X_t$, and estimate the distribution function F of V_t by the empirical distribution function of V_t. Because β and ϕ are unknown, one may estimate F by the empirical distribution function $\hat F$ of the residuals $\hat V_t = \hat U_t - \hat\phi \hat U_{t-1}$, where $\hat U_t = Y_t - \hat\beta X_t$ is the ith OLS residual and

$$\hat\phi = \frac{\sum_{t=1}^{n-1}\hat U_t \hat U_{t+1}}{\sum_{t=1}^{n}\hat U_t^2}$$

is the first-order autocorrelation coefficient of the OLS residuals. One may then modify step (3) of Algorithm 7.1 by drawing a sample $\hat V_2^*, \ldots, \hat V_n^*$ of size $n-1$ from $\hat F$, and then constructing pseudo data $\{(X_t, Y_t^*)\}$ through the recursion

$$Y_t^* = \hat\beta X_t + \hat\phi(Y_{t-1}^* - \hat\beta X_{t-1}) + \hat V_t^*, \qquad t = 2, \ldots, n,$$

starting from $Y_1^* = Y_1$. □

The previous example is easily generalized to the case of a linear model with AR(p) errors

$$(1 - \phi_1 L - \cdots - \phi_p L^p)(Y_t - \beta X_t) = V_t, \qquad \{V_t\} \sim \mathrm{IID}(0,\sigma^2).$$

Algorithm 7.2

(1) *Given parameter estimates $\hat\phi_1, \ldots, \hat\phi_p$ obtained from the OLS residuals $\{\hat U_t\}$, compute $\{\hat V_t\}$ recursively as*

$$\hat V_t = (1 - \hat\phi_1 L - \cdots - \hat\phi_p L^p)\hat U_t, \qquad t = p+1, \ldots, n,$$

starting from $\hat V_i = \hat U_i$, $i = 1, \ldots, p$.

(2) *Compute the empirical distribution function* $\hat{F}$ *of* $\hat{V}_t$.
(3) *Draw a sample* $\{\hat{V}_t^*\}$ *of size* $n - \max(p, q)$ *from* $\hat{F}$.
(4) *Construct pseudo data* $\{(X_t, Y_t^*)\}$ *through the recursion*

$$Y_t^* = \hat{\beta} X_t + \hat{\phi}_1 (Y_{t-1}^* - \hat{\beta} X_{t-1}) + \cdots + \hat{\phi}_p (Y_{t-q}^* - \hat{\beta} X_{t-p}) + \hat{V}_t^*, \qquad t = p+1, \ldots, n,$$

starting from $Y_i^* = Y_i$, $i = 1, \ldots, p$.
(5) *Compute the OLS estimate* $\hat{\beta}^*$ *for the pseudo data* $\{(X_t, Y_t^*)\}$.
(6) *Repeat steps* (2)–(5) *a sufficiently large number* B *of times, obtaining bootstrap replications* $\hat{\beta}^{*1}, \ldots, \hat{\beta}^{*B}$.
(7) *Use the empirical distribution of* $\hat{\beta}^{*1}, \ldots, \hat{\beta}^{*B}$ *to estimate any aspect of the sampling distribution of* $\hat{\beta}$.

Observe that Algorithm 7.2 and formula (7.11) rely crucially on the assumption that both the nature and the order of the stochastic process followed by the regression errors are known, and on the availability of estimates of the parameters of the process obtained from the OLS residuals.

7.6 NON-NORMALITY

This section discusses two issues. The first is the efficiency of the OLS estimator when the data are not Gaussian. The second is the existence of data transformations that help make the assumptions of the Gaussian linear model more plausible given the data at hand.

7.6.1 *EFFICIENCY OF THE OLS ESTIMATOR*

When the conditional distribution of Y belongs to a known parametric model, the ML method may be applied to obtain parameter estimates with good sampling properties in large samples.

Specifically, let the density of Y given $X = x$ be of the form

$$f(y \mid x; \theta) = \frac{1}{\sigma} f\left(\frac{y - \beta^\top x}{\sigma}\right), \qquad \theta = (\beta, \sigma^2).$$

The sample log-likelihood for a random sample $(X_1, Y_1), \ldots, (X_n, Y_n)$ from the distribution of (X, Y) is

$$L(\theta) = c - \frac{n}{2} \ln \sigma^2 + \sum_{i=1}^n \ln f\left(\frac{Y_i - \beta^\top X_i}{\sigma}\right),$$

where c is an arbitrary constant. If the parametric model is smooth, the likelihood equations are

$$0 = \frac{\partial L}{\partial \beta} = \frac{1}{\sigma} \sum_{i=1}^n s\left(\frac{Y_i - \beta^\top X_i}{\sigma}\right) X_i,$$

$$0 = \frac{\partial L}{\partial \sigma^2} = \frac{1}{2\sigma^2} \sum_{i=1}^n \left[s\left(\frac{Y_i - \beta^\top X_i}{\sigma}\right) \frac{Y_i - \beta^\top X_i}{\sigma} - 1 \right],$$

where $s(u) = -f'(u)/f(u)$. A local ML estimate of θ is a root of the likelihood equations corresponding to a local maximum of L.

If $\hat\beta$ and $\hat\sigma^2$ denote the local ML estimates of β and σ^2 and $\hat V_i = (Y_i - \hat\beta^\top X_i)/\hat\sigma$ denotes the ith standardized residual, then the likelihood equations are equivalent to the pair of conditions

$$0 = n^{-1}\sum_{i=1}^{n} s(\hat V_i)\, X_i, \qquad 1 = n^{-1}\sum_{i=1}^{n} s(\hat V_i)\, \hat V_i,$$

that is, $s(\hat V_i)$ and X_i must be orthogonal, implying that $s(\hat V_i)$ must have zero mean if the model contains an intercept, whereas $s(\hat V_i)$ and $\hat V_i$ must have unit covariance. In the Gaussian case, $s(u) = u$ and one obtains the results presented in Section 6.4. In general, however, the function $s(u)$ is nonlinear, which implies that the likelihood equations must be solved by numerical methods.

When the model for the data is not Gaussian, the OLS estimator remains BLU for β, but it is generally less efficient, at least in large samples, than the ML estimator based on the exact knowledge of the shape of the density f. Such efficiency loss depends, in turn, on how far the likelihood score $s(u)$ is from being linear.

Example 7.16 The likelihood score of the t-distribution with m degrees of freedom is

$$s_m(u) = \left(1 + \frac{1}{m}\right)\frac{u}{1 + m^{-1}u^2}, \qquad m = 1, 2, \ldots$$

(Figure 48). This may also be written as $s_m(u) = w_m(u)\, s_\infty(u)$, where $s_\infty(u) = u$ is the Gaussian score and

$$w_m(u) = \left(1 + \frac{1}{m}\right)\frac{m}{m + u^2}$$

is a decreasing function of u for m fixed. Notice that $w_m(u) \to 1$ as $m \to \infty$. Unlike the Gaussian score, the score of a t-distribution is not monotonic: it is strictly increasing over the interval $[-m, m]$, strictly decreasing outside this interval, and tends to zero as $u \to \pm\infty$. Score functions of this type are known as *redescending*.

The main advantage of regression models based on the t-distribution is their robustness to outliers among the Y_i. This is particularly important when the data exhibit thicker tails than would be the case under the Gaussian model. □

7.6.2 *TRANSFORMATIONS OF THE RESPONSE VARIABLE*

The classical linear model assumes that the CMF is linear in $\mathbf{X}$ and there is no functional relationship between the CMF and the CVF. This set of assumptions makes this model inappropriate in many situations. It is sometimes possible, however, to transform the data in order to restore the assumptions of the classical linear model. An example is the linear transformation introduced in Section 7.4.1. More generally, one may seek data transformations (not necessarily linear) in order to attain the following objectives: (i) linearity of the CMF; (ii) homoskedasticity; (iii) symmetry or even Gaussianity of the regression errors.

Figure 48 Score functions of t-distributions with $m = 1, 2, 3, 4$ degrees of freedom.

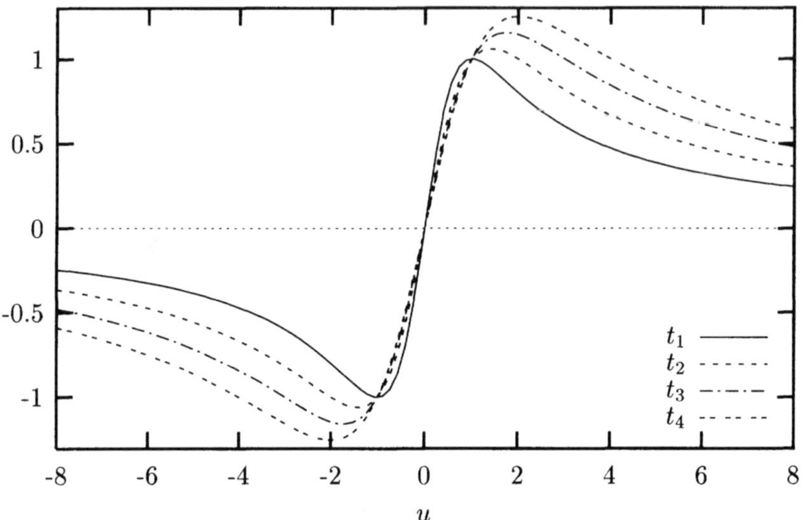

Example 7.17 Let the data $[\mathbf{X}, \mathbf{Y}]$ be a sample from the joint distribution of (X, Y). If $Y = \alpha X^{\beta} U$, where $\mathrm{E}(U \mid X) = 1$ and $\mathrm{Var}(U \mid X) = \sigma^2$, then the assumptions of the classical linear model are violated, for $\mu(x) = \alpha x^{\beta}$ and $\sigma^2(x) = \sigma^2 \mu(x)^2$. If X and Y are positive random variables, letting $X^* = \ln X$ and $Y^* = \ln Y$ gives

$$Y^* = \gamma + \beta X^* + U^*,$$

where $\gamma = \ln \alpha + \mathrm{E} \ln U$ and $U^* = \ln U - \mathrm{E} \ln U$. The transformed model satisfies all the assumptions of the classical linear model. Further, if the distribution of Y is log-normal, then the distribution of Y^* is Gaussian. □

The above example is rather special. When no transformation can be found that attains all three objectives, it is typically the last one (symmetry or Gaussianity of the regression errors) which ends up being sacrificed.

Example 7.18 Let Y be a continuous non-negative random variable that represents the duration of stay in a given state. A model based on the exponential distribution may specify the conditional hazard function of Y given $X = x$ as

$$h(y \mid x; \beta) = \exp(\beta^\top x).$$

A model based on the Weibull distribution may instead specify the conditional hazard function of Y as

$$h(y \mid x; \theta) = \alpha y^{\alpha - 1} \exp(\beta^\top x), \qquad \theta = (\alpha, \beta).$$

The exponential and Weibull models are special cases of the *proportional hazard model*

$$h(y \mid x; \theta) = h_0(y; \alpha) \exp(\beta^\top x), \qquad \theta = (\alpha, \beta), \tag{7.12}$$

where $h_0(y;\alpha)$ is a non-negative function called the ***baseline hazard function.*** Notice that the vector β does not include an intercept, which is instead absorbed into $h_0(y;\alpha)$. The baseline hazard is just the hazard for the case when $x = 0$. One has $h_0(y;\alpha) = 1$ for the exponential model and $h_0(y;\alpha) = \alpha y^{\alpha-1}$ for the Weibull model.

The proportional hazard model separates the effect of the duration from that of the covariates. The duration y only affects the baseline hazard, whereas the role of the covariates is to shift the hazard proportionally, leaving its basic shape unchanged. In fact, if x and x' are distinct values of X, then the ratio

$$\ln \frac{h(y \,|\, x;\theta)}{h(y \,|\, x';\theta)} = \beta^\top (x - x')$$

does not depend on y. On the other hand, if y and y' are distinct values of Y, then the ratio

$$\ln \frac{h(y \,|\, x;\theta)}{h(y' \,|\, x;\theta)} = \ln \frac{h_0(y;\alpha)}{h_0(y';\alpha)}$$

does not depend on x.

An important consequence of the proportional hazard model is that the integrated hazard takes the simple form

$$H(y \,|\, x;\theta) = \int_0^y h(u \,|\, x;\theta)\, du = \exp(\beta^\top x)\, H_0(y;\alpha),$$

where $H_0(y;\alpha) = \int_0^y h(u;\alpha)\, du$ is the integrated baseline hazard. Hence

$$\ln H_0(y;\alpha) = -\beta^\top x + \ln H(y \,|\, x;\theta).$$

Recall from Section 1.1.4 that the integrated hazard of a continuous non-negative random variable has a unit exponential distribution and therefore its logarithm has a standard Gumbel (Type 1 extreme value) distribution with mean and variance approximately equal to $-.577$ and 1.645 respectively. If $(X_1, Y_1), \ldots, (X_n, Y_n)$ is a sample from the joint distribution of (X, Y), then the proportional hazard model (7.12) leads to the linear model

$$\ln H_0(Y_i;\alpha) = -\beta^\top X_i + U_i, \qquad i = 1, \ldots, n, \tag{7.13}$$

where $U_i = \ln H(Y_i \,|\, X_i;\theta)$ has a standard Gumbel distribution independently of X_i. This result represents the basis for LS estimation of $\theta = (\alpha, \beta)$. In fact, for the exponential model $H_0(y;\alpha) = y$ and so (7.13) becomes

$$\ln Y_i = -\beta^\top X_i + U_i, \qquad i = 1, \ldots, n.$$

For the Weibull model $H_0(y;\alpha) = y^\alpha$ and so (7.13) becomes

$$\ln Y_i = -(\beta/\alpha)^\top X_i + V_i, \qquad i = 1, \ldots, n,$$

where V_i is distributed independently of X_i with mean and variance approximately equal to $-.577/\alpha$ and $1.645/\alpha^2$ respectively. If the mean of V_i is absorbed into the regression intercept, then an estimate of the parameter α is directly available from the OLS estimate of scale. □

In the previous example, knowledge of the conditional distribution of Y given X was used to transform the response variable so as to restore the assumptions of the classical linear model.

Suppose now that the available information is more limited. Specifically, suppose that it is only known that the relationship between the conditional mean $\mu(x)$ and the conditional standard deviation $\sigma(x)$ is of the form

$$\sigma(x) = \sigma\, \mu(x)^{1-\lambda}, \qquad \sigma > 0, \qquad 0 \le \lambda \le 1. \tag{7.14}$$

If $\lambda = 1$ then $\sigma^2(x) = \sigma^2$, as in the classical linear model; if $\lambda = 1/2$ then $\sigma^2(x) = \sigma^2 \mu(x)$, that is, the coefficient of variation $\sigma^2(x)/\mu(x)$ is constant; whereas if $\lambda = 0$ then $\sigma^2(x) = \sigma^2 \mu(x)^2$. Box and Cox (1964) considered the problem of finding a differentiable transformation g such that the conditional variance of $g(Y)$ given $X = x$ is constant. By the δ-method we get

$$\mathrm{Var}[g(Y) \,|\, X = x] = [g'(\mu(x))]^2 \sigma^2(x).$$

If $\sigma(x)$ is of the form (7.14), then

$$\mathrm{Var}[g(Y) \,|\, X = x] = \sigma^2 \left[g'(\mu(x))\, \mu(x)^{1-\lambda}\right]^2.$$

Hence, $\mathrm{Var}[g(Y) \,|\, X = x]$ is independent of x only if the function g satisfies the relation

$$g'(u) = cu^{\lambda - 1},$$

where c is an arbitrary constant. The latter is a first-order differential equation with the solution

$$g(u) = \begin{cases} u^\lambda/\lambda + c', & \text{if } 0 < \lambda \le 1, \\ \ln u + c', & \text{if } \lambda = 0, \end{cases}$$

where c' is another arbitrary constant. This result justifies the class of transformation of Y of the form

$$Y^{(\lambda)} = \begin{cases} (Y^\lambda - 1)/\lambda, & \text{if } 0 < \lambda \le 1, \\ \ln Y, & \text{if } \lambda = 0, \end{cases}$$

called the family of *Box–Cox transformations*. Thus, in the case of the Poisson model ($\lambda = 1/2$), the Box–Cox transformation of Y is the square-root transformation, whereas in the case of the exponential model ($\lambda = 0$) it is the logarithmic transformation, in agreement with the results in Example 7.18.

BIBLIOGRAPHIC NOTES

The model with polynomial distributed lags goes back to Almon (1965). The ridge-regression estimator was introduced by Hoerl and Kennard (1970a,b).

For a nice discussion of representative agent models and aggregation over a large number of heterogeneous individuals see Stoker (1993) and Hildenbrand (1998).

The infinitesimal jackknife is discussed in Efron and Tibshirani (1993). The formula for the infinitesimal jackknife estimate of the sampling variance of the OLS estimator goes back at least to Eicker (1967) and has been popularized in econometrics by White (1980a). An extension of formula (7.11) to the case when the regression errors follow a general stationary process has been proposed by Newey and West (1987). Künsch (1989) suggested an alternative approach based on a generalization of the jackknife and the nonparametric bootstrap to the case of arbitrary stationary processes. For a survey of bootstrap methods for time series models see Li and Maddala (1996).

For a generalization of the Prais–Winsten transformation to regression models with stationary AR(p) errors see Fuller (1976), Section 9.7. Computational ease helps explain the popularity of regression models with AR errors. In fact, when the regression errors are MA or stationary ARMA, the GLS transformation requires using nonlinear procedures in order to obtain estimates of the parameters of the regression error process (see Zinde-Walsh & Galbraith 1991).

Magnus (1978) discusses alternatives to the feasible GLS estimator based on the method of ML.

For a discussion of linear models based on the t-distribution see Lange, Little and Taylor (1989). Hjort (1994) discusses the advantages of using the Gaussian model when the true model is t but its number of degrees of freedom m is sufficiently large ($m \geq 1.458\sqrt{n}$).

The book by Carroll and Ruppert (1988) provides an extensive discussion of how weighting and transformations may reduce the impact of heteroskedasticity and non-normality on the OLS estimates.

For a discussion of the proportional hazard model see Cox and Oakes (1984). In addition to the family of transformations that bears their names, Box and Cox (1964) have proposed a ML estimator of (β, λ) for the case when $Y^{(\lambda)} \sim \mathcal{N}(X^\top \beta, \sigma^2)$.

PROBLEMS

7.1 Show that the posterior mean $\hat\beta$ in Example 7.3 also solves the penalized LS problem

$$\min_{\beta \in \Re^k} \|\mathbf{Y} - \mathbf{X}\beta\|^2 + \gamma \|R\beta\|^2,$$

for given $\gamma \geq 0$. Interpret this result.

7.2 Show that if A is a singular matrix, then there exists a number $\gamma^* > 0$ such that $A + \gamma I$ is a p.d. matrix for all $\gamma > \gamma^*$.

7.3 Given the classical linear model, show that a ridge-regression estimator $\tilde\beta_\gamma$ satisfies

$$\begin{aligned} \mathrm{E}\,\tilde\beta_\gamma &= (\mathbf{X}^\top\mathbf{X} + \gamma I_k)^{-1}\mathbf{X}^\top\mathbf{X}\beta, \\ \mathrm{Var}\,\tilde\beta_\gamma &= \sigma^2\,(\mathbf{X}^\top\mathbf{X} + \gamma I_k)^{-1}\mathbf{X}^\top\mathbf{X}(\mathbf{X}^\top\mathbf{X} + \gamma I_k)^{-1}. \end{aligned}$$

7.4 Given the classical linear model, show that the bias of a ridge-regression estimator $\tilde\beta_\gamma$ is increasing in γ, whereas its sampling variance is decreasing. Hence show that there exists a $\gamma_0 > 0$ such that $\tilde\beta_\gamma$ has smaller MSE than the OLS estimator.

7.5 Prove Theorem 7.2.

7.6 Suppose that the model adopted by the investigator assumes that $\mathrm{E}\,\mathbf{Y} = \mathbf{X}\beta + \mathbf{W}\gamma$ when in fact $\mathrm{E}\,\mathbf{Y} = \mathbf{X}\beta$ and $\mathrm{Var}\,\mathbf{Y} = \sigma^2 I_n$. Show that the OLS estimator $\tilde\beta$ in a regression of $\mathbf{Y}$ on $\mathbf{X}$ and $\mathbf{W}$ is unbiased for β, compute its sampling variance and show that it exceeds that of the efficient estimator $\hat\beta = (\mathbf{X}^\top\mathbf{X})^{-1}\mathbf{X}^\top\mathbf{Y}$ by a n.n.d. matrix.

7.7 A random sample of n households gives information about the number of cars owned N_i and the wealth W_i of each household. Given the assumption that

$$\ln N_i \sim \mathcal{N}(\alpha + \beta \ln W_i, \sigma^2), \qquad i = 1, \ldots, n,$$

an investigator estimates α and β by OLS using the subset of the data for which $N_i > 0$. Comment on the appropriateness of this procedure.

7.8 Suppose that the conditional distribution of Y given X is $\mathcal{N}(X^\top\beta, \sigma^2)$ and that (X, Y) may be observed only if $a \leq Y \leq b$. Given a sample $\{(X_i, Y_i)\}$ of size n from the joint distribution of (X, Y), derive the conditional mean of Y_i given $X_i = x$ and use this result to compute the bias of the OLS estimator in the regression of Y_i on X_i.

7.9 Let X_1 and X_2 be random variables with zero mean and suppose that the conditional distribution of Y given X_1 and X_2 is $\mathcal{N}(X_1\beta_1 + X_2\beta_2, \sigma^2)$. Consider a sampling scheme where X_2 is observable only for a fraction p of the sample. Compare the statistical properties of the following approaches with the problem of missing data.

(i) Estimate $\beta = (\beta_1, \beta_2)$ by OLS using only the complete data.
(ii) Assign to missing data the value $\hat{X}_{i2} = \hat{\alpha} X_{i1}$, where $\hat{\alpha}$ is the OLS coefficient in the regression of X_2 on X_1.

7.10 Consider the linear model with AR(1) errors introduced in Example 3.7. Given quadratic loss, compute the best unconditional predictor of Y_t and the best linear predictor given $Y_{t-1}, Y_{t-2}, \ldots$. Compare the properties of the prediction error in the two cases.

7.11 Compute the sampling variance of the OLS estimator of regression in a linear model with MA(q) errors.

7.12 Generalize Algorithm 7.2 to the case of a linear model with ARMA(p, q) errors.

7.13 (Goldberger 1962) Let $\mathrm{E}\,\mathbf{Y} = \mathbf{X}\beta$ and $\mathrm{Var}\,\mathbf{Y} = \Sigma$, a known p.d. matrix. Show that the BLU predictor of a new set $\mathbf{Y}^*$ of observations from the same model is given by $\hat{\mathbf{Y}}^* = \mathbf{X}^*\tilde{\beta} + \Psi\Sigma^{-1}(\mathbf{Y} - \mathbf{X}\tilde{\beta})$, where $\mathbf{X}^*$ is the design matrix associated with $\mathbf{Y}^*$, $\tilde{\beta}$ is the GLS estimator of β based on $[\mathbf{X}, \mathbf{Y}]$ and $\Psi = \mathrm{Cov}(\mathbf{Y}^*, \mathbf{Y})$, a supposedly known matrix. Derive necessary and sufficient conditions under which $\hat{\mathbf{Y}}^* = \mathbf{X}^*\tilde{\beta}$.

7.14 Consider the Gaussian model $\mathbf{Y} \sim \mathcal{N}_n(\mathbf{X}\beta, \Omega)$, where $\mathbf{X}$ is an $n \times k$ matrix of rank k and Ω is a nonsingular $n \times n$ matrix. Show that, if Ω is known, then the ML estimator of β coincides with the GLS estimator.

7.15 Compute Ω^{-1} for a linear model with MA(1) errors and use this result to derive the GLS estimator of the regression parameter.

7.16 Compute Ω and Ω^{-1} for a linear model with ARMA(1,1) errors and use this result to derive the GLS estimator of the regression parameter.

7.17 (Hjort 1994) Compute the Fisher information for a linear regression model with i.i.d. errors following a t-distribution with m degrees of freedom, separately for the case when m is known and the case when m is unknown and becomes one of the model parameters.

7.18 Show that the log-logistic hazard model in Problem 1.9 cannot be written as a proportional hazard model.

7.19 Show that $\lim_{\lambda \to 0}(z^\lambda - 1)/\lambda = \ln z$ (*Hint:* Use de L'Hopital rule).

8

Diagnostics Based on the OLS Estimates

A statistical analysis may be viewed as an iterative process consisting of three stages. The first one is *model specification*. This stage includes the formulation of the statistical problem, the choice of the response variable and the covariates, appropriate data transformations, and the choice of a functional form for the relationship between the response variable and the covariates. The second stage is estimation of the model using the data, or *model fitting*. The third stage is critical assessment of the model assumptions given the data and the fit, or *model criticism*. Model criticism may lead to modifications of the initial assumptions and to a new iteration of the process.

Important aspects of the criticism stage of the modelling cycle are:

- diagnostics that try to detect aspects of the data that are not adequately captured by the model;
- diagnostics that try to detect aspects of the fit that are too sensitive to a specific data configuration;
- examination of the structural part of the model in order to evaluate the effects of adding, dropping or modifying some of its elements;
- a study of the importance of particular covariates in "explaining" the response variable.

Residuals, defined as the difference between the observed data and their fitted values, contain important information on the model adequacy. In particular, the presence of systematic patterns in the residuals is an indication that the model may not be appropriate. Residual analysis may also help in locating *outliers*, that is, data points that appear surprising or discrepant to the investigator, and *influential observations*, that is, subsets of the data that appear to have a disproportionate influence on the fit.

Residual analysis includes both exploratory procedures (mainly graphical) to display general features of the residuals, and formal tests to detect specific departures from the underlying assumptions. The two approaches are complementary and both play a useful role. In this chapter we focus on exploratory procedures. Formal diagnostic tests are discussed in the following chapters.

Figure 49 Standard residual plot for the data in Figure 45: the x- and y-axis show, respectively, the fitted values $\hat{Y}_i$ and the residuals $\hat{U}_i$ of an OLS regression of Y_i on X_i.

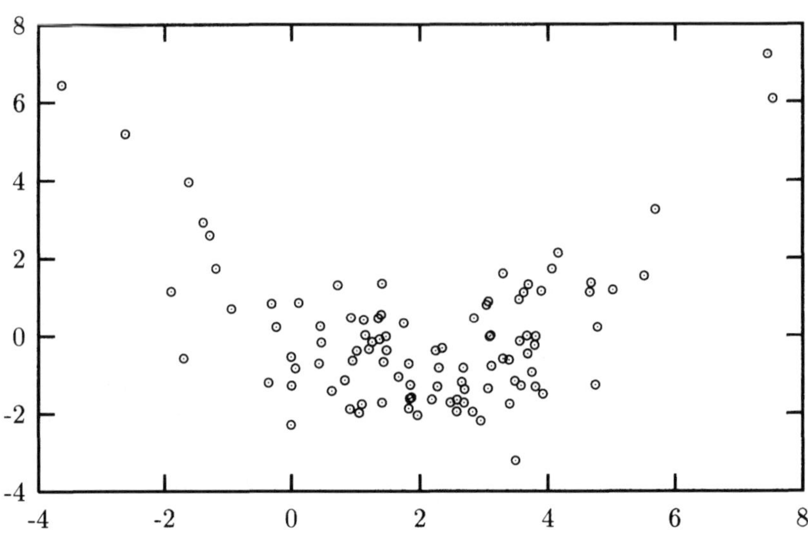

8.1 OLS RESIDUALS

Under the classical linear model, the vector $\mathbf{U} = \mathbf{Y} - \mathbf{X}\beta$ of regression errors has mean zero and variance equal to $\sigma^2 I_n$, that is, regression errors are homoskedastic and uncorrelated.

Regression errors are usually unobservable. What is observable are instead the OLS residuals $\hat{U}_i = Y_i - \hat{Y}_i$, where the $\hat{Y}_i$ are the OLS fitted values. The fundamental property of the vector $\hat{\mathbf{U}}$ of OLS residuals is its orthogonality to the columns of the design matrix $\mathbf{X}$, that is, $\mathbf{X}^\top \hat{\mathbf{U}} = 0$. Such a property is a direct consequence of the OLS normal equations. In particular, if the regression includes an intercept, then $\iota_n^\top \hat{\mathbf{U}} = \sum_i \hat{U}_i = 0$ and so the OLS residuals have zero mean and are uncorrelated with both the covariates and the fitted values.

A *standard residual plot* (Figure 49) is a scatterplot of the OLS residuals against the fitted values of Y_i. Although the residuals and the fitted values are uncorrelated by construction if the regression includes an intercept, such a plot tends to reveal the presence of systematic patterns arising from nonlinearity of the regression function or heteroskedasticity. Instead of the OLS fitted values one may also use other functions of X_i that are orthogonal to the residuals or approximately so. In time series analysis, residuals may also be plotted against time, as in Figure 50.

How closely do the statistical properties of the OLS residuals mimic those of the unobservable regression errors? If $\mathbf{X}^\top \mathbf{X}$ is a nonsingular matrix, then $\hat{\mathbf{U}} = M\mathbf{Y} = M\mathbf{U}$, where $M = I_n - \mathbf{X}(\mathbf{X}^\top \mathbf{X})^{-1}\mathbf{X}^\top$ is a symmetric idempotent matrix such that $M\mathbf{X} = 0$. Because M is a singular matrix, the OLS residual vector $\hat{\mathbf{U}}$ is a singular linear transformation of $\mathbf{U}$ and therefore has a singular distribution. Under the classical

Figure 50 Time series plot of the OLS residuals in a regression of Y_t on X_t. The data consist of $T = 100$ observations from the process $Y_t = 1 + 2X_t + V_t - .8V_{t-1}$, where $\{X_t\}$ and $\{V_t\}$ are independent Gaussian white noises.

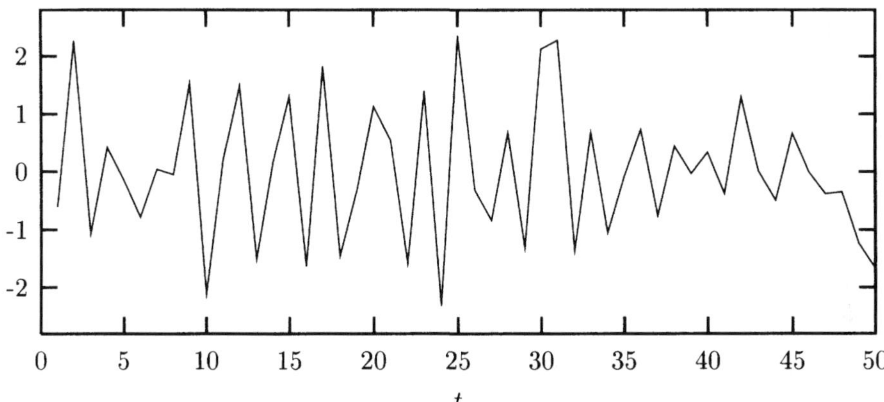

linear model, the first and second moments of the sampling distribution of $\hat{\mathbf{U}}$ are

$$\mathrm{E}\,\hat{\mathbf{U}} = M\mathbf{X}\beta = 0, \qquad \mathrm{Var}\,\hat{\mathbf{U}} = M(\sigma^2 I_n)M = \sigma^2 M.$$

Hence

$$\mathrm{Cov}(\hat{U}_i, \hat{U}_j) = \begin{cases} \sigma^2\,(1 - h_{ii}), & \text{if } j = i, \\ -\sigma^2\, h_{ij}, & \text{otherwise}, \end{cases}$$

where $h_{ij} = X_i^\top(\mathbf{X}^\top\mathbf{X})^{-1}X_j$ denotes the ijth element of the projection matrix $H = \mathbf{X}(\mathbf{X}^\top\mathbf{X})^{-1}\mathbf{X}^\top$. Thus, the OLS residuals have mean zero but are heteroskedastic and autocorrelated even when the regression errors are not. This feature complicates the task of examining the residuals to detect failures of the model assumptions. In fact, the behavior of the OLS residuals mirrors that of the regression errors if and only if $M \approx I_n$.

Theorem 8.1 $M \to I_n$ *if and only if* $\max_i\{h_{ii}\} \to 0$.

Proof. Because $M = I_n - H$, we have that $M \to I_n$ if and only if all elements h_{ij} of the matrix H tend to zero. From Section 6.2.3, the following relationship holds

$$h_{ii} = \sum_j h_{ij}^2, \qquad i = 1, \ldots, n.$$

Hence $\sum_j h_{ij}^2 \to 0$ if and only if $h_{ii} \to 0$. Since $h_{ij}^2 \geq 0$, we have that $\sum_j h_{ij}^2 \to 0$ if and only if $h_{ij} \to 0$ for all j. □

From Section 6.2.7, h_{ii} is a measure of the leverage effect of the ith case on the OLS estimate. By Theorem 8.1, $\hat{\mathbf{U}}$ provides a useful approximation to $\mathbf{U}$ if and only if all these leverage measures are small. In the presence of high leverage cases, the OLS residuals may give a highly distorted picture of the properties of the regression errors.

Figure 51 Scatterplot of $\hat{U}_t$ against $\hat{U}_{t-1}$ for the data of Figure 50.

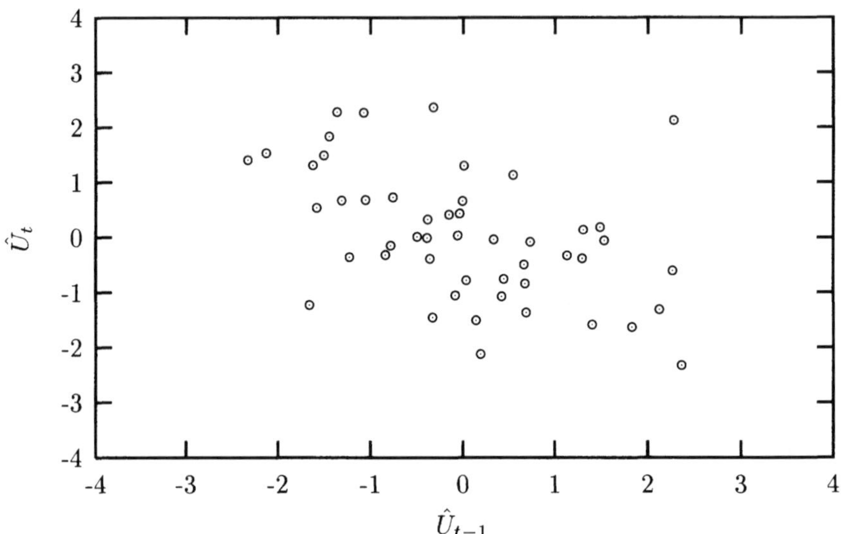

Example 8.1 Because $M = I_n - H$, we have

$$\hat{U}_i = U_i - \sum_{j=1}^{n} h_{ij}U_j = (1 - h_{ii})U_i - \sum_{j \neq i} h_{ij}U_j, \qquad i = 1, \ldots, n. \tag{8.1}$$

If $h_{ii} = 1$ for some i, then $h_{ij} = 0$ for all $j \neq i$ and so $\hat{U}_i = 0$, that is, the ith case lies exactly on the OLS hyperplane despite the fact that the ith regression error may be arbitrarily large. This implies that it may be dangerous to rely exclusively on the OLS residuals for outlier detection. □

Now consider the behavior of the OLS residuals when the assumptions of the classical linear model are violated. We first look to the case when $\mathrm{E}\,\mathbf{Y} = \mathbf{X}\beta$ but the observations on the response variable are heteroskedastic or autocorrelated, that is, $\mathrm{Var}\,\mathbf{Y} = \sigma^2\,\Omega$, where $\Omega \neq I_n$. In this case $\mathrm{E}\,\hat{\mathbf{U}} = 0$ and $\mathrm{Var}\,\hat{\mathbf{U}} = \sigma^2\,M\Omega M$. If $\max_i \{h_{ii}\} \approx 0$, then the OLS residuals have a pattern of heteroskedasticity or autocorrelation which mimics that of the regression errors.

In particular, to detect the presence of autocorrelation in the regression errors, residuals may be plotted against their lagged values. If the regression errors follow an MA(q) process, then a scatterplot of $\hat{U}_t$ against $\hat{U}_{t-h}$, with $h > q$, should reveal no pattern. The example of an MA(1) error process is presented in Figures 51 and 52.

Now consider the case when the regression function is misspecified. Thus, suppose that the true regression function is

$$\mathrm{E}\,\mathbf{Y} = \mathbf{X}\beta + \mathbf{W}\gamma, \qquad \mathrm{Var}\,\mathbf{Y} = \sigma^2 I_n, \tag{8.2}$$

where $\mathbf{W}$ is a nonstochastic $n \times q$ matrix of full column rank and $\gamma \neq 0$. This formulation is general enough to include both omitted variables and misspecification

Figure 52 Scatterplot of $\hat{U}_t$ against $\hat{U}_{t-2}$ for the data of Figure 50.

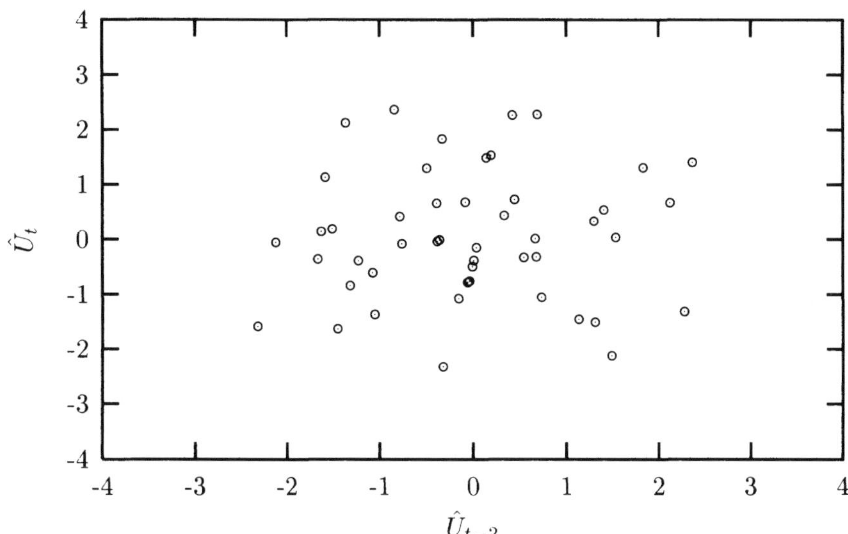

of the shape of the regression function (for example, **W** may contain powers of the variables in **X**). Model (8.2) may also be written as

$$\mathbf{Y} = \mathbf{X}\beta + \mathbf{U},$$

where the regression error vector $\mathbf{U} = \mathbf{Y} - \mathbf{X}\beta$ has mean $\mathrm{E}\,\mathbf{U} = \mathbf{W}\gamma$ and variance $\mathrm{Var}\,\mathbf{U} = \sigma^2 I_n$. Further

$$\mathrm{E}\,U_i^2 = \mathrm{Var}\,U_i + (\mathrm{E}\,U_i)^2 = \sigma^2 + (\gamma^\top W_i)^2, \qquad i = 1, \ldots, n,$$

where $W_i^\top$ is the ith row of **W**. This formula shows that the first moments and the noncentral second moments of the regression errors are no longer constant but depend on the covariates in **W**, their squares and their cross-products.

The OLS residual vector in the regression of **Y** on **X** is

$$\hat{\mathbf{U}} = M\mathbf{Y} = M(\mathbf{X}\beta + \mathbf{W}\gamma + \mathbf{U}) = M\mathbf{W}\gamma + M\mathbf{U},$$

where we used the fact that $M\mathbf{X} = 0$, and its first two moments are

$$\mathrm{E}\,\hat{\mathbf{U}} = M\mathbf{W}\gamma, \qquad \mathrm{Var}\,\hat{\mathbf{U}} = \sigma^2 M,$$

where $M\mathbf{W}\gamma$ is the OLS residual vector in the regression of $\mathbf{W}\gamma$ on **X**. The mean of $\hat{\mathbf{U}}$ is therefore equal to the part of the vector $\mathbf{W}\gamma$ that cannot be predicted from the knowledge of **X**. If **X** and **W** are orthogonal, then $\mathrm{E}\,\hat{\mathbf{U}} = \mathbf{W}\gamma$. Thus, the presence of a systematic relationship between $\hat{\mathbf{U}}$ and either $M\mathbf{W}$ or **W** is evidence that the regression function is misspecified.

For example, if **W** consists of a single variable, plotting the elements of $\mathrm{E}\,\hat{\mathbf{U}}$ against the elements of $M\mathbf{W}$ gives a straight line through the origin. The empirical counterpart

Figure 53 Added variable plot for the data in Figure 45: the x- and y-axes show, respectively, the OLS residuals $(M\mathbf{W})_i$ of the regression of W_i on X_i and the OLS residuals $\hat{U}_i$ of the regression of Y_i on X_i. The straight line is the OLS line in the regression of the first set of residuals on the second. Its slope is equal to the coefficient associated with W_i in the OLS regression of Y_i on X_i and W_i.

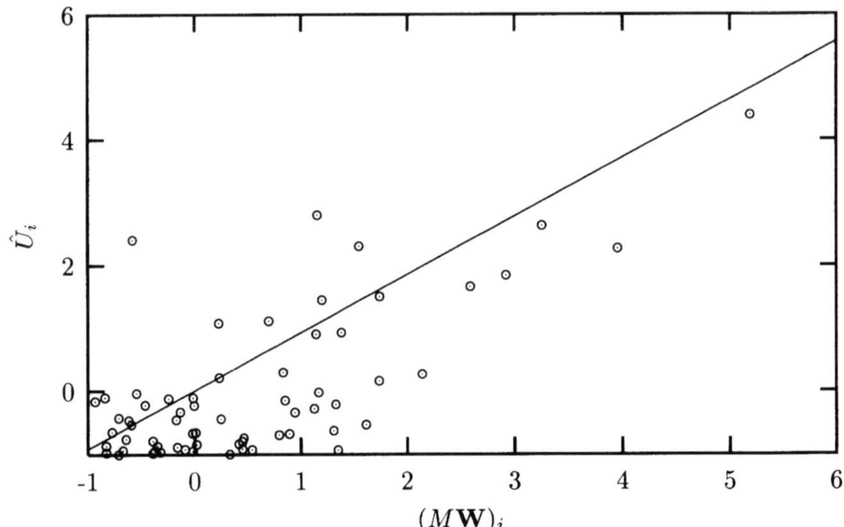

of this plot is a plot of the elements of $\hat{\mathbf{U}}$ against the elements of $M\mathbf{W}$, called an *added variable plot* (Figure 53). It is useful for studying the role of adding linearly a single variable to the model. Its general form gives an overall impression of the strength of the relationship.

If the data satisfy (8.2) we also have

$$\mathrm{E}\,\hat{U}_i^2 = \mathrm{Var}\,\hat{U}_i + (\mathrm{E}\,\hat{U}_i)^2 = (1 - h_{ii})\sigma^2 + [(1 - h_{ii})\gamma^\top W_i - \sum_{j \neq i} h_{ij}\gamma^\top W_j]^2,$$

Thus, the noncentral second moments of the OLS residuals display a pattern of dependence on the variables in $\mathbf{W}$, their squares and their cross-products. This suggests a set of scatterplots of the squared OLS residuals against the squares and the cross-products of the variables that one suspects have been omitted from the model (Figure 54).

A variety of techniques are commonly used to diagnose departures from the assumption of Gaussian errors. The basic idea is the following.

If U is a random variable with a continuous and strictly increasing distribution function F, then its $i/(n+1)$th quantile is equal to $F^{-1}(i/(n+1))$. If the regression errors $U_1, \ldots, U_n$ are a sample from the distribution of U, then the ordered value $U_{[i]}$ corresponds to the $i/(n+1)$th empirical quantile. Thus, if the regression errors were observable, plotting their ordered values against $F^{-1}(i/(n+1))$ should give approximately a 45^0 line. Such a plot is called a *quantile-quantile (Q–Q) plot* (Figure 55). In particular, if $\mathbf{U} \sim \mathcal{N}_n(0, \sigma^2 I_n)$, then the ordered values of the regression

Figure 54 Scatterplot of $\hat{U}_i^2$ and W_i^2 for the data in Figure 45.

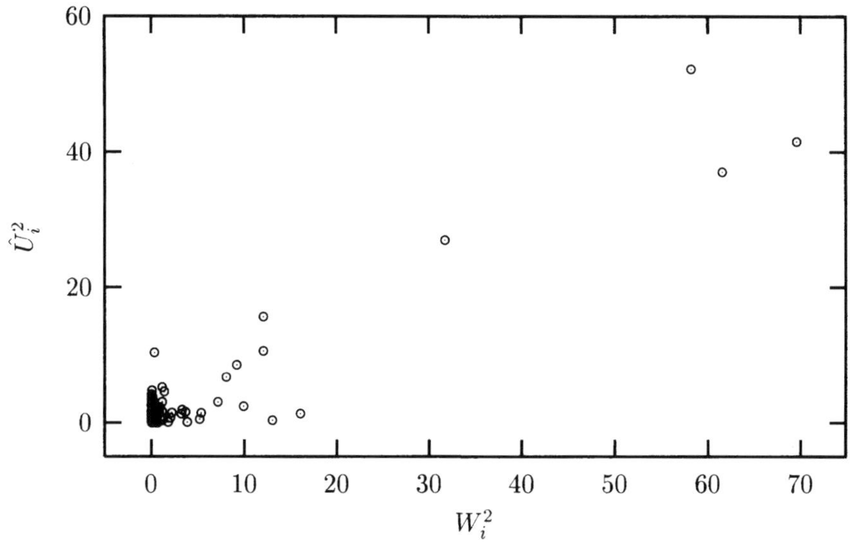

errors must satisfy

$$\frac{U_{[i]}}{\sigma} = \Phi^{-1}\left(\frac{i}{n+1}\right), \qquad i = 1, \ldots, n,$$

where Φ denotes the $\mathcal{N}(0,1)$ distribution function. Inverting this relationship gives

$$\Phi\left(\frac{U_{[i]}}{\sigma}\right) = \frac{i}{n+1}, \qquad i = 1, \ldots, n.$$

A scatterplot of $\Phi(U_{[i]}/\sigma)$ against $i/(n+1)$ is called a *normal probability plot* (Figure 56).

In practice, regression errors are unobservable and Q–Q or normal probability plots are based on the OLS residuals. This makes their interpretation somewhat complicated, especially in small samples, because OLS residuals tend to behave more like a normal sample than the true regression errors. This is because the OLS residuals are a weighted sum of the regression errors, as shown by (8.1). Therefore, by the CLT, they tend to have a distribution that, in sufficiently large samples, is closer to Gaussian than the regression error distribution.

8.2 TRANSFORMATIONS OF THE OLS RESIDUALS

For use in diagnostic procedures, several transformations of the OLS residuals have been suggested to overcome some of the shortcomings discussed in the previous section.

Figure 55 Q–Q plot of the residuals: the x- and y-axes show, respectively, the quantiles $\Phi^{-1}(i/(n+1))$ of the $\mathcal{N}(0,1)$ distribution and the ordered normalized residuals $\hat{U}_{[i]}/s$, where s is the classical estimate of scale. The residuals are computed for a regression where the error distribution is $\mathcal{N}(0,1)$ with probability π and $\mathcal{N}(0,25)$ with probability $1-\pi$, with $\pi = 2/3$.

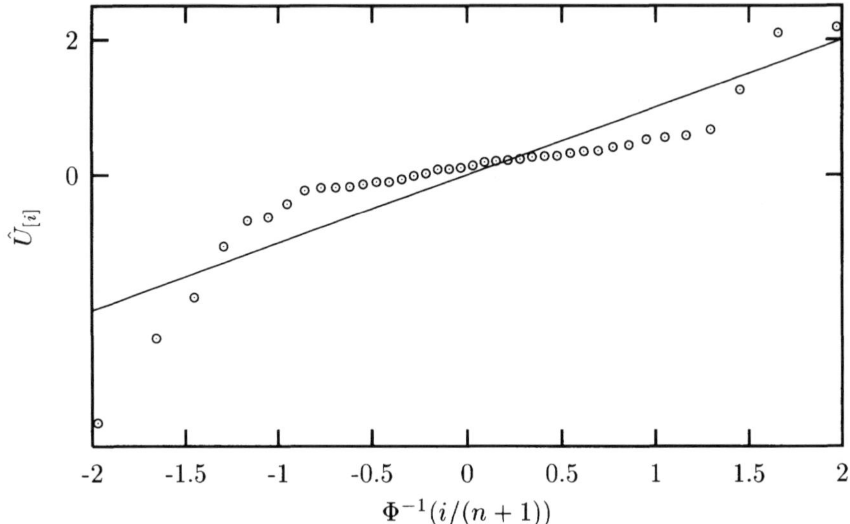

Figure 56 Normal probability plot of the residuals based on the data of the previous figure.

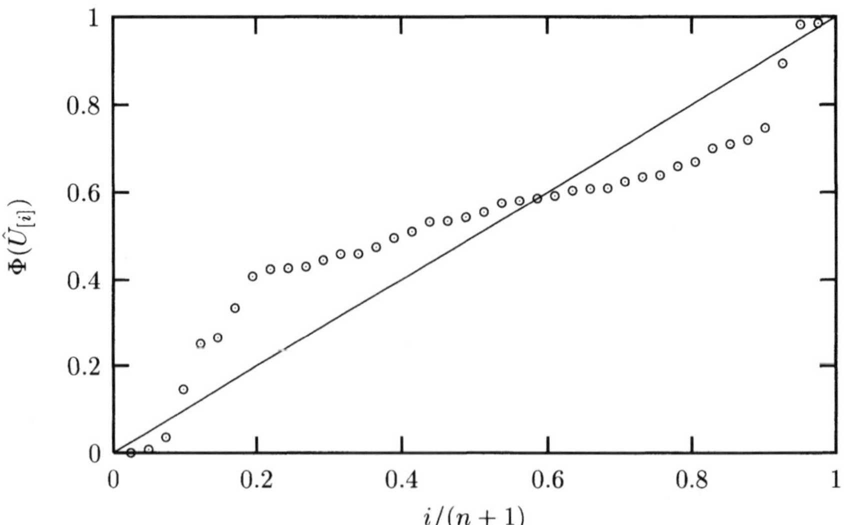

8.2.1 PREDICTED RESIDUALS

The OLS residuals are based on fitting all the data. On the contrary, the ith *predicted residual* $\hat{U}_{(i)}$ is based on fitting the ith jackknife sample, that is, the set of $n-1$ observations obtained by excluding the ith case. Thus

$$\hat{U}_{(i)} = Y_i - \hat{\beta}_{(i)}^\top X_i, \qquad i = 1, \ldots, n,$$

where $\hat{\beta}_{(i)}$ is the OLS estimate from the ith jackknife sample. From Section 6.2.7 we get

$$\hat{U}_{(i)} = Y_i - \hat{\beta}^\top X_i + \frac{\hat{U}_i X_i^\top (\mathbf{X}^\top \mathbf{X})^{-1} X_i}{1 - h_{ii}} = \frac{\hat{U}_i}{1 - h_{ii}}.$$

Because $0 \leq h_{ii} \leq 1$, we have that $\hat{U}_{(i)} \geq \hat{U}_i$. Thus, compared with the OLS residuals, the predicted residuals tend to give more emphasis to high leverage cases. The larger is the leverage effect of the ith case, the larger is the difference $\hat{U}_{(i)} - \hat{U}_i = h_{ii}/(1-h_{ii})$.

The statistical properties of the predicted residuals follow immediately from those of the OLS residuals. In particular

$$\mathrm{E}\,\hat{U}_{(i)} = 0, \qquad \mathrm{Var}\,\hat{U}_{(i)} = \frac{\sigma^2}{1 - h_{ii}}, \qquad \mathrm{Cov}(\hat{U}_{(i)}, \hat{U}_{(j)}) = -\frac{\sigma^2 \, h_{ij}}{(1 - h_{ii})(1 - h_{jj})},$$

where $j \neq i$.

8.2.2 STUDENTIZED RESIDUALS

Both the OLS and the predicted residuals are scale dependent, since their variance depends on σ^2 and h_{ii}. For many diagnostic procedures it is useful to adopt transformations of the residuals that do not depend on these quantities and are homoskedastic. Using this kind of residuals has the advantage that their pattern is not complicated by the presence of spurious heteroskedasticity. By *Studentization* we mean the division of a scale dependent statistic T by a scale estimate S, in such a way that the ratio T/S has a distribution that is free from nuisance parameters.

Internal Studentization corresponds to the case when S and T are derived from the same data and are therefore dependent. An internally Studentized version of OLS residuals is

$$\tilde{U}_i = \frac{\hat{U}_i}{s\sqrt{1 - h_{ii}}},$$

where s^2 is the OLS estimate of scale. It is easily verified that

$$\tilde{U}_i = \frac{\hat{U}_{(i)}}{s/\sqrt{1 - h_{ii}}},$$

that is, $\tilde{U}_i$ coincides with the internally Studentized version of the predicted residuals. Because $\hat{U}_i$ and s^2 are not independent, the distribution of $\tilde{U}_i$ is rather complicated. Cook and Weisberg (1982) derive the joint distribution of a subset of $m < n - k$ internally Studentized residuals under the assumption that $\mathbf{Y} \sim \mathcal{N}_n(\mathbf{X}\beta, \sigma^2 I_n)$. In particular, they show that

$$\mathrm{E}\,\tilde{U}_i = 0, \qquad \mathrm{Var}\,\tilde{U}_i = 1, \qquad \mathrm{Cov}(\tilde{U}_i, \tilde{U}_j) = -\frac{h_{ij}}{\sqrt{(1 - h_{ii})(1 - h_{jj})}},$$

for $j \neq i$. Although homoskedastic, the internally Studentized residuals are therefore autocorrelated.

A Studentization is called *external* when the statistics T and S are independent. In our case, consider the following estimator of scale

$$s_{(i)}^2 = \frac{1}{n-k-1} \sum_{j \neq i} (Y_j - \hat{\beta}_{(i)}^\top X_j)^2.$$

It may be shown (Cook & Weisberg 1982, Appendix A.2) that

$$s_{(i)}^2 = \frac{(n-k)s^2 - [\hat{U}_i^2/(1-h_{ii})]}{n-k-1} = s^2 \frac{n-k-\tilde{U}_i^2}{n-k-1}.$$

If observations are independent, then $\hat{U}_i$ and $s_{(i)}^2$ are also independent and so an externally Studentized version of the OLS residuals is

$$\bar{U}_i = \frac{\hat{U}_i}{s_{(i)}\sqrt{1-h_{ii}}} = \tilde{U}_i \left(\frac{n-k-1}{n-k-\tilde{U}_i^2} \right)^{1/2}.$$

Thus, $\bar{U}_i^2$ is a monotonic transformation of $\tilde{U}_i^2$. If $\mathbf{Y} \sim \mathcal{N}_n(\mathbf{X}\beta, \sigma^2 I_n)$, then $\bar{U}_i$ can be shown to have a t-distribution with $n-k-1$ degrees of freedom.

8.2.3 LUS AND BLUS RESIDUALS

While Studentization corrects the OLS residuals for heteroskedasticity, their autocorrelation structure is left unchanged. The objective of this section is to introduce a class of residuals that are *unbiased scalar*, that is, have mean zero and scalar variance matrix under the classical linear model. The main attraction of these kind of residuals is that they mimic more closely the behavior of the underlying regression errors.

A residual vector $\hat{\mathbf{V}}$ is said to be *linear* if $\hat{\mathbf{V}} = C\mathbf{Y}$, where the matrix C does not depend on $\mathbf{Y}$. Under the classical linear model, for the vector $\hat{\mathbf{V}}$ to be unbiased we must have

$$\mathrm{E}\,\hat{\mathbf{V}} = C\mathbf{X}\beta = 0,$$

which holds if and only if

$$C\mathbf{X} = 0. \tag{8.3}$$

Further, since $\mathrm{E}\,\hat{\mathbf{V}}\hat{\mathbf{V}}^\top = \sigma^2 CC^\top$, the vector $\hat{\mathbf{V}}$ has a scalar variance matrix if and only if $CC^\top$ is equal to the unit matrix.

Theorem 8.2 *If the classical linear model holds and $\hat{\mathbf{V}} = C\mathbf{Y}$ is a vector with zero mean and scalar variance matrix, then the matrix C cannot have more than $n-k$ rows.*

Proof. Let p be the number of rows of C. If $\mathrm{E}\,\hat{\mathbf{V}} = 0$, then (8.3) implies that the columns of C are subject to k linear constraints. Hence, the rank of C is at most $n-k$. If $\hat{\mathbf{V}}$ has a scalar variance matrix, then $\operatorname{rank} C = \operatorname{rank} CC^\top = \operatorname{rank} I_p = p$ and so $p \leq n-k$. □

The above theorem shows that, if a residual vector $\hat{\mathbf{V}}$ is to be *linear unbiased scalar (LUS)*, then it can represent at most $n-k$ elements of the regression error vector $\mathbf{U}$. Since the choice of which element to represent is essentially arbitrary, LUS residuals are not uniquely defined.

In order to choose a LUS residual vector optimally, consider the partition

$$\mathbf{U} = \begin{pmatrix} \mathbf{U}_1 \\ \mathbf{U}_2 \end{pmatrix}, \qquad \mathbf{X} = \begin{bmatrix} \mathbf{X}_1 \\ \mathbf{X}_2 \end{bmatrix}, \qquad C = [C_1, C_2],$$

where the suffix 1 corresponds to the k elements of $\mathbf{U}$ that are not represented by $\hat{\mathbf{V}}$ and the suffix 2 corresponds to the remaining $n-k$ elements. We assume that the $k \times k$ matrix $\mathbf{X}_1$ is nonsingular. Given a choice of C_2, it follows from (8.3) that

$$C_1\mathbf{X}_1 + C_2\mathbf{X}_2 = 0,$$

which implies that $C_1 = -C_2\mathbf{X}_2\mathbf{X}_1^{-1}$. A set of *best* LUS or BLUS residuals $\tilde{\mathbf{V}}$ is obtained by choosing C_2 to minimize the expected error sum-of-squares

$$\mathrm{E}(C\mathbf{Y} - \mathbf{U}_2)^\top(C\mathbf{Y} - \mathbf{U}_2).$$

Theil (1971), Section 5.2, shows that the solution to this problem is the vector

$$\tilde{\mathbf{V}} = \mathbf{U}_2 - \mathbf{X}_2\mathbf{X}_1^{-1}\left[\sum_{h=1}^{m} \frac{d_h}{1+d_h} q_h q_h^\top\right],$$

where $d_1, \ldots, d_m$, with $m \leq k$, denote the square roots of those eigenvalues of the matrix $\mathbf{X}_1(\mathbf{X}^\top\mathbf{X})^{-1}\mathbf{X}_1^\top$ that are smaller than one and $q_1, \ldots, q_m$ denote the corresponding eigenvectors. Theil also shows that $\tilde{\mathbf{V}}^\top\tilde{\mathbf{V}} = \hat{\mathbf{U}}^\top\hat{\mathbf{U}}$.

8.2.4 RECURSIVE RESIDUALS

Sometimes the data possess a natural ordering. For example, in a time series context a natural ordering is given by time. Other types of ordering are also possible. If one suspects that an important predictor has been omitted, ordering may be based on increasing values of that variable. In all these cases, a set of LUS residuals can easily be computed recursively.

For simplicity, let the data be indexed by time $t = 1, \ldots, n$. Define

$$\mathbf{Y}_t = \begin{pmatrix} Y_1 \\ \vdots \\ Y_t \end{pmatrix}, \qquad \mathbf{X}_t = \begin{bmatrix} X_1^\top \\ \vdots \\ X_t^\top \end{bmatrix}.$$

If $\mathbf{X}_t$ is of full rank k, which requires $t \geq k$, then the OLS estimate based on the first t observations is

$$\hat{\beta}_t = (\mathbf{X}_t{}^\top\mathbf{X}_t)^{-1}\mathbf{X}_t{}^\top\mathbf{Y}_t, \qquad t = k, \ldots, n.$$

Under the classical linear model, $\hat{\beta}_t$ is clearly unbiased for β with sampling variance equal to $\sigma^2(\mathbf{X}_t^\top\mathbf{X}_t)^{-1}$. In particular, if $\mathbf{X}_k$ is of full rank, then the estimate based on the first k observations is

$$\hat{\beta}_k = (\mathbf{X}_k{}^\top\mathbf{X}_k)^{-1}\mathbf{X}_k{}^\top\mathbf{Y}_k = \mathbf{X}_k^{-1}\mathbf{Y}_k,$$

with sampling variance equal to $\sigma^2 \mathbf{X}_k^{-1}$.

If $t > k$, the expressions derived in Section 6.2.7 for the empirical influence function of the OLS estimate give a pair of updating formulae relating $\hat{\beta}_t$ and $(\mathbf{X}_t^\top \mathbf{X}_t)^{-1}$ to Y_t, X_t, $\hat{\beta}_{t-1}$, and $(\mathbf{X}_{t-1}^\top \mathbf{X}_{t-1})^{-1}$. The updating formulae are

$$\hat{\beta}_t = \hat{\beta}_{t-1} + (\mathbf{X}_{t-1}^\top \mathbf{X}_{t-1})^{-1} X_t \frac{\hat{V}_t}{f_t} \tag{8.4}$$

and

$$(\mathbf{X}_t^\top \mathbf{X}_t)^{-1} = (\mathbf{X}_{t-1}^\top \mathbf{X}_{t-1})^{-1} - \frac{1}{f_t}(\mathbf{X}_{t-1}^\top \mathbf{X}_{t-1})^{-1} X_t X_t^\top (\mathbf{X}_{t-1}^\top \mathbf{X}_{t-1})^{-1}, \tag{8.5}$$

where

$$\hat{V}_t = Y_t - \hat{\beta}_{t-1}^\top X_t, \qquad f_t = 1 + X_t^\top (\mathbf{X}_{t-1}^\top \mathbf{X}_{t-1})^{-1} X_t.$$

Once $\hat{\beta}_k$ and $\mathbf{X}_k^{-1}$ have been computed from the first k observations, $\hat{\beta}_{k+1}, \ldots, \hat{\beta}_n$ and $(\mathbf{X}_{k+1}^\top \mathbf{X}_{k+1})^{-1}, \ldots, (\mathbf{X}_n^\top \mathbf{X}_n)^{-1}$ may be obtained by repeatedly applying formulae (8.4) and (8.5) without the need for further matrix inversions. The final estimate $\hat{\beta}_n$ is simply the OLS estimate based on the whole sample and $\hat{V}_n = \hat{U}_n$. The updating formulae (8.4)–(8.5) are a simple version of the *Kalman filter*.

Notice that $\hat{V}_t$ is the prediction error in predicting Y_t on the basis of X_t and the information available at time $t - 1 \geq k$. This one-step-ahead prediction error contains all that is needed to update the estimate of β on the basis of the new information contained in Y_t. The one-step-ahead prediction error also appears in the updating formula for the residual sum-of-squares

$$\mathrm{SSE}_t = \sum_{i=1}^{t} (Y_i - \hat{\beta}_t^\top X_i)^2 = \mathrm{SSE}_{t-1} + \frac{\hat{V}_t^2}{f_t}, \qquad t = k+1, \ldots, n,$$

starting from $\mathrm{SSE}_k = 0$. It follows that

$$\mathrm{SSE}_n = \sum_{t=1}^{n} \hat{U}_t^2 = \sum_{t=k+1}^{n} \frac{\hat{V}_t^2}{f_t}.$$

Writing the linear model in the form $Y_t = \beta^\top X_t + U_t$, it is easy to verify that

$$\hat{V}_t = (\beta - \hat{\beta}_{t-1})^\top X_t + U_t.$$

Thus, under the classical linear model, $\mathrm{E}\, \hat{V}_t = 0$ and $\mathrm{Var}\, \hat{V}_t = \sigma^2 f_t$. It can also be shown that

$$\mathrm{Cov}(\hat{V}_t, \hat{V}_s) = 0, \qquad t > s = k+1, \ldots, n-1.$$

Thus, the one-step-ahead prediction errors are uncorrelated. Heuristically, since $\hat{V}_t$ contains all the new information required to update the estimator, it must be uncorrelated with the previous prediction errors, as these are already incorporated in the current estimator $\hat{\beta}_{t-1}$.

The tth *recursive residual* is the Studentized prediction error

$$\tilde{V}_t = \frac{\hat{V}_t}{\sqrt{f_t}}, \qquad t = k+1, \ldots, n.$$

The recursive residuals form a set of $n-k$ LUS residuals because, under the classical linear model, they have zero mean, constant variance σ^2 and are uncorrelated.

Time series plots of the recursive residuals are frequently used to locate structural breaks in a statistical relationship.

Unlike the OLS residuals, the sum of the recursive residuals is not identically equal to zero. If the model is incorrectly specified, then there may be a tendency for a disproportionate number of recursive residuals to have the same sign. This suggests plotting against time (or against one of the covariates) their cumulative sum

$$\text{CUSUM}_t = \frac{1}{\hat{\sigma}} \sum_{i=k+1}^{t} \tilde{V}_i, \qquad t = k+1, \ldots, n,$$

where $\hat{\sigma}^2$ is the sample variance of the recursive residuals. This plot is known as the *CUSUM plot*. Omitted variables or structural breaks tend to show up in CUSUM_t moving away from the horizontal axis.

A useful complement to the CUSUM plot is the *CUSUMSQ plot*, based on the normalized cumulative sum of the squared recursive residuals

$$\text{CUSUMSQ}_t = \frac{\sum_{i=k+1}^{t} \tilde{V}_i^2}{\sum_{i=k+1}^{n} \tilde{V}_i^2}, \qquad t = k+1, \ldots, n.$$

Critical values for the CUSUM and CUSUMSQ plots are given in Brown, Durbin and Evans (1975).

8.3 INFLUENCE AND LEVERAGE

In this section we discuss techniques aimed at detecting influential observations, that is, subsets of the data that appear to have a disproportionate influence on the conclusions of a statistical analysis. Influential observations are often also outliers, that is, data points that appear surprising or discrepant to the investigator.

Outliers and influential observations may arise for several reasons: (i) local errors, such as round-off or grouping of the data; (ii) gross errors, such as incorrectly recorded data; (iii) legitimately occurring extreme observations; (iv) model misspecification, due for example to non-normality, nonlinearity of the CMF, or omitted variables.

Except for the brief remarks that follow, we leave open the question of how to *accommodate* these data, that is, how to treat them once they have been detected. If influential observations correspond to gross errors (e.g. recording or keypunch errors), then they should be corrected if possible or otherwise deleted. If the presence of influential observations reveals instead that the model is inadequate, then the way of accommodating them consists in respecifying the model. Using robust methods (Chapter 16) may be viewed as an attempt to treat the detection and the accommodation problem jointly instead of separately.

The problem of how to detect outliers is particularly important in the case of large data sets with many predictors, where simple bivariate scatterplots may not be sufficient. The sensitivity curve introduced in Section 6.2.7 is a useful tool for locating single influential data points, for it is easy to compute and has a very natural interpretation. However, because it is vector-valued, it does not give a ranking of the

Figure 57 Leverage plot for the data in Figure 45: the x- and y-axis show, respectively, the leverage measures $h_{ii}/(1-h_{ii})$ and the squares $\tilde{U}_i^2$ of the internally Studentized residuals.

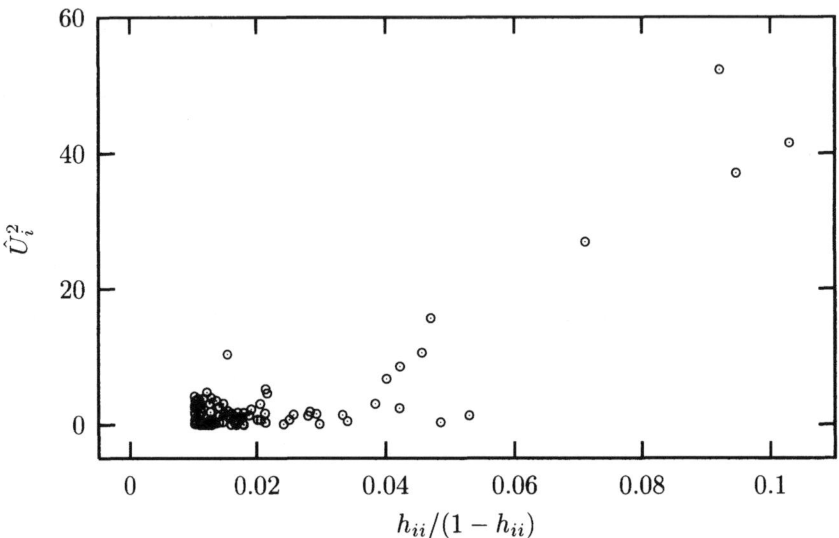

data points in terms of their degree of influence. Such a ranking may be obtained by introducing a norm for the vector $\hat{\beta} - \hat{\beta}_{(i)}$.

Cook (1977) proposed to measure the overall influence of the ith case by the norm of the vector $\hat{\beta} - \hat{\beta}_{(i)}$ in the metric of the matrix $\mathbf{X}^\top\mathbf{X}$. The result is *Cook's index*

$$D_i = \frac{(\hat{\beta} - \hat{\beta}_{(i)})^\top \mathbf{X}^\top \mathbf{X} (\hat{\beta} - \hat{\beta}_{(i)})}{ks^2} = \frac{(\hat{\mathbf{Y}} - \hat{\mathbf{Y}}_{(i)})^\top (\hat{\mathbf{Y}} - \hat{\mathbf{Y}}_{(i)})}{ks^2}$$
$$= \frac{h_{ii}}{1-h_{ii}} \frac{\tilde{U}_i^2}{k}, \qquad i = 1, \ldots, n,$$

where $\hat{\mathbf{Y}} = \mathbf{X}\hat{\beta}$, $\hat{\mathbf{Y}}_{(i)} = \mathbf{X}\hat{\beta}_{(i)}$ and $\tilde{U}_i$ is the ith OLS internally Studentized residual. The set of points in $\Re^k$ with constant D_i is an ellipsoid centered at $\hat{\beta}$ that passes through $\hat{\beta}_{(i)}$. A large value of D_i indicates that the ith case has a strong influence on the OLS estimate of β. Cook and Weisberg (1982) suggest choosing $D_i = 1$ as a cutoff.

A large value of D_i may be due either to a large Studentized residual $\tilde{U}_i$ or to large value of the ratio $h_{ii}/(1-h_{ii})$. The two components measure the importance of two different characteristics of each data point. The first is an outlier measure, the second is a leverage measure. To isolate these two components in Cook's index D_i, one may consider a scatterplot of $h_{ii}/(1-h_{ii})$ against $\tilde{U}_i^2$, called the *leverage plot* (Figure 57). The graph may be further enriched by superimposing the contour levels of D_i. Because the mean $\bar{h}$ of the h_{ii} is equal to k/n, one may also mark $\bar{h}/(1-\bar{h}) = k/(n-k)$ as a reference. Another possibility (Belsley, Kuh & Welsch 1980) is to use $2k/n$ as a cutoff value for $\bar{h}$ and mark instead $2k/(n-2k)$ as a reference.

Another measure of overall influence is the change in the OLS fitted values after excluding the ith case

$$\mathrm{DFFIT}_i = (\hat{\beta} - \hat{\beta}_{(i)})^\top X_i = \hat{U}_{(i)} - \hat{U}_i = \frac{h_{ii}}{1 - h_{ii}} \hat{U}_i, \qquad i = 1, \ldots, n.$$

Dividing by the estimate $s_{(i)}\sqrt{h_{ii}}$ of the standard deviation of Y_i gives

$$\mathrm{DFFITS}_i = \left(\frac{h_{ii}}{1 - h_{ii}} \right)^{1/2} \frac{\hat{U}_i}{s_{(i)}\sqrt{1 - h_{ii}}}, \qquad i = 1, \ldots, n.$$

Notice that diagnostic procedures based on the exclusion of a single observation at a time may fail to reveal subsets of influential cases. This effect is called *masking.* In principle, one could use procedures based on the exclusion of pairs, triples, etc. of observations, but these methods tend to be computationally more burdensome.

BIBLIOGRAPHIC NOTES

The books by Belsley, Kuh and Welsch (1980) and Cook and Weisberg (1982) present a variety of techniques for studying the influence of single cases. Another useful reference is Carroll and Ruppert (1988).

A good introduction to the Kalman filter is Harvey (1989).

The development of dynamic graphical methods, as a complement to the traditional techniques for static data representation, is increasing enormously the power of graphical methods to shed light on the structure of the data. On dynamic graphics see Becker, Cleveland and Wilks (1987).

PROBLEMS

8.1 Show that the OLS estimate $\hat{\beta}_{(i)}$ for the $n-1$ observations with the ith case deleted is equal to the OLS estimate of β in the regression $\mathrm{E}\,\mathbf{Y} = \mathbf{X}\beta + e_i\gamma$, where e_i is the ith unit vector.

8.2 Show that the OLS, the predicted and the internally Studentized residuals have the same autocorrelation structure, that is,

$$\mathrm{Corr}(\hat{U}_i, \hat{U}_j) = \mathrm{Corr}(\hat{U}_{(i)}, \hat{U}_{(j)}) = \mathrm{Corr}(\tilde{U}_i, \tilde{U}_j)$$

for all $i \neq j$.

8.3 Show that the ith externally Studentized OLS residual $\bar{U}_i$ is equal to the Studentized version of DFFIT_i obtained through dividing DFFIT_i by an estimate of its standard deviation.

8.4 Verify formulae (8.4) and (8.5).

8.5 Let $\hat{V}_t = Y_t - X_t^T \hat{\beta}_{t-1}$, where $\hat{\beta}_{t-1}$ is defined as in Section 8.2.4. Show that

$$\mathrm{SSE}_n = \sum_{t=1}^{n} \hat{U}_t^2 = \sum_{t=k+1}^{n} \frac{\hat{V}_t^2}{f_t},$$

where $\hat{U}_t$ is the OLS residual.

8.6 Let

$$\tilde{V}_t = \frac{\hat{V}_t}{\sqrt{f_t}}, \qquad t = k+1, \ldots, n,$$

where $\hat{V}_t$ and f_t are defined as in Section 8.2.4. Show that, under the classical linear model, $\{\tilde{V}_t\}$ is a set of LUS residuals.

9

The Classical Linear Model: Hypothesis Testing

This chapter considers various ways of testing statistical hypotheses about a regression model. In order to obtain exact results, we assume that the classical Gaussian linear model holds.

9.1 THE CLASSICAL t- AND F-TESTS

We first look at the classical way of testing a set of $q \geq 1$ linear equality constraints on the regression parameter β. The null hypothesis is H_0: $R\beta = r$, where R is a known $q \times k$ matrix of rank q and r is a known q-vector. Unless otherwise indicated, $\hat{\beta}$ and s^2 denote the OLS estimates of regression and scale in a regression of $\mathbf{Y}$ on $\mathbf{X}$, where $\mathbf{Y}$ is an n-vector and $\mathbf{X}$ is an $n \times k$ matrix of rank k.

9.1.1 THE t-TEST

The classical test of a single linear equality constraint is the t-test, which is based on the following result.

Theorem 9.1 *Let $R \neq 0$ be a k-dimensional row vector and let r be a scalar. Under the classical Gaussian linear model, the statistic*

$$T = \frac{R\hat{\beta} - r}{s[R(\mathbf{X}^\top\mathbf{X})^{-1}R^\top]^{1/2}}$$

has a noncentral t-distribution with $n - k$ degrees of freedom and noncentrality parameter

$$\mu = \frac{R\beta - r}{\sigma[R(\mathbf{X}^\top\mathbf{X})^{-1}R^\top]^{1/2}}. \tag{9.1}$$

Proof. Notice that $T = Z/\sqrt{S/(n-k)}$, where

$$Z = \frac{R\hat{\beta} - r}{\sigma[R(\mathbf{X}^\top\mathbf{X})^{-1}R^\top]^{1/2}}, \qquad S = \frac{\hat{\mathbf{U}}^\top\hat{\mathbf{U}}}{\sigma^2}.$$

Under the classical Gaussian linear model, Z is distributed as $\mathcal{N}(\mu, 1)$, where μ is given by (9.1). The conclusion then follows from the fact that, by Theorem 6.3, S is statistically independent of Z with a χ^2_{n-k}-distribution. □

Theorem 9.1 gives the sampling distribution of the statistic T both under the null hypothesis and any fixed alternative. In particular, its sampling distribution under H_0 is (central) t with $n-k$ degrees of freedom. This result is the basis for constructing the critical region of a classical t-test of given level.

Notice that, under the classical Gaussian linear model, the statistic T is the ratio between the random variable $R\hat{\beta}-r$ and the square root of the unbiased estimator of its sampling variance, whereas the noncentrality parameter μ is the ratio between the mean and the standard error of $R\hat{\beta}-r$.

A one-sided t-test of H_0 against the alternative that $R\beta > r$ rejects H_0 for large values of the statistic T. An α-level test rejects H_0 whenever $T > t_{(\alpha)}$, where $t_{(\alpha)}$ denotes the upper αth quantile of the (central) t-distribution with $n-k$ degrees of freedom. Notice that the critical value of the test statistic decreases as the number of degrees of freedom increases. When $R\beta \geq r$, the probability that the test statistic exceeds the critical value $t_{(\alpha)}$ is an increasing function of the noncentrality parameter μ. This result has two implications for the power of the test. First, the power is greater than α under any alternative, that is, the test is unbiased. Second, the power increases as the precision of $\hat{\beta}$ increases or the difference $R\beta - r$ increases. For alternatives such that $R\beta - r$ is sufficiently large, the test rejects the null hypothesis with probability arbitrarily close to one.

A two-sided t-test of H_0 against the alternative $R\beta \neq r$ rejects H_0 for large values of the statistic $|T|$. An α-level test rejects H_0 whenever $|T| > t_{(\alpha/2)}$. If $R\beta \neq r$, the probability that $|T|$ exceeds the critical value $t_{(\alpha/2)}$ is an increasing function of $|\mu|$. As a result, the test is also unbiased, for it has power greater than α under any alternative. Further, the power under any fixed alternative increases as the precision of $\hat{\beta}$ increases or the distance between $R\beta$ and r increases. For alternatives sufficiently far from H_0, the test rejects the null hypothesis with probability arbitrarily close to one.

Notice that $T = T(\mathbf{Y}; r)$, where $T(\mathbf{Y}; \cdot)$ is the statistic introduced in Section 6.4.4. Thus, rejecting H_0 whenever T falls in the critical region is equivalent to rejecting H_0 whenever the confidence interval for the given linear combination $R\beta$ of the elements of β does not contain the specific value r dictated by H_0.

Example 9.1 A *test of significance* of the jth covariate is a test of the hypothesis H_0: $\beta_j = 0$ that the jth element of β is equal to zero against the alternative that $\beta_j \neq 0$.

Because in this case $r = 0$ and $R = e_j^\top$, where e_j is the jth unit vector, a two-sided t-test rejects H_0 for large values of the statistic

$$|T| = \frac{|\hat{\beta}_j|}{s\sqrt{c_{jj}}},$$

where c_{jj} denotes the jth diagonal element of the matrix $(\mathbf{X}^\top\mathbf{X})^{-1}$. Because the noncentrality parameter of the statistic $|T|$ is

$$\mu = \frac{|\beta_j|}{\sigma\sqrt{c_{jj}}},$$

the power of the test under any fixed alternative increases with the precision of $\hat{\beta}_j$ or the distance of β_j from zero. □

Example 9.2 Suppose that one is interested in testing whether a single data point, say the last, is an outlier. Given a fixed design matrix $\mathbf{X}$, a useful model for $\mathbf{Y}$ is the *mean-shift outlier model*

$$\mathrm{E}\, Y_i = \begin{cases} \beta^\top X_i, & \text{if } i = 1, \ldots, n-1, \\ \gamma, & \text{if } i = n. \end{cases}$$

This model allows the mean of the first observation to be completely arbitrary. Under the assumption that $\mathbf{Y}$ has a Gaussian distribution with variance equal to $\sigma^2 I_n$, we obtain a Gaussian linear model with regression parameters γ and β. The hypothesis that the first data point is not an outlier corresponds to the hypothesis that $\gamma = \beta^\top X_n$ or, equivalently, that the linear combination $\gamma - \beta^\top X_n$ of the regression parameters is equal to zero.

The OLS estimator of (γ, β) is obtained by solving the normal equations

$$0 = \sum_{i=1}^{n-1} X_i(Y_i - \beta^\top X_i),$$

$$0 = Y_n - \gamma,$$

from which we see that the estimator of β coincides with the OLS estimator $\hat{\beta}_{(n)}$ in a regression of $\mathbf{Y}$ on $\mathbf{X}$ with the last case excluded, whereas the estimator of γ is equal to Y_n.

The estimator of the linear combination $\gamma - \beta^\top X_n$ is therefore $Y_n - \hat{\beta}_{(n)}^\top X_n$. This estimator coincides with the predicted residual $\hat{U}_{(nn)} = \hat{U}_n/(1 - h_{nn})$ from an OLS regression of $\mathbf{Y}$ on $\mathbf{X}$, and its sampling variance is equal to $\sigma^2/(1 - h_{nn})$, where h_{nn} denotes the last diagonal element of the matrix $H = \mathbf{X}(\mathbf{X}^\top\mathbf{X})^{-1}\mathbf{X}^\top$. Because the model residuals are equal to $Y_i - \hat{\beta}_{(n)}^\top X_i$, except for the last one which is equal to zero, the estimator of σ^2 coincides with the OLS estimator of scale $s_{(n)}^2$ in a regression of $\mathbf{Y}$ on $\mathbf{X}$ with the last case excluded.

Thus, a two-sided t-test rejects H_0 for large values of the statistic

$$|T| = \frac{|\hat{U}_{(n)}|}{s_{(n)}/\sqrt{1 - h_{nn}}} = \frac{|\hat{U}_n|}{s_{(n)}\sqrt{1 - h_{nn}}},$$

which coincides with the absolute value of the last externally Studentized residual from an OLS regression of $\mathbf{Y}$ on $\mathbf{X}$. Because $\mathrm{Var}\, \hat{U}_n = \sigma^2(1 - h_{nn})$, the noncentrality parameter of the statistic $|T|$ is

$$\mu = \frac{|\gamma - \beta^\top X_n|}{\sigma/\sqrt{1 - h_{nn}}}.$$

Thus, the power of the test under any fixed alternative decreases as h_{nn} increases. If $h_{nn} = 1$, then the test has no power. □

9.1.2 THE F-TEST

It is clear from the discussion in Section 6.4.4 that the critical region of a joint test of $q > 1$ constraints on the regression parameters is different from the Cartesian product of the critical regions of separate univariate tests, one for each constraint.

The classical joint test of a set of linear equality constraints is the F-test, which is based on the following result.

Theorem 9.2 *Let R be a $q \times k$ matrix of rank q and let r be a q-vector. Under the classical Gaussian linear model, the statistic*

$$F = \frac{(R\hat{\beta} - r)^\top [R(\mathbf{X}^\top\mathbf{X})^{-1}R^\top]^{-1}(R\hat{\beta} - r)}{qs^2}$$

has a noncentral F-distribution with $(q, n-k)$ degrees of freedom and noncentrality parameter

$$\lambda = \frac{(R\beta - r)^\top [R(\mathbf{X}^\top\mathbf{X})^{-1}R^\top]^{-1}(R\beta - r)}{\sigma^2}.$$

Proof. Notice that

$$F = \frac{W/q}{S/(n-k)},$$

where

$$W = \sigma^{-2}\,(R\hat{\beta} - r)^\top [R(\mathbf{X}^\top\mathbf{X})^{-1}R^\top]^{-1}(R\hat{\beta} - r), \qquad S = \sigma^{-2}\,\hat{\mathbf{U}}^\top\hat{\mathbf{U}}.$$

Under the classical Gaussian linear model

$$\sigma^{-1}\,[R(\mathbf{X}^\top\mathbf{X})^{-1}R^\top]^{-1/2}(R\hat{\beta} - r) \sim \mathcal{N}_q(\mu, I_q),$$

where $\mu = \sigma^{-1}\,[R(\mathbf{X}^\top\mathbf{X})^{-1}R^\top]^{-1/2}(R\beta - r)$. Hence $W \sim \chi^2_{q,\lambda}$, where $\lambda = \mu^\top\mu$. The conclusion then follows from the fact that, by Theorem 6.3, S is statistically independent of W with a χ^2_{n-k}-distribution. □

Theorem 9.2 gives the sampling distribution of the statistic F both under the null hypothesis and any fixed alternative. In particular, its sampling distribution under H_0 is a central F with $(q, n-k)$ degrees of freedom. This result is the basis for constructing critical regions of a classical F-test of a given level.

Notice that qF is an estimate of the squared Mahalanobis norm of the random vector $R\hat{\beta} - r$, and is therefore a measure of how far the OLS estimator $\hat{\beta}$ is from satisfying the constraints that define the null hypothesis. The noncentrality parameter λ is instead the squared norm of the vector $R\beta - r$ in the metric of the matrix $[R(\mathbf{X}^\top\mathbf{X})^{-1}R^\top]^{-1}/\sigma^2$, and is therefore a measure of how far the regression parameter β is from satisfying the constraints that define the null hypothesis.

A classical F-test of H_0 against the alternative that $R\beta \neq r$ rejects H_0 for large values of the statistic F. An α-level test rejects H_0 whenever $F > F_{(\alpha)}$, where $F_{(\alpha)}$ denotes the upper αth quantile of the $F_{q,n-k}$ distribution. If $q = 1$, the F statistic is equal to the square of the T statistic and therefore the F-test is equivalent to a two-sided t-test. Notice that $F = F(\mathbf{Y}; r)$, where $F(\mathbf{Y}; \cdot)$ is the statistic introduced in Section 6.4.4. Thus, rejecting H_0 whenever F falls in the critical region is equivalent to rejecting H_0 whenever the confidence ellipsoid for the q linear combinations $R\beta$ of the elements of β does not contain the specific value r specified by H_0. Figure 58 shows the behavior of the critical value of the statistic F for tests of level $\alpha = .05$ as

Figure 58 Critical value of an F-test of level $\alpha = .05$ as a function of the number q of constraints and the number $n - k$ of degrees of freedom.

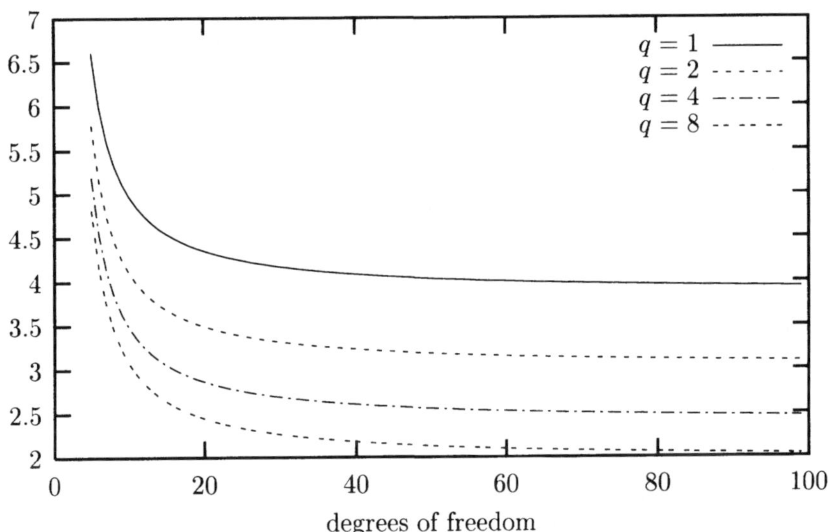

a function of the number q of constraints and the number $n - k$ of degrees of freedom. Notice that, for any q, the critical value decreases as the number of degrees of freedom increases.

When $R\beta \neq r$, the probability that the F-test statistic exceeds the critical value $F_{(\alpha)}$ is an increasing function of the noncentrality parameter λ. As a result, the test has power greater than α under any alternative, that is, the test is unbiased. Further, the power of the test under any fixed alternative increases with the precision of $\hat{\beta}$ or the distance between $R\beta$ and r. For alternatives sufficiently far from H_0, the test rejects the null hypothesis with probability arbitrarily close to one.

Example 9.3 Consider a test of the simple hypothesis H_0: $\beta = \beta_0$. Because in this case $R = I_k$ and $r = \beta_0$, an F-test rejects H_0 for large values of the statistic

$$F = \frac{(\hat{\beta} - \beta_0)^\top \mathbf{X}^\top \mathbf{X}(\hat{\beta} - \beta_0)}{ks^2}.$$

When $\beta_0 = 0$, the test statistic is simply

$$F = \frac{\hat{\beta}^\top \mathbf{X}^\top \mathbf{X}\hat{\beta}}{ks^2} = \frac{\mathbf{Y}^\top \mathbf{X}(\mathbf{X}^\top \mathbf{X})^{-1}\mathbf{X}^\top \mathbf{Y}}{ks^2}.$$

Because the noncentrality parameter of the F-test statistic is

$$\lambda = \frac{(\beta - \beta_0)^\top \mathbf{X}^\top \mathbf{X}(\beta - \beta_0)}{\sigma^2},$$

the test has low power under alternatives that are "too close" to β_0, where the precise meaning of "too close" depends on σ^2 and the design matrix $\mathbf{X}$. □

Example 9.4 Consider the model $\mathrm{E}\,\mathbf{Y} = \mathbf{X}\beta + \mathbf{W}\gamma$, where $[\mathbf{X}, \mathbf{W}]$ is an $n \times (k+q)$ matrix of full column rank. A *test of significance* of the subset of covariates in $\mathbf{W}$ is a test of the hypothesis H_0: $\gamma = 0$. Because in this case $R = [0, I_q]$, where 0 is the null matrix of order $q \times k$ and r is the q-dimensional null vector, an F-test rejects H_0 for large values of the statistic

$$F = \frac{\hat{\gamma}^\top \mathbf{W}^\top M \mathbf{W} \hat{\gamma}}{q s^2} = \frac{\mathbf{Y}^\top M \mathbf{W}(\mathbf{W}^\top M \mathbf{W})^{-1} \mathbf{W}^\top M \mathbf{Y}}{q s^2},$$

where $\hat{\gamma} = (\mathbf{W}^\top M \mathbf{W})^{-1} \mathbf{W}^\top M \mathbf{Y}$ and s^2 are, respectively, the OLS estimators of γ and σ^2 in the regression of $\mathbf{Y}$ on $\mathbf{X}$ and $\mathbf{W}$. □

We now give two other interpretations of the F-test statistic. From Section 6.5, the statistic may equivalently be written as

$$F = \frac{(\tilde{\mathbf{U}}^\top \tilde{\mathbf{U}} - \hat{\mathbf{U}}^\top \hat{\mathbf{U}})/q}{\hat{\mathbf{U}}^\top \hat{\mathbf{U}}/(n-k)},$$

where $\tilde{\mathbf{U}}$ and $\hat{\mathbf{U}}$ are, respectively, the constrained and the unconstrained OLS residual vectors. The F-test statistic is therefore proportional to the percentage increase in the residual sum of squares after imposing the constraints.

When the model includes an intercept, the F-test statistic may also be written as

$$F = \frac{(\hat{R}^2 - \tilde{R}^2)/q}{(1 - \hat{R}^2)/(n-k)},$$

where $\hat{R}^2$ and $\tilde{R}^2$ denote the coefficients of multiple correlation for the unconstrained and the constrained model respectively. The F-test statistic is therefore proportional to the percentage increase in the standard measure of goodness-of-fit after removing the constraints.

Example 9.5 The *null model* is the one where all regression coefficients except the intercept are equal to zero, that is, $\beta_j = 0$, $j = 2, \ldots, k$. A test of the null model is also called a *test of significance of a regression.* Because $q = k - 1$ and $\tilde{R}^2 = 0$ in this case, an F-test rejects the null model for large values of the statistic

$$F = \frac{\hat{R}^2/(k-1)}{(1 - \hat{R}^2)/(n-k)}.$$

□

Example 9.6 The *Chow test* (Chow 1960) of equality of the regression functions of two populations is a test of equality of β_1 and β_2 in the classical Gaussian linear models

$$\mathbf{Y}_1 \sim \mathcal{N}_{n_1}(\mathbf{X}_1\beta_1, \sigma^2 I_{n_1}),$$
$$\mathbf{Y}_2 \sim \mathcal{N}_{n_2}(\mathbf{X}_2\beta_2, \sigma^2 I_{n_2}),$$

where $\mathbf{Y}_j$ is an n_j-vector ($j = 1, 2$), $\mathbf{X}_j$ is an $n_j \times k$ matrix, and the columns of $\mathbf{X}_1$ and $\mathbf{X}_2$ contain exactly the same variables. Although the regression parameters β_1

and β_2 may be different in the two populations, the scale parameter is assumed to be the same. The null hypothesis corresponds to the set of k linear equality constraints H_0: $\beta_1 - \beta_2 = 0$.

First consider the case when both $\mathbf{X}_1$ and $\mathbf{X}_2$ are of full rank k, which requires that $k \leq \min(n_1, n_2)$. The unconstrained OLS estimator is in this case $(\hat{\beta}_1, \hat{\beta}_2)$, where $\hat{\beta}_j = (\mathbf{X}_j{}^\top \mathbf{X}_j)^{-1} \mathbf{X}_j{}^\top \mathbf{Y}_j$ is the OLS estimator in the regression of $\mathbf{Y}_j$ on $\mathbf{X}_j$, and the unconstrained residual sum-of-squares is $\hat{\mathbf{U}}_1 \hat{\mathbf{U}}_1 + \hat{\mathbf{U}}_2^\top \hat{\mathbf{U}}_2$, where $\hat{\mathbf{U}}_j = \mathbf{Y}_j - \mathbf{X}_j \hat{\beta}_j$. Imposing the constraint $\beta_1 = \beta_2 = \beta$ gives the model

$$\mathbf{Y} \sim \mathcal{N}_n(\mathbf{X}\beta, \sigma^2 I_n), \tag{9.2}$$

where $n = n_1 + n_2$ and

$$\mathbf{Y} = \begin{pmatrix} \mathbf{Y}_1 \\ \mathbf{Y}_2 \end{pmatrix}, \qquad \mathbf{X} = \begin{bmatrix} \mathbf{X}_1 \\ \mathbf{X}_2 \end{bmatrix}.$$

The constrained OLS estimator is clearly $\tilde{\beta} = (\mathbf{X}^\top \mathbf{X})^{-1} \mathbf{X}^\top \mathbf{Y}$, and the constrained residual sum-of-squares is denoted by $\tilde{\mathbf{U}}^\top \tilde{\mathbf{U}}$.

The Chow test is a classical F-test that rejects H_0 for large values of the statistic

$$F = \frac{(\tilde{\mathbf{U}}^\top \tilde{\mathbf{U}} - \hat{\mathbf{U}}_1^\top \hat{\mathbf{U}}_1 - \hat{\mathbf{U}}_2^\top \hat{\mathbf{U}}_2)/k}{(\hat{\mathbf{U}}_1^\top \hat{\mathbf{U}}_1 + \hat{\mathbf{U}}_2^\top \hat{\mathbf{U}}_2)/(n - 2k)}.$$

Construction of the test statistic does not require a particular ordering of the observations, but only their grouping into two groups each of size at least equal to k. The Chow test statistic is frequently used in time series analysis to detect the presence of discrete shifts or "structural breaks" in a regression relationship. Its validity for testing purposes requires, in addition to homoskedasticity, that there is at most one break and its date is known exactly. For the case of a single structural break with unknown date see Andrews (1993). For the case of multiple structural breaks with unknown dates see Bai and Perron (1998).

When one of the two matrices $\mathbf{X}_1$ or $\mathbf{X}_2$ is not of full rank k, the model is not identifiable under the alternative. A second version of the Chow test, called the *predictive Chow test,* is used in this case. Thus suppose that, given the particular ordering of the data, $[\mathbf{X}_2, \mathbf{Y}_2]$ contains the last $n_2 = n - n_1 < k$ observations. The predictive Chow test rejects H_0 for large values of the statistic

$$F^* = \frac{(\tilde{\mathbf{U}}^\top \tilde{\mathbf{U}} - \hat{\mathbf{U}}_1^\top \hat{\mathbf{U}}_1)/n_2}{\hat{\mathbf{U}}_1^\top \hat{\mathbf{U}}_1/(n_1 - k)}.$$

To understand the rationale for this test, consider the model

$$\mathrm{E}\, Y_i = \begin{cases} \beta^\top X_i, & \text{if } i = 1, \ldots, n_1, \\ \gamma_i, & \text{otherwise}. \end{cases} \tag{9.3}$$

This model generalizes the mean-shift outlier model (Example 9.2) by allowing the mean of the last n_2 observations to be completely arbitrary. Imposing the n_2 constraints $\gamma_i = \beta^\top X_i$, $i = n_1 + 1, \ldots, n$, results in model (9.2). We now show that

F^* is just the classical F-test statistic for testing model (9.2) against the alternative represented by model (9.3). Since the constrained residual sum-of-squares is equal to $\tilde{\mathbf{U}}^\top\tilde{\mathbf{U}}$, we only have to derive the unconstrained residual sum-of-squares.

The unconstrained OLS estimator of (β, γ), with $\gamma = (\gamma_1, \dots, \gamma_{n_2})$, is obtained by solving the normal equations

$$0 = \mathbf{X}_1^\top(\mathbf{Y}_1 - \mathbf{X}_1\beta),$$
$$0 = \mathbf{Y}_2 - \gamma.$$

This shows that the estimator of β is equal to $\hat{\beta}_1$, the estimator of γ is equal to $\mathbf{Y}_2$, and therefore the unconstrained residual sum-of-squares is equal to $\hat{\mathbf{U}}_1^\top\hat{\mathbf{U}}_1$. Finally notice that the constrained model contains $k + n_2$ regression parameters and therefore has $n - k - n_2 = n_1 - k$ degrees of freedom. □

The t- and F-tests remain valid when the covariates are stochastic. This follows from the fact that the conditional distribution of the test statistics under the null hypothesis does not depend on $\mathbf{X}$ and therefore coincides with the marginal distribution. The tests lose their validity, however, when the other assumptions of the Gaussian linear model are violated. As we shall see in Chapter 10, the t- and F-test remain approximately valid in large samples when the data are not Gaussian provided that all other assumptions of the linear model are satisfied.

9.1.3 RELATIONS WITH LIKELIHOOD-BASED TESTS

In Section 5.4 we introduced three general testing principles: the likelihood ratio principle, the Wald principle, and the score or Lagrange multiplier principle. We now establish the basic equivalence between these three principles and the classical F-test of linear equality constraints on the regression coefficients of a Gaussian linear model.

Consider the classical Gaussian linear model $\mathbf{Y} \sim \mathcal{N}_n(\mathbf{X}\beta, \sigma^2 I_n)$ and the hypothesis H_0: $R\beta = r$. We want to show that all three testing principles lead in this case to the classical F-test of H_0.

The sample log-likelihood may be written

$$L(\theta) = c - \frac{n}{2}\ln\sigma^2 - \frac{n}{2\sigma^2}Q(\beta), \qquad \theta = (\beta, \sigma^2),$$

where c is an arbitrary constant and $Q(\beta) = n^{-1}(\mathbf{Y} - \mathbf{X}\beta)^\top(\mathbf{Y} - \mathbf{X}\beta)$ is the OLS criterion. For a fixed β, the log-likelihood attains its unique maximum at $\sigma^2 = Q(\beta)$. If $\hat{\beta}$ and $\tilde{\beta}$ denote, respectively, the unconstrained and the constrained Gaussian ML estimators of β, then the corresponding ML estimators of σ^2 are $\hat{\sigma}^2 = Q(\hat{\beta})$ and $\tilde{\sigma}^2 = Q(\tilde{\beta})$. Hence

$$L(\hat{\theta}) = c' - \frac{n}{2}\ln\hat{\sigma}^2, \qquad L(\tilde{\theta}) = c' - \frac{n}{2}\ln\tilde{\sigma}^2,$$

where $c' = c - n/2$. The likelihood ratio test statistic is therefore

$$\xi^R = 2[L(\hat{\theta}) - L(\tilde{\theta})] = n\ln\frac{\tilde{\sigma}^2}{\hat{\sigma}^2},$$

with $\xi^R \geq 0$ since $\tilde{\sigma}^2 \geq \hat{\sigma}^2$. Notice that $\xi^R = g(F)$, where $F = [(n-k)/q][(\tilde{\sigma}^2 - \hat{\sigma}^2)/\hat{\sigma}^2]$ is the classical F-test statistic and g is the monotonically increasing function

$$g(x) = n \ln \left(\frac{1 + qx}{n - k} \right).$$

Thus, a likelihood ratio test is in this case equivalent to a classical F-test. In particular, the critical value of an α-level test based on ξ^R is equal to $g(F_{(\alpha)})$, where $F_{(\alpha)}$ is the critical value of an α-level test based on F.

Next notice that, since $R\hat{\beta} - r \sim \mathcal{N}_q(0, \sigma^2 R(\mathbf{X}^\top \mathbf{X})^{-1} R^\top)$ under H_0, the Wald test statistic is

$$\xi^W = \frac{(R\hat{\beta} - r)^\top [R(\mathbf{X}^\top \mathbf{X})^{-1} R^\top]^{-1} (R\hat{\beta} - r)}{\hat{\sigma}^2} = n \, \frac{\tilde{\sigma}^2 - \hat{\sigma}^2}{\hat{\sigma}^2}.$$

Because $\xi^W = nqF/(n-k)$, a Wald test is therefore also equivalent to a classical F-test.

Finally, since the scale parameter σ^2 is left unconstrained, we have

$$S_\beta(\tilde{\theta}) = \frac{1}{\tilde{\sigma}^2} \mathbf{X}^\top (\mathbf{Y} - \mathbf{X}\tilde{\beta}) = R^\top \tilde{\nu},$$

where $S_\beta = \partial L / \partial \beta$ is the element of the likelihood score corresponding to β and

$$\tilde{\nu} = \frac{1}{\tilde{\sigma}^2} [R(\mathbf{X}^\top \mathbf{X})^{-1} R^\top]^{-1} (R\hat{\beta} - r)$$

is the vector of Lagrange multipliers associated with the constraints. Exploiting the block-diagonality of the expected total information with respect to β and σ^2, and replacing the block corresponding to β by its estimate under H_0, that is, $\tilde{\sigma}^{-2}\mathbf{X}^\top\mathbf{X}$, we obtain three equivalent expressions for the score test statistic

$$\begin{aligned} \xi^S &= \frac{\tilde{\mathbf{U}}^\top \mathbf{X}(\mathbf{X}^\top \mathbf{X})^{-1} \mathbf{X}^\top \tilde{\mathbf{U}}}{\tilde{\sigma}^2} \\ &= \frac{(R\hat{\beta} - r)^\top [R(\mathbf{X}^\top \mathbf{X})^{-1} R^\top]^{-1} (R\hat{\beta} - r)}{\tilde{\sigma}^2} \\ &= n \, \frac{\tilde{\sigma}^2 - \hat{\sigma}^2}{\tilde{\sigma}^2}, \end{aligned}$$

where $\tilde{\mathbf{U}} = \mathbf{Y} - \mathbf{X}\tilde{\beta}$ denotes the constrained OLS residual vector and the last equality follows from (6.10). Because $\xi^S = \xi^W/(1 + n^{-1}\xi^W)$ is a monotonically increasing transformation of the Wald test statistic, the score principle also leads to the classical F-test.

Notice that the score test statistic may be rewritten as

$$\xi^S = n \frac{\tilde{\mathbf{U}}^\top \mathbf{X}(\mathbf{X}^\top \mathbf{X})^{-1} \mathbf{X}^\top \tilde{\mathbf{U}}}{\tilde{\mathbf{U}}^\top \tilde{\mathbf{U}}},$$

which is just n times the uncentered R^2 of a regression of the constrained OLS residuals $\tilde{\mathbf{U}}$ on the complete set of covariates. This suggests that, whenever H_0 specifies that certain covariates should be excluded from the model, then a score test may be implemented through a classical t- or F-test of significance of the excluded variables in an auxiliary regression of the constrained OLS residuals on the complete set of covariates.

Example 9.7 Consider the Gaussian linear model $\mathbf{Y} \sim \mathcal{N}_n(\mathbf{X}_1\beta_1 + \mathbf{X}_2\beta_2, \sigma^2 I_n)$ and the hypothesis H_0: $\beta_1 = 0$. In this case, the constrained OLS residual vector is equal to the vector of OLS residuals $\hat{\mathbf{U}}_1$ from the regression of $\mathbf{Y}$ on $\mathbf{X}_1$. The score test statistic is therefore equal to n times the R^2 of the regression of $\hat{\mathbf{U}}_1$ on $\mathbf{X}_1$ and $\mathbf{X}_2$. Because $\mathbf{X}_1^\top \hat{\mathbf{U}}_1 = 0$ by definition, the score test statistic turns out in this case to be simply equal to n times the R^2 of the regression of $\hat{\mathbf{U}}_1$ on $\mathbf{X}_2$. □

This approach to constructing the score test statistic may be generalized to all cases where maximizing the sample log-likelihood is equivalent, or approximately equivalent, to minimizing a sum of squared errors.

9.1.4 CLASSICAL PRE-TEST ESTIMATION

Suppose that the prior information on the regression parameter β in a classical Gaussian linear model takes the form of a set of $q \leq k$ linear equality constraints. When there is uncertainty about the quality of this prior information, a widely used procedure consists of choosing between the constrained and the unconstrained estimates on the basis of a preliminary test. What are the properties of this estimation method?

Specifically, let F be the statistic of a classical F-test of the hypothesis H_0: $R\beta = r$. If the constraints are valid, then $F \sim F_{q,n-k}$. Consequently, an α-level test rejects H_0 whenever $F > F_{(\alpha)}$, where $F_{(\alpha)}$ denotes the upper αth quantile of the $F_{q,n-k}$ distribution. A *classical pre-test estimator* of β is defined as

$$\bar{\beta}_\alpha = \begin{cases} \hat{\beta}, & \text{if } F > F_{(\alpha)}, \\ \tilde{\beta}, & \text{otherwise,} \end{cases}$$

that is, $\bar{\beta}_\alpha$ is equal to the unconstrained OLS estimator $\hat{\beta}$ if the F-test rejects H_0 and to the constrained OLS estimator $\tilde{\beta}$ if the test does not reject H_0. The pre-test estimator may be represented more compactly as

$$\bar{\beta}_\alpha = D_\alpha \hat{\beta} + (1 - D_\alpha)\tilde{\beta},$$

where $D_\alpha = 1\{F > F_{(\alpha)}\}$. Which estimate is obtained in a particular situation depends on the data $[\mathbf{X}, \mathbf{Y}]$, the particular hypothesis H_0 about β, and the level α of the test. Notice that the pre-test estimator is not a continuous function of the data, but has a sharp discontinuity at $F = F_{(\alpha)}$.

In order to evaluate the statistical properties of $\bar{\beta}_\alpha$, suppose that $R = I_k$ and $r = \beta_0$. In this case, the null hypothesis is H_0: $\beta = \beta_0$ and the F-test statistic is distributed as $F_{k,n-k}$ under H_0. For convenience, consider the linear model in its canonical form $\mathrm{E}\,\mathbf{Y} = \mathbf{W}\gamma$, where $\mathbf{W} = \mathbf{X}S^\top$, S is a nonsingular matrix such that $S^\top S = (\mathbf{X}^\top\mathbf{X})^{-1}$ and $\gamma = S^{-\top}\beta$. Under this reparametrization, the unconstrained OLS estimator is equal to $\hat{\gamma} = S^{-\top}\hat{\beta} = \mathbf{W}^\top\mathbf{Y}$, the null hypothesis becomes H_0: $\gamma = \gamma_0$, with $\gamma_0 = S^{-\top}\beta_0$, and the F-test statistic is $F = (\hat{\gamma} - \gamma_0)^\top(\hat{\gamma} - \gamma_0)/(ks^2)$.

The unconstrained OLS estimator is clearly unbiased for γ with sampling variance equal to $\sigma^2 I_k$. Under the quadratic loss function $\ell(u) = u^\top u$, where u is a k-vector, its risk is

$$r(\hat{\gamma}, \gamma) = \operatorname{tr} \operatorname{Var}(\hat{\gamma}) = k\sigma^2.$$

Because the constrained OLS estimator $\tilde{\gamma}$ is equal to γ_0 and does not depend on the data, its risk is

$$r(\tilde{\gamma}, \gamma) = (\gamma_0 - \gamma)^\top (\gamma_0 - \gamma) = \delta^\top \delta,$$

where the vector $\delta = \gamma_0 - \gamma$ represents the specification error in the constraints. The risk of the constrained estimator is equal to zero if the constraints are correct, that is, $\gamma = \gamma_0$, but becomes arbitrarily large as the specification error increases.

A classical pre-test estimator $\bar{\gamma}_\alpha$ is equal to $\hat{\gamma}$ if $F > F_{(\alpha)}$, and is equal to the constrained estimator $\tilde{\gamma} = \gamma_0$ otherwise. Its risk is given by the following theorem.

Theorem 9.3 *If the classical Gaussian linear model holds, then the risk of a classical pre-test estimator* $\bar{\gamma}_\alpha$ *is*

$$r(\bar{\gamma}_\alpha, \gamma) = [1 - \pi_2(\alpha)]\, r(\hat{\gamma}, \gamma) + [2\pi_2(\alpha) - \pi_4(\alpha)]\, r(\tilde{\gamma}, \gamma),$$

where

$$\pi_j(\alpha) = \Pr\left\{ F_{k+j, n-k, \lambda} \leq \frac{kF_{(\alpha)}}{k+j} \right\}, \qquad j = 2, 4,$$

and $\lambda = \delta^\top \delta / \sigma^2$.

Proof. A classical pre-test estimator may be represented compactly as $\bar{\gamma}_\alpha = \gamma_0 + D_\alpha(\hat{\gamma} - \gamma_0)$. Hence, its risk is

$$\begin{aligned} r(\bar{\gamma}_\alpha, \gamma) &= \mathrm{E}[\gamma_0 + D_\alpha(\hat{\gamma} - \gamma_0) - \gamma]^\top [\gamma_0 + D_\alpha(\hat{\gamma} - \gamma_0) - \gamma] \\ &= \delta^\top \delta + 2\delta^\top \mathrm{E}[D_\alpha(\hat{\gamma} - \gamma_0)] + \mathrm{E}[D_\alpha(\hat{\gamma} - \gamma_0)^\top (\hat{\gamma} - \gamma_0)]. \end{aligned}$$

In order to evaluate this expression we use the fact that, if $Z \sim \mathcal{N}_k(\mu, I_k)$, then

$$\mathrm{E}[Z\, 1\{Z^\top Z > c\}] = \mu + \Pr\{\chi^2_{k+2,\lambda} > c\}$$

and

$$\mathrm{E}[Z^\top Z\ 1\{Z^\top Z > c\}] = k \Pr\{\chi^2_{k+2,\lambda} > c\} + \lambda \Pr\{\chi^2_{k+4,\lambda} > c\},$$

where $\lambda = \mu^\top \mu$ (see Judge & Bock 1978). Thus let $Z = (\hat{\gamma} - \gamma_0)/\sigma$, $\mu = -\delta/\sigma$ and $c = ks^2 F_{(\alpha)}/\sigma^2$, and notice that $D_\alpha = 1$ if and only if $Z^\top Z > c$. For s^2 fixed, the previous formulae give

$$\mathrm{E}[D_\alpha(\hat{\gamma} - \gamma_0)] = -\delta\, [1 - \pi_2(\alpha)],$$

and

$$\mathrm{E}[D_\alpha(\hat{\gamma} - \gamma_0)^\top (\hat{\gamma} - \gamma_0)] = k\sigma^2[1 - \pi_2(\alpha)] + \delta^\top \delta[1 - \pi_4(\alpha)],$$

where

$$\pi_j(\alpha) = \Pr\left\{ \chi^2_{k+j,\lambda} \leq \frac{ks^2\, F_{(\alpha)}}{\sigma^2} \right\}, \qquad j = 2, 4,$$

Figure 59 Risk of the constrained and unconstrained OLS estimators and of a classical pre-test estimator under quadratic loss.

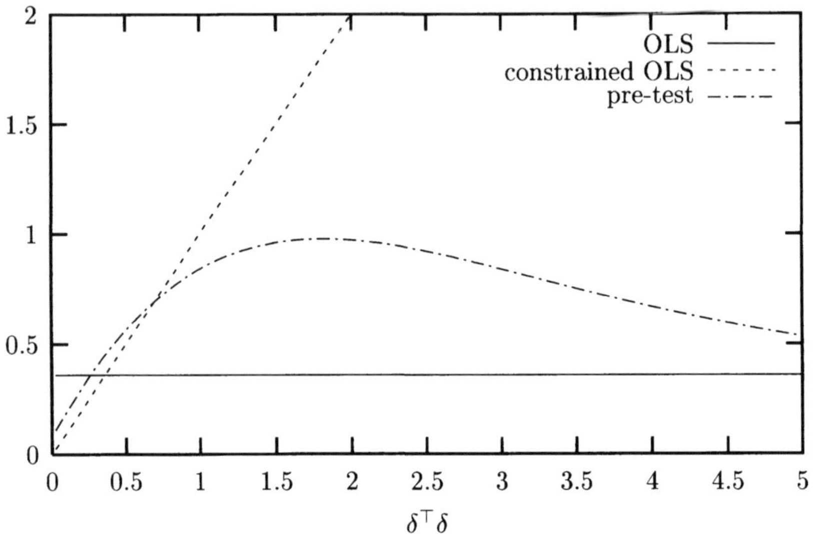

and $\lambda = \delta^\top\delta/\sigma^2$. For s^2 fixed, we therefore have

$$r(\bar{\gamma}_\alpha, \gamma) = k\sigma^2\,[1 - \pi_2(\alpha)] + \delta^\top\delta\,[2\pi_2(\alpha) - \pi_4(\alpha)].$$

Finally, since $(n-k)s^2/\sigma^2$ is distributed independently of $\hat{\gamma}$ as chi-square with $n-k$ degrees of freedom, we get

$$\pi_j(\alpha) = \Pr\left\{\frac{\chi^2_{k+j,\lambda}/(k+j)}{\chi^2_{n-k}/(n-k)} \le \frac{kF_{(\alpha)}}{k+j}\right\} = \Pr\left\{F_{k+j,n-k,\lambda} \le \frac{kF_{(\alpha)}}{k+j}\right\},$$

for $j = 2, 4$. □

The risk of a classical pre-test estimator is therefore a weighted sum of the risk of the constrained and unconstrained OLS estimators, with weights that depend on the number k of covariates, the level α of the test, and the noncentrality parameter $\lambda = (\gamma - \gamma_0)^\top(\gamma - \gamma_0)/\sigma^2$ of the sampling distribution of the F-test statistic.

As shown in Figure 59, none of the three estimators uniformly dominates the others. If the constraints are valid or nearly so, that is, $\delta^\top\delta$ is near zero, the classical pre-test estimator is better than the unconstrained estimator but worse than the constrained one, whereas the opposite is true for large values of the specification error $\delta^\top\delta$. More precisely, if the constraints are correct, then the risk of the pre-test estimator satisfies

$$0 < r(\bar{\gamma}_\alpha, \gamma_0) = [1 - \pi_2(\alpha)]\,r(\hat{\gamma}, \gamma_0) < r(\hat{\gamma}, \gamma_0).$$

As the specification error increases, that is, $\delta^\top\delta$ increases, the risk of the pre-test estimator first increases, reaching a peak after crossing from below the risk of the unconstrained estimator. It can be shown that the point in the space $\delta^\top\delta$ where the risk of the pre-test estimator crosses that of the unconstrained estimator is between $k\sigma^2/2$ and $k\sigma^2$. As $\delta^\top\delta \to \infty$, $\pi_j(\alpha)$ and $\pi_j(\alpha)\,\delta^\top\delta$, $j = 2, 4$, both tend to zero and so $r(\bar{\gamma}_\alpha, \gamma) \to r(\hat{\gamma}, \gamma)$, that is, the risk of the pre-test estimator declines monotonically towards the risk of the unconstrained estimator.

Notice that the pre-test estimator is better than the unconstrained OLS estimator only over a finite interval in the space of $\delta^\top\delta$. A more damaging result is the fact that, for moderate values of the specification error $\delta^\top\delta$, the classical pre-test estimator is actually worse than the other two estimators. This occurs, in particular, for values of $\delta^\top\delta$ near $k\sigma^2$ or, equivalently, for values of the noncentrality parameter λ near k.

9.2 SPECIFICATION TESTS

We use the term *specification test* or *pure significance test* to indicate cases where the alternative hypothesis is left deliberately vague. The specification tests that we consider are tests of the hypothesis that the linear regression specification is correct, H_0: $\mathrm{E}\,\mathbf{Y} = \mathbf{X}\beta$, against the general alternative that it is not, H_1: $\mathrm{E}\,\mathbf{Y} = \mathbf{X}\beta + \zeta$, where the precise structure of the specification error vector $\zeta = \mathrm{E}\,\mathbf{Y} - \mathbf{X}\beta$ is unknown.

If $\mathbf{Y}$ has a $\mathcal{N}_n(\mathbf{X}\beta + \zeta,\, \sigma^2 I_n)$ distribution, then the regression error vector $\mathbf{U} = \mathbf{Y} - \mathbf{X}\beta$ has a $\mathcal{N}_n(\zeta,\, \sigma^2 I_n)$ distribution, the OLS estimator $\hat{\beta} = (\mathbf{X}^\top\mathbf{X})^{-1}\mathbf{X}^\top\mathbf{Y}$ has a $\mathcal{N}_k(\beta + (\mathbf{X}^\top\mathbf{X})^{-1}\mathbf{X}^\top\zeta,\, \sigma^2 I_k)$ distribution, and the OLS residual vector $\hat{\mathbf{U}} = \mathbf{Y} - \mathbf{X}\hat{\beta}$ has a $\mathcal{N}_n(M\zeta,\, \sigma^2 M)$ distribution, with $M = I_n - \mathbf{X}(\mathbf{X}^\top\mathbf{X})^{-1}\mathbf{X}^\top$.

9.2.1 RESET

RESET (REgression Specification Error Test) was introduced by Ramsey (1969). To motivate this test, suppose that the possible source of model misspecification is known, namely it is known that $\zeta = \mathbf{W}\gamma$, where $\mathbf{W}$ is an $n \times q$ nonstochastic matrix of rank q. This formulation covers both omitted variables and misspecification of the shape of the regression function.

If the error vector $\mathbf{U} = \mathbf{Y} - \mathbf{X}\beta$ was observable, then the OLS estimator in the regression of $\mathbf{U}$ on $\mathbf{W}$ would be distributed as $\mathcal{N}_q(\gamma,\, \sigma^2\,(\mathbf{W}^\top\mathbf{W})^{-1})$ and a specification test would correspond to a classical F-test of significance of $\mathbf{W}$ in this regression. Because the error vector $\mathbf{U}$ is unobservable, consider instead a regression of the residual vector $\hat{\mathbf{U}} = M\mathbf{Y}$ on $\mathbf{W}$. It is easy to verify that the vector $\tilde{\gamma} = (\mathbf{W}^\top\mathbf{W})^{-1}\mathbf{W}^\top\hat{\mathbf{U}}$ is distributed as

$$\mathcal{N}_q((\mathbf{W}^\top\mathbf{W})^{-1}\mathbf{W}^\top M\mathbf{W}\gamma,\, \sigma^2\,(\mathbf{W}^\top\mathbf{W})^{-1}\mathbf{W}^\top M\mathbf{W}(\mathbf{W}^\top\mathbf{W})^{-1}).$$

It is appropriate to distinguish two cases, depending on whether $\mathbf{X}$ and $\mathbf{W}$ are orthogonal. If they are orthogonal, then $\tilde{\gamma}$ is unbiased for γ and its sampling variance is equal to $\sigma^2\,(\mathbf{W}^\top\mathbf{W})^{-1}$. Thus, a specification test corresponds to a classical F-test of significance of $\mathbf{W}$ in this regression.

If $\mathbf{X}$ and $\mathbf{W}$ are not orthogonal, then $\tilde{\gamma}$ is generally biased for γ, unless $\gamma = 0$, while the estimate of the precision of $\tilde{\gamma}$ based on the classical formula employed by most regression packages is proportional to $(\mathbf{W}^\top\mathbf{W})^{-1}$ and is therefore incorrect. Thus, although $\tilde{\gamma}$ is unbiased for γ under H_0, a classical F-test is no longer valid in this case. Further, the power of a test that rejects H_0 for large values of $\tilde{\gamma}$ may be a problem.

To see this notice that, if $\mathbf{W}\gamma$ lies in the null space of M, then $\mathrm{E}\,\tilde{\gamma} = 0$ and so a test based on $\tilde{\gamma}$ would not reject H_0 despite the fact that the model is misspecified.

Consider now an OLS regression of $\hat{\mathbf{U}}$ on $M\mathbf{W}$. The OLS coefficient in this regression is $\hat{\gamma} = (\mathbf{W}^\top M\mathbf{W})^{-1}\mathbf{W}^\top \mathbf{MY}$ and it is easy to verify that $\hat{\gamma} \sim \mathcal{N}_q(\gamma, \sigma^2\,(\mathbf{W}^\top M\mathbf{W})^{-1})$. In fact, from the results in Section 6.2.6, $\hat{\gamma}$ is simply the OLS estimator of γ in the regression of $\mathbf{Y}$ on $\mathbf{X}$ and $\mathbf{W}$. A test of significance of $M\mathbf{W}$ in the regression of $\hat{\mathbf{U}}$ on $M\mathbf{W}$ is therefore equivalent to a classical F-test of significance of $\mathbf{W}$ in the regression of $\mathbf{Y}$ on $\mathbf{X}$ and $\mathbf{W}$.

In RESET, the structure of ζ is unknown and $\mathbf{W}$ is just a matrix of variables that we presume may help explain the specification error vector ζ, that is, may be such that $\mathbf{W}^\top\zeta \neq 0$. In this case, the OLS coefficient $\tilde{\gamma}$ in the regression of $\hat{\mathbf{U}}$ on $\mathbf{W}$ is distributed as

$$\mathcal{N}_q((\mathbf{W}^\top\mathbf{W})^{-1}\mathbf{W}^\top M\zeta,\ \sigma^2\,(\mathbf{W}^\top\mathbf{W})^{-1}\mathbf{W}^\top M\mathbf{W}(\mathbf{W}^\top\mathbf{W})^{-1}),$$

while the OLS coefficient $\hat{\gamma}$ in the regression of Uh on $M\mathbf{W}$ is distributed as

$$\mathcal{N}_q((\mathbf{W}^\top M\mathbf{W})^{-1}\mathbf{W}^\top M\zeta,\ \sigma^2\,(\mathbf{W}^\top M\mathbf{W})^{-1}).$$

RESET rejects H_0 for large values of the distance from zero of either $\tilde{\gamma}$ or $\hat{\gamma}$. Because both estimators have mean zero under the null hypothesis, both may be used to construct a valid test. The power of RESET may be a problem, however. Suppose for example that $\zeta \neq 0$ but $\mathbf{W}^\top\zeta = 0$, that is, $\mathbf{W}$ is completely uninformative about ζ. If $\mathbf{X}^\top\mathbf{W} = 0$ or $\mathbf{X}^\top\zeta = 0$, then both estimators have mean zero and so RESET would not reject H_0 despite the fact that the model is misspecified.

Pagan and Hall (1983) show that, under mild regularity conditions, the same results are approximately valid in large samples when the data are not Gaussian and $\mathbf{X}$ and $\mathbf{W}$ are stochastic matrices.

9.2.2 THE DIFFERENCE TEST

We call a *difference test* one based on the difference between two alternative estimators of the regression parameter β.

In order to fix the ideas, suppose that $\mathbf{Y} \sim \mathcal{N}_n(\mathbf{X}\beta + \zeta, \sigma^2 I_n)$ and let $\mathbf{W}$ be a nonstochastic $n \times q$ matrix of rank q which consists of variables that are presumed to help explain the specification error vector ζ. Consider two different estimators of β. One is the OLS estimator in the regression of $\mathbf{Y}$ on $\mathbf{X}$, the other is the OLS estimator in the regression of $\mathbf{Y}$ on $\mathbf{X}$ and $\mathbf{W}$. If $M_W = I_n - \mathbf{W}(\mathbf{W}^\top\mathbf{W})^{-1}\mathbf{W}^\top$ and $\hat{\mathbf{X}} = M_W\mathbf{X}$ denotes the OLS residual matrix in the multivariate regression of $\mathbf{X}$ on $\mathbf{W}$, then the second estimator is just $\tilde{\beta} = (\hat{\mathbf{X}}^\top\hat{\mathbf{X}})^{-1}\hat{\mathbf{X}}^\top\mathbf{Y}$.

Under H_0: $\zeta = 0$, both estimators are unbiased for β. Of course, $\hat{\beta}$ is MVU. Under the alternative hypothesis that $\zeta \neq 0$, both estimators are biased but their bias is different

$$\mathrm{Bias}\,\hat{\beta} = (\mathbf{X}^\top\mathbf{X})^{-1}\mathbf{X}^\top\zeta, \qquad \mathrm{Bias}\,\tilde{\beta} = (\hat{\mathbf{X}}^\top\hat{\mathbf{X}})^{-1}\hat{\mathbf{X}}^\top\zeta,$$

where we used the fact that $\hat{\mathbf{X}}^\top\mathbf{X} = \mathbf{X}^\top M_W\mathbf{X} = \hat{\mathbf{X}}^\top\hat{\mathbf{X}}$ by the idempotency of M_W. This suggests a test that rejects H_0 for large values of the norm of the difference vector $\tilde{\delta} = \tilde{\beta} - \hat{\beta}$. Under our set of assumptions, $\tilde{\delta}$ has a k-variate Gaussian distribution with mean equal to zero under H_0 and $\delta = \text{Bias}\,\tilde{\beta} - \text{Bias}\,\hat{\beta}$ under the alternative. In order to determine the sampling variance of $\hat{\delta}$ we make use of the following result.

Theorem 9.4 *If $\hat{\theta}$ is a MVU estimator of a parameter θ and $\tilde{\theta}$ is any other unbiased estimator of θ, then:*

(i) *$\hat{\theta}$ and $\hat{\delta} = \tilde{\theta} - \hat{\theta}$ are uncorrelated;*
(ii) $\text{Var}(\tilde{\theta} - \hat{\theta}) = \text{Var}\,\tilde{\theta} - \text{Var}\,\hat{\theta}$.

Proof. Consider the linear combination $\bar{\theta} = (1-\alpha)\hat{\theta} + \alpha\tilde{\theta} = \hat{\theta} + \alpha\hat{\delta}$. Because $\hat{\theta}$ and $\tilde{\theta}$ are both unbiased for θ, $\bar{\theta}$ is also unbiased and coincides with $\hat{\theta}$ when $\alpha = 0$. The sampling variance of $\bar{\theta}$ is $\text{Var}\,\bar{\theta} = \text{Var}\,\hat{\theta} + \alpha^2\,\text{Var}\,\hat{\delta} + 2\alpha\,\text{Cov}(\hat{\theta}, \hat{\delta})$. For $\hat{\theta}$ to be MVU, $\text{Var}\,\bar{\theta}$ must attain its global minimum at $\alpha = 0$. Because

$$\frac{\partial}{\partial\alpha}\,\text{Var}\,\bar{\theta} = 2\alpha\,\text{Var}\,\hat{\delta} + 2\,\text{Cov}(\hat{\theta}, \hat{\delta})$$

must vanish at the point $\alpha = 0$, necessarily $\text{Cov}(\hat{\theta}, \hat{\delta}) = 0$ and therefore $\text{Var}\,\tilde{\theta} = \text{Var}(\hat{\theta} - \hat{\delta}) = \text{Var}\,\hat{\theta} + \text{Var}\,\hat{\delta}$. Part (ii) then follows immediately. □

In our case, Theorem 9.4 implies that

$$\text{Var}\,\hat{\delta} = \text{Var}\,\tilde{\beta} - \text{Var}\,\hat{\beta} = \sigma^2\,[(\hat{\mathbf{X}}^\top\hat{\mathbf{X}})^{-1} - (\mathbf{X}^\top\mathbf{X})^{-1}].$$

By the matrix inversion lemma in Appendix A.7

$$\begin{aligned}(\hat{\mathbf{X}}^\top\hat{\mathbf{X}})^{-1} &= [\mathbf{X}^\top\mathbf{X} - \mathbf{X}^\top\mathbf{W}(\mathbf{W}^\top\mathbf{W})^{-1}\mathbf{W}^\top\mathbf{X}]^{-1} \\ &= (\mathbf{X}^\top\mathbf{X})^{-1} + P(\mathbf{W}^\top M\mathbf{W})^{-1}P^\top,\end{aligned}$$

where $M = I_n - \mathbf{X}(\mathbf{X}^\top\mathbf{X})^{-1}\mathbf{X}^\top$ and $P = (\mathbf{X}^\top\mathbf{X})^{-1}\mathbf{X}^\top\mathbf{W}$ is the $k \times q$ matrix of OLS coefficients in the multivariate regression of $\mathbf{W}$ on $\mathbf{X}$. Hence

$$\text{Var}\,\hat{\delta} = \sigma^2\,P(\mathbf{W}^\top M\mathbf{W})^{-1}P^\top.$$

Inspection of this formula reveals that the variance matrix of $\hat{\delta}$ may be of rank less than k and therefore singular. Because the matrix $\mathbf{W}^\top M\mathbf{W}$ has rank q, this occurs when $q < k$, that is, the number of variables in $\mathbf{W}$ is less than the number of variables in $\mathbf{X}$. Another case is when $q \geq k$ but $\mathbf{X}^\top\mathbf{W} = 0$, that is, $\mathbf{X}$ and $\mathbf{W}$ are orthogonal, so that $\tilde{\beta} = \hat{\beta}$ and $\text{Var}\,\hat{\delta} = 0$.

If σ^2 is known, a difference test rejects H_0 for large values of the statistic

$$\xi^D = \hat{\delta}^\top(\text{Var}\,\hat{\delta})^-\,\hat{\delta} = \sigma^{-2}\,\hat{\delta}^\top[P(\mathbf{W}^\top M\mathbf{W})^{-1}P^\top]^-\,\hat{\delta},$$

where the use of a generalized inverse, denoted by $^-$, is necessary because the sampling variance of $\hat{\delta}$ may be a singular matrix. Under our set of assumptions, the distribution of ξ^D under H_0 is (central) chi-square with number of degrees of freedom equal to the rank of the matrix $P(\mathbf{W}^\top M\mathbf{W})^{-1}P^\top$. Under the alternative hypothesis, the distribution of ξ^D is noncentral chi-square with number of degrees of freedom equal to the rank of $P(\mathbf{W}^\top M\mathbf{W})^{-1}P^\top$ and noncentrality parameter

$$\nu = \sigma^{-2}\,\delta^\top\,[P(\mathbf{W}^\top M\mathbf{W})^{-1}P^\top]^-\,\delta.$$

One can show that the distribution of ξ^D does not depend on the choice of generalized inverse. Because the power of such a test is an increasing function of the noncentrality parameter ν, a difference test has high power whenever the average difference between the two estimators is large or the use of $\tilde{\beta}$ involves little loss of efficiency.

The same results are approximately valid in large samples when the data are not Gaussian and σ^2 is replaced by an estimator based on $\hat{\beta}$ or $\tilde{\beta}$.

We now show that, when $\operatorname{Var}\hat{\delta}$ is nonsingular, a difference test statistic may be computed through an auxiliary OLS regression. Because $\hat{\mathbf{X}}^\top\hat{\mathbf{X}} = \hat{\mathbf{X}}^\top\mathbf{X}$, we get

$$\hat{\mathbf{X}}^\top\hat{\mathbf{X}}\,\hat{\delta} = \hat{\mathbf{X}}^\top\hat{\mathbf{X}}(\tilde{\beta} - \hat{\beta}) = \hat{\mathbf{X}}^\top\mathbf{Y} - \hat{\mathbf{X}}^\top\hat{\mathbf{X}}(\mathbf{X}^\top\mathbf{X})^{-1}\mathbf{X}^\top\mathbf{Y} = \hat{\mathbf{X}}^\top M\mathbf{Y}.$$

Further

$$\begin{aligned}(\hat{\mathbf{X}}^\top\hat{\mathbf{X}})^{-1}(\operatorname{Var}\hat{\delta})^{-1}(\hat{\mathbf{X}}^\top\hat{\mathbf{X}})^{-1} &= \sigma^{-2}\,[\hat{\mathbf{X}}^\top\hat{\mathbf{X}} - \hat{\mathbf{X}}^\top\hat{\mathbf{X}}(\mathbf{X}^\top\mathbf{X})^{-1}\hat{\mathbf{X}}^\top\hat{\mathbf{X}}]^{-1} \\ &= \sigma^{-2}\,(\hat{\mathbf{X}}^\top M\hat{\mathbf{X}})^{-1}.\end{aligned}$$

The difference test statistic may therefore be written

$$\hat{\delta} = \sigma^{-2}\,\mathbf{Y}^\top M\hat{\mathbf{X}}(\hat{\mathbf{X}}^\top M\hat{\mathbf{X}})^{-1}\hat{\mathbf{X}}^\top M\mathbf{Y},$$

which is proportional to the statistic of a classical F-test of significance of $\hat{\mathbf{X}}$ in the OLS regression of $\mathbf{Y}$ on $\mathbf{X}$ and $\hat{\mathbf{X}}$. With this interpretation, a difference test corresponds to a version of RESET where $\hat{\mathbf{X}}$ is used to "explain" the vector ζ.

Example 9.8 Suppose that the data are the result of stratified random sampling. Specifically, partition the statistical population into S strata, let n_s be the size of the sample drawn from the sth stratum and let $n = \sum_s n_s$ be the total sample size. Also let π_s be the population weight of the sth stratum, let $p_s = n_s/n$ be the sample stratum weight and let $\omega_s = \pi_s/p_s$ be the inflation factor.

Consider two alternative linear models. The first model assumes that the population is perfectly homogeneous

$$\mathbf{Y}_s \sim \mathcal{N}_{n_s}(\mathbf{X}_s\beta,\, \sigma^2\, I_{n_s}), \qquad s = 1, \ldots, S,$$

whereas the second model allows for complete heterogeneity across strata

$$\mathbf{Y}_s \sim \mathcal{N}_{n_s}(\mathbf{X}_s\beta_s,\, \sigma_s^2\, I_{n_s}), \qquad s = 1, \ldots, S. \tag{9.4}$$

The target parameter is $\beta_* = \sum_s \pi_s\beta_s$. Clearly, $\beta_* = \beta$ under the homogeneous population model.

Consider two alternative estimators of β_*. One is the OLS estimator

$$\hat{\beta} = (\sum_s \mathbf{X}_s^\top\mathbf{X}_s)^{-1}\sum_s \mathbf{X}_s^\top\mathbf{Y}_s = (\mathbf{X}^\top\mathbf{X})^{-1}\mathbf{X}^\top\mathbf{Y},$$

where

$$\mathbf{Y} = \begin{pmatrix}\mathbf{Y}_1 \\ \vdots \\ \mathbf{Y}_S\end{pmatrix}, \qquad \mathbf{X} = \begin{bmatrix}\mathbf{X}_1 \\ \vdots \\ \mathbf{X}_S\end{bmatrix}.$$

The other is the WLS estimator

$$\tilde{\beta} = (\sum_s \omega_s \mathbf{X}_s^\top \mathbf{X}_s)^{-1} \sum_s \omega_s \mathbf{X}_s^\top \mathbf{Y}_s = (\mathbf{X}^\top D \mathbf{X})^{-1} \mathbf{X}^\top D \mathbf{Y},$$

where $D = \text{diag}[\omega_s I_{n_s}]$, a diagonal $n \times n$ matrix. This second estimator is based on the idea that the inflation factors represent how many population units each sample unit "stands for".

If the homogeneous population model holds, then both estimators are unbiased for $\beta_* = \beta$ with sampling variance

$$\text{Var}\,\hat{\beta} = \sigma^2\,(\mathbf{X}^\top \mathbf{X})^{-1}, \qquad \text{Var}\,\tilde{\beta} = \sigma^2\,(\mathbf{X}^\top D \mathbf{X})^{-1} \mathbf{X} D^2 \mathbf{X} (\mathbf{X}^\top D \mathbf{X})^{-1}.$$

Of course, $\hat{\beta}$ is efficient relative to $\tilde{\beta}$. If instead the heterogeneous population model holds, then

$$\text{E}\,\hat{\beta} = (\sum_s \mathbf{X}_s^\top \mathbf{X}_s)^{-1} \sum_s \mathbf{X}_s^\top \mathbf{X}_s \beta_s = (\sum_s p_s P_s)^{-1} \sum_s p_s P_s \beta_s,$$

where $P_s = \mathbf{X}_s^\top \mathbf{X}_s / n_s$. The OLS estimator $\hat{\beta}$ is therefore biased for β_* unless $p_s = \pi_s$ and $P_s = P$ for all s. The WLS estimator is also biased in this case since

$$\text{E}\,\tilde{\beta} = (\sum_s \pi_s P_s)^{-1} \sum_s \pi_s P_s \beta_s \neq \beta_*$$

unless $P_s = P$ for all s. Even in the latter case, though, $\tilde{\beta}$ is not fully efficient unless all strata have the same variance.

The fact that the two estimators have no bias under the homogeneous population model but different bias under the heterogeneous population model is the basis for the difference test of homogeneity proposed by DuMouchel and Duncan (1983). Let $\hat{\delta} = \tilde{\beta} - \hat{\beta}$. The null hypothesis of homogeneity implies that $\text{E}\,\hat{\delta} = 0$ and

$$\begin{aligned} \text{Var}\,\hat{\delta} &= \sigma^2\,[(\mathbf{X}^\top D \mathbf{X})^{-1} \mathbf{X}^\top D^2 \mathbf{X} (\mathbf{X}^\top D \mathbf{X})^{-1} - (\mathbf{X}^\top \mathbf{X})^{-1}] \\ &= \text{Var}\,\tilde{\beta} - \text{Var}\,\hat{\beta}. \end{aligned}$$

If σ^2 is known, then a difference test rejects the homogeneity assumption for large values of the statistic $\xi^D = \hat{\delta}^\top [\text{Var}\,\tilde{\beta} - \text{Var}\,\hat{\beta}]^{-1}\,\hat{\delta}$. It can be shown that, under the null hypothesis, ξ^D has a (central) chi-square distribution with k degrees of freedom. It is not hard to verify that the difference test statistic ξ^D may also be computed as the statistic of a classical F-test for the significance of $D\mathbf{X}$ in the auxiliary regression of $\mathbf{Y}$ on $\mathbf{X}$ and $D\mathbf{X}$. □

9.2.3 *RELATIONS WITH THE CLASSICAL TESTS*

Suppose as before that $\zeta = \mathbf{W}\gamma$, that is, the possible source of model misspecification is known. Suppose also that σ^2 is known and, without loss of generality, set it equal to one.

We saw in Section 9.2.1 that a version of RESET based on $\mathbf{W}$ coincides in this case with a classical F-test of the hypothesis H_0: $\gamma = 0$. We also saw in Section 9.2.2 that a difference test coincides in this case with a version of RESET where $\hat{\mathbf{X}} = M_W\mathbf{X}$ is used to "explain" the specification error vector ζ. Thus, it only remains to study the relation between a classical F-test and a difference test.

An F-test rejects $\mathrm{H_0}$ for large values of the statistic $F = \hat{\gamma}^\top \mathbf{W}^\top M \mathbf{W}\hat{\gamma}$, where $\hat{\gamma} = (\mathbf{W}^\top M\mathbf{W})^{-1}\mathbf{W}^\top M\mathbf{Y}$ is an unbiased estimator of γ. Under the alternative hypothesis, the F-test statistic has a noncentral chi-square distribution with q degrees of freedom and noncentrality parameter $\lambda = \gamma^\top V\gamma$, where $V = \mathbf{W}^\top M\mathbf{W}$. Because V is a p.d. matrix, the noncentrality parameter is equal to zero if and only if the null hypothesis holds. Therefore, a classical F-test is powerful under any alternative.

A difference test rejects instead $\mathrm{H_0}$ for large values of the statistic

$$\xi^D = \hat{\delta}^\top[(\hat{\mathbf{X}}^\top\hat{\mathbf{X}})^{-1} - (\mathbf{X}^\top\mathbf{X})^{-1}]^- \hat{\delta}, \hat{\delta}^\top[(\mathbf{X}^\top M_W\mathbf{X})^{-1} - (\mathbf{X}^\top\mathbf{X})^{-1}]^- \hat{\delta},$$

where

$$\begin{aligned} \mathrm{E}\,\hat{\delta} &= [(\mathbf{X}^\top M_W\mathbf{X})^{-1}\mathbf{X}^\top M_W - (\mathbf{X}^\top\mathbf{X})^{-1}\mathbf{X}^\top]\,(\mathbf{X}\beta + \mathbf{W}\gamma) \\ &= -(\mathbf{X}^\top\mathbf{X})^{-1}\mathbf{X}^\top\mathbf{W}\gamma \end{aligned}$$

under the alternative hypothesis. One interpretation of this result is that the difference test does not try to test $\mathrm{H_0}$ directly, but rather the hypothesis that $\mathbf{X}^\top\mathbf{W}\gamma = 0$. This is sometimes called the ***implicit null hypothesis*** of the difference test. It is only under special circumstances that the two hypotheses, that is, $\mathrm{H_0}$: $\gamma = 0$ and $\mathbf{X}^\top\mathbf{W}\gamma = 0$, coincide. This occurs when the matrix $\mathbf{X}^\top\mathbf{W}$ has rank equal to q, in which case $\mathbf{X}^\top\mathbf{W}\gamma = 0$ if and only if $\gamma = 0$. If instead $\mathbf{X}^\top\mathbf{W}$ has rank less than q, then the implicit null hypothesis of the difference test consists of $\mathrm{H_0}$ and all the vectors $\gamma \neq 0$ that lie in the null space of $\mathbf{X}^\top\mathbf{W}$.

Under the alternative hypothesis, the statistic ξ^D has a noncentral chi-square distribution with number of degrees of freedom less than or equal to $\min(k, q)$ and noncentrality parameter

$$\begin{aligned} \nu &= \gamma^\top\mathbf{W}^\top\mathbf{X}(\mathbf{X}^\top\mathbf{X})^{-1}\,[(\mathbf{X}^\top M_W\mathbf{X})^{-1} - (\mathbf{X}^\top\mathbf{X})^{-1}]^-\,(\mathbf{X}^\top\mathbf{X})^{-1}\mathbf{X}^\top\mathbf{W}\gamma \\ &= \gamma^\top\mathbf{W}^\top\mathbf{X}\,(\mathbf{X}^\top\mathbf{W}V^{-1}\mathbf{W}^\top\mathbf{X})^-\,\mathbf{X}^\top\mathbf{W}\gamma. \end{aligned}$$

The power of a difference test depends on the noncentrality parameter. Two cases are possible. The first is when the matrix $\mathbf{X}^\top\mathbf{W}$ has rank $q \leq k$. Because V is a p.d. matrix of rank q and $\mathrm{rank}(\mathbf{X}^\top\mathbf{W}V^{-1}\mathbf{W}^\top\mathbf{X}) = \mathrm{rank}\,V^{-1} = q$, it may be shown that $\nu = \gamma^\top V\gamma = \lambda$ in this case. A classical and a difference test therefore have the same power. The proof is immediate when $q = k$ and the matrix $\mathbf{X}^\top\mathbf{W}$ is nonsingular.

The second case is when the matrix $\mathbf{X}^\top\mathbf{W}$ has rank $k < q$. Now a classical and a difference test are not directly comparable, for the first has q degrees of freedom while the second has at most $k < q$. However, because the noncentrality parameter of the difference test is equal to zero for every $\gamma \neq 0$ that lies in the null space of $\mathbf{X}^\top\mathbf{W}$, there exist forms of misspecification under which a difference test has no power. In particular, a difference test never finds evidence of model misspecification when $\mathbf{X}$ and $\mathbf{W}$ are orthogonal.

9.2.4 THE DURBIN–WATSON TEST

Let $\mathbf{Y} = (Y_1, \ldots, Y_n)$ be a finite segment of a stochastic process $\{Y_t\}$ with time-varying mean $\beta^\top X_t$, where $\{X_t\}$ is a sequence of nonstochastic k-vectors, and consider the hypothesis that the regression errors $U_t = Y_t - \beta^\top X_t$ follow a white noise process against the alternative of a more general stationary process.

If the regression errors were observable, then a test may be based on their estimated autocorrelations. Because only the OLS residuals $\hat{U}_t = Y_t - X_t^\top \hat{\beta}$ are observable, it seems natural to consider their sample autocorrelations

$$\hat{\rho}_h = \frac{\sum_{t=1}^{n-h} \hat{U}_t \hat{U}_{t+h}}{\sum_{i=1}^{n} \hat{U}_t^2}, \qquad |h| = 1, 2, \ldots.$$

Deriving the exact sampling distribution of $\hat{\rho}_h$ is generally complicated. An exact result may be obtained when the regression errors follow a stable Gaussian AR(1) process with zero mean, that is

$$(1 - \phi L)(Y_t - \beta^\top X_t) = V_t,$$

where $|\phi| < 1$ and $\{V_t\}$ is a Gaussian white noise with mean zero and variance σ^2. In this case, a test of the hypothesis H_0: $\phi = 0$ may be based on the *Durbin–Watson statistic*

$$\xi^{DW} = \frac{\sum_{t=1}^{n-1} (\hat{U}_{t+1} - \hat{U}_t)^2}{\sum_{t=1}^{n} \hat{U}_t^2} = \frac{\mathbf{Y}^\top MAM\mathbf{Y}}{\mathbf{Y}^\top M\mathbf{Y}},$$

where $M = I_n - \mathbf{X}(\mathbf{X}^\top \mathbf{X})^{-1}\mathbf{X}^\top$ and A is the $n \times n$ matrix

$$A = \begin{bmatrix} 1 & -1 & & & & \\ -1 & 2 & -1 & & & \\ & -1 & 2 & -1 & & \\ & & \ddots & \ddots & \ddots & \\ & & & -1 & 2 & -1 \\ & & & & -1 & 1 \end{bmatrix}.$$

It is not difficult to show that the Durbin–Watson statistic may be written

$$\xi^{DW} = 2(1 - \hat{\rho}_1) - \frac{\hat{U}_1^2 + \hat{U}_n^2}{\sum_{t=1}^{n} \hat{U}_t^2}. \tag{9.5}$$

If n is large, then $\xi^{DW} \approx 2(1 - \hat{\rho}_1)$. Since $-1 \leq \hat{\rho}_1 \leq 1$, the Durbin–Watson statistic ranges between 0 and 4. The null hypothesis is rejected against the one-sided alternative that $\phi > 0$ whenever $\hat{\rho}_1$ is sufficiently close to one, that is, ξ^{DW} is sufficiently close to zero, and is rejected against the one-sided alternative that $\phi < 0$ whenever $\hat{\rho}_1$ is sufficiently close to -1, that is, ξ^{DW} is sufficiently close to 4.

In order to determine the critical region of an exact test, one needs to compute the sampling distribution of ξ^{DW} under H_0. Because

$$\Pr\{\xi^{DW} < c\} = \Pr\{\mathbf{Y}^\top MAM\mathbf{Y} < c\mathbf{Y}^\top M\mathbf{Y}\} = \Pr\{\mathbf{U}^\top B\mathbf{U} < 0\},$$

with $B = MAM - cM$ and $\mathbf{U} = \mathbf{Y} - \mathbf{X}\beta \sim \mathcal{N}_n(0, \sigma^2 I_n)$ under H_0, this requires computing the distribution of a linear combination of independent random variables, each distributed as chi-square with one degree of freedom, where the coefficients of the linear combination are the eigenvalues of B.

Exact critical values may be obtained by various methods, such as the one of Imhof (Johnson & Kotz 1972, pp. 150–153). These critical values depend on the design matrix $\mathbf{X}$. However, when the regression includes an intercept, they satisfy an upper bound d_U and a lower bound d_L that depend only on the sample size n, the number k of regression coefficients and the level α of the test. Durbin and Watson (1951) tabulated these bounds for different values of n, k and α, and suggested a type of test known as the *bounds test*. A bounds test of H_0 against the alternative that $\phi > 0$ rejects H_0 if $0 \leq \xi^{DW} < d_L$, does not reject H_0 if $d_U < \xi^{DW} \leq 2$, and has an undetermined outcome if $d_L \leq \xi^{DW} \leq d_U$. By the symmetry about 2 of the null distribution of ξ^{DW}, a bounds test of H_0 against the alternative that $\phi < 0$ rejects H_0 if $4 - d_L < \xi^{DW} \leq 4$, does not reject H_0 if $2 \leq \xi^{DW} < 2 + d_U$, and has an undetermined outcome if $2 + d_U \leq \xi^{DW} \leq 4 - d_U$.

Notice that the Durbin–Watson test is powerful not only under AR(1) regression errors, but also under other forms of dependence that result in nonzero first-order error autocorrelation. Also notice that a test of H_0: $\phi = 0$ against the alternative that $\phi \neq 0$ may be viewed as a test of the hypothesis that $\mathrm{E}(Y_t \,|\, Y_{t-1}) = \beta^\top X_t$ against the alternative that

$$\mathrm{E}(Y_t \,|\, Y_{t-1}) = \beta^\top X_t + \phi(Y_{t-1} - \beta^\top X_{t-1}),$$

that is, as a test of the hypothesis that the regression function is misspecified due to the omission of the term $Y_{t-1} - \beta^\top X_{t-1}$. Because error autocorrelation may also arise from other forms of misspecification of the regression function, the Durbin–Watson test may be applied to more general contexts than just time series regression. In particular, instead of ordering the data on the basis of a time index, one may order them on the basis of increasing values of the fitted values or some other linear combination of the covariates.

9.3 CLASSICAL MODEL SELECTION CRITERIA

As argued in Chapter 5, a crucial problem with classical hypothesis testing is the fact that it does not provide criteria for choosing the level of a test. In this section we show that no such problem arises if hypothesis testing is formulated as a decision problem. In this case, however, the intent is somewhat different from that of classical hypothesis testing, as the question is not how to determine whether a given set of constraints is consistent with the data, but rather how to select among the available models one that is best given the purposes of the analysis. Formulating the problem explicitly as a decision problem also avoids the pitfalls associated with classical pre-test estimation.

9.3.1 R^2 AND ADJUSTED R^2

In what follows, we shall consider regression models that include an intercept and have a fixed (nonstochastic) design.

First consider the case when the loss incurred by the investigator in selecting a model is measured by $1 - \hat{R}^2$, where $\hat{R}^2$ is the coefficient of determination of the regression. A comparison of $1 - \hat{R}^2$ does not provide a good way of selecting a model for, if noncollinear variables are added, this necessarily leads to a reduction of $1 - \hat{R}^2$. In particular, one can always make $1 - \hat{R}^2$ equal to zero by just selecting a model that contains as many noncollinear predictors as there are observations.

If one regards $1 - \hat{R}^2$ as an estimate of the ratio between the conditional and the unconditional variance of Y, then a natural measure of loss is

$$1 - \bar{R}^2 = \frac{s^2}{\sum_i (Y_i - \bar{Y})^2/(n-1)} = \frac{n-1}{n-k}(1 - \hat{R}^2), \tag{9.6}$$

where $\bar{R}^2$ is known as *adjusted* R^2. The following result provides a simple rule for boosting the adjusted R^2.

Theorem 9.5 *Omitting a single covariate from a regression increases the adjusted R^2 if and only if the F-test statistic for the significance of that covariate is less than one.*

Consider now the following classical linear models for the response vector $\mathbf{Y}$

$$\begin{aligned} \mathrm{H}_1: &\quad \mathrm{E}\,\mathbf{Y} = \mathbf{X}\beta, &\quad \mathrm{Var}\,\mathbf{Y} = \sigma^2 I_n, \\ \mathrm{H}_2: &\quad \mathrm{E}\,\mathbf{Y} = \mathbf{W}\gamma, &\quad \mathrm{Var}\,\mathbf{Y} = \omega^2 I_n, \end{aligned}$$

where $\mathbf{X}$ and $\mathbf{W}$ are nonstochastic matrices of order $n \times k$ and $n \times q$ respectively. It is clear from (9.6) that selecting the model with the highest adjusted R^2 is the same as selecting the one with the smallest s^2. The main justification for the latter criterion is given by the following theorem.

Theorem 9.6 *Let s_j^2 be the OLS estimators of scale for model* H_j, $j = 1, 2$. *If model* H_1 *holds, then* $\mathrm{E}\, s_1^2 \leq \mathrm{E}\, s_2^2$.

Proof. Observe that $s_1^2 = (n-k)^{-1}\mathbf{Y}^\top M_X \mathbf{Y}$ and $s_2^2 = (n-q)^{-1}\mathbf{Y}^\top M_W \mathbf{Y}$, where $M_X = I_n - \mathbf{X}(\mathbf{X}^\top\mathbf{X})^{-1}\mathbf{X}^\top$ and $M_W = I_n - \mathbf{W}(\mathbf{W}^\top\mathbf{W})^{-1}\mathbf{W}^\top$. Under H_1 we have

$$\begin{aligned} \mathrm{E}\,\mathbf{Y}^\top M_W \mathbf{Y} &= \beta^\top \mathbf{X}^\top M_W \mathbf{X}\beta + \mathrm{E}\,\mathbf{U}^\top M_W \mathbf{U} \\ &= \beta^\top \mathbf{X}^\top M_W \mathbf{X}\beta + (n-q)\sigma^2 \geq (n-q)\sigma^2. \end{aligned}$$

Hence $\mathrm{E}\, s_2^2 \geq \sigma^2 = \mathrm{E}\, s_1^2$ under H_1. □

The main problem with the residual sum-of-squares, and therefore with s^2, as a criterion for model selection is that it tends to overestimate a model's predictive accuracy. To see this, suppose that model H_1 holds and consider the problem of predicting an n-dimensional response vector $\tilde{\mathbf{Y}}$ corresponding to a new design matrix $\tilde{\mathbf{X}}$. Under quadratic loss, the performance of the OLS predictor $\tilde{\mathbf{X}}\hat{\beta}$ may be measured by the sum of squared prediction errors $(\tilde{\mathbf{Y}} - \tilde{\mathbf{X}}\hat{\beta})^\top(\tilde{\mathbf{Y}} - \tilde{\mathbf{X}}\hat{\beta})$. The *predictive risk* of $\tilde{\mathbf{X}}\hat{\beta}$ under H_1 is then

$$r(\tilde{\mathbf{X}}\hat{\beta}, \mathrm{H}_1) = \mathrm{E}(\tilde{\mathbf{Y}} - \tilde{\mathbf{X}}\hat{\beta})^\top(\tilde{\mathbf{Y}} - \tilde{\mathbf{X}}\hat{\beta}),$$

where the expectation is with respect to the joint distribution of $\mathbf{Y}$ and $\tilde{\mathbf{Y}}$. To evaluate $r(\tilde{\mathbf{X}}\hat{\beta}, \mathrm{H}_1)$ we use the law of iterated expectations. First, we take expectations with respect to the conditional distribution of $\tilde{\mathbf{Y}}$ given $\mathbf{Y}$

$$\begin{aligned} \mathrm{E}[(\tilde{\mathbf{Y}} - \tilde{\mathbf{X}}\hat{\beta})^\top(\tilde{\mathbf{Y}} - \tilde{\mathbf{X}}\hat{\beta}) \mid \mathbf{Y}] &= \mathrm{tr}[\mathrm{Var}(\tilde{\mathbf{Y}} \mid \mathbf{Y})] + (\tilde{\mathbf{X}}\beta - \tilde{\mathbf{X}}\hat{\beta})^\top(\tilde{\mathbf{X}}\beta - \tilde{\mathbf{X}}\hat{\beta}) \\ &= n\sigma^2 + (\hat{\beta} - \beta)^\top\tilde{\mathbf{X}}^\top\tilde{\mathbf{X}}(\hat{\beta} - \beta). \end{aligned}$$

Next, we take expectations with respect to $\mathbf{Y}$

$$\mathrm{E}(\hat{\beta}-\beta)^\top\tilde{\mathbf{X}}^\top\tilde{\mathbf{X}}(\hat{\beta}-\beta) = \mathrm{tr}[\tilde{\mathbf{X}}^\top\tilde{\mathbf{X}}\,\mathrm{E}(\hat{\beta}-\beta)(\hat{\beta}-\beta)^\top]$$
$$= \sigma^2\,\mathrm{tr}[\tilde{\mathbf{X}}^\top\tilde{\mathbf{X}}(\mathbf{X}^\top\mathbf{X})^{-1}].$$

The predictive risk of $\tilde{\mathbf{X}}\hat{\beta}$ under H_1 is therefore

$$r(\tilde{\mathbf{X}}\hat{\beta},\mathrm{H}_1) = \sigma^2\{n+\mathrm{tr}[\tilde{\mathbf{X}}^\top\tilde{\mathbf{X}}(\mathbf{X}^\top\mathbf{X})^{-1}]\}.$$

In particular, if $\tilde{\mathbf{X}}^\top\tilde{\mathbf{X}} = \mathbf{X}^\top\mathbf{X}$, then

$$r(\tilde{\mathbf{X}}\hat{\beta},\mathrm{H}_1) = (n+k)\sigma^2 > (n-k)\,\mathrm{E}\,s^2 = \mathrm{E}\,\mathbf{Y}^\top M_X\mathbf{Y},$$

that is, the residual sum-of-squares (and therefore s^2) is a downward biased estimator of the predictive risk. Its absolute bias is equal to $2k\sigma^2$ and therefore increases with the number of parameters in the regression model.

Now let $\hat{\gamma} = (\mathbf{W}^\top\mathbf{W})^{-1}\mathbf{W}^\top\mathbf{Y}$ be the OLS coefficient in the regression of $\mathbf{Y}$ on $\mathbf{W}$ and suppose for simplicity that $\tilde{\mathbf{X}}^\top\tilde{\mathbf{X}} = \mathbf{X}^\top\mathbf{X}$, $\tilde{\mathbf{W}}^\top\tilde{\mathbf{W}} = \mathbf{W}^\top\mathbf{W}$ and $\tilde{\mathbf{W}}^\top\tilde{\mathbf{X}} = \mathbf{W}^\top\mathbf{X}$. The predictive risk of $\tilde{\mathbf{W}}\hat{\gamma}$ under H_1 is

$$r(\tilde{\mathbf{W}}\hat{\gamma},\mathrm{H}_1) = \mathrm{E}(\tilde{\mathbf{Y}}-\tilde{\mathbf{W}}\hat{\gamma})^\top(\tilde{\mathbf{Y}}-\tilde{\mathbf{W}}\hat{\gamma}) = (n+q)\sigma^2 + \beta^\top\mathbf{X}^\top M_W\mathbf{X}\beta,$$

where $M_W\mathbf{X}\beta$ is the expectation of the OLS residual vector $\mathbf{Y}-\mathbf{W}\hat{\gamma}$. The second model is clearly misspecified under H_1. We would nevertheless select this model whenever $r(\tilde{\mathbf{W}}\hat{\gamma},\mathrm{H}_1) < r(\tilde{\mathbf{X}}\hat{\beta},\mathrm{H}_1)$, that is, whenever

$$k-q > \frac{\beta^\top\mathbf{X}^\top M_W\mathbf{X}\beta}{\sigma^2}. \tag{9.7}$$

A necessary condition for this to happen is that $q<k$, that is, the misspecified model H_2 must be more parsimonious than the true model H_1. Although (9.7) is not an operational criterion for model selection, for it depends on unknown parameters, it does illustrate the fact that selecting a simple parsimonious model may be a sensible thing to do, at least from the point of view of prediction.

The next three sections discuss three different operational criteria for selecting models on the basis of their predictive accuracy.

9.3.2 THE C_p PROCEDURE

Suppose again that the true model is H_1, defined in the previous section. Let $\mathbf{X} = [\mathbf{X}_1,\mathbf{X}_2]$ and $\beta = (\beta_1,\beta_2)$, where β_1 and β_2 are of dimension k_1 and $k_2 = k-k_1$ respectively, and consider the constrained model H_2: $\mathrm{E}\,\mathbf{Y} = \mathbf{X}_1\beta_1$, which is obtained from H_1 by imposing the constraint $\beta_2 = 0$. Let $\hat{\beta} = (\hat{\beta}_1,\hat{\beta}_2)$ be the unconstrained OLS estimator. The constrained OLS estimator is $\tilde{\beta} = (\tilde{\beta}_1, 0)$, where $\tilde{\beta}_1 = (\mathbf{X}_1{}^\top\mathbf{X}_1)^{-1}\mathbf{X}_1{}^\top\mathbf{Y}$.

First, we evaluate the accuracy of the two models in predicting an n-dimensional response vector $\tilde{\mathbf{Y}}$ corresponding to a new design matrix $\tilde{\mathbf{X}} = [\tilde{\mathbf{X}}_1,\tilde{\mathbf{X}}_2]$. Assuming for simplicity that $\tilde{\mathbf{X}}^\top\tilde{\mathbf{X}} = \mathbf{X}^\top\mathbf{X}$, it follows from the results in Section 9.3.1 that the predictive risk of the larger (unconstrained) model is $r(\tilde{\mathbf{X}}\hat{\beta}, \mathrm{H}_1) = (n+k)\sigma^2$, while the predictive risk of the smaller (constrained) model is

$$r(\tilde{\mathbf{X}}\tilde{\beta}, \mathrm{H}_1) = r(\tilde{\mathbf{X}}_1\tilde{\beta}_1, \mathrm{H}_1) = (n+k_1)\sigma^2 + \beta_2^\top \mathbf{X}_2^\top M_1 \mathbf{X}_2 \beta_2,$$

where $M_1 = \mathbf{X}_1(\mathbf{X}_1^\top \mathbf{X}_1)^{-1}\mathbf{X}_1^\top$ and we used the fact that $M_1\mathbf{X}\beta = M_1\mathbf{X}_2\beta_2$.

If the predictive risks were observable, then we would select the smaller model H_2 whenever $r(\tilde{\mathbf{X}}_1\tilde{\beta}_1, \mathrm{H}_1) < r(\tilde{\mathbf{X}}\hat{\beta}, \mathrm{H}_1)$, that is, whenever

$$k_2 > \frac{\beta_2^\top \mathbf{X}_2^\top M_1 \mathbf{X}_2 \beta_2}{\sigma^2},$$

where k_2 is the difference in the number of parameters between the two models. Because this expression depends on unknown parameters, Mallows (1973) suggested estimating the predictive risks unbiasedly, and then selecting the model having the smallest estimated predictive risk.

Because s^2 is an unbiased estimator of σ^2, an unbiased estimator of the predictive risk of the larger model H_1 is $C_1 = (n+k)s^2$. In order to find an unbiased estimator of the predictive risk of the smaller model H_2 notice that, since $\hat{\beta}_2$ is unbiased for β_2,

$$\begin{aligned}\mathrm{E}(\hat{\beta}_2^\top \mathbf{X}_2^\top M_1 \mathbf{X}_2 \hat{\beta}_2) &- \beta_2^\top \mathbf{X}_2^\top M_1 \mathbf{X}_2 \beta_2 \\ &= \mathrm{Var}[(\hat{\beta}_2 - \beta_2)^\top \mathbf{X}_2^\top M_1 \mathbf{X}_2 (\hat{\beta}_2 - \beta_2)] = k_2\sigma^2,\end{aligned}$$

where we used the fact that $\mathrm{Var}\,\hat{\beta}_2 = \sigma^2\,(\mathbf{X}_2^\top M_1 \mathbf{X}2)^{-1}$. Hence

$$\mathrm{E}(\hat{\beta}_2^\top \mathbf{X}_2^\top M_1 \mathbf{X}_2 \hat{\beta}_2 - k_2\sigma^2) = \beta_2^\top \mathbf{X}_2^\top M_1 \mathbf{X}_2 \beta_2,$$

which implies that the predictive risk of the smaller model H_2 may be estimated unbiasedly by

$$C_2 = (n + k_1 - k_2)s^2 + \hat{\beta}_2^\top \mathbf{X}_2^\top M_1 \mathbf{X}_2 \hat{\beta}_2.$$

Mallows' C_p *procedure* selects the smaller model if $C_2 < C_1$, that is, if

$$2k_2 > \frac{\hat{\beta}_2^\top \mathbf{X}_2^\top M_1 \mathbf{X}_2 \hat{\beta}_2}{s^2} \tag{9.8}$$

or, equivalently, if

$$F = \frac{\hat{\beta}_2^\top \mathbf{X}_2^\top M_1 \mathbf{X}_2 \hat{\beta}_2}{k_2 s^2} < 2,$$

where F is the statistic of an F-test of the hypothesis that $\beta_2 = 0$. Thus, the C_p procedure may be viewed as a rule for choosing the critical region, and therefore the level, of a test of H_2 against H_1. Notice that, unlike the classical F-test, the critical value of the test statistic does not decrease with the sample size but remains constant. As a result, the level of the test does not remain constant but decreases as the sample size increases.

The fact that $C_2 - C_1$ is unbiased for the difference in the predictive risk of the two models represents, however, only a weak justification for C_p. A stronger justification would require showing that, on average, the model selected by C_p is indeed that for which the predictive risk is smallest.

The C_p procedure may also be applied to the problem of selecting among more than two models, not necessarily nested within each other. For example, in addition to H_1 and H_2, also consider the model H_3: $\mathrm{E}\,\mathbf{Y} = \mathbf{X}_2\beta_2$. Letting $\tilde{\beta}_2 = (\mathbf{X}_2{}^\top\mathbf{X}_2)^{-1}\mathbf{X}_2{}^\top\mathbf{Y}$, an unbiased estimator of the predictive risk associated with this model is

$$C_3 = (n + k_2 - k_1)s^2 + \hat{\beta}_1^\top \mathbf{X}_1^\top M_2 \mathbf{X}_1 \hat{\beta}_1,$$

where $M_2 = \mathbf{X}_2(\mathbf{X}_2^\top\mathbf{X}_2)^{-1}\mathbf{X}_2^\top$. In this case, the C_p procedure selects model H_2 if, in addition to (9.8), we also have $C_2 < C_3$, that is,

$$2(k_2 - k_1)s^2 > \hat{\beta}_2^\top \mathbf{X}_2^\top M_1 \mathbf{X}_2 \hat{\beta}_2 - \hat{\beta}_1^\top \mathbf{X}_1^\top M_2 \mathbf{X}_1 \hat{\beta}_1.$$

9.3.3 CROSS-VALIDATION

The idea of cross-validation is to use a fraction of the data for estimating a model and the remaining fraction for assessing its predictive accuracy. One possibility is to divide the data in two halves, estimate the model on the first half and then use these estimates to predict the second half of the data.

In fact, there is no need to divide the data in two halves. Given a model, one possibility is to exclude $d < n$ cases at a time from the sample, estimate the model on the basis of the remaining $n - d$ observations and then use the resulting estimates to predict the excluded cases. When $d = 1$, this method is known as *leave-one-out cross-validation*. Notice that the sample obtained by excluding the ith case is just the ith jackknife sample. Denoting by $\hat{Y}_{(i)}$ a predictor of Y_i based on the ith jackknife sample, the prediction error is given by the difference $Y_i - \hat{Y}_{(i)}$. The sum of the squared prediction errors

$$\mathrm{CV} = \sum_{i=1}^{n} [Y_i - \hat{Y}_{(i)}]^2$$

is also called the *cross-validation criterion*. The *cross-validation procedure* selects the model for which CV is smallest.

Example 9.9 For a linear model estimated by OLS, the cross-validation criterion is

$$\mathrm{CV} = \sum_{i=1}^{n} [Y_i - \hat{\beta}_{(i)}^\top X_i]^2,$$

where $\hat{\beta}_{(i)}$ denotes the OLS estimate from the ith jackknife sample. The CV criterion is therefore equal to the sum of the squared predicted residuals introduced in Section 8.2.1. Because $Y_i - \hat{\beta}_{(i)}^\top X_i = \hat{U}_i/(1 - h_{ii})$, we have

$$\mathrm{CV} = \sum_{i=1}^{n} \left(\frac{\hat{U}_i}{1 - h_{ii}} \right)^2.$$

Under the classical linear model, CV is an approximately unbiased estimator of the predictive risk. To see this notice that, because $\mathrm{E}\,\hat{U}_i = (1 - h_{ii})\sigma^2$,

$$\mathrm{E(CV)} = \sigma^2 \sum_{i=1}^{n} \frac{1}{1 - h_{ii}}.$$

If n is sufficiently large and there are no high leverage points, then h_{ii} is small enough to justify a first-order Taylor series expansion of $(1 - h_{ii})^{-1}$ about $h_{ii} = 0$ yielding

$$\mathrm{E(CV)} \approx \sigma^2 \sum_{i=1}^{n} (1 + h_{ii}) = (n + k)\sigma^2,$$

where we used the fact that $\sum_i h_{ii} = \operatorname{tr} \mathbf{X}^\top \mathbf{X} = k$. □

9.3.4 INFORMATION CRITERIA

The procedure discussed in this section may be regarded as an extension of Mallows' C_p to general parametric problems. Given a parametric model $\mathcal{F}_\Theta = \{f(\mathbf{z}; \theta), \theta \in \Theta\}$ for the joint distribution of the observed data $\mathbf{Z}$, a measure of the model accuracy in predicting a new set $\tilde{\mathbf{Z}}$ of n observations is the Kullback–Leibler dissimilarity index

$$\mathcal{K}(\theta, f_0) = \mathrm{E}_0[\ln f_0(\tilde{\mathbf{Z}})] - \mathrm{E}_0[\ln f(\tilde{\mathbf{Z}}; \theta)],$$

where the expectation is with respect to the true density f_0 of $\tilde{\mathbf{Z}}$. Akaike (1973) proposed $2\,\mathcal{K}(\theta, f_0)$ as a measure of the loss due to approximating f_0 by an element of $\mathcal{F}_\Theta$. In particular, if $f_0(\mathbf{z})$ is approximated by $f(\mathbf{z}; \hat{\theta})$, where $\hat{\theta} = \hat{\theta}(\mathbf{Z})$ is the ML estimator of θ, then the risk of this decision rule is given by

$$r(\hat{\theta}, f_0) = 2\,\mathrm{E}_0\,\mathcal{K}(\hat{\theta}, f_0) = 2\,\mathrm{E}_0[\ln f_0(\tilde{\mathbf{Z}})] - 2\,\mathrm{E}_0[\ln f(\tilde{\mathbf{Z}}; \hat{\theta}(\mathbf{Z}))],$$

where the expectation is with respect to the joint distribution of $\mathbf{Z}$ and $\tilde{\mathbf{Z}}$. The best model is the one for which $r(\hat{\theta}, f_0)$ is smallest. Because $\mathrm{E}_0[\ln f_0(\tilde{\mathbf{Z}})]$, although unknown, is the same for all models, this selection procedure reduces to a comparison of

$$\tilde{r}(\hat{\theta}, f_0) = -2\,\mathrm{E}_0[\ln f(\tilde{\mathbf{Z}}; \hat{\theta}(\mathbf{Z}))]$$

for the various models. As an approximately unbiased estimator of $\tilde{r}(\hat{\theta}, f_0)$, Akaike (1973) proposed the *information criterion*

$$\mathrm{AIC}(\hat{\theta}) = -2\hat{L} + 2p,$$

where $\hat{L} = L(\hat{\theta})$ denotes the maximized value of the sample log-likelihood and p denotes the number of model parameters. The *minimum AIC procedure* selects the model for which AIC is smallest. This procedure may also be used to select among more than two models, possibly nonnested.

Because the term $2p$ may be interpreted as a penalty for lack of parsimony in the model parametrization, AIC provides one way of representing the trade-off between goodness-of-fit and parsimony.

If there are two models, one with p_1 and the other with $p_2 < p_1$ parameters, then the minimum AIC procedure selects the smaller model whenever $\hat{L}_1 - \hat{L}_2 < p_1 - p_2$, where $\hat{L}_j$ denotes the maximized value of the sample log-likelihood for the jth model. Of course, if both models have the same number of parameters, then the second model is selected whenever $\hat{L}_1 < \hat{L}_2$.

If the second model is nested within the first, then $2(\hat{L}_1 - \hat{L}_2)$ is the likelihood ratio statistic for testing the validity of the constraints that define the smaller model. In this case, the minimum AIC procedure may be viewed as a way of choosing the critical region, and therefore the level, of a likelihood ratio test of the constraints.

Figure 60 Critical value of the minimum AIC procedure for choosing between two Gaussian linear models as a function of the number k_1 of parameters in the larger model and the number $n - k_1$ of degrees of freedom. The number of parameters in the smaller model is $k_2 = k_1 - 1$.

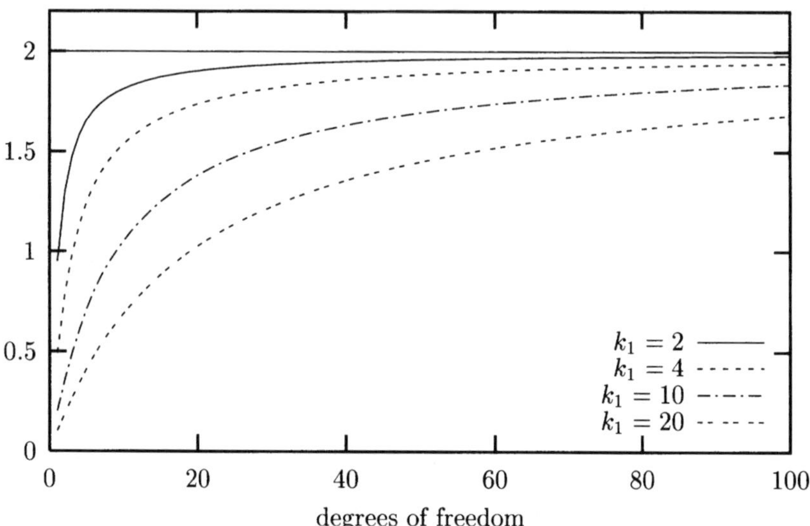

Example 9.10 In the case of two classical Gaussian linear models

$$\text{H}_j: \qquad \mathbf{Y} \sim \mathcal{N}_n(\mathbf{X}_j \beta_j, \sigma_j^2 I_n), \qquad j = 1, 2,$$

where β_j is a k_j-vector, we have that $\hat{L}_j = c - (n/2) \ln \hat{\sigma}_j^2$, $j = 1, 2$, where $\hat{\sigma}_j^2$ denotes the ML estimate of σ_j^2. Thus, the minimum AIC procedure selects H_2 whenever $n \ln(\hat{\sigma}_2^2/\hat{\sigma}_1^2) < 2(k_1 - k_2)$. If $k_1 = k_2$ or n is very large, then AIC selects H_2 whenever $\hat{\sigma}_2^2 < \hat{\sigma}_1^2$. If the second model is obtained from the first by imposing a set of q linear equality constraints, then the minimum AIC procedure selects the smaller model whenever

$$F = \frac{(\hat{\sigma}_2^2 - \hat{\sigma}_1^2)/q}{\hat{\sigma}_1^2/(n - k_1)} < \frac{n - k_1}{q} \left[\exp\left(\frac{2q}{n}\right) - 1 \right],$$

where F is the F-test statistic and $q = k_1 - k_2$. This procedure may therefore be viewed as another way of choosing the critical region, and therefore the level, of an F-test of the restrictions implied by the second model. Unlike the C_p procedure, the critical value of the test statistic depends now on n, k_1 and q (Figure 60). This critical value increases with the sample size and converges slowly from below to 2, which is also the critical value of the C_p procedure. Thus, the AIC selects the unconstrained model more frequently than C_p does, especially when the number of degrees of freedom is small.

Figure 61 shows the relationship between the number of degrees of freedom and the level of tests that reject the smaller model when the F-test statistic F exceeds the critical values implied by AIC or the C_p criterion for $k_1 = 10$ and $q = 1$. Notice

Figure 61 Relationship between the number of degrees of freedom and the level (vertical axis) of tests that reject the smaller model when the F-test statistic exceeds the critical values implied by AIC or the C_p criterion for $k_1 = 10$ and $q = 1$.

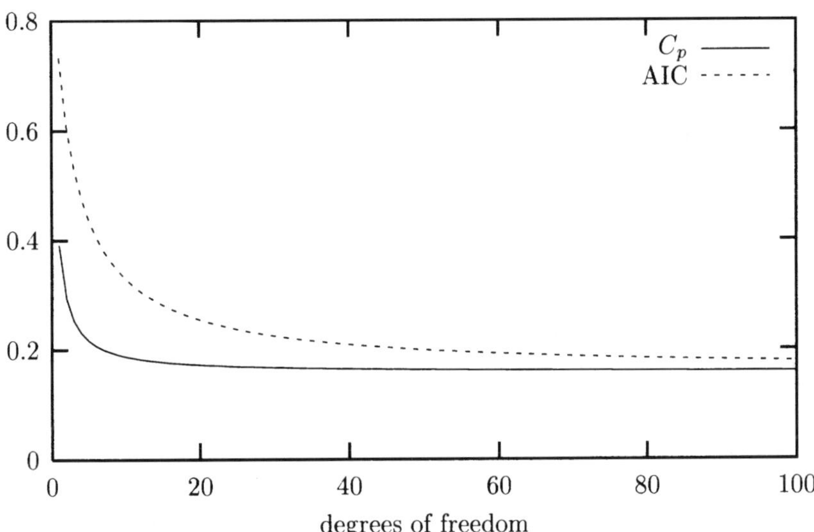

that the probabilities of Type I error implied by the AIC and the C_p criterion always exceed 10 percent. □

A problem with the minimum AIC procedure is the fact that it tends to favor the unconstrained model more than it should.

Example 9.11 Consider again the case of Section 9.3.2, but further suppose that the two models are Gaussian. Let $\hat{\theta}(\mathbf{Y}) = (\hat{\beta}, \hat{\sigma}^2)$ be the unconstrained ML estimate of $\theta = (\beta, \sigma^2)$ and let $\tilde{\theta}(\mathbf{Y}) = (\tilde{\beta}, \tilde{\sigma}^2)$ be the constrained estimate. Sawa (1978) showed that, although AIC is approximately unbiased for $-2\,\mathrm{E}_0[\ln f(\tilde{\mathbf{Y}}; \hat{\theta}(\mathbf{Y}))]$, it is a biased estimator of $-2\,\mathrm{E}_0[\ln f(\tilde{\mathbf{Y}}; \tilde{\theta}(\mathbf{Y}))]$. In this case, an approximately unbiased estimator is

$$\mathrm{BIC}(\tilde{\theta}) = -2L(\tilde{\theta}) + 2\left(\frac{\hat{\sigma}^2}{\hat{\sigma}_*^2}\right)\left[k + 1 - \left(\frac{\hat{\sigma}^2}{\hat{\sigma}_*^2}\right)\right],$$

where $\hat{\sigma}_*^2 = \hat{\sigma}^2 + n^{-1}\hat{\beta}_2^\top \mathbf{X}_2^\top M_1 \mathbf{X}_2 \hat{\beta}_2$. BIC tends to favor the constrained model more than AIC. □

This problem has generated an active line of research which resulted in several proposals in the general class of criteria of the form $C(\mathbf{Z}, p) = Q(\mathbf{Z}) + \alpha p$, $\alpha > 0$ (Smith & Spiegelhalter 1980), where $Q(\mathbf{Z})$ is some measure of goodness-of-fit and α is a penalty for the number p of model parameters. Typically $Q(\mathbf{Z}) = -2\hat{L}$, but the residual variance or other statistics have also been suggested. Most controversies concern the choice of the parameter α. If $\alpha = 2$, we obtain AIC. If $\alpha = \ln n$, we obtain the criterion of Schwarz (1978). If $\alpha = c\ln(\ln n)$, for $c > 2$, we obtain the criterion of Hannan and Quinn (1979).

9.4 BAYESIAN HYPOTHESIS TESTING

Consider J possible Gaussian linear models for $\mathbf{Y}$

$$\mathrm{H}_j\colon \mathbf{Y} \sim \mathcal{N}_n(\mathbf{X}_j\beta_j,\, \sigma_j^2 I_n), \qquad j = 1, \dots, J,$$

where β_j is a k_j-vector. Notice that these J models need not be nested within each other. Assume that prior probabilities have been attached to each of these models, and let p_j denote the prior probability attached to the jth one.

The sample likelihood for the jth model is of the form

$$f(\mathbf{Y} \,|\, \beta_j, \sigma_j) \propto \frac{1}{\sigma_j^n} \exp\left\{ -\frac{1}{2\sigma_j^2}[n\hat{\sigma}_j^2 + (\beta_j - \hat{\beta}_j)^\top \mathbf{X}_j^\top \mathbf{X}_j(\beta_j - \hat{\beta}_j)] \right\},$$

where $\hat{\beta}_j$ and $\hat{\sigma}_j^2$ are the usual ML estimates of β_j and σ_j^2 based on model H_j. Suppose that the prior distribution of (β_j, σ_j), $j = 1, \dots, J$, is gamma-Gaussian with parameter $(\bar{\beta}_j, \Sigma_j, m_j, \lambda_j)$, that is, the conditional prior distribution of β_j given σ_j is $\mathcal{N}_k(\bar{\beta}_j,\, \sigma_j^2 \Sigma_j^{-1})$, while the prior distribution of σ_j is an inverted gamma with parameter $(m_j/2, m_j\lambda_j/2)$ and density

$$p(\sigma_j) \propto \frac{1}{\sigma_j^{m_j+1}} \exp\left(-\frac{m_j \lambda_j}{2\sigma_j^2} \right).$$

The posterior odds-ratio between any two models, say the first and the second, is

$$\frac{p_1(\mathbf{Y})}{p_2(\mathbf{Y})} = \frac{p_1}{p_2} \frac{f(\mathbf{Y} \,|\, \mathrm{H}_i)}{f(\mathbf{Y} \,|\, \mathrm{H}_2)},$$

which is the product of the prior odds-ratio p_1/p_2 and the Bayes factor $f(\mathbf{Y} \,|\, \mathrm{H}_1)/f(\mathbf{Y} \,|\, \mathrm{H}_2)$. The data favor the first model over the second if the posterior odds-ratio $p_1(\mathbf{Y})/p_2(\mathbf{Y})$ is greater than one or, equivalently, if the Bayes factor is greater than one.

Computing the Bayes factor requires evaluating the marginal likelihoods

$$f(\mathbf{Y} \,|\, \mathrm{H}_j) = \int f(\mathbf{Y} \,|\, \beta_j, \sigma_j)\, p(\beta_j, \sigma_j)\, d\beta_j\, d\sigma_j, \qquad j = 1, 2.$$

We do this in two steps. First we obtain the conditional distribution of $\mathbf{Y}$ given σ_j. Then we integrate with respect to σ_j.

Under H_j and given the prior distribution of β_j, the conditional distribution of $\mathbf{Y}$ given σ_j is n-variate Gaussian with mean equal to $\mathbf{X}_j\bar{\beta}_j$ and variance equal to $\sigma_j^2(I_n + \mathbf{X}_j\Sigma_j\mathbf{X}_j^\top)$. Dropping the suffix j to simplify notation, the conditional density of $\mathbf{Y}$ given σ is therefore

$$f(\mathbf{Y} \,|\, \sigma) \propto \frac{1}{\sigma^n} \exp\left[-\frac{1}{2\sigma^2}(\mathbf{Y} - \mathbf{X}\bar{\beta})^\top M_*(\mathbf{Y} - \mathbf{X}\bar{\beta}) \right],$$

where $M_* = (I_n + \mathbf{X}\Sigma^{-1}\mathbf{X}^\top)^{-1} = I_n - \mathbf{X}(\mathbf{X}^\top\mathbf{X} + \Sigma^{-1})^{-1}\mathbf{X}^\top$. Given the prior distribution of σ, we then have

$$f(\mathbf{Y} \,|\, \sigma)\, p(\sigma) \propto \frac{1}{\sigma^{n+m+1}} \exp\left\{ -\frac{1}{2\sigma^2}[m\lambda + (\mathbf{Y} - \mathbf{X}\bar{\beta})^\top M_*(\mathbf{Y} - \mathbf{X}\bar{\beta})] \right\}.$$

Now integrating with respect to σ and using the integral formula in Section 6.6.1, we obtain

$$f(\mathbf{Y}) = \int_0^\infty f(\mathbf{Y} \mid \sigma)\, p(\sigma)\, d\sigma \propto [m\lambda + (\mathbf{Y} - \mathbf{X}\bar{\beta})^\top M_*(\mathbf{Y} - \mathbf{X}\bar{\beta})]^{-(n+m)/2},$$

which has the form of an n-variate t-density with m degrees of freedom. Hence

$$f(\mathbf{Y}) = c(m,n)\,[\det(M_*/\lambda)]^{1/2}\left(m + \frac{S}{\lambda}\right)^{-(n+m)/2},$$

where

$$S = (\mathbf{Y} - \mathbf{X}\bar{\beta})^\top M_*(\mathbf{Y} - \mathbf{X}\bar{\beta}) = n\hat{\sigma}^2 + (\hat{\beta} - \bar{\beta})^\top[(\mathbf{X}^\top\mathbf{X})^{-1} + \Sigma^{-1}]^{-1}(\hat{\beta} - \bar{\beta}).$$

Because $f(\mathbf{Y})$ is a monotonically decreasing function of S, the marginal likelihood of the model is reduced either when $\hat{\sigma}^2$ is large (or, equivalently, the regression $\hat{R}^2$ is small) or when there is a large discrepancy between $\hat{\beta}$ and the prior mean $\bar{\beta}$.

As $n \to \infty$, the behavior of S is dominated by the term $n\hat{\sigma}^2$. Further, because $\det M_* = \det(\Sigma)/\det(\mathbf{X}^\top\mathbf{X} + \Sigma)$, the behavior of $\det M_*$ is dominated by the one of $\det \mathbf{X}^\top\mathbf{X}$. Thus, in large samples, the Bayes factor of the first model relative to the second is well approximated by

$$\frac{f(\mathbf{Y} \mid \mathrm{H}_1)}{f(\mathbf{Y} \mid \mathrm{H}_2)} \approx c\left[\frac{\det(\mathbf{X}_2^\top\mathbf{X}_2)}{\det(\mathbf{X}_1^\top\mathbf{X}_1)}\right]^{1/2}\left(\frac{\hat{\sigma}_2^2}{\hat{\sigma}_1^2}\right)^{n/2},$$

where c does not depend on the sample size. If, in addition, $\mathbf{X}_1^\top\mathbf{X}_1/n$ and $\mathbf{X}_2^\top\mathbf{X}_2/n$ both converge to constant matrices, say P_1 and P_2, then

$$\frac{\det(\mathbf{X}_2^\top\mathbf{X}_2)}{\det(\mathbf{X}_1^\top\mathbf{X}_1)} \to \frac{\det(nP_2)}{\det(nP_1)} = n^{k_2-k_1}\frac{\det P_2}{\det P_1}.$$

In this case, a large sample approximation to the Bayes factor is

$$B = c'\, n^{(k_2-k_1)/2}\left(\frac{\hat{\sigma}_2^2}{\hat{\sigma}_1^2}\right)^{n/2},$$

where $c' = c\,(\det P_2/\det P_2)^{1/2}$. In particular, if the second model is obtained by excluding $q = k_1 - k_2$ covariates from the first, then the data favor the smaller model whenever $B < 1$, that is, whenever

$$F = \frac{(\hat{\sigma}_2^2 - \hat{\sigma}_1^2)/q}{\hat{\sigma}_1^2/(n-k_1)} < \left(\frac{n^{q/n}}{c'} - 1\right)\frac{n-k_1}{q},$$

where F denotes the classical F-test statistic. As shown in Table 4, the critical values on the right-hand side of the above expression do not decrease as in the classical approach, but rather increase with the sample size. As a result, the probability of Type I error is not constant but approaches zero as the sample size increases.

Table 4 Bayesian and classical critical values of an F-test of a single constraint ($q = 1$). The row corresponding to $\alpha = .05$ presents the critical values of a classical 5%-level test. The table is taken from Leamer (1978), p. 116.

	Degrees of freedom $(n-k)$				
	5	10	50	100	1,000
$k = 1$	1.74	2.44	4.01	4.68	6.93
$k = 2$	1.60	2.30	3.95	4.64	6.92
$k = 3$	1.48	2.18	3.89	4.60	6.91
$k = 4$	1.38	2.07	3.83	4.57	6.91
$k = 5$	1.29	1.98	3.78	4.53	6.90
$k = 10$	.99	1.62	3.53	4.37	6.87
$k = 20$	.69	1.20	3.13	4.07	6.81
$\alpha = .05$	6.60	4.96	4.03	3.94	3.85

BIBLIOGRAPHIC NOTES

An exact test of linear inequality constraints on the regression parameter of a Gaussian linear model is discussed in Gourieroux, Holly and Monfort (1982) and Wolak (1987).

On pre-testing see Judge and Bock (1978) and Giles and Giles (1993).

The difference test goes back to Durbin (1954) and Wu (1973). It has been made popular in econometrics by Hausman (1978). Thursby (1985) describes the relation between the difference test, RESET and the Chow test. Holly (1982) studies in detail the power properties of the difference test. Two good surveys on specification tests are Holly (1987) and Ruud (1984).

The Durbin–Watson test was introduced by Durbin and Watson (1950, 1951). See also Durbin and Watson (1971).

A good introduction to the general problem of model selection is the book by Linhart and Zucchini (1986). The idea of comparing models on the basis of their predictive risk goes back to Hotelling (1940). The C_p criterion was introduced by Mallows (1973). Methods for evaluating the precision of the C_p procedure are discussed in Efron (1984). A good introduction to cross-validation is Efron and Tibshirani (1993).

The main reference for Section 9.4 is Leamer (1978).

PROBLEMS

9.1 Consider the model introduced in Example 9.2. Show that the OLS estimator of β for this model coincides with the OLS estimator $\hat{\beta}_{(i)}$ for the sample with the ith case excluded.

9.2 Generalize the test of Example 9.2 to the case when $q < n$ observations are potential outliers.

9.3 You are interested in testing for the absence of heteroskedasticity given a sample of n independent observations. After ordering the observations on the basis of the norm of the vector X_i, keep the n_1 observations $[\mathbf{X}_1, \mathbf{Y}_1]$ for which $\|X_i\|$ is smallest and the n_2 observations $[\mathbf{X}_2, \mathbf{Y}_2]$ for which $\|X_i\|$ is largest, with $n_1 + n_2 < n$. Let SSE_j denote the residual sum-of-squares from an OLS regression of $\mathbf{Y}_j$ on $\mathbf{X}_j$. Show that, if

$$\mathbf{Y}_j \sim \mathcal{N}_{n_j}(\mathbf{X}_j\beta_j, \sigma_j^2 I_{n_j}), \qquad j = 1, 2,$$

then

$$\frac{\mathrm{SSE}_1/n_1}{\mathrm{SSE}_2/n_2} \sim F_{n_1,n_2}$$

under H_0: $\sigma_1^2 = \sigma_2^2$.

9.4 Show that the classical t- and F-test statistics are invariant under nonsingular linear transformations of the parameter space, that is, under reparametrizations of the form $\gamma = A\beta$, where A is a nonsingular matrix.

9.5 Let $Z \sim \mathcal{N}_k(\mu, I_k)$. Show that

$$\mathrm{E}[Z\,1\{Z^\top Z > c\}] = \mu + \Pr\{\chi^2_{k+2,\lambda} > c\}$$

and

$$\mathrm{E}[Z^\top Z\; 1\{Z^\top Z > c\}] = k\Pr\{\chi^2_{k+2,\lambda} > c\} + \lambda \Pr\{\chi^2_{k+4,\lambda} > c\},$$

where $\lambda = \mu^\top \mu$.

9.6 Suppose that $\mathbf{Y} \sim \mathcal{N}_n(\mathbf{X}\beta + \mathbf{W}\gamma, \sigma^2 I_n)$. Let $\mathbf{U} = \mathbf{Y} - \mathbf{X}\beta$, $M = I_n - \mathbf{X}(\mathbf{X}^\top\mathbf{X})^{-1}\mathbf{X}^\top$ and $\hat{\mathbf{U}} = M\mathbf{Y}$, and denote by $\tilde{\gamma}$, $\bar{\gamma}$ and $\hat{\gamma}$, respectively, the OLS coefficients in the regression of $\mathbf{U}$ on $\mathbf{W}$, of $\hat{\mathbf{U}}$ on $\mathbf{W}$, and of $\hat{\mathbf{U}}$ on $M\mathbf{W}$. Show that $\hat{\gamma}$ is the OLS estimator of γ in the regression of $\mathbf{Y}$ on $\mathbf{X}$ and $\mathbf{W}$, and that

$$\tilde{\gamma} \sim \mathcal{N}_q(\gamma, \sigma^2\,(\mathbf{W}^\top\mathbf{W})^{-1}),$$
$$\bar{\gamma} \sim \mathcal{N}_q((\mathbf{W}^\top\mathbf{W})^{-1}\mathbf{W}^\top M\mathbf{W}\gamma, \sigma^2\,(\mathbf{W}^\top\mathbf{W})^{-1}\mathbf{W}^\top M\mathbf{W}(\mathbf{W}^\top\mathbf{W})^{-1}),$$
$$\hat{\gamma} \sim \mathcal{N}_q(\gamma, \sigma^2\,(\mathbf{W}^\top M\mathbf{W})^{-1}).$$

9.7 Consider again Problem 9.6, and denote by $\tilde{\gamma}_*$, $\bar{\gamma}_*$ and $\hat{\gamma}_*$, respectively, the OLS coefficients in a regression of $\mathbf{U}$ on $\mathbf{Z}$, of $\hat{\mathbf{U}}$ on $\mathbf{Z}$, and of $\hat{\mathbf{U}}$ on $M\mathbf{Z}$, where $\mathbf{Z}$ is a matrix of constants different from $\mathbf{W}$. Show that

$$\tilde{\gamma}_* \sim \mathcal{N}_q((\mathbf{Z}^\top\mathbf{Z})^{-1}\mathbf{Z}^\top\mathbf{W}\gamma, \sigma^2\,(\mathbf{Z}^\top\mathbf{Z})^{-1}),$$
$$\bar{\gamma}_* \sim \mathcal{N}_q((\mathbf{Z}^\top\mathbf{Z})^{-1}\mathbf{Z}^\top M\mathbf{W}\gamma, \sigma^2\,(\mathbf{Z}^\top\mathbf{Z})^{-1}\mathbf{Z}^\top M\mathbf{Z}(\mathbf{Z}^\top\mathbf{Z})^{-1}),$$
$$\hat{\gamma}_* \sim \mathcal{N}_q((\mathbf{Z}^\top M\mathbf{Z})^{-1}\mathbf{Z}^\top M\mathbf{W}\gamma, \sigma^2\,(\mathbf{Z}^\top M\mathbf{Z})^{-1}).$$

9.8 Show that the difference test statistic in Example 9.8 may be computed through an auxiliary OLS regression of $\mathbf{Y}$ on $\mathbf{X}$ and $D\mathbf{X}$.

9.9 Show that the Durbin–Watson statistic may be written as (9.5).

9.10 Prove Theorem 9.5.

9.11 Consider an OLS regression of $\mathbf{Y}$ on $\mathbf{X}$ and let $\mathrm{CV} = \sum_i [Y_i - \hat{\beta}^\top X_i]^2$, where $\hat{\beta}_{(i)}$ denotes the OLS coefficient computed excluding the ith case. Compute the expectation of CV when $\mathrm{E}\,\mathbf{Y} = \mathbf{W}\gamma$ and $\mathrm{Var}\,\mathbf{Y} = \sigma^2 I_n$.

9.12 Consider the minimum AIC procedure for selecting between two Gaussian linear models, neither of which is necessarily the true one. Show that when the two models have the same number of parameters, this method selects the model for which $\hat{R}^2$ is larger or the scale estimate is smaller.

9.13 Consider the minimum AIC procedure for selecting between two Gaussian linear models, one of which is the true one. Show that when the conditional variance of **Y** given **X** is known, then AIC coincides with the C_p criterion.

10

Asymptotic Properties of Least Squares Methods

In this chapter we study the large sample properties of statistical procedures based on LS methods. As an introduction and a motivation, let the data consist of a random n-vector $\mathbf{Y}$ and a nonstochastic $n \times k$ matrix $\mathbf{X}$ of rank $k < n$. If $\mathrm{E}\,\mathbf{Y} = \mathbf{X}\beta$, where β is a k-vector of parameters to be estimated then, no matter what β is, the OLS estimator $\hat{\beta}_n = (\mathbf{X}^\top\mathbf{X})^{-1}\mathbf{X}^\top\mathbf{Y}$ is unbiased for β. If in addition $\mathrm{Var}\,\mathbf{Y} = \sigma^2 I_n$, with $0 < \sigma^2 < \infty$, then $\mathrm{Var}\,\hat{\beta}_n = \sigma^2\,(\mathbf{X}^\top\mathbf{X})^{-1}$. Now keep k fixed and let the sample size n grow without bounds. If all elements on the main diagonal of $(\mathbf{X}^\top\mathbf{X})^{-1}$ converge to zero as $n \to \infty$, then the sequence $\{\hat{\beta}_n\}$ of OLS estimators, corresponding to increasing sample sizes, converges in mean square to the regression parameter β. Since mean square convergence implies convergence in probability, $\hat{\beta}_n$ is a consistent estimator of β. Further, if $\mathbf{Y} \sim \mathcal{N}_n(\mathbf{X}\beta,\, \sigma^2 I_n)$, then the sampling distribution of $\hat{\beta}_n$ is $\mathcal{N}_k(\beta,\, \sigma^2\,(\mathbf{X}^\top\mathbf{X})^{-1})$ for every $n \geq k$ and therefore the rescaled difference $\sqrt{n}\,(\hat{\beta}_n - \beta)$ is asymptotically Gaussian with asymptotic variance $V_n = \sigma^2(\mathbf{X}^\top\mathbf{X}/n)^{-1}$.

In the remainder of this chapter we show that consistency and asymptotic normality of the OLS estimator hold under much weaker conditions. In particular, we do not need $\mathbf{X}$ to be nonstochastic and to have full rank for every $n \geq k$, nor the conditional distribution of $\mathbf{Y}$ given $\mathbf{X}$ to be Gaussian, nor the conditional variance of $\mathbf{Y}$ given $\mathbf{X}$ to be scalar or even finite.

10.1 CONSISTENCY OF THE OLS ESTIMATOR

Section 10.1.1 presents sufficient conditions for the sequence $\{\hat{\beta}_n\}$ of OLS estimators to converge in probability to the regression parameter β as $n \to \infty$. Section 10.1.2 introduces some primitive assumptions that guarantee that the OLS estimator is consistent for β. In fact, this set of assumptions can easily be modified to establish strong consistency of the OLS estimator. Section 10.1.3 discusses cases where the OLS estimator fails to be consistent. In all cases considered, the parameter space does not change with the sample size. An important situation where this does not hold is discussed in Chapter 12.

10.1.1 THE MAIN RESULT

In most practical cases, showing that $\hat{\beta}_n$ is a consistent estimator of β reduces to verifying the conditions of the following theorem.

Theorem 10.1 *Suppose that:*

(i) $n^{-1}\mathbf{X}^\top(\mathbf{Y}-\mathbf{X}\beta) \xrightarrow{\text{p}} 0$ *for some* $\beta \in \Re^k$*;*
(ii) $n^{-1}\mathbf{X}^\top\mathbf{X} - P_n \xrightarrow{\text{p}} 0$*, where the* $k \times k$ *matrix* P_n *is symmetric and* $O(1)$*, and* $\det P_n > \delta$ *for some* $\delta > 0$ *and all* n *sufficiently large.*

Then $\hat{\beta}_n$ *exists with probability approaching one and* $\hat{\beta}_n \xrightarrow{\text{p}} \beta$*.*

Proof. Let $\mathbf{U} = \mathbf{Y} - \mathbf{X}\beta$. Since P_n is $O(1)$, it follows that $\det(n^{-1}\mathbf{X}^\top\mathbf{X}) - \det(P_n) \xrightarrow{\text{p}} 0$. Because $\det P_n > \delta > 0$ for all n sufficiently large, the inverse matrix of $n^{-1}\mathbf{X}^\top\mathbf{X}$ exists with probability approaching one and so does

$$\hat{\beta}_n = \beta + \left(\frac{\mathbf{X}^\top\mathbf{X}}{n}\right)^{-1} \frac{\mathbf{X}^\top\mathbf{U}}{n}.$$

Finally, assumption (i) and the fact that $(\mathbf{X}^\top\mathbf{X}/n)^{-1} - P_n^{-1} \xrightarrow{\text{p}} 0$ imply

$$\hat{\beta}_n - \beta = \left[\left(\frac{\mathbf{X}^\top\mathbf{X}}{n}\right)^{-1} - P_n^{-1}\right] \frac{\mathbf{X}^\top\mathbf{U}}{n} + P_n^{-1}\frac{\mathbf{X}^\top\mathbf{U}}{n} \xrightarrow{\text{p}} 0,$$

that is, $\hat{\beta}_n \xrightarrow{\text{p}} \beta$. □

The matrix $n^{-1}\mathbf{X}^\top\mathbf{X}$ is the uncentered sample second moment matrix of the covariates in $\mathbf{X}$. Assumption (ii) requires $n^{-1}\mathbf{X}^\top\mathbf{X}$ to converge to a matrix P_n which, although not necessarily fixed, must be finite and "sufficiently nonsingular" for all n sufficiently large.

The fundamental assumption of Theorem 10.1 is (i), which implicitly defines the regression parameter β by requiring any correlation between $\mathbf{X}$ and the regression error vector $\mathbf{U} = \mathbf{Y} - \mathbf{X}\beta$ to vanish in large samples. This assumption is clearly satisfied when $\mathrm{E}(\mathbf{Y} \mid \mathbf{X}) = \mathbf{X}\beta$, because then $\mathrm{E}(\mathbf{U} \mid \mathbf{X}) = 0$, or when $\mathbf{X}\beta$ is the BLP of $\mathbf{Y}$ given $\mathbf{X}$, because then $\mathrm{E}\,\mathbf{X}^\top\mathbf{U} = 0$ by definition. Notice that no assumption is made about the second moments of the regression errors. The latter could therefore be heteroskedastic, autocorrelated or even have infinite variance with no effect on the consistency of $\hat{\beta}_n$.

Replacing convergence in probability with almost sure convergence in the assumptions of Theorem 10.1 gives the stronger result that $\hat{\beta}_n$ exists with probability one for all n sufficiently large and $\hat{\beta}_n \xrightarrow{\text{as}} \beta$, that is, $\hat{\beta}_n$ is a strongly consistent estimator of β.

10.1.2 SOME PRIMITIVE ASSUMPTIONS

Primitive assumptions typically differ in cross-section and time series settings. The simplest situation is when the observations are a sequence of i.i.d. random variables, as in the case of simple random sampling.

Theorem 10.2 *Suppose that:*

(i) $\{(X_i, Y_i)\}$ *is a sequence of i.i.d. random vectors;*
(ii) $\mathrm{E}\, X_i(Y_i - \beta^\top X_i) = 0$ *for some* $\beta \in \Re^k$*;*
(iii) $\mathrm{E}\, X_i X_i^\top = P$*, a finite p.d. matrix.*

Then $\hat\beta_n$ *exists with probability approaching one and* $\hat\beta_n \xrightarrow{\mathrm{p}} \beta$.

Proof. Let $U_i = Y_i - \beta^\top X_i$. Assumption (i) implies that the elements of the sequences $\{X_i U_i\}$ and $\{X_i X_i^\top\}$ are i.i.d. with finite mean. Hence, by Khinchine WLLN, $n^{-1}\mathbf{X}^\top \mathbf{U} = n^{-1}\sum_{i=1}^n X_i U_i \xrightarrow{\mathrm{p}} 0$ and $n^{-1}\mathbf{X}^\top\mathbf{X} = n^{-1}\sum_{i=1}^n X_i X_i^\top \xrightarrow{\mathrm{p}} P$, where the matrix P is p.d. by assumption (iii). All the conditions of Theorem 10.1 are therefore satisfied. □

Notice that assumption (i) allows the regression model to be conditionally heteroskedastic, that is, $\mathrm{Var}(Y_i \mid X_i)$ may depend on X_i.

It is often appropriate to regard the observations as independent but not identically distributed, as in the case of stratified sampling.

Theorem 10.3 *Suppose that:*

(i) $\{(X_i, Y_i)\}$ *is a sequence of independent random vectors;*
(ii) $\mathrm{E}\, X_i(Y_i - \beta^\top X_i) = 0$ *for some* $\beta \in \Re^k$*;*
(iii) $\mathrm{E}\,|X_{ij}^2|^\nu \le M < \infty$ *for some* $\nu > 1$*, all* $j = 1, \ldots, k$ *and every* i*;*
(iv) $\mathrm{E}(n^{-1}\mathbf{X}^\top\mathbf{X}) = P_n$*, with* $\det P_n > \delta$ *for some* $\delta > 0$ *and all* n *sufficiently large;*
(v) $\mathrm{E}\,|X_{ij}(Y_i - \beta^\top X_i)|^\nu \le M < \infty$ *for some* $\nu > 1$*, all* $j = 1, \ldots, k$ *and every* i*.*

Then $\hat\beta_n$ *exists with probability approaching one and* $\hat\beta_n \xrightarrow{\mathrm{p}} \beta$.

Proof. Let $U_i = Y_i - \beta^\top X_i$. Assumption (i) implies that the elements of the sequences $\{X_i U_i\}$ and $\{X_i X_i^\top\}$ are independent. Given (ii) and (v), $n^{-1}\mathbf{X}^\top\mathbf{U} = n^{-1}\sum_i X_i U_i \xrightarrow{\mathrm{p}} 0$ by the Markov SLLN. Cauchy–Schwarz inequality and assumption (iii) imply that

$$\mathrm{E}\,|X_{ij}X_{ih}|^\nu \le (\mathrm{E}\,|X_{ij}^2|^\nu\, \mathrm{E}\,|X_{ih}^2|^\nu)^{1/2} \le \sqrt{M}\sqrt{M} = M < \infty$$

for some $\nu > 1$, all $j, h = 1, \ldots, k$, and every i. Hence, $P_n = O(1)$ and therefore, by the Markov SLLN, $n^{-1}\mathbf{X}^\top\mathbf{X} - P_n = n^{-1}\sum_i X_i X_i^\top - P_n \xrightarrow{\mathrm{p}} 0$ where, under assumption (iv), $\det P_n > \delta > 0$ for all n sufficiently large. □

Theorem 10.3 differs from Theorem 10.2 in two respects. First, it weakens the assumption that the observations are identically distributed and that $n^{-1}\mathbf{X}^\top\mathbf{X}$ converges to a constant matrix. Second, it imposes more stringent conditions on the moments of the relevant distributions. In particular, if $U_i = Y_i - \beta^\top X_i$, then the absolute moments of $X_i U_i$ of order slightly higher than one must now be uniformly bounded. This trade-off between heterogeneity and moment restrictions is typical of asymptotic problems.

The case when the design matrix $\mathbf{X}$ is nonstochastic may be seen as a case of independent not identically distributed random variables whose probability distribution is degenerate and gives unit mass to the observed values of the covariates. Therefore, Theorem 10.3 may also be applied to the case when the covariates are fixed, provided that they are uniformly bounded.

Finally, we present a result for stationary ergodic time series.

Theorem 10.4 *Let $U_t = Y_t - \beta^\top X_t$, $t = 1, \ldots, n$, and suppose:*

(i) $\{(X_t, U_t)\}$ *is a stationary ergodic process;*
(ii) $\mathrm{E}\, X_t U_t = 0$;
(iii) $\mathrm{E}\, |X_t j U_t| < \infty$ *for all* $j = 1, \ldots, k$ *and every* t;
(iv) $\mathrm{E}\, |X_{tj}|^2 < \infty$ *for all* $j = 1, \ldots, k$ *and every* t;
(v) $\mathrm{E}\, X_t X_t^\top = P$, *a p.d. matrix.*

Then $\hat{\beta}_n$ exists almost surely as $n \to \infty$ and $\hat{\beta}_n \overset{\text{as}}{\to} \beta$.

Proof. See White (1984), Theorem 3.37. □

10.1.3 VIOLATIONS OF THE FUNDAMENTAL ASSUMPTION

The assumption that $n^{-1}\mathbf{X}^\top(\mathbf{Y} - \mathbf{X}\beta) \overset{\text{p}}{\to} 0$ is of fundamental importance because it implicitly defines the regression parameter β. Such a condition is satisfied in Theorems 10.2 and 10.3 through the assumption that $\mathrm{E}\, X_i(Y_i - \beta^\top X_i) = 0$ for every i. If instead $\mathrm{E}\, X_i(Y_i - \beta^\top X_i) \neq 0$ for some i, then the OLS estimate is not generally consistent for β.

We now present three important examples where this fundamental assumption is violated. The first example is a linear model with measurement errors in the covariates. The second is a linear simultaneous equation model. The third is a dynamic linear model with autocorrelated errors.

Example 10.1 The linear model with classical measurement errors was introduced in Section 2.5.1. It consists of a latent linear model, that for simplicity we assume to be $Y^* = \beta X^* + \epsilon$, and a measurement model $Y = Y^* + \nu$ and $X = X^* + \xi$, where X^*, ϵ, ν and ξ are uncorrelated random variables with mean zero and finite variance equal to σ_X^2, σ_ϵ^2, σ_ν^2 and σ_ξ^2, respectively. The researcher does not observe Y^* and X^* but only their error-ridden measures Y and X. The relationship between the observables may be represented as $Y = \beta X + U$, $U = \epsilon + \nu - \beta\xi$. The relevant moments are

$$\operatorname{Var} X = \operatorname{Var} X^* + \operatorname{Var} \xi = \sigma_X^2 + \sigma_\xi^2,$$
$$\operatorname{Cov}(X, Y) = \mathrm{E}(X^* + \xi)(\beta X^* + \epsilon + \nu) = \beta\sigma_X^2,$$

and

$$\mathrm{E}\, XU = \mathrm{E}(X^* - \xi)(\epsilon + \nu - \beta\xi) = -\beta\sigma_\xi^2,$$

where $\mathrm{E}\, XU = 0$ if either $\beta = 0$, that is, Y^* does not depend on X^*, or $\sigma_\xi^2 = 0$, that is, X^* is measured without error. The BLP of Y given X is $\mathrm{E}^*(Y \,|\, X) = \beta_* X$, where

$$\beta_* = \beta \frac{\sigma_X^2}{\sigma_X^2 + \sigma_\xi^2}$$

is different from β unless $\beta = 0$ or $\sigma_\xi^2 = 0$.

If $\{(X_i, Y_i)\}$ is a sample of size n from the distribution of (X, Y) then, by Khinchine WLLN, the OLS estimator $\hat\beta_n$ in the regression of Y_i on X_i satisfies

$$\hat\beta_n = \frac{n^{-1}\sum_i X_i Y_i}{n^{-1}\sum_i X_i^2} \xrightarrow{\text{p}} \beta\,\frac{\sigma_X^2}{\sigma_X^2 + \sigma_\xi^2}$$

and is therefore consistent for β_* but not for β in general. The reason for the inconsistency is the measurement errors in the covariate, not in the response variable. In particular, because $0 < \sigma_\xi^2/(\sigma_X^2 + \sigma_\xi^2) < 1$, the OLS estimator is asymptotically downward biased for β, and its asymptotic bias

$$\beta_* - \beta = -\beta\,\frac{\sigma_\xi^2}{\sigma_X^2 + \sigma_\xi^2} = -\beta\,\frac{1}{1 + (\sigma_X^2/\sigma_\xi^2)}$$

is a decreasing function of the signal-to-noise ratio σ_X^2/σ_ξ^2. □

Example 10.2 Suppose that the random variables (X, Y) are jointly determined through the pair of relations

$$Y = \beta X + U,$$
$$X = \gamma Y + V,$$

where U and V are uncorrelated random variables with mean zero and finite variance equal to σ^2 and ω^2 respectively. This model is known as a *linear simultaneous equation model* and will be discussed in more detail in Chapter 13. Solving for (X, Y) as a function of (U, V) gives

$$Y = \frac{U + \beta V}{1 - \beta\gamma}, \qquad X = \frac{\gamma U + V}{1 - \beta\gamma},$$

called the *reduced form* of the model. Thus, the relevant moments are

$$\operatorname{Var} X = \frac{\gamma^2\sigma^2 + \omega^2}{(1 - \beta\gamma)^2}, \qquad \operatorname{Cov}(X, Y) = \frac{\gamma\sigma^2 + \beta\omega^2}{(1 - \beta\gamma)^2},$$

and

$$\operatorname{E} XU = \frac{\gamma\sigma^2}{1 - \beta\gamma},$$

where $\operatorname{E} XU = 0$ if either $\gamma = 0$, that is, Y does not play any role in determining X, or $Y = \beta X$ because $\sigma^2 = 0$. The BLP of Y given X is $\operatorname{E}^*(Y \mid X) = \beta^* X$, where

$$\beta^* = \frac{\gamma\sigma^2 + \beta\omega^2}{\gamma^2\sigma^2 + \omega^2}$$

is different from β unless $\gamma = 0$ or $\sigma^2 = 0$.

If $\{(X_i, Y_i)\}$ is a sample of size n from the distribution of (X, Y), then Khinchine WLLN implies that the OLS estimator $\hat\beta_n$ in the regression of Y_i on X_i satisfies

$$\hat\beta_n = \frac{n^{-1}\sum_i X_i Y_i}{n^{-1}\sum_i X_i^2} \xrightarrow{\text{p}} \frac{\gamma\sigma^2 + \beta\omega^2}{\gamma^2\sigma^2 + \omega^2}$$

and is therefore consistent for β^* but not for β in general. □

Example 10.3 Consider the stable invertible ARMA(1,1) model

$$Z_t = \beta Z_{t-1} + V_t - \theta V_{t-1}, \qquad \{V_t\} \sim \mathrm{WN}(0, \sigma^2),$$

where $|\beta| < 1$ and $|\theta| < 1$. Putting $Y_t = Z_t$, $X_t = Z_{t-1}$ and $U_t = V_t - \theta V_{t-1}$, the model may be written as

$$Y_t = \beta X_t + U_t, \qquad \{U_t\} \sim \mathrm{MA}(1),$$

that is, as a linear model with MA(1) errors. From Example 3.18, the relevant moments are

$$\operatorname{Var} X_t = \operatorname{Var} Z_{t-1} = \sigma^2 \frac{1 + \theta^2 - 2\beta\theta}{1 - \beta^2},$$

$$\operatorname{Cov}(X_t, Y_t) = \operatorname{Cov}(Z_t, Z_{t-1}) = \sigma^2 \frac{(1 - \beta\theta)(\beta - \theta)}{1 - \beta^2},$$

and

$$\mathrm{E}\, X_t U_t = \mathrm{E}(\beta Z_{t-2} + V_{t-1} - \theta V_{t-2})(V_t - \theta V_{t-1}) = -\theta\sigma^2,$$

where $\mathrm{E}\, X_t U_t = 0$ only if $\theta = 0$, in which case the model reduces to an AR(1).

Since the process is stable, Theorem D.13 implies that the OLS estimator in the regression of Y_t on X_t satisfies

$$\hat{\beta}_n = \frac{n^{-1} \sum_{t=2}^n Y_{t-1} Y_t}{n^{-1} \sum_{t=2}^n Y_{t-1}^2} \overset{\mathrm{p}}{\to} \frac{(1 - \beta\theta)(\beta - \theta)}{1 + \theta^2 - 2\beta\theta}$$

and is therefore consistent for the first-order autocorrelation coefficient of Y_t but not for β, unless the process is AR(1), that is, $\theta = 0$. □

Example 10.3 generalizes straightforwardly to OLS estimation of models of the form

$$Y_t = \beta_1 Y_{t-1} + \cdots + \beta_p Y_{t-p} + \gamma_1 X_{t-1} + \cdots + \gamma_q X_{t-q} + U_t,$$

where $\{U_t\}$ is a stationary invertible ARMA process. The OLS estimator $\hat{\alpha}_n = (\hat{\beta}_n, \hat{\gamma}_n)$ in a regression of Y_t on $Y_{t-1}, \ldots, Y_{t-p}, X_{t-1}, \ldots, X_{t-q}$ is consistent for $\alpha = (\beta, \gamma)$ only if $\{U_t\}$ is a white noise.

10.1.4 TRENDS IN THE COVARIATES

Assumption (ii) of Theorem 10.1 requires $n^{-1}\mathbf{X}^\top\mathbf{X}$ to converge to a matrix P_n which, although not necessarily fixed, must be finite and "sufficiently nonsingular" for all n sufficiently large. This assumption is restrictive, because it rules out the case of trends in the data, but can be relaxed. In fact, if $\hat{\beta}_n$ is unbiased for β and has finite variance, then consistency only requires the largest element of $\operatorname{Var} \hat{\beta}_n$ to converge to zero as $n \to \infty$.

Example 10.4 Suppose that the data $Y_1, \ldots, Y_n$ are a finite segment of a time series $\{Y_t\}$ that follows the deterministic linear trend model

$$Y_t = \beta_1 + \beta_2 t + U_t, \qquad \{U_t\} \sim \mathrm{WN}(0, \sigma^2).$$

Figure 62 Rates of convergence to zero of $n^{-1/2}$, n^{-1}, and $n^{-3/2}$.

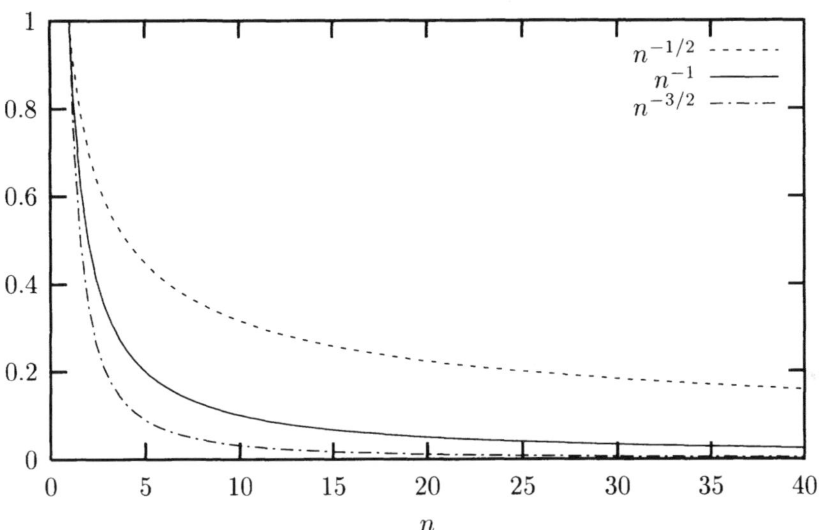

Putting $X_t = (1, t)$ gives

$$\mathbf{X}^\top \mathbf{X} = \begin{bmatrix} n & \sum_{t=1}^n t \\ \sum_{t=1}^n t & \sum_{t=1}^n t^2 \end{bmatrix} = n \begin{bmatrix} 1 & (n+1)/2 \\ (n+1)/2 & (n+1)(2n+1)/6 \end{bmatrix}.$$

Since $n^{-1}\mathbf{X}^\top\mathbf{X} = O(n^2)$, the conditions of Theorem 10.1 are not satisfied. Dividing instead $\mathbf{X}^\top\mathbf{X}$ by n^3 gives a matrix that is $O(1)$ but whose determinant vanishes as $n \to \infty$. Using Theorem 10.1 is really not necessary in this case, for

$$(\mathbf{X}^\top\mathbf{X})^{-1} = \frac{1}{n\sum_t t^2 - (\sum_t t)^2} \begin{bmatrix} \sum_t t^2 & -\sum_t t \\ -\sum_t t & n \end{bmatrix} = \begin{bmatrix} O(n^{-1}) & O(n^{-2}) \\ O(n^{-2}) & O(n^{-3}) \end{bmatrix},$$

that is, the sampling variance of the OLS estimator tends to zero as $n \to \infty$, which implies that the estimator is consistent.

Because a sequence of random variables is bounded in probability by the order of its standard deviation (see Appendix D.3), the estimator of β_1 is $O_p(n^{-1/2})$, whereas the estimator of β_2 is $O_p(n^{-3/2})$, that is, the estimator of β_2 converges in probability at a faster rate. The difference between these rates of convergence is illustrated in Figure 62. □

From the qualitative point of view, the presence of a stochastic trend in the covariates has effects that are similar to the presence of a deterministic trend. In either case, the rate at which the OLS estimator converges in probability to β is faster than in the absence of trends.

Example 10.5 Let $Y_1, \ldots, Y_n$ be a finite segment of the Gaussian AR(1) process

$$Y_t = \beta Y_{t-1} + U_t,$$

where $Y_0 = 0$ and $\{U_t\}$ is a Gaussian WN$(0, \sigma^2)$ process, and consider the properties of the OLS estimator $\hat{\beta}_n = \sum_{t=2}^n Y_t Y_{t-1} / \sum_{t=2}^n Y_{t-1}^2$ when $\beta = 1$, that is, $\{Y_t\}$ is a Gaussian random walk. The difference $\hat{\beta}_n - \beta$ is

$$\hat{\beta}_n - \beta = \frac{\sum_{t=2}^n Y_{t-1} U_t}{\sum_{t=2}^n Y_{t-1}^2},$$

where $Y_t = \sum_{i=1}^t U_i$ in this case. For the numerator and the denominator of this expression we have

$$\begin{aligned}
\operatorname{Var}(\sum_{t=2}^n Y_{t-1} U_t) &= \sum_{t=1}^{n-1} t\sigma^4 = \frac{1}{2} n(n-1)\sigma^4, \\
\operatorname{Var}(\sum_{t=2}^n Y_{t-1}^2) &= \sum_{t=1}^{n-1} 2(t\sigma^2)^2 + 2 \sum_{i=1}^{n-2} 2(n-1-i)(i\sigma^2)^2 \\
&= \frac{1}{3} n(n-1)(n^2 - n + 1)\sigma^4,
\end{aligned}$$

which are of order $O(n^2)$ and $O(n^4)$ respectively. Although Theorem 10.1 does not apply, Example 10.6 shows that $\hat{\beta}_n - 1 = O_p(n^{-1})$. Notice that $\hat{\beta}_n - \beta = O_p(n^{-1/2})$ when $|\beta| < 1$. Thus, in the presence of a stochastic trend, the OLS estimator converges in probability to β at a rate that is faster than the case when $|\beta| < 1$, but slower than the case of a deterministic trend. □

The fact that the OLS estimator is "superconsistent" when the covariates in a regression model are integrated is of practical importance in the estimation of cointegrated systems of order $(1, 1)$, for it ensures not only the consistency, but also the convergence in probability at a faster rate than $n^{-1/2}$ of the OLS estimator of the cointegrating vector.

10.2 ASYMPTOTIC NORMALITY OF THE OLS ESTIMATOR

When the sampling distribution of the OLS estimator is difficult to derive, being able to rely on some form of approximation is essential in order to construct confidence intervals and test statistical hypotheses. The simplest form of approximation is the Gaussian one.

10.2.1 THE MAIN RESULT

In most practical cases, showing that the limiting distribution of the OLS estimator $\hat{\beta}_n$ is Gaussian reduces to verifying the conditions of the following theorem.

Theorem 10.5 *Let* $\mathbf{U} = \mathbf{Y} - \mathbf{X}\beta$ *and suppose that:*

(i) $D_n^{-1/2} \mathbf{X}^\top \mathbf{U} / \sqrt{n} \xrightarrow{\mathrm{d}} \mathcal{N}_k(0, I_k)$, *where the matrix* D_n *is symmetric and* $O(1)$, *and* $\det D_n > \delta$ *for some* $\delta > 0$ *and all* n *sufficiently large;*

(ii) $n^{-1} \mathbf{X}^\top \mathbf{X} - P_n \xrightarrow{\mathrm{p}} 0$, *where the matrix* P_n *is symmetric and* $O(1)$, *and* $\det P_n > \delta$ *for some* $\delta > 0$ *and all* n *sufficiently large.*

Then $V_n^{-1/2}\sqrt{n}\,(\hat{\beta}_n - \beta) \xrightarrow{\mathrm{d}} \mathcal{N}_k(0, I_k)$, *where* $V_n = P_n^{-1} D_n P_n^{-1}$.

Proof. First notice that

$$\sqrt{n}\,(\hat{\beta}_n - \beta) = \left(\frac{\mathbf{X}^\top \mathbf{X}}{n}\right)^{-1} \frac{\mathbf{X}^\top \mathbf{U}}{\sqrt{n}},$$

where, by assumption (ii), $(n^{-1}\mathbf{X}^\top\mathbf{X})^{-1}$ exists with probability approaching one. Further, both D_n and $V_n = P_n^{-1} D_n P_n^{-1}$ are $O(1)$ and sufficiently far from singularity for all n sufficiently large. Hence

$$V_n^{-1/2}\sqrt{n}\,(\hat{\beta}_n - \beta) - V_n^{-1/2} P_n^{-1} \frac{\mathbf{X}^\top \mathbf{U}}{\sqrt{n}} = V_n^{-1/2} \left[\left(\frac{\mathbf{X}^\top \mathbf{X}}{n}\right)^{-1} - P_n^{-1}\right] D_n^{1/2} D_n^{-1/2} \frac{\mathbf{X}^\top \mathbf{U}}{\sqrt{n}}$$

for all n sufficiently large. Because

$$V_n^{-1/2} \left[\left(\frac{\mathbf{X}^\top \mathbf{X}}{n}\right)^{-1} - P_n^{-1}\right] D_n^{1/2} = O(1) \cdot o_p(1) \cdot O(1) = o_p(1)$$

and $D_n^{-1/2} n^{-1/2} \mathbf{X}^\top \mathbf{U} = O_p(1)$, we then have

$$V_n^{-1/2}\sqrt{n}\,(\hat{\beta}_n - \beta) - V_n^{-1/2} P_n^{-1} \frac{\mathbf{X}^\top \mathbf{U}}{\sqrt{n}} = o_p(1) \cdot O_p(1) = o_p(1).$$

Therefore, $V_n^{-1/2}\sqrt{n}\,(\hat{\beta}_n - \beta)$ and

$$V_n^{-1/2} P_n^{-1} \frac{\mathbf{X}^\top \mathbf{U}}{\sqrt{n}} = V_n^{-1/2} P_n^{-1} D_n^{1/2} \left(D_n^{-1/2} \frac{\mathbf{X}^\top \mathbf{U}}{\sqrt{n}}\right)$$

have the same limiting distribution which, under assumption (i), is multivariate Gaussian with mean zero and variance

$$V_n^{-1/2} P_n^{-1} D_n^{1/2} D_n^{1/2} P_n^{-1} V_n^{-1/2} = V_n^{-1/2} V_n V_n^{-1/2} = I_k.$$

□

If assumptions (i) and (ii) in Theorem 10.5 are replaced by the stronger assumptions that $P_n = P$, a finite nonsingular matrix, and $D_n = \sigma^2 P$, where $0 < \sigma^2 < \infty$, then the asymptotic variance of the OLS estimator becomes $V_n = P^{-1}(\sigma^2 P)P^{-1} = \sigma^2 P^{-1}$.

10.2.2 SOME PRIMITIVE ASSUMPTIONS

We now discuss some basic assumptions that guarantee that the conditions of Theorem 10.5 are satisfied. The simplest case is again when the observations are i.i.d.

Theorem 10.6 *Let* $U_i = Y_i - \beta^\top X_i$, $i = 1, \ldots, n$. *In addition to assumptions (i)–(iii) of Theorem 10.2 suppose:*

(iv) $\operatorname{Var} X_i U_i = D$, *a finite symmetric p.d. matrix.*

Then $\sqrt{n}\,(\hat\beta_n - \beta) \xrightarrow{d} \mathcal{N}_k(0, \mathrm{AV}(\hat\beta_n))$, *where* $\mathrm{AV}(\hat\beta_n) = P^{-1}DP^{-1}$.

Proof. It is enough to show that $n^{-1/2}\mathbf{X}^\top\mathbf{U} \xrightarrow{d} \mathcal{N}_k(0, D)$. Given a vector $\lambda \neq 0$, put $W_i = \lambda^\top X_i U_i$. Assumption (i) implies that $\{W_i\}$ is a sequence of i.i.d. random variables, while (ii) and (iv) imply that $\mathrm{E}\,W_i = 0$ and $\mathrm{Var}\,W_i = \lambda^\top D\lambda > 0$. Therefore $n^{-1/2}\sum_{i=1}^n W_i = n^{-1/2}\lambda^\top\mathbf{X}^\top\mathbf{U} \xrightarrow{d} \mathcal{N}(0,\, \lambda^\top D\lambda)$, by the Lindeberg–Lévy CLT. Since λ is arbitrary, $n^{-1/2}\mathbf{X}^\top\mathbf{U} \xrightarrow{d} \mathcal{N}_k(0, D)$ by the Cramér–Wold device. □

Now consider the case when the observations are independent but not identically distributed.

Theorem 10.7 *Let* $U_i = Y_i - \beta^\top X_i$, $i = 1, \ldots, n$. *In addition to assumptions (i)–(iv) of Theorem 10.3, suppose:*

(v) $\mathrm{E}\,|X_{ij}U_i|^\nu \le M < \infty$ *for some* $\nu > 2$, *all* $j = 1, \ldots, k$ *and every* i;
(vi) $\mathrm{Var}(n^{-1/2}\mathbf{X}^\top\mathbf{U}) = D_n$, *where* $\det D_n > \delta$ *for some* $\delta > 0$ *and all* n *sufficiently large.*

Then $V_n^{-1/2}\sqrt{n}\,(\hat\beta_n - \beta) \xrightarrow{d} \mathcal{N}_k(0, I_k)$, *where* $V_n = P_n^{-1}D_nP_n^{-1}$.

Asymptotic normality of the OLS estimator depends crucially on the asymptotic normality of the vector $n^{-1/2}\mathbf{X}^\top\mathbf{U}$. This requires imposing stronger moment restrictions than the ones needed for the OLS estimator to be consistent. Thus, both Theorems 10.6 and 10.7 require $n^{-1/2}\mathbf{X}^\top\mathbf{U}$ to have a finite variance. In addition, Theorem 10.7 requires the absolute moments $\mathrm{E}\,|X_{ij}U_i|^\nu$ to be uniformly bounded by some $\nu > 2$. A similar condition was also needed in Theorem 10.3, but only for some $\nu > 1$.

When the model for the data belongs to a general class of time series, establishing asymptotic normality of the OLS estimator requires knowledge that goes beyond the purposes of this book. Therefore, we shall only present a result that guarantees asymptotic normality of the conditional LS estimator when the data follow a stable AR(p) process driven by i.i.d. innovations.

Given a finite segment $Z_1, \ldots, Z_T$ of the process, such an estimator may be written as $\hat\beta_n = (\mathbf{X}^\top\mathbf{X})^{-1}\mathbf{X}^\top\mathbf{Y}$, where $n = T - p$ and

$$\mathbf{X} = \begin{bmatrix} Z_p & \cdots & Z_1 \\ \vdots & & \vdots \\ Z_{T-1} & \cdots & Z_{T-p} \end{bmatrix}, \qquad \mathbf{Y} = \begin{pmatrix} Z_{p+1} \\ \vdots \\ Z_T \end{pmatrix} \tag{10.1}$$

are, respectively, an $n \times p$ matrix and an n-vector.

Theorem 10.8 *Suppose that* $\{Z_t\}$ *follows the stable* AR(p) *process*

$$\mathrm{B}(L)\,Z_t = U_t, \qquad \{U_t\} \sim \mathrm{IID}(0, \sigma^2),$$

where $\mathrm{B}(z) = 1 - \beta_1 z - \cdots - \beta_p z^p \neq 0$ *for all* $|z| \le 1$. *Let* $\beta = (\beta_1, \ldots, \beta_p)$ *and let* $\hat\beta_n$ *be the conditional LS estimator based on* $n + p$ *consecutive observations of the process* $\{Z_t\}$. *Then* $\sqrt{n}\,(\hat\beta_n - \beta) \xrightarrow{d} \mathcal{N}_p(0,\, \sigma^2\,\Gamma_p^{-1})$, *where* Γ_p *is the autocovariance matrix associated with* $Z_1, \ldots, Z_p$.

Proof. Write the model for the data as $\mathbf{Y} = \mathbf{X}\beta + \mathbf{U}$, where $\mathbf{Y}$ and $\mathbf{X}$ are defined in (10.1). Notice first that the law of large numbers for linear processes (Theorem D.13) implies that $n^{-1}\mathbf{X}^\top\mathbf{X} \xrightarrow{\text{p}} \Gamma_p$. Now consider the expansion

$$\begin{aligned}\sqrt{n}\,(\hat{\beta}_n - \beta) &= \sqrt{n}\,[(\mathbf{X}^\top\mathbf{X})^{-1}\mathbf{X}^\top(\mathbf{X}\beta + \mathbf{U}) - \beta] \\ &= (n^{-1}\mathbf{X}^\top\mathbf{X})^{-1}(n^{-1/2}\mathbf{X}^\top\mathbf{U}) = (n^{-1}\mathbf{X}^\top\mathbf{X})^{-1}\frac{1}{\sqrt{n}}\sum_{t=1}^{n} V_t,\end{aligned}$$

where V_t is an n-vector whose jth element is equal to $Z_{t-j}U_t$. Since U_t is independent of $Z_{t-1}, Z_{t-2}, \ldots$, we have $\mathrm{E}\, V_t = 0$ and

$$\mathrm{E}\, V_t V_{t+h}^\top = \begin{cases} \sigma^2\,\Gamma_p, & \text{if } h = 0, \\ 0, & \text{otherwise.} \end{cases}$$

Because $\{Z_t\}$ is stable, it possesses the MA(∞) representation $Z_t = \sum_{j=0}^{\infty}\psi_j U_{t-j}$, where $\sum_{j=0}^{\infty}\psi_j z^j = 1/\mathrm{B}(z)$ for all $|z| \le 1$. For a fixed m, consider the MA(m) process $Z_t^{(m)} = \sum_{j=0}^{m}\psi_j U_{t-j}$, which is a truncated version of $\{Z_t\}$, and put

$$V_t^{(m)} = \begin{pmatrix} Z_{t-1}^{(m)}U_t \\ \vdots \\ Z_{t-p}^{(m)}U_t \end{pmatrix}.$$

For any $\lambda \in \Re^p$, the process $\{\lambda^\top V_t^{(m)}\}$ is strictly stationary and $(m+p)$-dependent with variance equal to $\sigma^2\,\lambda^\top\Gamma_p^{(m)}\lambda$, where $\Gamma_p^{(m)}$ is the autocovariance matrix associated with $Z_{t-1}^{(m)}, \ldots, Z_{t-p}^{(m)}$. Hence, by Hoeffding–Robbins CLT (Theorem D.18),

$$n^{-1/2}\sum_{t=1}^{n}\lambda^\top V_t^{(m)} \xrightarrow{\text{d}} \lambda^\top V^{(m)},$$

where $V^{(m)} \sim \mathcal{N}_p(0, \sigma^2\,\Gamma_p^{(m)})$. Further, since $\Gamma_p^{(m)} \to \Gamma_p$ as $m \to \infty$, we have

$$n^{-1/2}\sum_{t=1}^{n}\lambda^\top V_t^{(m)} \xrightarrow{\text{d}} \lambda^\top V,$$

where $V \sim \mathcal{N}_p(0, \sigma^2\,\Gamma_p)$. Finally, it is easy to verify that

$$n^{-1/2}\sum_{t=1}^{n}\lambda^\top V_t^{(m)} - n^{-1/2}\sum_{t=1}^{n}\lambda^\top V_t \xrightarrow{\text{ms}} 0.$$

Hence $n^{-1/2}\sum_{t=1}^{n} V_t \xrightarrow{\text{d}} \mathcal{N}_p(0, \Gamma_p)$, and therefore $\sqrt{n}\,(\hat{\beta}_n - \beta) \xrightarrow{\text{d}} \mathcal{N}_p(0, \sigma^2\,\Gamma_p^{-1})$. □

A straightforward generalization of Theorem 10.8 establishes asymptotic normality of the conditional LS estimator when the data follow a stable multivariate autoregressive (VAR) process.

When the data follow a nonstationary process, the results tend to be more complicated.

Example 10.6 Let $Y_1, \ldots, Y_n$ be a finite segment of the AR(1) process

$$Y_t = \beta Y_{t-1} + U_t, \qquad \{U_t\} \sim \mathrm{IID}(0, \sigma^2),$$

where $Y_0 = 0$, and consider the limiting distribution of the difference

$$\hat{\beta}_n - \beta = \frac{\sum_{t=2}^n Y_{t-1} U_t}{\sum_{t=2}^n Y_{t-1}^2} = \frac{\sum_{t=1}^n Y_{t-1} U_t}{\sum_{t=1}^n Y_{t-1}^2}.$$

If $|\beta| < 1$, then Theorem 10.8 implies that $\sqrt{n}\,(\hat{\beta}_n - \beta) \xrightarrow{\mathrm{d}} \mathcal{N}(0, 1 - \beta^2)$, and so the asymptotic variance of $\hat{\beta}_n$ tends to vanish as $\beta \to 1$. Indeed, for the case when $\beta = 1$, Fuller (1976) and Phillips (1987) show that $\sqrt{n}\,(\hat{\beta}_n - 1) \xrightarrow{\mathrm{p}} 0$, which implies that the limiting distribution of $\sqrt{n}\,(\hat{\beta}_n - 1)$ is degenerate.

To find a nondegenerate limiting distribution for the case when $\beta = 1$, consider the stochastic process $X_n(\cdot)$ defined on the closed unit interval $[0, 1]$ by

$$W_n(r) = \frac{Y_{[nr]}}{\sigma\sqrt{n}},$$

where $[a]$ denotes the integer part of a, that is, $[a]$ is the largest integer less than or equal to a. Because $Y_t = \sum_{i=1}^t U_i$ when $\beta = 1$, this process is formally the same as the partial sum process considered in Example D.1. Hence

$$n^{-2} \sum_{t=1}^n Y_{t-1}^2 = \int_0^1 W_n(r)^2\, dr \xrightarrow{\mathrm{d}} \sigma^2 \int_0^1 W(r)^2\, dr,$$

where $W(\cdot)$ denotes the standard Brownian motion. Further,

$$\sum_{t=1}^n Y_{t-1} U_t = \frac{1}{2}(Y_n^2 - \sum_{t=1}^n U_t^2),$$

where we used the fact that $Y_t^2 = (Y_{t-1} + U_t)^2 = Y_t^2 + 2Y_{t-1}U_t + U_t^2$ and so

$$Y_{t-1} U_t = \frac{1}{2}(Y_t^2 - Y_{t-1}^2 - U_t^2).$$

Because $Y_n^2 = W_n(1) \xrightarrow{\mathrm{d}} W(1)^2$ and $n^{-1} \sum_{t=1}^n U_i^2 \xrightarrow{\mathrm{p}} \sigma^2$, we have

$$n^{-1} \sum_{t=1}^n Y_{t-1} U_t = \frac{1}{2}[W_n(1)^2 - n^{-1} \sum_{t=1}^n U_t^2] \xrightarrow{\mathrm{d}} \frac{1}{2}[W(1)^2 - \sigma^2],$$

where $W(1)^2 \sim \chi_1^2$. Therefore, by the continuous mapping theorem (Theorem D.23),

$$n(\hat{\beta}_n - 1) \xrightarrow{\mathrm{d}} \frac{(1/2)[W(1)^2 - 1]}{\int_0^1 W(r)^2\, dr}.$$

This limiting distribution is clearly not Gaussian and is not available in closed form. Tables computed by Fuller (1976) and Evans and Savin (1981) show that it is skewed to the left, with negative values about twice as likely as positive values.

More generally, the limiting distribution of the OLS estimator in the nonstationary case depends on whether an intercept or a time trend are included in the model, and on whether the data are generated by a random walk with or without drift. See Sims, Stock and Watson (1990) for details. □

10.2.3 ESTIMATES OF STATISTICAL PRECISION

We have shown that, under suitable conditions, the OLS estimator is consistent for the regression parameter β, and is asymptotically normal with asymptotic mean equal to β and asymptotic variance equal to $V_n = P_n^{-1} D_n P_n^{-1}$. The practical usefulness of the latter result depends, however, on the availability of good estimates of V_n. Constructing these estimates is often straightforward.

For example, if assumption (iv) of Theorem 10.6 is replaced by the stronger assumption that the regression errors are conditionally homoskedastic, that is, $\operatorname{Var}(U_i \mid X_i) = \sigma^2$, then $D = \sigma^2 P$ and so the asymptotic variance of $\hat{\beta}_n$ is equal to $\sigma^2 P^{-1}$. In this case, the classical estimator of scale s_n^2 is consistent for σ^2 and therefore $\hat{V}_n = s_n^2(n^{-1}\mathbf{X}^\top\mathbf{X})^{-1} \xrightarrow{\mathrm{p}} \sigma^2 P^{-1}$.

More generally, if $n^{-1}\mathbf{X}^\top\mathbf{X} - P_n \xrightarrow{\mathrm{p}} 0$ and $\hat{D}_n$ is a symmetric p.d. matrix such that $\hat{D}_n - D_n \xrightarrow{\mathrm{p}} 0$, then a consistent estimator of V_n is

$$\tilde{V}_n = \left(\frac{\mathbf{X}^\top\mathbf{X}}{n}\right)^{-1} \hat{D}_n \left(\frac{\mathbf{X}^\top\mathbf{X}}{n}\right)^{-1}.$$

An important special case is when $\{(X_i, U_i)\}$ is a sequence of i.i.d. random vectors but the model is conditionally heteroskedastic, so that $D = \operatorname{Var} X_i U_i = \mathrm{E}\, U_i^2 X_i X_i^\top$. If the regression errors U_i were observable, then D could be estimated consistently by $\tilde{D}_n = n^{-1}\sum_{i=1}^n U_i^2 X_i X_i^\top$. Eicker (1967) showed that replacing the regression errors by the OLS residuals in the above formula gives an estimator that is consistent for D under assumptions only slightly more restrictive than the ones of Theorem 10.6.

Theorem 10.9 (Eicker) *Let* $\hat{U}_i = Y_i - \hat{\beta}_n^\top X_i$, $i = 1, \ldots, n$, *and* $\hat{D}_n = n^{-1}\sum_{i=1}^n \hat{U}_i^2 X_i X_i^\top$. *In addition to the assumptions of Theorem 10.6, suppose that* $\mathrm{E}\,|X_{ih} X_{ij}|^2 < \infty$ *for every* $h, j = 1, \ldots, k$. *Then* $\hat{D}_n \xrightarrow{\mathrm{p}} D$.

Proof. Assumptions (ii) and (iii) of Theorem 10.6 imply

$$\begin{aligned}
\hat{D}_n - D &= n^{-1}\sum_{i=1}^n \hat{U}_i^2 X_i X_i^\top - \mathrm{E}\, U_i^2 X_i X_i^\top \\
&= n^{-1}\sum_{i=1}^n [U_i - X_i^\top(\hat{\beta}_n - \beta)]^2 X_i X_i^\top - \mathrm{E}\, U_i^2 X_i X_i^\top \\
&= n^{-1}\sum_{i=1}^n [U_i^2 X_i X_i^\top - \mathrm{E}\, U_i^2 X_i X_i^\top] - \frac{2}{n}\sum_i (\hat{\beta}_n - \beta)^\top X_i U_i X_i X_i^\top \\
&\quad + n^{-1}\sum_{i=1}^n (\hat{\beta}_n - \beta)^\top X_i X_i^\top (\hat{\beta}_n - \beta) X_i X_i^\top.
\end{aligned}$$

We prove the theorem by showing that each of the terms on the right-hand side of the above expression converges to zero in probability.

Assumption (i) of Theorem 10.6 implies that $\{U_i^2 X_i X_i^\top\}$, $\{U_i X_{ij} X_{ir} X_{is}\}$ and $\{X_{ih} X_{ij} X_{ir} X_{is}\}$ are sequences of i.i.d. random variables. Assumptions (ii) and (iii) then imply that $n^{-1}\sum_i U_i^2 X_i X_i^\top - \mathrm{E}\, U_i^2 X_i X_i^\top \xrightarrow{\mathrm{p}} 0$, by Khinchine WLLN. Because the term $n^{-1}\sum_i(\hat\beta_n-\beta)^\top X_iU_iX_iX_i^\top$ may be written as the sum of k matrices, where the rsth element of the jth matrix is equal to $(\hat\beta_{nj}-\beta_j)n^{-1}\sum_i U_iX_{ij}X_{ir}X_{is}$, it follows from the Cauchy–Schwarz inequality that

$$\mathrm{E}\,|U_iX_{ij}X_{ir}X_{is}| \le (\mathrm{E}\,|X_{is}U_i|^2)^{1/2}(\mathrm{E}\,|X_{ij}X_{ir}|^2)^{1/2},$$

where $\mathrm{E}\,|X_{ij}U_i|^2$ and $\mathrm{E}\,|X_{ij}X_{ir}|^2$ are by assumption finite. Hence $\mathrm{E}\,|U_iX_{ij}X_{ir}X_{is}|$ is finite and therefore $n^{-1}\sum_i U_iX_{ij}X_{ir}X_{is} \xrightarrow{\mathrm{p}} \mathrm{E}\,U_iX_{ij}X_{ir}X_{is}$. Since $\hat\beta_n \xrightarrow{\mathrm{p}} \beta$, the assumptions of the theorem imply that

$$\frac{2}{n}\sum_{i=1}^{n}(\hat\beta_n-\beta)^\top X_iU_iX_iX_i^\top \xrightarrow{\mathrm{p}} 0.$$

Finally, the last term in $\hat D_n - D$ may be written as the sum of k^2 matrices, where the (r,s)th element of the hjth matrix is equal to

$$(\hat\beta_{nh}-\beta_h)(\hat\beta_{nj}-\beta_j)n^{-1}\sum_{i=1}^{n} X_{ih}X_{ij}X_{ir}X_{is}.$$

Because $\hat\beta_n \xrightarrow{\mathrm{p}} \beta$ and $\mathrm{E}\,|X_{ih}X_{ij}X_{ir}X_{is}|$ is finite, it follows from the Cauchy–Schwarz inequality that $n^{-1}\sum_i(\hat\beta_n-\beta)^\top X_iX_i^\top(\hat\beta_n-\beta)^\top X_iX_i^\top \xrightarrow{\mathrm{p}} 0$. □

A consistent estimator of the asymptotic variance of $\hat\beta_n$ under heteroskedasticity is therefore

$$\tilde V_n = \left(\frac{\mathbf{X}^\top\mathbf{X}}{n}\right)^{-1}\left(\frac{1}{n}\sum_i \hat U_i^2X_iX_i^\top\right)\left(\frac{\mathbf{X}^\top\mathbf{X}}{n}\right)^{-1}.$$

More generally, it is possible to construct a consistent estimator of the asymptotic variance of $\hat\beta_n$ even when $D_n = \mathrm{Var}(n^{-1/2}\mathbf{X}^\top\mathbf{U}) = \mathrm{E}(n^{-1}\mathbf{X}^\top\Omega_n\mathbf{X})$, where Ω_n is an unknown symmetric p.d. matrix. See for example White (1984) and Newey and West (1987).

The sampling variance of $\hat\beta_n$ under heteroskedasticity may be approximated by

$$n^{-1}\tilde V_n = (\mathbf{X}^\top\mathbf{X})^{-1}(\sum_i \hat U_i^2X_iX_i^\top)(\mathbf{X}^\top\mathbf{X})^{-1}, \tag{10.2}$$

which is the infinitesimal jackknife estimate introduced in Section 7.5.1. In small samples it may be preferable to correct for the number of degrees of freedom using instead

$$\frac{1}{n-k}\tilde V_n = \frac{n}{n-k}(\mathbf{X}^\top\mathbf{X})^{-1}(\sum_i \hat U_i^2X_iX_i^\top)(\mathbf{X}^\top\mathbf{X})^{-1}, \tag{10.3}$$

which is clearly greater than $\tilde V_n/n$.

Monte Carlo results (MacKinnon & White 1985) and exact calculations (Chesher & Jewitt 1987) show that both (10.2) and (10.3) may be severely biased, especially when the sample contains high-leverage points. To correct for this problem, Hinkley (1977) suggested estimating the sampling variance of $\hat\beta$ by

$$\tilde V_n^* = (\mathbf{X}^\top\mathbf{X})^{-1}(\sum_i \hat U_{(i)}^2X_iX_i^\top)(\mathbf{X}^\top\mathbf{X})^{-1},$$

where $\hat{U}_{(i)} = \hat{U}_i/(1 - h_{ii})$ is the ith predicted residual. This estimate may also be interpreted as an approximation to the jackknife.

The classical way of constructing approximate confidence intervals for a known linear combination $\lambda^\top \beta$ of the regression coefficients proceeds as follows. If V_n is the asymptotic variance of $\hat{\beta}_n$ and $\hat{V}_n$ is a symmetric p.d. matrix such that $\hat{V}_n - V_n \xrightarrow{\text{p}} 0$, then an asymptotic $(1 - 2\alpha)$-level confidence interval for $\lambda^\top \beta$ is

$$[\lambda^\top \hat{\beta}_n - z_{(\alpha)}(n^{-1}\lambda^\top \hat{V}_n \lambda)^{1/2},\ \lambda^\top \hat{\beta}_n + z_{(\alpha)}(n^{-1}\lambda^\top \hat{V}_n \lambda)^{1/2}], \tag{10.4}$$

where $z_{(\alpha)}$ denotes the upper αth quantile of the $\mathcal{N}(0,1)$ distribution. The problem with this approach is that the symmetric confidence interval (10.4) takes the Gaussian approximation too literally and is therefore quite unsatisfactory when the distribution of $\hat{\beta}_n$ exibits asymmetry or kurtosis. The bootstrap gives an automatic way of taking this into account. In order to obtain sufficiently accurate estimates of tail probabilities, however, a bootstrap confidence interval typically requires many more replications than a bootstrap estimate of variance.

Let $\hat{\beta}_n$ be the OLS estimate for the original sample $\{(X_i, Y_i)\}$ of size n and let $\hat{\beta}_n^*$ be the OLS estimate for a resample $\{(X_i^*, Y_i^*)\}$ of size n from the joint empirical distribution of (X_i, Y_i) (Algorithm 5.1). In this case, an asymptotic justification for the bootstrap is the following result.

Theorem 10.10 *If all the assumptions of Theorem 10.9 hold, then along almost all sample sequences, the conditional distribution of* $\sqrt{n}\,(\hat{\beta}_n^* - \hat{\beta}_n)$ *given the observations* $\{(X_i, Y_i)\}$ *converges weakly to the* $\mathcal{N}_k(0, P^{-1}DP^{-1})$ *distribution.*

Proof. See Freedman (1981). □

Theorem 10.10 implies that the bootstrap is asymptotically correct, that is, the (conditional) variability of the bootstrap estimates about the original estimate $\hat{\beta}_n$ closely mimics, for large n, the sampling variability of $\hat{\beta}_n$ about the target parameter β. An analogous result holds for regression models with a fixed design when resampling is from the empirical distribution of the centered OLS residuals (Algorithm 7.1). It is important to notice that the asymptotic results for the bootstrap estimate are conditional on the available data, whereas those for the original OLS estimate are unconditional.

10.3 ASYMPTOTIC PROPERTIES OF THE GLS ESTIMATOR

Consider the case when the regression function of $\mathbf{Y}$ on $\mathbf{X}$ is linear but $\mathbf{Y}$ has a nonscalar variance matrix. Specifically, suppose that $\text{Var}(\mathbf{Y} \mid \mathbf{X}) = \sigma^2\,\Omega_n$, where Ω_n is an $n \times n$ symmetric p.d. matrix.

When the matrix Ω_n is known, the asymptotic properties of the GLS estimator $\tilde{\beta}_n = (\mathbf{X}^\top \Omega_n^{-1} \mathbf{X})^{-1} \mathbf{X}^\top \Omega_n^{-1} \mathbf{Y}$ follow immediately under the next set of assumptions on $\mathbf{X}$ and the regression error vector $\mathbf{U} = \mathbf{Y} - \mathbf{X}\beta$.

Assumption 10.1

(i) $n^{-1}\mathbf{X}^\top \Omega_n^{-1} \mathbf{U} \xrightarrow{\text{p}} 0$;

(ii) $n^{-1}\mathbf{X}^\top \Omega_n^{-1} \mathbf{X} \xrightarrow{\text{p}} P$, *where P is a finite p.d. matrix;*

(iii) $n^{-1/2}\mathbf{X}^\top\Omega_n^{-1}\mathbf{U} \xrightarrow{\text{d}} \mathcal{N}_k(0, \sigma^2 P)$, *where* $0 < \sigma^2 < \infty$.

Assumption 10.1 is clearly sufficient for consistency and asymptotic normality of the OLS estimator in a regression of $\mathbf{Y}^* = H\mathbf{Y}$ on $\mathbf{X}^* = H\mathbf{X}$, where H is any nonsingular matrix such that $H^\top H = \Omega_n^{-1}$.

Theorem 10.11 *If Assumption 10.1 holds then:*

(i) $\tilde{\beta}_n \xrightarrow{\text{p}} \beta$;
(ii) $\sqrt{n}\,(\tilde{\beta}_n - \beta) \xrightarrow{\text{d}} \mathcal{N}_k(0, \sigma^2 P^{-1})$.

Proof. Part (i) follows immediately from the expansion

$$\tilde{\beta}_n - \beta = \left(\frac{\mathbf{X}^\top\Omega_n^{-1}\mathbf{X}}{n}\right)^{-1} \frac{\mathbf{X}^\top\Omega_n^{-1}\mathbf{U}}{n}.$$

To obtain (ii), just multiply by $\sqrt{n}$ and use Assumption 10.1 (ii) and (iii). □

Now suppose that $\Omega_n^{-1} = G_n(\psi)$, where $\psi \in \Psi$ is a finite-dimensional parameter and $G_n(\cdot)$ is an $n \times n$ symmetric p.d. matrix whose elements are functions of ψ. Given an estimate $\hat{\psi}_n$ of ψ, put $\hat{\Omega}_n^{-1} = G_n(\hat{\psi}_n)$ and consider the feasible GLS estimator

$$\bar{\beta}_n = (\mathbf{X}^\top\hat{\Omega}_n^{-1}\mathbf{X})^{-1}\mathbf{X}^\top\hat{\Omega}_n^{-1}\mathbf{Y}.$$

Exact statistical results for $\bar{\beta}_n$ are not generally available and one has to rely on asymptotic approximations. It may seem at first that only the condition $\hat{\psi}_n \xrightarrow{\text{p}} \psi$ is needed for the feasible GLS estimator to behave as the GLS estimator in large samples. This, however, is not always true. In fact, consistency of $\hat{\psi}_n$ for ψ does not imply that $\bar{\beta}_n$ is consistent for β, nor does it imply that $\tilde{\beta}_n$ and $\bar{\beta}_n$ have the same asymptotic distribution. For a nice example, see Schmidt (1976), pp. 69–70.

The next result gives sufficient conditions under which $\bar{\beta}_n$ is consistent for β.

Theorem 10.12 *Suppose that:*

(i) $n^{-1}\mathbf{X}^\top\hat{\Omega}_n^{-1}\mathbf{X} \xrightarrow{\text{p}} P$, *a finite p.d. matrix;*
(ii) $n^{-1}\mathbf{X}^\top\hat{\Omega}_n^{-1}\mathbf{U} \xrightarrow{\text{p}} 0$.

Then $\bar{\beta}_n \xrightarrow{\text{p}} \beta$.

The last theorem of this section gives sufficient conditions for $\tilde{\beta}_n$ and $\bar{\beta}_n$ to have the same asymptotic distribution.

Theorem 10.13 *In addition to Assumption 10.1, suppose that:*

(i) $n^{-1}\mathbf{X}^\top(\hat{\Omega}_n^{-1} - \Omega_n^{-1})\mathbf{X} \xrightarrow{\text{p}} 0$;
(ii) $n^{-1}\mathbf{X}^\top(\hat{\Omega}_n^{-1} - \Omega_n^{-1})\mathbf{Y} \xrightarrow{\text{p}} 0$.

Then $\sqrt{n}\,(\bar{\beta}_n - \beta) \xrightarrow{\text{d}} \mathcal{N}_k(0, \sigma^2 P^{-1})$.

Proof. Consider the difference

$$\sqrt{n}\,(\bar{\beta}_n - \tilde{\beta}_n) = \left(\frac{\mathbf{X}^\top \hat{\Omega}_n^{-1}\mathbf{X}}{n}\right)^{-1} \frac{\mathbf{X}^\top \hat{\Omega}_n^{-1}\mathbf{Y}}{\sqrt{n}} - \left(\frac{\mathbf{X}^\top \Omega_n^{-1}\mathbf{X}}{n}\right)^{-1} \frac{\mathbf{X}^\top \Omega_n^{-1}\mathbf{Y}}{\sqrt{n}}.$$

Assumptions (i) and (ii) imply that $\sqrt{n}\,(\bar{\beta}_n - \tilde{\beta}_n) = o_p(1)$. Hence, $\sqrt{n}\,(\bar{\beta}_n - \beta)$ and $\sqrt{n}\,(\tilde{\beta}_n - \beta)$ have the same limiting distribution. □

The conditions of Theorem 10.13 seem to be met in most cases where $\Omega_n^{-1} = G_n(\psi)$ and there exists a consistent estimator of ψ. However, they must always be checked.

Even when the sufficient conditions are satisfied for the feasible GLS estimator $\bar{\beta}_n$ to have the same limiting distribution as the GLS estimator, using $\bar{\beta}_n$ need not represent an improvement over the OLS estimator in finite samples. Indeed, there is enough Monte Carlo evidence to show that, unless the sample size is large, using $\bar{\beta}_n$ may lead to a considerable loss of efficiency with respect to the OLS estimator.

10.4 ASYMPTOTIC PROPERTIES OF t- AND F-TESTS

We now study the asymptotic properties of t- and F-tests of a hypothesis of the form H_0: $R\beta = r$, where R is a $q \times k$ matrix of rank q and r is a q-vector. When $q = 1$, a two-sided t-test rejects H_0 against the alternative H_1: $R\beta \neq r$ for large values of the statistic

$$|T_n| = \frac{|R\hat{\beta}_n - r|}{s_n[R(\mathbf{X}^\top\mathbf{X})^{-1}R^\top]^{1/2}}.$$

When $q \geq 1$, an F-test rejects H_0 for large values of the statistic

$$F_n = \frac{(R\hat{\beta}_n - r)^\top [R(\mathbf{X}^\top\mathbf{X})^{-1}R^\top]^{-1}(R\hat{\beta}_n - r)}{qs_n^2}$$

or, equivalently, of the statistic $F_n^* = qF_n$. Notice that $F_n^* = F_n = T_n^2$ when $q = 1$.

We first derive the asymptotic properties of t- and F-tests when $\mathbf{X}$ is a stochastic matrix and the distribution of the vector $\mathbf{U} = \mathbf{Y} - \mathbf{X}\beta$ of regression errors satisfies all the assumptions of the classical Gaussian linear model in large samples.

Assumption 10.2 $n^{-1}\mathbf{X}^\top\mathbf{X} \xrightarrow{\mathrm{p}} P$, *where P is a finite p.d. matrix.*

Assumption 10.3 $n^{-1}\mathbf{U}^\top\mathbf{U} \xrightarrow{\mathrm{p}} \sigma^2$, *where* $0 < \sigma^2 < \infty$.

Assumption 10.4 $n^{-1/2}\mathbf{X}^\top\mathbf{U} \xrightarrow{\mathrm{d}} \mathcal{N}_k(0,\, \sigma^2 P)$.

These three assumptions imply that $\hat{\beta}_n$ and s_n^2 exist with probability approaching one, are consistent for β and σ^2 respectively, and $\sqrt{n}\,(\hat{\beta}_n - \beta) \xrightarrow{\mathrm{d}} \mathcal{N}_k(0,\, \sigma^2 P^{-1})$. Notice that our set of assumptions rules out the case when the covariates in a regression model are integrated.

10.4.1 CONSISTENCY

The t- and F-tests are both *consistent*, that is, the probability that they reject H_0 under any fixed alternative approaches one as $n \to \infty$.

Theorem 10.14 *Let ξ_n be either of the test statistics T_n and F_n^*. If Assumptions 10.2–10.4 hold then, under any fixed alternative,* $\Pr\{|\xi_n| > c\} \to 1$ *as $n \to \infty$ for every $c > 0$.*

Proof. Under a fixed alternative $\delta = R\beta - r \neq 0$, we have

$$\sqrt{n}\,(R\hat{\beta}_n - r) = \sqrt{n}\,R(\hat{\beta}_n - \beta) + \sqrt{n}\,(R\beta - r) = \sqrt{n}\,R(\hat{\beta}_n - \beta) + \sqrt{n}\,\delta.$$

Since $\sqrt{n}\,R(\hat{\beta}_n - \beta) = O_p(1)$ under our set of assumptions and $\sqrt{n}\,\delta \to \infty$, it follows that $\Pr\{|\sqrt{n}\,(R\hat{\beta}_n - r)| > c\} \to 1$ for every $c > 0$, and therefore $\Pr\{|\xi_n| > c\} \to 1$. □

This result has two implications for classical tests of a given level. First, from the theoretical point of view, it makes no sense to study their asymptotic power under a fixed alternative, because this is always equal to one. Second, from the practical point of view, a null hypothesis that holds only approximately is always rejected if the sample size is large enough.

10.4.2 LOCAL ALTERNATIVES

One way of drawing nontrivial conclusions about the asymptotic power of a test of a given level is to consider, instead of a fixed alternative, a sequence of alternatives that are *local*, that is, converge to the null hypothesis at the same rate as the sequence of estimators $\{\hat{\beta}_n\}$ converges to a limiting Gaussian distribution centered about the regression parameter β. Thus consider the distribution of the test statistics T_n and F_n^* under a sequence $\{\beta_n\}$ of alternatives such that

$$R\beta_n = r + n^{-1/2}\delta,$$

where the q-vector δ represents a particular direction of departure from the null hypothesis H_0: $R\beta = r$.

Theorem 10.15 *If Assumptions 10.2–10.4 hold then, under a sequence $\{\beta_n\}$ of local alternatives:*

(i) $T_n \xrightarrow{d} \mathcal{N}(\mu_\delta, 1)$, *where* $\mu_\delta = \sigma^{-1}(RP^{-1}R^\top)^{-1/2}\delta$;
(ii) F_n^* *converges in distribution to a noncentral chi-square with q degrees of freedom and noncentrality parameter* $\lambda_\delta = \sigma^{-2}\delta^\top(RP^{-1}R^\top)^{-1}\delta$.

Proof. Under our set of assumptions,

$$\left[s_n^2 R \left(\frac{\mathbf{X}^\top \mathbf{X}}{n}\right)^{-1} R^\top\right]^{-1} \xrightarrow{p} (\sigma^2\, RP^{-1}R^\top)^{-1},$$

a finite p.d. matrix. If $q = 1$, then $T_n - (\sigma^2 RP^{-1}R^\top)^{-1/2}\sqrt{n}\,(R\hat{\beta}_n - r) = o_p(1)$. Part (i) then follows from the fact that, under the sequence $\{\beta_n\}$,

$$\begin{aligned}\sqrt{n}\,(R\hat{\beta}_n - r) &= \sqrt{n}\,(R\beta_n - r) + \sqrt{n}\,R(\mathbf{X}^\top\mathbf{X})^{-1}\mathbf{X}^\top\mathbf{U} \\ &= \delta + R\left(\frac{\mathbf{X}^\top\mathbf{X}}{n}\right)^{-1}\frac{\mathbf{X}^\top\mathbf{U}}{\sqrt{n}} \xrightarrow{\text{d}} \mathcal{N}_q(\delta,\, \sigma^2\, RP^{-1}R^\top).\end{aligned}$$

To prove part (ii), notice that

$$\begin{aligned}F_n^* &= \sqrt{n}\,(R\hat{\beta}_n - r)^\top \left[s_n^2 R\left(\frac{\mathbf{X}^\top\mathbf{X}}{n}\right)^{-1} R^\top\right]^{-1} \sqrt{n}\,(R\hat{\beta}_n - r) \\ &= g\left(\sqrt{n}\,(R\hat{\beta}_n - r),\, \frac{\mathbf{X}^\top\mathbf{X}}{n},\, s_n^2\right).\end{aligned}$$

Since $0 < \sigma^2 < \infty$ and the function g is continuous at all points where the matrix P is nonsingular, we have $F_n^* - \zeta^\top(\sigma^2\, RP^{-1}R^\top)^{-1}\zeta = o_p(1)$, where ζ is a random q-vector with a $\mathcal{N}_q(\delta,\, \sigma^2\, RP^{-1}R^\top)$ distribution under $\{\beta_n\}$. Therefore, F_n^* has the same limiting distribution as the random variable $Z^\top Z$, where $Z = (\sigma^2\, RP^{-1}R^\top)^{-1/2}\zeta$. Since the limiting distribution of Z is $\mathcal{N}_q(\mu_\delta, I_q)$, with $\mu_\delta = (\sigma^2\, RP^{-1}R^\top)^{-1/2}\delta$, the limiting distribution of F_n^* is $\chi^2_{q,\lambda_\delta}$, with $\lambda_\delta = \mu_\delta^\top \mu_\delta$. □

If we put $\delta = 0$, then Theorem 10.15 gives the limiting distribution of the t- and F-test statistics under H_0. Since $T_n \xrightarrow{\text{d}} \mathcal{N}(0,1)$ when $\delta = 0$, a one-sided asymptotic α-level t-test rejects H_0 against the alternative that $R\beta > r$ whenever $T_n > z_{(\alpha)}$, where $z_{(\alpha)}$ denotes the upper αth quantile of the $\mathcal{N}(0,1)$ distribution. A two-sided asymptotic α-level test rejects H_0 against the assumption that $R\beta \neq r$ whenever $|T_n| > z_{\alpha/2}$.

Since $F_n^* \xrightarrow{\text{d}} \chi^2_q$ when $\delta = 0$, an asymptotic α-level F-test rejects H_0 against the alternative that $R\beta \neq r$ whenever $F_n^* > c_{(\alpha)}$ or, equivalently, $F_n > qc_{(\alpha)}$, where $c_{(\alpha)}$ denotes the upper αth quantile of the χ^2_q-distribution.

Since $T_n \xrightarrow{\text{d}} \mathcal{N}(\mu_\delta, 1)$, the asymptotic power of a two-sided t-test with critical value k under a sequence of local alternatives is

$$\pi(\delta) = 2 - \Phi(k - \mu_\delta) - \Phi(k + \mu_\delta), \qquad \delta \in \Re,$$

where μ_δ is given in Theorem 10.15. Viewed as a function of δ, this is called the *asymptotic local power function* of the test. The function π has exactly the same shape as the power function in Example 5.11. The asymptotic local power function of an F-test is instead obtained from the limiting noncentral chi-square distribution of F_n^*. The asymptotic local power of t- and F-tests is an increasing function of the noncentrality parameter, and therefore depends on both the direction δ of departure from the null hypothesis and the asymptotic variance of the OLS estimator. Because the noncentrality parameter is equal to zero if and only if $\delta = 0$, the classical t- and F-tests have power under any departure from the null hypothesis.

The noncentrality parameter λ_δ is a quadratic form in the p.d. matrix $(RP^{-1}R^\top)^{-1}$. It then follows from Theorem A.6 that the set of local alternatives under which an F-test has constant asymptotic power is an ellipsoid centered at the origin, with jth axis having the same direction as the jth eigenvector of $RP^{-1}R^\top$ and length inversely proportional to the jth eigenvalue of $(RP^{-1}R^\top)^{-1}$. The asymptotic power of an F-test is therefore highest under alternatives that are in the same direction as the eigenvector associated with the largest eigenvalue of $(RP^{-1}R^\top)^{-1}$.

10.4.3 NONSCALAR VARIANCE

Now consider the limiting distribution of the t- and F-test statistics under H_0 when the variance matrix of the regression errors is nonscalar. Replace Assumption 10.4 by the following.

Assumption 10.5 $n^{-1/2}\mathbf{X}^\top\mathbf{U}\xrightarrow{\mathrm{d}}\mathcal{N}_k(0,D)$, *where D is a finite symmetric p.d. matrix.*

Under Assumptions 10.2 and 10.5, the asymptotic distribution of $\sqrt{n}\,(\hat\beta_n-\beta)$ is $\mathcal{N}_k(0,V)$, where $V=P^{-1}DP^{-1}$. The next result shows that when V is not a scalar multiple of the matrix P, as happens when the elements of $\mathbf{Y}$ are heteroskedastic or autocorrelated, critical regions based on the $\mathcal{N}(0,1)$ and chi-square distributions are no longer valid, not even asymptotically.

Theorem 10.16 *If Assumptions 10.2, 10.3 and 10.5 hold and $V=P^{-1}DP^{-1}$ then, under* H_0*:*

(i) $T_n\xrightarrow{\mathrm{d}}\mathcal{N}(0,[\sigma^2 RP^{-1}R^\top]^{-1}RVR^\top)$;

(ii) $F_n^*\xrightarrow{\mathrm{d}}\sum_{i=1}^q\lambda_iW_i$, *where $W_1,\ldots,W_q$ are independent random variables with a common χ_1^2-distribution and $\lambda_1,\ldots,\lambda_q$ are the eigenvalues of the p.d. matrix* $M=(\sigma^2 RP^{-1}R^\top)^{-1}RVR^\top$.

Proof. Under our set of assumptions, $s_n^2\xrightarrow{\mathrm{p}}\sigma^2$ and

$$\left[s_n^2R\left(\frac{\mathbf{X}^\top\mathbf{X}}{n}\right)^{-1}R^\top\right]^{-1}\xrightarrow{\mathrm{p}}(\sigma^2 RP^{-1}R^\top)^{-1}.$$

Hence, $T_n-(\sigma^2 RP^{-1}R^\top)^{-1/2}\sqrt{n}\,(R\hat\beta_n-r)=o_p(1)$. Part (i) then follows from the fact that, under H_0, $\sqrt{n}\,(R\hat\beta_n-r)=\sqrt{n}\,R(\hat\beta_n-\beta)\xrightarrow{\mathrm{d}}\mathcal{N}(0,\,RVR^\top)$.

Now consider the asymptotic distribution of F_n^*. An argument analogous to the one used in Theorem 10.15 shows that $F_n^*-\zeta^\top(\sigma^2 RP^{-1}R^\top)^{-1}\zeta=o_p(1)$, where ζ is a random q-vector with a $\mathcal{N}_q(0,\,RVR^\top)$ distribution. The conclusion of the theorem then follows from Result C.21. □

When $V=\sigma^2P^{-1}$, the matrix M in Theorem 10.16 is equal to the unit matrix and therefore $F_n^*\xrightarrow{\mathrm{d}}\chi_q^2$ under H_0. When $V\neq\sigma^2P^{-1}$, however, the matrix M is different from the unit matrix and so the limiting distribution of F_n^* under H_0 is a weighted sum of chi-squares.

10.4.4 TESTS BASED ON THE OLS CRITERION

Consider again a set of constraints on the regression parameter β of the form $R\beta = r$, where R is a $q \times k$ matrix of rank q. The OLS estimator $\hat{\beta}_n$ solves the problem

$$\min_{\beta \in \Re^k} Q_n(\beta) = (\mathbf{Y} - \mathbf{X}\beta)^\top (\mathbf{Y} - \mathbf{X}\beta).$$

The constrained OLS estimator $\tilde{\beta}_n$ solves instead the problem of minimizing $Q_n(\beta)$ subject to $R\beta = r$. From Section 6.5, the q-vector of Lagrange multipliers associated with the constraint is

$$\tilde{\nu}_n = -2\,[R(\mathbf{X}^\top \mathbf{X})^{-1} R^\top]^{-1} (R\hat{\beta}_n - r).$$

Notice that $Q_n(\tilde{\beta}_n) \geq Q_n(\hat{\beta}_n)$, with equality if and only if $\hat{\beta}_n$ satisfies the constraints exactly, in which case $\tilde{\beta}_n = \hat{\beta}_n$ and $\tilde{\nu}_n = 0$. By analogy with the discussion in Section 5.4, three natural measures of "discrepancy" between the null hypothesis H_0: $R\beta = r$ and the sample evidence are:

1. the difference $Q_n(\tilde{\beta}_n) - Q_n(\hat{\beta}_n)$ or, equivalently, the difference $\tilde{\sigma}_n^2 - \hat{\sigma}_n^2$, where $\tilde{\sigma}_n^2 = n^{-1} Q_n(\tilde{\beta}_n)$ and $\hat{\sigma}_n^2 = n^{-1} Q_n(\hat{\beta}_n)$;
2. the norm of the vector $R\hat{\beta}_n - r$;
3. the norm of the vector $\tilde{\nu}_n$.

When the conditional distribution of $\mathbf{Y}$ given $\mathbf{X}$ is not Gaussian, a test based on the difference $Q_n(\hat{\beta}_n) - Q_n(\tilde{\beta}_n) = n(\tilde{\sigma}_n^2 - \hat{\sigma}_n^2)$ is called a *pseudo likelihood ratio test.* From Section 6.5,

$$n(\tilde{\sigma}_n^2 - \hat{\sigma}_n^2) = (R\hat{\beta}_n - r)^\top [R(\mathbf{X}^\top \mathbf{X})^{-1} R^\top]^{-1} (R\hat{\beta}_n - r),$$

which is the numerator of the F-test statistic. Thus, by Theorem 10.16, the asymptotic distribution of a statistic based on the difference $Q_n(\hat{\beta}_n) - Q_n(\tilde{\beta}_n)$ is not easy to compute in the presence of heteroskedasticity or autocorrelation in $\mathbf{Y}$.

If Assumption 10.5 holds and $R\beta = r$, then $\sqrt{n}\,(R\hat{\beta}_n - r) \xrightarrow{\mathrm{d}} \mathcal{N}_q(0,\, RVR^\top)$, where $V = P^{-1} D P^{-1}$. If there exists a symmetric p.d. matrix $\hat{V}_n$ such that $\hat{V}_n \xrightarrow{\mathrm{p}} V$, then a test that rejects H_0 for large values of the statistic

$$\xi_n^W = n\,(R\hat{\beta}_n - r)^\top (R\hat{V}_n R^\top)^{-1} (R\hat{\beta}_n - r)$$

is called a *Wald test.* Under the same set of assumptions, $n^{-1/2}\tilde{\nu}_n \xrightarrow{\mathrm{d}} \mathcal{N}_q(0, \mathrm{AV}(\tilde{\nu}_n))$, where

$$\mathrm{AV}(\tilde{\nu}_n) = 4(RP^{-1}R^\top)^{-1} RVR^\top (RP^{-1}R^\top)^{-1}.$$

If there exists a symmetric p.d. matrix $\tilde{V}_n$ such that $\tilde{V}_n \xrightarrow{\mathrm{p}} V$ under H_0, then a test that rejects H_0 for large values of the statistic

$$\begin{aligned}\xi_n^{LM} &= \frac{1}{4n} \tilde{\nu}_n^\top \left[R \left(\frac{\mathbf{X}^\top \mathbf{X}}{n} \right)^{-1} R^\top (R\tilde{V}_n R^\top)^{-1} R \left(\frac{\mathbf{X}^\top \mathbf{X}}{n} \right)^{-1} R^\top \right] \tilde{\nu}_n \\ &= n\,(R\hat{\beta}_n - r)^\top (R\tilde{V}_n R^\top)^{-1} (R\hat{\beta}_n - r)\end{aligned}$$

is called a *Lagrange multiplier test.* In the special case when $D = \sigma^2 P$, and therefore $V = \sigma^2 P^{-1}$, the Wald and Lagrange multiplier test statistics reduce to

$$\xi_n^W = \frac{(R\hat{\beta}_n - r)^\top [R(\mathbf{X}^\top \mathbf{X})^{-1} R^\top]^{-1} (R\hat{\beta}_n - r)}{\hat{\sigma}_n^2} = n\, \frac{\tilde{\sigma}_n^2 - \hat{\sigma}_n^2}{\hat{\sigma}_n^2},$$

$$\xi_n^{LM} = \frac{(R\hat{\beta}_n - r)^\top [R(\mathbf{X}^\top \mathbf{X})^{-1} R^\top]^{-1} (R\hat{\beta}_n - r)}{\tilde{\sigma}^2} = n\, \frac{\tilde{\sigma}_n^2 - \hat{\sigma}_n^2}{\tilde{\sigma}_n^2}.$$

When V is unconstrained, construction of critical regions of given level may be based on the following result.

Theorem 10.17 *Suppose that Assumptions 10.2, 10.3 and 10.5 hold and let $\hat{V}_n$ be a symmetric p.d. matrix such that $\hat{V}_n \xrightarrow{\text{p}} V = P^{-1} D P^{-1}$ whenever $R\beta = r$. Then $\xi_n = n\,(R\hat{\beta}_n - r)^\top (R\hat{V}_n R^\top)^{-1} (R\hat{\beta}_n - r) \xrightarrow{\text{d}} \chi_q^2$ under* H_0.

Theorem 10.17 implies that the statistics ξ_n^W and ξ_n^{LM} have the same limiting distribution under H_0. In finite samples, however, critical regions based on the asymptotic chi-square approximation may result in conflicting inferences depending on what test statistic is used (see Berndt & Savin 1977, Evans & Savin 1982).

In finite samples, inference may also depend on the particular method with which V is estimated. Chesher (1989) considered a heteroskedastic linear model and established bounds on the exact level of Wald tests based on alternative consistent estimators of V. For a test of a single linear equality constraint of the form $R\beta = r$, where R is a k-dimensional row-vector, the statistic of a Wald test is

$$T_n = \frac{R\hat{\beta}_n - r}{\sqrt{R\hat{V}_n R^\top}},$$

where $\hat{V}_n$ is a consistent estimate of V. Chesher (1989) showed that, in finite samples, a test based on the jackknife estimate is conservative, that is, its exact level cannot exceed its asymptotic one. On the contrary, tests based on the infinitesimal jackknife or on Hinkley's (1977) estimates are never conservative, for they may reject the null hypothesis more frequently than desired.

The bounds on the exact level of a test depend also on the sample size n, the number k of covariates and the measures h_{ii} of leverage in the design. If the design matrix is perfectly balanced, that is, $h_{ii} = k/n$ for every i, then

$$\hat{V}_n^{(1)} = \hat{V}_n^{(2)} = \frac{n-k}{n-1}\, \hat{V}_n^{(3)},$$

where $\hat{V}_n^{(1)}$ is the infinitesimal jackknife estimate, $\hat{V}_n^{(2)}$ is Hinkley's (1977) estimate and $\hat{V}_n^{(3)}$ is the jackknife estimate. In this case, the exact level of a test is near the asymptotic one no matter which of the three estimates of V is used. The difference between the exact and the asymptotic level gets larger as the design becomes more unbalanced, that is, $\max\{h_{ii}\} \to 1$. Chesher's results highlight the influence of regression design on the quality of the asymptotic approximation to the distribution of a Wald test statistic. His results suggest calculating leverage measures whenever a Wald test is performed, and interpreting the results with caution if high leverage points are present.

10.4.5 NONLINEAR CONSTRAINTS

So far, we have only considered linear constraints on the regression parameter β. Sometimes one may also be interested in testing nonlinear constraints. For example, if $\beta = (\beta_1, \beta_2)$, one may be interested in testing the hypotheses that $\beta_1\beta_2 = 1$ or that $\beta_2 = \beta_1^2$. Thus consider a null hypothesis defined by a set of $q \leq k$ nonlinear equality constraints of the form H_0: $h(\beta) = 0$, where h: $\Re^k \to \Re^q$ is a known differentiable function with continuous Jacobian $h'(\beta)$. A set of linear equality constraints is a special case corresponding to $h(\beta) = R\beta - r$ and $h'(\beta) = R$.

Example 10.7 A linear model with AR(1) errors may be represented as

$$Y_t = \rho Y_{t-1} + \alpha X_t + \rho\alpha X_{t-1} + V_t, \qquad \{U_t\} \sim \mathrm{WN}(0, \sigma^2).$$

Testing this model against the more general specification

$$Y_t = \beta_1 Y_{t-1} + \beta_2 X_t + \beta_3 X_{t-1} + V_t, \qquad \{U_t\} \sim \mathrm{WN}(0, \sigma^2)$$

is equivalent to testing the nonlinear equality constraint $h(\beta) = \beta_3 - \beta_1\beta_2 = 0$. Because the unconstrained model is easily estimated by OLS, a Wald test is here the most convenient to carry out. □

A Wald test rejects H_0 for large values of the norm of the vector $h(\hat{\beta}_n)$. Construction of critical regions of a given asymptotic level may be based on the following result.

Theorem 10.18 *Suppose that Assumptions 10.2, 10.3 and 10.5 hold and assume:*

(i) h: $\Re^k \to \Re^q$ *is a continuously differentiable function;*
(ii) $H = h'(\beta)$ *has rank* q*;*
(iii) *there exists a symmetric p.d. matrix* $\hat{V}_n$ *such that* $\hat{V}_n \xrightarrow{\mathrm{p}} V = P^{-1}DP^{-1}$.

Then, under H_0, $\xi_n^W = n\, h(\hat{\beta}_n)^\top (\hat{H}_n \hat{V}_n \hat{H}_n^\top)^{-1} h(\hat{\beta}_n) \xrightarrow{\mathrm{d}} \chi_q^2$, *where* $\hat{H}_n = h'(\hat{\beta}_n)$.

Proof. Assumption (i) and the mean value theorem imply

$$h(\hat{\beta}_n) = h(\beta) + h'(\beta_n^*)(\hat{\beta}_n - \beta),$$

where $h(\beta) = 0$ under H_0 and $\beta_n^* = (1 - \lambda)\hat{\beta}_n + \lambda\beta$ for some $\lambda \in [0, 1]$. Since $\|\beta_n^*\| \leq \|\hat{\beta}_n\|$ and $\hat{\beta}_n \xrightarrow{\mathrm{p}} \beta$, it follows that $\beta_n^* \xrightarrow{\mathrm{p}} \beta$ and therefore $h'(\beta_n^*) \xrightarrow{\mathrm{p}} H$. Thus, under H_0, $\sqrt{n}\, h(\hat{\beta}_n) - H\sqrt{n}\,(\hat{\beta}_n - \beta) \xrightarrow{\mathrm{p}} 0$. The conclusion of the theorem then follows by noticing that $\hat{H}_n \xrightarrow{\mathrm{p}} H$, $\hat{V}_n \xrightarrow{\mathrm{p}} V$ and $H\sqrt{n}\,(\hat{\beta}_n - \beta) \xrightarrow{\mathrm{d}} \mathcal{N}_q(0,\, HVH^\top)$. □

A problem with Wald tests of nonlinear constraints is that, although the test statistic is easy to construct, it is not invariant to the particular algebraic form chosen to represent the null hypothesis. As pointed out by Gregory and Veall (1985) and Phillips and Park (1988), different representations of the same null hypothesis may lead to different test statistics and therefore to conflicting inferences in small samples if an asymptotic critical region is used.

10.5 LIKELIHOOD-BASED TESTS

In Section 5.4 we introduced three general testing principles for parametric models: the likelihood ratio principle, the Wald principle, and the score principle. In this section we discuss other regression problems where these three principles lead to tests that have a very natural interpretation.

Except for special cases, such as the one in Section 9.1.3, the exact distribution of the derived test statistics is complicated. Therefore, construction of critical regions usually relies on the fact that, under appropriate regularity conditions, the sampling distribution of the test statistics is well approximated in large samples by a chi-square distribution with number of degrees of freedom equal to the number of constraints that define the null hypothesis (Theorem 5.3). A viable alternative, however, is the parametric bootstrap discussed in Section 5.4.6.

10.5.1 LIKELIHOOD RATIO TESTS

A likelihood ratio test requires computing both the unconstrained and the constrained ML estimates. In some cases this is straightforward.

Example 10.8 Consider again Example 9.8 and suppose that we are interested in testing the null hypothesis

$$\mathbf{Y}_s \sim \mathcal{N}_{n_s}(\mathbf{X}_s\beta_s,\, \sigma^2\, I_{n_s}), \qquad s = 1, \ldots, S,$$

namely that heterogeneity is confined to the regression functions, against the alternative hypothesis (9.4) of complete heterogeneity across strata. Testing this null hypothesis is equivalent to testing the set of $S-1$ constraints $\sigma_1^2 = \cdots = \sigma_S^2$. Separate OLS regressions for each stratum give the estimates

$$\hat{\beta}_s = (\mathbf{X}_s{}^\top\mathbf{X}_s)^{-1}\mathbf{X}_s{}^\top\mathbf{Y}_s, \qquad s = 1, \ldots, S.$$

The unconstrained Gaussian ML estimate of σ_s^2 is therefore $\hat{\sigma}_s^2 = n_s^{-1}\hat{\mathbf{U}}_s^\top\hat{\mathbf{U}}_s$, where $\hat{\mathbf{U}}_s = \mathbf{Y}_s - \mathbf{X}_s\hat{\beta}_s$. The constrained estimate is instead $\tilde{\sigma}^2 = n^{-1}\sum_s \hat{\mathbf{U}}_s^\top\hat{\mathbf{U}}_s = \sum_s p_s\hat{\sigma}_s^2$, where $n = \sum_s n_s$ and $p_s = n_s/n$. Hence, the maximized values of the log-likelihood for the two models are $\hat{L} = c' - \frac{1}{2}\sum_s n_s \ln\hat{\sigma}_s^2$ and $\tilde{L} = c' - (n/2)\ln\tilde{\sigma}^2$. Therefore, a likelihood ratio test rejects H_0 for large values of the statistic

$$\xi^R = 2(\hat{L} - \tilde{L}) = n\ln\tilde{\sigma}^2 - \sum_s n_s \ln\hat{\sigma}_s^2 = n\ln\frac{\sum_s p_s\hat{\sigma}_s^2}{\prod_s(\hat{\sigma}_s^2)^{p_s}}.$$

This test, also known as the *Bartlett test*, compares the arithmetic mean of the estimated stratum variances $\hat{\sigma}_s^2$ with their geometric mean. The two means coincide only when all the $\hat{\sigma}_s^2$ are the same, otherwise the arithmetic mean is larger than the geometric mean. □

10.5.2 WALD TESTS

When the unconstrained ML estimate is easy to compute, a Wald test is undoubtedly attractive.

Example 10.9 Consider a longitudinal data set that consists of T observations on each of n sample units, and let $\mathbf{Y}_i$ denote the vector of T observations on the response variable for the ith sample unit. Our model for the data is a Gaussian SURE model where the design matrix $\bar{\mathbf{X}}$ is exactly the same for each sample unit. From Section 7.3.3, this model may be written $\mathbf{Y} \sim \mathcal{N}_{nT}((I_n \otimes \bar{\mathbf{X}})\beta, \Gamma \otimes I_T)$. The null hypothesis is H_0: $R\beta = r$.

The unconstrained Gaussian ML estimate of β is easily computed because it consists of n vectors, $\hat{\beta}_1, \ldots, \hat{\beta}_n$, one for each sample unit, where $\hat{\beta}_i$ is the OLS coefficient in the regression of $\mathbf{Y}_i$ on $\bar{\mathbf{X}}$. If we imposed the constraint $R\beta = r$, the resulting estimate of β would be more complicated to compute except for the special case when constraints are separable across equations, that is, there are no cross-equation constraints. It is therefore natural to use a Wald test in this case.

Given the model, the sampling variance of $\hat{\beta} = (\hat{\beta}_1, \ldots, \hat{\beta}_n)$ is

$$\operatorname{Var} \hat{\beta} = [(I_n \otimes \bar{\mathbf{X}})^\top (\Gamma \otimes I_T)^{-1} (I_n \otimes \bar{\mathbf{X}})]^{-1} = \Gamma \otimes (\bar{\mathbf{X}}^\top \bar{\mathbf{X}})^{-1}.$$

As an estimate of Γ consider

$$\hat{\Gamma} = \frac{1}{n} \begin{bmatrix} \hat{\mathbf{U}}_1^\top \hat{\mathbf{U}}_1 & \cdots & \hat{\mathbf{U}}_1^\top \hat{\mathbf{U}}_n \\ \vdots & & \vdots \\ \hat{\mathbf{U}}_n^\top \hat{\mathbf{U}}_1 & \cdots & \hat{\mathbf{U}}_n^\top \hat{\mathbf{U}}_n \end{bmatrix},$$

where $\hat{\mathbf{U}}_i = \mathbf{Y}_i - \bar{\mathbf{X}}\hat{\beta}_i$ is the OLS residual vector for the ith sample unit. Thus, a Wald test rejects H_0 for large values of the statistic

$$\xi^W = (R\hat{\beta} - r)^\top [R(\hat{\Gamma}^{-1} \otimes \bar{\mathbf{X}}^\top \bar{\mathbf{X}})R^\top]^{-1} (R\hat{\beta} - r).$$

□

10.5.3 SCORE TESTS

We illustrate regression applications of the score principle with some examples. These examples share three interesting features. First, all tests may be viewed as tests of the hypothesis H_0: $\lambda = 0$, where λ is a suitable vector of parameters added by augmenting the maintained Gaussian linear model. Second, the score test statistics have a strong intuitive appeal, for they generally look for inconsistency between the data and the null hypothesis by examining sample analogues of moment conditions which only hold under H_0. Third, the test statistics do not depend on the precise specification of the alternative hypothesis.

The latter feature may be a strength or a weakness depending on the quality of the available information. It is a strength when the class of alternatives is rather vague. It may be a weakness when the alternative is known precisely, for the test does not seem to be using all the available information. It turns out that this lack of sensitivity to the choice of the alternative hypothesis is a general feature of tests based on the score principle.

Example 10.10 Consider a heteroskedastic Gaussian linear model where the heteroskedasticity has a known parametric form. Following Breusch and Pagan (1979), suppose that

$$\sigma_i^2 = \operatorname{Var} Y_i = g(\alpha_0 + \alpha^\top W_i), \qquad i = 1, \ldots, n,$$

where g is some positive, smooth and invertible function, W_i is a nonstochastic q-vector whose first element is identically equal to one, and α is a parameter vector that is functionally independent of the regression parameter β. This specification is quite general and encompasses several models proposed in the literature (see Section 1.3.4). Because the first element of W_i is equal to one, the null hypothesis of homoskedasticity is equivalent to the set of $q-1$ constraints $\alpha_j = 0$, $j = 2, \ldots, q$.

The sample log-likelihood is in this case

$$L(\theta) = c - \frac{1}{2}\sum_{i=1}^n \ln g(\alpha^\top W_i) - \frac{1}{2}\sum_{i=1}^n \frac{(Y_i - \beta^\top X_i)^2}{g(\alpha^\top W_i)}, \qquad \theta = (\beta, \alpha),$$

where c is an arbitrary constant. Because the expected total information $I(\theta)$ can be shown to be block-diagonal with respect to β and α, constructing the score test statistic only requires the element $S_\alpha = \partial L/\partial\alpha$ of the likelihood score and the corresponding block $I_{\alpha\alpha}$ of the expected total information

$$S_\alpha(\theta) = \frac{1}{2}\sum_{i=1}^n \frac{g'(\alpha^\top W_i)}{\sigma_i^2} W_i \left[\left(\frac{Y_i - \beta^\top X_i}{\sigma_i}\right)^2 - 1\right],$$

$$I_{\alpha\alpha}(\theta) = \frac{1}{4}\sum_{i=1}^n \left[\frac{g'(\alpha^\top W_i)}{\sigma_i^2}\right]^2 W_i W_i^\top \operatorname{E}\left[\left(\frac{Y_i - \beta^\top X_i}{\sigma_i}\right)^2 - 1\right]^2$$

$$= \frac{1}{2}\sum_{i=1}^n \left[\frac{g'(\alpha^\top W_i)}{\sigma_i^2}\right]^2 W_i W_i^\top,$$

where we used the fact that, under the Gaussian model, $(Y_i - \beta^\top X_i)^2/\sigma_i^2 \sim \chi_1^2$ and therefore

$$\operatorname{E}\left[\left(\frac{Y_i - \beta^\top X_i}{\sigma_i}\right)^2 - 1\right]^2 = 2.$$

The constrained Gaussian ML estimate of θ is $\tilde\theta = (\hat\beta, \tilde\alpha_1, 0, \ldots, 0)$, where $\hat\beta$ is the OLS estimator of β, $\tilde\alpha_1 = g^{-1}(\hat\sigma^2)$ and $\hat\sigma^2$ is the average squared deviation of the OLS residuals. Evaluating the score for α at the constrained estimate gives

$$\tilde S_\alpha = S_\alpha(\tilde\theta) = \frac{1}{2}\frac{g'(\tilde\alpha_1)}{\hat\sigma^2}\mathbf{W}^\top\tilde{\mathbf{U}},$$

where $\tilde{\mathbf{U}}$ is an n-vector whose ith element is equal to $\tilde U_i = (\hat U_i^2/\hat\sigma^2) - 1$, a standardized version of the squared OLS residuals, and $\mathbf{W}$ is an $n \times q$ matrix whose ith row is equal to W_i. Evaluating the block corresponding to the expected information on α at the constrained ML estimate gives

$$\tilde I_{\alpha\alpha} = I_{\alpha\alpha}(\tilde\theta) = \frac{1}{2}\frac{g'(\tilde\alpha_1)^2}{\hat\sigma^4}\mathbf{W}^\top\mathbf{W}.$$

Thus, a score test rejects H_0 for large values of the statistic

$$\xi^S = \tilde{S}_\alpha^\top \tilde{I}_{\alpha\alpha}^{-1} \tilde{S}_\alpha = \frac{1}{2} \tilde{\mathbf{U}}^\top \mathbf{W}(\mathbf{W}^\top \mathbf{W})^{-1} \mathbf{W}^\top \tilde{\mathbf{U}},$$

which is equal to 1/2 the predicted sum of squares in the auxiliary regression of $\tilde{\mathbf{U}}$ on $\mathbf{W}$. A score test, therefore, looks for the presence of a linear relation between the squared OLS residuals (suitably standardized) and a set of variables that are supposed to help "explain" the heterosckedasticity of the data. Notice that the test statistic is invariant to the precise form of the function g. □

Example 10.11 Given a classical Gaussian linear model, one way of testing the Gaussian assumption is to consider some broader family of distributions that contains the Gaussian as a special case. There are several ways to do so. Here we follow Jarque and Bera (1980) and consider the *Pearson family of distributions*, which contains the Gaussian, the t, the beta, and the gamma (among others) as special cases. For each distribution in this family, the density function satisfies the differential equation

$$\frac{d}{du} \ln f(u) = \frac{c_1 - u}{c_0 + c_1 u + c_2 u^2} \tag{10.5}$$

(see for example Johnson & Kotz 1970). This differential equation may be solved using the condition that a density must integrate to one. The solution is

$$f(u) = \frac{\exp g(u)}{\int_{-\infty}^{\infty} \exp g(t)\, dt},$$

where

$$g(u) = \int_{-\infty}^{u} \frac{c_1 - t}{c_0 + c_1 t + c_2 t^2}\, dt.$$

In particular, when $c_1 = c_2 = 0$ and $c_0 = \sigma^2$, solving (10.5) gives

$$f(u) \propto \exp\left(-\frac{u^2}{2\sigma^2}\right),$$

which is the density of a $\mathcal{N}(0, \sigma^2)$ distribution. A test of the hypothesis of Gaussian data is therefore a test of the pair of constraints $c_1 = c_2 = 0$.

If the regression errors $U_i = Y_i - \beta^\top X_i$ are i.i.d. according to a distribution in the Pearson family having zero mean, then the sample log-likelihood is

$$L(\theta) = c + \sum_{i=1}^{n} \left[g(Y_i - \beta^\top X_i) - \ln \int \exp g(u)\, du \right], \qquad \theta = (\beta, c_0, c_1, c_2),$$

where c is an arbitrary constant. Thus, the components of the likelihood score are

$$S_\beta(\theta) = -\sum_{i=1}^{n} X_i \frac{c_1 - U_i}{c_0 + c_1 U_i + c_2 U_i^2},$$

$$S_{c_j}(\theta) = \sum_{i=1}^{n} \left[\frac{\partial g(U_i)}{\partial c_j} - \mathrm{E}\left(\frac{\partial g(U_i)}{\partial c_j} \right) \right], \qquad j = 0, 1, 2.$$

Evaluating at $c_1 = c_2 = 0$ gives

$$\frac{\partial g(u)}{\partial c_0} = \frac{u^2}{2c_0^2}, \qquad \frac{\partial g(u)}{\partial c_1} = \frac{u}{c_0} + \frac{u^3}{3c_0^2}, \qquad \frac{\partial g(u)}{\partial c_2} = \frac{u^4}{4c_0^2}.$$

Putting $c_0 = \sigma^2$, the components of the likelihood score evaluated under H_0 are therefore

$$\begin{aligned} S_\beta(\theta) &= \frac{1}{\sigma^2}\sum_{i=1}^n X_i U_i, \\ S_{\sigma^2}(\theta) &= \frac{1}{2\sigma^2}\sum_{i=1}^n (U_i^2 - \sigma^2), \\ S_{c_1}(\theta) &= \frac{1}{\sigma^2}\sum_{i=1}^n U_i + \frac{1}{3\sigma^4}\sum_i U_i^3, \\ S_{c_2}(\theta) &= \frac{1}{4\sigma^4}\sum_{i=1}^n (U_i^4 - 3\sigma^4), \end{aligned}$$

where we used the fact that, under the Gaussian null hypothesis, $\mathrm{E}\, U_i^2 = \sigma^2$, $\mathrm{E}\, U_i^3 = 0$ and $\mathrm{E}\, U_i^4 = 3\sigma^4$.

The constrained ML estimate is $\tilde\theta = (\hat\beta, \hat\sigma^2, 0, 0)$, where $\hat\beta$ is the OLS estimate and $\hat\sigma^2$ is the average squared deviation of the OLS residuals. The score test statistic is therefore obtained by combining the statistics

$$S_{c_1}(\tilde\theta) = \frac{1}{3\tilde\sigma^4}\sum_{i=1}^n \hat U_i^3, \qquad S_{c_2}(\tilde\theta) = \frac{1}{4\hat\sigma^4}\sum_{i=1}^n (\hat U_i^4 - 3\hat\sigma^4).$$

Thus, a score test looks for deviations of the third and fourth sample moments of the OLS residuals from what one would predict on the basis of the Gaussian hypothesis. For this reason, this type of test is likely to be powerful under other classes of distribution that have skewness and kurtosis different from the Gaussian. □

Example 10.12 Suppose that $Y_1, \ldots, Y_n$ are a finite segment of a Gaussian AR(p) process with time-varying mean $\beta^\top X_t$

$$\Phi(L)\,(Y_t - \beta^\top X_t) = V_t,$$

where $\Phi(L) = 1 - \phi_1 L - \cdots - \phi_p L^p$, $\{X_t\}$ is a sequence of nonstochastic vectors and $\{V_t\}$ is a Gaussian $\mathrm{WN}(0, \sigma^2)$ process. Because the deviations of Y_t from its mean follow an AR(p) process with mean zero, this model is often represented in the form

$$\begin{aligned} Y_t - \beta X_t &= U_t, \\ \Phi(L)\, U_t &= V_t, \end{aligned}$$

and called a *linear model with* AR(p) *errors*. We shall assume that the regression error process $\{U_t\}$ is stable. Testing for the validity of a classical Gaussian linear model is here equivalent to testing the hypothesis that the vector $\phi = (\phi_1, \ldots, \phi_p)$ is zero.

If the sample size is sufficiently large then, by an argument similar to the one used in Example 4.10, the sample log-likelihood may be approximated by

$$L(\theta) = c - \frac{n}{2}\ln\sigma^2 - \frac{1}{2\sigma^2}\sum_{t=p+1}^{n}(Y_t^* - \beta^\top X_t^*)^2, \qquad \theta = (\beta, \phi, \sigma^2),$$

where c is an arbitrary constant, and $Y_t^* = \Phi(L)\,Y_t$ and $X_t^* = \Phi(L)\,X_t$ are a simple generalization of the data transformation introduced in Example 7.11 for the case of a linear model with AR(1) errors. The components of the likelihood score are

$$S_\beta(\theta) = \frac{1}{\sigma^2}\sum_t X_t^* V_t,$$

$$S_{\phi_j}(\theta) = \frac{1}{\sigma^2}\sum_t V_t U_{t-j}, \qquad j = 1, \ldots, p,$$

$$S_{\sigma^2}(\theta) = -\frac{n}{2\sigma^2} + \frac{1}{2\sigma^4}\sum_t V_t^2,$$

where $X_t^* = \Phi(L)\,X_t$. The expected total information on θ is

$$I(\theta) = \frac{1}{\sigma^2}\begin{bmatrix} \mathbf{X}^{*\top}\mathbf{X}^* & & \\ & n\,\Gamma(\phi) & \\ & & n/(2\sigma^2) \end{bmatrix},$$

where $\Gamma(\phi)$ is the $p \times p$ matrix whose elements are the autocovariances of an AR(p) process. Notice the block-diagonality of the information matrix.

The constrained ML estimate is $\tilde\theta = (\hat\beta, 0, \hat\sigma^2)$, where $\hat\beta$ is the OLS estimate in the regression of $\mathbf{Y}$ on $\mathbf{X}$ and $\hat\sigma^2$ is the average squared deviation of the residuals of this regression. Further, under H$_0$: $\phi = 0$, the matrix $\Gamma(\phi)$ reduces to the scalar matrix $\sigma^2 I_p$. The score test statistic is therefore

$$\xi^S = \frac{1}{n}\sum_{j=1}^{p} S_{\phi_j}(\tilde\theta)^2.$$

Because

$$S_{\phi_j}(\tilde\theta) = n\frac{\sum_t \hat U_t \hat U_{t-j}}{\sum_t \hat U_t^2} = n\hat\rho_j, \qquad j = 1, \ldots, p,$$

where $\hat\rho_j$ is the jth sample autocorrelation of the OLS residuals, the score test statistic may be rewritten as

$$\xi^S = n\sum_{j=1}^{p}\hat\rho_j^2,$$

which is known as the *Box–Pierce statistic*. In particular, if the alternative is an AR(1) error process, then the score test statistic is simply $\xi^S = n\hat\rho_1^2$. The Durbin–Watson test may therefore be interpreted as a score test.

It can be shown that the Box–Pierce statistic is also the score test statistic for testing the hypothesis of no error autocorrelation against the alternative of a Gaussian MA(p) error process

$$Y_t - \beta^\top X_t = \Theta_p(L)\,V_t,$$

where $\Theta_p(L) = 1 - \theta_1 L - \cdots - \theta_p L^p$, $\{X_t\}$ is a sequence of nonstochastic vectors and $\{V_t\}$ is a Gaussian white noise process. □

10.6 TESTING NON-NESTED HYPOTHESES

In all cases discussed so far, the null hypothesis H_0 is *nested* within the alternative H_1, that is, H_0 can be obtained by imposing a set of constraints on the parameters of H_1. Two hypotheses H_1 and H_2 are said to be *non-nested* if neither H_1 is nested within H_2, nor H_2 is nested within H_1.

Non-nested hypotheses may arise for several reasons. For example, competing economic theories may lead to alternative sets of covariates in $\mathbf{X}$. Or, even when there is agreement on the set of covariates, there may be disagreement on the form of the CMF. For example, one theory may suggest that the CMF is linear in $\mathbf{X}$, another that it is log-linear.

Tests of non-nested hypotheses differ from those considered so far on two counts. First, there is complete symmetry in the treatment of the two hypotheses under investigation. Second, unlike a classical test, which has only two possible outcomes, namely "reject H_0" and "do not reject H_0", a non-nested test has four possible outcomes, namely "reject H_1 but not H_2", "reject H_2 but not H_1", "reject both H_1 and H_2", "reject neither H_1 nor H_2".

In this section, the two non-nested hypotheses correspond to two alternative classical Gaussian linear models

$$H_j: \qquad \mathbf{Y} \sim \mathcal{N}_n(\mathbf{X}_j \beta_j,\, \sigma_j^2\, I_n), \qquad j = 1, 2,$$

where β_j is a k_j-vector and $\mathbf{X}_j$ is an $n \times k_j$ matrix. For simplicity, we assume that there is no overlap between the variables in $\mathbf{X}_1$ and $\mathbf{X}_2$. The Gaussian ML estimate of (β_j, σ_j^2) is denoted by $(\hat\beta_j, \hat\sigma_j^2)$.

We consider three alternative approaches to non-nested testing. Although our focus is on testing H_1 against H_2, the procedure for testing H_2 against H_1 is symmetrically defined.

10.6.1 THE COMPREHENSIVE APPROACH

The basic idea is to postulate a "comprehensive" model which contains both H_1 and H_2 and then apply a classical test. One possibility is the model

$$\mathbf{Y} = \mathbf{X}_1 \beta_1^* + \mathbf{X}_2 \beta_2^* + \mathbf{U}_*. \tag{10.6}$$

A test of H_1 is a test of $\beta_2^* = 0$. If the error vector $\mathbf{U}_*$ has a Gaussian distribution with zero mean and scalar variance matrix, then an exact test may be based on the F-distribution. Let $\hat{\mathbf{U}}_1$ and $\hat{\mathbf{U}}_*$ denote the OLS residuals in the regression of $\mathbf{Y}$ respectively on $\mathbf{X}_1$ and on $\mathbf{X}_1$ and $\mathbf{X}_2$, and let $s_*^2 = \hat{\mathbf{U}}_*^\top \hat{\mathbf{U}}_*/(n - k_1 - k_2)$. Then the F-test statistic

$$\xi_1^F = \frac{\hat{\mathbf{U}}_1^\top \hat{\mathbf{U}}_1 - \hat{\mathbf{U}}_*^\top \hat{\mathbf{U}}_*}{k_2 s_*^2} = \frac{\mathbf{Y}^\top M_1 \mathbf{X}_2 (\mathbf{X}_2^\top M_1 \mathbf{X}2)^{-1} \mathbf{X}_2^\top M_1 \mathbf{Y}}{k_2 s_*^2},$$

where $M_1 = I_n - \mathbf{X}_1(\mathbf{X}_1^\top \mathbf{X}_1)^{-1}\mathbf{X}_1^\top$, is distributed as $F_{k_2, n-k_1-k_2}$ under H_1. If the error vector $\mathbf{U}_*$ has a scalar variance matrix but is not Gaussian, a test based on ξ_1^F

is valid only asymptotically.

Another possibility is to introduce an artificial nesting parameter that can be estimated and tested easily. For example, Davidson and MacKinnon (1981) suggest testing H_1 by testing for $\alpha = 0$ in the model

$$\mathbf{Y} = \mathbf{X}_1\beta_1^* + \alpha\mathbf{X}_2\hat{\beta}_2 + \mathbf{U}.$$

This test, called the *J-test*, rejects H_1 for large values of the statistic

$$\xi_1^J = \frac{\hat{\beta}_2^\top \mathbf{X}_2 M_1 \mathbf{Y}}{\hat{\sigma}_1(\hat{\beta}_2^\top \mathbf{X}_2 M_1 \mathbf{X}_2\hat{\beta}_2)^{1/2}}.$$

Under H_1, this test statistic can be shown to be approximately distributed as $\mathcal{N}(0,1)$ in large samples.

A simple modification of ξ_1^J, suggested by Fisher and MacAleer (1981), leads to an exact test. If we replace $\hat{\beta}_2$ in ξ_1^J by the OLS coefficient $\hat{\beta}_{21} = (\mathbf{X}_2{}^\top\mathbf{X}_2)^{-1}\mathbf{X}_2{}^\top\mathbf{X}_1\hat{\beta}_1$ in a regression of $\mathbf{X}\hat{\beta}_1$ on $\mathbf{X}_2$, then the resulting statistic

$$\xi_1^{JA} = \frac{\hat{\beta}_{21}^\top \mathbf{X}_2 M_1 \mathbf{Y}}{\hat{\sigma}_1(\hat{\beta}_{21}^\top \mathbf{X}_2 M_1 \mathbf{X}_2\hat{\beta}_{21})^{1/2}}$$

can be shown to have a t_{n-k_2} distribution under H_1. A test that rejects H_1 for large values of this statistic is called a *JA-test.* A problem with the *JA*-test is the fact that $\hat{\beta}_{21} = 0$ when $\mathbf{X}_1$ and $\mathbf{X}_2$ are orthogonal. In this case, the test statistic cannot be computed because both the numerator and the denominator vanish.

10.6.2 THE COX TEST

The test proposed by Cox (1961, 1962) is essentially a generalization of the likelihood ratio test. The test statistic for testing H_1 against H_2 is the difference between the ratio of the maximized value of the log-likelihoods and its expectation under H_1

$$\xi_1^C = \hat{L}_1 - \hat{L}_2 - \mathrm{E}_1(\hat{L}_1 - \hat{L}_2),$$

where $\hat{L}_j$ denotes the maximized value of the sample log-likelihood for model H_j and E_1 denotes the expectations under H_1.

When $\xi_1^C \approx 0$, the evidence favors H_1 because H_2 fits exactly as expected if H_1 were true. When the statistic ξ_1^C is significantly negative, then H_2 fits better than it should if H_1 were true. Finally, when ξ_1^C is significantly positive, then H_2 fits worse than it should. Thus, large values of $|\xi_1^C|$ are evidence against H_1.

To compute the test statistic, assume first that the scale parameters in the two models are known and, without loss of generality, set them both equal to one. The ratio of the maximized values of the sample log-likelihoods is in this case $\hat{L}_1 - \hat{L}_2 = (n/2)(\hat{\sigma}_2^2 - \hat{\sigma}_1^2)$. Under H_1 we have

$$\mathrm{E}_1\, n\hat{\sigma}_1^2 = \mathrm{E}_1\, \mathbf{Y}^\top M_1 \mathbf{Y} = n - k_1,$$
$$\mathrm{E}_1\, n\hat{\sigma}_2^2 = \mathrm{E}_1\, \mathbf{Y}^\top M_2 \mathbf{Y} = \mathrm{tr}[M_2(\mathrm{E}_1\, \mathbf{Y}\mathbf{Y}^\top)],$$

where $M_2 = I_n - \mathbf{X}_2(\mathbf{X}_2^\top\mathbf{X}_2)^{-1}\mathbf{X}_2^\top$. Because $\mathrm{E}_1(\mathbf{Y}\mathbf{Y}^\top) = I_n + \mathbf{X}_1\beta_1\beta_1^\top\mathbf{X}_1^\top$, we get

$$\mathrm{E}_1(\hat{L}_1 - \hat{L}_2) = k_1 - k_2 + \beta_1^\top\mathbf{X}_1^\top M_2\mathbf{X}_1\beta_1.$$

Replacing the unknown parameters by estimates leads to the test statistic

$$\hat{\xi}_1^C = \frac{1}{2}(n\hat{\sigma}_2^2 - n\hat{\sigma}_1^2 - k_1 + k_2 - \hat{\beta}_1^\top\mathbf{X}_1^\top M_2\mathbf{X}_1\hat{\beta}_1).$$

When the scale parameters in the two models are unknown, the ratio of the maximized values of the sample log-likelihoods becomes $\hat{L}_1 - \hat{L}_2 = (n/2)\ln(\hat{\sigma}_2^2/\hat{\sigma}_1^2)$ and computing its expected value is more complicated. Pesaran (1974) showed that, in large samples, a test of H_1 may be based on the statistic

$$\tilde{\xi}_1^C = \frac{n}{2}\ln\frac{\hat{\sigma}_2^2}{\hat{\sigma}_{21}^2},$$

where $\hat{\sigma}_{21}^2 = \hat{\sigma}_1^2 + n^{-1}\hat{\beta}_1^\top\mathbf{X}_1^\top M_2\mathbf{X}_1\hat{\beta}_1$. It can be shown that $\tilde{\xi}_1^C \xrightarrow{\mathrm{d}} \mathcal{N}(0, V_1)$ under H_1, where

$$V_1 = \operatorname{plim}_1 \frac{\sigma_1^2}{\hat{\sigma}_{21}^4}(n^{-1}\beta_1^\top\mathbf{X}_1^\top M_2 M_1 M_2\mathbf{X}_1\beta_1)$$

and plim_1 denotes the limit in probability under H_1. See Pesaran (1974) and White (1982b) for a full set of regularity conditions. A consistent estimate of V_1 is

$$\hat{V}_1 = \frac{\hat{\sigma}_1^2}{\hat{\sigma}_{21}^4}(n^{-1}\beta_1^\top\mathbf{X}_1^\top M_2 M_1 M_2\mathbf{X}_1\beta_1).$$

Therefore, in large samples, $\tilde{\xi}_1^C/\hat{V}_1^{1/2}$ is approximately distributed as $\mathcal{N}(0,1)$ under H_1.

10.6.3 ENCOMPASSING

The idea behind the encompassing principle is both simple and powerful at once. If H_1 is true, then it ought to be able to explain the evidence obtained by regressing $\mathbf{Y}$ on $\mathbf{X}_2$. Failure to do so provides evidence against H_1.

To simplify the presentation, suppose that $\mathbf{X}_1 = \mathbf{X}_2\Pi + \mathbf{V}$, where Π is a $k_2 \times k_1$ matrix and $\operatorname{vec}\mathbf{V}$ has an nk_1-variate Gaussian distribution with mean zero and variance $I_n \otimes \Sigma$. If H_1 is true, then it must be the case that

$$\mathbf{Y} \sim \mathcal{N}_n(\mathbf{X}_2\beta_2, \sigma_2^2 I_n),$$

where β_2 and σ_2^2 are now functions of the parameters of H_1 and the model for $\mathbf{X}_1$, namely $\beta_2 = \Pi\beta_1$ and $\sigma_2^2 = \sigma_1^2 + \beta_1\Sigma\beta_1$. Thus, the truth of H_1 implies the following relationships

$$\beta_2 - \Pi\beta_1 = 0 \tag{10.7}$$

and

$$\sigma_2^2 - \sigma_1^2 + \beta_1\Sigma\beta_1 = 0. \tag{10.8}$$

We say that H_1 *regression encompasses* H_2 if (10.7) holds, *variance encompasses* H_2 if (10.8) holds, and *completely encompasses* H_2 if both (10.7) and (10.8) hold. Therefore, a test of H_1 regression encompassing H_2 may be based on the statistic

$$\hat{\Delta}_\beta = \hat{\beta}_2 - \hat{\Pi}\hat{\beta}_1 = (\mathbf{X}_2^\top \mathbf{X}_2)^{-1}\mathbf{X}_2^\top M_1 \mathbf{Y},$$

where $\hat{\Pi} = (\mathbf{X}_2^\top \mathbf{X}_2)^{-1}\mathbf{X}_2^\top \mathbf{X}_1$ is the coefficient matrix in the multivariate OLS regression of $\mathbf{X}_1$ on $\mathbf{X}_2$, while a test of H_1 variance encompassing H_2 may be based on the statistic

$$\hat{\Delta}_\sigma = \hat{\sigma}_2^2 - \hat{\sigma}_1^2 - \hat{\beta}_1 \hat{\Sigma} \hat{\beta}_1,$$

where

$$\hat{\Sigma} = n^{-1}(\mathbf{X}_1 - \mathbf{X}_2\hat{\Pi})^\top (\mathbf{X}_1 - \mathbf{X}_2\hat{\Pi}) = n^{-1}\mathbf{X}_1^\top M_2 \mathbf{X}_1.$$

Under the truth of H_1, $\hat{\Delta}_\beta \sim \mathcal{N}(0, V)$, where

$$V = \sigma_1^2(\mathbf{X}_2^\top \mathbf{X}_2)^{-1}\mathbf{X}_2^\top M_1 \mathbf{X}_2 (\mathbf{X}_2^\top \mathbf{X}_2)^{-1}.$$

A consistent estimate $\hat{V}$ of V_Δ is simply obtained by replacing σ_1^2 with $\hat{\sigma}_1^2$. The resulting test statistic

$$\xi_1^E = \hat{\Delta}_\beta^\top \hat{V}^{-1}\hat{\Delta}_\beta = \hat{\sigma}_1^{-2}\mathbf{Y}^\top M_1 \mathbf{X}_2 (\mathbf{X}_2^\top M_1 \mathbf{X}2)^{-1}\mathbf{X}_2^\top M_1 \mathbf{Y}$$

is easily seen to be asymptotically distributed as chi-square with k_2 degrees of freedom under H_1. On the other hand, multiplying ξ_1^E by $\hat{\sigma}_1^2/(k_2 s_*^2)$ gives exactly the F-test statistic ξ_1^F for testing $\beta_2^* = 0$ in the comprehensive model (10.6). Thus, the encompassing principle provides a strong justification for using the classical F-test.

10.7 THE INFORMATION MATRIX TEST

Recall from Section 10.2.3 that, if the regression model is conditionally heteroskedastic, then the matrix

$$\tilde{V}_n = \left(\frac{\mathbf{X}^\top \mathbf{X}}{n}\right)^{-1} \left(\frac{1}{n}\sum_{i=1}^n \hat{U}_i^2 X_i X_i^\top\right) \left(\frac{\mathbf{X}^\top \mathbf{X}}{n}\right)^{-1}$$

is consistent for the asymptotic variance of $\hat{\beta}$, while this is not true in general for the classical estimator $\hat{V}_n = \hat{\sigma}_n^2(n^{-1}\mathbf{X}^\top \mathbf{X})^{-1}$. Based on this observation, White (1980a) suggested testing for correct specification of the CVF by looking at the difference $\tilde{V}_n - \hat{V}_n$ or, equivalently, at the $m = k(k+1)/2$ distinct elements of the symmetric matrix of differences

$$\frac{1}{n}\sum_{i=1}^n \hat{U}_i^2 X_i X_i^\top - \hat{\sigma}_n^2 \frac{\mathbf{X}^\top \mathbf{X}}{n} = n^{-1}\sum_{i=1}^n (\hat{U}_i^2 - \hat{\sigma}_n^2) X_i X_i^\top. \tag{10.9}$$

Letting W_i be the m-vector containing the lower triangle of the matrix $X_i X_i^\top$, a test that rejects the assumption of correct specification for large values of the norm of the vector

$$\hat{\delta}_n = n^{-1}\sum_{i=1}^n (\hat{U}_i^2 - \hat{\sigma}_n^2) W_i$$

is called an *OLS variance matrix test.*

Suppose that $\{(X_i, Y_i)\}$ are i.i.d. random vectors and the regression errors are conditionally homoskedastic. Under appropriate regularity conditions, $\sqrt{n}\,\hat{\delta}_n \xrightarrow{\text{d}} \mathcal{N}_m(0, \Delta)$, where the $m \times m$ matrix

$$\Delta = \mathrm{E}(U_i^2 - \sigma^2)^2 (W_i - \mathrm{E}(W_i))(W_i - \mathrm{E}(W_i))^\top$$

may be estimated consistently by

$$\hat{\Delta}_n = n^{-1} \sum_{i=1}^{n} (\hat{U}_i^2 - \hat{\sigma}_n^2)^2 (W_i - \bar{W}_n)(W_i - \bar{W}_n)^\top,$$

with the vector $\bar{W}_n = n^{-1} \sum_{i=1}^{n} W_i$ containing the elements of the lower triangle of the matrix $n^{-1}\mathbf{X}^\top\mathbf{X}$. This fact is the key to the following result.

Theorem 10.19 *Let $U_i = Y_i - \beta^\top X_i$, $i = 1, \ldots, n$, and suppose:*

(i) *$\{(X_i, U_i)\}$ is a sequence of i.i.d. random vectors with finite fourth moments;*
(ii) *$\mathrm{Var}(U_i \,|\, X_i) = \sigma^2$ for every i;*
(iii) $n^{-1} \sum_i \mathrm{E}(U_i^2 - \sigma^2)^2 > 0$.

Then $\xi_n = n\,\hat{\delta}_n^\top \hat{\Delta}_n^{-1} \hat{\delta}_n \xrightarrow{\text{d}} \chi_m^2$, where $m = k(k+1)/2$.

Proof. See White (1980a). □

The above theorem may be used to construct a test of the joint hypothesis that the first two moments of the conditional distribution of Y_i given X_i are correctly specified. This is a pure specification test because it only indicates that something is wrong with the fitted model, but not what. The test has power under a variety of sources of misspecification of the regression function (functional form misspecification, omitted variables, etc.). It is only when the specification of the regression function is not an issue that the test may be used as a test for heteroskedasticity of unknown form.

The test detects model misspecification only when the latter implies a difference with respect to the classical estimates of the OLS precision. Thus, there may be forms of misspecification under which the test has no power.

Example 10.13 Suppose that the regression errors are heteroskedastic but independent of the covariates in X_i. Further assume that the covariates are i.i.d. with $\mathrm{E}\, X_i X_i^\top = P$, a p.d. matrix, and put $\bar{\sigma}_n^2 = n^{-1} \sum_{i=1}^{n} \sigma_i^2$. In this case

$$n^{-1} \sum_{i=1}^{n} (\hat{U}_i^2 - \hat{\sigma}_n^2) X_i X_i^\top - n^{-1} \sum_{i=1}^{n} (\sigma_i^2 - \bar{\sigma}_n^2) P \xrightarrow{\text{p}} 0,$$

where

$$n^{-1} \sum_{i=1}^{n} (\sigma_i^2 - \bar{\sigma}_n^2) P = \frac{1}{n} (\bar{\sigma}_n^2 - \bar{\sigma}_n^2) P = 0$$

even when $\sigma_i^2 \neq \sigma_j^2$. Thus, the fact that the test does not reject the null hypothesis does not imply that heteroskedasticity is absent. □

White (1980a) also shows that, if the regression errors are homokurtic, that is, $\mathrm{E}\, U_i^4 = \mu_4$ for all i, then a test based on ξ_n is asymptotically equivalent under the null hypothesis of homoskedasticity to a test based on $n\hat{R}^2$, where $\hat{R}^2$ is the uncentered R^2 in the artificial regression

$$\hat{U}_i^2 = \alpha_0 + \sum_{r=1}^{k} \sum_{s \leq r} \alpha_s X_{ir} X_{is} + \epsilon_i, \qquad i = 1, \ldots, n.$$

This test is essentially an F-test of the joint hypothesis that $\alpha_1 = \cdots = \alpha_m$. Given the results in Section 8.1, the test is intuitively appealing because it looks for a systematic association between the squared OLS residuals and the regressors, their squares and their cross-products. If the assumption of homokurtosis fails, the size of a test based on $n\hat{R}^2$ is incorrect, but the test remains consistent.

The results in this section are easily generalized to testing the specification of a regular parametric model with log-likelihood $L(\theta)$ and likelihood score $s(z;\theta)$, where θ is a p-dimensional parameter. Recall from Theorem 1.2 that, if the model is correctly specified, then the information equality $\mathrm{Var}_\theta\, s(Z;\theta) = -\,\mathrm{E}_\theta\, s'(Z;\theta)$ holds. This equality no longer holds if the model is misspecified. If $\hat{\theta}$ denotes a ML estimator and $s_i(\hat{\theta}) = s(Z_i;\hat{\theta})$, then it is easy to verify that the analogue of the difference (10.9) is the difference

$$\tilde{\mathcal{I}} - \hat{\mathcal{I}} = n^{-1}[\sum_i s_i(\hat{\theta}) s_i(\hat{\theta})^\top + L''(\hat{\theta})] = n^{-1} \sum_i [s_i(\hat{\theta}) s_i(\hat{\theta})^\top + s_i'(\hat{\theta})] \tag{10.10}$$

between alternative estimates of the Fisher information. A test that rejects the hypothesis of correct specification when the difference (10.10) is large is called an *information matrix test.*

Lancaster (1984) showed that the test statistic of an information matrix test is easily computed as n times the uncentered R^2 in a regression of an n-vector of ones on S and D, where S is an $n \times p$ matrix with generic element $(\partial/\partial\theta_j) \ln f(Z_i;\theta)$ and D is an $n \times p(p+1)/2$ matrix with generic element

$$\frac{1}{f(Z_i;\hat{\theta})} \frac{\partial^2 f(Z_i;\hat{\theta})}{\partial\theta_j \partial\theta_h}, \qquad h \leq j = 1, \ldots, p.$$

White (1982a) showed that asymptotically valid critical values for such statistic may be based on the $\mathcal{N}(0,1)$ distribution.

BIBLIOGRAPHIC NOTES

For a more extensive treatment of the material presented in the first two sections of this chapter see White (1984).

For further references on the error-in-variables model see Fuller (1987) and Leamer (1987).

On the distribution of t- and F-test statistics for nonstationary autoregressive time series see Dickey and Fuller (1979, 1981).

For a survey of applications of likelihood-based tests (likelihood ratio, Wald and score) in econometrics see Engle (1984). Godfrey (1981) discusses the lack of sensitivity of score tests to the choice of alternatives, whereas Godfrey (1989) presents a systematic treatment of diagnostic tests based on the score principle.

The score test for heteroskedasticity in Section 10.10 is based on Breusch and Pagan (1979). For a related test see Cook and Weisberg (1983). The score test for normality in Section 10.11 is based on Jarque and Bera (1980). An alternative, based on Gram-Charlier expansions, has been proposed by Kiefer and Salmon (1983). Other tests for normality are discussed in White and MacDonald (1980), where some Monte Carlo evidence is also presented. A good survey of the literature on testing for univariate and multivariate normality is Mardia (1980).

All score tests discussed in Section 10.5.3 may be viewed as tests of the hypothesis H_0: $\lambda = 0$, where λ is a vector of parameters added through augmenting the maintained parametric model. Chesher and Smith (1997) argue in favor of adopting the LR principle to test the same hypothesis. The main advantage is the possibility of applying standard corrections to the test statistics in order to bring their sampling distribution closer to the asymptotic chi-square distribution.

On the invariance properties of asymptotic testing procedures for nonlinear models see Dagenais and Dufour (1991). The lack of invariance of Wald tests makes them unreliable in nonlinear models or when constraints are nonlinear. A related problem with Wald tests in nonlinear models is possible non-monotonicity of the exact power function (Nelson & Savin 1990), in contrast to monotonicity of their asymptotic local power function. This may yield incorrect inferences when power is extrapolated from the asymptotic power function.

Tests of linear and nonlinear inequality constraints are discussed in Wolak (1987, 1991).

On non-nested testing see the surveys by MacKinnon (1983) and Gourieroux and Monfort (1994). The artificial nesting approach is due to Atkinson (1970). For a generalization of the Cox test to multivariate nonlinear regression models see Pesaran and Deaton (1978). On the encompassing principle see Mizon and Richard (1986).

The information matrix test was proposed by White (1982a). See Chesher (1984) for an interpretation of this test as a score test for neglected heterogeneity. See Horowitz (1994) for the construction of critical values via the parametric bootstrap.

PROBLEMS

10.1 Compute the sampling variance of the OLS estimator of β_1 and β_2 in the model of Example 10.4.

10.2 Consider a classical linear model for the random n-vector $\mathbf{Y}$. Show that, if the elements of the jth column of the design matrix $\mathbf{X}$ are of the form $X_{ij} = \lambda^i$, where $|\lambda| < 1$, then the OLS estimator $\hat{\beta}_n$ is inconsistent for β although, for $h \neq j$, the hth element of $\hat{\beta}$ is consistent for the hth element of β.

10.3 Given a Gaussian AR(p) process, show that the conditional LS estimator is asympotically equivalent to the Yule–Walker estimator, and both are consistent for the model parameters.

10.4 Consider the model

$$Y_t = \beta_1 Y_{t-1} + \cdots + \beta_p Y_{t-p} + \gamma_1 X_{t-1} + \cdots + \gamma_q X_{t-q} + U_t,$$

where $\{U_t\}$ is a stationary invertible ARMA process. Show that the OLS estimator $\hat{\alpha}_n = (\hat{\beta}_n, \hat{\gamma}_n)$ in a regression of Y_t on $Y_{t-1}, \dots, Y_{t-p}, X_{t-1}, \dots, X_{t-q}$ is consistent for $\alpha = (\beta, \gamma)$ only if $\{U_t\}$ is a white noise.

10.5 Given the linear model $Y_i = \beta X_i + U_i$, $i = 1, \dots, n$, where $\{X_1\}$ is a sequence of constants and $\{U_i\}$ is a sequence of uncorrelated random variables with mean zero and variance $\operatorname{Var} U_i = \sigma^2 X_i^2$, consider the following estimators of β

$$\hat{\beta}_n = \frac{\sum_i X_i Y_i}{\sum_i X_i^2}, \qquad \tilde{\beta}_n = \frac{1}{n} \sum_i \frac{Y_i}{X_i}.$$

(i) What is a justification for the estimator $\tilde{\beta}_n$?
(ii) Show that both estimators are unbiased for β.
(iii) Assume that $\lim(n^{-1} \sum_i X_i^2) = m^2$ and $\lim(n^{-1} \sum_i X_i^4) = 3m^4$, where $m > 0$, and study the asymptotic efficiency of $\hat{\beta}_n$ relative to $\tilde{\beta}_n$.

10.6 Consider the heteroskedastic linear model $E(\mathbf{Y}) = \beta \iota_n$ and $\operatorname{Var} \mathbf{Y} = \sigma^2 \Omega_n$, where $\Omega_n^{-1} = G_n(\psi) = \operatorname{diag}[\psi^{i-1}, i = 1, \dots, n]$. Let $\tilde{\beta}_n$ be the GLS estimator and let $\bar{\beta}_n$ be the feasible GLS estimator based on the estimate $\hat{\Omega}_n^{-1} = G_n(\hat{\psi}_n)$, with $\hat{\psi}_n = 1 + n^{-1}$.

(i) Show that, if $\psi = 1$, then $\hat{\psi}_n^i \xrightarrow{\text{p}} \psi^i$ for every i.
(ii) Show that, if $\psi = 1$, then $\sqrt{n}\,(\hat{\beta}_n - \beta) \xrightarrow{\text{d}} \mathcal{N}(0, \sigma^2)$ while

$$\sqrt{n}\,(\bar{\beta}_n - \beta) \xrightarrow{\text{d}} \mathcal{N}\left(0,\ \sigma^2 \frac{e^2 - 1}{2(e-1)^2}\right).$$

(iii) Discuss this result.

10.7 Prove Theorem 10.12.

10.8 (Berndt & Savin 1977) Given the classical Gaussian linear model $\mathbf{Y} \sim \mathcal{N}_n(\mathbf{X}\beta, \sigma^2 I_n)$ and the hypothesis H$_0$: $R\beta = r$, show that the following inequalities hold

$$\xi^S \leq \xi^R \leq \xi^W,$$

where ξ^S, ξ^R and ξ^W are the score, likelihood ratio and Wald test statistics respectively (*Hint*: Put $Q(\beta) = n^{-1}(\mathbf{Y} - \mathbf{X}\beta)^\top (\mathbf{Y} - \mathbf{Y}\beta)$ and show that $n \ln[Q(\beta)/\sigma^2] \leq n[Q(\beta) - \sigma^2]/\sigma^2$ for every (β, σ^2)).

10.9 (Breusch 1979) Consider the Gaussian linear model $\mathbf{Y} \sim \mathcal{N}_n(\mathbf{X}\beta, \Sigma(\gamma))$, where $\Sigma(\cdot)$ is a known function, and β and γ are unknown vectors of dimension k and p respectively. Let $\hat{\beta}_n$ and $\hat{\gamma}_n$ be the ML estimates of β and γ respectively, and assume that

$$\sqrt{n} \left[\begin{pmatrix} \hat{\beta}_n \\ \hat{\gamma}_n \end{pmatrix} - \begin{pmatrix} \beta \\ \gamma \end{pmatrix} \right] \xrightarrow{\text{d}} \mathcal{N}_{k+p}\left(\begin{pmatrix} 0 \\ 0 \end{pmatrix}, \begin{bmatrix} \operatorname{AV}(\hat{\beta}_n) & 0 \\ 0 & \operatorname{AV}(\hat{\gamma}_n) \end{bmatrix} \right).$$

Let ξ_n^W, ξ_n^R and ξ_n^S denote, respectively, the Wald, likelihood ratio and score test statistics for testing the assumption H$_0$: $R\beta = r$, where R is a $q \times k$ matrix of rank q. Show that the following inequalities hold

$$\xi_n^S \leq \xi_n^R \leq \xi_n^W.$$

10.10 (Gregory & Veall 1985) Consider the linear model

$$\mathrm{E}(Y_i \mid X_i) = \beta_0 + \beta_1 X_{1i} + \beta_2 X_{2i}, \qquad i = 1, \ldots, n,$$

where $\mathrm{Var}(Y_i \mid X_i) = \sigma^2$ for every i.

(i) Derive the Wald test statistic of the hypothesis H_0^a: $\beta_1 = 1/\beta_2$.
(ii) Derive the Wald test statistic of the hypothesis H_0^b: $\beta_1 \beta_2 = 1$.
(iii) Compare the small and large sample properties of tests based on the two statistics.

10.11 (Nelson & Savin 1990) Let $Z_1, \ldots, Z_n$ be a random sample from a Gaussian distribution with mean e^θ and unit variance. Compute the exact power function of a Wald test of the hypothesis H_0: $\theta = \theta_0$ and compare it with the asymptotic local power function.

10.12 Prove Theorem 10.17.

10.13 Derive the score test statistic for testing the hypothesis of Gaussian errors in a classical linear model against the alternative that they have a generalized t-distribution with density

$$f(u) = \frac{p}{2q^{1/p}} \frac{\Gamma((q+1)/p)}{\Gamma(1/p)\,\Gamma(q/p)} \left(1 + \frac{|u|^p}{q}\right)^{-\frac{q+1}{p}},$$

where p and q are known integers and $\Gamma(p) = \int_0^\infty u^{p-1} e^{-u}\, du$ is the gamma function. Does the test satisfy the regularity conditions of Theorem 5.3?

10.14 Consider the model

$$Y_i = \beta_1 X_{i1} + \beta_2 (X_{i2} - \gamma)^{-1} + U_i, \qquad i = 1, \ldots, n,$$

where $U_1, \ldots, U_n$ are i.i.d. $\mathcal{N}(0, \sigma^2)$. Derive the score test statistic of H_0: $\gamma = 0$.

10.15 Derive the score test statistic for testing the absence of autocorrelation in a Gaussian linear model with MA(1) errors.

10.16 Derive the score test statistic for testing the absence of autocorrelation in a Gaussian linear model with MA(q) errors.

10.17 Suppose that the conditional distribution of Y given X is $\mathcal{N}(\beta^\top X, \sigma^2)$. Derive the exact sampling distribution of the likelihood ratio and score test statistics of the hypothesis H_0: $\sigma^2 = \sigma_0^2$. Compare your results with a χ_1^2-distribution.

10.18 Consider the J-test for testing the hypothesis H_1: $\mathbf{Y} \sim \mathcal{N}_n(\mathbf{X}_1\beta_1, \sigma_1^2 I_n)$ against the non-nested alternative H_2: $\mathbf{Y} \sim \mathcal{N}_n(\mathbf{X}_1\beta_1, \sigma_1^2 I_n)$. Show that when $\mathbf{X}_1$ and $\mathbf{X}_2$ are orthogonal, the J-test statistic is equal to the square root of the F-test statistic for testing H_1 against the alternative of a composite model that includes all the covariates in either H_1 or H_2.

10.19 Show that, for the classical Gaussian linear model, a test based on the difference (10.10) leads to a test based on the difference (10.9).

10.20 Given a parametric model $f(z; \theta)$ show that

$$\frac{1}{f} \frac{\partial^2 f}{\partial\theta \partial\theta^\top} = \frac{\partial^2 \ln f}{\partial\theta \partial\theta^\top} + \frac{\partial \ln f}{\partial\theta} \frac{\partial \ln f}{\partial\theta^\top}.$$

11

The Instrumental Variables Method

An OLS regression of $\mathbf{Y}$ on $\mathbf{X}$ gives a consistent estimator of the target parameter β only when $n^{-1}\mathbf{X}^\top(\mathbf{Y} - \mathbf{X}\beta) \xrightarrow{\text{P}} 0$ as $n \to \infty$. There are important cases where this condition is violated. Examples discussed in Chapter 10 include the errors-in-variables model, where some regressors are measured with errors, the dynamic regression model with autocorrelated errors, and the simultaneous equations model, where $\mathbf{X}$ contains variables that are jointly determined with $\mathbf{Y}$.

This chapter shows that, even when the OLS estimator is inconsistent, β may still be estimated consistently under certain conditions.

11.1 INSTRUMENTAL VARIABLES ESTIMATION

A key role in what follows is played by the existence of a random $n \times r$ data matrix $\mathbf{W}$, with r fixed and $n > r$, that satisfies the following properties.

Assumption 11.1 $n^{-1}\mathbf{W}^\top(\mathbf{Y} - \mathbf{X}\beta) \xrightarrow{\text{P}} 0$ *for some* $\beta \in \Re^k$.

Assumption 11.2 $n^{-1}\mathbf{W}^\top\mathbf{X} \xrightarrow{\text{P}} P$, *where* P *is a finite* $r \times k$ *matrix of rank* k.

Assumption 11.1 requires the columns of $\mathbf{W}$ and the error vector $\mathbf{U} = \mathbf{Y} - \mathbf{X}\beta$ to be uncorrelated, at least asymptotically. This assumption implicitly defines the parameter of interest through a system of r linear equations in the k-dimensional vector β

$$\operatorname{plim}\left(\frac{\mathbf{W}^\top\mathbf{Y}}{n} - \frac{\mathbf{W}^\top\mathbf{X}}{n}\beta\right) = 0. \tag{11.1}$$

Assumption 11.2 instead requires the columns of $\mathbf{W}$ and $\mathbf{X}$ to be asymptotically correlated. A matrix $\mathbf{W}$ that satisfies Assumptions 11.1 and 11.2 is called an *instrument matrix* for β, and the variables corresponding to its columns are called *instrumental variables* or simply *instruments*. Typically, it is the nature of the underlying model that suggests which variables should be included in $\mathbf{W}$ as instruments.

Example 11.1 Consider the linear regression representation of an ARMA(1,1) model, namely

$$Y_t = \phi X_t + U_t, \qquad \{U_t\} \sim \text{MA}(1),$$

where $Y_t = Z_t$, $X_t = Z_{t-1}$, $U_t = V_t - \theta V_{t-1}$, $\{V_t\}$ is a white noise and $\phi \neq \theta$. Notice that

$$\mathrm{E}\, Z_{t-2}(Y_t - \phi X_t) = \mathrm{E}\, Z_{t-2}(V_t - V_{t-1}) = 0,$$

whereas

$$\mathrm{E}\, Z_{t-2} X_t = \mathrm{E}\, Z_{t-2} Z_{t-1} = \frac{\sigma^2(1-\phi\theta)(\phi-\theta)}{1-\phi^2} \neq 0.$$

Because Assumptions 11.1 and 11.2 are both satisfied for $W_t = Z_{t-2}$, this is a valid instrument for the autoregressive parameter ϕ. In fact,

$$\phi = \frac{\mathrm{E}\, W_t Y_t}{\mathrm{E}\, W_t X_t} = \frac{\mathrm{E}\, Z_{t-2} Z_t}{\mathrm{E}\, Z_{t-2} Z_{t-1}}.$$

It is easy to verify that Z_{t-2} is not the only instrument, however, as other valid choices are $W_t = (Z_{t-2}, Z_{t-3})$ and, more generally, $W_t = (Z_{t-2}, \ldots, Z_{t-r-1})$ for $r > 1$. □

We distinguish between two cases, depending on the number of available instruments. The first, known as the *exactly identified case*, is when $r = k$, that is, the number of instruments is just equal to the number of parameters in β. The second, known as the *overidentified case*, is when $r > k$, that is, there are more instruments than parameters to be estimated.

11.1.1 THE SIMPLE IV ESTIMATOR

If $r = k$ and Assumption 11.2 holds, solving (11.1) for β gives an explicit definition of the target parameter

$$\beta = \left(\operatorname{plim} \frac{\mathbf{W}^\top \mathbf{X}}{n}\right)^{-1} \operatorname{plim} \frac{\mathbf{W}^\top \mathbf{Y}}{n}.$$

When $\mathbf{W}^\top \mathbf{X}$ is a nonsingular matrix, the method of moments suggests estimating β by its sample counterpart

$$\hat\beta = (\mathbf{W}^\top \mathbf{X})^{-1} \mathbf{W}^\top \mathbf{Y},$$

called a *simple instrumental variables estimator.* Notice that $\hat\beta$, being a linear transformation of $\mathbf{Y}$, is a linear estimator. In particular, $\hat\beta$ coincides with the OLS estimator when $\mathbf{W} = \mathbf{X}$.

Example 11.2 Consider the linear model

$$Y_i = \beta X_i^* + U_i, \qquad i = 1, \ldots, n,$$

where $\mathrm{E}(U_i \,|\, X_i^*) = 0$, and assume that only an error-ridden measurement of X_i^* is available, namely $X_i = X_i^* + V_i$, where V_i is a zero-mean random error distributed independently of X_i^*. Partition the data into two groups $\mathcal{A}_1$ and $\mathcal{A}_2$, of size n_1 and n_2 respectively, and let $\bar Y_j$ and $\bar X_j$ denote the sample averages of Y_i and X_i for group $\mathcal{A}_j$, $j = 1, 2$. The estimate

$$\hat\beta = \frac{\bar Y_1 - \bar Y_2}{\bar X_1 - \bar X_2} = \frac{\sum_i W_i Y_i}{\sum_i W_i X_i}$$

is a simple instrumental variables estimate with instrument vector $\mathbf{W} = (W_1, \ldots, W_n)$, where

$$W_i = \begin{cases} n/n_1, & \text{if } i \in \mathcal{A}_1, \\ -n/n_2, & \text{if } i \in \mathcal{A}_2. \end{cases}$$

The vector $\mathbf{W}$ is a valid instrument if

$$0 = \operatorname{plim} \frac{1}{n} \mathbf{W}^\top (\mathbf{Y} - \beta \mathbf{X}) = \operatorname{plim}(\bar{Y}_1 - \bar{Y}_2) - \beta \operatorname{plim}(\bar{X}_1 - \bar{X}_2)$$

and

$$0 \neq \operatorname{plim} \frac{1}{n} \mathbf{W}^\top \mathbf{X} = \operatorname{plim} \bar{X}_1 - \operatorname{plim} \bar{X}_2.$$

To interpret these two conditions notice that, if X_i^* has finite mean then, under random sampling,

$$\begin{aligned} \bar{Y}_j &\xrightarrow{\text{p}} \mathrm{E}(Y_i \,|\, \mathcal{A}_j) = \beta\, \mathrm{E}(X_i^* \,|\, \mathcal{A}_j) + \mathrm{E}(U_i \,|\, \mathcal{A}_j), \\ \bar{X}_j &\xrightarrow{\text{p}} \mathrm{E}(X_i \,|\, \mathcal{A}_j) = \mathrm{E}(X_i^* \,|\, \mathcal{A}_j) + \mathrm{E}(V_i \,|\, \mathcal{A}_j), \qquad j = 1, 2. \end{aligned}$$

Hence

$$n^{-1} \mathbf{W}^\top (\mathbf{Y} - \beta \mathbf{X}) \xrightarrow{\text{p}} \mathrm{E}(U_i \,|\, \mathcal{A}_1) - \mathrm{E}(U_i \,|\, \mathcal{A}_2) - \beta [\mathrm{E}(V_i \,|\, \mathcal{A}_1) - \mathrm{E}(V_i \,|\, \mathcal{A}_2)]$$

and

$$n^{-1} \mathbf{W}^\top \mathbf{X} \xrightarrow{\text{p}} \mathrm{E}(X_i^* \,|\, \mathcal{A}_1) - \mathrm{E}(X_i^* \,|\, \mathcal{A}_2) + \mathrm{E}(V_i \,|\, \mathcal{A}_1) - \mathrm{E}(V_i \,|\, \mathcal{A}_2).$$

Thus, $\hat{\beta}$ is consistent for β provided that: (i) grouping of the data is independent of U_i and V_i; (ii) $\mathrm{E}(X_i^* \,|\, \mathcal{A}_1) \neq \mathrm{E}(X_i^* \,|\, \mathcal{A}_2)$, that is, grouping is not based on the observed values of Y_i or X_i but on some other variable known to be correlated with X_i^*. □

11.1.2 THE CLASS OF IV ESTIMATORS

When $r > k$, both the equation system (11.1) and its sample counterpart are overdetermined. Therefore, the method of moments cannot be applied directly. Two alternatives are possible.

One is to discard $r - k$ instruments and then compute the simple IV estimate based on the remaining k instruments. It is not clear, however, which instruments to discard and, in any case, discarding relevant information generally leads to inefficient estimates.

The other, directly motivated by (11.1), is to choose as an estimator of β a point $\hat{\beta} \in \Re^k$ such that the distance between the vectors $\mathbf{W}^\top \mathbf{Y}$ and $\mathbf{W}^\top \mathbf{X} \hat{\beta}$ is the smallest possible or, equivalently, the norm of the vector $\mathbf{W}^\top (\mathbf{Y} - \mathbf{X} \hat{\beta})$ is as close to zero as possible.

Following the second approach, consider minimizing with respect to β the quadratic form

$$Q(\beta, A) = (\mathbf{Y} - \mathbf{X}\beta)^\top \mathbf{W} A \mathbf{W}^\top (\mathbf{Y} - \mathbf{X}\beta), \tag{11.2}$$

where A is a symmetric, p.d., possibly data-dependent $r \times r$ matrix. This quadratic form is just n^{-1} times the squared norm of the vector $\mathbf{W}^\top (\mathbf{Y} - \beta \mathbf{X})$ in the metric of the weight matrix A. Because the function Q is quadratic in β and $\mathbf{X}^\top\mathbf{W}A\mathbf{W}^\top\mathbf{X}$ is a n.n.d. matrix, a global minimum exists and necessarily satisfies the equation system

$$0 = \mathbf{X}^\top\mathbf{W}A\mathbf{W}^\top(\mathbf{Y} - \mathbf{X}\beta).$$

If $\mathbf{X}^\top\mathbf{W}A\mathbf{W}^\top\mathbf{X}$ is a nonsingular matrix, the above system has the unique solution

$$\hat{\beta}_A = (\mathbf{X}^\top\mathbf{W}A\mathbf{W}^\top\mathbf{X})^{-1}\mathbf{X}^\top\mathbf{W}A\mathbf{W}^\top\mathbf{Y}. \tag{11.3}$$

An estimator satisfying (11.3) for some choice of A is called an *instrumental variables (IV) estimator*. Notice that (11.3) defines a whole class of linear estimators, indexed by the choice of the weight matrix A. In order to simplify the notation, the dependence on the choice of weight matrix A is from now on omitted.

An estimator of the form (11.3) may be interpreted as a simple IV estimator based on the $n \times k$ instrument matrix $\mathbf{W}^* = \mathbf{W}A\mathbf{W}^\top\mathbf{X}$, whose columns are linear combinations of the r columns of $\mathbf{W}$. When $r = k$, we get

$$\hat{\beta} = (\mathbf{W}^\top\mathbf{X})^{-1}A^{-1}(\mathbf{X}^\top\mathbf{W})^{-1}\mathbf{X}^\top\mathbf{W}A\mathbf{W}^\top\mathbf{Y} = (\mathbf{W}^\top\mathbf{X})^{-1}\mathbf{W}^\top\mathbf{Y},$$

which does not depend on the choice of weight matrix and coincides with the simple IV estimator. It is easy to verify that in this case

$$Q(\hat{\beta}, A) = (\mathbf{Y} - \mathbf{X}\hat{\beta})^\top\mathbf{W}A\mathbf{W}^\top(\mathbf{Y} - \mathbf{X}\hat{\beta}) = 0$$

for every weight matrix A.

11.2 ASYMPTOTIC PROPERTIES OF IV ESTIMATORS

Exact results about the sampling distribution of an IV estimator are generally difficult to derive. In fact, it follows from (11.3) that

$$\hat{\beta} - \beta = (\mathbf{X}^\top\mathbf{W}A\mathbf{W}^\top\mathbf{X})^{-1}\mathbf{X}^\top\mathbf{W}A\mathbf{W}^\top\mathbf{U},$$

where $\mathbf{U} = \mathbf{Y} - \mathbf{X}\beta$. This shows that, unless $\mathrm{E}(\mathbf{U} \mid \mathbf{X}, \mathbf{W}) = 0$, the sampling distribution of $\hat{\beta}$ is a complicated function of the joint distribution of $\mathbf{X}$, $\mathbf{W}$ and $\mathbf{U}$.

This section provides simple approximations based on the asymptotic properties of a sequence $\{\hat{\beta}_n\}$ of IV estimators corresponding to increasing sample sizes. Because an IV estimator is a linear estimator, the presentation follows closely that of Chapter 10. Most of the proofs are similar and are therefore left to the reader as an exercise. In addition to Assumptions 11.1 and 11.2, our basic set of assumptions includes the following.

Assumption 11.3 $A_n \xrightarrow{\text{p}} A$, *where A is a finite, symmetric, p.d. $r \times r$ matrix.*

Assumption 11.4 $n^{-1/2}\mathbf{W}^\top(\mathbf{Y} - \mathbf{X}\beta) \xrightarrow{\text{d}} \mathcal{N}_r(0, D)$, *where D is a finite p.d. $r \times r$ matrix.*

11.2.1 CONSISTENCY

The first theorem gives sufficient conditions under which $\hat{\beta}_n$ is consistent for β. As usual, we limit ourselves to convergence in probability, although the arguments in this section are easily adapted to establish almost sure convergence.

Theorem 11.1 *If Assumptions 11.1–11.3 hold, then $\hat{\beta}_n$ exists with probability approaching one and $\hat{\beta}_n \xrightarrow{\text{p}} \beta$.*

Proof. The proof follows immediately from the expansion

$$\hat{\beta}_n = \beta + \left(\frac{\mathbf{X}^\top \mathbf{W}}{n} A_n \frac{\mathbf{W}^\top \mathbf{X}}{n} \right)^{-1} \frac{\mathbf{X}^\top \mathbf{W}}{n} A_n \frac{\mathbf{W}^\top \mathbf{U}}{n}.$$

□

A simple set of primitive assumptions is the following.

Theorem 11.2 *Let $U_i = Y_i - \beta^\top X_i$, $i = 1, \ldots, n$, and suppose:*

(i) *$\{(X_i, W_i, U_i)\}$ is a sequence of i.i.d. random vectors;*
(ii) *$\mathrm{E}\, W_i U_i = 0$;*
(iii) *$\mathrm{E}\, W_i X_i^\top = P$, a finite $r \times k$ matrix of rank k;*
(iv) *$A_n \xrightarrow{\text{p}} A$, where A is a finite, symmetric, p.d. $r \times r$ matrix.*

Then $\hat{\beta}_n$ exists with probability approaching and $\hat{\beta}_n \xrightarrow{\text{p}} \beta$.

11.2.2 ASYMPTOTIC NORMALITY

We now give sufficient conditions for asymptotic normality of a sequence $\{\hat{\beta}_n\}$ of IV estimators.

Theorem 11.3 *If Assumptions 11.1–11.4 hold, then $\sqrt{n}\,(\hat{\beta}_n - \beta) \xrightarrow{\text{d}} \mathcal{N}_k(0, \mathrm{AV}(\hat{\beta}_n))$, where $\mathrm{AV}(\hat{\beta}_n) = (P^\top A P)^{-1} P^\top A D A P (P^\top A P)^{-1}$. If, in addition, there exists a symmetric matrix $\hat{D}_n$ such that $\hat{D}_n \xrightarrow{\text{p}} D$, then*

$$\left(\frac{\mathbf{X}^\top \mathbf{W}}{n} A_n \frac{\mathbf{W}^\top \mathbf{X}}{n} \right)^{-1} \frac{\mathbf{X}^\top \mathbf{W}}{n} A_n \hat{D}_n A_n \frac{\mathbf{W}^\top \mathbf{X}}{n} \left(\frac{\mathbf{X}^\top \mathbf{W}}{n} A_n \frac{\mathbf{W}^\top \mathbf{X}}{n} \right)^{-1}$$

is consistent for $\mathrm{AV}(\hat{\beta}_n)$.

When $r = k$, the asymptotic variance of $\hat{\beta}_n$ becomes

$$\mathrm{AV}(\hat{\beta}_n) = P^{-1} D P^{-\top}.$$

A simple set of primitive assumptions for the first part of Theorem 11.3 is given by the following result.

Theorem 11.4 *Let $U_i = Y_i - \beta^\top X_i$, $i = 1, \ldots, n$. In addition to the assumptions of Theorem 11.2, suppose that $\mathrm{Var}\, W_i U_i = D$, a finite symmetric p.d. $r \times r$ matrix. Then $\sqrt{n}\,(\hat{\beta}_n - \beta) \xrightarrow{\text{d}} \mathcal{N}_k(0, \mathrm{AV}(\hat{\beta}_n))$, where $\mathrm{AV}(\hat{\beta}_n) = (P^\top A P)^{-1} P^\top A D A P (P^\top A P)^{-1}$.*

Generalizations of Theorems 11.3 and 11.4 to cases when the observations are not identically distributed or not independent may be found in White (1984).

11.2.3 ASYMPTOTIC EFFICIENCY

Now consider the problem of choosing an IV estimator that is *asymptotically efficient*, that is, has smallest asymptotic variance in its class.

Theorem 11.5 *Given symmetric p.d. matrices A_n and B_n, let*

$$\hat{\beta}_n = (\mathbf{X}^\top \mathbf{W} A_n \mathbf{W}^\top \mathbf{X})^{-1} \mathbf{X}^\top \mathbf{W} A_n \mathbf{W}^\top \mathbf{Y}$$

and

$$\tilde{\beta}_n = (\mathbf{X}^\top \mathbf{W} B_n \mathbf{W}^\top \mathbf{X})^{-1} \mathbf{X}^\top \mathbf{W} B_n \mathbf{W}^\top \mathbf{Y}.$$

If Assumptions 11.1–11.4 hold and $B_n \xrightarrow{p} D^{-1}$, then:

(i) $\mathrm{AV}(\tilde{\beta}_n) = (P^\top D^{-1} P)^{-1}$;
(ii) $\mathrm{AV}(\hat{\beta}_n) - \mathrm{AV}(\tilde{\beta}_n) \geq 0$, *with equality only if $A_n \xrightarrow{p} D^{-1}$.*

Proof. Since $B_n \xrightarrow{p} D^{-1}$, we get

$$\mathrm{AV}(\tilde{\beta}_n) = (P^\top D^{-1} P)^{-1} P^\top D^{-1} D D^{-1} P (P^\top D^{-1} P)^{-1} = (P^\top D^{-1} P)^{-1}.$$

If R is a nonsingular matrix such that $R^\top R = D^{-1}$, then

$$(P^\top AP)^{-1} P^\top ADAP (P^\top AP)^{-1} - (P^\top D^{-1} P)^{-1}$$

$$= (P^\top AP)^{-1} P^\top AR^{-1} [I_r - RP(P^\top R^\top RP)^{-1} P^\top R^\top] (R^\top)^{-1} AP (P^\top AP)^{-1}.$$

Part (ii) then follows from the fact that the matrix $I_r - RP(P^\top R^\top RP)^{-1} P^\top R^\top$ is idempotent and therefore n.n.d. □

Thus, an estimator $\tilde{\beta}_n$ in the class (11.3) is asymptotically efficient if it is based on a weight matrix B_n that converges to D^{-1} in probability. The asymptotic variance of $\tilde{\beta}_n$ may be estimated consistently by

$$\widehat{\mathrm{AV}}(\tilde{\beta}_n) = \left(\frac{\mathbf{X}^\top \mathbf{W}}{n} B_n \frac{\mathbf{W}^\top \mathbf{X}}{n} \right)^{-1}.$$

Example 11.3 Suppose that $D = \sigma^2 C$, where $C = \mathrm{plim}(n^{-1} \mathbf{W}^\top \mathbf{W})$ is a finite p.d. matrix. Since $\hat{C}_n = n^{-1} \mathbf{W}^\top \mathbf{W} \xrightarrow{p} \sigma^{-2} D$, an asymptotically efficient estimator in the class (11.3) is

$$\tilde{\beta}_n = \left[\mathbf{X}^\top \mathbf{W} \left(\frac{\mathbf{W}^\top \mathbf{W}}{n} \right)^{-1} \mathbf{W}^\top \mathbf{X} \right]^{-1} \mathbf{X}^\top \mathbf{W} \left(\frac{\mathbf{W}^\top \mathbf{W}}{n} \right)^{-1} \mathbf{W}^\top \mathbf{Y}$$
$$= [\mathbf{X}^\top \mathbf{W} (\mathbf{W}^\top \mathbf{W})^{-1} \mathbf{W}^\top \mathbf{X}]^{-1} \mathbf{X}^\top \mathbf{W} (\mathbf{W}^\top \mathbf{W})^{-1} \mathbf{W}^\top \mathbf{Y},$$

which does not depend on σ^2. This estimator is known as the *two-stage least squares (2SLS) estimator*. It may be interpreted as a simple IV estimator whose instrument matrix is $\tilde{\mathbf{X}} = \mathbf{W}(\mathbf{W}^\top \mathbf{W})^{-1} \mathbf{W}^\top \mathbf{X}$, the OLS predictor of $\mathbf{X}$ based on $\mathbf{W}$.

There are other interpretations of 2SLS. One follows from the fact that this estimator may also be written as

$$\tilde{\beta}_n = (\tilde{\mathbf{X}}^\top \tilde{\mathbf{X}})^{-1} \tilde{\mathbf{X}}^\top \mathbf{Y},$$

and therefore coincides with the OLS estimator in the regression of $\mathbf{Y}$ on $\tilde{\mathbf{X}}$. Because $n^{-1}\tilde{\mathbf{X}}^\top \mathbf{U} \xrightarrow{\text{p}} 0$, the matrix $\tilde{\mathbf{X}}$ is a version of $\mathbf{X}$ asymptotically "purged" of its correlation with $\mathbf{U}$. This was the original motivation of 2SLS.

Another interpretation of $\tilde{\beta}_n$ is in terms of GLS. Notice that

$$\frac{\mathbf{W}^\top \mathbf{Y}}{n} = \frac{\mathbf{W}^\top \mathbf{X}}{n}\beta + \frac{\mathbf{W}^\top \mathbf{U}}{n},$$

where, under our set of assumptions, $n^{-1}\mathbf{W}^\top \mathbf{U} \xrightarrow{\text{p}} 0$ and $n^{-1}\mathbf{W}^\top \mathbf{U}\mathbf{U}^\top \mathbf{W} \xrightarrow{\text{p}} \sigma^2 C$. This suggests a GLS regression of $\mathbf{W}^\top \mathbf{Y}$ on $\mathbf{W}^\top \mathbf{X}$, with $(n^{-1}\mathbf{W}^\top \mathbf{W})^{-1}$ as the weight matrix. It is easily seen that the resulting estimator coincides with 2SLS.

The asymptotic variance of the 2SLS estimator, and therefore its asymptotic efficiency, depends on the matrix D. If indeed $D = \sigma^2 C$, then

$$\text{AV}(\tilde{\beta}_n) = \sigma^2\, (P^\top C^{-1} P)^{-1}.$$

If instead $D \neq \sigma^2 C$, then

$$\text{AV}(\tilde{\beta}_n) = (P^\top C^{-1} P)^{-1} P^\top C^{-1} D C^{-1} P (P^\top C^{-1} P)^{-1}.$$

In this case, the 2SLS estimator is generally not asymptotically efficient in the class of IV estimators. □

The next result shows that when additional instruments are available, their use may lead to asymptotic efficiency gains.

Theorem 11.6 *Suppose that Assumptions 11.1–11.4 hold, and let* $\mathbf{W} = [\mathbf{W}_1, \mathbf{W}_2]$. *Partition P and D accordingly as*

$$P = \begin{bmatrix} P_1 \\ P_2 \end{bmatrix}, \qquad D = \begin{bmatrix} D_{11} & D_{12} \\ D_{21} & D_{22} \end{bmatrix}.$$

Let

$$\tilde{\beta}_n = (\mathbf{X}^\top \mathbf{W} B_n \mathbf{W}^\top \mathbf{X})^{-1} \mathbf{X}^\top \mathbf{W} B_n \mathbf{W}^\top \mathbf{Y},$$

where $B_n \xrightarrow{\text{p}} D^{-1}$, *and*

$$\hat{\beta}_n = (\mathbf{X}^\top \mathbf{W}_1 B_{11n} \mathbf{W}_1^\top X)^{-1} \mathbf{X}^\top \mathbf{W}_1 B_{11n} \mathbf{W}_1^\top \mathbf{Y},$$

where B_{11n} denotes the top-left submatrix of B_n. Then $\text{AV}(\hat{\beta}_n) - \text{AV}(\tilde{\beta}_n) \geq 0$, *with equality if and only if*

$$P_2 - D_{21} D_{11}^{-1} P_1 = 0. \tag{11.4}$$

Proof. The inequality $\text{AV}(\hat{\beta}_n) - \text{AV}(\tilde{\beta}_n) = (P_1^\top D_{11}^{-1} P_1)^{-1} - (P^\top D^{-1} P)^{-1} \geq 0$ holds if and only if $P^\top D^{-1} P - P_1^\top D_{11}^{-1} P_1 \geq 0$. By the rules for partitioned inverses

$$\begin{aligned} P^\top D^{-1} P &= [P_1^\top\ P_2^\top] D^{-1} \begin{bmatrix} P_1 \\ P_2 \end{bmatrix} \\ &= P_1^\top (D_{11}^{-1} + D_{11}^{-1} D_{12} E^{-1} D_{21} D_{11}^{-1}) P_1 - P_2^\top E^{-1} D_{21} D_{11}^{-1} P_1 \\ &\quad - P_1^\top D_{11}^{-1} D_{12} E^{-1} P_2 + P_2^\top E^{-1} P_2, \end{aligned}$$

where the matrix $E = D_{22} - D_{21}D_{11}^{-1}D_{12}$ is p.d. and symmetric because D is p.d. and symmetric. Hence

$$\begin{aligned} P^\top D^{-1}P - P_1^\top D_{11}^{-1}P_1 &= P_1^\top D_{11}^{-1}D_{12}E^{-1}D_{21}D_{11}^{-1}P_1 - P_2^\top E^{-1}D_{21}D_{11}^{-1}P_1 \\ &\quad - P_1^\top D_{11}^{-1}D_{12}E^{-1}P_2 + P_2^\top E^{-1}P_2 \\ &= (P_2^\top - P_1^\top D_{11}^{-1}D_{12})E^{-1}(P_2 - D_{21}D_{11}^{-1}P_1) \geq 0. \end{aligned}$$

Therefore, $\hat{\beta}_n$ and $\tilde{\beta}_n$ have the same asymptotic variance if and only if $P_2 - D_{21}D_{11}^{-1}P_1 = 0$. □

Example 11.4 Consider the 2SLS estimator introduced in Example 11.3. If $D = \sigma^2 C$, then the left-hand side of (11.4) may be estimated consistently (up to a scale factor) by

$$n^{-1}\mathbf{W}_2^\top\mathbf{X} - n^{-1}\mathbf{W}_2^\top\mathbf{W}_1(\mathbf{W}_1^\top\mathbf{W}_1)^{-1}\mathbf{W}_1^\top\mathbf{X} = n^{-1}\mathbf{W}_2^\top\hat{\mathbf{X}}_1,$$

where $\hat{\mathbf{X}}_1 = \mathbf{X} - \mathbf{W}_1(\mathbf{W}_1^\top\mathbf{W}_1)^{-1}\mathbf{W}_1^\top\mathbf{X}$ is the residual matrix in the multivariate OLS regression of $\mathbf{X}$ on $\mathbf{W}_1$. If $\mathbf{W}_2$ is asymptotically uncorrelated with $\hat{\mathbf{X}}_1$, then adding $\mathbf{W}_2$ to the instruments in $\mathbf{W}_1$ produces no gain in asymptotic efficiency. □

Notice that, unlike OLS, omitting valid instruments produces no bias, although it may lead to asymptotic efficiency losses.

Theorem 11.6 suggests that, even when the OLS estimator is consistent, there may exist IV estimators that are asymptotically more efficient than OLS. To construct these estimators, one has to find a valid set of instruments.

Example 11.5 If $U_i = Y_i - \beta^\top X_i$ and the regression model satisfies $\mathrm{E}(U_i \,|\, X_i) = 0$ then, by the law of iterated expectations, any transformation $g(X_i)$ is uncorrelated with U_i. Since the OLS estimator only relies on the lack of correlation between X_i and U_i, it may be improved upon asymptotically by an IV estimator that uses $W_i = (X_i, g(X_i))$ as a set of instruments. □

Example 11.6 Cragg (1983) considered a linear model with nonscalar variance matrix Ω_n and showed that it is possible to construct an estimator which is asymptotically more efficient than OLS even in cases when the structure of the matrix Ω_n is unknown.

Let $\mathrm{E}(\mathbf{Y} \,|\, \mathbf{X}) = \mathbf{X}\beta$ and $\mathrm{Var}(\mathbf{Y} \,|\, \mathbf{X}) = \Omega_n$, and suppose that one has available, in addition to $\mathbf{X}$, a matrix $\mathbf{Z}$ containing variables which help explain Ω_n. For example, in the case of pure heteroskedasticity, $\mathbf{Z}$ may contain squares and cross-products of the variables in $\mathbf{X}$.

Now suppose that the instrument matrix $\mathbf{W} = [\mathbf{X}, \mathbf{Z}]$ satisfies Assumptions 11.1–11.4. Let $B_n \xrightarrow{\mathrm{p}} D^{-1}$, and consider the asymptotically efficient IV estimator

$$\tilde{\beta}_n = (\mathbf{X}^\top\mathbf{W}B_n\mathbf{W}^\top\mathbf{X})^{-1}\mathbf{X}^\top\mathbf{W}B_n\mathbf{W}^\top\mathbf{Y}.$$

To establish conditions under which $\tilde{\beta}_n$ is asymptotically more efficient than the OLS estimator $\hat{\beta}_n = (\mathbf{X}^\top\mathbf{X})^{-1}\mathbf{X}^\top\mathbf{Y}$, partition P and D as

$$P = \begin{bmatrix} P_{XX} \\ P_{ZX} \end{bmatrix}, \qquad D = \begin{bmatrix} D_{XX} & D_{XZ} \\ D_{ZX} & D_{ZZ} \end{bmatrix}.$$

Condition (11.4) implies that $\hat{\beta}_n$ and $\tilde{\beta}_n$ have the same asymptotic variance if and only if

$$P_{ZX} - D_{ZX} D_{XX}^{-1} P_{XX} = 0.$$

Postmultiplying by the inverse of P_{XX} and taking the transpose gives the equivalent condition

$$D_{XX}^{-1} D_{XZ} = P_{XX}^{-1} P_{XZ}.$$

Notice that $D_{XX}^{-1} D_{XZ}$ is the coefficient matrix in the GLS projection of $\mathbf{Z}$ on $\mathbf{X}$, whereas $P_{XX}^{-1} P_{XZ}$ is the coefficient matrix in the OLS projection of $\mathbf{Z}$ on $\mathbf{X}$.

Unlike the feasible GLS estimator of β, which requires an estimate of Ω_n, the IV estimator $\tilde{\beta}_n$ only requires a consistent estimate of D^{-1}. In the case of pure heteroskedasticity, where Ω_n is a diagonal matrix, such an estimate is easily constructed as $B_n = (n^{-1} \sum_i \hat{U}_i^2 W_i W_i^\top)^{-1}$, where $\hat{U}_i^2$ are the squared OLS residuals. The Monte Carlo results in Cragg (1983) indicate that the efficiency gains from using $\tilde{\beta}_n$ may be substantial even in small samples. □

11.2.4 ESTIMATES OF PRECISION

Theorem 11.3 shows that a consistent estimate of the asymptotic variance of an IV estimator is readily available if one can find a consistent estimate of D. In some cases this is straightforward.

Example 11.7 Suppose that the assumptions of Theorem 11.4 hold. Further suppose that $\mathrm{E}(U_i \mid W_i) = 0$, $\mathrm{Var}(U_i \mid W_i) = \sigma^2$ and $\mathrm{E}\, W_i W_i^\top = C$, a finite p.d. matrix. In this case

$$D = \mathrm{Var}\, W_i U_i = \mathrm{E}[\mathrm{Var}(W_i U_i \mid W_i)] = \sigma^2\, \mathrm{E}\, W_i W_i^\top = \sigma^2 C,$$

and so the asymptotic variance of an estimator in the class (11.3) is

$$\mathrm{AV}(\hat{\beta}_n) = \sigma^2\, (P^\top A P)^{-1} P^\top A C A P (P^\top A P)^{-1}.$$

Since $n^{-1}\mathbf{W}^\top \mathbf{X} \xrightarrow{\mathrm{p}} P$ and $n^{-1}\mathbf{W}^\top \mathbf{W} \xrightarrow{\mathrm{p}} C$, the problem of consistently estimating the asymptotic variance of $\hat{\beta}_n$ reduces to that of consistently estimating σ^2. A natural candidate is

$$\hat{\sigma}_n^2 = n^{-1}(\mathbf{Y} - \mathbf{X}\hat{\beta}_n)^\top (\mathbf{Y} - \mathbf{X}\hat{\beta}_n) = n^{-1}\mathbf{U}^\top M \mathbf{U},$$

where the matrix $M = I_n - \mathbf{X}(\mathbf{X}^\top \mathbf{W} A_n \mathbf{W}^\top \mathbf{X})^{-1} \mathbf{X}^\top \mathbf{W} A_n \mathbf{W}^\top$ is idempotent (but not symmetric) and orthogonal to $\mathbf{X}$. It is easy to verify that $\hat{\sigma}_n^2 \xrightarrow{\mathrm{p}} \sigma^2$.

In particular, under our set of assumptions, the asymptotic variance of the 2SLS estimator $\tilde{\beta}_n$ can be estimated consistently by

$$\widehat{\mathrm{AV}}(\tilde{\beta}_n) = n\tilde{\sigma}_n^2 [\mathbf{X}^\top \mathbf{W}(\mathbf{W}^\top \mathbf{W})^{-1} \mathbf{W}^\top \mathbf{X}]^{-1},$$

where $\tilde{\sigma}_n^2 = n^{-1}(\mathbf{Y} - \mathbf{X}\tilde{\beta}_n)^\top (\mathbf{Y} - \mathbf{X}\tilde{\beta}_n)$. □

The next theorem shows that, by strengthening the assumptions of Theorem 11.4 only slightly, a consistent estimator of D can easily be constructed for more general situations than the one considered in the previous example.

Theorem 11.7 (Eicker–White) *Given an IV estimator $\hat{\beta}_n$, let*

$$\hat{D}_n = n^{-1} \sum_{i=1}^{n} \hat{U}_i^2 W_i W_i^\top,$$

where $\hat{U}_i = Y_i - \hat{\beta}_n^\top X_i$, $i = 1, \ldots, n$. Suppose, in addition to the assumptions of Theorem 11.4, that $\mathrm{E}\,|W_{ih} X_{ij}|^2 < \infty$ for every $h = 1, \ldots, r$ and all $j = 1, \ldots, k$. Then $\hat{D}_n \xrightarrow{\mathrm{p}} D$.

A generalization of Theorem 11.7 to the case of autocorrelation of unknown form may be found in Newey and West (1987).

The sampling variance of $\hat{\beta}_n$ may also be estimated using the jackknife. The jackknife estimate is

$$\widehat{\mathrm{Var}}_J\, \hat{\beta}_n = \frac{n-1}{n} \sum_i [\hat{\beta}_{(i)} - \hat{\beta}_{(\cdot)}][\hat{\beta}_{(i)} - \hat{\beta}_{(\cdot)}]^\top,$$

where $\hat{\beta}_{(i)}$ is the IV estimate obtained by leaving out the ith data point and $\hat{\beta}_{(\cdot)} = n^{-1} \sum_i \hat{\beta}_{(i)}$. In the case of the 2SLS estimator, the appropriate set of recursions for computing $\hat{\beta}_{(i)}$ is given in Phillips (1977). Although these expressions are more complicated than in the OLS case, still only one extra pass through the data is needed after computing $\hat{\beta}_n$.

Example 11.8 The expression for the leave-one-out estimate $\hat{\beta}_{(i)}$ simplifies considerably in the simple IV case and becomes

$$\hat{\beta}_n - \hat{\beta}_{(i)} = (\mathbf{W}^\top \mathbf{X})^{-1} \frac{W_i \hat{U}_i}{h_{ii}}, \qquad i = 1, \ldots, n, \tag{11.5}$$

where $h_{ii} = 1 - X_i^\top (\mathbf{W}^\top \mathbf{X})^{-1} W_i$ and $\hat{U}_i = Y_i - \hat{\beta}_n^\top X_i$. Notice the close analogy with the formula for OLS. Viewed as a function of i, the difference (11.5) is just the sensitivity curve of the simple IV estimate. The fact that this sensitivity curve is unbounded reveals the fundamental lack of robustness of linear IV estimators (see Chapter 15).

By analogy with Cook's (1977) statistic, an overall measure of the influence of the ith data point may be given by the statistic

$$D_i = \frac{h_{ii}}{1 - h_{ii}} \frac{\tilde{U}_i^2}{k}, \qquad i = 1, \ldots, n,$$

where $\tilde{U}_i = \hat{U}_i / (\hat{\sigma}\sqrt{1 - h_{ii}})$ and $\hat{\sigma}_n^2 = n^{-1} \sum_i \hat{U}_i^2$. As for OLS, $h_{ii}/(1 - h_{ii})$ may be interpreted as a measure of leverage and the standardized residual $\tilde{U}_i$ as a measure of consistency of the ith data point with the rest of the sample. □

The sampling variance of $\hat{\beta}_n$ may also be estimated by using the nonparametric bootstrap, with bootstrap replications obtained by sampling with replacement from the joint empirical distribution of (X_i, W_i, Y_i).

Freedman (1984) suggested the following variant for the case when $\{(X_i, W_i, Y_i)\}$ is a sequence of i.i.d. random vectors and the instruments are valid.

Algorithm 11.1

(1) *Let* $\tilde{\mathbf{U}} = \mathbf{Y} - \mathbf{X}\tilde{\beta}_n$ *be the 2SLS residual vector and let* $\tilde{\mathbf{V}}$ *be the part of* $\tilde{\mathbf{U}}$ *which is orthogonal to the instruments, that is,* $\tilde{\mathbf{V}} = M_W \tilde{\mathbf{U}}$ *where* $M_W = I_n - \mathbf{W}(\mathbf{W}^\top \mathbf{W})^{-1}\mathbf{W}^\top$.

(2) *Construct the empirical distribution function* F_n *of* $(X_i, W_i, \tilde{V}_i)$.

(3) *Draw a resample* $\{(X_i^*, W_i^*, \tilde{V}_i^*)\}$ *of size n from* F_n.

(4) *Construct bootstrap pseudo data* $Y_1^*, \ldots, Y_n^*$ *as*

$$Y_i^* = \tilde{\beta}_n^\top X_i^* + \tilde{V}_i^*, \qquad i = 1, \ldots, n.$$

(5) *Compute the 2SLS estimate* $\tilde{\beta}^*$ *from the pseudo sample* $\{(X_i^*, W_i^*, Y_i^*)\}$.

(6) *Independently repeat steps (3)–(5) a large number B of times, obtaining bootstrap replicates* $\tilde{\beta}_1^*, \ldots, \tilde{\beta}_B^*$.

(7) *Use the empirical distribution of* $\tilde{\beta}_1^*, \ldots, \tilde{\beta}_B^*$ *to estimate any aspect of the sampling distribution of* $\tilde{\beta}_n$.

Step (1) of the algorithm ensures that $\tilde{V}_i$ and W_i are orthogonal. Freedman (1984) shows that, if $\mathbf{W}$ is a valid instrument matrix, then this bootstrap algorithm is asymptotically correct under general conditions, that is, the (conditional) variability of the bootstrap estimates about the original estimate $\tilde{\beta}_n$ closely mimics, for large n, the sampling variability of $\tilde{\beta}_n$ about the population parameter β. In particular, the bootstrap estimator of variance is robust to heteroskedasticity.

When $W_i = X_i$, the OLS estimator $\hat{\beta}_n$ and the 2SLS estimator $\tilde{\beta}_n$ coincide, and the algorithm reduces to the one in Chapter 7. To see this notice that, because $Y_i = \hat{\beta}_n^\top X_i + \hat{U}_i$, drawing samples from the empirical distribution of $\{(X_i, Y_i)\}$ is equivalent to drawing samples from the empirical distribution of $\{(X_i, \hat{U}_i)\}$ and then constructing pseudo data $Y_i^* = \hat{\beta}_n^\top X_i^* + \hat{U}_i^*$. This method is therefore different from Algorithm 7.1 where, for each fixed X_i, a random draw is made from the (marginal) empirical distribution of $\{\hat{U}_i\}$.

11.2.5 THE GENERALIZED 2SLS ESTIMATOR

Recall that when $D \neq \sigma^2 C$, the 2SLS estimator $\tilde{\beta}_n$ is no longer asymptotically efficient in the class of IV estimators based on Assumption 11.1. When $\Omega_n = \text{Var}(\mathbf{U} \,|\, \mathbf{W})$ is known, one may try to improve upon $\tilde{\beta}_n$ by proceeding by analogy with GLS.

Thus, suppose that Ω_n is a finite p.d. matrix and let H be a nonsingular matrix such that $H^\top H = \Omega_n^{-1}$. Let $\bar{\mathbf{Y}} = H\mathbf{Y}$, $\bar{\mathbf{X}} = H\mathbf{X}$, and $\bar{\mathbf{W}} = H\mathbf{W}$ denote the transformed data. The variance of the transformed errors $\bar{\mathbf{U}} = \bar{\mathbf{Y}} - \bar{\mathbf{X}}\beta = H\mathbf{U}$ is

$$\text{Var}(\bar{\mathbf{U}} \,|\, \bar{\mathbf{W}}) = \text{Var}(H\mathbf{U} \,|\, \mathbf{W}) = H\Omega_n H^\top = I_n,$$

a scalar matrix. If the matrix $\bar{\mathbf{W}}^\top \bar{\mathbf{X}} = \mathbf{W}^\top \Omega_n^{-1} \mathbf{X}$ has rank k and the matrix $\bar{\mathbf{W}}^\top \bar{\mathbf{W}} = \mathbf{W}^\top \Omega_n^{-1} \mathbf{W}$ is p.d., then the 2SLS estimator for the transformed data is

$$\begin{aligned}\bar{\beta}_n &= [\bar{\mathbf{X}}^\top \bar{\mathbf{W}}(\bar{\mathbf{W}}^\top \bar{\mathbf{W}})^{-1}\bar{\mathbf{W}}^\top \bar{\mathbf{X}}]^{-1}\bar{\mathbf{X}}^\top \bar{\mathbf{W}}(\bar{\mathbf{W}}^\top \bar{\mathbf{W}})^{-1}\bar{\mathbf{W}}^\top \bar{\mathbf{Y}} \\ &= [\mathbf{X}^\top \Omega_n^{-1}\mathbf{W}(\mathbf{W}^\top \Omega_n^{-1}\mathbf{W})^{-1}\mathbf{W}^\top \Omega_n^{-1}\mathbf{X}]^{-1}\mathbf{X}^\top \Omega_n^{-1}\mathbf{W}(\mathbf{W}^\top \Omega_n^{-1}\mathbf{W})^{-1}\mathbf{W}^\top \Omega_n^{-1}\mathbf{Y},\end{aligned}$$

which is known as the *generalized 2SLS estimator*. Notice that this estimator does not belong to the class (11.3). Its asymptotic properties are given below.

Theorem 11.8 *Suppose that:*

(i) $n^{-1}\mathbf{W}^\top\Omega_n^{-1}(\mathbf{Y}-\mathbf{X}\beta)\xrightarrow{\text{p}}0$;
(ii) $n^{-1}\mathbf{W}^\top\Omega_n^{-1}\mathbf{X}\xrightarrow{\text{p}}\bar{P}$, *a finite $r\times k$ matrix of rank k;*
(iii) $n^{-1}\mathbf{W}^\top\Omega_n^{-1}\mathbf{W}\xrightarrow{\text{p}}\bar{C}$, *a finite p.d. matrix.*

Then $\bar{\beta}_n$ exists with probability approaching one and $\bar{\beta}_n\xrightarrow{\text{p}}\beta$.

Theorem 11.9 *Suppose that the assumptions of Theorem 11.8 hold. If*

$$n^{-1/2}\mathbf{W}^\top\Omega_n^{-1}(\mathbf{Y}-\mathbf{X}\beta)\xrightarrow{\text{d}}\mathcal{N}_r(0,\bar{C}),$$

then $\sqrt{n}\,(\bar{\beta}_n-\beta)\xrightarrow{\text{d}}\mathcal{N}_k(0,\,(\bar{P}^\top\bar{C}^{-1}\bar{P})^{-1})$.

We now verify our conjecture that the generalized 2SLS estimator $\bar{\beta}_n$ is at least as efficient as the 2SLS estimator $\tilde{\beta}_n$.

Theorem 11.10 *Let $\tilde{\beta}_n$ be the 2SLS estimator and let $\bar{\beta}_n$ be the generalized 2SLS estimator. If all the conditions of Theorems 11.3 and 11.9 are satisfied, then* $\mathrm{AV}(\tilde{\beta}_n)-\mathrm{AV}(\bar{\beta}_n)\geq 0$.

Proof. The linear projection of $\mathbf{X}$ onto the subspace spanned by the columns of $\mathbf{W}$ is of the form $\mathbf{X}=\mathbf{W}\Pi^\top+\mathbf{V}$, where

$$\Pi^\top=\left(\operatorname{plim}\frac{\mathbf{W}^\top\mathbf{W}}{n}\right)^{-1}\operatorname{plim}\frac{\mathbf{W}^\top\mathbf{X}}{n}=C^{-1}P$$

is an $r\times k$ matrix of rank k and $n^{-1}\mathbf{W}^\top\mathbf{V}=o_p(1)$ by construction. By using the fact that $n^{-1}\mathbf{W}^\top\Omega_n^{-1}\mathbf{V}=o_p(1)$, we get

$$\bar{P}=\operatorname{plim}\frac{1}{n}\mathbf{W}^\top\Omega_n^{-1}\mathbf{X}=\operatorname{plim}\frac{1}{n}\mathbf{W}^\top\Omega_n^{-1}(\mathbf{W}\Pi^\top+\mathbf{V})=\bar{C}\Pi^\top.$$

Hence

$$\begin{aligned}\mathrm{AV}(\tilde{\beta}_n)&=(P^\top C^{-1}P)^{-1}P^\top C^{-1}DC^{-1}P(P^\top C^{-1}P)^{-1}\\&=(\Pi C\Pi^\top)^{-1}\Pi D\Pi^\top(\Pi C\Pi^\top)^{-1},\end{aligned}$$

and

$$\mathrm{AV}(\bar{\beta}_n)=(\bar{P}^\top\bar{C}^{-1}\bar{P})^{-1}=(\Pi\bar{C}\Pi^\top)^{-1}.$$

If A is a symmetric p.d. $n\times n$ matrix, B is a $k\times n$ matrix of rank $k\leq n$, and R is a nonsingular matrix such that $R^\top R=A^{-1}$, then

$$BA^{-1}B^\top-BB^\top(BAB^\top)^{-1}BB^\top=AR^\top MRA^\top\geq 0,$$

since $M=I-R^{-\top}B^\top(BAB^\top)^{-1}BR^{-1}$ is an idempotent matrix. Applying this result with $A=\Omega_n$ and $B=n^{-1/2}\Pi\mathbf{W}^\top$ gives

$$n^{-1}[\Pi\mathbf{W}^\top\Omega_n^{-1}\mathbf{W}\Pi^\top-\Pi\mathbf{W}^\top\mathbf{W}\Pi^\top(\Pi\mathbf{W}^\top\Omega_n\mathbf{W}\Pi^\top)^{-1}\Pi\mathbf{W}^\top\mathbf{W}\Pi^\top]\geq 0.$$

Taking the limit in probability as $n \to \infty$ we get

$$\Pi\bar{C}\Pi^\top - \Pi C\Pi^\top(\Pi D\Pi^\top)^{-1}\Pi C\Pi^\top \geq 0,$$

which implies that $\mathrm{AV}(\tilde{\beta}_n) - \mathrm{AV}(\bar{\beta}_n) \geq 0$. □

In practice, Ω_n is rarely known. One obtains a feasible generalized 2SLS estimator when the matrix Ω_n is replaced by some consistent estimate. Under appropriate regularity conditions, the feasible estimator can be shown to be consistent for β and asymptotically equivalent to $\bar{\beta}_n$.

11.3 HYPOTHESIS TESTING

We now consider tests based on an IV estimator $\hat{\beta}_n$ in the class (11.3). Recall that, under Assumptions 11.1 and 11.4, $\hat{\beta}_n$ exists with probability approaching one as $n \to \infty$, is consistent for β and has an asymptotically normal distribution with asymptotic variance matrix $\mathrm{AV}(\hat{\beta}_n) = (P^\top AP)^{-1}P^\top ADAP(P^\top AP)^{-1}$. Further, under the same set of assumptions, $\hat{\beta}_n$ is asymptotically efficient provided that A_n is a consistent p.d. estimate of D^{-1}.

11.3.1 *WALD TESTS*

Consider the general problem of testing the hypothesis that the parameter β satisfies a set of $q \leq k$ nonlinear equality constraints, that is, H_0: $h(\beta) = 0$, where h: $\Re^k \to \Re^q$ is a known function. A Wald test rejects H_0 whenever the norm of the vector $h(\hat{\beta}_n)$ is large. Construction of a critical region of a given asymptotic level may be based on the following result, which parallels the one in Section 10.4.5.

Theorem 11.11 *In addition to Assumptions 11.1–11.4, suppose:*

(i) h: $\Re^k \to \Re^q$ *is a continuously differentiable function;*
(ii) $H = h'(\beta)$ *is a* $q \times r$ *matrix of rank* q*;*
(iii) *there exists a symmetric p.d. matrix* $\hat{V}_n$ *such that* $\hat{V}_n \xrightarrow{\mathrm{p}} \mathrm{AV}(\hat{\beta}_n)$.

Then $\xi_n^W = n\, h(\hat{\beta}_n)^\top(\hat{H}_n\hat{V}_n\hat{H}_n^\top)^{-1}h(\hat{\beta}_n) \xrightarrow{\mathrm{d}} \chi^2_q$ *under* H_0, *where* $\hat{H}_n = h'(\hat{\beta}_n)$.

If $\mathrm{AV}(\hat{\beta}_n)$ is estimated by

$$\hat{V}_n = \left(\frac{\mathbf{X}^\top\mathbf{W}}{n}A_n\frac{\mathbf{W}^\top\mathbf{X}}{n}\right)^{-1}\frac{\mathbf{X}^\top\mathbf{W}}{n}A_n\hat{D}_nA_n\frac{\mathbf{W}^\top\mathbf{X}}{n}\left(\frac{\mathbf{X}^\top\mathbf{W}}{n}A_n\frac{\mathbf{W}^\top\mathbf{X}}{n}\right)^{-1},$$

asymptotic validity of a test based on ξ_n^W requires that $\hat{D}_n \xrightarrow{\mathrm{p}} D$. Clearly, using an asymptotically efficient estimator leads to more powerful tests.

11.3.2 *TESTS OF OVERIDENTIFYING RESTRICTIONS*

Let $\tilde{\beta}_n$ be an IV estimator based on a weight matrix B_n which converges to D^{-1} in probability, and let $Q_n(\beta) = Q(\beta, B_n)$ denote the criterion which defines such an estimator. If the chosen instruments are valid, then $\tilde{\beta}_n$ is asymptotically efficient and $Q_n(\tilde{\beta}_n)$ must be arbitrarily close to zero for big enough n. On the other hand, $Q_n(\tilde{\beta}_n) > 0$ for any finite n whenever the number of available instruments is greater than the number of parameters to be estimated. Thus, large values of $Q_n(\tilde{\beta}_n)$ are evidence against the overall validity of the model. A test that rejects the assumed model whenever $Q_n(\tilde{\beta}_n)$ is large is called a *test of overidentifying restrictions.* Construction of a critical region for this test may be based on the following result.

Theorem 11.12 *If Assumptions 11.1–11.4 hold and $\tilde{\beta}_n$ is an asymptotically efficient IV estimator, then $n^{-1}Q_n(\tilde{\beta}_n) \xrightarrow{d} \chi^2_{r-k}$ whenever $r > k$.*

Proof. The idea of the proof is to show that $n^{-1}Q_n(\tilde{\beta}_n) \xrightarrow{p} Z^\top M Z$, where Z is a random vector with a $\mathcal{N}_r(0, I_r)$ distribution and M is an idempotent matrix of rank $r - k$.

First notice that

$$\begin{aligned} \mathbf{W}^\top(\mathbf{Y} - \mathbf{X}\tilde{\beta}_n) &= \mathbf{W}^\top[I_n - \mathbf{X}(\mathbf{X}^\top\mathbf{W}B_n\mathbf{W}^\top\mathbf{X})^{-1}\mathbf{X}^\top\mathbf{W}B_n\mathbf{W}^\top]\mathbf{Y} \\ &= [I_r - \mathbf{W}^\top\mathbf{X}(\mathbf{X}^\top\mathbf{W}B_n\mathbf{W}^\top\mathbf{X})^{-1}\mathbf{X}^\top\mathbf{W}B_n]\mathbf{W}^\top\mathbf{U}, \end{aligned}$$

where $\mathbf{U} = \mathbf{Y} - \mathbf{X}\beta$. Since $B_n \xrightarrow{p} D^{-1}$ and

$$I_r - \mathbf{W}^\top\mathbf{X}(\mathbf{X}^\top\mathbf{W}B_n\mathbf{W}^\top\mathbf{X})^{-1}\mathbf{X}^\top\mathbf{W}B_n \xrightarrow{p} I_r - P(P^\top D^{-1}P)^{-1}P^\top D^{-1} \equiv M,$$

we get that $n^{-1}Q_n(\tilde{\beta}_n) - n^{-1}\mathbf{U}^\top\mathbf{W}M^\top D^{-1}M\mathbf{W}^\top\mathbf{U} \xrightarrow{p} 0$. Next notice that

$$\begin{aligned} M^\top D^{-1}M &= D^{-1} - D^{-1}P(P^\top D^{-1}P)^{-1}P^\top D^{-1} \\ &= D^{-1/2}[I_r - D^{-1/2}P(P^\top D^{-1}P)^{-1}P^\top D^{-1/2}]D^{-1/2} \\ &= D^{-1/2}MD^{-1/2}, \end{aligned}$$

where $M = I_r - D^{-1/2}P(P^\top D^{-1}P)^{-1}P^\top D^{-1/2}$ is an idempotent matrix of rank $r-k$. The conclusion of the theorem then follows from the fact that

$$n^{-1}Q_n(\tilde{\beta}_n) - (n^{-1/2}D^{-1/2}\mathbf{W}^\top\mathbf{U})^\top M(n^{-1/2}D^{-1/2}\mathbf{W}^\top\mathbf{U}) \xrightarrow{p} 0,$$

where $n^{-1/2}D^{-1/2}\mathbf{W}^\top\mathbf{U} \xrightarrow{d} \mathcal{N}_r(0, I_r)$ by Assumption 11.4. □

Example 11.9 In the case of a model estimated by 2SLS, the test statistic of Theorem 11.12 reduces to

$$n^{-1}Q_n(\tilde{\beta}_n) = n\frac{\tilde{\mathbf{U}}^\top\mathbf{W}(\mathbf{W}^\top\mathbf{W})^{-1}\mathbf{W}^\top\tilde{\mathbf{U}}}{\tilde{\mathbf{U}}^\top\tilde{\mathbf{U}}}.$$

This test statistic may be interpreted as n times the uncentered R^2 in the OLS regression of the 2SLS residual vector $\tilde{\mathbf{U}}$ on $\mathbf{W}$. The validity of tests based on this statistic depends crucially on the validity of the assumption that $n^{-1/2}\mathbf{W}^\top\mathbf{U} \xrightarrow{d} \mathcal{N}_r(0, \sigma^2 C)$, which guarantees that the 2SLS estimator is asymptotically efficient. □

11.3.3 DIFFERENCE TESTS

Let $\mathbf{U} = \mathbf{Y} - \mathbf{X}\beta$, and consider the hypothesis that $\mathrm{H}_0: n^{-1}\mathbf{X}^\top\mathbf{U} \xrightarrow{\mathrm{p}} 0$ against the alternative H_1: $n^{-1}\mathbf{X}^\top(\mathbf{Y} - \mathbf{X}\beta) \xrightarrow{\mathrm{p}} c \neq 0$. H_1 may arise, for example, because of omitted variables or measurement errors in $\mathbf{X}$, or because $\mathbf{X}$ contains variables that are jointly determined with $\mathbf{Y}$. The OLS estimator $\hat{\beta}_n = (\mathbf{X}^\top\mathbf{X})^{-1}\mathbf{X}^\top\mathbf{Y}$ is consistent for β under H_0, but is inconsistent under H_1. On the other hand, a simple IV estimator $\tilde{\beta}_n = (\mathbf{W}^\top\mathbf{X})^{-1}\mathbf{W}^\top\mathbf{Y}$, based on some instrument matrix $\mathbf{W}$, is consistent for β under both H_0 and H_1. Thus, large differences between $\hat{\beta}_n$ and $\tilde{\beta}_n$ are evidence against H_0.

More generally, consider the following assumption.

Assumption 11.5 *Let $\hat{\theta}_n$ and $\tilde{\theta}_n$ be estimators of a p-dimensional parameter θ, and let H_0 be a statistical hypothesis such that:*

(i) *if H_0 is true, then* $\operatorname{plim}\hat{\theta}_n = \operatorname{plim}\tilde{\theta}_n = \theta$;
(ii) *if H_0 is not true, then* $\operatorname{plim}(\hat{\theta}_n - \tilde{\theta}_n) \neq 0$.

Under this set of assumptions, a difference test rejects H_0 for large values of the norm of the vector $\hat{\delta}_n = \tilde{\theta}_n - \hat{\theta}_n$. Construction of a critical region of a given asymptotic level may be based on the following result.

Theorem 11.13 *Suppose that Assumption 11.5 holds and assume that under H_0:*

(i) $\sqrt{n}\,\hat{\delta}_n = \sqrt{n}\,(\tilde{\theta}_n - \hat{\theta}_n) \xrightarrow{\mathrm{d}} \mathcal{N}_p(0, \Delta)$ *where Δ is a finite n.n.d. matrix of rank equal to $p_* \leq p$;*
(ii) *there exists a symmetric n.n.d. matrix $\hat{\Delta}_n$ such that $\hat{\Delta}_n \xrightarrow{\mathrm{p}} \Delta$.*

Then, under H_0, $\xi_n^D = n\,\hat{\delta}_n^\top\hat{\Delta}_n^-\,\hat{\delta}_n \xrightarrow{\mathrm{d}} \chi^2_{p_*}$ for any choice of generalized inverse.

In some cases $\mathrm{AV}(\hat{\delta}_n)$ has a particularly simple form. In particular, suppose that Assumption 11.5 may be replaced by the following.

Assumption 11.6 *Let $\hat{\theta}_n$ and $\tilde{\theta}_n$ belong to a class $\mathcal{T}$ of asymptotically normal estimators of a p-dimensional parameter θ and let the statistical hypothesis H_0 be such that:*

(i) *if H_0 is true, then $\hat{\theta}_n$ and $\tilde{\theta}_n$ are both consistent for θ, while $\hat{\theta}_n$ is asymptotically efficient in the class $\mathcal{T}$;*
(ii) *if H_0 is not true, then* $\operatorname{plim}(\hat{\theta}_n - \tilde{\theta}_n) \neq 0$.

As a consequence of Assumption 11.6 we get the following generalization of Theorem 9.4.

Theorem 11.14 *Suppose that Assumption 11.6 holds and let $\hat{V}_n$ and $\tilde{V}_n$ be symmetric p.d. matrices such that $\hat{V}_n \xrightarrow{\mathrm{p}} \mathrm{AV}(\hat{\theta}_n)$ and $\tilde{V}_n \xrightarrow{\mathrm{p}} \mathrm{AV}(\tilde{\theta}_n)$. Then, under H_0:*

(i) *$\hat{\theta}_n$ and $\hat{\delta}_n = \tilde{\theta}_n - \hat{\theta}_n$ are asymptotically independent;*
(ii) $\mathrm{AV}(\hat{\delta}_n) = \mathrm{AV}(\tilde{\theta}_n) - \mathrm{AV}(\hat{\theta}_n)$;
(iii) $\xi_n^D = n\,\hat{\delta}_n^\top(\tilde{V}_n - \hat{V}_n)^-\,\hat{\delta}_n \xrightarrow{\mathrm{d}} \chi^2_{p_*}$ *for any choice of generalized inverse, where p_* is the rank of $\mathrm{AV}(\hat{\delta}_n)$.*

Example 11.10 Consider computing the difference test statistic for the hypothesis $\mathrm{H}_0\colon n^{-1}\mathbf{X}^\top(\mathbf{Y} - \mathbf{X}\beta) \xrightarrow{\mathrm{p}} 0$. Let $\hat{\beta}_n$ be the OLS estimator of β and let $\tilde{\beta}_n = (\mathbf{W}^\top\mathbf{X})^{-1}\mathbf{W}^\top\mathbf{Y}$ be a simple IV estimator based on some instrument matrix $\mathbf{X}$. Then

$$\begin{aligned}\hat{\delta}_n &= [(\mathbf{W}^\top\mathbf{X})^{-1}\mathbf{W}^\top - (\mathbf{X}^\top\mathbf{X})^{-1}\mathbf{X}^\top]\mathbf{Y} \\ &= (\mathbf{W}^\top\mathbf{X})^{-1}[\mathbf{W}^\top - \mathbf{W}^\top\mathbf{X}(\mathbf{X}^\top\mathbf{X})^{-1}\mathbf{X}^\top]\mathbf{Y} \\ &= (\mathbf{W}^\top\mathbf{X})^{-1}\mathbf{W}M\mathbf{Y},\end{aligned}$$

where $M = I_k - \mathbf{X}(\mathbf{X}^\top\mathbf{X})^{-1}\mathbf{X}^\top$. If $\mathrm{AV}(\hat{\delta}_n)$ is estimated by

$$\begin{aligned}n\hat{\sigma}_n^2&[(\mathbf{W}^\top\mathbf{X})^{-1}\mathbf{W}^\top\mathbf{W}(\mathbf{X}^\top\mathbf{W})^{-1} - (\mathbf{X}^\top\mathbf{X})^{-1}] \\ &= n\,\hat{\sigma}_n^2(\mathbf{W}^\top\mathbf{X})^{-1}\mathbf{W}^\top M\mathbf{W}(\mathbf{X}^\top\mathbf{W})^{-1},\end{aligned}$$

where $\hat{\sigma}_n^2 = n^{-1}(\mathbf{Y} - \mathbf{X}\hat{\beta}_n)^\top(\mathbf{Y} - \mathbf{X}\hat{\beta}_n)$, then the difference test statistic becomes

$$\xi_n^D = \hat{\sigma}_n^{-2}\mathbf{Y}^\top M\mathbf{W}(\mathbf{W}^\top M\mathbf{W})^{-1}\mathbf{W}M\mathbf{Y},$$

which is proportional to the statistic of a classical F-test of significance of $\mathbf{W}$ in the OLS regression of $\mathbf{Y}$ on $\mathbf{X}$ and $\mathbf{W}$. Quite intuitively, H_0 is rejected if including the instrument matrix $\mathbf{W}$ in the regression significantly improves the fit. □

In order to study the asymptotic power of a difference test, consider a sequence of local alternatives such that

$$\hat{\delta}_n - n^{-1/2}\delta \xrightarrow{\mathrm{p}} 0. \tag{11.6}$$

Under this sequence of alternatives, the difference $\hat{\delta}_n$ between the two estimators goes to zero at the same rate of $n^{-1/2}$.

Theorem 11.15 *If the assumptions of Theorem 11.14 hold, then, under the sequence of local alternatives* (11.6), $\xi_n^D \xrightarrow{\mathrm{d}} \chi^2_{p_*,\nu}$, *where* p_* *is the rank of* $\mathrm{AV}(\hat{\delta}_n)$ *and* $\nu = \delta^\top[\mathrm{AV}(\tilde{\theta}_n) - \mathrm{AV}(\hat{\theta}_n)]^-\delta$.

The form of the noncentrality parameter ν suggests that a difference test is likely to have high power either under alternatives such that δ is large or in cases where the asymptotic efficiency loss from using $\tilde{\theta}_n$ is small. On the other hand, a difference test has no power under alternatives that belong to the null space of $\mathrm{AV}(\tilde{\theta}_n) - \mathrm{AV}(\hat{\theta}_n)$.

11.4 THE GENERALIZED METHOD OF MOMENTS

The instrumental variable method may be viewed as a special case of a more general method called the *generalized method of moments (GMM)*.

Let $\eta(Z;\theta)$ be a transformation of a random q-vector Z into $\Re^r$. Suppose that the mean of $\eta(Z;\theta)$ exists for all θ in a subset Θ of $\Re^p$ and satisfies

$$\mathrm{E}\,\eta(Z;\theta_0) = 0 \tag{11.7}$$

for some $\theta_0 \in \Theta$. The statistical problem is estimation and inference about the parameter point θ_0. Clearly, this only makes sense if θ_0 is unique, that is, $\mathrm{E}\,\eta(Z;\theta) = 0$ only if $\theta = \theta_0$, in which case we say that θ_0 is *identifiable*.

We refer to the function $\eta(z;\theta)$ as the *moment function* and to equation (11.7) as the *population moment conditions*. The latter may be viewed as implicitly defining the target parameter. The population moment conditions typically summarize the information contained in an econometric model.

Example 11.11 Let $s(z;\theta)$ be the likelihood score of a smooth parametric model. Then $\mathrm{E}\, s(Z;\theta) = 0$ corresponds to the population moment conditions underlying ML estimation. □

An important special case is when the moment function is linear in the parameters, that is, of the form $\eta(z;\theta) = b(z) + C(z)\,\theta$, where $b(z)$ is an r-vector and $C(z)$ an $r \times p$ matrix.

Example 11.12 As an example of linear moment function let $Z = (X, Y)$, $b(Z) = XY$ and $C(Z) = -XX^\top$. Then $\mathrm{E}\,\eta(Z;\theta) = \mathrm{E}\,X(Y - \theta^\top X) = 0$ corresponds to the population moment conditions underlying OLS estimation. As another example let $Z = (X, W, Y)$, $b(Z) = WY$ and $C(Z) = -WX^\top$. In this case $\mathrm{E}\,\eta(Z;\theta) = \mathrm{E}\,W(Y - \theta^\top X) = 0$ corresponds to the population moment conditions underlying IV estimation. □

Let $Z_1, \ldots, Z_n$ be a sample from the distribution of Z, and let $\eta_i(\theta) = \eta(Z_i;\theta)$. The sample counterpart of the population moment conditions (11.7) is the system of r equations

$$\bar{\eta}_n(\theta) = n^{-1} \sum_{i=1}^{n} \eta_i(\theta) = 0.$$

We refer to this equation system as the *sample moment conditions*. Three cases arise depending on the relationship between the number p of parameters to be estimated and the number r of population moment conditions.

When $r < p$, the sample moment conditions do not have a unique solution in general, and therefore consistent estimation of the populations parameter θ_0 is generally impossible.

When $r = p$, called the *exactly identified case*, any root $\hat{\theta}_n$ of the sample moment conditions that also belongs to Θ is a MM estimator of θ_0. Thus, a MM estimator is any point in the parameter space at which the sample counterpart of the population moment conditions is equal to zero. Unless $\eta_i(\theta)$ is linear in θ, numerical methods are needed to find $\hat{\theta}_n$. Notice that a local ML estimator fits this case with $\eta_i(\theta)$ equal to the likelihood score.

When $r > p$, called the *overidentified case*, the sample moment conditions have no solution. In this case an estimator of θ_0 may be obtained by first specifying a measure of distance of the sample moments from zero, and then selecting a point in the parameter space which minimizes such distance. A convenient choice is the generalized Euclidean distance in the metric of a symmetric p.d. $r \times r$ matrix A_n. This leads to the problem

$$\min_{\theta \in \Theta} Q_n(\theta) = \bar{\eta}_n(\theta)^\top A_n \bar{\eta}_n(\theta).$$

A solution to this problem, if it exists, is called a *generalized method of moments (GMM)* or *nonlinear IV estimator* of θ_0. By varying the weight matrix A_n, one obtains a whole class of GMM estimators based on the same population moment conditions. If $\bar{\eta}_n$ is continuously differentiable on Θ with Jacobian $P_n(\theta) = \bar{\eta}_n'(\theta)$, then a GMM estimator $\hat{\theta}_n$ necessarily satisfies

$$0 = Q_n'(\hat{\theta}_n) = P_n(\hat{\theta}_n)^\top A_n \bar{\eta}_n(\hat{\theta}_n).$$

Thus $\hat{\theta}_n$ may itself be viewed as a MM estimator based on the sample moment conditions $\eta_n^*(\theta) = 0$, where $\eta_n^*(\theta) = P_n(\theta)^\top A_n \bar{\eta}_n(\theta)$.

Since, $\bar{\eta}_n(\theta) \xrightarrow{\text{p}} \mathrm{E}\, \eta_i(\theta)$ by the WLLN, one may expect a GMM estimator to be consistent for θ_0 provided that θ_0 is identifiable and appropriate regularity conditions hold. We derive the asymptotic properties of a sequence $\{\hat{\theta}_n\}$ of GMM estimators under the following set of assumptions.

Assumption 11.7

(i) Θ *is a compact subset of* $\Re^p$.
(ii) η_i *is continuous on* Θ.
(iii) $\mathrm{E}\, |\eta_i(\theta)| < \infty$ *for all* $\theta \in \Theta$, *and* $\bar{\eta}_n(\cdot)$ *converges in probability uniformly on* Θ *to* $\mathrm{E}\, \eta_i(\cdot)$.
(iv) $\mathrm{E}\, \eta_i(\theta) = 0$ *for* $\theta \in \Theta$ *only if* $\theta = \theta_0$.
(v) $A_n \xrightarrow{\text{p}} A$, *where* A *is a finite symmetric p.d. matrix.*

Assumption 11.8

(i) $\sqrt{n}\, \bar{\eta}_n(\theta_0) \xrightarrow{\text{d}} \mathcal{N}_r(0, D)$, *where* D *is a finite symmetric p.d. matrix.*
(ii) *The function* η_i *is continuously differentiable in an open neighborhood of* θ_0 *and the matrix* $P = \mathrm{E}\, \eta_i'(\theta_0)$ *is finite with rank* $p \leq r$.

The next set of theorems, whose proof is based on the methods discussed in Chapter 15, generalizes to nonlinear settings the results obtained for linear IV estimators.

Theorem 11.16 *If Assumption 11.7 holds, then* $\hat{\theta}_n$ *exists with probability approaching one and* $\hat{\theta}_n \xrightarrow{\text{p}} \theta_0$.

Theorem 11.17 *If Assumptions 11.7 and 11.8 hold, then* $\sqrt{n}\,(\hat{\theta}_n - \theta_0) \xrightarrow{\text{d}} \mathcal{N}_p(0, AV(\hat{\theta}_n))$, *where* $\mathrm{AV}(\hat{\theta}_n) = (P^\top AP)^{-1} P^\top ADAP(P^\top AP)^{-1}$.

Theorem 11.18 *Given symmetric p.d. matrices* A_n *and* B_n, *let*

$$\hat{\theta}_n = \operatorname*{argmin}_{\theta \in \Theta} \bar{\eta}_n(\theta)^\top A_n \bar{\eta}_n(\theta)$$

and

$$\tilde{\theta}_n = \operatorname*{argmin}_{\theta \in \Theta} \bar{\eta}_n(\theta)^\top B_n \bar{\eta}_n(\theta).$$

If Assumptions 11.7 and 11.8 hold and $B_n \xrightarrow{\text{p}} D^{-1}$, *then:*

(i) $\mathrm{AV}(\tilde{\theta}_n) = (P^\top D^{-1} P)^{-1}$;
(ii) $\mathrm{AV}(\hat{\theta}_n) - \mathrm{AV}(\tilde{\theta}_n) \geq 0$, *with equality only if* $A_n \xrightarrow{\text{p}} D^{-1}$.

The above theorem characterizes an asymptotically best GMM estimator based on a given set of population moment conditions. This estimator corresponds to choosing D^{-1} as the asymptotic weight matrix. If $r = p$, then $\hat{\theta}_n$ satisfies $\bar{\eta}_n(\hat{\theta}_n) = 0$ for any p.d. matrix A_n and $\mathrm{AV}(\hat{\theta}_n) = P^{-1}DP^{-\top}$.

The next theorem provides a way of testing the overidentifying restrictions imposed by the model when $r > p$.

Theorem 11.19 *If Assumptions 11.7 and 11.8 hold and $\tilde{\theta}_n$ is a GMM estimator based on a weight matrix B_n such that $B_n \xrightarrow{\mathrm{p}} D^{-1}$, then $Q_n(\tilde{\theta}_n) = \bar{\eta}_n(\tilde{\theta}_n)^\top B_n \bar{\eta}_n(\tilde{\theta}_n) \xrightarrow{\mathrm{d}} \chi^2_{r-p}$ whenever $r > p$.*

This set of theorems can be generalized to more complicated sampling processes, including heterogeneous and dependent observations (Hansen 1982).

BIBLIOGRAPHIC NOTES

On the asymptotic properties of IV estimators under heteroskedasticity and autocorrelation see White (1984).

On the finite sample properties of IV estimators see the review article by Phillips (1983). Recent contributions focusing on the case when the instruments are weak include Nelson and Startz (1990), Bound, Jaeger and Baker (1995), and Staiger and Stock (1997).

On measures of goodness-of-fit for linear IV estimation and related model selection procedures see Pesaran and Smith (1994). The test of overidentifying restriction in Example 11.9 was originally proposed by Sargan (1958).

On the generalized method of moments see Hansen (1982).

PROBLEMS

11.1 Show that, if $r = k$, then $Q(\hat{\beta}, A) = (\mathbf{Y} - \mathbf{X}\hat{\beta})^\top \mathbf{W} A \mathbf{W}^\top (\mathbf{Y} - \mathbf{X}\hat{\beta}) = 0$ for any p.d. matrix A.

11.2 Show that the class of IV estimators based on the moment condition (11.1) is invariant to a nonsingular linear transformation of (11.1).

11.3 Given a sample $\{(X_i, Y_i, W_i)\}$, show that the simple IV estimator $\hat{\beta} = \sum_i W_i Y_i / \sum_i W_i X_i$ is equal to the ratio of two OLS estimators. Use this result to derive the exact sampling distribution of $\hat{\beta}$ under the assumption that $\{(X_i, Y_i, W_i)\}$ are a random sample from a trivariate normal distribution.

11.4 Prove Theorem 11.1.

11.5 Prove Theorem 11.2.

11.6 Prove Theorem 11.3.

11.7 Prove Theorem 11.4.

11.8 Derive (11.5).

11.9 Prove Theorem 11.8.

11.10 Suppose that the assumptions of Theorem 11.4 hold. Further assume that $\mathrm{E}(U_i \mid Wi) = 0$, $\mathrm{Var}(U_i \mid W_i) = \sigma^2$, and $\mathrm{E}\, W_i W_i^\top = C$, where C is a finite p.d. matrix. Given an IV estimator $\hat{\beta}_n$, show that $\hat{\sigma}_n^2 = n^{-1}(\mathbf{Y} - \mathbf{X}\hat{\beta})^\top(\mathbf{Y} - \mathbf{X}\hat{\beta}) \xrightarrow{\mathrm{p}} \sigma^2$.

11.11 Show that, when $\mathbf{W} = \mathbf{X}$, a generalized 2SLS estimator coincides with a GLS estimator.

11.12 Let $Z_1, \ldots, Z_n$ be a sample from the distribution of a random vector $Z = (X, W_1, W_2, Y)$. Suppose that Z has finite second moments and that

$$\mathrm{E}\, W_1(Y - \beta X) = \mathrm{E}\, W_2(Y - \beta X) = 0 \tag{11.8}$$

for some $\beta \in \Re$.

(i) Show that (11.8) suggests two simple IV estimators of the parameter β, say $\hat{\beta}_{1n}$ and $\hat{\beta}_{2n}$. Are these estimators consistent?

(ii) Show that the 2SLS estimator based on the instrument vector (W_1, W_2) is a convex combination of $\hat{\beta}_{1n}$ and $\hat{\beta}_{2n}$ (*Hint*: The 2SLS estimator may be viewed as a simple IV estimator that uses as instrument the OLS predictor of X, which is of the form $\hat{X} = \hat{\pi}_1 W_1 + \hat{\pi}_2 W_2$ of X).

(iii) Give sufficient conditions for $\hat{\beta}_n = (\hat{\beta}_{1n}, \hat{\beta}_{2n})$ to be asymptotically normal, with an asymptotic variance matrix V whose jkth element is

$$v_{jk} = \frac{\mathrm{E}(Y - \beta X)^2 W_j W_k}{(\mathrm{E}\, X W_j)(\mathrm{E}\, X W_k)}, \qquad j, k = 1, 2.$$

(iv) What conditions are necessary for the 2SLS estimator to be asymptotically efficient in the class of estimators based on the moment conditions (11.8)?

11.13 Let $\hat{\beta}_n$ be the OLS estimator, let $\tilde{\beta}_n$ be a simple IV estimator based on some instrument matrix $\mathbf{W}$, and let $\hat{\delta}_n = \tilde{\beta}_n - \hat{\beta}_n$. Show that, if $\mathrm{E}(\mathbf{Y} \mid \mathbf{X}, \mathbf{W}) = \mathbf{X}\beta$, then $\mathrm{E}(\hat{\delta}_n \mid \mathbf{X}, \mathbf{W}) = 0$. Also show that, if $\mathrm{Var}(\mathbf{Y} \mid \mathbf{X}, \mathbf{W}) = \sigma^2 I_n$, then $\mathrm{Cov}(\hat{\beta}_n, \hat{\delta}_n \mid \mathbf{X}, \mathbf{W}) = 0$ and therefore

$$\mathrm{Var}(\hat{\delta}_n \mid \mathbf{X}, \mathbf{W}) = \mathrm{Var}(\tilde{\beta}_n \mid \mathbf{X}, \mathbf{W}) - \mathrm{Var}(\hat{\beta}_n \mid \mathbf{X}, \mathbf{W}).$$

Under what conditions is the sampling variance of $\hat{\delta}_n$ a nonsingular matrix?

11.14 Prove Theorem 11.11.

11.15 Prove Theorem 11.13.

11.16 Prove Theorem 11.14.

11.17 Prove Theorem 11.15.

12

Linear Models for Panel Data

A *panel*, or longitudinal data set, consists of a sequence of observations, repeated through time, on a set of statistical units (individuals, households, firms, regions, countries, etc.). We focus on cases, such as household panels, where the observed units are sampled from a well defined population. This kind of panels combines features of both cross-section and time series data. As for time series, observations on the same unit tend to be autocorrelated. As for cross-sections, dependence across units may be neglected, at least to a first approximation, and modeling differences in the mean behavior is the crucial issue. At the same time, issues of sample design, sample selection, nonresponse and measurement error also arise, which may affect the representativeness of the underlying population.

Panel data offer two distinct advantages over pure cross-sections or time series. First, because the observed units are followed through time, panel data simplify the analysis of a variety of economic problems, such as intertemporal consumption and labor supply decisions, that would be more difficult to study using pure cross-sections. Second, unlike aggregate macroeconomic time series, panel data make it possible to analyze behavior at the level of the individual units while controlling for unobserved heterogeneity among them. One important source of heterogeneity is missing but relatively constant information on the individual units.

In most of this chapter we assume that the panel is *balanced*, that is, the data consist of T consecutive observations on n sample units. The parameter T is called the *length* of the panel. Further, we deal mainly with the ideal situation where the n sample units have been drawn at random from the population of interest and there are no issues of measurement error or missing data. Both these assumptions are very strong and their practical usefulness depends on the characteristics of the survey.

Many studies based on panel data face the simultaneous problem of unobserved heterogeneity and sample selection. A source of sample selection specific to panel surveys is *attrition*, that is, the fact that some of the units originally included in the panel may be lost through time. Attrition affects, more or less seriously, most microeconomic panels. For example, the NLS-Old Men is a U.S. panel of 5,020 men aged 45 to 59 in 1966, who were interviewed every two years between 1966 and 1983. Because of attrition, due mainly to geographical mobility and death, by 1983 the actual sample was reduced to 2,602 persons.

When attrition is exogenous, that is, unrelated to the response variable Y, it does not bias the information carried by the sample about the population regression function of Y. This is no longer true when attrition is endogenous, that is, systematically related to Y. For example, in household panels, attrition is typically related to important transitions in a person's life: going to college, finding a new job, marriage or divorce, retirement, death. These events are, at the same time, the main object of study using panel data. Attrition cannot therefore be ignored, for it may lead to invalid inference about the population of interest, even when attrition rates are modest. The study of attrition should therefore play a key role in evaluating what can be learned from a panel survey. Some of the relevant issues are addressed in Chapter 18.

12.1 THE BASIC MODEL

Let Y_{it} and X_{it} denote the observations on, respectively, the response variable and a k-vector of covariates for the ith sample unit in the tth period. We assume random sampling and treat observations on different sample units as mutually independent. Our basic model for the data is the following linear model

$$\begin{aligned} \mathrm{E}(Y_{it} \mid X_{i1}, \dots, X_{iT}, \alpha_i) &= \alpha_i + \beta^\top X_{it}, \\ \mathrm{Cov}(Y_{it}, Y_{is} \mid X_{i1}, \dots, X_{iT}, \alpha_i) &= \begin{cases} \sigma^2, & \text{if } s = t, \\ 0, & \text{otherwise}, \end{cases} \\ i = 1, \dots, n, &\qquad s, t = 1, \dots, T. \end{aligned} \tag{12.1}$$

Model (12.1) extends the classical linear model by introducing a set $\alpha_1, \dots, \alpha_n$ of unit-specific intercepts, or "individual effects", which are meant to capture time-invariant unobserved heterogeneity, that is, differences in the expected behavior of the sample units that cannot be attributed to the observed differences in their covariate vector. The model differs from the SURE model introduced in Section 7.3.3 for three reasons. First, it excludes any correlation between sample units. Second, it confines heterogeneity to the regression function. Third, it assumes that differences in the regression function across sample units with the same value of X_{it} only arise because of differences in the individual effects. Thus, the model may also be viewed as a special case of the one in Example 7.7, where all the coefficients and not just the intercepts are allowed to vary across sample units.

Model (12.1) may be written more compactly as

$$\begin{aligned} \mathrm{E}(\mathbf{Y}_i \mid \mathbf{X}_i, \alpha_i) &= \iota_T \alpha_i + \mathbf{X}_i \beta, \\ \mathrm{Var}(\mathbf{Y}_i \mid \mathbf{X}_i, \alpha_i) &= \sigma^2 I_T, \qquad i = 1, \dots, n, \end{aligned}$$

where ι_T is a T-vector with elements all equal to one and

$$\mathbf{Y}_i = \begin{pmatrix} Y_{i1} \\ \vdots \\ Y_{iT} \end{pmatrix}, \qquad \mathbf{X}_i = \begin{bmatrix} X_{i1}^\top \\ \vdots \\ X_{iT}^\top \end{bmatrix},$$

respectively a T-vector and a $T \times k$ matrix. Letting

$$\mathbf{D} = I_n \otimes \iota_T = \begin{bmatrix} \iota_T & & \\ & \ddots & \\ & & \iota_T \end{bmatrix}, \qquad \alpha = \begin{pmatrix} \alpha_1 \\ \vdots \\ \alpha_n \end{pmatrix},$$

respectively an $nT \times n$ matrix and an n-vector, the model may be written even more compactly as

$$\mathrm{E}(\mathbf{Y} \mid \mathbf{X}, \alpha) = \mathbf{D}\alpha + \mathbf{X}\beta,$$
$$\mathrm{Var}(\mathbf{Y} \mid \mathbf{X}, \alpha) = \sigma^2 I_{nT},$$

where

$$\mathbf{Y} = \begin{pmatrix} \mathbf{Y}_1 \\ \vdots \\ \mathbf{Y}_n \end{pmatrix}, \qquad \mathbf{X} = \begin{bmatrix} \mathbf{X}_1 \\ \vdots \\ \mathbf{X}_n \end{bmatrix},$$

respectively an nT-vector and an $nT \times k$ matrix. Notice that the columns of the matrix $\mathbf{D}$ correspond to a set of n dummy variables, one for each sample unit. The statistical problem is estimation and inference about the regression parameter β. The vector α of individual effects and the scale parameter σ^2 are treated as nuisance parameters.

This chapter discusses two different approaches to the problem of estimating β. The first approach treats α as a vector of parameters to be estimated jointly with β and σ^2. In this case, model (12.1) is known as the *fixed effects model.* The second approach treats the elements of α as n independent realizations of a latent random variable. With this interpretation, model (12.1) is known as the *random effects model.* Alternatively, the fixed effects model corresponds to the case when inference about β is conditional on the particular set α of realizations of the individual effects, whereas the random effects model corresponds to the case when inference is unconditional.

The choice between the two approaches depends on the phenomenon under examination, the way in which the data have been collected, the population from which they are drawn, and the purpose of the analysis. For example, in analyzing a panel consisting of a small number of regions or countries, one could be interested in assessing specific differences between them. In this case, the fixed effects model may be preferable. If the panel consists instead of a random sample from a large population, then the random effects model may be more appropriate. If the purpose of the analysis is out of sample predictions, then the fixed effects model is more problematic for, strictly speaking, it requires knowledge of the fixed effects.

12.2 THE FIXED EFFECTS MODEL AND THE WITHIN GROUP ESTIMATOR

When α is treated as a vector of parameters to be estimated, model (12.1) satisfies Assumptions 6.2 and 6.3 of the classical linear model. It is therefore natural to consider the OLS estimator of β in the regression of $\mathbf{Y}$ on $\mathbf{D}$ and $\mathbf{X}$. Notice that simply regressing $\mathbf{Y}$ on $\mathbf{X}$ gives a biased and inconsistent estimator of β because of the omission of $\mathbf{D}$. The bias of $\hat{\beta} = (\mathbf{X}^\top\mathbf{X})^{-1}\mathbf{X}^\top\mathbf{Y}$ is

$$\mathrm{E}\,\hat{\beta} - \beta = (\mathbf{X}^\top\mathbf{X})^{-1}\mathbf{X}^\top\mathbf{D}\alpha = (\sum_i \mathbf{X}_i^\top\mathbf{X}_i)^{-1}(T\sum_i \bar{X}_i\alpha_i),$$

where $\bar{X}_i = T^{-1}\sum_t X_{it}$, which is equal to zero only if $\mathbf{X}^\top\mathbf{D}\alpha = T\sum_i \bar{X}_i\alpha_i = 0$, that is, the individual effects and the average value of the covariates are orthogonal. This condition is clearly satisfied if $\bar{X}_i = 0$ for all i.

The OLS estimator of α and β in the regression of $\mathbf{Y}$ on $\mathbf{D}$ and $\mathbf{X}$ is well defined if the rank of the design matrix $[\mathbf{D}, \mathbf{X}]$ is equal to the dimension $n+k$ of the parameter vector (α, β). Since $[\mathbf{D}, \mathbf{X}]$ is of order $nT \times (n+k)$, a necessary (but not sufficient) condition is that $nT \geq n+k$. When $T = 1$ (the case of a pure cross-section), such a condition is always violated. When $T > 1$, the rank condition on the design matrix is violated if some of the columns of $\mathbf{X}$ can be represented as linear combinations of the columns of $\mathbf{D}$. This rules out the case when X_{it} contains time-invariant covariates.

Thus consider the case when $T \geq 2$ (a genuine panel) and $\text{rank}[\mathbf{D}, \mathbf{X}] = n+k$. Direct computation of the OLS estimator requires inverting an $(n+k) \times (n+k)$ cross-moment matrix, which is not to be recommended unless n is small. This can be avoided by using the Frisch–Waugh theorem (Section 6.2.6). The resulting estimator of β is

$$\hat{\beta}_w = (\mathbf{X}^\top M_D \mathbf{X})^{-1} \mathbf{X}^\top M_D \mathbf{Y},$$

where

$$\begin{aligned} M_D &= I_{nT} - \mathbf{D}(\mathbf{D}^\top \mathbf{D})^{-1} \mathbf{D}^\top \\ &= I_{nT} - (I_n \otimes \iota_T)[(I_n \otimes \iota_T)^\top (I_n \otimes \iota_T)]^{-1} (I_n \otimes \iota_T)^\top \\ &= I_{nT} - (I_n \otimes T^{-1} J_T) \\ &= I_n \otimes L \end{aligned}$$

is a symmetric idempotent $nT \times nT$ block-diagonal matrix, $J_T = \iota_T \iota_T^\top$ is a symmetric $T \times T$ matrix with elements all equal to one and $L = I_T - T^{-1} J_T$ is a symmetric idempotent matrix. The matrix L was introduced in Section 6.2.4 and transforms a vector into the deviations from the average of its elements. Applied to a vector of panel observations, the matrix M_D produces the vector of deviations from the individual-specific averages over the T periods. A typical element of the vector $M_D \mathbf{Y}$ is therefore equal to $Y_{it} - \bar{Y}_i$, with $\bar{Y}_i = T^{-1} \sum_t Y_{it}$, while a typical row of the matrix $M_D \mathbf{X}$ is equal to the vector $X_{it} - \bar{X}_i$. Hence

$$\mathbf{X}^\top M_D \mathbf{X} = \sum_{i=1}^{n} \mathbf{X}_i^\top L \mathbf{X}_i = \sum_{i=1}^{n} \sum_{t=1}^{T} (X_{it} - \bar{X}_i)(X_{it} - \bar{X}_i)^\top,$$

$$\mathbf{X}^\top M_D \mathbf{Y} = \sum_{i=1}^{n} \mathbf{X}_i^\top L \mathbf{Y}_i = \sum_{i=1}^{n} \sum_{t=1}^{T} (X_{it} - \bar{X}_i)(Y_{it} - \bar{Y}_i),$$

and so $\hat{\beta}_w$ corresponds to the OLS estimator in the regression of the deviations $Y_{it} - \bar{Y}_i$ on the deviations $X_{it} - \bar{X}_i$. This transformation eliminates the individual effects α_i, along with any other time-invariant variable. Because it only uses the time variation within each sample unit (added up over all sample units), $\hat{\beta}_w$ is called the *within group* estimator of β. When $T = 2$, the within group estimator corresponds to the OLS estimator in the regression of $\Delta Y_i = Y_{i2} - Y_{i1}$ on $\Delta X_i = X_{i2} - X_{i1}$.

Given model (12.1), $\hat{\beta}_w$ is unbiased for β and its conditional variance is

$$\text{Var}(\hat{\beta}_w \,|\, \mathbf{X}) = \sigma^2 \, (\mathbf{X}^\top M_D \mathbf{X})^{-1}.$$

By the Gauss–Markov theorem, $\hat{\beta}_w$ is in fact BLU for β.

To obtain an unbiased estimator of σ^2, notice that the residual vector $\hat{\mathbf{U}}_w = M_D\mathbf{Y} - M_D\mathbf{X}\hat{\beta}_w$ may be represented as $\hat{\mathbf{U}}_w = M_*\mathbf{Y}$, where

$$M_* = M_D - M_D\mathbf{X}(\mathbf{X}^\top M_D\mathbf{X})^{-1}\mathbf{X}^\top M_D$$

is a symmetric idempotent matrix such that $M_*\mathbf{X} = 0$ and

$$\operatorname{tr} M_* = \operatorname{tr}(M_D) - \operatorname{tr}[M_D\mathbf{X}(\mathbf{X}^\top M_D\mathbf{X})^{-1}\mathbf{X}^\top M_D] = nT - n - k.$$

Under the assumptions of the fixed effects model

$$\mathrm{E}(\hat{\mathbf{U}}_w^\top\hat{\mathbf{U}}_w \,|\, \mathbf{X}) = \mathrm{E}(\mathbf{Y}^\top M_*\mathbf{Y} \,|\, X) = \operatorname{tr}[M_*\,\mathrm{E}(\mathbf{Y}\mathbf{Y}^\top) \,|\, \mathbf{X}] = (nT - n - k)\sigma^2.$$

An unbiased estimator of σ^2 is therefore

$$s_w^2 = [n(T-1) - k]^{-1}\hat{\mathbf{U}}_w^\top\hat{\mathbf{U}}_w.$$

Finally, an unbiased estimator of α is $\hat{\alpha} = (\hat{\alpha}_1, \ldots, \hat{\alpha}_n)$, where

$$\hat{\alpha}_i = \bar{Y}_i - \hat{\beta}_w^\top\bar{X}_i, \qquad i = 1, \ldots, n.$$

As far as the asymptotic properties are concerned, it is useful to distinguish between the case in which $n \to \infty$ with T fixed, and the case in which $T \to \infty$ with n fixed. The first case represents situations where the panel is short but contains a large number of sample units, while the second case represents situations where the sample size is small but each sample unit is observed for a relatively long period.

When $n \to \infty$, there is an important difference between the fixed effects model and the linear models discussed in earlier chapters. Because the parameter vector to be estimated now includes α, the dimensionality of the parameter space is $n + k$ and grows with the sample size. This is known as an *incidental parameter problem.*

When $T \to \infty$ with n fixed, $\hat{\beta}_w$ is consistent for β provided that $T^{-1}\mathbf{X}^\top M_D\mathbf{U} \xrightarrow{p} 0$ and $T^{-1}\mathbf{X}^\top M_D\mathbf{X}$ converges in probability to a finite p.d. matrix. When $n \to \infty$ with T fixed, $\hat{\beta}_w$ is consistent for β provided that $n^{-1}\mathbf{X}^\top M_D\mathbf{U} \xrightarrow{p} 0$ and $n^{-1}\mathbf{X}^\top M_D\mathbf{X}$ converges in probability to a finite p.d. matrix. Thus, the within group estimator $\hat{\beta}_w$ is generally consistent for β either as $T \to \infty$ or $n \to \infty$. The estimator $\hat{\alpha}$ displays instead a different behavior in the two cases. Because

$$\operatorname{Var}(\hat{\alpha}_i \,|\, \mathbf{X}) = \frac{\sigma^2}{T} + \sigma^2\,\bar{X}_i^\top(\mathbf{X}^\top M_D\mathbf{X})^{-1}\bar{X}_i, \tag{12.2}$$

the sampling variance of $\hat{\alpha}$ does not vanish as $n \to \infty$ with T fixed, but tends instead to σ^2/T. For the sampling variance of $\hat{\alpha}$ to vanish, and therefore for $\hat{\alpha}$ to be consistent, it is necessary that $T \to \infty$ with n fixed.

12.3 THE RANDOM EFFECTS MODEL

We now consider the case when the individual effects α_i are treated as realizations of a latent random variable. Without loss of generality we assume the marginal distribution of the individual effects to have zero mean. In Section 12.3.1 we derive estimators of

β based on the assumption that the individual effects are mean independent of the observed covariates, that is,

$$\mathrm{E}(\alpha_i \mid \mathbf{X}_i) = 0, \qquad i = 1, \ldots, n. \tag{12.3}$$

In Section 12.3.3 we discuss ways of testing this assumption, while in Section 12.5 we present a method of estimating β that does not require (12.3) to hold.

12.3.1 THE GLS AND THE BETWEEN GROUP ESTIMATORS

Given model (12.1) and assumption (12.3), the law of iterated expectations implies

$$\mathrm{E}(Y_{it} \mid \mathbf{X}_i) = \mathrm{E}[\mathrm{E}(Y_{it} \mid \mathbf{X}_i, \alpha_i) \mid \mathbf{X}_i] = \beta^\top X_{it},$$

for every i and all t. Hence, both the OLS and the within group estimator are now unbiased for the regression parameter β.

Under the further assumption that $\mathrm{Var}(\alpha_i \mid \mathbf{X}_i)$ is finite and equal to σ_α^2, we also get

$$\mathrm{Cov}(Y_{it}, Y_{is} \mid \mathbf{X}_i) = \begin{cases} \sigma^2 + \sigma_\alpha^2, & \text{if } s = t, \\ \sigma_\alpha^2, & \text{otherwise.} \end{cases} \tag{12.4}$$

The presence of the random individual effects therefore has two consequences. First, observations corresponding to the same sample unit, although homoskedastic, are autocorrelated. Second, this autocorrelation does not die out as the time distance between Y_{it} and Y_{is} increases, but remains constant and equal to $\sigma^2/(\sigma^2 + \sigma_\alpha^2)$. For this reason, observations on the same sample unit are said to be *equicorrelated.*

Model (12.1)–(12.4) is known as the *variance component model* and represents a simple generalization of the model introduced in Example 3.8. It may be further generalized by introducing a third component of variance in order to capture unobserved temporal heterogeneity (see for example Hsiao 1986).

The variance component model may be represented more compactly as

$$\begin{aligned} \mathrm{E}(\mathbf{Y}_i \mid \mathbf{X}_i) &= \mathbf{X}_i\beta, \\ \mathrm{Var}(\mathbf{Y}_i \mid \mathbf{X}_i) &= \Sigma, \qquad i = 1, \ldots, n, \end{aligned}$$

where Σ is the $T \times T$ matrix

$$\Sigma = \begin{bmatrix} \sigma^2 + \sigma_\alpha^2 & \sigma_\alpha^2 & \cdots & \sigma_\alpha^2 \\ \sigma_\alpha^2 & \sigma^2 + \sigma_\alpha^2 & \cdots & \sigma_\alpha^2 \\ \vdots & \vdots & & \vdots \\ \sigma_\alpha^2 & \sigma_\alpha^2 & \cdots & \sigma^2 + \sigma_\alpha^2 \end{bmatrix} = \sigma^2 I_T + \sigma_\alpha^2 J_T.$$

An even more compact representation is

$$\begin{aligned} \mathrm{E}(\mathbf{Y} \mid \mathbf{X}) &= \mathbf{X}\beta, \\ \mathrm{Var}(\mathbf{Y} \mid \mathbf{X}) &= I_n \otimes \Sigma = \sigma^2 \Omega, \end{aligned}$$

where Ω is the $nT \times nT$ matrix

$$\Omega = I_{nT} + \frac{T\sigma_\alpha^2}{\sigma^2} H_D \tag{12.5}$$

and $H_D = I_n \otimes T^{-1}J_T = I_{nT} - M_D$ is a symmetric idempotent matrix.

Because the variance of $\mathbf{Y}$ is not a scalar matrix, the OLS and the within group estimators, although both unbiased for β, are inefficient. In addition, the classical formula for the sampling variance of the OLS estimator is incorrect.

The BLU estimator of β is the GLS estimator

$$\tilde{\beta} = (\sum_i \mathbf{X}_i^\top \Sigma^{-1}\mathbf{X}_i)^{-1} \sum_i \mathbf{X}_i^\top \Sigma^{-1}\mathbf{Y}_i = (\mathbf{X}^\top \Omega^{-1}\mathbf{X})^{-1}\mathbf{X}^\top \Omega^{-1}\mathbf{Y}.$$

In order to interpret this estimator, the following result is very useful.

Lemma 12.1 *If $\Omega = I + \lambda H$, where $\lambda \geq 0$ is a scalar and H is a symmetric idempotent matrix, then*

$$\Omega^{-1} = I + \left(\frac{1}{1+\lambda} - 1\right) H.$$

Applying Lemma 12.1 to (12.5) gives

$$\Omega^{-1} = I_{nT} + \left(\frac{\sigma^2}{\sigma^2 + T\sigma_\alpha^2} - 1\right) H_D = M_D + \psi H_D,$$

where $\psi = \sigma^2/(\sigma^2 + T\sigma_\alpha^2)$. Thus,

$$\tilde{\beta} = (\mathbf{X}^\top M_D \mathbf{X} + \psi \mathbf{X}^\top H_D \mathbf{X})^{-1}(\mathbf{X}^\top M_D \mathbf{Y} + \psi \mathbf{X}^\top H_D \mathbf{Y}), \tag{12.6}$$

where $H_D\mathbf{Y}$ is a vector whose typical element is equal to $\bar{Y}_i$, while $H_D\mathbf{X}$ is a matrix whose typical row is equal to the vector $\bar{X}_i$.

Notice that $0 < \psi \leq 1$ and consider first the two extreme cases. If $\psi = 1$, then $\Omega^{-1} = M_D + H_D = I_{nT}$ and so $\tilde{\beta} = (\mathbf{X}^\top\mathbf{X})^{-1}\mathbf{X}^\top\mathbf{Y}$, which is simply the OLS estimator in the pooled regression of $\mathbf{Y}$ on $\mathbf{X}$. This case occurs when $\sigma_\alpha^2 = 0$, that is, individual effects are absent. On the other hand, if $\psi = 0$, then $\tilde{\beta} = (\mathbf{X}^\top M_D\mathbf{X})^{-1}\mathbf{X}^\top M_D\mathbf{Y}$, which is simply the within group estimator. Because $\psi \to 0$ if $T \to \infty$, this shows that in long panels the GLS estimator tends to coincide with the within group estimator.

If $0 < \psi < 1$, then (12.6) shows that the GLS estimator may be represented as a matrix weighted average of two alternative estimators of β, that is,

$$\tilde{\beta} = C\hat{\beta}_w + (I_k - C)\hat{\beta}_b,$$

where $C = (\mathbf{X}^\top M_D \mathbf{X} + \psi \mathbf{X}^\top H_D \mathbf{X})^{-1}\mathbf{X}^\top M_D\mathbf{X}$ is a $k \times k$ matrix, $\hat{\beta}_w$ is the within group estimator and

$$\hat{\beta}_b = (\mathbf{X}^\top H_D\mathbf{X})^{-1}\mathbf{X}^\top H_D\mathbf{Y} = (\sum_i \bar{X}_i\bar{X}_i^\top)^{-1}\sum_i \bar{X}_i\bar{Y}_i$$

is the OLS estimator in the regression of $\bar{Y}_i$ on $\bar{X}_i$. Because it only uses the differences in the time averages between sample units, $\hat{\beta}_b$ is called the *between group* estimator.

The between group estimator is based on the fact that, under the assumptions of the variance component model,

$$\mathrm{E}(\bar{Y}_i \mid \mathbf{X}_i) = \beta^\top \bar{X}_i,$$
$$\mathrm{Var}(\bar{Y}_i \mid \mathbf{X}_i) = \sigma_\alpha^2 + T^{-1}\sigma^2, \qquad i = 1, \ldots, n.$$

Thus, under the model assumptions, the between group estimator is unbiased for β and its conditional variance is

$$\mathrm{Var}(\hat{\beta}_b \,|\, \mathbf{X}) = (\sigma_\alpha^2 + T^{-1}\sigma^2)(\mathbf{X}^\top H_D \mathbf{X})^{-1}.$$

Because the panel is balanced, the between group estimator is actually BLU for the grouped data.

It is easy to verify that $\Omega^{-1} = \Gamma^2$, where

$$\Gamma = M_D + \sqrt{\psi} H_D = I_{nT} - (1 - \sqrt{\psi}) H_D$$

is a symmetric p.d. matrix. If ψ was known, then the GLS estimator could simply be obtained by an OLS regression of $Y_{it} - (1 - \sqrt{\psi})\bar{Y}_i$ on $X_{it} - (1 - \sqrt{\psi})\bar{X}_i$. When ψ is replaced by some consistent estimator $\hat{\psi}$, the resulting feasible GLS estimator can be shown to be asymptotically equivalent to $\tilde{\beta}$.

In order to consistently estimate ψ as $n \to \infty$ with T fixed, one needs to estimate σ^2 and $\sigma^2 + T\sigma_\alpha^2$ consistently. A consistent estimator of σ^2 is the within group estimator s_w^2, while a consistent estimator of $\sigma_\alpha^2 + T^{-1}\sigma^2$ is the scale estimator obtained from the between group regression, that is,

$$s_b^2 = (n-k)^{-1} \sum_{i=1}^n (\bar{Y}_i - \bar{X}_i^\top \hat{\beta}_b)^2.$$

An estimator that is consistent for ψ as $n \to \infty$ is therefore $\hat{\psi} = s_w^2/(T s_b^2)$.

12.3.2 TESTING FOR INDIVIDUAL EFFECTS

In the fixed effects model, testing for the presence of individual effects amounts to testing the hypothesis $\mathrm{H}_0\colon \alpha_{i+1} - \alpha_i = 0$, $i = 1, \ldots, n-1$, that the individual effects do not differ from each other. A classical F-test rejects H_0 for large values of the statistic

$$F = \frac{(\hat{\mathbf{U}}^\top \hat{\mathbf{U}} - \hat{\mathbf{U}}_w^\top \hat{\mathbf{U}}_w)/(n-1)}{\hat{\mathbf{U}}_w^\top \hat{\mathbf{U}}_w / [n(T-1) - k]},$$

where $\hat{\mathbf{U}}$ is the residual vector from an OLS regression of $\mathbf{Y}$ on a constant and $\mathbf{X}$, and $\hat{\mathbf{U}}_w$ is the residual vector associated with the within group estimator. If the conditional distribution of $\mathbf{Y}$ is Gaussian, then the statistic F is distributed as $F_{n-1, n(T-1)-k}$ under H_0.

In the random effects model, testing for the presence of individual effects amounts instead to testing the hypothesis H_0: $\sigma_\alpha^2 = 0$ that their distribution is degenerate. A simple score test of this hypothesis has been proposed by Breusch and Pagan (1980).

Using the fact that the vectors $M_D \mathbf{Y}$ and $H_D \mathbf{Y}$ are orthogonal, the log-likelihood function for the Gaussian variance component model is easily seen to be

$$\begin{aligned} L(\theta) = c &+ \frac{nT}{2} \ln 2\pi - \frac{n(T-1)}{2} \ln \sigma^2 - \frac{n}{2} \ln \sigma_*^2 \\ &- \frac{1}{2\sigma^2} \sum_i (\mathbf{Y}_i - \mathbf{X}_i \beta)^\top L (\mathbf{Y}_i - \mathbf{X}_i \beta) - \frac{1}{2\sigma_*^2} \sum_i (\bar{Y}_i - \bar{X}_i^\top \beta)^2, \end{aligned}$$

where $\theta = (\beta, \sigma^2, \sigma_\alpha^2)$, c is an arbitrary constant and $\sigma_*^2 = \sigma^2 + T\sigma_\alpha^2$. The relevant components of the likelihood score are

$$\frac{\partial L(\theta)}{\partial \sigma^2} = -\frac{n(T-1)}{2\sigma^2} - \frac{n}{2\sigma_*^2} + \frac{1}{2\sigma^4}\sum_i (\mathbf{Y}_i - \mathbf{X}_i\beta)^\top L(\mathbf{Y}_i - \mathbf{X}_i\beta) + \frac{1}{2\sigma_*^4}\sum_i (\bar{Y}_i - \bar{X}_i^\top \beta)^2$$

and

$$\frac{\partial L(\theta)}{\partial \sigma_\alpha^2} = -\frac{nT}{2\sigma_*^2} + \frac{T^2}{2\sigma_*^4}\sum_i (\bar{Y}_i - \bar{X}_i^\top \beta)^2.$$

The information matrix is easily seen to be block-diagonal with respect to β and $(\sigma^2, \sigma_\alpha^2)$, and the block corresponding to $(\sigma^2, \sigma_\alpha^2)$ is

$$I^*(\theta) = \begin{bmatrix} \dfrac{T-1}{2\sigma^4} + \dfrac{1}{2\sigma_*^2} & \dfrac{T}{2\sigma_*^2} \\ \dfrac{T}{2\sigma_*^2} & \dfrac{T^2}{2\sigma_*^2} \end{bmatrix}.$$

Evaluating at the constrained ML estimator $\tilde{\theta} = (\hat{\beta}, \hat{\sigma}^2, 0)$, where $\hat{\beta}$ is the OLS estimator and $\hat{\sigma}^2$ is the mean squared deviation of the OLS residuals $\hat{U}_{it} = Y_{it} - X_{it}^\top \hat{\beta}$, gives

$$\frac{\partial L(\tilde{\theta})}{\partial \sigma^2} = -\frac{nT}{2\hat{\sigma}^2} - \frac{nT\hat{\sigma}^2}{2\hat{\sigma}_*^4} = 0,$$

$$\frac{\partial L(\tilde{\theta})}{\partial \sigma_\alpha^2} = -\frac{nT}{2\hat{\sigma}^2} + \frac{1}{2\hat{\sigma}^4}\sum_i \Big(\sum_t \hat{U}_{it}\Big)^2$$

and

$$I^*(\tilde{\theta}) = \frac{nT}{2\hat{\sigma}^4}\begin{bmatrix} 1 & 1 \\ 1 & T \end{bmatrix}.$$

Hence, a score test rejects the null hypothesis for large values of the statistic $\xi^S = a\,[\partial L(\tilde{\theta})/\partial \sigma_\alpha^2]^2$, where $a = 2\hat{\sigma}^4/[nT(T-1)]$ is the lower-right element of the inverse of $I^*(\tilde{\theta})$. Thus, the score test statistic is

$$\begin{aligned} \xi^S &= \frac{2\hat{\sigma}^4}{nT(T-1)}\left(\frac{nT}{2\hat{\sigma}^2}\right)^2 \left[\frac{1}{nT\hat{\sigma}^2}\sum_i \Big(\sum_t \hat{U}_{it}\Big)^2 - 1\right]^2 \\ &= \frac{nT}{2(T-1)}\left[\frac{\sum_i (\sum_t \hat{U}_{it})^2}{\sum_i \sum_t \hat{U}_{it}^2} - 1\right]^2. \end{aligned}$$

Under the null hypothesis, the asymptotic distribution of ξ^S is chi-square with one degree of freedom.

12.3.3 SPECIFICATION TESTS

In practice, different inferences about β are sometimes obtained depending on which of the three estimators is used: within group, between group or GLS. This is more often the case in short panels, where the sample units are only observed for a few periods.

The crucial problem is the validity of the assumption that $\mathrm{E}(\alpha_i \,|\, \mathbf{X}_i) = 0$ for all i, which underlies the variance component model. Under this assumption, the individual effects are uncorrelated with the covariates. If model (12.1) holds but $\mathrm{E}(\alpha_i \,|\, \mathbf{X}_i) \neq 0$, then the within group estimator remains unbiased but the GLS and the between group estimators are biased and inconsistent. Specification tests of the null hypothesis $\mathrm{H}_0\colon \mathrm{E}(\alpha \,|\, \mathbf{X}) = 0$ may therefore be based on any of the following differences

$$\hat{\delta}_1 = \hat{\beta}_w - \tilde{\beta}, \qquad \hat{\delta}_2 = \hat{\beta}_b - \tilde{\beta}, \qquad \hat{\delta}_3 = \hat{\beta}_w - \hat{\beta}_b.$$

Because $\tilde{\beta} = C\hat{\beta}_w + (I_k - C)\hat{\beta}_b$, we get

$$\hat{\delta}_1 = (I_k - C)(\hat{\beta}_w - \hat{\beta}_b) = (I_k - C)\hat{\delta}_3,$$
$$\hat{\delta}_2 = -C(\hat{\beta}_w - \hat{\beta}_b) = -C\hat{\delta}_3.$$

For a panel of fixed length T, the matrices $I_k - C$ and C are nonsingular and so the three statistics, being nonsingular linear transformations of each other, lead to the same test. Because $I_k - C \to 0$ as $T \to \infty$, tests based on $\hat{\delta}_1$ should however be used only when T is small.

Let $\hat{\delta}_n$ denote any of the differences $\hat{\delta}_1$, $\hat{\delta}_2$ or $\hat{\delta}_3$ for a fixed T. Because $\mathrm{E}(\hat{\delta}_n \,|\, \mathbf{X}) = 0$ if H_0 is true and $\mathrm{E}(\hat{\delta}_n \,|\, \mathbf{X}) \neq 0$ if H_0 is incorrect, large values of the norm of the vector $\hat{\delta}_n$ are evidence against H_0. Rejection of H_0, however, does not imply that the between group estimator is consistent, because the presence of measurement errors or, more generally, incorrect specification of (12.1) may invalidate this estimator as well.

Given mild regularity conditions, it can be shown that, as $n \to \infty$, $\sqrt{n}\,\hat{\delta}_n \xrightarrow{\mathrm{d}} \mathcal{N}_k(0, \mathrm{AV}(\hat{\delta}_n))$ under H_0. If $\hat{\Delta}_n$ is a consistent p.d. estimator of $\mathrm{AV}(\hat{\delta}_n)$, one can then reject H_0 for large values of the statistic

$$\xi_n = n\,\hat{\delta}_n^\top \hat{\Delta}_n^{-1} \hat{\delta}_n.$$

It is easy to verify that $\xi_n \xrightarrow{\mathrm{d}} \chi^2_k$ under H_0.

Hausman (1978) showed that, for short panels, a test based on ξ_n is asymptotically equivalent to a classical F-test of the hypothesis that $\gamma = 0$ in the artificial regression model

$$Y_{it} - (1 - \sqrt{\hat{\psi}})\bar{Y}_i = \beta^\top[X_{it} - (1 - \sqrt{\hat{\psi}})\bar{X}_i] + \gamma^\top(X_{it} - \bar{X}_i) + U^*_{it}.$$

To see this, consider the difference $\hat{\delta}_1 = \hat{\beta}_w - \tilde{\beta}$ between the within group and the GLS estimators. Because the GLS estimator is BLU for β under H_0, we get

$$\mathrm{Var}(\hat{\delta}_1 \,|\, \mathbf{X}) = \mathrm{Var}(\hat{\beta}_w \,|\, \mathbf{X}) - \mathrm{Var}(\tilde{\beta} \,|\, \mathbf{X}).$$

A consistent estimator of $\mathrm{Var}(\hat{\delta}_1 \,|\, \mathbf{X})$ under H_0 is therefore

$$\widehat{\mathrm{Var}}\,\hat{\delta}_1 = s_w^2\,[(\hat{\mathbf{X}}^\top\hat{\mathbf{X}})^{-1} - (\tilde{\mathbf{X}}^\top\tilde{\mathbf{X}})^{-1}],$$

where $\hat{\mathbf{X}} = M_D\mathbf{X}$, $\tilde{\mathbf{X}} = \hat{\Gamma}\mathbf{X}$ and $\hat{\Gamma} = M_D + \sqrt{\hat{\psi}}H_D$. Now let $\hat{\mathbf{Y}} = M_D\mathbf{Y}$ and $\tilde{\mathbf{Y}} = \hat{\Gamma}\mathbf{Y}$, and notice that $\hat{\mathbf{X}}^\top\hat{\mathbf{X}} = \hat{\mathbf{X}}^\top\tilde{\mathbf{X}}$ and $\hat{\mathbf{X}}^\top\hat{\mathbf{Y}} = \hat{\mathbf{X}}^\top\tilde{\mathbf{Y}}$ since $M_D H_D = 0$. Thus

$$\begin{aligned}
\hat{\mathbf{X}}^\top\hat{\mathbf{X}}\hat{\delta}_1 &= \hat{\mathbf{X}}^\top\hat{\mathbf{X}}[(\hat{\mathbf{X}}^\top\hat{\mathbf{X}})^{-1}\hat{\mathbf{X}}^\top\hat{\mathbf{Y}} - (\tilde{\mathbf{X}}^\top\tilde{\mathbf{X}})^{-1}\tilde{\mathbf{X}}^\top\tilde{\mathbf{Y}}] \\
&= \hat{\mathbf{X}}^\top\hat{\mathbf{Y}} - \hat{\mathbf{X}}^\top\hat{\mathbf{X}}(\tilde{\mathbf{X}}^\top\tilde{\mathbf{X}})^{-1}\tilde{\mathbf{X}}^\top\tilde{\mathbf{Y}} \\
&= \hat{\mathbf{X}}^\top\tilde{M}\tilde{\mathbf{Y}},
\end{aligned}$$

with $\tilde{M} = I_k - \tilde{\mathbf{X}}(\tilde{\mathbf{X}}^\top\tilde{\mathbf{X}})^{-1}\tilde{\mathbf{X}}^\top$. Furthermore

$$\begin{aligned}
(\hat{\mathbf{X}}^\top\hat{\mathbf{X}})^{-1}(\widehat{\operatorname{Var}}\,\hat{\delta}_1)^{-1}(\hat{\mathbf{X}}^\top\hat{\mathbf{X}})^{-1} &= s_w^{-2}[\hat{\mathbf{X}}^\top\hat{\mathbf{X}} - \hat{\mathbf{X}}^\top\hat{\mathbf{X}}(\tilde{\mathbf{X}}^\top\tilde{\mathbf{X}})^{-1}\hat{\mathbf{X}}^\top\hat{\mathbf{X}}]^{-1} \\
&= s_w^{-2}(\hat{\mathbf{X}}^\top\tilde{M}\hat{\mathbf{X}})^{-1}.
\end{aligned}$$

The difference test statistic

$$\xi_1 = n s_w^{-2}\,\tilde{\mathbf{Y}}^\top\tilde{M}\hat{\mathbf{X}}(\hat{\mathbf{X}}^\top\tilde{M}\hat{\mathbf{X}})^{-1}\hat{\mathbf{X}}^\top\tilde{M}\tilde{\mathbf{Y}}$$

is therefore proportional to the statistic of a classical F-test of significance of $M_D\mathbf{X}$ in the OLS regression of $\hat{\Gamma}\mathbf{Y}$ on $\hat{\Gamma}\mathbf{X}$ and $M_D\mathbf{X}$.

12.4 UNBALANCED PANELS

In this section we show how the within group and the GLS estimators can be generalized to the case of unbalanced panels where, because of sample attrition and new entry, the sample units are not all observed for the same number of periods.

Since the vector Y_i and the matrix X_i now have T_i rows, where $T_i \geq 2$ denotes the number of periods for which the ith sample unit is observed, the basic linear model (12.1) becomes

$$\begin{aligned}
\mathrm{E}(\mathbf{Y}_i \,|\, \mathbf{X}_i, \alpha_i) &= \iota_{T_i}\alpha_i + \mathbf{X}_i\beta, \\
\operatorname{Var}(\mathbf{Y}_i \,|\, \mathbf{X}_i, \alpha_i) &= \sigma^2 I_{T_i}, \qquad i = 1, \ldots, n,
\end{aligned}$$

where ι_{T_i} is a T_i-vector whose elements are all equal to unity. The model may be written more compactly as

$$\begin{aligned}
\mathrm{E}(\mathbf{Y} \,|\, \mathbf{X}, \alpha) &= \mathbf{D}\alpha + \mathbf{X}\beta, \\
\operatorname{Var}(\mathbf{Y} \,|\, \mathbf{X}, \alpha) &= \sigma^2 I_{n\bar{T}},
\end{aligned}$$

where $\mathbf{X}$ is an $n\bar{T} \times k$ matrix, with $\bar{T} = n^{-1}\sum_i T_i$, and $\mathbf{D}$ is the $n\bar{T} \times n$ matrix

$$\mathbf{D} = \begin{bmatrix} \iota_{T_1} & & \\ & \ddots & \\ & & \iota_{T_n} \end{bmatrix}.$$

The within group estimator is again $\hat{\beta}_w = (\mathbf{X}^\top M_D \mathbf{X}^\top)^{-1}\mathbf{X}^\top M_D \mathbf{Y}$, where now $M_D = I_{n\bar{T}} - \mathbf{D}(\mathbf{D}^\top\mathbf{D})^{-1}\mathbf{D}^\top$. Since $\mathbf{D}^\top\mathbf{D} = \operatorname{diag}[T_i, i = 1, \ldots, n]$ and therefore $(\mathbf{D}^\top\mathbf{D})^{-1} = \operatorname{diag}[1/T_i, i = 1, \ldots, n]$, it is easily seen that

$$M_D = \begin{bmatrix} L_1 & & \\ & \ddots & \\ & & L_n \end{bmatrix},$$

where $L_i = I_{T_i} - T_i^{-1}\iota_{T_i}\iota_{T_i}^\top$ is a symmetric idempotent matrix which takes the deviations from the individual-specific averages. The within group estimator may therefore be written

$$\hat\beta_w = (\sum_i \mathbf{X}_i^\top L_i \mathbf{X}_i)^{-1} \sum_i \mathbf{X}_i^\top L_i \mathbf{Y}_i.$$

Turning to the variance component model, the main change with respect to the balanced panel case lies in the conditional variance which is now

$$\operatorname{Var}(\mathbf{Y}_i \mid \mathbf{X}_i) = \sigma^2 \Omega_i, \qquad i = 1, \ldots, n,$$

where $\Omega_i = I_{T_i} + (T_i\sigma_\alpha^2/\sigma^2)\, H_i$ and $H_i = I_{T_i} - L_i = T_i^{-1}\iota_{T_i}\iota_{T_i}^\top$ is a symmetric and idempotent $T_i \times T_i$ matrix. By Lemma 12.1, the inverse of Ω_i is $\Omega_i^{-1} = L_i + \psi_i H_i$, where $\psi_i = \sigma^2/(\sigma^2 + T_i\sigma_\alpha^2)$. Thus,

$$\begin{aligned}\tilde\beta &= (\sum_i \mathbf{X}_i^\top \Omega_i^{-1} \mathbf{X}_i)^{-1} \sum_i \mathbf{X}_i^\top \Omega_i^{-1} \mathbf{Y}_i \\ &= [\sum_i \mathbf{X}_i^\top (L_i + \psi_i H_i)\mathbf{X}_i]^{-1} \sum_i \mathbf{X}_i^\top (L_i + \psi_i H_i)\mathbf{Y}_i,\end{aligned}$$

and again we conclude that $\tilde\beta = C\hat\beta_w + (I_k - C)\hat\beta_b$, where $\hat\beta_b = (\sum_i \bar X_i \bar X_i^\top)^{-1} \sum_i \bar X_i \bar Y_i$ is the between group estimator and

$$C = [\sum_i \mathbf{X}_i^\top (L_i + \psi_i H_i)\mathbf{X}_i]^{-1} \sum_i \mathbf{X}_i^\top L_i \mathbf{X}_i.$$

Notice that $\hat\beta_b$ is no longer BLU as $\operatorname{Var}(\bar Y_i \mid \mathbf{X}_i) = \sigma_\alpha^2 + T_i^{-1}\sigma^2$, which implies that the grouped data are now heteroskedastic.

The crucial issue, however, is not how to extend the various estimators encountered so far to the case of unbalanced panels but, instead, whether it makes sense to use the linear model (12.1) in this case. As shown in the example below, the answer depends on whether or not the probability of missing data is correlated with the response variable.

Example 12.1 Consider a two-period panel where, because of attrition or nonresponse, a fraction of the sample units is lost after the first interview. Let A_i be an indicator of attrition that takes value one or zero depending on whether the sample unit is lost or not. Suppose that the complete data obey a classical linear model without individual effects

$$Y_{it} = \alpha + \beta^\top X_{it} + U_{it}, \qquad t = 1, 2,$$

where $\mathrm{E}(U_{it} \mid \mathbf{X}_i) = 0$. If the complete data were available, then β could be estimated consistently by an OLS regression of Y_{i2} on a constant and X_{i2}. This estimator is not consistent in general when the data are incomplete because of attrition. The model for the data observed in the second period is in fact

$$\mathrm{E}(Y_{i2} \mid \mathbf{X}_i, A_i = 0) = \alpha + \beta^\top X_{i2} + h_i,$$

where $h_i = \mathrm{E}(U_{i2} \mid \mathbf{X}_i, A_i = 0)$. If X_{i2} and h_i are uncorrelated, then β can be estimated consistently by an OLS regression of Y_{i2} on a constant and X_{i2} using the observations for which $A_i = 0$. This is for example the case when h_i depends only on X_{i1} and X_{12} is independent of X_{i1}. On the other hand, if X_{i2} and h_i are correlated, then OLS gives biased and inconsistent estimates of β. The bias of the OLS estimator $\hat{\beta}$ is

$$\operatorname{Bias}\hat{\beta} = [\sum_0 (X_{i2} - \bar{X}_2)(X_{i2} - \bar{X}_2)^\top]^{-1} \sum_0 (X_{12} - \bar{X}_2)h_i,$$

where $\bar{X}_2$ denotes the average of X_{i2} and $\sum_0$ denotes summation, both over the observations for which $A_i = 0$.

To derive an expression for h_i, suppose that the ith unit attrites whenever the perceived net loss C_i of continuing panel participation becomes positive. Let $C_i = \mu_i + V_i$, where μ_i is a systematic component, which may depend on $\mathbf{X}_i$ and other covariates, and V_i is a random component which may be correlated with U_{it}. Assuming that (U_{it}, V_i) have a joint Gaussian distribution with zero mean and conditioning on μ_i, the probability of attrition is

$$\Pr\{A_i = 1\} = \Pr\{C_i > 0\} = \Pr\{V_i > -\mu_i\} = \Phi\left(\frac{\mu_i}{\omega}\right),$$

where $\omega^2 = \operatorname{Var} V_i$ and Φ denotes the $\mathcal{N}(0,1)$ distribution function. Further, by the results in Appendix C.9,

$$\begin{aligned} h_i &= \mathrm{E}(U_{i2} \mid \mathbf{X}_i, V_i \leq -\mu_i) \\ &= \frac{\sigma\omega\rho}{1 - \Phi(\mu_i/\omega)} \int_{-\mu_i}^{\infty} \frac{1}{\omega}\phi\left(\frac{v}{\omega}\right) dv \\ &= \sigma\rho \frac{\phi(\mu_i/\omega)}{1 - \Phi(\mu_i/\omega)}, \end{aligned}$$

where $\sigma^2 = \operatorname{Var} U_{it}$ and ρ denotes the correlation between U_{i2} and V_i. Thus, an OLS regression using the observations available in the second period gives biased and inconsistent estimates of β unless X_{i2} and μ_i are independent or $\rho = 0$. □

12.5 MINIMUM DISTANCE ESTIMATION

The assumptions of the variance component model are very strong, but can be relaxed in order to allow for heteroskedasticity or general forms of autocorrelation in the observations, and for possible correlation between the individual effects and the covariates. The basic idea, due to Chamberlain (1982, 1984), is to fix the panel length T and treat each time period as a single equation in a multivariate regression model. For simplicity we only consider the balanced panel case, although the results in this and the next section are easily generalized to unbalanced panels.

The linear model (12.1) may alternatively be represented as

$$\mathrm{E}(Y_i \mid X_i, \alpha_i) = \alpha_i \iota_T + (I_T \otimes \beta^\top)X_i, \qquad i = 1, \ldots, n,$$

where $Y_i = \operatorname{vec}\mathbf{Y}_i = \mathbf{Y}_i$ is a T-vector and $X_i = \operatorname{vec}\mathbf{X}_i = (X_{i1}, \ldots, X_{iT})$ is a kT-vector. We assume that $(Y_1, X_1), \ldots, (Y_n, X_n)$ are i.i.d. random vectors with finite second moments and $P = \mathrm{E}\, X_i X_i^\top$ is a p.d. matrix. Without loss of generality, we also assume the marginal distribution of α_i to have zero mean.

Because α_i and X_i may be correlated, consider the BLP of α_i given X_i

$$\mathrm{E}^*(\alpha_i \mid X_i) = \sum_{t=1}^{T} \gamma_t^\top X_{it} = \gamma^\top X_i,$$

where $\gamma = (\mathrm{E}\, X_i X_i^\top)^{-1} \mathrm{E}\, X_i \alpha_i$ is a kT-vector. If α_i and X_i are uncorrelated, then $\gamma = 0$ and so $\mathrm{E}^*(\alpha_i \mid X_i) = 0$. If $\mathrm{E}(\alpha_i \mid X_i)$ is linear in X_i, as is the case when the joint distribution of α_i and X_i is multivariate normal, then $\mathrm{E}^*(\alpha_i \mid X_i) = \mathrm{E}(\alpha_i \mid X_i)$. By the law of iterated projections (Exercise 12.12), the BLP of Y_i given X_i is

$$\begin{aligned} \mathrm{E}^*(Y_i \mid X_i) &= \mathrm{E}^*[\mathrm{E}(Y_i \mid X_i, \alpha_i) \mid X_i] \\ &= \iota_T\, \mathrm{E}^*(\alpha_i \mid X_i) + (I_T \otimes \beta^\top) X_i \\ &= \iota_T \gamma^\top X_i + (I_T \otimes \beta^\top) X_i \\ &= \Pi X_i, \end{aligned} \tag{12.7}$$

where $\Pi = \iota_T \gamma^\top + (I_T \otimes \beta^\top)$ is a $T \times kT$ matrix. Thus, if α_i and X_i are correlated, the matrix Π has a distinctive pattern, namely the off-diagonal elements within the same column are all equal. If $T \geq 3$, this restriction is testable. If α_i and X_i are uncorrelated, then $\gamma = 0$ and so $\Pi = I_T \otimes \beta^\top$ is a block-diagonal matrix, which provides the basis for an alternative to the specification tests in Section 12.3.3.

Example 12.2 If $k = 1$ and $T = 3$, then (12.7) becomes

$$\begin{aligned} \mathrm{E}^*(Y_{i1} \mid X_i) &= (\gamma_1 + \beta) X_{i1} + \gamma_2 X_{i2} + \gamma_3 X_{i3}, \\ \mathrm{E}^*(Y_{i2} \mid X_i) &= \gamma_1 X_{i1} + (\gamma_2 + \beta) X_{i2} + \gamma_3 X_{i3}, \\ \mathrm{E}^*(Y_{i3} \mid X_i) &= \gamma_1 X_{i1} + \gamma_2 X_{i2} + (\gamma_3 + \beta) X_{i3}. \end{aligned}$$

In this case, Π is the 3×3 matrix

$$\Pi = \begin{bmatrix} \gamma_1 + \beta & \gamma_2 & \gamma_3 \\ \gamma_1 & \gamma_2 + \beta & \gamma_3 \\ \gamma_1 & \gamma_2 & \gamma_3 + \beta \end{bmatrix},$$

where the off-diagonal elements within the same column are all equal. □

Relationship (12.7) and the fact that $\Pi X_i = \operatorname{vec} \Pi X_i = (I_T \otimes X_i^\top)\pi$, where $\pi = \operatorname{vec} \Pi$ is a vector of dimension $m = kT^2$, lead to the following multivariate regression model

$$Y_i = (I_T \otimes X_i)^\top \pi + V_i, \qquad i = 1, \ldots, n, \tag{12.8}$$

where, by definition of BLP, the prediction error $V_i = Y_i - \mathrm{E}^*(Y_i \mid X_i)$ is uncorrelated with the covariates, that is, $\mathrm{E}(V_i \otimes X_i) = 0$.

Because model (12.8) is a SURE model with exactly the same covariates in each equation, it follows from Example 7.12 that the vector π may simply be estimated by multivariate least squares. If the matrix $\sum_i X_i X_i^\top$ is nonsingular, then the multivariate OLS estimator of π is

$$\begin{aligned} \hat{\pi}_n &= [\sum_i (I_T \otimes X_i)(I_T \otimes X_i)^\top]^{-1} \sum_i (I_T \otimes X_i) Y_i \\ &= [\sum_i (I_T \otimes X_i X_i^\top)]^{-1} \sum_i (I_T \otimes X_i) Y_i. \end{aligned}$$

The subvector of $\hat{\pi}_n$ corresponding to the tth time period can simply be obtained by the OLS regression of Y_{it} on $X_{i1}, \ldots, X_{iT}$, that is, on the present, past and future values of X_{it}.

The asymptotic properties of $\hat{\pi}_n$ are given by the following theorem.

Theorem 12.1 *Let $V_i = Y_i - (I_T \otimes X_i)^\top \pi$, $i = 1, \ldots, n$, and suppose:*

(i) *$\{(X_i, V_i)\}$ is a sequence of i.i.d. random vectors;*
(ii) *$\mathrm{E}(V_i \otimes X_i) = 0$;*
(iii) *$\mathrm{E}\, X_i X_i^\top = P$, a finite p.d. matrix.*

Then $\hat{\pi}_n \xrightarrow{\mathrm{p}} \pi$ as $n \to \infty$ with T fixed. If, in addition,

$$n^{-1/2} \sum_i (V_i \otimes X_i) \xrightarrow{\mathrm{d}} \mathcal{N}_m(0, \mathrm{E}[V_i V_i^\top \otimes X_i X_i^\top]),$$

then $\sqrt{n}\,(\hat{\pi}_n - \pi) \xrightarrow{\mathrm{d}} \mathcal{N}_m(0, \mathrm{AV}(\hat{\pi}_n))$ where

$$\mathrm{AV}(\hat{\pi}_n) = \mathrm{E}(V_i V_i^\top \otimes P^{-1} X_i X_i^\top P^{-1}).$$

Proof. Assumptions (i)–(iii) imply that $n^{-1}\sum_i (V_i \otimes X_i) \xrightarrow{\mathrm{p}} \mathrm{E}(V_i \otimes X_i) = 0$ and $n^{-1}\sum_i (I_T \otimes X_i X_i^\top) \xrightarrow{\mathrm{p}} I_T \otimes P$, by the WLLN. The first part of the theorem then follows from the expansion

$$\begin{aligned}
\hat{\pi}_n - \pi &= [\sum_i (I_T \otimes X_i X_i^\top)]^{-1} \sum_i (I_T \otimes X_i) V_i \\
&= [n^{-1} \sum_i (I_T \otimes X_i X_i^\top)]^{-1} n^{-1} \sum_i (V_i \otimes X_i).
\end{aligned}$$

Asymptotic normality of $\hat{\pi}_n$ follows from the expansion

$$\sqrt{n}\,(\hat{\pi}_n - \pi) - (I_T \otimes P)^{-1} n^{-1/2} \sum_i (V_i \otimes X_i) = o_p(1)$$

and the fact that $n^{-1/2}\sum_i (V_i \otimes X_i)$ obeys a CLT. Finally

$$\begin{aligned}
\mathrm{AV}(\hat{\pi}_n) &= (I_T \otimes P)^{-1} [\mathrm{E}(V_i V_i^\top \otimes X_i X_i^\top)]\, (I_T \otimes P)^{-1} \\
&= \mathrm{E}(V_i V_i^\top \otimes P^{-1} X_i X_i^\top P^{-1}).
\end{aligned}$$

□

The next theorem provides a consistent estimator of the asymptotic variance of $\hat{\pi}_n$.

Theorem 12.2 *Let $\hat{V}_i = Y_i - (I_T \otimes X_i)^\top \hat{\pi}_n$, $i = 1, \ldots, n$, and*

$$\hat{V}_n = n^{-1} \sum_{i=1}^{n} (\hat{V}_i \hat{V}_i^\top \otimes S_{XX}^{-1} X_i X_i^\top S_{XX}^{-1}),$$

where $S_{XX} = n^{-1}\sum_i X_i X_i^\top$. If the assumptions of Theorem 12.1 hold and X_i has finite fourth moments, then $\hat{V}_n \xrightarrow{\mathrm{p}} \mathrm{AV}(\hat{\pi}_n)$ as $n \to \infty$ with T fixed.

The matrix $\hat{V}_n$ in Theorem 12.2 is the infinitesimal jackknife estimate of the asymptotic variance of $\hat{\pi}_n$. Theorems 12.1 and 12.2 provide the basis for Wald tests of hypotheses about the structure of the projection matrix Π in (12.7). In particular, a test of the hypothesis of lack of correlation between α_i and X_i is simply a test of significance of the leads and lags of X_i.

Consider the special case when $\mathrm{E}(\alpha_i \,|\, X_i)$ is linear in X_i and the prediction errors $\{V_i\}$ are conditionally homoskedastic, that is, $\mathrm{E}(V_i V_i^\top \,|\, X_i) = \Sigma$ does not depend on X_i. In this case

$$\mathrm{E}(V_i V_i^\top \otimes X_i X_i^\top) = \mathrm{E}[\mathrm{E}(V_i V_i^\top \otimes X_i X_i^\top) \,|\, X_i] = \Sigma \otimes P,$$

and the asymptotic variance of $\hat{\pi}_n$ becomes $\mathrm{AV}(\hat{\pi}_n) = \Sigma \otimes P^{-1}$, where Σ can be estimated consistently by $\hat{\Sigma}_n = n^{-1} \sum_i \hat{V}_i \hat{V}_i^\top$.

The multivariate LS estimator $\hat{\pi}_n$ is not fully efficient because it ignores the fact that the elements of the vector π are functions of the parameters in γ and β, namely

$$\pi = \operatorname{vec} \Pi = \operatorname{vec} [\iota_T \gamma^\top + (I_T \otimes \beta^\top)].$$

Because $I_T \otimes \beta^\top = [(\operatorname{vec} I_T) \otimes I_k] \beta$ and $\operatorname{vec}(\iota_T \gamma^\top) = (\iota_T \otimes I_{kt}) \gamma$, the relationship between π and (β, γ) may be written

$$\pi = [(\operatorname{vec} I_T) \otimes I_k,\ \iota_T \otimes I_{kT}] \begin{pmatrix} \beta \\ \gamma \end{pmatrix}, \tag{12.9}$$

where (β, γ) is a vector of dimension $p = k(1+T)$. The above relationship corresponds to a set of linear constraints on the parameter vector $\theta = (\beta, \gamma)$ of the form $R\theta - \pi = 0$, where $R = [(\operatorname{vec} I_T) \otimes I_k\ \iota_T \otimes I_{kT}]$ is a $kT^2 \times p$ matrix whose elements are either zero or one.

One may impose the set of constraints (12.9) by using the minimum distance method. Given a symmetric p.d. matrix A_n, a *minimum distance (MD) estimator* of θ is a solution $\hat{\theta}_n$ to the problem

$$\min_{\theta \in \Re^p} (R\theta - \hat{\pi}_n)^\top A_n (R\theta - \hat{\pi}_n).$$

The MD estimator of β corresponds to the first k elements of $\hat{\theta}_n$. Varying the weight matrix A_n gives a whole class of estimators indexed by the choice of A_n. An MD estimator $\hat{\theta}_n$ necessarily satisfies the normal equations

$$0 = R^\top A_n (R\hat{\theta}_n - \hat{\pi}_n).$$

If the matrix R has rank p, which requires that $T \geq 2$, the matrix $R^\top A_n R$ is nonsingular and so the normal equations have the unique solution

$$\hat{\theta}_n = (R^\top A_n R)^{-1} R^\top A_n \hat{\pi}_n.$$

Notice that $\hat{\theta}_n$ coincides with a GLS-type estimator in a regression of $\hat{\pi}_n$ on R.

The following theorem gives the asymptotic properties of the class of MD estimators when the model is correctly specified, that is, the parameter θ satisfies the set of constraints (12.9).

Theorem 12.3 *Assume that the parameter* θ *satisfies* (12.9). *If the assumptions of Theorem 12.1 hold and* $A_n \xrightarrow{p} A$, *where* A *is a symmetric p.d. matrix, then:*

(i) $\hat{\theta}_n \xrightarrow{p} \theta$;

(ii) $\sqrt{n}\,(\hat{\theta}_n - \theta) \xrightarrow{d} \mathcal{N}_p(0,\, \mathrm{AV}(\hat{\theta}_n))$, *where*

$$\mathrm{AV}(\hat{\theta}_n) = (R^\top AR)^{-1} R^\top A\ \mathrm{AV}(\hat{\pi}_n)\, A^\top R(R^\top AR)^{-1}.$$

Of special interest is the estimator

$$\tilde{\theta}_n = (R^\top \hat{V}_n^{-1} R)^{-1} R^\top \hat{V}_n^{-1} \hat{\pi}_n,$$

based on the weight matrix $A_n = \hat{V}_n^{-1}$, where $\hat{V}_n$ is a consistent p.d. estimator of the asymptotic variance of $\hat{\pi}_n$, such as the infinitesimal jackknife estimator. The fact that $\tilde{\theta}_n$ corresponds to a feasible GLS estimator in the regression of $\hat{\pi}_n$ on R suggests that it may have good efficiency properties in large samples.

Theorem 12.4 *Let* $\hat{\theta}_n = (R^\top A_n R)^{-1} R^\top A_n \hat{\pi}_n$ *and* $\tilde{\theta}_n = (R^\top \hat{V}_n^{-1} R)^{-1} R^\top \hat{V}_n^{-1} \hat{\pi}_n$. *If the assumptions of Theorems 12.2 and 12.3 hold then:*

(i) $\mathrm{AV}(\tilde{\theta}_n) = [R^\top\, \mathrm{AV}(\hat{\pi}_n)^{-1} R]^{-1}$;

(ii) $\mathrm{AV}(\hat{\theta}_n) - \mathrm{AV}(\tilde{\theta}_n) \geq 0$, *with equality only if* $A_n \xrightarrow{p} \mathrm{AV}(\hat{\pi}_n)^{-1}$;

(iii) $n(R\tilde{\theta}_n - \hat{\pi}_n)^\top \hat{V}_n^{-1} (R\tilde{\theta}_n - \hat{\pi}_n) \xrightarrow{d} \chi^2_{m-p}$, *with* $m = kT^2$ *and* $p = k(1+T)$.

The estimator $\tilde{\theta}_n$ is therefore asymptotically efficient in the class of MD estimators based on the set of constraints (12.9). If these constraints are correct, then the minimized value of the criterion that defines such an estimator is asymptotically distributed as chi-square with $k(T^2 - 1 + T)$ degrees of freedom. This result may be used to test the validity of the constraints (12.9) implied by model (12.1).

12.6 IV ESTIMATION

A simple generalization of the linear model (12.1) is

$$\mathrm{E}(Y_{it} \,|\, \mathbf{X}_i, D_i, \alpha_i) = \alpha_i + \beta^\top X_{it} + \gamma^\top D_i, \tag{12.10}$$

where D_i is a q-vector of covariates that represent observed time-invariant characteristics of the sample units. If α_i is correlated with either X_{it} or D_i, the GLS and the between group estimators are biased and inconsistent for β and γ. The within group estimator of β is instead consistent because the individual effects are eliminated when the data are transformed by taking deviations from the individual means over the T periods. This transformation, however, also eliminates all variables that are time-invariant and so γ cannot be estimated.

An alternative is to find appropriate instruments for the variables on the right-hand side of (12.10) and then apply the IV method. This requires prior information on the nature of the correlation between the covariates in the model and the individual effects α_i. In this section we consider cases that are somehow intermediate between the fixed effects model, where all covariates are potentially correlated with α_i, and the variance component model, where no covariate is correlated with α_i.

12.6.1 ASYMPTOTICALLY EFFICIENT IV ESTIMATION

A general framework for asymptotically efficient IV estimation of the linear model (12.10) has been proposed by Arellano and Bover (1995). Although our presentation is based on a static formulation of the statistical model, their framework can also deal with dynamic specifications.

Write model (12.10) as

$$\begin{aligned} Y_{it} &= \beta^\top X_{it} + \gamma^\top D_i + V_{it}, \\ V_{it} &= \alpha_i + U_{it}, \qquad i = 1, \ldots, n, \qquad t = 1, \ldots, T, \end{aligned}$$

where $U_{it} = Y_{it} - \mathrm{E}(Y_{it} \mid \mathbf{X}_i, \alpha_i)$ is a random error with mean zero and variance σ_U^2 conditionally on $(\mathbf{X}_i, \alpha_i)$. A more compact representation is

$$\begin{aligned} \mathbf{Y}_i &= \mathbf{X}_i\beta + \iota_T D_i^\top \gamma + \mathbf{V}_i \\ &= \mathbf{Z}_i\theta + \mathbf{V}_i, \\ \mathbf{V}_i &= \iota_T \alpha_i + \mathbf{U}_i, \qquad i = 1, \ldots, n, \end{aligned}$$

where $\theta = (\beta, \gamma)$ is a vector of dimension $p = k+q$, $\mathbf{Z}_i = [\mathbf{X}_i, \iota_T D_i^\top]$ is a $T \times p$ matrix, and $\mathbf{U}_i = \mathbf{Y}_i - \mathrm{E}(\mathbf{Y}_i \mid \mathbf{X}_i, \alpha_i)$ is a T-vector.

The classical decomposition into between and within group variation can be generalized by considering a nonsingular $T \times T$ matrix

$$M = \begin{bmatrix} H \\ h\iota_T^\top \end{bmatrix},$$

where h is a nonzero scalar and H is a $(T-1) \times T$ matrix of rank $T-1$ with the property that $H\iota_T = 0$. This implies that

$$M\iota_T = \begin{pmatrix} H\iota_T \\ hJ_T \end{pmatrix} = \begin{pmatrix} 0 \\ hT \end{pmatrix},$$

where $J_T = \iota_T\iota_T^\top$. The matrix H may be any of the transformations discussed in Verbeek (1995). For example, H could be the matrix of first differences

$$H = \begin{bmatrix} -1 & 1 & & & \\ & -1 & 1 & & \\ & & \ddots & \ddots & \\ & & & -1 & 1 \end{bmatrix},$$

or could correspond to the first $T-1$ rows of the matrix $I_T - T^{-1}J_T$ used by the within group estimator. As far as the scalar h is concerned, one possibility is to set it equal to T^{-1}.

Using the matrix M to transform the data gives

$$\mathbf{Y}_i^+ = \mathbf{Z}_i^+\theta + \mathbf{V}_i^+, \qquad i = 1, \ldots, n, \tag{12.11}$$

where $\mathbf{Y}_i^+ = M\mathbf{Y}_i$, $\mathbf{Z}_i^+ = M\mathbf{Z}_i$ and

$$\mathbf{V}_i^+ = M\mathbf{V}_i = \begin{pmatrix} H\mathbf{V}_i \\ hT\bar{V}_i \end{pmatrix},$$

with $\bar{V}_i = T^{-1}\sum_t V_{it}$. Because $H\iota_T = 0$, it follows that $H\mathbf{Z}_i = [H\mathbf{X}_i, 0]$ and $H\mathbf{V}_i = H\mathbf{U}_i$. Therefore, this transformation eliminates all individual effects and all time-invariant covariates from the first $T-1$ relationships in (12.11).

Now consider the $[kT(T-1)+m] \times T$ matrix

$$\mathbf{W}_i = \begin{bmatrix} I_{T-1} \otimes X_i & \\ & Z_i^* \end{bmatrix} = \begin{bmatrix} X_i & & & \\ & \ddots & & \\ & & X_i & \\ & & & Z_i^* \end{bmatrix},$$

where $X_i = \operatorname{vec} \mathbf{X}_i$ is a kT-vector and Z_i^* is an m-vector of instrumental variables that are assumed to be uncorrelated with α_i and every U_{it}. The choice of the variables in Z_i^* is discussed in Section 12.6.2. Because, under the model assumptions, the vector X_i is uncorrelated with every U_{it} and the vector Z_i^* is uncorrelated with α_i and every U_{it}, we get

$$0 = \mathrm{E}\, \mathbf{W}_i \mathbf{V}_i^+ = \mathrm{E}\, \mathbf{W}_i M \mathbf{V}_i.$$

If the model is correctly specified, then the parameter θ must satisfy the set of moment restrictions

$$\mathrm{E}\, \eta_i(\theta) = 0, \tag{12.12}$$

where $\eta_i(\theta) = \mathbf{W}_i M(\mathbf{Y}_i - \mathbf{Z}_i\theta)$ is a vector of dimension $r = kT(T-1) + m$ and the expectation is taken with respect to the joint distribution of $(\mathbf{Y}_i, \mathbf{Z}_i, \mathbf{W}_i)$. This set of moment restrictions represents the basis for constructing a class of IV estimators of θ.

The sample counterpart of $\mathrm{E}\, \eta_i(\theta)$ is

$$n^{-1}\sum_{i=1}^n \eta_i(\theta) = n^{-1}\sum_{i=1}^n \mathbf{W}_i M(\mathbf{Y}_i - \mathbf{Z}_i\theta) = n^{-1}\mathbf{W}\mathbf{M}(\mathbf{Y} - \mathbf{Z}\theta),$$

where $\mathbf{M} = I_n \otimes M$ is an $nT \times nT$ matrix, $\mathbf{W} = [\mathbf{W}_1, \ldots, \mathbf{W}_n]$ is an $r \times nT$ matrix, and

$$\mathbf{Y} = \begin{pmatrix} \mathbf{Y}_1 \\ \vdots \\ \mathbf{Y}_n \end{pmatrix}, \qquad \mathbf{Z} = \begin{bmatrix} \mathbf{Z}_1 \\ \vdots \\ \mathbf{Z}_n \end{bmatrix}$$

are, respectively, an nT-vector and an $nT \times p$ matrix. The class of IV estimators based on the moment restrictions (12.12) consists of the set of solutions to problems of the form

$$\min_{\theta \in \Re^p} [\sum_i \eta_i(\theta)]^\top A_n [\sum_i \eta_i(\theta)],$$

where A_n is a symmetric p.d. $r \times r$ matrix. By Theorem 11.5, an estimator is asymptotically efficient in this class if A_n is such that $A_n \xrightarrow{\mathrm{p}} [\operatorname{Var} \mathbf{W}_i \mathbf{V}_i^+]^{-1}$, where

$$\operatorname{Var} \mathbf{W}_i \mathbf{V}_i^+ = \mathrm{E}(\mathbf{W}_i M \Sigma M^\top \mathbf{W}_i^\top)$$

and $\Sigma = \operatorname{Var}(\mathbf{V}_i \,|\, \mathbf{X}_i)$.

Letting $\hat{\Sigma}_n$ be a consistent estimator of Σ, one can show that, under general conditions,

$$n^{-1}\sum_{i=1}^{n} \mathbf{W}_i M \hat{\Sigma}_n M^\top \mathbf{W}_i^\top = n^{-1}\mathbf{W}\mathbf{M}\hat{\Omega}_n\mathbf{M}^\top\mathbf{W}^\top \xrightarrow{\text{p}} \mathrm{E}(\mathbf{W}_i M \Sigma M^\top \mathbf{W}_i^\top),$$

where $\hat{\Omega}_n = I_n \otimes \hat{\Sigma}_n$. An asymptotically efficient IV estimator is therefore a solution to the problem

$$\min_{\theta\in\Re^p} (\mathbf{Y}-\mathbf{Z}\theta)^\top\mathbf{M}^\top\mathbf{W}^\top(\mathbf{W}\mathbf{M}\hat{\Omega}_n\mathbf{M}^\top\mathbf{W}^\top)^{-1}\mathbf{W}\mathbf{M}(\mathbf{Y}-\mathbf{Z}\theta),$$

and must therefore satisfy the set of linear equations

$$0 = \mathbf{Z}^\top\mathbf{M}^\top\mathbf{W}^\top(\mathbf{W}\mathbf{M}\hat{\Omega}_n\mathbf{M}^\top\mathbf{W}^\top)^{-1}\mathbf{W}\mathbf{M}(\mathbf{Y}-\mathbf{Z}\tilde{\theta}_n).$$

If the matrix $\mathbf{WMZ}$ has rank p and $\mathbf{W}\mathbf{M}\hat{\Omega}_n\mathbf{M}^\top\mathbf{W}^\top$ is a p.d. matrix, solving for $\tilde{\theta}_n$ gives the unique solution

$$\begin{aligned}\tilde{\theta}_n = {} & [\mathbf{Z}^\top\mathbf{M}^\top\mathbf{W}^\top(\mathbf{W}\mathbf{M}\hat{\Omega}_n\mathbf{M}^\top\mathbf{W}^\top)^{-1}\mathbf{WMZ}]^{-1} \\ & \times \mathbf{Z}^\top\mathbf{M}^\top\mathbf{W}^\top(\mathbf{W}\mathbf{M}\hat{\Omega}_n\mathbf{M}^\top\mathbf{W}^\top)^{-1}\mathbf{WMY}.\end{aligned}$$

If the model is correctly specified and the regularity conditions of Chapter 11 hold then $\sqrt{n}\,(\tilde{\theta}_n - \theta) \xrightarrow{\text{d}} \mathcal{N}_p(0, \mathrm{AV}(\tilde{\theta}_n))$, where

$$\mathrm{AV}(\tilde{\theta}_n) = \operatorname{plim}\, [n^{-1}\mathbf{Z}^\top\mathbf{M}^\top\mathbf{W}^\top(\mathbf{W}\mathbf{M}\hat{\Omega}_n\mathbf{M}^\top\mathbf{W}^\top)^{-1}\mathbf{WMZ}]^{-1}.$$

It is interesting to notice that an IV estimator based on the moment restrictions (12.12) is essentially invariant to the choice of the linear transformation M. To show this, notice first that

$$\eta_i(\theta) = \mathbf{W}_i M \mathbf{V}_i = \begin{pmatrix} H\mathbf{V}_i \otimes X_i \\ hT\bar{V}_i Z_i^* \end{pmatrix} = \begin{bmatrix} H \otimes I_{kT} & \\ & hT \end{bmatrix} \begin{pmatrix} \operatorname{vec}\mathbf{V}_i X_i^\top \\ \bar{V}_i Z_i^* \end{pmatrix},$$

where we used the fact that, if a and b are column vectors, then $a\otimes b = \operatorname{vec}(ab^\top)$. Now consider the linear transformation $\eta_i^*(\theta) = G\eta_i(\theta)$, where G is a nonsingular matrix. An IV estimator based on η_i^* solves the problem

$$\min_{\theta\in\Re^p} [\sum_i \eta_i^*(\theta)]^\top A_n^* [\sum_i \eta_i^*(\theta)].$$

If $A_n^* = G^{-\top}A_n G^{-1}$, this estimator is numerically the same as the one based on η_i. In particular, consider the data transformation defined by the nonsingular matrix

$$M^* = \begin{bmatrix} H^* \\ h^*\iota_T^\top \end{bmatrix}.$$

Letting $H^* = \Lambda H$ and $h^* = \lambda h$, one gets

$$\eta_i^*(\theta) = \begin{bmatrix} \Lambda H \otimes I_{kT} & \\ & \lambda hT \end{bmatrix} \begin{pmatrix} \operatorname{vec}\mathbf{V}_i X_i^\top \\ \bar{V}_i Z_i^* \end{pmatrix} = G\,\eta_i(\theta),$$

where

$$G = \begin{bmatrix} \Lambda \otimes I_{kT} & \\ & \lambda \end{bmatrix}.$$

Thus, any transformation M^* such that Λ is nonsingular and $\lambda \neq 0$ leads to the same IV estimator.

12.6.2 CHOICE OF INSTRUMENTS

In this section we discuss the choice of the instrument vector Z_i^* to include in the matrix $\mathbf{W}_i$. First notice that the assumption

$$\mathrm{E}\, X_i \mathbf{U}_i^\top = 0, \qquad i = 1, \ldots, n \tag{12.13}$$

and the fact that $H\iota_T = 0$ always make it possible to identify β. In this case, the moment function $\eta_i(\beta)$ is of the form

$$\begin{aligned}\eta_i(\beta) = (I_{T-1} \otimes X_i) H (\mathbf{Y}_i - \mathbf{X}_i \beta) &= (H \otimes X_i)(\mathbf{Y}_i - \mathbf{X}_i \beta) \\ &= (H \otimes I_{kT})(I_T \otimes X_i)(\mathbf{Y}_i - \mathbf{X}_i \beta),\end{aligned}$$

since $(I_{T-1} \otimes X_i) H = (H \otimes X_i)$, and an optimal weight matrix is

$$A_n = [\sum_i (I_{T-1} \otimes X_i) H \Sigma H^\top (I_{T-1} \otimes X_i^\top)]^{-1} = \frac{1}{\sigma_U^2} (HH^\top \otimes \sum_i X_i X_i^\top)^{-1},$$

where we used the fact that, because $H\iota_T = 0$ and $\mathrm{Var}(\mathbf{U}_i \,|\, X_i) = \sigma_U^2 \mathcal{I}_T$,

$$H \Sigma H^\top = \mathrm{Var}(H\mathbf{V}_i \,|\, X_i) = \mathrm{Var}(H\mathbf{U}_i \,|\, X_i) = \sigma_U^2\, HH^\top.$$

An asymptotically efficient IV estimator is therefore obtained by choosing β to minimize the quadratic form

$$[\sum_i (I_T \otimes X_i)(\mathbf{Y}_i - \mathbf{X}_i \beta)]^\top [L \otimes (\sum_i X_i X_i^\top)^{-1}] [\sum_i (I_T \otimes X_i)(\mathbf{Y}_i - \mathbf{X}_i \beta)], \tag{12.14}$$

where $L = H^\top (HH^\top)^{-1} H = I_T - T^{-1} J_T$. It can be shown that this estimator coincides with the within group estimator.

Identifiability of γ on the basis of the moment restrictions (12.12) depends on the choice of the variables in Z_i^* and the prior information about the joint distribution of $(X_i, D_i, \mathbf{U}_i, \alpha_i)$. If all variables in (X_i, D_i) are uncorrelated with α_i, then one can choose $Z_i^* = (X_i, D_i)$. It can be shown that, in this case, an asymptotically efficient IV estimator coincides with the GLS estimator for the variance component model.

Now assume that only some of the covariates are uncorrelated with α_i. Thus, partition the vector X_i as $X_i = (X_{i1}, X_{i2})$ and the vector D_i as $D_i = (D_{i1}, D_{i2})$, where X_{ij} is a vector of dimension $k_j T$ and D_{ji} is a vector of dimension q_j, with $k_1 + k_2 = k$ and $q_1 + q_2 = q$. Suppose, in addition to (12.13), that

$$\mathrm{E}\, X_{i1} \alpha_i = 0, \qquad \mathrm{E}\, D_{i1} \alpha_i = 0, \qquad i = 1, \ldots, n, \tag{12.15}$$

whereas the correlations between X_{i2} and α_i and between D_{i2} and α_i are left unconstrained. Under these assumptions, the moment restrictions (12.12) are satisfied by choosing $Z_i^* = (X_{i1}, D_{i1})$. The resulting IV estimator was originally proposed by Amemiya and MaCurdy (1986). This estimator is asymptotically more efficient than the one proposed by Hausman and Taylor (1981), which is based instead on the instrument vector $Z_i^* = (\bar{X}_{i1}, D_{i1})$, where $\bar{X}_{i1} = T^{-1} \sum_t X_{i1t}$ is the sample average over the T periods of the variables included in X_{i1}. On the other hand, it is quite possible that $\mathrm{E}\, \bar{X}_{i1} \alpha_i = 0$ even when $\mathrm{E}\, X_{i1t} \alpha_i \neq 0$. In this case, the estimator of

Hausman and Taylor is consistent despite the fact that the one of Amemiya and MaCurdy is not.

Stronger assumptions help generate further moment restrictions that can be exploited in estimation. If, for example, the correlation between X_{i2} and α_i is the same in all time periods, that is,

$$\mathrm{E}\, X_{i2t}\alpha_i = \mathrm{E}\, X_{i2s}\alpha_i, \qquad \text{for all } t, s, \tag{12.16}$$

then a further orthogonality condition is

$$\mathrm{E}\, \Delta X_{i2t}\alpha_i = 0, \qquad i = 1, \ldots, n,$$

with $\Delta X_{i2t} = X_{i2t} - X_{i2,t-1}$. In this case, a valid set of instruments is

$$Z_i^* = (X_{i1}, D_{i1}, \Delta X_{i22}, \ldots, \Delta X_{i2T}).$$

The asymptotically efficient estimator in the class of IV estimators based on this set of orthogonality conditions coincides with the one proposed by Breusch, Mizon and Schmidt (1989).

One can generate additional orthogonality conditions, and therefore potentially increase efficiency of estimation, by exploiting specific features of the problem under consideration. Notice, for example, that (12.16) is equivalent to the assumption that X_{i2t} contains a time-invariant component ξ_i that may be correlated with α_i, that is, $X_{i2t} = \xi_i + \epsilon_{it}$, where ϵ_{it} is uncorrelated with ξ_i and α_i for all t. As an alternative to this model, one may instead assume that the growth rate of X_{i2t} contains a time-invariant component ξ_i that may be correlated with α_i, that is,

$$\tilde{X}_{i2t} = \ln X_{i2t} - \ln X_{2i,t-1} = \xi_i + \epsilon_{it}.$$

In this case, a valid set of instruments is $Z_i^* = (X_{i1}, D_{i1}, \Delta\tilde{X}_{i23}, \ldots, \Delta\tilde{X}_{i2T})$, with $T \geq 3$.

The estimators discussed in this section may be ordered on the basis of the amount of prior information that they require to justify their consistency, and therefore on the basis of their degree of "robustness".

1. Estimators based on the moment restrictions (12.13) are the most robust because they only require information on the joint distribution of $(X_i, \mathbf{U}_i)$. In this case, only β is estimable, not γ.
2. Estimators based on $Z_i^* = (\bar{X}_{i1}, D_{i1})$ require, in addition to the validity of (12.13), that

$$\mathrm{E}\, D_i\mathbf{U}_i^\top = 0, \qquad \mathrm{E}\, \bar{X}_{i1}\alpha_i = 0, \qquad \mathrm{E}\, D_{i1}\alpha_i = 0. \tag{12.17}$$

3. Estimators based on $Z_i^* = (X_{i1}, D_{i1})$ require, in addition to the validity of (12.13) and (12.17), that $\mathrm{E}\, X_{i1}\alpha_i = 0$. Notice that cases 2. and 3. only require information on the joint distribution of (X_{i1}, α_i).
4. If further information is available on the joint distribution of (X_{i2}, α_i), then potentially more efficient estimators may be constructed. For example if, in addition to (12.13) and (12.15), (12.16) also holds, then one can choose $Z_i^* = (X_{i1}, D_{i1}, \Delta X_{i22}, \ldots, \Delta X_{2iT})$.

In general, it is the nature of the problem under investigation that suggests which variables in X_i are potentially correlated with the individual effect α_i and why.

The fact that models 1.–4. are obtained by imposing stronger and stronger constraints suggests a sequence of specification tests based on the difference between alternative estimators of β, or of β and γ.

12.6.3 AUTOREGRESSIVE MODELS FOR PANEL DATA

One way of allowing for persistence in a panel is to insert into the model lagged values of the response variable and the covariates. For simplicity, consider the following autoregressive model

$$Y_{it} = \alpha_i + \phi Y_{i,t-1} + \beta^\top X_{i,t-1} + U_{it}, \qquad \{U_{it}\} \sim \text{WN}(0, \sigma^2), \tag{12.18}$$

where β is a k-vector. This model assumes that, conditionally on the individual effect α_i, the BLP of Y_{it} based on the entire past history of the bivariate process $\{(Y_{it}, X_{it})\}$ depends only on the state of the process at time $t-1$. The model contains two sources of persistence: one is the dependence of Y_{it} on $Y_{i,t-1}$ and $X_{i,t-1}$, the other is the presence of the individual effect α_i.

Applying the within group transformation to (12.18) leads to the model

$$Y_{it} - \bar{Y}_i = \phi(Y_{i,t-1} - \bar{Y}_{i,-1}) + \beta^\top (X_{i,t-1} - \bar{X}_{i,-1}) + (U_{it} - \bar{U}_i),$$

where $\bar{Y}_{i,-1}$ and $\bar{X}_{i,-1}$ denote the individual-specific averages of $Y_{i,t-1}$ and $X_{i,t-1}$ respectively. When T is small, a regression of $Y_{it} - \bar{Y}_i$ on $Y_{i,t-1} - \bar{Y}_{i,-1}$ and $X_{i,t-1} - \bar{X}_{i,-1}$ would give biased estimates of ϕ and β because $U_{it} - \bar{U}_i$ is correlated with $Y_{i,t-1} - \bar{Y}_{i,-1}$ (and possibly $X_{i,t-1} - \bar{X}_{i,-1}$), due to the correlation between $\bar{U}_i$ and $\bar{Y}_{i,-1}$ (and possibly $\bar{X}_{i,-1}$). In fact, under the assumption that $\{X_{it}\}$ is strongly exogenous, Nickell (1981) and Sevestre and Trognon (1985) show that

$$\frac{1}{nT} \sum_i \sum_t (Y_{it} - \bar{Y}_i)(U_{it} - \bar{U}_i) \xrightarrow{\text{p}} \frac{1 - \phi^T - T(1-\phi)}{T^2(1-\phi)^2}\, \sigma^2 \neq 0$$

as $n \to \infty$ with T fixed. Notice that the bias of the within group estimator arises because of the short length of time over which the dynamic model (12.18) is estimated and vanishes as T increases.

As an alternative to the within group estimator, Holtz-Eakin, Newey and Rosen (1988) propose to estimate the transformed model by the IV method. They consider, more generally, the model

$$Y_{it} = \psi_t \alpha_i + \phi Y_{i,t-1} + \beta^\top X_{i,t-1} + U_{it}, \qquad \{U_{it}\} \sim \text{WN}(0, \sigma^2), \tag{12.19}$$

where ψ_t is a parameter allowed to vary over time. Lagging equation (12.19) once, multiplying by $r_t = \psi_t / \psi_{t-1}$ and subtracting the result from (12.19) gives

$$Y_{it} = c_{1t} Y_{i,t-1} + c_{2t} Y_{i,t-2} + d_1^\top X_{i,t-1} + d_2^\top X_{i,t-2} + V_{it}, \tag{12.20}$$

for $t = 3, \ldots, T$, where $V_{it} = U_{it} - r_t U_{i,t-1}$ and

$$\begin{aligned} c_{1t} &= r_t + \phi, & c_{2t} &= -r_t \phi, \\ d_1 &= \beta, & d_{2t} &= -r_t \beta. \end{aligned}$$

If $r_t = 1$, then (12.20) simplifies to

$$Y_{it} = (1+\phi)Y_{i,t-1} - \phi Y_{i,t-2} + \beta^\top X_{i,t-1} - \beta^\top X_{i,t-2} + V_{it},$$

which corresponds to taking first differences of equation (12.19).

Because the error V_{it} satisfies

$$\mathrm{E}\, V_{it} Y_{is} = 0, \qquad \mathrm{E}\, V_{it} X_{is} = 0, \qquad \text{for all } s < t-1,$$

a valid set of instruments for estimating the parameters of model (12.19) consists of all variables lagged two or more periods, that is,

$$W_{it} = [1, Y_{i,t-2}, \ldots, Y_{i1}, X_{i,t-2}, \ldots, X_{i1}].$$

In order to identify the parameters of (12.19), the transformed model (12.20) must contain at least the same number of free parameters as the original model. The simplest case is when $r_t = 1$ for all t, because the transformed model simply becomes

$$\Delta Y_{it} = \phi \Delta Y_{i,t-1} + \beta^\top \Delta X_{i,t-1} + V_{it}, \qquad t = 3, \ldots, T.$$

The original model is therefore identifiable if $T \geq 3$.

12.7 TIME SERIES OF REPEATED CROSS-SECTIONS

Many countries have no panel data but they do have *repeated cross-sections*, that is, a set of successive cross-sections of identical or at least very similar design and sample size. Even when panel data are available, their quality may be inferior to available cross-section data, for example because of the smaller sample size, the severity of attrition problems, the high rate of nonresponse to specific questions, etc. In cases when repeated cross-sections are available, grouping the data makes it possible to construct *pseudo panels* of group averages that may be used to estimate linear relationships, pretty much as if they were genuine panels.

Suppose that the available data consist of a sequence of T repeated cross-sections, and that the basic relationship at the individual level is given by (12.1). For each cross-section, partition the data into C groups or "cohorts", defined for example by the sex and the birth year of the individuals in the sample. Aggregating the observations at the cohort level gives the following model for the cohort averages

$$\bar{Y}_{ct} = \bar{\alpha}_{ct} + \beta^\top \bar{X}_{ct} + \bar{U}_{ct}, \qquad c = 1, \ldots, C; \qquad t = 1, \ldots, T, \tag{12.21}$$

where $\bar{Y}_{ct}$ indicates the sample average of Y_{it} for the cth cohort at time t, and so on. Because the cohort averages $\bar{\alpha}_{ct}$ of the individual effects are not time-invariant and are potentially correlated with the cohort averages $\bar{X}_{ct}$ of the covariates, applying the within group estimator to (12.21) would not eliminate the cohort effects and therefore would not give a consistent estimator of β.

On the other hand, if there is no migration or death, then population cohorts contain exactly the same individuals in each period and so the population cohort means of the individual effects, denoted by α_c^*, have the property of being time-invariant. The population counterpart of (12.21) is therefore

$$Y_{ct}^* = \alpha_c^* + \beta^\top X_{ct}^* + U_{ct}^*, \qquad c = 1, \ldots, C; \qquad t = 1, \ldots, T,$$

where the asterisk indicates population cohort means.

The sample cohort means $\bar{Y}_{ct}$ and $\bar{X}_{ct}$ may be viewed as error-ridden measurements of the population cohort means, that is,

$$\bar{Y}_{ct} = Y_{ct}^* + \epsilon_{ct},$$
$$\bar{X}_{ct} = X_{ct}^* + \eta_{ct}.$$

Following Deaton (1985) and Verbeek and Nijman (1993), assume that the measurement errors $\{(\epsilon_{ct}, \eta_{ct})\}$ are i.i.d. with mean zero and variance

$$\operatorname{Var}\begin{pmatrix} \epsilon_{ct} \\ \eta_{ct} \end{pmatrix} = \begin{bmatrix} \sigma_{YY} & \sigma_{YX} \\ \sigma_{YX} & \Sigma_{XX} \end{bmatrix},$$

which is assumed to be p.d. This last assumption is not unreasonable when the size of the samples drawn from each cohort is roughly the same. Of course, if the sample size for some cohort becomes arbitrarily large, then $\operatorname{Var}(\epsilon_{ct}, \eta_{ct}) \to 0$ for that cohort.

Now define the following matrices of sample second moments

$$P_{XX} = \frac{1}{CT} \sum_c \sum_t (\bar{X}_{ct} - \bar{X}_c)(\bar{X}_{ct} - \bar{X}_c)^\top,$$
$$p_{XY} = \frac{1}{CT} \sum_c \sum_t (\bar{X}_{ct} - \bar{X}_c)(\bar{Y}_{ct} - \bar{Y}_c)^\top,$$

with $\bar{X}_c = T^{-1} \sum_t \bar{X}_{ct}$ and $\bar{Y}_c = T^{-1} \sum_t \bar{Y}_{ct}$, and observe that

$$\bar{X}_{ct} - \bar{X}_c = X_{ct}^* - X_c^* + \eta_{ct} - \bar{\eta}_c,$$

where $X_c^* = T^{-1} \sum_t X_{ct}^*$, $\bar{\eta}_c = T^{-1} \sum_t \eta_{ct}$ and $\operatorname{Var}(\eta_{ct} - \bar{\eta}_c) = \tau \Sigma_{XX}$, with $\tau = (T-1)/T$. Further assume that the matrix

$$\Omega = \lim_{C \to \infty} \frac{1}{CT} \sum_c \sum_t (X_{ct}^* - X_c^*)(X_{ct}^* - X_c^*)^\top$$

is finite and p.d. Because $\{\eta_{ct} - \bar{\eta}_c\}$ is a sequence of i.i.d. random vectors with finite variance, Khinchine WLLN implies that $P_{XX} \xrightarrow{p} \Pi_{XX} = \Omega + \tau \Sigma_{XX}$ as $C \to \infty$ with T fixed. A similar argument shows that $p_{XY} \xrightarrow{p} \pi_{XY} = \Omega\beta + \tau \sigma_{XY}$ as $C \to \infty$ with T fixed. The target parameter β may therefore be defined as

$$\beta = \Omega^{-1}(\pi_{XY} - \tau\sigma_{XY}) = (\Pi_{XX} - \tau\Sigma_{XX})^{-1}(\pi_{XY} - \tau\sigma_{XY}).$$

If S_{XX} and s_{XY} are consistent estimators of Σ_{XX} and σ_{XY}, and $P_{XX} - \tau S_{XX}$ is a nonsingular matrix, then an estimator of β based on the analogy principle is

$$\hat{\beta}_C = (P_{XX} - \tau S_{XX})^{-1}(p_{XY} - \tau s_{XY}).$$

Under the model assumptions, $\hat{\beta}_C$ is indeed consistent for β as $C \to \infty$ with T fixed.

A consistent estimator of the second moments of the measurement errors may be obtained from the original cross-sectional data. For example, Σ_{XX} may be estimated by

$$S_{XX} = \frac{1}{nT} \sum_c \sum_t \sum_{i \in c} (X_{it} - \bar{X}_{ct})(X_{it} - \bar{X}_{ct})^\top.$$

Consider, more generally, the following class of estimators of β

$$\tilde{\beta}_\alpha = (P_{XX} - \alpha S_{XX})^{-1}(p_{XY} - \alpha s_{XY}), \tag{12.22}$$

where $\alpha \in [0,1]$. The estimator $\hat{\beta}_C$ belongs to this class for $\alpha = \tau$. When $\alpha = 0$, one obtains the within group estimator applied to the cohort averages. When $\alpha = 1$, one obtains the estimator originally proposed by Deaton (1985), namely

$$\tilde{\beta}_1 = (P_{XX} - S_{XX})^{-1}(p_{XY} - s_{XY}).$$

This estimator is consistent for β only in the limiting case when $T \to \infty$. When T is small, Deaton's estimator may be worse than the consistent estimator $\hat{\beta}_C$ (Verbeek & Nijman 1993). Notice that Deaton's estimator adjusts the sample second moments matrices by subtracting the estimated measurement error variance, whereas the consistent estimator subtracts only a fraction τ of the estimated measurement error variance.

The estimators in the class (12.22) are asymptotically normal under general conditions. The form of their asymptotic variance depends, however, on the distribution of the measurement errors $(\epsilon_{ct}, \eta_{ct})$. Deaton (1985) and Verbeek and Nijman (1993) assume, for convenience, that this is multivariate Gaussian.

BIBLIOGRAPHIC NOTES

Good introductions to econometric methods for the analysis of panel data are the books by Hsiao (1986) and Baltagi (1995a). A comprehensive treatment is Mátyás and Sevestre (1996).

A set of interesting contributions is contained in three special issues of the *Journal of Econometrics*, namely Heckman and Singer (1982), Carraro, Peracchi and Weber (1993) and Baltagi (1995b).

The incidental parameter problem was first addressed by Neyman and Scott (1948) who pointed out the possible inconsistency of the ML estimator in this case.

The result in Lemma 12.1 goes back to Balestra and Nerlove (1966) and Wallace and Hussain (1969). See also Maddala (1971) and Nerlove (1971). For a general class of decompositions of the matrix Ω in variance component models see Wansbeek and Kapteyn (1982).

The model in Section 12.4 is formally equivalent to the model of cluster or multistage sampling with common intercluster correlation discussed in Scott and Holt (1982). With this interpretation, n is the number of clusters (primary sample units) and T_i is the number of elements drawn from the ith cluster.

On specification and estimation of panel data models with sample selection and latent individual effects see Verbeek (1990), Verbeek and Nijman (1992), Wooldridge (1995) and Kyriazidou (1997).

The minimum distance (or minimum chi-square) method was introduced, in a different context, by Ferguson (1958).

PROBLEMS

12.1 In each period t, a farmer i combines his entrepreneurial ability A_i with labor input L_{it} in order to maximize expected profit $\pi_{it} = P_{it}Q_{it} - w_{it}L_{it}$, where P_t is the output price,

w_{it} is the wage rate and Q_{it} is the amount of output produced. The production function is

$$Q_{it} = L_{it}^{\beta} A_i^{\gamma} V_{it},$$

where V_{it} is a random variable that represents the uncertain amount of rain and is such that $\mathrm{E}\, V_{it} = \alpha$ for all t.

(i) Given P_{it} and w_{it}, what is the labor input level that maximizes expected profit?
(ii) Given observations on $(Q_{it}, L_{it}, P_{it}, w_{it})$, but not on A_i, for a random sample of n farmers at time t, how would you estimate the coefficient β?
(iii) Given a panel survey, how would you estimate β?

12.2 Show that, when $T = 2$, the within group estimator coincides with the OLS estimator in the regression of $Y_{i2} - Y_{i1}$ on $X_{i2} - X_{i1}$.

12.3 Consider the Gaussian fixed effects model with parameter vector $\theta = (\alpha, \beta, \sigma^2)$, where $\alpha = (\alpha_1, \ldots, \alpha_n)$.

(i) Show that the likelihood score for (α, β) is uncorrelated with the likelihood score for σ^2.
(ii) Show that, in general, the likelihood score for α is correlated with the likelihood score for β. What are the conditions under which they are uncorrelated?

12.4 Derive (12.2) (*Hint*: $\hat{\alpha}_i - \alpha_i = \bar{Y}_i - \alpha_i - \beta^\top \bar{X}_i - (\hat{\beta}_w - \beta)^\top \bar{X}_i$).

12.5 Show that, under the assumptions of the variance component model, the within group estimator is unbiased for β.

12.6 Derive (12.4) (*Hint*: Use the law of iterated expectations for covariances).

12.7 Prove Lemma 12.1 (*Hint*: Assume that $\Omega^{-1} = I + \gamma P$ for some γ and then obtain γ by equating the coefficients of P on both sides of the identity $I = (I + \lambda P)(I + \gamma P)$).

12.8 Show that the between group estimator is BLU for the grouped data in the balanced panel case. Also show how the estimator should be modified in order to retain this property when the panel is unbalanced.

12.9 Show that the OLS and the GLS estimators are both matrix weighted averages of the within group and the between group estimators, but the GLS estimator gives more weight to the within group estimator than OLS does.

12.10 Verify directly that, if the assumptions of the variance component model hold and $\hat{\beta}_w$ and $\tilde{\beta}$ denote respectively the within group and the GLS estimator, then the difference $\mathrm{Var}(\hat{\beta}_w \,|\, \mathbf{X}) - \mathrm{Var}(\tilde{\beta} \,|\, \mathbf{X})$ is a n.n.d. matrix.

12.11 Given the matrix Ω, defined in (12.5), show that $\Omega^{-1} = \Gamma^2$, where $\Gamma = M_D + \sqrt{\psi} H_D$ is a symmetric p.d. matrix.

12.12 Let Y, X and Z be random variables defined on the same probability space. Show that if $\mathrm{E}^*(Y \,|\, X, W)$ is the BLP of Y given X and W, then the BLP of Y given X is

$$\mathrm{E}^*(Y \,|\, X) = \mathrm{E}^*[\mathrm{E}^*(Y \,|\, X, W) \,|\, X].$$

This result is known as the *law of iterated projections*.

12.13 Prove Theorem 12.3.

12.14 Prove Theorem 12.4.

12.15 Show that the IV estimator obtained by minimizing the criterion function (12.14) coincides with the within group estimator.

12.16 Show that applying the within group estimator to panel data generated by model (12.19) would give inconsistent estimates of the model parameter.

13

Linear Simultaneous Equation Models

In this chapter we assume that the data $[\mathbf{X}, \mathbf{Y}]$ are a sample from the distribution of (X, Y), where X and Y are random vectors of dimension k and m respectively. A *structural econometric model* describes in causal ("if, then") terms the relationship between the variables in X, now called *exogenous variables*, and the variables in Y, now called *endogenous variables.*

From a statistical point of view, the dependence of Y on X is modeled by assuming that m specific linear combinations BY of the endogenous variables in Y have a conditional distribution given X whose mean is $\mathrm{E}(BY \mid X) = \Gamma X$, where Γ is an $m \times k$ matrix of parameters, and whose variance is $\mathrm{Var}(BY \mid X) = \Sigma$, where Σ is an $m \times m$ finite p.d. matrix. We further assume that $\mathrm{E}\, XX^\top = P$, a finite p.d. matrix. The model may also be written

$$BY = \Gamma X + U, \tag{13.1}$$

where the error vector $U = BY - \Gamma X$ satisfies

$$\mathrm{E}(U \mid X) = 0, \qquad \mathrm{Var}(U \mid X) = \Sigma. \tag{13.2}$$

Model (13.1)–(13.2) is called a *linear simultaneous equation model in structural form* and the parameters in the matrices (B, Γ, Σ) are called the *structural parameters* of the model. The statistical problem is estimation and inference about the structural parameters.

The structure of the matrices B, Γ and Σ embodies constraints that are often derived from some more or less developed economic model. In fact, causal relationships only make sense in the context of an economic model. At the same time, as we shall see, these restrictions are essential in order to achieve identifiability.

13.1 THE STATISTICAL PROBLEM

The following example illustrates the nature of the statistical problem arising with linear simultaneous equation models. Suppose that the data are a sample from the distribution of the bivariate random variable $Y = (Y_1, Y_2)$, where

$$\begin{aligned} Y_1 &= \gamma_1 + \beta_1 Y_2 + U_1, \\ Y_2 &= \gamma_2 + \beta_2 Y_1 + U_2, \end{aligned} \tag{13.3}$$

and the random vector (U_1, U_2) has a standard bivariate Gaussian distribution. This system of simultaneous equations is interpreted as structural, that is, as a representation of the process that generated the data. For concreteness, suppose that the two equations in (13.3) represent the market demand and the (inverse) supply function of a specific good, Y_1 and Y_2 represent respectively the quantity exchanged and the market price, and U_1 and U_2 represent the combined effect of several other variables that affect market demand and supply.

The structural form of this model is $BY \sim \mathcal{N}_2(\gamma, I_2)$, with $\gamma = (\gamma_1, \gamma_2)$ and

$$B = \begin{bmatrix} 1 & -\beta_1 \\ -\beta_2 & 1 \end{bmatrix}.$$

The structural parameters are γ_1, γ_2, β_1 and β_2. If $\beta_1\beta_2 \neq 1$, the distribution of the random vector Y is $\mathcal{N}_2(\mu, \Omega)$, with

$$\mu = \frac{1}{1 - \beta_1\beta_2} \begin{pmatrix} \gamma_1 + \beta_1\gamma_2 \\ \beta_2\gamma_1 + \gamma_2 \end{pmatrix}$$

and

$$\Omega = \frac{1}{(1 - \beta_1\beta_2)^2} \begin{bmatrix} 1 + \beta_1^2 & \beta_1 + \beta_2 \\ \beta_1 + \beta_2 & 1 + \beta_2^2 \end{bmatrix}.$$

Notice that $\mathrm{E}(Y_1 \mid Y_2) = \gamma_1^* + \beta_1^* Y_2$, where

$$\gamma_1^* = \frac{1}{1 - \beta_1\beta_2}[\gamma_1 + \beta_1\gamma_2 - \beta_1(\beta_2\gamma_1 + \gamma_2)], \qquad \beta_1^* = \frac{\beta_1 + \beta_2}{1 + \beta_2^2}. \tag{13.4}$$

Hence, in general, the first equation in model (13.3) cannot be interpreted as a conditional expectation. We conclude that an OLS regression of Y_1 on a constant and Y_2 gives good estimates of γ_1^* and β_1^* but, in general, not of γ_1 and β_1. The only exception is when $\beta_2 = 0$, that is, the market supply function is perfectly price elastic.

In fact, this is not simply an estimation problem. Even if we knew γ_1^* and β_1^*, it is clear from (13.4) that this would not be enough to uniquely determine the structural parameters γ_1 and β_1. Suppose now that both $\mathrm{E}(Y_1 \mid Y_2)$ and $\mathrm{E}(Y_2 \mid Y_1) = \gamma_2^* + \beta_2^* Y_1$ are known. Is knowledge of the four parameters γ_1^*, γ_2^*, β_1^* and β_2^* enough to recover the four structural parameters in γ and B? The answer is again negative, as we can see from the equation system

$$\beta_1^* = \frac{\beta_1 + \beta_2}{1 + \beta_2^2}, \qquad \beta_2^* = \frac{\beta_1 + \beta_2}{1 + \beta_1^2}.$$

Because this is a system of quadratic equations, the solution is not unique in general.

13.2 IDENTIFIABILITY

Consider again model (13.1)–(13.2). If the parameter matrix B is nonsingular then, under our set of assumptions, the first two moments of the conditional distribution of Y given X are $\mathrm{E}(Y \mid X) = \Pi X$ and $\mathrm{Var}(Y \mid X) = \Omega$, where

$$\Pi = B^{-1}\Gamma, \qquad \Omega = B^{-1}\Sigma B^{-\top}. \tag{13.5}$$

Equivalently, Y may be represented as

$$Y = \Pi X + V, \tag{13.6}$$

where $V = Y - \mathrm{E}(Y \mid X) = B^{-1}U$ satisfies $\mathrm{E}(V \mid X) = 0$ and $\mathrm{Var}(V \mid X) = \Omega$. The system of equations (13.6) corresponds to a SURE system and is called the *reduced form* of model (13.1)–(13.2). If $B = I_m$, then the structural form and the reduced form coincide.

The parameters in the matrices (Π, Ω) are called the *reduced form parameters* of the model and can be estimated consistently by GLS. Because the variables on the right-hand side of each equation in (13.6) are always the same, GLS here simply reduces to multivariate OLS. The resulting estimator of Π is indeed BLU.

A triple (B, Γ, Σ), where B is a nonsingular matrix and Σ is a symmetric p.d. matrix, is called a *structure* of model (13.1)–(13.2). A structure implies a complete specification of the first and second moments of the conditional distribution of Y given X through the relationships in (13.5). An important question is whether the converse is also true, that is, whether knowledge of Π and Ω is sufficient to uniquely recover a structure (B, Γ, Σ) through the factorization (13.5).

Two structures (B, Γ, Σ) and $(B_*, \Gamma_*, \Sigma_*)$ are said to be *indistinguishable* if they imply the same first and second moments of the conditional distribution of Y given X. A structure (B, Γ, Σ) is said to be *identifiable* if there exists no other structure $(B_*, \Gamma_*, \Sigma_*)$ that is indistinguishable from (B, Γ, Σ). A model is said to be *identifiable* if all its structures are identifiable. We now show that, in the absence of further constraints, a linear simultaneous equation model is not identifiable.

Given a structure (B, Γ, Σ) of model (13.1)–(13.2), consider another structure $(B_*, \Gamma_*, \Sigma_*)$ such that

$$B_* = GB, \qquad \Gamma_* = G\Gamma, \qquad \Sigma_* = G\Sigma G^\top,$$

where G is a nonsingular $m \times m$ matrix. The structure $(B_*, \Gamma_*, \Sigma_*)$ implies that the first two moments of the conditional distribution of Y given X are

$$B_*^{-1}\Gamma_* = B^{-1}G^{-1}G\Gamma = B^{-1}\Gamma$$

and

$$B_*^{-1}\Sigma_* B_*^{-\top} = B^{-1}G^{-1}G\Sigma G^\top (B^{-1}G^{-1})^\top = B^{-1}\Sigma B^{-\top},$$

that is, they coincide with the ones implied by (B, Γ, Σ). Hence, the structure (B, Γ, Σ) is indistinguishable from $(B_*, \Gamma_*, \Sigma_*)$. Because this is true for every other structure that corresponds to a nonsingular transformation of (B, Γ, Σ), a linear simultaneous equation model is not in general identifiable. If $B = I_m$, no identifiability problem arises because in this case a structure of the model is defined by the pair of matrices (Γ, Σ), and two different structures (Γ, Σ) and (Γ_*, Σ_*) give, in general, different first and second moments of the conditional distribution of Y given X.

13.2.1 CONDITIONS FOR IDENTIFIABILITY: FIRST METHOD

The existence of prior information plays a crucial role in ensuring that a linear simultaneous equation model is identifiable. When such information takes the form of a set of constraints on the model parameters (B, Γ, Σ), a reparametrization defined by a transformation G is said to be ***admissible*** if the resulting structure $(GB, G\Gamma, G\Sigma G^\top)$ satisfies all the constraints implied by the model. Thus, a structure is identifiable if and only if the unique reparametrization that is model admissible is the trivial one defined by the identity transformation $G = I_m$.

Assume, for simplicity, that prior information is only available on the $m \times (m + k)$ matrix

$$A = [B, \Gamma] = \begin{bmatrix} a_1^\top \\ \vdots \\ a_m^\top \end{bmatrix},$$

where a_j is the vector of the $m + k$ structural parameters in the jth equation. We do not discuss the case when constraints are also imposed on the conditional variance of BY given X. Further assume that the prior information may be represented by a set of q linear equality constraints on the matrix A of the form

$$Ra = r, \tag{13.7}$$

where R is a known $q \times m(m + k)$ matrix of rank q, r is a known q-vector and

$$a = \operatorname{vec} A = \begin{pmatrix} a_1 \\ \vdots \\ a_m \end{pmatrix}$$

is the $m(m + k)$-vector of structural parameters. This representation is quite general and allows for cross-equation constraints, that is, constraints linking parameters in more than one equation of the model.

Now assume that a structure A satisfies the constraints (13.7) implied by the model. A reparametrization $A_* = GA$ is model admissible if and only if it also satisfies the constraints (13.7), that is, $R \operatorname{vec}(A_*) = R \operatorname{vec}(GA) = r$ or, equivalently, $R \operatorname{vec}[(G - I_m)A] = 0$. Since $\operatorname{vec}[(G - I_m)A] = (I_m \otimes A^\top) \operatorname{vec}(G - I_m)$, the above condition becomes

$$[R(I_m \otimes A^\top)] \operatorname{vec}(G - I_m) = 0.$$

The structure A is identifiable if and only if the unique reparametrization that is also model admissible is the trivial one defined by the identity transformation $G = I_m$. A necessary and sufficient condition is that the $q \times m^2$ matrix $[R(I_m \otimes A^\top)]$ be of full column rank, that is,

$$\operatorname{rank}[R(I_m \otimes A^\top)] = m^2. \tag{13.8}$$

A necessary condition is the ***order condition***

$$q \geq m^2. \tag{13.9}$$

If (13.8) does not hold, then the model is not identifiable. Whenever the model is identifiable, we say that it is ***exactly identifiable*** if $q = m^2$ and that it is ***overidentifiable*** if $q > m^2$.

13.2.2 SEPARABLE CONSTRAINTS

An important special case is when the constraints are *separable*, that is, each of them only links the parameters of one particular equation in the model. In this case, the set of linear constraints (13.7) becomes

$$R_j a_j = r_j, \qquad j = 1, \ldots, m,$$

where R_j is a known $q_j \times (m+k)$ matrix, r_j is a known q_j-vector and $q = \sum_{i=1}^m q_j$. The rank condition (13.8) now becomes

$$m^2 = \operatorname{rank}[R(I_m \otimes A^\top)] = \operatorname{rank}\begin{bmatrix} R_1 A^\top & & \\ & \ddots & \\ & & R_m A^\top \end{bmatrix},$$

that is,

$$\operatorname{rank} R_j A^\top = m, \qquad j = 1, \ldots, m, \tag{13.10}$$

and the necessary order condition (13.9) becomes

$$q_j \geq m, \qquad j = 1, \ldots, m. \tag{13.11}$$

If (13.10) is satisfied by the jth equation, then this equation is identifiable even when all the others are not. If the jth equation is identifiable, we say that it is *exactly identifiable* when $q_j = m$ and that it is *overidentifiable* when $q_j > m$. Notice that checking the rank condition for identifiability of even a single equation requires all the other model equations to be specified.

13.2.3 NORMALIZATION AND EXCLUSION CONSTRAINTS

Another important special case is when the constraints are separable and consist of either normalization or exclusion of variables. Without loss of generality, consider the first equation of the model. The normalization constraint sets equal to one the coefficient a_{11} associated with Y_1, whereas the exclusion constraints specify that $m - m_1$ of the endogenous variables and $k - k_1$ of the exogenous variables do not feature in the first equation. The total number of constraints imposed on the first equation is therefore $q_1 = 1 + m - m_1 + k - k_1$. In this case

$$R_1 = \begin{bmatrix} 1 & 0 \\ 0 & R_1^* \end{bmatrix}, \qquad r_1 = \begin{pmatrix} 1 \\ 0 \end{pmatrix},$$

where R_1^* is the $(q_1 - 1) \times (m + k - 1)$ matrix

$$R_1^* = \begin{bmatrix} 0 & I_{m-m_1} & 0 & 0 \\ 0 & 0 & 0 & I_{k-k_1} \end{bmatrix},$$

and the first row of the matrix $[R_1, r_1]$ corresponds to the normalization constraint on the coefficient of Y_1. Partition the matrix $A^\top$ as

$$A^\top = \begin{bmatrix} a_{11} & a_{(1)}^\top \\ A_{(1)}^* & A_1^{*\top} \end{bmatrix},$$

where a_{11} is the coefficient associated with Y_1 in the first equation, $a_{(1)}$ is the row-vector consisting of the other parameters in the first equation, $A^*_{(1)}$ is the column-vector of the coefficients associated with Y_1 in the other $m-1$ equations of the model, and $A_1^{*\top}$ is the matrix of all the other parameters in A. Then

$$R_1 A^\top = \begin{bmatrix} a_{11} & a_{(1)} \\ R_1^* A^*_{(1)} & R_1^* A_1^{*\top} \end{bmatrix},$$

where $R_1^* A_1^{*\top}$ is a $(q_1 - 1) \times (m - 1)$ matrix which consists of the coefficients, in the other $m - 1$ equations of the model, associated with the variables excluded from the first equation. Because $a_{11} \neq 0$, the rank condition (13.10) becomes

$$\operatorname{rank} R_1^* A_1^{*\top} = m - 1,$$

while the order condition (13.11) becomes

$$m - m_1 + k - k_1 \geq m - 1,$$

that is, at least $m - 1$ variables must be excluded from the first equation. The order condition may equivalently be expressed as

$$k \geq (m_1 - 1) + k_1,$$

that is, the number of exogenous variables in the model must be at least equal to the number of variables included on the right-hand side of the first equation. As we shall see below, the order condition for identifiability of a single equation via normalization and exclusion constraints is closely related to the conditions under which the parameters of such an equation can be estimated consistently by the IV method.

13.2.4 CONDITIONS FOR IDENTIFIABILITY: SECOND METHOD

An alternative but equivalent approach to identifiability of a linear simultaneous equation model starts from the fact that, by the results in Section 1.4.2, the reduced form parameters in Π are always identifiable provided that the matrix $P = \operatorname{E} X X^\top$ is nonsingular. The identifiability of $A = [B, \Gamma]$ is then equivalent to the existence of a one-to-one correspondence between Π and A. The relationship $\Pi = B^{-1}\Gamma$ between the reduced form and the structural parameters may be represented as

$$0 = B\Pi - \Gamma = A \begin{bmatrix} \Pi \\ -I_k \end{bmatrix}$$

or, equivalently,

$$0 = \operatorname{vec}(B\Pi - \Gamma) = \operatorname{vec}\left(A \begin{bmatrix} \Pi \\ -I_k \end{bmatrix}\right) = [I_m \otimes (\Pi^\top, -I_k)]\, a, \tag{13.12}$$

where $a = \operatorname{vec} A$ is the $m(m+k)$-vector of structural parameters. Given the matrix Π, (13.12) consists of mk linear equations in the $m(m+k)$ structural parameters. Because $mk < m(m+k)$, this linear system can only have a unique solution if enough constraints are placed on A. Thus, knowledge of Π is not sufficient to recover the structural parameters in the model and prior information on A becomes necessary.

Combining now equation (13.12) with the set of linear equality constraints (13.7) gives the following system of $q + mk$ linear equations in the $m(m+k)$ elements of the vector a

$$\begin{bmatrix} R \\ I_m \otimes (\Pi^\top, -I_k) \end{bmatrix} a = \begin{pmatrix} r \\ 0 \end{pmatrix}. \tag{13.13}$$

Model identifiability is therefore equivalent to the existence of a unique solution to the linear system (13.13) with respect to the structural parameters in a. A necessary and sufficient condition is

$$\operatorname{rank} \begin{bmatrix} R \\ I_m \otimes (\Pi^\top, -I_k) \end{bmatrix} = m(m+k).$$

A necessary condition is the order condition

$$q + mk \geq m(m+k),$$

which requires $q \geq m^2$, exactly as in (13.11).

When the constraints are separable, (13.13) reduces to

$$\begin{bmatrix} R_j \\ (I_m, -I_k) \end{bmatrix} a_j = \begin{pmatrix} r_j \\ 0 \end{pmatrix}, \qquad j = 1, \ldots, m.$$

The jth equation is therefore identifiable if and only if

$$\operatorname{rank} \begin{bmatrix} R_j \\ (I_m, -I_k) \end{bmatrix} = m + k.$$

A necessary condition is the order condition

$$q_j + k \geq m + k,$$

which requires $q_j \geq m$, exactly as in (13.11).

13.3 SINGLE EQUATION ESTIMATION

This section examines the problem of estimating the parameters of a single equation in a linear simultaneous equation model where identifiability has been attained through normalization and exclusion constraints. Without loss of generality, consider again the first equation of the model

$$\beta_1^\top Y = \gamma_1^\top X + U_1,$$

where $U_1 = \beta_1^\top Y - \gamma_1^\top X$ is a random error assumed to be mean independent of X and homoskedastic, and β_1 and γ_1 are vectors of structural parameters of dimension m and k respectively. After normalizing to one the coefficient associated with Y_1 and after imposing enough exclusion constraints to ensure identifiability, this equation may equivalently be written

$$Y_1 = \alpha_1^\top Z_1 + U_1,$$

where the vector Z_1 consists of the $m_1 - 1$ endogenous variables Y_1^* and the k_1 exogenous variables X_1^* included on the right-hand side of the first equation, and α_1 is a vector of $p_1 = m_1 - 1 + k_1$ parameters. The model for the observed data is therefore

$$Y_{i1} = \alpha_1^\top Z_{i1} + U_{i1}, \qquad i = 1, \ldots, n,$$

where $Z_{i1} = (Y_{i1}^*, X_{i1}^*)$ and $\mathrm{E}(U_{i1} \mid X_i) = 0$. Stacking the n observations on the variable Y_1 into the vector $\mathbf{Y}_1$, the model for $\mathbf{Y}_1$ may be written more compactly as

$$\mathbf{Y}_1 = \mathbf{Y}_1^* \beta_1 + \mathbf{X}_1^* \gamma_1 + \mathbf{U}_1 = \mathbf{Z}_1 \alpha_1 + \mathbf{U}_1,$$

where $\mathbf{Z}_1 = [\mathbf{Y}_1^*, \mathbf{X}_1^*]$ is an $n \times p_1$ matrix and $\mathbf{U}_1 = \mathbf{Y}_1 - \mathbf{Z}_1 \alpha_1$. The statistical problem is estimation and inference about the vector α_1 of structural parameters.

13.3.1 OLS ESTIMATION

If $\mathbf{Z}_1$ is a matrix of rank p_1, then the OLS estimator of α_1 is

$$\hat{\alpha}_{1n} = (\mathbf{Z}_1{}^\top \mathbf{Z}_1)^{-1} \mathbf{Z}_1{}^\top \mathbf{Y}_1 = \alpha_1 + (n^{-1} \mathbf{Z}_1^\top \mathbf{Z}_1)^{-1} (n^{-1} \mathbf{Z}_1^\top \mathbf{U}_1).$$

This estimator is consistent for α_1 if $n^{-1} \mathbf{Z}_1^\top \mathbf{Z}_1$ converges in probability to a finite and p.d. matrix and $n^{-1} \mathbf{Z}_1^\top \mathbf{U}_1 \xrightarrow{\text{p}} 0$. In order to evaluate the relevant probability limits, notice first that under our set of assumptions $n^{-1} \mathbf{Z}_1^\top \mathbf{U}_1 \xrightarrow{\text{p}} \mathrm{E}\, Z_1 U_1$ and $n^{-1} \mathbf{Z}_1^\top \mathbf{Z}_1 \xrightarrow{\text{p}} \mathrm{E}\, Z_1 Z_1^\top$ by Khinchine WLLN. Next observe that $Y_1^* = C_1 Y$ and $X_1^* = D_1 X$, where C_1 and D_1 are selection matrices (that is, matrices whose elements consist only of zeros and ones) of rank $m_1 - 1$ and k_1 respectively, that pick the endogenous and exogenous variables featuring on the right-hand side of the first equation, and notice that

$$\mathrm{E} \begin{bmatrix} YY^\top & YX^\top \\ XY^\top & XX^\top \end{bmatrix} = \begin{bmatrix} \Pi P \Pi^\top + \Omega & \Pi P \\ P \Pi^\top & P \end{bmatrix}$$

and

$$\mathrm{E} \begin{pmatrix} YU^\top \\ XU^\top \end{pmatrix} = \begin{bmatrix} B^{-1} \Sigma \\ 0 \end{bmatrix},$$

where $P = \mathrm{E}\, XX^\top$, and $\Pi = B^{-1} \Gamma$ and $\Omega = B^{-1} \Sigma B^{-\top}$ are the matrices of reduced form parameters. Thus, we have

$$\mathrm{E}\, Z_1 U^\top = \mathrm{E} \begin{bmatrix} Y_1^* U^\top \\ X_1^* U^\top \end{bmatrix} = \begin{bmatrix} C_1 B^{-1} \Sigma \\ 0 \end{bmatrix},$$

$$\mathrm{E}\, Z_1 Z_1^\top = \mathrm{E} \begin{bmatrix} Y_1^* Y_1^{*\top} & Y_1^* X_1^{*\top} \\ X_1^* Y_1^{*\top} & X_1^* X_1^{*\top} \end{bmatrix} = \begin{bmatrix} C_1 (\Pi P \Pi^\top + \Omega) C_1^\top & C_1 \Pi P D_1^\top \\ C_1 P \Pi^\top D_1 & C_1 P D_1^\top \end{bmatrix},$$

and

$$\mathrm{E}\, Z_1 X^\top = \mathrm{E} \begin{bmatrix} Y_1^* X^\top \\ X_1^* X^\top \end{bmatrix} = \begin{bmatrix} C_1 \Pi \\ D_1 \end{bmatrix} P.$$

The OLS estimator is therefore inconsistent for α_1 because, although $n^{-1} \mathbf{Z}_1^\top \mathbf{Z}_1$ converges in probability to a finite p.d. matrix, the vector $n^{-1} \mathbf{Z}_1^\top \mathbf{U}_1$ does not converge in probability to zero due to the presence of endogenous variables on the right-hand side of the equation.

13.3.2 IV ESTIMATION

Although the OLS estimator is inconsistent, the parameter α_1 may be estimated consistently. The key is the existence of an $n \times r$ instrument matrix $\mathbf{W}$ such that $n^{-1}\mathbf{W}^\top \mathbf{U}_1 \xrightarrow{p} 0$ and $n^{-1}\mathbf{W}^\top \mathbf{Z}_1$ converges in probability to an $r \times p_1$ matrix of rank p_1. An obvious candidate instrument matrix is $\mathbf{W} = \mathbf{X}$, the $n \times k$ matrix of the exogenous variables in the model. This is a valid instrument matrix because, by the results in Section 13.3.1, $n^{-1}\mathbf{X}^\top \mathbf{U}_1 \xrightarrow{p} \mathrm{E}\, XU_1 = 0$ and $n^{-1}\mathbf{X}^\top \mathbf{Z}_1 \xrightarrow{p} \mathrm{E}\, XZ_1^\top = PS_1$, where $S_1 = [\Pi^\top C_1^\top, D_1^\top]$ is a finite $k \times p_1$ matrix of rank p_1.

We distinguish two cases, depending on the number of exogenous variables in the model. The first case is when the first equation is exactly identifiable, that is, the number k of exogenous variables is equal to the number p_1 of parameters in α_1. The second case is when the equation is overidentifiable, that is, the number of exogenous variables is greater than the number of parameters in α_1.

When $k = p_1$, a consistent estimator of α_1 is the simple IV estimator

$$\tilde{\alpha}_{1n} = (\mathbf{X}^\top \mathbf{Z}_1)^{-1} \mathbf{X}^\top \mathbf{Y}_1.$$

When $k > p_1$, one may consider the 2SLS estimator

$$\tilde{\alpha}_{1n} = [\mathbf{Z}_1^\top \mathbf{X}(\mathbf{X}^\top \mathbf{X})^{-1} \mathbf{X}^\top \mathbf{Z}_1]^{-1} \mathbf{Z}_1^\top \mathbf{X}(\mathbf{X}^\top \mathbf{X})^{-1} \mathbf{X}^\top \mathbf{Y}_1.$$

The asymptotic properties of a sequence $\{\tilde{\alpha}_{1n}\}$ of 2SLS estimators, corresponding to increasing sample sizes, are given by the following result.

Theorem 13.1 *Let* $\mathbf{U}_1 = \mathbf{Y}_1 - \mathbf{Z}_1 \alpha_1$ *and assume that:*

(i) $n^{-1}\mathbf{X}^\top \mathbf{U}_1 \xrightarrow{p} 0$;
(ii) $n^{-1}\mathbf{X}^\top \mathbf{X} \xrightarrow{p} P$, *a finite p.d. matrix;*
(iii) $n^{-1}\mathbf{X}^\top \mathbf{Z}_1 \xrightarrow{p} PS_1$, *where* S_1 *is a finite* $k \times p_1$ *matrix of rank* p_1.

Then $\tilde{\alpha}_{1n}$ *exists with probability approaching one and* $\tilde{\alpha}_{1n} \xrightarrow{p} \alpha_1$. *If, in addition,* $n^{-1/2}\mathbf{X}^\top \mathbf{U}_1 \xrightarrow{d} \mathcal{N}_{k_1}(0, \sigma_{11}^2\, P)$, *then* $\sqrt{n}\,(\tilde{\alpha}_{1n} - \alpha_1) \xrightarrow{d} \mathcal{N}_{k_1}(0, \mathrm{AV}(\tilde{\alpha}_{1n}))$, *where* $\mathrm{AV}(\tilde{\alpha}_{1n}) = \sigma_{11}^2 (S_1^\top P S_1)^{-1}$. *Further,*

$$\widehat{\mathrm{AV}}(\tilde{\alpha}_{1n}) = n\tilde{\sigma}_{11n}^2 [\mathbf{Z}_1^\top \mathbf{X}(\mathbf{X}^\top \mathbf{X})^{-1} \mathbf{X}^\top \mathbf{Z}_1]^{-1} \xrightarrow{p} \mathrm{AV}(\tilde{\alpha}_{1n}),$$

where $\tilde{\sigma}_{11n}^2 = n^{-1}(\mathbf{Y}_1 - \mathbf{Z}_1^\top \tilde{\alpha}_{1n})^\top (\mathbf{Y}_1 - \mathbf{Z}_1 \tilde{\alpha}_{1n})$.

Asymptotic efficiency of $\tilde{\alpha}_{1n}$ and consistency of $\widehat{\mathrm{AV}}(\tilde{\alpha}_{1n})$ for $\mathrm{AV}(\tilde{\alpha}_{1n})$ only hold if the asymptotic variance of $n^{-1/2}\mathbf{X}^\top \mathbf{U}_1$ is equal to $\sigma_{11}^2 P$, which rules out heteroskedasticity or autocorrelation in the elements of $\mathbf{U}_1$.

Now consider adding to the original instrument matrix $\mathbf{X}$ a new $n \times q$ matrix $\mathbf{X}^+$ which consists of observations on variables that are uncorrelated with $\mathbf{U}_1$ but are not part of the structural representation of the process under study. Let $\mathbf{W} = [\mathbf{X}, \mathbf{X}^+]$ denote the enlarged instrument matrix and consider the 2SLS estimator based on $\mathbf{W}$, that is,

$$\bar{\alpha}_{1n} = [\mathbf{Z}_1^\top \mathbf{W}(\mathbf{W}^\top \mathbf{W})^{-1} \mathbf{W}^\top \mathbf{Z}_1]^{-1} \mathbf{Z}_1^\top \mathbf{W}(\mathbf{W}^\top \mathbf{W})^{-1} \mathbf{W}^\top \mathbf{Y}_1.$$

The next result shows that using $\bar{\alpha}_{1n}$ gives no asymptotic efficiency gain over $\tilde{\alpha}_{1n}$.

Theorem 13.2 *Let $\hat{\alpha}_{in}$ and $\tilde{\alpha}_n$ be the 2SLS estimators based on the instrument matrices* $\mathbf{X}$ *and* $\mathbf{W} = [\mathbf{X}, \mathbf{X}^+]$ *respectively. Suppose that the assumptions of Theorem 13.1 hold and assume that:*

(i) $n^{-1}\mathbf{W}^\top \mathbf{U}_1 \xrightarrow{p} 0$;
(ii) $n^{-1}\mathbf{W}^\top \mathbf{X} \xrightarrow{p} P$, *a finite matrix of rank k;*
(iii) $n^{-1/2}\mathbf{W}^\top \mathbf{U}_1 \xrightarrow{d} \mathcal{N}_{k+q}(0, D)$, *where* $D = \sigma_{11}^2 \, \mathrm{E}\, WW^\top$ *is a finite p.d. matrix.*

Then $\bar{\alpha}_{1n}$ and $\tilde{\alpha}_{1n}$ both exist with probability approaching one and they have the same asymptotic variance.

Proof. Notice that

$$P = \begin{bmatrix} P_1 \\ P_2 \end{bmatrix} = \mathrm{E}\begin{bmatrix} XX^\top \\ X^+X^\top \end{bmatrix},$$

and

$$D = \begin{bmatrix} D_{11} & D_{12} \\ D_{21} & D_{22} \end{bmatrix} = \sigma_{11}^2 \, E \begin{bmatrix} XX^\top & X(X^+)^\top \\ X^+X^\top & X^+(X^+)^\top \end{bmatrix}.$$

Since

$$P_2 - D_{21}D_{11}^{-1}P_1 = (\mathrm{E}\, X^+X^\top) - (\mathrm{E}\, X^+X^\top)(\mathrm{E}\, XX^\top)^{-1}(\mathrm{E}\, XX^\top) = 0,$$

Theorem 11.6 implies that $\mathrm{AV}(\bar{\alpha}_{1n}) - \mathrm{AV}(\tilde{\alpha}_{1n}) = 0$. □

13.4 SYSTEM ESTIMATION

The methods considered in the previous section are *limited information* procedures, for they enable one to estimate an identifiable equation in isolation from the other equations in the model. This may be viewed as a strength when there is uncertainty about the precise specification of the rest of the model, but it becomes a weakness when the structure of the model is known exactly.

This section considers *full information* estimators, that is, estimators which take into account the complete structure of the model. After imposing a set of normalization and exclusion constraints sufficient to identify all the structural parameters, the complete model may be represented as

$$Y_j = \alpha_j^\top Z_j + U_j, \qquad j = 1, \ldots, m,$$

where the vector Z_j consists of the $m_j - 1$ endogenous variables and the k_j exogenous variables included on the right-hand side of the jth equation, and α_j is a vector of $p_j = m_j - 1 + k_j$ parameters. Stacking the n observations on the variable Y_j into the vector $\mathbf{Y}_j$, the model for the observed data may be written

$$\mathbf{Y}_j = \mathbf{Z}_j\alpha_j + \mathbf{U}_j, \qquad j = 1, \ldots, m.$$

A more compact representation is

$$\mathbf{Y} = \mathbf{Z}\alpha + \mathbf{U}, \tag{13.14}$$

where

$$\mathbf{Y} = \begin{pmatrix} \mathbf{Y}_1 \\ \vdots \\ \mathbf{Y}_m \end{pmatrix}, \qquad \mathbf{Z} = \begin{bmatrix} \mathbf{Z}_1 & & \\ & \ddots & \\ & & \mathbf{Z}_m \end{bmatrix}, \qquad \alpha = \begin{pmatrix} \alpha_1 \\ \vdots \\ \alpha_m \end{pmatrix},$$

and $\mathbf{U} = \mathbf{Y} - \mathbf{Z}\alpha$. Notice that $\mathbf{Y}$ and $\mathbf{U}$ are mn-vectors, $\mathbf{Z}$ is an $mn \times p$ matrix and α is a vector of dimension $p = \sum_{j=1}^{m} p_j$. Under the model assumptions, $\mathrm{E}(\mathbf{U} \,|\, \mathbf{X}) = 0$ and $\Omega_n = \mathrm{Var}(\mathbf{U} \,|\, \mathbf{X}) = \Sigma \otimes I_m$, a finite p.d. matrix.

13.4.1 IV ESTIMATION

Because the $n \times k$ matrix $\mathbf{X}$ of exogenous variables will be used as instrument matrix for all the model equations, the instrument matrix for the complete system is the $mn \times mk$ matrix

$$\mathbf{W} = \begin{bmatrix} \mathbf{X} & & \\ & \ddots & \\ & & \mathbf{X} \end{bmatrix} = I_m \otimes \mathbf{X}.$$

We assume that $\mathbf{Z}^\top \Omega_n^{-1} \mathbf{W}$ is a matrix of full column rank and $\mathbf{W}^\top \Omega_n^{-1} \mathbf{W}$ is a p.d. matrix. From Section 11.2.5, the generalized 2SLS estimator of α is

$$\bar{\alpha}_n = [\mathbf{Z}^\top \Omega_n^{-1} \mathbf{W} (\mathbf{W}^\top \Omega_n^{-1} \mathbf{W})^{-1} \mathbf{W}^\top \Omega_n^{-1} \mathbf{Z}]^{-1} \mathbf{Z}^\top \Omega_n^{-1} \mathbf{W} (\mathbf{W}^\top \Omega_n^{-1} \mathbf{W})^{-1} \mathbf{W}^\top \Omega_n^{-1} \mathbf{Y},$$

where

$$\mathbf{W}^\top \Omega_n^{-1} \mathbf{W} = (I_m \otimes \mathbf{X}^\top)(\Sigma^{-1} \otimes I_n)(I_m \otimes \mathbf{X}) = (\Sigma^{-1} \otimes \mathbf{X}^\top \mathbf{X})$$

and

$$\mathbf{W}^\top \Omega_n^{-1} \mathbf{Z} = (I_m \otimes \mathbf{X}^\top)(\Sigma^{-1} \otimes I_n)\mathbf{Z} = (\Sigma^{-1} \otimes \mathbf{X}^\top)\mathbf{Z}.$$

Hence, the generalized 2SLS estimator of α is

$$\bar{\alpha}_n = \{\mathbf{Z}^\top [\Sigma^{-1} \otimes \mathbf{X}(\mathbf{X}^\top \mathbf{X})^{-1} \mathbf{X}^\top] \mathbf{Z}\}^{-1} \mathbf{Z}^\top [\Sigma^{-1} \otimes \mathbf{X}(\mathbf{X}^\top \mathbf{X})^{-1} \mathbf{X}^\top] \mathbf{Y}.$$

To determine the asymptotic properties of $\bar{\alpha}_n$, we need to establish the probability limit of the matrix $n^{-1} \mathbf{W}^\top \Omega_n^{-1} \mathbf{Z}$. Let σ^{ij} denote a generic element of Σ^{-1} and notice that

$$\mathbf{W}^\top \Omega_n^{-1} \mathbf{Z} = (\Sigma^{-1} \otimes \mathbf{X}^\top)\mathbf{Z} = \begin{bmatrix} \sigma^{11} \mathbf{X}^\top \mathbf{Z}_1 & \cdots & \sigma^{1m} \mathbf{X}^\top \mathbf{Z}_m \\ \vdots & & \vdots \\ \sigma^{m1} \mathbf{X}^\top \mathbf{Z}_1 & \cdots & \sigma^{mm} \mathbf{X}^\top \mathbf{Z}_m \end{bmatrix}.$$

From Section 13.3.2, $n^{-1} \mathbf{X}^\top \mathbf{Z}_j \xrightarrow{\mathrm{p}} P S_j$, $j = 1, \ldots, m$, where $S_j = [\Pi^\top C_j^\top, D_j^\top]$ is a $k \times p_j$ matrix, and C_j and D_j are selection matrices, of rank $m_j - 1$ and k_j respectively, that pick the endogenous and exogenous variables that feature on the right-hand side of the jth equation. Therefore

$$n^{-1}\mathbf{W}^\top\Omega_n^{-1}\mathbf{Z} \xrightarrow{\text{p}} \begin{bmatrix} \sigma^{11}PS_1 & \cdots & \sigma^{1m}PS_m \\ \vdots & & \vdots \\ \sigma^{11}PS_1 & \cdots & \sigma^{mm}PS_m \end{bmatrix}$$

$$= \begin{bmatrix} \sigma^{11}P & \cdots & \sigma^{1m}P \\ \vdots & & \vdots \\ \sigma^{11}P & \cdots & \sigma^{mm}P \end{bmatrix} \begin{bmatrix} S_1 & & \\ & \ddots & \\ & & S_m \end{bmatrix} = (\Sigma^{-1} \otimes P)S,$$

where S is a block-diagonal $mk \times p$ matrix of rank equal to p, whose jth diagonal block is equal to S_j.

Theorem 13.3 *Let* $\mathbf{U} = \mathbf{Y} - \mathbf{Z}\alpha$ *and suppose that:*

(i) $n^{-1}\mathbf{W}^\top\Omega_n^{-1}\mathbf{U} \xrightarrow{\text{p}} 0$;
(ii) $n^{-1}\mathbf{W}^\top\Omega_n^{-1}\mathbf{W} \xrightarrow{\text{p}} \Sigma^{-1} \otimes P$, *where P is a finite p.d. matrix;*
(iii) $n^{-1}\mathbf{W}^\top\Omega_n^{-1}\mathbf{Z} \xrightarrow{\text{p}} (\Sigma^{-1} \otimes P)S$, *where S is a finite matrix of rank equal to* p.

Then $\bar{\alpha}_n$ exists with probability approaching one and $\bar{\alpha}_n \xrightarrow{\text{p}} \alpha$. If, in addition, $n^{-1/2}\mathbf{W}^\top\Omega_n^{-1}\mathbf{U} \xrightarrow{\text{d}} \mathcal{N}_{mk}(0, \Sigma^{-1} \otimes P)$, then $\sqrt{n}\,(\bar{\alpha}_n - \alpha) \xrightarrow{\text{d}} \mathcal{N}_p(0, \text{AV}(\bar{\alpha}_n))$, where $\text{AV}(\bar{\alpha}_n) = [S^\top(\Sigma^{-1} \otimes P)S]^{-1}$.

It is easy to verify that the generalized 2SLS estimator is asymptotically at least as efficient as the estimator

$$\begin{aligned} \tilde{\alpha}_n &= [\mathbf{Z}^\top\mathbf{W}(\mathbf{W}^\top\mathbf{W})^{-1}\mathbf{W}^\top\mathbf{Z}]^{-1}\mathbf{Z}^\top\mathbf{W}(\mathbf{W}^\top\mathbf{W})^{-1}\mathbf{W}^\top\mathbf{Y} \\ &= \{\mathbf{Z}^\top[I_m \otimes \mathbf{X}(\mathbf{X}^\top\mathbf{X})^{-1}\mathbf{X}^\top]\mathbf{Z}\}^{-1}\mathbf{Z}^\top[I_m \otimes \mathbf{X}(\mathbf{X}^\top\mathbf{X})^{-1}\mathbf{X}^\top]\mathbf{Y}, \end{aligned}$$

obtained by applying 2SLS to each equation in isolation.

Because Σ is generally unknown, some consistent estimate of it is necessary for feasible system estimation. The usual procedure consists of first applying 2SLS to each equation in isolation and then using the 2SLS residuals to construct an estimate $\tilde{\Sigma}_n = n^{-1}\sum_i \tilde{U}_i\tilde{U}_i^\top$ of Σ, where the jth element of the m-vector $\tilde{U}_i$ is equal to $\tilde{U}_{ij} = Y_{ij} - Z_{ij}^\top\tilde{\alpha}_j$ and $\tilde{\alpha}_{jn}$ is the 2SLS estimate from the jth equation. If $\tilde{\Sigma}_n$ is a p.d. matrix, replacing Σ by $\tilde{\Sigma}_n$ gives the feasible generalized 2SLS or *three-stage least squares (3SLS) estimator*

$$\bar{\alpha}_n^* = \{\mathbf{Z}^\top[\tilde{\Sigma}_n^{-1} \otimes \mathbf{X}(\mathbf{X}^\top\mathbf{X})^{-1}\mathbf{X}^\top]\mathbf{Z}\}^{-1}\mathbf{Z}^\top[\tilde{\Sigma}_n^{-1} \otimes \mathbf{X}(\mathbf{X}^\top\mathbf{X})^{-1}\mathbf{X}^\top]\mathbf{Y}.$$

It can be shown that $\bar{\alpha}_n^* - \bar{\alpha}_n \xrightarrow{\text{p}} 0$ under general conditions, that is, the 3SLS estimator is asymptotically equivalent to the generalized 2SLS estimator. It can also be shown that the asymptotic variance of the 3SLS estimator may be estimated consistently by

$$\widehat{\text{AV}}(\bar{\alpha}_n^*) = \{\mathbf{Z}^\top[\tilde{\Sigma}_n^{-1} \otimes \mathbf{X}(\mathbf{X}^\top\mathbf{X})^{-1}\mathbf{X}^\top]\mathbf{Z}\}^{-1}.$$

Notice that asymptotic efficiency of $\bar{\alpha}_n^*$ and consistency of $\widehat{\text{AV}}(\bar{\alpha}_n^*)$ for $\text{AV}(\bar{\alpha}_n^*)$ only hold if the asymptotic variance of $n^{-1/2}\mathbf{X}^\top\Omega_n^{-1}\mathbf{U}$ is equal to $\Sigma^{-1} \otimes P$, which excludes the presence of heteroskedasticity or autocorrelation in the elements of $\mathbf{U}$.

13.4.2 MINIMUM DISTANCE ESTIMATION

The minimum distance (MD) method was introduced in Section 12.5. We now show how this method may be applied to the problem of estimating the vector α of structural parameters in a linear simultaneous equation model.

The basic idea is quite simple. Suppose that the data are a sample from the linear simultaneous equation model (13.1)–(13.2) and the constraints imposed to achieve identifiability are valid. Then the mk-vector $\pi = \operatorname{vec}\Pi$ of reduced form parameters is a function of the p-vector α of structural parameters in the representation (13.14). Let $\pi = g(\alpha)$ denote this relationship. Given a symmetric p.d. weight matrix A_n, a MD estimator of α is a solution $\hat{\alpha}_n$ to the problem

$$\min_{\alpha \in \Re^p} [\hat{\pi}_n - g(\alpha)]^\top A_n [\hat{\pi}_n - g(\alpha)],$$

where $\hat{\pi}_n = \operatorname{vec}[I_m \otimes (\mathbf{X}^\top \mathbf{X})^{-1} \mathbf{X}^\top]\mathbf{Y}$ is the mk-vector of reduced form parameters estimated by multivariate OLS. Chamberlain (1982) shows that, under mild regularity conditions, $\hat{\alpha}_n$ is $\sqrt{n}$-consistent for α and asymptotically normal with asymptotic variance

$$\operatorname{AV}(\hat{\alpha}_n) = (G^\top AG)^{-1} G^\top A \operatorname{AV}(\hat{\pi}_n) A^\top G (G^\top AG)^{-1},$$

where $A = \operatorname{plim} A_n$ and G denotes the Jacobian of g evaluated at the target parameter α. Varying the matrix A_n gives a whole class of MD estimators indexed by the choice of A_n.

Like in Section 12.5, an estimator is asymptotically efficient in the class of MD estimators if the inverse of its weight matrix converges in probability to the asymptotic variance of $\hat{\pi}_n$. The asymptotic variance of such estimator is equal to $[G^\top \operatorname{AV}(\hat{\pi}_n)^{-1} G]^{-1}$. It is easily seen, by an argument analogous to that in the proof of Theorem 12.1, that

$$\operatorname{AV}(\hat{\pi}_n) = \operatorname{E}(V_i V_i^\top \otimes P^{-1} X_i X_i^\top P^{-1}),$$

where $V_i = (V_{i1}, \ldots, V_{im})$ is the m-vector of reduced form errors for the ith observation and $X_i = (X_{i1}, \ldots, X_{ik})$. In the special case when V_i is homoskedastic, that is, $\operatorname{Var}(V_i \mid X_i)$ does not depend on X_i and is equal to the constant matrix $\Omega = B^{-1}\Sigma B^{-\top}$, the asymptotic variance of $\hat{\pi}_n$ simplifies to $\operatorname{AV}(\hat{\pi}_n) = \Omega \otimes P^{-1}$.

To find an explicit expression for the MD estimator notice that, since $\Pi = B^{-1}\Gamma$, we have

$$\pi = \operatorname{vec}(B^{-1}\Gamma) = (B^{-1} \otimes I_k)\gamma,$$

where the matrix B and the vector $\gamma = \operatorname{vec}\Gamma$ are both functions of α. Thus, a MD problem may be written

$$\min_{\alpha \in \Re^p} [\hat{\pi}_n - (B^{-1} \otimes I_k)\gamma]^\top A_n [\hat{\pi}_n - (B^{-1} \otimes I_k)\gamma] \tag{13.15}$$

for some choice of the matrix A_n. Next notice that, since the data are assumed to satisfy (13.1), we must also have

$$\mathbf{Y} - \mathbf{Z}\alpha = \mathbf{U} = (B \otimes I_m)\mathbf{Y} - (I_m \otimes \mathbf{X})\gamma.$$

Hence, premultiplying the above identity by $I_m \otimes \mathbf{X}^\top$ and using the definition of $\hat{\pi}_n$, gives

$$(I_m \otimes \mathbf{X}^\top)(\mathbf{Y} - \mathbf{Z}\alpha) = (I_m \otimes \mathbf{X}^\top)[(B \otimes I_m)\mathbf{Y} - (I_m \otimes \mathbf{X})\gamma]$$
$$= (B \otimes \mathbf{X}^\top\mathbf{X})\hat{\pi}_n - (I_m \otimes \mathbf{X}^\top\mathbf{X})\gamma$$
$$= (I_m \otimes \mathbf{X}^\top\mathbf{X})[(B \otimes I_k)\hat{\pi}_n - \gamma].$$

Letting $s_{XY} = n^{-1}(I_m \otimes \mathbf{X}^\top)\mathbf{Y}$ and $S_{XZ} = n^{-1}(I_m \otimes \mathbf{X}^\top)\mathbf{Z}$, we then have

$$s_{XY} - S_{XZ}\alpha = (I_m \otimes S_{XX})[(B \otimes I_k)\hat{\pi}_n - \gamma] = (B \otimes S_{XX})[\hat{\pi}_n - (B^{-1} \otimes I_k)\gamma],$$

where $S_{XX} = n^{-1}\mathbf{X}^\top\mathbf{X}$. Because the matrix $B \otimes S_{XX}$ is nonsingular, problem (13.15) is equivalent to the following problem

$$\min_{\alpha \in \Re^p} \; [s_{XY} - S_{XZ}\alpha]^\top A_n^*[s_{XY} - S_{XZ}\alpha] \tag{13.16}$$

for some choice of the matrix A_n^*. The solution to problem (13.16) is easily seen to be of the form

$$\hat{\alpha}_n = (S_{ZX}\, A_n^*\, S_{XZ})^{-1} S_{ZX}\, A_n^*\, s_{XY}$$
$$= [\mathbf{Z}^\top(I_m \otimes \mathbf{X})A_n^*(I_m \otimes \mathbf{X}^\top)\mathbf{Z}]^{-1}\mathbf{Z}^\top(I_m \otimes \mathbf{X})A_n^*(I_m \otimes \mathbf{X}^\top)\mathbf{Y}.$$

Notice that the 3SLS estimator may be viewed as a MD estimator based on the weight matrix $A_n^* = (\tilde{\Sigma}_n^{-1} \otimes S_{XX})^{-1}$.

For asymptotic efficiency, the inverse of the weight matrix A_n in problem (13.15) must be a consistent estimate of $\mathrm{AV}(\hat{\pi}_n)$, such as

$$\hat{V}_n = n^{-1} \sum_{i=1}^{n} (\hat{V}_i \hat{V}_i^\top \otimes S_{XX}^{-1}\, X_i X_i^\top\, S_{XX}^{-1}),$$

where $\hat{V}_i$ is the m-vector of reduced form residuals. Because

$$(B \otimes P)\; \mathrm{AV}(\hat{\pi}_n)\, (B^\top \otimes P) = \mathrm{E}(U_i U_i^\top \otimes X_i X_i^\top),$$

where $U_i = BV_i$ is the m-vector of structural form errors, an asymptotically optimal choice of weight matrix for problem (13.16) is

$$A_n^* = [n^{-1} \sum_i (\hat{U}_i \hat{U}_i^\top \otimes X_i X_i^\top)]^{-1},$$

where $\hat{U}_i$ is the m-vector of structural residuals obtained from some consistent but inefficient procedure, such as 2SLS applied to each equation in isolation. It is easy to verify that if the structural form errors are homoskedastic, that is, $\mathrm{Var}(U_i \,|\, X_i) = \Sigma$, then an optimal weight matrix is $A_n^* = (\hat{\Sigma}_n \otimes S_{XX})^{-1}$, where $\hat{\Sigma}_n$ is some consistent estimator of Σ. If Σ is estimated by the matrix $\tilde{\Sigma}_n$ in Section 13.4.1, then the asymptotically efficient MD estimator coincides with the 3SLS estimator.

BIBLIOGRAPHIC NOTES

In this chapter we deliberately avoided parametric assumptions about the distribution of the data and only relied on information about their first and second moments. For a more advanced treatment, including pseudo maximum likelihood methods based on the Gaussian distribution, see Hausman (1975, 1983), Hendry (1976), Magnus and Neudecker (1988) and Sargan (1988). For an alternative approach based on the multivariate t-distribution see Prucha and Kelejian (1984). For an application of the LAD method to the estimation of a single equation in a linear simultaneous equation model see Amemiya (1982) and Powell (1983).

Hsiao (1983) presents conditions for the identifiability of dynamic linear simultaneous equation models. For a discussion of identifiability via constraints on the model second moment matrix see Hausman and Taylor (1983) and Hausman, Newey and Taylor (1987).

For a discussion of the "incredible" nature of the exclusion constraints traditionally imposed to attain identifiability of macroeconomic models see Sims (1980).

The material in Section 13.4.2 is based on Chamberlain (1982). A general review of the finite sample properties of simultaneous equation estimators is Phillips (1983).

PROBLEMS

13.1 Consider the following reduced form of a linear simultaneous equation model

$$\begin{aligned} Y_1 &= 5 + 6X_1 + 3X_2 + 2X_3 + V_1, \\ Y_2 &= 2 + 3X_1 + 4X_2 + X_3 + V_2, \\ Y_3 &= X_1 + X_3 + V_3. \end{aligned}$$

Assume that the structural form of the model incorporates the following constraints

$$\begin{aligned} \beta_{11} &= \beta_{22} = \beta_{33} = 1, \\ \beta_{12} &= \beta_{21} = \beta_{32} = 0, \\ \gamma_{11} &= \gamma_{22} = \gamma_{33} = 0, \\ \gamma_{31} &= -2. \end{aligned}$$

For each equation, determine whether such constraints are sufficient to identify the structural parameters or they are inconsistent with the reduced form coefficients.

13.2 Consider the linear simultaneous equation model

$$\begin{aligned} Y_1 + \beta_{12} Y_2 + \gamma_1 X &= U_1, \\ Y_2 + \gamma_2 X &= U_2, \\ Y_3 + \gamma_3 X &= U_3, \end{aligned}$$

where $U = (U_1, U_2, U_3)$ is a random vector with mean zero and variance $\Sigma = [\sigma_{ij}]$.

(i) Are β_{12} and γ_1 identifiable in the absence of further information?

(ii) If it is known that $\sigma_{13} = 0$, are β_{12} and γ_1 identifiable? (*Hint*: There is no need to know the conditions for identifiability through covariance constraints. Just think in terms of instrumental variables.)

(iii) If $\sigma_{13} \neq 0$ but $\sigma_{12} = 0$, are β_{12} and γ_1 identifiable?

13.3 Consider the linear simultaneous equation model

$$\begin{aligned} \beta_{11}Y_1 + \beta_{12}Y_2 + \beta_{13}Y_3 + \gamma_1 X &= U_1, \\ \beta_{21}Y_1 + \beta_{22}Y_2 + \beta_{23}Y_3 + \gamma_2 X &= U_2, \\ \beta_{31}Y_1 + \beta_{32}Y_2 + \beta_{33}Y_3 + \gamma_3 X &= U_3, \end{aligned}$$

where $U = (U_1, U_2, U_3)$ is a random vector with mean zero and variance $\Sigma = [\sigma_{ij}]$.

(i) If it is known that $\beta_{12} = \beta_{13} = \beta_{23} = 0$, which equations are identifiable?
(ii) If, in addition, it is known that $\sigma_{12} = \sigma_{23} = 0$, which equations are now identifiable?
(iii) If it is also known, in addition to (i) and (ii), that $\sigma_{13} = 0$, which equations are identifiable? What special property has the model in this case?

13.4 Consider the linear simultaneous equation model

$$\begin{aligned} Y_1 + \beta_{12}Y_2 + \gamma_{11}X_1 + \gamma_{12}X_2 &= U_1, \\ \beta_{21}Y_1 + Y_2 + \gamma_{21}X_1 + \gamma_{22}X_2 &= U_2, \end{aligned}$$

where $U = (U_1, U_2)$ is a random vector with mean zero. Discuss model identifiability under the following constraints:

(i) $\gamma_{12} = 0$;
(ii) $\gamma_{12} = 0$ and $\gamma_{11} = -\gamma_{21}$;
(iii) $\beta_{21} = \gamma_{21} = 0$.

13.5 Consider the linear simultaneous equation models

$$\begin{aligned} Y_1 + \beta_{12}Y_2 + \gamma_1 X &= U_1, \\ Y_1 + \beta_{22}Y_2 + \gamma_2 &= U_2, \end{aligned} \tag{13.17}$$

and

$$\begin{aligned} Y_1 + \beta_{12}Y_2 &= U_1, \\ Y_1 + \beta_{22}Y_2 + \gamma_{21} + \gamma_2 X &= U_2, \end{aligned}$$

where $U = (U_1, U_2)$ is a random vector with mean zero. Show that the second model implies constraints on the reduced form, while this is not true for the first.

13.6 Consider the Gaussian linear simultaneous equation model $BY + \Gamma X = U$, where $U \sim \mathcal{N}(0, \Sigma)$. Given a random sample of size n from the distribution of (X, Y):

(i) derive the log-likelihood of the model in structural form;
(ii) derive the log-likelihood of the model in reduced form and the ML estimator of the reduced form parameters.

13.7 Consider the Gaussian linear simultaneous equation model

$$\begin{aligned} Y_1 + \beta_{12}Y_2 &= U_1, \\ Y_1 + \beta_{22}Y_2 + \gamma_2 &= U_2. \end{aligned}$$

Construct an estimator of γ_2 from the OLS estimate of the reduced form. Show that this estimator is consistent and coincides with the 2SLS estimator. Repeat this exercise for the first equation in model (13.17) and comment on the results obtained.

13.8 Prove Theorem 13.1.

13.9 Prove Theorem 13.3.

13.10 Given a linear simultaneous equation model, show that the generalized 2SLS estimator is asymptotically at least as efficient as the estimator obtained by applying 2SLS to each equation in isolation.

13.11 Given a linear simultaneous equation model, show that the 3SLS estimate reduces to the set of 2SLS estimates for each equation in isolation when:

(i) the errors in each equation are contemporaneously uncorrelated, or
(ii) each equation is exactly identifiable.

13.12 (Nelson & Startz 1990) Let the data be a random sample from the linear simultaneous equation model

$$Y_1 = \beta Y_2 + U_1,$$
$$Y_2 = \gamma^{-1} U_1 + U_2,$$
$$X = \delta U_2 + U_3,$$

where U_1, U_2 and U_3 are independent Gaussian random variables with zero mean and finite variance, and $\sum_i U_{i2} U_{i3} = 0$.

(i) Derive the asymptotic distribution of the 2SLS estimator $\hat{\beta}_n$ of β.
(ii) What happens to the asymptotic distribution of $\hat{\beta}_n$ as $\delta \to 0$?
(iii) Derive the exact distribution of $\hat{\beta}_n$ and compare it with the asymptotic one.

13.13 Give sufficient conditions for the 3SLS estimator to be asymptotically equivalent to the generalized 2SLS estimator.

14

Nonparametric Methods

In this chapter we assume that the data $(X_1, Y_1), \ldots, (X_n, Y_n)$ are a sample from the distribution of a continuous random vector (X, Y) and we discuss nonparametric methods for estimating the CMF or regression function $\mu(x) = \mathrm{E}(Y \mid X = x)$ of Y. These methods are useful not only for exploratory data analysis, that is, for an informal study of the properties of a particular data set, but also for estimating certain aspects of the CMF, such as its derivatives, its maxima and minima, etc., as well as for the specification and testing of parametric models.

We begin with the problem of estimating a density function. Besides being interesting in itself, a solution to this problem may be used to construct a nonparametric estimate of the CMF for, given an estimate $\hat{f}(x, y)$ of the joint density of (X, Y), the analogy principle suggests estimating $\mu(x)$ by

$$\hat{\mu}(x) = \int y \, \frac{\hat{f}(x, y)}{\hat{f}_X(x)} \, dy, \tag{14.1}$$

where $\hat{f}_X(x) = \int \hat{f}(x, y) \, dy$. More generally, many statistical problems involve estimation of a statistical functional $T(f)$ of the population density f. In all these cases, if $\hat{f}$ is a good estimate of f, then a plausible estimate of $\theta = T(f)$ is simply $\hat{\theta} = T(\hat{f})$.

14.1 DENSITY ESTIMATION

Although the distribution function and the density function are equivalent ways of representing a probability distribution, there are certain advantages in analyzing a density. For example, the graphic of a density is easier to interpret than that of a distribution function, especially with regard to aspects such as symmetry or multimodality. Further, estimates of certain population parameters, such as the mode, can more easily be obtained from an estimate of the density.

14.1.1 EMPIRICAL DENSITIES

Let $Z_1, \ldots, Z_n$ be a sample from the distribution of a random variable Z. What method is appropriate for estimating the population density depends on the nature of Z. If Z is a discrete random variable, with a distribution that assigns positive probability mass to the points $z_1, z_2, \ldots$, a plausible estimate of the probability $f(z_j) = \Pr\{Z = z_j\}$ is the fraction of sample points for which $Z_i = z_j$

$$\hat{f}(z_j) = n^{-1} \sum_{i=1}^{n} 1\{Z_i = z_j\},$$

called the *empirical probability* that $Z_i = z_j$. Formally, $\hat{f}(z_j)$ is the size of the jump of the empirical distribution function at the point z_j.

The above estimate only works if the distribution of Z is discrete. If Z is a continuous random variable and z is any point in a sufficiently small interval $(a, b]$ then, by the definition of probability density,

$$f(z) \approx \frac{\Pr\{a < Z \leq b\}}{b-a} = \frac{F(b) - F(a)}{b-a}.$$

Because the empirical distribution function $\hat{F}$ is a reasonable estimate of the parent distribution function F, a natural estimate of $f(z)$ is

$$\hat{f}(z) = \frac{\hat{F}(b) - \hat{F}(a)}{b-a} = \frac{\sum_i 1\{a < Z_i \leq b\}}{n(b-a)}, \qquad a < z \leq b, \tag{14.2}$$

called the *empirical probability density* of Z_i at the point z. Notice that $\hat{f}(z)$ is the fraction of sample points falling into the interval $(a, b]$ divided by the length $b - a$ of such an interval. If no sample value is repeated and the interval $(a, b]$ is small enough, then it contains at most one data point and so $\hat{f}(z)$ is equal either to zero or to $[n(b-a)]^{-1}$.

The sampling properties of $\hat{f}(z)$ follow immediately from the fact that the numerator of (14.2) is the average of n i.i.d. random variables, each having a Bernoulli distribution with mean equal to $F(b) - F(a)$. In particular,

$$\mathrm{E}\, \hat{f}(z) = \frac{F(b) - F(a)}{b-a},$$

that is, the estimator $\hat{f}(z)$ is generally biased for $f(z)$, although the bias is negligible when the interval $(a, b]$ is sufficiently small. Further

$$\begin{aligned}\operatorname{Var} \hat{f}(z) &= \frac{[F(b) - F(a)][1 - F(b) + F(a)]}{n(b-a)^2} \\ &= \frac{1}{n(b-a)} \frac{F(b) - F(a)}{b-a} - \frac{1}{n} \left[\frac{F(b) - F(a)}{b-a}\right]^2,\end{aligned}$$

which shows that, for a fixed sample size n, choosing a small interval $(a, b]$ around z tends to reduce the bias but also to increase the sampling variability of the empirical density. This trade-off between bias (systematic error) and sampling variability (random error) is typical of nonparametric estimation problems with n fixed.

A *histogram* is a classical example of an empirical probability density. Let $(a_0, b_0]$ be an interval that contains the range of the data, and partition $(a_0, b_0]$ into m subintervals or *bins* $(c_{j-1}, c_j]$ of equal width $\delta = (b_0 - a_0)/m$, with

$$c_j = c_{j-1} + \delta = a_0 + j\delta, \qquad j = 1, \ldots, m-1,$$

Figure 63 Histograms computed for a sample of 200 observations from a distribution that is $\mathcal{N}(0,1)$ with probability 3/5 and $\mathcal{N}(4,4)$ with probability 2/5. The histograms are computed for $m = 5$, $m = 25$ and $m = 50$ bins of equal width. The broken curve denotes the population density f.

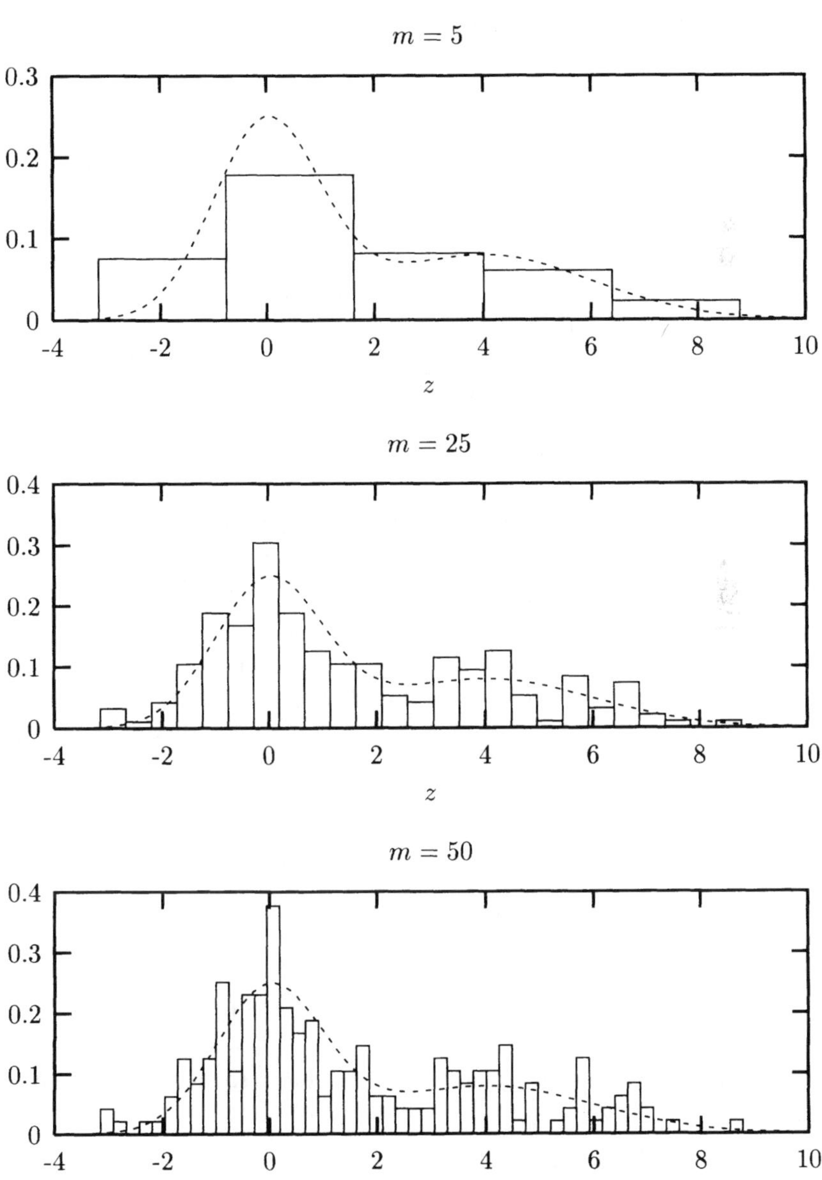

and $c_m = b_0$. The ith sample point belongs to the jth bin if $c_{j-1} < Z_i \leq c_j$. A histogram estimate of $f(z)$ is the fraction of observations falling in the bin containing z divided by the bin width δ. Formally, for all z in $(c_{j-1}, c_j]$, we have

$$\tilde{f}(z) = \frac{\hat{F}(c_j) - \hat{F}(c_{j-1})}{\delta} = \frac{1}{n\delta} \sum_{i=1}^{n} 1\{c_{j-1} < Z_i \leq c_j\}.$$

It is easy to verify that $\tilde{f}$ is a proper density, that is, $\tilde{f}(z) \geq 0$ and $\int \tilde{f}(z)\, dz = 1$.

Although widely used, the histogram method has four important drawbacks.

1. The results depend on the choice of the range $(a_0, b_0]$.
2. The results also depend on the bin width and the number of cells (Figure 63). For example, given the data, increasing the number m of bins tends to give a histogram that is only informative about the location of the distinct sample points. By contrast, reducing the number of bins eventually leads to a completely uninformative rectangle. It is intuitively clear, however, that as the sample size n increases, the histogram may be made more informative by increasing the number of bins.
3. The histogram is a step function with jumps at the end of each bin. Thus, not only it is impossible to incorporate prior information on the degree of smoothness of a density, but the use of this method may create difficulties when estimates of the derivatives of the density are needed as input of other statistical procedures.
4. The fact that the bin width is kept fixed over the range of the data may lead to loss of detail where the data are most concentrated. If the bin width is reduced to deal with this problem, then spurious noise may appear in regions of low density of the data.

To illustrate the sampling properties of the histogram, let $Z_1, \ldots, Z_n$ be a sample from a continuous distribution on the interval $(0, 1]$, with distribution function F and probability density f. Put $a_0 = 0$, $b_0 = 1$, and partition the interval $(0, 1]$ into m bins of equal width $\delta = 1/m$. If X_j denotes the number of observations falling in the jth bin and z is any point in the jth bin, then the histogram estimator of $f(z)$ is $\tilde{f}(z) = X_j/(n\delta)$. The random m-vector $(X_1, \ldots, X_m)$ has a multinomial distribution with index n and parameter $\pi = (\pi_1, \ldots, \pi_m)$, where

$$\pi_j = F(c_j) - F(c_{j-1}) = F(c_j) - F(c_j - \delta), \qquad j = 1, \ldots, m.$$

Hence

$$\Pr\{X_1 = x_1, \ldots, X_m = x_m\} = \frac{n!}{x_1! \cdots x_m!} \prod_{j=1}^{m} \pi_j^{x_j},$$

where $x_j = 0, 1, \ldots, n$. By the properties of the multinomial distribution, X_j has mean equal to $n\pi_j$ and variance equal to $n\pi_j(1 - \pi_j)$ and therefore

$$\mathrm{E}\, \tilde{f}(z) = \frac{\pi_j}{\delta}, \qquad \mathrm{Var}\, \tilde{f}(z) = \frac{\pi_j(1 - \pi_j)}{n\delta^2}.$$

Thus, the histogram estimator is biased for $f(z)$ in general and its bias is just the error made in approximating $f(z)$ by π_j/δ.

What happens when the number of bins $m = m_n$ increases with the sample size or, equivalently, the bin width $\delta_n = 1/m_n$ decreases? First notice that

$$\frac{F(z) - F(z - \delta_n)}{\delta_n} \to f(z),$$

provided that $\delta_n \to 0$ as $n \to \infty$. If we denote by $\{(a_{j_n-1}, a_{j_n}]\}$ the sequence of bins that contain the point z and let $\pi_{j_n} = F(a_{j_n}) - F(a_{j_n-1})$, then $\mathrm{E}\,\tilde{f}(z) = \pi_{j_n}/\delta_n \to f(z)$ as $\delta_n \to 0$, that is, the bias of $\tilde{f}(z)$ tends to vanish if the bin width is progressively reduced as the sample size grows. On the other hand, because

$$\operatorname{Var} \tilde{f}(z) = \frac{1}{n\delta_n} \frac{\pi_{j_n}}{\delta_n} - \frac{1}{n} \left(\frac{\pi_{j_n}}{\delta_n} \right)^2 \to \frac{1}{n\delta_n} f(z)$$

as $\delta_n \to 0$, the precision of $\tilde{f}(z)$ increases with the sample size only if $n\delta_n \to \infty$ or, equivalently, only if $m_n/n \to 0$, that is, the number m_n of bins grows at a slower rate than n.

14.1.2 THE KERNEL METHOD

The histogram method is a very useful tool for exploratory data analysis, but it has some undesirable features. Among these are the need to choose a partition of the range of Z into cells, and the fact that the resulting estimates of f are not continuous. We now present a related method that tries to overcome these two problems.

Consider the empirical density (14.2). Putting $a = z - \delta$ and $b = z + \delta$, where δ is a small positive number, gives

$$\tilde{f}(z) = \frac{\sum_i 1\{z - \delta < Z_i \le z + \delta\}}{2\delta n}$$

(Figure 64). The product $2\delta\tilde{f}(z)$ is just the fraction of sample points that lie in the interval $(z - \delta,\, z + \delta]$. Because $z - \delta < Z_i \le z + \delta$ if and only if $Z_i - \delta \le z < Z_i + \delta$, another way of interpreting the estimate $\tilde{f}(z)$ is the following:

1. place a "box" of width equal to 2δ and height equal to $(2n\delta)^{-1}$ around each observation Z_i;
2. add up the heights of the "boxes" that contain the point z; the result is equal to $\tilde{f}(z)$.

If we contructed a histogram of constant cell width 2δ having z as the center of one of its cells, then $\tilde{f}(z)$ would coincide with the histogram estimate. The advantage over the histogram method is that there is no need to partition the range of Z into cells, although we still have the dependence of the estimate on the constant δ and the fact that $\tilde{f}$ is a step function with jumps at the points $z = Z_i \pm \delta$.

It is simple, however, to modify $\tilde{f}$ in order to obtain estimates of f that are smooth. Notice that $\tilde{f}(z)$ may also be written

$$\tilde{f}(z) = \frac{1}{n\delta} \sum_{i=1}^{n} w\left(\frac{z - Z_i}{\delta} \right),$$

Figure 64 Empirical density $\tilde{f}(z)$ of the data in Figure 63 for $\delta = .5$, $\delta = 1$ and $\delta = 1.5$. The broken curve denotes the true density of the data.

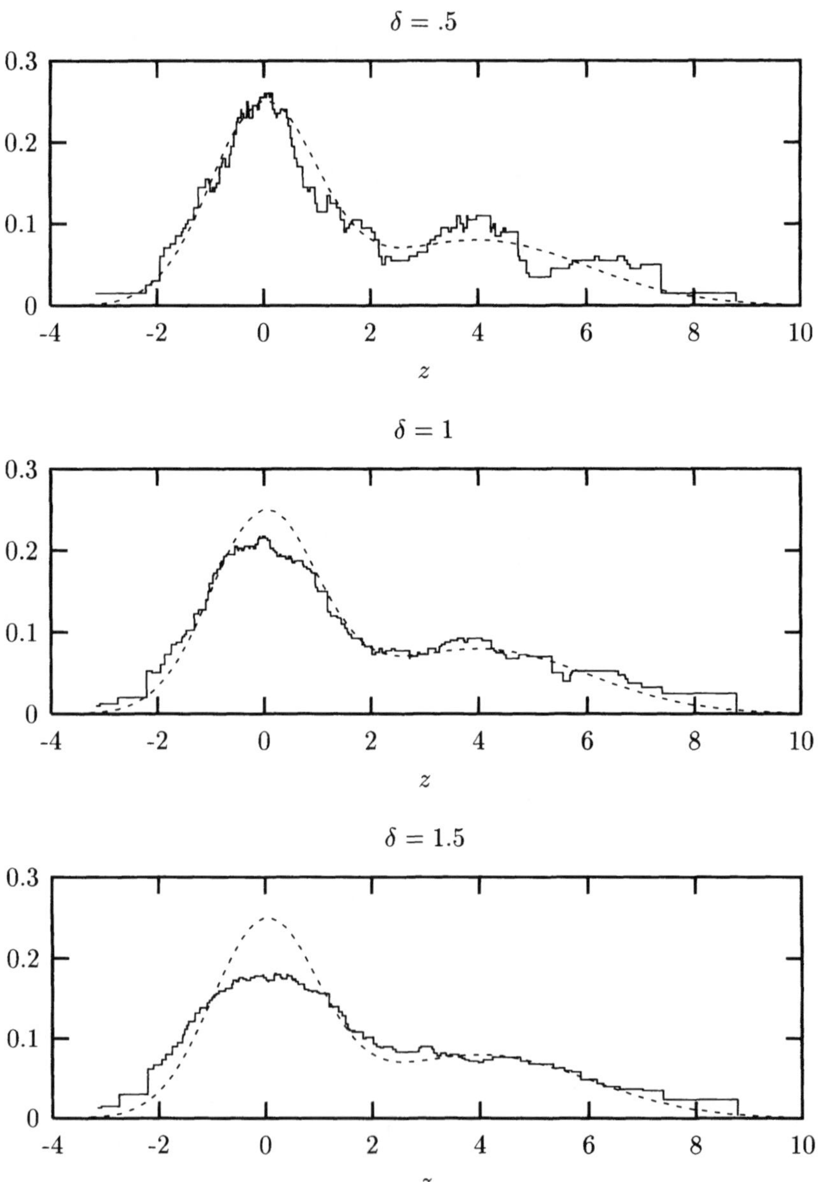

where

$$w(u) = \begin{cases} 1/2, & \text{if } -1 \le u < 1, \\ 0, & \text{otherwise} \end{cases} \tag{14.3}$$

is a symmetric bounded non-negative function that integrates to one and corresponds to the density of a uniform distribution on the interval $[-1, 1]$. This representation makes it clear that the unsatisfactory nature of $\tilde{f}$ is due to its being a sum of step functions. Since the sum of smooth functions is itself smooth, replacing w by a smooth function K gives an estimate of f which inherits all the continuity and differentiability properties of K. This leads to the class of estimates of $f(z)$ of the form

$$\hat{f}(z) = \frac{1}{n\delta} \sum_{i=1}^{n} K\left(\frac{z - Z_i}{\delta}\right),$$

where K is a bounded function called the *kernel* and δ is a positive constant called the *bandwidth.* An estimate in this class is called a *kernel estimate* of $f(z)$. If K integrates to one, then $\hat{f}$ also integrates to one, if K is a proper density, that is, $K \ge 0$ and $\int K(u)\, du = 1$, then $\hat{f}$ is also a proper density, and if K is differentiable up to order r, so is $\hat{f}(z)$. The bandwidth δ controls the degree of smoothness or regularity of a density estimate. Small values of δ tend to produce estimates that are irregular, while high values of δ correspond to very smooth estimates.

If K corresponds to the density of a random variable U, then $\delta^{-1}K((v - Z_i)/\delta)$ corresponds to the density of the location and scale transformation $V_i = Z_i + \delta U$ of U. In this case, the kernel estimate of $f(z)$ may be viewed as the average height at the point z of n densities with the same spread and the same shape, each centered around one of the observations. The smaller is δ, the more concentrated is each density and therefore the smaller is the number of observations that contribute in an appreciable way to form $\hat{f}(z)$ and the more irregular is the resulting estimate of $f(z)$.

Example 14.1 If $K = \phi$, where ϕ denotes the density of the $\mathcal{N}(0, 1)$ distribution, then the kernel estimate of f is continuous and has continuous derivates of every order (Figure 65). Such an estimate may be viewed as the average of n Gaussian densities, each centered about one of the observations and with common variance equal to the squared bandwidth δ^2 (Figure 66).

Unlike the uniform kernel (14.3), which takes constant positive value in the interval $[Z_i - \delta,\ Z_i + \delta)$ and vanishes outside this interval, the Gaussian kernel is always positive, assumes its maximum when $z = Z_i$ and tends to zero as $|z - Z_i| \to \infty$. Hence, while the uniform kernel estimate of $f(z)$ is based only on the observations that are within δ distance from the evaluation point z and assigns them a constant weight, the Gaussian kernel estimate is based on all the observations but assigns them a weight that declines exponentially as the distance from the evaluation point increases. □

The fact that the bandwidth is independent of the point where the density is estimated is a nuisance, for it tends to produce spurious effects in regions where the data are very sparse. If a sufficiently large bandwidth is chosen to eliminate this phenomenon, we may end up losing important detail in regions where the data are more concentrated. Other methods, such as the one discussed in Section 14.3.1, allow the bandwidth to vary with the local density of the data.

Figure 65 Density estimates based on a Gaussian kernel for the data in Figure 63. The broken curve denotes the true density of the data.

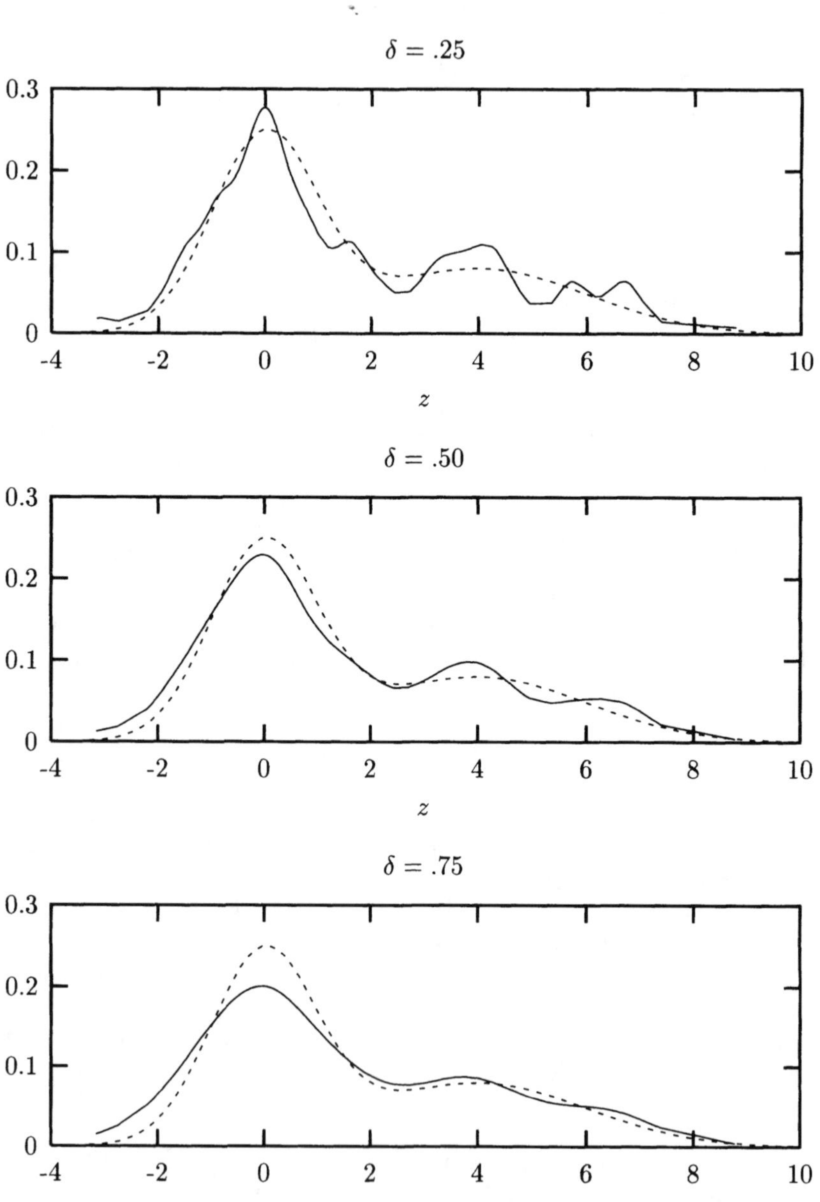

Figure 66 Decomposition of a kernel density estimate based on a Gaussian kernel. The data are denoted by a small vertical line. The broken curve denotes the density estimate $\hat{f}(z)$, while the solid curves represent its individual components $(n\delta)^{-1}K((z - Z_i)/\delta)$, $i = 1, \ldots, 6$.

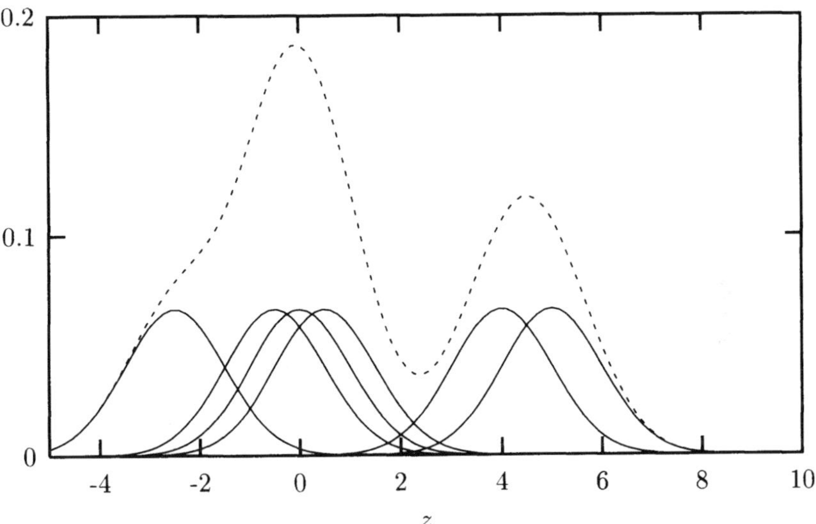

Given an estimate $\hat{f}$ of f, one may easily estimate other aspects of the distribution of Z. For example, a natural estimate of the mode of Z is the mode of $\hat{f}$.

Example 14.2 Recall that an alternative characterization of the distribution of a continuous non-negative random variable Z is the hazard function $\lambda(z) = f(z)/[1 - F(z)]$, where F denotes the distribution function of Z. If $Z_1, \ldots, Z_n$ is a sample from the distribution of Z and $\hat{f}$ is a kernel estimate of f, then an estimate of $\lambda(z)$ is simply obtained by replacing f with $\hat{f}$ and F with the empirical distribution function $\hat{F}$. Alternatively, if K is a smooth kernel, F may be replaced by the smooth estimate

$$\tilde{F}(z) = \int_{-\infty}^{z} \hat{f}(u)\, du = n^{-1} \sum_{i=1}^{n} \mathcal{K}\left(\frac{z - Z_i}{\delta}\right),$$

where $\mathcal{K}(u) = \int_{-\infty}^{u} K(v)\, dv$. If K corresponds to a proper density, then $\mathcal{K}$ is the associated distribution function, and so $\hat{F}$ is itself a proper distribution function. □

The kernel method may be generalized without conceptual difficulty to the case when $Z = (X, Y)$ is a bivariate random variable with density f. Given a sample $(X_1, Y_1), \ldots, (X_n, Y_n)$ from the distribution of (X, Y), a bivariate kernel density estimate of f is of the form

$$\hat{f}(x, y) = \frac{1}{n\delta_X \delta_Y} \sum_{i=1}^{n} K\left(\frac{x - X_i}{\delta_X}, \frac{y - Y_i}{\delta_Y}\right), \tag{14.4}$$

where $K\colon \Re^2 \to \Re$ is a bivariate kernel.

14.2 STATISTICAL PROPERTIES OF THE KERNEL METHOD

In evaluating the statistical accuracy of a density estimator $\hat{f}$, it is important to distinguish between its local and global properties. The first kind of property refers to the accuracy of $\hat{f}(z)$ as an estimator of the value of f at a given point z, the second refers to the degree of statistical "closeness" between the two functions $\hat{f}$ and f. To stress its dependence on the bandwidth δ, a kernel density estimator will henceforth be denoted by $\hat{f}_\delta$.

14.2.1 LOCAL PROPERTIES

Consider, for simplicity, the kernel estimator of a univariate density. As a local measure of performance, consider the MSE of $\hat{f}_\delta(z)$

$$\mathrm{MSE}[\hat{f}_\delta(z)] = \mathrm{E}[\hat{f}_\delta(z) - f(z)]^2 = \mathrm{Var}\,\hat{f}_\delta(z) + [\mathrm{Bias}\,\hat{f}_\delta(z)]^2.$$

Because $\hat{f}_\delta(z)$ may be represented as a sample average, assuming that the data are a sample from the distribution of Z immediately gives

$$\mathrm{E}\,\hat{f}_\delta(z) = \frac{1}{\delta}\,\mathrm{E}\,K\left(\frac{z-Z}{\delta}\right), \qquad \mathrm{Var}\,\hat{f}_\delta(z) = \frac{1}{n\delta^2}\,\mathrm{Var}\,K\left(\frac{z-Z}{\delta}\right).$$

The estimator $\hat{f}_\delta(z)$ is therefore biased for $f(z)$ in general. For δ fixed, its bias does not depend on the sample size, whereas its sampling variance tends to zero as n increases.

Under additional assumptions about the density f and the kernel K, it is possible to study in more detail the sampling properties of $\hat{f}_\delta(z)$.

Assumption 14.1
(i) *The density f is twice continuously differentiable.*
(ii) *The kernel K satisfies*

$$\int K(u)\,du = 1, \qquad \int uK(u)\,du = 0, \qquad 0 < \int u^2 K(u)\,du < \infty.$$

If K is a non-negative function, then Assumption 14.1 requires K to be the density of some nondegenerate probability distribution with zero mean and finite variance.

The bias of $\hat{f}_\delta(z)$ is

$$\begin{aligned}\mathrm{Bias}\,\hat{f}_\delta(z) &= \frac{1}{\delta}\int K\left(\frac{z-x}{\delta}\right) f(x)\,dx - f(z)\\ &= \int K(u)\,[f(z-\delta u) - f(z)]\,du,\end{aligned}$$

after a change of variable from $(z-x)/\delta$ to u and using the fact that K integrates to one. Because the density f is twice differentiable, a Taylor's series expansion of $f(z-\delta u)$ about $\delta = 0$ gives

$$f(z-\delta u) - f(z) = -\delta u f'(z) + \frac{1}{2}\delta^2 u^2 f''(z) + O(\delta^3).$$

If δ is sufficiently small, then

$$\text{Bias}\,\hat{f}_\delta(z) \approx -\delta f'(z) \int uK(u)\,du + \frac{1}{2}m_2\delta^2 f''(z) = \frac{1}{2}m_2\,\delta^2 f''(z), \tag{14.5}$$

where $m_2 = \int u^2K(u)\,du$ is finite and we used the fact that K has mean zero.

Formula (14.5) shows that the bias of $\hat{f}_\delta(z)$ depends on the degree of curvature $f''(z)$ of the density at the point z, and on the amount of smoothing of the data through the bandwidth δ and the spread m_2 of the kernel, but not directly on the sample size. In particular, the bias is approximately zero when $f''(z) = 0$, that is, when the density is linear in a neighborhood of z. Further, Bias $\hat{f}_\delta(z) \to 0$ as $\delta \to 0$. Thus, if the bandwidth depends on the sample size in such a way that $\delta \to 0$ as $n \to \infty$, then the bias of $\hat{f}_\delta(z)$ tends to vanish in large samples.

Because the bias of $\hat{f}_\delta(z)$ is at most of order δ^2, we have

$$\begin{aligned}\text{Var}\,\hat{f}_\delta(z) &= \frac{1}{n\delta^2}\int K\left(\frac{z-x}{\delta}\right)^2 f(x)\,dx - \frac{1}{n}\,[f(z) + \text{Bias}\,\hat{f}_\delta(z)]^2 \\ &= \frac{1}{n\delta}\int f(z-\delta u)\,K(u)^2\,du - \frac{1}{n}\,[f(z) + O(\delta^2)]^2,\end{aligned}$$

after a change of variable from $(z-x)/\delta$ to u. Expanding $f(z-\delta u)$ in Taylor's series around $\delta = 0$ gives

$$\begin{aligned}\text{Var}\,\hat{f}_\delta(z) &= \frac{1}{n\delta}\int [f(z) - \delta u f'(z)]\,K(u)^2\,du + O(n^{-1}) \\ &= \frac{f(z)}{n\delta}\int K(u)^2\,du - \frac{f'(z)}{n}\int uK(u)^2\,du + O(n^{-1}).\end{aligned}$$

In large samples and for δ sufficiently small, we therefore have

$$\text{Var}\,\hat{f}_\delta(z) \approx \frac{1}{n\delta}f(z)\int K(u)^2\,du.$$

If the sample size is fixed, increasing the bandwidth reduces the sampling variability of $\hat{f}_\delta(z)$ but, from (14.11), it also increases its bias. On the other hand, if the sample size increases and smaller bandwidths are chosen for larger n, then both the bias and the sampling variance of $\hat{f}_\delta(z)$ may be reduced. Notice that consistency of $\hat{f}_\delta(z)$ for $f(z)$ requires not only $\delta \to 0$ as $n \to \infty$, but also $n\delta \to \infty$, that is, the bandwidth must decrease at a slower rate than n.

To conclude, in large samples and for δ sufficiently small, the MSE of $\hat{f}_\delta(z)$ is approximately equal to

$$\frac{f(z)}{n\delta}\int K(u)^2\,du + \frac{1}{4}m_2^2\,\delta^4\,f''(z)^2. \tag{14.6}$$

14.2.2 GLOBAL PROPERTIES

We now study some global properties of $\hat{f}_\delta$ as an estimator of the function f. Common measures of distance between two functions f and g are the L_1 distance

$$d_1(f,g) = \int_{-\infty}^{\infty} |f(g) - g(z)|\,dz,$$

the L_2 distance

$$d_2(f,g) = \int_{-\infty}^{\infty} [f(z) - g(z)]^2 \, dz,$$

and the uniform or L_∞ distance

$$d_\infty(f,g) = \sup_{-\infty<z<\infty} |f(z) - g(z)|.$$

In the case of the L_2 distance, a global measure of performance of $\hat{f}_\delta$ as an estimator of f is the *mean integrated squared error (MISE)*

$$\text{MISE}(\hat{f}_\delta) = \text{E}\, d_2(\hat{f}_\delta, f) = \text{E} \int_{-\infty}^{\infty} [\hat{f}_\delta(z) - f(z)]^2 \, dz,$$

where the expectation is with respect to joint distribution of $Z_1, \ldots, Z_n$. Under appropriate regularity conditions, interchanging the order of integration gives

$$\text{MISE}(\hat{f}_\delta) = \int_{-\infty}^{\infty} \text{E}[\hat{f}_\delta(z) - f(z)]^2 \, dz = \int_{-\infty}^{\infty} \text{MSE}[\hat{f}(z)] \, dz,$$

that is, the MISE is equal to the integrated MSE. In large samples and for δ sufficiently small, one may therefore approximate the MISE by integrating expression (14.6) under the further assumption that the second derivative of f is square integrable, that is,

$$R(f) = \int f''(z)^2 \, dz < \infty.$$

Our global measure of performance is therefore

$$\text{MISE}(\hat{f}_\delta) \approx \frac{1}{n\delta} \int K(u)^2 \, du + \frac{1}{4} m_2^2 \, \delta^4 \, R(f). \tag{14.7}$$

14.2.3 OPTIMAL CHOICE OF BANDWIDTH AND KERNEL FUNCTION

As a way of choosing an optimal bandwidth for a fixed sample size, consider minimizing the right-hand side of (14.7) with respect to δ. Assuming that $0 < R(f) < \infty$, it is easily seen that the optimal bandwidth is

$$\delta_* = \left[\frac{\int K(u)^2 \, du}{m_2^2 \, R(f)} \right]^{1/5} n^{-1/5} = O(n^{-1/5}), \tag{14.8}$$

which convergences to zero as $n \to \infty$ but at the rather slow rate of $n^{-1/5}$. Notice that smaller values of δ_* are appropriate for densities that are more wiggly, that is, such that $R(f)$ is high, or kernels that are more spread out, that is, such that m_2 is high.

Example 14.3 If f is a $\mathcal{N}(\mu, \sigma^2)$ density and K is a standard Gaussian kernel, then

$$R(f) = \sigma^{-5} \int \phi''(z)^2 \, dz = \frac{3}{8\sqrt{\pi}} \sigma^{-5}$$

and

$$\int K(u)^2\,du = \frac{1}{2\sqrt{\pi}}.$$

The optimal bandwidth in this case is $\delta_* = (4/3)^{1/5}\sigma n^{-1/5} \approx 1.059\,\sigma n^{-1/5}$. □

Substituting the optimal bandwidth δ_* into (14.7) gives

$$\text{MISE}(\hat{f}_{\delta_*}) \approx \frac{5}{4}\,C(K)\,R(f)^{1/5}\,n^{-4/5},$$

where

$$C(K) = m_2^{2/5}\left[\int K(u)^2\,du\right]^{4/5}.$$

Given the optimal bandwidth, the MISE depends on the choice of kernel function only through the term $C(K)$. Suppose that we confine our attention to kernels that correspond to densities of distributions with mean zero and finite variance. An optimal kernel may then be obtained by minimizing $C(K)$ under the side conditions

$$K(u) \geq 0 \text{ for all } u, \qquad \int K(u)\,du = 1,$$

$$\int u\,K(u)\,du = 0, \qquad \int u^2\,K(u)\,du = 1,$$

where the last condition is an innocuous normalization. It may be shown that the optimal kernel is

$$K_*(u) = \frac{3}{4}(1-u^2)\;1\{|u| \leq 1\},$$

called the *Epanechnikov kernel* (Figure 73). The efficiency loss from using suboptimal kernels, however, is modest. For example, using the uniform kernel w only implies an efficiency loss of about 7 percent with respect to K_*. Thus, "it is perfectly legitimate, and indeed desirable, to base the choice of kernels on other considerations, for example the degree of differentiability or the computational effort involved" (Silverman 1986, p. 43).

It turns out that the crucial choice is not what kernel to use, but rather how much to smooth. This choice partly depends on the purpose of the analysis. If we are only interested in exploring the data, then a subjective choice of the bandwidth δ may be appropriate. A natural way of proceeding is to plot several curves, each corresponding to a different amount of smoothing, and choose the one that comes closest to one's prior ideas about the density. If we are interested in presenting conclusions, it may be desirable to undersmooth somewhat rather than oversmooth, because the human eye can always eliminate the irregularity of a curve, but certainly cannot unsmooth.

14.2.4 AUTOMATIC BANDWIDTH SELECTION

It is often convenient to be able to rely on some procedure for choosing the bandwidth automatically rather than subjectively. This is especially important when a density estimate is used as an input to other statistical procedures.

The simplest approach, motivated by the result in Example 14.3, consists of choosing $\delta = 1.059\hat{\sigma}/n^{1/5}$, where $\hat{\sigma}$ is some estimate of the standard deviation of the data. This approach works reasonably well for Gaussian kernels and data that are not too far from Gaussian.

A second approach (Sheater & Jones 1991) is based on formula (14.8) and chooses

$$\delta = \left[\frac{\int K(u)^2 \, du}{m_2^2 \, R(\tilde{f})} \right]^{1/5} n^{-1/5},$$

where $\tilde{f}$ is a preliminary kernel estimate of f based on some initial bandwidth choice.

A third approach starts from the observation that the MISE of a kernel density estimator $\hat{f}_\delta$, based on a given kernel K, may be decomposed as

$$\text{MISE}(\hat{f}_\delta) = M(\delta) + \int f(z)^2 \, dz,$$

where

$$M(\delta) = \mathrm{E} \int \hat{f}_\delta(z)^2 \, dz - 2 \int \hat{f}_\delta(z) f(z) \, dz.$$

Hence, the MISE of $\hat{f}_\delta$ depends on the choice of the bandwidth only through the term $M(\delta)$. Minimizing the MISE with respect to δ is therefore equivalent to minimizing the function $M(\cdot)$ with respect to δ. Because such a function is unknown, a possibility is minimizing with respect to δ an unbiased estimate of $M(\cdot)$.

In order to construct such an unbiased estimate, notice first that $\int \hat{f}_\delta(z)^2 \, dz$ is clearly unbiased for $\mathrm{E} \int \hat{f}_\delta(z)^2 \, dz$. Now consider the estimate of $f(z)$ obtained by excluding the ith observation

$$\hat{f}_{(i)}(z) = \frac{1}{(n-1)\delta} \sum_{j \neq i} K\left(\frac{z - Z_j}{\delta} \right). \tag{14.9}$$

If the data are a sample from the distribution of Z, then

$$\mathrm{E} \left[\frac{1}{n} \sum_{i=1}^{n} \hat{f}_{(i)}(Z_i) \right] = \mathrm{E}\, \hat{f}_{(i)}(Z_i) = \mathrm{E} \int \hat{f}_{(i)}(z) f(z) \, dz = \mathrm{E} \int \hat{f}_\delta(z) f(z) \, dz,$$

where we used the fact that $\mathrm{E}\, \hat{f}_\delta(z)$ does not depend on the sample size. Thus, an unbiased estimate of $M(\delta)$ is the cross-validation criterion

$$\hat{M}(\delta) = \int \hat{f}_\delta(z)^2 \, dz - \frac{2}{n} \sum_{i=1}^{n} \hat{f}_{(i)}(Z_i). \tag{14.10}$$

The cross-validation procedure selects the bandwidth for which $\hat{M}(\delta)$ is smallest.

The calculation of $\hat{M}(\delta)$ is simplified if the kernel K corresponds to a symmetric density. It can be shown in this case (see for example Silverman 1986, p. 50) that

$$\int \hat{f}_\delta(z)^2 \, dz = \frac{1}{\delta n^2} \sum_{i=1}^{n} \sum_{j=1}^{n} K^{(2)} \left(\frac{Z_i - Z_j}{\delta} \right),$$

where $K^{(2)}(x) = \int K(x-u)\, K(u)\, du$ denotes the convolution of the kernel with itself, and

$$n^{-1} \sum_{i=1}^{n} \hat{f}_{(i)}(Z_i) = \frac{1}{n(n-1)\delta} \left[\sum_{i=1}^{n} \sum_{j=1}^{n} K\left(\frac{Z_i - Z_j}{\delta}\right) - nK(0) \right].$$

Replacing the factor $(n-1)^{-1}$ in (14.9) by n^{-1} gives the even simpler expression

$$\tilde{M}(\delta) = \frac{1}{\delta n^2} \left[\sum_{i=1}^{n} \sum_{j=1}^{n} K_*\left(\frac{X_i - X_j}{\delta}\right) + 2nK(0) \right],$$

where $K_*(u) = K^{(2)}(u) - 2K(u)$.

An asymptotic justification for choosing the bandwidth by minimizing the cross-validation criterion (14.10) has been given by Stone (1984). Let $I_{CV}(Z_1, \ldots, Z_n)$ denote the integrated squared error when the bandwidth is chosen to minimize (14.10) with respect to $\delta \geq 0$ for a given sample $Z_1, \ldots, Z_n$, and let $I_*(Z_1, \ldots, Z_n)$ denote the integrated squared error when the bandwidth is chosen optimally, that is,

$$I_*(Z_1, \ldots, Z_n) = \min_{\delta > 0} \int [\hat{f}_\delta(z) - f(z)]^2\, dz.$$

Stone (1984) showed that, if f is bounded and some other mild regularity conditions hold then

$$\frac{I_{CV}(Z_1, \ldots, Z_n)}{I_*(Z_1, \ldots, Z_n)} \to 1$$

as $n \to \infty$, that is, cross-validation achieves asymptotically the best choice of smoothing parameter in the sense of minimizing the integrated squared error for a given sample.

The main drawback of cross-validation is that the resulting kernel estimates tend to be highly variable and to undersmooth the data.

14.2.5 ASYMPTOTIC PROPERTIES

In this section we present some large sample properties of multivariate density estimators based on the kernel method. Given a sample of size n from the distribution of a random m-vector Z, we consider kernel estimators of the form

$$\hat{f}_n(z) = \frac{1}{n\delta_n^m} \sum_{i=1}^{n} K\left(\frac{z - Z_i}{\delta_n}\right),$$

where $K\colon \Re^m \to \Re$ is an m-variate kernel, and we make explicit the dependence of both the bandwidth and the density estimator on the sample size n. This type of kernel density estimator is a special case of (14.4), obtained by using the same bandwidth δ for each component of Z. This may be appropriate when the data have being previously rescaled using some preliminary estimate of scale.

The next two theorems provide sufficient conditions for a sequence $\{\hat{f}_n(z)\}$ of kernel density estimators to be consistent for the population density $f(z)$ and asymptotically normal. Both results rely on the fact that $\hat{f}_n(z)$ may be represented as an average of the n random variables

$$K_i(z) = \frac{1}{\delta_n^m} K\left(\frac{z - Z_i}{\delta_n}\right), \qquad i = 1, \dots, n.$$

If the kernel function K integrates to one and satisfies $\int uK(u)\,du = 0$ and $M_2 = \int uu^\top K(u)\,du < \infty$, then the mean of each of these random variables is

$$\mathrm{E}\, K_i(z) = f(z) + \frac{1}{2}\delta_n^2\, b(z) + O(\delta_n^3), \tag{14.11}$$

where $b(z) = \mathrm{tr}[f''(z)M_2]$, and the variance is

$$\mathrm{Var}\, K_i(z) = \frac{1}{\delta_n^m}\left[f(z)\int K(u)^2\,du + \delta_n f'(z)^\top \int uK(u)^2\,du\right] + O(\delta_n^4). \tag{14.12}$$

Results (14.11) and (14.12) are straightforward generalizations of the ones derived in Section 14.2.1.

Theorem 14.1 *Let $\{Z_i\}$ be a sequence of i.i.d. continuous random m-vectors with a twice continuously differentiable density f, and suppose that the sequence $\{\delta_n\}$ of bandwidths and the kernel $K\colon \Re^m \to \Re$ satisfy:*

(i) $\delta_n \to 0$;
(ii) $n\delta_n^m \to \infty$;
(iii) $\int K(u)\,du = 1$, $\int uK(u)\,du = 0$ *and* $\int uu^\top K(u)\,du = M_2$, *a finite* $m \times m$ *matrix.*

Then $\hat{f}_n(z) \xrightarrow{p} f(z)$ for every z in the support of f.

Proof. The result follows directly from the Chebyshev inequality since $\mathrm{E}\,\hat{f}_n(z) = \mathrm{E}\, K_i(z) = f(z)$ as $\delta_n \to \infty$ and $\mathrm{Var}\,\hat{f}_n(z) = n^{-1}\,\mathrm{Var}\, K_i(z) \to 0$ as $n\delta_n^m \to \infty$. □

The next theorem could in principle be used to construct confidence intervals for $f(z)$ based on the asymptotically normal distribution.

Theorem 14.2 *In addition to the assumptions of Theorem 14.1, suppose:*

(iv) $\delta_n^2(n\delta_n^m)^{1/2} \to \lambda$, *where* $0 \le \lambda < \infty$.

Then

$$\sqrt{n}\,\delta_n^{m/2}\,[\hat{f}_n(z) - f(z)] \xrightarrow{d} \mathcal{N}\left(\frac{1}{2}\lambda\, b(z),\ f(z)\int K(u)^2\,du\right)$$

for every z in the support of f, where $b(z) = \mathrm{tr}[f''(z)M_2]$.

Proof. Since $\{Z_i\}$ is a sequence of i.i.d. random vectors, $\{K_i(z)\}$ is a sequence of i.i.d. random variables with mean equal to (14.11) and finite p.d. variance matrix equal to (14.12). For δ_n fixed and sufficiently small, the Lindeberg–Lévy CLT then implies

$$\sqrt{n}\,\delta_n^{m/2}\,\frac{[\hat{f}_n(z) - f(z) - \frac{1}{2}\delta_n^2 b(z)]}{[f(z)\int K(u)^2\,du + \delta_n f'(z)^\top \int uK(u)^2\,du]^{1/2}} \xrightarrow{d} \mathcal{N}(0,1).$$

Figure 67 Rates of convergence to 0 of $n^{-1/2}$, $n^{-2/5}$, $n^{-1/3}$ and $n^{-1/4}$. The last three are equal to the rate of convergence to the asymptotic normal distribution of m-variate kernel density estimates for $m = 1$, $m = 2$ and $m = 4$ respectively.

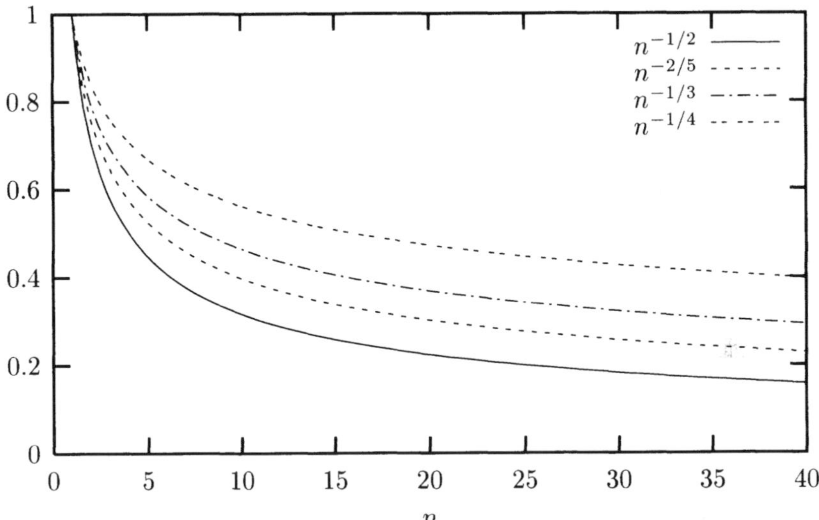

The conclusion then follows from assumptions (i) and (iv). □

Some remarks about the last result are in order. First, the speed of convergence of $\hat{f}_n(z)$ to its asymptotically normal distribution is inversely related to the dimension m of the random vector whose density is to be estimated. This essentially reflects the "curse of dimensionality" problem discussed in Section 14.6.1.

Second, although consistent, $\hat{f}_n(z)$ is generally asymptotically biased for $f(z)$. There are three cases when no asymptotic bias arises: (i) when δ_n is chosen such that $\lambda = 0$; (ii) when $f''(z) = 0$, that is, the density of Z is linear at the point z; (iii) when $\int uu^\top K(u)\,du = 0$, in which case the kernel K may assume negative values and therefore the estimate $\hat{f}_n$ may fail to be a proper density.

Third, when $\lambda > 0$, assumption (iv) implies that $\delta_n = O(n^{-1/(m+4)})$. In this case, putting $\delta_n = cn^{-1/(m+4)}$, where c is a positive constant, gives $\lambda = c^{(m+4)/2}$ and $\sqrt{n}\,\delta_n^{m/2} = c^{m/2} n^{2/(m+4)}$, and therefore

$$n^{2/(m+4)}\,[\hat{f}_n(z) - f(z)] \xrightarrow{\text{d}} \mathcal{N}\left(\frac{1}{2}c^2 b(z),\; c^{-m} f(z) \int K(u)^2\,du\right).$$

In particular, in the univariate case ($m = 1$) we have that $\delta_n = O(n^{-1/5})$, which is the rate of convergence to zero of the optimal bandwidth derived in Section 14.2.3. In this case, $\hat{f}_n(z)$ converges to the Gaussian distribution at the rate of $n^{-2/5}$, which is slower than the rate $n^{-1/2}$ achieved in regular parametric problems (Figure 67).

Fourth, when $\lambda = 0$, the bandwidth tends to zero at a faster rate than $O(n^{-1/(m+4)})$ but the convergence of $\hat{f}_n(z)$ to the Gaussian distribution is slower than the optimal rate.

14.3 OTHER METHODS FOR DENSITY ESTIMATION

We now consider other methods for estimating a density f nonparametrically. Section 14.3.1 presents the nearest neighbor method, while Section 14.3.2 presents the maximum penalized likelihood method.

14.3.1 THE NEAREST NEIGHBOR METHOD

One of the problems with the kernel method is the fact that the bandwidth is independent of the point at which the density is evaluated. This tends to produce too much smoothing in some regions of the data and too little in others. The nearest neighbor method is a way of making the bandwidth depend on the density of the data in a neighborhood of the evaluation point.

For each point evaluation z, let $d_1(z) \leq d_2(z) \leq \ldots \leq d_n(z)$ be the distances, arranged in ascending order, between z and each of the n data points. The kth *nearest neighbor estimate* of $f(z)$ is defined as

$$\hat{f}(z) = \frac{k}{2n\, d_k(z)}, \qquad k < n.$$

To understand the rationale for this estimate notice that, if the sample is large enough, then we would expect approximately $2n\delta f(z)$ observations to fall in a small interval $[z - \delta,\, z + \delta]$ around z. Since the closed interval $[z - d_k(z),\, z + d_k(z)]$ contains by definition exactly k observations, an estimate $\hat{f}$ of the density may be obtained by inverting the relation $k = 2n\, d_k(z)\hat{f}(z)$. Unlike the rectangular kernel estimator which is based on the number of observations falling in a box of fixed width centered at the point z, the nearest neighbor estimate is inversely proportional to the width of the box needed to exactly contain the k observations nearest to z. The smaller is the density of the data around z, the larger is this width. The number k regulates the degree of smoothness of the estimates, with larger values of k corresponding to smoother estimates. The fraction $\lambda = k/n$ of sample points in each neighborhood is called the *span*.

There are two problems with the nearest neighbor method. First, $\hat{f}$ does not integrate to one and so it is not a proper density. Second, although continuous, $\hat{f}$ is not smooth, for its derivatives are discontinuous at all points of the form $(Z_{[i]} + Z_{[i+k]})/2$, where $Z_{[i]}$ denotes the ith order statistic of the sample.

One way of overcoming the second problem is to notice that $\hat{f}(z)$ may alternatively be represented as

$$\hat{f}(z) = \frac{1}{nd_k(z)} \sum_{i=1}^{n} w\left(\frac{z - Z_i}{d_k(z)}\right),$$

where w is the uniform kernel (14.3). Thus, the nearest neighbor estimate may be regarded as a uniform kernel estimate with a bandwidth $d_k(z)$ which varies with z. The lack of smoothness of the nearest neighbor estimate depends therefore on the use of a kernel that is not continuous and a bandwidth $d_k(z)$ that varies in a nonsmooth fashion with the evaluation point z. Substituting the uniform kernel w with a general kernel K gives a *generalized nearest neighbor estimate*, defined as

$$\tilde{f}(z) = \frac{1}{nd_k(z)} \sum_{i=1}^{n} K\left(\frac{z - Z_i}{d_k(z)}\right).$$

If K is a smooth kernel and the bandwidth $d_k(z)$ is a continuously differentiable function, then $\tilde{f}$ is a smooth estimate of f.

14.3.2 THE MAXIMUM PENALIZED LIKELIHOOD METHOD

The log-likelihood of a sample $Z_1, \ldots, Z_n$ from a distribution with strictly positive density f is defined as

$$L(f) = c + \sum_{i=1}^{n} \ln f(Z_i),$$

where c is an arbitrary constant. Thus, one may think of estimating f by selecting a function $\hat{f}$, out of some class $\mathcal{F}$ of probability density functions, which maximizes the sample log-likelihood. If the class $\mathcal{F}$ is a parametric family of densities, then we obtain the classical ML estimate. At the other extreme, if the class $\mathcal{F}$ includes all densities on the real line, then the sample likelihood can be shown to be maximized by

$$\hat{f}(z) = n^{-1} \sum_{i=1}^{n} \delta(z - Z_i),$$

where $\delta(u)$ is the Dirac delta function, which is equal to ∞ if $u = 0$ and is equal to zero otherwise. Thus, the nonparametric ML estimate of f is a function whose value is equal to infinity at each of the sample points and is equal to zero otherwise. This ought not to be surprising, for $\hat{f}$ may be regarded as the derivative of the empirical distribution function which, in turn, is the nonparametric ML estimate of the parent distribution function.

The function $\hat{f}$ is infinitely irregular and therefore provides a rather unsatisfactory solution to the problem of estimating f. If one is unwilling to make parametric assumptions, an alternative is to introduce a penalty for the lack of smoothness of an estimate and then maximize the likelihood function subject to this constraint. Assuming that the second derivative of the population density f is square integrable, a functional that may be used to quantify the degree of smoothness of f is $R(f) = \int f''(z)^2 dz$. Densities that are wiggly result in large values of $R(f)$. On the other hand, if the support of the distribution is an interval and the density is linear, then $R(f) = 0$. For other types of penalty see Good and Gaskins (1971).

Introducing this criterion for lack of smoothness, one may consider maximizing the *penalized log-likelihood*

$$L_\lambda(f) = \sum_{i=1}^{n} \ln f(Z_i) - \lambda R(f),$$

where $\lambda > 0$ is a parameter that represents the trade-off between smoothness and fidelity to the data. A *maximum penalized likelihood density estimate* is a solution $\hat{f}$ to the problem of maximizing L_λ over the class of density functions with continuous first derivative and square integrable second derivative. Clearly, the smaller is λ, the rougher in terms of $R(\hat{f})$ is the maximum penalized likelihood estimator.

The maximum penalized likelihood method has several attractive features. First, it makes explicit two often conflicting goals in density estimation: one is maximizing fidelity to the data, represented here by the term $\sum_i \ln f(Z_i)$, the other is avoiding densities that are too wiggly, represented here by the term $-\lambda R(f)$. Second, the method places density estimation within the context of a unified approach to curve estimation. Third, the method can be given a nice Bayesian interpretation. A disadvantage of the method is that the estimate $\hat{f}$ is defined only implicitly, as the solution to a maximization problem.

14.4 REGRESSION SMOOTHERS

Let $\mathbf{Y}$ be an n-vector of observations on a response variable and let $\mathbf{X}$ be a matrix of n observations on k covariates. We call a *regression smoother* any statistical method for summarizing the dependence of $\mathbf{Y}$ on $\mathbf{X}$. Using a regression smoother produces a vector $\hat{\boldsymbol{\mu}} = (\hat{\mu}_1, \ldots, \hat{\mu}_n)$ of fitted values of the elements of $\mathbf{Y}$ that is usually less variable than $\mathbf{Y}$ itself.

A regression smoother is said to be *linear* if it can be represented as $\hat{\boldsymbol{\mu}} = S\mathbf{Y}$, where $S = [s_{ij}]$ is an $n \times n$ matrix, called the *smoother matrix*, that depends on $\mathbf{X}$ but not on $\mathbf{Y}$. Thus, the class of linear regression smoothers coincides with the class of linear predictors of $\mathbf{Y}$. If $\hat{\boldsymbol{\mu}}$ is a linear regression smoother, then its ith element is a linear combination or weighted average $\hat{\mu}_i = \sum_{j=1}^n s_{ij} Y_j$ of the elements of $\mathbf{Y}$, and the generic element s_{ij} of the matrix S represents the weight assigned to the jth element of $\mathbf{Y}$ in the construction of $\hat{\mu}_i$. An example of a linear regression smoother is the OLS projection vector $\hat{\mathbf{Y}} = H\mathbf{Y}$, where $H = \mathbf{X}(\mathbf{X}^\top\mathbf{X})^{-1}\mathbf{X}^\top$ is a symmetric idempotent matrix.

A smoother matrix is not necessarily symmetric or idempotent. A matrix S is said to *preserve the constant* if $S^\top \iota = \iota$, where ι is a vector of ones. If a smoother matrix S preserves the constant, then

$$n^{-1} \sum_{i=1}^n \hat{\mu}_i = n^{-1} \iota_n^\top S\mathbf{Y} = n^{-1} \iota_n^\top \mathbf{Y} = \bar{Y},$$

where $\bar{Y}$ is the sample mean of the Y_i. For example, the OLS smoother matrix preserves the constant if the design matrix $\mathbf{X}$ contains a column of ones.

Regression smoothers may be used for several purposes, including (i) exploration and description of the data, (ii) estimation of the conditional mean of $\mathbf{Y}$ given $\mathbf{X}$, and (iii) diagnostic checking of a parametric regression model. The second purpose is the object of this section. Using regression smoothers for diagnostic checking of a parametric regression model will be discussed briefly in Section 14.5.4.

Assume that the data $[\mathbf{X}, \mathbf{Y}]$ are a sample from the joint distribution of (X, Y), for which the CMF $\mu(x) = \mathrm{E}(Y \mid X = x)$ is well defined. The statistical problem is estimating the function $\mu(x)$. Consider the class of estimates that are nonparametric, that is, do not depend on parametric assumptions about the shape of $\mu(x)$, and linear, that is, of the form

$$\hat{\mu}(x) = \sum_{j=1}^{n} S_j(x)\, Y_j, \tag{14.13}$$

where the weight $S_j(x)$ assigned to Y_j depends only on $X_1, \ldots, X_n$ and the evaluation point x. Letting $\hat{\mu}_i = \hat{\mu}(X_i)$ and $s_{ij} = S_j(X_i)$, we may represent a linear nonparametric estimate of $\mu(x)$ as a linear smoother. This fact is useful for at least two reasons. First, it simplifies considerably the task of evaluating the statistical properties of linear nonparametric estimators. Second, it enables one to compare estimates produced by methods that may apparently be quite far from each other.

The remainder of this section is devoted to some examples of linear nonparametric regression estimates. Many of these estimates are regression analogues of the ones introduced in the previous sections. For ease of presentation, we assume that X is a scalar random variable.

14.4.1 REGRESSION SPLINES

A polynomial regression represents a parsimonious and relatively flexible way of approximating an unspecified CMF. A k-degree polynomial regression approximates $\mu(x)$ by a function of the form

$$h(x) = \alpha + \beta_1 x + \cdots + \beta_k x^k.$$

Polynomial approximations are frequently used because they can be evaluated, integrated, differentiated, etc., very easily. However, if the CMF is very irregular, even on small regions of the approximation range, then a polynomial approximation tends to be poor everywhere. For an example, see de Boor (1978), pp. 22–26.

One way of avoiding global dependence on local properties of the function $\mu(x)$ is to consider piecewise polynomial functions. A ***regression spline*** approximates $\mu(x)$ by a smooth piecewise polynomial function and therefore represents a very flexible way of approximating $\mu(x)$ (the term spline denotes a flexible strip of wood or metal used to draw curves).

Example 14.4 The simplest kind of spline is the linear one. Select p distinct points or ***knots***, $c_1 < \cdots < c_p$, on the support of X. These points define a partition of $\Re$ in $p+1$ intervals. To simplify the notation, also define two boundary knots $c_0 < c_1$ and $c_{p+1} > c_p$. A ***linear spline*** is a continuous piecewise linear function, that is, of the form

$$h(x) = \alpha_j + \beta_j x, \qquad c_{j-1} < x \le c_j, \qquad j = 1, \ldots, p+1.$$

For the function h to be continuous at each point c_j, the model parameters must satisfy the constraints

$$\alpha_j + \beta_j c_j = \alpha_{j+1} + \beta_{j+1} c_j, \qquad j = 1, \ldots, p.$$

On the interval $(c_0, c_2]$, we therefore have

$$h(x) = \begin{cases} \alpha_1 + \beta_1 x, & \text{if } c_0 < x \le c_1, \\ \alpha_1 + (\beta_1 - \beta_2)c_1 + \beta_2 x, & \text{if } c_1 < x \le c_2. \end{cases}$$

Figure 68 Sample of 200 observations from the model $Y = \mu(X) + .06\,U$, where $\mu(x) = 1 - x + \exp[-50(x - .5)^2]$ and $U \sim \mathcal{N}(0, 1)$.

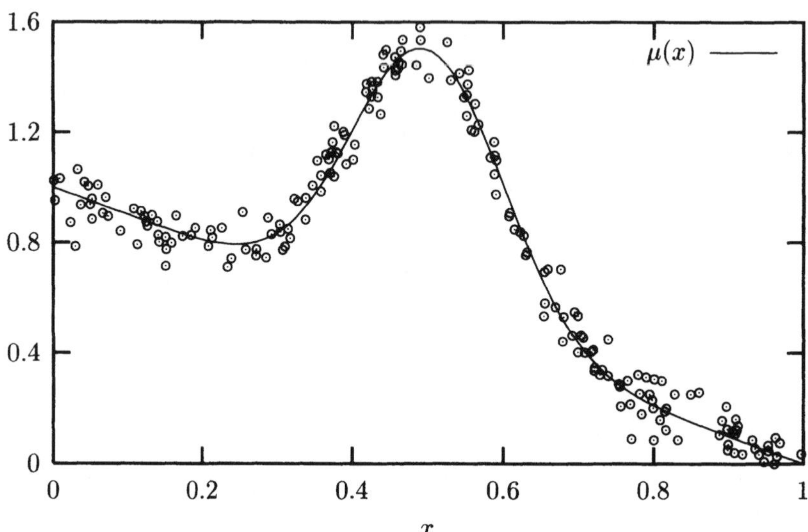

Letting $\alpha = \alpha_1$, $\beta = \beta_1$ and $\gamma_1 = \beta_2 - \beta_1$, a more compact representation of h on the interval $(c_0, c_2]$ is

$$h(x) = \alpha + \beta x + \gamma_1 (x - c_1)_+, \qquad c_0 < x \leq c_2,$$

where $(x - c_1)_+ = \max(0, x - c_1)$. Repeating this argument for all the other interior knots, a linear spline may be represented more compactly as

$$h(x) = \alpha + \beta x + \sum_{j=1}^{p} \gamma_j (x - c_j)_+,$$

where $\gamma_j = \beta_{j+1} - \beta_j$. The number of free parameters of a linear spline is only $p + 2$, which is less than the number $2(p+1)$ of parameters of an unrestricted piecewise linear function. The difference $2(p + 1) - (p + 2)$ is equal to the number of constraints that must be imposed to ensure continuity. Notice that although continuous, a linear spline is not differentiable for its derivative is a step function with jumps at $c_1, \ldots, c_p$.

Given a sample, an estimate of h is easily obtained by an OLS regression of Y_i on a constant, X_i and the p auxiliary variables $(X_i - c_j)_+$. A linear spline is therefore a linear smoother defined by a symmetric idempotent smoother matrix which depends on the sample values X_i and the number and position of the knots. The latter effectively control the flexibility and smoothness of a linear spline. As the number of knots increases, the approximation becomes more flexible, but also more choppy.

Given the sequence of knots, both the flexibility and the smoothness of a spline may be enhanced if the line segments are replaced by higher degree polynomials. One example, based on the data shown in Figure 68, is presented in Figures 69–71. □

Figure 69 Linear OLS regression and linear spline estimates for the data in Figure 68. The spline has three knots at the points $x = .25$, $x = .50$, and $x = .75$.

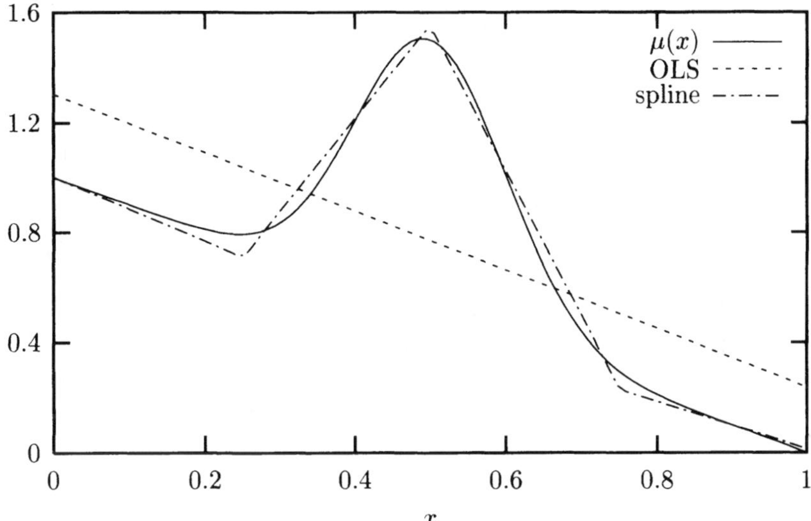

Figure 70 Quadratic OLS regression and quadratic spline estimates for the data in Figure 68. The spline has three knots at the points $x = .25$, $x = .50$, and $x = .75$.

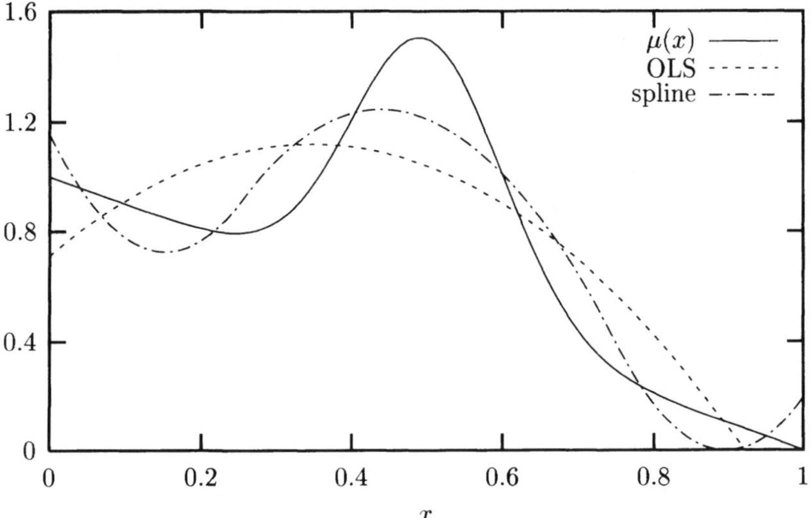

Figure 71 Cubic OLS regression and cubic spline estimates for the data in Figure 68. The spline has three knots at the points $x = .25$, $x = .50$, and $x = .75$.

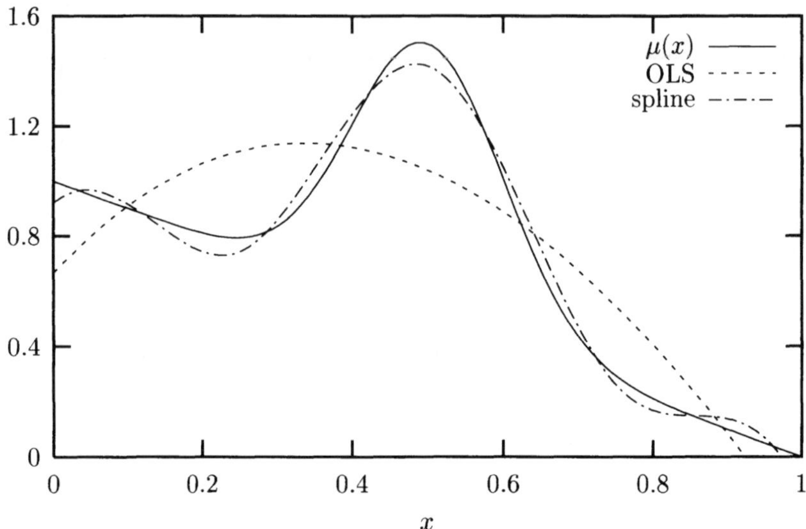

A common choice is a cubic spline, that is, a twice continuously differentiable piecewise cubic function. Given p distinct knots $c_1 < \cdots < c_p$ in the support of X, a cubic spline possesses the parametric representation

$$h(x) = \alpha + \beta_1 x + \beta_2 x^2 + \beta_3 x^3 + \sum_{j=1}^{p} \gamma_j (x - c_j)_+^3, \tag{14.14}$$

which contains $p + 4$ free parameters. It is easy to verify that the function h indeed satisfies all properties of a cubic spline, namely: (i) h is a cubic polynomial in each subinterval $[c_j, c_{j+1}]$; (ii) h is twice continuously differentiable; (iii) the third derivative of h is a step function with jumps at the points $c_1, \ldots, c_p$.

The representation (14.14) lends itself directly to estimation by the OLS method. This in turn shows that a cubic spline is a linear smoother defined by a symmetric idempotent smoother matrix. As in the case of a linear spline (Example 14.4), the number and position of the knots control the flexibility and smoothness of the approximation.

If we force the cubic spline to be linear outside the boundary knots c_0 and c_{p+1}, then we obtain a *natural cubic spline*. The number of free parameters in this case is equal to $p + 2$.

In general, given the sequence of knots and the degree of the polynomial, a regression spline may be estimated by an OLS regression of $\mathbf{Y}$ on an appropriate set of vectors that represent a basis for the selected family of piecewise polynomial functions evaluated at the sample values of X.

One problem with regression splines is how to select the number and the position of the knots. Another problem is the considerable increase in the degree of complexity of the problem when there are two or more covariates.

14.4.2 THE KERNEL METHOD

Given nonparametric estimates of the bivariate density $f(x,y)$ of (X,Y), an estimate of the CMF $\mu(x)$ may be obtained by applying formula (14.1). An advantage of the kernel method is that, under certain conditions, such an estimate may be computed directly from estimates of the marginal density $f_X(x)$ and of

$$c(x) = \int y\, f(x,y)\, dy,$$

without any need for estimating the joint density $f(x,y)$. Consider the estimate (14.4) based on a bivariate kernel K_*. If $\delta_X = \delta_Y = \delta$, putting $K(x) = \int K_*(x,y)\,dy$ gives $\int \hat{f}(x,y)\,dy = \hat{f}_X(x)$, where $\hat{f}_X(x)$ is the estimate of $f_X(x)$ based on the kernel K and the bandwidth δ. If, in addition, $K_*(x,y)$ satisfies $\int y\, K_*(x,y)\,dy = 0$, then it can be shown that

$$\hat{c}(x) = \int y\, \hat{f}(x,y)\, dy = \frac{1}{n\delta} \sum_{i=1}^{n} Y_i\, K\left(\frac{x - X_i}{\delta}\right).$$

Substituting these two expressions in (14.1) gives

$$\hat{\mu}(x) = \frac{\hat{c}(x)}{\hat{f}_X(x)} = \left[\sum_{i=1}^{n} K\left(\frac{x - X_i}{\delta}\right)\right]^{-1} \sum_{i=1}^{n} K\left(\frac{x - X_i}{\delta}\right) Y_i, \tag{14.15}$$

which is called the *Nadaraya–Watson kernel regression estimate* (Figure 72). Notice that $\hat{\mu}(x)$ is simply a weighted average of the Y_j with non-negative weights

$$w_j(x) = \left[\sum_{i=1}^{n} K\left(\frac{x - X_i}{\delta}\right)\right]^{-1} K\left(\frac{x - X_j}{\delta}\right), \qquad j = 1, \ldots, n,$$

which add up to one. The Nadaraya–Watson estimate is therefore a linear smoother whose smoother matrix $S = [w_j(X_i)]$ depends on the sample values X_i, the selected kernel K, and the bandwidth δ. If the kernel corresponds to a unimodal density with mode at zero, then the closer X_j is to x, the bigger is the weight assigned to Y_j in forming $\hat{\mu}(x)$. If the kernel vanishes outside the interval $[-1,1]$, then only values of Y for which $|x - X_j| < \delta$ enter the summation. This fact may be exploited to speed up the computations.

Example 14.5 A family of kernels with bounded support which contains many kernels used in practice is

$$K_\alpha(u) = c_\alpha (1 - u^2)^\alpha\, 1\{0 \le |u| \le 1\}, \qquad \alpha = 0, 1, 2, \ldots,$$

where the constant c_α, chosen such that K_α is a proper density, is

$$c_\alpha = 2^{-2\alpha-1}\Gamma(2\alpha+2)\,\Gamma(\alpha+1)^{-2}$$

Figure 72 Nadaraya–Watson kernel density estimates for the data in Figure 68. The kernel is the Epanechnikov kernel and the estimates correspond to two different bandwidths: $\delta = .1$ and $\delta = .2$.

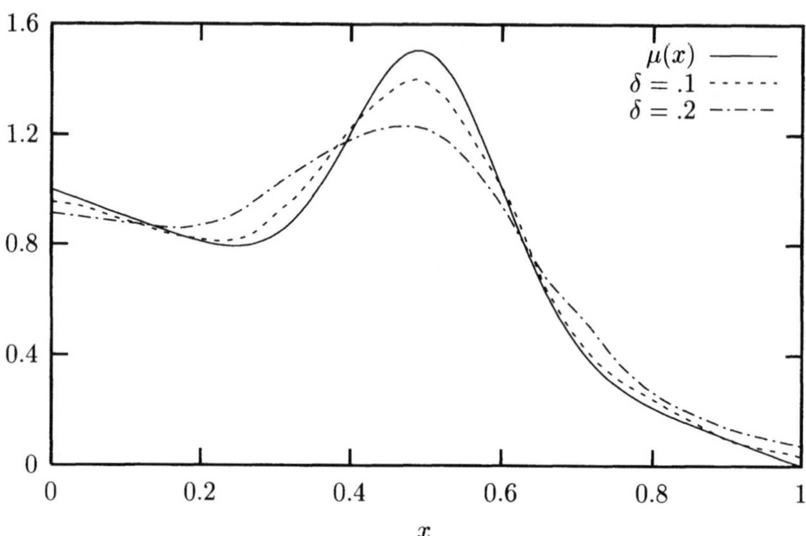

and $\Gamma(z)$ is the gamma function. Some members of this family of kernels are presented in Figure 73. The uniform kernel corresponds to $\alpha = 0$. If $\alpha = 1$, we obtain the Epanechnikov kernel. If $\alpha = 2$, we obtain the quartic kernel

$$K(u) = \frac{15}{16}(1-u^2)^2\ 1\{0 \le |u| \le 1\}.$$

If $\alpha \to \infty$, then K_α converges to the Gaussian kernel. □

Now suppose that the CMF is sufficiently smooth and consider estimating its slope

$$\mu'(x) = \frac{c'(x) - \mu(x)\, f_X'(x)}{f_X(x)}$$

and its average slope or *average derivative* $\delta = \mathrm{E}\,\mu'(X)$. If the kernel K is differentiable, then an analogue estimator of $\mu'(x)$ is

$$\hat{\mu}'(x) = \frac{\hat{c}'(x) - \hat{\mu}(x)\, \hat{f}_X'(x)}{\hat{f}_X(x)}.$$

An estimator of the average derivative δ is therefore

$$\hat{\delta} = n^{-1} \sum_{i=1}^{n} D_i\, \hat{\mu}'(X_i),$$

where $D_i = 1\{\hat{f}_X(X_i) > c_n\}$ for some trimming constant c_n that goes to zero as $n \to \infty$. The lower bound on $\hat{f}_X$ is introduced to avoid erratic behavior when the value of $\hat{f}_X(x)$ is very small.

Figure 73 Kernels from the family $\{K_\alpha(u)\}$ for different values of α.

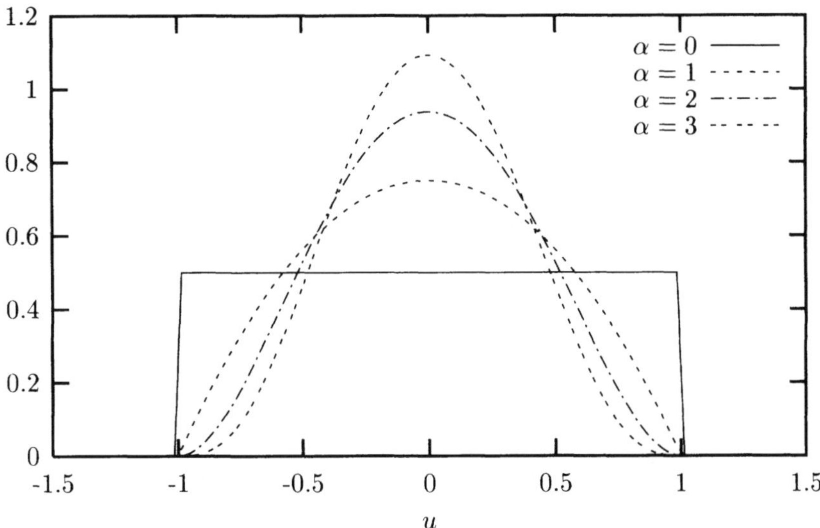

An alternative estimator may be based on the fact that, if $\mu(x)$ is a smooth function then, by part (ii) of Theorem 1.2, $\mathrm{E}\,\mu(X)s(X)$ where $s(x) = -f'_X(x)/f_X(x)$ is the score of the marginal density of X. Hence, by the law of iterated expectations,

$$\delta = \mathrm{E}\,\mu(X)\,s(X) = \mathrm{E}[s(X)\;\mathrm{E}(Y \mid X)] = \mathrm{E}\,s(X)\,Y.$$

The sample counterpart of this expression is

$$\tilde{\delta} = n^{-1} \sum_{i=1}^{n} D_i\,\hat{s}(X_i)\,Y_i,$$

where $\hat{s}(x) = -\hat{f}'_X(x)/\hat{f}_X(x)$ is the estimated score.

14.4.3 THE NEAREST NEIGHBOR METHOD

In the regression case, the nearest neighbor method suggests considering the X_i that are closest to the evaluation point x and estimating $\mu(x)$ by taking an average of the corresponding values of Y. A kth nearest neighborhood of x, written $\mathcal{O}_k(x)$, consists of the k points that are closest to x. The corresponding nearest neighbor estimate of $\mu(x)$ is

$$\hat{\mu}(x) = \frac{1}{k} \sum_{j \in \mathcal{O}_k(x)} Y_j,$$

which is just a *running average* or moving average of the Y_i. This regression estimate is clearly a linear smoother and its degree of smoothness depends on the value of k or, equivalently, on the span $\lambda = k/n$ of the neighborhood.

When X is a vector, the choice of the metric is of some importance, for it determines the shape of the neighborhoods in the covariate space. One possibility is the Euclidean distance $d(x,x') = [(x-x')^\top(x-x')]^{1/2}$. Another possibility is the Mahalanobis distance

$$d(x,x') = [(x-x')^\top \hat{\Omega}^{-1}(x-x')]^{1/2},$$

where $\hat{\Omega}$ is some p.d. estimate of the dispersion matrix of the covariates.

Using a running average may result in severe biases near the boundaries of the data, where neighborhoods tend to be highly asymmetric. A way of reducing this bias is to replace the running average by a *running line*

$$\hat{\mu}(x) = \hat{\alpha}(x) + \hat{\beta}(x)x, \tag{14.16}$$

where $\hat{\alpha}(X)$ and $\hat{\beta}(x)$ are the intercept and the slope of the OLS line computed for the k points ($k > 2$) in the neighborhood $\mathcal{O}_k(x)$. Computation of (14.16) for the n sample points may be based on the recursive formulae introduced in Section 6.2.7 and therefore requires a number of operations of order $O(n)$. This method tends to produce ragged curves but it can be improved through replacing OLS by locally weighted LS, with weights that decline as the distance of X_i from x increases. To gain flexibility, the linear specification (14.16) may be replaced by a quadratic one.

The estimates $\hat{\alpha}(x)$ and $\hat{\beta}(x)$ in (14.16) are the solution to the locally weighted LS problem

$$\min_{(\alpha,\beta)\in\Re^2} \sum_{i=1}^{n} w_i(x)(Y_i - \alpha - \beta X_i)^2,$$

where the weight $w_i(x)$ is equal to one if the ith point belongs to $\mathcal{O}_k(x)$ and to zero otherwise. By considering more general weights, we obtain different types of locally weighted running line.

Example 14.6 An example of a locally weighted running line is the *lowess* (LOcally WEighted Scatterplot Smoother) estimate introduced by Cleveland (1979) and generalized by Cleveland and Devlin (1988) to the case when X is multidimensional. A lowess estimate is computed as follows.

Algorithm 14.1

(1) *Identify the* kth *nearest neighborhood* $\mathcal{O}_k(x)$ *of* x.

(2) *Compute the distance* $\Delta(x) = \max_{i\in\mathcal{O}_k(x)} d(X_i,x)$ *of the point in* $\mathcal{O}_k(x)$ *that is farthest from* x.

(3) *Assign weights* $w_i(x)$ *to each point in* $\mathcal{O}_k(x)$ *according to the* tricube function

$$w_i(x) = W\left(\frac{d(X_i,x)}{\Delta(x)}\right),$$

where

$$W(u) = \begin{cases} (1-u^3)^3, & \text{if } 0 \le u < 1, \\ 0, & \text{otherwise.} \end{cases}$$

(4) *Compute* $\hat{\mu}(x)$ *as the predicted value of* Y *corresponding to* x *from a WLS regression that uses the observations in* $\mathcal{O}_k(x)$ *and the weights defined in step (3).*

Figure 74 Lowess estimates for the data in Figure 68. The estimates correspond to two different neighborhood spans: $\lambda = .2$ and $\lambda = .4$.

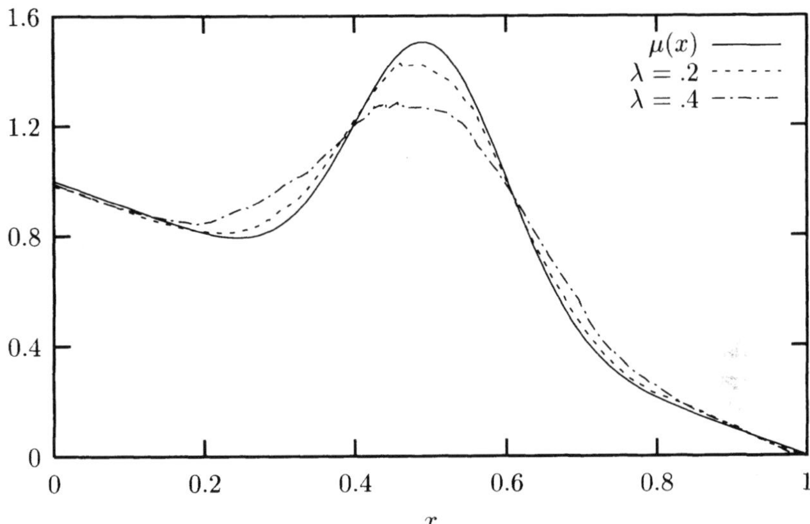

Notice that the weight $w_i(x)$ is maximum when $X_i = x$, it decreases as the distance of X_i from x increases, and becomes zero if X_i is the kth nearest neighbor of x.

Two examples of lowess estimates are presented in Figure 74. □

14.4.4 SMOOTHING SPLINES AND PENALIZED LS

The regression analogue of the maximum penalized likelihood problem introduced in Section 14.3.2 is the problem of finding a smooth function that best interpolates the observations on Y without fluctuating too wildly. This problem may be formalized as follows

$$\min_{h \in C^2[a,b]} Q(h) = \sum_{i=1}^{n} [Y_i - h(X_i)]^2 + \lambda \int_a^b h''(u)^2\, du, \tag{14.17}$$

where $C^2[a,b]$ is the class of functions defined on the closed interval $[a,b]$ that have continuous first derivative and integrable second derivative, a and b are the limits of a finite interval that contains the observed values of X, and $\lambda \geq 0$ is a fixed parameter. The function space $C^2[a,b]$ is also called a *Sobolev space*. The residual sum of squares in the functional Q corresponds to the Gaussian log-likelihood and measures fidelity to the data, whereas the second term penalizes for excessive fluctuations of the estimated CMF.

It can be shown (Reinsch 1967) that a solution $\hat{h}$ to problem (14.17) exists, is unique and can be represented as a natural cubic spline with not more than $n - 2$ interior points corresponding to the distinct sample values of X. Such a solution is called a *cubic smoothing spline*.

Because of its equivalence to a natural cubic spline, a cubic smoothing spline is clearly a linear smoother. Its definition is however only indirect, through the solution of a minimization problem that depends on the value of the parameter λ. Large values of λ tend to produce solutions that are smoother, whereas smaller values tend to produce solutions that are more wiggly. In particular, when $\lambda \to \infty$, the penalty would become arbitrarily large unless $h'' = 0$, that is, unless h is linear. Thus, when $\lambda \to \infty$, problem (14.17) reduces to the OLS problem. When $\lambda = 0$, there is no penalty for curvature and the solution $\hat{h}$ is a twice differentiable function that exactly interpolates the data.

Knowledge of the form of the solution to (14.17) makes it possible to define its smoother matrix. If we consider the representation of $\hat{h}$ as a cubic spline, then the required number of basis functions is $n-2+4 = n+2$. The solution to problem (14.17) may therefore be written

$$\hat{h}(x) = \sum_{j=1}^{n+2} \alpha_j B_j(x),$$

where $\alpha_1, \ldots, \alpha_{n+2}$ are coefficients to be determined and $B_1(x), \ldots, B_{n+2}(x)$ is a set of twice differentiable basis functions. Now define the $n \times (n+2)$ matrix $\mathbf{B} = [B_{ij}]$, where $B_{ij} = B_j(X_i)$ is the value of the jth basis function at the point X_i, and the $(n+2) \times (n+2)$ matrix $\Omega = [\Omega_{ij}]$, where

$$\Omega_{ij} = \int_a^b B_i''(x) B_j''(x)\, dx.$$

Problem (14.17) is then equivalent to the penalized LS problem

$$\min_\alpha\, (\mathbf{Y} - \mathbf{B}\alpha)^\top (\mathbf{Y} - \mathbf{B}\alpha) + \lambda \alpha^\top \Omega \alpha,$$

where $\alpha = (\alpha_1, \ldots, \alpha_{n+2})$. The problem of minimizing the functional R over a Sobolev space of functions is therefore reduced to the much simpler problem of minimizing a quadratic form in the $(n+2)$-dimensional vector α. A solution to this problem exists and must satisfy the normal equation

$$0 = -2\mathbf{B}^\top (\mathbf{Y} - \mathbf{B}\tilde{\alpha}) + 2\lambda\Omega\tilde{\alpha}.$$

If $\mathbf{B}^\top\mathbf{B} + \lambda\Omega$ is a nonsingular matrix, then

$$\tilde{\alpha} = (\mathbf{B}^\top\mathbf{B} + \lambda\Omega)^{-1}\mathbf{B}^\top\mathbf{Y}.$$

Because $\tilde{\alpha}$ formally coincides with a ridge-regression estimate, it may also be interpreted as the posterior mean of a Gaussian linear model given a prior Gaussian distribution for the regression parameter α. With this interpretation, the estimator is closely related to the one presented in Example 7.3. Since $\hat{\boldsymbol{\mu}} = \mathbf{B}\tilde{\alpha}$, the smoother matrix of a cubic smoothing spline is

$$S = \mathbf{B}(\mathbf{B}^\top\mathbf{B} + \lambda\Omega)^{-1}\mathbf{B}^\top,$$

and is symmetric but not idempotent.

14.5 STATISTICAL PROPERTIES OF LINEAR SMOOTHERS

As we have seen in the previous section, the smoother matrix of a linear smoother depends on the sample values of X and a parameter (or set of parameters) which regulates the amount of smoothing of the data. To emphasize this dependence, the smoother matrix is denoted by $S_\lambda = [s_{ij}]$, where λ is the smoothing parameter. We adopt the convention that larger values of λ correspond to more smoothing.

14.5.1 MEASURES OF ACCURACY

Let the data be a sample from the distribution of (X, Y), and suppose that the CMF $\mu(x) = \mathrm{E}(Y \mid X = x)$ and the CVF $\sigma^2(x) = \mathrm{Var}(Y \mid X = x)$ are both well defined. Let $\boldsymbol{\mu}$ and Σ denote, respectively, an n-vector with generic element $\mu_i = \mu(X_i)$ and a diagonal $n \times n$ matrix with generic element $\sigma_i^2 = \sigma^2(X_i)$. For a linear smoother $\hat{\boldsymbol{\mu}} = S_\lambda \mathbf{Y}$, with generic element $\hat{\mu}_i = \hat{\mu}(X_i)$, we have $\mathrm{E}(\hat{\boldsymbol{\mu}} \mid \mathbf{X}) = S_\lambda \boldsymbol{\mu}$ and $\mathrm{Var}(\hat{\boldsymbol{\mu}} \mid \mathbf{X}) = S_\lambda \Sigma S_\lambda^\top$. The bias of $\hat{\boldsymbol{\mu}}$ is therefore

$$\mathrm{Bias}(\hat{\boldsymbol{\mu}} \mid \mathbf{X}) = \mathrm{E}(\hat{\boldsymbol{\mu}} \mid \mathbf{X}) - \boldsymbol{\mu} = (S_\lambda - I_n)\boldsymbol{\mu}.$$

A case when $\hat{\boldsymbol{\mu}}$ is unbiased for $\boldsymbol{\mu}$ is when $\boldsymbol{\mu} = \mathbf{X}\beta$ and S_λ is such that $S_\lambda \mathbf{X} = \mathbf{X}$.

Given an estimate $\hat{\Sigma}$ of the matrix Σ, we may estimate the sampling variance of $\boldsymbol{\mu}$ by $S_\lambda \hat{\Sigma} S_\lambda^\top$. The result may then be used to construct pointwise standard error bands for the regression estimates. If the smoother is approximately unbiased, then these standard error bands also represent pointwise confidence intervals. An alternative way of constructing confidence intervals is the bootstrap.

Example 14.7 In the special case when the observations are conditionally homoskedastic, that is, $\sigma^2(x) = \sigma^2$ for all x, Σ may be estimated by $\hat{\sigma}^2 I_n$, where $\hat{\sigma}^2 = n^{-1} \sum_i (Y_i - \hat{\mu}_i)^2$. The sampling variance of $\hat{\mu}_i$ may then be estimated by $\hat{\sigma}^2 \sum_{j=1}^n s_{ij}^2$. □

As a global measure of accuracy of a linear smoother, we may consider the average conditional MSE

$$\begin{aligned}\mathrm{AMSE}(\lambda) &= n^{-1} \sum_{i=1}^n \mathrm{E}(\hat{\mu}_i - \mu_i)^2 \\ &= n^{-1}[\mathrm{tr}(S_\lambda \Sigma S_\lambda^\top) + \boldsymbol{\mu}^\top (S_\lambda - I_n)^\top (S_\lambda - I_n)\boldsymbol{\mu}].\end{aligned}$$

When the data are conditionally homoskedastic, this expression reduces to

$$\mathrm{AMSE}(\lambda) = n^{-1}[\sigma^2 \ \mathrm{tr}(S_\lambda S_\lambda^\top) + \boldsymbol{\mu}^\top (S_\lambda - I_n)^\top (S_\lambda - I_n)\boldsymbol{\mu}].$$

As a measure of predictive accuracy, we may instead consider the average mean squared error of prediction or average predictive risk

$$n^{-1} \sum_{i=1}^n \mathrm{E}(Y_i - \hat{\mu}_i)^2 = n^{-1} \sum_{i=1}^n \sigma_i^2 + \mathrm{AMSE}(\lambda).$$

In general, increasing the amount of smoothing tends to increase the bias and to reduce the sampling variance of a smoother. One method for choosing the smoothing parameter optimally is to minimize the average predictive risk with respect to λ. It may be shown, using an argument similar to the one in Section 9.3.3, that an approximately unbiased estimator of the predictive risk is the cross-validation criterion

$$\mathrm{CV}(\lambda) = n^{-1} \sum_{i=1}^{n} [Y_i - \hat{\mu}_{(i)}(X_i)]^2,$$

where $\hat{\mu}_{(i)}(X_i)$ denotes the value of the smoother at the point X_i, computed by excluding the ith observation, and $Y_i - \hat{\mu}_{(i)}(X_i)$ denotes the ith predicted residual. Minimizing $\mathrm{CV}(\lambda)$ represents an automatic method for choosing the smoothing parameter λ.

Cross-validation requires computing the sequence $\hat{\mu}_{(1)}(X_1), \ldots, \hat{\mu}_{(n)}(X_n)$. This is very simple if the smoother matrix preserves the constant. Because $\sum_i s_{ij} = 1$ in this case, $\hat{\mu}_{(i)}(X_i)$ may be computed by setting the weight of the ith observation equal to zero and then dividing all the other weights by $1 - s_{ii}$ in order for them to add up to one. This gives

$$\hat{\mu}_{(i)}(X_i) = \sum_{j \neq i} \frac{s_{ij}}{1 - s_{ii}} Y_j = \frac{\sum_{j=1}^{n} s_{ij} Y_j - s_{ii} Y_i}{1 - s_{ii}} = \frac{\hat{\mu}_i - s_{ii} Y_i}{1 - s_{ii}}.$$

Hence, the ith predicted residual is $Y_i - \hat{\mu}_{(i)}(X_i) = \hat{U}_i / (1 - s_{ii})$, where $\hat{U}_i = Y_i - \hat{\mu}_i$, and the cross-validation criterion becomes

$$\mathrm{CV}(\lambda) = \frac{1}{n} \sum_{i=1}^{n} \left(\frac{\hat{U}_i}{1 - s_{ii}} \right)^2,$$

which coincides with the result obtained for OLS in Section 9.3.3.

14.5.2 EQUIVALENT KERNELS AND EQUIVALENT DEGREES OF FREEDOM

Using the representation (14.13), it becomes easy to compare linear smoothers obtained from different methods. The set of weights $S_1(x), \ldots, S_n(x)$ assigned to the sample values of Y in the construction of $\hat{\mu}(x)$ is called the *equivalent kernel* evaluated at the point x. The ith row of the smoother matrix S_λ is just the equivalent kernel evaluated at the point X_i. A comparison of the equivalent kernels is therefore a simple and effective way of comparing different linear smoothers.

A synthetic index of the amount of smoothing of the data is the *effective number of parameters* defined, by analogy with OLS, as $k_* = \operatorname{tr} S_\lambda$. The number $df = n - k_*$ is called *equivalent degrees of freedom*. The effective number of parameters is equal to the sum of the eigenvalues of the matrix S_λ. If S_λ is a projection matrix, that is, is symmetric and idempotent as in the case of a regression spline, then $k_* = \operatorname{rank} S_\lambda$. The effective number of parameters depends mainly on the value of the smoothing parameter λ, while the configuration of the predictors tends to have a much smaller effect. As λ increases, we usually observe a decrease in k_* and a corresponding increase in *df*.

14.5.3 ASYMPTOTIC PROPERTIES OF KERNEL REGRESSION ESTIMATORS

In this section we present some asymptotic properties of regression smoothers. For simplicity, we confine our attention to estimators based on the kernel method.

Given a sample of size n from the distribution of (X,Y), where X is a random k-vector and Y is a scalar random variable, a Nadaraya–Watson estimator of the CMF of Y is

$$\hat{\mu}_n(x) = \left[\sum_{i=1}^{n} K\left(\frac{x - X_i}{\delta_n}\right)\right]^{-1} \sum_{i=1}^{n} K\left(\frac{x - X_i}{\delta_n}\right) Y_i.$$

Pointwise convergence to the CMF $\mu(x)$ of a sequence $\{\hat{\mu}_n(x)\}$ of Nadaraya–Watson regression estimators follows immediately under assumptions analogous to the ones of Theorem 14.1.

Theorem 14.3 *Suppose that the sequence $\{\delta_n\}$ of bandwidths and the kernel $K\colon \Re^k \to \Re$ satisfy:*

(i) $\delta_n \to 0$;
(ii) $n\delta_n^k \to \infty$;
(iii) $\int K(u)\,du = 1$, $\int uK(u)\,du = 0$, *and* $\int uu^\top K(u)\,du$ *is a finite* $k \times k$ *matrix.*

Then $\hat{\mu}_n(x) \xrightarrow{\text{p}} \mu(x)$ *for every* x *in the support of* X.

Proof. If $f(x)$ denotes the marginal density of X, then

$$\hat{f}_n(x) = \frac{1}{n\delta_n^k} \sum_{i=1}^{n} K\left(\frac{x - X_i}{\delta_n}\right) \xrightarrow{\text{p}} f(x).$$

Further

$$\frac{1}{n\delta_n^k} \sum_{i=1}^{n} Y_i K\left(\frac{x - X_i}{\delta_n}\right) \xrightarrow{\text{p}} \int y\, f(x,y)\,dy.$$

The conclusion then follows from Slutzky's theorem, provided that $f(x) > 0$. □

The next result establishes asymptotic normality of $\hat{\mu}_n(x)$ under general conditions.

Theorem 14.4 *In addition to the assumptions of Theorem 14.3, suppose:*

(iv) $\delta_n^2 (n\delta_n^k)^{1/2} \to \lambda$, *where* $0 \le \lambda < \infty$.

If the CMF $\mu(x)$ and the CVF $\sigma^2(x)$ are smooth and X has a twice continuously differentiable density f then

$$(n\delta_n^k)^{1/2}\, [\hat{\mu}_n(x) - \mu(x)] \xrightarrow{\text{d}} \mathcal{N}\left(\lambda \frac{b(x)}{f(x)},\ \frac{\sigma^2(x)}{f(x)} \int K(u)^2\,du\right)$$

for every x in the support of X, where $b(x)$ is defined below in the proof. Further, $(n\delta_n^k)^{1/2}[\hat{\mu}_n(x) - \mu(x)]$ and $(n\delta_n^k)^{1/2}[\hat{\mu}_n(x') - \mu(x')]$ are asymptotically independent for $x \neq x'$.

Proof. We only sketch the proof of the first part of the theorem. The details may be found in Bierens (1994). First notice that $\hat{\mu}_n(x)$ and $\hat{f}_n(x)$ are consistent estimators of $\mu(x)$ and $f(x)$ respectively, and therefore

$$[\hat{\mu}_n(x) - \mu(x)] - [\hat{\mu}_n(x) - \mu(x)]\frac{\hat{f}_n(x)}{f(x)} \xrightarrow{\mathrm{p}} 0.$$

Hence, $\hat{\mu}_n(x) - \mu(x)$ has the same limiting distribution as $[\hat{\mu}_n(x) - \mu(x)]\hat{f}_n(x)/f(x)$. Next notice that

$$\begin{aligned}[\hat{\mu}_n(x) - \mu(x)]\hat{f}_n(x) &= (n\delta_n^k)^{-1}\sum_{i=1}^n [Y_i - \mu(x)]K\left(\frac{x - X_i}{\delta_n}\right) \\ &= \hat{q}_1(x) + \hat{q}_2(x) + \hat{q}_3(x),\end{aligned}$$

where

$$\begin{aligned}\hat{q}_1(x) &= (n\delta_n^k)^{-1}\sum_{i=1}^n [Y_i - \mu(X_i)]\, K\left(\frac{x - X_i}{\delta_n}\right), \\ \hat{q}_2(x) &= (n\delta_n^k)^{-1}\sum_{i=1}^n [\mu(X_i) - \mu(x)]\, K\left(\frac{x - X_i}{\delta_n}\right) \\ &\quad - \frac{1}{\delta_n^k}\,\mathrm{E}\left\{[\mu(X_i) - \mu(x)]\, K\left(\frac{x - X_i}{\delta_n}\right)\right\}, \\ \hat{q}_3(x) &= \frac{1}{\delta_n^k}\,\mathrm{E}\left\{[\mu(X_i) - \mu(x)]\, K\left(\frac{x - X_i}{\delta_n}\right)\right\},\end{aligned}$$

with $\hat{q}_3(x)$ nonstochastic. If $\mu(x)$ and $\sigma^2(x)$ are smooth, one can show that

$$\begin{aligned}&(n\delta_n^k)^{1/2}\,\hat{q}_1(x) \xrightarrow{\mathrm{d}} \mathcal{N}\left(0,\, \sigma^2(x)f(x)\int K(u)^2\,du\right), \\ &(n\delta_n^k)^{1/2}\hat{q}_2(x) \xrightarrow{\mathrm{ms}} 0, \\ &\delta_n^{-2}\,\hat{q}_3(x) \to b(x) < \infty.\end{aligned}$$

Since assumption (iv) implies that $\delta_n^2(n\delta_n^k)^{1/2} \to \lambda < \infty$, we get

$$(n\delta_n^k)^{1/2}[\hat{\mu}_n(x) - \mu(x)]\hat{f}_n(x) - (n\delta_n^k)^{1/2}\hat{q}_1(x) - \lambda[\hat{q}_3(x)/\delta_n^2] \xrightarrow{\mathrm{p}} 0,$$

which completes the proof. □

Notice that $\hat{\mu}_n(x)$ is asymptotically biased for $\mu(x)$ unless δ_n is chosen such that $\lambda = 0$. In this case, however, the convergence of $\hat{\mu}_n(x)$ to its limiting distribution is slower than in the case when $\lambda > 0$.

The convergence rate of $\hat{\mu}_n(x)$ is inversely related to the number k of covariates, reflecting the "curse of dimensionality" problem. For k fixed, the maximal rate is achieved when $\delta_n = cn^{-1/(k+4)}$, for some $c > 0$. In this case, $\lambda = c^{(k+4)/2}$ and therefore

$$n^{2/(k+4)}\,[\hat{\mu}_n(x) - \mu(x)] \xrightarrow{\mathrm{d}} \mathcal{N}\left(c^2\frac{b(x)}{f(x)},\, c^{-k}\frac{\sigma^2(x)}{f(x)}\int K(u)^2\,du\right).$$

Even when there is a single covariate ($k = 1$), the fastest convergence rate is only equal to $n^{-2/5}$ and is lower than the rate of $n^{-1/2}$ achieved by a regular estimator of $\mu(x)$ in a parametric context.

These problems have generated two active lines of research. One seeks ways of eliminating the asymptotic bias of $\hat{\mu}_n(x)$ while retaining the maximal convergence rate of $n^{-2/(k+4)}$. A proposal by Schucany and Sommers (1977) and Bierens (1987) is to consider a weighted average of two estimators with different bandwidths chosen such that the resulting estimator is asymptotically centered at $\mu(x)$.

The other seeks ways of improving the speed of convergence of $\hat{\mu}_n(x)$ which, from the proof of Theorem 14.4, depends on the convergence rate of $\hat{q}_3(x)$. If the kernel K is chosen such that $\int uu^\top K(u)\, du = 0$, allowing therefore for negative values of K, then $\lim_{n\to\infty} \delta_n^{-3} \hat{q}_3(x) < \infty$ and so the optimal convergence rate becomes $n^{-3/(k+6)}$. More generally, if one chooses a kernel with zero moments up to order m, then the optimal bandwidth becomes $\delta_n = cn^{-1/(k+2m)}$, and the maximal convergence rate becomes $n^{-m/(k+2m)}$ which, as $m \to \infty$, tends to the rate $n^{-1/2}$ typical of a parametric estimator. See Robinson (1988) for further details.

14.5.4 TESTS OF PARAMETRIC MODELS

Nonparametric regression may be used to test the validity of a parametric model. For this purpose one may employ both informal methods, especially graphical ones, and more formal tests.

In this section we confine our attention to a test for the goodness-of-fit of a linear regression model. Let $[\mathbf{X}, \mathbf{Y}]$ be a sample of size n from the distribution of the random vector (X, Y), and assume for simplicity that the conditional distribution of Y given $X = x$ is $\mathcal{N}(\mu(x), \sigma^2)$. The null hypothesis H_0: $\mu(x) = \alpha + \beta^\top x$ specifies the CMF as linear in x, whereas the alternative hypothesis specifies $\mu(x)$ as a smooth nonlinear function of x.

Let $\hat{\mathbf{U}} = M\mathbf{Y}$ be the OLS residual vector and let $\tilde{\mathbf{U}} = (I_n - S_\lambda)\mathbf{Y}$ be the residual vector associated with some other linear smoother $\hat{\mu} = S_\lambda \mathbf{Y}$. Because the null hypothesis may be viewed as nested within the alternative, an F-type test would reject H_0 for large values of the statistic

$$F = \frac{\hat{\mathbf{U}}^\top\hat{\mathbf{U}} - \tilde{\mathbf{U}}^\top\tilde{\mathbf{U}}}{\tilde{\mathbf{U}}^\top\tilde{\mathbf{U}}} = \frac{\mathbf{Y}^\top M\mathbf{Y} - \mathbf{Y}^\top M_*\mathbf{Y}}{\mathbf{Y}^\top M_*\mathbf{Y}},$$

where $M_* = (I_n - S_\lambda)^\top (I_n - S_\lambda)$. If the smoother is a smoothing spline, as in Eubank and Spiegelman (1990), the sampling distribution of the statistic F under H_0 may be derived. For more general types of linear smoother, the distribution of F under H_0 is difficult to derive as it depends on the unknown parameter (α, β).

Azzalini and Bowman (1993) suggest replacing H_0 by the hypothesis that the OLS residual vector has mean zero. The alternative is now that the mean of $\hat{\mathbf{U}}$ is a smooth function of the covariates. This leads to a test that rejects the null hypothesis for large values of the statistic

$$F_* = \frac{\hat{\mathbf{U}}^\top\hat{\mathbf{U}} - \hat{\mathbf{U}}^\top M_*\hat{\mathbf{U}}}{\hat{\mathbf{U}}^\top M_*\hat{\mathbf{U}}}.$$

It turns out that the statistic F_* depends only on the data and the value of the smoothing parameter λ. Rejecting the null hypothesis for large values of F_* is equivalent to rejecting for small values of the statistic

$$\xi = \frac{1}{F_* + 1} = \frac{\hat{\mathbf{U}}^\top M_* \hat{\mathbf{U}}}{\hat{\mathbf{U}}^\top \hat{\mathbf{U}}},$$

which has the same form as the Durbin–Watson test statistic. In order to determine the critical value of a test based on F_*, one needs to compute probabilities such as

$$\Pr\{F_* > c\} = \Pr\{\hat{\mathbf{U}}^\top \hat{\mathbf{U}} - \hat{\mathbf{U}}^\top M_* \hat{\mathbf{U}} > c\,\hat{\mathbf{U}}^\top M_* \hat{\mathbf{U}}\} = \Pr\{\hat{\mathbf{U}}^\top A \hat{\mathbf{U}} > 0\},$$

where $A = I_n - (1+c)M_*$. Hence, the problem reduces to calculating the distribution of the quadratic form $\hat{\mathbf{U}}^\top A \hat{\mathbf{U}}$ under the null hypothesis. Azzalini and Bowman (1993) offer some suggestions. As far as the power of the test is concerned, their simulation results show that, although the amount of smoothing influences the power of a test based on F_*, the observed significance level seems to change little over a fairly broad range of values of the smoothing parameter λ.

14.6 OTHER METHODS FOR HIGH-DIMENSIONAL DATA

We now review a few nonparametric approaches that try to overcome some of the problems encountered in trying to extend univariate nonparametric methods to multivariate situations.

14.6.1 THE CURSE OF DIMENSIONALITY PROBLEM

Although conceptually straightforward, extending univariate nonparametric methods to higher dimensions is problematic for at least two reasons.

First, there is the neglected but practically important problem of how to represent the results of a nonparametric analysis involving two or more variables.

Second, when one-dimensional nonparametric methods are generalized to higher dimensions, their statistical properties deteriorate quite rapidly because of the so-called *curse of dimensionality* problem, namely the fact that the volume of data required to maintain a tolerable degree of statistical precision grows much faster than the number of variables under examination.

For these reasons, simple generalizations of one-dimensional methods, such as histograms or kernel estimates, to the case of more than two or three variables tend to produce results that are difficult to represent and are too irregular unless the size of the available data is very large.

Example 14.8 A simple way of illustrating the curse of dimensionality problem is to consider a multivariate histogram constructed for a sample from the distribution of a random m-vector Z, whose components are independently and uniformly distributed on the interval $(0, 1)$. The random vector Z therefore has a uniform distribution on the m-dimensional unit hypercube.

If we partition the unit hypercube into hypercubical cells of side equal to α, then each cell contains, on average, only α^m percent of the data. Assuming that at least 30 observations per cell are needed for a tolerably accurate histogram estimate, then

Table 5 The table is constructed under the assumption that the data are a sample from the distribution of a random vector Z with a uniform distribution on the unit hypercube in $\Re^m$ and that each hypercubical cell has side equal to α. The expected total sample size $\mathrm{E}\, n$ is determined by assuming that 30 observations per cell are necessary, on average, for a sufficiently precise histogram estimate.

	Number m of variables in Z				
	1	2	3	4	5
$\alpha = .10$					
number of cells	10	100	1,000	10,000	100,000
$\mathrm{E}\, n$	300	3,000	30,000	300,000	3,000,000
$\alpha = .05$					
number of cells	20	400	8,000	160,000	3,200,000
$\mathrm{E}\, n$	600	12,000	240,000	4,800,000	96,000,000

an adequate sample should have an average size at least equal to $n = 30(1/\alpha)^m$. Table 5 presents some calculations for $m = 1, \ldots, 5$, and for α equal to .10 and .05. Leaving aside the nontrivial problem of how it could be represented, a five-dimensional histogram is likely to be estimated too imprecisely to be of practical use, unless the sample size is truly gigantic. □

The next three sections discuss methods that try to deal with the curse of dimensionality problem. A common feature of all these methods is that, although nonparametric in nature, they do impose a certain amount of structure on the estimation problem.

14.6.2 PROJECTION PURSUIT DENSITY ESTIMATION

One approach to nonparametric estimation of multivariate densities is the method of *projection pursuit (PP)*, introduced by Friedman, Stuetzle and Schroeder (1984). This method assumes that the density of a random m-vector Z may well be approximated by a density f_* of the form

$$f_*(z) = f_0(z) \prod_{j=1}^{p} f_j(\alpha_j^\top z), \tag{14.18}$$

where f_0 is a known m-variate density, α_j is a vector with unit norm which specifies a particular direction in $\Re^m$, $\alpha_j^\top z = \sum_{h=1}^m \alpha_{jh} z_h$ is a linear combination or "projection" of the variables in Z, and $f_1, \ldots, f_p$ are smooth univariate functions, called *ridge functions*, to be determined empirically.

Thus, the PP method approximates the multivariate density f by the product of a known multivariate density f_0 and a set of p arbitrary functions of linear combinations of the elements of z. The choice of f_0 is left to the investigator and should reflect the prior information available about the problem.

The estimation algorithm determines the number p of terms and the directions α_j in (14.18), and constructs nonparametric estimates of the ridge functions by minimizing a suitably chosen index of goodness-of-fit or *projection index*. The curse of dimensionality problem is by-passed by using linear projections and nonparametric estimates of univariate ridge functions. As a by-product of this method, the graphical information provided by the shape of the estimated ridge functions may be useful for exploring and interpreting the multivariate distribution of the data.

The PP method may be seen as a generalization of the principal components method, where multidimensional data are projected linearly onto subspaces of much smaller dimension, chosen to minimize the variance of the projections.

14.6.3 PROJECTION PURSUIT REGRESSION ESTIMATION

The PP method was originally introduced in the regression context by Friedman and Stuetzle (1981). Specifically, given a random variable Y and a random k-vector X, they proposed to approximate the CMF of Y by a function of the form

$$h(x) = \alpha + \sum_{j=1}^{p} h_j(\beta_j^\top x), \tag{14.19}$$

where β_j is a vector with unit norm that specifies a particular direction in $\Re^k$, $\beta_j^\top x = \sum_{i=1}^k \beta_{ij} x_i$ is a linear combination or "projection" of the variables in X, and $h_1, \ldots, h_p$ are smooth univariate "ridge functions" to be determined empirically. By representing the CMF as a sum of arbitrary functions of linear combinations of the elements of x, this method allows for quite complex patterns of interaction among the covariates. Single-index models may be viewed as special cases corresponding to $p = 1$, and linear regression as a special case corresponding to $p = 1$ and $h_1(u) = u$. The curse of dimensionality problem is by-passed by using linear projections and nonparametric estimates of univariate ridge functions.

PP regression works as follows.

Algorithm 14.2

(1) *Given estimates* $\hat\beta_j$ *of the projection directions and estimates* $\hat h_j$ *of the ridge functions for the first* $m - 1$ *terms of* (14.19), *compute the approximation errors*

$$r_i = \tilde Y_i - \sum_{j=1}^{m-1} \hat h_j(\hat\beta_j^\top X_i), \qquad i = 1, \ldots, n,$$

where $\tilde Y_i = Y_i - \bar Y$.

(2) *Given a vector* $b \in \Re^k$ *such that* $\|b\| = 1$, *construct a linear smoother* $\hat h(b^\top X_i)$ *based on the errors* r_i *and compute the residual sum-of-squares*

$$S(b) = \sum_{i=1}^{n} [r_i - \hat h(b^\top X_i)]^2.$$

(3) *Determine* b_* *and the corresponding smooth function* $\hat h_*$ *for which* $S(b)$ *is minimized.*

(4) *Insert* b_* *and the corresponding function* $\hat h_*$ *as the* m*th terms into the approximating sum* (14.19).

(5) *Iterate steps* (1)–(4) *until the decrease in the residual sum-of-squares becomes negligible.*

As has been stressed by Huber (1985), PP regression "emerge as the most powerful method yet invented to lift one-dimensional statistical techniques to higher dimensions". However, it is not without problems. First, interpretability of the individual terms of (14.19) is difficult when $p > 1$. Second, PP regression has problems in dealing with highly nonlinear structures. In fact, there exist functions that cannot be represented as a finite sum of ridge functions. A simple example is the function $\mu(x) = \exp(x_1 x_2)$. Third, the sampling theory of PP regression is still lacking. Fourth, the choice of the amount of smoothing in constructing the nonparametric estimates of the ridge functions is delicate. Finally, the PP method tends to be computationally expensive.

The next section discusses an approach that may be regarded as a simplification of PP regression.

14.6.4 ADDITIVE REGRESSION

An important property of the linear regression model $h(x) = \alpha + \beta^\top x$ is additivity. This property makes it possible to "separate" the effect of the different covariates and to interpret the jth element of the parameter vector β as the partial derivative of $\mu(x)$ with respect to the jth covariate.

An *additive regression model* approximates the CMF of Y by a function of the form

$$h(x) = \alpha + \sum_{j=1}^{k} h_j(x_j),$$

where $h_1, \ldots, h_k$ are univariate smooth functions, one for each covariate. The linear regression model corresponds to $h_j(u) = \beta_j u$ for all j. Because $h_j'(x_j) = \partial h(x)/\partial x_j$, additive regression retains the interpretability of the effect of the individual covariates. Interactions between categorical covariates and continuous ones may be modeled by estimating separate versions of the model for each value of the categorical variable. Interactions between continuous covariates may be modelled by creating compound variables, such as products of pairs.

The problem of approximating the CMF $\mu(x)$ by an additive function may be viewed as a projection problem, whose solution is characterized in the next theorem. In turn, this leads to a general iterative procedure for estimating additive regression models.

Theorem 14.5 *Let $Z = (X_1, \ldots, X_k, Y)$ be a random $(k+1)$-vector with finite second moments. Let $\mathcal{H}$ be the Hilbert space of zero-mean functions of Z, with the inner product defined as $\langle \psi \mid \phi \rangle = \mathrm{E}\, \psi(Z)\phi(Z)$. For any $j = 1, \ldots, k$, let $\mathcal{H}_j$ be the subspace of zero-mean square integrable functions of X_j and let $\mathcal{H}^a = \mathcal{H}_1 + \cdots + \mathcal{H}_k$ be the subspace of zero-mean square integrable additive functions of $X = (X_1, \ldots, X_k)$. Then a solution to the following problem*

$$\min_{h \in \mathcal{H}^a} \mathrm{E}\, |Y - h(X)|^2 \qquad (14.20)$$

exists, is unique and is of the form

$$h_*(X) = \sum_{j=1}^{k} h_j(X_j), \tag{14.21}$$

where $h_1, \ldots, h_k$ *are univariate functions such that*

$$h_j(X_j) = \mathrm{E}[Y - \sum_{l \neq j} h_l(X_l) \,|\, X_j], \qquad j = 1, \ldots, k. \tag{14.22}$$

Proof. We only sketch the proof. The details can be found in Stone (1985). If we endow the Hilbert space $\mathcal{H}$ with the norm $\|\psi\| = [\mathrm{E}\,\psi(Z)^2]^{1/2}$, then problem (14.20) is equivalent to the minimum norm problem

$$\min_{h \in \mathcal{H}^a} \|Y - h\|^2.$$

Under some technical conditions, $\mathcal{H}^a$ and $\mathcal{H}_1, \ldots, \mathcal{H}_k$ are closed subspaces of $\mathcal{H}$. Thus, by the classical projection theorem (Theorem A.8), there exists a unique vector $h_* \in \mathcal{H}^a$ that solves (14.20). Moreover, h_* is characterized by the orthogonality condition $Y - h_* \perp \mathcal{H}^a$ or equivalently, given that $\mathcal{H}^a = \mathcal{H}_1 + \cdots + \mathcal{H}_k$, by the set of orthogonality conditions

$$Y - h_* \perp \mathcal{H}_j, \qquad j = 1, \ldots, k.$$

Because $h_* \in \mathcal{H}^a$, it must be of the form (14.21). Further, since the conditional expectation $\mathrm{E}(\cdot \,|\, X_j)$ is an orthogonal projection onto $\mathcal{H}_j$, we must have

$$\mathrm{E}[Y - \sum_{j=1}^{k} h_j(X_j) \,|\, X_j] = 0, \qquad j = 1, \ldots, k,$$

that is,

$$h_j(X_j) = \mathrm{E}[Y - \sum_{l \neq j} h_l(X_l) \,|\, X_j], \qquad j = 1, \ldots, k.$$

□

Denote now by S_j a smoother matrix for univariate smoothing on the jth covariate. Because the univariate smoother $S_j \mathbf{Y}$ is the sample analogue of the conditional mean $\mathrm{E}(Y \,|\, X_j)$, the analogy principle suggests the following equation system as the sample counterpart of (14.22)

$$\mathbf{h}_j = S_j(\tilde{\mathbf{Y}} - \sum_{l \neq j} \mathbf{h}_l), \qquad j = 1, \ldots, k,$$

where $\mathbf{h}_j = (h_j(X_1), \ldots, h_j(X_n))$ and $\tilde{\mathbf{Y}}$ is the n-vector of deviations of Y_i from its sample mean. This results in the system of $nk \times nk$ linear equations

$$\begin{bmatrix} I_n & S_1 & S_1 & \cdots & S_1 \\ S_2 & I_n & S_2 & \cdots & S_2 \\ \vdots & \vdots & \vdots & & \vdots \\ S_k & S_k & S_k & \cdots & I_n \end{bmatrix} \begin{pmatrix} \mathbf{h}_1 \\ \mathbf{h}_2 \\ \vdots \\ \mathbf{h}_k \end{pmatrix} = \begin{pmatrix} S_1 \tilde{\mathbf{Y}} \\ S_2 \tilde{\mathbf{Y}} \\ \vdots \\ S_k \tilde{\mathbf{Y}} \end{pmatrix}. \tag{14.23}$$

If $(\hat{\mathbf{h}}_1, \ldots, \hat{\mathbf{h}}_k)$ is a solution to the above system and we put $\hat{\alpha} = \bar{Y}$, then an estimate of $\boldsymbol{\mu} = (\mu(X_1), \ldots, \mu(X_n))$ is $\hat{\boldsymbol{\mu}} = \hat{\alpha}\iota_n + \sum_{j=1}^k \hat{\mathbf{h}}_j$.

One way of solving system (14.23) is the *Gauss–Seidel method.* This method solves iteratively for each vector $\mathbf{h}_j$ from the relationship

$$\mathbf{h}_j = S_j(\tilde{\mathbf{Y}} - \sum_{l \neq j} \mathbf{h}_l),$$

using the latest values of $\{\mathbf{h}_l, l \neq j\}$ at each step. The process is repeated for $j = 1, \ldots, k, 1, \ldots, k, \ldots$, until convergence. The result is the *backfitting algorithm*:

Algorithm 14.3

(1) *Compute the univariate smoother matrices* $S_1, \ldots, S_k$.

(2) *Initialize the algorithm by setting* $\mathbf{h}_j = \mathbf{h}_j^{(0)}$, $j = 1, \ldots, k$.

(3) *Cycle for* $j = 1, \ldots, k$, $\mathbf{h}_j = S_j(\tilde{\mathbf{Y}} - \sum_{l \neq j} \mathbf{h}_l)$, *where the smoother matrix* S_j *for univariate smoothing on the* jth *covariate is applied to the residual vector* $\tilde{\mathbf{Y}} - \sum_{l \neq j} \mathbf{h}_l$ *obtained from the previous step.*

(4) *Iterate step* (3) *until the changes in the individual functions become negligible.*

The smoother matrices S_j can be computed using any of the univariate linear smoothers discussed in Section 14.4 (OLS, regression splines, cubic smoothing splines, lowess, etc.), and do not change through the backfitting algorithm. To ensure that $\tilde{\mathbf{Y}} - \sum_{l \neq j} \mathbf{h}_l$ has mean zero at every stage, S_j may be replaced by the centered smoother matrix $S_j(I_n - n^{-1}\iota_n\iota_n^\top)$. A possible starting point for the algorithm is the fitted value of $\mathbf{Y}$ from an OLS regression of $\mathbf{Y}$ on $\mathbf{X}$. In this case $\mathbf{h}_j^{(0)} = \mathbf{X}_j\hat{\beta}_j$, where $\mathbf{X}_j$ and $\hat{\beta}_j$ denote respectively the jth column of $\mathbf{X}$ and the jth element of the OLS coefficient vector.

It can be shown that convergence of the backfitting algorithm is guaranteed if the chosen linear smoother is a projection operator, that is, defined by a symmetric idempotent smoother matrix. Convergence of the algorithm is also guaranteed in the case of smoothing splines (see Hastie & Tibshirani 1990, where the connection between the backfitting algorithm and penalized LS is also discussed).

Example 14.9 Consider the *partially linear model*

$$\mathrm{E}(Y \mid X, W) = h_1(X) + h_2(W),$$

where X and W are scalar random variables, $h_1(X) = \beta X$, and h_2 is an unknown univariate smooth function. More generally, X may consist of a vector of covariates. Such a model was used by Engle *et al.* (1986) to model in a flexible way the relationship between residential demand for electricity (Y), temperature (W) and other predictors (X).

If $\mathrm{E}\, X\, h_2(W) = 0$, then β may be estimated consistently and efficiently by an OLS regression of Y on X. This is typically the case when X has mean zero and is independent of W. In general, however, X and $h_2(W)$ are correlated and so a regression of Y on X gives biased and inconsistent estimates of β. As an alternative, consider applying the backfitting algorithm. Because in this case h_1 is linear, two different smoothers may be employed. One is an OLS smoother, with smoother matrix $S_1 = \mathbf{X}(\mathbf{X}^\top\mathbf{X})^{-1}\mathbf{X}^\top$, which produces estimates of the form $\hat{\mathbf{h}}_1 = \mathbf{X}\hat{\beta}$. The other is a nonparametric smoother, with smoother matrix S_2 obtained by univariate smoothing on the single variable $\mathbf{W}$, which produces estimates of the vector $(h_2(W_1), \ldots, h_2(W_n))$ of the form $\hat{\mathbf{h}}_2 = S_2\mathbf{W}$. The steps of the backfitting algorithm are therefore

$$\hat{\mathbf{h}}_1 = \mathbf{X}(\mathbf{X}^\top\mathbf{X})^{-1}\mathbf{X}^\top(\mathbf{Y} - \hat{\mathbf{h}}_2) = \mathbf{X}\hat{\beta},$$
$$\hat{\mathbf{h}}_2 = S_2(\mathbf{Y} - \mathbf{X}\hat{\beta}).$$

Premultiplying the first of the above equations by $\mathbf{X}^\top$ and substituting the expression for $\hat{\mathbf{h}}_2$ from the second equation gives

$$\mathbf{X}^\top\hat{\mathbf{h}}_1 = \mathbf{X}^\top(\mathbf{Y} - \hat{\mathbf{h}}_2) = \mathbf{X}^\top(I_n - S_2)\mathbf{Y} + \mathbf{X}^\top S_2\mathbf{X}\hat{\beta} = \mathbf{X}^\top\mathbf{X}\hat{\beta},$$

from which

$$\mathbf{X}^\top(I_n - S_2)\mathbf{Y} = \mathbf{X}^\top(I_n - S_2)\mathbf{X}\hat{\beta}.$$

Solving for $\hat{\beta}$ we then get

$$\hat{\beta} = [\mathbf{X}^\top(I_n - S_2)\mathbf{X}]^{-1}\mathbf{X}^\top(I_n - S_2)\mathbf{Y}.$$

In this case, no iteration is necessary. This method may be viewed as a generalization of the double residual regression method in Section 6.2.6. □

BIBLIOGRAPHIC NOTES

For a broad introduction to nonparametric methods in econometrics see the review articles by Blundell and Duncan (1997), Härdle and Linton (1994), Yatchew (1998) and the recent book by Pagan and Ullah (1999). Good introductions to nonparametric methods for density and regression estimation are Silverman (1986) and Härdle (1990).

Criteria for selecting the number of bins in a histogram are discussed in Linhart and Zucchini (1986). The kernel method for density estimation goes back to Rosenblatt (1956). For results based on the L_1 distance, as opposed to the L_2, see Devroye and Györfi (1985). For a review of bandwidth selection methods for density estimation see Jones, Marron and Sheather (1996).

The Nadaraya–Watson estimator was independently proposed by Nadaraya (1964) and Watson (1964). The average derivative estimator has been proposed by Stoker (1986). Its large sample properties are investigated in Härdle and Stoker (1989).

Useful monographs on splines are de Boor (1978) and Eubank (1988), while a more advanced one is Wahba (1990). On the relationship between smoothing splines and the distributed lag model of Shiller (1973) see Corradi (1977). On multivariate splines see Chui (1988).

On the method of locally weighted LS see Hastie and Loader (1993). For a generalization of the idea of local linear fitting to local polynomial fitting see Fan (1992) and Fan and Gijbels (1996). On the idea of locally fitting parametric models see Tibshirani and Hastie (1987).

Using the boostrap to derive confidence intervals for a linear smoother is discussed in Efron and Tibshirani (1986) and Di Ciccio and Romano (1988).

The main references for Section 14.5.4 are Azzalini, Bowman and Härdle (1989), Azzalini and Bowman (1993) and Eubank and Spiegelman (1990).

The results of Section 14.5.3 may be generalized to the case of linear smoothers. General conditions for their consistency may be found in Stone (1977). A linear smoother is asymptotically normal under general conditions. Results on the optimal rate of convergence to the asymptotically normal distribution have been obtained by Stone (1982).

Projection pursuit regression was introduced by Friedman and Stuetzle (1981), the method for density estimation by Friedman, Stuetzle and Schroeder (1984). A good survey is Huber (1985).

On additive regression see the book by Hastie and Tibshirani (1990). Robinson (1988) establishes $\sqrt{n}$-consistency and asymptotic normality of the estimator of the regression parameter β in Example 14.9.

PROBLEMS

14.1 Given a sample from a uniform distribution on the interval $(a, b]$, show that the empirical density is unbiased for the population density.

14.2 Show that, in large samples, the MSE of the empirical density is equal to its squared bias. Interpret this result.

14.3 Show that the histogram estimate $\tilde{f}$ is a proper density, that is, it satisfies $\tilde{f} \geq 0$ and $\int \tilde{f}\, dz = 1$.

14.4 Let $\hat{f}$ be a kernel density estimate based on the kernel function K. Show that if K integrates to one, then $\hat{f}$ also integrates to one, and that if K is a proper density, then $\hat{f}$ is also a proper density.

14.5 Given a sample of size n from the $\mathcal{N}(\mu, \sigma^2)$ distribution, use the formulae in Section 14.2.1 to evaluate the bias and the sampling variance of kernel density estimates based, respectively, on a uniform and a Gaussian kernel.

14.6 Let f be a $\mathcal{N}(\mu, \sigma^2)$ density and let K be a Gaussian kernel. Show that

$$\int f''(z)^2\, dz = \frac{3}{8\sqrt{\pi}}\sigma^{-5}, \qquad \int K(u)^2\, du = \frac{1}{2\sqrt{\pi}}.$$

14.7 Verify the formula for the bandwidth that minimizes the MISE of a kernel density estimator.

14.8 (Marron & Nolan 1988) When density estimates based on different kernels are compared, the same value of the bandwidth may result in very different amounts of smoothing. To eliminate this phenomenon, consider rescaling kernels of different shape through the transformation $K_s(z) = s^{-1}K(z/s)$, where the parameter s is chosen in such a way that $\int K_s(z)^2\, dz = [\int z^2 K_s(z)\, dz]^2$ for each kernel K. Discuss the effects of this proposal on the asymptotic properties of the estimates.

14.9 Verify that a nearest neighbor density estimate corresponds to a generalized kernel density estimate based on a uniform kernel.

14.10 Derive expressions (14.11) and (14.12).

14.11 Discuss ways of estimating the asymptotic mean and the asymptotic variance of $\hat{f}_n(z)$ given in Theorem 14.2.

14.12 Verify that representation (14.14) satisfies all three conditions for a cubic spline.

14.13 Show that the Nadaraya–Watson kernel regression estimate may be obtained by minimizing $\sum_i W_i(x)\,(Y_i - \mu)^2$, where $W_i(x) = \delta^{-1}K((x - X_i)/\delta)$. Interpret this result.

14.14 Discuss the behavior of a Nadaraya–Watson kernel regression estimate when a single observation (X_i, Y_i) tends to assume extreme values. Specifically, discuss the case when $(X_i, Y_i) \to (\pm c, X_i)$ and $(X_i, Y_i) \to (Y_i, \pm c)$ with $c \to \infty$ for a fixed i.

14.15 Let $(X_1, Y_1), \ldots, (X_n, Y_n)$ be a sample from the distribution of a bivariate random variable (X, Y) with density f, and consider the estimate (14.4) of f based on a bivariate kernel K_* and let $K(x) = \int K_*(x, y)\,dy$. Show that $\int \hat{f}(x, y)\,dy = \hat{f}_X(x)$, where $\hat{f}_X(x)$ is the estimate of the marginal density of X based on kernel K. Next show that if $K_*(x, y)$ satisfies $\int y\,K_*(x, y)\,dy = 0$, then

$$\int y\,\hat{f}(x, y)\,dy = \frac{1}{n\delta}\sum_{i=1}^{n} Y_i\,K\left(\frac{x - X_i}{\delta}\right).$$

14.16 This problem provides the updating formulae for computing the running line (14.16) for the n sample points in $O(n)$ operations. Consider adding a point (Y_{k+1}, X_{k+1}) to a neighborhood containing k points. Let $\bar{y}_k$, $\bar{x}_k$, S_k^x and S_k^{xy} denote, respectively, the means of Y and X, the variances of X and the covariance of X and Y for the k points of the neighborhood. Show that

$$\bar{y}_{k+1} = \frac{k\bar{y}_k + y_{k+1}}{k+1}, \qquad \bar{x}_{k+1} = \frac{k\bar{x}_k + x_{k+1}}{k+1},$$

and

$$\begin{aligned}(k+1)S_{k+1}^x &= kS_k^x + \frac{k+1}{k}(x_{k+1} - \bar{x}_{k+1})^2,\\ (k+1)S_{k+1}^{xy} &= kS_k^{xy} + \frac{k+1}{k}(x_{k+1} - \bar{x}_{k+1})(y_{k+1} - \bar{y}_{k+1}).\end{aligned}$$

Derive the corresponding formulae for eliminating a single point from the neighborhood.

14.17 Compare the properties of the first and second derivatives of the nonparametric regression estimates obtained, respectively, with the kernel method and the method of locally weighted LS.

14.18 This exercise establishes a relation between linear smoothers and penalized LS. Let S be a symmetric n.n.d. matrix. Show that $\hat{\boldsymbol{\mu}} = S\mathbf{Y}$ is a solution to the problem

$$\min_{\mathbf{h}}\,(\mathbf{Y} - \mathbf{h})^\top(\mathbf{Y} - \mathbf{h}) + \lambda\mathbf{h}^\top(S^- - I_n)\mathbf{h},$$

where $\mathbf{h}$ is a vector that does not belong to the null space of S and S^- is a generalized inverse of S. Interpret this result.

14.19 Let $(X_1, Y_1), \ldots, (X_n, Y_n)$ be a sample from the joint distribution of (X, Y), and suppose that the conditional distribution of Y given $X = x$ is $\mathcal{N}(\mu(x), \sigma^2)$. Construct Wald and likelihood ratio tests of the hypothesis that $\mu(x)$ is linear in x against the following alternatives:

(i) $\mu(x)$ is a cubic function of x;
(ii) $\mu(x)$ is a piecewise linear function of x;
(iii) $\mu(x)$ is cubic spline with two knots at the points $x = c_1$ and $x = c_2$.

14.20 Discuss ways of estimating the asymptotic mean and the asymptotic variance of $\hat{\mu}_n(x)$ given in Theorem 14.4.

14.21 Discuss the asymptotic properties of the Nadaraya–Watson kernel regression estimator when the random variable X is discrete. In particular, what restrictions must be imposed on the bandwidth? What is the rate of convergence of the estimator to its limiting distribution?

14.22 Give sufficient conditions for the solution in Example 14.9 to be unique.

14.23 Given an $n \times (k+1)$ data matrix $[\mathbf{Y}, \mathbf{X}]$, derive the k-vector β that minimizes

$$Q(\beta) = [\mathbf{Y} - \mathbf{X}\beta - S(\mathbf{Y} - \mathbf{X}\beta)]^\top [\mathbf{Y} - \mathbf{X}\beta - S(\mathbf{Y} - \mathbf{X}\beta)].$$

Compare the result with the estimator of β proposed in Example 14.9.

14.24 Consider again Example 14.9. Show that when both S_1 and S_2 are OLS smoother matrices, then the backfitting algorithm gives exactly the formulae for partitioned regression in Section 6.2.6.

15

M-Estimators

In this chapter we consider the sampling properties of the class of estimators obtained by maximizing a data-dependent criterion function over a finite-dimensional parameter space. This class of estimators is very broad and includes most common estimators, such as least squares (LS), least absolute deviations (LAD), maximum likelihood (ML), pseudo or quasi ML, method of moments (MM), generalized method of moments (GMM), minimum distance (MD) and Bayes estimators.

15.1 THE CLASS OF M-ESTIMATORS

Let $Q_n(\theta) = Q(\mathbf{Z}; \theta)$ be a real function of an $n \times m$ data matrix $\mathbf{Z} = [Z_1, \ldots, Z_n]^\top$ and a p-dimensional parameter $\theta \in \Theta$. An *M-estimator* is any solution $\hat{\theta}_n$ to the problem of maximizing Q over the parameter space Θ, that is, $\hat{\theta}_n = \operatorname{argmax}_{\theta \in \Theta} Q(\theta)$. The term *extremum estimator* is also used in the literature.

Example 15.1 The OLS estimator is an M-estimator corresponding to $\mathbf{Z} = [\mathbf{X}, \mathbf{Y}]$ and $Q_n(\theta) = (\mathbf{Y} - \mathbf{X}\theta)^\top (\mathbf{Y} - \mathbf{X}\theta)$. The 2SLS estimator is an M-estimator corresponding to $\mathbf{Z} = [\mathbf{X}, \mathbf{Y}, \mathbf{W}]$ and $Q_n(\theta) = -(\mathbf{Y} - \mathbf{X}\theta)^\top \mathbf{W}(\mathbf{W}^\top \mathbf{W})^{-1} \mathbf{W}^\top (\mathbf{Y} - \mathbf{X}\theta)$. In both cases, the function Q_n is quadratic in θ, which leads to simple closed form expressions for these estimators.

Given a parametric model $\{f(\mathbf{z}; \theta), \theta \in \Theta\}$ for $\mathbf{Z}$, a ML estimator of θ is an M-estimator corresponding to $Q_n(\theta) = c + \ln f(\mathbf{Z}; \theta)$, where c is an arbitrary constant. A Bayes point estimator with respect to the loss function ℓ is an M-estimator corresponding to $Q_n(\theta) = -\int \ell(t, \theta)\, p(t \mid \mathbf{Z})\, dt$, where $p(t \mid \mathbf{Z})$ is the posterior density of θ given $\mathbf{Z}$. Except in special cases, no closed form expression is available for the last two types of estimator. □

One may distinguish between two classes of M-estimator. The first class consists of estimators obtained by maximizing a criterion function of the form

$$Q_n(\theta) = n^{-1} \sum_{i=1}^{n} \rho_i(\theta),$$

where $\rho_i(\theta)$ is a real function that depends on the data only through Z_i. This class contains LS, LAD, ML and pseudo ML estimators. The second class consists of estimators obtained by minimizing the quadratic form $\bar{\eta}_n(\theta)^\top D_n \bar{\eta}_n(\theta)$ or, equivalently, by maximizing a criterion function of the form

$$Q_n(\theta) = -\bar{\eta}_n(\theta)^\top D_n \bar{\eta}_n(\theta),$$

where $\bar{\eta}_n(\theta)$ is a vector of dimension $r \geq p$ that typically consists of sample averages, and D_n is a symmetric p.d. matrix that may depend on the data. A solution to this problem may be viewed as minimizing the distance of $\bar{\eta}_n(\theta)$ from the zero vector. This class contains MM, GMM and MD estimators.

If Q_n is a quadratic function of θ, then an M-estimator admits an explicit representation, which greatly simplifies the task of obtaining its sampling distribution or some large sample approximation to it. This is indeed the case for most estimators considered in the earlier chapters of this book. In general, however, the function Q_n need not be quadratic. When it is not, an M-estimator is usually defined only implicitly and computing an M-estimate for a given sample requires iterative procedures, such as the ones reviewed in Appendix B.

Being able to obtain a closed form expression for an M-estimator is useful but not necessary in order to establish its large sample properties. It turns out that, under appropriate regularity conditions, consistency for the target parameter θ_0 follows directly from the limiting properties of the criterion function Q_n which defines the estimator, whereas asymptotic normality follows from the fact that, just like a ML estimator (see Section 4.6.2), an M-estimator generally possesses a linear asymptotic representation of the form

$$\hat{\theta}_n = \theta_0 + \frac{1}{n}\sum_{i=1}^{n} \psi(Z_i) + o_p(n^{-1/2}), \tag{15.1}$$

where $\psi(Z_i)$ is a zero mean random vector called the *influence function* of the estimator. As shown in Section 15.4, the influence function also plays a crucial role in the study of robustness, for it provides a description of the local robustness properties of an estimator.

15.2 CONSISTENCY

This section presents a set of conditions sufficient to guarantee that a sequence $\{\hat{\theta}_n\}$ of M-estimators is consistent for the target parameter. The basic argument is very similar to the one used in Section 4.6.1 to establish consistency of a ML estimator: if, after a suitable normalization, the sequence of random functions $\{Q_n\}$ converges in an appropriate sense to a nonrandom function Q and Q attains its unique maximum on Θ at the point $\theta = \theta_0$ then, under mild regularity conditions, the estimator sequence $\{\hat{\theta}_n\}$ is consistent for θ_0.

15.2.1 SUFFICIENT CONDITIONS FOR CONSISTENCY

First recall the following definitions from real analysis. Let $\{f_n\}$ be a sequence of real functions defined on $\mathcal{S}$. The sequence $\{f_n\}$ is said to *converge pointwise on* $\mathcal{S}$ to a function f if, given any $x \in \mathcal{S}$ and any $\epsilon > 0$, there exists an N such that $|f_n(x) - f(x)| < \epsilon$ for all $n \geq N$. The sequence $\{f_n\}$ is said to *converge uniformly on* $\mathcal{S}$ to a function f if, given any $\epsilon > 0$, there exists an N such that $|f_n(x) - f(x)| < \epsilon$ for

Figure 75 Graph of the function in Example 15.2.

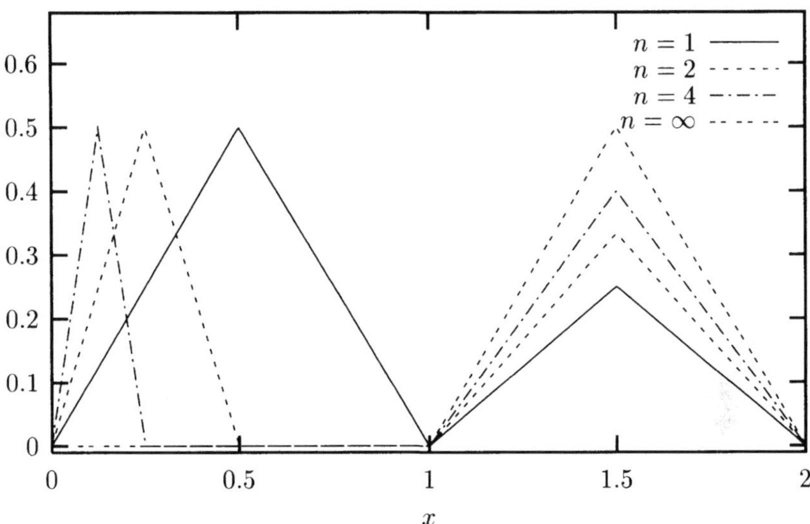

all $n \geq N$ and all $x \in \mathcal{S}$. If $\mathcal{S}$ is discrete, then pointwise convergence implies uniform convergence.

Example 15.2 Consider the function f_n defined on the interval $[0, 2]$ by

$$f_n(x) = \begin{cases} nx, & \text{if } 0 \leq x \leq (2n)^{-1}, \\ 1 - nx, & \text{if } (2n)^{-1} < x \leq n^{-1}, \\ 0, & \text{if } n^{-1} < x \leq 1, \\ [n/(n+1)](x-1), & \text{if } 1 < x \leq 3/2, \\ [n/(n+1)](2-x), & \text{otherwise} \end{cases}$$

(Figure 75). As $n \to \infty$, the sequence $\{f_n\}$ converges pointwise to the function

$$f(x) = \begin{cases} 0, & \text{if } 0 \leq x \leq 1, \\ x - 1, & \text{if } 1 < x \leq 3/2, \\ 2 - x, & \text{otherwise.} \end{cases}$$

It does not converge uniformly, however, for $\sup_{x \in [0,1]} |f_n(x) - f(x)| = 1/2$ for all n. Notice that the function f_n attains its maximum at $x = (2n)^{-1}$, which converges to zero as $n \to \infty$, while the function f attains its maximum at $x = 3/2$. □

We now generalize the above definitions to sequences of random functions.

Definition 15.1 A sequence $\{Q_n\}$ of random functions defined on a set Θ is said to *converge in probability pointwise on* Θ to a function Q if, given any $\theta \in \Theta$ and any $\epsilon > 0$,

$$\Pr\{|Q_n(\theta) - Q(\theta)| < \epsilon\} \to 1$$

as $n \to \infty$. □

Pointwise convergence in probability of $\{Q_n\}$ to Q is typically the consequence of some law of large numbers.

Example 15.3 Given a sequence $\{Z_i\}$ of i.i.d. random vectors and a function $\rho(z;\theta)$, let $Q_n(\theta) = n^{-1}\sum_i \rho_i(\theta)$, where $\rho_i(\theta) = \rho(Z_i;\theta)$. If $\mathrm{E}\,|\rho_i(\theta)| < \infty$ for all $\theta \in \Theta$, then Khinchine's WLLN implies that $Q_n(\theta) \xrightarrow{\mathrm{p}} Q(\theta) = \mathrm{E}\,\rho_i(\theta)$ for all $\theta \in \Theta$. □

Definition 15.2 A sequence $\{Q_n\}$ of random functions defined on a set Θ is said to *converge in probability uniformly on* Θ to a function Q if, for any $\epsilon > 0$,

$$\Pr\{\sup_{\theta\in\Theta} |Q_n(\theta) - Q(\theta)| < \epsilon\} \to 1$$

as $n \to \infty$. □

Conditions for uniform convergence in probability of $\{Q_n\}$ to Q will be given in Section 15.2.2.

The main consistency result for M-estimators is the following.

Theorem 15.1 *Suppose that:*

(i) Θ *is a compact subset of* $\Re^p$*;*
(ii) *the sequence of random functions* $\{Q_n\}$ *converges in probability uniformly on* Θ *to a continuous function* Q*;*
(iii) Q *attains a unique maximum on* Θ *at* θ_0.

Then $\hat\theta_n = \mathrm{argmax}_{\theta\in\Theta}\, Q_n(\theta)$ *exists and is unique with probability approaching one, and* $\hat\theta_n \xrightarrow{\mathrm{p}} \theta_0$.

Proof. First notice that, since Θ is a compact set and Q_n converges to a continuous function with probability approaching one, $\hat\theta_n$ exists with probability approaching one. Given $\delta > 0$, let $\mathcal{O} = \{\theta \in \Theta\colon \|\theta - \theta_0\| > \delta\}$. Since $\mathcal{O}$ is a compact set, Q attains a maximum on $\mathcal{O}$. Define $\epsilon = Q(\theta_0) - \max_{\theta\in\mathcal{O}} Q(\theta)$, and let A_n denote the event that $\hat\theta_n$ exists and $|Q_n(\theta) - Q(\theta)| < \epsilon/2$, for all $\theta \in \Theta$. Clearly, A_n implies that

$$Q_n(\theta) - \frac{\epsilon}{2} < Q(\theta) < Q_n(\theta) + \frac{\epsilon}{2}$$

for all $\theta \in \Theta$. In particular, it implies that

$$Q_n(\theta_0) > Q(\theta_0) - \frac{\epsilon}{2}. \tag{15.2}$$

Because $Q_n(\hat\theta_n) \geq Q_n(\theta_0)$ if $\hat\theta_n$ exists, the event A_n also implies that

$$Q(\hat\theta_n) > Q_n(\hat\theta_n) - \frac{\epsilon}{2} \geq Q_n(\theta_0) - \frac{\epsilon}{2}. \tag{15.3}$$

By adding both sides of (15.2) and (15.3), the event A_n implies that

$$Q(\hat\theta_n) > Q(\theta_0) - \epsilon = \max_{\theta\in\mathcal{O}} Q(\theta).$$

Thus, occurrence of A_n implies that $\hat{\theta}_n$ does not belong to $\mathcal{O}$, that is, the distance between $\hat{\theta}_n$ and θ_0 is less than δ. Therefore $\Pr\{A_n\} \leq \Pr\{\|\hat{\theta}_n - \theta_0\| < \delta\}$. Since $\Pr\{A_n\} \to 1$, it follows that $\Pr\{\|\hat{\theta}_n - \theta_0\| < \delta\} \to 1$. Because δ is arbitrary, $\hat{\theta}_n \xrightarrow{\text{p}} \theta_0$. Finally, the fact that θ_0 is unique implies that $\hat{\theta}_n$ is unique with probability approaching one. □

Assumption (i) requires the parameter space Θ to be bounded and rules out the incidental parameters case, where the dimensionality of Θ increases with the sample size. Assumption (ii) can be verified using the results presented in the next section. Assumption (iii) ensures that the target parameter θ_0 is identifiable. For ML and pseudo ML estimators, this condition is automatically satisfied if the assumed parametric model is identifiable for, in this case, the target parameter corresponds to the unique maximum on Θ of the expected log-likelihood.

In practice, the problem of maximizing Q_n over Θ is often replaced by the easier problem of maximizing Q_n over $\Re^p$. In this case we have the following.

Corollary 15.1 *In addition to the conditions of Theorem 15.2, suppose that*

$$\Pr\{Q_n(\theta_0) > \sup_{\theta \notin \Theta} Q_n(\theta)\} \to 1 \tag{15.4}$$

as $n \to \infty$. Then $\tilde{\theta} = \operatorname{argmax}_{\theta \in \Re^p} Q_n(\theta)$ exists and is unique with probability approaching one and $\tilde{\theta} \xrightarrow{\text{p}} \theta_0$.

Proof. If $\tilde{\theta}$ exists, then $Q_n(\tilde{\theta}) \geq Q_n(\theta_0)$. If $Q_n(\theta_0) > \sup_{\theta \notin \Theta} Q_n(\theta)$, then $Q_n(\tilde{\theta}) > \sup_{\theta \notin \Theta} Q_n(\theta)$, and so $\tilde{\theta}$ belongs to Θ. Hence, condition (15.4) implies that $\tilde{\theta}$ belongs to Θ with probability approaching one. □

15.2.2 CONDITIONS FOR UNIFORM CONVERGENCE IN PROBABILITY

Recall that a sequence $\{f_n\}$ of real functions is said to be *equicontinuous on $\mathcal{S}$* if, given any $\epsilon > 0$, there exists a $\delta > 0$ such that $\|x' - x\| < \delta$ implies $|f_n(x') - f_n(x)| < \epsilon$ for all $x', x \in \mathcal{S}$ and all n. Equicontinuity requires that small perturbations of x should have uniformly small effects on the sequence of function values $\{f_n(x)\}$. If $\mathcal{S}$ is a compact set, then the sequence $\{f_n\}$ converges uniformly on $\mathcal{S}$ to a continuous function f if and only if $\{f_n\}$ is equicontinuous on $\mathcal{S}$ and converges pointwise on $\mathcal{S}$ to f.

We now consider generalizations to a sequence of random functions.

Definition 15.3 A sequence $\{Q_n\}$ of random functions defined on a set Θ is said to be *stochastically equicontinuous on $\mathcal{S}$* if, for any $\epsilon, \eta > 0$ and $\theta \in \Theta$, there exist an integer N, an open neighborhood $\mathcal{O}$ of θ and a sequence $\{D_n\}$ of random variables such that $\Pr\{|D_n| > \epsilon\} < \eta$ and

$$\sup_{\theta' \in \mathcal{O}} |Q_n(\theta') - Q_n(\theta)| \leq D_n$$

for all $n \geq N$. □

The next theorem characterizes uniform convergence in probability to a continuous function on a compact set.

Theorem 15.2 *A sequence* $\{Q_n\}$ *of random functions defined on a compact set* Θ *converges in probability uniformly on* $\mathcal{S}$ *to a continuous function* Q *if and only if the sequence* $\{Q_n\}$ *is stochastically equicontinuous on* Θ *and converges in probability pointwise on* Θ *to* Q.

Proof. See Newey (1991), Theorem 2.1. □

Verifying the stochastic equicontinuity assumption is not always straightforward. Because of this, uniform laws of large numbers are an active area of research. The results in the remainder of this section imply stochastic equicontinuity and provide relatively simple sufficient conditions for uniform convergence in probability.

Theorem 15.3 *Let* $\{Z_i\}$ *be a sequence of i.i.d. random vectors and let* $Q_n(\theta) = n^{-1}\sum_i \rho_i(\theta)$, *where* $\rho_i(\theta) = \rho(Z_i;\theta)$. *Suppose that:*

(i) Θ *is a compact subset of* $\Re^p$;
(ii) $\rho_i(\cdot)$ *is continuous on* Θ *with probability one;*
(iii) $\mathrm{E}\sup_{\theta\in\Theta}|\rho_i(\theta)| < \infty$.

Then $\{Q_n\}$ *converges in probability uniformly on* Θ *to* $\mathrm{E}\,\rho_i(\cdot)$, *and* $\mathrm{E}\,\rho_i(\cdot)$ *is continuous on* Θ.

Proof. See Hansen (1982). □

Recall that a real function f defined on a set $\mathcal{S}$ satisfies a *Lipschitz condition of order* α *on* $\mathcal{S}$ if there exists an $M > 0$ such that

$$|f(x') - f(x)| \le M\,\|x' - x\|^\alpha$$

for all $x', x \in \mathcal{S}$. The function f is continuous on $\mathcal{S}$ if $\alpha > 0$, and is differentiable if $\alpha > 1$. For a sequence of random functions, we have the following generalization.

Definition 15.4 A sequence $\{Q_n\}$ of random functions defined on a subset Θ of $\Re^p$ is said to satisfy a *Lipschitz condition of order* α *on* Θ if there exist $\alpha > 0$ and a sequence $\{D_n\}$ of random variables such that $D_n = O_p(1)$ and

$$|Q_n(\theta') - Q_n(\theta)| \le D_n\,\|\theta' - \theta\|^\alpha$$

for all $\theta', \theta \in \Theta$ and all n. □

Theorem 15.4 *Suppose that:*

(i) Θ *is a compact subset of* $\Re^p$;
(ii) $\{Q_n\}$ *satisfies a Lipschitz condition on* Θ;
(iii) $\{Q_n\}$ *converges in probability pointwise on* Θ *to a continuous function* Q.

Then $\{Q_n\}$ *converges in probability uniformly on* Θ *to* Q.

Proof. See Newey (1991), Theorem 2.1 and Corollary 2.2. □

Corollary 15.2 *Let $\{Z_i\}$ be a sequence of i.i.d. random vectors and let $Q_n(\theta) = n^{-1} \sum_i \rho_i(\theta)$, where $\rho_i(\theta) = \rho(Z_i; \theta)$. Suppose that:*

(i) *Θ is a compact subset of $\Re^p$;*
(ii) *$\mathrm{E}\,|\rho_i(\theta)| < \infty$ for all $\theta \in \Theta$;*
(iii) *there exist $\alpha > 0$ and a function d such that $\mathrm{E}\,|d(Z_i)| < \infty$ and*

$$|\rho_i(\theta') - \rho_i(\theta)| \le d(Z_i)\, ||\theta' - \theta||^{\alpha}$$

for all $\theta', \theta \in \Theta$.

Then $\{Q_n\}$ converges in probability uniformly on Θ to $\mathrm{E}\,\rho_i(\cdot)$, and $\mathrm{E}\,\rho_i(\cdot)$ is continuous on Θ.

Proof. See Newey (1991), Corollary 3.1. □

The next result does not require compactness of the parameter space Θ but replaces continuity or Lipschitz conditions on Q_n by the stronger condition that Q_n is concave.

Theorem 15.5 *Suppose that:*

(i) *Θ is an open convex subset of $\Re^p$;*
(ii) *for all n, Q_n is concave on Θ;*
(iii) *$\{Q_n\}$ converges in probability pointwise on Θ to Q.*

Then, for any compact subset K of Θ, $\{Q_n\}$ converges in probability uniformly on K to Q. Further, Q is concave on Θ.

Proof. See Pollard (1991). □

15.3 ASYMPTOTIC NORMALITY

An estimator sequence $\{\hat{\theta}_n\}$ such that the rescaled difference $\sqrt{n}\,(\hat{\theta}_n - \theta_0)$ has a nondegenerate limiting distribution is said to be *$\sqrt{n}$-consistent for θ_0*. Under regularity conditions, $\sqrt{n}$-consistent M-estimators can be shown to converge to a limiting Gaussian distribution. The standard case (Section 15.3.1) is when the criterion function Q_n is twice differentiable, which implies that a CLT can be applied to a linearized version of $\hat{\theta}_n$. This is not an innocuous assumption, however, for it rules out important estimators such as LAD. More recently, asymptotic normality results have been established that only require the weaker assumptions that the asymptotic criterion function Q is twice differentiable (Section 15.3.3).

15.3.1 THE STANDARD CASE

The basic argument is similar to that in Section 4.6.2 for asymptotic normality of a ML estimator and relies on a second-order Taylor expansion of the criterion function defining the estimator.

Theorem 15.6 *Let $\hat\theta_n = \operatorname{argmax}_{\theta\in\Theta} Q_n(\theta)$ and suppose that:*

(i) $\hat\theta_n \xrightarrow{p} \theta_0$;
(ii) *θ_0 is in the interior of Θ;*
(iii) *the function Q_n is twice continuously differentiable on a neighborhood $\mathcal{O}$ of θ_0;*
(iv) $\sqrt{n}\, Q_n'(\theta_0) \xrightarrow{d} \mathcal{N}_p(0, C_0)$;
(v) *the sequence of random matrix functions $\{-Q_n''\}$ converges in probability uniformly on $\mathcal{O}$ to a matrix function B that is symmetric and continuous on $\mathcal{O}$;*
(vi) *$B_0 = B(\theta_0)$ is a finite p.d. matrix.*

Then $\sqrt{n}\,(\hat\theta_n - \theta_0) \xrightarrow{d} \mathcal{N}_p(0, B_0^{-1} C_0 B_0^{-1})$.

Proof. By (i)–(iii), with probability approaching one, $\hat\theta_n$ is a root of the equation $0 = Q_n'(\theta)$. By the mean value theorem

$$0 = Q_n'(\hat\theta_n) = \sqrt{n}\, Q_n'(\theta_0) + Q_n''(\theta_n^\star)\sqrt{n}\,(\hat\theta_n - \theta_0),$$

where $\theta_n^\star = (1-\lambda_n)\theta_0 + \lambda_n\hat\theta_n$ and $\lambda_n \in [0,1]$. Since $||\theta_n^\star - \theta_0|| \le ||\hat\theta_n - \theta_0||$ and $\hat\theta_n \xrightarrow{p} \theta_0$, $\theta_n^\star$ converges in probability to θ_0. Thus, for n sufficiently large,

$$\begin{aligned} ||Q_n''(\theta_n^\star) + B_0|| &\le ||Q_n''(\theta_n^\star) + B(\theta_n^\star)|| + ||B_0 - B(\theta_n^\star)|| \\ &\le \sup_{\theta\in\mathcal{O}} ||Q_n''(\theta) + B(\theta)|| + ||B_0 - B(\theta_n^\star)||, \end{aligned}$$

where the first term on the right side of the inequality converges in probability to zero by (v). Hence $Q_n''(\theta_n^\star) \xrightarrow{p} -B_0$, and therefore $\sqrt{n}\, Q_n'(\theta_0) - B_0\sqrt{n}\,(\hat\theta_n - \theta_0) = o_p(1)$. Because B_0 is nonsingular, we have $\sqrt{n}\,(\hat\theta_n - \theta_0) - B_0^{-1}\sqrt{n}\, Q_n'(\theta_0) = o_p(1)$. Thus $\sqrt{n}\,(\hat\theta_n - \theta_0)$ and $B_0^{-1}\sqrt{n}\, Q_n'(\theta_0)$ have the same limiting distribution, namely $\mathcal{N}_p(0, B_0^{-1} C_0 B_0^{-1})$. □

We refer to the conditions of Theorem 15.6 as the *standard conditions for asymptotic normality* of an M-estimator. Condition (ii) is convenient because it allows the estimator to be represented as a root of a set of first-order conditions. This assumption is essential for asymptotic normality, which usually does not hold when θ_0 is on the boundary of the parameter space. On the other hand, as shown in Section 15.3.3, condition (iii) is not necessary for asymptotic normality. Condition (iv) is typically the result of a CLT applied to the asymptotically linear representation (15.1). If the sequence of random functions $\{Q_n\}$ converges uniformly on a neighborhood $\mathcal{O}$ of θ_0 to a twice differentiable function Q, then the matrix $B(\theta)$ in condition (v) is equal to minus the Hessian of Q for each $\theta \in \mathcal{O}$. In this case, condition (vi) guarantees that Q has a local maximum on $\mathcal{O}$ at $\theta = \theta_0$, which implies that θ_0 is locally identifiable.

Estimates of the asymptotic variance of $\hat\theta_n$ are typically of the form

$$\widehat{\mathrm{AV}}(\hat\theta_n) = \hat B_n^{-1} \hat C_n \hat B_n^{-1},$$

where $\hat B_n$ and $\hat C_n$ are consistent estimates of B_0 and C_0 respectively. In standard situations, $\hat B_n = -Q''(\hat\theta_n)$ and

$$\hat C_n = n^{-1} \sum_{i=1}^{n} Q_n'(\hat\theta_n)\, Q_n'(\hat\theta_n)^\top.$$

It is easy to verify that, under the assumptions of Theorem 15.6, $\hat{B}_n$ is p.d. with probability approaching one and $\widehat{\mathrm{AV}}(\hat{\theta}_n) \xrightarrow{\mathrm{p}} \mathrm{AV}(\hat{\theta}_n)$. The sampling variance of $\hat{\theta}_n$ may therefore be estimated by $n^{-1}\,\widehat{\mathrm{AV}}(\hat{\theta}_n)$. Of course, an alternative estimate may be obtained by the bootstrap.

15.3.2 ONE-STEP M-ESTIMATORS

Consider the general class of Newton-type algorithms of the form

$$\theta^{(r+1)} = \theta^{(r)} + B_n(\theta^{(r)})^{-1}\,Q_n'(\theta^{(r)}), \qquad r = 0, 1, 2, \ldots, \tag{15.5}$$

where B_n is minus the Hessian of Q_n, as in the Newton–Raphson method, or some approximation to it, as in the scoring or the BHHH method (see Appendix B.3). A *one-step M-estimator* is obtained by starting from some initial value $\theta^{(0)}$ and taking only one step of (15.5) in the direction of a local maximum of Q_n. The resulting estimator is also called a *linearized M-estimator*. The main advantage of this type of estimator is that they are simpler to compute than fully iterated ones.

The next theorem shows that, under appropriate conditions, the limiting distribution of a one-step M-estimator is the same as that of a fully iterated M-estimator. The crucial requirements are: (i) the starting point $\theta_n^{(0)}$ must be a $\sqrt{n}$-consistent estimator of the target parameter θ_0, and (ii) $B_n(\theta)$ must be a consistent estimator of the matrix $B(\theta)$ defined in Theorem 15.6. A similar result holds for one-step M-estimators obtained by carrying out only one iteration of the Gauss–Newton method in the direction of a maximum of Q_n.

Theorem 15.7 *Let $\tilde{\theta}_n = \theta_n^{(0)} + (B_n^{(0)})^{-1} Q_n'(\theta_n^{(0)})$, where $B_n^{(0)} = B_n(\theta_n^{(0)})$, and suppose that the assumptions of Theorem 15.6 hold with $-Q_n''$ replaced by B_n. Further suppose that $\hat{\theta}_n^{(0)} - \theta_0 = o_p(n^{-1/2})$. Then $\tilde{\theta}_n - \hat{\theta}_n \xrightarrow{\mathrm{p}} 0$.*

Proof. From the definition of a one-step estimator

$$\sqrt{n}\,(\tilde{\theta}_n - \theta_0) = \sqrt{n}\,(\hat{\theta}_n^{(0)} - \theta_0) + (B_n^{(0)})^{-1}\sqrt{n}\,Q_n'(\hat{\theta}_n^{(0)}). \tag{15.6}$$

Expanding $\sqrt{n}\,Q_n'(\hat{\theta}_n^{(0)})$ about the target parameter θ_0 gives

$$\sqrt{n}\,Q_n'(\hat{\theta}_n^{(0)}) = \sqrt{n}\,[Q_n'(\theta_0) + B_n(\theta_0)(\hat{\theta}_n^{(0)} - \theta_0)] + o_p(1).$$

Substituting back into (15.6) gives

$$\sqrt{n}\,(\tilde{\theta}_n - \theta_0) = \sqrt{n}\,(\hat{\theta}_n^{(0)} - \theta_0) + \sqrt{n}\,(B_n^{(0)})^{-1}[Q_n'(\theta_0) + B_n(\theta_0)(\hat{\theta}_n^{(0)} - \theta_0)] + o_p(1),$$

where, under the stated assumptions, $B_n^{(0)} = B_0 + o_p(n^{-1/2})$ and $B_n(\theta_0) = B_0 + o_p(1)$. Thus we get

$$\begin{aligned}\sqrt{n}\,(\tilde{\theta}_n - \theta_0) &= \sqrt{n}\,(\hat{\theta}_n^{(0)} - \theta_0) + \sqrt{n}\,B_0^{-1}[Q_n'(\theta_0) + B_0(\hat{\theta}_n^{(0)} - \theta_0)] + o_p(1) \\ &= B_0^{-1}\sqrt{n}\,Q_n'(\theta_0) + o_p(1).\end{aligned}$$

The conclusion then follows from the fact that $\sqrt{n}\,(\hat{\theta}_n - \theta_0) - B_0^{-1}\sqrt{n}\,Q_n'(\theta_0) = o_p(1)$, using the proof of Theorem 15.6. □

Example 15.4 Consider a classical Gaussian linear model with nonscalar error covariance matrix $\Sigma_0 = \Sigma(\delta_0)$, where δ_0 is a finite-dimensional parameter, functionally unrelated to the regression parameter β_0. It is easily seen that the likelihood score for β is

$$\frac{\partial L}{\partial \beta} = n^{-1}\mathbf{X}^\top \Sigma^{-1}(\mathbf{Y} - \mathbf{X}\beta), \qquad \theta = (\beta, \delta).$$

Further, the Fisher information $\mathcal{I}$ is block-diagonal with respect to β and δ, and the block corresponding to β is $\mathcal{I}_\beta(\theta) = n^{-1}\mathbf{X}^\top\Sigma^{-1}\mathbf{X}$. The rth iteration of the scoring method is therefore

$$\begin{aligned}\beta^{(r+1)} &= \beta^{(r)} + [\mathbf{X}^\top(\Sigma^{(r)})^{-1}\mathbf{X}]^{-1}\mathbf{X}^\top(\Sigma^{(r)})^{-1}(\mathbf{Y} - \mathbf{X}\beta^{(r)}) \\ &= [\mathbf{X}^\top(\Sigma^{(r)})^{-1}\mathbf{X}]^{-1}\mathbf{X}^\top(\Sigma^{(r)})^{-1}\mathbf{Y},\end{aligned}$$

where $\Sigma^{(r)} = \Sigma(\delta^{(r)})$. The one-step estimator of β in this case is the feasible GLS estimator based on a consistent estimate of δ_0. □

15.3.3 ASYMPTOTIC NORMALITY UNDER NONSTANDARD CONDITIONS

Let $\{\hat\theta_n\}$ be a sequence of M-estimators defined by maximizing a random criterion function Q_n. We assume that the conditions of Theorem 15.2 hold. In particular, Q_n is assumed to converge in probability uniformly on Θ to a continuous function Q which attains its unique maximum at θ_0. When Q_n is smooth, as assumed in Theorem 15.3, $\hat\theta_n$ has the same limiting distribution as the (unfeasible) linearized estimator $\tilde\theta_n = \theta_0 - Q_n''(\theta_0)^{-1}Q_n'(\theta_0)$ obtained by maximizing the following local quadratic approximation to Q_n

$$\tilde Q_n(\theta) = Q_n(\theta_0) + Q_n'(\theta_0)^\top(\theta - \theta_0) + \frac{1}{2}(\theta - \theta_0)^\top Q_n''(\theta_0)(\theta - \theta_0).$$

When Q_n is not smooth, an argument for asymptotic normality of $\hat\theta_n$ may be constructed as follows. Suppose that θ_0 lies in the interior of the parameter space Θ. If Q is smooth, then $Q'(\theta_0) = 0$ and so $Q(\theta)$ may be approximated by the quadratic function

$$Q^*(\theta) = Q(\theta_0) - \frac{1}{2}(\theta - \theta_0)^\top B_0(\theta - \theta_0),$$

where $B_0 = -Q''(\theta_0)$ and the approximation error is of order $o(\|\theta - \theta_0\|^2)$. Now consider approximating $Q_n(\theta)$ by the locally quadratic function

$$Q_n^*(\theta) = Q_n(\theta_0) + D_n^\top(\theta - \theta_0) - \frac{1}{2}(\theta - \theta_0)^\top B_0(\theta - \theta_0),$$

where D_n is the gradient of Q_n or some approximation to it. If this approximation is good enough for large n and the matrix B_0 is p.d., then we may be able to obtain the limiting distribution of $\hat\theta_n$ from the asymptotic properties of

$$\hat\theta_n^* = \operatorname*{argmax}_{\theta\in\Theta} Q_n^*(\theta) = \theta_0 + B_0^{-1}D_n.$$

Suppose in particular that $D_n = n^{-1}\sum_i \Delta(Z_i)$, with $\mathrm{E}_F\,\Delta(Z_i) = 0$ and $\mathrm{Var}_F\,\Delta(Z_i) = C_0$. Then $\sqrt{n}\,D_n \xrightarrow{\mathrm{d}} \mathcal{N}_p(0, C_0)$ by the CLT and so, if we are able to show that $\sqrt{n}\,(\hat\theta_n - \hat\theta_n^*) = o_p(1)$, we can conclude that $\sqrt{n}\,(\hat\theta_n - \theta_0) \xrightarrow{\mathrm{d}} \mathcal{N}_p(0, B_0^{-1}C_0B_0^{-1})$.

The remainder of this section tries to make the above argument a little more precise. Let $\{Z_i\}$ be a sequence of i.i.d. random m-vectors with distribution function F and let $\{\hat{\theta}_n\}$ be a sequence of M-estimators defined by maximizing over a subset Θ of $\Re^p$ a random criterion function of the form

$$Q_n(\theta) = n^{-1} \sum_{i=1}^{n} \rho(Z_i; \theta),$$

where $\mathrm{E}\, \rho(Z_i;\theta)^2 < \infty$ for all $\theta \in \Theta$. We assume that $Q(\theta) = \mathrm{E}_F\, \rho(Z_i;\theta)$ is twice differentiable, although $\rho(\cdot;\theta)$ need not be. This assumption is much less restrictive than assuming twice differentiability of Q_n, for taking expectations often smooths out kinks or discontinuities.

Following Pollard (1984, 1985) and van der Vaart (1998), we use linear functional notation and write

$$F\rho(\cdot;\theta) = \mathrm{E}_F\, \rho(Z_i;\theta) = Q(\theta)$$

and

$$\hat{F}_n\rho(\cdot;\theta) = \mathrm{E}_{\hat{F}}\, \rho(Z_i;\theta) = Q_n(\theta),$$

where $\hat{F}_n$ is the empirical distribution function of the first n observations in the sequence $\{Z_i\}$. The rescaled difference $\nu_n(z) = \sqrt{n}\,[\hat{F}_n(z) - F(z)]$ is a function of z for any given sample and is a random variable for any given $z \in \Re^m$. The collection

$$\nu_n = \{\nu_n(z), z \in \Re^m\}$$

of all such random variables is therefore a stochastic process with index set $\Re^m$ and is called the *empirical process*. Applying the empirical process μ_n to $\rho(\cdot;\theta)$ gives

$$\nu_n\rho(\cdot;\theta) = \sqrt{n}\,[\hat{F}_n\rho(\cdot;\theta) - F\rho(\cdot;\theta)] = \sqrt{n}\,[Q_n(\theta) - Q(\theta)].$$

By the CLT, $\nu_n\rho(\cdot;\theta)$ has an asymptotically normal distribution and is therefore of order $O_p(1)$. Thus, the decomposition $\hat{F}_n = F + n^{-1/2}\nu_n$ gives the following decomposition of Q_n

$$Q_n(\theta) = Q(\theta) + n^{-1/2}\nu_n\rho(\cdot;\theta),$$

where $Q(\theta)$ is a deterministic component and $n^{-1/2}\nu_n\rho(\cdot;\theta)$ is a stochastic perturbation of order $O_p(n^{-1/2})$.

We now introduce a notion of differentiability in a weak (or average) sense which is similar to the notion of differentiability in probability of a stochastic process.

Definition 15.5 A function $\rho(z;\theta)$ is said to be *stochastically differentiable at* θ_0 if there exists a function $\Delta\colon \Re^m \to \Re^p$, which does not depend on θ_0, such that

$$\rho(z;\theta) = \rho(z;\theta_0) + (\theta - \theta_0)^\top \Delta(z) + \|\theta - \theta_0\| r(z;\theta), \tag{15.7}$$

where

$$\frac{|\nu_n r(\cdot;\theta)|}{1 + \sqrt{n}\,\|\theta - \theta_0\|} \xrightarrow{\mathrm{p}} 0$$

uniformly on any sequence $\{\mathcal{O}_n\}$ of neighborhoods shrinking to θ_0 as $n \to \infty$. □

If a function $\rho(z;\theta)$ is stochastically differentiable at θ_0, the function $\Delta(z)$ is called the *gradient* of $\rho(z;\theta)$ at θ_0.

The next theorem gives sufficient conditions for asymptotic normality of a sequence $\{\hat{\theta}_n\}$ of M-estimators.

Theorem 15.8 (Pollard) *Let $\{Z_i\}$ be a sequence of i.i.d. random q-vectors with distribution function F, let $\hat{F}_n$ be the empirical distribution function of the first n elements of $\{Z_i\}$, let $Q_n(\theta) = \hat{F}_n\rho(\cdot;\theta)$, $Q(\theta) = F\rho(\cdot;\theta)$ and $\hat{\theta}_n = \text{argmax}_{\theta\in\Theta} Q_n(\theta)$, where $\Theta \subseteq \Re^p$. Suppose that:*

(i) $\hat{\theta}_n \xrightarrow{\text{p}} \theta_0$;
(ii) *θ_0 is in the interior of Θ;*
(iii) *the function Q is twice differentiable at θ_0 and the matrix $B_0 = -Q''(\theta_0)$ is p.d.;*
(iv) *the function ρ is stochastically differentiable at θ_0 and its gradient Δ satisfies $F\Delta = 0$ and $F\|\Delta\|^2 < \infty$.*

Then $\sqrt{n}\,(\hat{\theta}_n - \theta_0) \xrightarrow{\text{d}} \mathcal{N}_p(0, B_0^{-1}C_0B_0^{-1})$, where $C_0 = F\Delta\Delta^\top$.

Proof. The proof proceeds in two parts. The first part improves the rate of convergence of $\hat{\theta}_n$ to θ_0 from $o_p(1)$ to $O_p(n^{-1/2})$. The second part shows that the limiting distribution of the rescaled difference $\sqrt{n}\,(\hat{\theta}_n - \theta_0)$ is Gaussian. We consider for simplicity the scalar parameter case and, without loss of generality, we let $\theta_0 = 0$.

By the definition of M-estimator

$$0 \le Q_n(\hat{\theta}_n) - Q_n(0) = Q(\hat{\theta}_n) - Q(0) + n^{-1/2}\nu_n[\rho(\cdot;\theta) - \rho(\cdot;0)].$$

Since Q is twice differentiable at $\theta = 0$ with a nonsingular gradient, there exists a constant $c > 0$ (for example, $c = B_0/4$) such that, with probability approaching one as $n \to \infty$, $Q(\hat{\theta}_n) - Q(0) \le -c|\hat{\theta}_n|^2$. Hence

$$0 \le Q_n(\hat{\theta}_n) - Q_n(0) \le -c|\hat{\theta}_n|^2 + n^{-1/2}\nu_n[\rho(\cdot;\theta) - \rho(\cdot;0)].$$

Stochastic differentiability of ρ implies

$$\begin{aligned} |\,\nu_n[\rho(\cdot;\hat{\theta}_n) - \rho(\cdot;0)]\,| &= |\,\hat{\theta}_n\nu_n\Delta + |\hat{\theta}_n|\,\nu_n r(\cdot;\hat{\theta}_n)\,| \\ &\le |\hat{\theta}_n|\,\{|\nu_n\Delta| + o_p(1 + \sqrt{n}\,|\hat{\theta}_n|)\}. \end{aligned}$$

Because $\nu_n\Delta \xrightarrow{\text{d}} \mathcal{N}_p(0, C_0)$ by (iv) and the CLT, assuming $\Pr\{\hat{\theta}_n = 0\} = 0$ gives

$$\begin{aligned} c\sqrt{n}\,|\hat{\theta}_n| \le \frac{|\,\nu_n[\rho(\cdot;\hat{\theta}_n) - \rho(\cdot;0)]\,|}{|\hat{\theta}_n|} &\le |\nu_n\Delta| + o_p(1 + \sqrt{n}\,|\hat{\theta}_n|) \\ &= O_p(1) + o_p(\sqrt{n}\,|\hat{\theta}_n|). \end{aligned}$$

We now show that the limiting distribution of $\sqrt{n}\,\hat{\theta}_n$ is Gaussian. Without loss of generality let $B_0 = 1$. Twice differentiability of Q implies

$$Q(\theta) - Q(0) = -\frac{1}{2}|\theta^2| + o(|\theta|^2)$$

for all θ near zero. Since $\hat{\theta}_n = O_p(n^{-1/2})$, the sequence $\{\hat{\theta}_n\}$ belongs with probability approaching one to a sequence of neighborhoods of zero shrinking at the rate of $O(n^{-1/2})$. Stochastic differentiability of ρ then implies

$$|\hat{\theta}_n|\,|\nu_n r(\cdot;\hat{\theta}_n)| = O_p(n^{-1/2})\,o_p(1 + n^{1/2}O_p(n^{-1/2})) = o_p(n^{-1/2}).$$

Therefore

$$\begin{aligned} Q_n(\hat{\theta}_n) &= Q_n(0) + Q(\hat{\theta}_n) - Q(0) + n^{-1/2}\nu_n[\rho(\cdot;\hat{\theta}_n) - \rho(\cdot;0)] \\ &= Q_n(0) - \frac{1}{2}|\hat{\theta}_n|^2 + o_p(n^{-1}) + n^{-1/2}[\hat{\theta}_n\Delta + o_p(n^{-1/2})] \\ &= Q_n(0) - \frac{1}{2}|\hat{\theta}_n|^2 + \hat{\theta}_n\hat{\delta}_n + o_p(n^{-1}), \end{aligned}$$

where $\hat{\delta}_n = n^{-1/2}\hat{\theta}_n\nu_n\Delta$. Exactly the same argument applied to the sequence $\{\hat{\delta}_n\}$ gives

$$Q_n(\hat{\delta}_n) = Q_n(0) - \frac{1}{2}|\hat{\delta}_n|^2 + \hat{\delta}_n^2 + o_p(n^{-1}) = Q_n(0) + \frac{1}{2}|\hat{\delta}_n|^2 + o_p(n^{-1}).$$

Because $\theta_0 = 0$ is an interior point of Θ, $\hat{\delta}_n$ belongs to Θ with probability approaching one. Hence $Q_n(\hat{\delta}_n) \le Q_n(\hat{\theta}_n)$, that is,

$$Q_n(0) + \frac{1}{2}|\hat{\delta}_n|^2 + o_p(n^{-1}) \le Q_n(0) - \frac{1}{2}|\hat{\theta}_n|^2 + \hat{\theta}_n\hat{\delta}_n + o_p(n^{-1}),$$

from which $\frac{1}{2}|\hat{\delta}_n - \hat{\theta}_n|^2 \le o_p(n^{-1})$. Thus $\sqrt{n}\,\hat{\theta}_n = \nu_n\Delta + o_p(1)$ and therefore $\sqrt{n}\,\hat{\theta}_n \xrightarrow{d} \mathcal{N}(0, C_0)$. □

Pointwise smoothness, namely condition (iii) in Theorem 15.3, is clearly sufficient for stochastic differentiability. A weaker set of conditions was given by Huber (1967), but his conditions may be hard to verify. Recent results in the theory of empirical processes provide simpler ways of verifying the stochastic differentiability assumption. These results establish conditions on the family $\mathcal{R} = \{r(\cdot;\theta\}, \theta \in \Theta\}$ of remainder functions in the expansion (15.7) under which, given any $\epsilon > 0$, there exists a $\delta > 0$ such that

$$\lim_{n\to\infty}\sup\, \Pr\{\sup_{\|r\|<\delta} |\nu_n r| > \epsilon\} < \epsilon, \tag{15.8}$$

with $\|r\| = (Fr^2)^{1/2}$. Condition (15.8) may be regarded as a stochastic equicontinuity condition on the class of remainder functions in the expansion (15.7). It is easy to verify that if the family $\mathcal{R}$ satisfies condition (15.8) and $\|r(\cdot;\theta)\| \to 0$ as $\theta \to 0$, then $\sup_{\theta\in\mathcal{O}_n} |\nu_n r(\cdot;\theta)| \xrightarrow{p} 0$ uniformly on any sequence of neighborhoods $\{\mathcal{O}_n\}$ shrinking to 0 as $n \to \infty$. This conclusion is actually stronger than the stochastic differentiability condition and allows one to absorb the remainder term into the coefficient of the linear term in the quadratic approximation to Q_n.

We now discuss one technique that may be useful in order to verify (15.8). Recall that the *graph* of a real function g is defined as the set

$$\{(x,\lambda)\colon g(x) \ge \lambda > 0 \text{ or } g(x) < \lambda \le 0\}.$$

Definition 15.6 A class of sets $\mathcal{D}$ is called a *polynomial class* or a *Vapnik–Červonenkis class* if given $D \in \mathcal{D}$ there exists a polynomial g such that for every finite set A with $\#A$ elements there are at most $g(\#A)$ distinct subsets of the form $A \cap D$. A collection $\mathcal{G}$ of real functions is called a *polynomial class* if the graphs of all the functions in $\mathcal{G}$ form a polynomial class. □

Theorem 15.9 *Let $\mathcal{G}$ be a class of functions equipped with the $L_2(F)$ norm $\|g\| = (Fg^2)^{1/2}$ and such that $F(\sup_{g\in\mathcal{G}} g^2) < \infty$. Then $\mathcal{G}$ satisfies (15.8) if it is a polynomial class or each member of $\mathcal{G}$ can be expressed as a sum of a fixed number of functions from a polynomial class.*

Proof. See Pollard (1984), Lemma VII.19. □

Thus, one way of verifying the stochastic differentiability assumption consists of verifying that the remainder function in the expansion (15.7) belongs to a polynomial class or can be expressed as a sum of a fixed number of functions from a polynomial class.

The following result gives a set of criteria for checking whether a collection of sets (e.g. the graphs of a class of functions) is a polynomial class.

Theorem 15.10 (Vapnik–Červonenkis)

(i) *The indicator functions of the members of a polynomial class of sets form a polynomial class of sets.*

(ii) *If $\mathcal{D}$ is a polynomial class of sets, then so is the collection of all pairwise unions and pairwise intersections of sets from $\mathcal{D}$.*

(iii) *If $\mathcal{G}$ is a finite-dimensional vector space of functions then it is a polynomial class and the collection of all sets of the form $\{g \geq 0\}$ or $\{g > 0\}$, with $g \in \mathcal{G}$, is a polynomial class of sets.*

(iv) *If $\mathcal{G}$ is a polynomial class, then so is the collection of all pairwise maxima and pairwise minima of functions in $\mathcal{G}$.*

(v) *The collection of all translates of a fixed right-continuous, monotone function on the real line is a polynomial class.*

Proof. See Pollard (1984), Section II.4. □

The next two examples are important because they help establish the asymptotic normality of several estimators discussed in Chapter 16.

Example 15.5 The sample median is an M-estimator corresponding to the choice $\rho(z;\theta) = -|z-\theta|$. Formal differentiation, which is not valid at $z = \theta$, suggests putting

$$\Delta(z) = \text{sign}(z-\theta) = 1\{z \geq \theta\} - 1\{z < \theta\}.$$

Let $\theta_0 = 0$ for simplicity. Then the remainder function is

$$r(z;\theta) = \frac{|z| - |z-\theta| - \theta\, 1\{z \geq \theta\} + \theta\, 1\{z < \theta\}}{|\theta|}, \qquad \theta \neq 0.$$

It is easy to see that, for any given $\theta \neq 0$, the graph of $r(\cdot;\theta)$ is a triangular region in $\Re^2$, defined as the intersection of three closed half-spaces. A half-space is representable as $\{g \geq 0\}$, where g is linear. Since a linear function in $\Re^2$ belongs to the three-dimensional vector space of first-degree real polynomials in $\Re^2$, the remainder functions form a polynomial class. If Θ is a bounded interval, then $|r(z;\theta)|$ is uniformly bounded and so $F(\sup_{\theta\in\Theta} |r(z;\theta)|^2) < \infty$. □

Example 15.6 The Huber estimator of location (Huber 1964) is an M-estimator corresponding to the choice

$$\rho(z;\theta) = \begin{cases} -(1/2)(z-\theta)^2, & \text{if } |z-\theta| \leq 1, \\ -|z-\theta| - (1/2)(z-1)^2, & \text{otherwise.} \end{cases}$$

Let $\theta_0 = 0$ for simplicity. The function is everywhere differentiable with derivative

$$\Delta(z) = z\ 1\{|z| \leq 1\} + \text{sign}(z))\ 1\{|z| > 1\}.$$

If $\Theta = [-1, 1]$, then $|r(z;\theta)|$ is uniformly bounded and $F(\sup_{\theta\in\Theta} |r(z;\theta)|^2) < \infty$. For each $\theta \neq 0$, the graph of $r(z;\theta)$ consists of three pieces, each piece being the intersection of at most four sets of the form $\{g \geq 0\}$, where g belongs to the six-dimensional vector space of second-degree real polynomials in $\Re^2$. Thus, the remainder functions form a polynomial class. □

15.4 ROBUSTNESS

The aim of robust estimation is to develop estimators that perform well when the assumed model is correctly specified, while being relatively insensitive to small departures from the model assumptions. Robust estimation makes use of parametric assumptions, thereby attaining high efficiency at the assumed model, but deals in a formal way with the fact that these assumptions are almost never literally true.

In what follows, we consider M-estimators of a p-dimensional parameter. We confine our attention to estimators that may be represented, either exactly or asymptotically, by a statistical functional that does not depend on the sample size n. This is not very restrictive because, as $n \to \infty$, most M-estimators converge to a functional T that does not depend on n and defines the parameter of interest.

Example 15.7 A GMM estimator $\hat{\theta}_n$ is a solution to a minimization problem of the form

$$\min_{\theta\in\Theta} \bar{\eta}_n(\theta)^\top D_n \bar{\eta}_n(\theta),$$

where $\bar{\eta}_n(\theta) = n^{-1}\sum_i \eta(Z_i;\theta)$ is a random vector of dimension $q \geq p$ and D_n is a p.d. symmetric random matrix. If $\bar{\eta}_n(\theta) \xrightarrow{p} \mathrm{E}_F\, \eta(Z;\theta)$ and $D_n \xrightarrow{p} D$, a p.d. symmetric matrix, then $\hat{\theta}_n$ is asymptotically implicitly defined by the functional $T(F)$ that solves the problem

$$\min_{\theta\in\Theta} [\mathrm{E}_F\, \eta(Z;\theta)]^\top D\, [\mathrm{E}_F\, \eta(Z;\theta)].$$

A GMM estimator is an example of a nonlinear functional. □

15.4.1 QUALITATIVE AND QUANTITATIVE ROBUSTNESS

Qualitative robustness is essentially a continuity requirement on the sampling distribution of an estimator $\hat{\theta}_n$: small changes in the population distribution (identified with its distribution function F defined on the sample space $\mathcal{Z}$) should only have small effects on the sampling distribution of $\hat{\theta}_n$. More formally.

Definition 15.7 (Hampel) A sequence of estimators $\{\hat{\theta}_n\}$ is said to be ***qualitatively robust at a distribution*** F if, for every $\epsilon > 0$, there exists $\delta > 0$ such that, for all n and all distributions G, $d(F, G) < \delta$ implies $d(\mathcal{L}_F(\hat{\theta}_n), \mathcal{L}_G(\hat{\theta}_n)) < \epsilon$, where d is some distance between probability distributions and $\mathcal{L}_F(\hat{\theta}_n)$ is the sampling distribution of $\hat{\theta}_n$ under F. □

Hampel's definition is not easy to verify directly. Further, it does not provide a way of ordering estimators according to their "degree of robustness". However, as we shall see in the next sections, there exists an easily verifiable definition of quantitative robustness which, for a broad class of estimators, is also sufficient for qualitative robustness. This second definition of robustness essentially measures the effects on an estimator of a certain type of small perturbation of the model assumptions. A third definition of robustness, discussed in Section 15.4.7, measures how big these perturbations can be before the estimator "breaks down", that is, ceases to be informative about the target parameter.

15.4.2 THE INFLUENCE FUNCTION

We consider an estimator $\hat{\theta}_n = T(\hat{F}_n)$, where $\hat{F}_n$ denotes the empirical distribution function for a random sample of n observations, and ask the following question. What are the effects on the sampling distribution of $\hat{\theta}_n$ of small changes in the population distribution function F? In particular, what is the asymptotic bias of $\hat{\theta}_n$ as an estimator of $\theta = T(F)$ when the observations come from some distribution function G "close" to F?

To answer the above questions one would need to compute the difference $T(G) - T(F)$. This is straightforward when T is a linear functional, that is of the form $T(F) = \int \psi(z)\, dF(z)$ for some function ψ: $\mathcal{Z} \to \Re^p$, because in this case

$$T(G) - T(F) = \int \psi(z)\, dG(z) - \int \psi(z)\, dF(z) = T(G - F).$$

If T is nonlinear, as in Example 15.7 or in the case of general M-estimators, then it is often possible to replace T by an asymptotically equivalent linear functional.

A statistical functional T is said to be ***asymptotically linear*** if it possesses the following *von Mises expansion* (von Mises 1947)

$$T(G) - T(F) = \delta T(F, G - F) + o(d(G, F)), \tag{15.9}$$

where $\delta T(F, \cdot)$ is a linear functional and the remainder on the right-hand side of (15.9) is of smaller order than the distance $d(G, F)$ between G and F. The von Mises expansion is essentially a Taylor expansion applied to the functional T. Because δT is a linear functional, it is of the form

$$\delta T(F, G-F) = \int \psi(z;F)\, d(G-F) = \int \psi(z;F)\, dG - \int \psi(z;F)\, dF$$

for some function $\psi(\cdot;F)$: $\mathcal{Z} \to \Re^p$. The vector-valued function

$$\text{IF}(z;F) = \psi(z;F) - \int \psi(x;F)\, dF(x),$$

viewed as a function of z for F given, is called the *influence function* of T at F. Clearly,

$$\int \text{IF}(z;F)\, dF(z) = 0,$$

that is, the influence function has mean zero. If $d(G,F) \approx 0$, then (15.9) and the definition of influence function give the following answer to our initial question about the asymptotic bias of $\hat{\theta}_n$

$$T(G) - T(F) \approx \delta T(F, G-F) = \int \text{IF}(z;F)\, dG.$$

The von Mises expansion (15.9) and the existence of the IF are closely related to the differentiability of a statistical functional. To see this, consider the case when $G = F_{\epsilon,z}$, where $F_{\epsilon,z}$ is an ϵ-contaminated version of F defined as

$$F_{\epsilon,z} = (1-\epsilon)F + \epsilon\Delta_{(z)} = F + \epsilon(\Delta_{(z)} - F), \qquad 0 \le \epsilon < 1,$$

and $\Delta_{(z)}$ is a degenerate distribution giving unit mass to the point z. This model is known as the *gross-error model* and was introduced in Section 2.5.3. Because $F_{\epsilon,z} - F = \epsilon(\Delta_{(z)} - F)$, it follows from (15.9) and the definition of influence function that

$$T(F_{\epsilon,z}) - T(F) = \int \text{IF}(x;F)\, dF_{\epsilon,z}(x) + o(d(F_{\epsilon,z}, F)),$$

with

$$\int \text{IF}(x;F)\, dF_{\epsilon,z}(x) = (1-\epsilon)\int \text{IF}(x;F)\, dF + \epsilon \int \text{IF}(x;F)\, d\Delta_{(z)} = \epsilon\, \text{IF}(z;F),$$

where we used the fact that $\int \text{IF}(x;F)\, d\Delta_{(z)} = \text{IF}(z;F)$. For a given z,

$$\|T(F_{\epsilon,z}) - T(F) - \epsilon\, \text{IF}(z;F)\| \to 0$$

as $\epsilon \to 0$, where $\|\cdot\|$ denotes the Euclidean norm of a vector. Thus, ϵ IF$(z;F)$ provides an approximation to the asymptotic bias of $\hat{\theta}_n$ under a small amount of contamination of the distribution F by a point-mass distribution centered at z. This shows that, formally,

$$\text{IF}(z;F) = \lim_{\epsilon \to 0+} \frac{T(F_{\epsilon,z}) - T(F)}{\epsilon} = \frac{\partial}{\partial \epsilon} T(F_{\epsilon,z})\bigg|_{\epsilon=0}, \qquad (15.10)$$

that is, the IF is the collection of Gateaux differentials of the functional T (see e.g. Luenberger 1969, p. 171) with increment $\Delta_{(z)} - F$.

An alternative derivation of the IF provides additional insight. Given the estimate $\hat{\theta}_n = T(\hat{F}_n)$ computed for a sample of n observations, add to the sample an extra point z and consider the difference $\hat{\theta}_{n+1} - \hat{\theta}_n = T(\hat{F}_{n+1}) - T(\hat{F}_n)$, where $\hat{F}_{n+1}$ is the empirical distribution function for the new sample of $n+1$ observations. Notice that $\hat{F}_{n+1} = (1-\delta_n)\,\hat{F}_n + \delta_n\,\Delta_{(z)}$, where $\delta_n = (n+1)^{-1}$. The standardized difference

$$\mathrm{EIF}_n(z) = n(\hat{\theta}_{n+1} - \hat{\theta}_n) = n[T((1-\delta_n)\hat{F}_n + \delta_n\Delta_{(z)}) - T(\hat{F}_n)]$$

is called the *empirical influence function* of $\hat{\theta}_n$, a concept already introduced in Section 6.2.7 with reference to the OLS estimator. Under regularity conditions, $\mathrm{EIF}_n(z)$ converges to the influence function defined by (15.10). This is easily verified for linear functionals.

Example 15.8 Consider the linear functional $T(F) = \int x\,dF(x)$, which defines the sample mean. Evaluating T at the gross-error model $F_{\epsilon,z} = (1-\epsilon)F + \epsilon\Delta_{(z)}$ gives

$$T(F_{\epsilon,z}) = (1-\epsilon)\int x\,dF + \epsilon\int x\,d\Delta_{(z)} = (1-\epsilon)\,T(F) + \epsilon z,$$

where we used the fact that $\int x\,d\Delta_{(z)} = z$. Therefore $\mathrm{IF}(z;F) = z - T(F)$.

Now consider the mean $\hat{\theta}_n = n^{-1}\sum_i Z_i$ of a sample of n observations from F. If an extra point z is added to the sample, then the mean of the new set of $n+1$ observations is

$$\hat{\theta}_{n+1} = \frac{1}{n+1}(\sum_{i=1}^{n} Z_i + z) = \frac{1}{n+1}(n\hat{\theta}_n + z).$$

Hence,

$$\mathrm{EIF}_n(z) = \frac{n}{n+1}(z - \hat{\theta}_n) \xrightarrow{\mathrm{p}} z - T(F) = \mathrm{IF}(z;F)$$

by the WLLN. □

Example 15.9 Let $F(z) = F(x,y)$ and consider the functional

$$T(F) = \left(\int xx^\top\,dF\right)^{-1}\int xy\,dF,$$

which defines the OLS estimator. Evaluating at the gross-error model $F_{\epsilon,z}$, where now $z = (x,y)$, gives

$$T(F_{\epsilon,z}) = [(1-\epsilon)\,Q + \epsilon\,xx^\top]^{-1}[(1-\epsilon)\;\mathrm{E}_F\,XY + \epsilon\,xy],$$

with $P = \mathrm{E}_F\,XX^\top$. Straightforward manipulations show that

$$\frac{T(F_{\epsilon,z}) - T(F)}{\epsilon} = \frac{1}{1-\epsilon(1-h)}\,P^{-1}x(x - \theta^\top x),$$

where $h = x^\top P^{-1}x$ and $\theta = T(F)$. Taking the limit as $\epsilon \to 0$, the influence function of the OLS estimator is

$$\mathrm{IF}(z;F) = P^{-1}x(y - \theta^\top x).$$

This influence function may be viewed as the product of two components: one is equal to $y - \theta^\top x$ and may be called "influence of the regression errors", the other is equal to $P^{-1}x$ and may be called "influence of the covariates".

From Section 6.2.7 we also have

$$\mathrm{EIF}_n(z) = \left(\frac{\mathbf{X}^\top \mathbf{X}}{n}\right)^{-1} \frac{x(y - \hat{\theta}_n^\top x)}{1 + h_n},$$

where $h_n = n^{-1}x^\top(\mathbf{X}^\top\mathbf{X}/n)^{-1}x$. Thus,

$$\mathrm{EIF}_n(z) = n^{-1}(\hat{\theta}_n - \hat{\theta}_{n-1}) \xrightarrow{\mathrm{p}} P^{-1}x(y - \theta^\top x) = \mathrm{IF}(z; F)$$

by the WLLN. □

Besides providing information on the asymptotic bias of $\hat{\theta}_n$, the von Mises expansion (15.9) can be used as a heuristic tool for deriving the asymptotic variance of an asymptotically linear estimator $\hat{\theta}_n$. If the data are a sample from a distribution F, then (15.9) implies

$$\begin{aligned} \hat{\theta}_n - \theta = T(\hat{F}_n) - T(F) &= \mathrm{E}_{\hat{F}_n} \mathrm{IF}(Z; F) + o_p(n^{-1/2}) \\ &= n^{-1} \sum_{i=1}^{n} \mathrm{IF}(Z_i; F) + o_p(n^{-1/2}), \end{aligned} \tag{15.11}$$

where $n^{-1/2}$ is the rate of convergence of the empirical distribution function $\hat{F}_n$ to F. Because $\{\mathrm{IF}(Z_i; F)\}$ is a sequence of i.i.d. random variables with mean zero and variance

$$\mathrm{Var}_F \mathrm{IF}(Z; F) = \mathrm{E}_F \mathrm{IF}(Z; F)\, \mathrm{IF}(Z; F)^\top,$$

application of a CLT gives

$$\sqrt{n}\,[T(\hat{F}_n) - T(F)] \xrightarrow{\mathrm{d}} \mathcal{N}_p(0, \mathrm{AV}(\hat{\theta}; F)),$$

where $\mathrm{AV}(\hat{\theta}; F) = \mathrm{Var}_F \mathrm{IF}(Z; F)$. The essential requirements for this result are that the first term of the expansion (15.11) is not vanishing and the remainder is $o_p(n^{-1/2})$.

15.4.3 B-ROBUSTNESS

Certain properties of an estimator may be described more conveniently by a few scalar summaries of its influence function. Denoting by $\|\cdot\|$ the Euclidean norm of a vector (or some generalization of it), the most important of such summaries is its L_∞ or sup-norm

$$\gamma^*(F) = \sup_{z \in \mathcal{Z}} \|\mathrm{IF}(z; F)\|,$$

called the *gross-error sensitivity* of the estimator. Because the difference $T(F_{\epsilon,z}) - T(F)$ is approximately equal to $\epsilon\, \mathrm{IF}(z; F)$ for small ϵ, we have

$$\sup_{z \in \mathcal{Z}} \|T(F_{\epsilon,z}) - T(F)\| \approx \epsilon \gamma^*(F),$$

that is, $\epsilon\gamma^*(F)$ provides an approximation to the maximum asymptotic bias of $\hat{\theta}$ under contamination of the model distribution of the gross-error type. More generally, if F and G are close to each other, then

$$T(G) - T(F) \approx \int \mathrm{IF}(z;F)\, dG(z) \leq \sup_{z \in \mathcal{Z}} \mathrm{IF}(z;F).$$

Therefore, in a small neighborhood of F,

$$\sup_G \|T(G) - T(F)\| \leq \gamma^*(F).$$

This justifies calling an estimator *bias-* or *B-robust* if $\gamma^*(F) < \infty$, that is, if its influence function is bounded. Estimators of this type are also called *bounded influence estimators.* For a B-robust estimator, the maximum asymptotic bias over a small neighborhood of the assumed model cannot be arbitrarily large. This is a desirable property, but one that is not satisfied by many common estimators.

Example 15.10 It was shown in Example 15.8 that the influence function of the sample mean is $\mathrm{IF}(z;F) = z - T(F)$. Because this is an unbounded function, the sample mean is not B-robust.

A similar conclusion holds for the OLS estimator, whose influence function (derived in Example 15.9) is $\mathrm{IF}(z;F) = P^{-1}x[y - T(F)^\top x]$. Notice that the influence function of the OLS estimator is unbounded because both its components, namely the influence of the regression errors and the influence of the covariates, are unbounded. This simply reflects the fact that a single large regression error or a single large x-value can have an arbitrarily large effect on the OLS estimate. □

It can be shown that, for M-estimators with a continuous IF, B-robustness is equivalent to qualitative robustness (see Hampel *et al.* 1986). Further, using the gross-error sensitivity we can now rank estimators according to their degree of robustness.

15.4.4 THE INFLUENCE FUNCTION OF M-ESTIMATORS

As is clear from Examples 15.8 and 15.9, deriving the influence function of a linear functional is straightforward. If the functional is nonlinear, other methods must be applied.

Our next result gives the influence function of an M-estimator based on a criterion function which satisfies the regularity conditions of Theorem 15.1 and converges uniformly to a twice differentiable function Q whose unique point of maximum lies in the interior of Θ. Asymptotically, such an estimator corresponds to the statistical functional $T(F)$ implicitly defined on $\mathcal{F}$ by the equation

$$\int \psi(z;\theta)\, dF(z) = 0, \tag{15.12}$$

where the function $\psi(z;\theta) = Q'(z;\theta)$ is called the *score function* associated with the estimator and $\mathcal{F}$ is the set of distributions for which (15.12) has a unique root. Here and in what follows, $g'(z;\theta)$ denotes the gradient of a function $g(z;\theta)$ with respect to θ.

Definition 15.8 Let $\hat{\theta}_n$ be an M-estimator with associated score function $\psi(z;\theta)$ and let $\mathcal{F}$ be the set of distributions for which the equation $\int \psi(z;\theta)\,dF(z) = 0$ has a unique root $T(F)$. Then $\hat{\theta}_n$ is said to be *regular* if:

(i) for all $F \in \mathcal{F}$, $\hat{\theta}_n$ is consistent for $T(F)$ and asymptotically normal;
(ii) the function $\psi(z;\theta)$ is continuously differentiable with respect to θ for almost all z;
(iii) the matrix $B(F) = -\operatorname{E}_F \psi'(Z;T(F))$ is nonsingular for all $F \in \mathcal{F}$.

□

Theorem 15.11 *The influence function of a regular M-estimator with associated score function $\psi(z;\theta)$ is*

$$\operatorname{IF}(z;F) = B(F)^{-1}\,\psi(z;T(F)).$$

Proof. Evaluating (15.12) at the gross-error model $F_{\epsilon,z} = F + \epsilon(\Delta_{(z)} - F)$ gives

$$0 = \int \psi(x;T(F_{\epsilon,z}))\,dF_{\epsilon,z}(x).$$

Under regularity conditions which allowi passing the derivative under the integral sign, differentiating the above identity with respect to ϵ gives

$$0 = \int \left[\frac{\partial}{\partial\theta}\,\psi(x;T(F_{\epsilon,z}))\right]\left[\frac{\partial}{\partial\epsilon}\,T(F_{\epsilon,z})\right]\,dF_{\epsilon,z}(x) + \int \psi(x;T(F_{\epsilon,z}))\,[d\Delta_{(z)}(x) - dF(x)].$$

Evaluating at $\epsilon = 0$ and using (15.10) and (15.12) gives

$$0 = -B(F)\,\operatorname{IF}(z;F) + \psi(z;T(F)).$$

Finally, solving for the influence function using the assumption that $B(F)$ is nonsingular yields $\operatorname{IF}(z;F) = B(F)^{-1}\,\psi(z;T(F))$. □

Thus, the influence function of a regular M-estimator is simply a nonsingular linear transformation of the score function that asymptotically defines the estimator. Intuitively, the score and the influence function of a regular M-estimator contain the same information.

By the heuristic argument in Section 15.4.1, the asymptotic variance of a regular M-estimator may be obtained from its influence function as

$$\operatorname{AV}(\hat{\theta};F) = \operatorname{Var}_F \operatorname{IF}(Z;F) = B(F)^{-1}\,C(F)\,B(F)^{-\top},$$

where

$$C(F) = \operatorname{Var}_F \psi(Z;T(F)) = \operatorname{E}_F \psi(Z;T(F))\,\psi(Z;T(F))^{\top}.$$

This agrees nicely with the results in Section 15.3.

For distributions in a regular parametric family $\{F_\theta, \theta \in \Theta\}$ and estimators that are Fisher consistent, namely such that $T(F_\theta) = \theta$, we have

$$\mathrm{IF}(z; F_\theta) = B(F_\theta)^{-1}\, \psi(z; \theta).$$

In particular, if $\hat{\theta}$ is a ML estimator, then $\psi(z;\theta)$ is equal to the likelihood score $s(z;\theta)$ and so, by the information equality,

$$B(F_\theta) = -\,\mathrm{E}_\theta\, s'(Z;\theta) = \mathcal{I}(\theta),$$

where $\mathcal{I}(\theta)$ is the Fisher information. Hence

$$\mathrm{IF}(z; F_\theta) = \mathcal{I}(\theta)^{-1}\, s(z;\theta).$$

If ψ is the score function of any other M-estimator that is Fisher consistent, then part (ii) of Theorem 1.2 gives

$$B(F_\theta) = \mathrm{E}_\theta\, \psi(Z;\theta) s(Z;\theta)^\top = \mathrm{Cov}[\psi(Z;\theta), s(Z;\theta)]. \tag{15.13}$$

In the light of our previous results, it is clear that any estimator $\hat{\theta}$ which possesses an IF is asymptotically equivalent to an M-estimator whose score function is equal to the influence function of $\hat{\theta}$. Thus, from an asymptotic viewpoint, there is little loss of generality in focusing on the class of M-estimators.

15.4.5 ASYMPTOTIC EFFICIENCY

We now give a formal proof of the claim made earlier in Section 4.6.2 that the ML estimator of a correctly specified parametric model is asymptotically efficient. To rule out cases that are somewhat pathological, such as the one in Problem 15.11, we place restrictions on both the class of parametric models and the class of estimators considered by requiring the parametric model to be regular and by confining our attention to regular M-estimators.

The next result shows that ML estimators of regular parametric models are asymptotically efficient in the class of regular M-estimators.

Theorem 15.12 *Let $\mathcal{F}_\Theta$ be a regular parametric model with likelihood score $s(z;\theta)$ and Fisher information $\mathcal{I}(\theta)$. If $\hat{\theta}_n$ is the ML estimator of θ and $\tilde{\theta}_n$ is a regular M-estimator with associated score function $\psi(z;\theta)$, then $\mathrm{AV}(\tilde{\theta}_n) - \mathrm{AV}(\hat{\theta}_n) \geq 0$.*

Proof. To simplify the notation, let $\Psi = \psi(Z;\theta)$ and $S = s(Z;\theta)$. Since the parametric model is regular, the asymptotic variance of the ML estimator $\hat{\theta}_n$ is

$$\mathrm{AV}(\hat{\theta}_n) = \mathcal{I}(\theta)^{-1} = (\mathrm{E}_\theta\, SS^\top)^{-1}.$$

Regularity of the M-estimator $\tilde{\theta}_n$ implies that its influence function is equal to $\mathrm{IF}(z;F_\theta) = B(F_\theta)^{-1}\psi(z;\theta)$, where $B(F_\theta) = \mathrm{E}_\theta\, \Psi S^\top$. Hence, its asymptotic variance is

$$\begin{aligned}\mathrm{AV}(\tilde{\theta}_n) &= B(F_\theta)^{-1}\, C(F_\theta)\, B(F_\theta)^{-\top} \\ &= (\mathrm{E}_\theta\, \Psi S^\top)^{-1}(\mathrm{E}_\theta\, \Psi\Psi^\top)(\mathrm{E}_\theta\, S\Psi\top)^{-1}.\end{aligned}$$

Now consider the difference $\Delta = \mathrm{AV}(\tilde{\theta}_n) - \mathrm{AV}(\hat{\theta}_n)$. We have

$$\begin{aligned}\Delta &= (\mathrm{E}_\theta\, \Psi S^\top)^{-1}(\mathrm{E}_\theta\, \Psi\Psi^\top)(\mathrm{E}_\theta\, S\Psi^\top)^{-1} - (\mathrm{E}_\theta\, SS^\top)^{-1} \\ &= (\mathrm{E}_\theta\, \Psi S^\top)^{-1}[(\mathrm{E}_\theta\, \Psi\Psi^\top) - (\mathrm{E}_\theta\, \Psi S^\top)^{-1}(\mathrm{E}_\theta\, SS^\top)^{-1}(\mathrm{E}_\theta\, S\Psi^\top)^{-1}](\mathrm{E}_\theta\, S\Psi^\top) \\ &= (\mathrm{E}_\theta\, \Psi S^\top)^{-1}(\mathrm{E}_\theta\, UU^\top)(\mathrm{E}_\theta\, S\Psi^\top),\end{aligned}$$

where $U = \Psi - (\mathrm{E}_\theta\, \Psi S^\top)(\mathrm{E}_\theta\, SS^\top)^{-1}S$ and we used the fact that, by definition, $\mathrm{E}_\theta\, \Psi = 0$. The conclusion of the theorem then follows from the fact that the matrix $\mathrm{E}_\theta\, UU^\top$ is n.n.d. □

Notice that the random vector U in the proof of Theorem 15.12 is just the residual in the orthogonal projection of the random p-vector $\psi(Z;\theta)$ on the random p-vector $s(Z;\theta)$. Thus, an M-estimator is asymptotically efficient if its associated score, and therefore its influence function, is equal to the likelihood score up to a linear transformation. Less formally, an M-estimator is asymptotically efficient at a given parametric model if it uses all the information contained in the likelihood score.

15.4.6 OPTIMAL B-ROBUST ESTIMATORS

In general, a B-robust estimator is asymptotically less efficient than a ML estimator based on a correctly specified parametric model. This is because B-robustness requires the influence function to be bounded, while asymptotic efficiency requires the influence function to coincide with the likelihood score (up to a linear transformation). When the latter is unbounded, B-robustness necessarily implies a loss of asymptotic efficiency. This loss can be minimized by considering estimators that are "optimally robust", that is, consistent and asymptotically efficient at the assumed model among all estimators with the same degree of robustness.

An optimality result for M-estimators with a bounded influence function was first derived by Hampel (1968). Given a parametric model indexed by a one-dimensional parameter θ, he managed to construct an estimator that is consistent at the assumed model and has minimum asymptotic variance among all estimators with the same gross-error sensitivity. Such an estimator can be interpreted as a weighted ML estimator and is obtained by censoring and recentering the likelihood score so as to satisfy the robustness constraint while ensuring consistency at the assumed model.

In what follows we generalize Hampel's (1968) approach to the case of multidimensional estimators. We restrict our attention to regular M-estimators of the parameter of a regular parametric model $\mathcal{F}_\Theta = \{F_\theta, \theta \in \Theta \subseteq \Re^p\}$ with likelihood score $s(z;\theta)$, and define an estimator's efficiency in terms of an asymptotic MSE criterion of the form $\mathrm{AMSE}(\hat{\theta}; F) = \mathrm{tr}\,\mathrm{AV}(\hat{\theta}; F)$. Among all estimators that are Fisher consistent and satisfy the robustness constraint $\gamma^*(F_\theta) \leq \gamma$, we want to pick one that has minimum asymptotic MSE at the assumed model. Such an estimator, if it exists, is said to be *optimal B-robust with respect to* γ. More general results may be obtained by varying the metric in which the asymptotic MSE and the estimator's sensitivity are defined (for details, see Peracchi 1990a).

In order to establish a one-to-one correspondence between the set of regular M-estimators and the set of associated score functions, we impose a normalization condition on the score function $\psi(z;\theta)$ by requiring that $B(F_\theta) = I_p$, where I_p is the identity matrix of order p. Under this normalization, $\mathrm{IF}(z;F_\theta) = \psi(z;\theta)$ and

$$\mathrm{AV}(\hat{\theta};F_\theta) = \mathrm{E}_\theta\, \psi(Z;\theta)\, \psi(Z;\theta)^\top.$$

An estimator that is optimal B-robust with respect to γ is then associated with the score function which solves the following problem

$$\min_{\psi(\cdot;\theta)\in\Psi} \mathrm{E}_\theta\, \psi(Z;\theta)^\top \psi(Z;\theta),$$

subject to the constraints

$$\mathrm{E}_\theta\, \psi(Z;\theta) = 0, \tag{15.14}$$

$$\mathrm{E}_\theta\, \psi(Z;\theta)\, s(Z;\theta)^\top = I_p, \tag{15.15}$$

$$\sup_{z\in\mathcal{Z}} \|\psi(z;\theta)\| \leq \gamma, \tag{15.16}$$

where $\mathcal{Z}$ is the sample space. The set Ψ is the set of functions that are square integrable with respect to any F_θ. Constraint (15.14) is necessary for Fisher consistency. Because of (15.13), constraint (15.15) corresponds to the normalization condition discussed above. Given the first two constraints, the criterion functional is the asymptotic MSE of the M-estimator associated with the score function $\psi(z;\theta)$. Finally, constraint (15.16) is the bound on the estimator's sensitivity. When this constraint is not imposed, that is, γ is not required to be finite, the problem reduces to the asymptotic optimality problem of classical parametric statistics, whose solution was given in Theorem 15.12.

The solution to the above problem is given by the following.

Theorem 15.13 *Let $\mathcal{F}_\Theta$ be a regular parametric model and suppose that, for all θ in an open subset Θ_0 of Θ, there exists a solution $(A(\theta), a(\theta))$ to the equation system*

$$\mathrm{E}_\theta\, w(Z;\theta)[As(Z;\theta) - a] = 0,$$

$$\mathrm{E}_\theta\, w(Z;\theta)\,[As(Z;\theta) - a]\, s(Z;\theta)^\top - I_p = 0,$$

where $w(z;\theta)$ is a scalar weight function defined by

$$w(z;\theta) = \min\left(1, \frac{\gamma}{\|As(z;\theta) - a\|}\right).$$

If $\tilde{\theta}$ is an M-estimator with associated score function

$$\tilde{\psi}(z;\theta) = w(z;\theta)\,[A(\theta)\, s(z;\theta) - a(\theta)],$$

then $\tilde{\theta}$ is Fisher consistent and B-robust with respect to γ. Further, $\mathrm{AMSE}(\tilde{\theta};F_\theta) \leq \mathrm{AMSE}(\hat{\theta};F_\theta)$ for any other regular M-estimator $\hat{\theta}$ that is Fisher consistent and B-robust with respect to γ.

Proof. The set Ψ is a Hilbert space with respect to the inner product $\langle\psi\,|\,\psi\rangle = \mathrm{E}_\theta\, \psi(Z)^\top\psi(Z)$. The induced norm of a vector $\psi \in \Psi$ is given by $\mathrm{E}_\theta\, \psi(Z)^\top\psi(Z)^{1/2}$. The set of points in Ψ that satisfy the robustness constraint is convex and may be viewed, heuristically, as a closed hypersphere with center at the origin and radius γ. The feasible set for the problem is therefore the intersection between this set of points and the hyperplane defined by the first two constraints. The feasible set is therefore closed and convex but can be empty. We show below that it is not empty provided that γ is large enough.

For a given θ, the problem is therefore one of finding a vector of minimum norm in a closed and convex subset of a Hilbert space. It then follows by standard results (see e.g. Luenberger 1969, Theorem 1, p. 69) that, if the feasible set is not empty, an optimal solution exists and is unique.

To characterize the solution, we introduce a non-negative p-vector λ of Lagrange multipliers associated with the constraint (15.14), a $p \times p$ n.n.d. matrix Γ of Lagrange multipliers associated with constraint (15.15), and a non-negative Lagrange multiplier function $\mu(z)$ associated with constraint (15.16). The dependence of all Lagrange multipliers on θ is omitted for simplicity. The optimal solution $(\tilde{\psi}(\cdot;\theta), \lambda, \Gamma, \mu(\cdot))$ is then characterized by

$$2\tilde{\psi}(z;\theta) + \lambda - \Gamma s(z;\theta) + \mu(z)\,\frac{\tilde{\psi}(z;\theta)}{||\tilde{\psi}(z;\theta)||} = 0 \tag{15.17}$$

$$\mu(z)\,(||\tilde{\psi}(z;\theta)|| - \gamma) = 0 \tag{15.18}$$

for all z, except possibly a set with zero probability under F_θ. If $|\tilde{\psi}(z;\theta)| < \gamma$ for some z, then $\mu(z) = 0$ and so

$$\tilde{\psi}(z;\theta) = As(z;\theta) - a,$$

where $A = \Gamma/2$ and $a = \lambda/2$. If $\mu(z) > 0$ at some point z, then $|\tilde{\psi}(z;\theta)| = \gamma$. In this case, solving equation (15.18) for $\tilde{\psi}(z;\theta)$ gives

$$\tilde{\psi}(z;\theta) = \frac{2\gamma}{2\gamma + \mu(z)}\,[As(z;\theta) - a].$$

Since $\mu(z)$ is a non-negative root of the equation

$$\frac{2\gamma}{2\gamma + \mu(z)}\,||As(z;\theta) - a|| = \gamma,$$

we get

$$\frac{2\gamma}{2\gamma + \mu(z)} = \frac{\gamma}{||As(z;\theta) - a||}.$$

Hence $\tilde{\psi}(z;\theta) = w(z;\theta)\,[As(z;\theta) - a]$, where

$$w(z;\theta) = \min\left(1, \frac{\gamma}{||As(z;\theta) - a||}\right).$$

The matrix A and the vector a are determined implicitly by the first two constraints. The existence of the optimal score function is therefore equivalent to the existence of a solution to the equation system

$$\mathrm{E}_\theta\, w(Z;\theta)[As(Z;\theta) - a] = 0,$$

$$\mathrm{E}_\theta\, w(Z;\theta)[As(Z;\theta)-a]\,s(Z;\theta)^\top - I_p = 0,$$

where $w(z;\theta)$ depends on (A, a). If a solution $(A(\theta),\, a(\theta))$ exists for all θ in an open set Θ_0 (the necessary conditions are provided below), the function $\tilde{\psi}(\cdot;\theta)\colon \mathcal{Z} \to \Re^q$ can be extended to a function $\tilde{\psi}\colon \mathcal{Z} \times \Theta_0 \to \Re^q$. □

An optimal B-robust estimator $\tilde{\theta}$ may be interpreted as a weighted ML estimator, obtained by applying the weight matrix $w(z;\theta)A(\theta)$ to the likelihood score and then subtracting the vector $w(z;\theta)\,a(\theta)$ in order to correct for the asymptotic bias. Geometrically, this corresponds to shrinking and twisting the likelihood score vector until it is entirely contained in a p-dimensional hypersphere with center at the origin and radius γ, while at the same time satisfying condition (15.14) which ensures consistency at the assumed model. If γ is finite, then the optimal B-robust estimator $\tilde{\theta}$ is qualitatively robust provided that the likelihood score is continuous in z. Unlike the ML estimator, however, $\tilde{\theta}$ is optimal only in a weak sense, namely with respect to the given MSE criterion.

In some cases the expression for the optimal score function simplifies considerably. For example, if $a(\theta) = 0$ then $\tilde{\psi}(z;\theta) = w(z;\theta)\,A(\theta)\,s(z;\theta)$, where

$$w(z;\theta) = \min\left(1, \frac{\gamma}{\|A(\theta)s(z;\theta)\|}\right)$$

and $A(\theta)$ is a symmetric p.d. matrix implicitly defined by the equation

$$\mathrm{E}_\theta[w(Z;\theta)\,s(Z;\theta)\,s(Z;\theta)^\top] - A(\theta)^{-1} = 0.$$

This case typically arises in regression models where disturbances are symmetrically distributed around zero, conditionally on the covariates. The optimal B-robust estimator in this case is the same as that based on the score function $\psi^*(z;\theta) = w(z;\theta)\,s(z;\theta)$, which makes its interpretation as a weighted ML estimator even clearer.

Example 15.11 Consider the Gaussian location model $\mathcal{N}(\mu, \sigma^2)$, with σ^2 known. Because $s(z;\mu) = (z-\mu)/\sigma^2$ and $b(\mu) = 0$ in this case, an optimal B-robust estimator of μ is associated with the score function

$$\psi(z;\mu) = \min\left(1, \frac{\gamma\sigma}{A(\mu)\,|(z-\mu)/\sigma|}\right)\frac{z-\mu}{\sigma^2},$$

where $A(\mu)$ is a positive root of the equation

$$\frac{1}{A} = \frac{1}{\sigma^2}\int \min\left(u^2, \frac{\gamma\sigma}{A}|u|\right)\phi(u)\,du = \frac{1}{\sigma^2}\left[2\Phi\left(\frac{\gamma\sigma}{A}\right) - 1\right],$$

and ϕ and Φ denote, respectively, the density and the distribution function of the $\mathcal{N}(0,1)$ distribution. The optimal score may also be written

$$\psi(z;\mu) = \frac{1}{\sigma}\,\min\left(\frac{z-\mu}{\sigma}, c\ \mathrm{sign}(z-\mu)\right) = \frac{1}{\sigma}\,h_c\left(\frac{z-\mu}{\sigma}\right),$$

where $c = \gamma\sigma/A(\mu)$ and the function $h_c(u) = \max(-c, \min(u, c))$ is called the *Huber function*. This estimator coincides with the Huber estimator of location introduced in Example 15.6. □

In specific applications, consistency and asymptotic normality of $\tilde{\theta}$ must be established formally using the results in Sections 15.2 and 15.3.

Theorem 15.13 generates a whole family of estimators indexed by the value of the sensitivity bound γ. If there is no bound on an estimator's sensitivity, that is $\gamma = \infty$, then the optimal estimator is the ML estimator. In this case, $a(\theta) = 0$ because the Fisher consistency constraint is no longer binding. Further, $A(\theta) = \mathcal{I}(\theta)^{-1}$ and so the information matrix is equal to the inverse of the matrix of Lagrange multipliers associated with the second constraint.

If γ is finite then, by a simple continuity argument, the optimal estimator $\tilde{\theta}$ exists and is unique provided that γ is sufficiently large. A necessary lower bound on γ is given below. The proof is straightforward and is therefore omitted.

Theorem 15.14 *Suppose that* $\mathrm{E}_\theta \|s(Z;\theta)\|$ *exists and is nonzero. Then* $A(\theta)$ *and* $a(\theta)$ *defined in Theorem 15.13 exist only if* $\gamma \geq p/[\mathrm{E}_\theta \|s(Z;\theta)\|]$.

Geometrically, when the number p of parameters to be estimated is greater than $\gamma \, \mathrm{E}_\theta \|s(Z;\theta)\|$, the hyperplane defined by the first two constraints does not intersect the convex set defined by the third one, and so the feasible set is empty. Notice that the lower bound on γ depends on θ.

If the lower bound of Theorem 15.14 is satisfied, varying γ describes a trade-off between efficiency (relative to the Cramér–Rao bound) and protection against bias (the sup-norm of the influence function). In some cases, such as linear regression, this trade-off can be easily characterized. When both this trade-off and the econometrician's preferences between efficiency and protection against bias are known, solving for the optimal choice of γ is straightforward.

Example 15.12 Under the Gaussian location model

$$\mathrm{E}_\theta |s(Z;\theta)| = \mathrm{E}_\theta \frac{|Z-\mu|}{\sigma^2} = 2\sigma^{-1} \int_0^\infty u\,\phi(u)\,du = \sigma^{-1}\sqrt{2/\pi}.$$

Hence, an optimal B-robust estimator of μ exists only if

$$\gamma \geq \frac{\sigma^2}{\mathrm{E}_\theta |Z-\mu|} = \sigma\sqrt{\pi/2}.$$

□

The payoff from using bounded influence estimators might be quite large. By construction, they offer protection against data inadequacies (e.g. gross measurement and recording errors) and mild forms of model misspecification. The available evidence shows that these methods can lead to significant differences with respect to conventional ML methods in terms of point estimates, inference and forecasts. In particular, tests based on these estimators are also robust, that is, their power function has certain desirable stability properties (Peracchi 1991, Heritier & Ronchetti 1994). Finally, the robust weights obtained as a by-product of estimation often provide valuable diagnostic information.

15.4.7 THE BREAKDOWN POINT

Loosely speaking, the ***breakdown point*** of an estimator is the largest fraction of gross errors that the estimator may tolerate before becoming completely uninformative about the parameter of interest.

This definition may be formalized in several ways. Here we follow Donoho and Huber (1983) and consider a sample $\mathbf{Z} = (Z_1, \ldots, Z_n)$ of n observations and an estimator $\hat{\theta} = T(\mathbf{Z})$. Consider all possible corrupted samples $\mathbf{Z}'$ that are obtained by replacing a given fraction m/n of the original data points by arbitrary values. Let

$$B(m; \mathbf{Z}) = \sup_{\mathbf{Z}'} \|T(\mathbf{Z}') - T(\mathbf{Z})\|$$

denote the maximum bias that can be caused by such contamination. The estimator T is said to ***break down*** if $B(m; \mathbf{Z}) = \infty$. The (finite sample) breakdown point of T at the sample $\mathbf{Z}$ is defined as

$$\epsilon(\mathbf{Z}) = \min \left\{ \frac{m}{n} \colon B(m; \mathbf{Z}) = \infty \right\}.$$

Thus, the breakdown point is the smallest fraction of contamination of the original data that can cause the estimator T to take on values arbitrary far from $T(\mathbf{Z})$.

Example 15.13 From Section 6.2.7, the breakdown point of the OLS estimator is equal to $1/n$. From Example 11.8, the breakdown point of a simple IV estimator is also equal to $1/n$. This again reflects the extreme sensitivity of LS and linear IV methods to outliers.

It is not difficult to verify that the breakdown point of the sample median is equal to $1/2$ if the sample size n is even and to $(n-1)/(2n)$ if the sample size is odd. □

BIBLIOGRAPHIC NOTES

A general reference for this chapter is van der Vaart (1998).

Sections 15.2 and 15.3 are based on Newey and McFadden (1994). Other useful references are Andrews (1994) and Pötscher and Prucha (1994). Section 15.3.3 is based on Pollard (1985). Newey and McFadden (1994) generalize Theorem 15.8 to the case of an arbitrary criterion function Q_n. For the asymptotic distribution of M-estimators when the target parameter is on the boundary of the parameter space see Andrews (1999). On the properties of M-estimators under a variety of stratified sampling schemes see Wooldridge (1999).

The definitions of qualitative robustness and breakdown point are due to Hampel (1971). The influence function was introduced by Hampel (1974). A similar concept for the asymptotic variance of an estimator has been proposed by Hampel, Rousseeuw and Ronchetti (1981). For a general introduction to the infinitesimal approach to robustness see Hampel *et al.* (1986). For a detailed discussion of the breakdown point of various estimators see Rousseeuw and Leroy (1987). For the relationship between breakdown point and tail behavior of an estimator see He *et al.* (1990). For a thorough discussion of the relationships between the various concepts of robustness see Jurečková and Sen (1995).

On von Mises expansions, see Chapter 6 of Serfling (1980). On the differentiability of statistical functionals see Fernholz (1983).

An optimality result for M-estimators with a bounded influence function was first derived by Hampel (1968). The presentation in Section 15.4.6 is based on Peracchi (1990a).

PROBLEMS

15.1 Let $\{Q_n\}$ be a sequence of nonstochastic functions defined on $\Theta = [-2, 1]$ by

$$Q_n(\theta) = \begin{cases} (1 - 2^{1-n})\theta + 2 - 2^{2-n}, & \text{if } -2 \leq \theta < -1, \\ -(1 - 2^{1-n})\theta, & \text{if } -1 \leq \theta < 0, \\ \dfrac{2^{n+1} - 2}{2^{n+1} - 1}\theta, & \text{if } 0 \leq \theta < 1 - 2^{-n-1}, \\ \dfrac{2^{n+1} - 2}{2^{n+1} - 1}\theta + 2 - 2^{1-n}, & \text{if } 1 - 2^{-n-1} \leq \theta < 1, \\ 0, & \text{if } \theta = 1. \end{cases}$$

Does the sequence $\{Q_n\}$ converge pointwise? Does it converge uniformly? If not, why?

15.2 Consider again the convergence properties of the sequence $\{Q_n\}$ of nonstochastic functions introduced in the previous problem, but now let $\Theta = [-2, 1)$. Does the sequence $\{Q_n\}$ converge pointwise? Does it converge uniformly? If not, why?

15.3 Let $Z_1, \ldots, Z_n$ be a sample from a $\mathcal{N}(\mu, \sigma^2)$ distribution. Compute the constrained ML estimator $\hat{\theta}_n$ of μ under the constraint that $\mu > 0$. Show that, for every n, the distribution of $\hat{\theta}_n$ is a mixture of a spike at zero with probability 1/2 and the positive half-normal distribution.

15.4 Show that if, for each z, the function $\rho(z; \cdot)$ has a continuous second derivative matrix whose elements are bounded in absolute value by a function with finite mean, then $\rho(\cdot; \theta)$ is stochastically differentiable.

15.5 The OLS estimator is an M-estimator corresponding to $\rho(z; \theta) = -(z - \theta)^2/2$. Find the remainder function in the expansion (15.7) and verify that it belongs to a polynomial class.

15.6 Use the asymptotically linear representation (15.1) to show that the influence function of a regular M-estimator is approximately equal to the normalized difference $n(\hat{\theta}_n - \hat{\theta}_{n,(i)})$ between the value of the estimator for a sample of size n and the value for a sample of size $n - 1$ with the ith observation excluded.

15.7 Compute the influence function of a simple IV estimator and compare it with the limit, as $n \to \infty$, of its empirical influence function.

15.8 Show that, for a linear functional, the influence function is the limit, as $n \to \infty$, of the empirical influence function.

15.9 Discuss the use of metrics different from the Euclidean one for alternative definitions of gross-error sensitivity.

15.10 Use integration by parts to prove the score identity (15.13).

15.11 Given a sample $Z_1, \ldots, Z_n$ from a $\mathcal{N}(\mu, 1)$ distribution, let $\bar{Z}_n$ be the sample mean and define the estimator

$$\hat{\mu}_n = \begin{cases} \bar{Z}_n, & \text{if } |\bar{Z}_n| \geq n^{-1/4}, \\ b\bar{Z}_n, & \text{otherwise,} \end{cases}$$

for some b such that $|b| < 1$.

(i) Show that $\sqrt{n}\,(\bar{Z}_n - \mu) \xrightarrow{\text{d}} \mathcal{N}(0,1)$ for any μ.
(ii) Show that $\sqrt{n}\,(\hat{\mu}_n - \mu) \xrightarrow{\text{d}} \mathcal{N}(0,1)$ if $\mu > 0$, but $\sqrt{n}\,(\hat{\mu}_n - \mu) \xrightarrow{\text{d}} \mathcal{N}(0,b^2)$ if $\mu = 0$.
(iii) Comment on this result.

15.12 Compute the influence function and the gross-error sensitivity of the ML estimator of the variance σ^2 for a $\mathcal{N}(\mu, \sigma^2)$ distribution with μ known, and use Theorem 15.13 to derive an optimal B-robust estimator.

15.13 Compute the influence function and the gross-error sensitivity of the ML estimator of the scale parameter σ for a gamma distribution with density parametrized as $f(z) = [\sigma\Gamma(p)]^{-1} z^{p-1} \exp(-z/\sigma)$, with p fixed. Use Theorem 15.13 to derive an optimal B-robust estimator.

15.14 The density of the Cauchy model with scale parameter σ is given by

$$f(z;\sigma) = \frac{1}{\sigma\pi[1 + (z/\sigma)^2]}.$$

Compute the influence function and the gross-error sensitivity of the ML estimator of σ and use Theorem 15.13 to derive an optimal B-robust estimator.

15.15 Prove Theorem 15.14.

15.16 Derive the breakdown point of the sample median.

16

Adaptive and Robust Regression Estimators

The linear regression model is the workhorse of applied econometrics and OLS is by far the most common estimation technique. Inference based on OLS, however, is known to be very sensitive to small departures of the distribution of the observed responses from the Gaussian one.

In this chapter we review three classes of alternative to OLS. The first class consists of estimators that are "efficiency robust" (Martin & Yohai 1985), in the sense that they attain higher asymptotic efficiency than OLS under a broad set of alternatives to the Gaussian model. The other two classes consist of estimators that are "bias robust" in the sense of being not too sensitive to violations of the normality assumption.

16.1 ADAPTIVE ESTIMATORS

Let the data $(X_1, Y_1), \ldots, (X_n, Y_n)$ be i.i.d. random vectors that satisfy the linear model

$$Y_i = \beta^\top X_i + \sigma V_i, \qquad i = 1, \ldots, n,$$

where the V_i are standardized regression errors distributed independently of X_i with zero mean, unit variance and density f. If we do not want to impose strong parametric assumptions on f, then we may consider estimating the model parameter $\theta = (\beta, \sigma)$ by methods that try to "adapt" to characteristics of the data which cannot be accommodated by the Gaussian distribution, such as tail weight, broad shoulders, asymmetry, etc.

16.1.1 PARTIALLY ADAPTIVE ESTIMATORS

Partially adaptive estimators of θ are pseudo ML estimators based on some flexible family of distributions for the regression errors. This family typically includes the Gaussian as a special case. Two examples already encountered are the family of t-distributions (Example 7.16) and the Pearson family (Example 10.11). Here we consider three other families of continuous distributions which take values on the whole real line and include the Gaussian as a special case. The three families correspond to increasingly rich parametrizations and therefore afford increasing flexibility. Notice that the scale parameter of each distribution is always set equal to one and, with the exception of the third example, the location parameter is set equal to zero.

Our first example is the *generalized power-exponential* or *Box–Tiao (BT)* family of distributions with density

$$f(v) = \frac{p}{2\Gamma(1/p)} \exp(-|v|^p), \qquad p = 1, 2, \ldots,$$

where Γ is the gamma function. The BT family is a one-parameter family of symmetric distributions which generates a regression model with parameter $\theta = (\beta, \sigma, p)$. It contains the Laplace distribution for $p = 1$ and the $\mathcal{N}(0,1)$ for $p = 2$. The BT density is not differentiable unless p is even. Given p, maximizing the BT likelihood with respect to β leads to the L_p norm problem

$$\min_{\beta \in \Re^k} \sum_{i=1}^{n} |Y_i - \beta^\top X_i|^p.$$

The second example is the *generalized t (GT)* family of distributions with density

$$f(v) = \frac{p}{2q^{1/p} B(1/p, q)} \left(1 + \frac{|v|^p}{q}\right)^{-\frac{q+1}{p}}, \qquad p, q = 1, 2, \ldots,$$

where $B(1/p, q)$ is the beta function (Appendix C.5). The GT family is a two-parameter family of symmetric distributions which generates a regression model with parameter $\theta = (\beta, \sigma, p, q)$. It contains the BT distribution as $q \to \infty$, the t-distribution for $p = 2$ and the $\mathcal{N}(0,1)$ for $p = 2$ and $q \to \infty$. The likelihood score of the GT model is

$$s(v) = (pq + 1) \frac{(\operatorname{sign} v)|v|^{p-1}}{q + |v|^p}.$$

This score is bounded for $1 < p, q < \infty$ and redescending for $|v| > [(p-1)/q^p]^{1/p}$.

The third example is the *exponential generalized beta of the second kind (EGB2)* or *log-logistic* family of distributions with density

$$f(v; \delta) = \frac{\exp[p(v - \delta)]}{B(p, q)\,[1 + \exp(v - \delta)]^{p+q}}, \qquad p, q = 1, 2, \ldots.$$

This is a three-parameter family of distributions that arise by taking the logarithm of non-negative random variables distributed as generalized F or generalized beta of the second kind, and generates a regression model with parameter $\theta = (\beta, \sigma, p, q, \delta)$. The EGB2 family allows not only for thicker tails than Gaussian, but also for asymmetry. An EGB2 distribution is symmetric about zero if $p = q$. The likelihood score of the EGB2 model is

$$s(v) = \frac{q \exp(v - q) - p}{1 - \exp(\delta - v)},$$

and is bounded above by q and below by p.

If estimation is approached within a pseudo ML framework, the asymptotic properties of the resulting estimators follow straightforwardly from the results in Chapter 15.

16.1.2 FULLY ADAPTIVE ESTIMATORS

Fully adaptive estimators are asymptotically efficient, as would be a ML estimator based upon knowledge of the actual distribution of the regression errors.

We distinguish between two approaches. The first one (Bickel 1982, Manski 1984) is based on nonparametric estimation of the density of the regression errors. Given the regression residuals from an initial estimate $\hat{\theta}_n = (\hat{\beta}_n, \hat{\sigma}_n)$, the kernel method produces estimates

$$\hat{f}_n(v) = \frac{1}{n\delta_n} \sum_{i=1}^{n} K\left(\frac{v - \hat{V}_i}{\delta_n}\right),$$

where K is a smooth kernel function, δ_n is the bandwidth and $\hat{V}_i = (Y_i - \hat{\beta}_n^\top X_i)/\hat{\sigma}_n$ denotes the ith standardized residual. The density estimate $\hat{f}_n(v)$ is used to produce an estimate $\hat{s}_n(v) = -\hat{f}_n'(v)/\hat{f}_n(v)$ of the likelihood score associated with the distribution of the regression errors. From this estimate, an updated estimate of θ is obtained by solving the likelihood equations

$$0 = \sum_{i=1}^{n} \hat{s}_n\left(\frac{Y_i - \beta^\top X_i}{\sigma}\right) X_i,$$

$$0 = n - \sum_{i=1}^{n} \hat{s}_n\left(\frac{Y_i - \beta^\top X_i}{\sigma}\right) \frac{Y_i - \beta^\top X_i}{\sigma}.$$

The process is then iterated until convergence. To reduce the impact of outliers and influential observations, the estimated score is often trimmed by setting $\hat{s}_n(v) = 0$ whenever $|v| > t_1$, or $\hat{f}_n(v) < t_2$, or $\hat{f}_n'(v)/\hat{f}_n(v) > t_3$, where t_1, t_2 and t_3 are trimming constants selected by the user.

The other approach (Newey 1988) exploits the assumptions of independence between the covariates and the regression errors to form GMM estimators of β. The independence assumption implies that functions of the regression errors are uncorrelated with functions of the covariates. Newey (1988) investigates two types of function of the errors

$$g_1(v) = \left(\frac{v}{1+|v|}\right)^j, \qquad j = 1, 2, \ldots,$$

and

$$g_2(v) = v^j\, e^{-v^2/2}, \qquad j = 1, 2, \ldots.$$

He also investigates the relationship between precision of estimation, the number of moments used, and the sample size.

16.2 QUANTILE REGRESSION

Quantile regression, already introduced in Chapters 1 and 4, generalizes the notion of quantiles to regression settings. It can be motivated in two ways. The first motivation is that it leads to estimators which are robust to heavy tailed regression errors (this is in fact the reason for which it was originally introduced). The second is that it provides summaries of intrinsic interest of the conditional distribution of a continuous random variable Y given a random k-vector X. In fact, knowledge of the family $\{\zeta_p(x), p \in (0,1)\}$ of condtional quantiles and knowledge of the conditional distribution function $F(y \mid x)$ are equivalent because of the relationship

$$p = \Pr\{Y \leq \zeta_p(x) \mid x\} = F(\zeta_p(x) \mid x).$$

16.2.1 DEFINITIONS AND ALGEBRAIC PROPERTIES

Recall from Chapter 4 that, given a sample of n observations $\{(X_i, Y_i)\}$ and a linear model $\zeta_p(x) = \beta^\top x$ for the pth $(0 < p < 1)$ conditional quantile of Y_i given $X_i = x$, an estimate of β may be obtained by solving the asymmetric least absolute deviations (ALAD) problem

$$\min_{\beta \in \Re^k} n^{-1} \sum_{i=1}^{n} \ell_p(Y_i - \beta^\top X_i), \tag{16.1}$$

where

$$\ell_p(u) = [p\, 1\{u \geq 0\} + (1-p)\, 1\{u < 0\}]\, |u| = [p - 1\{u < 0\}]\, |u|$$

is the asymmetric absolute loss function. Any solution to (16.1) is called an ALAD estimate. Given an ALAD estimate $\tilde{\beta}_p$, the pth conditional quantile may be estimated by $\hat{\zeta}_p(x) = \tilde{\beta}_p^\top x$. The set of points $\{(x,y) \in \Re^{k+1} \colon \hat{\zeta}_p(x) = p\}$ is the estimated pth quantile regression hyperplane.

When $p = 1/2$, problem (16.1) reduces to the LAD problem

$$\min_{\beta \in \Re^k} n^{-1} \sum_{i=1}^{n} |Y_i - \beta^\top X_i|. \tag{16.2}$$

A solution to (16.2) is called a LAD or median regression estimate. It is easily verified that a LAD estimate is a ML estimate for a linear regression model where the regression errors are independent of the covariates and i.i.d. with a common Laplace distribution.

Notice that the derivative of the asymmetric absolute loss function is

$$\ell_p'(u) = \begin{cases} p \operatorname{sign}(u), & \text{if } u > 0, \\ (1-p) \operatorname{sign}(u), & \text{if } u < 0, \end{cases}$$

and is not defined when $u = 0$. Thus, absolute loss differs from quadratic loss in two respects. First, it is not differentiable at the origin. Second, whenever its derivative $\ell_p'(u)$ exists, it is bounded above by p and below by $p-1$. As we shall see, this has a number of theoretical and practical implications for the estimates obtained from problem (16.1).

We now state some algebraic properties of ALAD estimates which generalize corresponding properties of sample quantiles. We refer to Koenker and Bassett (1978) for a proof. The design matrix $\mathbf{X}$ is henceforth assumed to have full column rank k.

First, a solution to problem (16.1) always exists, but need not be unique unless a selection rule is chosen.

Second, if $\mathcal{B}_p$ denotes the set of solutions to (16.1) and $[\mathbf{X}_s, \mathbf{Y}_s]$ is any of the $S = \binom{n}{k}$ subsets of k observations that can be obtained from the data matrix $[\mathbf{X}, \mathbf{Y}]$, then $\mathcal{B}_p$ has at least one element $\tilde{\beta}_p$ for which $\mathbf{Y}_s = \mathbf{X}_s \tilde{\beta}_p$. Thus, a quantile regression hyperplane fits exactly at least k data points and so at least k of the ALAD residuals $\tilde{U}_i = Y_i - \tilde{\beta}_p^\top X_i$ are exactly equal to zero. This property is known as *exact fit.*

Third, if the design matrix contains a column of ones, and n_p^+, n_p^- and n_p^0 denote the number of ALAD residuals that are respectively positive, negative and zero, then

$$n_p^- \leq np \leq n - n_p^+ = n_p^- + n_p^0.$$

These inequalities are strict if $\tilde{\beta}_p$ is unique.

Fourth, an ALAD estimate has equivariance properties similar to those of the OLS estimate. Let $\tilde{\beta}_p$ and $\tilde{\alpha}_p$ denote the ALAD estimates for the original and the transformed data respectively. If $\tilde{\mathbf{Y}} = \mathbf{Y} + \mathbf{X}\gamma$, then $\tilde{\alpha}_p = \tilde{\beta}_p + \gamma$ (regression equivariance). If $\tilde{\mathbf{Y}} = \sigma\mathbf{Y}$, then

$$\tilde{\alpha}_p = \begin{cases} \sigma\tilde{\beta}_p, & \text{if } \sigma > 0, \\ \sigma\tilde{\beta}_{1-p}, & \text{if } \sigma < 0 \end{cases}$$

(scale equivariance). Finally, if the design matrix is transformed as $\mathbf{W} = \mathbf{X}A$, where A is a nonsingular matrix, then $\tilde{\alpha}_p = A^{-1}\tilde{\beta}_p$.

16.2.2 COMPUTATIONAL ASPECTS

From the point of view of computation, the lack of smoothness of the ALAD criterion function implies that gradient methods cannot be employed. An ALAD estimate may however be computed efficiently using linear programming algorithms (Barrodale & Roberts 1973, Koenker & d'Orey 1987). This is due to the fact that the ALAD problem (16.1) may be reformulated as the following linear program

$$\begin{aligned} \min_{\beta \in \Re^k} \quad & p\iota^\top \mathbf{U}^+ + (1-p)\iota^\top \mathbf{U}^- \\ \text{subject to} \quad & \mathbf{Y} = \mathbf{X}\beta + \mathbf{U}^+ - \mathbf{U}^- \\ & \mathbf{U}^+, \mathbf{U}^- \in \Re^n, \end{aligned}$$

where ι is the n-vector whose elements are all equal to one, and $\mathbf{U}^+$ and $\mathbf{U}^-$ are n-vectors with generic elements equal to $U_i^+ = \max(0, Y_i - \beta^\top X_i)$ and $U_i^- = -\min(0, Y_i - \beta^\top X_i)$ respectively. The dual formulation of the problem is

$$\begin{aligned} \max_{\delta \in [p-1,p]^n} \quad & \mathbf{Y}^\top \delta \\ \text{subject to} \quad & \mathbf{X}^\top \delta = 0 \end{aligned}$$

or, setting $\alpha = \delta + (1-p)\iota_n$,

$$\begin{aligned} \max_{\alpha \in [0,1]^n} \quad & \mathbf{Y}^\top \alpha \\ \text{subject to} \quad & \mathbf{X}^\top \alpha = (1-p)\mathbf{X}^\top \iota_n. \end{aligned}$$

The solution $\hat{\alpha}_p$ to the dual problem connects quantile regression to the regression generalization of classical rank scores proposed by Gutenbrunner and Jurečková (1992).

Simpler but cruder algorithms based on iterative WLS may also be employed. To see this, consider the LAD problem where $p = 1/2$. In large samples, a LAD estimate may be defined as a root of the asymptotic first order conditions

$$0 = \mathrm{E}[\mathrm{sign}(Y_i - \beta^\top X_i)\, X_i] = \mathrm{E}\left[\frac{Y_i - \beta^\top X_i}{|Y_i - \beta^\top X_i|}\, X_i\right].$$

This suggests the iterative scheme

$$\tilde\beta^{(r+1)} = [\sum_i w_i^{(r)} X_i X_i^\top]^{-1} \sum_i w_i^{(r)} X_i Y_i, \qquad r = 0, 1, 2, \ldots,$$

where either

$$w_i^{(r)} = \frac{1\{|Y_i - \tilde\beta^{(r)\top} X_i| > \epsilon\}}{|Y_i - \tilde\beta^{(r)\top} X_i|}$$

(Schlossmacher 1973) or $w_i^{(r)} = \min(|Y_i - \tilde\beta^{(r)\top} X_i|^{-1}, \epsilon^{-1})$ (Fair 1974), and ϵ is some small positive number chosen by the investigator. One should avoid setting $w_i^{(r)} = |Y_i - \tilde\beta^{(r)\top} X_i|^{-1}$ because, in the k-parameter case, at least k LAD residuals are exactly equal to zero.

16.2.3 ROBUSTNESS PROPERTIES

Suppose that $\{(X_i, Y_i)\}$ are i.i.d. random vectors with distribution function F. If the conditional distribution of Y_i given X_i has a continuous and strictly positive density $f(y \,|\, x)$, then an ALAD estimate may also be defined asymptotically as the unique root of the asymptotic first-order conditions

$$\begin{aligned} 0 &= \mathrm{E}_F[p\, 1\{Y_i > \beta^\top X_i\}\, X_i - (1-p)\, 1\{Y_i < \beta^\top X_i\}\, X_i] \\ &= \mathrm{E}_F[(p - 1\{Y_i < \beta^\top X_i\})\, X_i]. \end{aligned} \tag{16.3}$$

If $T(F)$ denotes the solution to (16.3) then, by Theorem 15.11, the influence function of the ALAD estimator is defined at all points for which $y \neq T(F)^\top x$ and is given by

$$\mathrm{IF}(z; F) = B^{-1}\, [p - 1\{y < T(F)^\top x\}]\, x, \tag{16.4}$$

where

$$B = \mathrm{E}_F[f(T(F)^\top X_i \,|\, X_i)\, X_i X_i^\top].$$

This influence function is the product of two components: the influence of the regression errors, equal to $p - 1\{y - T(F)^\top x\}$, and the influence of the covariates, equal to $B^{-1} x$. Unlike OLS, the influence of the regression errors is bounded above by p and below by $p-1$, which ensures good robustness properties when the regression errors have thick tails. However, because the influence of the covariates is unbounded, ALAD estimators are not qualitatively robust and their breakdown point is equal to zero.

It follows immediately from (16.3) that the influence function (16.4) has zero mean. Further

$$\mathrm{Var}_F\, \mathrm{IF}(Z_i; F) = B^{-1}\, C\, B^{-1},$$

where

$$C = \mathrm{Var}_F[(p - 1\{Y_i < T(F)^\top X_i\})\, X_i].$$

To evaluate the matrix C, notice that

$$\mathrm{Var}(1\{Y_i < y\} \mid X_i = x) = F(y \mid x)\,[1 - F(y \mid x)],$$

where $F(y \mid x)$ denotes the conditional distribution function of Y_i given $X_i = x$. Also notice that $F(T(F)^\top x \mid x) = p$ if the pth conditional quantile of Y_i is indeed linear. If $P = \mathrm{E}\, X_i X_i^\top$ then, by the law of total variance, $C = p(1-p)\, P$ and therefore

$$\mathrm{Var}_F\, \mathrm{IF}(Z_i; F) = p(1-p)\, B^{-1}\, P\, B^{-1}. \tag{16.5}$$

L-estimators, that is, linear combinations of sample quantiles such as the trimmed mean and the interquartile range, are known to possess good robustness properties. Except for lack of robustness to contamination in the x-space, all these properties carry over to L-estimators of regression. This class includes trimmed LS estimators and other analogues of linear combinations of sample quantiles (Ruppert & Carroll 1980).

16.2.4 ASYMPTOTIC DISTRIBUTION

If conditional quantiles are linear, namely of the form $\zeta_p(x) = \beta_p^\top x$, ALAD estimators can be shown to be $\sqrt{n}$-consistent and asymptotically normal under general conditions. Because one may be interested in estimating linear combinations of conditional quantiles, we focus on the joint asymptotic distribution of a finite set of ALAD estimators. Thus consider a set of J distinct points $0 < p_1 < \cdots < p_J < 1$, and let $\tilde{\boldsymbol{\beta}}_n$ denote the vector of ALAD estimators of the Jk-dimensional parameter $\boldsymbol{\beta} = (\beta_{p_1}, \ldots, \beta_{p_J})$ for a sample of size n.

The next theorem establishes the asymptotic behavior of the sequence $\{\tilde{\boldsymbol{\beta}}_n\}$ when the conditional distribution of Y_i given $X_i = x$ retains the same shape as x varies, only shifting linearly in location.

Theorem 16.1 *Let $(X_1, Y_1), \ldots, (X_n, Y_n)$ be i.i.d. random vectors and suppose that:*

(i) *the conditional distribution function of Y_i given $X_i = x$ is of the form $F(y - \beta_0^\top x)$ for some $\beta_0 \in \Re^k$;*

(ii) *F has a continuous and strictly positive density f at all u such that $0 < F(u) < 1$;*

(ii) *$\mathrm{E}\, X_i X_i^\top = P$, where P is a finite p.d. $k \times k$ matrix.*

Then $\sqrt{n}\,(\tilde{\boldsymbol{\beta}}_n - \boldsymbol{\beta}) \xrightarrow{\mathrm{d}} \mathcal{N}_{Jk}(0,\, \Omega \otimes P^{-1})$, where Ω is a $J \times J$ matrix with generic element

$$\omega_{rs} = \frac{\min(p_r, p_s) - p_r p_s}{f(\zeta_{p_r})\, f(\zeta_{p_s})}$$

and $\zeta_p = F^{-1}(p)$.

Proof. See Ruppert and Carroll (1980). □

In particular, under the assumptions of Theorem 16.1, the asymptotic variance of the ALAD estimator of β_p is

$$\mathrm{AV}(\tilde{\beta}_{pn}) = \frac{p(1-p)}{f(\zeta_p)^2}\, P^{-1},$$

which coincides with the variance (16.5) of the influence function after noticing that $f(y\,|\,x) = f(y - \beta_0^\top x)$ in this case. For the LAD estimator $\tilde{\beta}_n$, corresponding to $p = 1/2$, we get

$$\mathrm{AV}(\tilde{\beta}_n) = \frac{1}{[2f(\zeta_{1/2})]^2}\, P^{-1},$$

where $\zeta_{1/2}$ is the median of F. If Y_i is symmetrically distributed about $\beta_0^\top X_i$, then $\mathrm{AV}(\tilde{\beta}_n) = [2f(0)]^{-2} P^{-1}$. In this latter case, the asymptotic efficiency of the LAD estimator relative to the OLS estimator $\hat{\beta}_n$ is

$$\mathrm{ARE}(\tilde{\beta}_n, \hat{\beta}_n) = \frac{\operatorname{tr} \mathrm{AV}(\hat{\beta}_n)}{\operatorname{tr} \mathrm{AV}(\tilde{\beta}_n)} = [2f(0)\sigma]^2,$$

which is the same as the asymptotic relative efficiency of the sample median relative to the sample mean (Example 4.6). This implies that the LAD estimator dominates the OLS estimator for all error distributions where the median is superior to the mean as a location estimator, in particular, for distribution with heavy tails. These properties have been supported by extensive Monte Carlo evidence.

The asymptotic normality result (16.1) may be used to construct asymptotic tests of hypotheses about the effects of covariates on the spread, the symmetry, the tail behavior and other characteristics of the conditional distribution of Y (Koenker & Bassett 1982). Notice that, in order to use (16.1) to construct estimates of the asymptotic variance of ALAD estimators, we need estimates of the density f of the regression errors $U_i = Y_i - \beta_0^\top X_i$.

16.2.5 SOME DRAWBACKS OF ALAD ESTIMATORS

Linear models for conditional quantiles are increasingly used in empirical work to describe the conditional distribution of a variable of interest. However, they have some drawbacks which arise from the way their estimates behave under heteroskedasticity. Two issues are relevant here. The first is the validity of the linearity assumption. The second is the form of the asymptotic variance of ALAD estimators when conditonal quantiles are in fact nonlinear.

The first issue has already been discussed in Chapter 1, where it was shown that when the conditional distribution of Y_i given $X_i = x$ is of the form

$$F(y\,|\,x) = F\left(\frac{y - \beta^\top x}{\sigma(x)}\right), \qquad \sigma(x) > 0,$$

then $\zeta_p(x) = \sigma(x)\zeta_p + \beta^\top x$, where $\zeta_p = F^{-1}(p)$. Thus, unless the function $\sigma(x)$ is linear, the only conditional quantile which is linear in x is that for which $\zeta_p = 0$. This result is troubling, for it implies that linear models for a family of conditonal quantiles may be inadequate when the data are conditionally heteroskedastic. More seriously, in the general case when $\mu(x)$ is an arbitrary function, the conditional quantiles of Y are of the form $\zeta_p(x) = \mu(x) + \sigma^2(x)\zeta_p$. In the absence of prior information, it is now impossible to determine whether nonlinearity of the conditional quantile function $\zeta_p(x)$ is due to nonlinearity of $\mu(x)$, heteroskedasticity, or both.

From the practical point of view, the presence of heteroskedasticity implies that the estimated quantile regression hyperplanes may cross each other, thus violating one of the fundamental properties of conditional quantiles and complicating the interpretation of the results of a statistical analysis.

Turning now to the second issue, if conditional quantiles are nonlinear in x, then the asymptotic variance matrix of $\tilde{\beta}_n$ is no longer given by (16.1). By the heuristic argument in Section 16.2.3, the block corresponding to the asymptotic covariance between the estimates of β_{p_r} and β_{p_s} is instead equal to

$$[\min(p_r, p_s) - p_r p_s]\, B_r^{-1} P\, B_s^{-1},$$

where

$$B_r = \mathrm{E}[f(\beta_{p_r}^\top X_i \mid X_i)\, X_i X_i^\top]$$

and $\beta_{p_r} = \operatorname{plim} \hat{\beta}_{p_r,n}$. Bootstrap methods are typically used to carry out inference in this case.

16.3 ROBUST ESTIMATORS

Although the OLS estimator is UMVU at the Gaussian linear model (Theorem 6.4), it is far from optimal on robustness grounds. From Example 15.9, its influence function is $\mathrm{IF}(z; F) = P^{-1}\, x(y - T(F)^\top x)$, where $z = (x, y)$ and $P = \mathrm{E}\, X_i X_i^\top$. This influence function may be viewed as the product of two components: the influence $y - T(F)^\top x$ of the regression errors and the influence $P^{-1}x$ of the covariates. Since neither component is bounded, the OLS estimator is not qualitatively robust and its breakdown point is essentially equal to zero. Thus, either a single large x-value or a single large regression error can have an arbitrarily large effect on the OLS estimates.

In this section we assume that the data $\{(X_i, Y_i)\}$ are a random sample from a linear model and consider three classes of robust estimator of the regression parameter β. The first class consists of estimators for which the influence of the regression errors is optimally bounded. The second class consists of B-robust or bounded influence estimators which attain the best trade-off between asymptotic efficiency and robustness. The third class consists of estimators with a high breakdown point.

16.3.1 HUBER ESTIMATOR OF REGRESSION

Building on the optimal B-robust score for the Gaussian location model (Example 15.11), Huber (1973) suggested bounding the influence of the regression errors by weighting the Gaussian score with a weight function of the form

$$w(z; \theta) = \min\left(1, \frac{c\sigma}{|y - \beta^\top x|}\right), \qquad \theta = (\beta, \sigma),$$

where $c > 0$ is chosen to control the degree of robustness of the estimator. The resulting estimator is known as a *Huber estimator of regression*. Varying the constant c gives a whole class of estimators, with OLS as the limiting case corresponding to $c \to \infty$.

The score function associated with a Huber estimator of regression is

$$\psi(z;\theta) = w(z;\theta)\left(\frac{y-\beta^\top x}{\sigma}\right)x = h_c\left(\frac{y-\beta^\top x}{\sigma}\right)x,$$

where $h_c(u) = \max(-c, \min(u, c))$ is the Huber function introduced in Example 15.11. This estimator may therefore be interpreted as a MM estimator obtained by equating to zero the sample covariance between the covariates and the symmetrically censored residuals $h_c((Y_i - \beta^\top X_i)/\sigma)$.

It is easily verified that the Huber estimator is the ML estimator for a linear regression model where the standardized regression errors are independent of the covariates and follow *Huber's least informative distribution*, whose density is

$$f(v) = \begin{cases} (1-\epsilon)\,\phi(v), & \text{if } |v| \le c, \\ (1-\epsilon)\,\phi(c)\,\exp(c^2 - c|v|), & \text{otherwise,} \end{cases}$$

where $0 \le \epsilon < 1$, the constants c and ϵ are connected through the relationship

$$\frac{2\phi(c)}{c} - 2\Phi(-c) = \frac{\epsilon}{1-\epsilon},$$

and ϕ and Φ denote the $\mathcal{N}(0,1)$ density and distribution functions. Notice that $f(v)$ behaves like a Gaussian density in the center and like a Laplace density in the tails. This distribution is called least informative because it can be shown to have minimum Fisher information measure over all symmetric distributions in an ϵ-contamination neighborhood of the Gaussian model (Huber 1981). Thus, the Huber estimator is optimal in the minimax sense of having smallest asymptotic variance under the worst symmetric local alternative to the Gaussian model.

Simple calculations show that, under the assumption of a linear model, the influence function of the Huber estimator is

$$\text{IF}(z) = B^{-1}\,h_c\left(\frac{y-\beta^\top x}{\sigma}\right)x,$$

where

$$B = \sigma^{-1}\,\text{E}[1\{V_i \le c\}\,X_i X_i^\top]$$

and $V_i = (Y_i - \beta^\top X_i)/\sigma$ is the standardized regression error. Thus, the Huber estimator of regression has properties similar those of the LAD estimator. Being the ML estimator for Huber's least informative distribution, it has good robustness and efficiency properties if the regression errors have thick tails. On the other hand, because its influence function is unbounded in x, it is not qualitatively robust and its breakdown point is equal to zero.

Although exact sampling results are not available, the fact that the Huber function is odd, that is $h_c(-u) = h_c(u)$, implies that the Huber estimator is median unbiased, that is, its sampling distribution is symmetric about the regression parameter β whenever Y_i is symmetrically distributed about $\beta^\top X_i$ conditionally on X_i.

If $\mathrm{E}(Y_i \mid X_i) = \beta^\top X_i$, then the Huber estimator $\tilde{\beta}_n$ can be shown to be consistent and asymptotically normal under general conditions (Huber 1973). In particular, if the standardized regression errors V_i are independent of X_i, then its asymptotic variance matrix is

$$\mathrm{AV}(\tilde{\beta}_n) = \frac{\sigma^2}{\varphi_c(F)} P^{-1}$$

where F denotes the distribution function of V_i and

$$\varphi_c(F) = \frac{[2F(c) - 1]^2}{\mathrm{E}\, h_c(V_i)^2}.$$

In this case, the asymptotic efficiency of the Huber estimator $\tilde{\beta}_n$ relative to the OLS estimator $\hat{\beta}_n$ is

$$\mathrm{ARE}(\tilde{\beta}_n, \hat{\beta}_n) = \frac{\mathrm{tr}\, \mathrm{AV}(\hat{\beta}_n)}{\mathrm{tr}\, \mathrm{AV}(\tilde{\beta}_n)} = \varphi_c(F),$$

which can be shown to be monotonically decreasing in c for F fixed, and is the same as the asymptotic efficiency of the Huber estimator of location relative to the sample mean.

16.3.2 OPTIMAL BOUNDED INFLUENCE ESTIMATORS

We now consider regression estimators whose influence function (and not just one component of it) is bounded and continuous. Such estimators are qualitatively robust and have nonzero breakdown point.

From Section 15.4.6, an M-estimator which is optimal B-robust at the Gaussian linear model given a bound γ on its gross-error sensitivity is associated with the score function

$$w(z;\theta) = \min\left(1, \frac{c(x)\sigma}{|y - \beta^\top x|}\right),$$

where $c(x) = \gamma/\|Ax\|$ and A is a p.d. matrix which satisfies the implicit equation

$$\mathrm{E}\left[2\Phi\left(\frac{\gamma}{\|AX_i\|}\right) - 1\right] X_i X_i^\top - A^{-1} = 0. \tag{16.6}$$

This estimator is known as *Hampel–Krasker estimator* (Hampel 1978, Krasker 1980). When $c(x)$ is constant for all x we obtain the Huber estimator and when $\gamma = \infty$ we obtain the OLS estimator. Notice that the matrix A only depends on the marginal distribution of X_i under the "reference" model but not on model parameters. By Theorem 15.14, the matrix A exists only if

$$\gamma \geq \frac{k\sigma\sqrt{\pi/2}}{\mathrm{E}\,\|X_i\|},$$

where the lower bound on γ depends on the number k of regression parameters.

The score function associated with the Hampel–Krasker estimator is

$$\psi(z;\theta) = h_{c(x)}\left(\frac{y - \beta^\top x}{\sigma}\right) x.$$

Thus, the Hampel–Krasker estimator may also be interpreted as a MM estimator obtained by equating to zero the sample covariance between the covariates and the censored residuals. Unlike the Huber estimator, however, the degree of censoring is not constant but varies with x.

The Hampel–Krasker estimator is median unbiased for β whenever Y_i is symmetrically distributed about $\beta^\top X_i$ conditionally on X_i. If $\mathrm{E}(Y_i \mid X_i) = \beta^\top X_i$, then the Hampel–Krasker estimator is consistent for β and asymptotically normal under general conditions (Maronna & Yohai 1981) with asymptotic variance matrix of the form $\sigma^2 B^{-1} C\, B^{-1}$, where

$$B = \mathrm{E}[1\{V_i \leq c\} X_i X_i^\top], \qquad C = \mathrm{E}[\min(c_i^2, V_i^2)\, X_i X_i^\top],$$

and $c_i = c(X_i)$.

The asymptotic efficiency of the Hampel–Krasker estimator relative to OLS is a monotonically decreasing function of the sensitivity bound γ. Thus, given the distribution of the covariates, γ may be chosen to attain a prespecified asymptotic relative efficiency at the Gaussian linear model. Typically, an asymptotic efficiency loss of 5 percent is enough to ensure good robustness properties against outliers and gross errors.

One problem with the Hampel–Krasker estimator is its lack of equivariance under (nonsingular) reparametrizations of the model. An equivariant estimator is the Krasker–Welsch estimator (Krasker & Welsch 1982), which is the optimal B-robust estimator when the gross-error sensitivity is defined in the metric of the inverse asymptotic variance matrix of the estimator itself.

The weight function of all robust estimators discussed so far is such that the influence of large regression errors is finite and bounded away from zero. However, for some distributions with heavy tails, such as the t-distribution, the likelihood score tends to zero for large values of the errors (Example 7.16). This suggests that *redescending estimators*, that is, estimators with a redescending influence function, may have good robustness properties against thick-tailed distributions. Examples include Hampel's (1974) three-part redescending estimator, Tukey's biweight estimator (Beaton & Tukey 1974) and the hyperbolic tangent estimator of Hampel, Rousseeuw and Ronchetti (1981).

16.3.3 COMPUTATIONAL ASPECTS

All estimators discussed in the previous two sections are easily obtained by iterative WLS, with iterations of the form

$$\tilde{\beta}^{(r+1)} = [\sum_i w_i^{(r)} X_i X_i^\top]^{-1} \sum_i w_i^{(r)} X_i Y_i, \qquad r = 0, 1, 2, \ldots,$$

where $w_i^{(r)} = w(X_i, Y_i; \tilde{\beta}^{(r)})$, starting from some preliminary estimate $\tilde{\beta}^{(0)}$, such as OLS. In the case of the Hampel–Krasker estimator, the matrix A in the robust weights may be computed, before starting the iterations, by numerically solving the sample counterpart of the implicit equation (16.6).

The estimators discussed so far also require a concomitant estimate of scale. A robust possibility is to use the median absolute deviation of the residuals from the previous iteration. Another possibility is to follow Huber's (1964) Proposal 2, and derive joint estimates of $\theta = (\beta, \sigma)$ by minimizing a criterion of the form

$$Q_n(\theta) = \sigma \sum_{i=1}^{n} \left[\rho_{c_i} \left(\frac{Y_i - \beta^\top X_i}{\sigma} \right) + \nu \right],$$

where c_i is constant in the Huber case and equal to $\gamma / \|AX_i\|$ in the Hampel–Krasker case, $\rho_c(v)$ is the convex function

$$\rho_c(v) = \begin{cases} v^2/2, & \text{if } |v| \le c, \\ c|v| - c^2/2, & \text{otherwise,} \end{cases}$$

and ν is a constant chosen to guarantee asymptotic unbiasedness of the scale estimator at the assumed model. Notice that $\rho_c'(v) = h_c(v)$.

If the regression errors are i.i.d. and symmetrically distributed about zero, then the regression and scale estimators are asymptotically normal and asymptotically independent. If $(\tilde\beta_n, \tilde\sigma_n)$ are any of the above estimates, and $\tilde V_i = (Y_i - \tilde\beta_n^\top X_i)/\tilde\sigma_n$ denotes the standardized residuals, then a consistent estimate of the asymptotic variance of $\hat\beta_n$ is $\widehat{\mathrm{AV}}(\tilde\beta_n) = \tilde\sigma_n^2\, \tilde B_n^{-1} \tilde C_n \tilde B_n^{-1}$, where

$$\tilde B_n = n^{-1} \sum_{i=1}^{n} 1\{\tilde V_i < c_i\}\, X_i X_i^\top$$

and

$$\tilde C_n = n^{-1} \sum_{i=1}^{n} \min(c_i^2, \tilde V_i^2)\, X_i X_i^\top .$$

In the OLS case, where $c_i = \infty$, $\widehat{\mathrm{AV}}(\tilde\beta_n)$ corresponds to the infinitesimal jackknife estimate of the sampling variance. Consistent estimates of the sampling variance of $\tilde\beta_n$ may also be obtained by jackknife or bootstrap methods.

The robust weights derived as a by-product of bounded influence estimation represent useful diagnostics for detecting outliers and influential observations. They provide an alternative to methods, such as those discussed in Chapter 8, that are based on deleting a subset of observations at a time and then comparing the resulting estimates with those obtained from the full sample. Robust weights are jointly computed with the parameter estimates and require no additional calculations. They are also easy to interpret, because of the WLS nature of the estimators. Further, the form of the robust weights enables one to easily distinguish between the effects of outlying x-values and large residuals.

The difference between OLS and a bounded influence estimator may be used to construct a difference test for the hypothesis that the Gaussian linear model is correctly specified. Tests of this type are likely to be quite powerful, for the difference between the two estimators can be quite large under model misspecification, whereas the bounded influence estimator is only slightly less efficient than OLS when the model is correctly specified.

16.3.4 HIGH-BREAKDOWN ESTIMATORS

A drawback of M-estimators is the fact that their breakdown point decreases as the number of estimated parameters increases (Maronna, Bustos & Yohai 1979). This is somewhat unsatisfactory, because it means that these estimators tend to have low breakdown point when there are many covariates.

The class of *S-estimators*, that is, estimators obtained by minimizing some estimate of scale (Rousseeuw & Yohai 1984), includes a number of estimators with a high breakdown point. Here we briefly mention two of them.

Rousseeuw's (1984) *least median of squares (LMS)* estimator is based on the median of the squared residuals and minimizes

$$Q_n(\beta) = \mathrm{Med}_{1 \le i \le n}\, (Y_i - \beta^\top X_i)^2.$$

For the simple linear regression model, this corresponds to finding the narrowest strip covering half of the observations. It can be shown that the LMS estimator is regression, scale and affine equivariant.

The LMS breakdown point converges to $1/2$ as $n \to \infty$, which is the best that can be achieved. However, even if the assumed linear model is correct, the LMS estimator is not asymptotically normal and is only $n^{1/3}$-consistent for β (Kim & Pollard 1991), implying very low efficiency relative to standard $\sqrt{n}$-consistent M-estimators. Further, its computation is burdensome because the function Q_n tends to have a high number of local minima and only approximate algorithms are currently available for locating the global minimum (Rousseeuw & Leroy 1987).

Rousseeuw (1984) also introduced the *least trimmed squares (LTS)* estimator, based instead on the criterion function

$$Q_n(\beta) = m_n^{-1} \sum_{i=1}^{m_n} U_{[i]}^2(\beta),$$

where $U_{[i]}^2(\beta)$ denotes the ith ordered squared residual (residuals are first squared and then ordered), and $m_n \le n$ depends on some trimming proportion $\alpha \in [0, 1)$. The LTS estimator is also regression, scale and affine equivariant.

The LTS estimator can be shown to be $\sqrt{n}$-consistent and asymptotically normal under general conditions. If $m_n = (n+1)/2$, then it has the same breakdown point as the LMS estimator. It is, however, computationally more burdensome because its criterion function requires $O(n \ln n)$ steps as opposed to $O(n)$ steps for LMS.

High-breakdown estimators provide excellent starting values for one-step regression estimators based on more efficient bounded influence scores (Yohai 1987). Estimators of this type combine a high breakdown point with high efficiency at the Gaussian model.

BIBLIOGRAPHIC NOTES

The Box–Tiao family of distributions is discussed in Box and Tiao (1973), the generalized t in McDonald and Newey (1988), the generalized beta of the second kind in McDonald (1984) and the EGB2 in McDonald and Xu (1995). Monte Carlo evidence in Hsieh and Manski (1987), Newey (1988), McDonald and White (1993) and Ng (1995) shows that partially adaptive or fully adaptive estimators can outperform OLS in many cases. Even at the Gaussian model, the finite sample efficiency loss from using adaptive estimators tends to be small.

For a thorough discussion of LAD methods see Bloomfield and Steiger (1983). Portnoy and Koenker (1997) discuss alternatives to simplex-based methods for solving LAD problems and ways of reducing the computational burden of quantile regression. For alternative proofs of asymptotic normality of LAD estimators see Phillips (1991) and Pollard (1991). Horowitz (1998a) presents general results for an asymptotically equivalent class of estimators, called smoothed LAD estimators, obtained by smoothing the absolute loss function. On the assessment of goodness-of-fit of quantile regression models see Koenker and Machado (1999). On using the bootstrap to carry out inference about regression quantiles see De Angelis, Hall and Young (1993). For a review of empirical applications of quantile regression see Buchinsky (1997).

For an introduction to robust regression estimation see Huber (1981), Hampel *et al.* (1986) and Rousseeuw and Leroy (1987). For a robust version of IV estimators for simultaneous equation models see Krasker (1986), Krasker and Welsch (1985) and Krishnakumar and Ronchetti (1997).

PROBLEMS

16.1 Prove (16.4).

16.2 (Huber 1981) Show that Huber's least informative distribution has minimum Fisher information measure over an ϵ-contamination neighborhood $\mathcal{G}_\epsilon$ of symmetric distributions around the Gaussian, that is $\mathcal{G}_\epsilon$ is the family of mixtures of the form $F = (1-\epsilon)\Phi + \epsilon G$, where $0 < \epsilon < 1$, Φ is the $N(0,1)$ distribution and G is any distribution whose density is symmetric about zero and strictly positive everywhere.

16.3 Show that the Huber estimator is the ML estimator for a linear regression model where the standardized regression errors follow Huber's least informative distribution.

16.4 (Andrews 1986) Show that the Huber and the Hampel–Krasker estimators are median unbiased if the regression errors are i.i.d. and their distribution is symmetric about zero.

16.5 Derive the asymptotic variance of an the Huber estimator of regression.

16.6 Show that, under the Gaussian linear model, the asymptotic variance matrices of the Huber and the Hampel–Krasker estimators are of the form $\sigma^2 B^{-1} C B^{-1}$, where

$$B = \mathrm{E}[2\Phi(c_i) - 1]\, X_i X_i^\top,$$

$$C = B + 2\,\mathrm{E}[c_i^2(1-\Phi(c_i)) - c_i\phi(c_i)]\, X_i X_i^\top,$$

and ϕ and Φ denote the $N(0,1)$ density and distribution function respectively.

16.7 Given the linear model $\mathrm{E}(Y_i \mid X_i) = \alpha + \beta X_i$, evaluate the breakdown properties of the following estimators of β and α

$$\hat\beta = \mathrm{Med}_{1 \le i < j \le n} \frac{Yj - Y_i}{X_j - X_i}, \qquad \hat\alpha = \mathrm{Med}_i(Y_i - \hat\beta X_i).$$

16.8 Show that the OLS estimator is also an S-estimator.

16.9 Show that the LMS and LTS estimators are regression, scale and affine equivariant.

17

Models for Discrete Responses

In this chapter we consider a broad class of models that may be viewed as a generalization of the classical Gaussian linear model. This class of models includes, among others, logit and probit models for binary responses, multinomial models for categorical data, and Poisson regression models for count data. Recognizing the common structure of these models sharpens our understanding of their properties. It also has important implications for statistical modeling, because many ideas and tools developed for the Gaussian linear model can easily be adapted to a variety of other situations.

17.1 MODELS FOR BINARY RESPONSES

Suppose that the response variable Y_i can only take two values, say 1 ("success") and 0 ("failure"). In general, Y_i is an indicator of occurrence of a particular event. For example, Y_i may be an indicator of employment status (e.g. employed or unemployed), or the indicator of default on a bank loan, or represent the decision whether or not to buy a certain good. The statistical problem is estimation and inference about the relationship between the response probabilities $\pi_i = \Pr\{Y_i = 1\}$, $0 < \pi_i < 1$, and a k-vector X_i of covariates.

It follows from the nature of the response variable that $\mathrm{E}\, Y_i = \Pr\{Y_i = 1\} = \pi_i$ and $\mathrm{Var}\, Y_i = \pi_i(1 - \pi_i)$. For simplicity, we assume in most of this chapter assumes that the data are sampled at random. The observed responses $Y_1, \ldots, Y_n$ may then be modeled as independent 0–1 random variables, each having a Bernoulli distribution with parameter π_i which may vary across observations. Because the general shape of the distribution of the data is known, a natural approach is to parametrize the response probabilities $\pi_1, \ldots, \pi_n$ in terms of a finite-dimensional parameter α and then estimate α by the method of maximum likelihood. Alternative nonparametric and semiparametric approaches will also be discussed.

17.1.1 BINOMIAL REGRESSION MODELS

A *binomial regression model* specifies the response probabilities as a function $\pi_i = \pi(X_i)$ of the covariate vector X_i. Since $0 < \pi_i < 1$, the function $\pi(\cdot)$ must take values in the unit interval $(0, 1)$.

The *linear probability model* corresponds to the linear specification $\pi(x) = \alpha^\top x$. This model is inadmissible for it can take values outside the unit interval, thus violating the restriction on π_i. On the other hand, the *logit model*

$$\pi(x) = \Lambda(\alpha^\top x), \tag{17.1}$$

where $\Lambda(u) = e^u/(1+e^u)$ denotes the distribution function of the standard logistic, the *probit model*

$$\pi(x) = \Phi(\alpha^\top x), \tag{17.2}$$

where $\Phi(u)$ denotes the $\mathcal{N}(0,1)$ distribution function, and the *complementary log–log model*

$$\pi(x) = 1 - \exp(-\exp(\alpha^\top x)), \tag{17.3}$$

all take values in $(0,1)$ and therefore are all admissible.

Inverting the previous relationships shows that the logit model (17.1) corresponds to the assumption that

$$\ln \frac{\pi(x)}{1-\pi(x)} = \alpha^\top x.$$

Because the log-odds is the canonical parameter of the Bernoulli model, the logit model corresponds to a linear model for the canonical parameter. On the other hand, the probit model (17.2) corresponds to the assumption that

$$\Phi^{-1}(\pi(x)) = \alpha^\top x,$$

where $\Phi^{-1}(u)$ is the quantile function of the $\mathcal{N}(0,1)$ distribution, while the complementary log–log model (17.3) corresponds to the assumption that

$$\ln[-\ln(1-\pi(x))] = \alpha^\top x.$$

In all three cases (Figure 76) we have a monotonic function that relates the conditional mean of Y_i to a linear predictor, that is a linear combination of the covariates, which represents the systematic part of the model.

More generally, an invertible function g: $(0,1) \to \Re$ such that

$$g(\pi(x)) = \alpha^\top x$$

is called a *link function* (Figure 76). Associated with g is another function $h = g^{-1}$, called the *inverse link*, such that

$$\pi(x) = h(\alpha^\top x).$$

By varying the function g we obtain a whole class of models indexed by the choice of link function. Since $\alpha^\top x$ is continuously differentiable on $\Re$ and $\pi(x)$ ranges on $(0,1)$, it is natural to require a link to have a continuously differentiable inverse that maps $\Re$ back into $(0,1)$. In fact, a link g is said to be *admissible* if it corresponds to the quantile function F^{-1} of a continuous distribution or, equivalently, its inverse h corresponds to the cumulative distribution function F of a continuous distribution. This is indeed the case with all link functions considered so far. The inverse logit and probit links correspond to distribution functions – respectively, the standard logistic and the standard Gaussian – which are symmetric about zero, that is, $1 - F(u) = F(-u)$. This implies that their link function $g = F^{-1}$ satisfies $g(\pi) = -g(1-\pi)$. This

Figure 76 Link functions.

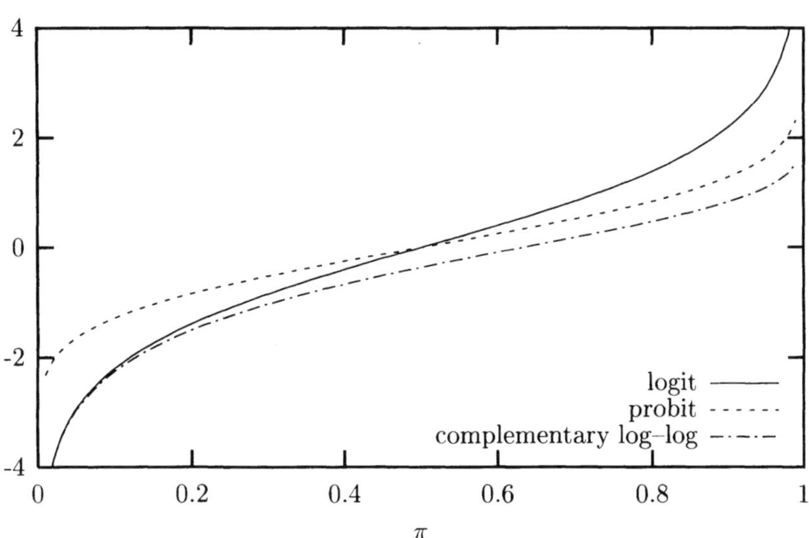

symmetry is not appropriate when, for example, $\pi(x)$ increases from zero fairly slowly but then approaches one quite rapidly. The inverse of the complementary log–log link corresponds instead to the distribution function of the standard Gumbel (Type 1 extreme value) distribution, which is not symmetric.

The logit and probit links are related almost linearly over the interval $.1 \leq \pi_i \leq .9$. For this reason, it is usually difficult to discriminate between these two functions on the basis of goodness-of-fit. On the other hand, as $\pi(x) \to 1$, the complementary log–log link approaches infinity much more slowly than the logit or probit links.

17.1.2 ML ESTIMATION

The sample log-likelihood, viewed as a function of the n-vector $\pi = (\pi_1, \ldots, \pi_n)$, is

$$L(\pi) = c + \sum_{i=1}^{n} [Y_i \ln \pi_i + (1 - Y_i) \ln(1 - \pi_i)],$$

where c is an arbitrary constant. The components of the likelihood score are

$$\frac{\partial L}{\partial \pi_i} = \frac{Y_i - \pi_i}{\pi_i(1 - \pi_i)}, \qquad i = 1, \ldots, n,$$

whereas

$$\frac{\partial^2 L}{\partial \pi_i^2} = -\left[\frac{Y_i - \pi_i}{\pi_i(1 - \pi_i)}\right]^2, \qquad i = 1, \ldots, n.$$

Given a parametric model for the response probabilities π_i, we can apply the chain rule to get the likelihood score in terms of the model parameters. If h denotes the inverse link and $h_i(\alpha) = h(\alpha^\top X_i)$, then

$$h_i'(\alpha) = H_i(\alpha)\, X_i,$$

where $H_i(\alpha) = h'(\alpha^\top X_i)$. For example, in the probit case $H_i(\alpha) = \phi(\alpha^\top X_i)$, where ϕ denotes the $\mathcal{N}(0,1)$ density, while in the logit case $H_i(\alpha) = h_i(\alpha)[1 - h_i(\alpha)]$. The likelihood score for α is then

$$L'(\alpha) = \sum_{i=1}^n \frac{\partial L}{\partial \pi_i}\, h_i'(\alpha) = \sum_{i=1}^n \frac{H_i(\alpha)}{h_i(\alpha)[1 - h_i(\alpha)]}[Y_i - h_i(\alpha)]X_i. \qquad (17.4)$$

A ML estimate of α is obtained by solving the likelihood equation $L'(\alpha) = 0$. Except for the linear probability model, this equation does not have a closed form solution and numerical methods become necessary. For all link functions considered here, the log-likelihood is concave, and so the Newton–Raphson (NR) and the scoring method are particularly convenient.

The NR method (see Appendix B.3.1) consists of iterations of the form

$$\alpha^{(r+1)} = \alpha^{(r)} - [L''(\alpha^{(r)})]^{-1}\, L'(\alpha^{(r)}), \qquad r = 0, 1, 2, \ldots,$$

where L'' is the Hessian of the sample log-likelihood. The method of scoring (Appendix B.3.2) consists instead of iterations of the form

$$\alpha^{(r+1)} = \alpha^{(r)} + [I(\alpha^{(r)})]^{-1}\, L'(\alpha^{(r)}), \qquad r = 1, 2, \ldots,$$

where

$$I(\alpha) = \sum_{i=1}^n \frac{H_i^2}{h_i(1 - h_i)} X_i X_i^\top \qquad (17.5)$$

is the expected total information on α conditional on the design matrix $\mathbf{X}$, and the dependence of h_i and H_i on α has been omitted for simplicity. Combining (17.4) and (17.5), the scoring iterations may be written

$$\alpha^{(r+1)} = \left[\sum_{i=1}^n \frac{H_i^2}{h_i(1 - h_i)} X_i X_i^\top\right]^{-1} \sum_{i=1}^n \frac{H_i^2}{h_i(1 - h_i)} X_i \left(X_i^\top \alpha^{(r)} + \frac{Y_i - h_i}{H_i}\right),$$

where the h_i and the H_i are all evaluated at $\alpha^{(r)}$. Notice that these iterations are of the form

$$\alpha^{(r+1)} = [\sum_i W_i^{(r)} X_i X_i^\top]^{-1} \sum_i W_i^{(r)} X_i Y_i^{(r)},$$

where

$$Y_i^{(r)} = X_i^\top \alpha^{(r)} + \frac{Y_i - h_i}{H_i}$$

is called the *adjusted dependent variable*, and

$$W_i^{(r)} = \frac{H_i^2}{h_i(1 - h_i)}.$$

Thus, the updated estimate $\alpha^{(r+1)}$ is just the coefficient vector in a weighted least squares (WLS) regression of the adjusted dependent variable $Y_i^{(r)}$ on X_i, with weights equal to $W_i^{(r)}$. As a result, the ML estimate is easily computed by iterative WLS.

17.1.3 ASYMPTOTIC PROPERTIES OF ML ESTIMATORS

We now consider the asymptotic properties of a sequence $\{\hat{\alpha}_n\}$ of ML estimators corresponding to increasing sample sizes.

Suppose first that the model for the response probabilities is correctly specified and identifiable, and let α_0 be the true value of α, that is, $\pi_i = h_i(\alpha)$ only if $\alpha = \alpha_0$. It follows from the results in Chapter 4 that, under mild regularity conditions, $\hat{\alpha}_n$ is $\sqrt{n}$-consistent for α_0 and asymptotically normal with asymptotic variance equal to the inverse of the Fisher information matrix

$$\mathcal{I}(\alpha_0) = n^{-1}\,\mathrm{E}\, I(\alpha_0) = \mathrm{E}\left[\frac{H_i^2}{\sigma_i^2}\, X_i X_i^\top\right],$$

where H_i is evaluated at α_0, $\sigma_i^2 = \pi_i(1-\pi_i)$ and the expectation is with respect to the marginal distribution of X_i. It can be shown that $\mathcal{I}(\alpha_0)$ is p.d. provided that the second moment matrix $\mathrm{E}\, X_i X_i^\top$ is p.d. If the assumed model is correctly specified, then a consistent estimator of the asymptotic variance of $\hat{\alpha}_n$ is

$$\left[n^{-1} \sum_{i=1}^n \frac{\hat{H}_i^2}{\hat{h}_i(1-\hat{h}_i)} X_i X_i^\top\right]^{-1},$$

where $\hat{h}_i = h_i(\hat{\alpha}_n)$ and $\hat{H}_i = H_i(\hat{\alpha}_n)$.

Now consider the case when the response probabilities are misspecified, for example because the assumed link function is incorrect or relevant covariates have been omitted. In this case, we generally obtain inconsistent estimates of the response probabilities because $\pi_i \neq h_i(\alpha)$ for all $\alpha \in \Re^k$. One way of guarding against the possibility that the link function is incorrectly specified is to follow the approach in Section 16.1.1 and consider some flexible family of links that includes the most common ones (probit, logit and complementary log–log) as special cases (see e.g. Chen, Dey & Shao 1999).

If the model is misspecified, then $\hat{\alpha}_n$ becomes a pseudo ML estimator. The relevant parameter in this case is the pseudo true parameter α_*, namely the root of the asymptotic first-order condition

$$0 = \mathrm{E}\left[\frac{H_i(\alpha)}{h_i(\alpha)(1-h_i(\alpha))}(Y_i - h_i(\alpha))\, X_i\right].$$

Assuming that α_* exists and is unique, it follows from the results in Chapter 15 that, under mild regularity conditions, $\hat{\alpha}_n$ is $\sqrt{n}$-consistent for α_* and asymptotically normal with asymptotic variance $\mathrm{AV}(\hat{\alpha}_n) = B_*^{-1}\, C_*\, B_*^{-1}$, where

$$B_* = \mathrm{E}\left[\frac{H_i^2}{h_i(1-h_i)} X_i X_i^\top\right], \qquad C_* = \mathrm{E}\left[\frac{H_i^2}{h_i^2(1-h_i)^2}\,(Y_i - h_i)^2\, X_i X_i^\top\right],$$

and h_i and H_i are both evaluated at α_*. Consistent estimates of B_* and C_* are readily obtained by replacing expectations with sample averages, and using $\hat{h}_i$ and $\hat{H}_i$ instead of h_i and H_i. A viable alternative is the nonparametric bootstrap.

17.1.4 THE LOGIT LINK

Using the logit link has several advantages. First, the logit link corresponds to the assumption that the log-odds are linear in x, implying that

$$\alpha_j = \frac{\partial}{\partial x_j} \ln \frac{\pi(x)}{1-\pi(x)}, \qquad j = 1, \ldots, k.$$

This allows a simple interpretation of the jth element of α as the proportional change in the odds if the jth covariate changes by one unit.

Second, since $H_i = h_i(1-h_i)$ for the logit link, the likelihood score simply becomes

$$L'(\alpha) = \sum_{i=1}^{n} [Y_i - h_i(\alpha)] X_i.$$

Thus, the likelihood equation may be viewed as equating to zero the correlation between the prediction error $Y_i - \hat{h}_i$ and the covariate vector X_i, which is also what OLS does. Equivalently, the logit ML estimator may be interpreted as a MM estimator that equates the vector $\sum Y_i X_i$ of sufficient statistics to its conditional mean $\sum \hat{h}_i X_i$ under the estimated model. In particular, if the model includes an intercept, then the likelihood equation implies that the prediction errors have zero mean or, equivalently, that the estimated response probabilities are on average equal to the sample frequency of successes.

Third, minus the Hessian of the sample log-likelihood is equal to the expected total information

$$-L''(\alpha) = \sum_{i=1}^{n} h_i(1-h_i) X_i X_i^\top = I(\alpha),$$

and so the NR and scoring iterations coincide. Notice that the expected total information may also be written

$$I(\alpha) = \sum_{i=1}^{n} V_i(\alpha)\, X_i X_i^\top,$$

where $V_i(\alpha) = h_i(1-h_i)$ is the conditional variance of Y_i given X_i under the logit model.

Fourth, the updated estimate $\alpha^{(r+1)}$ is just the coefficient in a WLS regression of the adjusted dependent variable $Y_i^{(r)}$ on X_i, with weights $W_i^{(r)} = V_i(\alpha^{(r)})$ that are equal to the conditional variance of Y_i under the model.

If the logit model is correctly specified and identifiable then the sequence $\{\hat{\alpha}_n\}$ of logit ML estimators corresponding to increasing sample size is $\sqrt{n}$-consistent for the target parameter α_0 and asymptotically normal with asymptotic variance equal to the inverse of the Fisher information matrix

$$\mathcal{I}(\alpha_0) = n^{-1}\,\mathrm{E}\, I(\alpha_0) = \mathrm{E}[V_i(\alpha_0)\, X_i X_i^\top].$$

If the logit model is misspecified then, under mild regularity conditions, there exists a unique root α_* of the asymptotic first-order condition

$$0 = \mathrm{E}[Y_i - h_i(\alpha)]\, X_i.$$

In this case, the logit ML estimator is $\sqrt{n}$-consistent for α_* and asymptotically normal with asymptotic variance matrix $\mathrm{AV}(\hat{\alpha}_n) = B_*^{-1} C_* B_*^{-1}$, where

$$B_* = \mathrm{E}[h_i(1-h_i) X_i X_i^\top], \qquad C_* = \mathrm{E}[(Y_i - h_i)^2 X_i X_i^\top],$$

with h_i evaluated at α_*.

17.1.5 DISCRIMINANT ANALYSIS AND LOGIT

We now consider the relationship between the logit specification and a popular technique for classification known as *discriminant analysis.*

The problem of discriminant analysis consists of classifying a unit from a given population into one of two mutually exclusive groups using the information contained in a k-vector of observed characteristics X. For example, one may want to classify a bank loan into the categories of "default" and "nondefault" and the vector X may include observed characteristics of the borrower.

Let Y be a binary indicator that takes value one if the unit belongs to the first group ("default") and value zero if it belongs to the second group ("nondefault"), let $\pi = \Pr\{Y = 1\}$ be the unconditional probability of belonging to the first group, and let the density of the random k-vector X be $f_1(x)$ for the first group and $f_2(x)$ for the second.

We seek a partition of the support of X into two regions, $\mathcal{A}_1$ and $\mathcal{A}_2$, such that, if X falls in $\mathcal{A}_j$, then we classify the unit into group $j = 1, 2$. For any proposed partition, misclassification is possible, that is, "defaulting" units may be classified as "nondefaulting" and vice versa. An optimal partition is one that minimizes the expected total cost of misclassification.

If C_j denotes the cost of incorrectly classifying a unit belonging to group j, then the expected total cost of misclassification is

$$\begin{aligned}
C &= C_1\pi \Pr\{X \in \mathcal{A}_2 \mid Y = 1\} + C_2(1-\pi)\Pr\{X \in \mathcal{A}_1 \mid Y = 2\} \\
&= C_1\pi(1 - \Pr\{X \in \mathcal{A}_1 \mid Y = 1\}) + C_2(1-\pi)\Pr\{X \in \mathcal{A}_1 \mid Y = 2\} \\
&= C_1\pi + \int_{\mathcal{A}_1} [C_2(1-\pi)f_2(x) - C_1\pi f_1(x)]\, dx.
\end{aligned}$$

This is minimized if $\mathcal{A}_1$ consists of all points in the support of X such that

$$C_2(1-\pi)f_2(x) - C_1\pi f_1(x) < 0,$$

or equivalently

$$\frac{f_1(x)}{f_2(x)} > \frac{C_2(1-\pi)}{C_1\pi}, \tag{17.6}$$

where $C_2(1-\pi)/(C_1\pi)$ is the ratio between the expected cost of misclassification in the two groups.

In particular, if $X_j \sim \mathcal{N}_k(\mu_j, \Sigma_j)$, $j = 1, 2$, then

$$f_j(x) = c\,|\Sigma_j|^{-1/2} \exp[-\frac{1}{2}(x-\mu_j)^\top \Sigma_j^{-1}(x-\mu_j)], \qquad j = 1, 2,$$

where c is a constant. If in addition $\Sigma_1 = \Sigma_2 = \Sigma$, then

$$\begin{aligned}\frac{f_1(x)}{f_2(x)} &= \exp[-\frac{1}{2}(x-\mu_1)^\top\Sigma^{-1}(x-\mu_1) + \frac{1}{2}(x-\mu_2)^\top\Sigma^{-1}(x-\mu_2)] \\ &= \exp[(\mu_1-\mu_2)^\top\Sigma^{-1}x - \frac{1}{2}(\mu_1-\mu_2)^\top\Sigma^{-1}(\mu_1+\mu_2)].\end{aligned}$$

Hence, after taking logs, condition (17.6) becomes

$$(\mu_1-\mu_2)^\top\Sigma^{-1}x > \ln\frac{C_2(1-\pi)}{C_1\pi} + \frac{1}{2}(\mu_1-\mu_2)^\top\Sigma^{-1}(\mu_1+\mu_2).$$

Letting

$$\delta = \Sigma^{-1}(\mu_1-\mu_2), \tag{17.7}$$

the optimal choice of $\mathcal{A}_1$ is defined by the condition that $\delta^\top x > c$, where the linear combination $\delta^\top x$ is known as the *linear discriminant function* or *z-score* and the critical value c is

$$c = \ln\frac{C_2(1-\pi)}{C_1\pi} + \frac{1}{2}\delta^\top(\mu_1+\mu_2).$$

If the expected cost of misclassification is the same for the two groups, that is $C_1\pi = C_2(1-\pi)$, then the critical value for the z-score is

$$c_0 = \frac{1}{2}\delta^\top(\mu_1+\mu_2).$$

The crucial assumptions behind this result are: (i) both $f_1(x)$ and $f_2(x)$ are multivariate normal, and (ii) the covariance matrices are the same for the two groups. If the second assumption is violated, then the discriminant function becomes quadratic in x, that is, of the form $x^\top\Lambda x + \lambda^\top x$ for some matrix Λ and some vector λ.

There is an interesting relationship between linear discriminant analysis and the logit model. By Bayes theorem, the conditional (or posterior) probability that $Y = 1$ given $X = x$ is

$$\pi(x) = \Pr\{Y = 1 \,|\, X = x\} = \frac{f_1(x)\pi}{f_1(x)\pi + f_2(x)(1-\pi)}.$$

It is easily verified that, if $f_j(x)$ is the multivariate normal density with mean μ_j and variance Σ (the same for the two groups), then the posterior odds-ratio is

$$\frac{\pi(x)}{1-\pi(x)} = \frac{f_1(x)}{f_2(x)}\frac{\pi}{1-\pi} = \exp(\gamma + \delta^\top x),$$

where δ is given by (17.7) and $\gamma = \ln[\pi/(1-\pi)] - c_0$. Hence

$$\ln\frac{\pi(x)}{1-\pi(x)} = \gamma + \delta^\top x,$$

which is the logit specification. Notice that this model implies

$$\ln\frac{\pi(x)}{1-\pi(x)} - \ln\frac{\pi}{1-\pi} = \delta^\top x - c_0,$$

that is, the difference between the z-score and the cutoff c_0 is equal to the gain in terms of log-odds from using the information contained in x.

17.1.6 OTHER LINKS

Although the logit link is attractive, there are cases where using other links is more natural. A typical situation is the following ***threshold crossing model.*** Let Y_i^* be a latent continuous random variable that obeys the linear model

$$Y_i^* = \beta^\top X_i - \sigma U_i,$$

where $\beta \in \Re^k$, $\sigma > 0$, and U_i is distributed independently of X_i with zero mean, unit variance and distribution function F. Also suppose that the observable response Y_i is related to the latent variable Y_i^* through the observation rule $Y_i = 1$ if $Y_i^* > c$ and $Y_i = 0$ otherwise, that is, $Y_i = 1\{Y_i^* > c\}$, where c is some threshold. If the model contains a fixed intercept, then there is no loss of generality in putting $c = 0$. In this case we have

$$\pi_i = \Pr\{U_i < \alpha^\top X_i \mid X_i\} = F(\alpha^\top X_i), \tag{17.8}$$

where $\alpha = \beta/\sigma$. One obtains the logit link if F is logistic, the probit link if F is Gaussian, and the complementary log–log link if F is Gumbel. Notice that β and σ are not separately identifiable, only their ratio is.

Threshold crossing models are often interpreted as behavioral. Suppose, for example, that the data describe the choices made by a set of individuals facing two alternatives. Each individual is assumed to evaluate the utility (payoff) associated with the available alternatives and to select the one which gives the highest utility. A ***binary choice model*** specifies the utility to the ith individual from choosing the jth alternative as $V_{ij} = \xi_{ij} - \epsilon_{ij}$, $j = 1, 2$, where ξ_{ij} is a systematic component and ϵ_{ij} is a random component representing unobservable individual characteristics or random taste variations. The systematic component ξ_{ij} is either a constant or a random variable independent of ϵ_{ij}.

Let $Y_i = 1$ if the ith individual chooses the first alternative and $Y_i = 0$ otherwise. Then $Y_i = 1$ if and only if $Y_i^* = V_{i1} - V_{i2} = \xi_{i1} - \xi_{i2} - \epsilon_{i1} + \epsilon_{i2} > 0$. Hence

$$\Pr\{Y_i = 1\} = \Pr\{\epsilon_{i1} - \epsilon_{i2} < \xi_{i1} - \xi_{i2}\}.$$

Denoting by $F(\cdot/\sigma)$ the distribution function of $\epsilon_{i1} - \epsilon_{i2}$ and letting $\xi_{i1} - \xi_{i2} = \beta^\top X_i$ gives (17.8). In particular, if ϵ_{i1} and ϵ_{i2} are i.i.d. with a standard Gumbel distribution then, by Result C.5, we obtain the logit model. If they are Gaussian, but not necessarily independently or identically distributed, then we obtain the probit model. The fact that the probit model does not require the random utility components to be independent or identically distributed helps explain its widespread use in empirical econometrics. No matter what is the distribution of the unobservables, an attractive feature of the binary choice specification is that the elements of the parameter vector $\alpha = \beta/\sigma$ have a natural interpretation as normalized differences in marginal utilities.

17.1.7 GROUPED DATA

Sometimes, the data do not record the individual sample values but consist instead of counts or proportions for a number of population strata. Suppose that there are S such strata, let n_s be the sample size from stratum s, and let π_s and p_s denote, respectively, the probability of "success" in stratum s and the fraction of "successes" in the sample drawn from stratum s.

Under stratified random sampling, the sample frequencies of success are independent across strata and have a $\mathrm{Bi}(n_s, \pi_s)$ distribution. We may also write

$$p_s = \pi_s + U_s, \qquad s = 1, \dots, S, \tag{17.9}$$

where U_i is a random error with mean zero and variance equal to $\pi_s(1-\pi_s)/n_s$.

Given a parametric model $\pi_s = h(\alpha^\top X_s) = h_s(\alpha)$ for π_s, where h is the inverse link and X_s is a vector of covariates, the above observations suggest two alternative methods for estimating α. The first method consists in maximizing the binomial log-likelihood

$$L(\alpha) = c + \sum_{s=1}^{S} n_s[p_s \ln h_s(\alpha) + (1-p_s)\ln(1-h_s(\alpha))],$$

where c is an arbitrary constant.

The second method is based instead on the regression specification (17.9). If $g = h^{-1}$ denotes the link function, differentiating the identity $g(h(\alpha^\top X_s)) = \alpha^\top X_s$ with respect to α gives $g'(\pi_s) = 1/H_s(\alpha)$, where $H_s = h'(\alpha^\top X_s)$. Expanding $g(p_s)$ about π_s then gives

$$g(p_s) \approx g(\pi_s) + g'(\pi_s)\, U_s = \alpha^\top X_s + \frac{U_s}{H_s} = \alpha^\top X_s + V_s$$

where $V_s = U_s/H_s$ is a random error with mean zero and heteroskedastic variance

$$\mathrm{Var}\, V_s = \frac{\pi_s(1-\pi_s)}{n_s H_s^2}.$$

The model parameter α may then be estimated by a feasible WLS regression of the transformed sample proportions $g(p_s)$ on X_s, with weights equal to the reciprocal of some consistent estimate $\widehat{\mathrm{Var}}\, V_s$ of $\mathrm{Var}\, V_s$. This WLS estimate is just the minimizer of the criterion

$$Q(\alpha) = \sum_{s=1}^{S} \frac{[g(p_s) - \alpha^\top X_s]^2}{\widehat{\mathrm{Var}}\, V_s}.$$

In particular, in the logistic case, $g(\pi_s) = \ln[\pi_s/(1-\pi_s)]$ and $H_s = \pi_s(1-\pi_s)$. Hence, α may be estimated by a feasible WLS regression of the "logits" $\ln[p_s/(1-p_s)]$ on X_s, with weights equal to $n_s p_s(1-p_s)$.

17.1.8 UNOBSERVED HETEROGENEITY

Suppose again that the data $Y_1, \dots, Y_S$ consist of the observed number of "successes" for S strata. If $Y_s \sim \mathrm{Bi}(n_s, \pi_s)$, then $\mathrm{E}\, Y_s = n_s\pi_s$ and $\mathrm{Var}\, Y_s = n_s\pi_s(1-\pi_s)$. *Overdispersion* is said to occur when $\mathrm{Var}\, Y_s > n_s\pi_n(1-\pi_n)$, and *underdispersion* when $\mathrm{Var}\, Y_s < n_s\pi_s(1-\pi_s)$. In either case, we maintain the assumption that $\mathrm{E}\, Y_s = n_s\pi_s$. Overdispersion typically occurs because of unobserved heterogeneity.

Example 17.1 Suppose that the population within a given stratum is clustered, for example by neighborhood. Suppose that there are p clusters within each stratum and, for simplicity, let the sample size from each cluster be constant and equal to q. For each cluster j, the number Z_j of "successes" has a $\mathrm{Bi}(q, \pi_j)$ distribution, where π_j

is allowed to vary across clusters. This variability may be modeled by treating the π_j as unobserved i.i.d. random variables with common mean π and variance equal to $\tau^2\pi(1-\pi)$, where $0 \le \tau^2 \le 1$.

Let $n = pq$ be the total sample size from the given stratum and let $Y = \sum_{j=1}^p Z_j$ be the total sample frequency of "successes". By the law of iterated expectations

$$\mathrm{E}\, Y = \mathrm{E} \sum_{j=1}^p q\pi_j = q \sum_{j=1}^p \mathrm{E}\, \pi_j = n\pi,$$

and by the law of total variance

$$\begin{aligned}\operatorname{Var} Y &= \mathrm{E} \sum_{j=1}^p q\pi_j(1-\pi_j) + \operatorname{Var} \sum_{j=1}^p q\pi_j \\ &= \sum_{j=1}^p q\pi(1-\pi)(1-\tau^2) + q^2 \sum_{j=1}^p \tau^2\pi(1-\pi) \\ &= n\pi(1-\pi)[1+(q-1)\tau^2],\end{aligned}$$

where $\omega^2 = 1 + (q-1)\tau^2$ is known as the *overdispersion parameter*. The value of ω^2 depends on both the sample size q from each cluster and the variance τ^2 between clusters, but not on the total sample size n. If $q = 1$, as in the case of ungrouped data, then $\omega^2 = 1$ and no problems arise. □

When $\mathrm{E}\, Y_s = n_s\pi_s$ but $\operatorname{Var} Y_s = n_s\pi_s(1-\pi_s)\omega^2$, with $\omega^2 \ne 1$, the model parameters may still be estimated consistently as before, as the ML estimator only requires $\mathrm{E}(Y_s - n_s\pi_s) = 0$ for consistency. Care however is needed in estimating the Fisher information matrix, for using $\hat\sigma_s^2 = n_s\hat\pi_s(1-\hat\pi_s)$ as an estimate of $\operatorname{Var} Y_s$ would lead to incorrect inference. It can be shown that if the assumed link is correct and the number k of coefficients in α is small relative to the number S of strata, then

$$\hat\omega^2 = \frac{1}{S-k} \sum_{s=1}^S \frac{(Y_s - n_s\hat\pi_s)^2}{n_s\hat\pi_s(1-\hat\pi_s)}$$

is approximately unbiased for ω^2 (McCullagh & Nelder 1989, Section 4.5.2).

An alternative is to treat $\pi_1, \ldots, \pi_S$ as random draws from a common probability distribution with a known shape. This information may then be used to derive the unconditional response probabilities as

$$\Pr\{Y_s = y\} = \mathrm{E}[\Pr\{Y_s = y \,|\, \pi_s\}],$$

where the expectation is with respect to the marginal distribution of π_s.

Example 17.2 Suppose that the conditional distribution of Y_s given $\pi_s = p$ is $\mathrm{Bi}(n_s, p)$, and let π_s have a $\mathcal{B}(\gamma, \delta)$ distribution with density

$$f(p) = \frac{p^{\gamma-1}(1-p)^{\gamma-1}}{B(\gamma,\delta)}, \qquad \gamma, \delta > 0,$$

for $0 \leq p \leq 1$. The beta distribution (Appendix C.5) is attractive for several reasons. First, because its support is the unit interval, it is an appropriate distribution for probabilities. Second, it has only two parameters. Third, it is flexible enough to accommodate a variety of shapes. The marginal distribution of Y_i is beta-logistic with frequency function

$$\begin{aligned} \Pr\{Y_s = y\} &= \int_0^1 \binom{n_s}{y} p^y (1-p)^{n_s - y} \frac{p^{\gamma-1}(1-p)^{\gamma-1}}{B(\gamma,\delta)}\, dp \\ &= \binom{n_s}{y} \frac{1}{B(\gamma,\delta)} \int_0^1 p^{\gamma+y-1}(1-p)^{n_s+\delta-y-1}\, dp \\ &= \binom{n_s}{y} \frac{B(\gamma+y, n_s+\delta-y)}{B(\gamma,\delta)}, \end{aligned}$$

for $y = 0, 1, 2, \ldots$. It can be verified that $\mathrm{E}\, Y_s = n_s\pi$ and $\mathrm{Var}\, Y_s = n_s\pi(1-\pi)[1 + (n_s - 1)\tau^2]$, where π and τ are functions of γ and δ. As an example of application, Heckman and Willis (1977) used the beta-logistic as a model for labor force transitions in a heterogeneous population. □

17.1.9 SEMIPARAMETRIC ESTIMATION

In the nonparametric approach, conditional response probabilities are left completely unspecified, except for the assumption that $\pi(x)$ is a smooth function of x. The methods discussed in Chapter 14 may then be employed to obtain estimates of the function $\pi(x)$.

In the semiparametric approach, conditional response probabilities are specified instead as $\pi(x) = h(\alpha^\top x)$, where h is a monotonic function with values in the unit interval, but one seeks to estimate the parameter α without making any assumption about the precise shape of h. One attractive feature of this approach is that, by retaining the single-index assumption, it avoids the curse of dimensionality problem that plagues fully nonparametric estimation.

This section discusses two examples. The first is based on quantile restrictions, the second is a semiparametric ML estimator based on nonparametric estimation of the conditional distribution of the unobservables. Both examples are easier to motivate by assuming that the data $(X_1, Y_1), \ldots, (X_n, Y_n)$ are a sample from the threshold crossing model

$$\begin{aligned} Y_i^* &= \alpha^\top X_i - U_i, \\ Y_i &= 1\{Y_i^* > 0\}, \end{aligned} \tag{17.10}$$

where $\alpha \in \Re^k$ and U_i is distributed independently of X_i with mean zero, unit variance and distribution function F. The constraints on the moments of U_i are introduced to guarantee that α is identifiable.

The *maximum score (MS) estimator* of Manski (1975, 1985) is an M-estimator based on the criterion function

$$Q_n(\alpha) = n^{-1} \sum_{i=1}^n [Y_i\, 1\{\alpha^\top X_i > 0\} + (1 - Y_i)\, 1\{\alpha^\top X_i \leq 0\}].$$

A positive contribution to Q_n comes from the observations for which $Y_i = 1$ and $\alpha^\top X_i > 0$, or $Y_i = 0$ and $\alpha^\top X_i \leq 0$, whereas zero contribution comes from the observations for which $Y_i = 1$ but $\alpha^\top X_i \le 0$, or $Y_i = 0$ but $\alpha^\top X_i > 0$. Thus, the MS estimate is the parameter value which maximizes a measure of concordance between the data and the predictions based on $\alpha^\top X_i$, namely the frequency of cases for which either $\alpha^\top X_i > 0$ and $Y_i = 1$, or $\alpha^\top X_i \le 0$ and $Y_i = 0$.

If $\alpha_0 \in \Re^k$ denotes the target parameter, then the MS estimator is consistent for α_0 whenever the conditional median of the latent response Y_i^* is unique and equal to $\alpha_0^\top X_i$ or, equivalently, the conditional median of the latent regression errors $U_i = Y_i^* - \alpha_0^\top X_i$ is unique and equal to zero. A sufficient condition is that the distribution function of the latent regression errors is continuous and strictly increasing at the origin. Notice that the threshold model (17.10) is much stronger than necessary. In fact, U_i need not be independent of X_i: only its conditional median is required not to depend on X_i. In particular, U_i may well be heteroskedastic without the consistency of the MS estimator being affected.

More formally, to establish consistency of the MS estimator by the methods in Chapter 15, one has to verify that the criterion function $Q_n(\alpha)$ converges uniformly in α to a nonstochastic function $Q(\alpha)$ which attains its global maximum at $\alpha = \alpha_0$. Here we sketch the main ideas of the proof. Under mild regularity conditions $Q_n(\alpha) \xrightarrow{\text{p}} \mathrm{E}\,\rho_i(\alpha)$ uniformly in α, where

$$\rho_i(\alpha) = 1\{\alpha^\top X_i > 0\}\, F(\alpha_0^\top X_i) + 1\{\alpha^\top X_i \le 0\}\,[1 - F(\alpha_0^\top X_i)].$$

Let $\mu = \alpha^\top X_i$ and $\mu_0 = \alpha_0^\top X_i$, and notice that

$$\begin{aligned}
\rho_i(\alpha_0) - \rho_i(\alpha) & \\
&= [1\{\mu_0 > 0\} - 1\{\mu > 0\}]F(\mu_0) + [1\{\mu_0 \le 0\} - 1\{\mu \le 0\}][1 - F(\mu_0)] \\
&= [1\{\mu_0 > 0\}\, 1\{\mu \le 0\} - 1\{\mu_0 \le 0\}\, 1\{\mu > 0\}]F(\mu_0) \\
&\quad + [1\{\mu_0 \le 0\}\, 1\{\mu > 0\} - 1\{\mu_0 > 0\}\, 1\{\mu \le 0\}][1 - F(\mu_0)] \\
&= 1\{\mu_0 > 0\}\, 1\{\mu \le 0\}[2F(\mu_0) - 1] + 1\{\mu_0 \le 0\}\, 1\{\mu > 0\}[1 - 2F(\mu_0)] \ge 0
\end{aligned}$$

for, if U_i has a unique median at zero, then $F(\mu_0) > 1/2$ if $\mu_0 > 0$, and $F(\mu_0) \le 1/2$ if $\mu_0 \le 0$. Also notice that $\rho_i(\alpha_0) - \rho_i(\alpha) = 0$ if $\alpha_0^\top X_i$ and $\alpha^\top X_i$ have the same sign. Now let $\mathcal{X}_\alpha = \{x\colon \mathrm{sign}(\alpha^\top x) \ne \mathrm{sign}(\alpha_0^\top x)\}$. If we impose the condition that $\Pr\{X_i \in \mathcal{X}_\alpha\} > 0$, then

$$Q(\alpha_0) = \mathrm{E}\,\rho_i(\alpha_0) > \mathrm{E}\,\rho_i(\alpha) = Q(\alpha)$$

for every $\alpha \ne \alpha_0$, that is, Q achieves a unique global maximum at $\alpha = \alpha_0$. A similar, but more involved argument, may be used for the case when the U_i are independently but not identically distributed conditionally on X_i.

The MS criterion Q_n, being a step function, is neither continuous nor differentiable. This has a number of implications. Theoretically, it can be shown that the sequence $\{\hat\alpha_n\}$ of MS estimators is not $\sqrt{n}$-consistent and is not asymptotically normal. Kim and Pollard (1991) show that $n^{1/3}(\hat\alpha_n - \alpha_0)$ converges in distribution to a random variable that maximizes a particular Gaussian process. This result cannot be used for inference, however, since the properties of the limiting distribution are largely unkown. Inference about the MS estimator, therefore, is usually based on the bootstrap (Manski & Thompson 1986).

Computationally, maximization of Q_n differs from the usual econometric optimization problems. Since the criterion function is not smooth, local analysis provides no information useful to select a fruitful search direction. Thus, given an initial candidate, it is difficult to identify a good direction along which to search for a better estimate. However, it is easy to maximize Q_n along any given direction.

To overcome the difficulties with the MS estimator, Horowitz (1992) suggests smoothing the MS criterion in order to make it continuous and differentiable. The resulting smoothed MS estimator is consistent, with a convergence rate equal to at least $n^{-2/5}$, and asymptotically normal. Further, the parameters of its limiting Gaussian distribution may be estimated consistently.

A different approach to consistent estimation of α_0 under weak distributional assumptions has been proposed by Klein and Spady (1993). They notice that if we knew the distribution F of the latent errors in the threshold crossing model (17.10), then the ML estimate of α_0 would be obtained by maximizing the sample log-likelihood

$$L_n(\alpha) = \sum_{i=1}^{n} [Y_i \ln \pi_i(\alpha) + (1 - Y_i) \ln(1 - \pi_i(\alpha))],$$

where $\pi_i(\alpha) = F(\alpha^\top X_i)$. Their basic idea is to replace the function π_i, which cannot be computed without knowledge of F, by a function π_i^* which can be estimated, and then maximize with respect to α the resulting feasible pseudo log-likelihood.

To construct the function π_i^* notice that, by Bayes rule,

$$\begin{aligned}\pi_i(\alpha) &= \Pr\{U_i < \alpha^\top X_i \mid X_i\} \\ &= \frac{\Pr\{U_i < \alpha^\top X_i\}\, f_c(\alpha^\top X_i \mid U_i < \alpha^\top X_i)}{f(\alpha^\top X_i)},\end{aligned}$$

where f_c and f denote, respectively, the conditional and unconditional densities of $\alpha^\top X_i$ and we used the fact that $\Pr\{U_i < \alpha^\top X_i \mid X_i\} = \Pr\{U_i < \alpha^\top X_i \mid \alpha^\top X_i\}$. The event that $U_i < \alpha_0^\top X_i$ is equivalent to the event that $Y_i = 1$, and is therefore observable. Thus define

$$\begin{aligned}\pi_i^*(\alpha) &= \frac{\Pr\{U_i < \alpha_0^\top X_i\}\, f_c(\alpha_0^\top X_i \mid U_i < \alpha_0^\top X_i)}{f(\alpha^\top X_i)} \\ &= \frac{\Pr\{Y_i = 1\}\, f_c(\alpha_0^\top X_i \mid Y_i = 1)}{f(\alpha^\top X_i)},\end{aligned}$$

and notice that $\pi_i^*(\alpha_0) = \pi_i(\alpha_0)$. The resulting pseudo log-likelihood is given by

$$Q_n(\alpha) = n^{-1} \sum_{i=1}^{n} [Y_i \ln \pi_i^*(\alpha) + (1 - Y_i) \ln(1 - \pi_i^*(\alpha))],$$

which coincides with L_n when $\alpha = \alpha_0$.

The pseudo log-likelihood Q_n cannot be employed directly since $\pi_i^*(\alpha)$ is unknown. Notice, however, that $\Pr\{Y_i = 1\}$ can be estimated consistently by $\bar{Y}_n = n^{-1} \sum_i Y_i$, while both the conditional and unconditional densities f_c and f can be estimated nonparametrically as smooth functions of α. Further, since $\alpha^\top X_i$ aggregates the information contained in the vector X_i into a scalar random variable, the problem involves only univariate density estimation. For example, if we use the kernel method with kernel function K and a fixed bandwidth δ_n, then $f(\alpha^\top X_i)$ may be estimated consistently by

$$\hat{f}(\alpha^\top x) = (n\delta_n)^{-1} \sum_{i=1}^{n} K\left(\frac{\alpha^\top (x - X_i)}{\delta_n}\right),$$

while $f_c(\alpha^\top x \,|\, Y_i = 1)$ may be estimated consistently by

$$\begin{aligned}\hat{f}_c(\alpha^\top x \,|\, Y_i = 1) &= (n\delta_n)^{-1} \sum_{i=1}^{n} Y_i K\left(\frac{\alpha^\top (x - X_i)}{\delta_n}\right) \\ &= (n\delta_n)^{-1} \sum_{1} K\left(\frac{\alpha^\top (x - X_i)}{\delta_n}\right),\end{aligned}$$

where $\sum_1$ denotes summation over the observations for which $Y_i = 1$. Thus, $\pi_i^*(\alpha)$ may be estimated consistently by

$$\hat{\pi}_i(\alpha) = \bar{Y}_n \, \frac{\hat{f}_c(\alpha^\top X_i \,|\, Y_i = 1)}{\hat{f}(\alpha^\top X_i)}.$$

The resulting feasible pseudo log-likelihood is given by

$$\hat{Q}_n(\alpha) = n^{-1} \sum_{i=1}^{n} [Y_i \ln \hat{\pi}_i(\alpha) + (1 - Y_i) \ln(1 - \hat{\pi}_i(\alpha))],$$

which can now be maximized with respect to α.

Klein and Spady (1993) show that the resulting estimator is $\sqrt{n}$-consistent for α_0 and asymptotically normal, and provides a consistent estimator of its asymptotic variance. The key steps in the consistency proof involve showing that $\hat{Q}_n$ behaves asymptotically as Q_n, and that Q_n converges, uniformly in α, to a nonstochastic function which has a unique global maximum at $\alpha = \alpha_0$.

17.2 MODELS FOR MULTINOMIAL RESPONSES

Suppose that the response variable Y can take $J \geq 2$ possible values, called *response categories*. We shall write $Y = j$ if the response variable falls in the jth category, with $j = 1, \ldots, J$. We are interested in modelling the J-vector $\mathbf{Y} = (Y_1, \ldots, Y_J)$, where Y_j denotes the number of times the response falls in the jth category.

An important distinction is between *ordered* categorical data, where the response categories possess a natural ordering (e.g. low income, mid-level income or high income), and *unordered* categorical data, where the response categories are mere labels totally devoid of structure (e.g. traveling by bus, by train or by car). Different models are used in the two cases. Before discussing them, we consider the general form of the log-likelihood for multinomial response models.

17.2.1 THE MULTINOMIAL LOG-LIKELIHOOD

In constructing the log-likelihood for multinomial response models, a key role is played by the multinomial distribution with index m and parameter $\boldsymbol{\pi} = (\pi_1, \ldots, \pi_J)$, where $\pi_j = \Pr\{Y = j\}$ is the jth response probability.

We write the probability mass function of the $\mathcal{M}_J(m, \boldsymbol{\pi})$ distribution as

$$f(\mathbf{y}; \boldsymbol{\pi}) = \Pr\{\mathbf{Y} = \mathbf{y}\} = \exp\left(\sum_{j=1}^{J} y_j \ln \pi_j + \ln \frac{m!}{y_1! \cdots y_J!}\right),$$

where $\mathbf{y} = (y_1, \ldots, y_J)$. Since $\sum_{j=1}^{J} y_j = m$ and $\sum_{j=1}^{J} \pi_j = 1$, we have

$$\sum_{j=1}^{J} y_j \ln \pi_j = \sum_{j=2}^{J} y_j \ln \frac{\pi_j}{\pi_1} + m \ln \pi_1 = \sum_{j=2}^{J} y_j \eta_j - m \ln \left(1 + \sum_{j=2}^{J} \exp \eta_j\right),$$

where $\eta_j = \ln(\pi_j/\pi_1)$ is the jth log odds-ratio and we used the fact that $\pi_1 = (1 + \sum_{j=2}^{J} \exp \eta_j)^{-1}$. Hence $f(\mathbf{y}; \boldsymbol{\pi})$ may equivalently be represented as

$$f(y_2, \ldots, y_J; \boldsymbol{\eta}) = \exp\left[\sum_{j=2}^{J} y_j \eta_j - b(\boldsymbol{\eta}) + c(m, y_2, \ldots, y_J)\right], \tag{17.11}$$

where $\boldsymbol{\eta} = (\eta_2, \ldots, \eta_J)$ is the $(J-1)$-vector of log-odds and $b(\boldsymbol{\eta})$ is the convex function

$$b(\boldsymbol{\eta}) = m \ln \left(1 + \sum_{j=2}^{J} \exp \eta_j\right).$$

This shows that the multinomial distribution is a $(J-1)$-parameter exponential family model with canonical parameter $\boldsymbol{\eta}$.

It can be shown that the moment generating function of $(Y_2, \ldots, Y_J)$ exists in an open neighborhood of $\mathbf{t} = (t_2, \ldots, t_J) = 0$ and is given by

$$M(\mathbf{t}) = \mathrm{E}\left(\exp \sum_{j=2}^{J} y_j t_j\right) = \exp[b(\boldsymbol{\eta} + \mathbf{t}) - b(\boldsymbol{\eta})].$$

Hence $\mathrm{E}\, Y_j = \partial b / \partial \eta_j = m\pi_j$ and

$$\mathrm{Cov}(Y_h, Y_j) = \frac{\partial^2 b}{\partial \eta_h \partial \eta_j} = \begin{cases} m\pi_j(1 - \pi_j), & \text{if } h = j, \\ -m\pi_h \pi_j, & \text{otherwise.} \end{cases}$$

Setting $\mathbf{t} = (t_2, 0, \ldots, 0)$ shows that the marginal distribution of Y_2 is $\mathrm{Bi}(m, \pi_2)$. Setting $\mathbf{t} = (t_2, t_3, 0, \ldots, 0)$ shows that the joint distribution of (Y_2, Y_3) is $\mathcal{M}_2(m, (\pi_2, \pi_3))$. The latter property extends to any number of components.

Now consider the distribution of the entire vector $\mathbf{Y} = (Y_1, \ldots, Y_J)$. Its first two moments are $\operatorname{E}\mathbf{Y} = m\boldsymbol{\pi}$ and $\operatorname{Var}\mathbf{Y} = \Sigma$, where

$$\Sigma = m \begin{bmatrix} \pi_1(1-\pi_1) & -\pi_1\pi_2 & \cdots & -\pi_1\pi_J \\ -\pi_2\pi_1 & \pi_2(1-\pi_2) & \cdots & -\pi_2\pi_J \\ \vdots & \vdots & & \vdots \\ -\pi_J\pi_1 & -\pi_J\pi_2 & \cdots & \pi_j(1-\pi_J) \end{bmatrix} = m[\operatorname{diag}(\pi_j) - \boldsymbol{\pi}\boldsymbol{\pi}^\top].$$

The distribution of $\mathbf{Y}$ is degenerate, since $\sum_j Y_j = m$ and therefore $\operatorname{Var}(\sum_j Y_j) = 0$. In fact, the rank of Σ is equal to $J-1$ as its rows add up to zero

$$\pi_j(1-\pi_1) - \pi_j\pi_2 - \cdots - \pi_j\pi_J = \pi_j(1 - \sum_i \pi_i) = 0,$$

since $\sum_i \pi_i = 1$. It is easy to verify that the matrix $\Sigma^- = \operatorname{diag}[1/(m\pi_j)]$ is a generalized inverse of Σ, that is, $\Sigma\Sigma^-\Sigma = \Sigma$. In fact, since $\Sigma\iota = 0$, any matrix of the form $\Sigma^- - c\iota\iota^\top$, where c is a constant and ι is a J-vector of ones, is a generalized inverse of Σ. When $c = 1$, we get the Moore–Penrose generalized inverse (Appendix A.10).

Let $\mathbf{Y}_1, \ldots, \mathbf{Y}_n$ be a sequence of independent random vectors, each having a $\mathcal{M}_J(m_i, \boldsymbol{\pi}_i)$ distribution with $\boldsymbol{\pi}_i = (\pi_{i1}, \ldots, \pi_{iJ})$. As usual, we first consider the log-likelihood as a function of the $J \times n$ matrix $[\boldsymbol{\pi}_1, \ldots, \boldsymbol{\pi}_n]$ and parametrize the response probabilities only later as functions $\pi_{ij} = \pi_j(X_i)$ of a covariate vector X_i. Because the observations are independent, the sample log-likelihood is

$$L(\boldsymbol{\pi}_1, \ldots, \boldsymbol{\pi}_n) = c + \sum_{i=1}^n \sum_{j=1}^J Y_{ij} \ln \pi_{ij},$$

where c is an arbitrary constant, $\sum_{j=1}^J Y_{ij} = m_i$ and $\sum_{j=1}^J \pi_{ij} = 1$. The differential of the log-likelihood is

$$dL = \sum_{i=1}^n \sum_{j=1}^J \frac{Y_{ij}}{\pi_{ij}}\, d\pi_{ij} = \sum_{i=1}^n \sum_{j=1}^J \frac{Y_{ij} - m_i\pi_{ij}}{\pi_{ij}}\, d\pi_{ij},$$

where we used the fact that $\sum_{j=1}^J d\pi_{ij} = 0$ for all i. Hence the derivatives of the log-likelihood with respect to π_{ij} are

$$\frac{\partial L}{\partial \pi_{ij}} = \frac{Y_{ij} - m_i\pi_{ij}}{\pi_{ij}}, \qquad j = 1, \ldots, J.$$

In matrix notation, we have

$$\frac{\partial L}{\partial \boldsymbol{\pi}_i} = m_i\Sigma_i^-(\mathbf{Y}_i - m_i\boldsymbol{\pi}_i), \qquad i = 1, \ldots, n,$$

where $\Sigma_i^- = \operatorname{diag}[1/(m_i\pi_{ij})]$. Using (17.11), the sample log-likelihood may equivalently be written in terms of the log-odds as

$$L(\boldsymbol{\eta}_1, \ldots, \boldsymbol{\eta}_n) = c + \sum_{i=1}^n \left[\sum_{j=2}^J Y_{ij}\eta_{ij} - m_i \ln(1 + \sum_{j=2}^J \exp \eta_{ij}) \right],$$

where $\boldsymbol{\eta}_i = (\eta_{i2}, \ldots, \eta_{iJ})$. The resulting derivatives of the log-likelihood are

$$\frac{\partial L}{\partial \eta_{ij}} = Y_{ij} - m_i \pi_{ij}, \qquad j = 2, \ldots, J.$$

Given a parametric model for the conditional response probabilities $\pi_{ij} = \pi_j(X_i)$, or equivalently for the conditional log-odds $\eta_{ij} = \eta_j(X_i)$, applying the chain rule yields the likelihood score for the model parameters. The next sections present four alternative models.

17.2.2 ORDERED CATEGORICAL RESPONSES

When categories are ordered, one may work with either the response probabilities $\pi_j(x) = \Pr\{Y = j \,|\, X = x\}$ or the cumulative response probabilities

$$\gamma_j(x) = \Pr\{Y \leq j \,|\, X = x\} = \sum_{h=1}^{j} \pi_h(x).$$

Clearly, $\gamma_J(x) = \sum_{j=1}^{J} \pi_j(x) = 1$, for the response must fall in one of the J categories.

The simplest conceivable models specify the response probabilities as a family of parallel hyperplanes after a suitably chosen transformation. Thus, in the case of the logit link, we may consider the *ordered logit model*

$$\ln \frac{\gamma_j(x)}{1 - \gamma_j(x)} = \alpha_j - \beta^\top x, \qquad j = 1, \ldots, J-1.$$

This model is also known as the *proportional odds model*, for it implies that

$$\frac{\gamma_j(x)}{1 - \gamma_j(x)} \bigg/ \frac{\gamma_j(x')}{1 - \gamma_j(x')} = \exp[-\beta^\top (x - x')],$$

independently of j. The Gaussian link gives the *ordered probit model*

$$\gamma_j(x) = \Phi(\alpha_j - \beta^\top x),$$

whereas the complementary log–log link gives

$$\ln[-\ln(1 - \gamma_j(x))] = \alpha_j - \beta^\top x, \qquad j = 1, \ldots, J-1,$$

which is also known as the *proportional hazard model.* Derivation of the corresponding models in terms of response probabilities is straightforward using the fact that $\pi_j(x) = \gamma_j(x) - \gamma_{j-1}(x)$. For example, in the ordered probit case we get

$$\pi_j(x) = \begin{cases} \Phi(\alpha_1 - \beta^\top x), & \text{if } j = 1, \\ \Phi(\alpha_j - \beta^\top x) - \Phi(\alpha_{j-1} - \beta^\top x), & \text{otherwise.} \end{cases}$$

All three models may be derived, much like the threshold crossing model in Section 17.1.6, by treating the response as a categorical observation on a latent continuous random variable Y^*, that is, the observable response Y is related to Y^*

through the observation rule $Y = j$ if $Y^* \in (c_{j-1}, c_j]$, where $j = 1, \ldots, J-1$ and $c_0 = -\infty$. If the latent regression model is $Y^* = \alpha + \beta^\top X + U$, where U is independent of X with distribution function F, then we obtain

$$\gamma_j(x) = \Pr\{Y^* \le c_j \mid X = x\} = \Pr\{U \le c_j - \alpha - \beta^\top x\} = F(\alpha_j - \beta^\top x),$$

where $\alpha_j = c_j - \alpha$. It is easy to verify that one obtains the ordered logit model when $F = \Lambda$ (the standard logistic distribution function), the ordered probit model when $F = \Phi$ (the standard Gaussian distribution function), and the proportional hazard model when F is the Gumbel distribution function.

The threshold crossing formulation of these models suggests simple generalizations that allow for over- or underdispersion. Suppose, for example, that $U/[\exp(\tau^\top x)]$ has a standard logistic distribution. Then the log-odds become

$$\ln \frac{\gamma_j(x)}{1 - \gamma_j(x)} = \frac{\alpha_j - \beta^\top x}{\exp(\tau^\top x)}, \qquad j = 1, \ldots, J-1.$$

This model may be a useful alternative if one is interested in testing the proportional odds assumption.

17.2.3 MULTINOMIAL LOGIT

When categories are not ordered, one is forced to work directly with the response probabilities or the log-odds. If the log-odds are parametrized as

$$\eta_{ij} = \ln \frac{\pi_{ij}}{\pi_{i1}} = \alpha_j^\top X_i, \qquad j = 2, \ldots, J,$$

where X_i is a vector of characteristics specific to the ith individual and α_j is a vector of coefficients specific to the jth alternative, then we obtain the so-called *multinomial logit (MNL)* model. If

$$\eta_{ij} = \ln \frac{\pi_{ij}}{\pi_{i1}} = \beta^\top X_{ij}, \qquad j = 2, \ldots, J,$$

where X_{ij} is a vector of characteristics specific to the jth alternative as perceived by the ith individual, then we obtain the so-called *conditional logit (CL)* model.

The two models are formally equivalent but differ in their interpretation and their use for prediction. The MNL model can be used to predict the choice probabilities, among a given set of J alternatives, of a randomly chosen individual with known characteristics X_i. The CL model can be used to predict the probability that a randomly chosen individual will select an alternative not previously available, given knowledge of β and the vector X_{ij} of alternative specific characteristics. The vector β may here be interpreted as a vector of hedonic prices.

Of course, one may combine the MNL and the CL models by specifying the log-odds as

$$\eta_{ij} = \ln \frac{\pi_{ij}}{\pi_{i1}} = \beta_j^\top X_{ij}, \qquad j = 2, \ldots, J.$$

The likelihood score for this model takes the simple form

$$\frac{\partial L}{\partial \beta_j} = \sum_{i=1}^n X_{ij}(Y_{ij} - m_i \pi_{ij}), \qquad j = 2, \ldots, J,$$

and a ML estimator $\hat{\beta} = (\hat{\beta}_2, \ldots, \hat{\beta}_J)$ may be interpreted as a MM estimator that equates the vector of sufficient statistics to its conditional mean under the estimated model.

Despite the simplicity and interpretability of the logit link, there are several reasons why one may want to consider other links. Some of them are discussed in the next two sections.

17.2.4 NESTED LOGIT

One reason for considering noncanonical links is that the logit link places strong restrictions on choice behavior, for it implies that $\pi_{ij}/\pi_{ik} = \exp[(\alpha_j - \alpha_k)^\top X_i]$ in the MNL model, and $\pi_{ij}/\pi_{ik} = \exp[\beta^\top (X_{ij} - X_{ik})]$ in the CL model, independently of all other available alternatives. This property, called *independence of irrelevant alternatives (IIA)*, may lead to unreasonable conclusions in certain cases.

Example 17.3 Let there be $J = 3$ alternatives: car (C), blue bus (B) and red bus (R), and suppose that a person is indifferent between car and bus, that is, $\Pr\{C \mid C, B\} = \Pr\{C \mid C, R) = .5$. Since the person is indifferent between car and bus, it would be reasonable to assume that $\Pr\{C \mid C, B, R\} = .5$. In this case, however, the logit link implies that

$$\frac{\Pr\{B \mid C, B, R\}}{\Pr\{C \mid C, B, R\}} = \frac{\Pr\{B \mid C, B\}}{\Pr\{C \mid C, B\}} = 1$$

and

$$\frac{\Pr\{R \mid C, B, R\}}{\Pr\{C \mid C, B, R\}} = \frac{\Pr\{R \mid C, R\}}{\Pr\{C \mid C, R\}} = 1.$$

Hence

$$\Pr\{C \mid C, B, R\} = \left[1 + \frac{\Pr\{B \mid C, B\}}{\Pr\{C \mid C, B\}} + \frac{\Pr\{R \mid C, R\}}{\Pr\{C \mid C, R\}}\right]^{-1} = \frac{1}{3} < \frac{1}{2}.$$

□

A simple alternative to MNL is the *nested logit (NL)* model, which may be regarded as a model of sequential choice. For example, if there are $J = 3$ alternatives, one first decides whether or not to choose alternative 1. If alternative 1 is not chosen, one then chooses between alternatives 2 and 3. The NL model specifies the choice probabilities as

$$\pi_1 = \Pr\{1\} = \frac{\exp(\eta_1)}{\exp(\eta_1) + \exp(\lambda\vartheta)}$$

and

$$\begin{aligned} \pi_j &= \Pr\{j \mid 2 \text{ or } 3\} \Pr\{2 \text{ or } 3\} \\ &= \frac{\exp(\eta_j/\lambda)}{\exp(\eta_2/\lambda) + \exp(\eta_3/\lambda)} \, \frac{\exp(\lambda\vartheta)}{\exp(\eta_1) + \exp(\lambda\vartheta)} \\ &= \frac{\exp(\eta_j/\lambda)\exp(\lambda\vartheta)}{\exp(\vartheta)[\exp(\eta_1) + \exp(\lambda\vartheta)]}, \qquad j = 2, 3, \end{aligned}$$

where $\lambda > 0$ and

$$\vartheta = \ln[\exp(\eta_2/\lambda) + \exp(\eta_3/\lambda)] \tag{17.12}$$

is called the *inclusive value*. The log-odds are $\ln(\pi_2/\pi_3) = \eta_2 - \eta_3$ and $\ln(\pi_j/\pi_1) = \eta_j - \eta_1 + (\lambda - 1)\vartheta$ if $j = 2, 3$.

If the η_j are parametrized as $\eta_j = \beta^\top X_j$, the model parameters (β, λ) may be estimated by a two-step procedure. The first step consists of estimating the ratio β/λ from the logit model applied to the choice between alternatives 2 and 3, and then estimates ϑ from (17.12). The second step consists of applying the logit model to the choice between alternative 1 and 2 or 3. Because this is a two-step procedure, care is needed in computing valid standard errors.

Testing for $\lambda = 1$ in the NL model provides a test of the IIA assumption. Another test may be based on the difference between the CL estimates of β and the estimates obtained by applying logit to the choice between a subset of the alternatives (Hausman & McFadden 1984).

17.2.5 MULTINOMIAL CHOICE MODELS

Another reason for considering noncanonical links is when the data describe the choices made by individuals facing $J \geq 2$ alternatives. Let $V_j = \xi_j - \epsilon_j$ denote the utility associated with the jth alternative. Because the first alternative is chosen if $V_1 \geq V_j$ for all $j = 2, \ldots, J$, we get

$$\begin{aligned}\pi_1 = \Pr\{Y_1 = 1\} &= \Pr\{V_1 \geq V_2, \ldots, V_1 \geq V_J\} \\ &= \Pr\{U_2 \leq \Delta_2, \ldots, U_J \leq \Delta_J\} \\ &= F(\Delta_2, \ldots, \Delta_J),\end{aligned}$$

where $U_j = \epsilon_1 - \epsilon_j$, $\Delta_j = \xi_1 - \xi_j$ and F is the distribution function of the random $(J-1)$-vector $U = (U_2, \ldots, U_J)$. This shows that the choice of link function is equivalent to the choice of a joint distribution for the random utility components ϵ_j or, equivalently, for the differences U_j between random utility components. Any particular multinomial response model may be derived from specific assumptions on these multivariate distributions and on the differences Δ_j between systematic utility components.

For example, McFadden (1974) showed that the MNL model is equivalent to the assumption that the ϵ_j are i.i.d. with a common Gumbel distribution. Here we only prove the "if" part of this result.

Without loss of generality, let the ϵ_j be i.i.d. with a standard Gumbel distribution. It follows from (C.5) that the random variables $-V_j = \epsilon_j - \xi_j$ are independent Gumbel with parameter $(1, \psi_j)$, where $\psi_j = \exp(\xi_j)$. Next notice that the first alternative is chosen if $V_* - V_1 < 0$, where $V_* = \max(V_2, \ldots, V_J) = -\min(-V_2, \ldots, -V_J)$. By Result C.4, the distribution of $-V_*$ is Gumbel with parameter $(1, \psi_*)$, where $\psi_* = \sum_{j=2}^J \psi_j$. Because V_* and V_1 are independent, Result C.5 implies that the distribution of $U = V_* - V_1 = -V_1 - (-V_*)$ is logistic with distribution function

$$F(u) = \frac{e^{\delta+u}}{1 + e^{\delta+u}} = \frac{1}{1 + e^{-\delta-u}},$$

where

$$-\delta = \ln \psi_* - \ln \psi_1 = \ln \left[\sum_{j=2}^{J} \exp(\xi_j - \xi_1) \right] = \ln \left[\sum_{j=2}^{J} \exp(-\Delta_j) \right].$$

Therefore

$$\pi_1 = F(0) = \frac{1}{1 + e^{-\delta}} = \frac{1}{1 + \sum_{j=2}^{J} \exp(-\Delta_j)} = \frac{\exp(\xi_1)}{\sum_{j=1}^{J} \exp(\xi_j)}.$$

The NL model follows from the multinomial choice model under the assumptions that $0 < \lambda \leq 1$ and the joint distribution of $\epsilon_1, \ldots, \epsilon_J$ is the generalized extreme value (McFadden 1974) with distribution function

$$F(u_1, \ldots, u_J) = 1 - \exp\left[-g\left(e^{u_1}, \ldots, e^{u_J}\right)\right],$$

where the function $g(x_1, \ldots, x_J)$ is non-negative, homogeneous of degree one in $(x_1, \ldots, x_J) \geq 0$, satisfies $\lim_{x_j \to \infty} g(x_1, \ldots, x_J) = \infty$, $j = 1, \ldots, J$, and is such that, for any distinct set of indices $(i_1, \ldots, i_J)$,

$$\frac{\partial^J g}{\partial x_{i_1} \cdots \partial x_{i_J}} \begin{cases} \geq 0, & \text{if } k \text{ is odd,} \\ \leq 0, & \text{if } k \text{ is even.} \end{cases}$$

The special case $g(x_1, \ldots, x_p) = \sum_{j=1}^{J} x_j$ gives the joint distribution function of J i.i.d. random variables with a common Gumbel distribution, and therefore the MNL or the CL model.

When the joint distribution of the ϵ_j is Gaussian we have instead the so-called *multinomial probit (MNP)* model. In general, computing the choice probabilities for this model requires evaluating a set of integrals whose dimension is equal to the number of alternatives minus one. Unless it is assumed that the random utility components are independent, direct numerical integration is only practical for $J \leq 4$ (see e.g. Hausman & Wise 1978).

17.2.6 THE METHOD OF SIMULATED MOMENTS

The general form of the log-likelihood of a multinomial response model is

$$L(\theta) = c + \sum_{i=1}^{n} \sum_{j=1}^{J} Y_{ij} \ln \pi_{ij}(\theta),$$

where c is an arbitrary constant and $\theta \in \Theta$ denotes the p-dimensional vector of model parameters. The resulting likelihood equation is

$$0 = \sum_{i=1}^{n} \sum_{j=1}^{J} X_{ij}(\theta)[Y_{ij} - \pi_{ij}(\theta)],$$

where $Y_{ij} - \pi_{ij}(\theta)$ is the prediction error and $X_{ij}(\theta) = \pi'_{ij}(\theta)$ is a p-vector. More compactly, the likelihood equation may be written

$$0 = \sum_{j=1}^{J} \mathbf{X}_j(\theta)[\mathbf{Y}_j - \boldsymbol{\pi}_j(\theta)],$$

where $\mathbf{X}_j = [X_{1j}, \ldots, X_{nj}]$ is a $p \times n$ matrix, and $\mathbf{Y}_j = (Y_{1j}, \ldots, Y_{nj})$ and $\boldsymbol{\pi}_j = (\pi_{1j}, \ldots, \pi_{nj})$ are n-vectors. An even more compact notation is

$$0 = \mathbf{X}(\theta)^\top [\mathbf{Y} - \boldsymbol{\pi}(\theta)],$$

where

$$\mathbf{X} = \begin{bmatrix} \mathbf{X}_1 \\ \vdots \\ \mathbf{X}_J \end{bmatrix}, \qquad \mathbf{Y} = \begin{pmatrix} \mathbf{Y}_1 \\ \vdots \\ \mathbf{Y}_J \end{pmatrix}, \qquad \boldsymbol{\pi} = \begin{pmatrix} \boldsymbol{\pi}_1 \\ \vdots \\ \boldsymbol{\pi}_J \end{pmatrix},$$

respectively an $nJ \times p$ matrix, an nJ-vector and another nJ-vector. Finding a root of the likelihood equation is the same as minimizing with respect to $\theta \in \Theta$ the criterion function

$$Q_n(\theta) = [\mathbf{Y} - \boldsymbol{\pi}(\theta)]^\top \mathbf{X}(\theta)\, \mathbf{X}(\theta)^\top [\mathbf{Y} - \boldsymbol{\pi}(\theta)].$$

This suggests estimating instead the general multinomial model by an IV method, using an $nJ \times r$ instrument matrix $\mathbf{W}$ of rank $r \geq p$ which satisfies the following conditions:

1. the instruments are asymptotically correlated with the matrix of likelihood scores evaluated at the "true" parameter θ_0, that is, $n^{-1}\mathbf{W}^\top \mathbf{X}(\theta_0) \xrightarrow{\text{p}} P$, where P is a matrix of full rank p;
2. $\mathrm{E}[\mathbf{Y} - \boldsymbol{\pi}(\theta) \,|\, \mathbf{W}] = 0$ if and only if $\theta = \theta_0$.

An asymptotically efficient IV estimator in this class is one for which $\mathbf{W} = \mathbf{X}(\theta_0)$, where θ_0 may be replaced by some consistent estimate.

McFadden (1989) introduced an alternative IV estimator obtained by replacing response probabilities that require numerical integration with unbiased estimates obtained by Monte Carlo simulation. This method, called the *method of simulated moments (MSM)*, is particularly attractive when computing the exact response probabilities is unfeasible or too expensive relative to the unbiased simulations, as in the MNP case. The resulting estimator can be shown to be $\sqrt{n}$-consistent and asymptotically normal under general conditions. Typically there is some loss of efficiency, caused by noise in the simulations. The method is quite general and can be applied to many other estimation problems.

As an illustration, consider again the multinomial choice model in Section 17.2.5. The MNP specification assumes that the utility to individual i of choosing alternative j is equal to $V_{ij} = \xi_{ij}(\alpha) - \epsilon_{ij}$, where $\epsilon_i = (\epsilon_{i1}, \ldots, \epsilon_{iJ})$ is distributed as $\mathcal{N}_J(0, \Sigma(\sigma))$. The vector of model parameters is $\theta = (\alpha, \sigma)$. Unless strong assumptions are placed on the covariance matrix Σ, numerical computation of $\boldsymbol{\pi}(\theta)$ is generally impractical for $J > 4$.

A MSM estimator avoids direct numerical computation of $\boldsymbol{\pi}(\theta)$ by using a *simulator* $\mathbf{p}(\theta) = [p_{ij}(\theta)]$ which is asymptotically unbiased for $\boldsymbol{\pi}(\theta)$, independent across observations, and "well behaved" in θ. An example, based on the *simple frequency simulator*, is the following.

Algorithm 17.1

(1) *For any trial vector $\theta \in \Theta$ and each observation $i = 1, \ldots, n$, use Monte Carlo methods to independently draw one or more vectors ϵ_i^* from the $\mathcal{N}_J(0, \Sigma(\sigma))$ distribution.*

(2) *Given the Monte Carlo draws* ϵ_i^*, *compute* $V_{ij}^* = \xi_{ij}(\alpha) - \epsilon_{ij}^*$, $j = 1, \ldots, J$.
(3) *Let* $p_{ij}(\theta)$ *be the frequency with which the* jth *alternative is chosen for the* ith *observation, that is, the frequency of the event* $V_{ij}^* > V_{ik}^*$, *for all* $k \neq j$.
(4) *A MSM estimator* $\bar{\theta}_n$ *is a solution to the problem*

$$\min_{\theta \in \Theta} [\mathbf{Y} - \mathbf{p}(\theta)]^\top \mathbf{W} \mathbf{W}^\top [\mathbf{Y} - \mathbf{p}(\theta)].$$

McFadden (1989) gives sufficient conditions for a MSM estimator to be $\sqrt{n}$-consistent for the "true" parameter θ_0 and asymptotically normal. One critical condition on the simulator $\mathbf{p}(\theta)$ is asymptotic unbiasedness.

Assumption 17.1 *The simulation bias* $B_n(\theta) = n^{-1/2}\mathbf{W}^\top[\mathrm{E}\,\mathbf{p}(\theta) - \boldsymbol{\pi}(\theta)]$ *satisfies* $\sup_{\theta \in \Theta} |B_n(\theta)| \to 0$ *as* $n \to \infty$.

This assumption is satisfied if the simulator is unbiased, that is, $\mathrm{E}[\mathbf{p}(\theta) \,|\, \mathbf{X}, \mathbf{Y}] = \boldsymbol{\pi}(\theta)$ for all θ, and the random numbers used to compute $\mathbf{p}(\theta)$ are independent of the vector $\mathbf{Y}$ of observed responses and of any simulator used to compute the instrument matrix $\mathbf{W}$.

Define the simulation residual

$$\zeta_n(\theta) = n^{-1/2}\mathbf{W}^\top[\mathbf{p}(\theta) - \mathrm{E}\,\mathbf{p}(\theta)].$$

The simulation residuals $\zeta_n(\theta)$ are by construction a normalized sum of i.i.d. terms that are independent of $\mathbf{Y}$, have mean zero and are uniformly bounded. The second critical condition is the following.

Assumption 17.2 *The simulation residual process* $\{\zeta_n(\theta), \theta \in \Theta\}$ *is uniformly stochastically bounded and equicontinuous, that is,* $\sup_{\theta \in \Theta} |\zeta_n(\theta)| = O_p(1)$ *and* $\sup_{\theta \in A_n} |\zeta_n(\theta) - \zeta_n(\theta_0)| = o_p(1)$, *where, for a given* $\delta > 0$, $A_n = \{\theta \in \Theta\colon n^{1/2}|\theta - \theta_0| \leq \delta\}$.

This condition is generally satisfied if the Monte Carlo random numbers used to construct $\mathbf{p}(\theta)$ are not redrawn when θ is changed.

Under the above set of assumptions, McFadden (1989) shows that $n^{1/2}(\bar{\theta}_n - \theta_0) \xrightarrow{d} \mathcal{N}_p(0, \mathrm{AV}(\bar{\theta}_n))$, where

$$\mathrm{AV}(\bar{\theta}_n) = (P^\top P)^{-1} P^\top (G_m + G_s) P (P^\top P)^{-1},$$

$$G_m = \operatorname{plim} \frac{1}{n} \sum_{i=1}^{n} \sum_{j=1}^{J} [\pi_{ij}(\theta) X_{ij} X_{ij}^\top - \bar{X}_i \bar{X}_i^\top],$$

$$G_s = \operatorname{plim} \frac{1}{n} \sum_{i=1}^{n} \sum_{j=1}^{J} X_{ii} X_{ij}^\top \, \mathrm{E}(e_{ii} e_{ij}),$$

with $\bar{X}_i = \sum_{j=1}^{J} \pi_{ij}(\theta) X_{ij}$ and $e_{ij} = p_{ij}(\theta) - \pi_{ij}(\theta)$.

If $\bar{\theta}_n$ is a simple frequency simulator (Algorithm 17.1) obtained by r Monte Carlo draws for each observation, then $G_s = r^{-1} G_m$ and so $\mathrm{AV}(\bar{\theta}_n) = (1 + r^{-1})\,\mathrm{AV}(\tilde{\theta}_n)$, where $\tilde{\theta}_n$ is the MM estimator based on $\pi_{ij}(\theta)$ rather than $p_{ij}(\theta)$. Thus, the asymptotic efficiency of $\bar{\theta}_n$ relative to $\tilde{\theta}_n$ is given by

$$\text{ARE}(\bar{\theta}_n, \tilde{\theta}_n) = \frac{\det \text{AV}(\tilde{\theta}_n)}{\det \text{AV}(\bar{\theta}_n)} = \frac{r}{r+1}.$$

Notice that $\text{ARE}(\bar{\theta}_n, \tilde{\theta}_n) \to 1$ as $r \to \infty$. If $r = 1$, then $\text{ARE}(\bar{\theta}_n, \tilde{\theta}_n) = .5$, and if $r = 10$, then $\text{ARE}(\bar{\theta}_n, \tilde{\theta}_n) \approx .91$.

17.3 PANEL DATA MODELS

Consider the following threshold crossing model for binary panel data

$$\begin{aligned} Y_{it}^* &= \alpha_i + \beta^\top X_{it} + U_{it}, \\ Y_{it} &= 1\{Y_{it}^* > 0\}, \qquad t = 1, \ldots, T, \end{aligned} \tag{17.13}$$

where α_i is an individual specific effect and $U_{i1}, \ldots, U_{iT}$ are i.i.d. random errors with zero mean and unit variance. The statistical problem is estimation and inference about the target parameter β given a balanced panel of T observations $\{(X_{it}, Y_{it})\}$ on each of the n sample units. We assume that T is small and n large.

When $\operatorname{Var} \alpha_i = 0$ (no individual specific effects), choice in each period is independent of the choices made in all other periods. In this case it is appropriate to use a univariate binary response model for the pooled observations. In general, however, model (17.13) implies that $\Pr\{Y_{it} = 1 \mid Y_{i,t-1}, X_{it}\} \neq \Pr\{Y_{it} = 1 \mid X_{it}\}$. In this simple model, dependence on the past does not arise from dependence of Y_{it}^* on its own past or on past values of Y_{it}. Instead, it reflects the fact that the latent regression errors $V_{it} = \alpha_i + U_{it}$ are equicorrelated due to the presence of the individual specific effects.

As in Chapter 12, we consider two alternative approaches. The first is the fixed effects approach, where the α_i are treated as nuisance parameters to be eliminated. The second is the random effects approach, where the elements of α_i are treated as n random draws from some probability distribution.

17.3.1 THE FIXED EFFECTS APPROACH

The basic idea (Chamberlain 1980) is to consider the likelihood conditional on sufficient statistics for the incidental parameters $\{\alpha_i\}$. If the link is logit, then a sufficient statistic for α_i is the individual specific mean $\bar{Y}_i = T^{-1} \sum_{t=1}^T Y_{it}$ or, equivalently, $\sum_{t=1}^T Y_{it}$.

Consider first the case when $T = 2$. The event $\sum_{t=1}^T Y_{it} = 1$ occurs if either the event $(1,0) = \{Y_{i1} = 1, Y_{i2} = 0\}$ or the event $(0,1) = \{Y_{i1} = 0, Y_{i2} = 1\}$ occur. Since $(1,0)$ and $(0,1)$ are mutually exclusive, we have

$$\Pr\{(0,1) \mid (1,0) \text{ or } (0,1)\} = \frac{\Pr\{(0,1)\}}{\Pr\{(1,0)\} + \Pr\{(0,1)\}}.$$

Under the logit assumption

$$\Pr\{Y_{it} = 1 \mid \alpha_i\} = \frac{\exp(\eta_{it})}{1 + \exp(\eta_{it})}, \qquad t = 1, 2,$$

where the log-odds are specified as

$$\eta_{it} = \alpha_i + \beta^\top X_{it}, \qquad t = 1, 2.$$

Thus, conditionally on the individual effects,

$$\Pr\{(1,0)\} = \frac{\exp(\eta_{i1})}{1+\exp(\eta_{i1})}\,\frac{1}{1+\exp(\eta_{i2})},$$
$$\Pr\{(0,1)\} = \frac{1}{1+\exp(\eta_{i1})}\,\frac{\exp(\eta_{i2})}{1+\exp(\eta_{i2})}.$$

Hence, conditionally on the individual effects,

$$\Pr\{(0,1)\,|\,(1,0) \text{ or } (0,1)\} = \frac{\exp(\eta_{i2})}{\exp(\eta_{i1})+\exp(\eta_{i2})} = \frac{\exp(\eta_{i2}-\eta_{i1})}{1+\exp(\eta_{i2}-\eta_{i1})},$$

where $\eta_{i2} - \eta_{i1} = \beta^\top(X_{i2} - X_{i1})$. Notice that the fixed effects have been eliminated and we have a standard logit model in which the two outcomes are $(0, 1)$ and $(1, 0)$, and in which changes in X between the two periods are used to predict changes in Y. Thus, the conditional likelihood approach is the analogue of first differencing. Notice that in this model only the observations for which $\sum_{t=1}^T Y_{it} = 1$ carry information about β.

For the case when $T = 3$, we can condition on two different events, namely $\sum_{t=1}^T Y_{it} = 1$ and $\sum_{t=1}^T Y_{it} = 2$. The first event occurs if $(1, 0, 0)$ or $(0, 1, 0)$ or $(0, 0, 1)$ occur. Thus, under the logit specification,

$$\Pr\{(0,1,0)\,|\,\sum_{t=1}^T Y_{it} = 1\} = \frac{\exp(\eta_{i2}-\eta_{i1})}{1+\exp(\eta_{i2}-\eta_{i1})+\exp(\eta_{i3}-\eta_{i1})}$$

and

$$\Pr\{(0,0,1)\,|\,\sum_{t=1}^T Y_{it} = 1\} = \frac{\exp(\eta_{i3}-\eta_{i1})}{1+\exp(\eta_{i2}-\eta_{i1})+\exp(\eta_{i3}-\eta_{i1})}.$$

The second event occurs if $(1, 1, 0)$ or $(0, 1, 1)$ or $(1, 0, 1)$ occur. Thus, under the logit specification,

$$\Pr\{(0,1,1)\,|\,\sum_{t=1}^T Y_{it} = 2\} = \frac{\exp(\eta_{i3}-\eta_{i1})}{1+\exp(\eta_{i3}-\eta_{i1})+\exp(\eta_{i3}-\eta_{i2})}$$

and

$$\Pr\{(1,0,1)\,|\,\sum_{t=1}^T Y_{it} = 2\} = \frac{\exp(\eta_{i3}-\eta_{i2})}{1+\exp(\eta_{i3}-\eta_{i1})+\exp(\eta_{i3}-\eta_{i2})}.$$

Again, the fixed effects have been eliminated through a transformation that represents the analogue of differencing. For general T, we have to consider the events $\sum_{t=1}^T Y_{it} = 1, 2, \ldots, T-1$. Chamberlain (1980) shows how the model can be extended to MNL.

The main problems with the conditional likelihood approach are, first, that only a fraction of the sample is used in estimation and, second, that the approach only applies to the logit case. If the link is not canonical, as in the probit case, no simplification is obtained because the fixed effects do not cancel out. Further, since all the fixed effects $\{\alpha_i\}$ must be estimated jointly with β, the estimates of β are inconsistent because of the incidental parameter problem. This leads inevitably to the random effects specification.

17.3.2 THE RANDOM EFFECTS APPROACH

Let $V_{it} = \alpha_i + U_{it}$ be the latent error in model (17.13) and suppose that the conditional distribution of $V_i = (V_{i1}, \ldots, V_{iT})$ given $X_i = (X_{i1}, \ldots, X_{iT})$ does not depend on X_i. Because the event $\{Y_{it} = 1\}$ is equivalent to the event $\{V_{it} > -\beta^\top X_{it}\}$, in order to compute the choice probabilities we need to assume a multivariate distribution for V_{it} and evaluate a T-dimensional integral. For example,

$$\Pr\{Y_{i1} = 1, \ldots, Y_{iT} = 1\} = \int_{-\beta^\top X_{i1}}^{\infty} \cdots \int_{-\beta^\top X_{iT}}^{\infty} f(v_1, \ldots, v_T)\, dv_1 \cdots dv_T,$$

where f denotes the multivariate density of V_i. Estimation is not generally feasible computationally for $T > 4$, unless special assumptions are made on f, such as independence or special functional forms. A useful approach for the general case is the method of simulated moments discussed in Section 17.2.6.

Example 17.4 Suppose that α_i and $U_{i1}, \ldots, U_{iT}$ are mutually independent and distributed independently of the covariates as $\alpha_i \sim \mathcal{N}(0, \sigma_\alpha^2)$ and $U_{it} \sim \mathcal{N}(0, \sigma^2)$. Because the event $\{Y_{it} = 1\}$ is equivalent to the event $\{U_{it}/\sigma > c(\alpha_i)\}$, where $U_{it}/\sigma \sim \mathcal{N}(0,1)$ and $c(\alpha_i) = -(\alpha_i + \beta^\top X_{it})/\sigma$, the conditional frequency function of a sample of T observations is easily derived given the value of α_i

$$f(y_1, \ldots, y_T \,|\, \alpha_i) = \prod_{t=1}^{T} [1 - \Phi(c(\alpha_i))]^{y_t}\, \Phi(c(\alpha_i))^{1-y_t}.$$

The unconditional frequency function is obtained by integrating the conditional frequency function with respect to the distribution of α_i. This gives

$$f(y_1, \ldots, y_T) = \int \prod_{t=1}^{T} [1 - \Phi(c(a))]^{y_t}\, \Phi(c(a))^{1-y_t}\, \frac{1}{\sigma_\alpha} \phi\left(\frac{a}{\sigma_\alpha}\right) da,$$

from which the log likelihood function is easily constructed using the quadrature method proposed by Butler and Moffitt (1982). □

If the assumption of independence between the errors and the regressors is relaxed, an approach similar to the one in Section 12.5 may be followed by assuming that

$$\alpha_i = \sum_{t=1}^{T} \gamma_t^\top X_{it} + \epsilon_i = \gamma^\top X_i + \epsilon_i, \tag{17.14}$$

where $\gamma = (\gamma_1, \ldots, \gamma_T)$ and ϵ_i is independent of X_i. Under this specification, the random effects are assumed to depend on all current, future and past values of the covariates (Chamberlain 1980, 1984). Notice that, unlike Section 12.5, model (17.14) can no longer be interpreted as a BLP. Substituting back into (17.13) gives the model

$$Y_{it} = 1\{\beta^\top X_{it} + \gamma^\top X_i + \epsilon_i + U_{it} > 0\}, \qquad t = 1, \ldots, T.$$

If ϵ_i and $U_{i1}, \ldots, U_{iT}$ are independent Gaussian random variables, we obtain a set of T probit models, one for each time period, which can be estimated separately of each other. As in Section 12.5, the implied cross-equation constraints may then be imposed using the minimum distance method.

17.4 GENERALIZED LINEAR MODELS

Despite their differences, the Gaussian linear model and the categorical response models discussed in the previous sections share some common features, such as the interpretation of the likelihood equation and the relationship between ML and LS methods. In fact, the analogy between these two types of model runs deep as a consequence of their common nature of exponential families. This makes it possible to unify regression methodologies for discrete and continuous responses.

17.4.1 ONE-PARAMETER EXPONENTIAL FAMILIES

Let Z be a scalar random variable whose distribution belongs to a parametric family $\mathcal{F}_\Theta$ of densities or frequency functions of the form

$$f(z;\theta) = \exp\left[\frac{\eta z - b(\eta)}{\gamma} + c(z,\gamma)\right], \qquad \theta = (\eta, \gamma), \tag{17.15}$$

at all points in the support of the distribution, where η and $\gamma > 0$ are scalar parameters. The parameter of interest is η while γ, called the *dispersion parameter*, is usually treated as a nuisance parameter. We henceforth assume that the family $\mathcal{F}_\Theta$ is regular in the following sense:

Assumption 17.3 *The parametric family $\mathcal{F}_\Theta$ satisfies:*

(i) $\Theta = \mathcal{H} \times \Re_+$, *where $\mathcal{H}$ is an open subset of $\Re$;*
(ii) *the support $\mathcal{S}$ does not depend on θ;*
(iii) *the function $b(\cdot)$ is strictly convex and twice continuously differentiable;*
(iv) *for all $z \in \mathcal{S}$, the function $c(z, \cdot)$ is twice continuously differentiable.*

Under this assumption, $\mathcal{F}_\Theta$ is a one-parameter (linear) exponential family with canonical parameter η and natural sufficient statistic Z.

Example 17.5 Using the results in Example 1.19, the family of $\mathrm{Bi}(m,\pi)$ distributions is a one-parameter exponential family with $\eta = \ln[\pi/(1-\pi)]$, $b(\eta) = m\ln(1+e^\eta)$, $\gamma = 1$ and $c(z,\gamma) = \ln\binom{m}{z}$.

The family of $\mathcal{P}(\lambda)$ distributions is a one-parameter exponential family with $\eta = \ln\lambda$, $b(\eta) = e^\eta$, $\gamma = 1$ and $c(z,\gamma) = -\ln(z!)$.

The family of $\mathcal{E}(\gamma)$ distributions is a one-parameter exponential family with $\eta = -\gamma$, $b(\eta) = -\ln(-\eta)$, $\gamma = 1$ and $c(z,\gamma) = 0$.

The family of $\mathcal{N}(\mu, \sigma^2)$ distributions is a one-parameter exponential family with $\eta = \mu$, $b(\eta) = \mu^2/2$, $\gamma = \sigma^2$ and

$$c(z, \gamma) = -\frac{1}{2}\left[\frac{z^2}{\gamma} + \ln(2\pi\gamma)\right].$$

□

All the distributions in this class share two common features. First, the canonical parameter η is a strictly increasing function of the mean of Z. Second, the mean and the variance of Z are related (except in the Gaussian case). As we shall see, both are general properties of the parametric family (17.15) and follow from the next result.

Theorem 17.1 *If the random variable Z has a distribution that belongs to a one-parameter exponential family with a density of the form (17.15), then the moment generating function of Z exists in an open neighborhood of $t = 0$ and is*

$$M(t) = \exp\left[\frac{b(\eta + \gamma t) - b(\eta)}{\gamma}\right].$$

Proof. If Z is a continuous random variable, then

$$\begin{aligned} M(t) = E(e^{tZ}) &= \int \exp\left[\frac{z(\eta + \gamma t) - (\eta)}{\gamma} + c(z, \gamma)\right] dz \\ &= \exp\left[-\frac{b(\eta)}{\gamma}\right] \int \exp\left[\frac{z(\eta + \gamma t)}{\gamma} + c(z, \gamma)\right] dz \\ &= \exp\left[\frac{b(\eta + \gamma t) - b(\eta)}{\gamma}\right] \end{aligned}$$

using the fact that densities integrate to one. In the discrete case the same result is obtained by replacing integration with summation. □

Theorem 17.1 has a number of important consequences. Because $M(t)$ exists in an open neighborhood of $t = 0$, all moments of Z exist and can easily be recovered by differentiation. In particular the following holds.

Corollary 17.1 *If the random variable Z has a distribution that belongs to a one-parameter exponential family with density of the form (17.15), then $\mathrm{E}_\theta Z = b'(\eta)$ and $\mathrm{Var}_\theta Z = \gamma\, b''(\eta)$.*

Since the function b' is strictly increasing and continuously differentiable, it has a continuously differentiable inverse, called the *canonical link* and denoted by g^*, which relates the canonical parameter η to the mean μ of Z.

Example 17.6 From Example 17.5, the canonical link for the binomial model is the logit link $g^*(\mu) = \ln(\mu/(1-\mu))$, for the Poisson model it is the logarithmic link $g^*(\mu) = \ln \mu$, for the exponential model it is the inverse link $g^*(\mu) = 1/\mu$, and for the Gaussian model it is the identity link $g^*(\mu) = \mu$. □

Notice that the variance of Z depends on the canonical parameter η only through $b''(\eta)$. The assumption that γ is strictly positive and $b(\cdot)$ is strictly convex guarantees that Z has a nondegenerate distribution. Finally, the relationship

$$b''(\eta) = \frac{d}{d\eta} b'(\eta) = \frac{d\mu}{d\eta}$$

implicitly defines the variance of Z as a function of the mean of Z. The function relating μ to $b''(\eta)$ is written $V(\mu)$ and called the *variance function.* Thus, $\mathrm{Var}_\theta\, Z = \gamma V(\mu)$.

Example 17.7 From Example 17.5, $V(\mu) = m\mu(1-\mu)$ for the binomial model, $V(\mu) = \mu$ for the Poisson model, $V(\mu) = 1/\mu^2$ for the exponential model, and $V(\mu) = 1$ for the Gaussian model. □

Corollary 17.2 *If the random variable Z has a distribution that belongs to a one-parameter exponential family with density of the form (17.15), then*

$$\mathrm{E}_\theta \frac{\partial^2}{\partial\eta^2} \ln f(Z;\eta,\gamma) = -\frac{b''(\eta)}{\gamma} \qquad \mathrm{E}_\theta \frac{\partial^2}{\partial\gamma\partial\eta} \ln f(Z;\eta,\gamma) = 0.$$

Proof. The partial derivatives of the log-density are

$$\frac{\partial \ln f}{\partial\eta} = \frac{z - b'(\eta)}{\gamma}, \qquad \frac{\partial^2 \ln f}{\partial\eta^2} = -\frac{b''(\eta)}{\gamma}, \qquad \frac{\partial^2 \ln f}{\partial\gamma\partial\eta} = -\frac{z-b'(\eta)}{\gamma^2},$$

where $\mathrm{E}\, Z = b'(\eta)$ by Corollary 17.1. □

Corollary 17.2 implies that the Fisher information on θ is diagonal with respect to η and γ, and so there is no loss of generality in treating γ as known. Further, the Fisher information on η is

$$\mathcal{I}_\eta(\theta) = \frac{b''(\eta)}{\gamma} = \frac{\mathrm{Var}\, Z}{\gamma^2}.$$

The next corollary gives the exact sampling distribution of the sample mean $\bar{Z} = n^{-1}\sum_{i=1}^n Z_i$ which is the natural sufficient statistic for a sample of n observations from a distribution in this class.

Corollary 17.3 *If $Z_1, \ldots, Z_n$ is a sample from a distribution that belongs to a one-parameter exponential family with density of the form (17.15), then the density (frequency) function of the sample mean $\bar{Z} = n^{-1}\sum_{i=1}^n Z_i$ is*

$$f(z;\theta) = \exp\left[\frac{\eta z - b(\eta)}{\gamma/n} + c(z,\gamma)\right].$$

Proof. Since $Z_1, \cdots, Z_n$ are independent, the moment generating function of $\bar{Z}$ is

$$M_{\bar{Z}}(t) = [M(t/n)]^n = \left[\exp\left(\frac{b(\eta+\gamma t/n) - b(\eta)}{\gamma}\right)\right]^n$$
$$= \exp\left[\frac{b(\eta+\gamma t/n) - b(\eta)}{\gamma/n}\right].$$

□

17.4.2 ELEMENTS OF A GLM

Now suppose that the conditional distribution of a scalar random variable Y given a random k-vector X belongs to a one-parameter exponential family with density of the form (17.15). The chosen parametric model represents the first element of a *generalized linear model (GLM),* while the choice of which covariates to include in X represents its second element.

Let $\mu(x)$ and $\sigma^2(x)$ denote, respectively, the CMF and the CVF of Y given $X = x$. We model the dependence of Y on X by assuming that there exists a link function g such that, for all x in the support of X,

$$g(\mu(x)) = \beta^\top x \tag{17.16}$$

for a unique $\beta \in \Re^k$. The link function g connects the CMF of Y to the linear predictor $\beta^\top x$ which represents the systematic part of the model. The link function is assumed to satisfy the following.

Assumption 17.4 *The function g has a continuously differentiable inverse which maps $\Re$ onto the range space of $\mu(\cdot)$.*

Any link function g that satisfies Assumption 17.4 is said to be *admissible.* The choice of an admissible link represents the third element of a GLM.

To summarize, the elements of a GLM are: (i) the choice of a parametric model in the one-parameter exponential family (the random part of the model); (ii) the choice of which covariates to include in X (the systematic part of the model); (iii) the choice of a link function g, linking the systematic and the random part of the model.

If g is an admissible link, inverting (17.16) gives

$$\mu(x) = h(\beta^\top x),$$

where $h = g^{-1}$ is a monotonic function called the *inverse link.* Because $\mu(x)$ depends on x and β only through the linear predictor $\beta^\top x$, a GLM is an example of a single-index model. This implies that

$$\frac{\beta_j}{\beta_l} = \frac{\partial \mu(x)/\partial x_j}{\partial \mu(x)/\partial x_l},$$

just like the linear model. The canonical parameter $\eta(x)$ itself depends on the linear predictor through the relationship $b'(\eta(x)) = \mu(x) = h(\beta^\top x)$. This implies that

$$\eta(x) = g^*(h(\beta^\top x)),$$

where g^*, equal to the inverse of b', is the canonical link. Finally, since $\sigma^2(x) = \gamma\, b''(\eta(x)) = \gamma\, V(\mu(x))$, where the dispersion parameter γ is usually assumed not to depend on x, the CVF of Y also depends on the linear predictor $\beta^\top x$ through the relationship

$$\sigma^2(x) = \gamma\, V(h(\beta^\top x)).$$

When the link is canonical, the inverse link h is equal to b' and so $\eta(x) = \beta^\top x$, that is, the canonical parameter is linear in x. In this case, the conditional density (frequency) function of Y given $X = x$ is of the form

$$f(y \mid x; \theta) = \exp\left[\frac{\beta^\top xy - b(\beta^\top x)}{\gamma} + c(y, \gamma)\right], \qquad \theta = (\beta, \gamma),$$

which implies that XY is the natural sufficient statistic for β. Up to an additive constant, the conditional log-density is therefore

$$\ln f(y \mid x; \theta) = \frac{\beta^\top xy - b(\beta^\top x)}{\gamma} + c(y, \gamma),$$

the conditional likelihood score for β is

$$s(y \mid x; \theta) = \frac{y - b'(\beta^\top x)}{\gamma}\, x,$$

and the conditional Fisher information on β given $X = x$ is

$$\mathcal{I}_\beta(x) = \frac{b''(\beta^\top x)}{\gamma}\, xx^\top = \sigma^2(x)\, xx^\top,$$

where we used the fact that, from Corollary 17.2, the conditional Fisher information on θ is block-diagonal with respect to β and γ.

17.5 ESTIMATION OF A GLM

Estimation of the parameter β in a GLM may be carried out either by ML or by LS methods. Pseudo ML methods are also available. Because of Corollary 17.2, there is no loss of generality in assuming $\gamma = 1$.

17.5.1 ML ESTIMATION

Suppose that the conditional distribution of Y given the random k-vector X belongs to a one-parameter exponential family. If $(X_1, Y_1), \ldots, (X_n, Y_n)$ is a sample from the distribution of (X, Y), then the sample log-likelihood is

$$L(\eta) = c + \sum_{i=1}^{n} [\eta_i Y_i - b(\eta_i)],$$

where c is an arbitrary constant, η_i is the canonical parameter for the ith observation and $\eta_i = (\eta_{i1}, \ldots, \eta_{in})$. The components of the likelihood score are of the form

$$\frac{\partial L}{\partial \eta_i} = Y_i - b'(\eta_i), \qquad i = 1, \ldots, n.$$

Now parametrize the model explicitly by assuming that $g(\mu(x)) = \beta^\top x$, where g is an admissible link function with inverse $h = g^{-1}$. Let $h_i(\beta) = h(\beta^\top X_i)$ and $V_i(\beta) = V(h_i(\beta))$. Since the canonical parameter η_i satisfies $b'(\eta_i) = h_i(\beta)$, we get

$$b''(\eta_i)\, d\eta_i = H_i(\beta) X_i\, d\beta,$$

where $b''(\eta_i) = V_i(\beta)$ and $H_i(\beta) = h'(\beta^\top X_i)$. Hence

$$\frac{\partial \eta_i}{\partial \beta} = \frac{H_i}{V_i} X_i.$$

By the chain rule, the likelihood equation defining a ML estimator of β is

$$0 = L'(\beta) = \sum_{i=1}^{n} \frac{H_i}{V_i}(Y_i - h_i)X_i.$$

If the link is canonical, then $H_i = V_i$. In this case the likelihood score becomes

$$L'(\beta) = \sum_{i=1}^{n} (Y_i - h_i)X_i,$$

and a ML estimator $\hat{\beta}$ satisfies

$$\sum_{i=1}^{n} Y_i X_i = \sum_{i=1}^{n} \hat{h}_i X_i,$$

where $\hat{h}_i = h(\hat{\beta}^\top X_i)$. Thus, $\hat{\beta}$ may be interpreted as equating the sufficient statistic $\sum_{i=1}^n Y_i X_i$ to its conditional expectation under the estimated model. The likelihood equation also implies that the residuals $Y_i - \hat{h}_i$ have mean zero if the model includes an intercept.

Except in special cases, such as the Gaussian linear model, computing the ML estimate of β, either by maximizing the sample log-likelihood or by solving the likelihood equation, requires numerical methods. This task is straightforward, however, because strict convexity of the function b implies strict concavity of the log-likelihood provided that the design matrix is of full rank k.

The NR method requires the Hessian $L''(\beta)$ of the sample log-likelihood. When the link is not canonical, this is somewhat complicated (see e.g. McCullagh & Nelder 1989) and the scoring method is easier to use, for it only requires an estimate of the expected total information on β

$$I(\beta) = \mathrm{E}[L'(\beta)\, L'(\beta)^\top] = \sum_{i=1}^{n} \frac{H_i^2}{V_i^2} V_i X_i X_i^\top = \sum_{i=1}^{n} W_i(\beta) X_i X_i^\top,$$

where $W_i(\beta) = H_i^2/V_i$. Since the likelihood score may be written

$$L'(\beta^{(r)}) = \sum_{i=1}^{n} W_i^{(r)} \frac{Y_i - h_i(\beta^{(r)})}{H_i(\beta^{(r)})} X_i,$$

where $W_i^{(r)} = W_i(\beta^{(r)})$, the scoring iteration is

$$\begin{aligned}\beta^{(r+1)} &= \beta^{(r)} + [\sum_i W_i^{(r)} X_i X_i^\top]^{-1} \sum_i W_i^{(r)} \frac{Y_i - h_i(\beta^{(r)})}{H_i(\beta^{(r)})} X_i \\ &= [\sum_i W_i^{(r)} X_i X_i^\top]^{-1} \sum_i W_i^{(r)} X_i Y_i^{(r)},\end{aligned}$$

where

$$Y_i^{(r)} = X_i^\top \beta^{(r)} + \frac{Y_i - h_i(\beta^{(r)})}{H_i(\beta^{(r)})}$$

is called the *adjusted dependent variable*. The updated estimate $\beta^{(r+1)}$ is just the coefficient in a WLS regression of the adjusted dependent variable $Y_i^{(r)}$ on X_i, with weights equal to $W_i^{(r)}$. Thus, the ML estimate of β can easily be computed by iterative WLS.

For a canonical link, the Hessian of the sample log-likelihood is simply

$$L''(\beta) = -\sum_{i=1}^n V_i(\beta)\, X_i X_i^\top,$$

and it is easy to verify that $-L''(\beta)$ is equal to the expected total information. In this case, therefore, the NR and the scoring method coincide. Further, since $H_i = V_i$, the weight $W_i^{(r)}$ and the adjusted dependent variable $Y_i^{(r)}$ simply become

$$W_i^{(r)} = V_i^{(r)}, \qquad Y_i^{(r)} = X_i^\top \beta^{(r)} + \frac{Y_i - h_i(\beta^{(r)})}{V_i^{(r)}},$$

with $V_i^{(r)} = V_i(\beta^{(r)})$.

Suppose that the assumed GLM is correctly specified and identifiable, and let β_0 be the true value of β, that is, $\mu(x) = h(\beta^\top x)$ and $\sigma^2(x) = V(h(\beta^\top x))$ only if $\beta = \beta_0$. If $\{\hat\beta_n\}$ is a sequence of ML estimators corresponding to increasing sample sizes then, under mild regularity conditions, $\hat\beta_n$ is $\sqrt{n}$-consistent for β_0 and asymptotically normal with asymptotic variance equal to the inverse of the Fisher information matrix

$$\mathcal{I}(\beta_0) = \mathrm{E}[W_i(\beta_0)\, X_i X_i^\top].$$

Hence, a consistent estimator of the asymptotic variance of $\hat\beta_n$ is

$$[n^{-1} \sum_i W_i(\hat\beta_n)\, X_i X_i^\top]^{-1}.$$

If the link is canonical, then $W_i = V_i$ and the Fisher information matrix simplifies to

$$\mathcal{I}(\beta_0) = \mathrm{E}[V_i(\beta_0)\, X_i X_i^\top].$$

The properties of a ML estimator when the GLM is misspecified are discussed in Section 17.5.4.

17.5.2 RESIDUALS AND DIAGNOSTICS

Given a ML estimate $\hat\beta$ of the k-parameter β, let $\hat\mu_i = h(\hat\beta^\top X_i)$ denote the estimated mean for the ith observation and let $\hat L$ denote the maximized value of the sample log-likelihood of the working model.

A *null* model is one with a common mean for all observations and no covariate effects. The ML estimate of such a mean is the sample average $\bar Y$ and the maximized value of the sample log-likelihood of this model is denoted by $\bar{L}$. A comparison of $\hat{L}$ and $\bar{L}$ provides a natural measure of the significance of the covariates in the model. For a given γ, such a comparison may be based on the statistic

$$2(\hat{L} - \bar{L}) = 2\sum_{i=1}^{n} \frac{(\hat{\eta}_i - \bar{\eta})Y_i - [b(\hat{\eta}_i) - b(\bar{\eta})]}{\gamma},$$

where $\hat{\eta}_i = g^*(\hat{\mu}_i)$ and $\bar{\eta} = g^*(\bar{Y})$. This is just the likelihood ratio test statistic for testing the null model against the alternative of the working model with k parameters. Under appropriate regularity conditions, this statistic can be shown to be asymptotically distributed under the null model as chi-square with $k - 1$ degrees of freedom.

A *full* or *saturated* model is instead one that has $k = n$ parameters, one for each observation. In this case, the data are interpolated exactly and the estimated mean for the ith observation is simply equal to Y_i. If $\tilde{L}$ denotes the maximized value of the log-likelihood of the full model, then a comparison of $\tilde{L}$ and $\hat{L}$ provides a natural measure of goodness-of-fit. For a given γ, such a comparison may be based on the *scaled deviance*

$$\hat{D}^* = 2(\tilde{L} - \hat{L}) = \frac{\hat{D}}{\gamma},$$

where the statistic

$$\hat{D} = \sum_{i=1}^{n} (\tilde{\eta}_i - \hat{\eta}_i)Y_i - [b(\tilde{\eta}_i) - b(\hat{\eta}_i)],$$

with $\tilde{\eta}_i = g^*(Y_i)$, is called the *deviance*. The scaled deviance is simply the likelihood ratio test statistic for testing the working model against the alternative of a full model.

Example 17.8 For the binomial model with index m, the deviance is

$$\hat{D} = 2\sum_{i=1}^{n} \left[Y_i \ln \frac{Y_i}{\hat{\mu}_i} + (m - Y_i) \ln \frac{m - Y_i}{m - \hat{\mu}_i} \right],$$

whereas for the Gaussian model it is equal to the residual-sum-of-squares. □

An alternative measure of goodness-of-fit is the generalized Pearson statistic

$$\hat{G} = \sum_{i=1}^{n} \frac{(Y_i - \hat{\mu}_i)^2}{\hat{V}_i},$$

where $\hat{V}_i = V_i(\hat{\beta})$ is the estimated value of the variance function for the ith observation. In the Gaussian linear model, $V_i(\beta)$ is identically equal to one and so the generalized Pearson statistic coincides with the deviance. On the other hand, for the binomial model, $\hat{G}$ coincides with the original Pearson statistic.

As for the classical linear model, the differences between the observed data and their fitted values or "residuals" contain important information on the model adequacy. In particular, the presence of systematic patterns in the residuals is an indication that the model may not be appropriate.

For GLMs, two types of residual play a useful role. The first are the *Pearson residuals*

$$\hat{U}_i = \frac{Y_i - \hat{\mu}_i}{\hat{V}_i^{1/2}}, \qquad i = 1, \ldots, n$$

which, for the Gaussian linear model, coincide with the ordinary residuals. The generalized Pearson statistic is just the sum of the squared Pearson residuals.

The second type of residuals are the *deviance residuals.* Letting

$$d_i = (\tilde{\eta}_i - \hat{\eta}_i)Y_i - [b(\tilde{\eta}_i) - b(\hat{\eta}_i)],$$

the deviance residuals are defined as

$$\tilde{U}_i = \operatorname{sign}(Y_i - \hat{\mu}_i)\sqrt{d_i}, \qquad i = 1, \ldots, n.$$

Notice that the deviance is just the sum of the squared deviance residuals.

17.5.3 LEAST SQUARES ESTIMATION

Suppose that the conditional distribution of Y given the random k-vector X belongs to a one-parameter exponential family. Assume that $g(\mu(x)) = \beta^\top x$ for some admissible link function g and let $h = g^{-1}$ denote the inverse link. If the data $(X_1, Y_1), \ldots, (X_n, Y_n)$ are a sample from the distribution of (X, Y), then

$$Y_i = h_i(\beta) + U_i, \qquad i = 1, \ldots, n, \tag{17.17}$$

where $h_i(\beta) = h(\beta^\top X_i)$ and $U_i = Y - h_i(\beta)$ is a random error such that $\mathrm{E}(U_i \mid X_i) = 0$. The regression formulation (17.17) suggests two alternative estimators of the target parameter β. One is a nonlinear least squares (NLLS) estimator defined as a solution to the problem

$$\min_{\beta \in \Re^k} \sum_{i=1}^n [Y_i - h_i(\beta)]^2. \tag{17.18}$$

The other is a MM estimator defined as a root of the equation

$$0 = \sum_{i=1}^n [Y_i - h_i(\beta)]X_i.$$

Although both estimators are $\sqrt{n}$-consistent and asymptotically normal under general conditions, they are generally asymptotically less efficient than a ML estimator, for they neglect the information contained in the conditional variance $\gamma V_i(\beta)$ of Y_i. If this conditional variance does not depend on β, as in the classical Gaussian linear model, then both estimators are asymptotically equivalent to a ML estimator. Otherwise, both could be made asymptotically more efficient by taking into account the dependence of $V_i(\beta)$ on β. For example, we may consider the weighted NLLS estimator defined as a solution to the problem

$$\min_{\beta \in \Re^k} \sum_{i=1}^n \frac{[Y_i - h_i(\beta)]^2}{V_i(\beta)}. \tag{17.19}$$

A weighted version of the MM estimator may also be considered.

17.5.4 PSEUDO ML METHODS

The NLLS estimator that solves problem (17.18) may be viewed as a pseudo ML estimator based on the assumption that the conditional distribution of Y_i given X_i is $\mathcal{N}(h_i(\beta), \sigma^2)$. The weighted NLLS estimator that solves (17.19) may instead be viewed as a pseudo ML estimator based on the assumption that the conditional distribution of Y_i given X_i is $\mathcal{N}(h_i(\beta), V_i(\beta))$. Their consistency is a consequence of the following general property of pseudo ML estimators based on distributions in the exponential family.

Theorem 17.2 *Let $\hat{\beta}_n$ maximize any regular log-likelihood function of the form*

$$L_n(\beta) = c + \sum_{i=1}^{n} [\eta_i(\beta)\, Y_i - b(\eta_i(\beta))],$$

where c is an arbitrary constant, and let $h_i(\beta) = b'(\eta_i(\beta))$. If $\mu_i = \mathrm{E}(Y_i \,|\, X_i) = h_i(\beta)$ if and only if $\beta = \beta_0$, then $\hat{\beta}_n \xrightarrow{\mathrm{p}} \beta_0$.

Proof. A pseudo ML estimator $\hat{\beta}_n$ based on L_n is a root of the likelihood equation

$$0 = L_n'(\beta) = \sum_{i=1}^{n} [Y_i - h_i(\beta)]\, \eta_i'(\beta).$$

Since L_n is regular, $n^{-1} L_n'(\beta) \xrightarrow{\mathrm{p}} \mathrm{E}[Y_i - h_i(\beta)]\, \eta_i'(\beta)$ uniformly over compact sets. Since $\eta_i'(\beta) = (H_i/V_i)X_i$, the equation

$$0 = \mathrm{E}[Y_i - h_i(\beta)]\, \eta_i'(\beta) = \mathrm{E}\left\{\mathrm{E}\left[\frac{H_i}{V_i}(Y_i - h_i)X_i \,|X_i\right]\right\} = \mathrm{E}\left[\frac{H_i}{V_i}(\mu_i - h_i)X_i\right]$$

is satisfied if and only if $\beta = \beta_0$. Hence $\hat{\beta}_n \xrightarrow{\mathrm{p}} \beta_0$. □

Thus, consistency of a pseudo ML estimator $\hat{\beta}_n$ requires only correct specification of the CMF and does not depend on what particular model in the exponential family is chosen. Of course, the choice of model generally affects the asymptotic efficiency of the resulting pseudo ML estimator and the way in which its precision is estimated. Under mild regularity conditions (see for example Gourieroux, Monfort & Trognon 1984a), a pseudo ML estimator based on a correctly specified CMF is asymptotically normal with asymptotic variance $\mathrm{AV}(\hat{\beta}_n) = B_0^{-1}\, C_0\, B_0^{-1}$, where

$$B_0 = \mathrm{E}\left[\frac{H_i^2}{V_i}\, X_i X_i^\top\right], \qquad C_0 = \mathrm{E}\left[\frac{H_i^2}{V_i^2}\, \sigma_i^2\, X_i X_i^\top\right],$$

with $\sigma_i^2 = \mathrm{Var}(Y_i \,|\, X_i)$, and h_i, H_i and V_i are all evaluated at β_0. If the link is the canonical one for the assumed model, then $H_i = V_i$ and so

$$B_0 = \mathrm{E}[V_i\, X_i X_i^\top], \qquad C_0 = \mathrm{E}[\sigma_i^2\, X_i X_i^\top].$$

Notice that the matrix B_0 depends on the assumed conditional variance of Y_i, whereas the matrix C_0 depends on the true one. Thus, if both the CMF and the CVF of Y_i

are correctly specified, then the pseudo ML estimator is asymptotically equivalent to the ML estimator based on a correctly specified model.

Now consider the case when the CMF is misspecified. If the equation

$$0 = \mathrm{E}[Y_i - b'(\eta_i)]\,\eta_i'(\beta)$$

admits a unique solution β_* then, under mild regularity conditions, the pseudo ML estimator $\hat{\beta}_n$ is $\sqrt{n}$-consistent for the pseudo true parameter β_* and asymptotically normal with asymptotic variance $\mathrm{AV}(\hat{\beta}_n) = B_*^{-1}\, C_*\, B_*^{-1}$, where

$$B_* = \mathrm{E}\left[\frac{H_i^2}{V_i} X_i X_i^\top\right], \qquad C_* = \mathrm{E}\left[\frac{H_i^2}{V_i^2}(Y_i - h_i)^2\, X_i X_i^\top\right],$$

and h_i, H_i and V_i are all evaluated at β_*.

Irrespective of whether the CMF of Y_i is correctly specified, a consistent estimator of the asymptotic variance of $\hat{\beta}_n$ is given by $\hat{B}_n^{-1}\hat{C}_n\hat{B}_n^{-1}$, where

$$\hat{B}_n = n^{-1}\sum_{i=1}^n \frac{\hat{H}_i^2}{\hat{V}_i} X_i X_i^\top, \qquad \hat{C}_n = n^{-1}\sum_{i=1}^n \frac{\hat{H}_i^2}{\hat{V}_i^2}(Y_i - \hat{h}_i)^2\, X_i X_i^\top,$$

with $\hat{h}_i = h_i(\hat{\beta}_n)$, $\hat{H}_i = H_i(\hat{\beta}_n)$ and $\hat{V}_i = V_i(\hat{\beta}_n)$. A viable alternative to "plug-in" estimates is the nonparametric bootstrap.

17.6 POISSON REGRESSION

To illustrate the results obtained in the last two sections, consider the case when the discrete response Y_i is a non-negative integer. The typical situation is when Y_i counts the number of times that a certain event occurs during a specified time unit. For example, Y_i may record the number of withdrawals from a cash machine during a week, or the number of job offers received by an unemployed person during a month, or the number of patents applied for by a firm during a year.

The basic model for this kind of data is the Poisson distribution with natural parameter λ (equal to the mean and the variance of the distribution), canonical parameter $\eta = \ln\lambda$, canonical link $g^*(\mu) = \ln\mu$ and variance function $V(\mu) = \mu$.

A natural way of modeling the dependence of Y_i on a k-vector of covariates X_i is to allow the canonical parameter to depend on X_i. The *Poisson regression model* corresponds to the case when the canonical parameter depends linearly on X_i and the link is canonical, that is, $\mu(x) = \exp(\beta^\top x)$ for some $\beta \in \Re^k$, ensuring non-negativity of $\mu(x)$. This specification implies that

$$\beta_j = \frac{\partial}{\partial x_j}\ln\mu(x) \qquad j = 1,\ldots,k,$$

which allows a simple interpretation of the jth element of β as the proportional change in the CMF if the jth covariate changes by one unit.

Given a random sample $(X_1, Y_1), \ldots, (X_n, Y_n)$ from a Poisson regression model, the conditional log-likelihood is

$$L(\beta) = c + \sum_{i=1}^n [\beta^\top X_i Y_i - \exp(\beta^\top X_i)],$$

where c is an arbitrary constant, the conditional likelihood score is

$$L'(\beta) = \sum_{i=1}^{n} [Y_i - \exp(\beta^\top X_i)]\, X_i,$$

and the expected total information on β is

$$I(\beta) = \sum_{i=1}^{n} \exp(\beta^\top X_i)\, X_i X_i^\top.$$

Notice that the log-likelihood is strictly concave provided that the design matrix is nonsingular. Hence, if a ML estimator $\hat{\beta}$ exists, then it is unique. Also notice that, for this model,

$$h_i(\beta) = H_i(\beta) = V_i(\beta) = \exp(\beta^\top X_i).$$

Because the link is canonical, the NR and scoring iterations coincide. The iterations for locating a ML estimator compute the updated estimate $\beta^{(r+1)}$ as the coefficient vector in a WLS regression of the adjusted dependent variable

$$Y_i^{(r)} = X_i^\top \beta^{(r)} + \frac{Y_i - h_i(\beta^{(r)})}{h_i(\beta^{(r)})}$$

on X_i, with weights equal to $W_i^{(r)} = h_i(\beta^{(r)})$.

In evaluating the asymptotic properties of a sequence $\{\hat{\beta}_n\}$ of ML estimators we distinguish between three cases. The first case is when the Poisson model is correctly specified and identifiable. If β_0 is the true value of β, then $\hat{\beta}_n$ is $\sqrt{n}$-consistent for β_0 and asymptotically normal with asymptotic variance equal to the inverse of the Fisher information matrix

$$\mathcal{I}(\beta_0) = \mathrm{E}[\mu_i\, X_i X_i^\top],$$

where $\mu_i = h_i(\beta_0)$. A consistent estimator of the asymptotic variance of $\hat{\beta}_n$ is

$$[n^{-1} \sum_i \hat{\mu}_i\, X_i X_i^\top]^{-1},$$

where $\hat{\mu}_i = h_i(\hat{\beta}_n) = \exp(\hat{\beta}_n X_i)$, and the deviance statistic is

$$\hat{D} = 2 \sum_{i=1}^{n} \left[Y_i \ln \frac{Y_i}{\hat{\mu}_i} + (Y_i - \hat{\mu}_i) \right],$$

which coincides with the original Pearson statistic.

The second case is when the distribution of the data is not Poisson, but the CMF is correctly specified and identifiable. A typical situation is when $\mu(x) = \exp(\beta_0^\top x)$ but $\sigma^2(x) > \mu(x)$ because of neglected heterogeneity resulting in overdispersion. It is not difficult to show that, in this case, the probability of zero is higher relative to the prediction of the Poisson model, a complication known as the "excess zeros" problem.

Example 17.9 Suppose that the Poisson regression model is true but the CMF varies across sample units, that is,

$$\mu_i(x) = \exp(\beta_0^\top x)\, U_i, \qquad i = 1, \ldots, n,$$

where U_i is introduced to capture unobserved heterogeneity arising from failure to control for all relevant covariates. A typical approach in this case consists of treating the U_i as i.i.d. random variables distributed independently of X_i with unit mean. If the model includes an intercept, the unit mean assumption is only an innocuous normalization. In this case

$$\mu(x) = \mathrm{E}\, \mu_i(x) = \exp(\beta_0^\top x),$$

where the expectation is with respect to the distribution of U_i. The resulting model is not generally Poisson, however, for

$$\sigma^2(x) = \mathrm{E}\, \mu_i(x) + \mathrm{Var}\, \mu_i(x) = \mu(x)[1 + \omega^2\, \mu(x)] \geq \mu(x),$$

with equality only if $\omega^2 = \mathrm{Var}\, U_i = 0$. Thus, unobserved heterogeneity leads to overdispersion. If g denotes the common density of the U_i, then

$$f(y \,|\, x) = \Pr\{Y_i = y \,|\, X_i = x\} = \int \exp[-\mu(x)u]\, \frac{[\mu(x)u]^y}{y!}\, g(u)\, du,$$

with $y = 0, 1, 2, \ldots$. The precise form of the conditional model for Y_i depends on the assumptions made about the mixing distribution g. In particular, suppose that g is the density of a $\mathcal{G}(p, \gamma)$ distribution. The assumption that $\mathrm{E}\, U_i = 1$ implies that $p = \gamma$ and therefore $\omega^2 = \mathrm{Var}\, U_i = 1/p$. It is not difficult to show that the conditional distribution of Y_i is negative binomial with probability mass function

$$\begin{aligned} f(y \,|\, x) &= \frac{\Gamma(p+y)}{\Gamma(p)\, y!}\, [p^{-1}\mu(x)]^y\, [1 + p^{-1}\mu(x)]^{-(p+y)} \\ &= \frac{\Gamma(p+y)}{\Gamma(p)\, y!} \left[\frac{p}{p+\mu(x)}\right]^p \left[\frac{\mu(x)}{p+\mu(x)}\right]^y, \end{aligned}$$

where Γ is the gamma function (Appendix C.5). □

In this case the Poisson pseudo ML estimator $\hat{\beta}_n$ is $\sqrt{n}$-consistent for the true value β_0 and asymptotically normal with asymptotic variance matrix $\mathrm{AV}(\hat{\beta}_n) = B_0^{-1}\, C_0\, B_0^{-1}$, where

$$B_0 = \mathrm{E}[\mu_i\, X_i X_i^\top], \qquad C_0 = \mathrm{E}[\sigma_i^2\, X_i X_i^\top].$$

It is not difficult to show that, in this case, $\mathrm{AV}(\hat{\beta}_n) - \mathcal{I}(\beta_0) \geq 0$.

The third case is when the CMF is also misspecified. If the equation

$$0 = \mathrm{E}[Y_i - h_i(\beta)]\, X_i$$

admits a unique solution β_* then, under mild regularity conditions, the Poisson pseudo ML estimator $\hat{\beta}_n$ is $\sqrt{n}$-consistent for the pseudo true parameter β_* and asymptotically normal with asymptotic variance $\mathrm{AV}(\hat{\beta}_n) = B_*^{-1}\, C_*\, B_*^{-1}$, where

$$B_* = \mathrm{E}[h_i(\beta_*)\, X_i X_i^\top], \qquad C_* = \mathrm{E}[(Y_i - h_i(\beta_*))^2\, X_i X_i^\top].$$

Whether or not the CMF of Y_i is correctly specified, a consistent estimator of the asymptotic variance of $\hat{\beta}_n$ is given by $\hat{B}_n^{-1}\hat{C}_n\hat{B}_n^{-1}$, where

$$\hat{B}_n = n^{-1}\sum_{i=1}^{n} \hat{\mu}_i X_i X_i^\top, \qquad \hat{C}_n = n^{-1}\sum_{i=1}^{n} (Y_i - \hat{\mu}_i)^2 X_i X_i^\top.$$

BIBLIOGRAPHIC NOTES

For a broad introduction to models for discrete responses see Maddala (1983), Amemiya (1985) and Agresti (1990). Ben-Akiva and Lerman (1985) focus on the case when the discrete response represents the choice among a discrete set of alternatives.

Identifiability of binary response models is discussed in Manski (1988a). On semiparametric estimation of binary choice models see also Ichimura (1993), Matzkin (1992) and the reviews by Powell (1994), Horowitz (1998b) and Pagan and Ullah (1999).

For an alternative proof of consistency and asymptotic normality of a MSM estimator see Pakes and Pollard (1989). On other applications of the MSM see Hajivassiliou and Ruud (1994) and Gourieroux and Monfort (1996).

GLMs were introduced by Nelder and Wedderburn (1972). A comprehensive treatment is the book by McCullagh and Nelder (1989).

For a detailed discussion of the sampling properties of the quasi ML estimator for the Poisson model see Gourieroux, Monfort and Trognon (1984b). On panel data models for count data see Hausman, Hall and Griliches (1984), on semiparametric methods see Delgado and Kniesner (1997). A thorough account of statistical models for count data is the book by Cameron and Trivedi (1998). A compact survey is Winkelmann and Zimmermann (1995).

All estimators discussed in this chapter are not B-robust since their influence function is unbounded. On B-robust estimation of GLM see Künsch, Stefanski and Carroll (1989).

During the last decade, GLMs have been extended along several directions. The first direction is weakening of parametric assumptions. One approach (Hastie & Tibshirani 1990) extends additive regression (Section 14.6.4) to GLM by replacing the linear predictor with an additive one. A second approach (Tibshirani & Hastie 1987, Fan, Heckman & Wand 1995) extends the notion of locally linear fitting to GLM fitted locally over neighborhoods in the covariate space. This approach is equivalent to maximizing a kernel weighted sample log-likelihood. A third approach (Green & Silverman 1994) is similar to smoothing splines and consists of maximizing a penalized log-likelihood which trades off fidelity to the data and excessive fluctuations of the estimated relationship.

The second direction (Liang & Zeger 1986, Prentice & Zhao 1991) is estimation of GLM for panel data. The key here is the fact, already noticed by Robinson (1982), that the "naive" NLLS estimator that does not account for autocorrelation remains consistent even when the observations are autocorrelated, provided that the CMF is correctly specified. In this case, however, care is needed in estimating the asymptotic variance of $\hat{\beta}$. A general reference is the survey article by Fitzmaurice, Laird and Rotnitzky (1993).

PROBLEMS

17.1 Given a random sample $Y_1, \ldots, Y_n$, where Y_i is a 0–1 random variable with $\Pr\{Y_i = 1\} = \pi_i$, write down the log-likelihood as a function of the log-odds $\eta_i = \ln[\pi_i/(1-\pi_i)]$, $i = 1, \ldots, n$. Compute the gradient and the Hessian of the log-likelihood.

17.2 Let the random variables X_1 and X_2 be independent Gumbel with parameters (α, γ_1) and (α, γ_2) respectively. Show that the distribution of the difference $Y = X_1 - X_2$ is logistic.

17.3 Show that the logit model $\pi(x) = \Lambda(\alpha + \beta x)$ has steepest slope when $\pi(x) = 1/2$.

17.4 Consider the logit model $\pi(x) = \Pr\{Y = 1 \mid X = x\} = \Lambda(\alpha + \beta x)$. Show that, if X is a 0–1 binary random variable, then this model can also be written as a linear probability model $\pi(x) = \gamma + \delta x$. Determine the parameter (γ, δ) as a function of (α, β) and show that the ML estimator of (γ, δ) is equal to the OLS estimator in a regression of Y_i on a constant term and X_i.

17.5 Verify that if $f_1(x)$ and $f_2(x)$ are multivariate normal densities with mean μ_1 and μ_2 and common variance Σ, then the posterior odds-ratio $[f_1(x)/f_2(x)][\pi/(1-\pi)]$ has the logit form.

17.6 Let Y_1 and Y_2 be 0–1 binary random variables. Show that if $\Pr\{Y_1 = 1 \mid X, Y_2\} = \Lambda(\alpha X + \beta Y_2)$ and $\Pr\{Y_2 = 1 \mid X, Y_1\} = \Lambda(\gamma X + \delta Y_1)$, then $\beta = \delta$.

17.7 Verify the formulae for the mean and the variance of Y_i in Example 17.2.

17.8 Suppose that the dependence of response probabilities on X is of the form $\pi(x) = \frac{1}{2} + (1/\pi)\tan^{-1}(\alpha + \beta x)$. What distribution has a distribution function of this form? When would you expect this model to be more appropriate than logit or probit?

17.9 Derive the influence function of the probit and logit ML estimator.

17.10 Suppose that the random vector $Y = (Y_1, \ldots, Y_J)$ has a $\mathcal{M}_J(m, \pi)$ distribution where $\pi = (\pi_1, \ldots, \pi_J)$. Let $\Sigma = \operatorname{Var} Y$ and show that the matrix $\Sigma^- = \operatorname{diag}[1/(m\pi_j), j = 1, \ldots, J]$ is a generalized inverse of Σ.

17.11 Derive a set of conditions sufficient to guarantee that the log-likelihood of a GLM is strictly concave in β.

17.12 Prove Corollary 17.1.

17.13 Use the regression formulation (17.17) of a GLM to derive GMM estimators of β. Evaluate the sampling properties of the proposed estimators.

17.14 Show that unobserved heterogeneity in a Poisson model implies a higher probability of zero relative to the Poisson model.

17.15 Show that the log-likelihood of a Poisson regression model coincides with that of a duration model based on the exponential distribution with hazard function of the form $h(y \mid x; \beta) = \exp(\beta^\top x)$.

18

Models for Truncated and Censored Data

In this chapter we discuss models for cases where the range of the response variable is limited due to partial observability or selection problems, such as those discussed in Chapter 2. To model this kind of situation, we introduce a partially observable continuous random variable (or vector) Y_i^*, which obeys a classical linear model with covariate vector X_i, and assume that the observed Y_i coincides with Y_i^* only over a known range C_i. When the latent variable Y_i^* is unobservable, the covariate vector X_i may or may not be observed. We also introduce a binary indicator D_i which takes value one when $Y_i^* \in C_i$ and zero otherwise. Thus, D_i is the indicator of the event that Y_i^* is observed. This model differs from the threshold crossing model in Chapter 17 where Y_i^* is never observed and $Y_i = D_i$. Following Chapter 2, we say that the data are *truncated* if $D_i = 1$ for all sample units, that is, the data only contain cases for which Y_i^* is observed. We say that the data are *censored* if they contain both cases for which Y_i^* is observed and cases for which it is not.

Most of this chapter is concerned with situations where Y_i^* is a scalar random variable and $C_i = (a_i, b_i)$ is a known interval, that is, Y_i^* is only observed if $a_i < Y_i^* < b_i$. We distinguish between the *fixed censoring* case where a_i and b_i may be treated as constants, possibly after conditioning on some set of exogenous covariates, and the *random censoring* case where a_i and b_i are better viewed as random. The last part of the chapter deals with cases where Y_i^* is a vector of latent variables.

18.1 DISTRIBUTION AND MOMENTS OF TRUNCATED AND CENSORED DATA

Our basic model for the latent random variable Y_i^* is

$$Y_i^* = \mu_i + \sigma V_i, \qquad i = 1, \ldots, n, \tag{18.1}$$

where $\mu_i \in \Re$ is a location parameter that may depend on a k-vector X_i of covariates, $\sigma > 0$ is a scale parameter, and V_i is a continuous random variable distributed independently of X_i with zero mean, unit variance, distribution function F and density function $f = F'$. Under this set of assumptions, the latent response Y_i^* has mean μ_i, variance σ^2, distribution function $F((y - \mu_i)/\sigma)$ and density function $f((y - \mu_i)/\sigma)/\sigma$.

The remainder of this section summarizes a number of results about the distribution and the moments of truncated and censored data. These results will prove useful later on when we shall address the question of how to estimate μ_i and σ.

When $C_i = (a_i, b_i)$, the event that $D_i = 1$ is equivalent to the event that

$$c_i = \frac{a_i - \mu_i}{\sigma} < V_i < \frac{b_i - \mu_i}{\sigma} = d_i,$$

where both c_i and d_i depend on X_i through the dependence of μ_i (and possibly of a_i and b_i) on the covariates. Conditional on X_i, the probability of the event that $D_i = 1$ is therefore

$$\Pr\{D_i = 1\} = \mathrm{E}\, D_i = F(d_i) - F(c_i).$$

We consider the case of truncated and censored data separately.

18.1.1 TRUNCATED DATA

Truncated data only contain cases for which $D_i = 1$. Hence, the conditional distribution function of a single sample observation Y_i is

$$G(y \,|\, D_i = 1) = \begin{cases} 0, & \text{if } y < a_i, \\ \dfrac{F((y - \mu_i)/\sigma) - F(c_i)}{F(d_i) - F(c_i)}, & \text{if } a_i \le y < b_i, \\ 1, & \text{if } b_i \le y, \end{cases}$$

where the dependence on the covariate vector X_i has been omitted for simplicity. Conditionally on X_i and $D_i = 1$, the density of Y_i is

$$g(y \,|\, D_i = 1) = 1\{a_i < y < b_i\}\, \frac{1}{\sigma} \frac{f((y - \mu_i)/\sigma)}{F(d_i) - F(c_i)},$$

the mean of Y_i is

$$\mathrm{E}(Y_i \,|\, D_i = 1) = \mu_i + \sigma\, \psi_i, \tag{18.2}$$

with

$$\psi_i = \mathrm{E}(V_i \,|\, c_i < V_i < d_i) = \int_{c_i}^{d_i} v\, \frac{f(v)}{F(d_i) - F(c_i)}\, dv, \tag{18.3}$$

and the variance of Y_i is

$$\mathrm{Var}(Y_i \,|\, D_i = 1) = \sigma^2\, \mathrm{Var}(V_i \,|\, c_i < V_i < d_i), \tag{18.4}$$

with

$$\mathrm{Var}(V_i \,|\, c_i < V_i < d_i) = \int_{c_i}^{d_i} v^2\, \frac{f(v)}{F(d_i) - F(c_i)}\, dv - \psi_i^2. \tag{18.5}$$

The precise form of the integrals (18.3) and (18.5), and whether or not they possess a closed form expression, depends on the distribution of V_i.

Example 18.1 If $V_i \sim \mathcal{N}(0, 1)$, it follows from the results in Appendix C.9 that

$$\psi_i = \mathrm{E}(V_i \,|\, c_i < V_i < d_i) = -\frac{\phi(d_i) - \phi(c_i)}{\Phi(d_i) - \Phi(c_i)}$$

and

$$\operatorname{Var}(V_i \mid c_i < V_i < d_i) = 1 - \frac{d_i\,\phi(d_i) - c_i\,\phi(c_i)}{\Phi(d_i) - \Phi(d_i)} - \left[\frac{\phi(d_i) - \phi(c_i)}{\Phi(d_i) - \Phi(c_i)}\right]^2,$$

where Φ and ϕ denote, respectively, the distribution function and the density of the standard Gaussian distribution. If $a_i = -\infty$, namely truncation is only on the right, then

$$\mathrm{E}(V_i \mid V_i < d_i) = -\lambda(d_i)$$

where $\lambda(d_i) = \phi(d_i)/\Phi(d_i)$ is the inverse Mill's ratio and

$$\operatorname{Var}(V_i \mid V_i < d_i) = 1 - d_i\,\lambda(d_i) - \lambda(d_i)^2.$$

If $b_i = \infty$, namely truncation is only on the left, then

$$\mathrm{E}(V_i \mid V_i > c_i) = \lambda(-c_i)$$

where $\lambda(-c_i) = \phi(c_i)/[1 - \Phi(c_i)]$, and

$$\operatorname{Var}(V_i \mid V_i > c_i) = 1 + c_i\,\lambda(-c_i) - \lambda(-c_i)^2.$$

□

18.1.2 *CENSORED DATA*

Censored data contain both cases for which Y_i^* is observable ($D_i = 1$) and cases for which it is not ($D_i = 0$). In what follows, we adopt the convention of putting $Y_i = a_i$ whenever $Y_i^* \le a_i$ and $Y_i = b_i$ whenever $Y_i^* \ge b_i$. Under this convention, Y_i may be related to the latent variable Y_i^* through the observation rule

$$Y_i = \max(a_i, \min(Y_i^*, b_i)).$$

Notice that $Y_i = \min(Y_i^*, b_i)$ in the case of right-censoring ($a_i = -\infty$), whereas $Y_i = \max(a_i, Y_i^*)$ in the case of left-censoring ($b_i = \infty$). An example of right-censoring is the top-coding case discussed in Example 2.2, whereas an example of left-censoring is the tobit model introduced in Example 1.33.

Conditionally on X_i, the distribution function of a single observation Y_i is

$$G(y) = \begin{cases} 0, & \text{if } y < a_i, \\ F\left(\dfrac{y - \mu_i}{\sigma}\right), & \text{if } a_i \le y < b_i, \\ 1, & \text{if } b_i \le y. \end{cases}$$

This distribution function is of the mixed continuous–discrete type with two mass points at $y = a_i$ and $y = b_i$, whose probabilities are $F((a_i - \mu_i)/\sigma)$ and $1 - F((b_i - \mu_i)/\sigma)$ respectively. Unlike the case of truncated data, the distribution function of Y_i coincides with that of the latent variable Y_i^* over the interval $[a_i, b_i)$ (Figure 77). Conditionally on X_i, the density function of Y_i is

$$g(y) = 1\{a_i < y < b_i\}\,\frac{1}{\sigma}\,f\left(\frac{y - \mu_i}{\sigma}\right),$$

Figure 77 Distribution functions of truncated and censored data. The latent variable Y_i^* is distributed as $\mathcal{N}(0,1)$ and $D_i = 1\{-1 < Y_i^* < 1\}$. The broken line in the left graph denotes the $\mathcal{N}(0,1)$ distribution function.

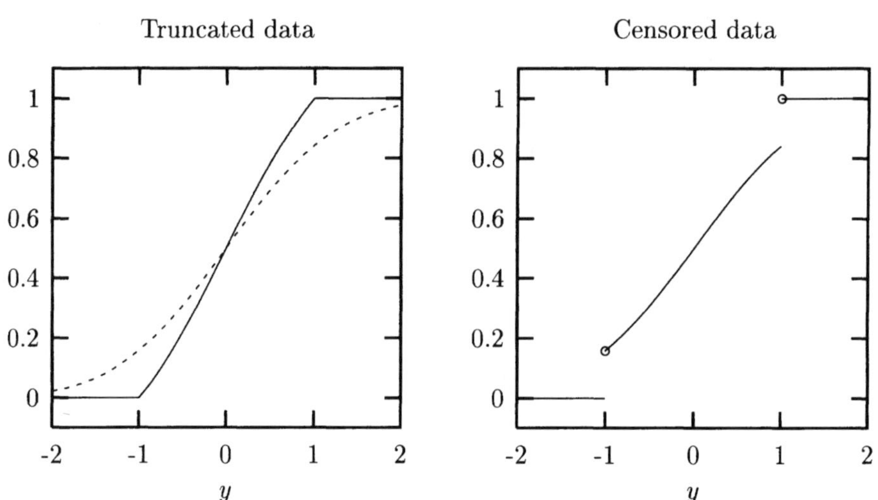

the mean of Y_i is the weighted sum

$$\mathrm{E}\, Y_i = \mathrm{E}(Y_i \,|\, D_i = 1)\, \Pr\{D_i = 1\} + a_i\, \Pr\{Y_i^* \leq a_i\} + b_i\, \Pr\{Y_i^* \geq b_i\}, \tag{18.6}$$

where

$$\mathrm{E}(Y_i \,|\, D_i = 1)\, \Pr\{D_i = 1\} = \mu_i[F(d_i) - F(c_i)] + \sigma \int_{c_i}^{d_i} v\, f(v)\, dv$$

and

$$\Pr\{Y_i^* \leq a_i\} = F(c_i), \qquad \Pr\{Y_i^* \geq b_i\} = 1 - F(d_i),$$

and the variance of Y_i is

$$\mathrm{Var}\, Y_i = \mathrm{Var}(Y_i \,|\, D_i = 1)\, \mathrm{E}\, D_i + \mathrm{E}(Y_i \,|\, D_i = 1)^2\, \mathrm{Var}\, D_i,$$

where $\mathrm{Var}\, D_i = \mathrm{E}\, D_i\, (1 - \mathrm{E}\, D_i)$.

Example 18.2 If $Y_i^* \sim \mathcal{N}(\mu_i, \sigma^2)$, then

$$\mathrm{E}\, Y_i = \mu_i[\Phi(d_i) - \Phi(c_i)] - \sigma[\phi(d_i) - \phi(c_i)] + a_i\, \Phi(c_i) + b_i[1 - \Phi(d_i)].$$

In particular,

$$\mathrm{E}\, Y_i = \mu_i\, \Phi(d_i) + \sigma\, \phi(d_i) + b_i[1 - \Phi(d_i)]$$

for right-censored data ($a_i = -\infty$), and

$$\mathrm{E}\, Y_i = \mu_i[1 - \Phi(c_i)] + \sigma\, \phi(c_i) + a_i\, \Phi(c_i)$$

for left-censored data ($b_i = \infty$). □

The set of results in this section represents the basis for consistent estimation of the model parameters by least squares or maximum likelihood methods. Before discussing estimation issues, in the next section we present a simple model which represents the prototype of a wide class of models for truncated and censored data.

18.2 THE ROY MODEL

The Roy model (Roy 1951) is the prototypical economic model of *self-selection*. Examples of applications include a woman's choice between market and nonmarket work, a worker's choice between union and nonunion sector, interfirm job mobility, migration, etc. Here we only discuss the static version of the model.

Following Heckman and Honorè (1990), consider a two-sector economy populated by income maximizing individuals who possess positive amounts s_1 and s_2 of two skills, with associated skill prices p_1 and p_2. Skill j is only useful in sector j, $j = 1, 2$. Individuals differ in their skill endowments and everybody knows his own endowment. People can work only in one sector, there are no mobility costs, and sector specific skills cannot be augmented by personal investments. People make their sectoral choice after skill prices are revealed. A person chooses sector 1 if his earnings are greater there, that is $W_1 = p_1 S_1 > p_2 S_2 = W_2$, and sector 2 otherwise. Let $D = 1$ if sector 1 is chosen and $D = 0$ otherwise.

To model the variability of skill endowments, (S_1, S_2) is represented as a non-negative continuous random vector with density $f(s_1, s_2)$. The proportion of the population working in sector 1 is

$$\pi = \Pr\{D = 1\} = \Pr\{p_1 S_1 > p_2 S_2\} = \int_0^\infty \int_0^{s_1 p_1 / p_2} f(s_1, s_2)\, ds_2\, ds_1 .$$

Because $\partial\pi/\partial(p_1/p_2) > 0$, the proportion of the population that works in sector 1 increases with an increase in the relative price of skill 1.

We now derive the sectoral distribution of skills and earnings, and their distribution in the whole economy. The population densities of the two skills are, respectively,

$$f_1(s_1) = \int_0^\infty f(s_1, s_2)\, ds_2, \qquad f_2(s_2) = \int_0^\infty f(s_1, s_2)\, ds_1,$$

while the density of skill 1 in sector 1 is

$$f_1(s_1 \,|\, D = 1) = \frac{1}{\pi} \int_0^{s_1 p_1 / p_2} f(s_1, s_2)\, ds_2,$$

and the density of skill 2 in sector 2 is

$$f_2(s_2 \,|\, D = 0) = \frac{1}{1 - \pi} \int_0^{s_2 p_2 / p_1} f(s_1, s_2)\, ds_1 .$$

Thus, the distribution of skills in each sector differs from the population distribution of skills. Since $W_j = p_j S_j$, the density of earnings in the two sectors is respectively

$$g_1(w) = \frac{1}{p_1} f_1(w/p_1 \,|\, D = 1),$$

$$g_2(w) = \frac{1}{p_2} f_2(w/p_2 \,|\, D = 0),$$

whereas the density of earnings in the economy is the weighted average

$$g(w) = \pi g_1(w) + (1-\pi) g_2(w).$$

Now suppose that the first two moments of the joint distribution of log of skills exist and let

$$\mathrm{E}\begin{pmatrix} \ln S_1 \\ \ln S_2 \end{pmatrix} = \begin{pmatrix} \mu_1 \\ \mu_2 \end{pmatrix}, \qquad \mathrm{Var}\begin{pmatrix} \ln S_1 \\ \ln S_2 \end{pmatrix} = \begin{bmatrix} \sigma_1^2 & \sigma_{12} \\ \sigma_{21} & \sigma_2^2 \end{bmatrix}.$$

Then $\ln W_j$ may be represented as

$$\ln W_j = \ln p_j + \ln S_j = \ln p_j + \mu_j + U_j, \qquad j = 1, 2,$$

where $U_j = \ln S_j - \mu_j$ is a zero-mean random error with variance σ_j^2. Therefore, sector 1 is chosen $(D = 1)$ whenever

$$0 < \ln W_1 - \ln W_2 = \ln p_1 - \ln p_2 + \mu_1 - \mu_2 + U_1 - U_2,$$

that is, whenever

$$V = U_1 - U_2 > \ln \frac{p_2}{p_1} + \mu_2 - \mu_1 = c,$$

where the random variable V has mean zero and variance equal to $\sigma_1^2 + \sigma_2^2 - 2\sigma_{12}$.

Notice that U_1 may be represented more conveniently as $U_1 = \alpha_1 V + U_*$, where U_* is a zero-mean random variable uncorrelated with V and

$$\alpha_1 = \frac{\mathrm{Cov}(V, U_1)}{\mathrm{Var}\, V} = \frac{\mathrm{Var}\, U_1 - \mathrm{Cov}(U_2, U_1)}{\mathrm{Var}\, V}.$$

It is easily verified that U_2 can be represented as $U_2 = \alpha_2 V + U_*$, where $\alpha_2 = \alpha_1 - 1$. Hence

$$\begin{aligned} \ln S_j &= \mu_j + \alpha_j V + U_*, \\ \ln W_j &= \ln p_j + \mu_j + \alpha_j V + U_*, \qquad j = 1, 2. \end{aligned}$$

Therefore

$$\begin{aligned} \mathrm{E}(\ln S_j \mid D = 1) &= \mu_j + \alpha_j\, \mathrm{E}(V \mid V > c) + \mathrm{E}(U_* \mid V > c), \\ \mathrm{E}(\ln W_j \mid D = 1) &= \ln p_j + \mu_j + \alpha_j\, \mathrm{E}(V \mid V > c) + \mathrm{E}(U_* \mid V > c), \end{aligned}$$

and

$$\begin{aligned} \mathrm{Var}(\ln S_j \mid D = 1) &= \mathrm{Var}(\ln W_j \mid D = 1) \\ &= \alpha_j^2\, \mathrm{Var}(V \mid V > c) + \mathrm{Var}(U_* \mid V > c) - 2\alpha_j\, \mathrm{Cov}(V, U_* \mid V > c), \end{aligned}$$

where $\mathrm{E}(V \mid V > c) \geq \mathrm{E}\, V = 0$ and $\mathrm{E}(U_* \mid V > c) \geq \mathrm{E}\, U_* = 0$. Thus, the properties of the Roy model, in particular the effects of changes in relative prices on the population and sectoral distributions of skills and earnings, depend on α_1, α_2, and the conditional distribution of V and U_* given $V > c$. The case when $\alpha_1 > 0$ is regarded as the standard case for it implies that $\mathrm{E}(\ln S_1 \mid D = 1) \geq \mu_1$, that is, people who work in sector 1 have on average a higher level of (log of) skill 1.

Assume, as in Roy's original paper, that the distribution of skills is log-normal. This implies that V and U_* are independent, and therefore

$$\mathrm{E}(\ln W_1 \mid D=1) = \ln p_1 + \mu_1 + \alpha_1 \, \mathrm{E}(V \mid V > c).$$

Further, under the normalization $\mathrm{Var}\, V = 1$, we have

$$\begin{aligned}\mathrm{Var}(\ln W_1 \mid D=1) &= \alpha_1^2 \, \mathrm{Var}(V \mid V > c) + \mathrm{Var}\, U_* \\ &= \sigma_1^2 [\rho_1^2 \, \mathrm{Var}(V \mid V > c) + 1 - \rho_1^2],\end{aligned}$$

where $\rho_1 = \mathrm{Corr}(V, U_1) = \alpha_1/\sigma_1$. The effects of a change in skill prices on the conditional distribution of log of earnings are easily derived from the results in Appendix C.9. In particular, because

$$\mathrm{E}(V \mid V > c) = \frac{\phi(c)}{1-\Phi(c)} = \lambda(-c)$$

and

$$\mathrm{Var}(V \mid V > c) = 1 + c\,\lambda(-c) - \lambda(-c)^2,$$

it follows that

$$\mathrm{E}(V \mid V > c) > \max(0, c), \qquad 0 < \mathrm{Var}(V \mid V > c) < 1,$$

and

$$0 < \frac{d}{dc} \mathrm{E}(V \mid V > c) < 1, \qquad \frac{d}{dc} \mathrm{Var}(V \mid V > c) < 0.$$

Although the qualitative results obtained for the log-normal Roy model are not valid for a general distribution of (U_1, U_2), many of them remain valid when the distribution of $V = U_1 - U_2$ is *log-concave*, that is, its density $f(v)$ is such that

$$\ln f(\lambda v + (1-\lambda)v') \geq \lambda \ln f(v) + (1-\lambda) \ln f(v'),$$

for all v, v' in the support of V and $0 \leq \lambda \leq 1$. If V is log-concave and the above inequality is strict for $0 < \lambda < 1$, then V is said to be *strictly log-concave*. Notice that log skills need not be log-concave, just their difference. The class of log-concave distributions includes the linear exponential family, the beta with bounded density, the logistic, the Gumbel and the Box–Tiao family (Section 16.1.1) with density proportional to $\exp(-|v|^p)$ for $p = 1, 2, \ldots$.

Heckman and Honorè (1990) establish the following result.

Theorem 18.1 *If the random variable V is log-concave, then*

$$0 \leq \frac{d}{dc} \mathrm{E}(V \mid V > c) \leq 1, \qquad 0 \leq \frac{d}{dc} \mathrm{E}(V \mid V \leq c) \leq 1,$$

$$\frac{d}{dc} \mathrm{Var}(V \mid V > c) \leq 0, \qquad \frac{d}{dc} \mathrm{Var}(V \mid V \leq c) \geq 0.$$

If V is strictly log-concave, then the inequalities are strict, except possibly at the boundaries of the support.

Proof. See Heckman and Honorè (1990), Proposition 1. □

18.3 LEAST SQUARES ESTIMATION

We now consider the case when $\mu_i = \beta^\top X_i$ in the latent regression model (18.1). The statistical problem is estimation and inference about the regression parameter β from data subject to truncation or censoring. We first examine the nature of the bias that results from using OLS to estimate β. We then show that, if the conditional distribution of the latent response Y_i^* has a known shape, then β can be estimated consistently by nonlinear least squares (NLLS). It is worth stressing that the OLS estimator retains all its desirable properties if interest is not in the CMF of the latent response Y_i^* but only in the BLP of the observed Y_i.

18.3.1 OLS ESTIMATION

Let $(X_1, Y_1, D_1), \ldots, (X_n, Y_n, D_n)$ be the observed data, which we treat as a set of i.i.d. random vectors, and let

$$\hat{\beta} = (\sum_i X_i X_i^\top)^{-1} \sum_i X_i Y_i$$

be the OLS estimator in the regression of Y_i on X_i. The sampling properties of $\hat{\beta}$ as an estimator of β depend on both the distribution of the latent variable Y_i^* and the nature of the truncation/censoring process.

Consider first the truncated case, where $D_i = 1$ for all i. Conditionally on the observed covariates, we have

$$\mathrm{E}\,\hat{\beta} = (\sum_i X_i X_i^\top)^{-1} \sum_i X_i \,\mathrm{E}(Y_i \,|\, D_i = 1),$$

where $\mathrm{E}(Y_i \,|\, D_i = 1)$ is given by (18.2). Assuming that $\mu_i = \beta^\top X_i$, we then have

$$\mathrm{E}\,\hat{\beta} = \beta + \sigma(\sum_i X_i X_i^\top)^{-1} \sum_i X_i \,\psi_i, \tag{18.7}$$

where $\psi_i = \mathrm{E}(V_i \,|\, c_i < V_i < d_i)$. Hence, $\hat{\beta}$ is a biased estimator of β in general. Since the bias does not vanish asymptotically, $\hat{\beta}$ is also inconsistent for β. The bias arises because we only observe a portion of the conditional distribution of Y_i^*. It is useful to interpret the bias of the OLS estimator as an omitted variables bias due to omission from the regression of the term ψ_i, which is correlated with X_i in general (Heckman 1979).

To get further insight into the properties of the OLS estimator in the case of truncated data, consider the partial derivative of $\mathrm{E}(Y_i \,|\, D_i = 1)$ with respect to μ_i

$$\frac{\partial}{\partial \mu_i} \mathrm{E}(Y_i \,|\, D_i = 1) = 1 + \sigma \frac{\partial \psi_i}{\partial \mu_i}.$$

In the Gaussian case we get

$$\frac{\partial \psi_i}{\partial \mu_i} = -\frac{1}{\sigma} \left\{ \frac{d_i\,\phi(d_i) - c_i\,\phi(c_i)}{\Phi(d_i) - \Phi(c_i)} + \left[\frac{\phi(d_i) - \phi(c_i)}{\Phi(d_i) - \Phi(c_i)} \right]^2 \right\}.$$

Thus, from the results in Appendix C.9,

$$\frac{\partial}{\partial \mu_i} \mathrm{E}(Y_i \mid D_i = 1) = \frac{\operatorname{Var}(Y_i \mid D_i = 1)}{\sigma^2} = \frac{\operatorname{Var}(Y_i \mid D_i = 1)}{\operatorname{Var}(Y_i^*)}.$$

In the special case when $\mu_i = \beta^\top X_i$, it follows that $\mathrm{E}\,\hat{\beta}$ and β have the same sign. However, $|\mathrm{E}\,\hat{\beta}| < |\beta|$ since $\operatorname{Var}(Y_i \mid D_i = 1) < \operatorname{Var} Y_i^*$, a result known as the *attenuation bias* due to truncation. Because increasing the degree of truncation reduces $\operatorname{Var}(Y_i \mid D_i = 1)$, the attenuation bias rises with truncation.

The same qualitative result holds for the censored case. Under our set of assumptions, and conditionally on the covariates, the mean of the observed data is given by (18.6), which is different from $\beta^\top X_i$ in general. Thus, the OLS estimator is again biased and inconsistent for β in general. The next result by Chung and Goldberger (1984) shows that, in the special case when the "reverse regression" $\mathrm{E}(X_i \mid Y_i^*)$ is also linear in Y_i^*, the OLS estimator is approximately proportional to β in large samples.

Theorem 18.2 *Let $\hat{\beta}_n$ be the vector of slope coefficients in an OLS regression of the censored observations Y_i on X_i. If $\mathrm{E}(Y_i^* \mid X_i) = \alpha + \beta^\top X_i$ and $\mathrm{E}(X_i \mid Y_i^*) = \gamma + \delta Y_i^*$, then $\hat{\beta}_n \xrightarrow{\mathrm{p}} \eta\beta$, where $\eta = \operatorname{Cov}(Y_i^*, Y_i)/\operatorname{Var} Y_i^*$.*

Proof. Since $\beta = (\operatorname{Var} X_i)^{-1} \operatorname{Cov}(X_i, Y_i^*)$, we have

$$\delta = \frac{\operatorname{Cov}(X_i, Y_i^*)}{\operatorname{Var} Y_i^*} = \frac{1}{\operatorname{Var} Y_i^*} (\operatorname{Var} X_i)\beta.$$

Next notice that

$$\operatorname{Cov}(X_i, Y_i) = \mathrm{E}\{E[(X_i - \mu_X)Y_i \mid Y_i^*]\} = \mathrm{E}[Y_i\, \mathrm{E}(X_i - \mu_X \mid Y_i^*)],$$

where $\mu_X = \mathrm{E}\, X_i$ and

$$E(X_i - \mu_X \mid Y_i^*) = \mathrm{E}(X_i \mid Y_i^*) - \mu_X = \delta(Y_i^* - \mathrm{E}\, Y_i^*).$$

Hence

$$\operatorname{Cov}(X_i, Y_i) = \mathrm{E}[\delta Y_i(Y_i^* - \mathrm{E}\, Y_i^*)] = \delta \operatorname{Cov}(Y_i^*, Y_i) = \eta(\operatorname{Var} X_i)\beta,$$

where $\eta = \operatorname{Cov}(Y_i^*, Y_i)/(\operatorname{Var} Y_i^*)$. Therefore $\hat{\beta}_n \xrightarrow{\mathrm{p}} (\operatorname{Var} X_i)^{-1} \operatorname{Cov}(X_i, Y_i) = \eta\beta$, where we used the fact that censoring does not affect the variance of X_i. □

Under the conditions of Theorem 18.2, $\hat{\beta}_{jn}/\hat{\beta}_{hn} \xrightarrow{\mathrm{p}} \beta_j/\beta_h$, that is, the ratio of elements of β is consistently estimated by the ratio of the corresponding elements of the OLS coefficient vector. One case where the conditions of the theorem are satisfied is when the joint distribution of (X_i, Y_i^*) is Gaussian. Notice that η in Theorem 18.2 is the slope of the BLP of Y_i given Y_i^*.

18.3.2 NONLINEAR LEAST SQUARES

If $D_i = 1\{a_i < Y_i^* < b_i\}$ then, assuming a latent linear model for Y_i^*, we have

$$h_i^*(\theta) = \mathrm{E}(Y_i \mid X_i, D_i = 1) = \beta^\top X_i + \sigma \psi_i(\theta)$$

and

$$h_i(\theta) = \mathrm{E}(Y_i \mid X_i) = h_i^*(\theta)\,[F(d_i(\theta)) - F(c_i(\theta))] + a_i\, F(c_i(\theta)) + b_i\,[1 - F(d_i(\theta))],$$

where $\theta = (\beta, \sigma)$, $\psi_i(\theta) = \mathrm{E}(V_i \mid X_i, D_i = 1)$, $c_i(\theta) = (a_i - \beta^\top X_i)/\sigma$ and $d_i(\theta) = (b_i - \beta^\top X_i)/\sigma$. This suggests estimating the model parameters by solving either the NLLS problem

$$\min_{\theta \in \Theta} \sum_{i=1}^{n} D_i [Y_i - h_i^*(\theta)]^2, \tag{18.8}$$

or the NLLS problem

$$\min_{\theta \in \Theta} \sum_{i=1}^{n} [Y_i - h_i(\theta)]^2, \tag{18.9}$$

where $\Theta = \Re^k \times \Re_+$. If the assumed model is correctly specified and identifiable, then the resulting estimators of θ can be shown to be $\sqrt{n}$-consistent and asymptotically normal under general conditions.

Because Y_i is heteroskedastic, asymptotic efficiency gains may be obtained by using weighted NLLS instead. If $v_i^*(\theta) = \mathrm{Var}(Y_i \mid X_i, D_i = 1)$ and $v_i(\theta) = \mathrm{Var}(Y_i \mid X_i)$, then the weighted counterparts of problems (18.8) and (18.9) are

$$\min_{\theta \in \Theta} \sum_{i=1}^{n} D_i \frac{[Y_i - h_i^*(\theta)]^2}{v_i^*(\theta)},$$

or the NLLS problem

$$\min_{\theta \in \Theta} \sum_{i=1}^{n} \frac{[Y_i - h_i(\theta)]^2}{v_i(\theta)}.$$

All these estimators rely crucially on the knowledge of the functional form of the conditional mean and possibly the conditional variance of Y_i, and therefore their sampling properties depend on the validity of the assumptions made about the probability distribution of the latent variable Y_i^*. Linearity of the CMF of Y_i^* is not enough and inconsistencies may now arise also from heteroskedasticity or failure to correctly specify the shape of the probability distribution of Y_i^*.

18.3.3 TWO-STEP ESTIMATION

To keep the presentation as simple as possible, consider the case when data from a Gaussian latent linear model are left-censored at zero, that is, $a_i = 0$ and $b_i = \infty$ for all i. Since in this case $c_i = -\alpha^\top X_i$, where $\alpha = \beta/\sigma$, we may represent the positive values of Y_i as

$$Y_i = \beta^\top X_i + \sigma\, \lambda_i(\alpha) + U_i, \tag{18.10}$$

where $\lambda_i(\alpha) = \lambda(\alpha^\top X_i)$ and $U_i = Y_i - \mathrm{E}(Y_i \mid X_i, D_i = 1)$ is a heteroskedastic regression error with zero mean conditionally on X_i. The regression representation (18.10) suggests estimating the model parameters $\theta = (\beta, \sigma)$ by a simple two-step procedure.

1. Estimate α by probit using D_i as the response variable. This corresponds to estimating the probability that $Y_i > 0$ conditionally on X_i.
2. Estimate β and σ by an OLS regression of the positive values of Y_i on X_i and $\tilde{\lambda}_i = \lambda_i(\tilde{\alpha})$, where $\tilde{\alpha}$ denotes the probit estimate of α.

Despite its simplicity, there are a number of problems with this estimator. First, the two-step approach only works for censored data, as it depends on the possibility of estimating the probability of censoring in the first stage. Second, because the two-step estimator relies crucially on the knowledge of the functional form of $\mathrm{E}(Y_i \mid X_i, D_i = 1)$, it is only consistent for θ if the Gaussian latent linear model is correctly specified. Violations of the model assumptions, such as heteroskedasticity or departures from the Gaussian distribution, lead to inconsistent estimates. Third, the two-step estimator is asymptotically less efficient than the weighted NLLS estimators discussed in the previous section. Fourth, care is needed in estimating its sampling variance.

To see the last point, notice that the two-step method is really based on the regression equation

$$Y_i = \beta^\top X_i + \sigma\tilde{\lambda}_i + U_i^*,$$

where $U_i^* = U_i + \sigma(\lambda_i - \tilde{\lambda}_i)$ is a heteroskedastic regression error with zero mean conditionally on X_i. If $\hat{\theta}^* = (\hat{\beta}^*, \hat{\sigma}^*)$ denotes the two-step estimator, then consistent estimates of the sampling variance of $\hat{\beta}^*$ may be obtained by the heteroskedasticity robust methods discussed in Section 7.5.1.

18.4 ML ESTIMATION

Least squares methods for truncated/censored data require specifying the conditional distribution of the latent variable Y_i^* in order to obtain the conditional mean and possibly the conditional variance of the observed response Y_i. An alternative, therefore, is to apply the method of ML directly.

Up to an additive constant, the log-likelihood for a truncated sample is of the form

$$L(\theta) = \sum_1 \ln g(Y_i \mid D_i = 1),$$

where θ is the vector of model parameters, $\sum_1$ denotes summation over the observations for which $D_i = 1$, and the conditional density of Y_i was derived in Section 18.1.1. By the argument in Example 4.11, the log-likelihood for a censored sample is instead of the form

$$\begin{aligned} L(\theta) &= \sum_1 \ln[g(Y_i \mid D_i = 1)\ \Pr\{D_i = 1\}] + \sum_0 \ln \Pr\{D_i = 0\} \\ &= \sum_1 \ln g(Y_i \mid D_i = 1) + [\sum_0 \ln \Pr\{D_i = 0\} + \sum_1 \ln \Pr\{D_i = 1\}], \end{aligned} \tag{18.11}$$

where $\sum_0$ denotes summation over the observations for which $D_i = 0$. Notice that this log-likelihood is the sum of the log-likelihood for the truncated sample and the log-likelihood of a binary response model.

The nature of the estimators obtained and their sampling properties depend crucially on the assumption made about the distribution of the latent variable Y_i^*. The most common assumption is that, conditionally on X_i, Y_i^* obeys a classical Gaussian linear model.

18.4.1 GAUSSIAN ML ESTIMATORS

Suppose that $Y_i^* \sim \mathcal{N}(\beta^\top X_i, \sigma^2)$ conditionally on X_i and, for simplicity, consider the case when $D_i = 1\{Y_i^* > 0\}$. Because

$$\Pr\{D_i = 1\} = 1 - \Phi\left(-\frac{\beta^\top X_i}{\sigma}\right) = \Phi\left(\frac{\beta^\top X_i}{\sigma}\right),$$

the log-likelihood for a truncated sample is

$$L(\theta) = \sum_1 \left[-\frac{1}{2}\ln\sigma^2 + \ln\phi\left(\frac{Y_i - \beta^\top X_i}{\sigma}\right) - \ln\Phi\left(\frac{\beta^\top X_i}{\sigma}\right)\right],$$

where $\theta = (\beta, \sigma^2)$. The resulting ML estimator $\tilde{\theta} = (\tilde{\beta}, \tilde{\sigma}^2)$ is a root of the likelihood equations

$$0 = \frac{\partial L}{\partial \beta} = \frac{1}{\sigma^2}\sum_1 [Y_i - \beta^\top X_i - \sigma\lambda_i(\alpha)]\, X_i,$$

$$0 = \frac{\partial L}{\partial \sigma^2} = \frac{1}{2\sigma^2}\sum_1 \left[\left(\frac{Y_i - \beta^\top X_i}{\sigma}\right)^2 + \alpha^\top X_i\lambda_i(\alpha) - 1\right],$$

where $\alpha = \beta/\sigma$ and $\lambda_i(\alpha) = \lambda(\alpha^\top X_i)$. The first equation gives

$$\tilde{\beta} = (\sum_1 X_i X_i^\top)^{-1}\sum_1 X_i(Y_i - \tilde{\sigma}\tilde{\lambda}_i) = \hat{\beta} - \tilde{\sigma}(\sum_1 X_i X_i^\top)^{-1}\sum_1 X_i\tilde{\lambda}_i, \qquad (18.12)$$

where $\hat{\beta}$ is the OLS estimator applied to the observations for which $D_i = 1$ and $\tilde{\lambda}_i = \lambda_i(\tilde{\alpha})$. Premultiplying the first equation by the transpose of $\tilde{\beta}/(2\tilde{\sigma}^2)$ and adding the result to the second equation gives the ML estimator of σ^2

$$\tilde{\sigma}^2 = \frac{1}{n_1}\sum_1 (Y_i - \tilde{\beta}^\top X_i)Y_i, \qquad (18.13)$$

where n_1 denotes the number of cases for which $D_i = 1$.

Formulae (18.12) and (18.13) suggest a simple iterative least squares method for computing the ML estimate of β. Given an initial estimate $\beta^{(r)}$, an estimate $\sigma^{(r)}$ of σ is computed using (18.13). An updated estimate of β is then obtained by subtracting from $\hat{\beta}$ the OLS coefficient in a regression of $\sigma^{(r)}\lambda_i(\alpha^{(r)})$ on X_i, with $\alpha^{(r)} = \beta^{(r)}/\sigma^{(r)}$. The comparison with (18.7) shows that this adjustment may be interpreted as a way of correcting the OLS estimator for its bias. The analogue of this method for the case of a censored sample is easily seen to be an application of the EM method discussed in Appendix B.4.

Turning to the asymptotic properties of the Gaussian ML estimator, Amemiya (1973) showed that it is $\sqrt{n}$-consistent and asymptotically normal provided that:

1. β and σ^2 belong to a compact parameter space;
2. $\{V_i\}$ is a sequence of i.i.d. $\mathcal{N}(0,1)$ random variables;
3. the X_i are uniformly bounded;
4. $n^{-1}\sum_1 X_i X_i^\top \xrightarrow{\text{p}} P$, a finite p.d. matrix.

In general, if the distribution of the errors in the latent linear model (18.1) is not Gaussian, or is Gaussian but heteroskedastic, then the Gaussian ML estimator is inconsistent. This result is very different from the case of a classical linear model and arises from the fact that the conditional mean of the likelihood score is no longer equal to zero under these two types of model misspecification. To see this, notice that the Gaussian score for β is of the form

$$\frac{\partial L}{\partial \beta} = \frac{1}{\sigma} \sum_{i=1}^{n} s_i(\theta)\, X_i,$$

where

$$s_i(\theta) = D_i \left[\frac{Y_i - \beta^\top X_i}{\sigma} - \lambda\left(\frac{\beta^\top X_i}{\sigma} \right) \right].$$

If the errors in the latent linear model are i.i.d. with common distribution function $F \neq \Phi$, then

$$\mathrm{E}[s_i(\theta) \mid X_i = x] = \int_{-\alpha^\top x}^{\infty} v\, f(v)\, dv - \lambda(\alpha^\top x)\, [1 - F(-\alpha^\top x)],$$

which is different from zero for all α. A similar result is obtained if the latent errors are Gaussian but heteroskedastic.

The available evidence (see e.g. Hurd 1979 and Arabmazar & Schmidt 1981, 1982) shows that the bias of Gaussian ML estimators under heteroskedasticity or non-normality can be very large, particularly if the scale parameter is unknown and the degree of censoring is high. The estimator for the censored model is generally less biased than the one for the truncated model, which suggests that the censored observations should be used whenever available. However, most of the available Monte Carlo studies restrict attention to symmetric distributions and do not investigate explicitly the relationship between the bias and the skewness and tail weight of the error distribution.

18.4.2 AN ALTERNATIVE PARAMETRIZATION

The parametrization considered so far, namely $\theta = (\beta, \sigma^2)$, is of course not unique. A convenient alternative is to parametrize the model in terms of $\eta = (\alpha, \gamma)$, where $\alpha = \beta/\sigma$ and $\gamma = 1/\sigma$. This is in fact the parametrization initially adopted by Tobin

(1958). The transformation $\eta = g(\theta)$ is clearly one-to-one with nonsingular Jacobian matrix

$$G(\theta) = \frac{1}{\sigma^2} \begin{bmatrix} \sigma & -\beta \\ 0 & -1 \end{bmatrix}.$$

Under the new parametrization, the Gaussian log-likelihood for the truncated model is

$$L(\eta) = \sum_1 [\ln \gamma + \ln \phi(\gamma Y_i - \alpha^\top X_i) - \ln \Phi(\alpha^\top X_i)].$$

Because L is the sum of strictly concave functions, it is itself strictly concave. This implies that, if a maximum of L exists, then it is unique and standard iterative methods, such as NR or the method of scoring, always converge to it. Given ML estimates $\tilde{\alpha}$ and $\tilde{\gamma}$ of α and γ, the ML estimates of β and σ^2 are easily obtained as $\tilde{\beta} = \tilde{\alpha}/\tilde{\gamma}$ and $\tilde{\sigma}^2 = 1/\tilde{\gamma}^2$. The NR method requires the likelihood score and the Hessian of the log-likelihood. The components of the likelihood score are

$$\frac{\partial L}{\partial \alpha} = \sum_1 [\gamma Y_i - \alpha^\top X_i - \lambda_i(\alpha)] X_i,$$

$$\frac{\partial L}{\partial \gamma} = \frac{n_1}{\gamma} - \sum_1 (\gamma Y_i - \alpha^\top X_i) Y_i,$$

where $\lambda_i(\alpha) = \lambda(\alpha^\top X_i)$. The elements of the Hessian of L are

$$\frac{\partial^2 L}{\partial \alpha \partial \alpha^\top} = -\sum_1 [1 + \lambda_i^*(\alpha)]\, X_i X_i^\top,$$

$$\frac{\partial^2 L}{\partial \gamma \partial \alpha} = \sum_1 X_i Y_i,$$

$$\frac{\partial^2 L}{\partial \gamma^2} = -\frac{n_1}{\gamma^2} - \sum_1 Y_i^2,$$

where $\lambda_i^*(\alpha) = \lambda'(\alpha^\top X_i)$, with

$$\lambda'(v) = -\frac{\phi(v)}{\Phi(v)^2} [v\Phi(v) + \phi(v)] = -\frac{\phi(v)}{\Phi(v)^2} \int_{-\infty}^{v} \Phi(u)\, du < 0.$$

Under the new parametrization, the Gaussian log-likelihood for the censored model is instead

$$L(\eta) = \sum_1 [\ln \gamma + \ln \phi(\gamma Y_i - \alpha^\top X_i)] + \sum_0 \ln[1 - \Phi(\alpha^\top X_i)],$$

which is also a strictly concave function. In this case

$$\frac{\partial L}{\partial \alpha} = \sum_1 (\gamma Y_i - \alpha^\top X_i) X_i - \sum_0 \lambda_i(-\alpha) X_i$$

and

$$\frac{\partial^2 L}{\partial \alpha \partial \alpha^\top} = -\sum_1 X_i X_i^\top + \sum_0 \lambda_i^*(-\alpha)\, X_i X_i^\top,$$

while the other components of the likelihood score and of the Hessian of L are exactly as in the truncated case.

18.4.3 NONGAUSSIAN ML ESTIMATORS

There are cases when the Gaussian model is not a good representation of the distribution of the latent response. One important example is the case of censored duration data.

For concreteness, consider a random sample of individuals who enter unemployment at time t_0 and are followed for a period of length b_i. At the end of the follow-up period, some of the people in the sample may have completed their unemployment spell, but some may have not. The actual length of a completed unemployment spell is only observed in the first case, whereas in the second case we only know that this length must be at least equal to b_i. If the non-negative random variable Y_i^* denotes the unobserved duration of a completed unemployment spell, then the observed duration may be represented by $Y_i = \min(Y_i^*, b_i)$. Thus, the log-likelihood for a censored sample has exactly the same form as (18.11) with $D_i = 1\{Y_i^* < b_i\}$.

The fact that spell lengths are non-negative has two important implications. First, the Gaussian distribution is not a good model for such data. More appropriate models are, for example, the exponential or the Weibull distribution. Second, the distribution of the data may equivalently be characterized in terms of the hazard function $h(y) = f(y)/S(y)$, where $S(y) = 1 - F(y) = \exp[-H(y)]$ is the survivor function and $H(y) = \int_0^y h(u)\,du$ is the integrated hazard. Because $\Pr\{D_i = 0\} = S(b_i)$, the log-likelihood for a censored sample may be written

$$L(\theta) = \sum_{1} \ln[h(Y_i)\, S(Y_i)] + \sum_{0} \ln S(b_i) = \sum_{i=1}^{n} [D_i \ln h(Y_i) - H(Y_i)],$$

where $h(y) = \gamma$ and $H(y) = \gamma y$ in the exponential case, and $h(y) = \gamma \alpha y^{\alpha-1}$ and $H(y) = \gamma y^{\alpha}$ in the Weibull case.

The proportional hazard model introduced in Example 7.18 provides a simple way of allowing h to depend on a k-vector of covariates X_i. In this case, the scale parameter γ varies across sample units and is specified as $\gamma_i(\beta) = \exp(\beta^\top X_i)$. The model may be further generalized to the case when the follow-up period is stochastic but distributed independently of Y_i^*. The resulting log-likelihood for a censored sample from the exponential model is of the form

$$L(\beta) = \sum_{i=1}^{n} [D_i \ln \gamma_i(\beta) - \gamma_i(\beta)\, Y_i],$$

where $Y_i = \min(Y_i^*, b_i)$ are the observed durations, while for a censored sample from the Weibull model it is of the form

$$L(\theta) = \sum_{1} [\ln \gamma_i(\beta) + \ln \alpha + (\alpha - 1) \ln Y_i] - \sum_{i=1}^{n} \gamma_i(\beta)\, Y_i^{\alpha}, \qquad \theta = (\alpha, \beta).$$

18.5 SEMIPARAMETRIC ESTIMATION

The lack of robustness of ML estimators in models with truncation/censoring motivates the search for consistent estimators based on weak distributional assumptions. This section considers three alternative approaches to estimation of the standard tobit model, that is, a latent linear model with fixed left-censoring at $a_i = 0$. The first approach relies on independence between the covariates and the latent regression errors, the second approach relies on linearity of the median regression function or, more generally, of the regression quantiles of the latent response variable Y_i^*, while the third approach relies on symmetry of the conditional distribution of Y_i^*.

18.5.1 SEMIPARAMETRIC LEAST SQUARES

If Y_i^* were observed, then β could equivalently be estimated by minimizing the OLS criterion $\sum_i (Y_i^* - \beta^\top X_i)^2$ or by solving the OLS normal equations $0 = \sum_i X_i(Y_i^* - \beta^\top X_i)$. The methods discussed in this section are derived by modifying either the OLS criterion or the OLS normal equations to account for censoring.

Our key assumption is that the latent regression errors are independent of the covariates and i.i.d. with a continuous distribution function F. For a given parameter value β, we denote by $\tilde{F}(u;\beta)$ the Kaplan–Meier (KM) estimate of the distribution function of the regression residuals $U_i(\beta) = Y_i - \beta^\top X_i$, $i = 1, \ldots, n$. The basic idea is to replace sample averages by expectations with respect to the KM estimate $\tilde{F}(u;\beta)$ which, from Section 2.3.2, is the natural nonparametric estimate of F in case of censoring.

Miller (1976) suggested estimating β by minimizing the sum-of-squares

$$Q(\beta) = n \int u^2 \, d\tilde{F}(u;\beta).$$

In the absence of censoring, the problem reduces to classical OLS. The sampling properties of this estimator are difficult to obtain because the objective function Q is discontinuous. In general, consistency only holds under strong restrictions on the censoring process.

Buckley and James (1979) modify instead the OLS normal equations by replacing each censored observation by its conditional expectation computed from the KM estimate $\tilde{F}(u;\beta)$. Notice that

$$\mathrm{E}(Y_i^* \mid X_i) = \mathrm{E}[D_i Y_i + (1 - D_i)\,\mathrm{E}(Y_i^* \mid Y_i^* > 0, X_i) \mid X_i],$$

where

$$\mathrm{E}(Y_i^* \mid Y_i^* > 0, X_i) = \beta^\top X_i + \frac{\int_{-\beta^\top X_i}^{\infty} u \, dF(u)}{1 - F(-\beta^\top X_i)}.$$

Replacing $F(u)$ by the KM estimate gives, as an estimate of $\mathrm{E}(Y_i^* \mid Y_i^* > 0, X_i)$,

$$\hat{Y}_i(\beta) = \beta^\top X_i + \sum_{k=1}^{n} D_k w_{ik}(\beta)(Y_k - \beta^\top X_k),$$

where

$$w_{ik}(\beta) = \begin{cases} v_k(\beta)/[1 - \tilde{F}(-\beta^\top X_i;\beta)], & \text{if } U_i(\beta) < U_k(\beta), \\ 0, & \text{otherwise,} \end{cases}$$

and $v_k(\beta)$ is the probability mass assigned by the KM estimate to the uncensored residual $U_i(\beta)$. If $\sum_i X_i X_i^\top$ is a p.d. matrix, replacing the censored values of the response by $\hat{Y}_i(\beta)$ in the OLS normal equations leads to the implicit equation

$$\beta = (\sum_{i=1}^{n} X_i X_i^\top)^{-1} \sum_{i=1}^{n} X_i [D_i Y_i + (1 - D_i)\hat{Y}_i(\beta)],$$

which can be solved iteratively by successive substitions. The rth step of this iterative scheme is of the form

$$\beta^{(r+1)} = (\sum_{i=1}^{n} X_i X_i^\top)^{-1} \sum_{i=1}^{n} X_i [D_i Y_i + (1 - D_i)\hat{Y}_i(\beta^{(r)})].$$

This approach may be viewed as a semiparametric version of the EM algorithm (Appendix B.4). Consistency and asymptotic normality of a slightly modified version of the Buckley–James estimator have been obtained by Ritov (1990) and Lai and Ying (1991).

A third approach, proposed by Horowitz (1986), is based on the fact that integrating by parts gives

$$\begin{aligned} \mathrm{E}(Y_i \mid X_i) &= \mathrm{E}(Y_i^* \mid Y_i^* \geq 0, X_i)\ \Pr(Y_i^* > 0 \mid X_i) \\ &= \beta^\top X_i [1 - F(-\beta^\top X_i)] + \int_{-\beta^\top X_i}^{\infty} u\, dF(u) \\ &= \int_{-\beta^\top X_i}^{\infty} [1 - F(u)]\, du. \end{aligned}$$

This suggests minimizing with respect to β the least squares criterion

$$\sum_{i=1}^{n} \left\{ Y_i - \int_{-\beta^\top X_i}^{\infty} [1 - \tilde{F}(u;\beta)]\, du \right\}^2.$$

Horowitz (1986) establishes consistency of the resulting estimator under the assumption that the parameter space is finite and the latent regression errors have bounded support and are distributed independently of X_i.

18.5.2 QUANTILE RESTRICTIONS

When there is less than 50 percent censoring, the sample median is consistent for the population median, whereas the sample mean is not consistent for the population mean. Powell (1984) exploited this idea to construct a semiparametric estimator for the censored regression model.

Suppose that the conditional median of the latent response Y_i^* is equal to $\beta^\top X_i$. To derive the conditional median of the observed data Y_i, notice that if $\beta^\top X_i > 0$, then $\mathrm{Med}(Y_i \mid X_i) = \beta^\top X_i$, whereas if $\beta^\top X_i \leq 0$, then $\mathrm{Med}(Y_i \mid X_i) = 0$. Thus

$$\mathrm{Med}(Y_i \mid X_i) = \max(0, \beta^\top X_i).$$

This observation leads to the *censored least absolute deviations (CLAD) estimator*, defined as a solution to the nonlinear LAD problem

$$\min_{\beta \in \Re^k} \sum_{i=1}^{n} |Y_i - \max(0, \beta^\top X_i)|.$$

Unlike the standard LAD criterion, that defining the CLAD estimator is not convex in β.

It can be shown that the CLAD estimator is $\sqrt{n}$-consistent and asymptotically normal provided that the conditional median of Y_i^* is linear in X_i. Notice that homoskedasticity is not required. In addition to the original proof by Powell (1984), an alternative proof based on the arguments in Section 15.3.3 may be found in Pollard (1990). A consistent estimate of the asymptotic variance of the CLAD estimator $\hat\beta_n$ is $\widehat{\mathrm{AV}}(\hat\beta_n) = \hat B_n^{-1}\,\hat C_n\,\hat B_n^{-1}$, where

$$\hat B_n = n^{-1}\sum_{i=1}^n 1\{\hat\beta_n^\top X_i > 0\}\,X_i X_i^\top,$$

$$\hat C_n = n^{-1}\sum_{i=1}^n \hat f_i(0\,|\,X_i)\;1\{\hat\beta_n^\top X_i > 0\}\,X_i X_i^\top,$$

and $\hat f_i(0\,|\,X_i)$ is a consistent estimate of the conditional density of the latent regression errors at the median.

For a generalization to the case of censored regression quantiles see Powell (1986a).

18.5.3 SYMMETRY RESTRICTIONS

The bias of the OLS estimator is due to the fact that, unless $\beta^\top X_i$ is large, the conditional distribution of Y_i is not centered at $\beta^\top X_i$. Powell (1986b) noticed that, if the distribution of the latent response Y_i^* were symmetric about $\beta^\top X_i$, and if β were known and $\beta^\top X_i > 0$, then the conditional symmetry of Y_i could be restored by artificially right-censoring Y_i at $2\beta^\top X_i$. In other words, the conditional distribution of the random variable

$$\tilde Y_i = 1\{\beta^\top X_i > 0\}\,\min(Y_i, 2\beta^\top X_i)$$

is centered at $\beta^\top X_i$, whereas the conditional distribution of the random variable

$$\eta_i(\beta) = \tilde Y_i - \beta^\top X_i = 1\{\beta^\top X_i > 0\}\,[\min(Y_i, 2\beta^\top X_i) - \beta^\top X_i]$$

is centered at zero. In particular, since $\mathrm{E}[\eta_i(\beta)\,|\,X_i] = 0$, we have that

$$\mathrm{E}\,\eta_i(\beta)\,X_i = 0.$$

This set of k unconditional moment conditions leads to the *symmetrically censored least squares (SCLS) estimator* $\tilde\beta_n$, defined as a root of the implicit equation

$$n^{-1}\sum_{i=1}^n \eta_i(\beta)\,X_i = 0.$$

The SCLS estimator $\tilde\beta_n$ may easily be computed by iterative WLS.

It can be shown that $\tilde\beta_n$ is $\sqrt{n}$-consistent and asymptotically normal provided that the latent regression errors are symmetrically distributed about zero (homoskedasticity is not required). It is easy to see that a consistent estimate of the asymptotic variance of $\hat\beta_n$ is $\widehat{\mathrm{AV}}(\tilde\beta_n) = \hat B_n^{-1}\,\hat C_n\,\hat B_n^{-1}$, where

$$\hat B_n = n^{-1}\sum_{i=1}^n 1\{\hat\beta_n^\top X_i > 0\}\,X_i X_i^\top$$

and

$$\hat C_n = n^{-1}\sum_{i=1}^n \eta_i(\hat\beta_n)^2\,X_i X_i^\top .$$

A version of the SCLS estimator is also available for the truncated regression model. A test of the symmetry assumption was proposed by Newey (1987). Newey's test compares the SCLS estimator with a more efficient estimator under symmetry.

Interestingly, neither the CLAD nor the SCLS estimator requires a knowledge of the scale parameter, which may help explain their robustness properties. However, Monte Carlo evidence indicates that both the CLAD and the SCLS estimator may be very inefficient relative to the ML estimator based on the correctly specified model. See Paarsch (1984) for the CLAD estimator and Powell (1986b) for the SCLS estimator. This raises the question of whether too much information is ignored in order to attain consistency under very general conditions.

18.6 BIVARIATE MODELS

The truncated and censored regression models discussed so far are models for univariate responses. Hence, they do not provide an adequate representation of various empirical problems involving more than one response variable, such as the joint decision whether to purchase and how much to purchase of a certain good, or the joint determination of wages and hours worked.

Example 18.3 Cragg (1971) first pointed out that the standard tobit model does not distinguish between the decision whether or not to purchase a certain good, represented by the binary indicator D_i, and the decision of how much to purchase, represented by the censored random variable Y_i (see also Blundell & Meghir 1987). To see this notice that both

$$\Pr\{D_i = 1\} = \Pr\{V_i > -\beta^\top X_i/\sigma\}$$

and

$$\mathrm{E}(Y_i \mid D_i = 1) = \beta^\top X_i + \sigma\,\mathrm{E}(V_i \mid V_i > -\beta^\top X_i/\sigma)$$

depend on the same set of variables and parameters. Thus, the model places strong restrictions on the way in which changes in one explanatory variable affect the probability of purchase and the mean of a positive value of Y_i. □

These considerations lead to multivariate models with truncation/censoring. Here we confine our attention to the bivariate case and discuss two classes of model. In the first class, one response variable is a binary indicator while the other is truncated or censored. In the second class, both variables are censored. Following Amemiya (1985), we refer to these two classes as, respectively, type-2 and type-3 tobit models.

18.6.1 TYPE-2 TOBIT MODELS

A *type-2 tobit model* consists of the following relationships

$$\begin{aligned} Y_{ij}^* &= \beta_j^\top X_i + \sigma_j V_{ij}, \qquad j = 1, 2, \\ Y_{i1} &= 1\{Y_{i1}^* > 0\}, \\ Y_{i2} &= Y_{i1}\, Y_{i2}^*, \end{aligned} \tag{18.14}$$

where V_{i1} and V_{i2} are correlated random variables distributed independently of X_i with zero mean and unit variance. Notice that Y_{i1}^* is unobservable, whereas Y_{i2}^* is observable only when $Y_{i1}^* > 0$. In general, Y_{i2}^* is the latent variable of interest, while Y_{i1}^* is only introduced to capture the sample selection process.

Example 18.4 The model of self-selection in Example 2.3 is a type-2 tobit model where Y_{i1} is a binary indicator equal to one or zero depending on whether or not a person works, Y_{i2} is the observed wage, and $Y_{i1}^* = Y_{i2}^* - W_i^* > 0$ is the difference between the offered wage Y_{i2}^* and the reservation wage W_i^*. □

For the type-2 tobit model, the mean of Y_{i1} is

$$\mathrm{E}\, Y_{i1} = \Pr\{Y_{i1} = 1\} = \Pr\{V_{i1} > -\alpha_1^\top X_i\},$$

where $\alpha_1 = \beta_1/\sigma_1$, while the conditional mean of the nonzero values of Y_{i2} is

$$\mathrm{E}(Y_{i2} \,|\, Y_{i1} = 1) = \beta_2^\top X_i + \sigma_2\, \mathrm{E}(V_{i2} \,|\, V_{i1} > -\alpha_1^\top X_i). \tag{18.15}$$

In both cases, the dependence on X_i has been omitted for simplicity. If the joint distribution of the latent regression errors has a known form, then the model parameters may be estimated by a two-step procedure, like in Section 18.3.3.

Example 18.5 If V_{i1} and V_{i2} are bivariate normal then $\mathrm{E}\, Y_{i1} = \Phi(\alpha_1^\top X_i)$ and

$$\begin{aligned} \mathrm{E}(Y_{i2} \,|\, Y_{i1} = 1) &= \beta_2^\top X_i + \sigma_2 \rho\, \mathrm{E}(V_{i1} \,|\, V_{i1} > -\alpha_1^\top X_i) \\ &= \beta_2^\top X_i + \sigma_2 \rho\, \lambda(\alpha_1^\top X_i), \end{aligned}$$

where $\rho = \mathrm{Corr}(V_{i1}, V_{i2})$ and $\lambda(v) = \phi(v)/\Phi(v)$. This suggests a two-step procedure where an estimate $\hat\alpha_1$ of α_1 is first obtained by probit, and then an estimate $\hat\beta_2$ of β_2 is obtained by an OLS regression of the positive values of Y_{i2} on X_i and $\hat\lambda_i = \lambda(\hat\alpha_1^\top X_i)$. As an estimate of σ_2^2, Heckman (1979) proposed

$$\hat\sigma_2^2 = n_1^{-1} \sum_1 [\hat U_{i2}^2 + \hat\gamma^2 \hat\lambda_i^(\hat\alpha_1^\top X_i + \hat\lambda_i)],$$

where n_1 is the number of cases for which $Y_{i1} = 1$, $\hat U_{i2} = Y_{i2} - \hat\beta_2^\top X_i - \hat\gamma \hat\lambda_i$ and $\hat\gamma$ is the OLS coefficient on the estimated correction term $\hat\lambda_i$. This estimate can be shown to be positive and consistent for σ_2^2 under the model assumptions. Finally, an estimate of the correlation coefficient ρ is given by $\hat\rho = \hat\gamma/\hat\sigma_2^2$. □

Alternatively, the whole vector of model parameters may be jointly estimated by ML. The sample log-likelihood of a type-2 tobit model is of the form

$$L(\theta) = \sum_1 [\ln f(Y_{i2} \,|\, Y_{i1} = 1) + \ln \Pr\{Y_{i1} = 1\}] + \sum_0 \ln \Pr\{Y_{i1} = 0\},$$

where $\sum_1$ and $\sum_0$ denote summation over the observations for which $Y_{i1} = 1$ and $Y_{i1} = 0$ respectively.

Notice that when Y_{i1}^* depends on a single covariate which does not affect Y_{i2}^*, model (18.15) is formally equivalent to the partially linear model discussed in Example 14.9. The parameter β_2 may therefore be estimated semiparametrically by the backfitting algorithm.

Despite the relative simplicity with which a type-2 tobit model may be estimated, identifiability of its parameters is likely to be an issue. First of all, only the ratio $\alpha_1 = \beta_1/\sigma_1$ is identifiable, not β_1 and σ_1 separately. Further, as is clear from Example 18.5, identifiability of the other parameters of the model depends crucially on the fact that the linear function $\beta_2^\top X_i$ and the nonlinear function $\lambda(\alpha_1^\top X_i)$ affect the conditional mean of Y_{i2} in different ways. In the extreme case when $\beta_1 = \beta_2$, identifiability entirely depends on the nonlinearity of λ. Because λ is nonlinear only for extreme values of the index $\alpha_1^\top X_i$ and, in any case, using nonlinearities to identify relationships is not very satisfactory, exclusion restrictions are typically imposed on the models for the two latent responses. Unfortunately, the justification for these exclusion restrictions is often weak (see Little 1985).

Another drawback of model (18.14) is the fact that Y_{i2} is not restricted to be non-negative, which may be undesirable in some cases. To take care of this problem, straightforward modifications of the basic model are available.

Example 18.6 Cragg (1971) proposed a "double hurdle" model of durable goods expenditure, where the purchase decision is represented by $Y_{i1} = 1\{Y_{i1}^* > 0\}$ but the actual amount purchased is represented by a censored regression model, thereby avoiding negativity of Y_{i2}. In this case

$$Y_{i2} = Y_{i1} \max(0, Y_{i2}^*).$$

One interpretation of this model is that observed demand Y_{i2} is zero either because an individual genuinely does not consume the good (that is, $Y_{i1}^* \leq 0$), or because for some reason (infrequency of purchase, misreporting, etc.) zero expenditure was recorded (that is, $Y_{i2}^* \leq 0$). If Y_{i1}^* and Y_{i2}^* are independent, then

$$\begin{aligned} \Pr\{Y_{i2} = 0\} &= \Pr\{Y_{i2}^* \leq 0\} + \Pr\{Y_{i1}^* \leq 0\} \Pr\{Y_{i2}^* > 0\} \\ &= 1 - \Pr\{Y_{i1}^* > 0\} \Pr\{Y_{i2}^* > 0\}, \end{aligned}$$

and the sample log-likelihood is of the form

$$L(\theta) = \sum_1 [\ln f(Y_{i2}) + \ln \Pr\{Y_{i1} = 1\}] + \sum_0 \ln[1 - \Pr\{Y_{i1} = 0\} \Pr\{Y_{i2} > 0\}].$$

The model reduces to censored regression when $\Pr\{Y_{i1} = 1\} = 1$ for all sample units. This restriction can easily be tested, for example by the score test of Deaton and Irish (1984).

The position of the two "hurdles" may be reversed. First a binary choice model may determine whether a purchase is to be made. The amount purchased may then be determined by a truncated regression model. This is equivalent to replacing the censored values of Y_{i2}^* in the previous model by truncated values. If Y_{i1}^* and Y_{i2}^* are independent, then the sample log-likelihood for this model is of the form

$$L(\theta) = \sum_1 [\ln f(Y_{i2} \mid Y_{i2} > 0) + \ln \Pr\{Y_{i1} = 1\}] + \sum_0 \ln \Pr\{Y_{i1} = 0\}.$$

The model reduces to censored regression when $\Pr\{Y_{i1}^* > 0\} = \Pr\{Y_{i2}^* > 0\}$. This restriction can easily be tested, for example by the score test of Lin and Schmidt (1984). □

The standard tobit model may be regarded as a special case of a type-2 model, corresponding to $Y_{i1}^* = Y_{i2}^*$, that is, complete dependence between Y_{i1}^* and Y_{i2}^*. Another special case is the so-called *two-part model*, where Y_{i1}^* and Y_{i2}^* are independent conditionally on X_i. The two-part model is particularly convenient to analyze and estimate, for the conditional mean (18.15) simply becomes

$$\mathrm{E}(Y_{i2} \mid Y_{i1} = 1) = \beta_2^\top X_i,$$

which justifies estimating β_2 by an OLS regression of the positive values of Y_{i2} on X_i. Further, the log-likelihood of this model is

$$L(\theta) = \sum_1 [\ln f(Y_{i2}) + \ln \Pr\{Y_{i1} = 1\}] + \sum_0 \ln \Pr\{Y_{i1} = 0\}.$$

Thus, under the normality assumption, an efficient procedure for this model consists of separately estimating α_1 and β_2, the first by probit and the second by an OLS regression of the positive values of Y_{i2} on X_i. Although the two-part model is generally regarded as "unrealistic", Monte Carlo evidence in Manning, Duan and Rogers (1987) shows that it predicts no worse than a type-2 tobit model where exclusion restrictions have not been imposed.

18.6.2 TYPE-3 TOBIT MODELS

Type-2 tobit models can only represent the decision whether or not to participate in the labor market. If attention focuses on the number of hours worked, then an alternative is a *type-3 tobit model*, which is of the following form

$$\begin{aligned} Y_{ij}^* &= \beta_j^\top X_i + \sigma_j V_{ij}, \qquad j = 1, 2, \\ Y_{i1} &= \max(0, Y_{i1}^*), \\ Y_{i2} &= 1\{Y_{i1}^* > 0\}\, Y_{i2}^*. \end{aligned}$$

Now Y_{i1}^* and Y_{i2}^* are both observed when $Y_{i1}^* > 0$. The sample log-likelihood for this model is of the form

$$L(\theta) = \sum_1 \ln f(Y_{i1}, Y_{i2}) + \sum_0 \ln \Pr\{Y_{i1} = 0\},$$

where $\sum_1$ denotes summation over the observations for which $Y_{i1} > 0$ and $f(y_1, y_2)$ denotes the joint density of (Y_{i1}^*, Y_{i2}^*).

Example 18.7 Heckman (1974) used a version of the type-3 tobit model to represent the joint determination of wages and labor supply. In this case, Y_{i1}^* and Y_{i2}^* represent respectively the desired hours of work and the offered wage. The reservation wage depends on the desired hours of work and is given by $W_i^* = \mu_i + \delta Y_{i1}^* + V_i$, where μ_i may depend on covariates. If the offered wage exceeds the reservation wage at zero hours of work, that is $Y_{i2}^* - \mu_i - V_i > 0$, then participation occurs and the model jointly determines the observed wage and the number of hours worked. □

BIBLIOGRAPHIC NOTES

For a broad introduction to models for truncated and censored data see Maddala (1983) and Amemiya (1985). For a recent survey of estimation methods for models with sample selection see Vella (1997).

The presentation of the Roy model follows Heckman and Honorè (1990). The two-step estimator from censored data was first proposed by Heckman (1976). The result in Section 18.4.2 is due to Olsen (1978). Conditions for identifiability of type-2 tobit models are discussed by Olsen (1980). For a derivation of the limiting distribution of the Gaussian ML estimators in Sections 18.4 and 18.6.1 see Dhrymes (1986).

All the estimators discussed in this chapter are not B-robust since their influence function is unbounded. On B-robust estimation of the Gaussian tobit model see Peracchi (1990b).

For a review of various semiparametric alternatives to estimators based on the Gaussian assumption see Powell (1994) and Pagan and Ullah (1999). See Chay and Honorè (1997) for an interesting application. On the use of locally linear regression smoothers after a suitable transformation of the data see Fan & Gijbels (1994).

PROBLEMS

18.1 Let $\phi(z)$ and $\Phi(z)$ denote the $\mathcal{N}(0,1)$ density and distribution function respectively. Show that $\ln\phi(x)$ and $\ln\Phi(z)$ are strictly concave.

18.2 Show that if a density is log-concave, so is the associated distribution function F and the survivor function $S = 1 - F$.

18.3 Consider the doubly-truncated Gaussian regression model, where Y_i is only observed if $a_i < Y_i < b_i$, in which case $Y_i = Y_i^*$. Show that the OLS estimator in the regression of the observed values of Y_i on X_i is unbiased for β whenever $\mu_i = \beta^\top X_i$ and $\mu_i - a_i = b_i - \mu_i$.

18.4 Generalize the procedures in Section 18.3.3 to the case when all observations are used, not only those for which $D_i = 1$.

18.5 Compute the conditional mean of the likelihood score for the model in Section 18.4.1 and show that it is not generally equal to zero when the latent regression errors are Gaussian but heteroskedastic.

18.6 Write down the log-likelihood function and the likelihood equations for the Gaussian tobit model parametrized in terms of $\theta = (\beta, \sigma^2)$.

18.7 Write down the Newton–Raphson iterations for the Gaussian tobit model parametrized in terms of $\theta = (\beta, \sigma^2)$ and compare them with those of the EM algorithm.

18.8 Derive the influence function of the ML estimator for the Gaussian tobit model.

18.9 Derive the Hessian of the sample log-likelihood and the Fisher information matrix for the classical Gaussian linear model parametrized in terms of $(\beta/\sigma, 1/\sigma)$. Verify that the Hessian matrix is n.d. at all points in the parameter space. Is the Fisher information matrix block-diagonal?

18.10 Show that concavity of the log-likelihood is not generally preserved under nonsingular reparametrizations.

18.11 Verify that, under the reparametrization in Section 18.4.2, the Hessian of the Gaussian log-likelihood for the truncated regression model is n.d. at all points in the parameter space.

18.12 Verify that, under the reparametrization in Section 18.4.2, the Hessian of the Gaussian log-likelihood for the censored regression model is n.d. at all points in the parameter space.

18.13 Derive and interpret the likelihood equations for a censored sample from the exponential and the Weibull model.

18.14 Consider a type-2 tobit model and suppose that the conditional distribution of V_{i2} given $V_{i1} = v_1$ is $\mathcal{N}(\rho v_1, 1 - \rho^2)$, whereas the marginal distribution of V_{i1} is uniform on the interval $(-\sqrt{3}, \sqrt{3})$. Show that the model is not identifiable if all components of β_1 and β_2 are different from zero. Derive conditions sufficient to guarantee that the model is identifiable.

18.15 Propose likelihood ratio, Wald and score tests of a two-part model against the alternative of a type-2 tobit model.

18.16 Suppose that the latent variables

$$Y_j^* = \beta_j^\top X_j + U_j, \qquad j = 1, 2$$

are related to the observable variable Y through the rule

$$Y = \begin{cases} Y_1^*, & \text{with probability } \lambda, \\ Y_2^*, & \text{with probability } 1 - \lambda. \end{cases}$$

This model is called the *switching regression model.* Write down the log-likelihood for a random sample of n observations from this model.

References

Agresti A. (1990) *Categorical Data Analysis*, Wiley, New York.

Aigner D.J., Hsiao C., Kapteyn A. and Wansbeek T. (1984) Latent Variable Models in Econometrics. In Griliches Z. and Intriligator M.D. (eds.) *Handbook of Econometrics*, Vol. 2, pp. 1321–1393, North-Holland, Amsterdam.

Aitcheson J. and Silvey S.D. (1958) Maximum Likelihood Estimation of Parameters Subject to Restraints. *Annals of Mathematical Statistics*, 29: 813–828.

Akaike H. (1973) Information Theory and an Extension of the Maximum Likelihood Principle. In Petrov B.N. and Csaki F. (eds.) *2nd International Symposium on Information Theory*, Akademiai Kiado, Budapest.

Almon S. (1965) The Distributed Lag Between Capital Appropriations and Expenditures. *Econometrica*, 33: 178–196.

Amemiya T. (1973) Regression Analysis When the Dependent Variable Is Truncated Normal. *Econometrica*, 41: 997–1016.

Amemiya T. (1982) Two Stage Least Absolute Deviations Estimators. *Econometrica*, 50: 689–711.

Amemiya T. (1985) *Advanced Econometrics*, Harvard University Press, Cambridge, MA.

Amemiya T. and MaCurdy T.E. (1986) Instrumental-Variable Estimation of an Error-Component Model. *Econometrica*, 54: 869–881.

Anderson T.W. (1971) *The Statistical Analysis of Time Series*, Wiley, New York.

Andrews, D.W.K. (1986) A Note on the Unbiasedness of Feasible GLS, Quasi-Maximum Likelihood, Robust, Adaptive, and Spectral Estimators of the Linear Model. *Econometrica*, 54: 687–698.

Andrews, D.W.K. (1993) Tests for Parameter Instability and Structural Change with Unknown Change Point. *Econometrica*, 61: 821–856.

Andrews D.W.K. (1994) Empirical Process Methods in Econometrics. In Engle R.F. and McFadden D.L. (eds.) *Handbook of Econometrics*, Vol. 4, pp. 2247–2294, North-Holland, Amsterdam.

Andrews, D.W.K. (1997) A Stopping Rule for the Computation of Generalized Method of Moments. *Econometrica*, 65: 913–931.

Andrews, D.W.K. (1999) Estimation When a Parameter is on a Boundary. *Econometrica*, 67: 1341–1383.

Apostol T.M. (1974) *Mathematical Analysis* (2nd ed.), Addison Wesley, Reading, MA.

Arabmazar A. and Schmidt P. (1981) Further Evidence on the Robustness of the Tobit Estimator to Heteroskedasticity. *Journal of Econometrics*, 17: 253–258.

Arabmazar A. and Schmidt P. (1982) An Investigation of the Robustness of the Tobit Estimator to Non-normality. *Econometrica*, 50: 1055–1063.

Arellano M. and Bover O. (1995) Another Look at the Instrumental-Variable Estimation of Error-Components Models. *Journal of Econometrics*, 68: 29–51.

Atkinson A.C. (1970) A Method for Discriminating Between Models. *Journal of the Royal Statistical Society*, Series B, 32: 211–243.

Azzalini A. and Bowman A.W. (1993) On the Use of Nonparametric Regression for Checking a Linear Relationship. *Journal of the Royal Statistical Society*, Series B, 55: 549–557.

Azzalini, A., Bowman A.W. and Härdle W. (1989) On the Use of Nonparametric Regression for Model Checking. *Biometrika*, 76: 1–12.

Bahadur R.R. (1971) *Some Limit Theorems in Statistics*, SIAM, Philadelphia, PA.

Bai J. and Perron P. (1998) Estimation and Testing Linear Models with Multiple Structural Changes. *Econometrica*, 66: 47–78.

Balestra P. and Nerlove M. (1966) Pooling Cross-Section and Time Series Data in the Estimation of a Dynamic Model. *Econometrica*, 34: 585–612.

Baltagi B. (1995a) *Econometric Analysis of Panel Data*, Wiley, New York.

Baltagi B. (1995b) (ed.) *Panel Data, Journal of Econometrics, Annals*, 68, No. 1.

Barndorff-Nielsen O.E. (1978) *Information and Exponential Families in Statistical Theory*, Wiley, New York.

Barndorff-Nielsen O.E. and Cox D.R. (1989) *Asymptotic Techniques for Use in Statistics*, Chapman and Hall, London.

Barrodale I. and Roberts F. (1973) An Improved Algorithm for Discrete l_1 Linear Approximation. *SIAM Journal of Numerical Analysis*, 10: 839–848.

Basu A.P. (1984) Censored Data. In Krishnaiah P.R. and Sen P.K. (eds.) *Handbook of Statistics*, Vol. 4, Elsevier Science Publishers, Amsterdam.

Beach C.M. and MacKinnon J.G. (1978) A Maximum Likelihood Procedure for Regression with Autocorrelated Errors. *Econometrica*, 45: 51–58.

Beaton A.E. and Tukey J.W. (1974) The Fitting of Power Series, Meaning Polynomials, Illustrated on Band-Spectroscopic Data. *Technometrics*, 16: 147–185.

Becker R.A., Cleveland W.S. and Wilks A.R. (1987) Dynamic Graphics for Data Analysis. *Statistical Science*, 2: 355–395.

Belsley D.A., Kuh E. and Welsch R.E. (1980) *Regression Diagnostics: Identifying Influential Data and Sources of Collinearity*, Wiley, New York.

Ben-Akiva M. and Lerman S.R. (1985) *Discrete Choice Analysis: Theory and Application to Travel Demand*, MIT Press, Cambridge, MA.

Bera A.K. and Higgins M.L. (1993) ARCH Models. Properties, Estimation and Testing. *Journal of Economic Surveys*, 7: 305–366.

Berndt E. and Savin N.E. (1977) Conflict Among Criteria for Testing Hypotheses in the Multivariate Linear Regression Model. *Econometrica*, 45: 1263–1278.

Berndt E., Hall B., Hall R., and Hausman J.A. (1974) Estimation and Inference in Nonlinear Structural Models. *Annals of Economic and Social Measurement*, 3/4, 653–665.

Beveridge S. and Nelson C.R. (1981) A New Approach to Decomposition of Economic Time Series into Permanent and Transitory Components with Particular Attention to Measurement of the Business Cycle. *Journal of Monetary Economics*, 2: 151-174.

Bhattacharya R.N. and Rao R.R. (1976) *Normal Approximation and Asymptotic Expansions*, Wiley, New York.

Bickel P. (1982) On Adaptive Estimation. *Annals of Statistics*, 10: 647–671.

Bierens H.J. (1987) Kernel Estimators of Regression Functions. In Bewley T.F. (ed.) *Advances in Econometrics, Fifth World Congress*, Vol. 1, pp. 99–144, Cambridge University Press, New York.

Bierens H.J. (1994) *Topics in Advanced Econometrics*, Cambridge University Press, New York.

Billingsley P. (1968) *Convergence of Probability Measures*, Wiley, New York.

Billingsley P. (1979) *Probability and Measure*, Wiley, New York.

Bloomfield P. and Steiger W. (1983) *Least Absolute Deviations: Theory, Applications, Algorithms*, Birkhäuser, Boston, MA.

Blundell R. and Duncan A. (1997) Kernel Regression in Empirical Microeconomics. *Journal of Human Resources*, 33: 62–87.

Blundell R.W. and Meghir C. (1987) Bivariate Alternatives to the Univariate Tobit Model. *Journal of Econometrics*, 33: 179–200.

Bollerslev T. (1986) Generalized Autoregressive Conditional Heteroskedasticity. *Journal of Econometrics*, 31: 307–327.

Bollerslev T., Chou R.Y. and Kroner K.F. (1992) ARCH Modeling in Finance: a Review of the Theory and Empirical Evidence. *Journal of Econometrics*, 52: 5–59.

Bollerslev T., Engle R.F. and Nelson D.B. (1994) ARCH Models. In Engle R.F. and McFadden D.L. (eds.) *Handbook of Econometrics*, Vol. 4, pp. 2959–3038, North-Holland, Amsterdam.

Bound J.D., Jaeger A. and Baker R. (1995) Problems with Instrumental Variables Estimation When the Correlation Between the Instruments and the Endogenous Explanatory Variable is Weak. *Journal of the American Statistical Association*, 90: 443–450.

Bowden R. (1973) The Theory of Parametric Identification. *Econometrica*, 41: 1069–1074.

Box G.E.P. and Cox D.R. (1964) An Analysis of Transformations. *Journal of the Royal Statistical Society*, Series B, 26: 211–246.

Box G.E.P. and Jenkins G.M. (1977) *Time Series Analysis, Forecasting and Control* (revised edition), Holden-Day, Oakland, CA.

Box G.E.P. and Tiao G.C. (1973) *Bayesian Inference in Statistical Analysis*, Addison-Wesley, Reading, MA.

Breusch T.V. (1979) Conflict Among Criteria for Testing Hypotheses: Extensions and Comments. *Econometrica*, 47: 203–207.

Breusch T.V. and Pagan A.R. (1979) A Simple Test for Heteroskedasticity and Random Coefficient Variation. *Econometrica*, 47: 1287–1294.

Breusch T.V. and Pagan A.R. (1980) The Lagrange Multiplier Test and Its Applications to Model Specification in Econometrics. *Review of Economic Studies*, 47: 239–254.

Breusch T.V., Mizon G.E. and Schmidt P. (1989) Efficient Estimation Using Panel Data. *Econometrica*, 57: 695–700.

Brockwell P.J. and Davis R.A. (1987) *Time Series: Theory and Methods*, Springer, New York.

Brown L.D. (1986) Fundamentals of Statistical Exponential Families with Applications in Statistical Decision Theory, Institute of Mathematical Statistics, Hayward, CA.

Brown R.L., Durbin J. and Evans J.M. (1975) Techniques for Testing the Constancy of Regression Relationships over Time (with discussion). *Journal of the Royal Statistical Society*, Series B, 37: 149–192.

Buchinsky M. (1997) Recent Advances in Quantile Regression Models: A Practical Guideline for Empirical Research. *Journal of Human Resources*, 33: 88–126.

Buckley J. and James I. (1979) Linear Regression with Censored Data. *Biometrika*, 66: 429–436.

Butler J.S. and Moffitt R. (1982) A Computationally Efficient Quadrature Procedure for One-Factor Multinomial Probit Models. *Econometrica*, 50: 761–768.

Cameron A.C. and Trivedi P.K. (1998) *Regression Analysis of Count Data*, Cambridge University Press, New York.

Carraro C., Peracchi F. and Weber G. (1993) (eds.) *The Econometrics of Panels and Pseudo Panels, Journal of Econometrics, Annals*, 59, No. 1/2.

Carroll R.J. and Ruppert D. (1988) *Transformation and Weighting in Regression*, Chapman and Hall, New York.

Chamberlain G. (1980) Analysis of Covariance with Qualitative Data. *Review of Economics Studies*, 47: 225–238.

Chamberlain G. (1982) Multivariate Regression Models for Panel Data. *Journal of Econometrics*, 18: 5–46.

Chamberlain G. (1984) Panel Data. In Griliches Z. and Intriligator M.D. (eds.) *Handbook of Econometrics*, Vol. 2, pp. 1248–1318, North-Holland, Amsterdam.

Chamberlain G. and Leamer E. (1976) Matrix Weighted Averages and Posterior Bounds. *Journal of the Royal Statistical Society*, Series B, 38: 73–84.

Chambers J.M. and Hastie T.J. (1992) *Statistical Models in S*, Wadsworth & Brooks/Cole, Pacific Grove, CA.

Chay K.Y. and B.E. Honorè (1997) Estimation of Semiparametric Censored Regression

Models. An Application to Changes in Black-White Earnings Inequality During the 1960s. *Journal of Human Resources*, 33: 4–38.

Chen M.-H., Dey D.K. and Shao Q.-M. (1999) A New Skewed Link Model for Dichotomous Quantal Response Data. *Journal of the American Statistical Association*, 94: 1172–1186.

Chesher A. (1984) Testing for Neglected Heterogeneity. *Econometrica*, 52: 865–872.

Chesher A. (1989) Hájek Inequalities, Measures of Leverage and the Size of Heteroskedasticity Robust Wald Tests. *Econometrica*, 57: 971–977.

Chesher A. (1991) The Effect of Measurement Error, *Biometrika*, 78: 451–462.

Chesher A. and Jewitt I. (1987) The Bias of a Heteroskedasticity Consistent Covariance Matrix Estimator. *Econometrica*, 55: 1217–1222.

Chesher A. and Smith R. (1997) Likelihood Ratio Specification Tests. *Econometrica*, 65: 627–646.

Chow G. (1960) Tests of the Equality Between Two Sets of Coefficients in Two Linear Regressions. *Econometrica*, 28: 561–605.

Chow Y.S. and Teicher H. (1988) *Probability Theory. Independence, Interchangeability, Martingales* (2nd ed.), Springer, New York.

Chui C.K. (1988) *Multivariate Splines*, SIAM, Philadelphia, PA.

Chung C.F. and Goldberger A.S. (1984) Proportional Projections in Limited Dependent Variable Models. *Econometrica*, 52: 531–534.

Chung K.L. (1974) *A Course in Probability Theory* (2nd ed.), Academic Press, Orlando, FL.

Cleveland W.S. (1979) Robust Locally Weighted Regression and Smoothing Scatterplots. *Journal of the American Statistical Association*, 74: 829–836.

Cleveland W.S. and Devlin S.J. (1988) Locally Weighted Regression: An Approach to Regression Analysis by Local Fitting. *Journal of the American Statistical Association*, 93: 596–610.

Cochran W.G. (1977) *Sampling Techniques* (3rd ed.), Wiley, New York.

Cook R.D. (1977) Detection of Influential Observations in Linear Regression. *Technometrics*, 19: 15–18.

Cook R.D. and Weisberg S. (1982) *Residuals and Influence in Regression*, Chapman and Hall, New York.

Cook R.D. and Weisberg S. (1983) Diagnostics for Heteroskedasticity in Regression. *Biometrika*, 70: 1–10.

Corradi C. (1977) Smooth Distributed Lag Estimators and Smoothing Spline Functions in Hilbert Spaces. *Journal of Econometrics*, 5: 211–219.

Cox D.R. (1961) Tests of Separate Families of Hypotheses. In *Proceedings of the Fourth Berkeley Symposium on Mathematical Statistics and Probability*, Vol. 1, pp. 105–123, University of California Press, Berkeley, CA.

Cox D.R. (1962) Further Results on Tests of Separate Families of Hypotheses. *Journal of the Royal Statistical Society*, Series B, 24: 363–370.

Cox D.R. and Hinkley D.V. (1974) *Theoretical Statistics*, Chapman and Hall, London.

Cox D.R. and Oakes D. (1984) *Analysis of Survival Data*, Chapman and Hall, London.

Cragg J. (1971) Some Statistical Models for Limited Dependent Variables with Applications to the Demand for Durable Goods. *Econometrica*, 39: 829–844.

Cragg J.G. (1983) More Efficient Estimation in the Presence of Heteroskedasticity of Unknown Form. *Econometrica*, 51: 751–764.

Cramér H. (1946) *Mathematical Methods of Statistics*, Princeton University Press, Princeton, NJ.

Crowder M.J. (1976) Maximum Likelihood Estimation for Dependent Observations. *Journal of the Royal Statistical Society*, Series B, 38: 45–53.

Dagenais M.G. and Dufour J.-M. (1991) Invariance, Nonlinear Models and Asymptotic Tests. *Econometrica*, 59: 1601–1615.

Davidson R. and MacKinnon J.G. (1981) Several Tests for Model Specification in the Presence of Alternative Hypotheses. *Econometrica*, 49: 781–793.

De Angelis D., Hall P. and Young G.A. (1993) Analytical and Bootstrap Approximations to Estimator Distributions in L^1 Regression. *Journal of the American Statistical Association*, 88: 1310–1316.

de Boor C. (1978) *A Practical Guide to Splines*, Springer, New York.

Deaton A. (1985) Panel Data from Time Series of Cross Sections. *Journal of Econometrics*, 30: 109–126.

Deaton A. (1997) *The Analysis of Household Surveys: A Microeconometric Approach to Development Policy*, Johns Hopkins University Press, Baltimore, MD.

Deaton A. and Irish M. (1984) Statistical Models for Zero Expenditures in Household Budgets. *Journal of Public Economics*, 23: 59–80.

Delgado M.A. and Kniesner T.J. (1997) Count Data Models with Variance of Unknown Forms: An Application to a Hedonic Model of Worker Absenteeism. *Review of Economics and Statistics*, 41–49.

Dempster A.P., Laird N.M. and Rubin D.B. (1977) Maximum Likelihood Estimation from Incomplete Data via the EM Algorithm (with discussion). *Journal of the Royal Statistical Society*, Series B, 39: 1–38.

Devroye L. and Györfi L. (1985) *Nonparametric Density Estimation: The L_1 View*, Wiley, New York.

Dhrymes P.J. (1986) Limited Dependent Variables. In Griliches Z. and Intriligator M.D. (eds.) *Handbook of Econometrics*, Vol. 3, pp. 1567–1631, North-Holland, Amsterdam.

Di Ciccio T.J. and Efron B. (1996) Bootstrap Confidence Intervals. *Statistical Science*, 11: 189–228.

Di Ciccio T.J. and Romano J. (1988) A Review of Bootstrap Confidence Intervals. *Journal of the Royal Statistical Society*, Series A, 151: 338–354.

Dickey D.A. and Fuller W.A. (1979) Distribution of the Estimator for Autoregressive Time Series with a Unit Root. *Journal of the American Statistical Association*, 74: 427–431.

Dickey D.A. and Fuller W.A. (1981) Likelihood Ratio Statistics for Autoregressive Time Series with a Unit Root. *Econometrica*, 49: 1057–1072.

Donoho D.L. and Huber P.J. (1983) The Notion of Breakdown Point. In Bickel P., Doksum K. and Hodges J.L. (eds.) *Festschrift for Erich Lehmann*, Wadsworth, Belmont, CA.

Doob J.L. (1953) *Stochastic Processes*, Wiley, New York.

Dufour J.-M. and Renault E. (1998) Short Run and Long Run Causality in Time Series: Theory. *Econometrica*, 66: 1099–1125.

DuMouchel W.H. and Duncan G.J. (1983) Using Sample Survey Weights in Multiple Regression Analysis of Stratified Samples. *Journal of the American Statistical Association*, 78: 535–543.

Durbin J. (1954) Errors in Variables. *Review of the International Statistical Institute*, 22: 23–32.

Durbin J. and Watson G.S. (1950) Testing for Serial Correlation in Least Squares Regression. I. *Biometrika*, 37: 409–428.

Durbin J. and Watson G.S. (1951) Testing for Serial Correlation in Least Squares Regression. II. *Biometrika*, 38: 159–178.

Durbin J. and Watson G.S. (1971) Testing for Serial Correlation in Least Squares Regression. III. *Biometrika*, 58: 1–19.

Efron B. (1979) Bootstrap Methods: Another Look at the Jackknife. *Annals of Statistics*, 7: 1–26.

Efron B. (1982) *The Jackknife, the Bootstrap and Other Resampling Plans*, SIAM, Philadelphia, PA.

Efron B. (1984) Comparing Non-Nested Linear Models. *Journal of the American Statistical Association*, 79: 791–803.

Efron B. (1987) Better Bootstrap Confidence Intervals (with discussion). *Journal of the American Statistical Association*, 82: 171–200.

Efron B. and Hinkley D.V. (1978) Assessing the Accuracy of the Maximum Likelihood

Estimator: Observed Versus Expected Fisher Information (with discussion). *Biometrika*, 65: 457–487.

Efron B. and Morris C. (1973) Stein's Estimation Rule and Its Competitors: An Empirical Bayes Approach. *Journal of the American Statistical Association*, 68: 117–130.

Efron B. and Stein C. (1981) The Jackknife Estimate of Variance. *Annals of Statistics*, 9: 586–596.

Efron B. and Tibshirani R. (1986) Bootstrap Methods for Standard Errors, Confidence Intervals, and Other Measures of Statistical Accuracy. *Statistical Science*, 1: 54–77.

Efron B. and Tibshirani R. (1993) *An Introduction to the Bootstrap*, Chapman and Hall, New York.

Eicker F. (1967) Limit Theorems for Regressions with Unequal and Dependent Errors. In LeCam L.M. and Neyman J. (eds.) *Proceedings of the Fifth Berkeley Symposium on Mathematical Statistics and Probability*, University of California Press, Berkeley, CA.

Engle R.F. (1982) Autoregressive Conditional Heteroskedasticity with Estimates of the Variance of U.K. Inflation. *Econometrica*, 55: 391–407.

Engle R.F. (1984) Wald, Likelihood Ratio and Lagrange Multiplier Tests in Econometrics. In Griliches Z. and Intriligator M.D. (eds.) *Handbook of Econometrics*, Vol. 2, pp. 776–826, North-Holland, Amsterdam.

Engle R.F. and Bollerslev T. (1986) Modeling the Persistence of Conditional Variances. *Econometric Reviews*, 5: 1–50.

Engle R.F. and Granger C.W.J. (1987) Cointegration and Error Correction: Representation, Estimation and Testing. *Econometrica*, 55: 251–276.

Engle R.F. and Granger C.W.J. (1991) (eds.) *Long-Run Economic Relationships. Readings in Cointegration*, Oxford University Press, Oxford.

Engle R.F., Hendry D.F. and Richard J.F. (1983) Exogeneity. *Econometrica*, 51: 277-304.

Engle R.F., Granger C.W.J., Rice J.A. and Weiss A. (1986) Semiparametric Estimates of the Relationship Between Weather and Electricity Sales. *Journal of the American Statistical Association*, 81: 310–320.

Eubank R.L. (1988) *Spline Smoothing and Nonparametric Regression*, Dekker, New York.

Eubank R.L. and Spiegelman C.H. (1990) Testing the Goodnes of Fit of a Linear Model Via Nonparametric Regression Techniques. *Journal of the American Statistical Association*, 85: 387–392.

Evans G.B.A. and Savin E. (1981) Testing for Unit Roots: I. *Econometrica*, 49: 753–779.

Evans G.B.A. and Savin E. (1982) Conflict Among the Criteria Revisited: The W, LR and LM Tests. *Econometrica*, 50: 737–748.

Fair R. (1974) On the Robust Estimation of Econometric Models. *Annals of Economic and Social Measurement*, 3: 667–677.

Fan J. (1992) Design-adaptive Nonparametric Regression. *Journal of the American Statistical Association*, 87: 998–1004.

Fan J. and Gijbels I. (1994) Censored Regression: Local Linear Approximations and Their Applications. *Journal of the American Statistical Association*, 89: 560–570.

Fan J. and Gijbels I. (1996) *Local Polynomial Modelling and Its Applications*, Chapman and Hall, London.

Fan J., Heckman N.E. and Wand M.P. (1995) Local Polynomial Regression for Generalized Linear Models and Quasi-likelihood Functions. *Journal of the American Statistical Association*, 90: 141–150.

Feller W. (1971) *Introduction to Probability Theory and Its Applications*, Vol. 2 (2nd ed.), Wiley, New York.

Ferguson T.S. (1958) A Method of Generating Best Asymptotically Normal Estimates with Application to the Estimation of Bacterial Densities. *Annals of Mathematical Statistics*, 29: 1046–1062.

Ferguson T.S. (1967) *Mathematical Statistics: A Decision Theoretic Approach*, Academic Press, New York.

Ferguson T.S. (1996) *A Course in Large Sample Theory*, Chapman and Hall, London.

Fernholz L.T. (1983) *Von Mises Calculus for Statistical Functionals*, Springer, New York.

Fisher G.R. and MacAleer M. (1981) Alternative Procedures and Associated Tests of Significance for Non-Nested Hypotheses. *Journal of Econometrics*, 16: 103–119.

Fitzmaurice G.M., Laird N.M. and Rotnitzky A.G. (1993) Regression Models for Discrete Longitudinal Responses. *Statistical Science*, 8: 284–309.

Flinn C. and Heckman J. (1982) New Methods for Analyzing Structural Models of Labor Force Dynamics. *Journal of Econometrics*, 18: 115–168.

Forni M. and Lippi M. (1997) *Aggregation and the Microfoundations of Dynamic Macroeconomics*, Oxford University Press, Oxford.

Freedman D.A. (1981) Bootstrapping Regression Models. *Annals of Statistics*, 9: 1218–1228.

Freedman D.A. (1984) On Bootstrapping Two-Stage Least-Squares Estimates in Stationary Linear Models. *Annals of Statistics*, 12: 827–842.

Friedman J.H. and Stuetzle W. (1981) Projection Pursuit Regression. *Journal of the American Statistical Association*, 76: 817–823.

Friedman J.H., Stuetzle W. and Schroeder A. (1984) Projection Pursuit Density Estimation. *Journal of the American Statistical Association*, 79: 599–608.

Fuller W.A. (1976) *Introduction to Statistical Time Series*, Wiley, New York.

Fuller W.A. (1987) *Measurement Error Models*, Wiley, New York.

Giles J.A. and Giles D.E.A. (1993) Pre-test Estimation and Testing in Econometrics: Recent Developments, *Journal of Economic Surveys*, 7: 145–197.

Gill P.E., Murray W. and Wright M.H. (1981) *Practical Optimization*, Academic Press, San Diego, CA.

Godfrey L.G. (1981) On the Invariance of the Lagrange Multiplier Test with Respect to Certain Changes in the Alternative Hypothesis. *Econometrica*, 49: 1443–1455.

Godfrey L.G. (1989) *Misspecification Tests in Econometrics. The Lagrange Multiplier Principle and Other Approaches*, Cambridge University Press, New York.

Goldberger A.S. (1962) Best Linear Unbiased Prediction in the Generalized Linear Regression Model. *Journal of the American Statistical Association*, 57: 369–375.

Goldfeld S., Quandt R. and Trotter H. (1966) Maximization by Quadratic Hill Climbing. *Econometrica*, 34: 541–551.

Good I.J. and R.A. Gaskins (1971) Nonparametric Roughness Penalties for Probability Densities. *Biometrika*, 58, 255-277.

Gourieroux C. (1997) *ARCH Models and Financial Applications*, Springer, New York.

Gourieroux C. and Monfort A. (1994) Testing Non-Nested Hypotheses. In Engle R.F. and McFadden D.L. (eds.) *Handbook of Econometrics*, Vol. 4, pp. 2583–2637, North-Holland, Amsterdam.

Gourieroux C. and Monfort A. (1996) *Simulation-Based Econometric Methods*, Oxford University Press, Oxford.

Gourieroux C., Holly A. and Monfort A. (1982) Likelihood Ratio, Wald Test, and Kuhn-Tucker Test in Linear Models with Inequality Constraints on the Regression Parameters. *Econometrica*, 50: 63–80.

Gourieroux C., Monfort A. and Trognon A. (1984a) Pseudo Maximum Likelihood Method: Theory. *Econometrica*, 52: 681–700.

Gourieroux C., Monfort A. and Trognon A. (1984b) Pseudo Maximum Likelihood Method: Applications to Poisson Models. *Econometrica*, 52: 701–720.

Granger C.W.J. (1969) Investigating Causal Relations by Econometric Models and Cross-Spectral Methods. *Econometrica*, 37: 424–438.

Granger C.W.J. (1981) Some Properties of Time-Series Data and Their Use in Econometric Model Specification. *Journal of Econometrics*, 16: 121-130.

Granger C.W.J. and Joyeux R. (1980) An Introduction to Long-Memory Time Series Models and Fractional Differencing. *Journal of Time Series Analysis*, 1: 15–29.

Granger C.W.J. and Newbold R. (1986) *Forecasting Economic Time Series* (2nd ed.),

Academic Press, Orlando, FL.

Green P.J. and Silverman B.W. (1994) *Nonparametric Regression and Generalized Linear Models*, Chapman and Hall, London.

Gregory A.W. and Veall M.R. (1985) Formulating Wald Tests of Nonlinear Restrictions. *Econometrica*, 53: 1465–1468.

Griliches Z. (1986) Economic Data Issues. In Griliches Z. and Intriligator M.D. (eds.) *Handbook of Econometrics*, Vol. 3, pp. 1465–1514. North-Holland, Amsterdam.

Gronau R. (1973) The Effects of Children on the Housewife's Value of Time. *Journal of Political Economy*, 81: S168–S199.

Gutenbrunner C. and Jurečková J. (1992) Regression Quantile and Regression Rank Score Process in the Linear Model and Derived Statistics. *Annals of Statistics*, 20: 305–330.

Hajivassiliou V.A. and Ruud P.A. (1994) Classical Estimation Methods for LDV Models Using Simulation. In Engle R.F. and McFadden D.L. (eds.) *Handbook of Econometrics*, Vol. 4, pp. 2384–2441, North-Holland, Amsterdam.

Hall P.J. (1992) *The Bootstrap and Edgeworth Expansions*, Springer, New York.

Hall P.J. (1994) Methodology and Theory for the Bootstrap. In Engle R.F. and McFadden D.L. (eds.) *Handbook of Econometrics*, Vol. 4, pp. 2341–2381, North-Holland, Amsterdam.

Hall W.J. and Wellner J.A. (1980) Confidence Bands for a Survival Curve from Censored Data. *Biometrika*, 67: 133–143.

Hamilton J.D. (1994) *Time Series Analysis*, Princeton University Press, Princeton, NJ.

Hampel F.R. (1968) Contribution to the Theory of Robust Estimation. Ph.D. Thesis, University of California, Berkeley, CA.

Hampel F.R. (1971) A General Qualitative Definition of Robustness. *Annals of Mathematical Statistics*, 42: 1887–1896.

Hampel F.R. (1974) The Influence Curve and Its Role in Robust Estimation. *Journal of the American Statistical Association*, 69: 383–393.

Hampel F.R. (1978) Optimally Bounding the Gross-Error Sensitivity and the Influence of Position in Factor Space. In *Proceedings of the ASA Statistical Computing Section*, American Statistical Association, Washington, DC.

Hampel F.R., Rousseeuw P.J. and Ronchetti E.M. (1981) The Change-of-Variance Curve and Optimal Redescending M-Estimators. *Journal of the American Statistical Association*, 76: 643–648.

Hampel F.R., Ronchetti E.M., Rousseeuw P.J. and Stahel W.A. (1986) *Robust Statistics: The Approach Based on Influence Functions*, Wiley, New York.

Hannan E.J. (1970) *Multiple Time Series*, Wiley, New York.

Hannan E.J. and Quinn B.G. (1979) The Determination of the Order of an Autoregression. *Journal of the Royal Statistical Society*, Series B, 41: 190–195.

Hansen L.P. (1982) Large Sample Properties of Generalized Method of Moments Estimators. *Econometrica*, 50: 1029–1054.

Härdle W. (1990) *Applied Nonparametric Regression*, Cambridge University Press, New York.

Härdle W. and Linton O. (1994) Applied Nonparametric Methods. In Engle R.F. and McFadden D.L. (eds.) *Handbook of Econometrics*, Vol. 4, pp. 2297–2339, North-Holland, Amsterdam.

Härdle W. and Stoker T. (1989) Investigating Smooth Multiple Regression by the Method of Average Derivatives. *Journal of the American Statistical Association*, 84: 986–995.

Harvey A.C. (1989) *Forecasting, Structural Time Series Models and the Kalman Filter*, Cambridge University Press, New York.

Hastie T.J. and Loader C.L. (1993) Local Regression: Automatic Kernel Carpentry (with discussion). *Statistical Science*, 8: 120–143.

Hastie T.J. and Tibshirani R.J. (1990) *Generalized Additive Models*, Chapman and Hall, London.

Hausman J.A. (1975) An Instrumental Variable Approach to Full Information Estimators for Linear and Certain Nonlinear Econometric Models. *Econometrica*, 43: 728–738.

Hausman J.A. (1978) Specification Tests in Econometrics. *Econometrica*, 46: 1251–1272.

Hausman J.A. (1983) Specification and Estimation of Simultaneous Equation Models. In Griliches Z. and Intriligator M.D. (eds.) *Handbook of Econometrics*, Vol. 1, pp. 391–448, North-Holland, Amsterdam.

Hausman J.A. and McFadden D.L. (1984) Specification Tests for the Multinomial Logit Model. *Econometrica*, 52: 1219–1240.

Hausman J.A. and Taylor W.E. (1981) Panel Data and Unobservable Individual Effects. *Econometrica*, 49: 1377–1398.

Hausman J.A. and Taylor W.E. (1983) Identification in Linear Simultaneous Equation Models with Covariance Restrictions: an Instrumental Variables Interpretation. *Econometrica*, 51: 1527–1550.

Hausman J.A. and Wise D.A. (1978) A Conditional Probit Model for Qualitative Choice: Discrete Decisions Recognizing Interdependence and Heterogeneous Preferences. *Econometrica*, 46: 403–426.

Hausman J.A., Hall B.H. and Griliches Z. (1984) Econometric Models for Count Data with an Application to the Patents–R&D Relationship. *Econometrica*, 52: 909–938.

Hausman J.A., Newey W.K. and Taylor W.E. (1987) Efficient Estimation and Identification of Simultaneous Equation Models with Covariance Restrictions. *Econometrica*, 55: 849–874.

He X., Jurečková J., Koenker R. and Portnoy S. (1990) Tail behavior of regression estimators and their breakdown points. *Econometrica*, 58: 1195–1214.

Heckman J.J. (1974) Shadow Prices, Market Wages, and Labour Supply. *Econometrica*, 42: 679–693.

Heckman J.J. (1976) The Common Structure of Statistical Models of Truncation, Sample Selection and Limited Dependent Variables and a Simple Estimator for Such Models. *Annals of Economic and Social Measurement*, 5: 475–492.

Heckman J.J. (1979) Sample Selection Bias as a Specification Error. *Econometrica*, 47: 153–161.

Heckman J.J. and Honorè B.E. (1990) The Empirical Content of the Roy Model. *Econometrica*, 58: 1121–1149.

Heckman J.J. and Singer B. (1982) (eds.) *Econometric Analysis of Longitudinal Data*, *Journal of Econometrics*, *Annals*, 18, No. 1.

Heckman J.J. and Singer B. (1984) A Method for Minimizing the Impact of Distributional Assumptions in Econometric Models for Duration Data. *Econometrica*, 52: 271–320.

Heckman J.J. and Willis R.J. (1977) A Beta-Logistic Model for the Analysis of Sequential Labor Force Participation by Married Women. *Journal of Political Economy*, 85: 27–58.

Hendry D.F. (1976) The Structure of Simultaneous Equation Estimators. *Journal of Econometrics*, 4: 51–68.

Heritier S. and Ronchetti E.M. (1994) Robust Bounded-Influence Tests in General Parametric Models. *Journal of the American Statistical Association*, 88: 897–904.

Hildenbrand W. (1998) How Relevant Are Specifications of Behavioral Relations on the Micro-Level for Modelling the Time Path of Population Aggregates? *European Economic Review*, 42: 437–458.

Hinkley D.V. (1977) Jackknifing in Unbalanced Situations. *Technometrics*, 19: 285–292.

Hjort N.L. (1994) The Exact Amount of t-ness That the Normal Model Can Tolerate. *Journal of the American Statistical Association*, 89: 665–675.

Hoadley B. (1971) Asymptotic Properties of Maximum Likelihood Estimators for the Independent Not Identically Distributed Case. *Annals of Mathematical Statistics*, 42: 1977–1991.

Hoerl A.E. and Kennard R.W. (1970a) Ridge Regression: Biased Estimation of Nonorthogonal Problems. *Technometrics*, 12: 55-67.

Hoerl A.E. and Kennard R.W. (1970b) Ridge Regression: Application to Nonorthogonal Problems. *Technometrics*, 12: 69–82.

Holly A. (1982) A Remark on Hausman's Specification Test. *Econometrica*, 50: 749–759.

Holly A. (1987) Specification Tests: an Overview. In Bewley T.F. (ed.) *Advances in Econometrics, Fifth World Congress*, Vol. 1, pp. 59–97, Cambridge University Press, New York.

Holtz-Eakin D., Newey W.K. and Rosen H.S. (1988) Estimating Vector Autoregressions with Panel Data. *Econometrica*, 56: 1371–1395.

Horowitz, J.L. (1986) A Distribution-Free Least Squares Estimator for Censored Linear Regression Models. *Journal of Econometrics*, 32: 59–84.

Horowitz J.L. (1992) A Smoothed Maximum Score Estimator for the Binary Response Model. *Econometrica*, 60: 505–531.

Horowitz J.L. (1994) Bootstrap Based Critical Values of the Information Matrix Test. *Journal of Econometrics*, 61: 395–411.

Horowitz J.L. (1998a) Bootstrap Methods for Median Regression Models. *Econometrica*, 66: 1327–1351.

Horowitz J.L. (1998b) *Semiparametric Methods in Econometrics*, Springer, New York.

Hosking J.R.M. (1981) Fractional Differencing. *Biometrika*, 68: 165–176.

Hotelling H. (1940) The Selection of Variates for Use in Prediction with Some Comments on the General Problem of Nuisance Parameters. *Annals of Mathematical Statistics*, 11: 271–283.

Hsiao C. (1983) Identification. In Griliches Z. and Intriligator M.D. (eds.) *Handbook of Econometrics*, Vol. 1, pp. 223–283, North-Holland, Amsterdam.

Hsiao C. (1986) *Analysis of Panel Data*, Cambridge University Press, New York.

Hsieh D. and Manski C.F. (1987) Monte Carlo Evidence on Adaptive Maximum Likelihood Estimation of a Regression. *Annals of Statistics*, 15: 541–551.

Huber P.J. (1964) Robust Estimation of a Location Parameter. *Annals of Mathematical Statistics*, 35: 73–101.

Huber P. (1967) The Behavior of Maximum Likelihood Methods under Nonstandard Conditions. In *Proceedings of the Fifth Berkeley Symposium on Mathematical Statistics and Probability*, Vol. 1, pp. 221–233, University of California Press, Berkeley, CA.

Huber P.J. (1973) Robust Regression: Asymptotics, Conjectures and Monte-Carlo. *Annals of Statistics*, 1: 799–821.

Huber P.J. (1981) *Robust Statistics*, Wiley, New York.

Huber P.J. (1985) Projection Pursuit (with discussion). *Annals of Statistics*, 13: 435–525.

Hurd M. (1979) Estimation in Truncated Samples When There Is Heteroskedasticity. *Journal of Econometrics*, 11: 247–258.

Ichimura H. (1993) Semiparametric Least Squares (SLS) and Weighted SLS Estimation of Single-Index Models. *Journal of Econometrics*, 58: 71–120.

Jarque C.M. and Bera A.K. (1980) Efficient Tests for Normality, Homoschedasticity and Serial Independence of Regression Residuals. *Economic Letters*, 6: 255–259.

Jeffreys H. (1961) *Theory of Probability* (3rd ed.), Oxford University Press, London.

Johnson N.L. and Kotz S. (1970) *Distributions in Statistics. Continuous Univariate Distributions*, Vols. 1 and 2, Wiley, New York.

Johnson N.L. and Kotz S. (1972) *Distributions in Statistics. Continuous Multivariate Distributions*, Wiley, New York.

Jones M.C., Marron J.S. and Sheather S.J. (1996) A Brief Survey of Bandwidth Selection for Density Estimation *Journal of the American Statistical Association*, 91: 401–407.

Judge G.C. and Bock M.E. (1978) *The Statistical Implications of Pre-Test and Stein-Rule Estimators in Econometrics*, North-Holland, New York.

Judge G.C. and Takayama T. (1966) Inequality Restrictions in Regression Analysis. *Journal of the American Statistical Association*, 61: 166–181.

Jurečková J. and Sen P.K. (1995) *Robust Statistical Procedures. Asymptotics and Interrelations*, Wiley, New York.

Karlin S. and Taylor H.M. (1975) *A First Course in Stochastic Processes* (2nd ed.), Academic Press, New York.

Keating J.P., Mason R.L. and Sen P.K. (1993) *Pitman's Measure of Closeness. A Comparison of Statistical Estimators*, SIAM, Philadelphia, PA.

Kiefer N.M. and Salmon M. (1983) Testing Normality in Econometric Models. *Economic Letters*, 11: 123–127.

Kim J. and Pollard D. (1991) Cube Root Asymptotics. *Annals of Statistics*, 18: 191–219.

Klein R.W. and Spady R.H. (1993) An Efficient Semiparametric Estimator for Discrete Choice Models. *Econometrica*, 61: 387–421.

Koenker R. and Bassett G. (1978) Regression Quantiles. *Econometrica*, 46: 33–50.

Koenker R. and Bassett G. (1982) Robust Tests for Heteroskedasticity Based on Regression Quantiles. *Econometrica*, 50: 43–61.

Koenker R. and d'Orey V. (1987) Computing Regression Quantiles. *Applied Statistics*, 36: 383–393.

Koenker R. and Machado J.A.F. (1999) Goodness of Fit and Related Inference Processes for Quantile Regression. *Journal of the American Statistical Association*, 94: 1296–1310.

Krasker W.S. (1980) Estimation in Linear Regression Models with Disparate Data Points. *Econometrica*, 48: 1333–1346.

Krasker W.S. (1986) Estimation in Linear Regression Models with Disparate Data Points. *Journal of Business and Economic Statistics*, 4: 437–444.

Krasker W.S. and Welsch R.E. (1982) Efficient Bounded-Influence Regression Estimation. *Journal of the American Statistical Association*, 77: 595–604.

Krasker W.S. and Welsch R.E. (1985) Resistant Estimation for Simultaneous-Equations Models Using Weighted Instrumental Variables. *Econometrica*, 53: 1475–1488.

Krishnakumar J. and Ronchetti E.M. (1997) Robust Estimators for Simultaneous-Equations Models using Weighted Instrumental Variables. *Journal of Econometrics*, 78: 295–314.

Kullback S. and Leibler R.A. (1951) On Information and Sufficiency. *Annals of Mathematical Statistics*, 22: 79–86.

Künsch H.R. (1989) The Jackknife and the Bootstrap for General Stationary Observations. *Annals of Statistics*, 17: 1217–1241.

Künsch H.R., Stefanski L.A. and Carroll R.Y. (1989) Conditionally Unbiased Bounded-Influence Estimation in General Regression Models. *Journal of the American Statistical Association*, 84: 460–466.

Kyriazidou E. (1997) Estimation of a Panel Data Sample Selection Model. *Econometrica*, 65: 1335–1364.

Lai T.L. and Ying Z. (1991) Large Sample Theory of a Modified Buckley–James Estimator for Regression Analysis with Censored Data. *Annals of Statistics*, 19: 1370–1402.

Lancaster T. (1984) *Econometrica*, 52: 1051–1053.

Lancaster T. (1990) *The Econometric Analysis of Transition Data*, Cambridge University Press, Cambridge.

Lange K.L., Little R.J.A. and Taylor J.M.G. (1989) Robust Statistical Modeling Using the t Distribution. *Journal of the American Statistical Association*, 84: 881–896.

Leamer E.E. (1978) *Specification Searches*, Wiley, New York.

Leamer E.E. (1987) Errors in Variables in Linear Systems. *Econometrica*, 55: 893–909.

LeCam L. (1986) *Asymptotic Methods in Statistical Decision Theory*, Springer, New York.

Lee M. (1989) Mode Regression. *Journal of Econometrics*, 42: 337–349.

Lehmann E.L. (1983) *Theory of Point Estimation*, Wiley, New York.

Lehmann E.L. (1988) *Testing Statistical Hypotheses* (2nd ed.), Wiley, New York.

Lessler J.T. and Kalsbeek W.D. (1992) *Nonsampling Error in Surveys*, Wiley, New York.

Li H. and Maddala G.S. (1996) Bootstrapping Time Series Models (with discussion). *Econometric Reviews*, 15: 115–195.

Liang, K.Y. and Zeger S.L. (1986) Longitudinal Data Analysis Using Generalized Linear Models. *Biometrika*, 73: 13–22.

Liew C.K. (1976) Inequality Constrained Least-Squares Estimation. *Journal of the American Statistical Association*, 71: 746–751.

Lin T.F. and Schmidt P. (1984) A Test of the Tobit Specification Against an Alternative Suggested by Cragg. *Review of Economics and Statistics*, 66: 174–177.
Lindley D.V. (1972) *Bayesian Statistics, A Review*, SIAM, Philadelphia, PA.
Linhart H. and Zucchini W. (1986) *Model Selection*, Wiley, New York.
Little R.J.A. (1985) A Note About Models for Selectivity Bias. *Econometrica*, 53: 1469–1474.
Little R.J.A. and Rubin D.B. (1987) *Statistical Analysis with Missing Data*, Wiley, New York.
Luenberger D. (1969) *Optimization by Vector Space Methods*, Wiley, New York.
Lukacs E. (1975) *Stochastic Convergence*, Academic Press, New York.
Lütkepohl H. (1991) *Introduction to Multiple Time-Series Analysis*, Springer, Berlin.
Maasumi E. (1993) A Compendium to Information Theory in Economics and Econometrics. *Econometric Reviews*, 12, 137–181.
MacKinnon D. (1983) Model Specification Tests Against Non-Nested Alternatives. *Econometric Reviews*, 2: 85–110.
MacKinnon D. and White H. (1985) Some Heteroskedasticity-Consistent Covariance Matrix Estimators with Improved Finite Sample Properties. *Journal of Econometrics*, 29: 305–325.
Maddala G.S. (1971) The Use of Variance Components Models in Pooling Cross Section and Time Series Data. *Econometrica*, 39: 341–358.
Maddala G.S. (1983) *Limited-Dependent and Qualitative Variables in Econometrics*, Cambridge University Press, New York.
Magnus J.R. (1978) Maximum Likelihood Estimation of the GLS Model with Unknown Parameters in the Disturbance Covariance Matrix. *Journal of Econometrics*, 7: 281–312.
Magnus J.R. and Durbin J. (1999) Estimation of Regression Coefficients of Interest When Other Regression Coefficients Are of No Interest. *Econometrica*, 67: 639–643.
Magnus J.R. and Neudecker H. (1988) *Matrix Differential Calculus with Applications in Statistics and Econometrics*, Wiley, Chichester, UK.
Mallows C.L. (1973) Some Comments on C_p. *Technometrics*, 15: 661–675.
Mann H.B. and Wald A. (1943) On Stochastic Limit and Order Relationships. *Annals of Mathematical Statistics*, 14: 217–226.
Manning W.G., Duan N. and Rogers W.H. (1987) Monte Carlo Evidence on the Choice Between Sample Selection and Two-Part Models. *Journal of Econometrics*, 35: 59–82.
Manski C.F. (1975) Maximum Score Estimation of the Stochastic Utility Model of Choice. *Journal of Econometrics*, 3: 205–228.
Manski C.F. (1984) Adaptive Estimation of Non-Linear Regression Models. *Econometric Reviews*, 3: 145–194.
Manski C.F. (1985) Semiparametric Analysis of Discrete Response: Asymptotic Properties of the Maximum Score Estimator. *Journal of Econometrics*, 27: 313–334.
Manski C.F. (1988a) Identification of Binary Response Models. *Journal of the American Statistical Association*, 83: 729–738.
Manski C.F. (1988b) *Analogue Estimation Methods in Econometrics*, Chapman and Hall, New York.
Manski C.F. (1989) Anatomy of the Selection Problem. *Journal of Human Resources*, 24: 343–360.
Manski C.F. (1991) Regression. *Journal of Economic Literature*, 29: 34–50.
Manski C.F. (1994) Analog Estimation of Econometric Models. In Engle R.F. and McFadden D.L. (eds.) *Handbook of Econometrics*, Vol. 4, pp. 2559–2582, North-Holland, Amsterdam.
Manski C.F. (1995) *Identification Problems in the Social Sciences*, Harvard University Press, Cambridge, MA.
Manski C.F. and Lerman S.R. (1977) The Estimation of Choice Probabilities from Choice Based Samples. *Econometrica*, 45: 1977–1988.
Manski C.F. and McFadden D.L. (1981) *Structural Analysis of Discrete Data with Econometric Applications*, MIT Press, Cambridge, MA.
Manski C.F. and Thompson S. (1986) Operational Characteristics of Maximum Score Estimation. *Journal of Econometrics*, 32: 65–108.

Mardia K.V. (1980) Tests of Univariate and Multivariate Normality. In Krishnaiah P.R. (ed.) *Handbook of Statistics*, Vol. 1, North-Holland, Amsterdam.

Maronna R.A. and Yohai V. (1981) Asymptotic Behavior of General M-Estimates for Regression and Scale with Random Carriers. *Zeitschrift für Wahrscheinlichkeitstheorie und Verwandte Gebiete*, 58: 7–20.

Maronna R.A., Bustos O.H. and Yohai V.J. (1979) Bias- and Efficiency-Robustness of General M-estimators for Regression with Random Carriers. In Gasser T. and Rosenblatt M. (eds) *Smoothing Techniques for Curve Estimation*, Springer, Berlin.

Marron J.S. and Nolan D. (1988) Canonical Kernels for Density Estimation. *Statistics and Probability Letters*, 7: 195–199.

Martin D.R. and Yohai V.J. (1985) Robustness in Time Series and Estimating ARMA Models. In Hannan E.J., Krisnaiah P.R. and Rao M.M. (eds.) *Handbook of Statistics*, Vol. 5, pp. 119–155, North-Holland, Amsterdam.

Mátyás L. and Sevestre P. (1996) (eds.) *The Econometrics of Panel Data: Handbook of Theory with Applications* (2nd ed.), Kluwer, Dordrecht.

Matzkin R. (1992) Nonparametric and Distribution-Free Estimation of the Binary Threshold Crossing Model and the Binary Choice Model. *Econometrica*, 60: 239–270.

McCullagh P. and Nelder J.A. (1989) *Generalized Linear Models* (2nd ed.), Chapman and Hall, London.

McDonald J.B. (1984) Some Generalized Functions for the Size Distributions of Income. *Econometrica*, 52: 647–663.

McDonald J.B. and W.K. Newey (1988) Partially Adaptive Estimation of Regression Models via the Generalized t Distribution. *Econometric Theory*, 4: 428–457.

McDonald J.B. and White S.B. (1993) A Comparison of Some Robust, Adaptive, and Partially Adaptive Estimators of Regression Models. *Econometric Reviews*, 12: 103–124.

McDonald J.B. and Y.J. Xu (1995) A Generalization of the Beta Distribution with Applications. *Journal of Econometrics*, 66: 133–152.

McFadden D.L. (1974) Conditional Logit Analysis of Qualitative Choice Behavior. In P. Zarembka (ed.) *Frontiers in Econometrics*, Academic Press, New York.

McFadden D.L. (1989) A Method of Simulated Moments for Estimation of Discrete Response Models without Numerical Integration. *Econometrica*, 57: 995–1026.

McLachlan G.J. and Krishnan T. (1997) *The EM Algorithm and Extensions*, Wiley, New York.

Miller R. (1976) Least Squares Regression with Censored Data. *Biometrika*, 63: 521–531.

Mizon G. and Richard J.F. (1986) The Encompassing Principle and Its Application to Testing Non-Nested Regression Models. *Econometrica*, 54: 657–678.

Nadaraya E.A. (1964) On Estimating Regressions. *Theory of Probability and Its Applications*, 9: 141–142.

Nelder J.A. and Wedderburn R.W.M. (1972) Generalized Linear Models. *Journal of the Royal Statistical Society*, Series A, 135: 370–384.

Nelson C.R. and Startz R. (1990) Some Further Results on the Exact Small Sample Properties of the Instrumental Variable Estimator. *Econometrica*, 58: 967–976.

Nelson F.D. and Savin N.E. (1990) The Danger of Extrapolating Asymptotic Local Power. *Econometrica*, 58: 977–981.

Nerlove M. (1971) A Note on Error Components Models. *Econometrica*, 39: 359–382.

Newey W.K. (1987) Specification Tests for Distributional Assumptions in the Tobit Model. *Journal of Econometrics*, 34: 125–145.

Newey W.K. (1988) Adaptive Estimation of Regression Models Via Moment Restrictions. *Journal of Econometrics*, 38: 301–339.

Newey W.K. (1991) Uniform Convergence in Probability and Stochastic Equicontinuity. *Econometrica*, 59: 1161–1167.

Newey W.K. and McFadden D.L. (1994) Large Sample Estimation and Hypothesis Testing. In Engle R.F. and McFadden D.L. (eds.) *Handbook of Econometrics*, Vol. 4, pp. 2111–2245,

North-Holland, Amsterdam.

Newey W.K. and Powell J.L. (1987) Asymmetric Least Squares Estimation and Testing. *Econometrica*, 55: 819–847.

Newey W.K. and West K. (1987) A Simple, Positive Semi-Definite, Heteroskedasticity and Autocorrelation Consistent Covariance Matrix. *Econometrica*, 55: 703–708.

Neyman J. and Scott E.L. (1948) Consistent Estimation from Partially Consistent Observations, *Econometrica*, 16, 1–32.

Ng P.T. (1995) Finite Sample Properties of Adaptive Regression Estimators. *Econometric Reviews*, 14: 267–297.

Nickell S. (1981) Biases in Dynamic Models with Fixed Effects. *Econometrica*, 49: 1417–1426.

Oehlert G.W. (1992) A Note on the Delta Method. *American Statistician*, 46: 27–29.

Olsen R.J. (1978) Note on the Uniqueness of the Maximum Likelihood Estimator for the Tobit Model. *Econometrica*, 46: 1211–1215.

Olsen R.J. (1980) A Least Squares Correction for Selectivity Bias. *Econometrica*, 48: 1815–1820.

Paarsch H.J. (1984) A Monte Carlo Comparison of Estimators for Censored Regression Models. *Journal of Econometrics*, 24: 197–213.

Pagan A.R. and Hall A.D. (1983) Diagnostic Tests as Residual Analysis. *Econometric Reviews*, 2: 159–218.

Pagan A.R. and Ullah A. (1999) *Nonparametric Econometrics*, Cambridge University Press, New York.

Pakes A. and Pollard D. (1989) Simulation and the Asymptotics of Optimization Estimators. *Econometrica*, 57: 1027–1058.

Peracchi F. (1990a) Robust M-Estimators (with discussion). *Econometric Reviews*, 9: 1–35.

Peracchi F. (1990b) Bounded-Influence Estimators for the Tobit Model. *Journal of Econometrics*, 44: 107–126.

Peracchi F. (1991) Robust M-Tests. *Econometric Theory*, 7: 69–84.

Percival D.B. (1993) Three Curious Properties of the Sample Variance and Autocovariance for Stationary Processes with Unknown Mean. *American Statistician*, 47: 274–276.

Pesaran M.H. (1974) On the General Problem of Model Selection. *Review of Economic Studies*, 41: 153–171.

Pesaran M.H. and Deaton A. (1978) Testing Non-Nested Non-Linear Regression Models. *Econometrica*, 46: 677–694.

Pesaran M.H. and Smith R.J. (1994) A Generalized R^2 Criterion for Regression Models Estimated by the Instrumental Variables Method. *Econometrica*, 62: 705–710.

Phillips G.D.A. (1977) Recursions for the Two-Stage Least-Squares Estimators. *Journal of Econometrics*, 6: 65–77.

Phillips P.C.B. (1983) Exact Small Sample Theory in the Simultaneous Equations Model. In Griliches Z. and Intriligator M.D. (eds.) *Handbook of Econometrics*, Vol. 1, pp. 449–516, North-Holland, Amsterdam.

Phillips P.C.B. (1987) Time Series Regression with a Unit Root. *Econometrica*, 55: 277-301.

Phillips P.C.B. (1991) A Shortcut to LAD Estimator Asymptotics. *Econometric Theory*, 7: 450–463.

Phillips P.C.B. and Park J.Y. (1988) On the Formulation of Wald Tests of Nonlinear Restrictions. *Econometrica*, 56: 1065–1083.

Pollard D. (1984) *Convergence of Stochastic Processes*, Springer, New York.

Pollard D. (1985) New Ways to Prove Central Limit Theorems. *Econometric Theory*, 1: 295–314.

Pollard D. (1990) *Empirical Processes: Theory and Applications*, NSF-CBMS Regional Conference Series in Probability and Statistics, Institute of Mathematical Statistics, Hayward, CA.

Pollard D. (1991) Asymptotics for Least Absolute Deviation Regression Estimators. *Econometric Theory*, 7: 186–199.

Portnoy S. and Koenker R. (1997) The Gaussian Hare and the Laplacian Tortoise: Computability for Squared-Error versus Absolute-Error Estimators (with discussion). *Statistical Science*, 12: 279–300.

Pötscher B.M. and Prucha I.R. (1994) Generic Uniform Convergence and Equicontinuity Concepts for Random Functions. An Exploration of the Basic Structure. *Journal of Econometrics*, 60: 23–63.

Powell J.L. (1983) The Asymptotic Normality of Two-Stage Least Absolute Deviations Estimators. *Econometrica*, 51: 1569–1575.

Powell J.L. (1984) Least Absolute Deviations Estimation for the Censored Regression Model. *Journal of Econometrics*, 25: 303–325.

Powell J.L. (1986a) Censored Regression Quantiles. *Journal of Econometrics*, 32: 143–155.

Powell J.L. (1986b) Symmetrically Trimmed Least Squares Estimation for Tobit Models. *Econometrica*, 54: 1435–1460.

Powell J.L. (1994) Estimation of Semiparametric Models. In Engle R.F. and McFadden D.L. (eds.) *Handbook of Econometrics*, Vol. 4, pp. 2443–2521, North-Holland, Amsterdam.

Prentice R.L. and Zhao L.P. (1991) Estimating Equations for Parameters in Means and Covariances of Multivariate Discrete and Continuous Responses. *Biometrics*, 47: 825–839.

Priestley M.B. (1981) *Spectral Analysis and Time-Series*, Academic Press, London.

Prucha I.R. and Kelejian H.R. (1984) The Structure of Simultaneous Equation Estimators: A Generalization Towards Nonnormal Disturbances. *Econometrica*, 52: 721–736.

Quandt R.E. (1983) Computational Problems and Methods. In Griliches Z. and Intriligator M.D. (eds.) *Handbook of Econometrics*, Vol. 1, North-Holland, Amsterdam.

Quenouille M. (1949) Approximate Tests of Correlation in Time Series. *Journal of the Royal Statistical Society*, Series B, 11: 18–84.

Raiffa H. and Schlaifer R. (1961) *Applied Statistical Decision Theory*, Harvard University Press, Cambridge, MA.

Ramsey J.B. (1969) Tests for Specification Errors in Classical Linear Least Squares Regression Analysis. *Journal of the Royal Statistical Society*, Series B, 31: 350-371.

Rao C.R. (1948) Large Sample Tests of Statistical Hypotheses Concerning Several Parameters with Application to Problems of Estimation. *Proceedings of the Cambridge Philosophical Society*, 44: 50–57.

Rao C.R. (1973) *Linear Statistical Inference and Its Applications* (2nd ed.), Wiley, New York.

Rao C.R. and Mitra S.K. (1971) *Generalized Inverse of Matrices and Its Applications*, Wiley, New York.

Reinsch C. (1967) Smoothing to Spline Functions. *Numerical Mathematics*, 10: 177–183.

Ritov Y. (1990) Estimation in a Linear Regression Model with Censored Data. *Annals of Statistics*, 18: 303–328.

Robinson P.M. (1982) On the Asymptotic Properties of Estimators Containing Limited Dependent Variables. *Econometrica*, 50: 27–41.

Robinson P. (1988) Root-N Consistent Semiparametric Regression. *Econometrica*, 56: 931–954.

Romano J.P. and Siegel A.F. (1986) *Counterexamples in Probability and Statistics*, Wadsworth & Brooks/Cole, Monterey, CA.

Rosenblatt M. (1956) Remarks on Some Nonparametric Estimates of a Density Function. *Annals of Mathematical Statistics*, 27: 832–837.

Rothenberg T.J. (1971) Identification in Parametric Models. *Econometrica*, 39: 577–592.

Rousseeuw P.J. (1984) Least Median of Squares Regression. *Journal of the American Statistical Association*, 79: 871–880.

Rousseeeuw P.J. and Leroy A.M. (1987) *Robust Regression and Outlier Detection*, Wiley, New York.

Rousseeuw P.J. and Yohai V.J. (1984) Robust Regression by Means of S-Estimators. In Franke J., Härdle W. and Martin R.D. (eds.) *Robust and Nonlinear Time Series Analysis*, Springer, New York.

Roy, A.D. (1951) Some Thoughts on the Distribution of Earnings. *Oxford Economic Papers*, 3: 135–146.

Ruppert D. and Carroll R.J. (1980) Trimmed Least Squares Estimation in the Linear Model. *Journal of the American Statistical Association*, 75: 828–838.

Ruud P.A. (1984) Tests of Specification in Econometrics (with discussion). *Econometric Reviews*, 3: 211–276.

Sargan J.D. (1958) The Estimation of Econometric Relationships Using Instrumental Variables. *Econometrica*, 26: 393–415.

Sargan J.D. (1988) *Lectures on Advanced Econometric Theory*, Blackwell, Oxford.

Särndal C.E., Swensson B. and Wretman J. (1992) *Model Assisted Survey Sampling*, Springer, New York.

Savage L.J. (1972) *The Foundations of Statistics* (2nd ed.), Dover, New York.

Sawa T. (1978) Information Criteria for Discriminating among Alternative Regression Models. *Econometrica*, 46: 1273–1291.

Schafer J.L. (1997) *Analysis of Incomplete Multivariate Data*, Chapman and Hall, New York.

Schlossmacher E.G. (1973) An Iterative Technique for Absolute Deviation Curve Fitting. *Journal of the American Statistical Association*, 68: 857–865.

Schmidt P. (1976) *Econometrics*, Dekker, New York.

Schucany W.R. and Sommers J.P. (1977) Improvement of Kernel Type Density Estimators. *Journal of the American Statistical Association*, 70: 420–423.

Schwarz G. (1978) Estimating the Dimension of a Model. *Annals of Statistics*, 6: 461–464.

Scott A.J. and Holt D. (1982) The Effect of Two-Stage Sampling on Ordinary Least Squares Methods. *Journal of the American Statistical Association*, 77: 848–854.

Serfling R.J. (1980) *Approximation Theorems of Mathematical Statistics*, Wiley, New York.

Sevestre P. and Trognon A. (1985) A Note on Autoregressive Error Components Models. *Journal of Econometrics*, 29: 231–245.

Shao J. and Tu D. (1995) *The Jackknife and Bootstrap*, Springer, New York.

Sheater S.C. and Jones M.C. (1991) A Reliable Data-Based Bandwidth Selection Method for Kernel Density Estimation. *Journal of the Royal Statistical Society*, Series B, 53: 683–690.

Shiller R.J. (1973) A Distributed Lag Estimator Derived from Smoothness Priors. *Econometrica*, 41: 775–788.

Silverman, B.W. (1986) *Density Estimation for Statistics and Data Analysis*, Chapman and Hall, New York.

Silvey S.D. (1959) The Lagrangean Multiplier Test. *Annals of Mathematical Statistics*, 30: 389–407.

Silvey S.D. (1975) *Statistical Inference*, Chapman and Hall, London.

Sims C.A. (1980) Macroeconomics and Reality. *Econometrica*, 48: 1–48.

Sims C.A., Stock J.H. and Watson M.W. (1990) Inference in Linear Time Series Models with Some Unit Roots. *Econometrica*, 58: 1113–1144.

Smith A.F.M. and Spiegelhalter D.J. (1980) Bayes Factors and Choice Criteria for Linear Models. *Journal of the Royal Statistical Society*, Series B, 42: 213–220.

Staiger D. and Stock J.H. (1997) Instrumental Variables Regression with Weak Instruments. *Econometrica*, 65: 557–586.

Stein C. (1956) Inadmissibility of the Usual Estimator for the Mean of a Multivariate Distribution. In *Proceedings of the Third Berkeley Symposium on Mathematical Statistics and Probability*, Vol. 1, pp. 197–206, University of California Press, Berkeley, CA.

Stock J.H. and Watson M.W. (1988) Variable Trends in Economic Time Series. *Journal of Economic Perspectives*, 2: 147–174.

Stoker T.M. (1986) Consistent Estimation of Scaled Coefficients. *Econometrica*, 54: 1461–1481.

Stoker T.M. (1993) Empirical Approaches to the Problem of Aggregation over Individuals. *Journal of Economic Literature*, 31: 1827–1874.

Stone C.J. (1977) Consistent Nonparametric Regression (with discussion). *Annals of*

Statistics, 5: 549–645.

Stone C.J. (1982) Optimal Global Rates of Convergence for Nonparametric Regression. *Annals of Statistics*, 10: 1040–1053.

Stone C.J. (1984) An Asymptotically Optimal Window Selection Rule for Kernel Density Estimates. *Annals of Statistics*, 12: 1285–1297.

Stone, C.J. (1985) Additive regression and other nonparametric models. *Annals of Statistics*, 13: 689–705.

Tanner M.A. (1993) *Tools for Statistical Inference. Methods for the Exploration of Posterior Distributions and Likelihood Functions*, Springer, New York.

Theil H. (1971) *Principles of Econometrics*, Wiley, New York.

Thursby J.G. (1985) The Relationship among the Specification Tests of Hausman, Ramsey, and Chow. *Journal of the American Statistical Association*, 80: 926–928.

Tibshirani R. and Hastie T. (1987) Local Likelihood Estimation. *Journal of the American Statistical Association*, 82: 559–567.

Tobin J. (1958) Estimation of Relationships for Limited Dependent Variables. *Econometrica*, 26: 24–36.

Tukey J. (1958) Bias and Confidence in Not Quite Large Samples. *Annals of Mathematical Statistics*, 29: 614.

Tukey J. (1977) *Exploratory Data Analysis*, Addison-Wesley, Reading, MA.

Turnbull B.W. (1974) The Empirical Distribution Function with Arbitrarily Grouped, Censored and Truncated Data. *Journal of the American Statistical Association*, 69: 169–173.

van der Vaart A.W. (1998) *Asymptotic Statistics*, Cambridge University Press, Cambridge.

van der Vaart A.W. and Wellner J.A. (1996) *Weak Convergence and Empirical Processes*, Springer, New York.

Vapnik V. (1982) *Estimation of Dependences Based on Empirical Data*, Springer, New York.

Vella F. (1997) Estimating Models with Sample Selection Bias: A Survey. *Journal of Human Resoruces*, 33: 127–169.

Verbeek M. (1990) On the Estimation of a Fixed Effects Model with Selectivity Bias. *Economics Letters*, 34: 267–270.

Verbeek M. (1995) Alternative Transformations to Eliminate Fixed Effects. *Econometric Reviews*, 14: 205–211.

Verbeek M. and Nijman T. (1992) Testing for Selectivity Bias in Panel Data Models. *International Economic Review*, 33: 681–703.

Verbeek M. and Nijman T. (1993) Minimum MSE Estimation of a Regression Model with Fixed Effects from a Series of Cross-Sections. *Journal of Econometrics*, 59: 125–136.

von Mises R. (1947) On the Asymptotic Distribution of Differentiable Statistical Functionals. *Annals of Mathematical Statistics*, 18: 309–348.

Vuong Q. (1989) Likelihood Ratio Tests for Model Selection and Non-Nested Hypotheses. *Econometrica*, 57: 307–333.

Wahba G. (1990) *Spline Models for Observational Data*, SIAM, Philadelphia, PA.

Wald A. (1943) Tests of Statistical Hypotheses Concerning Several Parameters When the Number of Observations is Large. *Transactions of the American Mathematical Society*, 54: 426–482.

Wald A. (1947) *Sequential Analysis*, Wiley, New York.

Wald A. (1949) Note on the Consistency of the Maximum Likelihood Estimate. *Annals of Mathematical Statistics*, 20: 595–601.

Wald A. (1950) *Statistical Decision Functions*, Wiley, New York.

Wallace T.D. and Hussain A. (1969) The Use of Error Component Models in Combining Cross Section with Time Series Data. *Econometrica*, 37: 55–68.

Wansbeek T. and Kapteyn A. (1982) A Class of Decompositions of the Variance-Covariance Matrix of a Generalized Error Component Model, *Econometrica*, 50: 713–724.

Watson G. (1964) Smooth Regression Analysis. *Sankhya*, Series A, 359–372.

White H. (1980a) A Heteroskedasticity-Consistent Covariance Matrix Estimator and a Direct Test for Heteroskedasticity. *Econometrica*, 48: 817–838.

White H. (1980b) Using Least Squares to Approximate Unknown Regression Functions. *International Economic Review*, 21: 149–170.

White H. (1982a) Maximum Likelihood Estimation of Misspecified Models. *Econometrica*, 50: 1–24.

White H. (1982b) Regularity Conditions for Cox's Test of Non-Nested Hypotheses. *Journal of Econometrics*, 19: 301–318.

White H. (1984) *Asymptotic Theory for Econometricians*, Academic Press, Orlando, FL.

White H. and MacDonald G.M. (1980) Some Large-Sample Tests for Nonnormality in the Linear Regression Model (with discussion). *Journal of the American Statistical Association*, 75: 16–31.

Winkelmann R. and Zimmermann K.F. (1995) Recent Developments in Count Data Modelling: Theory and Application. *Journal of Economics Surveys*, 9: 1–24.

Wolak F. (1987) An Exact Test for Multiple Equality and Inequality Constraints in the Linear Regression Model. *Journal of the American Statistical Association*, 82: 782–793.

Wolak F. (1991) The Local Nature of Hypothesis Tests Involving Inequality Constraints in Nonlinear Models. *Econometrica*, 59: 981–995.

Wolfe M.A. (1978) *Numerical Methods for Unconstrained Optimization*, Van Nostrand, New York.

Wolter K.M. (1985) *Introduction to Variance Estimation*, Springer, New York.

Wooldridge J.M. (1995) Selection Corrections for Panel Data Models under Conditional Mean Independence Assumptions. *Journal of Econometrics*, 68: 115–132.

Wooldridge J.M. (1999) Asymptotic Properties of Weighted M-Estimators for Variable Probability Samples. *Econometrica*, 67: 1385–1406.

Wu D.M. (1973) Alternative Tests of Independence Between Stochastic Regressors and Disturbances. *Econometrica*, 41: 733–750.

Yatchew A. (1998) Nonparametric Regression Techniques in Economics. *Journal of Economic Literature*, 36: 669-721.

Yohai V.J. (1987) High Breakdown-Point and High Efficiency Robust Estimates for Regression. *Annals of Statistics*, 15: 642–656.

Zaman A. (1996) *Statistical Foundations for Econometric Techniques*, Academic Press, San Diego, CA.

Zellner A. (1962) An Efficient Method of Estimating Seemingly Unrelated Regressions and Tests for Aggregation Bias. *Journal of the American Statistical Association*, 57: 348–368.

Zellner A. (1971) *An Introduction to Bayesian Inference in Econometrics*, Wiley, New York.

Zellner A. (1988) Optimal Information Processing and Bayes's Theorem (with discussion). *American Statistician*, 42: 278–284.

Zinde-Walsh V. and Galbraith J.W. (1991) Estimation of a Linear Regression Model with Stationary ARMA(p, q) Errors. *Journal of Econometrics*, 43: 333–357.

Appendix A

Review of Linear Algebra

A.1 VECTOR SPACES AND LINEAR TRANSFORMATIONS

Given the field $\Re$ of real numbers, a (real) *vector space* is a set $\mathcal{X}$ of elements, called *vectors*, for which the following operations are defined.

1. **Addition.** To each pair of vectors $y, x \in \mathcal{X}$ is associated a vector $x + y \in \mathcal{X}$ such that:
   (i) (commutative property) $x + y = y + x$;
   (ii) (associative property) $x + (y + z) = (x + y) + z$;
   (iii) there exists a unique vector $\emptyset \in \mathcal{X}$, called the *null vector*, such that $x + \emptyset = x$;
2. **Scalar multiplication.** To each $x \in \mathcal{X}$ and any $c \in \Re$ is associated a vector $cx \in \mathcal{X}$ such that:
   (i) (distributive property) $c(x + y) = cx + cy$;
   (ii) $(b + c)x = bx + cx$;
   (iii) (associative property) $(bc)x = b(cx)$;
   (iv) $1\,x = x$ and $0\,x = \emptyset$.

An important example of vector space is $\Re^n$, the real n-dimensional Euclidean space.

Given a vector space $\mathcal{X}$, a *linear combination* of vectors $x_1, \ldots, x_n$ in $\mathcal{X}$ is a sum of the form $\sum_{i=1}^{n} a_i x_i = a_1 x_1 + \cdots + a_n x_n$, where the a_i are real numbers. A set of vectors $x_1, \ldots, x_n$ in $\mathcal{X}$ is said to be *linearly independent* if $\sum_{i=1}^{n} a_i x_i = 0$ implies that $a_i = 0$ for all $i = 1, \ldots, n$. It is said to be *linearly dependent* otherwise.

Given two subsets $\mathcal{R}$ and $\mathcal{S}$ of $\mathcal{X}$, the *sum* of $\mathcal{R}$ and $\mathcal{S}$ consists of all the vectors of the form $r + s$, where $r \in \mathcal{R}$ and $s \in \mathcal{S}$. A nonempty subset $\mathcal{M}$ of $\mathcal{X}$ is called a *subspace of $\mathcal{X}$* if, for every $y, x \in \mathcal{M}$, any vector of the form $ax + by$ also belongs to $\mathcal{M}$. Given a vector $x \in \mathcal{X}$ and a subspace $\mathcal{M}$ of $\mathcal{X}$, the set $x + \mathcal{M}$ is called an *affine subspace*.

Given a subspace $\mathcal{S}$ of $\mathcal{X}$, the subspace *generated* by $\mathcal{S}$ consists of all vectors in $\mathcal{X}$ that are linear combinations of vectors in $\mathcal{S}$. A finite set $\mathcal{S}$ of linearly independent vectors in $\mathcal{X}$ forms a *basis* for $\mathcal{X}$ if $\mathcal{S}$ generates $\mathcal{X}$. A vector space is called *finite-dimensional* if it has a finite basis. In particular, if such a basis consists of n elements, then the vector space is called *n-dimensional*. Two different bases for the same n-dimensional vector space contain the same number n of elements.

Let $\mathcal{X}$ and $\mathcal{Y}$ be vector spaces and let $\mathcal{D}$ be a subset of $\mathcal{X}$. A rule that associates with any element $x \in \mathcal{D}$ an element $y \in \mathcal{Y}$ is called a *transformation from $\mathcal{X}$ to $\mathcal{Y}$*

with domain $\mathcal{D}$ and range $\mathcal{Y}$, written $y = T(x)$ or $T\colon \mathcal{D} \to \mathcal{Y}$. A transformation from a vector space $\mathcal{X}$ to $\Re$ is called a *functional on* $\mathcal{X}$. A transformation $T\colon \mathcal{X} \to \mathcal{Y}$ is said to be *linear* if $T(ax + by) = aT(x) + bT(y)$ for all pairs of vectors $y, x \in \mathcal{X}$ and every pair of real numbers a, b.

Let $\mathcal{S} = \{x_1, \ldots, x_n\}$ be a basis for an n-dimensional vector space $\mathcal{X}$, let $\mathcal{R} = \{y_1, \ldots, y_m\}$ be a basis for an m-dimensional vector space $\mathcal{Y}$, and let $T\colon \mathcal{X} \to \mathcal{Y}$ be a linear transformation. Since every vector in $\mathcal{Y}$ may be represented as a linear combination of the y_j, there exists a set of real numbers $\{a_{ij}\}$ such that

$$T(x_j) = \sum_{i=1}^{m} a_{ij} y_i, \qquad j = 1, \ldots, n.$$

The double array

$$A = [a_{ij}] = \begin{bmatrix} a_{11} & a_{12} & \cdots & a_{1n} \\ a_{21} & a_{22} & \cdots & a_{2n} \\ \vdots & \vdots & & \vdots \\ a_{m1} & a_{m2} & \cdots & a_{mn} \end{bmatrix}$$

is called the $m \times n$ *matrix of the linear transformation T in the coordinate system* $\mathcal{R}$.

Because every vector $x \in \mathcal{X}$ may be represented as a linear combination $\sum_j b_j(x)\, x_j$ of the x_j, the matrix A characterizes the linear transformation T. In fact, by the linearity of the transformation T we get

$$T(x) = T\left(\sum_{j=1}^{n} b_j(x)\, x_j\right) = \sum_{j=1}^{n} b_j(x)\, T(x_j) = \sum_{j=1}^{n} \sum_{i=1}^{m} b_j(x)\, a_{ij} y_i,$$

for all $x \in \mathcal{X}$. This result establishes a one-to-one correspondence between the class of matrices of order $m \times n$ and the class of linear transformations from $\mathcal{X}$ to $\mathcal{Y}$. If $\mathcal{Y} = \Re^m$ and $\mathcal{R}$ is the set of unit vectors in $\Re^m$, then the ith column of A is the image under T of the ith basis vector in $\mathcal{X}$.

A.2 MATRICES AND MATRIX OPERATIONS

An $m \times n$ matrix is called *square* if $m = n$. A square matrix is called *upper (lower) triangular* if all elements below (above) the main diagonal are equal to zero. A square matrix $[a_{ij}]$ is called *diagonal* if it is both upper and lower triangular, that is, $a_{ij} = 0$ for every $i \neq j$. A diagonal matrix is also denoted by $\mathrm{diag}[a_{ii}]$.

A *unit* or *identity matrix* of order n, written I_n or simply I, is a diagonal $n \times n$ matrix whose diagonal elements are all equal to one. Equivalently, $A = [a_{ij}]$ is a unit matrix if $a_{ij} = \delta_{ij}$ for every i, j, where δ_{ij} is Kronecker's delta

$$\delta_{ij} = \begin{cases} 1, & \text{if } i = j, \\ 0, & \text{otherwise.} \end{cases}$$

A *zero* or *null matrix* is a matrix whose elements are all equal to zero.

Two $m \times n$ matrices $A = [a_{ij}]$ and $B = [b_{ij}]$ are said to be *equal*, written $A = B$, if $a_{ij} = b_{ij}$ for every i, j. If A is not equal to B, then we write $A \neq B$.

Given $m \times n$ matrices $A = [a_{ij}]$ and $B = [b_{ij}]$, their *sum* $C = A + B$ is the $m \times n$ matrix whose ijth element is equal to $c_{ij} = a_{ij} + b_{ij}$.

Given a matrix $A = [a_{ij}]$ and a real number λ, their *scalar product* $C = \lambda A$ is the matrix whose ijth element is equal to $c_{ij} = \lambda a_{ij}$. Given a unit matrix I and a real number λ, the matrix $C = \lambda I$ is called a *scalar* matrix.

Given an $m \times p$ matrix $A = [a_{ij}]$ and a $p \times n$ matrix $B = [b_{ij}]$, their *product* $C = AB$ is the $m \times n$ matrix whose ijth element is equal to $c_{ij} = \sum_{k=1}^{p} a_{ik} b_{kj}$. Unlike scalar multiplication, matrix multiplication is not commutative, that is $AB \neq BA$, although it satisfies the associative law, that is $(AB)C = A(BC) = ABC$, and the distributive law, that is $A(B + C) = AB + AC$.

Given a square matrix $A = [a_{ij}]$, its *transpose* is the matrix $A^\top$ whose ijth element is equal to the jith element of A. If $C = A + B$ then $C^\top = A^\top + B^\top$, if $C = AB$ then $C^\top = B^\top A^\top$, and if $C = A^\top$ then $C^\top = A$.

A square matrix A is called *symmetric* if $A = A^\top$. A symmetric $n \times n$ matrix contains at most $n(n + 1)/2$ distinct elements.

A.3 DETERMINANT AND INVERSE OF A MATRIX

The *determinant* of a square matrix A is implicitly defined through the recursion

$$\det A = \sum_i a_{ij} \, (-1)^{i+j} \det A_{ij} = \sum_j a_{ij} \, (-1)^{i+j} \det A_{ij},$$

where A_{ij} is the matrix obtained by deleting the ith row and the jth column of A. The determinant $\det A_{ij}$ is called a *minor* of the matrix A, whereas $a^+_{ij} = (-1)^{i+j} \det A_{ij}$ is called a *cofactor*. The matrix $A^+ = [a^+_{ji}]$ is called the *adjoint* of A and satisfies

$$AA^+ = A^+ A = (\det A)\, I. \tag{A.1}$$

By the definition of the determinant of a matrix:

(i) $\det A^\top = \det A$;
(ii) if A is $n \times n$, then $\det(\lambda A) = \lambda^n \det A$;
(iii) if $A = \operatorname{diag}[a_{ii}]$, then $\det A = \prod_i a_{ii}$;
(iv) given square matrices A and B, $\det AB = (\det A)(\det B)$.

Given a square matrix A, if there exists a square matrix A^{-1} such that $A^{-1} A = A A^{-1} = I$, then A^{-1} is called the *inverse* of A. If A has an inverse, then this inverse is unique and, by (A.1), is equal to $A^{-1} = A^+/(\det A)$. Thus, a matrix A has an inverse if and only if $\det A \neq 0$. Further, the ijth element of the inverse of A is equal to $a^+_{ji}/(\det A)$. A matrix whose inverse exists is called *nonsingular*, otherwise it is called *singular*.

If A is a nonsingular matrix, then:

(i) $(A^{-1})^{-1} = A$;
(ii) $\det A^{-1} = 1/(\det A)$;
(iii) $(A^{-1})^\top = (A^\top)^{-1}$ and so A^{-1} is symmetric whenever A is;
(iv) if $A = \operatorname{diag}[a_{ii}]$, then $A^{-1} = \operatorname{diag}[1/a_{ii}]$;
(v) if both A and B are nonsingular, then $(AB)^{-1} = B^{-1} A^{-1}$.

A.4 RANK AND TRACE OF A MATRIX

The (column) *rank* of a matrix A, written $\operatorname{rank} A$, is the maximum number of linearly independent columns of A. It can be shown that:

(i) $\operatorname{rank} A = \operatorname{rank} A^\top$;
(ii) an $n \times n$ matrix A is nonsingular if and only if $\operatorname{rank} A = n$;
(iii) $\operatorname{rank} AB \leq \min(\operatorname{rank} A, \operatorname{rank} B)$;
(iv) if P and Q are nonsingular matrices, then $\operatorname{rank} PAQ = \operatorname{rank} PA = \operatorname{rank} AQ = \operatorname{rank} A$.

The *trace* of a square $n \times n$ matrix $A = [a_{ij}]$ is the number $\operatorname{tr} A = \sum_{i=1}^n a_{ii}$. By the definition of the trace of a matrix:

(i) $\operatorname{tr} A^\top = \operatorname{tr} A$;
(ii) given $n \times n$ matrices A and B, $\operatorname{tr}(\alpha A + \beta B) = \alpha(\operatorname{tr} A) + \beta(\operatorname{tr} B)$;
(iii) if $A = [a_{ij}]$ is an $m \times n$ matrix and $B = [b_{ij}]$ is an $n \times m$ matrix, then

$$\operatorname{tr} AB = \operatorname{tr} BA = \sum_{i=1}^{m} \sum_{j=1}^{n} a_{ij} b_{ji}.$$

A.5 EIGENVALUES AND EIGENVECTORS

Given an $n \times n$ matrix A, an *eigenvalue* of A is a real or complex number λ such that $\det(A - \lambda I_n) = 0$. The equation $\det(A - \lambda I_n) = 0$ is called the *characteristic equation* of A. Given a matrix A and an eigenvalue λ of A, an *eigenvector* of A associated with λ is a vector $x \neq 0$ such that $Ax = \lambda x$. If the matrix A has n distinct eigenvalues, then for each of them there exists a unique eigenvector x such that $x^\top x = 1$.

Theorem A.1 *Given an $n \times n$ matrix A:*

(i) *the characteristic equation of A is a polynomial equation of degree n that may be written as $\det(A - \lambda I_n) = \prod_{i=1}^n (\lambda_i - \lambda) = 0$, hence A has the n eigenvalues $\lambda_1, \ldots, \lambda_n$;*
(ii) *A and $A^\top$ have the same characteristic equation and therefore the same eigenvalues;*
(iii) *given a nonsingular $n \times n$ matrix P, A and $P^{-1}AP$ have the same characteristic equation and therefore the same eigenvalues;*
(iv) *$\det A = \prod_{i=1}^n \lambda_i$ and $\operatorname{tr} A = \sum_{i=1}^n \lambda_i$, hence A is nonsingular if and only if all its eigenvalues are nonzero;*
(v) *if A is nonsingular, then the eigenvectors of A^{-1} are the same as those of A and the eigenvalues of A^{-1} are the reciprocal of those of A;*
(vi) *if A is a symmetric matrix, then its eigenvalues are real and its rank is equal to the number of nonzero eigenvalues;*
(vii) *if A is a triangular matrix, then the elements on its main diagonal are its eigenvalues.*

Theorem A.2 *If A is a symmetric $n \times n$ matrix with eigenvalues $\lambda_1, \ldots, \lambda_n$, then there exists a matrix Q such that:*

(i) $Q^\top AQ = \text{diag}[\lambda_i]$;
(ii) $Q^\top Q = I_n$;
(iii) *the columns of* Q *are the normalized eigenvectors associated with* $\lambda_1, \ldots, \lambda_n$.

Theorem A.3 *Given an* $n \times n$ *matrix* A*, there exists a nonsingular matrix* P *such that* $P^{-1}AP = T$*, where* T *is a triangular matrix with the eigenvalues of* A *on its main diagonal.*

A.6 QUADRATIC FORMS AND DEFINITE MATRICES

Given a symmetric $n \times n$ matrix A and an n-vector x, the function $f(x) = x^\top Ax$ is called a *quadratic form.*

Definition A.1 A symmetric matrix A and the associated quadratic form are called:

(i) *positive definite* (p.d.) if $x^\top Ax > 0$ for all $x \neq 0$,
(ii) *non-negative definite* (n.n.d.) if $x^\top Ax \geq 0$ for all $x \neq 0$,
(iii) *negative definite* (n.d.) if $x^\top Ax < 0$ for all $x \neq 0$,
(iv) *nonpositive definite* (n.p.d.) if $x^\top Ax \leq 0$ for all $x \neq 0$,

and are called *indefinite* otherwise. □

Theorem A.4 *If* A *is a symmetric* $n \times n$ *matrix with eigenvalues* $\lambda_1, \ldots, \lambda_n$*, then* A *is:*

(i) *p.d. if* $\lambda_i > 0$ *for all* i,
(ii) *n.n.d. if* $\lambda_i \geq 0$ *for all* i,
(iii) *n.d. if* $\lambda_i < 0$ *for all* i,
(iv) *n.p.d. if* $\lambda_i \leq 0$ *for all* i,

and is indefinite otherwise.

Theorem A.5 *If* A *is a symmetric p.d.* $n \times n$ *matrix, then there exists a nonsingular matrix* H *such that* $H^\top H = A^{-1}$.

Proof. Since the matrix A is symmetric and p.d., its eigenvalues $\lambda_1, \ldots, \lambda_n$ are all real and positive. By Theorem A.2, we have that $Q^\top AQ = \Lambda$, where $\Lambda = \text{diag}[\lambda_i]$ and $Q = [q_1, \ldots, q_n]$ is the matrix of the corresponding eigenvectors. Since A and Λ are nonsingular matrices, Q is necessarily nonsingular and therefore $A^{-1} = Q\Lambda^{-1}$. The conclusion is then immediate if we put $H = \Lambda^{-1/2}Q^\top$, where $\Lambda^{-1/2} = \text{diag}[1/\sqrt{\lambda_i}]$. □

Given an $n \times n$ matrix A, the set $\{x \in \Re^n \colon x^\top Ax = r^2\}$ is called a *quadratic surface* in $\Re^n$ and the family of *concentric quadratic surfaces* is defined by all the equations of the form $x^\top Ax = r^2$, where $r \geq 0$.

Theorem A.6 *If* A *is a symmetric p.d.* $n \times n$ *matrix and* r *is a real number, then the quadratic surface* $x^\top Ax = r^2$ *is an ellipsoid in* $\Re^n$ *with center at the origin and axes equal to* $q_i r/\sqrt{\lambda_i}$*, where* λ_i *is an eigenvalue of* A *and* q_i *is the corresponding eigenvector.*

Proof. Since A is symmetric and p.d., it follows from Theorem A.2 that $Q^\top AQ = \Lambda$, where $\Lambda = \text{diag}[\lambda_i]$, with $\lambda_i > 0$ for all i, and $Q = [q_1, \ldots, q_n]$ is the orthonormal matrix of the corresponding eigenvectors. The quadratic surface $x^\top Ax = r^2$ may therefore be represented in the canonical form

$$z^\top \Lambda z = \sum_{i=1}^{n} \lambda_i z_i^2 = r^2, \tag{A.2}$$

where $z = Q^\top x$. Equation (A.2) defines an ellipsoid in $\Re^n$ with center at the origin and orthogonal axes equal to $e_i r/\sqrt{\lambda_i}$, where e_i is the ith unit vector. Transforming back into the original coordinate system using the transformation $x = Qz$, the quadratic surface $x^\top Ax = r^2$ is also an ellipsoid in $\Re^n$ with center at the origin and axes equal to $Qe_i r/\sqrt{\lambda_i} = q_i r/\sqrt{\lambda_i}$. □

The ith axis of the ellipsoid $\{x\colon x^\top Ax = r^2\}$ has the same direction as the ith eigenvector of A and its length is equal to $r/\sqrt{\lambda_i}$, the longest axis being associated with the smallest eigenvalue of A.

A.7 PARTITIONED MATRICES

If A and D are nonsingular matrices, then

$$\det \begin{bmatrix} A & B \\ C & D \end{bmatrix} = (\det A)(\det E) = (\det D)(\det F)$$

and

$$\begin{bmatrix} A & B \\ C & D \end{bmatrix}^{-1} = \begin{bmatrix} A^{-1} + A^{-1}BE^{-1}CA^{-1} & -A^{-1}BE^{-1} \\ -E^{-1}CA^{-1} & E^{-1} \end{bmatrix}$$
$$= \begin{bmatrix} F^{-1} & -F^{-1}BD^{-1} \\ -D^{-1}CF^{-1} & D^{-1} + D^{-1}CF^{-1}BD^{-1} \end{bmatrix},$$

where $E = D - CA^{-1}B$ and $F = A - BD^{-1}C$. This result may be used to prove the following.

Lemma A.1 *If A and D are nonsingular matrices, then*

$$(A + BDC)^{-1} = A^{-1} - A^{-1}B(D^{-1} + CA^{-1}B)^{-1}CA^{-1}.$$

A.8 KRONECKER PRODUCT AND VEC OPERATOR

Given any two matrices A and B, of order $m \times n$ and $p \times q$ respectively, the *Kronecker product* of A and B is the $mp \times nq$ matrix

$$A \otimes B = \begin{bmatrix} a_{11}B & \cdots & a_{1n}B \\ \vdots & & \vdots \\ a_{m1}B & \cdots & a_{mn}B \end{bmatrix}.$$

By the definition of Kronecker product:

(i) $A \otimes B \otimes C = (A \otimes B) \otimes C = A \otimes (B \otimes C)$;
(ii) $(A + B) \otimes (C + D) = A \otimes C + A \otimes D + B \otimes C + B \otimes D$;
(iii) if α is a real number, then $\alpha \otimes A = \alpha A = A\alpha = A \otimes \alpha$;
(iv) if a and b are (column) vectors, then $a^\top \otimes b = ba^\top = b \otimes a^\top$;
(v) $(A \otimes B)^\top = A^\top \otimes B^\top$;
(vi) if A and B are square matrices, then $\operatorname{tr}(A \otimes B) = (\operatorname{tr} A)(\operatorname{tr} B)$;
(vii) if A and B are nonsingular matrices, then $(A \otimes B)^{-1} = A^{-1} \otimes B^{-1}$;
(viii) $(A \otimes B)(C \otimes D) = AC \otimes BD$.

Given an $m \times n$ matrix

$$A = \begin{bmatrix} a_1^\top \\ \vdots \\ a_m^\top \end{bmatrix},$$

where a_j is an n-vector, we define

$$\operatorname{vec} A = \begin{pmatrix} a_1 \\ \vdots \\ a_m \end{pmatrix}$$

the nm-vector obtained by stacking the *rows* of A on top of each other. By the definition of vec operator:

(i) $\sum_{i=1}^m a_i^\top a_i = (\operatorname{vec} A)^\top (\operatorname{vec} A)$;
(ii) if a is a vector, then $\operatorname{vec} a^\top = \operatorname{vec} a = a$;
(iii) if a and b are (column) vectors, then $\operatorname{vec}(ab^\top) = a \otimes b$;
(iv) $\operatorname{vec} ABC = (A \otimes C^\top)(\operatorname{vec} B)$.

A.9 DIFFERENTIATION OF MATRICES AND VECTORS

If f: $\Re^p \to \Re$ is a twice differentiable function, then its *gradient* at x is the p-vector

$$f'(x) = \begin{pmatrix} \partial f(x)/\partial x_1 \\ \vdots \\ \partial f(x)/\partial x_p \end{pmatrix},$$

and its *Hessian* at x is the symmetric $p \times p$ matrix

$$f''(x) = \begin{bmatrix} \partial^2 f(x)/\partial x_1^2 & \cdots & \partial^2 f(x)/\partial x_1 \partial x_p \\ \vdots & & \vdots \\ \partial^2 f(x)/\partial x_p \partial x_1 & \cdots & \partial^2 f(x)/\partial x_p^2 f(x) \end{bmatrix}.$$

If f: $\Re^p \to \Re^q$ is a differentiable function, then its *Jacobian* at x is the $p \times q$ matrix

$$f'(x) = \begin{bmatrix} \partial f_1(x)/\partial x_1 & \cdots & \partial f_q(x)/\partial x_1 \\ \vdots & & \vdots \\ \partial f_1(x)/\partial x_q & \cdots & \partial f_q(x)/\partial x_p \end{bmatrix}.$$

In particular, if $f(x) = Ax$, then $f'(x) = A^\top$. If $f(x) = x^\top Ax$, then $f'(x) = (A + A^\top)x$ and $f''(x) = A + A^\top$. If $f(x) = x^\top Ax$ and A is a symmetric matrix, then $f'(x) = 2Ax$ and $f''(x) = 2A$.

A.10 GENERALIZED INVERSES

Given an $m \times n$ matrix A, its *generalized inverse* is an $n \times m$ matrix A^- such that

$$AA^-A = A.$$

The concept of generalized inverse extends that of the inverse of a nonsingular matrix A, because A^{-1}, if it exists, necessarily satisfies the above properties.

The definition of generalized inverse implies the following:

(i) a generalized inverse of an idempotent matrix A is A itself;
(ii) if A^- is a generalized inverse of A, then AA^- and A^-A are idempotent matrices;
(iii) if the matrix A has full column rank, then $A^- = (A^\top A)^{-1}A^\top$ is a generalized inverse of A;
(iv) if A is nonsingular and B has full column rank, then $A^{-1} = B^\top(BAB^\top)^-B$.

By the definition of generalized inverse, if B is a nonsingular matrix and C is a singular square matrix, then

$$\begin{bmatrix} B & 0 \\ 0 & 0 \end{bmatrix}^- = \begin{bmatrix} B^{-1} & 0 \\ 0 & 0 \end{bmatrix}, \qquad \begin{bmatrix} C & 0 \\ 0 & C \end{bmatrix}^- = \begin{bmatrix} C^- & 0 \\ 0 & C^- \end{bmatrix}.$$

Now consider the system of m linear equations

$$Ab = c, \tag{A.3}$$

where b is an n-vector with $n \geq m$. Multiplying $Ab - c$ by AA^- gives

$$AA^-Ab - AA^-c = Ab - AA^-c = (I_p - AA^-)c.$$

If A^- is such that $(I_p - AA^-)c = 0$, then

$$0 = Ab - AA^-c = A(b - A^-c).$$

Hence, the system (A.3) possesses a solution equal to $b^* = A^-c$. If A is a nonsingular matrix, then the solution is unique and is equal to $b^* = A^{-1}c$.

Result A.1 *Given a matrix A,*

$$A(A^\top A)^-A^\top A = A, \qquad A^\top A(A^\top A)^-A^\top = A^\top$$

for any choice of generalized inverse.

Result A.2 *If A and B are such that* $\operatorname{rank} ABA^\top = \operatorname{rank} A$, *then $A^\top(ABA^\top)^-A$ is a generalized inverse of B for any choice of generalized inverse.*

Result A.3 *If A and B are such that* $\operatorname{rank} ABA^\top = \operatorname{rank} A$, *then $A^\top(ABA^\top)^-A$ is invariant to the choice of generalized inverse.*

Result A.4 *The matrix $A(A^\top A)^-A$ and the matrix $A(A^\top A)^-A - AB(B^\top A^\top AB)^-B^\top A$ are idempotent for any choice of generalized inverse.*

Result A.5 *If B is a p.d. matrix, then* $\text{rank}[A^\top(ABA^\top)^- A] = \text{rank}\, A$ *for any choice of generalized inverse.*

A generalized inverse is not unique unless further conditions are imposed. A generalized inverse A^* that satisfies the properties

$$A^*AA^* = A^*, \qquad (A^*A)^\top = A^*A, \qquad (AA^*)^\top = AA^*$$

is called a *Moore–Penrose inverse* of A.

Theorem A.7 *If A is an $m \times n$ matrix, $n \leq m$, with rank equal to $r \leq n$, then:*

(i) *A^* exists and is unique;*
(ii) *$A^* = (A^\top A)^* A^\top = HD^{-1}H^\top A^\top$, where D is a diagonal matrix $r \times r$ whose diagonal elements are the positive eigenvalues of $A^\top A$ and H is the $n \times r$ matrix of the corresponding eigenvectors.*

A.11 PROJECTION THEOREMS

A *normed vector space* $\mathcal{X}$ is a (real) vector space on which is defined a transformation that associates with each $x \in \mathcal{X}$ a real number $||x||$ called the *norm* of x. The norm must satisfy the following axioms:

(i) $||x|| \geq 0$, and $||x|| = 0$ for all $x = 0$;
(ii) (**triangle inequality**) $||x + y|| \leq ||x|| + ||y||$ for all $y, x \in \mathcal{X}$;
(iii) $||\alpha x|| = |\alpha|||x||$ for all real numbers α.

In a normed vector space, an infinite sequence of vectors $\{x_n\}$ is said to *converge* to a vector x, written $x_n \to x$, if the sequence $\{||x - x_n||\}$ of real numbers converges to zero. An infinite sequence $\{x_n\}$ is called a *Cauchy sequence* if $||x_n - x_m|| \to 0$ for $n, m \to \infty$. A normed vector space $\mathcal{X}$ is said to be *complete* if every Cauchy sequence in $\mathcal{X}$ has a limit in $\mathcal{X}$. A complete vector space is called a *Banach space*.

Given a vector space $\mathcal{X}$, an *inner product* is a transformation, defined on $\mathcal{X} \times \mathcal{X}$, that associates with any pair of vectors $x, y \in \mathcal{X}$ a real number $\langle x \,|\, y\rangle$, called the inner product of x and y, which satisfies the following axioms:

(i) $\langle x \,|\, y\rangle = \langle y \,|\, x\rangle$;
(ii) $\langle x + y \,|\, z\rangle = \langle x \,|\, z\rangle + \langle y \,|\, z\rangle$;
(iii) $\langle \alpha x \,|\, z\rangle = \alpha\langle x \,|\, z\rangle$ for all scalar α;
(iv) $\langle x \,|\, x\rangle \geq 0$, and $\langle x \,|\, x\rangle = 0$ if and only if $x = 0$.

Two vectors x, y in a vector space $\mathcal{H}$ with inner product $\langle\cdot \,|\, \cdot\rangle$ are said to be *orthogonal*, written $x \perp y$, if $\langle x \,|\, y\rangle = 0$. A vector $x \in \mathcal{H}$ is said to be *orthogonal to a subset* $\mathcal{S}$ of $\mathcal{H}$, written $x \perp \mathcal{S}$, if $x \perp s$ for all $s \in \mathcal{S}$.

On a vector space with inner product $\langle\cdot \,|\, \cdot\rangle$, the function $||x|| = \sqrt{\langle x \,|\, x\rangle}$ is a norm. A complete vector space on which an inner product is defined is called a *Hilbert space*. Hence, a Hilbert space is a Banach space equipped with an inner product which induces a norm.

Example A.1 An important example of a Hilbert space is the space $\mathcal{H}$ of all random variables with finite variance defined on a probability space $(\Omega, \mathcal{A}, P)$. In this case, given two random variables $Y, X \in \mathcal{H}$, we define $\langle X \mid Y \rangle = \text{Cov}(Y, X)$. Viewed as elements of $\mathcal{H}$, two uncorrelated random variables are therefore orthogonal. The inner product thus defined induces the norm $\|X\| = [\text{Cov}(X, X)]^{1/2} = [\text{Var}(X)]^{1/2}$. □

Theorem A.8 (Classical projection theorem) *Let $\mathcal{M}$ be a closed subspace of a Hilbert space $\mathcal{H}$. For any vector $x \in \mathcal{H}$ there exists a unique vector $m_0 \in \mathcal{M}$ such that $\|x - m_0\| \leq \|x - m\|$ for all $m \in \mathcal{M}$. Further, a necessary and sufficient condition for $m_0 \in \mathcal{M}$ to be such a vector is that $x - m_0 \perp \mathcal{M}$.*

The vector $m_0 \in \mathcal{M}$ such that $x - m_0 \perp \mathcal{M}$ is called the *orthogonal projection of x onto $\mathcal{M}$*. The next result is just a restatement of the classical projection theorem.

Theorem A.9 *Let $\mathcal{M}$ be a closed subspace of a Hilbert space. Let $x \in \mathcal{H}$ and let $\mathcal{V}$ be the affine subspace $x + \mathcal{M}$. Then, there exists a unique vector x_0 in $\mathcal{V}$ with minimum norm. Further, $x_0 \perp \mathcal{M}$.*

Two types of minimum norm problem in Hilbert spaces may be reduced to the solution of a finite system of linear equations. In the first type of problem, the vectors $y_1, \ldots, y_n$ are elements of a Hilbert space $\mathcal{H}$ and $\mathcal{M}$ is a finite-dimensional closed subspace of $\mathcal{H}$ generated by these vectors. Given any element $x \in \mathcal{H}$, one seeks a vector $\hat{x} \in \mathcal{M}$ that is as close as possible to x. Since $\hat{x}$ may be represented as $\hat{x} = \sum_{i=1}^{n} \alpha_i y_i$, the problem is one of finding n scalars $\alpha_1, \ldots, \alpha_n$ such that $\|x - \sum_i \alpha_i y_i\|$ is minimized. By Theorem A.9, the unique solution $\hat{x}$ is the orthogonal projection of x on $\mathcal{M}$ and is characterized by the orthogonality between the vector $x - \hat{x}$ and each of the vectors y_i. Hence

$$\langle x - \sum_{i=1}^{n} \alpha_i y_i \mid y_j \rangle = 0, \qquad j = 1, \ldots, n,$$

or equivalently

$$\sum_{i=1}^{n} \alpha_i \langle y_i \mid y_j \rangle = \langle x \mid y_j \rangle, \qquad j = 1, \ldots, n.$$

These n equations in the n coefficients α_i are called the *normal equations* of the minimum norm problem. Let $\alpha = (\alpha_1, \ldots, \alpha_n)$ and define

$$G = \begin{bmatrix} \langle y_1 \mid y_1 \rangle & \langle y_1 \mid y_2 \rangle & \cdots & \langle y_1 \mid y_n \rangle \\ \langle y_2 \mid y_1 \rangle & \langle y_2 \mid y_2 \rangle & \cdots & \langle y_2 \mid y_n \rangle \\ \vdots & \vdots & & \vdots \\ \langle y_n \mid y_1 \rangle & \langle y_n \mid y_2 \rangle & \cdots & \langle y_n \mid y_n \rangle \end{bmatrix}, \qquad g = \begin{pmatrix} \langle x \mid y_1 \rangle \\ \langle x \mid y_2 \rangle \\ \vdots \\ \langle x \mid y_n \rangle \end{pmatrix},$$

respectively a symmetric $n \times n$ matrix, called the *Gram matrix* of $y_1, \ldots, y_n$, and an n-vector. Then the normal equations may be written more compactly as

$$G\alpha = g.$$

The vector α of coefficients is therefore unique if the Gram matrix is nonsingular, in which case $\alpha = G^{-1} g$.

The second type of problem consists of finding a vector of minimum norm among those that lie on a given hyperplane.

Theorem A.10 *Let $\mathcal{H}$ be a Hilbert space and let $y_1, \ldots, y_n$ be a finite set of linearly independent vectors in $\mathcal{H}$. Among all vectors $x \in \mathcal{H}$ that satisfy*

$$\langle x \,|\, y_i \rangle = c_i, \qquad i = 1, \ldots, n,$$

let x_0 have minimum norm. Then $x_0 = \sum_{i=1}^{n} \beta_i y_i$, where the coefficients β_i satisfy the normal equations

$$\sum_{i=1}^{n} \beta_i \langle y_i \,|\, y_j \rangle = c_j, \qquad j = 1, \ldots, n. \tag{A.4}$$

Letting $\beta = (\beta_1, \ldots, \beta_n)$ and $c = (c_1, \ldots, c_n)$, the equation system (A.4) may be represented more compactly as

$$G\beta = c,$$

where G is the Gram matrix of $y_1, \ldots, y_n$. The vector β of coefficients is therefore unique if the Gram matrix is nonsingular, in which case $\beta = G^{-1}c$.

BIBLIOGRAPHIC NOTES

On matrix differential calculus with econometric and statistical applications see Magnus and Neudecker (1988). On generalized inverses see Rao and Mitra (1971). Section A.11 is largely based on Luenberger (1969).

Appendix B

Methods of Numerical Maximization

This appendix reviews some numerical methods for locating a maximum of a continuous function $f\colon \Re^p \to \Re$. Without loss of generality we only consider maximization problems, for minimizing a function f corresponds to maximizing $-f$. Thus, $f(\theta)$ may correspond either to a sample log-likelihood or, more generally, to the criterion function defining an M-estimator.

We are concerned exclusively with unconstrained maximization problems. As shown in the next two examples, constrained problems can sometimes be turned easily into unconstrained ones.

Example B.1 Suppose that maximization is subject to the constraint $R(\theta) = 0$. If the conditions of the implicit function theorem are satisfied, one may partition θ as $\theta = (\theta_1, \Theta_2)$, solve $R(\theta_1, \theta_2) = 0$ for $\theta_2 = h(\theta_1)$, and then solve the unconstrained problem of maximizing $f_*(\theta_1) = f(\theta_1, h(\theta_1))$ with respect to θ_1. □

Example B.2 Inequality constraints can sometimes be handled by a suitable reparametrization. Thus, under the constraint that $\theta \geq 0$, the model may be reparametrized in terms of $\psi = \sqrt{\theta}$, under the constraint that $\theta > 0$ it may be reparametrized in terms of $\psi = \ln \theta$, and under the constraint that $0 < \theta < 1$ it may be reparametrized in terms of $\psi = \ln[\theta/(1-\theta)]$. □

B.1 ALGORITHMS

An *algorithm* is an iterative procedure or sequence of steps, with the rth step typically defined as

$$\theta^{(r+1)} = \theta^{(r)} + \lambda^{(r)}\Delta^{(r)}, \qquad r = 0, 1, 2, \ldots,$$

where $\lambda^{(r)}$ is a non-negative scalar called *step length* and $\Delta^{(r)}$ is a p-vector called the *search direction*. Algorithms differ in the way $\lambda^{(r)}$ and $\Delta^{(r)}$ are selected.

The role of the step length $\lambda^{(r)}$ is to guarantee that the value of g does not decrease by taking a step of the algorithm. To see this, let $\theta^{(r)}$ and $\Delta^{(r)}$ be the value of θ and the search direction at the rth iteration, and consider the linear combination

$$(1-\lambda)\theta^{(r)} + \lambda(\theta^{(r)} + \Delta^{(r)}) = \theta^{(r)} + \lambda\Delta^{(r)}.$$

Then there exists a step length $\lambda^{(r)}$ such that

$$f(\theta^{(r+1)}) = f(\theta^{(r)} + \lambda^{(r)}\Delta^{(r)}) \geq f(\theta^{(r)}).$$

Most algorithms can only find local maxima. If the criterion function can be shown to be strictly concave, then it has a unique local maximum which is also its global maximum. In this case, convergence of an algorithm to the global maximum is typically guaranteed no matter what the starting point is. If the criterion function is nonconcave, then the choice of the starting point is an important issue. An easy and tractable method is the *multistart* algorithm, where the iterations are started from several different points chosen either subjectively or randomly. If all starting points lead to the same local maximum θ^*, this is declared to be the global maximum. If the procedure locates several local maxima, the "maximum maximorum" is declared to be the global maximum.

Another important aspect of an algorithm is the criterion for terminating the iterations or *stopping rule*. If the sequence $\{\theta^{(r)}\}$ converges to a maximum of f, then $||\theta^{(r+1)} - \theta^{(r)}|| \rightarrow 0$ and $|f(\theta^{(r+1)}) - f(\theta^{(r)})| \rightarrow 0$. Although either criterion may be used, it is more common to base the stopping rule on relative changes. Thus, iterations may stop when either of the following conditions are met:

1. $||\theta^{(r+1)} - \theta^{(r)}|| < \epsilon \max(\delta, ||\theta^{(r)}||)$,
2. $f(\theta^{(r+1)}) - f(\theta^{(r)}) < \epsilon \max(\delta, |f(\theta^{(r)})|)$,

where ϵ and δ are preassigned positive constants. Theoretically, it is possible for either difference to be small while the other is large. It is therefore advisable to use both criteria and continue iterating until both are satisfied.

Achieving convergence may not be straightforward. Two typical problems are: (a) the function f may not have a unique maximum, and (b) the function f may be relatively flat around a local maximum.

B.2 DIRECT SEARCH METHODS

Direct search methods employ no derivatives. These methods are appealing, for the computation of derivatives, analytically or numerically, tends to be expensive. Other advantages are the assurance of eventual convergence, and the independence of the concavity or convexity of the function f.

A simple method is *grid search*. In the univariate case, one starts at some point $\theta^{(0)}$ and evaluates the function f over a grid of $2k + 1$ points

$$\theta^{(0)} - h^{(0)}k < \cdots < \theta^{(0)} < \cdots < \theta^{(0)} + h^{(0)}k,$$

where $h^{(0)}$ is a preassigned interval width. A step is taken from $\theta^{(0)}$ to $\theta^{(1)}$, where $\theta^{(1)}$ is the point on the grid at which f is maximized. The search is then repeated starting from $\theta^{(1)}$, with the width reduced to $h^{(1)} < h^{(0)}$. The algorithm continues until a maximum of f is located with sufficient accuracy.

This method may be difficult to use if the search interval is not known or is the whole real line. In the latter case, a natural approach involves reparametrizing the model in terms of $\psi = e^{\theta}/(1 + e^{\theta})$ and then searching over the interval $(0, 1)$.

Univariate direct search is often an important part of other algorithms, for a common problem consists of choosing a step length λ given a search direction $\Delta^{(r)}$ in order to maximize $f(\theta^{(r)} + \lambda\Delta^{(r)})$.

B.3 NEWTON-TYPE METHODS

Newton-type methods require the criterion function f to be smooth and employ its first and, possibly, second derivatives. The search direction for this class of methods is typically of the form $\Delta = -H^{-1}g$, where $g = f'$ is the gradient of f and $H = f''$ is the Hessian of f, or some approximation to it.

B.3.1 NEWTON-RAPHSON

The idea of the *Newton-Raphson (NR) method* is to locally approximate f by a quadratic function obtained by taking a second-order Taylor series expansion of f about a given point $\theta^{(r)}$

$$f^{(r)}(\theta) = f(\theta^{(r)}) + g^{(r)\top}(\theta - \theta^{(r)}) + \frac{1}{2}(\theta - \theta^{(r)})^\top H^{(r)}(\theta - \theta^{(r)}),$$

where $g^{(r)} = g(\theta^{(r)})$ and $H^{(r)} = H(\theta^{(r)})$. The error in approximating $f(\theta)$ by $f^{(r)}(\theta)$ may be neglected when θ is near $\theta^{(r)}$.

A stationary point of $f^{(r)}$ is a root of the system of linear equations

$$0 = g^{(r)} + H^{(r)}(\theta - \theta^{(r)}).$$

If the Hessian matrix $H^{(r)}$ is n.d., then the quadratic approximation $f^{(r)}(\theta)$ attains its maximum at the point

$$\theta^{(r+1)} = \theta^{(r)} - [H^{(r)}]^{-1}g^{(r)}. \tag{B.1}$$

The NR method consists of a sequence of iterations of the form (B.1) for $r = 0, 1, 2, \ldots$, starting from some initial guess $\theta^{(0)}$. Notice that the search direction is $\Delta^{(r)} = -[H^{(r)}]^{-1}g^{(r)}$ and the step length is $\lambda^{(r)} = 1$.

It is easy to verify that if f is quadratic, that is, $f(\theta) = a + b^\top\theta + \theta^\top C\theta$ and C is a n.d. matrix, then the NR method converges to the unique maximum $\theta^* = -C^{-1}b$ in a single iteration, no matter what the starting point is. If f is not quadratic, substituting (B.1) back into the quadratic approximation $f^{(r)}$ gives

$$f(\theta^{(r+1)}) \approx f(\theta^{(r)}) - \frac{1}{2}g^{(r)\top}[H^{(r)}]^{-1}g^{(r)}.$$

This shows two important limitations of the NR method. First, an iteration leads to an improvement in f only when $H^{(r)}$ is a n.d. matrix. If instead $H^{(r)}$ is p.d., then the value of f actually decreases, whereas if $H^{(r)}$ is singular and its null space contains $g^{(r)}$, then no improvement is possible. If $H^{(r)}$ is nearly singular, that is, $f(\theta)$ is relatively flat near the point $\theta^{(r)}$, then the algorithm tends to proceed very slowly.

A simple way of dealing with this first problem is to replace $-H^{(r)}$ by the identity matrix I_p. The resulting method is known as *steepest ascent.* Another possibility

(Goldfeld, Quandt & Trotter 1966) is to replace $H^{(r)}$ by the matrix $H^{(r)} - \alpha^{(r)} I_p$, where $\alpha^{(r)}$ is a scalar chosen (possibly at each iteration) in such a way that $H^{(r)} - \alpha^{(r)} I_p$ is n.d. The resulting method is known as *quadratic hill climbing.*

The second problem is that, even when $H^{(r)}$ is n.d., the difference $\theta^{(r+1)} - \theta^{(r)}$ may be too large or too small. If it is too large, then the algorithm overshoots the target. If it is too small, then the speed of convergence is too slow. This problem may be solved by introducing a variable step length.

B.3.2 METHOD OF SCORING

An alternative to the NR method exploits the fact that if the criterion to be maximized is the log-likelihood $L(\theta)$ of a correctly specified and regular parametric models then the information matrix $I(\theta)$ is p.d. on Θ and, by the information equality, $I(\theta) = \mathrm{E}_\theta[-L''(\theta)]$. Replacing the Hessian of the log-likelihood by $I(\theta)$ gives iterations of the form

$$\theta^{(r+1)} = \theta^{(r)} - I(\theta^{(r)})^{-1} S^{(r)}, \tag{B.2}$$

where $S^{(r)} = L'(\theta^{(r)})$. An advantage of this method, called *method of scoring*, is that $I(\theta)$ is often easier to compute than the Hessian of the log-likelihood. This may more than offset the slower rate of convergence of this algorithm.

B.3.3 BHHH

Another alternative to NR exploits the fact that $I(\theta) = \mathrm{E}_\theta[S(\theta)\, S(\theta)^\top]$, where $S(\theta) = L'(\theta)$. This suggests replacing $I(\theta^{(r)})$ in the scoring iteration by its consistent estimate $S^{(r)}\, S^{(r)\top}$, which is usually a p.d. matrix. With the introduction of a variable step length $\lambda^{(r)}$, we obtain the method of Berndt, Hall, Hall and Hausmann (1974) or *BHHH method*, based on iterations of the form

$$\theta^{(r+1)} = \theta^{(r)} + \lambda^{(r)} [S^{(r)} S^{(r)\top}]^{-1} S^{(r)}.$$

Notice that the BHHH method only employs first derivatives of the log-likelihood.

B.3.4 GAUSS-NEWTON

For GMM and NLLS problems, the criterion function is of the general form

$$f(\theta) = -g(\theta)^\top D\, g(\theta),$$

where g is a continuously differentiable function and D is a weight matrix.

The *Gauss-Newton (GN)* method exploits the special form of the criterion function f by considering a linear approximation to g obtained by taking a first-order Taylor series expansion of g about a given point $\theta^{(r)}$, namely

$$g^{(r)}(\theta) = g^{(r)} + G^{(r)}(\theta^{(r)} - \theta),$$

where $G^{(r)} = g'(\theta^{(r)})$. The resulting quadratic approximation to f is

$$f^{(r)}(\theta) = -[g^{(r)} + G^{(r)}(\theta^{(r)} - \theta)]^\top D\, [g^{(r)} + G^{(r)}(\theta^{(r)} - \theta)].$$

If $G^{(r)\top} D\, G^{(r)}$ is a p.d. matrix, then the quadratic approximation attains a unique maximum at

$$\theta^{(r+1)} = \theta^{(r)} - [G^{(r)\top} D\, G^{(r)}]^{-1} G^{(r)\top} D\, g^{(r)}, \tag{B.3}$$

where the difference $\theta^{(r+1)} - \theta^{(r)}$ is the vector of coefficients in a GLS regression of $g^{(r)}$ on $G^{(r)}$ with weight matrix equal to D^{-1}. Thus, the GN method corresponds to iterated GLS. If $D = I_p$, as in standard NLLS problems, the GN method corresponds to iterated LS.

It is easy to verify that if g is a linear function of θ, that is, $g(\theta) = b + C\theta$, then the GN iteration reduces to a single GLS regression of b on C, with weight matrix equal to D^{-1}.

If the vector function g is of the same dimension as θ, as in the case of exactly identified models, then G is a square matrix and (B.3) becomes

$$\theta^{(r+1)} = \theta^{(r)} - [G^{(r)}]^{-1} g^{(r)},$$

which is the same as the NR iteration with $H^{(r)} = G^{(r)}$.

B.4 THE EM ALGORITHM

The EM algorithm is a useful method for iteratively computing the ML estimator in latent variable models.

Let $\mathbf{Z}^*$ be a vector of latent data whose distribution is known to belong to a parametric family with distribution function $F(\mathbf{z};\theta)$ and density function $f(\mathbf{z},\theta)$. The parameter θ is assumed to lie in a compact subset Θ of $\Re^p$. Suppose that $\mathbf{Z}^*$ is related to the observed data vector $\mathbf{Z}$ through the *observation rule* $\mathbf{Z} = \tau(\mathbf{Z}^*)$, where τ is a noninvertible function which is assumed to be piecewise continuous, but not necessarily monotonic. We further assume that τ does not depend on θ. The distribution function of $\mathbf{Z}$ is

$$G(\mathbf{z};\theta) = \int_{\{\mathbf{u}:\tau(\mathbf{u})\le\mathbf{z}\}} f(\mathbf{u};\theta)\, d\mathbf{u},$$

and the associated density is denoted by $g(\mathbf{z};\theta)$.

Using this latent structure, the EM algorithm provides an iterative method for maximizing the observed-data log-likelihood $L(\theta) = \ln g(\mathbf{z};\theta)$ over Θ. The algoritm consists of two steps: The E- or expectation-step, and the M- or maximization-step.

In the E-step, one takes the expectation of the log-likelihood for the latent data $\mathbf{Z}^*$ conditional on the observed data $\mathbf{Z}$ and a preliminary estimate of θ, say $\theta^{(0)}$. The conditional distribution function of $\mathbf{Z}^*$ given $\mathbf{Z} = \mathbf{z}$ is

$$F(\mathbf{z}^* \mid \mathbf{z};\theta^{(0)}) = \lim_{\epsilon\to 0+} \frac{\Pr\{\mathbf{Z}^* \le \mathbf{z}^*, \mathbf{z} < \tau(\mathbf{Z}^*) \le \mathbf{z}+\epsilon\}}{\Pr\{\mathbf{z} < \tau(\mathbf{Z}^*) \le \mathbf{z}+\epsilon\}}.$$

This conditional distribution function, called *predictive distribution of* $\mathbf{Z}^*$ *given* $\theta^{(0)}$, may consist of a continuous and a discrete part. The expectation of the latent-data log-likelihood is

$$Q(\theta,\theta^{(0)}) = \int \ln f(\mathbf{z}^*;\theta)\, dF(\mathbf{z}^* \mid \mathbf{z};\theta^{(r)}).$$

In the M-step, one maximizes $Q(\theta, \theta^{(0)})$ with respect to θ obtaining

$$\theta^{(1)} = M(\theta^{(1)}) = \underset{\theta \in \Theta}{\text{argmax}}\ Q(\theta, \theta^{(0)}).$$

Under appropriate regularity conditions, iterating the two steps of the algorithm yields a sequence $\{\theta^{(r)}\}$ of values of θ which converges to a fixed point of the mapping M, that is, a value $\hat{\theta}$ such that $\hat{\theta} = M(\hat{\theta})$. It turns out that the fixed point $\hat{\theta}$ is also a local maximum of the observed-data log-likelihood $L(\theta)$. Here, we just sketch the basic idea.

Let

$$H(\theta, \theta^{(r)}) = Q(\theta, \theta^{(r)}) - L(\theta) \tag{B.4}$$

be the difference between the expectation $Q(\theta, \theta^{(r)})$ of the latent-data log-likelihood and the observed-data log-likelihood $L(\theta)$ and notice that

$$\begin{aligned} H(\theta, \theta^{(r)}) &= \int \ln \frac{f(\mathbf{z}^*; \theta)}{g(\mathbf{z}; \theta)}\, dF(\mathbf{z}^* \mid \mathbf{z}; \theta^{(r)}) \\ &= \int \ln f(\mathbf{z}^* \mid \mathbf{z}; \theta)\, dF(\mathbf{z}^* \mid \mathbf{z}; \theta^{(r)}). \end{aligned}$$

Thus

$$\begin{aligned} L(\theta^{(r+1)}) - L(\theta^{(r)}) = {} & Q(\theta^{(r+1)}, \theta^{(r)}) - Q(\theta^{(r)}, \theta^{(r)}) \\ & + H(\theta^{(r)}, \theta^{(r)}) - H(\theta^{(r+1)}, \theta^{(r)}), \end{aligned}$$

where

$$Q(\theta^{(r+1)}, \theta^{(r)}) - Q(\theta^{(r)}), \theta^{(r)}) \geq 0,$$

by the definition of $\theta^{(r+1)}$. Further, if the parametric model is identifiable then, by the Kullback-Leibler inequality,

$$H(\theta^{(r)}, \theta^{(r)}) - H(\theta, \theta^{(r)}) \geq 0$$

for all θ, and in particular for $\theta = \theta^{(r+1)}$. Hence, $L(\theta^{(r+1)}) - L(\theta^{(r)}) \geq 0$, that is, maximizing the expectation of the latent-data log-likelihood also improves the observed-data log-likelihood. In regular problems, iterating the EM algorithm eventually leads to the ML estimator of θ based on the observed-data log-likelihood.

Notice that the parameter vector θ need not be identifiable with respect to the distribution of the observed data $\mathbf{Z}$ for the EM algorithm to work.

Example B.3 The EM algorithm is particularly suited for models where the distribution of the latent-data $\mathbf{Z}^*$ belongs to the linear exponential family with density

$$f(\mathbf{z}; \eta) = \exp\left[\eta^\top T(\mathbf{z}) + d(\eta) + c(\mathbf{z})\right],$$

where η is the canonical parameter for the model and $T(\mathbf{z})$ is a vector of sufficient statistics. The latent-data log-likelihood is of the form

$$L^*(\eta) = \eta^\top T^* + d(\eta) + c,$$

where $T^* = T(\mathbf{Z}^*)$ is the vector of latent-data sufficient statistics and c is an arbitrary constant. The expectation of the latent-data log-likelihood is therefore

$$Q(\eta, \eta^{(r)}) = \eta^\top \operatorname{E}[T^* \mid \mathbf{Z} = \mathbf{z}; \eta = \eta^{(r)}] + d(\eta) + c,$$

where $E[T^* \mid \mathbf{Z} = \mathbf{z}; \eta = \eta^{(r)}]$ is often available in closed form. Hence, maximizing with respect to η gives the equation system

$$E[T^* \mid \mathbf{Z} = \mathbf{z}; \eta = \eta^{(r)}] = -d'(\eta),$$

which often can also be solved in closed form. □

In practice, the computational efficiency of the EM algorithm is somewhat mixed. In favor of the EM algorithm are the fact that it does not require calculation of the log-likelihood of $\mathbf{Z}$, a line search in the parameter space, or the Hessian of the log-likelihood at each iteration. Against it is the fact that the speed of each iteration may be more than compensated by the extra iterations required, especially in a neighborhood of the critical values of the log-likelihood.

We now show that both the likelihood score and estimates of the Fisher information for the observed-data model are readily available from the EM algorithm.

Let $Q_1(\theta, \hat{\theta}) = (\partial/\partial\theta)Q(\theta, \hat{\theta})$ and $Q_{11}(\theta, \hat{\theta}) = (\partial/\partial\theta)Q_1(\theta, \hat{\theta})$. Suppose that f is a smooth function of θ, and the function τ does not depend on θ. Differentiating the identity (B.4) with respect to θ gives

$$H_1(\theta, \hat{\theta}) = Q_1(\theta, \hat{\theta}) - L'(\theta),$$

where $H_1(\theta, \hat{\theta}) = (\partial/\partial\theta)H(\theta, \hat{\theta})$. Replacing $\hat{\theta}$ by θ and using the fact that $H_1(\theta, \theta) = 0$ gives

$$L'(\theta) = Q_1(\theta, \theta).$$

Thus, the EM algorithm provides a direct calculation of the likelihood score. Given the likelihood score, one may estimate the information matrix either by the outer-product $Q_1(\hat{\theta}, \hat{\theta})\, Q_1(\hat{\theta}, \hat{\theta})^\top$ or by the observed information $Q_{11}(\hat{\theta}, \hat{\theta})$.

The above result also provides an interesting comparison between the EM and the NR method. Suppose that Q_{11} and L'' are both nonsingular. To a first approximation, the EM iteration is of the form

$$\theta^{(r+1)} = \theta^{(r)} - Q_{11}^{-1}\, Q_1,$$

where Q_{11} and Q_1 are evaluated at $\theta = \theta^{(r)}$. The NR iteration is instead of the form

$$\theta^{(r+1)} = \theta^{(r)} - (L'')^{-1}\, L',$$

where L'' and L' are also evaluated at $\theta = \theta^{(r)}$. Differentiating the identity (B.4) twice gives

$$H_{11} = Q_{11} - L''.$$

Since $L' = Q_1$, the EM iteration can be written

$$\theta^{(r+1)} = \theta^{(r)} - (L'' + H_{11})^{-1}\, L'.$$

Thus, the EM algorithm is also a gradient method, but it substitutes the Hessian of the log-likelihood with a matrix that exceeds the Hessian by the symmetric n.n.d. H_{11}, which may be interpreted as a measure of the information loss due to partial observability of $\mathbf{Z}^*$. This explains both the remarkable numerical stability and the slow rate of convergence of the EM algorithm.

B.5 NUMERICAL DERIVATIVES

In all cases discussed so far, analytic derivatives may be replaced by numeric derivatives. For example, the partial derivative of f with respect to the jth component of θ may be replaced by either the one-sided derivative

$$\frac{f(\theta + \delta e_j) - f(\theta)}{\delta},$$

where δ is a small, positive scalar and e_j is the jth unit vector, or by the two-sided derivative

$$\frac{f(\theta + \delta e_j) - f(\theta - \delta e_j)}{2\delta}.$$

BIBLIOGRAPHIC NOTES

The article by Quandt (1983) reviews numerical methods for solving ML problems when the log-likelihood is not quadratic. Other useful references are Wolfe (1978) and Gill, Murray and Wright (1981). Tanner (1993) gives a unified treatment of a variety of numerical algorithms for solving ML and Bayes problems.

Andrews (1997) proposes a stopping rule for ensuring $\sqrt{n}$-consistency and asymptotic normality in nonconcave maximization problems where a multi-start algorithm is employed.

The EM algorithm was introduced by Dempster, Laird and Rubin (1977). The presentation in Section B.4 is based on Schafer (1997). Another useful monograph is McLachlan and Krishnan (1997).

Appendix C

Review of Probability

C.1 CONDITIONAL DISTRIBUTIONS

Let X and Y be random variables defined on the same probability space $(\Omega, \mathcal{A}, P)$. If X is discrete and x is such that $P\{X = x\} > 0$, then the *conditional probability given* $X = x$ is a probability measure P_x on $(\Omega, \mathcal{A})$ defined by

$$P_x\{A\} = \frac{P\{A, X = x\}}{P\{X = x\}}$$

for all $A \in \mathcal{A}$. Instead of $P_x\{A\}$ we more frequently write $P\{A \mid X = x\}$. The *conditional distribution of* Y *given* $X = x$ is the distribution of Y if P_x is the probability on $(\Omega, \mathcal{A})$.

In particular, if X and Y are both discrete with joint probability function $f(x, y)$, then we define

$$P\{Y = y \mid X = x\} = \frac{P\{Y = y, X = x\}}{P\{X = x\}} = \frac{f(x, y)}{f_X(x)}$$

if $f_X(x) = P\{X = x\} > 0$, and define $P\{Y = y \mid X = x\} = 0$ otherwise. Viewed as a function of y for given x, $P\{Y = y \mid X = x\}$ is called the *conditional probability function of* Y *given* $X = x$, written $f_{Y|X}(y \mid x)$ or simply $f(y \mid x)$. The conditional probability function of X given $Y = y$ is analogously defined and denoted by $f_{X|Y}(x \mid y)$ or simply by $f(x \mid y)$.

By the multiplicative law of probability

$$f(x, y) = f_{Y|X}(y \mid x)\, f_X(x) = f_{X|Y}(x \mid y)\, f_Y(y)$$

where, by the law of total probability,

$$f_Y(y) = \sum_x f_{Y|X}(y \mid x)\, f_X(x), \qquad f_X(x) = \sum_y f_{X|Y}(x \mid y)\, f_Y(y).$$

The conditional probability of Y given $X = x$ is easy to compute in two special cases. If Y is a function of X, namely $Y = h(X)$, then

$$f_{Y|X}(y \mid x) = \begin{cases} 1, & \text{if } y = h(x), \\ 0, & \text{otherwise.} \end{cases} \tag{C.1}$$

If X and Y are independent, then

$$f_{Y|X}(y \mid x) = \frac{f_X(x)\, f_Y(y)}{f_X(x)} = f_Y(y).$$

By analogy with the discrete case, if X and Y are continuous random variables with joint density $f(x, y)$ and marginal densities $f_X(x)$ and $f_Y(y)$ respectively, then the conditional density of Y given $X = x$ is defined as

$$f_{Y|X}(y \mid x) = \begin{cases} \dfrac{f(x,y)}{f_X(x)}, & \text{if } f_X(x) > 0, \\ 0, & \text{otherwise.} \end{cases}$$

Integrating with respect to x both sides of the identity

$$f(x, y) = f_{Y|X}(y \mid x)\, f_X(x)$$

gives

$$f_Y(y) = \int f_{Y|X}(y \mid x)\, f_X(x)\, dx.$$

If X and Y are independent, then

$$f_{Y|X}(y \mid x) = f_Y(y), \qquad f_{X|Y}(x \mid y) = f_X(x).$$

C.2 CONDITIONAL EXPECTATIONS

If X and Y are discrete random variables defined on the same probability space and Y is such that $\mathrm{E}\,|Y| < \infty$, then the *conditional mean* or *conditional expectation of* Y *given* $X = x$ is defined as

$$\mathrm{E}(Y \mid X = x) = \sum_y y\, f(y \mid x),$$

where $f(y \mid x)$ is the conditional probability function of Y given $X = x$. Since $f(x, y) \le \sum_x f(x, y) = f_Y(y)$, we have that $f(y \mid x) \le f_Y(y)/f_X(x)$ and therefore

$$\sum_y |y|\, f(y \mid x) \le \sum_y |y| \frac{f_Y(y)}{f_X(x)} = \frac{\mathrm{E}\,|Y|}{f_X(x)}.$$

Hence, $\mathrm{E}(Y \mid X = x)$ is well defined whenever $f_X(x) > 0$.

Given the function $\mu(x) = \mathrm{E}(Y \mid X = x)$, the random variable $\mu(X)$ is called the *conditional mean* or *conditional expectation of* Y *given* X, also denoted by $\mathrm{E}(Y \mid X)$. The conditional mean of X given Y, denoted by $\mathrm{E}(X \mid Y)$, is analogously defined.

Since the conditional mean of Y given $X = x$ is just the mean of the conditional distribution of Y given $X = x$, it satisfies all the properties of a mean. In particular

$$\mathrm{E}(aY + b \mid X = x) = a\mu(x) + b.$$

Because this must be true for all x such that $f_X(x) > 0$, we have

$$\mathrm{E}(aY + b \mid X) = a\mu(X) + b.$$

The conditional expectation of Y given X is easy to compute in two special cases. If $Y = h(X)$, then (C.1) implies that

$$\mathrm{E}[h(X) \mid X] = h(X). \tag{C.2}$$

If X and Y are independent, then $f(y \mid x) = f_Y(y)$ for all y and therefore

$$\mathrm{E}(Y \mid X) = \sum_y y\, f_Y(y) = \mathrm{E}\, Y. \tag{C.3}$$

More generally, when $\mathrm{E}(Y \mid X)$ does not depend on X, then we say that Y is *mean independent of* X. While independence implies mean independence, the converse is not true in general.

By a similar argument, if $\mathrm{E}\,|g(X,Y)| < \infty$, then

$$\mathrm{E}[g(X,Y) \mid X = x] = \mathrm{E}[g(x,Y) \mid X = x]. \tag{C.4}$$

In particular, if $g(x,y) = [y - \mu(x)]^2$, then $\mathrm{E}[g(X,Y) \mid X = x]$ is called the *conditional variance of* Y *given* $X = x$ and denoted by $\mathrm{Var}(Y \mid X = x)$. Given the non-negative function $\sigma^2(x) = \mathrm{Var}(Y \mid X = x)$, the random variable $\sigma^2(X)$ is called the *conditional variance of* Y *given* X, also denoted by $\mathrm{Var}(Y \mid X)$.

If Y and X are continuous random variables then, by analogy with the discrete case, the conditional mean of Y given $X = x$ is defined as the mean of a random variable with probability density $f(y \mid x)$ (for a more rigorous definition see for example Chung 1974). More generally, if $\mathrm{E}\,|g(Y)| < \infty$, then the conditional mean of $g(Y)$ given $X = x$ is defined as

$$\mathrm{E}[g(Y) \mid X = x] = \int g(y)\, f(y \mid x)\, dy.$$

As in the discrete case, if $h(x) = \mathrm{E}[g(Y) \mid X = x]$, then the random variable $h(X)$ is called the conditional mean of $g(Y)$ given X, written $\mathrm{E}[g(Y) \mid X]$. One can show that, with this definition, properties (C.3) and (C.4) hold for the continuous case as well. If Y and X are random vectors defined on the same probability space, $\mathrm{E}(Y \mid X)$ and $\mathrm{E}[g(Y) \mid X]$ are analogously defined.

The next theorem collects further results about conditional means.

Theorem C.1 *Let X and Y be random variables defined on the same probability space.*

(i) *If* $\mathrm{E}\,|Y| < \infty$, *then* $\mathrm{E}\,\mu(X) = \mathrm{E}\,Y$.

(ii) *If* $h(X)$ *is bounded and* $\mathrm{E}\,|g(Y)| < \infty$, *then*

$$\mathrm{E}[h(X)\, g(Y) \mid X] = h(X)\, \mathrm{E}[g(Y) \mid X],$$

$$\mathrm{E}\, h(X)\, g(Y) = \mathrm{E}\{h(X)\, \mathrm{E}[g(Y) \mid X]\}.$$

(iii) *If* $\mathrm{E}\{[Y - g(X)]^2\} < \infty$, *then*

$$\mathrm{E}[Y - g(X)]^2 = \mathrm{E}\,\sigma^2(X) + \mathrm{E}[g(X) - \mu(X)]^2.$$

Proof. See for example Chung (1974). □

Part (i), called the *law of iterated expectations*, implies that the mean of the random variable $\mu(X)$ is equal to $\mathrm{E}\,Y$. If $\mathrm{Var}\,Y$ exists and we put $g(x) = \mathrm{E}\,Y$ for all x, then part (iii) implies the *law of total variance*

$$\mathrm{Var}\,Y = \mathrm{E}\,\sigma^2(X) + \mathrm{Var}\,\mu(X),$$

where $\mathrm{Var}\,\mu(X) = \mathrm{E}[\mu(X) - \mathrm{E}\,Y]^2$.

It follows from the law of iterated expectations that if X, Y and W are random variables defined on the same probability space and $f_{W\,|\,X}(w\,|\,x)$ is the conditional density of W given $X = x$, then

$$\begin{aligned}\mathrm{E}[\mathrm{E}(Y\,|\,X,W)\,|\,X=x] &= \int \mathrm{E}(Y\,|\,X=x, W=w)\, f_{W\,|\,X}(w\,|\,x)\, dw \\ &= \mathrm{E}(Y\,|\,X=x),\end{aligned}$$

and therefore $\mathrm{E}[\mathrm{E}(Y\,|\,X,W)\,|\,X] = \mathrm{E}(Y\,|\,X)$.

C.3 STOCHASTIC INEQUALITIES

This section lists some useful inequalities from probability theory. Proofs may be found in Lukacs (1975) or Chow and Teicher (1988). The random variables X and Y are defined on the same probability space $(\Omega, \mathcal{A}, P)$.

Theorem C.2 (Jensen inequality) *Let g be a convex function defined on $\Re$. If X is such that $\mathrm{E}\,|X| < \infty$ and $\mathrm{E}\,|g(X)| < \infty$, then $g(\mathrm{E}\,X) \le \mathrm{E}\,g(X)$.*

Theorem C.3 (Chebyshev inequality) *If X is such that $\mathrm{E}\,|X|^r < \infty$ for some $r > 0$ then, for all $\epsilon > 0$ and any finite c, $P\{|X - c| \ge \epsilon\} \le \mathrm{E}\,|X - c|^r/\epsilon^r$.*

Theorem C.4 (Cauchy–Schwarz inequality) *If X and Y are such that $\mathrm{E}\,|X| < \infty$ and $\mathrm{E}\,|Y| < \infty$, then $\mathrm{E}\,|XY| \le (\mathrm{E}\,X^2)^{1/2}(\mathrm{E}\,Y^2)^{1/2}$, with equality if and only if $Y = aX$ for some a.*

Theorem C.5 (Hölder inequality) *Let p and q be positive numbers such that $p > 1$ and $p^{-1} + q^{-1} = 1$. If X and Y are such that $\mathrm{E}\,|X|^p < \infty$ and $\mathrm{E}\,|Y|^q < \infty$, then $\mathrm{E}\,|XY| \le (\mathrm{E}\,|X|^p)^{1/p}(\mathrm{E}\,|Y|^q)^{1/q}$.*

Theorem C.6 (Triangle inequality) *If X and Y are such that $\mathrm{E}\,|X| < \infty$ and $\mathrm{E}\,|Y| < \infty$, then $\mathrm{E}\,|X + Y| \le \mathrm{E}\,|X| + \mathrm{E}\,|Y|$.*

Theorem C.7 (Minkowski inequality) *If X and Y are such that $\mathrm{E}\,|X|^p < \infty$ and $\mathrm{E}\,|Y|^p < \infty$ for some $p \ge 1$, then $(\mathrm{E}\,|X + Y|^p)^{1/p} \le (\mathrm{E}\,|X|^p)^{1/p} + (\mathrm{E}\,|Y|^p)^{1/p}$.*

Theorem C.8 (c_r inequality) *If X and Y are such that $\mathrm{E}\,|X|^r < \infty$ and $\mathrm{E}\,|Y|^r < \infty$ for some $r > 0$, then $\mathrm{E}\,|X + Y|^r \le c_r(\mathrm{E}\,|X|^r + \mathrm{E}\,|Y|^r)$, where $c_r = 1$ if $0 < r \le 1$ and $c_r = 2^{r-1}$ otherwise.*

C.4 MOMENT GENERATING AND CHARACTERISTIC FUNCTIONS

Given a random variable Z, its *moment generating function* is a real non-negative function M defined by

$$M(t) = \mathrm{E}\, e^{tZ}$$

for all t such that the expectation is finite. Clearly $M(t)$ exists and is equal to one for $t = 0$, but need not exist for $t \neq 0$ because e^{tz} is not a bounded function of z.

Theorem C.9 *If $M(t)$ exists in an open neighborhood of $t = 0$, then:*

(i) *$M(t)$ uniquely determines the distribution of Z;*
(ii) *Z possesses moments of any order, and we have the expansion*

$$M(t) = \sum_{k=0}^{\infty} \frac{t^k}{k!} \mathrm{E}\, Z^k,$$

where $\mathrm{E}\, Z^0 = 1$.

It follows from (i) that if two random variables have the same moment generating function in an open interval containing zero, then they have the same distribution. By (ii), the moment generating function gives a compact and convenient way of recording the (noncentral) moments of Z, for the kth moment $\mathrm{E}\, Z^k$ is just the coefficient associated with $t^k/k!$ in a Taylor series expansion of $M(t)$ about $t = 0$ and can be recovered easily by differentiation

$$\mathrm{E}\, Z^k = \frac{d^k}{dt^k} M(t) \,|_{t=0} \,.$$

If Z has moment generating function M, then the moment generating function of $X = aZ + b$ exists and is

$$M_X(t) = \mathrm{E}\, e^{t(aZ+b)} = e^{bt}\, \mathrm{E}\, e^{atZ} = e^{bt}\, M(at).$$

In particular, if $a = 1$ and $b = -\mu$, where $\mu = \mathrm{E}\, Z$, then the moment generating function of $X = Z - \mu$ exists and is

$$M_X(t) = \mathrm{E}\, e^{t(Z-\mu)} = \sum_{k=0}^{\infty} \frac{t^k}{k!} \mathrm{E}(Z-\mu)^k = \sum_{k=0}^{\infty} \frac{t^k}{k!} \mu_k,$$

where $\mu_0 = 1$, $\mu_1 = 0$, and $\mu_k = \mathrm{E}(Z-\mu)^k$ for $k \geq 2$. Thus, the kth central moment of Z is the coefficient associated with $t^k/k!$ in a Taylor series expansion of $M_X(t)$ about $t = 0$.

Example C.1 If $Z \sim \mathcal{N}(0,1)$ then, by completing the square in the exponential,

$$M(t) = \frac{1}{\sqrt{2\pi}} \int e^{tz} e^{-z^2/2}\, dz = \frac{e^{t^2/2}}{\sqrt{2\pi}} \int e^{-(z-t)^2/2}\, dz = e^{t^2/2},$$

which exists for all t. The moments of Z can be read off easily from the power expansion

$$e^{t^2/2} = \sum_{k=0}^{\infty} \frac{1}{k!}\left(\frac{t^2}{2}\right)^k = \sum_{k=0}^{\infty} \frac{1 \times 3 \times \cdots \times (2k-1)}{(2k)!} t^{2k}.$$

In particular, the even-order moments are given by

$$\mathrm{E}\, Z^{2k} = (2k-1)(2k-3)\cdots 5 \cdot 3 \cdot 1,$$

whereas the odd-order moments are all equal to zero. If $Z \sim \mathcal{N}(0,1)$, then the distribution of $X = \mu + \sigma Z$ is $\mathcal{N}(\mu, \sigma^2)$ and its moment generating function is

$$M_X(t) = e^{\mu t}\, e^{\sigma^2 t^2/2} = \exp\left(\mu t + \frac{1}{2}\sigma^2 t^2\right).$$

□

If X and Y are independent random variables with moment generating function M_X and M_Y, then the moment generating function of the sum $X + Y$ exists and is

$$M_{X+Y}(t) = \mathrm{E}\, e^{t(X+Y)} = (\mathrm{E}\, e^{tX})(\mathrm{E}\, e^{tY}) = M_X(t)\, M_Y(t),$$

that is, the moment generating function of the sum of two independent random variables is equal to the product of their moment generating functions. This result generalizes to the sum of any finite number of independent random variables.

Example C.2 If $Z_1, \ldots, Z_n$ are i.i.d. with common moment generating function $M(t)$, then the moment generating function of their sum is equal to $[M(t)]^n$ and the moment generating function of their average $\bar{Z} = n^{-1} \sum_{i=1}^n Z_i$ is $M_{\bar{Z}}(t) = [M(t/n)]^n$. In particular, if $Z_1, \ldots, Z_n$ are i.i.d. with common $\mathcal{N}(\mu, \sigma^2)$ distribution, then

$$M_{\bar{Z}}(t) = \left[\exp\left(\frac{\mu t}{n} + \frac{1}{2}\frac{\sigma^2 t^2}{n^2}\right)\right]^n = \exp\left(\mu t + \frac{1}{2}\frac{\sigma^2}{n} t^2\right).$$

Thus, $\bar{Z} \sim \mathcal{N}(\mu, \sigma^2/n)$. □

The *characteristic function* of Z is the complex valued function ψ defined by

$$\psi(t) = \mathrm{E}\, e^{itZ},$$

where $i^2 = -1$. Unlike the moment generating function, the characteristic function is defined for all distributions since $|e^{itz}| \leq 1$ for all t and all z, and therefore $|\psi(t)| \leq 1$ for all t. If the moment generating function M of Z exists in a neighborhood of $t = 0$, then $\psi(t) = M(it)$. For example, if $Z \sim \mathcal{N}(\mu, \sigma^2)$, then its characteristic function is

$$\psi(t) = \exp\left[\mu i t + \frac{1}{2}\sigma^2 (it)^2\right] = \exp\left(\mu i t - \frac{1}{2}\sigma^2 t^2\right).$$

It can be shown that the characteristic function uniquely determines the distribution of Z (see e.g. Cramér 1946, Sections 10.6 and 10.7). Thus, two distributions are identical if and only if their characteristic functions are identical.

It can also be shown that if the moments of Z exist up to order r, then

$$\psi(t) = \sum_{k=0}^{r} \mathrm{E}\, Z^k \frac{(it)^k}{k!} + R_r,$$

where $R_r = o(t^r)$, that is, $\lim_{t\to 0} R_r/t^r = 0$. In particular, if Z has mean zero and variance $0 < \sigma^2 \infty$, then

$$\psi(t) = 1 - \frac{1}{2}\sigma^2 t^2 + o(t^2).$$

If Z has characteristic function ψ, then the characteristic function of $X = aZ + b$ is

$$\psi_X(t) = \mathrm{E}\, e^{it(aZ+b)} = e^{ibt}\, \mathrm{E}\, e^{iatZ} = e^{ibt}\, \psi(at).$$

If X and Y are independent, then the characteristic function of the sum $X + Y$ is

$$\psi_{X+Y}(t) = \mathrm{E}\, e^{it(X+Y)} = (\mathrm{E}\, e^{itX})(\mathrm{E}\, e^{itY}) = \psi_X(t)\, \psi_Y(t).$$

This result generalizes to the sum of any finite number of independent random variables.

Finally, if $Z = (Z_1, \ldots, Z_n)$ is a random n-vector, then its characteristic function is defined as

$$\psi(t) = \mathrm{E}\, e^{it^\top Z},$$

where $t = (t_1, \ldots, t_n)$. This characteristic function has a number of properties that are analogues of those derived in the univariate case. In particular, if $Z_1, \ldots, Z_n$ are independent, each with characteristic function ψ_{Z_i}, then

$$\psi(t) = \sum_{i=1}^{n} \psi_{Z_i}(t_i).$$

Further, if A is an $n \times n$ matrix and b is an n-vector, then the characteristic function of $X = AZ + b$ is

$$\psi_X(t) = \mathrm{E}\, e^{it^\top(AZ+b)} = e^{it^\top b}\, \psi(A^\top t).$$

C.5 THE GAMMA AND BETA DISTRIBUTIONS

Let $p > 0$. A non-negative random variable Z is said to have a *standard gamma distribution with parameter p* if its distribution is absolutely continuous with density

$$f(z) = \frac{1}{\Gamma(p)} z^{p-1} e^{-z}, \qquad z \geq 0,$$

where

$$\Gamma(p) = \int_0^\infty z^{p-1} e^{-z}\, dz$$

is the *gamma function*, which satisfies $\Gamma(p+1) = p\Gamma(p)$, and $\Gamma(p+1) = p!$ if p is a positive integer. If p is large, then the gamma function can be approximated by Stirling's formula $\Gamma(p) \approx e^{-p} p^{p-1/2} \sqrt{2\pi}$. If $p \geq 1$, Z is unimodal with mode equal

Figure 78 Densities of gamma distributions for different values of (p, γ).

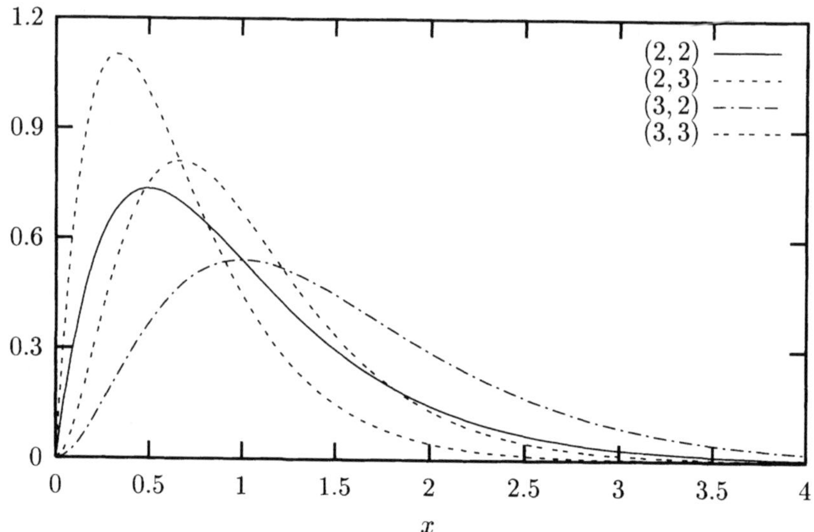

to $p-1$. Its moment generating function is $M(t) = (1-t)^{-p}$. Hence, the first two moments of Z are $\mathrm{E}\, Z = \mathrm{Var}\, Z = p$.

If Z has a standard gamma distribution with parameter p, the non-negative random variable $X = Z/\gamma$, where $\gamma > 0$, is said to have a *gamma distribution with parameter* (p, γ), written $X \sim \mathcal{G}(p, \gamma)$. The density of X (Figure 78) is

$$f(x) = \frac{\gamma^p}{\Gamma(p)} x^{p-1} e^{-\gamma x}, \qquad x \geq 0,$$

and its moment generating function is

$$M(t) = \left(1 - \frac{t}{\gamma}\right)^{-p} = \left(\frac{\gamma}{\gamma - t}\right)^p.$$

Hence, $\mathrm{E}\, X = p/\gamma$ and $\mathrm{Var}\, X = p/\gamma^2$. If $p \geq 1$, then X is unimodal with mode equal to $(p-1)/\gamma$.

Result C.1 *If* $X_1 \sim \mathcal{G}(p_1, \gamma)$ *and* $X_2 \sim \mathcal{G}(p_2, \gamma)$ *are independent, then* $X_1 + X_2 \sim \mathcal{G}(p_1 + p_2, \gamma)$.

If $X \sim \mathcal{G}(p, \gamma)$, the non-negative random variable $Y = 1/\sqrt{X}$ is said to have an *inverted gamma distribution with parameter* (p, γ). The density of Y is

$$f(y) = \frac{2\gamma^p}{\Gamma(p)} y^{-(2p+1)} \exp\left(-\frac{\gamma}{y^2}\right), \qquad y \geq 0.$$

Figure 79 shows densities of inverted gamma distributions for different values of (p, γ).

Figure 79 Densities of inverted gamma distributions for different values of (p, γ).

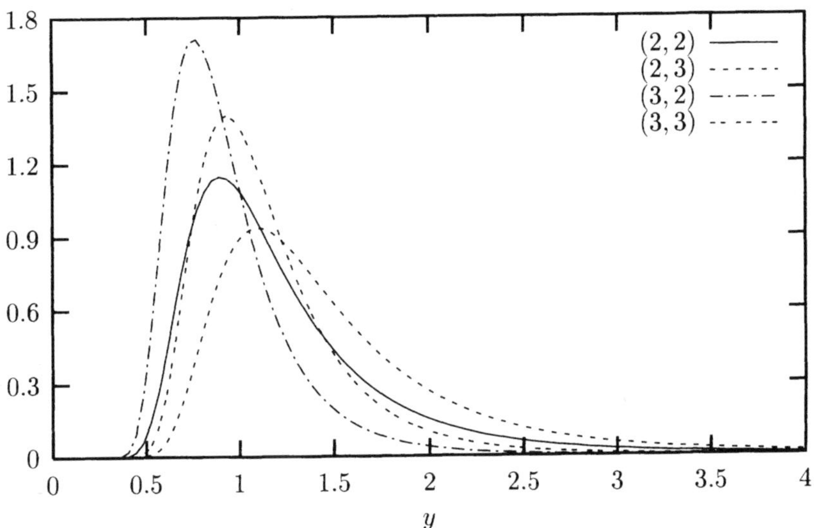

If $X_1 \sim \mathcal{G}(p, \gamma)$ and $X_2 \sim \mathcal{G}(q, \gamma)$ are independent, then $Z = X_1/(X_1 + X_2)$ is said to have a *beta distribution with parameter* (p, q), written $Z \sim \mathcal{B}(p, q)$. The random variable Z takes values in the interval $[0, 1]$ and its distribution is absolutely continuous with density (Figure 80)

$$f(z) = \frac{1}{B(p, q)} z^{p-1}(1 - z)^{q-1}, \qquad 0 \leq z \leq 1,$$

where

$$B(p, q) = \frac{\Gamma(p)\,\Gamma(q)}{\Gamma(p + q)}$$

is the *beta function*. The uniform distribution on $[0, 1]$ corresponds to the case when $p = q = 1$. A beta distribution is symmetric about zero if $p = q$, right-skewed if $p < q$, and left-skewed if $p > q$. It is U-shaped if $p, q < 1$, and J-shaped if $p > 1$ and $q < 1$ or $p < 1$ and $q > 1$.

Result C.2 *If $Z \sim \mathcal{B}(p, q)$, then* $\mathrm{E}\,Z = p/(p + q)$ *and*

$$\mathrm{Var}\,Z = \frac{pq}{(p + q)^2(p + q + 1)} = \frac{(\mathrm{E}\,Z)(1 - \mathrm{E}\,Z)}{p + q + 1}.$$

C.6 DISTRIBUTIONS RELATED TO THE EXPONENTIAL

The $\mathcal{E}(\gamma)$ distribution corresponds to the $\mathcal{G}(1, \gamma)$. Therefore, its moment generating function is $M(t) = (1 - t/\gamma) - 1$.

Figure 80 Densities of beta distributions for different values of (p, q).

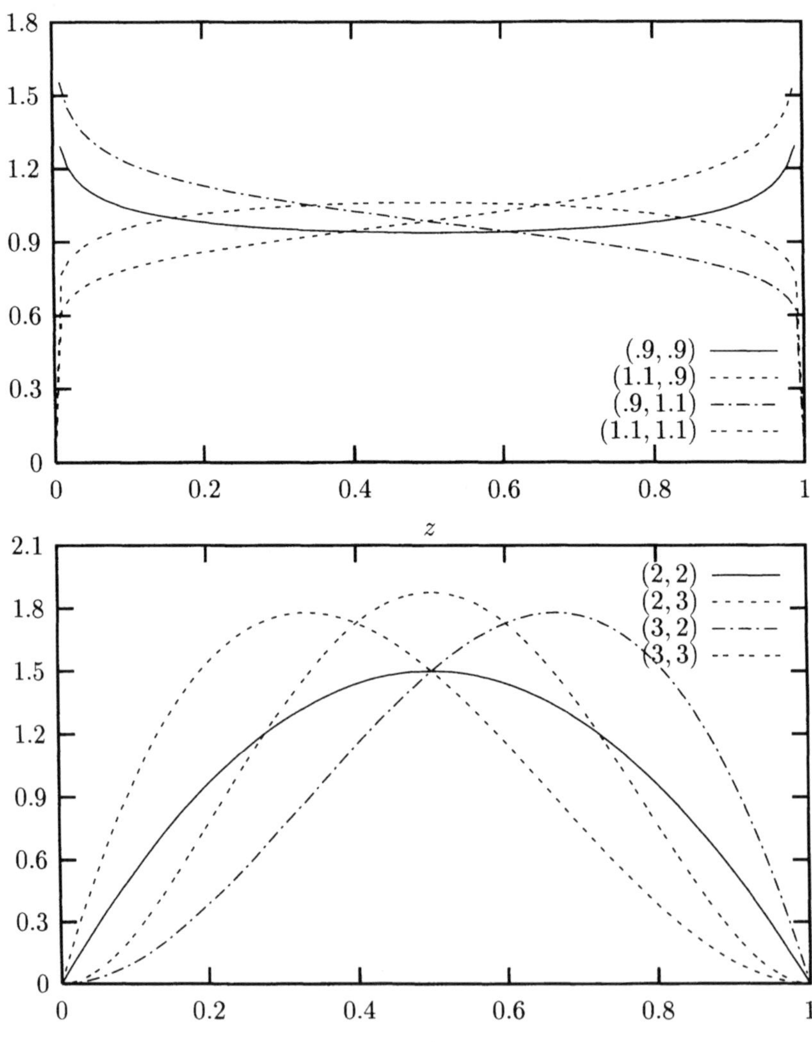

Figure 81 Densities of Laplace distributions for different values of γ.

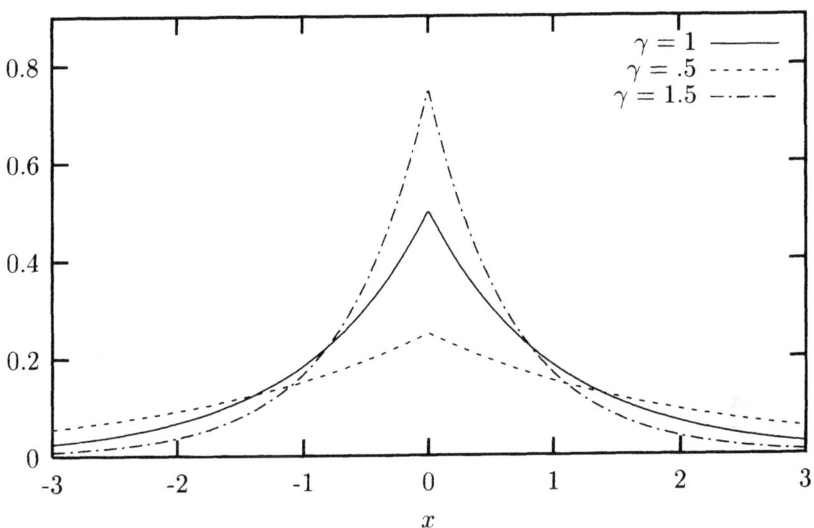

Result C.3 *If Z_1 and Z_2 are independent random variables with a common $\mathcal{E}(\gamma)$ distribution, then the difference $X = Z_1 - Z_2$ has a Laplace distribution with density function*

$$f(x) = \frac{\gamma}{2} e^{-\gamma|x|}.$$

Figure 81 show densities of Laplace distributions for different values of γ.

If $Z \sim \mathcal{E}(1)$, then $V = \ln Z$ is said to have a *standard Gumbel* or *standard Type 1 extreme value distribution* with distribution function $F(v) = 1 - \exp(-e^v)$, density function $f(v) = \exp(v - e^v)$, and moment generating function $M(t) = \Gamma(t+1)$. The distribution of V is skewed with a single mode at 0, and its first two moments are

$$\begin{aligned} \operatorname{E} V &= M'(0) = \Gamma'(1), \\ \operatorname{E} V^2 &= M''(0) = \Gamma''(1), \\ \operatorname{Var} V &= \operatorname{E} V^2 - (\operatorname{E} V)^2 = \Gamma''(1) - [\Gamma'(1)]^2, \end{aligned}$$

where $\Gamma'(1) \approx -0.577$ and $\Gamma''(1) - [\Gamma'(1)]^2 = \pi^2/6 \approx 1.645$.

A random variable X is said to have a Gumbel (Type 1 extreme value) distribution with parameter (α, γ) if it is obtained from V through the affine transformation

$$X = \frac{V - \ln \gamma}{\alpha}, \qquad \alpha, \gamma > 0, \tag{C.5}$$

where $-(\ln \gamma)/\alpha$ is the location parameter and $1/\alpha$ is the scale parameter. Clearly, $X = \ln[(Z/\gamma)^{1/\alpha}]$ where $Z \sim \mathcal{E}(1)$ or, equivalently, $X = \ln(Y^{1/\alpha})$ where $Y \sim \mathcal{E}(\gamma)$. The distribution function of X is $F(x) = 1 - \exp(-\gamma e^{\alpha x})$ and its density function (Figure 82) is $f(x) = \gamma\alpha \exp(\alpha x - \gamma e^{\alpha x})$.

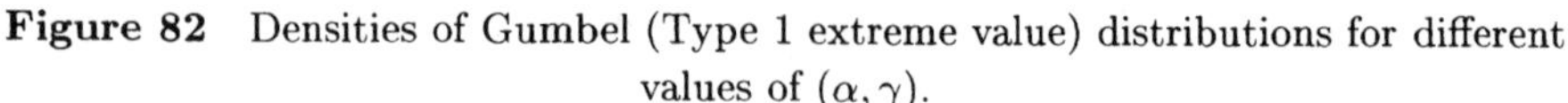

Figure 82 Densities of Gumbel (Type 1 extreme value) distributions for different values of (α, γ).

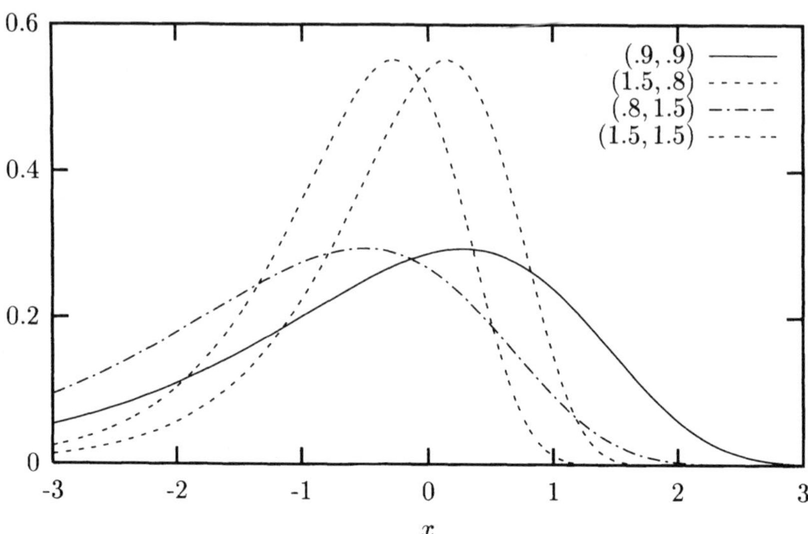

If X has a Gumbel distribution with parameter (α, γ), then the distribution of $U = -X$ is also called Gumbel. The distribution function of U is $F(u) = \exp(-\gamma e^{-\alpha u})$ and its density function is $f(u) = \gamma\alpha \exp(-\alpha u - \gamma e^{-\alpha u})$.

An alternative parametrization of the Gumbel distribution is obtained by putting $\beta = \ln \gamma$, in which case the distribution function of X is $F(x) = 1 - \exp(-e^{\beta + \alpha x})$ and its density function is $f(x) = \alpha \exp(\beta + \alpha x - e^{\beta + \alpha x})$.

The next result shows that the family of Gumbel distributions is closed under minimization.

Result C.4 *If the random variables $X_1, \ldots, X_n$ are independent Gumbel with parameters $(\alpha, \gamma_1), \ldots, (\alpha, \gamma_n)$ respectively, then the distribution of the random variable $X = \min(X_1, \ldots, X_n)$ is Gumbel with parameter (α, γ), where $\gamma = \sum_{i=1}^{n} \gamma_i$.*

Because $\min(X_1, \ldots, X_n) = -\max(U_1, \ldots, U_n)$, where $U_j = -X_j$, it follows from Result C.4 that the random variable $U = \max(U_1, \ldots, U_n)$ has the distribution function $F(u) = \exp(-\gamma e^{-\alpha u})$.

Result C.5 *If the random variables X_1 and X_2 are independent Gumbel with parameters (α, γ_1) and (α, γ_2) respectively, then the difference $Y = X_1 - X_2$ has a logistic distribution with distribution function*

$$F(y) = \frac{\exp(\beta + \alpha y)}{1 + \exp(\beta + \alpha y)},$$

where $\beta = \ln \gamma_1 - \ln \gamma_2$.

Figure 83 Densities of Weibull distributions for different values of (α, γ).

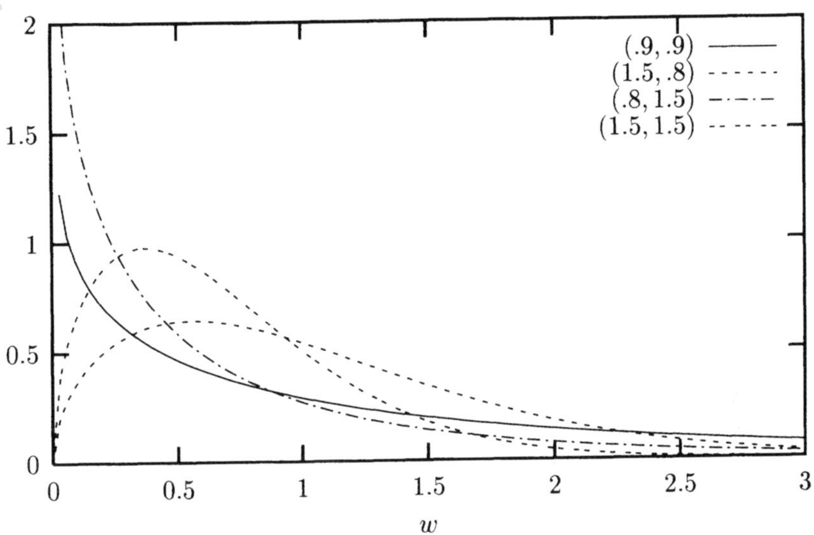

Equivalently, Result C.5 says that a random variable Y has a logistic distribution if it can be represented as $Y = \ln[(Y_1/Y_2)^{1/\alpha}]$, where $Y_1 \sim \mathcal{E}(\gamma_1)$ and $Y_2 \sim \mathcal{E}(\gamma_2)$ are independent.

If the random variable X has a Gumbel distribution with parameter (α, γ), then the non-negative random variable $W = e^X$ is said to have a ***Weibull*** or ***Type 3 extreme value distribution*** with parameter (α, γ). The standard Weibull distribution corresponds to $\gamma = 1$. Clearly, $W = (Z/\gamma)^{1/\alpha}$ where $Z \sim \mathcal{E}(1)$ or, equivalently, $W = Y^{1/\alpha}$ where $Y \sim \mathcal{E}(\gamma)$. Hence, when $\alpha = 1$, the distribution of W reduces to the $\mathcal{E}(\gamma)$ distribution. The distribution function of the Weibull distribution with parameter (α, γ) is

$$F(w) = 1 - \exp(-\gamma w^\alpha), \qquad w \geq 0,$$

and its density function is

$$f(w) = \gamma \alpha w^{\alpha-1} \exp(-\gamma w^\alpha), \qquad w \geq 0.$$

Figure 83 shows densities of Weibull distributions for different values of (α, γ).

C.7 DISTRIBUTIONS RELATED TO THE GAUSSIAN

Let n be a positive integer. The $\mathcal{G}(n/2, 1/2)$ distribution is called the *(central) chi-square distribution with n degrees of freedom* or simply the χ^2_n*-distribution*. Hence, the density of the χ^2_n-distribution is

$$f(x) = \frac{1}{2^{n/2}\Gamma(n/2)} x^{(n/2)-1} e^{-x/2}, \qquad x \geq 0$$

Figure 84 Densities of χ^2_n-distributions for different values of n.

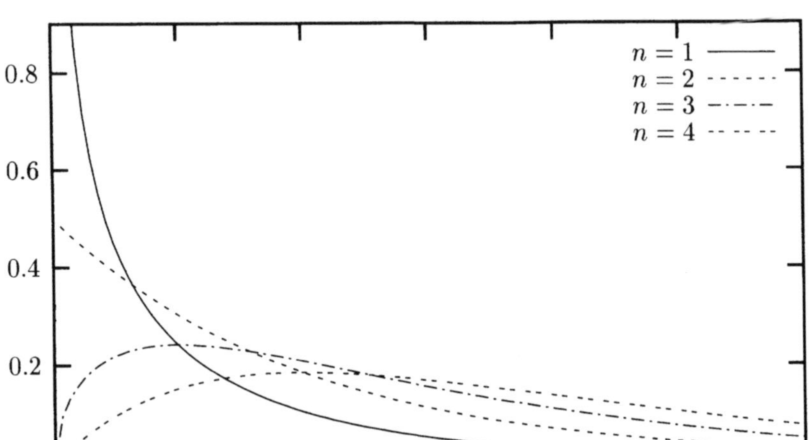

(Figure 84), and its moment generating function is $M(t) = (1-2t)^{-n/2}$. The χ^2_n-distribution is unimodal, with mode equal to zero for $n = 1, 2$ and $(n-1)/2$ for $n > 2$, mean equal to n, and variance equal to $2n$.

Result C.6 *If $Z \sim \mathcal{N}_n(0, I_n)$, then $X = Z^\top Z \sim \chi^2_n$.*

If the random n-vector Z has a $\mathcal{N}_n(\mu, I_n)$ distribution, then the random variable $X = Z^\top Z$ is said to have a *noncentral chi-square distribution with n degrees of freedom and noncentrality parameter* $\lambda = \mu^\top \mu$, written $X \sim \chi^2_{n,\lambda}$. The moment generating function of the $\chi^2_{n,\lambda}$ distribution is

$$M(t) = (1-2t)^{-n/2} \exp\left(\frac{\lambda t}{1-2t}\right).$$

It follows if $X \sim \chi^2_{n,\lambda}$, then $E(X) = n + \lambda$ and $\operatorname{Var} X = 2n + 4\lambda$.

Result C.7 *If $X \sim \chi^2_{n,\lambda}$, then $\Pr\{X \geq c\}$ is a strictly increasing function of λ.*

Result C.8 *If $X_1 \sim \chi^2_{n_1,\lambda_1}$ and $X_2 \sim \chi^2_{n_2,\lambda_2}$ are independent, then $X_1 + X_2 \sim \chi^2_{n,\lambda}$ with $n = n_1 + n_2$ and $\lambda = \lambda_1 + \lambda_2$.*

A random variable Y is said to have a *(central) t-distribution with n degrees of freedom*, written $Y \sim t_n$, if its distribution is absolutely continuous with density (Figure 85)

$$f(y) = \frac{\Gamma[(n+1)/2]}{\sqrt{n\pi}\,\Gamma(n/2)} \left(1 + \frac{y^2}{n}\right)^{-(n+1)/2}, \qquad -\infty < y < \infty.$$

Figure 85 Densities of t_n distributions for different values of n.

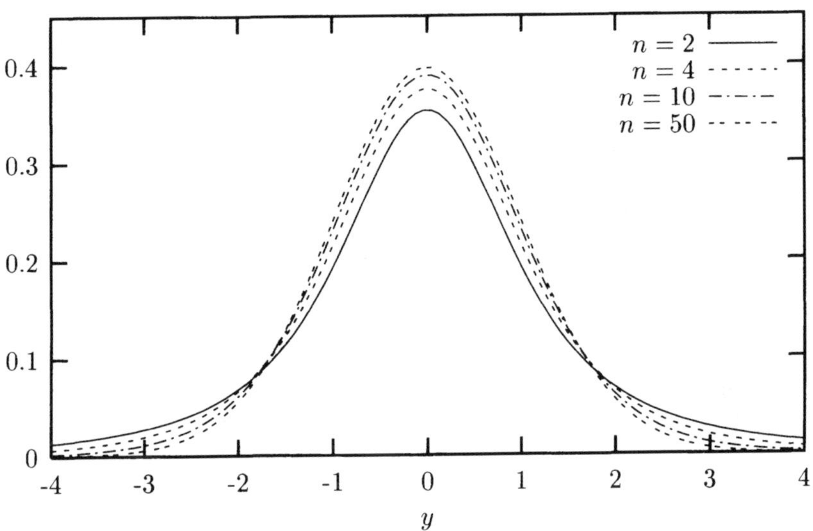

The density f is symmetric about zero and unimodal. The t-distribution with one degree of freedom is called the *Cauchy distribution* and is a standard example of heavy tailed distribution for none of its moments exists. On the other hand, the t_n distribution converges to the $\mathcal{N}(0,1)$ as $n \to \infty$.

Result C.9 *Let $Y \sim t_n$. If $n > 1$, then the mean of Y exists and is equal to zero. If $n > 2$, then the variance of Y exists and is equal to $n/(n-2)$.*

Result C.10 *If $Z \sim \mathcal{N}(0,1)$ and $X \sim \chi^2_n$ are independent, then*

$$Y = \frac{Z}{\sqrt{X/n}} \sim t_n.$$

Result C.11 *If X_1 and X_2 are independent $\mathcal{N}(0,1)$ random variables, then the ratio $Y = X_1/X_2$ has the Cauchy distribution.*

If $Z \sim \mathcal{N}(\mu, 1)$ and $X \sim \chi^2_n$ are independent, then the random variable

$$Y = \frac{Z}{\sqrt{X/n}}$$

is said to have a *noncentral t-distribution with n degrees of freedom and noncentrality parameter* μ, written $Y \sim t_{n,\mu}$.

Result C.12 *If $Y \sim t_{n,\mu}$, then* $\Pr\{Y \geq c\}$ *is a strictly increasing function of μ.*

A random m-vector Y is said to have a *multivariate t-distribution with n degrees of freedom* if its distribution is absolutely continuous with density

$$f(y) = \frac{n^{n/2}\Gamma[(m+n)/2]}{\pi^{m/2}\Gamma(n/2)}(n + y^\top y)^{-(m+n)/2}.$$

Figure 86 Densities of $F_{m,n}$ distributions for different values of (m, n).

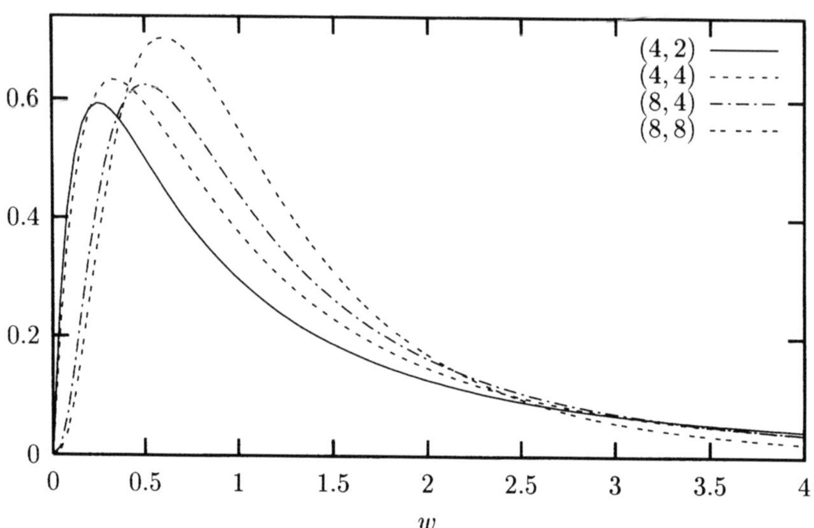

The density f is symmetric about zero and unimodal.

Result C.13 *Let the random vector Y have an m-variate t-distribution with n degrees of freedom. If $n > 1$, then the mean of Y exists and is equal to zero. If $n > 2$, then the variance (dispersion matrix) of Y exists and is equal to*

$$\operatorname{Var} Y = \frac{n}{n-2} I_n.$$

Result C.14 *If $Z \sim \mathcal{N}_m(0, I_m)$ and $X \sim \chi^2_n$ are independent, then the random m-vector*

$$Y = \frac{Z}{\sqrt{X/n}}$$

has an m-variate t-distribution with n degrees of freedom.

If a random vector Y has an m-variate t-distribution with n degrees of freedom and Λ is a $k \times m$ matrix of rank $k \leq m$, then the random vector $X = \mu + \Lambda Y$ is said to have a *k-variate t-distribution with parameter* (μ, Σ, n), where $\Sigma^{-1} = \Lambda\Lambda^\top$, and its density is

$$f(x) = \frac{n^{n/2}\Gamma[(n+m)/2]}{\pi^{m/2}\Gamma(n/2)} (\det \Sigma)^{1/2} [n + (x-\mu)^\top \Sigma (x-\mu)]^{-(m+n)/2}.$$

Let m and n be positive integers. A non-negative random variable W is said to have a *(central) F-distribution with* (m, n) *degrees of freedom*, written $W \sim F_{m,n}$, if its distribution is absolutely continuous with density (Figure 86)

$$f(w) = \frac{1}{B(m/2, n/2)} \left(\frac{m}{n}\right)^{m/2} w^{(m/2)-1} \left(1 + \frac{m}{n} w\right)^{-(m+n)/2}, \qquad w \geq 0.$$

Result C.15 *If $X \sim \chi^2_m$ and $Y \sim \chi^2_n$ are independent, then*

$$W = \frac{X/m}{Y/n} \sim F_{m,n}.$$

Result C.16 *If the random vector Y has an m-variate t-distribution with n degrees of freedom, then*

$$W = \frac{Y^\top Y}{n} \sim F_{m,n}.$$

It follows from Result C.13 that if $W \sim F_{m,n}$, then its mean exists if $n > 2$ and is equal to $n/(n-2)$. Notice that $\mathrm{E}\, W \to 1$ as $n \to \infty$.

If $X \sim \chi^2_{m,\lambda}$ and $Y \sim \chi^2_n$ are independent, then the random variable

$$W = \frac{X/m}{Y/n}$$

is said to have a *noncentral F-distribution with (m, n) degrees of freedom and noncentrality parameter λ*, written $W \sim F_{m,n,\lambda}$.

Result C.17 *If $W \sim F_{m,n,\lambda}$, then $\Pr\{W \geq c\}$ is a strictly increasing function of λ.*

C.8 QUADRATIC FORMS IN GAUSSIAN RANDOM VARIABLES

Result C.18 *If $Z \sim \mathcal{N}_n(0, I_n)$, Q is a symmetric idempotent matrix, and B is a matrix such that $BQ = 0$, then BZ and QZ are independent.*

Result C.19 *If $Z \sim \mathcal{N}_n(0, I_n)$ and Q is a symmetric idempotent matrix, then the random variable $X = Z^\top QZ$ has a chi-square distribution with $\operatorname{tr} Q$ degrees of freedom.*

Result C.20 *If $Z \sim \mathcal{N}_n(\mu, I_n)$ and Q is a symmetric idempotent matrix, then the random variable $X = Z^\top QZ$ has a noncentral chi-square distribution with $\operatorname{tr} Q$ degrees of freedom and noncentrality parameter equal to $\mu^\top Q\mu$.*

If $Z_1, \ldots, Z_n$ are i.i.d. $\mathcal{N}(0,1)$ random variables and $\lambda = (\lambda_1, \ldots, \lambda_n)$ is an n-vector, then the random variable $X = \sum_{i=1}^n \lambda_i Z_i^2$ is said to be distributed as a *weighted sum of chi-squares with parameter (n, λ)*. The next result appears as Lemma 3.2 in Vuong (1989).

Result C.21 *Let $Z \sim \mathcal{N}_n(0, \Sigma)$, with $\operatorname{rank}(\Sigma) \leq n$, and let Q be a symmetric matrix. Then the random variable $X = Z^\top QZ$ is distributed as a weighted sum of chi-squares with parameter (n, λ), where λ is the vector of eigenvalues of $Q\Sigma$. Moreover, the eigenvalues are all real, and they are all non-negative if Q is n.n.d.*

C.9 MOMENTS OF THE TRUNCATED GAUSSIAN DISTRIBUTION

Let Z be a random variable with distribution function F. If a and b are real numbers such that $a < b$, then

$$F(z \mid a < Z < b) = \begin{cases} 0, & \text{if } z < a, \\ \dfrac{F(z) - F(a)}{F(b) - F(a)}, & \text{if } a \leq z < b, \\ 1, & \text{if } b \leq z. \end{cases}$$

If Z is a continuous random variable with density function f, then

$$f(z \mid a < Z < b) = 1(a < z < b)\,\frac{f(z)}{F(b) - F(a)}.$$

If Z has a finite variance, then

$$0 \leq \operatorname{Var}(Z \mid a < Z < b) \leq \operatorname{Var} Z.$$

The next two results give the mean and variance of a truncated Gaussian distribution. We denote by ϕ and Φ, respectively, the density and distribution function of the standard Gaussian.

Result C.22 *If $Z \sim \mathcal{N}(0,1)$, then*

$$\mathrm{E}(Z \mid a < Z < b) = -\frac{\phi(b) - \phi(a)}{\Phi(b) - \Phi(a)}$$

and

$$\operatorname{Var}(Z \mid a < Z < b) = 1 - \frac{b\,\phi(b) - a\,\phi(a)}{\Phi(b) - \Phi(a)} - \left[\frac{\phi(b) - \phi(a)}{\Phi(b) - \Phi(a)}\right]^2.$$

As special cases of Result C.22 we have

$$\mathrm{E}(Z \mid Z > a) = \lambda(-a), \qquad \operatorname{Var}(Z \mid Z > a) = 1 + a\,\lambda(-a) - \lambda(-a)^2,$$

where $\lambda(-a) = \phi(a)/[1 - \Phi(a)]$, and

$$\mathrm{E}(Z \mid Z < b) = -\lambda(b), \qquad \operatorname{Var}(Z \mid Z < b) = 1 - b\,\lambda(b) - \lambda(b)^2,$$

where $\lambda(b) = \phi(b)/\Phi(b)$. Notice that $\mathrm{E}(Z \mid Z < b) < \mathrm{E}\,Z < \mathrm{E}(Z \mid Z > a)$.

BIBLIOGRAPHIC NOTES

The main references for Sections C.5–C.9 are Johnson and Kotz (1970, 1972).

Appendix D

Elements of Asymptotic Theory

D.1 CONVERGENCE OF SEQUENCES OF RANDOM VARIABLES

Recall that an infinite sequence $\{c_n\} = (c_1, c_2, \ldots)$ of real numbers is said to converge to a real number c, written $c_n \to c$ as $n \to \infty$ or $\lim_{n\to\infty} c_n = c$, if for any $\epsilon > 0$ there exists a number N_ϵ such that $|c_n - c| < \epsilon$ for every $n > N_\epsilon$. The next definitions provide different ways of generalizing this concept to the case of an infinite sequence $\{Z_n\} = (Z_1, Z_2, \ldots)$ of random variables defined on the same probability space. Unless otherwise indicated, all convergence statements hold for $n \to \infty$.

Definition D.1 A sequence $\{Z_n\}$ of random variables is said to *converge in probability* to a constant c, written $Z_n \overset{\mathrm{p}}{\to} c$ or $\operatorname{plim} Z_n = c$, if for every $\epsilon > 0$ we have $\lim \Pr\{|Z_n - c| \leq \epsilon\} = 1$ or, equivalently, $\lim \Pr\{|Z_n - c| > \epsilon\} = 0$. □

If $Z_n \overset{\mathrm{p}}{\to} c$, then the probability that Z_n takes values in an arbitrarily small neighborhood $[c - \epsilon, c + \epsilon]$ of c approaches one as $n \to \infty$.

Definition D.2 A sequence $\{Z_n\}$ of random variables is said to *converge almost surely* to a constant c, written $Z_n \overset{\mathrm{as}}{\to} c$, if $\Pr\{\lim Z_n = c\} = 1$. □

The following result facilitates comparison with convergence in probability.

Theorem D.1 $Z_n \overset{\mathrm{as}}{\to} c$ *if and only if* $\Pr\{|Z_m - c| \leq \epsilon, \text{ for all } m \geq n\} \to 1$, *or, equivalently,* $\Pr\{|Z_m - c| > \epsilon, \text{ for some } m \geq n\} \to 0$.

Proof. See Chung (1974), Theorem 4.1.1. □

Almost sure convergence is stronger than convergence in probability, for if $Z_n \overset{\mathrm{as}}{\to} c$ then, with probability approaching one as $n \to \infty$, $|Z_n - c| > \epsilon$ only a finite number of times.

Definition D.3 A sequence $\{Z_n\}$ of random variables with finite rth order moments is said to *converge in rth mean* to a constant c, written $Z_n \overset{r\mathrm{th}}{\to} c$, if $\mathrm{E}\,|Z_n - c|^r \to 0$. □

By Jensen inequality, $Z_n \overset{r\mathrm{th}}{\to} c$ implies that $Z_n \overset{s\mathrm{th}}{\to} c$ for all $0 < s < r$. The higher the value of r, the more stringent is the condition for convergence. The case when $r = 2$ is called *convergence in mean square* or *in quadratic mean* and denoted by $\overset{\mathrm{ms}}{\to}$. It is clear from Definition D.3 that $Z_n \overset{\mathrm{ms}}{\to} c$ whenever $\operatorname{Var} Z_n \to 0$ and $\mathrm{E}\, Z_n \to c$.

If $\{Z_n\}$ and Z are random variables defined on the same probability space and $Z_n - Z \xrightarrow{\text{P}} 0$, then the sequence $\{Z_n\}$ is said to converge in probability to Z, written $Z_n \xrightarrow{\text{P}} Z$. Almost sure convergence and convergence in rth mean to a random variable are defined analogously.

We have the following implications from the above three types of convergence.

Theorem D.2

(i) *If* $Z_n \xrightarrow{\text{as}} Z$, *then* $Z_n \xrightarrow{\text{P}} Z$.

(ii) *If* $Z_n \xrightarrow{\text{rth}} Z$ *for some* $r > 0$, *then* $Z_n \xrightarrow{\text{P}} Z$.

(iii) *If* $Z_n \xrightarrow{\text{P}} Z$, *then there exists a subsequence* $\{Z_{n_j}\}$ *such that* $Z_{n_j} \xrightarrow{\text{as}} Z$.

Proof. Part (i) follows from Theorem D.1. Part (ii) follows from Chebyshev inequality. For a proof of part (iii), see Billingsley (1979), Theorem 20.5. □

If $\{Z_n\}$ is a sequence of random vectors or matrices, the above definitions are valid if $|\cdot|$ is interpreted as Euclidean norm. In this case, a necessary and sufficient condition for Z_n to converge in any of the above modes is that all elements of Z_n converge in the given mode.

Let $\{\hat{\theta}_n\} = (\hat{\theta}_1, \hat{\theta}_2, \ldots)$ be a sequence of estimators of a parameter θ, corresponding to increasing sample sizes. If $\hat{\theta}_n \xrightarrow{\text{P}} \theta$, no matter what θ is, then the sequence $\{\hat{\theta}_n\}$ is said to be *(weakly) consistent* for θ or, equivalently, $\hat{\theta}_n$ is called a *(weakly) consistent* estimator for θ. If $\hat{\theta}_n \xrightarrow{\text{as}} \theta$, no matter what θ is, then the sequence $\{\hat{\theta}_n\}$ is said to be *strongly consistent* for θ or, equivalently, $\hat{\theta}_n$ is called a *strongly consistent* estimator of θ. If $\mathrm{E}\,\hat{\theta}_n \to \theta$ and $\mathrm{Var}\,\hat{\theta}_n \to 0$, then $\hat{\theta}_n \xrightarrow{\text{ms}} \theta$ and therefore, from Theorem D.2, $\hat{\theta}_n \xrightarrow{\text{P}} \theta$.

D.2 WEAK CONVERGENCE

Definition D.4 A sequence $\{F_n\} = (F_1, F_2, \ldots)$ of distribution functions is said to *converge weakly* to a distribution function F, written $F_n \Rightarrow F$, if F_n converges pointwise to F at all continuity points of F, that is,

$$F_n(z) \to F(z) \tag{D.1}$$

at all points z where F is continuous. □

An important question regarding the convergence of F_n to F is whether pointwise convergence holds uniformly.

Theorem D.3 (Pólya) *If* $F_n \Rightarrow F$ *and* F *is continuous, then*

$$\sup_z |F_n(z) - F(z)| \to 0.$$

The next result gives equivalent characterizations of weak convergence.

Theorem D.4 *If* ψ *and* $\{\psi_n\}$ *are the characteristic functions associated with the distribution functions* F *and* $\{F_n\}$, *respectively, then the following statements are equivalent:*

(i) $F_n \Rightarrow F$;
(ii) $\psi_n(t) \to \psi(t)$ *for every* $t \in \Re$;
(iii) $\int g(z)\,dF_n(z) \to \int g(z)\,dF(z)$ *for every bounded continuous function* g.

Proof. See Serfling (1980), Section 1.5. □

The implications (i) ⇔ (ii) and (i) ⇔ (iii) are known together as the *Helly–Bray theorem.*

Let F and $\{F_n\}$ be the distribution functions of the random variables Z and $\{Z_n\}$. Notice that $Z_1, Z_2, \ldots$ and Z need not be defined on the same probability space. If $F_n \Rightarrow F$, then $\{Z_n\}$ is said to *converge in distribution* to Z, written $Z_n \xrightarrow{d} Z$. In this case, the distribution function F is called the *asymptotic* or *limiting distribution* of the sequence $\{Z_n\}$. The moments of F, if they exist, are called the *asymptotic moments* of the sequence $\{Z_n\}$. Even when all moments of Z exist, the fact that $Z_n \xrightarrow{d} Z$ implies neither the existence nor the convergence of the moments of Z_n.

One is often interested in approximating the sampling distribution of an estimator $\hat{\theta}_n$ of a parameter θ. If there exists a sequence $\{\sigma_n\}$ of positive constants such that $(\hat{\theta}_n - \theta)/\sigma_n$ has a nondegenerate asymptotic distribution with mean zero, then the estimator $\hat{\theta}_n$ is said to be *asymptotically unbiased* for θ.

A sequence $\{Z_n\}$ of random variables is said to be *asymptotically normal (Gaussian)* with *asymptotic mean* μ_n and *asymptotic variance* σ_n^2, written $(Z_n - \mu_n)/\sigma_n \xrightarrow{d} \mathcal{N}(0,1)$, if $\sigma_n > 0$ for all n sufficiently large and the distribution function of the standardized random variable $(Z_n - \mu_n)/\sigma_n$ converges pointwise to the standardized Gaussian distribution function. The constants μ_n and σ_n need not be the mean and the standard deviation of Z_n, nor does Z_n need to possess such moments. However, Theorem D.3 implies that

$$\sup_z \left| \Pr\left\{ \frac{Z_n - \mu_n}{\sigma_n} \le z \right\} - \Phi(z) \right| \to 0,$$

where Φ denotes the $\mathcal{N}(0,1)$ distribution function. The quantiles of the distribution of Z_n may then be approximated by those of the $\mathcal{N}(\mu_n, \sigma_n^2)$ distribution. Sufficient conditions for a sequence of random variables to be asymptotically normal are discussed in Section D.5.

In many cases, $\sigma_n^2 = V/c_n V$, where c_n is an increasing function of n, for example $c_n = n$. We then say that V is the asymptotic variance of $\sqrt{c_n}(Z_n - \mu_n)$ or, with slight abuse, that V is the asymptotic variance of Z_n, written $V = \mathrm{AV}(Z_n)$.

Convergence in probability, in rth mean, and almost sure each represent a sense in which, for n sufficiently large, the random variables Z_n and Z approximate each other as measurable functions defined on the same probability space. This means that the probability distributions of Z_n and Z cannot be too far apart, so that weak convergence should follow. On the other hand, convergence in distribution depends only on the distribution functions involved and does not require that the relevant random variables approximate each other. As a result we have the following.

Theorem D.5
(i) *If* $Z_n \xrightarrow{p} Z$, *then* $Z_n \xrightarrow{d} Z$.

(ii) *If* $Z_n \xrightarrow{d} c$, *where c is a constant, then* $Z_n \xrightarrow{p} c$.

Proof. See Serfling (1980), Section 1.3. □

If $\{Z_n\}$ is a sequence of random vectors, then convergence in distribution requires convergence of the joint distribution function of the elements of Z_n. Convergence of their marginal distribution functions is generally not enough, for the marginals do not generally determine the joint. The last result of this section allows one to reduce convergence of multivariate distributions to convergence of univariate ones.

Theorem D.6 (Cramér–Wold device) *A sequence* $\{Z_n\}$ *of random vectors converges in distribution to a random vector* Z *if and only if* $\lambda^\top Z_n \xrightarrow{d} \lambda^\top Z$ *for every vector* λ.

Proof. See Serfling (1980), Section 1.5. □

A sequence $\{Z_n\}$ of random p-vectors is said to be *asymptotically multivariate normal* with asymptotic mean μ_n and asymptotic variance Σ_n if the matrix Σ_n is symmetric and n.n.d. for all n sufficiently large and

$$\frac{\lambda^\top(Z_n - \mu_n)}{(\lambda^\top \Sigma_n \lambda)^{1/2}} \xrightarrow{d} \mathcal{N}(0,1)$$

for every vector λ such that $\lambda^\top \Sigma_n \lambda > 0$. If μ_n and Σ_n do not depend on n, we also write $Z_n \xrightarrow{d} \mathcal{N}_p(\mu, \Sigma)$.

More generally, let P and $\{P_n\}$ be the probability measures of the random variables Z and $\{Z_n\}$ on the Borel sets $\mathcal{B}$ of $\Re$. Weak convergence can equivalently be expressed in terms of the probability measures P and $\{P_n\}$. For any set A, its *boundary* ∂A is defined as the closure minus the interior. For any measure P, a set $A \in \mathcal{B}$ such that $P\{\partial A\} = 0$ is called a *P-continuity set.* With these definitions, (D.1) is equivalent to the condition

$$P_n\{A\} \to P\{A\} \tag{D.2}$$

for all P-continuity sets A. If (D.2) holds, we write $P_n \Rightarrow P$.

The advantage of (D.2) over (D.1) is that it can be defined in much more general situations. Specifically, the random variables Z and $\{Z_n\}$ may take values in an arbitrary normed vector space $\mathcal{Z}$, and the probability measures P and $\{P_n\}$ may be defined on the Borel sets of $\mathcal{Z}$, that is, the σ-field generated by the open sets with respect to the norm associated with $\mathcal{Z}$. In particular, if $\mathcal{Z}$ is a normed vector space of functions defined on a set $\mathcal{T}$, then $P_n \Rightarrow P$ denotes convergence in distribution of a sequence of stochastic processes $\{Z_n(t), t \in \mathcal{T}\}$ to a limit process $\{Z(t), t \in \mathcal{T}\}$.

D.3 ORDERS IN PROBABILITY

It is often useful to compare the behavior of a sequence of random variables with that of a sequence of powers of n.

Recall that a sequence $\{c_n\}$ of real numbers is said to be of *smaller order than* n^λ, written $c_n = o(n^\lambda)$, if $c_n/n^\lambda \to 0$. The sequence $\{c_n\}$ is said to be *at most of order*

n^λ or to be *bounded by* n^λ, written $c_n = O(n^\lambda)$, if $\{c_n/n^\lambda\}$ is a bounded sequence, that is, there exists $M > 0$ and an integer m such that $|c_n|/n^\lambda \leq M$ for all $n \geq m$. The next definitions generalize these two concepts to the case of sequences of random variables.

Definition D.5 A sequence $\{Z_n\}$ of random variables is said to be of *smaller order in probability than* n^λ, written $Z_n = o_p(n^\lambda)$, if $Z_n/n^\lambda \xrightarrow{\text{p}} 0$. □

In particular, $Z_n = c + o_p(1)$ means that $Z_n \xrightarrow{\text{p}} c$.

Definition D.6 A sequence $\{Z_n\}$ of random variables is said to be *bounded in probability*, written $Z_n = O_p(1)$, if for every $\epsilon > 0$ there exist $M > 0$ and an integer m such that $\Pr\{|Z_n| \leq M\} \geq 1 - \epsilon$ for all $n \geq m$.

A sequence $\{Z_n\}$ of random variables is said to be *at most of order* n^λ *in probability* or to be *bounded in probability by* n^λ, written $Z_n = O_p(n^\lambda)$, if $Z_n/n^\lambda = O_p(1)$. □

If $Z_n \xrightarrow{\text{d}} Z$, then for every $\epsilon > 0$ one can find positive numbers M and $\delta \leq \epsilon$ and an integer m such that

$$\Pr\{|Z| \leq M\} + \delta \geq \Pr\{|Z_n| \leq M\} \geq \Pr\{|Z| \leq M\} - \delta \geq 1 - \epsilon$$

for all $n \geq m$. Hence $Z_n = O_p(1)$.

Let $\{Z_n\}$ be a sequence of random variables with mean μ_n and variance $0 < \sigma_n^2 \leq v/n$, where v is a finite number. Chebyshev inequality implies

$$\Pr\{|Z_n - \mu_n| > \sqrt{\epsilon}\} \leq \frac{\sigma_n^2}{\epsilon} \leq \frac{v/n}{\epsilon}$$

for every $\epsilon > 0$ and all n, and so $\Pr\{\sqrt{n}\,|Z_n - \mu_n| > \sqrt{\epsilon}\} \leq v/\epsilon$. Hence, $Z_n - \mu_n = O_p(n^{-1/2})$, that is, the sequence $\{Z_n - \mu_n\}$ is bounded in probability by the order $n^{-1/2}$ of its standard deviation. Further, if $\mu_n = \mu + O(n^{-1/2})$, then $Z_n = \mu + O_p(n^{-1/2})$. This result specifies the rate of convergence in probability of Z_n to the constant μ.

A random vector or a random matrix is $O_p(n^\lambda)$ or $o_p(n^\lambda)$ if all its elements are $O_p(n^\lambda)$ or $o_p(n^\lambda)$. If $Z_n = o_p(n^\lambda)$, then $Z_n = O_p(n^\nu)$ for all $\nu \geq \lambda$. Further, if $Z_n = O_p(n^\lambda)$, then $Z_n = o_p(n^\nu)$ for all $\nu > \lambda$. Thus, for example, $Z_n = O_p(n^{-1/2})$ implies that $Z_n = o_p(n^0) = o_p(1)$ and also $Z_n = O_p(1)$.

The next result shows that orders in probability can be manipulated in much the same way as orders of magnitude in real analysis.

Theorem D.7

(i) *If* $X_n = o_p(n^\lambda)$ *and* $Y_n = o_p(n^\nu)$, *then* $X_nY_n = o_p(n^{\lambda+\nu})$ *and* $X_n + Y_n = o_p(n^\mu)$, *where* $\mu = \max(\lambda, \nu)$.

(ii) *If* $X_n = O_p(n^\lambda)$ *and* $Y_n = O_p(n^\nu)$, *then* $X_nY_n = O_p(n^{\lambda+\nu})$ *and* $X_n + Y_n = O_p(n^\mu)$, *where* $\mu = \max(\lambda, \nu)$.

(iii) *If* $X_n = O_p(n^\lambda)$ *and* $Y_n = o_p(n^\nu)$, *then* $X_nY_n = o_p(n^{\lambda+\nu})$ *and* $X_n + Y_n = O_p(n^\mu)$, *where* $\mu = \max(\lambda, \nu)$.

D.4 LAWS OF LARGE NUMBERS

Given a sequence $\{Z_i\} = (Z_1, Z_2, \ldots)$ of random variables defined on the same probability space, let $\bar{Z}_n = n^{-1} \sum_i Z_i$ be the average of the first n elements of $\{Z_i\}$. A law of large numbers gives conditions for convergence of the sequence of random variables $\{\bar{Z}_n\} = (\bar{Z}_1, \bar{Z}_2, \ldots)$. There is a variety of laws of large numbers, differing in the assumptions made and the chosen modes of convergence. A *weak law of large numbers (WLLN)* refers to convergence in probability of $\{\bar{Z}_n\}$, whereas a *strong law of large numbers (SLLN)* refers to almost sure convergence.

We begin by stating a strong and a weak law of large numbers for the case when $\{Z_i\}$ is a sequence of i.i.d. random variables.

Theorem D.8 (Kolmogorov) *Let $\{Z_i\}$ be a sequence of i.i.d. random variables. Then $\bar{Z}_n \overset{\text{as}}{\to} \mu$ if and only if $\mathrm{E}\, Z_i$ exists and is equal to μ.*

Proof. See Rao (1973), pp. 115–116. □

Theorem D.8 provides a characterization of almost sure convergence. As a corollary, we obtain the following WLLN.

Theorem D.9 (Khinchine) *If $\{Z_i\}$ is a sequence of i.i.d. random variables with finite mean μ, then $\bar{Z}_n \overset{\text{p}}{\to} \mu$.*

Proof. For a direct proof, see Rao (1973), pp. 112–114. □

We now present a SLLN for the case when $\{Z_i\}$ is a sequence of random variables that are independent but not identically distributed. This weaker assumption requires stronger conditions on the existence of moments.

Theorem D.10 (Markov) *Let $\{Z_i\}$ be a sequence of independent random variables with mean μ_i. If $\mathrm{E}\,|Z_i|^\nu \leq M < \infty$ for some $\nu > 1$ and every i, then $\bar{Z}_n - \bar{\mu}_n \overset{\text{as}}{\to} 0$.*

Proof. See Chung (1974), pp. 124–126. □

By imposing even stronger conditions on the existence of moments and their behavior as n increases, we obtain a WLLN valid for sequences of random variables that are uncorrelated but not necessarily independent.

Theorem D.11 (Chebyshev) *Given a sequence $\{Z_i\}$ of uncorrelated random variables with mean μ_i and finite variance σ_i^2, let $\bar{\mu}_n = n^{-1} \sum_i \mu_i$ be the average of the first n elements of the sequence $\{\mu_i\}$. If $n^{-2} \sum_{i=1}^n \sigma_i^2 \to 0$, then $\bar{Z}_n - \bar{\mu}_n \overset{\text{p}}{\to} 0$.*

Proof. Since $\mathrm{E}\,\bar{Z}_n = \bar{\mu}_n$ and $\mathrm{Var}\,\bar{Z}_n = n^{-2} \sum_i \sigma_i^2$, Chebyshev inequality implies

$$\Pr\{|\bar{Z}_n - \bar{\mu}_n| > \epsilon\} \leq \epsilon^{-2} n^{-2} \sum_{i=1}^{n} \sigma_i^2.$$

Hence, $\Pr\{|\bar{Z}_n - \bar{\mu}_n| > \epsilon\} \to 0$. □

If $\{Z_i\}$ is a sequence of uncorrelated random variables with the same (finite) variance σ^2, then the conditions of Theorem D.11 are automatically satisfied and we conclude that $\bar{Z}_n - \bar{\mu}_n \xrightarrow{\text{p}} 0$.

Given a stationary time series $\{Z_t\}$ with mean μ and autocovariance function $\{\gamma_h\}$, let $\bar{Z}_n = n^{-1} \sum_{t=1}^{n} Z_t$ be the average of a finite segment $Z_1, \ldots, Z_n$ of the process. From Section 4.2.2, $\bar{Z}_n \xrightarrow{\text{ms}} \mu$ if and only if

$$\operatorname{Var} \bar{Z}_n = \frac{1}{n} \sum_{h=1-n}^{n-1} \left(1 - \frac{|h|}{n}\right) \gamma_h \to 0,$$

that is, if and only if $\operatorname{Var} \bar{Z}_n = o(1)$. The next theorem generalizes this result to almost sure convergence.

Theorem D.12 (Doob) *Let $\{Z_t\}$ be a stationary time series with mean μ and autocovariance function $\{\gamma_h\}$. If there exists a constant $\alpha > 0$ such that $\operatorname{Var} \bar{Z}_n = O(n^{-\alpha})$, then $\bar{Z}_n \xrightarrow{\text{as}} \mu$.*

Proof. See for example Hannan (1970), Theorem 5, pp. 206–207. □

We now give a SLLN for the sample autocovariances $\tilde{\gamma}_{hn} = (n-h)^{-1} \sum_{t=1}^{n-h} Z_t Z_{t+h}$, which are just sample averages of the products $Z_t Z_{t+h}$.

Theorem D.13 *If $\{Z_t\}$ is a linear process with autocovariance function $\{\gamma_h\}$ then, for any h, $\tilde{\gamma}_{hn} \xrightarrow{\text{as}} \gamma_h$.*

Proof. See for example Hannan (1970), Theorem 6, pp. 210-211. □

D.5 CENTRAL LIMIT THEOREMS

A *central limit theorem (CLT)* gives conditions under which the Gaussian distribution may be used to approximate the distribution of normalized sums of the first n elements of a sequence of random variables. Multivariate versions of the CLT presented in this section are straightforward to obtain using the Cramér–Wold device.

The simplest version of CLT deals with sequences of i.i.d. random variables with finite variance.

Theorem D.14 (Lindeberg–Lévy) *If $\{Z_i\}$ is a sequence of i.i.d. random variables with mean μ and variance $\sigma^2 > 0$ then*

$$S_n = \frac{\sqrt{n}\,(\bar{Z}_n - \mu)}{\sigma} = \frac{\sum_i (Z_i - \mu)}{\sigma\sqrt{n}} \xrightarrow{\text{d}} \mathcal{N}(0, 1).$$

Proof. Let $\psi(t)$ and $\psi_n(t)$ be the characteristic functions of $Z_i - \mu$ and S_n respectively. By the properties of characteristic functions

$$\psi_n(t) = \left[\psi\left(\frac{t}{\sigma\sqrt{n}}\right)\right]^n = \left[1 - \frac{t^2}{2n} + o(n^{-1})\right]^n.$$

Taking the logarithm of both sides of this relation and using the fact that $\ln(1+x) = x + o(|x|)$ gives

$$\ln \psi_n(t) = -n \left[\frac{t^2}{2n} + o(n^{-1}) \right] \to -\frac{t^2}{2}.$$

The conclusion then follows after noticing that $\exp(-t^2/2)$ is the characteristic function of the $\mathcal{N}(0,1)$ distribution. □

The next theorem gives a uniform bound for the absolute error of the Gaussian approximation implied by the Lindeberg–Lévy theorem.

Theorem D.15 (Berry–Esséen) *Let $\{Z_i\}$ be a sequence of i.i.d. random variables with mean μ, positive variance σ^2 and finite absolute third moment $\rho = \mathrm{E}\,|Z_i|^3$. If F_n is the distribution function of $X_n = \sqrt{n}\,(\bar{Z}_n - \mu)/\sigma$ then, for all n,*

$$\sup_x |F_n(x) - \Phi(x)| \leq .7975 \frac{\rho}{\sigma^3 \sqrt{n}}.$$

Proof. See Feller (1971), p. 543, or Serfling (1980), p. 33. □

The Berry–Esséen bound depends on the first three moments of Z_i, but can be generalized to the case of distributions without third moments. This bound is not very sharp, however, except in very large samples.

Notice that the approximation error in Theorem D.15 is of order $O(n^{-1/2})$. An *asymptotic expansion* is a way of improving upon the Gaussian approximation by considering approximations to the distribution function of $X_n = \sqrt{n}\,(\bar{Z}_n - \mu)/\sigma$ of the form

$$\Phi(x) + \frac{A_1(x)}{n^{1/2}} + \frac{A_2(x)}{n} + \cdots + \frac{A_s(x)}{n^{s/2}},$$

where the leading term in the expansion is the standard normal distribution function and the (absolute or relative) approximation error is of order $O(n^{-(s+1)/2})$, that is, the same order of magnitude as the first neglected term. Asymptotic expansions typically allow for skewness and kurtosis in the distribution of X_n.

We now state two CLTs valid for cases where $\{Z_i\}$ is a sequence of random variables that are independent but not identically distributed.

Theorem D.16 (Lindeberg–Feller) *Let $\{Z_i\}$ be a sequence of independent random variables with mean μ_i, finite variance σ_i^2 and distribution function F_i. Suppose that $B_n^2 = \sum_i \sigma_i^2$ satisfies*

$$\sigma_n^2 / B_n^2 \to 0, \qquad B_n \to \infty. \tag{D.3}$$

Then $S_n = B_n^{-1} \sum_i (Z_i - \mu_i) \xrightarrow{\mathrm{d}} \mathcal{N}(0,1)$ if and only if for every $\epsilon > 0$,

$$\frac{1}{B_n^2} \sum_{i=1}^{n} \int_{\{|z-\mu_i| > \epsilon B_n\}} (z - \mu_i)^2 \, dF_i(z) \to 0. \tag{D.4}$$

Proof. See Feller (1971), Section VIII.4. □

Condition (D.4) is also known as the *Lindeberg condition.* The pair of conditions in (D.3) is equivalent to the single condition

$$\max_{1 \le i \le n} \frac{\sigma_i^2}{B_n^2} \to 0,$$

called the *asymptotic negligibility condition.* This condition ensures that none of the individual variances σ_i^2 dominates the variance B_n^2 of the sum of the first n elements of $\{Z_i\}$. The Lindeberg condition completely characterizes the conditions of asymptotic normality and asymptotic negligibility.

Since the Lindeberg condition may be difficult to verify directly, we present a simpler set of sufficient conditions.

Theorem D.17 (Liapunov) *Let $\{Z_i\}$ be a sequence of independent random variables with mean μ_i, finite variance σ_i^2 and such that $\mathrm{E}\,|Z_i|^\nu \le M < \infty$ for some $\nu > 2$ and every i. If $n^{-1}B_n^2 > \delta$ for some $\delta > 0$ and every n sufficiently large then $S_n = B_n^{-1} \sum_i (Z_i - \mu_i) \xrightarrow{\mathrm{d}} \mathcal{N}(0, 1)$.*

Proof. See Serfling (1980), Section 1.9. □

Compare this result with the one in Theorem D.10. In both cases a uniform bound on the absolute moments $\mathrm{E}\,|Z_i|^\nu$ is imposed. If $\nu > 1$ we obtain a SLLN. Under the stronger conditions that $\nu > 2$ and $n^{-1}B_n^2 > 0$ we also obtain convergence to the standardized Gaussian distribution.

We now present a CLT valid for the case of a time series $\{Z_t\}$ which is strictly stationary and *m-dependent*, that is, such that the two sets of random variables $\{Z_r, r \le t\}$ and $\{Z_s, s \ge t + m + 1\}$ are independent for every t. If a time series is m-dependent, then elements of the process that are further away from each other by more than m periods are independent. An example is a strictly stationary MA(m) process.

Theorem D.18 (Hoeffding–Robbins) *Let $\{Z_t\}$ be a strictly stationary m-dependent time series with mean zero and autocovariance function $\{\gamma_h\}$. If $v_m = \gamma_0 + 2\sum_{h=1}^m \gamma_h \ne 0$, then $n\,\mathrm{Var}(\bar{Z}_n) \to v_m$ and $\sqrt{n}\,\bar{Z}_n \xrightarrow{\mathrm{d}} \mathcal{N}(0, v_m)$.*

Proof. See Brockwell and Davis (1987), Theorem 6.4.2. □

The condition that $v_m \ne 0$ is essential. If $v_m = 0$, then we may have that $\sqrt{n}\,\bar{Z}_n \xrightarrow{\mathrm{p}} 0$ and so $n\,\mathrm{Var}\,\bar{Z}_n \to 0$.

D.6 CONVERGENCE OF SEQUENCES OF TRANSFORMED RANDOM VARIABLES

This section considers the following problem. What conditions are needed for the convergence of a sequence of random variables to be preserved under a transformation h?

Theorem D.19 (Mann and Wald) *If $\{Z_n\}$ and Z are random p-vectors defined on the same probability space and the function $h\colon \Re^p \to \Re^q$ is continuous except on a set $\mathcal{D}$ such that $\Pr\{Z \in \mathcal{D}\} = 0$, then:*

(i) $Z_n \xrightarrow{\text{as}} Z$ *implies* $h(Z_n) \xrightarrow{\text{as}} h(Z)$;
(ii) $Z_n \xrightarrow{\text{p}} Z$ *implies* $h(Z_n) \xrightarrow{\text{p}} h(Z)$;
(iii) $Z_n \xrightarrow{\text{d}} Z$ *implies* $h(Z_n) \xrightarrow{\text{d}} h(Z)$.

Proof. See Serfling (1980), Section 1.7. □

Corollary D.1 *Let $Z_n = (X_n, Y_n)$ and $Z = (X, Y)$. If Z_n converges to Z in probability (or almost surely), then $X_n + Y_n \to X + Y$ and $X_n Y_n \to XY$ in the given mode of convergence.*

Corollary D.2 *Let $\{Z_n\}$ be a sequence of random vectors that converges in probability (or almost surely or in distribution) to a random vector Z. If A and B are conformable matrices, then $AZ_n \to AZ$ and $Z_n^\top BZ_n \to Z^\top BZ$ in the given mode of convergence.*

Other useful corollaries of Theorem D.19 are given below.

Corollary D.3 *Let $h\colon \Re^2 \to \Re$ be a continuous function. If $X_n \xrightarrow{\text{d}} X$ and $Y_n \xrightarrow{\text{p}} c$, where c is a constant, then $h(X_n, Y_n) \xrightarrow{\text{d}} h(X, c)$.*

Proof. The result follows from part (ii) of Theorem D.19, because one may interpret convergence in probability to a constant as convergence in distribution to a degenerate random variable. □

Corollary D.4 (Slutzky's lemma) *If $X_n \xrightarrow{\text{d}} X$ and $Y_n \xrightarrow{\text{p}} c$, where c is a constant, then:*

(i) $X_n + Y_n \xrightarrow{\text{d}} X + c$;
(ii) $X_n Y_n \xrightarrow{\text{d}} cX$;
(iii) $X_n/Y_n \xrightarrow{\text{d}} X/c$ *whenever* $c \neq 0$.

The assumptions of Slutzky's lemma imply that $X_n = O_p(1)$ and $Y_n = c + o_p(1)$. If F is the distribution function of X, then the distribution function of $X_n + Y_n$ converges to $F(x - c)$. If $c > 0$, then the distribution functions of $X_n Y_n$ and X_n/Y_n converge, respectively, to $F(x/c)$ and $F(cx)$.

Corollary D.5 *If $X_n \xrightarrow{\text{d}} X$ and $Y_n - X_n \xrightarrow{\text{p}} 0$, then $Y_n \xrightarrow{\text{d}} X$.*

Two sequences $\{X_n\}$ and $\{Y_n\}$ of random variables are said to be *asymptotically equivalent* if $X_n - Y_n \xrightarrow{\text{p}} 0$. By Corollary D.5, if $\{X_n\}$ and $\{Y_n\}$ are asymptotically equivalent and $\{X_n\}$ converges in distribution to X, then $\{X_n\}$ and $\{Y_n\}$ have the same limiting distribution, namely that of X. This result is useful when it is not easy to derive the limiting distribution of $\{Y_n\}$, but there exists an asymptotically equivalent sequence $\{X_n\}$ whose limiting distribution is either known or easier to derive.

If assuming that the sequence $\{Z_n\}$ converges to a constant limit is too restrictive, then the following result may be useful.

Theorem D.20 *Let h be a continuous function defined on a compact set $\mathcal{S} \subseteq \Re^{\checkmark}$. If $\{Z_n\}$ is a sequence of random p-vectors defined on the same probability space and $\{c_n\}$ is a sequence of p-vectors such that c_n is in the interior of $\mathcal{S}$ for all n sufficiently large, then:*

(i) $Z_n - c_n \stackrel{\text{as}}{\to} 0$ *implies* $h(Z_n) - h(c_n) \stackrel{\text{as}}{\to} 0$;
(ii) $Z_n - c_n \stackrel{\text{p}}{\to} 0$ *implies* $h(Z_n) - h(c_n) \stackrel{\text{p}}{\to} 0$.

Proof. See White (1984), Propositions 2.16 and 2.30. □

D.7 THE ASYMPTOTIC DELTA METHOD

The method of local linearization, or *asymptotic delta method*, plays a crucial role in approximating the distribution of transformations of random variables.

If $\{Z_n\}$ is a sequence of random variables such that $\sqrt{n}\,(Z_n - c) \stackrel{\text{d}}{\to} Z$, then

$$\sqrt{n}\,(Z_n - c) = O_p(1) = Z + o_p(1).$$

Let h: $\Re \to \Re$ be a twice continuously differentiable function whose first derivative h' does not vanish at the point c, and consider the random variable

$$\begin{aligned} X_n = \sqrt{n}\,[h(Z_n) - h(c)] &= h'(c)\sqrt{n}\,(Z_n - c) + R_n \\ &= h'(c)Z + o_p(1) + R_n, \end{aligned} \tag{D.5}$$

where $R_n = \frac{1}{2}h''(Z_n^*)\sqrt{n}\,(Z_n - c)^2$ is the remainder in a first-order Taylor expansion of $\sqrt{n}\,h(Z_n)$ about the point c, and Z_n^* is a point between Z_n and c. The remainder is determined by the second derivative of h at Z_n^*. If $R_n \stackrel{\text{p}}{\to} 0$, then (D.5) implies $X_n - h'(c)Z = o_p(1)$ and therefore $X_n \stackrel{\text{d}}{\to} h'(c)Z$. If $Z \sim \mathcal{N}(0, \sigma^2)$, then $X_n \stackrel{\text{d}}{\to} \mathcal{N}(0, h'(c)^2\sigma^2)$.

More generally, let h: $\mathcal{S} \to \Re^q$ be a function defined on a set $\mathcal{S} \subseteq \Re^p$, let c be an interior point of $\mathcal{S}$ and let $\mathcal{O}$ be an open neighborhood of c. The function h is said to be *differentiable* at c if there exists a $q \times p$ matrix $H(a)$ such that

$$h(z) = h(c) + H(c)\,(z - a) + o(\| z - c \|) \tag{D.6}$$

for every $z \in \mathcal{O}$, where $o(\| z - c \|) \to 0$ as $z \to c$. In this case, the partial derivatives of h exist at c and the Jacobian h' of h, that is, the matrix $q \times p$ of partial derivatives of h, is equal to $H(c)$. Vice versa, if h has continuous partial derivatives in a neighborhood of c, then h is differentiable at c.

Theorem D.21 (Cramér) *Let h: $\Re^p \to \Re^q$ be differentiable at the point $c \in \Re^q$ and assume that the rank of $h'(c)$ is equal to $q \le p$. If $\sqrt{n}\,(Z_n - c) \stackrel{\text{d}}{\to} \mathcal{N}_p(0, \Sigma)$, then*

$$\sqrt{n}\,[h(Z_n) - h(c)] \stackrel{\text{d}}{\to} \mathcal{N}_q(0, h'(c)\,\Sigma\,h'(c)^\top).$$

Proof. From (D.6) we have

$$\sqrt{n}\,[h(Z_n) - h(c)] = h'(c)\sqrt{n}\,(Z_n - c) + R_n,$$

where $R_n = o_p(\sqrt{n}\,|Z_n - c|) \stackrel{\text{p}}{\to} 0$. Hence $\sqrt{n}\,[h(Z_n) - h(c)] - h'(c)\sqrt{n}\,(Z_n - c) = o_p(1)$, where $h'(c)\sqrt{n}\,(Z_n - c) \stackrel{\text{d}}{\to} \mathcal{N}_q(0, h'(c)\,\Sigma\,h'(c)^\top)$. □

D.8 THE FUNCTIONAL CENTRAL LIMIT THEOREM

Let $\{Z_i\}$ be a sequence of i.i.d. random variables, defined on a probability space $(\Omega, \mathcal{A}, P)$, having mean μ and finite positive variance σ^2. Given a particular realization $Z_1(\omega), \ldots, Z_n(\omega)$, let $\{S_j(\omega)\}$ be the sequence of partial sums

$$S_j(\omega) = \sum_{i=1}^{j} [Z_i(\omega) - \mu], \qquad j = 1, \ldots, n,$$

and let $Y_n(\omega, \cdot)$ be a function defined on the closed unit interval $[0,1]$ by

$$Y_n(\omega, 0) = 0,$$
$$Y_n\left(\omega, \frac{j}{n}\right) = \frac{S_j(\omega)}{\sigma\sqrt{n}}, \qquad j = 1, \ldots, n,$$

and by linear interpolation elsewhere on $[0,1]$. For each event $\omega \in \Omega$, $Y_n(\omega, t)$ is a continuous function of t whereas, for any given $t \in [0,1]$, $Y_n(t) = Y_n(\cdot, t)$ is a random variable on $(\Omega, \mathcal{A}, P)$. The collection

$$Y_n(\cdot) = \{Y_n(t), t \in [0,1]\}$$

of all such random variables is therefore a stochastic process with index set $\mathcal{T} = [0,1]$, called the *standardized partial sum process.* In terms of the random variables $Z_1, \ldots, Z_n$, the process $Y_n(\cdot)$ is explicitly defined as

$$Y_n(t) = \frac{\sum_{i=1}^{[nt]}(Z_i - \mu) + (nt - [nt])(Z_{[nt]+1} - \mu)}{\sigma\sqrt{n}}, \qquad t \in [0,1],$$

where $[a]$ denotes the integer part of a. The sequence $\{Z_i\}$ generates a whole sequence $\{Y_n(\cdot)\}$ of such processes. Also notice that

$$Y_n(1) = \frac{\sum_i (Z_i - \mu)}{\sigma\sqrt{n}} = \frac{\bar{Z}_n - \mu}{\sigma/\sqrt{n}}.$$

It is convenient to analyze a stochastic process as a random element of a space of functions. Let $Z(\cdot) = \{Z(\cdot, t), t \in \mathcal{T}\}$ be a stochastic process on a probability space $(\Gamma, \mathcal{G}, P)$. If all sample paths $\{Z(\omega, \cdot)\}$ of the process lie in some space $\mathcal{Z}$ of real functions on $\mathcal{T}$, then each sample path is a single function in $\mathcal{Z}$ and the process can be thought of as a mapping from Γ into $\mathcal{Z}$, that is, as a random element of $\mathcal{Z}$.

The appropriate function space for $Y_n(\cdot)$ is the vector space $C[0,1]$ of all continuous functions on the unit interval $[0,1]$. Define on $C = C[0,1]$ the norm

$$\rho(g,h) = \sup_{t\in[0,1]} |g(t) - h(t)|$$

for $g, h \in C$. Let $\mathcal{B}$ be the class of Borel sets in C relative to the norm ρ, and let Q_n be the probability measure of $Y_n(\cdot)$ in C induced by the measure P through the relationship $Q_n\{B\} = P\{\omega\colon Y_n(\omega, \cdot) \in B\}$ for $B \in \mathcal{B}$. The new probability space $(C, \mathcal{B}, Q_n)$ is the appropriate probability model for the process $Y_n(\cdot)$. We are interested in finding a measure Q on $(C, \mathcal{B})$ such that $Q_n \Rightarrow Q$.

An important probability measure on $(C, \mathcal{B})$ is the (unique) measure associated with a stochastic process $W(\cdot) = \{W(t), t \in [0,1]\}$ which satisfies:

1. $W(0) = 0$ with probability 1;
2. $W(t) \sim \mathcal{N}(0, t)$ for each $t \in (0, 1]$;
3. for any $0 \leq t_0 \leq t_1 \leq \cdots \leq t_k \leq 1$, the increments $W(t_1) - W(t_0), \ldots, W(t_k) - W(t_{k-1})$ are uncorrelated.

Such a process is called *standard Brownian motion* or the *Wiener process* and the corresponding probability measure is called the *Wiener measure*, denoted by W.

Theorem D.22 (Donsker) *If $\{Z_i\}$ are i.i.d. random variables with mean μ and finite variance σ^2, then $Q_n \Rightarrow W$.*

The Donsker theorem is also known as the *functional central limit theorem*. It implies that $Y_n(\cdot) \xrightarrow{\mathrm{d}} W(\cdot)$ and so $Y_n(t) \xrightarrow{\mathrm{d}} W(t) \sim \mathcal{N}(0, t)$ for all $t \in [0, 1]$. In particular,

$$Y_n(1) = \frac{\bar{Z}_n - \mu}{\sigma/\sqrt{n}} \xrightarrow{\mathrm{d}} W(1) \sim \mathcal{N}(0, 1),$$

which is the classical CLT.

Weak convergence to the standard Brownian motion also holds for a related kind of partial sum process defined on the closed unit interval $[0, 1]$ by

$$X_n(t) = \begin{cases} 0, & \text{if } t = 0, \\ \dfrac{S_j}{\sigma\sqrt{n}}, & \text{if } \dfrac{j}{n} \leq t < \dfrac{j+1}{n}, \; j = 1, \ldots, n-1, \\ \dfrac{S_n}{\sigma\sqrt{n}}, & \text{if } t = 1 \end{cases}$$

or, more compactly,

$$X_n(t) = \frac{S_{[nt]}}{\sigma\sqrt{n}}. \tag{D.7}$$

Clearly, $X_n(t)$ coincides with $Y_n(t)$ at $t = 0, 1/n, 2/n, \ldots, 1$. Unlike the $Y_n(\cdot)$ process, however, the sample paths of $X_n(\cdot)$ are step functions that contain finitely many discontinuities of the first kind. The appropriate function space for $X_n(\cdot)$ is no longer $C[0, 1]$ but is instead the vector space $D[0, 1]$ of all functions on the unit interval $[0, 1]$ that are right-continuous and have left-hand limits.

The next result generalizes the Mann and Wald theorem to weak convergence on general metric spaces. Given a measurable transformation h from a probability space $(S, \mathcal{B})$ to $(S', \mathcal{B}')$ and a probability measure P on S, we denote by Ph^{-1} the unique probability measure on S' defined by $Ph^{-1}\{A\} = P\{h^{-1}A\}$ for $A \in \mathcal{B}'$.

Theorem D.23 (Continuous mapping theorem) *Let P and $\{P_n\}$ be probability measures on a metric space S and let h be a continuous transformation from S to another metric space S'. If $P_n \Rightarrow P$, then $P_n h^{-1} \Rightarrow Ph^{-1}$.*

Theorem D.23 implies that if h is a continuous transformation and $\{Z_n(\cdot)\}$ is a sequence of stochastic processes converging weakly to a limit process $Z(\cdot)$, then the process $h(Z_n(\cdot))$ converges weakly to the process $h(Z(\cdot))$.

Example D.1 Let $\{Z_i\}$ be a sequence of i.i.d. random variables with mean zero and finite positive variance σ^2 and consider approximating the distribution of the sum of partial sums $\sum_{j=1}^n S_j$, where $S_j = \sum_{i=1}^j Z_i$. In terms of the standardized partial sum process (D.7) we have

$$\int_0^1 X_n(t)\,dt = \frac{S_1}{\sigma\sqrt{n}}\frac{1}{n} + \cdots + \frac{S_n}{\sigma\sqrt{n}}\frac{1}{n} = \frac{1}{\sigma n^{3/2}}\sum_{j=1}^n S_j.$$

By the functional CLT, $X_n(\cdot) \xrightarrow{\text{d}} W(\cdot)$ and so, by the continuous mapping theorem, $n^{-3/2}\sum_j S_j \xrightarrow{\text{d}} \sigma \int_0^1 W(t)\,dt$.

Now consider approximating the distribution of $\sum_{j=1}^n S_j^2$. In this case

$$\int_0^1 X_n(t)^2\,dt = \frac{S_1^2}{\sigma^2 n}\frac{1}{n} + \cdots + \frac{S_n^2}{\sigma n}\frac{1}{n} = \frac{1}{\sigma^2 n^2}\sum_{j=1}^n S_j^2.$$

Hence, the continuous mapping theorem gives $n^{-2}\sum_j S_j^2 \xrightarrow{\text{d}} \sigma^2 \int_0^1 W(t)^2\,dt$. Notice that one of the main advantages of working with the $X_n(\cdot)$ process is the ease with which it can be integrated over $[0,1]$. □

BIBLIOGRAPHIC NOTES

Section D.1 relies heavily on Chapter 1 of Serfling (1980). For a number of interesting counterexamples see Chapter 6 of Romano and Siegel (1986).

Orders in probability were introduced by Mann and Wald (1943). For a thorough discussion see Fuller (1976).

Useful references on asymptotic expansions are Bhattacharya and Rao (1976) and Barndorff-Nielsen and Cox (1989). On the relationship between asymptotic expansions and the bootstrap see Hall (1992) and van der Vaart and Wellner (1996).

The material in Section D.8 is based on Billingsley (1968).

Index